M000223065

THE OXFORD HISTORY OF THE NOVEL IN ENGLISH

English and British Fiction 1750–1820

The Oxford History of the Novel in English

GENERAL EDITOR: PATRICK PARRINDER
ADVISORY EDITOR (US VOLUMES): JONATHAN ARAC

Volumes Published and in Preparation

1. *Prose Fiction in English from the Origins of Print to 1750*, edited by Thomas Keymer
2. *English and British Fiction 1750–1820*, edited by Peter Garside and Karen O'Brien
3. *The Nineteenth-Century Novel 1820–1880*, edited by John Kucich and Jenny Bourne Taylor
4. *The Reinvention of the British and Irish Novel 1880–1940*, edited by Patrick Parrinder and Andrzej Gąsiorek.
5. *The American Novel from its Beginnings to 1870*, edited by J. Gerald Kennedy and Leland S. Person
6. *The American Novel 1870–1940*, edited by Priscilla Wald and Michael A. Elliott
7. *British and Irish Fiction since 1940*, edited by Peter Boxall and Bryan Cheyette
8. *American Fiction since 1940*, edited by Cyrus R. K. Patell and Deborah Lindsay Williams
9. *World Fiction in English to 1950*, edited by Ralph Crane, Jane Stafford, and Mark Williams
10. *The Novel in English in South and South-East Asia since 1945*, edited by Alex Tickell
11. *The Novel in Africa and the Atlantic World since 1950*, edited by Simon Gikandi
12. *The Novel in Australia, Canada, New Zealand, and the South Pacific since 1950*, edited by Coral Ann Howells, Paul Sharrad, and Gerry Turcotte

THE OXFORD HISTORY OF THE NOVEL IN ENGLISH

Volume Two

English and British Fiction 1750–1820

EDITED BY

Peter Garside and Karen O'Brien

LIBRARY OF
CONGRESS
SURPLUS
DUPLICATE

OXFORD
UNIVERSITY PRESS

OXFORD
UNIVERSITY PRESS

Great Clarendon Street, Oxford, OX2 6DP,
United Kingdom

Oxford University Press is a department of the University of Oxford.
It furthers the University's objective of excellence in research, scholarship,
and education by publishing worldwide. Oxford is a registered trade mark of
Oxford University Press in the UK and in certain other countries

© Oxford University Press 2015

The moral rights of the authors have been asserted

First Edition published in 2015

Impression: 1

All rights reserved. No part of this publication may be reproduced, stored in
a retrieval system, or transmitted, in any form or by any means, without the
prior permission in writing of Oxford University Press, or as expressly permitted
by law, by licence or under terms agreed with the appropriate reprographics
rights organization. Enquiries concerning reproduction outside the scope of the
above should be sent to the Rights Department, Oxford University Press, at the
address above

You must not circulate this work in any other form
and you must impose this same condition on any acquirer

Published in the United States of America by Oxford University Press
198 Madison Avenue, New York, NY 10016, United States of America

British Library Cataloguing in Publication Data
Data available

Library of Congress Control Number: 2014946471

ISBN 978–0–19–957480–3

Printed and bound by
CPI Group (UK) Ltd, Croydon, CR0 4YY

Links to third party websites are provided by Oxford in good faith and
for information only. Oxford disclaims any responsibility for the materials
contained in any third party website referenced in this work.

Contents

Part III: Generic Variations and Narrative Structures

Part IV: Contexts

Part V: Alternative Forms of Fiction

Part VI: Assimilation and Cultural Interchanges

Afterword

Acknowledgements

THE editors are enormously grateful to Dr Anthony Mandal for his assistance and advice at every stage of this book's production. We would also like to thank Professor Emma Clery, of the Southampton Centre for Eighteenth Century Studies and the Chawton House Library Centre for the Study of Early English Women's Writing, for organizing and hosting the conference on the British novel which helped us to share ideas and shape our thinking.

This volume is dedicated to the memory of Susan Manning who died in January 2013 and whose scholarship has been a source of inspiration to many of its contributors.

List of Contributors

David Allan, University of St Andrews

Ros Ballaster, University of Oxford

James Chandler, University of Chicago

E. J. Clery, University of Southampton

Stephen Colclough, Bangor University, Wales

Deirdre Coleman, University of Melbourne

Claire Connolly, University College, Cork

Simon Dickie, University of Toronto

Ian Duncan, University of California, Berkeley

Ina Ferris, University of Ottawa

Lynn Festa, Rutgers University

Caroline Franklin, Swansea University

Michael Gamer, University of Pennsylvania

Peter Garside, University of Edinburgh

M. O. Grenby, Newcastle University

Gillian Hughes, Independent Scholar

Anthony Jarrells, University of South Carolina

Vivien Jones, University of Leeds

Thomas Keymer, University of Toronto

Deidre Lynch, Harvard University

Anthony Mandal, Cardiff University

Jenny Mander, University of Cambridge

Jon Mee, University of York

Robert Miles, University of Victoria

Karen O'Brien, King's College, London

Ruth Perry, Massachusetts Institute of Technology

James Raven, University of Essex

Gillian Russell, University of Melbourne

Betty A. Schellenberg, Simon Fraser University
Clifford Siskin, New York University
Helen Thompson, Northwestern University
Clara Tuite, University of Melbourne
Wil Verhoeven, Groningen University, Netherlands
Nicola J. Watson, Open University

List of Figures and Tables

Figures

Tables

General Editor's Preface

UNLIKE poetry and drama, the novel belongs entirely within the sphere of recorded history. Novels, like historical records, are written texts superseding the worlds of myth, of epic poetry, and oral storytelling. Typically they are commercial products taking advantage of the technology of printing, the availability of leisure time among potential readers, and the circulation of books. The growth of the novel as an art form would have been unthinkable without the habit of silent, private reading, a habit that we now take for granted although its origins are much disputed among scholars. While novels are not always read silently and in private, they are felt to belong in the domestic sphere rather than in the public arenas associated with music, drama, and the other performance arts. The need for separate histories of the novel form has long been recognized, since the distinctiveness of fictional prose narrative is quickly lost sight of in more general accounts of literary history.

The *Oxford History of the Novel in English* is a multi-volume series offering a comprehensive, worldwide history of English-language prose fiction, and drawing on the knowledge of a large, international team of scholars. Our history spans more than six centuries, firmly rejecting the simplified view that the novel in English began with Daniel Defoe's *Robinson Crusoe* in 1719. Fifteenth- and sixteenth-century prose fiction has, in fact, been surveyed by many earlier historians, including Ernest A. Baker whose *History of the English Novel* appeared in ten volumes between 1924 and 1939. Unlike Baker's strictly chronological account, the *Oxford History* broadens out as it approaches the present, recognizing the spread of the English language across the globe from the seventeenth century onwards. The 'English' (or British) novel becomes the novel in English. While we aim to offer a comprehensive account of the anglophone novel, our coverage cannot of course be exhaustive; that is a task for the bibliographer rather than the literary historian. All history has a commemorative function, but cultural memory is unavoidably selective. Selection, in the case of books, is the task of literary criticism, and criticism enters literary history the moment that we speak of 'the novel' rather than, simply, of the multitude of individual novels. Nevertheless, this *Oxford History* adopts a broader definition of 'the novel' than has been customary in earlier histories. Thus we neither focus exclusively on the so-called literary novel, nor on the published texts of fiction at the expense of the processes of production, distribution, and reception. Every volume in this series contains sections on relevant aspects of book history and the history of criticism, together with sections on popular fiction and the fictional subgenres, in addition to the sequence of chapters outlining the work of major novelists, movements, traditions, and tendencies. Novellas and short stories are regarded for our purposes (we would stress 'for our purposes') both as subgenres of the novel and as aspects of its material history.

Our aim throughout these volumes is to present the detailed history of the novel in a way that is both useful to students and specialists, and accessible to a wide and varied readership. We hope to have conveyed our understanding of the distinctiveness, the continuity, and the social and cultural resonance of prose fiction at different times and places. The novel, moreover, is still changing. Reports of its death—and there have been quite a few—are, as Mark Twain might have said, an exaggeration. At a time when new technologies are challenging the dominance of the printed book and when the novel's 'great tradition' is sometimes said to have foundered, we believe that the *Oxford History* will stand out as a record of the extraordinary adaptability and resilience of the novel in English, its protean character, and its constant ability to surprise.

Patrick Parrinder

Introduction

KAREN O'BRIEN

THE period 1750–1820 encompasses an extraordinarily eventful and decisive phase in the development of the British novel. The chronological arrangement of this volume of the *Oxford History of the Novel in English* starts in the middle of the eighteenth century, a century usually treated as a single era in the initial 'rise' of the British novel. Our period begins in the afterglow of the mid-century novels of Henry Fielding and Samuel Richardson. At this point, British fiction appeared to be in the doldrums, dismissed by many commentators as a briefly dazzling but ephemeral genre. By the end of our period, the British novel had taken its place among the pre-eminent genres of literary writing, had exhibited unprecedented thematic and technical range, and had come to dominate the international market for fiction. The suspicion of dubious respectability and uncertain factual status which hung over earlier novels had largely been replaced by public acceptance, even national pride, supported by a publishing infrastructure of review periodicals, anthologies, reprint series, fiction-orientated magazines, and lending libraries. The periodical in particular, and the category of the 'literary' developed alongside this phase in the novel's history. The development of the novel also paralleled developments in the writing of history, so that history became increasingly available to novelists as a knowable socio-economic backdrop to the individual life stories they sought to tell. The cultural assimilation of the novel reached such a level of sophistication by the end of the eighteenth century that it is difficult, even now, to distance ourselves from the terms within which contemporary commentators described its journey towards stability and success.

Although printed novels grew in number from 1750–1820, capitalizing upon and also creating a growing middle-class readership for all forms of print, their trajectory was not simply an upward one. A drought in the 1750s was followed by further drying up of interest and production in the late 1770s. As E. J. Clery's chapter shows, before the major reorientation of fiction by Laurence Sterne in the later 1760s, the legacies of the towering mid-century figures of Richardson and Fielding did not initially seem to offer a secure future for the novel. Nor can the trajectory of the British novel in this period be gauged in terms of its British readership. The works of Richardson and Sterne exerted an influence in the rest of Europe still greater than at home, and were, by the logic of cosmopolitan literary circulation, reimported as translated imitations. In this volume of the *Oxford History of the Novel in English*, we take as our starting point a borderless and mobile European and transatlantic culture of fiction, and observe, in the later part of the period, the growing association—at the level of theme rather than of audience—between the British novel and British national culture. Despite the large numbers of novels concerned with the themes of love, courtship, and marriage, this is not an inward or a nationally self-reflexive era for the novel, but one profoundly shaped by the economic and political transformations of the time, encompassing decades of continental and imperial warfare—warfare that came closer than ever to home in the French Revolutionary and Napoleonic Wars. The volume offers a collective account of the novel within this process of transformation, and evaluates the literary achievement of a huge range of major and less well-known novelists against a backdrop of the second 'rise' of the novel. It seeks to balance substantial treatments of influential authors, including Tobias Smollett, Sterne, Frances Burney, Jane Austen, and Walter Scott, with a broad engagement with most of the kinds of fictional writing at work in this period.

The term 'rise', as Clifford Siskin argues in his Afterword, is an artificial, organizing term which overlays the wider market and aesthetic phenomena which coalesced during this period. If we are to understand the novel's emergence, we must recognize that the discourse of rising was implicated, from the outset, in the self-positioning of the form. Writers of fiction and commentators were highly self-conscious in the ways in which they sought to associate the novel with 'literature' which was itself elaborated as a category during this period. Novelists and critics described and historicized the novel's journey from 'romance' to fictional verisimilitude, and from formal experimentation with epistolary, fragmentary, and other kinds of narrative, to more condensed first- or third-person kinds of delivery. Towards the end of our period, as Michael Gamer explains, there appeared the first book-length history of prose fiction, as well as numerous anthologies and reprint series which gave coherence to decades of diverse fictional achievement. Notable among these was Anna Barbauld's *The British Novelists* (1810), a fifty-volume collection. In her remarkable introduction 'On the Origin and Progress of Novel-Writing', Barbauld made the case for the seriousness and cultural stature of the modern novel as containing 'more of character and less (indeed in modern novels nothing) of the supernatural machinery'. Blithely ignoring the contemporary popularity of Gothic, supernatural fiction, Barbauld equates seriousness and modernity with realism, and situates the modern realist British novel within a long global tradition of fictional writing that stretched back to ancient Greece and classical Arabia.

By emphasizing the centrality of 'character' and of 'natural painting' (as she describes Daniel Defoe's writing), Barbauld deliberately sidelines not only Gothic but also other kinds of recent fiction which did not deal in psychological complexity but in a social realism of a different kind. In her chapter Lynn Festa gives a fascinating overview of the 'it' narrative, a fictional form that flourished in the 1750–80s, that was told from the perspective of guineas, rupees, atoms, lapdogs, and shillings. Like their cousin tradition of 'spy' novels (that examined European society from the perspective of the foreign out-sider), these works opened a window onto the structures of society, showing how they were held together by trade, transport networks, customs, and the law. Ros Ballaster explores the similar workings of oriental and philosophical tales; these were already well established before 1750, but continued to develop and thrive during this period. Oriental tales such as Samuel Johnson's *Rasselas* (1759) took up many of the same themes as novels—the search for happiness, the foundations of morality, the delusions of love—but approached them through plot rather than through character. Although some of these works approximated to 'natural painting' by adopting an ethnographic stance towards their non-European subject matter, they nevertheless reminded readers of the 'origin and progress' of fiction in traditions of representation outside those of modern Europe. Equally persistent from a much earlier period, and similarly international in origin, was Rabelasian and Cervantesque fictional comic writing. Recast in the eight-eenth century in the form of picaresque and 'ramble' novels, this kind of writing had no pretensions to psychological depth or plot plausibility, no interest in the new sentimen-tal modes of reader engagement, and no sympathetic regard for women (with the hon-ourable exception of Charlotte Lennox's *The Female Quixote*, 1752). Simon Dickie gives a fresh account of a much neglected tradition and its pre-eminent exponents Smollett and Edward Kimber, reminding us of its repertoire of perforated chamber pots, itching powder, attempted rapes, embarrassing injuries, and old lady races (the latter in Frances Burney's *Evelina*, 1778, a novel much indebted to this kind of comedy).

Barbauld could not have foreseen the enduring nineteenth-century popularity of Ramble fiction. She undoubtedly preferred apparently outdated epistolary fiction, and she celebrated the beneficial influence of Samuel Richardson, even though novels in let-ters were no longer fashionable in the early 1800s. Nicola Watson explains that epistolary fiction had enjoyed a spectacular flourishing in the second half of the eighteenth century, to the point where, in the 1770s, 40 per cent of all new novels appeared in letter form. Most were sentimental and intense accounts of the dilemmas of love. Although works such as Burney's comic masterpiece *Evelina* and Smollett's multi-vocal epistolary trav-elogue, *The Expedition of Humphry Clinker* (1771), temporarily revivified the form, they were not sufficient to avert its demise in the later eighteenth century. Watson speculates that the reasons for the steep and terminal decline were in some way connected to the widening repertoire of reality effects exemplified in other new novels: epistolary fiction had become technically exhausted; the novel, perhaps, no longer needed the alibi that it was an assemblage of 'real' letters; and the psychological realism to which it aspired might be better captured in portraits of characters making retrospective sense of their experiences and emotions. Jane Austen's early fictional experiments included parodies of epistolary fiction. Even though she provides the supreme instance in this period of the realism of mental retrospective—the self-conversing heroine making private sense of the day's encounters and emotions—we must beware of regarding even this as a rise above and beyond existing kinds of character representation. As Vivien Jones observes, Austen's relationship to other writers and genres was as much one of 'seamless absorption of popular forms within her rigorously unassuming realist aesthetic' as it was one of 'rejection' (274). Like Sterne before her, Austen's journey towards her own kinds of 'natural painting' was proceeded by an eclectic, sometimes even parodic, assimilation of earlier modes and techniques.

Austen published all of her fiction under the confident category of 'A Novel', a term widely contrasted in this period with 'romance', for example by Clara Reeve in her earlier history of the novel *The Progress of Romance* (1785). The revival, in the 1760s, of scholarly and popular interest in the medieval and Renaissance past cemented the association of romance with the distant, the heroic, and the marvellous: as Reeve comments, romance 'describes what never happened nor is likely to happen'. Yet, as Anthony Jarrells shows, this apparently straightforward divergence of novels and romance was complicated by the emergence of a new fictional category, the tale. This label, made famous by Walter Scott's *Tales of My Landlord* series (1816–31) was by the 1820s so dominant as to appear to have supplanted all other designations. The word tale, with its associations of oral recounting, regional location, overt moral purpose, and elements of the marvellous, as Jarrells argues, both challenged and consolidated the realist protocols of the novel. Writers of the tales which came 'after novels', particularly of shorter tales, embraced the designation for purposes of aesthetic and market differentiation. In doing so they affirmed that fiction was a dynamic and evolving system of writing, but they also helped to define for the next generation of writers the boundaries of the novel in terms of length, subject matter, verisimilitude, and depth of characterization.

If we have not, then, accepted the Enlightenment vocabularies of 'origin' and 'progress' to describe the trajectories of the novel in this period, we have sought to capture a dual process of generic consolidation around certain more privileged notions of realism and of fragmenting specialization by subgenres and segmented readerships. We have endeavoured to place this within the context of recent scholarship on the material history of print culture, including the conditions of production, authorship, British and international consumption, and reviewing. The new fictional output of this period rose steadily from around 231 new titles in the 1750s to 667 in the 1810s (Chapter 1, Table 1.1), an impressive growth that has been bibliographically mapped elsewhere by James Raven and Peter Garside and others. These numbers sat alongside swelling numbers of reprinted titles, particularly after a relaxation in copyright law in 1774 led to a republishing boom, creating a lagged reading culture in which writers such as Sterne, Fielding, Eliza Haywood, Smollett, and Defoe were dominant. Around one tenth of all new novels were continental novels, mainly from France but increasingly from Germany. Jenny Mander shows how widely these circulated, their mobility facilitated by the self-consciously borderless aesthetic of the sentimental, Richardsonian narrative or the oriental tale. The expansion in novel publication partook of a revolution in book production across all genres, and, more broadly, of the growing social significance of print culture. By the end of our period, this expansion enabled the rise of specialized fiction publishers, such the Minerva Press, and of publishing houses outside of London, notably in Edinburgh. However, it was not until after 1820 that novelists themselves were able to make an independent living out of publishing their work (with the underpaid exception of the hard-working Charlotte Smith). Smith, like Scott, was as much a poet as a novelist, and at a time when, as Gillian Russell points out, 'authorship itself had not yet been defined or delimited by genre' (515), the notion of a 'novelist' as a specialist kind of literary function had yet to take hold. Authors themselves were often unnamed on title pages, with male authors (Scott among them) adopting anonymity to avoid compromising their professional status. At the other end of the spectrum, Clara Tuite shows how the period also witnessed the rise of celebrity authors such as Sterne, Jean-Jacques Rousseau, and Mary Robinson, whose well-known public personae coloured readers' interpretations of their novels. The expansion in novel publication and the financial opportunity for a lump sum from the sale of copyright undoubtedly beckoned more women writers than ever before into the literary marketplace. Some recent commentators have somewhat overstated the prominence of female novelists in this period, and for the earlier decades they were outnumbered by male counterparts. But in the 1810s, women novelists did outperform their male rivals, and Jane Austen published her works during a period of 'reinvigorated female engagement' with novel production (Garside, 46).

Despite increases in publication volume and higher sales figures for successful authors (at the height of Scott's popularity, print runs of 12,000 would sell out in weeks), the industry itself remained largely rooted in what Raven calls its *ancien régime*: expensive books issuing from hand-operated presses before the adoption, in the 1820s, of steam-driven print and papermaking technology. In addition to these constraints on expansion, literacy rates grew only slowly, and novel reading and writing remained the preserve of the relatively wealthy. Although Britain was some way off having the broadly-based reading public of the nineteenth century, one institution that did make a significant difference was the new lending or 'circulating' library. David Allan argues that these and other kinds of libraries grew at an extraordinary rate from the later eighteenth century, and sowed the seeds of a more democratized relationship between the British people and fiction. Serial and extract publication in newspapers, magazines, anthologies, and chapbooks also expanded access to affordable fiction. Gillian Hughes gives an overview of the vibrant and generically fluid world of magazine fiction, some of it custom-written in short fictional formats, much of it consisting of serializations, extracts, and abridgements. Magazine publishers became more sophisticated in their approach, to the point where, at the end our period, William Blackwood fostered original works by major writers such as James Hogg and John Galt.

Stephen Colclough examines the social composition and habits of readers themselves, and demonstrates how these can, to a limited extent, be reconstructed from annotations, lending records, private journals, and other sources. These records evoke reading habits that hovered between the 'pleasures of familiarity' with old favourites and a desire for novelty (Lynch 2009: 98). And while extracts and serializations promoted a rapid, sampling approach to novel consumption, the very pace of reading, the extent to which it needed to be slow, silent, linear, and serious was itself a matter of public debate (Price 2000: 96–8). If, as Ina Ferris has argued, weighty works such as Scott's *Waverley* series implicitly demanded a shift of reading from 'the sofa to the study', other works led from the study to the boudoir (in the case of the thinly disguised portraits of the rich and fashionable discussed by Clara Tuite) or from the sofa to the nursery (Ferris 2009b: 474). This period, as M. O. Grenby demonstrates, was important for the development of children's writing, at a time when, demographically speaking, Britain was becoming a young country. During this period, fiction for the young first started to emerge as a separate literary form, most famously in the case of Thomas Day's *History of Sandford and Merton, a Work Intended for the Use of Children* (1783–9). However, as Grenby shows, writers had yet to distinguish between adult and child target readerships in the way they would do later in the nineteenth century.

In the era before mass literacy and mass readership in Britain, and before the large-scale, consolidated, and mechanized publishing of the later nineteenth century, there were inevitably real limits to the social reach of the novel. There was some market segmentation of fictional subgenres by age, gender, and social class. But the social reach of fiction was just as much enabled, in this period, by the relative flexibility of generic boundaries and the lack of authorial specialization. Gillian Russell observes that, for most of this period, the dominant form of public artistic culture was the theatre which had a close relationship both to print and to fiction. It was not only that novels and the stage were mutually fascinated with each other—for example, the amateur theatricals in Austen's *Mansfield Park* (1814), and Lydia Languish's addiction to novels in Sheridan's play *The Rivals* (1775). Writers and stories operated across their boundaries, and the very term 'to dramatize' dates from this time. Scott was one of the most 'dramatized' authors of this era; Gothic operated as a trans-generic fictional and melodramatic mode; and the reading public was also a watching public. Although literary categories were not firmly differentiated, the rising tide of print buoyed up a more general expansion in the infrastructure for literary writing, notably in the form of reviews and collections. The review periodical was invented and developed in this period, from Ralph Griffiths's *Monthly Review* and Smollett's *Critical Review* in the mid-eighteenth century to the *Edinburgh Review* and *Blackwood's Magazine* in the early nineteenth century. These, as Michael Gamer shows, would ultimately promote the novel as a separate and credible literary category, and increasingly enable readers to sift the worthwhile from the ephemeral by reviewing fewer novels at greater length. The second rising of the British novel, then, was accompanied by a constant process of assessment and assimilation by reviewers, anthologizers, and collectors; Walter Scott's own involvement with a publishing venture for a reprint series at the very time when he was commencing *Waverley* is, as Gamer suggests, indicative of the close connection between the cultural processing of existing novels and the creation of new ones.

The growth of print culture was enmeshed with the demographic, economic, and geopolitical expansion of Britain in the second half of the eighteenth century. Britain as an entity in itself underwent a process of national consolidation; after the defeat of the Jacobite Rebellion in 1746, a sense of dynastic security enabled those on the winning side in Scotland and England to forge a stronger British identity. The Scottish economy, its printing industry, and its intellectual life flourished, but the accompanying 'fictions of the Union', as Thomas Keymer demonstrates, were not without undercurrents of dissent. Smollett in his final, dazzling novel *Humphry Clinker* (1771) orchestrates his scepticism about the cultural unity of the Union through a series of diverse epistolary voices. The haunting of unionist consciousness by the voices of the marginal, defeated and obsolete, according to Ian Duncan, gave creative impetus to Scott. Not only in *Waverley*, in which the defeat of the Jacobite Highlanders is the overt subject matter, but also in other novels such as *Guy Mannering* (1815), *Old Mortality* (1816), and *Ivanhoe* (1820), Scott poises his protagonists between two unequal worlds, one aligned to the progressive history of civil society, the other to the past and to an uncertain future. Yet, far from proclaiming the triumph of 'history' over 'romance', Duncan argues that Scott's novels activate in their readers both scepticism and emotional attachment to the romance of common life. Scott negotiates the Union itself by repositioning both Scotland and England within an international frame of reference, and his novels become British by being at once Scottish and international.

Scott's poised fictions were, to a degree, anticipated by Welsh writers tackling the clash of cultural backwardness and industrialization within the context of a much older Union. Caroline Franklin uncovers this dynamic within a largely forgotten body of later eighteenth-century novels set in Wales, including works such as *Anna; or, Memoirs of a Welch Heiress* (1785) by the once-popular novelist Anna Maria Bennett. Irish writers confronting the crises at the end of the eighteenth century and the Acts of Union of 1800 similarly rose to the task of reimagining Britishness through what Claire Connolly calls a 'culturally sensitive form of realism' (217). She describes how the 'national tales' of novelists such as Maria Edgeworth and Sydney Owenson maintained a commitment to cultural specificity, through dialect, precise visual description, and detailed renditions of national customs, while dramatizing political union via romantic plots of courtship, dispossession, and rightful inheritance.

Both Scottish and Irish novelists reframed the dilemmas of Union within the wider context of European development and of Britain's growing global empire; here Scottish and Irish troops, engineers, and emigrants had started to play such a significant part. Following Britain's spectacular territorial gains during the Seven Years' War, growing numbers of novelists adopted the empire as their geographical canvas, and presented stories of courtship and self-development as narratives of colonial migration and return. These stories gave prominence to the 'fiction of bourgeois ubiquity' and mobility that would become more dominant in the later nineteenth century (Siskind 2010: 337). Frances Brooke's *Emily Montague* (1769), for example, was the first novel set in British-controlled Quebec, from which the heroine eventually returns; Phebe Gibbes's *Hartly House, Calcutta* (1789) charts its heroine's literal and inner journey from England and selfish ignorance, to India, cultural sympathy, and romantic reward with an English marriage; and Scott's *Guy Mannering* tells how its elder protagonist's return to Scotland from India eventually precipitates his future son-in-law's repossession of his rightful home. Deirdre Coleman shows how this plot motif of colonial exodus and return also became the means by which novelists both confronted and contained the horrors of slavery in the West Indies and North America. The much-discussed case of Sir Thomas Bertram's visit to his plantation in Antigua in Austen's *Mansfield Park* was one of a number of instances of this motif: many, such as Sarah Scott's *History of Sir George Ellison* (1766) or Henry Mackenzie's *Julia de Roubigné* (1777), described a West Indian interlude and tried to convey the voices of slaves themselves. Sterne's compassionate imagining of the predicament of the enslaved, as Helen Thompson shows, was influential in enabling novelists to project a limited degree of cross-cultural and cross-racial sentiment, as well as providing a direct source of inspiration for the former slave and anti-slavery writer Ignatius Sancho.

The 'sentimental' mode of writing, influentially shaped by Sterne, Oliver Goldsmith, and Mackenzie in the 1760s and 1770s, was as well attuned to political and international topics, as it was more obviously adapted to rendering intimate inner life. Properly 'sentimental' novels (the adjective is a contemporary one to which Sterne's *A Sentimental Journey*, 1768, first gave currency) allowed for a remarkably elastic approach to their subject matter. With moorings in the advanced philosophical thinking of the eighteenth century, sentimental novels were particularly effective in the service of an international, de-territorialized, and humanitarian sensibility. Lynn Hunt (2007) has explained the connection between fiction's humanitarian regard for the feelings of coerced or injured individuals and the Enlightenment elaboration of modern theories of human rights and obligations. James Chandler in his chapter argues that Sterne's intellectual connections both to Scottish Enlightenment philosophy and to the liberal, Enlightened latitudinarian Anglicanism of his day were readily apparent, if playfully reprised, in his fiction. For other writers, the connection between humanitarian sentimentality and Enlightenment ideals resided in a more generalized opposition to cruelty, coercion, and war-mongering. From Uncle Toby's garden re-enactments of the Siege of Namur in Sterne's *Tristram Shandy* (1760–7), sentimental fiction became a means of managing the divisiveness and trauma of war. The most successful war novel of the period, Samuel Jackson Pratt's *Emma Corbett; or, The Miseries of Civil War* (1780), a sentimental, epistolary account of a family torn apart by opposing loyalties during the American Revolutionary War, was a publishing sensation on both sides of the Atlantic. Caroline Franklin shows how Pratt adroitly conveyed the shock of colonial civil strife and recalled his readers to a common Britishness through the image of the dismembered family, even as he conceded the triumph of separatist violence and militarism. Wil Verhoeven's chapter enlarges upon the pan-Atlanticism of fiction before, during, and after the American Revolution when the American market was saturated with imported novels from the London and Dublin presses. In this domain, at least, there was no fictional declaration of independence after 1776, and there persisted, to the great frustration of the pioneering American novelist Charles Brockden Brown, an Atlantic literary system that was, in Franco Moretti's phrase, 'one, and unequal', and that favoured the dominance in America of British books and British taste (Moretti 2000). American readers continued to favour novels in the internationalist, sentimental mode of Pratt, most famously Susanna Rowson's best-selling tale of seduction and premature death, *Charlotte Temple* (1791, American edition 1794). Pratt's novel had many other imitators in the 1780s and 1790s who sought to 'realign England's relationship with its various colonial spaces' (Franklin, 168), notably Charlotte Smith; her *The Old Manor House* (1793) uses the retrospective setting of the American War to raise highly contemporary questions about the justice of revolutionary insurrection.

In both metropolitan and postcolonial settings, the novel of sensibility emphasized the outward turning of the sensitive gaze towards the sufferings of others. In the hands of Robert Bage or the commercially successful Smith, it readily lent itself to social critique. In the decade of the 'French Revolution controversy', political fiction first came of age. Jon Mee gives an assessment of the achievement of the reformist, 'Jacobin' novelists of 1792–6, among them Smith, Bage, William Godwin, Thomas Holcroft, Mary Hays, and Elizabeth Inchbald. With the exception of Godwin's psychological masterpiece, *Caleb Williams* (1794), few of their novels were particularly original or technically innovative. But their collective political achievement was, by their narrative sorting of authentic, feeling characters from those of false, conventional or corrupted sensibility, to give legitimacy to the sincere individual—male or female—as the instinctive arbiter of social justice. Mary Wollstonecraft's radical, international feminism was certainly shaped by this kind of methodological individualism, and, as a novelist herself, by this new confidence in the political efficacy of fiction.

Flourishing alongside and cross-fertilizing with the radical political novels of the 1790s, was Gothic fiction. These fictions of extreme psychological states and situations, ghostly hauntings, benighted locations, and erotic sadism enjoyed enormous popularity in two distinct waves: in the 1790s, when a third of all new novels were in this mode, and again between 1800–18, before falling away, or rather migrating downmarket into magazines, chapbooks, and melodramas. Despite the Gothic preoccupation with the violent and the supernatural, Deidre Lynch challenges the notion that it constituted a reaction to emergent forms of realism, or that there was a simple dichotomy between the Gothic and realism. Beginning with Horace Walpole's *Castle of Otranto* in 1765, and ascending through the works of William Beckford, Ann Radcliffe, and Matthew ('Monk') Lewis, she argues that the Gothic helped to 'define the frontiers of the fictive' by showing that superstition and the diabolical arts belonged to Catholic, Eastern, and pre-modern worlds, and by simultaneously redirecting readers' indignation to the real cruelties of their own world (Lynch, 185). In Godwin's *Caleb Williams*, in which the hero struggles against his aristocratic enemy, Robert Miles shows how Gothic provides both an atmosphere of cruelty and corruption and the literal residue of medieval feudal tyranny which his enemy exploits. Many Gothic plots culminated in the rational explanations of forgery, concealed machinery, and devices. In this way they provided a rehearsal space for what Lynch calls the 'receptive competencies' of their readers, who might or might not have been able to guess the truth all along. Gothic was certainly open to parody and pastiche. Jane Austen's *Northanger Abbey* (1818) and Thomas Love Peacock's *Nightmare Abbey* (1818) are the best known works among a body of 'anti-Gothic' writing, in which Gothic itself features as a kind of pathologized reading of reality, a failure to guess at the prosaic, unreassuring truth. Despite such discouragements, Miles tells how three late masterpieces opened out new avenues for succeeding Gothic writers. Godwin's daughter Mary Shelley transformed the supernatural into science fiction in *Frankenstein* (1818), pitting the perverted intellect of the scientist against the pathological sensibility of the monster. And, at the end of our period, Charles Robert Maturin's *Melmoth the Wanderer* (1820) and James Hogg's *Confessions of a Justified Sinner* (1824) mined Gothic's Protestant sectarian foundations, and cemented its nineteenth-century associations with the non-metropolitan periphery.

Just as Gothic writers were attacked by typically more politically conservative anti-Gothic writers, Jacobin novelists were countered by a number of lacklustre 'anti-Jacobin' opponents. However, Mee contends that this binary opposition was less significant than the cross-fictional dialogues that took place between radical and moderate writers, particularly about the place of feeling, rationality, and education in British life. Maria Edgeworth and the Scottish writer Elizabeth Hamilton voiced their distrust of revolutionary change, and caricatured radical figures such as Wollstonecraft and Rousseau in their novels. Yet they did so in the context of works, such as Edgeworth's *Belinda* (1801), that emphasized the need for critical rationality, especially female rationality, for a healthy distrust of aristocratic and paternal authority, and for a degree of social reform enabled by better public education. In Edgeworth and Hamilton, with their close ties to Scottish Enlightenment circles, as well as in the Jacobin writers, we see the rise of the novelist as public intellectual. Jane Austen praised *Belinda*, alongside the novels of Burney, as a work of intellectual substance embodied in style, character, and humour, 'in which the greatest powers of the mind are displayed'. Austen's own literary formation took place during the ideological ferment of the 1790s, and, as Vivien Jones argues, she ultimately put '1790s enlightenment ideals at the service not of revolutionary change, but of a gender-inflected vision of gradualist reform' (288). By the time her novels were published, female-centred stories about courtship, the pitfalls of high society, inheritance, and marriage had undoubtedly acquired an intellectual and political resonance which Austen did not need or choose to overemphasize. This resonance was certainly amplified by the mass experience of the French Revolution and Napoleonic Wars, when the social cohesion that comes from successful marriages and good mothers certainly seemed more important to the nation than ever before. But, as the chapters by Ruth Perry and Betty Schellenberg explain, this resonance long pre-dates the 1790s.

Perry explains how the basic plot and character types of even the most apparently domestic and conventionally romantic novels—prohibiting fathers, overbearing brothers and dependent sisters, thwarted young couples, financially disadvantaged second sons—were, from the beginning of this period, bound up with highly contemporary debates about property, civil rights, and inheritance. Sarah Fielding, a key figure in the development of sentimental fiction in the 1740s and 1750s, drew attention, as Perry points out, to the harsh English legal environment in which her well-meaning characters are so often defeated. Fielding exposed the increasing devaluation (financial and hence familial and social) of sisters relative to their brothers by means of legal devices such as 'strict settlement'. E. J. Clery also elucidates the similarities between Sarah Fielding's novels and the portraits of the 'institutionalised difference' or systematic cruelty of the law in her brother Henry's last great novel *Amelia* (1752). Austen's account of the ousting of the Dashwood sisters by their half-brother in *Sense and Sensibility* (1811) thus recapitulates more than half a century of fictional protest. In addition to her fraternal connection, Sarah Fielding was also a leading member of the intellectual circle of women writers which Richardson gathered round him, and which in turn nurtured a second generation of Anglican 'Bluestocking' women writers. These women, as Schellenberg makes clear, self-consciously addressed the questions which Richardson had raised, particularly in his last novel *Sir Charles Grandison* (1753–4): can individual benevolence help society to overcome self-indulgent sentimentality and base passions, in order to create 'a new order founded on moral sentiments', and can virtuous, rational women change society? (Clery, 88). Sarah Scott's fictional portrait of a calm, self-contained yet influential utopian community of women in *A Description of Millenium Hall* (1762) certainly attempted to answer that question in the affirmative. Schellenberg appraises the achievement of Frances Burney who self-consciously developed the unsentimental, 'capacious realism' of the Bluestockings that 'enabled women to look squarely at the realities of female lives' (150). Burney's mature novels, *Cecilia* (1782), *Camilla* (1796), and *The Wanderer; or Female Difficulties* (1814) are all fundamentally concerned with themes of courtship, inheritance, and economic survival, and the psychological and moral pressures on female characters—even, at times, to the point of madness—who try to remain rational and benevolent whilst searching for love and marriage in an unjust society.

Austen's focus upon the 'female difficulties' of courtship, money, and marriage thus came out of a socially and philosophically resonant tradition of realism that, though minute, was never narrow. Her novels were, as Jones indicates, highly topical in the 1810s, not only in their references to the Napoleonic Wars, the Navy, and the slave trade, but also in their alertness to the ways in which this realist inheritance was being challenged by new fictional modes such as the historical novel, the Evangelical novel, and the national tale. Anthony Mandal (2007) has argued that we should regard *Emma* (1816) as an English 'national tale' of a kind, and he also, in this volume, gives an overview of the Evangelical novels with which Austen's work sometimes directly competed. The Evangelical revival of the later eighteenth and early nineteenth century brought with it a new wave of novels with unenticing, abstract titles such as *Discipline, Temper, Duty, Self-Denial,* and *Integrity,* designed to recall men and women to moral seriousness. Many had clear continuities with the Anglican seriousness of the Bluestockings. The Bluestocking Evangelical campaigner Hannah More set the tone in her best-selling *Coelebs in Search of a Wife* (1808), a polite, mildly pious account of a young man's developing sense of his moral and social responsibilities. The most successful of these novels, Mary Brunton's still readable *Self-Control* (1811), presents a heroine for whom female rationality, piety, and self-knowledge are an end in themselves and not just a means to a better marriage (although, after many extreme incidents, she gets both). In *Mansfield Park*, Austen carefully skirts the borders of this Evangelical vogue, with its serious-minded heroine and clergyman hero, but nevertheless asserts, in the interests of a more thoroughgoing realism, a contrasting 'Anglican pragmatics of a liveable morality' (Jones, 291).

In this instance, Austen's originality is thrown into relief by setting her novels within the topography of her own fictional era. While acknowledging the formal, technical, and stylistic innovativeness of her particular kind of 'domestic realism', the volume also situates that realism within the wider context of what Mark Salber Phillips has called the contemporary 'historicisation of everyday life' (2000: 295). Scott himself was one of the first to praise the vividness and precision of Austen's renditions of contemporary common life. He recognized, at least indirectly, that, after generations of courtship novels set in a textureless, generalized 'novel time', there was something new about the tangible surface of Austen's contemporary provincial world. In this sense, Austen's novels partook of his own project to realize temporal depth in fiction, and to recreate the flavour of what were called in this period 'manners', meaning the whole, reticulated social way of being that defines particular groups of people at particular times. 'Manners' were the means by which the later eighteenth- and early nineteenth-century novel became properly 'historical'. Earlier novels had incorporated history as an atmosphere, as an allegory for contemporary times, or as process of change, by representing generational conflict and transition, or orphans and disinherited children creating a new life from their ruptured past. In this period, however, historical writing, in Scotland especially, underwent a process of spectacular development, and historians such as David Hume, William Robertson, and Edward Gibbon presented the past, not as a series of political events, but as a dynamic, stage-by-stage process of economic, social, and cultural evolution. Historians offered novelists a richer account of the past, in which domestic relationships, family structure, courtship, and artistic culture became more intelligible as part of the fabric of earlier forms of society. Ina Ferris shows how, well before Scott, novelists embraced a more vivid, discriminating, and less anachronistic sense of the past. Novels such as Clara Reeve's *The Old English Baron* (1777), Sophia Lee's *The Recess; or, A Tale of Other Times* (1783, 1785), and Jane Porter's *The Scottish Chiefs* (1810) pioneered a new kind of antiquarian romance in which factual detail and fictional elaboration could coexist without danger of cross-contamination. Scott owed something to these fictional portraits of long-gone times and manners, as well as to Gothic and national tales with their more dichotomized or spatially flattened representations of the pre-modern past. Yet Ian Duncan demonstrates that his achievement was qualitatively vastly different, not only on account of his far more encompassing sense of history (reaching out to the social margins of vagrants, Gypsies, outlaws, and Highlanders), but also because of his dynamic sense of historical stages as being always on the cusp of transition from one form of social life to another. Enlightenment history positioned critical retrospection on the evolution of civil society as, in itself, a condition of modernity. In both embracing and complicating this mode of historical consciousness, as Duncan argues, Scott created historical fiction of rare sophistication in which both history and fiction have a role to play in recreating social consensus and attachment to the modern world.

Chronologically speaking, Scott's novels belong both to this volume and to the third volume of the *Oxford History of the Novel*, in which the account of the historical novel continues in a chapter by Richard Maxwell. Scott's fictions were the high-water mark of the British novel as an international phenomenon in terms of subject matter, market reach, and influence, but they also strengthened enormously an association between fiction and national culture. With Scott, the British reading public came into possession of a fictional literature in which it could hear its own voice in the voices of history.

Editorial Note

THE referencing system in this volume employs a combination of footnotes and parenthetical references within the main text. Footnotes are used for first citations of primary texts, comprising original works (novels, memoirs, letters, etc.) and other key works originating from the period covered or earlier: in such instances full descriptions (including date and place of publication) are supplied in this way. Subsequent references to quotations from primary texts are normally given in parenthesis within the text. For the convenience of readers using different editions, volume, book, and chapter numbers are supplied where feasible in addition to the edition-specific page reference (for example, vol. 1, bk 2, ch. 3; 76). This does not apply however to cases in which no such clear divisions exist, nor with regard to citations from original editions (where numbering can be erratic).

In the case of secondary texts (notably modern critical works) a version of the 'MLA system', with parenthetical author–date references keyed to full descriptions in the end Bibliography, is used throughout.

Publication dates given after titles in the text for primary works follow date as found on original editions, even though in a few instances (owing to the then not uncommon practice of post-dating imprints) the first release might have occurred in the preceding year.

Note on the British Currency before Decimalization

B EFORE the introduction of decimal currency into the United Kingdom in 1971, the pound sterling was divided into twenty shillings, with twelve pence (pennies) to the shilling. A guinea was twenty-one shillings. In the present volume we use the conventional abbreviations 's.' for shillings and 'd.' for pence, and prices are given as follows: £1 3s. 6d. (one pound three shillings and sixpence, or more loosely one pound three and six). In decimal terms £1 3s. 6d. is £1.17½p.

Part I

===

Book Production and Distribution

I

Production

JAMES RAVEN

OF the two dozen or so new titles published in Britain in 1750 that might reasonably be categorized as 'novels', only one, the *Revived Fugitive*, actually styled itself 'a novel' on the title page. Printed and sold by J. Sadleir in Liverpool, this slight performance of seventy pages was also the only one of that year's new novels (and of the seventeen further editions of older novels issued that year) to be published in England outside London.[1] One other of the new novels of 1750 was published in Glasgow, and six reprinted titles were issued from Dublin. Most 1750 novels styled themselves not a 'Novel', but 'Memoirs of', a 'History of' (or 'True History of'), a 'Life of', and 'Adventures of' (or 'Life and Adventures of'). Lasting literary fame was rarely the aim. Writers, purveyors, and customers pursued amusement, diversion, fashion, and, all ostentatiously argued, moral instruction. However obvious the antecedents, all contributed to a type of publication declared to be wholly new—and regularly regarded as slipshod and shocking.

By far the most celebrated 'History' of the 1750 season was Henry Fielding's *Tom Jones*, first advertised in December 1749 in four volumes and published by the celebrated Andrew Millar of the Strand. Much humbler, although achieving two separate London editions in that year, was *The Adventures of Mr Loveill*. *Loveill* was more typical of mid-century novels in that it was issued anonymously (by the popular and prolific trade publisher, Mary Cooper of Paternoster Row) and because it has rarely been heard of since.[2] Like the *Nominal Husband*, also issued anonymously that year,[3] the author of *Loveill* thought it necessary to introduce the novel with a defensive and anxious preface, fretting over its potential reception, seeking to persuade of its authenticity, and excusing the motivation of the author. Such prefaces usually positioned the novel in what was trumpeted as an expanding market and often offered self-serving references to other, rival examples of an increasingly popular literary form. As the author of *Loveill* opened the preface, 'A Motive

---

[1] Anon., *Revived Fugitive. A Novel. Translated from the French* (Liverpool: J. Sadleir, 1750).
[2] *The Adventures of Mr Loveill, Interspers'd with many real amours of the modern polite world*, 2 vols (London: M. Cooper, 1750).
[3] *The Nominal Husband: or, Distress'd Innocence* (London: W. Owen, 1750).

extremely different from that of the whole race of modern writers of Memoirs, from the author of *Tom Jones*, down to the gentleman who has lately favoured us with the History of *Charlotte Summers*,[4] has influenced the drawing up of these [adventures]'. The 'story', insists the writer, 'is built not on the rovings of a luxuriant fancy, but on real occurrences'. 'I do confess myself a woman', the writer continues, whether or not this was true (presentation as a woman had proven commercial advantage), and assures readers that 'all that I have aimed at is, to inform the succeeding race of lovers, that vice is folly; and to guard the rest of my own sex from misfortunes'. Her characterizations are presented 'for the public good; as examples and as warnings to ten thousand people, who seem at present sufficiently to want them' (1.[iii], iv, vi). 'A Preface to a new Book is become almost equally customary with a Prologue to a new Play, and is little less expected by the Public', confirmed the author of the *Nominal Husband*. The novel might then respectably be added to 'the Load of Productions with which the Press is continually teeming' (i–ii, ii).

The teeming offspring of the 1750 printing houses had tripled by 1820. Some seventy-three new titles, all reviewed as 'novels' in the periodical reviews, were published in the 1819–20 season. Sixty of the novels were published in London, and included Mrs Meeke's *The Veiled Protectress*, William Parnell's *Maurice and Berghetta*, dedicated 'to the Catholic Priesthood of Ireland', and John William Polidori's *The Vampyre*. Despite the enduring dominance of London, the proportion of new titles published elsewhere in England and Britain had markedly increased since 1750. A single new novel, the anonymous but provocatively titled *The United Irishman*, appeared in Dublin. The Irish reprint industry of the eighteenth century had mostly collapsed after the 1800 Acts of Union (effective from 1 January 1801) and seems also to have deterred the launch of new titles in Dublin. The six new novels issued from Edinburgh included the third series of Walter Scott's *Tales of My Landlord* (the earlier series having appeared in 1816 and 1818). The thirteen 1819–20 titles published in England outside London included imprints from King's Lynn, Derby (two titles), Battle (in Sussex), Gloucester, and Bath. This is an eclectic list, reflecting the new social topography of the novel. A few novels now first appeared (and mostly in very small editions) in resorts, spa towns, and provincial communities, but not so obviously in more ancient and erudite publishing centres outside London, including Oxford, Cambridge, and York.

The broader revolution in book production across all genres is dramatic. Before 1700 up to about 1,800 different printed titles (including the most minor items) were issued annually; by 1820 up to 5,500—and this is simply a crude title count that does not consider the huge increases in the edition sizes of certain types of publication, increases that escalated sharply after 1820. A simple count of titles (including different editions of the same title) based on the online *English Short-Title Catalogue* suggests an average publication

---

[4] *The History of Charlotte Summers, the Fortunate Parish Girl*, 2 vols (London: Corbett, 1749–50).

growth rate of just over 2 per cent per annum for the years between 1740 and 1800, with an exceptional spurt of 3½ per cent in the 1780s. It was only in the 1810s that the production of literature, and notably the novel, temporarily faltered. Many of these new books achieved a fleeting prominence that seemed more voguish than literary. As one observer put it, 'a fashionable writer makes a fashionable book, and creates a number of fashionable readers—readers, who pay more attention to the fashion of the writer, than to the fashion of the book'.[5] According to an even more dismissive reviewer, many new book promotions were nothing less than 'insidious attempts at the purses of the Public'.[6]

The great majority of the new novels of 1819–20 carried either 'novel' or 'tale' in their title. The novel was now an established genre (if, as a result, even more attractive to writers who wished to redirect or subvert the form). Early nineteenth-century British reviewers and advertising booksellers accepted and promoted the 'novel' as a distinct literary category, even though it encompassed a great many narrative forms: fables, romances, biographical and autobiographical memoirs and histories, satirical tales, and exchanges in letters. 'The word novel', wrote the Rev. Edward Mangin in 1808, 'is a generical term; of which romances, histories, memoirs, letters, tales, lives, and adventures, are the species.'[7]

By 1820 also, readers might enjoy an accumulation of critical studies of the novels and even accounts of their production history and domestic and foreign influences. As early as 1785, Clara Reeve, already an accomplished fiction writer, set about chronicling the history of the English novel in her *Progress of Romance*. 'We had early translations of the best Novels of all other Countries,' she concluded, 'but for a long time produced very few of our own.'[8] With exquisite confidence, Reeve argued that English novel writing had reached critical maturity and that this offered the conclusion to her 'investigation of Novels' (1.108). During the next half-century, however, the achievement of Samuel Richardson, Henry Fielding, Eliza Haywood, Tobias Smollett, and Laurence Sterne was massively extended in quantity and range. Quality was a different matter. As already evident to Reeve, these were to be years in which 'the press groaned under the weight of Novels, which sprung up like Mushrooms every year' (2.7).

Unsurprisingly, most novelists during these seventy years belonged to the propertied classes, but among them also numbered humble vicars and curates, sea captains, destitute merchants' wives, high-class prostitutes, overachieving adolescents, and sanctimonious autodidacts. The diversity of writers and circumstances (as described by Peter Garside in the following chapter) corresponded to a range of success and failure. A few novels were

---

[5] Samuel Paterson, *Joineriana: or The Book of Scraps* (London: Joseph Johnson, 1772), 41.

[6] *Biographical and Imperial Magazine*, 3 (1790), 113.

[7] Edward Mangin, *An Essay on Light Reading, as it May Be Supposed to Influence Moral Conduct on Literary Taste* (London: James Carpenter, 1808), 5.

[8] Clara Reeve, *The Progress of Romance, through Times, Countries, and Manners*, 2 vols (Colchester: W. Keymer, 1785), 1.117.

quickly reprinted; others were revived after a few seasons or achieved a limited success in the writer's own circle or locality. Most novels were destined for either a very dusty or a very brief shelf life following a few polite readings by friendly subscribers or meagre outings from a fashionable circulating library (a subject also examined in greater detail by David Allan in Chapter 3).

Quantities

The production history of the novel during these years can be charted by various statistical lists, all of which require strict health warnings for the unwary. The tables below have been compiled from eighteenth- and nineteenth-century review notices, booksellers' and printers' records, advertisements, and term catalogues, followed by extensive searches of *ESTC*, *OCLC World-Cat*, and hands-on stack work in many hundreds of libraries worldwide.[9]

Given that many volumes reviewed as novels no longer survive, additional archival trawls are needed to reconstruct as far as possible details of missing books. Resources range from newspaper advertisements and periodical reviews to references in other surviving works by the same author or publishing bookseller. Where no copy of an edition survives, any bookseller's advertisement has to be supported by other firm evidence of publication (most notably by periodical review verification) before the edition can be included in the title and edition count. Past attempts at compiling these sorts of listings have often been deceived by the puffs of eighteenth-century booksellers, by generic titles in circulating library catalogues, and by attempts of writers of the period to persuade of the existence of an unwritten or unpublished book. The tallies given below exclude former identifications that cannot be proved to have been published, but also include, after consultation of reviews and printing records, novels certainly published but no longer surviving in extant copy. On that basis, we can assert that about 7 per cent of all new novel titles published between 1770 and 1800 are completely lost to us (although publication of these historical bibliographies continues to inspire private collectors to announce ownership of publications thought to be lost and certainly not shelved in an institutional library—often with astonishing results in Internet auction sales).

Statistical graphs charting the 'rise of the novel' are simple but also simplistic. For every general statement there is a caveat. Retrospective bibliography offers profiles of the number of separately (and usually surviving) published titles, but these are no sure indication

---

[9] All are derived and updated from the research offered in Raven (1987) and Garside, Raven, and Schöwerling (2000) (the post-1800 totals as revised by Garside et al. 2004). These also provide the basis for further statistical evidence in this chapter. For the period from 1700 to 1749, see McBurney (1960) and Beasley (1972).

of the total volume of publication given the extreme variation in the size of print runs. The enlargement of the book trade can be very generally plotted by the increase in the publication of separate titles, but estimates based on title counts very rarely take account of the continuing trade in all books, including imported and second-hand books. If it were possible to produce a snapshot of all books and magazines circulating in any given year, it would reveal a mix of new and old, foreign and home-produced, finely bound, incomplete, and damaged.

An additional and evident concern in the counting of novels, including newly published ones, is one of definition. The head-counting of people is fairly reliable, whatever the size and shape of the heads. Novels are not so easy to define. When Charlotte Palmer entitled her publication *It Is and It Is Not a Novel*,[10] she anticipated what now would be called 'crossover fiction' as well as novels commenting on the process of fiction writing. An obvious approach that both simplifies the problem and has the advantage of introducing a particular historical perspective is to follow contemporary designations of the 'novel'. We can at least count the number of different editions of new books that were labelled novels by their authors, booksellers, or reviewers (who contributed to 'novel' sections of latest book listings), even if the word 'novel' did not always appear on the title page itself. Such counts are those provided in the tables below.[11]

The broadly ascendant course of publication is obvious, but the number of new novels issued each year also fluctuated markedly (see Table 1.1). Statistical presentations must also allow for differences between the year cited in the imprints and the actual times of publication. The practice of post-dating was common, designed to extend the currency of the novel. In some cases, novels printed and published in August or even as early as April carried the date of the following year.[12] In addition, a publishing season extended from November to May, spanning the division of the calendar year. Even so, bumper 'imprint years' like 1771 stand out before a steep decline in novel production in the late 1770s followed by a strong rally from the late 1780s. A slight dip in the mid-1790s precedes a late-century surge in novel output. A decline in 1801–2 was followed a few seasons later by an unprecedented peak in 1808.

The annual output of new novel production by title charted in Figure 1.1 shows the general trends. The malaise in new production lasted from about 1775 to 1783, coterminous, it seems, with the American War of Independence. This downturn was perhaps a reaction to a decade of poorly produced novels or to a flood of reprints in the late 1770s

---

[10] Charlotte Palmer, *It Is and It Is Not a Novel*, 2 vols (London: Hookham and Carpenter, 1792).

[11] The criteria by which the novel is defined are discussed in Garside, Raven, and Schöwerling (2000: 1.1–5, 21–39); the totals generally include first editions of novels for juveniles and young persons, but exclude publications more clearly intended to be read to young children.

[12] See, for example, *The Happy Release* (London: F. Noble, 1787), and *The Minor* (London: W. Lane, 1788).

Table 1.1. Publication of new novel titles in Britain and Ireland, 1750–1819

Year	Total	Year	Total	Year	Total	Year	Total	Year	Total	Year	Total	Year	Total
1750	23	1760	35	1770	40	1780	24	1790	74	1800	82	1810	91
1751	23	1761	20	1771	60	1781	22	1791	74	1801	74	1811	80
1752	19	1762	19	1772	41	1782	22	1792	58	1802	61	1812	67
1753	19	1763	18	1773	39	1783	24	1793	45	1803	79	1813	64
1754	30	1764	26	1774	35	1784	24	1794	56	1804	75	1814	63
1755	22	1765	18	1775	31	1785	47	1795	50	1805	76	1815	53
1756	25	1766	27	1776	17	1786	40	1796	91	1806	72	1816	59
1757	26	1767	33	1777	18	1787	51	1797	79	1807	69	1817	55
1758	16	1768	37	1778	16	1788	80	1798	75	1808	111	1818	62
1759	28	1769	44	1779	18	1789	71	1799	99	1809	79	1819	73
1750–9	231	1760–9	277	1770–9	315	1780–9	405	1790–9	701	1800–9	778	1810–19	667
												1750–1819	3374

satisfying the market. More certainly, we can chart the rise and development of novel production in Britain from the late 1780s in relation to six general considerations: a new generation of writers, the way in which certain reprints grew stale, the development of new circulating libraries, the increase in translated and cheap borrowings from foreign novels, the greater emphasis on the female and on the country market, and finally the marketing practices of a new generation of bookseller-publishers. All these features continued to sustain novel publication in the early decades of the nineteenth century, although the 'rise' posited in so many general surveys was by no means linear or without severe setbacks and troughs. The decline in the 1810s (a total production 15 per cent lower than that of the previous decade) clearly related to the economic downturn and social disturbances of the long war years. Moreover, the high price of paper and production continued to constrain the market.

In many ways the seventy-year period considered here might be regarded as a continuing publishing 'ancien régime' in which the apparent technological breakthrough of the steam-driven printing press in the 1810s was so slowly adopted and was so circumscribed by high production costs that no real market advance was possible before 1820, and, indeed, in many ways not until the transport and distribution revolution of the 1830s. The introduction of steam-driven papermaking machines and printing presses shattered the principal technological constraint on the expansion of publishing. Mechanized papermaking first became commercially viable in 1807, and by 1825 half of all paper in England was manufactured by machine. In 1814, the year that Jane Austen's *Mansfield Park* was

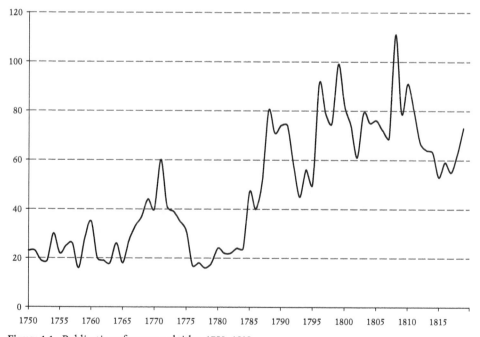

Figure 1.1. Publication of new novel titles, 1750–1819

published, *The Times* became the first publication printed by Koenig's new steam press, allowing the printing of 1,000 impressions each hour. The bookseller Charles Knight declared that 'what the printing press did for the instruction of the masses in the fifteenth century, the printing machine is doing for the nineteenth' (see Weedon 2003: 64–76, 70). In the two decades after 1820, new industrial processes and the use of cheaper raw materials hugely improved the return on publishing booksellers' invested capital and lowered their unit costs. Nevertheless, what *The Times* called 'the greatest improvement connected with printing since the discovery of the art itself' was not used for many other such publications until the 1820s.

Given the cost of paper, type, and labour, publication remained a risky enterprise, and especially the publication of novels. Unsold copies represented capital tied up in expensive material outlay and only assured market custom allowed the publication of larger editions. As a result, small editions characterized most publication of new novels (and indeed even most subsequent editions). Before 1820 most editions of novels continued to be produced in editions of no more than 500. Commercial prudence certainly affected the size of novel editions and even some of the most successful titles were issued in editions of 750 or 800. Risks were taken with an 1801 2,000-copy edition of Samuel Jackson Pratt's *Pity's Gift*, first published in 1798, and with an 1802 edition of the anonymous *Village Orphan* (1799), printed in 1,500 copies. Even so, publishers of many later editions remained generally cautious. The Longman 1804 fifth edition of Jane West's *Gossip's Story* (first printed in 1796) was limited to a standard 500 copies.[13] Risk had to be measured carefully. All remembered the sorry history of Andrew Millar's first 1751–2 edition of Fielding's *Amelia* issued in two impressions totalling 8,000 copies. Millar had hoped to emulate the runaway success of *Tom Jones* (10,000 copies printed between 1749 and 1750), but was left embarrassed, with copies still for sale ten years later. It was Mary Robinson's own decision that Thomas Hookham should have 1,500 copies printed of her 1794 *Widow*, a misjudgement that, despite initial sales, brought eventual disaster (Fergus and Thaddeus 1988: 196).

Between 1770 and 1800 about 60 per cent of all novel titles (and in some years, two-thirds) were never reprinted, even in Ireland where many novels were reprinted in Dublin (and occasionally elsewhere). Because, before the first day of 1801, Ireland was outside the Union of England and Scotland, with no copyright law in force, Dublin booksellers were able to publish reprints more cheaply than elsewhere. These were apparently for illegal import to England and Scotland, but many Irish publishers also supplied to an Irish home market. Most second editions also seemed to satisfy demand with ease. Of the 40 per cent of new novel titles reprinted in this period, fewer than 5 per cent reached a third edition or further edition, and, at least before 1800, the majority of 'second' editions were simply unauthorized Dublin reprints.

---

[13] University of Reading, Longman Archives, Impression Book H5, fols 8, 27, 104, 117.

Some of the demand for further editions came from overseas. Until the early 1790s, the overwhelming strength of book exports to North America, the Caribbean, and India, together with the handicapped state of colonial publishing, ensured that both individuals and institutions were supplied by London and other British booksellers. Only from the 1790s were American editions of British novels published in significant numbers. Between 1770 and 1790 a mere three novels were reprinted on the other side of the Atlantic, but some thirty-five novels first printed in Britain during the 1790s (or 5 per cent of the total) appeared in an American edition in the same season as their London publication. Thereafter, same- or next-season American reprintings increased to nearly 10 per cent of all novels first printed in Britain in the 1800s and 18 per cent in the 1810s (Garside 2000: 98; see also Verhoeven, Chapter 31).

This technological and economic regime does at least mean that distortions to calculations of overall book production caused by the variation in the size of editions (and particularly of successful later editions) are less damaging to estimates of novel publication than to those of some other genres. The commercial guardedness in the novel market contrasts remarkably with the monster and repeatedly reprinted editions of successful school and service books of the time. Playbooks might reach editions of 2,000 copies or more. *Emma*, Jane Austen's largest first edition, was also of 2,000. Histories with proven appeal might also in some cases be issued in 4,000-copy editions, but these pall before the huge printings commissioned, for example, by Thomas Longman II for staple titles like Isaac Watts's *Hymns*, Samuel Johnson's *Dictionary* in quarto, and numerous instruction books, such as an 18,000-copy edition of Daniel Fenning's spelling manual.

The sentimental novel, the 'spy' novel, and, from the 1780s, the Gothic novel, counted heavily in these tallies. Gothic novels, in particular, amounted to about a third of all new novels published between 1796 and 1806 and a quarter of all those published between 1800 and 1810. Thereafter, the genre joined the spy and sentimental novels in steady decline. In many ways, however, the most distinctive subset of novels before 1800 was of those written in letters. As more fully described by Nicola Watson in Chapter 20, the epistolary novel in English enjoyed a distinguished history from the early models of Richardson to the translations of Françoise, Madame de Grafigny, Jeanne Marie le Prince de Beaumont, and Marie-Jeanne Riccoboni. Between 1750 and 1760 new novels in letters averaged no more than a tenth of the annual total of new fiction, but by the mid-1760s a quarter and by 1767 more than a third of the annual crop of new novels were epistolary. During the 1770s and 1780s over 40 per cent of all novels were published in letter form (and in seven of the years between 1776 and 1784 comprised at least half the annual novel output). In 1776, a year of relatively few publications, more than two-thirds of the novels were epistolary. A turning point seems to have been reached in 1791 when only fifteen (or about a fifth) of the seventy-four novels published that year were in letters, and this proportion remained about the same until a further decline to some 10 per cent of the total between 1797 and 1799. By the final years of the century, the epistolary form had lost its popularity, swamped it seems by the diversity and directness of new historical and Gothic narratives that were ill-suited to relation by letters.

Such title counting also revises histories of the relative popularity of novelists and the creation of a particular literary canon. Among the most reprinted novels of the period were those mimicking the most fêted and also well-promoted offerings from a range of prolific but now forgotten writers. Undistinguished imitations of Richardson notably proliferated in the 1750s and 1760s, but even more remarkable (and almost unnoticed by later commentators) was a later flock of would-be Frances Burneys. Of many examples, *Harcourt: A Sentimental Novel* (1780) was falsely claimed to be 'by the authoress of Evelina', and the *Critical's* reviewer identified *Oswald Castle* (1788) as 'a production of the Cecilia school'. Other Burneyana of the 1788 season included Anne Hughes's *Henry and Isabella* and Anna Maria Mackenzie's *Retribution*. A year later, even Elizabeth Bonhote, according to her *Critical* reviewer, 'steps too nearly in the steps of Cecilia'.[14] By contrast, admitted imitation of Fielding and Smollett was slender.

In production terms, relative rankings of the leading novelists will always be imprecise. Further editions varied in size, and many, where no extant copy survives, might only have been bookseller's puffs. We can at least show (as later chapters will amplify) that the most reprinted novelists of the third quarter of the eighteenth century were Sterne, Fielding, Haywood, Smollett, Defoe, Riccoboni, Kimber, and Sarah Fielding (probably in that order), while succeeding generations of novel readers favoured Ann Radcliffe, Burney, Henry Mackenzie, and Walter Scott. The roll call of the most productive novelists, however, suggests quite another cast—one led by, among others, Stéphanie Genlis, Barbara Hofland, Isabella Kelly Hedgeland, August Lafontaine, Francis Lathom, Mrs Meeke, and Henry Summersett (see also Garside, Chapter 2).

It is hardly surprising that the great majority of novels were first published in London. By the early nineteenth century some 90 per cent of all new British books were published in the capital and the mushrooming numbers of provincial booksellers mostly served not as publishers but as the distribution agents of new books. Many were also newspaper printers (and the same newspapers acted as advertising platforms for the London publishers). Nevertheless, as the survey of the 1819–20 season has already shown, novel printing in Scotland and especially in some English provincial towns had developed, if modestly. Publishing and book trade activity in Edinburgh and Glasgow certainly advanced during the second half of the eighteenth century, and, after 1800, general book and magazine publication increased in Manchester, Liverpool, Aberdeen, Perth, Newcastle, Leeds, and many other cities. The position of London in both book distribution and manufacture was rearranged for the first time since the Restoration Printing Acts (also known as the 'Licensing Laws') and arguably since the invention of printing. Scots like Millar,

---

[14] *Critical Review*, 66 (December 1788), 503; 68 (November 1789), 407.

Alexander and John Donaldson, John [Mc]Murray I, and William Strahan made their fortunes in the eighteenth-century London book trade, and by 1800 cross-border partnerships flourished. The first two John Murrays cooperated with William Creech, Charles Elliot, and later William Blackwood in Edinburgh. Scottish branch shops and agencies were established in London, including Elliot and Kay operating in the Strand from 1787, and the later enterprise of Baldwin, Cradock, and Coat, London agents to Blackwood (who had himself started out as agent to John Murray II in 1811). English provincial novel publishing in the 1790s was led by Bath, but also included the work of publishing booksellers in Brentford, Birmingham, Bristol, Chelsea, Newcastle, Norwich, Shrewsbury, Southampton, Wakefield, and York, among others. Even so, relatively few novels originated from presses in English towns other than London. To put the strength of London novel publishers more simply: in 1775, the year of Jane Austen's birth, only one of the season's thirty-one new novel titles was not printed in London, and in 1817, the year of her death, only three of fifty-five.

In order to expand their trade, many novel publishers and booksellers expertly practised what today would be called product branding. Presentational strategies, together with innovative advertising techniques, played an important part in encouraging demand, both among those already accustomed to acquiring literature and also among those new to the purchase of print, or at least unfamiliar with books other than the penny chapbook, church Bible, or prayer book. The juxtaposition of advertisements for very different titles is striking testimony to booksellers' awareness of the diversity of readers' tastes. The increasing influence of critical reviewing could also be turned to advertising advantage. Many of the brasher booksellers 'puffed' works by citing from recent or imaginary notices. Critics certainly claimed that booksellers were fabricating the tributes.[15] By the late 1780s the great novel entrepreneur, William Lane, had so perfected the technique that end-page or prefatory advertisements to his works bear a striking resemblance to the modern book-jacket with its battery of short but glorious quotations from respected authorities. As practised by almost all publishers, the reliable and eye-catching line 'This Day is Published' represented (to the confusion of many modern readers) an announcement in the continuous present usually to be repeated the next day, next week, or even in successive weeks thereafter.

Advertising was expensive. Henry Woodfall, publishing his *Public Advertiser* from his large shop at the corner of Ivy Lane and Paternoster Row, took in advertisements 'of moderate length' at three shillings each. If 'moderate' was average and charging remained proportionate to size, then many of the full column booksellers' advertisements must have cost more than a guinea. Historians of the newspaper industry have argued that the direct profits accruing from advertisements were vital to newspapers

---

[15] *Monthly Review*, 80 (March 1789), 288.

unable to survive by sales alone. Even so, the costs of advertising in newspapers, catalogues, and separate notices proved a shock for many authors. In 1816 John Murray II charged Jane Austen the extraordinary sum of £50 for advertising *Emma* in the first nine months of publication, some of which was a charge for advertising in Murray's own catalogue (Fergus 1991: 21).

Given the booksellers' need to sell as quickly as possible the whole edition in which they had usually invested so much, the efficiency and cost of distribution remained critical. By catalogues, reviews, advertisements, and a variety of ingenious puffs, print itself was instrumental in promoting print across a range of prices and formats as a commodity. The newspaper advertisements were pivotal to such marketing, and many booksellers adopted the public postal service to assist with newsprint distribution. Even so, for more than a century, the fastest, most direct means of sending stock to provincial retailers and customers remained the common London carriers. Books and magazines left on the coaches leaving Ludgate and the Poultry to travel to distant parts. The great coaching inns acted in some respects as the models for the great Victorian train stations from the mid-century, located on each side of London and serving their own distinct routes. Much of the direct retailing also centred on the active second-hand market (the grander end nurtured by auctions and fixed-price catalogue sales) as well as on the sales of lesser productions, notably the thousands of almanacs, pamphlets, and chapbooks peddled by chapmen and general traders.

Publishers, Booksellers, and Printers

Almost all publishing booksellers of the period partly or wholly financed the publication of novels at some point in their careers. But it is also important (particularly given imprecision about this in the past) to consider the distinctions between eighteenth-century publishing booksellers, printers, and non-printing publishing booksellers. Differences within the different trades as practised from the late fifteenth to the mid-seventeenth century are somehow lost in the descriptions of the hugely enlarged and innovative trade of the eighteenth century. Many publishing booksellers issuing new novels did operate a printing press, but other notable publishers of novels, from the Nobles in the mid-eighteenth century to Thomas Norton Longman at the close of the century, did not undertake their own printing. Many novel publishers might be seen as commodity producers and sellers, given that most of them did not operate a printing press in their own premises (nor knew how to operate one). Rather, these entrepreneurs employed contract printers. Many of those associated with novel publication, such as John and Francis Noble, John Cooke, John Coote, James Harrison, and William Lane, had not been trained within and were not members of the traditional book trade guild, the Stationers' Company. Some belonged to other companies or to no company at all.

Unfortunately, we cannot now identify the majority of the contract printers who were employed on the common novel, although a few significant partnerships are apparent (and more will be so in the future, as comparative research continues). The Nobles, Cooke, and Coote, for example, favoured the printers Dryden Leach (father and son) of Chancery Lane and then Fleet Street, and William Adlard also of Fleet Street. The Leachs and Adlard produced beautiful presswork, with distinctive and innovative ornamentation, generous spacing and wide margins, even if these also became the butt of reviewers' jokes about more blank space and frippery than text. Thomas Egerton used Charles Roworth, a popular printer trading on his own from at least 1799 until 1832 and then with his sons for at least a decade more. Roworth was to print fourteen of the twenty-seven volumes of the various editions of Jane Austen's novels published in her lifetime. The first editions of both *Pride and Prejudice* and *Mansfield Park* were printed by both Roworth and George Sidney of the Strand, each taking responsibility for different volumes in the set. John Murray II, publishing *Emma* in 1816, continued to employ Roworth, but again, as was common, shared the work with another printer, in this case J. Moyes of Hatton Garden. When, from 1794, Thomas Norton Longman began occasional publication of novels (perhaps as a result of the retirement of his father and his recent partnership with Owen Rees), he employed many of the leading printers of London, notably Andrew Strahan and George Woodfall. In the case of Pratt's 1797 *Family Secrets*, Longman divided the manuscript between four different printers who produced the five different volumes in an edition of more than 1,000 copies. William Chapman, stationer of Cheapside, supplied all the paper, with Longman acting as distributor.

Some novel publishers prospered; many novel printers did not. It was John Cooke's publisher son Charles, not his printers, Leach or Adlard, who built a grand folly of a mansion at Walthamstow. Although modest compared to both James Dodsley, who died in 1797 worth more than £70,000 and the owner of a landed estate near Chislehurst, and to Thomas Cadell whose effects were estimated to have been worth at least £150,000 at his death in 1802, Lane, the specialist novel producer, died with a fortune of about £17,500. The further and crucial feature of the businesses founded by Hookham, Lane, and then Henry Colburn (at least until the end of the 1810s) was the extent to which their publishing and retail operations turned on the success of their own circulating libraries and the supply of ready-made fiction and belles lettres libraries to other booksellers and new proprietors. In 1770 one author, making an optimistic estimate of total edition size, suggested that 400 of every 1,000 copies of novels were sold to circulating libraries.[16] In 1790 Lane claimed 10,000 volumes in an advertisement for his 'General and Encreasing Circulating Library', increasing a year later to 60,000 volumes after his purchase of the

---

[16] Elizabeth and Richard Griffith, *A Series of Genuine Letters between Henry and Frances*, 6 vols (London: W. Johnston, 1767–70), 5.15.

stock of John Walter's Logographic Press. Lane's *Minerva Catalogue* of 1802 lists 17,000 separate titles. Hookham's 1794 *Catalogue* lists 8,866 titles, 14 per cent of which are fiction. As David Allan demonstrates in Chapter 3, and as Jane Austen wrote in 1814, given the high price of new novels, readers were 'more ready to borrow & praise, than to buy'.[17]

Despite the promotion of new literature as fashionable and expensive delicacies, authors (and especially novelists) and their publishers also suffered from much poor-quality printing. Examples of badly executed novel printing are common. Only a single copy survives of Judith Alexander's 1789 *The Young Lady of Fortune*, printed in two volumes 'for the Author' by Levy Alexander, a Jewish printer of Bishopsgate Street. The printing is execrable. At the beginning of every gathering the pages are illegible, suggesting a damaged printing press at that position on the forme. Even where the printed impression was satisfactory, other evidence of rushed production can be found from almost all booksellers. Somehow, the Fleet Street bookshop of Thomas Lowndes (or the printers he contracted) managed to transpose some final gatherings from one volume to the other when sewing and binding Miss Elliott's 1780 *Relapse*. 'The printer's blunders, added to the author's, render the story often unintelligible,' wrote the *Critical* in 1789 of *The Ill Effects of a Rash Vow*, an anonymous Minerva Press publication of that year.[18]

Other horrors resulted from accidents in the press room or from the ill-conceived intervention of editing booksellers. Writing for the *Monthly Review*, Samuel Badcock reported that Lady Mary Hamilton had complained that seventy-five pages of the original manuscript for what proved to be her last novel, *The Life of Mrs Justman* (1782), had been accidentally burnt by the printer. 'We have seldom seen any thing so mangled and mutilated', lamented Badcock.[19] Even distinguished authors of these quickly produced novels enjoyed little apparent influence over typographical matters and book design. Many writers, the victims of unintentional outcomes, blamed the booksellers. The more informed held the printers to be solely responsible, even though it might be argued that financing (or part-financing) publishing booksellers might have supervised their printers more carefully. John Murray II's literary adviser, William Gifford, wrote to him in on 29 September 1815 in praise of *Pride and Prejudice* (sent to Murray by Austen), but found it 'wretchedly printed, and so pointed as to be almost unintelligible' (see Smiles 1891: 1.282). After *Emma* was published by Murray in December 1815, he issued a second edition of *Mansfield Park* in the New Year, improving on the badly printed 1814 Egerton edition.

Whatever the failings of certain printers and the hardships of certain novelists, for consumers of these novels, possession of a beautiful thing had its own importance. Botched printing was a recurrent disappointment, but well-executed typographical

---

[17] Letter to Fanny Knight, 30 November 1814, in Deirdre Le Faye (ed.), *Jane Austen's Letters*, 3rd edn (Oxford and New York: Oxford University Press, 1995), 287.

[18] *Critical Review*, 67 (February 1789), 153.

[19] *Monthly Review*, 66 (June 1782), 474.

design elevated the representation of dialogue or offered distinctive running heads, chapter breaks, and page layouts. All added to the appreciation of the novel. To read was to be involved in a tactile experience of handling the text, of valuing and actually feeling a good binding, good paper, and good type impression. Both the high price of new novels and the limits of literacy determined readership boundaries, but these can never be clear-cut. Purchases of non-essential goods depend upon individual taste as much as supply, opportunity, alternative spending attractions, and the fundamental level of income. What is at least clear is that the lure of novel publication attracted—with a few important exceptions—all enterprising booksellers in late eighteenth- and early nineteenth-century London and many towns besides.

More than sixty different booksellers were the first-named publishers in the imprints of novels published between 1750 and 1770, and 200 others were listed as partners or in other ways that implied financial involvement. In the following decades the number of different firms involved continued to increase, although many booksellers also claimed more specialist associations and about twenty booksellers became known as leading novel producers. In total, more than 500 firms were involved in the publication of novels between 1770 and 1820, many of them short-lived and many responsible for the printing or publication of no more than one novel title. During the final quarter of the eighteenth century, four particular firms, all in London, boosted publication totals: Thomas Hookham, the Robinsons, the long-established Noble brothers John and Francis (Francis until 1789), and, from 1775 itself, the newcomer and greatest novel manufacturer of all, William Lane.

Certain important publishing houses are poorly represented among listed booksellers of novels. Only three novels were issued in this period by the devoutly Anglican Rivington family, publishers of more than 7,000 different titles between 1711 and 1810. This select trio included Charles Moser's 1797 *Moral Tales*, said by the *Monthly* to 'uniformly tend to promote the cause of good morality',[20] and the even more pious and influential *Emily* written by Henry Kett and published in 1809. Thomas Longman II, nephew to the founder of the house, issued only one work that can count as a novel (a highly moralistic tale 'for the benefit of intelligent servants' in 1787), and that was produced in combination with the publishing booksellers Thomas Cadell and the family firm of George Robinson in Paternoster Row (Garside, Raven, and Schöwerling 2000: 1.391—entry 1787: 4). This was followed by some twenty-four Longman novel titles between 1794 and 1799, all following the withdrawal of Thomas II from business in about 1792. By contrast, the novels published by Cadell and by his successors, his son Thomas and his partner William Davies, are a select group (which Jane Austen, of course, hoped to join) and included the novels of Henry Mackenzie, Charles Johnstone, and Charlotte Smith, translations of Wieland

---

[20] *Monthly Review*, n.s., 25 (March 1798), 346–7.

and Grafigny, Burney's *Cecilia* and *Camilla*, and almost no completely anonymous or poorly reviewed volumes. Cadell also sustained a spirited list of authors thought worthy of encouragement, including Alexander Bicknell, Elizabeth Blower, Frances Brooke, Sophia Lee, Charlotte Lennox, Dr John Moore, and Helen Maria Williams.

Table 1.2 lists the most productive of those primarily responsible for the publication of the novels. All were London booksellers, with one nineteenth-century exception (William Blackwood of Edinburgh, prefiguring the continuing advance of Edinburgh publishers after 1820). This is hardly surprising, given the long-standing dominance of London in publishing, but the neighbourhoods of the booksellers are also significant.

Table 1.2. Leading British novel publishers, 1750–1819, by publication of new novel titles

Publishing concern	1750–9	1760–9	1770–9	1780–9	1790–9	1800–9	1810–19
Thomas Becket / Abraham de Hondt		25	17				
(Becket)				3			
John Bell			9		30	3	
John Bew			21	24	10		
William Blackwood							7
Thomas Cadell			16	14	4		
(Cadell and Davies)				14	9	7	
Henry Colburn and Co.						16	43
Mary Cooper	18	2					
Benjamin Crosby and Co.				12	43	13	
Robert / James Dodsley	6	19	11	8	1		
Thomas Hookham			5	41	19		
(and Carpenter)					35		
(Thomas Hookham Jr & Co.)							9
James Fletcher Hughes						77	16
William Lane / A. K. Newman			3	80	217	214	163
Thomas Longman and Co.				1	24	53	60
Thomas Lowndes and Co.	2	19	22	8	6		
John and Francis Noble	24	38	38	21			
George Robinson and Co.			14	34	54	23	9
John Roson			18				
Sherwood and Co.						4	37
Henry Symonds				6	23	16	
Thomas Vernor		1	9	4	5		
(and Thomas Hood)					27	13	1
George Whittaker and Co.							4

Excluding the appearance of these booksellers' names in the 'sold by' advertisements in novels when not also cited in the actual imprint. Some of the novels, jointly financed, appear more than once in this table.

Some, like the firms of George Robinson and John Bew, operated from Paternoster Row, by 1800 the main novel-publishing street in London, close to the traditional stationery and bookselling centre of St Paul's Churchyard. Other booksellers, like Hookham (with his partner James Carpenter) and the Nobles, set up shop in the newly built and fashionable squares and lanes of the West End. Still others, like Lane and his Minerva Press in Leadenhall Street, made an address famous despite an unusual site. Some of the leading publishers of novels worked within the established network and even as prominent members of the Stationers' Company; others seemed to relish challenging the book trade establishment and made the popular novel a weapon in their battle for commercial and public success. Self-publicists like the Nobles, Lane, and Hookham and Carpenter can be credited with pioneering efforts in the establishment of commercial circulating libraries and in the publication of fashionable, almost production line novels. The success of the Nobles, Hookham, and their rivals was carried forward in the next century by James Fletcher Hughes (until his 1808 bankruptcy) and by Lane's underrated successor at the Minerva, A. K. Newman, challenged by Henry Colburn from the 1810s and especially during the 1820s. Although much of the published writing was formulaic, it is also important to recognize the variety of the productions from these houses, and especially from the Minerva Press, whose authors included Robert Bage and whose later productions at least gained some excellent (as well as some excoriating) critical reviews. As *The Morning Chronicle* wrote in 1793, 'That this may be called the Novel Age, we have copied the List of one Publisher only, in London, within the space of a year, namely, Lane, at the Minerva, Leadenhall Street' (see Neiman 2012). In response to the development of the novel market, certain of the more established and reputable firms, most notably Longmans, also made significant investments in fiction publication.

The majority of booksellers were apparently not averse to publishing novels when the purchase of rights was so cheap or the pockets of certain authors so deep. It was certainly one reason for the establishment of William Lane as the leading novel publisher in Britain in the 1780s. A decade later, his dominance was overwhelming. During the 1790s, Lane's Minerva Press published one third of all new novel titles in London, even if few were reprinted. By the 1810s the firm, directed by A. K. Newman after Lane's retirement and then death in 1814, was responsible for almost a quarter of all new fiction titles of the decade. The Minerva's nearest competitor, Longmans, published some 9 per cent of the total. Newman, who retired in 1848, continued the 'Minerva' name until 1820. During the 1790s, non-fiction comprised more than a quarter of all Lane titles, but the writing was rarely distinguished and continuing attacks on circulating libraries and popular novels ensured that the Minerva remained an easy target. In Jane Austen's *Northanger Abbey* (1818) the nine 'horrid' novels enthused over by the foolish Isabella Thorpe were all authentic titles and six of them were published by Lane.

Although circumstantial evidence is scarce, few booksellers seem to have turned down a novel if financing were available. We cannot, of course, know for certain how many manuscripts of authors looking for booksellers' support were refused, and the majority of negotiations over publication where the bookseller acted wholly or even in part as financing publisher are obscure. Few letters survive between first-time or even popular novelists and booksellers, and refusals (such as that of Joseph Trapp's 'Perverted Clergyman', declined and confiscated by the notorious bookseller, the Rev. Dr John Trusler) are rarely glimpsed. In his own novel, Trusler even suggested that underhand booksellers might agree to print a novel at the author's expense and then print half as many again, selling, moreover, the booksellers' portion first and then claiming unsold copies as entirely from the number paid for by the author.[21] Where a novel was 'printed for the author' the bookseller often acted as little more than a vanity press, although in some cases authorial risk-taking did pay off. Although often disguised in part or whole by the wording of the imprint, many publications were vanity productions in which the author underwrote all or most of the edition of some 500 or (more daringly) 750 copies. To most booksellers, the acceptance of such a commission must have seemed like jobbing printing. Of the total number of first editions of novels published in the 1780s and 1790s, 7 per cent were described as 'printed for the author'. These must also be minimum figures, when many title pages, such as Mary Robinson's *Widow* of 1794, hide known commission agreements 'on account of the author' where the publisher-writer assumed responsibility for any loss. The most common agreements, at least before the early nineteenth century, and certainly for first-time writers, were outright copyright sale, fully self-financing deals (authors acting as publishers themselves) in which the author bore liability for all losses, and varied subscription schemes. These arrangements are further discussed in the following chapter on 'Authorship'.

Borrowing from abroad—that is, translation—is the final important feature of novel publication in these years. Although associated with imported fiction from Continental Europe (more fully considered in Mander, Chapter 32), declared but sometimes also brazen and silent translation remained a separate operation and resort. We can only guess at the exact number of novels directly translated from or very largely based on foreign originals. Elizabeth Helme, for example, insisted that in addition to being the acknowledged author of ten novels and three translations, she had 'translated sixteen volumes for different booksellers without my name'.[22] Some translations were also made indirectly (a German novel via a French translation, for example) with conflicting evidence about the text used for the translation, whatever the title page or puffing advertisement declared. We can at least show that more than a tenth of all novel titles first published in Britain in

---

[21] John Trusler, *Modern Times, or the Adventures of Gabriel Outcast*, 3 vols (London: Logographic Press, 1785), 3.39.

[22] Papers of the Royal Literary Fund (British Library), case 97, item 2, letter of 20 October 1803.

this period were translations from Continental novels. Some of the source fiction was elderly and obscure, almost all translation from the 1750s until the mid-1790s was from the French, and foreign dependency was especially marked in the early years. At least 95 (or 18 per cent) of the 531 novels (including further editions) published in Britain between 1750 and 1769 were translations. Of these, eighty-four were from the French, two from the Spanish, and only nine from other languages.

In the 1770s and 1780s a few more novels were translated from the German, but it was a popular source only at the end of the eighteenth century and at the beginning of the next. In 1794 translations from the German exceeded those from other languages for the first time, but the revolution was short-lived. Within a few seasons French translations resumed ascendancy, accounting for at least seventy-four of the total 778 new novels published in English between 1800 and 1809, and twenty-one of the 667 new titles published in the 1810s. Many translations hid attempts by authors to disguise plagiarism (and lack of imagination), but their attraction to bookseller-publishers was also evident. Second-rate novels could be translated by ill-paid hacks with relative ease and cheapness. Booksellers paid most novel writers a pittance for their original manuscript, after which they had no rights to any further profit, but even this expense was avoided if the text was borrowed from abroad. Much translation was the resort of indigent writers and scholars huddled in Grub Street garrets or moonlighting from poorly paid clerical positions. Although beyond the remit of this chapter, we should also note that the literary traffic across the English Channel was far from one way. Indeed, in reviewing one of the imports—*The Innocent Rivals* (1786)—the *Critical* referred to a cross-Channel battle, each side capturing each other's voguish texts. Many English novels of the late eighteenth century were quickly translated into German, French, and other languages, and of the 1,421 new novel titles known to have been published in Britain between 1770 and 1800, 500 are known to have been translated into French or German before 1850. Of the 1,445 new novel titles known to have been published in Britain between 1800 and 1819, 167 (at least) were translated into French or German before 1850. Translations into French outnumber those into German by nearly two-to-one in the 1800s, and by more than two-to-one in the 1810s.

Prices and Properties

The production of novels in small editions minimized risks, but constriction also enabled artful price setting. Not that printing and efforts at typographical distinctiveness came cheaply—and one production cost, that of paper, proved a further critical variable. The prices of new novels increased gradually from the late 1780s until a far steeper acceleration in nominal prices after 1800. The 2*s*. 6*d*. norm for sewed (unbound) novel volumes continued through most of the 1780s, but during 1787 a handful of volumes, in sets or separately, were advertised at 3*s*. and even 3*s*. 6*d*. sewed. What was to be a long-running increase in the price of novels resulted from the increase by about a third in the labour costs of composition and press work between about 1785 and 1810, but more importantly from the doubling in the price of quality paper between about 1793 and 1801. The average price for a new three-volume novel rose from 12s. (1802–5), 13s. 6d. (1806–7), and 15s. (1808–12) to 18s. (1813–17).

In the fashionable novel market, other production decisions followed from high retail pricing. Duodecimo proved the favoured format for popular book production, but octavo was also adopted when booksellers aimed to give publications a certain distinction, even though this format still accounted for only just over 4 per cent of total novel output in the 1810s. In the same decade, the three-decker (three-volume) novel also began an ascendancy that dominated almost to the end of the century. In some cases, the three-decker promoted more efficient as well as more elegant typographical composition when, in difficult times, the amount of text per page was increased. A three-volume novel advertised as sewed in blue paper wrapping or in boards might cost an additional 2s. bound in calf and lettered (and, if available, a further shilling or more with gilt edges). By the end of the eighteenth century more volumes seem to have been sold already bound. Titles were often marketed as 'sold, bound, unless otherwise stated', but even in the 1810s a common advertised price remained that of the volume sewed in paper or boards, allowing the purchaser to have the book bound according to his or her choice. The other conspicuous production decision resulting from high pricing was the distribution of the text over more than one volume. The greater spacing of text attempted to ensure, at standard pricing per volume, greater returns from retail or from library subscriptions and charges, but it was achieved at great critical cost. Complaints about bloated novels pepper the reviews.

The additional costs of attempting to maintain elegant presentation explain John Aikin's 1812 caution that 'typographical luxury…joined to the necessary increase of expence in printing, has so much enhanced the price of new books as to be a material obstacle to the indulgence of a laudable and reasonable curiosity by the reading Publick'.[23] In 1811, Egerton priced Austen's three-volume *Sense and Sensibility* (printed in a modest edition of 750) at 15s.; the same bookseller sold *Pride and Prejudice* two years later for 18s. for the three volumes (as he did *Mansfield Park* the year after that). In 1816, during difficult economic conditions and at a low point in general novel production, John Murray II reflected both rising costs and his own higher pricing by selling *Emma*, also in three volumes, for 21s. In 1818 (against a general recovery in economic fortunes) the four-volume set of *Northanger Abbey* and *Persuasion* retailed at 24s. in boards. As a result of such high pricing, the increasing number of new novels sold in the first decades of the nineteenth century represented a notable expansion of the numbers of books bought by and for an

[23] In John Nichols, *Literary Anecdotes of the Eighteenth Century*, 9 vols (London: Nichols, Son, and Bentley, 1812–15), 3.464.

already book-reading section of the population, rather than simply a great expansion in at least new book purchasing among those of small income. For those of modest means, book-buying was increasingly concentrated on a few prized purchases—perhaps an instruction manual, a recommended work of improvement or biblical commentary, or, certainly by the 1810s, cheaper reprints, often of ancient origin. In the publication of novels, the obvious exceptions to these production and market profiles were first, the cheap and serial republication from the final quarter of the eighteenth century of older novel titles, and second, new publications by instalment, increasing at the end of this period and designed to distribute both production costs and the outlay on the purchase over a longer period.

The alterations in production also resulted from changing considerations of the holding of literary property. During the second half of the eighteenth century, increased demand for books boosted commerce within the book trade in the copyright sales relating to particular titles. Such sales were almost exclusively post-publication between publishing booksellers. One contemporary commentator, Thomas Mortimer, despaired of calculating ownership of shares in copyrights because they were so greatly divided and exchanged hands so rapidly.[24] Familiar as well as more obscure names featured as powerful investors in copyright, including Jacob Robinson, Thomas Longman, the Rivingtons, Millar, Thomas Cadell, Benjamin Dod, and later Joseph Johnson. The worth of these rights accumulated remarkably. The total value of John Rivington's share in trade books amounted to £3,906 in 1760, £3,909 in 1761, £3,636 in 1762, and £5,324 in 1772 (Rivington 1919: 71). We shall never be sure of the worth of the investment in copyrights in total. The most helpful estimate is Cadell's 1785 report that the total value of all copyrights then owned by British booksellers amounted to £200,000 (of which he and Strahan, he said, owned more than a quarter).[25]

In the production of novels, the outstanding feature of the book trade copyright sales was the non-appearance of novel titles for all but a handful of unusually successful titles. The value of individual titles ranged hugely, from immensely valuable copyrights (as well as certain publications still protected by patent), to a long tail of books with little economic worth. As noted, many authors of fiction were paid paltry sums for an initial surrender of rights to works which booksellers knew were very unlikely to be reprinted or to return much profit in their own right. Sometimes such cheap initial purchases proved to have a surprising long-term value at the auctions of reprint rights (and might have encouraged some authors in negotiating one-edition-only agreements), but the majority of titles published did not reach a further edition. Titles that did offer good reprint value were to feature significantly in literary market development and to be a key encouragement to new booksellers (as well as a major temptation for them to overreach).

[24] *The Universal Director* (London: J. Coote, 1763).
[25] Sheila Lambert (ed.), *House of Commons Sessional Papers of the Eighteenth Century*, 147 vols (Wilmington, DE: Scholarly Resources, 1975–6), 52.359.

The focus of copyright history in this period remains the upheavals of the challenges by Alexander and John Donaldson, Thomas Carnan, and John Bell who infuriated many of the associations built up through the London closed copyright auctions, still central to the trade in the 1760s. The 1662 (and successive) licensing laws have been characterized as typical of the 'ill-drafted legislation in which royal order was restored' (Treadwell 1996: 6); but by comparison, the 1710 Copyright Act created even more confusion. Confusion, however, can easily be exploited by those with the greatest economic clout. Immediately following the mid-century technical expiration of rights to older works and works first protected under this statute, the booksellers' associations seemed successful in arguing that the Act's spirit sanctioned perpetual copyright under Common Law. A 1768 King's Bench ruling and then the injunction by the Court of Chancery against the Donaldson brothers in November 1772 resulted from the action brought by Thomas Becket against the Donaldsons' cheap Edinburgh edition of James Thomson's *The Seasons*. The 1768 restraining injunction in King's Bench marked the high-water mark of the efforts by closed associations of booksellers to control copyright. In July 1773, Alexander Donaldson and two others successfully challenged the injunction before the Scottish Court of Session, foreshadowing the House of Lords reversal of the *Donaldson v. Becket* injunction in February 1774. This Lords ruling extinguished the booksellers' invocation of common law to sanction perpetual copyright, and it established, in good measure, a modern concept of limited, statutory copyright.

Nonetheless, changes before the 1774 pronouncement and continuities after it suggest less a watershed than a point in a much longer and more complex course of development. It is true that in terms of legal rulings, the assault on the publishing domination of the leading booksellers' associations was finally successful only in 1774 (after the House of Lords ruling on *Donaldson v. Becket*). In terms of actual arrangements, however, cheap reprinting had flourished for several decades, the framework for the protection of sale and investment in rights to *new* works remained intact in the final decades of the century, and leading booksellers' de facto extended copyright continued as securely as ever. Competition increased, certainly, but the advance of new cheap editions was in addition to, not in substitution of, major publishing undertakings by booksellers' associations. Clarified rather than undermined by the earlier legal battles, copyright trading brought new riches to those with the skill to favour the right authors and publications (for the legal developments, largely arising from the poor drafting of the 1710 Act, see Deazley 2004).

Following the events of 1774, robust bookselling associations regrouped, but an increasing number of those outside the charmed circle of major copyright-holding booksellers published cheap reprinted library editions and part-issues of classic or best-selling works. During the 1780s, reprints of newly declared out-of-copyright best-sellers flourished. Many of these efforts—launched by single booksellers or by a simple partnership of two—benefited from new promotional techniques, advertising, and reorganized retail and distribution. The changing conditions of the market undermined cooperative publishing associations designed not only to share risk but also to exclude competitors from trade sales and favoured distributive networks.

Although the Donaldsons are rightly credited with the initial actions that resisted booksellers' claims to perpetual copyright, it was John Bell who captured the initiative in cheaper, part-issued, and reprinted popular literature. Between 1776 and 1778, Bell issued twenty-one volumes of *Bell's British Theatre* in 6*d.* weekly parts, pitted against the *New English Theatre* issued in twelve volumes (1776–7) by a syndicate of twenty-seven book-sellers. In cheap reprints and weekly numbers, James Harrison and then John Cooke and Alexander Hogg established themselves as the clear rivals to Bell. James Harrison was an author and literary innovator as well as a highly successful entrepreneur. Among his 120 or so eighteenth-century titles were several part-book periodicals and weekly maga-zines, some of which hugely boosted the sale of and market for fiction. In November 1779, Harrison commenced his *Novelist's Magazine* in octavo with double columns and stitched in small weekly numbers. Echoes of mid-century anthologies by Dodsley and others were clear,[26] but at their peak, ten thousand copies or more of the *Novelist's Magazine* sold each week, with twenty-three volumes extant by the date of completion.[27] The *Novelist's Magazine* opened with John Hawkesworth's oriental *Almoran and Hamet* and Henry Fielding's *Joseph Andrews* and *Amelia* (the numbers for these three comprised the first volume). Elegant engraved plates commissioned by Harrison added significantly to the appeal of his publications. Later reprinted works included Tobias Smollett's *Peregrine Pickle* and *Humphry Clinker* and Samuel Richardson's *Pamela* and *Clarissa* (among sixty-one novels in all) (Taylor 1993). Harrison's *New Novelist's Magazine* ran monthly from May 1786 to early 1788,[28] and Harrison himself contributed at least four tales to his *New Novelist's Magazine*, which printed short fiction only with no well-known novels (in contrast, there-fore, to the *Novelist's Magazine*).

Broader Profiles

The publishing history of the British eighteenth-century and early nineteenth-century novel confirms the advance of specialist booksellers and commercial circulating librar-ians, as well as new advertising techniques and promotional ploys. Novels, like other leisure and fashion goods, were advanced by a variety of entrepreneurs, many modestly financed but eager to exploit fresh markets. For good or ill, the novel was recognized as a

---

[26] Notably Robert Dodsley, *A Select Collection of Old Plays*, 12 vols (London: Dodsley, 1744).

[27] See Rees and Britton (1896: 22), suggesting 12,000 copies a week (not implausible but 10,000 is more likely); and Taylor (1993).

[28] Existing dating of its part publication is problematic: most surviving copies are bound in two vol-umes, making monthly dating difficult.

new cultural force, as distinctive as the theatre or newspaper. Reviewers might find a tale that 'affords many lessons to the youth of both sexes' but also—and far more usually—a novel deemed to be 'one of those pernicious incentives to vice that are a scandal to decency'.[29] Most critics regarded the novel as a separate and definable class of books.[30] In an age when Linnaeus and others categorized natural phenomena, many observers described novels according to their 'order', 'species', 'kind', 'race', or 'tribe'. In more military fashion, novels were assigned a 'rank' or placed within a 'list'.[31] Commentators of the time were certainly not averse to their own exercises in novel counting and classification.

The escalating output shocked many contemporaries. Only when entertainment was combined with useful instruction might the novel escape charges of insignificance or depravity. Concern about the effects of novel-mania was a serious one, and should not be dismissed with retrospective levity, however much we now enjoy the reviewers' wit and scorn. For many, the writing of a novel was an apprentice piece—and one from which they did not always recover. Much of this fiction slavishly followed model forms or lionized writers, predictably and with restrained ambition. Several novels even seem to have been put together above the printing room—a few chapters from a hack writer, other parts culled from an old romance, something more translated from a foreign potboiler.

Books, print, and novels notably contributed to a new age of conspicuous consumption in the late eighteenth and early nineteenth centuries. Book trade entrepreneurs like Thomas Longman, John Murray I and II, Charles Rivington, Thomas Cadell, James Lackington, and George Robinson ranked with Hogarth, Boulton, Watt, and Wedgwood as the promoters and beneficiaries of an evolving 'consumer society'. It was not just that printed advertisements and other promotional publications advanced a great range of consumer goods, but books, magazines, and prints themselves became prominent exemplars of the new decencies adorning the homes of propertied men and women. James Lackington proclaimed his 'Temple of the Muses' bookshop to be the largest second-hand and remaindered bookshop in the world and it attracted lively contemporary comment. Nor was this a solely English development (despite the continuing production dominance of London); in many ways the social penetration of print in Scotland and the much smaller but fast-developed domestic market for books and newspapers in eighteenth-century Ireland are the more remarkable.

---

[29] *Critical Review*, 33 (February 1772), 180, and 55 (March 1783), 234, on *The Cautious Lover* (London, 1772), and *Frailties of Fashion* (London, 1782).

[30] Of many examples, *Monthly Review*, 44 (February 1771), 173; *Critical Review*, 63 (April 1787), 308; *Monthly Review*, n.s., 14 (August 1794), 465.

[31] Of many examples, *Critical Review*, 33 (February 1772), 181–2; 34 (July 1772), 77; 44 (August 1777), 154; 65 (March 1788), 236–7; 67 (June/July 1789), 505–6, 554; n.s., 9 (September 1793), 118; and *Monthly Review*, 45 (December 1771), 503; 59 (September 1778), 233–4; 78 (June 1788), 531; 79 (November 1788), 466.

There were constants. Throughout these seventy years, publishing remained, as it had been since the late seventeenth century, dominated by questions of monopoly price fixing, centralized production and control, technological constraints (and breakthroughs), and the efficiency of distribution networks. The British book production regime was characterized by the extreme variability of the size and price of the printed text, by multiple but modestly sized reprintings of successful titles (instead of ambitious single print runs), and by the manufacture of many non-commercial books where full costs were not always recovered from sale. Above all, the price of new and reprinted books had been modulated for most of the eighteenth century by the effective cartelization of the trade in which booksellers' protection of reprinting rights maintained monopoly prices in England (although not in Ireland and only ineffectively in Scotland, whose booksellers led the challenge against English claims to perpetual copyright).

The increased output of novels in separate volumes and by instalment by publishing booksellers was not necessarily propelled by the pursuit of more efficient production, especially when publishing responded to investment opportunity as much as to the possibility of immediate returns on work in hand. The publishing syndicates and partnerships organized from the late seventeenth century were driven by both long-term and speculative investment, and lessened the extent to which the rate of product sale determined price and the economic development of book and allied trades. The ranks of booksellers were fundamentally divided between those who invested and dealt in the ownership of the copyright to publication, and those who either printed, sold, or distributed books for the copyholders or who traded entirely outside the bounds of copyright materials. This division remained in effect in the early nineteenth century, even after new freedoms to reprint out-of-copyright titles following legal decisions weakened leading booksellers' monopolistic control of copyright in 1768 and 1774. The successful challenge was followed by a great outpouring of anthologies and abridgements (including even the Bible). New restrictions were reimposed by further Copyright Acts in 1808 and 1814, and after these Acts the number of titles coming out of copyright fell sharply. A raft of cheaper reprints had certainly contributed to the fourfold increase in publication in the three decades after 1770, but most new in-copyright publications were more expensive than ever and by the 1810s the reproduction of obsolescent literature for lower-income book buyers was renewed.

What the buyers of both new (and to a lesser extent) second-hand novels did experience was a more competitive and expanding market for books, together with more efficient technologies (especially in illustration) and expanding distributive systems. For most of this period, however, the novel did not constitute cheaper literature. New productivity was based on financial and organizational innovation, but very much within a trading structure dominated by cartels of large, powerful publishing booksellers investing in copyrights under legal copyright protection (as they conveniently interpreted it). Those in the book trade who had benefited most from new financial mechanisms and opportunities were well-resourced London publishing booksellers, such as Thomas Cadell, the family firms of the Robinsons, Rivingtons, Longmans, and John Murray II. The new book trade leviathans were all able to command the respect and trust of a far-flung commercial elite. By contrast, the customer (like so many writers) was often as much a victim as beneficiary. The 1774 defeat of certain booksellers' protective associations together with new competition and new reprinting practices probably forced a cut in the relative price of books, but it was a short-term reprieve. Notwithstanding the cheapening of certain out-of-copyright books, recent assessment of change in the relative prices of books suggests that by the very early nineteenth century the book (despite the many difficulties in calculating any 'average' price) was more and not less a luxury item than it had been a hundred years earlier (see Raven 2009).

Publishers' pricing of books and other print was based not only on the evaluation of production costs, but also on the sort of mark-ups that a luxury and protected market might support. Where publishing booksellers took on the full financial risk, the production expenses of paper, labour, and type were balanced against monopoly printing rights at least until 1774 and, for many publishing ventures, through the lifetimes of both Austen and Scott. Expansion in retailing and allied services (as well as in the amount and length of credit offered) derived from the changing commercial potential of the audience, while prices of many books—and notably, novels—had often been inflated, not discounted, in order to attract. The supply as much as the demand for new novels related to the costliness of the product. That, after all, is the basis of decisions by specialist manufacturers to produce fewer goods when the price is too low and, conversely, for their encouragement of exclusivity by a generous dose of overpricing.

It was within this development of the book trade that novel publication so famously increased from the mid-eighteenth century. In 1775, the year of Jane Austen's birth, thirty-one new novels are known to have been published in Britain; in 1811, the year that *Sense and Sensibility* appeared, eighty new titles were published; and in the year after her death, the joint publication of *Northanger Abbey* and *Persuasion* joined sixty-one other new novel titles with an 1818 imprint. Altogether, British publishing booksellers issued over 2,500 new novels between 1775 and 1818. Output rose sharply before 1800 before a trough in the mid-1810s (with a strong recovery in the 1820s). The early dominance of the epistolary novel (almost three-quarters of all titles published in 1776) had declined by the 1790s. The epistolary form was replaced in part by new interest in the Gothic, just as translations from the French (eight of all forty new titles in 1786) dimmed before advancing interest in the German (ten of ninety-nine in 1799). More than a tenth of all novel titles first published in Britain between 1770 and 1810 were translations from Continental novels. Of Samuel Noble's circulating library catalogue (*c*.1773) about a quarter of its 4,484 titles were French. What, however, was most distinctive about novels in terms of their publishing history was their high retail price, the production of ephemeral editions in very small print runs, and the poverty and exploitation of novelists (even more, perhaps, than of other writers).

2

Authorship

PETER GARSIDE

ONE of the advantages of the new bibliographies of fiction lies in their full transcription of title page details, wherever copies of first editions are to be found, allowing a much clearer view of the way in which novels were projected at their original readers.[1] Using this information as a main basis for analysis can offer a strikingly different view of authorship as it appeared in its time, not least with regard to anonymity and the naming of authors. Out of 3,374 novels first published from 1770–1819, some 2,045 (representing just over 60 per cent) were published without the name of an author on the title page. Nor does this simply reflect a large underbelly of supposedly 'indiscriminate' titles. Amongst authors who appeared anonymously on title pages in their own time can be counted Samuel Richardson, Tobias Smollett, Henry Mackenzie, Frances Burney, Walter Scott, and Jane Austen (even if, to varying degrees, their authorship was publicly known by other means). In the first four decades under view an overwhelming majority of over 80 per cent of new titles were published anonymously, making this the norm for the genre over those years. Pseudonymous authorship is virtually unheard of up to 1800, though a shift in this direction is evident in the new century. Novels carrying the author's name on the title page come more fully into view with the 1790s, actually outnumbering anonymous and pseudonymous titles in the 1800s. However, the resilience of anonymity is again apparent in the 1810s, when unattributed titles once more outnumber those with names on the title page, albeit narrowly so.

Compared with this, modern bibliographers are able to attribute authorial names to more than two-thirds of the novels belonging to the period, with a residue of just over 1,100 titles (32.8 per cent) still classifiable as anonymous. Identifications have come to light in a variety of ways, some occurring within or shortly after the period itself. Occasionally, full author names are found within a novel—as in a signed preface, or

---

[1] Statistical information in this chapter is based on a revision of Raven (1987) and Garside, Raven, and Schöwerling (2000), supplemented by the new findings in the online *Database of British Fiction, 1800–29 (DBF)*: Garside et al. (2004).

through the inclusion of an engraved portrait or additional title page—when the main title page offers no direct authorial description. It was also a fairly common procedure for authors to declare themselves after several works had been written anonymously, especially if the latter had proved successful, this having the effect of identifying the earlier titles (which, if reprinted, would then be likely to bear the author's name). In some instances circumstantial factors determined full exposure, as in the case of the decision of Mackenzie's publishers to announce his authorship to ward off rival claims in favour of a deceased Mr Eccles of Bath, or the more celebrated outing of Scott at a public dinner in 1827 in the wake of his insolvency. Collections of fictions, after the fashion of *Harrison's Novelist's Magazine* (1779–88), were also given to naming authors who had been anonymous in their own day, while in some instances extending the compliment to near-contemporary figures such as Robert Bage. An increasing awareness of the author–work relationship in the Victorian period, and more particularly its embedded nature in library catalogues and literary history, led in turn to more concerted exercises in author identification, notably Allibone's monumental *Critical Dictionary of English Literature, and British and American Authors* (1859–71). Identification has also been enhanced for modern bibliographers through wider accessibility of archival sources, including the publishing records of a number of concerns with a significant commitment to fiction (Robinsons, Longmans, etc.), as well as the papers of the Royal Literary Fund, providing detailed information on a wide band of authors (see Cross 1985). A significant input in recent years has also been achieved through the retrieval of biographical and bibliographical information about individual women novelists, as now available in reference works compiled by Todd (1987), Blain, Clements, and Grundy (1990), and Shattock (1993), as well as through the online *Orlando* database.[2]

Compared with more traditional accounts, much of the later work described above shows a commendable sense of the materiality of cultural production, depicting authors likely to operate through a variety of personas, and necessarily responsive to external conditions relating to contemporary book production and publishing priorities. Dangers still remain, however, in viewing the conditions of authorship from a present-day vantage point. This chapter offers an overview of issues relating to output and popularity, anonymity and pseudonymity, gender distribution, and author dealings vis-à-vis publishers, seen as far as is possible from within the period itself. In passing, it also observes a number of transitions which have been instrumental in determining later perceptions.

---

[2] Susan Brown, Patricia Clements, and Isobel Grundy, *Orlando: Women's Writing in the British Isles from the Beginnings to the Present* (Cambridge University Press), available online at <www.arts.ualberta.ca/orlando>, last accessed 22 May 2014.

Author Numbers and Output

Although a number of factors, notably the high proportion of still unidentified anonymous titles, make any kind of absolute statement impossible, all the evidence points to a growing body of authors involved in the production of novels during the period. James Raven in his *British Fiction 1750–1770* (1987) identifies 236 authors and translators of novels published or republished during the twenty years covered by that bibliography, although if the procedure is limited just to new titles then the count reduces to a smaller phalanx of about 140 figures, of which some forty are foreign writers, and another ten translators of fiction only. The first volume of *The English Novel 1770–1829*, covering the last three decades of the eighteenth century, identifies about 500 authors and translators of new fiction, of whom some forty apparently operated as translators only, with over 100 foreign-born writers among the total count. An analysis of the twenty years from 1800–19, as found in the second volume of *The English Novel*, reveals approximately 580 original author names (of which some twenty-five are actual or probable pseudonyms), about fifty-five of these being foreign writers, with an additional body of thirty or so specialist translators of fiction. Taking into account crossovers between the different time spans, it is possible to claim in the region of 1,100 distinguishable authors and translators involved in the production of fiction from 1750 to 1820, a figure which would no doubt expand beyond 1,500 if the writers of the considerable residue of unidentified titles were also known.

Identifiable authors range between some of the most prolific in the history of fiction and others whose engagement with the genre appears to have been only momentary. As many as 600 authors, as far as is known, produced only one novel within the confines of the period. Among these can be counted a number of high-profile titles, the product usually of an established author stepping into the genre on a one-off basis, as in the case of Samuel Johnson's *The Prince of Abissinia* [*Rasselas*] (1759) and Horace Walpole's *The Castle of Otranto* (1765); or, in the later period, Hannah More's *Coelebs in Search of a Wife* (1808). In some other instances the tightness of the time restraints in operation limits an otherwise productive novelist to a single work, with Henry Fielding's *Amelia* (1752) being thus isolated near the beginning of the survey, and Mary Shelley's *Frankenstein* (1818) being separated off from her later output at its end. As a whole, however, a large proportion of the singleton works in evidence would have represented an unavailing attempt to make a mark in and/or profit by a field of writing littered with failures, the author's sometimes self-proclaimed 'first literary attempt' not infrequently proving to be their last.

Of the remaining authors identified, just under 130 are known to have produced five titles or more during the period. Authors contributing to this level within the earlier period include Eliza Haywood, Edward Kimber, Charlotte Lennox, and (allowing for co-authorship) Sarah Scott. In the case of Haywood, her five titles produced in the 1750s represent the tail-end of an exceptionally prolific career, involving up to forty previous works of fiction, not even counting collected works, though many of the earlier of these were relatively short pieces. Significantly productive writers whose contribution was centred in the later eighteenth century include Anna Maria Bennett, Thomas Holcroft, Samuel Jackson Pratt, and Ann Radcliffe. Among writers whose main output began early in the new century can be counted Maria Edgeworth, Amelia Opie, and Sydney Owenson (Lady Morgan), all of whom achieved at least seven titles within the period, though their output was to stretch further. From a later starting point, both Jane Austen and Walter Scott had entered the category of significant producers by the end of the 1810s: the former through her five 'mature' works of fiction, all published during that decade (the last posthumously); Scott through his initial sequence of Scottish novels, from *Waverley* (1814) to the third series of *Tales of My Landlord* (1819), comprising seven titles in twenty-four volumes.

Between 1750 and 1820, twenty of the above authors stand out by virtue of having produced ten or more original titles.[3] Table 2.1 lists the number of novels originating from each of these writers during the period, followed by the amount of volumes generated, and by their inclusive imprint dates (with 1819 an absolute cut-off point). As in the cases of Haywood and Scott, there is inevitably an element of arbitrariness in view of a number of authors whose main output is not containable within these parameters. However, the results point usefully towards new kinds of authorial output which developed during the period and remained characteristic well into the Victorian era. Unlike the smaller amatory fictions of Haywood, the bulk of novels produced by regular authors were in multi-volume form, and most were issued as single unitary publications, in contrast with the more elaborate method, evident in publications such as Henry Brooke's *The Fool of Quality* (five vols, 1766–70), of accumulating volumes over a succession of years. Amongst prolific authors, the generation of novels on a yearly basis was not uncommon, with in exceptional cases two or three titles being issued under the same imprint year. It is also possible to distinguish different levels of authorship, most notably between those novelists who operated predominantly as manufacturers of fiction for the circulating libraries, and those aspiring to some degree of autonomy as independent writers.

At the head of the list, and most prominent in the first category, is Mrs [Elizabeth] Meeke, all of whose twenty-six original novels (including a final title issued in 1823) were published by the Minerva Press, under the proprietorship of William Lane, and by his successor A. K. Newman.[4] With its own circulating library and multiplying offshoots to feed, and a market share of close to a third of total output of fiction for most years between 1790 and 1815, the Minerva enterprise stood in need of reliable suppliers, capable of sustaining their readers' attention through recognizable kinds of material. Other

---

[3] The list excludes authors with totals swelled by questionable titles, notably Phebe Gibbes, who claimed in 1804 to have written in all 'twenty-two' sets of novels (see Raven 2003: 153–4).

[4] For a new identification of Mrs Meeke as Elizabeth Meeke, née Allen, a stepsister of the novelist Frances Burney, see Macdonald (2013).

Table 2.1. Most productive authors of novels, 1750–1819

Authors	Novels	Volumes	Imprint Dates
Meeke, Mrs [Elizabeth] [a]	25	91	1795–1819
Lafontaine, August	23	60	1797–1813
Genlis, Stéphanie	21	55	1783–1819
Parsons, Eliza [b]	18	62	1790–1807
Lathom, Francis [c]	13	38	1795–1809
Green, Sarah [d]	13	35	1790–1814
Mackenzie, Anna Maria	13	34	1783–1809
Smith, Charlotte [e]	12	44	1787–1802
Holstein, Anthony [pseud.]	12	41	1808–1815
Gunning, Susannah [f]	12	40	1764–1803
Gunning, Elizabeth [g]	11	36	1794–1815
Hofland, Barbara	11	25	1809–1817
Roche, Regina Maria [h]	10	34	1789–1814
Thomas, Elizabeth	10	33	1803–1817
Helme, Elizabeth [i]	10	32	1787–1814
Kelly, Isabella	10	31	1794–1813
Porter, Anna Maria	10	28	1793–1818
Foster, Mrs E. M.	10	25	1795–1803
Summersett, Henry [j]	10	19	1794–1811
Riccoboni, Marie-Jeanne	10	16	1759–1803

(a) excludes 4 translations (13 vols)
(b) excludes 1 translation (3 vols)
(c) excludes 2 translations (3 vols)
(d) excludes 1 translation (2 vols)
(e) excludes 1 translation (2 vols)
(f) includes 3 co-authored works and 1 questionable title (13 vols)
(g) includes 1 co-authored work (3 vols), but excludes 3 translations (8 vols)
(h) includes 1 questionable work (2 vols)
(i) excludes 1 translation (2 vols)
(j) includes 1 questionable work (1 vol.)

females in the list who wrote under the Minerva imprint include Eliza Parsons, Anna Maria Mackenzie, Regina Maria Roche, and Isabella Kelly (later Hedgeland), all of whom appeared alongside Meeke as one of ten 'particular and favourite Authors' in a Minerva Prospectus of 1798 (Blakey 1939: appendix IV). Another regular producer in this category was Anthony Frederick Holstein (the Germanic-sounding name is almost certainly a pseudonym), ten of whose rapidly produced twelve titles bear the Minerva imprint. In some instances there is evidence of authors moving downmarket to find a kind of refuge in Minerva, while others moved on to form more prestigious links with other publishers. Following the first path, Francis Lathom published five of his first six titles elsewhere, before committing himself more fully to the Minerva Press with *The Impenetrable Secret* (1805), itself to be followed by a succession of similar Gothic potboilers to 1809. After this Lathom disappears as a producer of fiction until 1820, when he re-emerges as an exclusive Minerva author, achieving a total output of twenty-seven titles with *Mystic Events* (which lists no less than half of its predecessors on the title page) in 1830. In a reverse direction, Barbara Hofland, writing to support her family, published the majority of her first eleven titles with Minerva, before turning to Longmans as her main publisher in the 1820s, her career total amounting to some twenty-five works of fiction by 1835, discounting a number of additional children's tales.

Writers whose careers involved a more intermittent relationship with the Minerva Press include Sarah Green, whose two novels from the 1790s were both published there, but whose varied, satirical, politically engaged output between 1808–14 found a number of alternative outlets in the London trade, though her four novels belonging to the 1820s were all published by A. K. Newman. A different kind of authorship is indicated by the numerous 'fashionable' fictions generated collaboratively and independently by Susannah Gunning [née Minifie] and her daughter Elizabeth, beginning with Susannah's *The Histories of Lady Frances S ——, and Lady Caroline S ——* (1763) (co-authored with her sister Margaret) and ending with Elizabeth's *The Victims of Seduction* (1815), a body of work involving a large array of booksellers and varying publishing arrangements. Elizabeth Helme, whose career as a novelist began with the runaway success of her sentimental novel *Louisa; or, The Cottage on the Moor* (1787), likewise published with a number of London concerns, apparently confining her Minerva output to one original title, *The Farmer of Inglewood Forest* (1796), though some of her other titles were reissued by that Press. In the new century she features briefly as a Longmans author with the historical romance *St. Clair of the Isles* (1803), prior to the last of her three novels appearing under the imprint of Norbury, a bookseller in Brentford, where her husband kept a school, the last of these, *Modern Times* (1814), being described on its title page as a 'A Posthumous Novel'.

Probably the strongest example in the listing of an attempted independence in authorship, however, is provided by Charlotte Smith, who entered the genre with a reputation as a poetess, but who desperately sought funds to support her large family after separation from her husband. In spite of early diffidence, Smith managed to negotiate profitably with a number of mainstream publishers, first establishing a relationship with Thomas Cadell, who had built up a cohort of respected novelists, and then alternating the procedure for her later works by engaging rival publishers, such as George Robinson, all of whom promoted the end product as belonging to a higher sphere than 'common' circulating-library fiction. A different pattern still is evident in the case of Anna Maria Porter, another purely non-Minerva author in the listing, all of whose works from *Octavia* (1798) were managed by Longmans, where Porter prospered alongside a number of other house authors, including the conservative novelist Jane West, Amelia Opie, and her own sister Jane, publishing a further thirteen titles with the firm (including two co-authored with Jane) ending in 1830.

Another aspect of authorship, reflecting the high proportion of imported foreign titles over the period (see also Mander, Chapter 32), is apparent in the presence of three non-native authors in the listing, Marie-Jeanne Riccoboni, Madame de Genlis, and August Lafontaine. The first nine of Riccoboni's sentimental fictions were published in original translations shortly after their first appearance in France, beginning in 1759 with the *History of the Marquis de Cressy* and *Letters of Lady Julia Catesby* and ending with *The History of Christina, Princess of Swabia* (1784), a number of London booksellers being involved in the process. Original translations of Madame de Genlis, highly regarded for the moral integrity of her writing, stretch from *Adelaide and Theodore* (1783) to two rival editions of *Petrarch and Laura* in 1820. As relatively high-prestige articles, especially in the 1780s and 1790s, these involved a number of leading publishing houses, with the author's celebrity name invariably appearing on the titles. The sentimental domestic fictions of August Lafontaine, commencing in 1797, likewise commonly display the author's name and German origin on the titles as selling points. As a more 'middle-market' phenomenon, his output eventually became a specialism of the Minerva Press, with as many as ten titles carrying its imprint from 1802–5. Translation was also a way of generating income for a number of original novelists, including (from those in the present listing) Elizabeth Gunning, Eliza Parsons, Elizabeth Meeke, Sarah Green, and Elizabeth Helme.

An element of uncertainty exists about the three remaining figures in the listing. Six of the ten titles accorded to Henry Summersett were published by the Minerva Press; eight carried his name on the title page; but a faint question mark still hangs over his authorship of *Jaqueline of Olzeburg* (1800), and little appears to be known about Summersett himself. The main body of Elizabeth Thomas's work consists of eight titles published by Minerva between 1806 and 1817, all as by Mrs Bridget Bluemantle; however, another Thomas pseudonym, Martha Homely, is found on *Maids as They Are Not, and Wives as They Are*, published by W. Earle in 1803; and Thomas near the end of her career appears to have taken a new tack with *Purity of Heart* (1816), marketed by Simpkin & Marshall as by 'An Old Wife of Twenty Years', a counter-narrative to Caroline Lamb's *Glenarvon* of that same year. Perhaps the greatest mystery of all is provided by Mrs E. M. Foster, the most shadowy figure in the listing. The ten novels ascribed to her there appeared under a number of guises, with 'E. M. F.' representing the fullest exposure on the titles. Four appeared with the same Minerva year imprint of 1800, a rate of output matched only by the same concern's Lafontaine titles in 1804. Compounding the difficulty is a connection through title linkage between the last in this grouping, *Light and Shade* (1803), and another body of some twenty novels stretching to 1817, components of which have also been associated with Mrs Foster, as well as (somewhat implausibly) with two other authors. Recent research has had the effect of altering the bibliographic record relating to a number of other authors in the period, significantly extending the output of Laetitia-Matilda Hawkins, while diminishing that previously attributed to Mrs Ross, and undoubtedly there are other authors and bodies of writing waiting to be discovered (see Fergus 2007; Garside 1998).

Anonymity, Pseudonymity, and Named Authorship

A number of reasons have been adduced for authors choosing to hide under the mask of anonymity (Raven 2003; Mullan 2007). Many women writers evidently felt a threat to their respectability in avowing authorship, and so associating themselves with trade and the pursuit of financial gain, not least in relation to a form generally held to have low literary status. Among male authors association with what was increasingly being perceived as a female form may equally have proved a strong disincentive. Male writers might also have wished to avoid compromising their professional life through open engagement with a relatively frivolous pursuit. This is one of several plausible reasons posited by Scott for anonymity in the Preface to the Third Edition (1814) of *Waverley*; others included the unwillingness of a literary novice to avow authorship and the shame of a 'hackneyed author' at 'too frequent appearance', none of these approaching too closely to the complexity of his own situation (1.vii).

In more run-of-mill cases, it was often the publisher rather than the author who decided the final wording of the title page. Usually printed last in the production process, this not only provided the text for the headings of review notices but also helped determine the positioning of a work in circulating-library catalogues. In the case of a new or relatively unknown author, an arresting title, or one likely to connect with already popular novels, must often have seemed the best way of attracting interest and generating sales. As William St Clair has suggested, publishers whose main output went to the libraries had good reason to prioritize generic characteristics over authorial origin, thereby turning 'novels into uniform and mutually substitutable commodities' (2008: 40).

At the same time, it is important to recognize the existence of varying degrees of anonymity. Out of the total of 2,045 anonymous titles, over 360 provide a measure of information by listing a previous work or works by the same author, while some 225 offer descriptive indications of gender and/or social standing in lieu of a direct attribution. The use of the formula 'By the Author of' was already established by the 1750s, exponents of the method including Smollett, Charlotte Lennox, and Sarah Fielding, the latter's adoption of 'by the Author of David Simple' providing an unusually prominent 'badge of achievement' among contemporary female authors, according to Schellenberg (2005: 99). An interesting shift is perceptible in the later 1770s with the careers of Henry Mackenzie and Frances Burney, both of whom were to exert a strong influence on succeeding novelists. Mackenzie's *The Man of Feeling* (1771) and *The Man of the World* (1773) were both published anonymously, without any other form of embellishment in the titles, though their status as cousin works would have been self-evident. *Julia de Roubigné* (1777), on the other hand, openly gathers its forerunners into a larger unit by proclaiming itself as 'Published by the Author of The Man of Feeling, and The Man of the World'. Burney's first novel *Evelina* (1778) was likewise published anonymously, the first linkage in her career occurring with the description of *Cecilia* (1782) as 'by the Author of Evelina'. By this time however her authorship, already an open secret, was rapidly advancing into a kind of celebrity. Nevertheless the same formula, accumulating previous titles, was followed for both *Camilla* (1796) and *The Wanderer* (1814), though the former as a subscription novel would have involved its author's personal circumstances being widely broadcast, and the latter included a signed dedication by the author.

From the 1780s the practice became more common, with over 20 per cent of anonymous works in the 1790s providing title information of this kind. A variety of options for manipulating this information also came into play, ranging between the choice of one key title, the selection of several works with an affinity to the present one, and a progressive piling-up to show a full oeuvre. In a few instances works other than novels were selected, with Charles Robert Maturin's *Women* (1818), evidently at the behest of its publisher Constable, displaying only his successful play *Bertram*, instead of any of three previous novels. Other authors of this period whose works were issued exclusively or predominantly according to the 'by the author' method include Robert Bage and Jane West. By far its most spectacular and influential exponent however was Walter Scott, who first appeared as 'the Author of Waverley' on the titles of *Guy Mannering* (1815), then again as 'the Author of Waverley and Guy Mannering' on those of *The Antiquary* (1816). Notwithstanding the parallel series founded by *Tales of My Landlord* (1816), his fourth work of fiction, ostensibly collected by the schoolmaster Jedediah Cleishbotham, authorship of *Waverley* became the main token binding together an accelerating output, providing a vital link with the shift to medieval English subject matter in *Ivanhoe* (1820) and featuring (alone or in combination) on each of the following titles through the 1820s, by which time Scott's authorship had effectively become public knowledge. The 1820s as whole, too, saw a distinct upturn in the use of this species of anonymity, especially among male authors, many of them no doubt influenced by the example of Scott.

Most common by far amongst gender/social descriptors is the designation 'By a Lady' and close variant forms ('Young Lady' etc.), which over the period occur on more than 150 occasions. Less than twenty instances appear between 1750–69, the earliest being Susan Smythies' *The History of Lucy Wellers* (1754), 'Written by a Lady', a slight surge being perceptible with four such titles at the end of the second decade. After a fairly steady occurrence of some thirty titles in the 1770s, a major explosion becomes apparent in the 1780s, especially in the middle years, with over 25 per cent of novels in 1785 following this form, at a time of accelerating output generally. One feature here is the growing number of cases where youthful apprenticeship is suggested ('The First Literary Attempt of a Young Lady'), indicating a significant intake of new women novelists at this point. Alongside this must be set the suspicion, expressed by a number of contemporaries, that many such novelists were only female in name. The image of male hacks cashing in on the craze for 'intimate' women's fiction has proved durable and can be found reasonably intact in a number of modern commentaries. Raven supplies an array of supportive evidence, but apparently only two clear instances of such misnaming on the actual titles of novels (2000: 42, 2003: 145). Against this might be set over forty cases where novels originally described as being by a Lady have since been identified as the work of known women novelists. In the 1790s usage of the label is still fairly common, representing almost 5 per cent of output, but only a thin trickle is to be found after the turn of the century. One outstanding example in the later period, however, is the use of 'By a Lady' for Austen's *Sense and Sensibility* (1811), an indication of the term still having applicability for an unknown female from a respectable background just setting out as a published novelist.

Of seventy or so broader social descriptors male occurrences outnumber female ones by approximately two to one, with a handful of gender-indeterminate cases. Female descriptors usually point to familial situation ('A Clergyman's Daughter'), while in the case of male equivalents institutional links are most frequent, with the clergymen and officers in the armed services especially visible. There are also a few lawyers and a number of needy or ambitious undergraduates ('A Student of Trinity College, Cambridge', 'A Gentleman at the University of Oxford': identifiable as a Mr Lyttleton and Percy Bysshe Shelley respectively). Age-related cases are usually found at both ends of the spectrum ('A Youth of Seventeen', 'An Old Maid of Distinction'). Whereas there is always the possibility that 'A Bengal Officer' is 'An English-Woman', or vice versa, with unidentified titles, the only clear case of title page gender-switching discovered in the later period amongst indigenous authors is Barbara Hofland's use of 'An Old-Fashioned Englishman' for her *Says She to Her Neighbour, What?* (1812), a choice more obviously determined by its relation to Edward Nares's highly popular *Think's-I-To-Myself* of the previous season, than by any concerted effort to assume a male identity.

The use of a pseudonym—in the sense of an assumed name distinct from the main narrative—is relatively rare in the earlier period, with more than two-thirds of the 150 pseudonymous titles noted belonging to the nineteenth century. A possible exception might be claimed in Eliza Haywood's choice of 'Mira, One of the Authors of The Female Spectator, and Epistles for Ladies' for her *The Wife* (1756), but this is far from a simple case and there are no obvious parallels in surrounding years. One also looks hard for anything similar in the 1760s, the most notable examples there being Horace Walpole's antiquarian-style naming of William Marshal as the 'translator' of *The Castle of Otranto* (1765), and Sterne's representation of his *Sentimental Journey* (1768) as 'By Mr. Yorick', an ultra-conscious reprising of an older kind of protagonist-authorship by a writer of celebrity. In the following decade, the most telling example is Samuel Jackson Pratt's consecutive use of 'Courtney Melmoth' (a name adopted when he was an actor) for four of works of fiction, running from *Liberal Opinions* (1775–7) to *Shenstone-Green* (1779). Nearer the end of the century instances become slightly more frequent, though the majority are one-off cases leaving little doubt as to their fictionality (Dr Typo, Sylvania Pastorella, Lemuel Gulliver).

One feature in the new century is the manufacture of apparent pseudonyms echoing well-known established writers, this being especially evident in the pool of authors assembled by J. F. Hughes, among whom might be counted 'Miss West' and a spurious Caroline Burney. The same period also sees the emergence of a number of more regular pseudonymous forms, some effectively operating in the market as proper author names. Noteworthy female examples include: Rosa Matilda [Charlotte Dacre], Emma de Lisle [Emma Parker], and Anne of Swansea [Anne Hatton]. Among the jokier male equivalents may be counted: Cervantes Hogg [Eaton Stannard Barrett], Humphry Hedgehog [John Agg], and Scott's own Jedediah Cleishbotham. Of the 150 pseudonymous titles counted, some fifty indicate a female origin and eighty-five a male one, with the remainder being gender-indeterminate.

Originally very much the exception, the practice of directly naming authors on title pages (found in just under 35 per cent of cases overall) likewise accelerated over the period, gaining significant momentum late in the eighteenth century, and in the 1800s achieving a brief dominance. Naming potentially held out a number of advantages for authors, enabling the assembly of a visible corpus of work, while making more tangible any proprietary rights that they might command. A rise in the general critical standing of the novel as a genre, too, particularly noticeable in the 1790s, undoubtedly encouraged a number of already active novelists to begin naming (and in the process reclaiming) their works.

Though the overall pattern is complex, it is possible to distinguish a number of key moments in relation to named authorship, which for much of the first thirty years was more likely to be granted to foreign rather than domestic writers. The 1780s especially proved to be pivotal. In the imprint years 1781–2 only two authors were named on the title page, out of a total of forty-four novels, both of them male and one deceased ('the late Henry Mansel, Esq.'). In 1788 (from a larger pool of eighty titles) as many as twelve novels named authors, ten of whom were indigenous female writers. Another key year is 1796, when more than a third of new novels (thirty-one out of ninety-one) displayed an author name, notable examples being M. G. Lewis's *The Monk* and Mary Hays's semi-autobiographical *Memoirs of Emma Courtney*. Also evident in this decade is a new kind of assertiveness among certain women novelists in publicly committing themselves to the genre, as apparent in Charlotte Smith's declaration (in the Preface to *Desmond* (1792)) that she had 'become an *Author by profession*' (1.v). Amongst males, one distinct feature is the readiness of Jacobin novelists such as Holcroft and William Godwin to acknowledge authorship on key titles such as *Anna St. Ives* (1792) and *Things as They Are* [*Caleb Williams*] (1794), no doubt as a token of the openness of their intent, though this had not always been their previous practice.

Notwithstanding the buffeting suffered by the genre through the anti-Jacobin reaction, the beginning of the century witnessed fresh assertions of authorship. Two telling examples are found in 1801 with Maria Edgeworth's *Belinda* and Amelia Opie's *The Father and Daughter* (both authors had published anonymously beforehand), with Opie in her Dedication figuring herself as 'an avowed Author at the bar of public opinion' ([vi]). From 1801–9, then again in 1811 and 1813, over 50 per cent of new novels carried an author name on the titles. In 1814 the anonymous *Waverley* found itself in the company of acknowledged titles by Margaret Cullen, Selina Davenport, Maria Edgeworth, Jane Harvey, Laetitia Matilda Hawkins, Elizabeth Helme, Barbara Hofland, Elizabeth Meeke, Lady Morgan, Anna Maria Porter, and Regina Maria Roche, several of whom published with Longmans, the London managers of Scott's own novel. Later in the same decade the picture becomes less distinct, partly one suspects as a result of Scott's own early impact, and in the 1820s named authorship again finds itself in retreat. At same time it is useful to bear in mind the flexibility involved in naming and not naming over the period as a whole, when anonymity could coexist with national acclaim, and known authors might appear before their readers in a variety of forms.

Gender Distribution

In spite of some remaining uncertainties, it is now possible to chart the gender distribution of authorship over the full period with new authority. One result is a substantiation, and sophistication, of previous claims in favour of the novel representing a predominantly female field of writing at this time. A strong push in this direction came from feminist literary historians such as Dale Spender (1986) and Cheryl Turner (1992), both of whom drew up long lists of women novelists and novels prior to Jane Austen, with the former estimating that 'at least half' of eighteenth-century novels were by women (117). Approaching from a different direction, other such commentators pointed to a male capturing of the novel from the mid-1810s (Ferris 1991), and a more concerted appropriation of the novel from the 1840s, leading to a full-scale 'edging out' of women (Tuchman and Fortin 1989). All such assertions however were to a degree hypothetical in the absence of hard data concerning output, a situation ameliorated by the new bibliographies, though in some areas this has had the effect of complicating rather than corroborating matters. According to Raven in *British Fiction 1750–1770* 'the case for a predominance of women writers of early fiction is far from overwhelming' (1987: 18). Male writers too in his assessment 'hugely outnumber' (2000: 41) female writers during the period covered by the first volume of *The English Novel 1770–1829*, that is to the end of the century, while the second volume points to an unexpected flowering of female authorship during the 1810s. One remaining difficulty in coordinating such results lies in the somewhat different criteria used for analysing output in gender terms. It is also important to bear in mind a difference between calculations based on the number of male and female authors active during the period and those which survey the number of new titles generated annually in gender terms.

As a whole, counts based on authors tend to be less conducive to the idea of the novel as a specially female form. Of the 140 identifiable novelists and translators producing new titles in the years 1750–69, a breakdown shows 106 male authors, thirty-one female equivalents, and two gender-uncertain names. For 1770–99, Raven counts 292 male writers as opposed to 189 female ones, with twenty-five identified authors of unknown sex (2000: 41). Adding the thirty or so specialist translators to 580 original authors for 1800–19 similarly reveals a male superiority, though a diminished one, with some 300 male writers just outnumbering 295 female counterparts, and twelve or so gender-uncertain names. If however the above figures are stripped of foreign writers and specialist translators, then the figures become more favourable to female authorship. This is especially telling in the case of the 1810s, itself marked by a decreasing proportion of translated fiction, where 172 native female novelists clearly outnumber 124 males. Another factor is the greater productivity of female novelists, especially in the later periods. Out of fifty-nine novelists producing five or more new titles from 1800–19, almost two-thirds (thirty-nine) were women.

This in itself offers a main reason why analysis by title numbers normally generates a more favourable representation of the contribution made by female novelists. Table 2.2 gives a numerical breakdown of new fiction over the period, employing three sub-categories within gender: (i) 'named', which applies to cases where the author's proper name appeared on the title page; (ii) 'identified', referring to cases where a work appeared anonymously or pseudonymously, but where the author has been identified; and (iii) 'implied', which relates to unidentified pseudonyms and gender-implicit tags such as 'By a Clergyman'. The final 'Unknown' category, while consisting mainly of unidentified anonymous works, also contains a number of instances where a name given is gender-indeterminate. The most obvious difference in the present procedure compared to the figures given by Raven lies in the inclusion in a broader gender count of 'implied' titles, which arguably risks distorting the outcome, granted gender-switching was prevalent at any stage. For reasons already outlined, however, this seems unlikely on any large scale; and in any case the figures can be reduced back to the 'firmer' named/identified groupings if required. Unlike the first volume of the *English Novel*, too, the 'named' category excludes cases where an author name is only to be found in prefatory matter, most of which instances however are almost certain to be incorporated under 'identified'. One overall result is that the same methodology is applied here across the full seventy years under view, with the option of extension into the 1820s.

Table 2.2. Authorship of new novels by gender, 1750–1819

Imprint Year	Female			Male			Unknown	Total
	Named	Identified	Implied	Named	Identified	Implied		New Titles
1750	–	2	–	4	4	–	13	23
1751	–	1	–	2	9	1	10	23
1752	–	3	–	–	5	–	11	19
1753	1	4	–	1	5	–	8	19
1754	–	4	–	3	8	–	15	30
1755	1	2	–	1	6	–	12	22
1756	–	4	–	1	6	1	13	25
1757	–	1.5	–	–	3.5	1	20	26
1758	–	2	1	–	3	–	10	16
1759	–	5	3	3	5	–	12	28
1750s	2	28.5	4	15	54.5	3	124	231
	(0.9%)	(12.3%)	(1.7%)	(6.5%)	(23.6%)	(1.3%)	(53.7%)	
1760	–	4	2	2	4	1	22	35
1761	–	2	–	1	7	–	10	20
1762	2	3	–	1	7	–	6	19
1763	1	1	–	0	3	–	13	18
1764	3	4	–	1	6	–	12	26
1765	1	2	1	2	5	–	7	18
1766	4	1.5	–	2	4.5	–	15	27
1767	2	5	2	2	6	–	16	33
1768	1	–	–	6	4	1	25	37
1769	1	4	3	3	10	–	23	44
1760s	15	26.5	8	20	56.5	2	149	277
	(5.4%)	(9.6%)	(2.9%)	(7.2%)	(20.4%)	(0.7%)	(53.8%)	
1770	1	1.5	5	5	10.5	1	16	40
1771	4	3	4	6	11	–	32	60
1772	1	5	3	3	4	2	23	41
1773	2	2	2	4	8	–	21	39
1774	1	1	4	3	5	3	18	35
1775	1	4	1	–	10	–	15	31
1776	1	3	1	2	5	–	5	17
1777	1	4	2	1	3	1	6	18
1778	1	4	3	1	1	1	5	16
1779	2	2	1	2	7	–	4	18
1770s	15	29.5	26	27	64.5	8	145	315
	(4.7%)	(9.4%)	(8.3%)	(8.6%)	(20.5%)	(2.5%)	(46%)	
1780	4.5	2	1	1.5	4	1	10	24
1781	–	2	4	–	5	–	11	22
1782	–	3	1	2	6	1	9	22
1783	1	8	1	4	5	–	5	24
1784	2	3	4	2	8	–	5	24
1785	4	12	6	4	5	1	15	47

(continued)

Table 2.2. CONTINUED

Imprint Year	Female			Male			Unknown	Total
	Named	Identified	Implied	Named	Identified	Implied		New Titles
1786	3	12	2	2	11	–	10	40
1787	5	9	5	1	9	1	21	51
1788	10	11	10	2	16	1	30	80
1789	10	16	6	2	12	1	24	71
1780s	39.5	78	40	20.5	81	6	140	405
	(9.7%)	(19.3%)	(9.9%)	(5.0%)	(20%)	(1.5%)	(34.6%)	
1790	11	13	5	2	11	1	31	74
1791	8	13	5	16	9	–	23	74
1792	7	7	5	8	8	–	23	58
1793	11	4	1	6	8	–	15	45
1794	14	11	2	11	4	–	14	56
1795	6	12	1	8	12	–	11	50
1796	25	11	3	16	15	1	20	91
1797	18	13	2	15	8	–	23	79
1798	17	21	2	15	6	1	13	75
1799	24	15	4	24	14	–	18	99
1790s	141	120	30	121	95	3	191	701
	(20.1%)	(17.1%)	(4.3%)	(17.3%)	(13.6%)	(0.4%)	(27.2%)	
1800	17	22	2	18	10	–	13	82
1801	27	15	2	13	4	1	12	74
1802	17	11	1	12	8	2	10	61
1803	18	14	1	27	8	–	11	79
1804	22	6	2	22	12	3	8	75
1805	22	9	3	24	6	–	12	76
1806	25	12	2	15	6	2	10	72
1807	24	6	–	18	7	6	8	69
1808	33	14	2	28	8	6	20	111
1809	22	13	2	20	7	5	10	79
1800s	227	122	17	197	76	25	114	778
	(29.2%)	(15.7%)	(2.2%)	(25.3%)	(9.8%)	(3.2%)	(14.6%)	
1810	28	16	7	12	7	3	18	91
1811	21	12	3	21	9	2	12	80
1812	12	21	–	6	5	6	17	67
1813	25	13	1	10	6	3	6	64
1814	22	18	1	7	7	3	5	63
1815	18	5	–	7	7	4	12	53
1816	19	11	–	6	9	1	13	59
1817	22	8	–	4	9	3	9	55
1818	16	11	3	5	10	4	13	62
1819	22	8	2	7	12	1	21	73
1810s	205	123	17	85	81	30	126	667
	(30.7%)	(18.4%)	(2.6%)	(12.7%)	(12.2%)	(4.5%)	(18.9%)	

Figure 2.1 supplies a supplementary view of the broad gender breakdown, with the three sub-gender categories brought together, by decades and in percentage terms. For the years 1750–69 new fiction by women authors is very much in a minority. Of the 508 titles first published then, 84 (16.5 per cent) can be counted as female in broad gender terms, and 151 (29.7 per cent) as male, with a considerable body of 273 (53.8 per cent) 'unknown' titles. (With 'implied' titles omitted, the female/male percentages are 14.2 per cent and 28.7 per cent respectively.) Male titles are predominant in sixteen of the twenty years, outweighing female equivalents by two-to-one or more in no less than eight of these. Female titles prevail only in 1767, and achieve equivalence in 1758, 1759, and 1764. If any shift towards female output is apparent it occurs during the late 1750s and in the later 1760s. Raven (1987: 18) observes a peak of sorts in 1763–4, boosted by the success of Frances Brooke's *The History of Lady Julia Mandeville*, but in this case the rapidity of reprints (an element not considered in the present survey) is a leading factor.

Little change is apparent in the 1770s, a decade marked by diminishing output in its later years, with female titles outnumbering males only in 1777 and 1778. As a whole, 31.6 per cent male titles outweigh 22.4 per cent female ones, with a high proportion of 'unknown' cases (46 per cent). A more even distribution can be discerned in the early 1780s, though the figures are small owing to a continuing low rate of production. The first major shift in favour of female authors coincides with a surge in production, first visible in 1785, when annual output doubled, accelerating once more to nearly twice as many

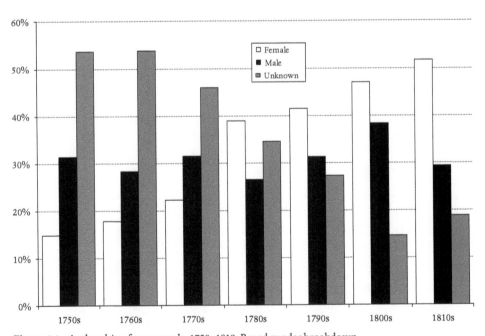

Figure 2.1. Authorship of new novels, 1750–1819: Broad gender breakdown

again nearer the end of the decade. In 1785 for the first time the female count is double that of the male (twenty-two as opposed to ten titles). Women authors predominate for the rest of the decade, with 1789 again showing twice as many female titles (32/15). Even excluding a marked increase in the 'implied' category, female titles outnumber male ones for all years from 1785–9. In broader gender terms for these five years, 121 female titles (41.9 per cent) substantially outweigh sixty-eight male equivalents (23.5 per cent), with 100 gender-unknown titles (a slightly reduced proportion of 34.6 per cent). One particular impetus here undoubtedly came from the success of Frances Burney's *Cecilia* (1782), whose potency as a model is attested by the large number of imitations in immediately following years. The accelerating number of female titles later in the decade also coincides with the emergence of new subgenres, strongly associated with female authorship, notably the sentimental domestic romance.

In the following decade, the pattern becomes more variegated. Male-authored works approach a level of parity in 1791–3, and just exceed female titles in 1795, at a time when total output momentarily dips. Distinct 'female' peaks are nevertheless apparent in 1794 and in 1798 (when forty out a total seventy-five novels for that year represents the attainment of a clear outperformance by women authors). The year 1796, noteworthy for a fresh leap to over ninety titles in all, is especially interesting in showing a rough parity, with thirty-nine female and thirty-two male titles, both numbers exceeding any preceding year, indicative of an influx of new or returning authors of each gender to the genre. Near parity is again achieved in 1799, when production almost touches 100, with thirty-eight male titles nearly matching forty-three female ones (an outcome aided no doubt by a reduced proportion of less than 20 per cent unknown titles). The increased willingness of both male and female authors to declare their names on title pages (twenty-four instances apiece in 1799) is also a distinct feature at this juncture, while the proportion of gender-implied titles (notably 'By a Lady') dwindles. For the 1790s as a whole the broad gender figures for titles are 291 female (41.5 per cent), 219 male (31.3 per cent), and 191 unknown (27.2 per cent).

An equivalently variegated pattern is apparent in the 1800s, when gender proportions are more visible than in any previous decade, with less than 15 per cent of titles in the 'unknown' category. During the first three years the trajectory towards female ascendancy again picks up, with 114 female- as opposed to sixty-eight male-authored titles, and an outnumbering by more than two-to-one in 1801. One contributing factor could be the continuing popularity of the Radcliffian romance, at a time when up to a third of total output was Gothic in character. In 1803 and 1804 however male titles are predominant, outnumbering female counterparts over the two years by seventy-two to sixty-three. One might trace here a delayed effect of the anti-Jacobin reaction in the late 1790s, with excoriating attacks on sentimental and 'radical' female novelists such as Smith and Wollstonecraft in the *Anti-Jacobin Review* and in ultra-conservative fictions such as Robert Bisset's *Douglas* (1800). Female-authored works are again ascendant from

1805–6 (seventy-three to fifty-three), but male titles narrowly exceed female ones in 1807 (thirty-one to thirty), followed by a slight female predominance in 1808–9 (eighty-six to seventy-four). The bumper year of 1808 (111 titles) includes forty-nine female and forty-two male works, the largest number over the whole period for both genders, indicating a shared readiness to engage with the genre, though sometimes in angularly different ways. Boosting the male total in 1807–8 are two types of sensationalist fiction as marketed by J. F. Hughes: Lewisian *Monk*-like 'horror' fictions, such as Edward Montague's *The Demon of Sicily* (1807), and a new kind of acerbic scandal fiction, a speciality of the pseudonymous Charles Sedley. Authorship of this kind in turn helps inflate the 'male-implied' subcategory, which at this time starts to exceed its female equivalent.

The 1810s by contrast show a relatively even pattern of female dominance, with women novelists outproducing their male counterparts annually over the decade, and accounting for over 50 per cent of output in five of the years between 1810 and 1817. This matches the prevalence of female authorship in two fashionable modes: the historical romance (prior to Scott's disruptive intervention in mid-decade) and the polite evangelical domestic novel, after the fashion of Mary Brunton's *Self-Control*, itself an unexpected success in 1811. Male-authored works generally hover below the 30 per cent mark, a low ebb (25.4 per cent) occurring in 1812. In numerical terms female titles outmatch male ones by more than two-to-one in 1810 (51/22), 1813 (39/19), and 1814 (41/17), female production in the last year reaching an unprecedented level of over 65 per cent of output. Another feature in the 1810s is the continuing high number of novels by named female authors, representing over 30 per cent of output, compared with just under 13 per cent of instances where male authors are named. Seen in such terms, the *publication* of Jane Austen's novels was achieved not against the grain but during a period of reinvigorated female engagement. Conversely, Scott's earliest historical novels were launched when male authorship of fiction stood at a low point. However, it is also important to bear in mind the decline in production generally during this decade, one reflection of which is that numerically female production actually fell to an average of around thirty a year between 1816 and 1819. Also potentially significant in the later 1810s is an increase in male-identified as well as 'unknown' titles, indicative arguably of a return to the genre of male authors, albeit under the guise of anonymity.

The 1820s in turn were marked by yet another shift in the gender balance of authorship. As a whole in that decade male-authored novels outnumber female counterparts by 426 to 289, with 122 gender-unknown cases, the male category thus claiming more than half of the total number of titles overall. Evidently women novelists found it harder to prosper in this environment, as publishers sought out a new breed of male authors, and as new modes such as the Scottian historical novel overtook older female favourites. Nevertheless there can be little doubt that the period as a whole provided an unprecedented opportunity for women novelists, especially between 1785 and 1819, when nearly half (46.1 per cent) of new fiction is categorizable as female in broad gender terms.

Publishers and Author Remuneration

According to the Copyright Act of 1710 authors stood in a pole position over the sale of their works. In practical terms, however, booksellers bargained from a position of strength in all but exceptional cases. Accounts of the difficulties faced by novice writers of fiction are legion in the period, both in anecdotal records and within novels themselves. In *A Series of Letters* (1789), the Scottish author Jean Marishall describes her difficulties in trying to dispose of her first novel, *The History of Miss Clarinda Cathcart* (1766), while living in London: the shock at being offered just 'five guineas' by the publisher/library proprietor Noble; an abortive effort on her behalf to place it with other London booksellers, including 'an eminent bookseller who lives in the Strand', all of whom had declared that 'they never purchased the productions of ladies'; and a reluctant return to the original terms offered. Noble's reported reasons for not offering more—the need for heavy correction of grammar, his offer of 'five guineas for a first performance' representing 'a very great price', and the willingness of established novelists to accept even less—must have been repeated frequently to those in similar positions.[5]

For authors living outside London, the difficulties in securing a suitable publisher must have been even greater. Normally too most authors would have been required to provide their own writing materials as well as any carriage costs involved. Women authors could also find the hurdle of direct bargaining difficult if not impossible to surmount, preferring to act through third parties, often male members of their own family. Even at the end of our period, with the novel apparently in ascendancy, Shelley experienced difficulty in securing a publisher for his wife's *Frankenstein*, with rejections from John Murray II, Charles Ollier, and at least one other concern, before the reaching agreement with Lackington & Co. on far from spectacular terms.[6] Many novels never saw publication at all. Jane Austen's first attempt at placement, through her father in 1797, met with instant rejection from Cadell, with *Susan* (a prototype of *Northanger Abbey*) then suffering the perhaps more aggravating fate of remaining unpublished after being sold in 1803 to Crosby & Co. for £10, leading eventually to its repurchase at the same price by her brother Henry in 1816 (Mandal 2007: 57, 63–4). The records of established publishing houses early in the nineteenth century are flecked with rejections of incoming proposals for novels.

Even after acceptance, authors could face a variety of difficulties. Normally they had little or no control over the production process: house readers and compositors enjoyed considerable licence in making changes; manuscripts were usually discarded after setting into type; and proofs were rarely provided. More mystifying for some would have been the financial arrangements involved. The present-day system of royalty payments,

---

[5] *A Series of Letters*, 2 vols (Edinburgh: C. Elliot, 1789), 2.157–60.
[6] See the record for *Frankenstein* in the *DBF* (Garside et al. 2004), 1818A057. Information relating to the publishing history of further titles below is also indebted to this resource.

calculated as a proportion of retail price or the publisher's net receipts, was virtually unheard of in the period. Apart from rudimentary cases, payment came in the form of post-dated promissory notes, which could be converted at banks to cash at a discount, calculated according to the considered reliability of the issuer. In some cases, publishers would withhold any kind of payment until a certain number had been sold. Bankruptcies, hardly infrequent in the trade, could lead to some expectant authors getting nothing.

As a whole, four main types of financial arrangement are in evidence:

(i) Publication for the author. In these circumstances the cost of production and advertising was borne by the author, with the publisher taking a commission on copies sold and the author claiming any remaining profit. The most visible sign of this method having been employed is the appearance of 'Printed/Published for the Author [or Editor]' on title pages. In all nearly two hundred such cases can be found, representing 5.8 per cent of total output of new titles. In view of the number of additional instances where publication by the author is known to have taken place, this almost certainly underestimates the extent of this practice in operation. By reputation the system was peculiarly open to abuse by the trade; while even honest publishers had no large incentive to push works where at best they stood to gain small amounts themselves, and which did not carry their own regular imprint. Conversely, in principle at least, the author stood to gain the largest proportion of receipts by this method, and there were some successes. After opting for sale of copyright with *Pride and Prejudice* (1813), Austen returned to this method for the two remaining novels published in her lifetime. One notable beneficiary was Hannah More, who claimed to have cleared £2,000 after an outlay of £5,000 on the multiple editions of *Coelebs*, retaining copyright in the process (Copeland 1995: 248). For those without capital resources, however, the results could prove devastating, the author having full financial responsibility in the event of a loss, with some booksellers demanding payment to cover materials at the outset. By the end of the period, with an increasing professionalization of the trade, the number of titles visibly published 'for the author' had diminished to a trickle (just 2 per cent in the 1820s compared with over 8 per cent during the 1780s).

(ii) Publication by subscription. By this method, the author effectively guaranteed the sale of the work by procuring in advance promises to pay for copies from subscribers. This was especially useful for novice writers, particularly women, who otherwise might have been rejected, and also offered a lever for those hoping to persuade a local bookseller to contact a London publisher. A palpable downside for some lay in the public exposure and appearance of solicitation that a subscription normally entailed. As with publication by the author, with which this method sometimes blurs, authors could face a humiliating lack of support and the prospect of being left with costs. In all just over 140 novels belonging to the period include lists of subscribers, a figure which excludes a number of instances where there is evidence of a subscription but no list has been found in a surviving copy. Sizeable lists are found virtually from the beginning, one early instance

being the Miss Minifies' *The Histories of Lady Frances S——, and Lady Caroline S——*, with over 750 subscriptions. A notable bulge is distinguishable in the 1790s, with some thirty instances between 1796 and 1799 representing nearly 10 per cent of output for those years. A major influence here undoubtedly was Burney's decision to turn to this method with *Camilla* (1796), in support of herself and her émigré husband, leading to a spectacular list containing 1,058 subscribers vouching for 1,194 copies, and profits to the author of £2,000 (half from the subscription, half by the commercial sale). Where gender is known, female-authored subscription titles outnumber male equivalents by more than three-to-one (ninety-two to thirty). Novelists who cut their teeth this way, before proving prolific in the commercial field, include Anna Maria Mackenzie, Eliza Parsons, and Anna Maria Porter. In the case of lesser-known authors, bereft daughters, widows of officers, and dutiful sons are conspicuous among the supplicants, some of whom appear to have been badly disappointed. As in the case of 'for the author' publication, works of this kind are likely to have provided little incentive for their publishers once the subscribers had been satisfied. A fair proportion were remaindered, the Minerva Press reissuing several with replacement title pages. In the later years the number of subscription novels declined, representing less than 4 per cent of output (twenty-five cases) during the 1810s and with just eleven instances (1.3 per cent) in the following decade.

(iii) *Dividing profits.* More common for novels in the later period, this system involved a sharing of profits between author and publisher based on the trade or 'sale' price of the novel (usually two-thirds of the retail price), after the deduction of production and advertising costs. In most cases, payments were made at yearly or bi-annual intervals in the wake of publication, causing authors to wait for any proceeds. Most commonly, the division was on a 'half-profits' basis, leading to the expression 'going half-and-half'. This was the system most commonly offered by Longmans to works by untried novelists, instances including Anna Maria Porter's early *A Sailor's Friendship, and a Sailor's Love* (1805) and Maturin's first two novels, *Fatal Revenge* (1807) and *The Wild Irish Boy* (1808). Generally the sums generated were on the small side, the most considerable inflow usually coming with the initial sale, and the account sometimes being concluded by a remaindering of unsold copies. Sometimes the result was a loss, in which circumstance an author was likely to be dropped. Notwithstanding the apparent disadvantages involved, a handful of more established authors can also be seen opting for this method. Amelia Opie, one of Longmans' regular novelists, chose half profits for more than half of her titles, achieving returns at least equivalent to those where she had sold copyright. An even more striking exception is Walter Scott, who insisted on contracting his novels on a half-profits basis, limiting the initial agreement to a certain number of copies, with the prospect of enhanced profits on the less costly subsequent editions, which could be negotiated separately, with a change of publishers if need be. By the 1820s Scott was generating sums approaching £4,000 for a single title, much of it in the form of bills in anticipation of profits. A number of other novelists, following in Scott's wake, also managed to generate advance payments after this fashion, Godwin contriving to extract as much as £750 from Constable for *Mandeville* (1817). Others with less clout endured long waits for pitiful returns calculated in a way that could seem mystifying. Hogg struggled to secure a final settlement on *The Brownie of Bodsbeck* (1818) that he felt still owed to him by its co-publisher, Murray. His last novel, *Confessions of a Justified Sinner* (1824), accounted for on a strict half-profits basis by Longmans, had generated just £16 1s. 2d. after four years, the profits being sent to the publisher Blackwood, who had by then taken over the rights.

(iv) *Sale of copyright.* Probably the most common method overall, this involved the disposal of the copyright for a lump sum, the publisher being left to exploit the commercial sale without other involvement. For needy authors the attraction of cash in hand was obvious, though several were to rue an outright sale later. Variations to the pattern include: allowance of extra copies to the author; subsequent *ex gratia* payment; and the limitation of the sale to single editions. All the signs point to payments being small for much of the later eighteenth century, with £5 a fairly normal outlay from circulating-library publishers such as Lane. Some authors were able to bargain higher. Having accepted 20 guineas for *Evelina* (1778), Burney had learned enough of her value to the trade to sell *Cecilia* (1782) for £250; though even then she had to endure rumours that it had cleared £1,500 in its first year. As more general publishing houses entered the market in the 1790s, prices were raised for some authors, as a more distinct double-tiered system came into operation. The George Robinson archive shows sums in the region of 10 guineas a volume being paid regularly for novels; though this could be exceeded in the case of an outstanding author, with Ann Radcliffe reportedly being offered a sum of £500 for her *Mysteries of Udolpho* (1794). By the 1810s Longmans were regularly paying a select body of female authors comparably large sums as a one-off payment for copyright, sometimes even allowing generous advances before delivery of the manuscript. Jane West was offered 200 guineas for *The Loyalists* (1812), having received a similar amount for *The Refusal* (1810); while Jane Porter was paid £315 for a first edition of 2,000 of her *The Scottish Chiefs* (1810). Even allowing for inflation, these sums reflect the growing value of reputable fiction in publishers' eyes at this time. The apex of the Longmans' payments came with Burney's *The Wanderer* (1814), where the author was to be paid £1,500 for the first edition, and another £1,500 for five subsequent editions. By this point a number of novelists had become adept in their bargaining, Sydney Owenson successfully playing off Joseph Johnson and Richard Phillips against each other before accepting £300 from the latter for her *Wild Irish Girl* (1806). In the case of *O'Donnel* (1814) she settled with Henry Colburn, himself then becoming conspicuous by paying large sums for copy. Another Irish novelist, Maria Edgeworth, enjoyed an exponential rise in the proceeds for her fiction during these years, with sums of £300 for *Belinda* (1801), £1,050 for the second series (1812) of *Tales of Fashionable Life*, and £2,100 for her less popular *Patronage* (1814). By the end of the decade news of the sums being generated by Scott had filtered through, further raising the financial bar. William Blackwood's offer of £150 for Susan Ferrier's

Marriage (1818) was followed by the £1,000 given for her second novel, *The Inheritance* (1824). A similar sum was offered by Blackwood for J. G. Lockhart's third work of fiction *Reginald Dalton* (1823), one of a number of novels produced by male members of the Blackwoodian circle in the 1820s.

Notwithstanding the increasingly high sums on record, it is hard to find any clear instance of a writer achieving financial independence as a professional novelist. Charlotte Smith perhaps comes closest to the mark among women authors, achieving an annual income of between £370 and £570 in the literary market during her more productive years, with a lifetime total of over £4,000, primarily from fiction though also from poetry and children's books (Stanton 1987: 378, 390–2). Such sums however were hardly excessive for those from the middling ranks (probably the largest constituency in the pool of authors then) wishing to maintain an element of respectability at this time. Frances Burney's proceeds from her four novels, stretched over a thirty-six-year period, Copeland calculates, would only have brought a yearly income of around £160 if invested in government funds, approximating the basic income of a country curate (1995: 194). As in Austen's case, the earnings of many relatively successful female novelists would have come as a welcome personal addition to an already secure (if cramping) familial situation. Successful male novelists, for their part, were likely to operate in a variety of genres, some more profitable than fiction, as well as holding on to their professional careers. Scott kept his main legal posts until almost the end of his life, gaining by these both social standing and reliable income, as well as a useful life raft after his bankruptcy in 1826.

At the other end of the scale, there is plenty of evidence of novelists writing out of dire necessity. A valuable window here is provided by the archives of the Royal Literary Fund, which began making donations to needy authors in 1790. In all, some seventy-five authors (thirty-eight female, thirty-seven male) who wrote fiction within the period are to be found there, despite the difficulties some clearly felt making a claim based on novel-writing. While some only dabbled in the genre, the list includes several prolific novelists, among them Eliza Parsons, Regina Maria Roche, and Isabella Kelly. In the case of male supplicants, a not uncommon theme is the need for a quick injection of cash to escape debtor's gaol. Amongst women novelists two common types are the widowed mother with a large family and the single woman having to survive without parental support. A notable instance of the first is Eliza Parsons, as a widow with eight children, whose appeals began in 1792, when a fractured leg thwarted her efforts at self-sufficiency. By 1796, though able to claim 'five and Twenty Volumes', she was again desperately in need of support, having been obliged to take temporary lodgings, and without any flow of income for her efforts: 'as Necessity always obliges me to Sell the Copy rights, my Advantages are trifling to what the Publisher gains'. An instance of the difficulties faced by single women is provided by the case of Sarah Isdell, 'reduced' in 1810 'to the necessity of procuring a subsistence for herself' after her father's death in Ireland. With two works of fiction already to her name, she had come to London with a new novel and some theatrical pieces, only to meet with frustration at every turn. While praising the novel as 'of a superior description', Stockdale had rejected it as 'not of the *very first order*'; it had lain with Newman at the Minerva Press for a month prior to rejection for being 'in letters'; Longmans were known to prioritize works received through their own connexions; and Crosby was only prepared to publish if it could be deferred for another year. In the event, Isdell was granted 5 guineas, which allowed her to return home.[7]

As a whole, however, it is possible to point to a considerable shift over the period from a situation where the author, if distinct at all from the narrative, remained at best a shadowy figure, to one where a known authorial identity could be vital in defining a whole body of work. The use of proper names on title pages increased significantly from the 1790s; and if the end of the period saw a return to anonymity, it was of a uniquely new kind, with journalistic puffing rapidly supplying any gaps in the public's knowledge. An equivalent movement can be found in circulating-library catalogues, where a tendency to use author names as a peg in alphabetical lists, rather than just titles, becomes more apparent in the new century. A mounting interest in the private lives of novelists is likewise evident in contemporary reviews. More telling still perhaps, at the close of the period, is the appearance of two works of fiction containing substantial biographical accounts of their recently deceased authors: Jane Austen's *Northanger Abbey: And Persuasion* (1818), containing Henry Austen's 'Biographical Notice of the Author', and Mary Brunton's *Emmeline* (1819), with its long prefatory 'Memoir' by her husband (also a frontispiece portrait). From here it was not a long step to Scott's extensive personal engagement through the new Introductions and Notes to the Magnum Opus collected edition of the Waverley Novels, commencing in 1829, and the biographical emphasis, as applied to recently published fiction, in Bentley's *Standard Novels* from 1831. Both of these in turn were hugely influential in establishing a new sense of the centrality of the novelist, one capable of both informing and distorting the fiction of this earlier period.

[7] Papers of the Royal Literary Fund (British Library), case 21, item 8, letter of 7 July 1796; case 246, item 1, letter of 20 February 1810.

3

Circulation

DAVID ALLAN

B Y the 1750s the reading of novels had become an important cultural experience shared repeatedly and enthusiastically by large numbers of English-speaking men and women. Frequently it seemed enjoyable to contemporaries precisely because it brought them together: 'We are much entertained in reading the expedition of Humphry Clinker', purred the Lancaster teenager Mary Chorley in 1778, recording in her diary what was evidently a mutual pleasure created by the prevalence of reading aloud within her household.[1] Yet reading novels also seemed rather more than mere entertainment. It actually promised edification, even moral improvement: what he earnestly described as 'Walter Scott's most excellent advice to <u>all</u> young men of landed prop^y', in fact simply a passage from *The Fortunes of Nigel* (1822), was copied out in April 1823 by Richard Hoare, a Wiltshire squire, confident that reflecting carefully on Scott's words would be of direct practical benefit to his own son Henry.[2] Such faith in the benefits of novel-reading, however, begs a series of questions about the conditions that made these contrasting acts of textual reception possible in the first place. How extensively did narrative fiction really circulate among readers between the eighteenth and the early nineteenth centuries? Quite simply, how easy was it to get one's hands on a novel in the ages of Smollett or of Scott? And what factors determined whether an individual in Georgian Britain would come into direct contact with this intensely seductive but also relatively new kind of imaginative literature?

Having and Holding

The personal ownership of books was in fact far from unknown at the time and indeed even attracted much comment in certain circumstances. The period undoubtedly

---

[1] Lancaster Public Library: MS 8752–3, Mary Chorley's diaries, 18 May 1778.
[2] Trowbridge: Wiltshire and Swindon RO: 383/940, Extract from *The Fortunes of Nigel*.

produced a number of legendary individual collectors. Samuel Johnson's friend Topham Beauclerk, for example, owned more than 30,000 volumes when he died in 1780.[3] The obsessive bibliophile Richard Heber, meanwhile, had accumulated an almost unimaginable 150,000 forty years later (Hunt 2001). Acquisitiveness on this scale, however, was not typical. Most book-buyers, even by the early nineteenth century, owned just a small handful, or at most a few dozen—mainly because they still laboured under the same constraints that had dogged committed book-lovers for generations.

The biggest hindrance to individual ownership was simply the gulf between high retail prices and low personal incomes. For large printed texts remained expensive items both to create and to replicate in any quantity. Decisive technological changes in the second quarter of the nineteenth century—involving the introduction of stereotyping, steam-powered printing, machine-produced paper, and new inks—which slashed production costs and made much cheaper books feasible, would change this situation forever. But for all of the period under consideration, the substantial printed text, including the novel in its most familiar contemporary formats, remained a relatively expensive proposition for most readers to contemplate.

The size of the resulting obstacle facing those who wished to buy the latest novels is evident in some of the exorbitant prices charged for first-edition copies. *Sense and Sensibility* (1811), for example, came in at fifteen shillings in the standard 'three-decker' edition; *Guy Mannering* (1815), meanwhile, cost the customer twenty-one shillings; and by the end of the decade *The Monastery* (1820) was priced at twenty-four (St Clair 2004: 203). Such tariffs invariably made for difficult, maybe impossible, decisions: as Richard Altick pointed out, the average Georgian reader, even if utterly besotted with a particular title, faced the prospect of parting company with an entire week's wage, and so would in practice be choosing 'between buying a newly published quarto volume and a good pair of breeches . . . or between a volume of essays and a month's supply of tea and sugar' (1957: 51–2). Even second-hand copies remained prohibitively expensive and did not adequately solve the problem of affordability.

A further impediment to widespread ownership of novels arose quite naturally from the problem of pricing. The combination of high manufacturing costs and the understanding by publishing booksellers that their sales were likely to be low ensured that print runs were for the most part also strikingly unambitious. *Emma*, for example, first appeared in December 1815 in a mere 2,000 copies at the height of the author's reputation in her lifetime, and even then one quarter needed to be remaindered five years later; and when *Persuasion* and *Northanger Abbey* (1818) were produced it was in just 1,750 copies, of which 282 were unsold as late as 1821 (St Clair 2004: 579–80). Whichever way one

---

[3] *Bibliotheca Beauclerkiana. A Catalogue of the Large and Valuable Library of the Late Honourable Topham Beauclerk . . .* (London, [1781]).

looks at such figures, it is hard not to be struck by the tiny numbers of copies of these novels—today definitively canonical texts but then only just starting to make their way in the world—that actually existed at the time and so were accessible in *any* context by a contemporary reader.

The evidence confirms, however, that some readers did nonetheless manage to procure the latest English novels as they appeared—invariably, and predictably, by dint of unusual levels of personal wealth. Robert Gordon, for example, who lived at Leweston in Dorset and who was an MP and government minister, was an avid collector of Scott's poetry even before he also purchased *Waverley* (1814), shortly after its publication.[4] Charles, Lord Dormer, a Catholic squire from Warwickshire, had not previously acquired any of Scott's work but then followed Gordon in snapping up an early copy of *Waverley*, which was still in his personal possession when he died shortly afterwards.[5] Richard Watson, Bishop of Llandaff, and his family, went further. Living at Calgarth in Westmorland they continued to buy Scott's novels even after Watson's death in 1816—though seemingly with the singular exception of *The Heart of Mid-Lothian* (1818), missing when the collection was eventually catalogued.[6] Occasionally the evidence of ownership even hints at a more intimate relationship having arisen at the time between a contemporary reader and a particular novel. For example, it is tempting to think that the purchase of *Peveril of the Peak* (1822) by the Derbyshire gentleman John Longden—*Waverley* apart, the sole prose work by Scott that he ever owned—was related to the fact that it was the novelist's only narrative production to focus on that reader's native county.[7]

For most people, of course, such indulgence, involving buying an expensive new publication probably only because it piqued personal or local interest, was beyond their wildest dreams. Instead, the only sense in which somewhat larger numbers of readers might realistically hope to own a substantial work of narrative fiction for themselves was by relying on serialization and number publication. It is clear, however, that even the latter (involving the marketing of complete works broken up into discrete parts) would not always have been particularly helpful to the poor reader. After all, a typical instalment of a popular eighteenth-century novel—*Robinson Crusoe* (1719) received this treatment repeatedly—would still have retailed at around sixpence (St Clair 2004: 205–6, 568). Nor were the major booksellers all that keen, especially as far as the more lucrative copyrighted titles were concerned, since they feared that too much number publication would undermine the traditional market for complete texts at full cover price.

---

[4] Dorchester: Dorset Record Office: D/FFO 17/68, 'Catalogue of Leweston Library', 105.

[5] Warwick: Warwickshire County Record Office: CR895/49, 'Inventory of the Furniture and Effects at Grove Park Bequeathed as Heir Looms by The Rt Hon. Charles Lord Dormer 1819', fol. 18r.

[6] Kendal: Cumbria Archive Service: WD/K/210, 'Catalogue of the Library at Calgarth Park', 123–4.

[7] *Catalogue of [an] Extensive Sale...on the Premises of John Longden, Esq., Ashbourne...* (Ashbourne, 1827), 53, 56.

Serialization, though, the trade as a whole deemed rather less threatening. Accordingly it was relatively widely pursued, from the sequential appearance of sections of *Moll Flanders* (1722) in issues of the *Kentish Post* and the *London Post* shortly after its first appearance in book form, through the releasing of Charlotte Lennox's *Sophia* (1762) in separate parts in *The Lady's Museum* even before the book's initial publication, until at least the weekly appearance of successive portions of *Great Expectations* (1860–1) in the pages of Dickens's own periodical *All The Year Round*. Serialization was therefore regarded as an established and accepted practice by authors and publishers alike, bringing the latest novels to unprecedented numbers of people, albeit at the inconvenience of readers having their own progress through the story—arguably an essential part of the novel-consuming experience—interrupted by the exasperating waits between instalments.

Equally frustrating for some even as it also cast tantalizing shafts of light onto a new literary landscape, the practice also emerged of printing choice extracts from certain novels in the magazines and newspapers—themselves a ubiquitous presence in the coffee houses and taverns and a staple of many ordinary readers' lives. The belief was that this whetted appetites and stirred up wider public interest: to cite just a couple of the leading examples, *Tristram Shandy* (1760–7), itself published in a succession of volumes issued over the best part of a decade, justified repeated serialization and extraction through the late eighteenth century, while sample passages from the newly published *Humphry Clinker* (1771) were reproduced immediately in both the *Town and Country Magazine* and the *Critical Review*.[8] Abridgement and anthologization, too, with early novels like *Clarissa* (1748–9) and *Sir Charles Grandison* (1753–4) among the works quickly subjected to these techniques, extended at least partial exposure to their texts even more widely among the literate public—though again at the expense of fundamentally altering an individual's experience of a complex narrative, and not necessarily always for the better (Price 2000: 13–27).

Not surprisingly, a further consequence of the practical difficulties most people faced in buying the more sizeable printed works for themselves was frequent recourse to interpersonal borrowing. Robust historical evidence for this entirely informal mechanism is unsurprisingly slight. But we do occasionally catch glimpses of it productively at work in allusions made by contemporary correspondents as well as in fleeting anecdotal references which by chance have come down to us. Certainly this practice was both endemic and mundane in Georgian society and many of the period's best-known figures took full advantage. Wordsworth, for example, loaned his own books to friends like Coleridge when they came to see him at Rydal Mount: we know this because he took the wise precaution of keeping a book recording the borrowers' names and the volumes they had taken away (Shaver and Shaver 1979: xxiii–xxv). Keats too borrowed from his brother

---

[8] *Town and Country Magazine*, 3 (1771): 317; *Critical Review*, 32 (August 1771): 88.

Tom as well as from John Taylor, a bookseller friend: the poet's frank letters disclose a lax borrower with a guilty conscience as well as an acute literary intelligence at work dissecting the respective merits of the novelists whose writings he knew best, like Fielding, Smollett, Godwin, and Scott.[9] Coleridge, for his part, even found himself in August 1817 having to apologize for having had the bad manners to write all over one book, borrowed from his good friend George Frere, that he had simply been unable to resist covering with his own scrawl (the book, Duncan Forbes's *Works*, is now in the British Library).

Yet ad hoc lending was not the exclusive preserve of the wealthy and the well-connected. The poor, many of whom could read and many more of whom could at least listen to a story being read aloud by a literate friend, workmate, or family member if he or she had somehow got hold of a copy of the text, also benefited directly from such informal arrangements. Thomas Carter, an Essex apprentice tailor, and Thomas Bewick, then working for a Newcastle engraver, were both lent books by enlightened employers; William Dodd, a Kendal textile worker, was given reading materials by his masters; John Cannon, a Somerset farm labourer, was allowed to borrow from a friendly local gardener; and young John Clare, the son of a Northamptonshire agricultural worker, encountered *Robinson Crusoe*, 'the first book of any merit I got hold of after I could read', when he was able to borrow it from a school friend (Vincent 1981: 117; Brewer 1997: 186–7).[10] Indeed, as the cases of Dodd and Clare in particular make clear, the lending of a literary text might potentially trigger momentous changes in a susceptible beneficiary: the young Mary Ann Evans, too, the future George Eliot, was apparently first inspired to become a novelist when a kindly neighbour allowed her family to borrow a copy of *Waverley* (Haldane 2004: 22).

Not all book owners, of course, were conscious of the part that they were playing in the increasing circulation of texts through different readers' hands—and nor would they necessarily have approved of what was happening if they had known. If his own testimony is to be believed, the Bath servant John Jones surreptitiously read his employers' books behind their backs,[11] while Robert Dodsley was in part catapulted from domestic servitude to man of consequence in the republic of letters by the privileges afforded him as a young man working as a footman in the book-filled household of the daughter of Lord Lonsdale (Irwin 1958: 211). But such casual, unstructured and therefore largely untraceable forms of access to books can inevitably form only part of the story of how relatively scarce and forbiddingly expensive texts, including considerable numbers of novels, became known to growing numbers of readers. Properly organized lending, expressly

---

[9] *The Letters of John Keats 1814–1821*, ed. Hyder Edward Rollins, 2 vols (Cambridge, MA: Harvard University Press, 1958), 1.295–6; 2.111, 234–5.

[10] William Dodd, *The Factory System Illustrated...* (London: J. Murray, 1842), 288; *John Clare's Autobiographical Writings*, ed. Eric Robinson (Oxford: Oxford University Press, 1983), 13.

[11] Robert Southey, *Attempts in Verse, By John Jones, An Old Servant* (London: J. Murray, 1831), 173.

designed to enrich as well as merely to extend the reading experiences of contemporaries, was also becoming an increasingly influential feature of British book culture.

The Joy of Borrowing

The Georgian expansion and diversification of fully fledged lending collections is of more than merely technical interest. For they exemplify better than any other institutional development the progressive cultural forces that were steadily transforming society. In nurturing and facilitating reading, libraries consciously encouraged literacy and promoted the spread of knowledge and understanding: the aim, according to those who founded one collection in the industrial town of Sunderland in 1812, was nothing less than to 'furnish the ready means of useful information to many who could not otherwise obtain it, and, by diffusing instruction, equally serve to improve their manners and their taste'.[12] In attracting sponsorship and patronage, many libraries also provided a focus for the sort of public-spirited philanthropy in which people from a wide variety of backgrounds could join forces in a common enterprise. At the same time, regular library attendance, especially if reinforced by active participation in its communal management, allowed individuals both to practise sociability and to hone their politeness: such vigorous associational behaviour was a striking illustration of the Earl of Shaftesbury's dictum in 1711 that it was precisely by such voluntary activities, unforced and unconstrained, that 'we polish one another and rub off our corners and rough sides by a sort of amicable collision'.[13] Nor was even this the end of the benefits. For in granting unprecedented access to large numbers of books, and even, in many cases, conferring the chance to play a role in choosing new acquisitions, libraries allowed readers themselves to help shape taste and to define the emerging canon. Consequently the extraordinary growth of libraries in the eighteenth century could hardly avoid being implicated in some way in the successful establishment of the novel as a popular—in time, *the* popular—literary form among the reading public.

Not that all Georgian lending collections were bold new departures. Cathedral libraries, for example, long established by this time, were an important cultural force in certain localities. Most opened their holdings to readers who were known to them or who could procure a recommendation: Coleridge, that inveterate consulter of other people's books, borrowed items from Carlisle Cathedral and Durham Cathedral, and Johnson, during a final visit to his native town in 1784, was lent books at Lichfield Cathedral (Kaufman 1960, 1973: 112–13). More widespread in their impact were the parish libraries, of which,

---

[12] *A Catalogue of the Sunderland Subscription Library...* (Sunderland, 1812), iii.
[13] Lord Shaftesbury, *Characteristics of Men, Manners, Opinions, Times*, ed. Lawrence E. Klein (Cambridge: Cambridge University Press, 1999), 31.

not least because of Rev. Thomas Bray's far-sighted national scheme, many additional examples were now emerging. Collections ostensibly instituted purely to improve the professional expertise of clerical incumbents were in many instances transformed into a resource that was freely available to literate parishioners. Symbolizing this new emphasis on wider access in the parish libraries, the last volume to be physically chained up to prevent its being easily taken away suffered this fate in 1752, while no further collections using this device were started in England after 1710.

In many of these Anglican collections, moreover, modern English literature, either ordered by *avant-garde* clergymen or else donated by enlightened local worthies, increasingly made its presence felt. At Lichfield, for example, Johnson would also, had he looked, have found the works of Fielding and Swift, while anyone inspecting the library at Canterbury Cathedral in the late eighteenth century would have seen both Swift and Sterne (Botfield 1849: 266, 40). That crucial context to the growing public consumption of narrative fiction, the polite literature and critical reviews that helped frame readers' perceptions of the novel and highlighted notable examples worth seeking out, were also often extending their influence within the cathedral closes: the *Gentleman's Magazine*, for example, could be perused at Lincoln and Lichfield; the *Edinburgh Review* at Gloucester; the *Quarterly* at Worcester; and the literary scholarship of Thomas Warton, together with the works of Sterne, at Norwich (Botfield 1849: 296, 266, 170, 500, 343).

Parish libraries too were frequently useful in these respects, both exposing local readers to critical literature and making available loan copies of important novels. Readers at Whitchurch in Shropshire, for example, would have been able to imbibe the parish's copies of Johnson's criticism and the literary guidance of the *Annual Register*, while at Bridgnorth in the same county the *Gentleman's* would once more have informed and educated the ambitious parishioner.[14] At Elham in Kent, meanwhile, the browser interested in imaginative literature would have taken satisfaction in having *Gulliver's Travels* (1726), *Robinson Crusoe*, and *Tristram Shandy* all available to read; at Ribbesford in Worcestershire, too, the literary-minded parishioner would have been able to get his or her hands on Swift's works and *Tristram Shandy*.[15]

Modern secular literature presented in an avowedly religious setting was by the early nineteenth century even more visible in the non-Anglican libraries. Most of the Dissenters' collections were in fact attached to chapels, invariably relying on the subscriptions as well as on the purchasing proposals of their congregations. This lent them an essentially voluntaristic air and made them more responsive to their readers' own tastes

---

[14] *Catalogue of Books from Parochial Libraries in Shropshire* (Shrewsbury: Shropshire County Council, 1971), 298, 603, 604.

[15] *A Catalogue of Mr Lee Warley's Library Bequeathed by Him to the Parish of Elham* . . . (London, 1845), 13, 24, 26; *Catalogue of the Library of the Rev. Thomas Wigan, Given to the Parish of Ribbesford* . . . (Middle Hill, 1859), 6.

than were the Church of England collections. Obvious results include the concessions made to the contemporary novel, nicely captured in the slightly contradictory declaration of the Wesleyans of the Brunswick Chapel Library in Newcastle: 'It will therefore naturally follow', they announced in 1809, 'that the majority of Books, will be of a nature calculated to inculcate "the fear of the Lord, which is the beginning of wisdom"; at the same time it is not meant to be exclusively a Religious Library, and useful Books, containing nothing inimical to the interests of Religion, will readily be admitted'.[16]

At Blackburn in Lancashire, too, the Congregationalists insisted that their lending collection would be properly subservient to the chapel's religious purposes, including announcing library business from the pulpit on Sundays, but even they still bought popular novels, such as Elizabeth Hamilton's influential satire on Scottish manners and mores *The Cottagers of Glenburnie* (1808).[17] The consequence of such accommodations with secular culture and especially with the ungovernable literary tastes of ordinary believers in the pews is particularly well seen in the Portsmouth Unitarian Chapel Library, founded in 1816. For despite their pious intentions, those who ran it soon went on to purchase all of Scott's intensely fashionable novels, clearly unable to resist the most sensational literary phenomenon of the first half of the nineteenth century.[18]

The principal associational focus among the incurably bookish, however, was the properly secular lending collection which tended to occur, especially in a veritable tidal wave of new foundations from the 1750s onwards, in two separate but related forms—the book club and the subscription library. Both variants had common origins in the desire to gather together with like-minded other readers and to begin purchasing a significant number of books for private circulation amongst themselves. Indeed, many if not most subscription libraries actually started life as book clubs, with proven success over time and growing ambitions gradually encouraging their metamorphosis into something grander: thousands of the basic book clubs had probably existed by the 1820s but perhaps only 260 of the more complicated subscription libraries. The main functional difference, at least in theory, was that the book club's holdings were expected to be transitory, each text being sold off once it had been read. The subscription library, by contrast, was supposed to develop a permanent collection—hence the elaborate and expensive paraphernalia that they usually evolved, such as a published catalogue, membership rolls, an elected subcommittee for routine decision-making, and often, by the 1820s, a prominently positioned library building erected at considerable cost to the subscribers. Clearly

[16] Newcastle upon Tyne: Tyne and Wear Archives Service: 1041/6: Brunswick Chapel Library, minute book, 1808–, 7.

[17] *Rules and Catalogue of the Subscription Library, Established at the Independent Chapel, Blackburn...* (Blackburn, 1827), 3.

[18] *Catalogue of the Congregational Library at the Unitarian Chapel, Portsmouth...* ([Portsmouth], 1823), 111–12.

if we wish to get a sense of how widely and easily novels were circulating among the contemporary reading public, these dynamic membership-based organizations are another obvious place to look.

Fortunately the subscription libraries' habit of compiling detailed printed catalogues, and even of preserving coherent minutes of internal discussions, makes this a relatively straightforward exercise. And from this evidence it is very clear that the admission of the novel was not entirely without difficulty—because many participants were understandably sensitive to the suggestion that narrative fiction, or at least a great deal of it, was both trashy in character and incorrigibly manipulative in its wider effects. Accordingly the records sometimes capture defensive-sounding rhetoric gesturing at a crucial distinction between the decent and uplifting fictional narrative, with which sustained contact by respectable readers was broadly acceptable, and the merely dangerous potboiler or titillating page-turner, with which it most certainly was not. The founders of the Literary Society in Leicester exemplified this line of reasoning in 1790, ruling that 'No Novel, or Play, shall be admitted into the Library, but such as have stood the test of time, and are of established reputation'.[19] Even so, as a proportion of total holdings, the part of the collection comprising modern narrative fiction was generally high. At Lancaster, for example, no less than 30 per cent of the Amicable Society's Library collection in 1812 was made up of creative literature of various kinds—327 titles all told.[20] At both the Shrewsbury Subscription Library that same year and the Union Library in Liverpool six years earlier, novels also formed comfortably the second-largest category in the respective catalogues.[21]

We see this same pattern replicated again and again when we look in detail at the collections of individual libraries. One that could stand for many is the Macclesfield Subscription Library (confusingly, it sometimes called itself the Circulating Library), which, by the time that one of the three surviving catalogues was issued in 1796, had been in existence for more than twenty years and had built up a mixed-sex membership of sixty-four people drawn from the merchants, professionals, landowners, and clergy of this prosperous Cheshire silk-manufacturing town.[22] The collection that they had constructed over two decades of careful purchasing was richly varied, with narrative fiction representing around one-quarter of the 565 numbered items. Described here as 'Novels and Romances' (18–21), this section contained 130 separate titles, all but four octavo volumes having been produced in the smaller duodecimo format. Several different kinds of imaginative fiction were present, including most of the experimental types that had recently helped push back the boundaries of the genre —the 'it-narrative' about the lives

---

[19] *Laws for the Regulation of the Literary Society. Leicester* ([Leicester], [1790]), 11.
[20] *A Catalogue of the Amicable Society's Library*... (Lancaster, 1812).
[21] *Catalogue of Books Belonging to the Subscription Library in Shrewsbury*... (Shrewsbury, 1812); *A Catalogue of Books in the Union Library, Liverpool, 1806* (Liverpool, n.d.).
[22] *A Catalogue of the Books in the Macclesfield Subscription Library*... (Macclesfield, 1796), 41–2.

of inanimate objects in the form of Thomas Bridges' *Adventures of a Bank Note* (1770–1) and Smollett's *Adventures of an Atom* (1769); the epistolary novel exemplified in very different tones by *Humphry Clinker* and *Evelina* (1778); comedy variously represented by *Tom Jones* (1749) and by *Peregrine Pickle* (1751); tragic moralism typified by *Clarissa*; the sentimental by *The Man of Feeling* (1771) and Harriet Lee's *The Errors of Innocence* (1786); the Gothic, and much else besides, by Charlotte Smith's *Emmeline* (1788); the deliberately unclassifiable by *Tristram Shandy*. It is deeply disappointing that the absence of any surviving loan records at Macclesfield—as virtually everywhere with the subscription libraries—means that we cannot say how often any of these titles was actually borrowed, much less by whom. But it is difficult to avoid the conclusion that the people who founded and ran such institutions expended their precious funds on these works of narrative fiction only because they genuinely wanted to own them and to read them.

Notwithstanding the relative paucity of printed catalogues produced by the generally less formalized book clubs, comparable enthusiasm for the novel can nevertheless be securely documented. Scrutiny of handwritten minutes and ledgers reveals that, for example, the members of the Fairford Society in Gloucestershire ordered *The Mysteries of Udolpho* (1794) on 21 July that year, within weeks of its first appearance; the Ely Pamphlet Club in Cambridgeshire, belying its name, enthusiastically bought *The Man of Feeling*, *The Vicar of Wakefield* (1766), and *Clarissa*; and at Luddenden near Halifax the copies of *Roderick Random* (1748) and *Tom Jones* were actually so well-thumbed that they were the only titles owned by this local book club ever to need repairing (Kaufman 1969a: 69, 45, 56). Their zeal for narrative fiction extended even to assistance with publication: the Colchester Book Society, the Cheshire Book Society at Chester, the Repton Book Society in Nottinghamshire, the Sheffield Book Society, and the Sutton Book Society in Surrey all subscribed to Burney's *Camilla* (1796); while the George Book Club and the Fountain Book Club, whose very names, identifying the Huntingdon inns at which they habitually met, are a useful reminder that bibulousness and bibliophilia often went enjoyably hand in hand in polite society, both sponsored Sarah Cobbe's *Julia St. Helen* (1800).[23] No clearer proof could be imagined of the determination of the members of these book clubs to help increase the quantity and quality of novels in circulation by whatever means were available to them.

It should also be emphasized that the many benefits of associational lending were not restricted to the prosperous and the genteel. Indeed, these structures also provided an admirable means by which humble readers of limited means could hope to sate at least some of their no less ravenous hunger for books. Some lending collections, admittedly, were created and managed on their users' behalf by benign employers and patrons,

---

[23] Frances Burney, *Camilla*, 5 vols (London: Cadell and Davies, 1796), 1.xii, xv, xxxvii, xxxix, xli; Sarah Cobbe, *Julia St. Helen*, 2 vols (London: Earle and Hemet, 1800), 1.xii.

apparently seeking to edify as well as to educate the lower classes at whom they were explicitly aimed: the Hexham Mechanics' and Scientific Institution in Northumberland, which gave local workers the opportunity to borrow the Waverley Novels, and the Liverpool Mechanics' and Apprentices' Library, where the first book accessioned was none other than that classic fare for the nineteenth-century proletarian autodidact, *Robinson Crusoe*, were typical of many such organizations by the late 1820s and early 1830s (Rose 2001: 93–7, 104–11).[24]

Associationalism, however, generally implied a propensity for self-organization, and so it often proved with the literate poor. The Liberals, for example, were a London book club founded and run by working men in 1821: the printer and later Chartist activist William Lovitt was a member, and reasonably credited it with much of his own intellectual awakening (St Clair 2004: 672). William Heaton, a tanner's son, helped found a membership-based lending collection in the West Riding of Yorkshire specifically for people like himself: again the episode may well have been transformational, as he later became a notable working-class poet. Christopher Thomson, another Yorkshireman, who began work in a shipyard but subsequently took up the occupation of domestic painter, was actively involved in setting up an artisans' library at Edwinstowe in Nottinghamshire: when he subsequently penned his autobiography, Thomson was self-aware enough to attribute his profound veneration of the demi-gods of English literature—chiefly Shakespeare and Johnson—to that life-changing experience.[25]

Eating the Apple

If one kind of Georgian lending institution above all is associated with the apotheosis of the English novel, it is, of course, the circulating library. This was also true at the time. Sir Anthony Absolute in Sheridan's *The Rivals* (1775) was characteristically scathing: 'A circulating library in a town is as an evergreen tree of diabolical knowledge!', he complained colourfully; 'It blossoms through the year! — and depend on it, Mrs Malaprop, that they who are so fond of handling the leaves, will long for the fruit at last'.[26] The playwright George Colman, meanwhile, in *Polly Honeycombe* (1760), allowed a desperate character, alarmed by the corrupting effects on young women of their now being able to borrow and read anything they wanted, to warn that 'a man might as well turn his Daughter loose in Covent-garden, as trust the cultivation of her mind to A CIRCULATING LIBRARY'.[27]

---

[24] *A Catalogue of the Hexham Mechanics' and Scientific Institution* (Hexham, 1835), 14–15; *An Account of the Liverpool Mechanics' and Apprentices' Library* (Liverpool, 1824), 22.

[25] Christopher Thomson, *The Autobiography of an Artisan* (London: J. Chapman, 1847), 65–7.

[26] Richard Sheridan, *The Rivals*, ed. Elizabeth Duthie (London: Benn, 1979), 26.

[27] George Colman, *Polly Honeycombe: A Dramatick Novel of One Act* (London: T. Becket and T. Davies, 1760), 44.

And there was no doubt that it was the ability that the rise of book-renting had given to women, servants, and young people in particular to gain unsupervised access to the novel—too often racy, titillating, manipulative, or just plain cynical—that most concerned purse-lipped moralists. Henry Mackenzie, for instance, who knew a thing or two about writing best-selling narrative fiction, frantically distanced himself from 'That common herd of Novels (the wretched offspring of circulating libraries), which are despised for their insignificance, or proscribed for their immorality'.[28]

The institutions which formed the focus for such concentrated and consistent sniping had initially had no direct connection with the emergent novel. Indeed, they clearly originated as an experimental outgrowth of the retail book trade during the late seventeenth century, when creative booksellers like Francis Kirkman and Enoch Wyer in London had realized that additional income could be raised by allowing readers to pay to borrow as well as simply to purchase from their stock. This had, however, been a slow and halting beginning. Worried that renting might displace purchasing and also that the resale of old lending stock would depress retail prices, the trade did not properly expand into organized book-renting until the second quarter of the eighteenth century.

Eventually, though, a more nuanced and responsive business model evolved, with some proprietors—like Samuel Fancourt, who traded in Salisbury from 1735 and moved to the metropolis in 1742—giving themselves over entirely to lending activities, which increasingly looked commercially viable in their own right. This in turn necessitated the invention of a specialist infrastructure: printed catalogues and rulebooks were issued, as by the private subscription libraries; advertising and promotional activities became ever more ingenious (owners usually had other goods and services to showcase in parallel, ranging from printing and stationery to insurance, patent medicines, ornamental stonemasonry, and umbrellas); and complex systems of fees were devised as the growing market increasingly segmented, with different kinds of book, varying loan periods, diverse entitlements, and even readers situated nearby or further away from the library all receiving separate consideration. It was the circulating library in this mature and often highly organized form that ultimately acquired a symbiotic relationship with the English novel.

By 1800, and for all the venomous criticism it had attracted, the circulating library had become a deeply entrenched cultural institution—an irreplaceable resource in the reading lives of many, as affectionate soubriquets like 'Southey's Bodleian' for Lewis Bull's library in Bath, where the poet, a draper's son, dallied in his youth, should remind us (Stewart-Murphy 1992: 31). No exact figure can be offered but there were certainly dozens in existence at some point during the eighteenth and early nineteenth centuries

---

[28] *The Lounger*, no. 20: Saturday, 18 June 1785.

in every one of the substantial towns—forty-one in Manchester, for example, and at least seventy-eight in Bristol. There were literally hundreds throughout this period in the capital itself. As a result it seems certain that the total number of Georgian circulating libraries active at one time or another must have run comfortably into the thousands.

We can also be confident that the critics, so quick to draw attention to the sheer scale of this burgeoning phenomenon, were correct about at least one other aspect of the commercial libraries' activities: that they were making an important contribution to the circulation of narrative fiction in particular. Indeed, a significant number were even active in commissioning, or at least in supporting, the production of additional novels. Businessmen such as Thomas Hookham of Hanover Square, who published works like *Anna: A Sentimental Novel* (1782), William Lane, owner of the famous Minerva Library on Leadenhall Street, who printed Susannah Gunning's *Anecdotes of the Delborough Family* (1792), and James Lackington, the celebrated retail bookseller who also ran a circulating library on Chiswell Street in Finsbury and who brought out Alicia Tyndal Palmer's *The Husband and the Lover* (1809), all physically helped to create as well as merely to circulate new narrative fiction, keenly aware as they were of its commercial value to their library operations as much as to their bookselling interests (Skelton-Foord 2002: 141, 146). Even so, and despite its key role in their businesses, the novel was certainly not all that such entrepreneurs offered in order to satisfy customer demand. In fact, a notable study by Paul Kaufman showed that across a sample of late eighteenth-century libraries the average holding of novels was around 20 per cent of the overall stock, though with widely differing approaches being taken by individual proprietors—just 5 per cent at John Allen's library at Hereford and yet 95 per cent at James Corkhill's establishment at Whitehaven (1967: 14).

It is obvious, however, that there must have been very many library owners who did indeed seek to build their businesses on a novel-oriented model that was broadly similar to the one exemplified by Corkhill. William Harrod of Stamford in Lincolnshire was evidently one of those who appreciated the public's appetite for narrative fiction: in 1790 his collection of a thousand separate works was actually itemized in a published catalogue which bore the simple and self-explanatory subtitle 'comprising 700 NOVELS, &c. and 300 PLAYS'.[29] Many such collections, especially in the decades immediately after 1800, could not have been more appropriately composed if their very purpose had been to lend credence to the grim stereotype of the circulating library proprietor as nothing more or less than a socially irresponsible novel-renter whose business was parasitic upon the worst instincts of the most inexperienced and vulnerable parts of the literate population.

---

[29] *A Catalogue of Harrod's Circulating Library...* (Stamford, 1790).

At Chesterfield, for example, John Ford's circulating library at the end of this period was plainly dominated by its owner's desire to satisfy the demand for such work: it had 531 novels and plays in a collection that ran to only 575 items.[30] The Waters family's operation at Kettering in 1813 also offered its Northamptonshire customers only 188 titles, almost entirely comprising narrative fiction.[31] Anthony Soulby at Penrith in Cumberland in 1808 was another who followed what was clearly an entirely viable strategy: although Gibbon and Locke did feature on his shelves, his customers were largely treated to the work of the English novelists.[32] We see the same again at John Rogers' circulating library. Trading on Greengate Street at Stafford in the early 1820s, its 350 books (though, by a stroke of predatory genius, Rogers made sure to claim on the title page that he offered more than 2,000 volumes) were once again effectively all novels.[33] These sorts of numbers all help us to make somewhat better sense of the often-quoted advice of Thomas Wilson, a proprietor at Bromley in Kent, whose *The Use of Circulating Libraries Considered* (1797) explicitly recommended that the stock in trade of the circulating library should indeed be narrative fiction—the prudent owner ideally offering, proposed Wilson with interesting precision, a selection of 1,050 novels and 130 romances in a collection of around 1,500 titles all told (Varma 1972: 66).

It is crucial to note, however, that such data on library holdings are in fact fraught with difficulty for use in measuring the relative importance of a single genre in the working life of an individual commercial collection. To state the obvious, they give no concrete insight into actual borrowing levels—though they do, unfortunately, invite us wrongly to imagine a simple linear relationship between the proportion of novels held and the proportion of lending for which they must have accounted. Moreover, the almost total absence of borrowing records for libraries, allied to the desperate lack of detailed customer information (regrettably it is possible to recover a substantial number of readers' names for fewer than half a dozen Georgian commercial libraries), means that we simply cannot tell how much use the novels in a proprietor's stock actually received, much less identify the sort of literate contemporary who would have exhibited a marked preference for one title (or author or genre) over another. As significant is the likelihood that overconcentration on raw figures of this kind, derived from catalogues which usually went no further than listing authors and titles, also masks the dramatic effect of multiple copies. For it is clear that circulating libraries were indeed willing to provide additional copies of the most popular texts, the better to mop up excess demand: a novel carried by the Minerva Library, for example, where Shelley and Leigh Hunt—the second

---

[30] *A Catalogue of the New and Increasing Circulating Library Belonging to John Ford* (Chesterfield, [1821?]).
[31] *Catalogue of J. & S. Waters' Circulating Library* (Kettering, 1813).
[32] *Catalogue of the Circulating Library of Anthony Soulby, Printer & Bookseller . . .* (Penrith, 1808).
[33] *Catalogue of the Circulating Library of John Rogers* (Stafford, 1825).

a self-confessed 'glutton for novels'—were regular customers, would apparently have been available in as many as twenty-five copies, while the public enthusiasm for Scott reportedly led some circulating library owners by the 1820s to buy between fifty and seventy copies of each of the Waverley Novels (Kaufman 1967: 15; St Clair 2004: 245; Varma 1972: 83).

It is therefore impossible to be at all precise about who was actually reading what in the circulating libraries of the late eighteenth and early nineteenth centuries. Yet it is nonetheless tenable to say something about the aggregate profile of certain libraries' customers—and so about the sorts of people increasingly in a position to be exposed to novels through the commercial collections—by extrapolation from the financial arrangements that these collections demonstrably put in place. Certainly in some cases the price structures allow us safely to discount the possibility that poorer people could ever have used the library: neither William Earle's establishment on Albemarle Street in Piccadilly in 1799, which demanded three guineas as an annual subscription and bestowed the right for London residents to borrow twelve books at a time (country-based customers, though, could have twenty-four), nor William Sams's library on St James's Street in Westminster in 1820, which charged an eye-watering five guineas per annum for membership, can have done anything to introduce artisans, craftsmen, and labourers to the novel.[34] Yet at the other end of the scale there were clearly plenty of circulating libraries whose much more affordable charges indicate that they could and did open their doors to the less well-off—especially if the pricing also permitted the most cash-conscious customers to ration themselves to intermittent and ruthlessly selective borrowing.

The best-known example, partly because of the rare survival of high-quality documentary records, is Samuel Clay's library at Warwick: in the early 1770s Clay was offering three-week loans for just two pence per volume—a sum well within the compass of literate workers at a time when a journeyman might be earning anywhere between fifteen and twenty shilling each week and a country craft worker between six and twelve (Fergus 1984; Allan 2008: 151–2). Other circulating library proprietors similarly pitched their wares at the less fortunate, usually by setting an attractively low subscription rate: in 1813 the Waters at Kettering were charging fourteen shillings per annum for membership but also advertised a flat-rate loan fee for non-subscribers at a mere two pence for a duodecimo and three pence for an octavo—an arrangement palpably aimed directly at the un-moneyed novel-lover.[35] James Brown, who ran a library at Wigan, seems to have had much the same idea, unambiguously tailoring his business towards the particular reading needs (and, crucially, the much shallower pockets) of working people interested

---

[34] *Earle's New Catalogue of English Books...* (n.p., n.d.); *Catalogue of Sams's Public Subscription Library...* (London, n.d.).
[35] *Catalogue of J. & S. Waters' Circulating Library.*

in narrative fiction in particular: in 1821 he was offering a flat-rate charge of just two pence for the five-day loan of a duodecimo volume and three pence for a full week in possession of an octavo.[36]

These would clearly still not be cheap experiences entered into by readers without a second thought. But nor—and quite purposely on the part of the proprietors who had so carefully calibrated them—were these kinds of fees intended to deny access to working people with a serious interest in the sorts of books, often novels, that these collections tended to carry. In the final analysis this calculation by many circulating library owners explains why it was that at least some ordinary readers from ordinary backgrounds were able to develop a functioning relationship with the English novel. It tells us how it was that the fourteen-year-old William Cobbett, an innkeeper's son, using William Taylor's library at Brompton, was in a position, as he later recollected, to pore over 'novels, plays, history and poetry . . . with equal avidity', and why it was that Thomas Chatterton, a teenaged customer of Green's library at Bristol, came to read Eliza Haywood's novels with similar devotion (Varma 1972: 84). It also begins to make sense of how it was possible for an obscure adolescent apprentice cutler like Joseph Hunter in 1798 to pick up a text, evidently borrowed for just two days at a cost of a single penny, from Thomas Lindley's circulating library on Church Street in Sheffield—and, as he recorded in his diary, to plunge headlong, though with ultimately not wholly positive results, into the Gothic fantasy world laid out in Martha Hugill's *The Castle of Mowbray* (1788) (Colclough 2000: 26–7).

The Novel as Novelty

The circulation of texts was plainly central to the broader culture of this period as well as to the social history of its literature. In fact, it performed many important functions in a rapidly changing environment. The mechanisms employed provided ample opportunities for sociability, for the cultivation and display of politeness, and even for genuine philanthropy. They also gave scope for the determined pursuit of self-improvement, for personal education, and, not least, for deep inward satisfaction. In all of this the novel was a crucial factor—helping, as it also benefited from, these vital transformational processes. Above all, its extraordinary cultural and commercial success between 1750 and 1820 confirms much about the scale and sophistication of the methods by which texts were now becoming available to readers.

The novel's relationship with commercial lending in particular was certainly as close as some people feared at the time and many have wanted to believe ever since. A large part

---

[36] *Catalogue of Brown's Circulating Library . . .* (Wigan, 1821), A2r.

of the mass of narrative fiction now being produced was truly the 'offspring of circulating libraries', wretched or not. Yet the novel's parentage was actually more mixed than Mackenzie's barb suggested. Its circulation, as we have seen, was by no means restricted to the commercial libraries. And nor was there a shortage of other effective means by which novels, like many different kinds of texts, could go on to become an integral part of the inner lives of significant numbers of literate contemporaries. Throughout this period of growth and change in the literary marketplace, readers' engagement with narrative fiction was shaped as much by the continually shifting contexts in which reception was able to occur as it was by the talents and energies of individual authors and the intrinsic literary merits of what they wrote.

Part II

Major Authors and Traditions

4

The Novel in the 1750s

E. J. CLERY

IN a preface to the reader, the anonymous author of *The Campaign* (1759) candidly admits that his motive for writing was mercenary: 'I wanted money. I wrote a book to get it, and that book is a novel'.[1] He (the tone and content make it clear that the author is male) then goes on to describe the blow dealt to his naive expectations: 'Far from immediately filling my purse; I found my performance rejected by every bookseller in town: rejected, as absurd, stupid, low, unworthy even the expence of printing.' How could this be, he wonders, given the abysmal standard set by similar works 'that have appeared in these five or six last years' (1.iv)? He goes on to relate that he eventually succeeded in selling copyright to the reputable bookseller Thomas Harrison, albeit for a much smaller sum than he had anticipated.

The author's complaints are typical of the late 1750s. The genre had started the decade with its reputation riding high on the remarkable success of Richardson's *Clarissa* (1748–9), Smollett's *Roderick Random* (1748), and especially *Tom Jones* (1749) by Henry Fielding. In the immediate aftermath of the last work, it was almost obligatory for other fiction writers to pay tribute to the great Fielding in their prefaces; Edward Kimber in *Joe Thompson* (1750), the anonymous *Charlotte Summers; or, The Fortunate Parish Girl* (1750), and Francis Coventry in *Pompey the Little* (1751) are notable examples. Men of letters, chief among them Samuel Johnson, hastened to analyse the potency of the 'works of fiction, with which the present generation seems more particularly delighted' and legislate for its future.[2] Other significant statements on fiction at this moment include the anonymous *An Essay on the New Species of Writing founded by Mr Fielding* (1751); the prefatory essay to *Constantia; or, A True Picture of Human Life* (1751), also anonymous; John Hawkesworth, *The Adventurer*, no. 4 (18 November 1752); and William Whitehead, *The World*, no. 19 (10 May 1753) (see Nixon 2009 for extracts from three of these).

---

[1] Anon., *The Campaign; A True Story*, 2 vols (London: T. Harrison, 1759), 1.ii.
[2] Samuel Johnson, *The Rambler*, no. 4 (31 March 1750), in the *Yale Edition of the Works of Samuel Johnson*, vol. 3, ed. W. J. Bate and Albrecht B. Strauss (New Haven: Yale University Press, 1969), 19–23 (19).

The critical hits of the late 1740s also enjoyed best-seller status: there were four author-ized editions of *Clarissa* by 1751; five of *Roderick Random* by 1750; and *Tom Jones* went through no less than four large editions in its year of publication. Yet just a few years later the healthy market position of the genre had apparently declined along with its cultural capital. Fielding's next work, *Amelia* (1752), was widely declared to be a failure, much of the first edition (albeit a massive 5,000 copies) remained unsold, and he felt driven to defend it with embarrassing intensity in the pages of the *Covent Garden Journal*. Smollett's *Adventures of Peregrine Pickle* (1751) similarly fell flat after a sensational start, any merit it had as fiction overshadowed by the opportunistic inclusion of the true-life scandalous mem-oirs of Lady Vane at its centre. It would be seven years until a second edition was called for, and the author undertook substantial revisions to meet initial criticisms that it was 'immoral' and 'libellous' (Buck 1925: 8–10). *The History of Sir Charles Grandison* (1753–4) was a slightly different case. Three editions appeared rapidly before the middle of 1754. A brief notice in the *Monthly Review*, ignominiously placed in the 'Miscellaneous' section rather than as a leading article, acknowledges that this is a work which 'every body reads, and every body talks of' but for that very reason gives it short shrift, registering merely the reviewer's '*disgust*' at the improbability of the letter-writing form, the prolixity and 'studied formality' of method, the 'frequent affectation' of the language, and 'inconsist-ency' of characterization.[3] Richardson's final work took fiction down a path that few other writers, as yet, were prepared to follow. His day would come, posthumously, in the 1760s with the resurgence of epistolary works in the sentimental mode.

In the meantime, the trade in new fiction remained in the doldrums. As James Raven's research has shown, the average over the 1750s was around twenty-three new novels per year, ranging from a high of thirty in 1754 to a low of sixteen in 1758, compared with an average twenty-eight per annum for the 1760s (see Table 1.1 in Chapter 1 on 'Production'). There was nothing like the spike in novel production that marked the brilliant success of *Pamela* in 1740. Richardson and Fielding retired from fiction writing, as did Smollett, tem-porarily, following the poorly received *Ferdinand Count Fathom* in 1753. For the remainder of the decade Smollett channelled his prodigious energies into other projects: a transla-tion of *Don Quixote* (1755), the founding of the *Critical Review* (1756), and preparation of a *Complete History of England* (1757–8). Eliza Haywood, that grand old veteran who had monitored and responded to the ups and downs of the novel scene for over three dec-ades, published five works of fiction in the earlier 1750s as well as diversifying prior to her death in 1756, as she had done in previous fallow periods, into hybrid forms. Sarah Scott produced promising novels in 1750 and 1754, but did not resume until *Millenium Hall* in 1762. It is interesting to note that the activities of two prominent hack writers and controversialists of the day, Sir John Hill (*The Adventures of Mr. George Edwards, A Creole,*

---

[3] *Monthly Review*, 10 (January 1754), 70–1.

1751) and John Shebbeare (*The Marriage Act*, 1754; *Lydia*, 1755), are, like those of Smollett and Haywood, redirected away from the novel by the mid-point of the decade. No professional writer seemed to consider writing novels alone to be a viable career. Charlotte Lennox, the most professional of female authors following Haywood, produced three works of fiction in this decade only within a mixed economy of publication.

While the author of *The Campaign* was doing the rounds of the booksellers with his manuscript, even Richardson was having difficulty placing, on behalf of a friend, *The Histories of Some of the Penitents in the Magdalen House* (1759; dated 1760; published anonymously and still without firm attribution).[4] Back in 1751 he had succeeded in persuading the bookseller Andrew Millar to take on Charlotte Lennox's *The Female Quixote* (1752), but had to report to Lady Barbara Montagu his lack of success in the same quarter with the *Penitents*: 'There was a Time, when every Man of that Trade published a Novel, 'till the Public (in this Mr. Millar says true) became tired of them.' He offered to try Robert Dodsley, though he too was 'one of those Booksellers, who think the Day of Novels is over' (see Eaves and Kimpel 1971: 463). Eventually Richardson printed it himself. It was a similar story with another of his protégées, Susan Smythies. Her third novel, *The Brothers* (1758), was turned down by every bookseller in spite of the success of *The Stage-Coach* (1753; enthusiastically reviewed). Her second work, *The History of Lucy Wellers* (1754), had done less well, the remainder of the edition reissued as new in 1755. Richardson recommended publication by subscription. With his energetic assistance the results (a total of 675 names appear, including those of Smollett, Garrick, and Joseph Spence) 'succeeded beyond her Hopes' (see Eaves and Kimpel 1971: 464; cf. Sherbo 2004).

The new breed of periodical reviewers, like a Greek chorus, regularly predicted the demise of the novel. The *Monthly Review*, founded in 1749, included John Cleland—author of *Fanny Hill* (1749) and *Memoirs of a Coxcomb* (1751)—in its roster of critics, and featured some fair-minded and substantial assessments, particularly in its first years. In a review of *Peregrine Pickle* in 1751 Cleland went so far as to pronounce fictions founded on nature 'public benefits'. The following year, however, another *Monthly Review* critic was announcing that 'all the variety of which this species of literary entertainment is capable, seems almost exhausted, and even novels themselves no longer charm us with novelty'.[5] The *Monthly* was joined in 1756 by the rival *Critical Review*, founded by Tobias Smollett, and together they formed a 'regulatory institution' that contributed to the sense of exhaustion with its 'crushingly comparative' habit of judgement, dismissing new arrivals as sad indications of a genre in decline (Keymer 2002: 54).

---

[4] See Introduction, Anon., *The Histories of Some of the Penitents in the Magdalen House*, ed. Jennie Batchelor and Megan Hiatt, Chawton House Library Series (London: Pickering and Chatto, 2007), xx–xxiii.

[5] *Monthly Review*, 6 (March 1752), 231.

The evidence of the eighteenth-century British fiction market disrupts the notion of a steady, unstoppable commercial and cultural 'rise' of the novel suggested by Ian Watt's famous 1957 title. Very early, John Richetti observed that to talk in these terms represents a 'teleological bias' (1969: 2). Thomas Keymer's *Sterne, The Moderns, and the Novel* is an important revaluation that identifies the 1750s as 'a crucial decade in the history of the novel, and one that poses an interesting challenge to our assumptions about the genre' (2002: 53; see also Burditt 2005). But although he persuasively situates *Tristram Shandy* (1760–7) as a response to the novel 'hiatus' of the late 1750s, his argument concerning the modernity, or modishness, of Sterne's work leads him to concur with the established view that by mid-century the novel was 'securely established' as 'the quintessential mode ... of commercialized modern writing' (2002: 50, 7–8).

The statistics might lead to other conclusions. The 1750s was not a unique case; there were similar novel droughts in the 1730s and 1770s. In addition, according to Raven's calculations (which he admits are difficult to verify exactly), through much of the century novels constitute a tiny share of total book and pamphlet production, increasing gradually from 1 per cent in 1700–9 to 4 per cent through the 1740s, 1750s, and 1760s, as Richardson, Fielding, and Sterne came and went, only accelerating (with an initial stutter) 'towards the end of the 1760s' (1987: 10). We may be led to share the realization of the author of *The Campaign* that, against expectations, the novel is vulnerable, at the margins of print culture, even *un*commercial. Several critical points stem from this recognition, challenging earlier preconceptions about eighteenth-century English fiction.

The profit motive for publishing fiction has been taken for granted. But if writers wanted to make money, novels were not the thing to write. In spite of Fielding's fabled copyright fees, for most who tried their hand at fiction the rewards were not great. The going rate for copyright remained low. It has been estimated that the average was an astonishingly paltry £5 to £27, 'lower than payments for almost any other category of publication, and certainly the lowest in proportion to length' (Schellenberg 2005: 99).

Theories of the 'raising' of the novel, the 'licensing' of it as entertainment by the addition of moral instruction, depend upon the assumption that there is a buoyant cycle of supply and demand (see Skinner 2001; Warner 1998). Scholars have tended to favour evidence of the novel's popularity, and Richardson and Fielding's varied responses to the imperative of *utile dulci* have been understood as clever strategies to harness the powerful energies of fiction-making, and ensure greater cultural legitimacy and hence superior profits. But what if the majority of the reading public were simply indifferent and disinclined to buy, regardless of whether a novel appeared in 'legitimate' guise?

Similar questions surround the proposition that novelists in the 1750s were forced to innovate to escape the long shadows of Richardson and Fielding. Keymer, taking as his point of departure the success of the wildly inventive *Tristram Shandy* at the end of the decade, has demonstrated a considerable degree of experimentation in the preceding years from novelists presumably spurred on by the jibes of reviewers. Examples can certainly be found: Smollett's *Ferdinand Count Fathom* (1753) with its proto-Gothic scenes, *The Cry* (1754) by Jane Collier and Sarah Fielding, John Kidgell's *The Card* (1755), and the anonymous *Ephraim Tristram Bates* (1756, often identified as precursor to *Tristram Shandy*) which led the reviewer in the *Monthly* to concede that 'the chapter of Novels is not yet quite exhausted'.[6]

Like the critical focus on legitimation, however, this emphasis on novelty presupposes a buoyant market, responsive to the new and fashionable. What has largely been neglected by scholars, but is revealed in Raven's bibliographical work, is the strong undertow of the already known at this time: the prevalence of reprints even before the freeing up of copyright law from 1774 (of sixty novels published in 1759, thirty-two were reprints; 1987: 8). The runaway best-seller of the 1750s, with a total of six new editions, was Daniel Defoe's *Robinson Crusoe*, first published in 1719. In the course of the decade *Moll Flanders* and *Roxana* both enjoyed two new editions, and the full list of output for 1750–70 reveals the frequent reappearance of other works of the 1720s and 1730s by, notably, Haywood, Mary Davys, and Marivaux; the last indicative of the frequent recourse of London publishers to translations of earlier foreign works outside copyright law (Raven 1987: 15). The late 1740s and the 1750s have been identified as the start of a rise in the format of 'select collections' of reprinted writings, including novels (Gamer 2008). There is scope for exploring more fully the persistence of trends untouched by the influence of Richardson and Fielding: spy fiction, imaginary travels, secret histories. In addition there was the drag of popular traditions, the jest book, the harlequinade, the scandal broadsheet, the chapbook; new research on comic fiction addresses this populist aspect of mid-century fiction (Dickie 2011; see also Chapter 5 by Dickie in this volume).

A stagnant market makes it difficult to claim that the profit motive was uppermost; similarly that production was driven by demand for novelty. There cannot, in fact, have been a lot of incentive to write fiction in the 1750s. Although fiction writing might appeal as an easy option for novices, not requiring a classical education, some degree of wit and fancy was essential to success and these might be hard to conjure up for writers living hand to mouth. Fiction was marginal, a tiny niche within the overall economy of print. It was risky. The reviewers gave it their attention mainly to lash it. Booksellers increasingly discouraged it. The reading public was still small, and for the most part conservative, with a strong appetite for tried and tested favourites.

Given this gloomy outlook it seems valid to ask: How was it that the novel survived the 1750s? One possible answer is that the growth and development of the novel, in spite of adverse circumstances, was dependent not on commercial incentives but on what the novel could do: opportunities for thought experiments, debate, and the discharge of spleen that no other form of writing offered. Still without generic fixity or a clear market

---

[6] *Monthly Review*, 15 (October 1756), 426.

position, fiction continued to operate as 'wild space' (Gallagher 1994: xvi). What was the 'work' of novels in the 1750s? It goes without saying that a primary function of novels was entertainment, but what did the entertainment consist of, and how did it have its effect?

The impression left by the best-known prose fiction of the 1750s—the cruelty and mockery that is the stuff of Smollett's world, the bleak landscape of urban degradation and corruption in *Amelia*, the one hundred and one wrongs to be righted by Sir Charles Grandison, modernity stripped of romantic idealism in Lennox, the ubiquity of psychological torture revealed by Sarah Fielding and Jane Collier—is of rancour, in most cases barely alleviated by humour and only uneasily resolved by the contrivance of a happy ending. The general run of little-known and anonymous novels does little to alter the picture. Paula Backscheider has coined the phrase 'Mid-Century Anger' to sum up the relationship between the novel and widespread outrage at the emerging shape of British society (2005: 513). It is difficult, indeed, to find the sort of complacent congruence with the rise of capitalism and the middle classes posited by Watt and many later literary critics.

This was a time of unease culminating in a war that seemed to expose the nation's inner rottenness and signal its imminent downfall. Kathleen Wilson has described the early 1750s as an epoch 'marked by a deepening sense of national malaise, stimulated by xenophobia and tinged by sharpening anti-aristocratic sensibilities' (1994: 145). The continuing ascendancy of the Whig oligarchy after Robert Walpole's fall in 1742 had been widely accepted as the price of stability, but now the stench of corruption was growing too strong to tolerate. In the economic sphere, Britain was undergoing a gear change. A long period of stagnation, low prices, limited population increase, and 'profitless prosperity' was quickening into a new phase of 'capital accumulation and risk-taking', creating opportunities for the few, but disruption and immiseration for many (Little 1976: 100, 101).

This was the juncture that gave rise to some of Hogarth's most searing images, *Gin Lane* (1751) and *The Four Stages of Cruelty* (1751). The London earthquake of 1750, which provoked questions about providence, was followed by the Lisbon earthquake of November 1755, killing 30,000 and deepening the mood of pessimism throughout Europe. In Britain, the perception of a diseased body politic was articulated with increasing belligerence by the 'Patriot' opposition led by William Pitt. Once the Seven Years' War with France broke out in 1756, there would be self-lacerating diatribes on modern British manners and mores such as John Brown's *An Estimate of the Manners and Principles of the Times* (seven editions in its year of publication, 1757). It was only in 1759, the *Annus Mirabilus*, with Pitt now in control, that Britain decisively gained the upper hand and a restored sense of national destiny, poised to acquire its 'second empire'.

Popular revolt against authority in this decade centred on the Penlez riots (1749), the strange case of Elizabeth Canning (1753–4; Fielding was directly involved in both as magistrate, and produced shilling pamphlets to defend his position), the Jew Bill (1753), the

Marriage Act (1753), and the court martial and execution of Admiral Byng for abandoning Minorca to the French (1757). These events were rarely referred to directly in novels, although it would be possible to read the fiction of the 1750s as one extended debate on the aims and consequences of Hardwicke's Marriage Act, designed to prevent clandestine marriages but having broad implications (see also Shebbeare's propagandist novel, mentioned above). Agitation for the recuperation of prostitutes can be traced through Mary Collyer's *The History of Betty Barnes* (1752) and *Sir Charles Grandison*, culminating in the foundation of the Magdalen House charity in 1758 and publication of the *Histories of Some of the Penitents in the Magdalen House* (see Ellis 1996: 165–85; Grossman 2001; also Thompson, Chapter 7).

The basis of the novel tradition in casuistry suited it to a role of ethical dispute on questions of manners and mores rather than topical interventions (see Starr 1971; Keymer 1992). Narrative and mimesis lend themselves to religious/philosophical questions of reward and punishment, causality and justification, chance and providence. Nowhere else was so appropriate for the 'testing' of contemporary values through imaginary case histories, bringing to bear verities of human nature, motivation, and moral responsibility. The analysis and representation of human nature, and beyond this the appeal to the passions of the reader in the name of virtue: these were the skills that the mid-century novelists primarily lay claim to—certainly Richardson and Fielding, but equally the obscure pretender, such as the author of *The Campaign*, who declares his intention of 'turning the passions on the side of truth' (1.iii). The language in which novelists justify this project, in digressions and commentaries, suggests continuity rather than the turning point at 1740 that has often been assumed. The mid-century writers' understanding of what they were doing with fiction, and of what fiction was for, does not differ in this fundamental way from that of Aphra Behn, Delarivier Manley, Daniel Defoe, or Eliza Haywood as revealed in their prefaces. Mary Davys in the introduction to her 1725 *Works* commented of her own fiction that it offered an 'important Service to the Publick' in showing that 'since Passions will ever have a Place in the Actions of Men, and Love a principal one, what cannot be removed or subdu'd, ought at least to be regulated'. Anticipating Richardson she adds that it is women who can best begin this reformation, reclaiming their 'Empire' over the realm of feeling (see Nixon 2009: 82).

Davys's model of selfhood is elaborated through the neo-classical discourse of the passions, and this too continues into the 1750s, notwithstanding the growing influence of Locke's alternative empirical theory of selfhood at this time. The decade is bracketed by important publications which build on Locke: David Hartley's seminal associationist treatise *Observations on Man* (1749) and Adam Smith's *Theory of the Moral Sentiments* (1759). Influential literary and cultural historians—Ian Watt, Nancy Armstrong, Dror Wahrman, among others—have discussed the novel as a primary locus for the elaboration of Locke's model of selfhood. At times the references in fiction or contemporary commentary on the novel are unmistakably Lockean; and yet the effect at mid-century is one of superimposition, a coexistence of belief systems. The discourse of the passions had its roots in Stoic and early Christian suspicion of feeling; during the Renaissance it evolved into a quasi-scientific method of analysis, with the aim of penetrating the irrational side of human nature in order the more effectively to control it or channel it towards desirable ends. Bernard Mandeville had given the question of whether the passions could serve moral ends a new and controversial relevance with *The Fable of the Bees* (1714), where he had argued that pride, envy, and acquisitiveness were the engines of social and economic progress. Novelists constantly revisit the troubling notion that private vices could be a public benefit.

In an essay entitled 'Standard Novels', first published in the *Edinburgh Review* for February 1815, William Hazlitt hailed the roster of 'first-rate of writers' led by Cervantes and Le Sage, and followed by Fielding, Richardson, Smollett, and Sterne: 'a certain set' of writers 'who, as it were, take their rank by the side of reality, and are appealed to as evidence on all questions of human nature'. By means of their art 'moral impressions [are] called out, and our moral judgements exercised' more often than in real life (see Nixon 2009: 164, 163). At the distance of fifty or sixty years, these writers might appear united in wisdom. But at the time the skirmishes for the cherished ground of human nature were often bitter.

The ongoing rivalry between Richardson and Fielding is the place to get the measure of what was at stake. The antagonism between the two authors has generally been put down to personal enmity; William Warner has alternatively proposed that it was 'less about literary fame than it was about shaping the contemporary terms for licensing entertainment' (1998: 241). But if we were to take the ammunition, the actual rhetoric, of the war of words seriously—the acerbic remarks in private letters, the coded attacks of a title page or preface—the basis of the argument comes to appear more consequential still.

The challenge was not just a matter of depicting the play of the passions accurately through the medium of characterization. The project was also to reach and transform the reader's passions. The reader identifies with the action and the protagonists not via sympathy, the category that becomes familiar with the discourse of sensibility, but by the trans-subjective contagion of the passions. Moral instruction is to operate through the passions of the readers; it is not simply an appeal to reason. The Preface to *Pamela* states that the aim of the publication is to 'engage the Passions of every sensible Reader and strongly interest them in the edifying Story', and the 'Editor' expresses confidence that this will be fulfilled because 'he can Appeal from his *own* Passions (which have been uncommonly moved in perusing these engaging Scenes) to the Passions of *Every one* who shall read them with the least Attention'.[7] Smollett concurs that it is the job

---

[7] Samuel Richardson, *Pamela; or, Virtue Rewarded*, ed. Thomas Keymer and Alice Wakely (Oxford: Oxford University Press, 2001), 3–4.

of the novelist to 'inflame' the 'humane passions' of the reader, in response to their engagement with the adventures of a central character.[8] In *The Adventures of Ferdinand Count Fathom* he announced an experiment to test the theory that, fear being 'the most violent and interesting of all the passions', a reader will be better instructed by their anticipation of the punishment due to a villainous main protagonist than by their hopes for a virtuous one.[9]

Fielding appears to hand Richardson the laurels with his high praise of the first instalment of *Clarissa* in *The Jacobite's Journal* (1 January 1747, 5 March 1748), and his blow-by-blow account of his tumultuous feelings at reading Volume Five before publication in a personal letter to its author (Battestin and Battestin 1989: 442–3). But the truce was no doubt ruptured by the claim in the first chapter of *Tom Jones* that the 'Provision' offered to the reader 'is no other than HUMAN NATURE'. Bystanders got drawn in to adjudicate. The Bluestocking writers Elizabeth Carter and Catherine Talbot squabbled, for the most part amicably, over the relative merits of the two as painters of human nature. Carter was to persist as one of the most doughty defenders of *Amelia* (Paulson and Lockwood 1969: nos 115, 129, 132–3; cf. Bree 2010: 22–3). Smollett comes down on the side of Richardson in his *History of England*, though acknowledging Fielding as the heir of Cervantes: 'The laudable aim of enlisting the passions on the side of Virtue was successfully pursued by Richardson in *Pamela*, *Clarissa* and *Grandison*; a species of writing equally new and extraordinary, where, mingled with much superfluity, we find a sublime system of ethics, an amazing knowledge and command of human nature'.[10]

Sarah Fielding, friend of one and sister of the other, gets caught in the crossfire. In *Critical Remarks on Sir Charles Grandison, Clarissa and Pamela* by 'A Lover of Virtue' (1754) which Hester Mulso (later Chapone) suspected to have been written by Fielding or one of his supporters, Richardson is accused of encouraging amorous passion and is unfavourably compared with 'the moral and ingenious authoress of David Simple...perhaps the best moral romance we have' (see Eaves and Kimpel 1971: 409). Richardson's remark to her in a letter might be seen as retaliation:

> What a knowledge of the human heart! Well might a critical judge of writing say, as he did to me, that your late brother's knowledge of it was not (fine writer as he was) comparable to your's. His was but as the knowledge of the outside of a clock-work machine, while your's was that of all the finer springs and movements of the inside. (1 December 1756; quoted in Eaves and Kimpel 1971: 305)

---

[8] Tobias Smollett, *The Adventures of Roderick Random*, ed. Paul-Gabriel Boucé (Oxford: Oxford University Press, 1979), Preface, xxxiii.

[9] Tobias Smollett, *The Adventures of Ferdinand Count Fathom*, ed. O. M. Brack Jr, introd. Jerry C. Beasley (Athens, GA: University of Georgia Press, 1988), Dedication, 5.

[10] Tobias Smollett, *The History of England, from the Revolution in 1688, to the Death of George the Second*, 5 vols (London: Talboys and Pickering, 1827), 5.285.

The most famous judgement of all on this matter appeared in Boswell's *The Life of Samuel Johnson* (1791), relating to the year 1768 and transferring the terms of Richardson's praise of Sarah Fielding to Johnson's judgement on Richardson himself:

> 'Sire, (continued he,) there is all the difference in the world between characters of nature and characters of manners; and *there* is the difference between the characters of Fielding and those of Richardson. Characters of manners are very entertaining; but they are to be understood by a more superficial observation than characters of nature, where a man must dive into the recesses of the human heart ... there was as great a difference between them as between a man who knew how a watch was made, and a man who could tell the hour by looking on the dial plate'.[11]

Ian Donaldson has traced the clock image to Locke's *Essay on Human Understanding* and sees it as typical of eighteenth-century use of analogies drawn from 'human craftsmanship' rather than nature (1970: 14–15). La Mettrie's *L'Homme machine* (1747; translated as *Man a Machine* in 1749) takes the analogy to its furthest extreme. But there is a mechanistic element already apparent in the discourse of the passions, with its taxonomy of opposing passions, ruling passions, and countervailing passions. It was a knowledge based on systemic analysis which could also be applied, in the case of novel-writing, through deliberately exercising the passions of the reader in the way in which Fielding noted in himself in response to *Clarissa*. If we were to ask, where else within the range of generic options available to writers was it possible to say the things said in fiction about people and society, the answer must be 'Nowhere', especially if we add that in the saying, the passions of the reader must be engaged, to bring the force of the presentation home inwardly. The novel survived the 1750s not because it was saleable, but because it was necessary.

Picturing Human Nature

In the 1750s both Fielding and Richardson appear to turn their backs on a successful formula, heedless of alienating their established constituencies, seemingly intent on extending their own fictional empires through incursions on each other's territory. Fielding chooses the Richardsonian title *Amelia*. Richardson in his title foregrounds the hero, in Fielding mode, rather than heroine. Fielding broaches for the first time domestic drama, minutely portrayed, and gives serious attention to Richardson's *leitmotif* of sexual threat. Richardson for the first time sets himself the question, 'What is a good man?', that had been the light-hearted preoccupation of Fielding's previous works. In terms of formal method, Fielding's transition may appear the more radical. He drastically cuts back the apparatus of the intrusive omniscient narrator which had been so popular with professional critics,

---

[11] James Boswell, *The Life of Samuel Johnson*, ed. G. Birkbeck Hill, rev. and enl. edn ed. L. F. Powell, 6 vols (Oxford: Clarendon Press, 1934), 2.48.

readers, and imitators alike, the source of endless effects of comic dissonance between low action and elevated retelling, and a reassuring mark of cultural authority placed on the subject matter of popular realist fiction. The narrator continues from time to time to comment, address the reader, and mischievously manipulate the higher discursive registers, but overall the action is permitted greater immediacy for the purposes of exploring a world of pathos and empathy formerly the monopoly of Richardson. The letter format of *Sir Charles Grandison* may give the appearance of business as usual for Richardson, but he too was striking out in a new direction, sacrificing the powerful intensity generated by the limited cast of correspondents in *Clarissa* in favour of a more dispersed group, approaching the open, panoramic prospect of Fielding. At the same time he broadens the field of action to encompass Italy (he himself never left England), and borrows from *Tom Jones* the backdrop of the Jacobite rising of 1745 for Sir Charles's inset narrative.

But it would be a mistake to insist too far on a convergence of means and ends. The first three Books of *Amelia* that constitute Volume I are as virtuoso a stretch of writing as Fielding ever produced, and it is here that he establishes the ethical problems and questions about human nature that he will wrestle with for the remainder of the narrative. Richardson, in letters to female friends, declared that he left off reading at the end this volume, unable to relate to 'characters and situations so wretchedly dirty and low' (Paulson and Lockwood 1969: 335, no. 122). He is unable to recognize a compulsion to anatomize social evils as fervent as his own.

What Fielding addresses is systemic cruelty and suffering: wrongs unrelieved, even exacerbated, by the fact that they are not personal and deliberate but rather the product of the institutionalized indifference of the law. The scenes come directly from his own experience, beginning in 1749, as Justice of the Peace for Westminster and Middlesex, an office described by his biographers as 'among the most cheerless and despicable in the kingdom' (Battestin and Battestin 1989: 458). Nevertheless it is Fielding's characteristic strategy to play injury and suffering for laughs. At the start of the action, the ignorant and bellicose Justice Thrasher is unable to recognize the genuine testimony of innocent plaintiffs who lack the wherewithal for bribes because he has 'too great an Honour for Truth to suspect that she ever appeared in sordid Apparel'.[12] The inmates of Newgate 'instead of wailing and repining at their Condition, were laughing, singing and diverting themselves with various kinds of Sports and Gambols' (bk 1, ch. 3; 27). Fielding will not permit the reader to readily discharge emotions of anger or of empathy; initially he holds indignation in suspension the better to navigate injustice and its consequences as an intellectual problem.

Captain William Booth, an army officer on half pay, has been wrongfully imprisoned for assault. His encounter with Miss Mathews, convicted of murder, towards the end of Book One, serves a number of functions in the novel. At the level of plot, after it emerges

---

[12] Henry Fielding, *Amelia*, ed. Martin C. Battestin (Oxford: Clarendon Press, 1983), bk 1, ch. 3; 27.

she is an old acquaintance, their conversational exchanges fill in much of the backstory since their last meeting 'eight or nine years' previously: his own account of his relationship with Amelia, before and after marriage, stretching over three Books. Miss Mathews subsequently facilitates the release of Booth only to embroil him later in clandestine dealings that will threaten his marriage and his life. At the level of narrative, by ensnaring Booth in a short-lived adulterous affair even before the main story has begun she gives him a burden of guilt to carry through the ensuing action that is one of several factors complicating the reader's sympathy for the 'hero', and also prepares for the spectrum of female characters in which Amelia, Booth's wife, features as the paragon, Mrs Atkinson as a faulty but forgivable middle point, and Miss Mathews herself as a lost cause. But in thematic terms, Miss Mathews' most important function is to champion Bernard Mandeville's theory of the passions.

Booth in telling his life story relates the case of Colonel James, who in spite of scoffing at 'Virtue and Religion' shows great compassion when Booth lies mortally ill from a wound sustained at the siege of Gibraltar. He takes from this the doctrine that 'Men act entirely from their Passions'. Miss Mathews immediately makes the connection: Virtue and Religion 'serve only as Cloaks under which Hypocrisy may be the better enabled to cheat the World. I have been of that Opinion ever since I read that charming Fellow *Mandevil*'. Booth is uncomfortable: Mandeville has left out of his system Love, 'the best Passion which the Mind can possess', and explained it away as a product of 'base Impulses of Pride or Fear'; in doing so he represents 'human Nature in a Picture of the highest Deformity'. Although Miss Mathews concurs that the denial of the existence of the passion of Love is an oversight—'I am afraid I can give him the Lye myself'—she nevertheless avers, 'This I know, that when I read *Mandevil*, I thought all he said was true' (bk 3, ch. 5; 114–15).

It might be supposed that Mandeville's ideas are straightforwardly discredited by the advocacy of a wicked character, but in fact the challenge lingers. After all, the reader will see the appearance of moral integrity repeatedly stripped away in the course of the novel, from institutions and also from characters including Booth himself, to reveal the turbulent and dangerous workings of the passions. Fielding risks following Mandeville in representing 'human Nature in a Picture of the highest Deformity'. Amelia is apparently the exception, the redeeming example, above the fray. Like Miss Mathews, however, she is motivated by the passion of love, and to an even more improbable degree. In spite of her superior understanding and moral stature, there is nothing she will not forgive in her beloved Billy: reckless expenditure that plunges the young family (two children under the age of seven) into desperate poverty; drunken gambling that leads to further imprisonment for debt; foolish acts of bravado that threaten to remove him permanently from the family as provider and protector; groundless suspicions and accusations against her; and of course, sexual betrayal. After each misdemeanour she welcomes him back to some squalid lodging house or other, and very explicitly into her bed, with open arms.

This leaves the cleric Doctor Harrison, friend, mentor, and benefactor to the Booths, as the sole rock against which the doctrine of the selfish passions collides. It is Dr Harrison's refusal to bail out Booth from a sponging house for the second time which results in the latter's conversion. Booth's reading of Dr Isaac Barrow's sermons during this period of forced isolation has convinced him of the existence of future reward and punishment as the support of virtue in this world. The Doctor approves, yet his elaboration of this point is worryingly close to the moral relativism Booth expressed in conversation with Miss Mathews: 'if Men act, as I believe they do, from their Passions, it would be fair to conclude that Religion to be true which applies immediately to the strongest of these Passions, Hope and Fear'; in other words, the truth of the Christian religion is proven by its successful manipulation of human behaviour through the promise of either salvation or damnation (bk 12, ch. 5; 511–12).

Ultimately the world of *Amelia* is a Mandevillian one, and in this it is characteristic of the fiction of the 1750s, which painfully relinquishes the dream of an order free of the passions through ritual humiliation and defeat of a scapegoat figure, the stoic or rationalist. The most elaborate example is the tricking of the misanthropic Cadwallader Crabtree in *Peregrine Pickle*. Similar exorcisms can be found in *Amelia* (the freethinker Mr Robinson in bk 1, ch. 3), Sarah Fielding's *Volume the Last*, the continuation of *David Simple* (1753; Mr Orgueil), Samuel Johnson's *Rasselas* (1759; the sage in chapter 18), and Charlotte Lennox's *Henrietta* (1758) where an unnamed low-bred learned lady parrots the motto of Pope and the deist Bolingbroke 'whatever is, is right'. It is observed of the latter that she reads the Stoic philosopher Epictetus for directions on how to 'regulate her passions' while her maid is dressing her hair but 'closes her book to storm at the poor trembling creature for hurting her with the comb'.[13] The trope indicates the growing acceptance of emotion and desire as a crucial lever for good behaviour, in spite of the risks posed by the rampant self-interest and pleasure-seeking of the modern age.

In a respectful appraisal in the *Monthly Review*, John Cleland hails *Amelia*'s main subject, marriage rather than a courtship, as 'the boldest stroke that has been yet attempted in this species of writing'.[14] It was indeed a brave move to leave behind the familiar quixotic masculine narrative structure, still adhered to by Smollett and a mass of anonymous authors. Yet in pursuing this course, Fielding was not entirely alone. Interpolated tales of difficult marriages had long been a feature in fiction, *Pamela* Part 2 (1741) had brought conjugal issues to the fore, and in the fiction of the 1750s the wedded state begins to take the main stage. Sarah Fielding's *Volume the Last* concerns the troubles besetting three married couples. Haywood's *The History of Betsy Thoughtless*, published just two months before *Amelia* in 1751, is one of several novels at the start of the decade that dwell on ill-fated matches.

---

13 Charlotte Lennox, *Henrietta*, 2 vols (London: A. Millar, 1758), 2.110, 112.
14 *Monthly Review*, 5 (December 1751), 510–17 (510).

Amelia; or The Distrest Wife (1751), a fictionalized memoir of the separated and now impecunious author Elizabeth Justice, forms a counter-narrative to Fielding's portrait of an
ideal marriage of the same name; although, in the latter, the inclusion of Mrs Bennet's
account of how she was violently beaten after her husband's discovery that she has been
infected with syphilis having been drugged and raped brings home social realities more
sharply. *The Nominal Husband* (1750) is an account of domestic abuse in curious Saxon
disguise.

Further exposures of the cruelties practised under cover of domestic intimacy can be
found in unexpected places. 'The Memoirs of a Lady of Quality' included in *Peregrine
Pickle* is not just a salacious account of Lady Vane's amours, but also a notable example
of that feature of the arranged marriage system, usually alluded to only covertly, which
Ruth Perry has identified as 'the invention of sexual disgust' (2004: 254–9; and for an
account of how and why this short autobiography found its way into Smollett's novel, see
Flanders 1975). Lady Vane describes a wedded life of perpetual petty harassment, in bed
and out of it, beginning with the account of her wedding night when the attentions of
her husband strike her memorably as like 'the pawings of an imp, sent from hell to teize
and torment some guilty wretch'.[15] The opportunistic, anonymous *History of Tom Jones
the Foundling in His Married State* (1750) contains accounts of a string of cautionary bad
marriages, while *The Adventures of Jack Smart* (1756), also anonymous, to all appearances a
simple tale of a young man on the make, contains the history of Mrs McAdams, prey to an
Irish fortune hunter, who complains of inequality of the sexes before the law.

The Marriage Act of 1753 was one of a succession of bold measures introduced by the
Lord Chancellor, Philip Yorke, Lord Hardwicke, ostensibly with the aim of improving
the morals of the nation. Furious debate surrounded the passage of the Bill, inside and
outside Parliament. The opposition focused on the way in which the tightening of regulations for marriage would create barriers to the union of young men and women in love,
with consequences for population, and condemned its likely tendency to benefit the high
nobility by giving parents greater control over minors. Both sides declared the welfare of
women as a primary object. But the law did nothing to alter the dynamics of the conjugal household (see Perry, Chapter 22). The happiness and well-being of married women
were left, as before, to chance, dependent on the personalities of husbands generally little
known to them beforehand. Society promised women that men would reliably be kind
and wise masters and companions. Such was the order of things. Yet the brutal social
practices surrounding male identity formation, vividly evoked in a coming-of-age novel
such as *Peregrine Pickle*, seemed to ensure that men would reach adulthood as damaged
goods, destined to cause damage to those subordinate to them.

---

[15] Tobias Smollett, *The Adventures of Peregrine Pickle*, ed. James L. Clifford (Oxford: Oxford University
Press, 1983), ch. 88; 451.

This is the problem that Richardson seeks to address in his final, visionary novel of social regeneration, *Sir Charles Grandison*. His main aim was the creation of a portrait of a 'good and agreeable man' and it is a measure of the perceived difficulty of the task that he enlisted the help of a veritable committee of learned women, including the prominent Bluestocking writers Elizabeth Carter, Catherine Talbot, and Hester Mulso. The opening two volumes present the predicament of a spirited, intelligent young woman, Harriet Byron, an inveterate letter writer faced with an array of worthless suitors at home in Northamptonshire, to which she adds in her new situation on a visit to relatives in London. The story reaches a crisis with the abduction of the heroine from a masquerade by a rejected lover, the libertine Sir Harcourt Pollexfen.

Masquerade is a device used in English fiction throughout the century. In *Amelia* and *Peregrine Pickle* its depiction serves both to critique luxurious urban modernity and, paradoxically, to unmask illicit desire, concealed by the banal forms of polite society. In *Grandison*, this moment of ultimate iniquity leads directly to the introduction of the hero as quite literally the answer to Harriet's prayers. The courtship plot is effectively ended at this point. Harriet is taken to Grandison Hall to recuperate and put in the care of Sir Charles's two sisters, with whom she is soon on the terms of highest friendship. Before long she openly admits in her letters that she is in love with Sir Charles and it is apparent that he loves her too, although something holds him back. The uncertainty lies in the past: a prior engagement between the hero and a beautiful Italian aristocrat, Clementina, whom he had met after saving her brother from bandits while on the Grand Tour. The tortuous marriage negotiations with Clementina's Catholic family emerge in a series of letters between Sir Charles and Dr Bartlett, which Harriet is eventually given permission to read. It is only when Clementina heroically renounces her love in favour of her religion in the third volume that the path is cleared for the predestined British union.

Such are the general outlines of the narrative. But there is another drama at stake: Sir Charles returns to England not just to carry out the opportune rescue of the heroine, but to set to rights every aspect of his world following the death of his father, Sir Thomas, an extravagant rake who had wreaked havoc on family and estate. He neglected his gentle, steadfast, high-minded wife and gave the final blow to her delicate constitution when she heard that he had been killed in a duel. Lady Mary Wortley Montagu was a reader who found the account of this marriage compelling for personal reasons which must have applied to a good proportion of the aristocracy, although she was no fan of what she regarded as Richardson's vulgar puritanism: 'I heartily despise him and eagerly read him, nay, sob over his works in a most scandalous manner.'[16]

---

[16] Lady Mary Wortley Montagu, *The Complete Letters of Lady Mary Wortley Montagu*, ed. Robert Halsband, 3 vols (Oxford: Clarendon Press, 1967), 3.90.

Sir Charles has been shaped by adoration of his mother: 'my Mother was my oracle'.[17] He carries the legacy of her influence into the next generation, undoing case by case with infinite attention to detail the consequences of Sir Thomas's misdeeds. The fact that he is handsome, charming, astute, and rich, and goes about his business with consummate ease, detracts in some measure from the interest of the ensuing action. But there is fascination in the method. Sir Charles is like a virtuous Peregrine Pickle in his penetration into human nature and ability to manipulate it; where Peregrine uses his knowledge to create chaos through 'practical satire' (ch. 89; 540), Sir Charles seeks the improvement of all around him. On every occasion he understands what makes his adversaries tick. The scene in which he humours and flatters into virtuous behaviour Lady Beauchamp, the erring mother of one of his protégés, is a tour de force (2.272–84).

Yes, Richardson is minute. His works are consequently a remarkable storehouse of information about the texture of everyday life in the period. But there is an epic dimension to his work, most apparent in *Clarissa*, but also present in this final novel, where we are given a historical allegory of the overcoming of a society based on the passions in favour of a new order founded on moral sentiments. Other novelists of the period accepted the inevitability of the passions, and could see hope of improvement only in the countervailing effect of the more beneficial passions over the more malign. In *Grandison*, to a far greater extent than in *Clarissa*, Richardson adopts a zero tolerance stance on the passions. On many occasions he curbs the prevailing discourse by reducing 'the passions', with all their complexity of interaction, to undifferentiated 'passion'. In *A Collection of the Moral and Instructive Sentiments . . . Contained in the Histories of 'Pamela', 'Clarissa', and 'Sir Charles Grandison'* (1755), he abstracts from his final work a series of reflections on the passions that emphasize subordination and control, for the most part, rather than the inevitable and sometimes ameliorative ascendancy of self-love. In the same volume, with Fielding perhaps in his sights, and Mandeville, Pope, and Swift almost certainly, he presents two other related reflections from *Grandison*: 'Libertinism, by some, is called a knowledge of the world, a knowledge of Human Nature; but the character of Human Nature, it is hoped, is not to be taken from the overflowings of dirty imaginations'; and 'Human Nature in general, is not so bad a thing as some disgracers of their own species have seemed to imagine it'.[18] What is striking here is the close connection indicated between imagination and models of human nature; it illustrates Richardson's belief in the vital role of fiction in defining the capacities as well as the duties of the individual.

In the 1740s with the first instalment of *The Adventures of David Simple* (1744) Sarah Fielding had pre-empted Richardson in setting out to depict a good man, and had

---

[17] Samuel Richardson, *The History of Sir Charles Grandison*, ed. Jocelyn Harris, 3 vols (London: Oxford University Press, 1972), 1.261.

[18] *A Collection of the Moral and Instructive Sentiments, Maxims, Cautions, and Reflexions, Contained in the Histories of 'Pamela', 'Clarissa', and 'Sir Charles Grandison'* (London: S. Richardson, 1755), 293.

anticipated *Amelia* also in thematizing the search for true friendship. One might venture to say she becomes the quintessential novelist of the 1750s, due to a number of features: her conscious and explicit foregrounding of human nature as subject matter; the underlying pessimism of her writing; and her formal and thematic experimentalism, which gives the impression of an inner compulsion rather than a strategy for material gain, much as she needed money. In *Volume the Last* of *David Simple*, ferocious hatred of the hypocrisy and callous indifference to suffering of the complacently wealthy is barely containable within the conventions of narrative realism, as she rapidly (and with a savage disregard for the feelings of the reader) lays one by one the deaths of almost every member of the hero's family circle at the door of the fair-weather man of means Mr Ratcliff, the moneylender Mr Nichols, and the allegorically-named Mr and Mrs Orgueil. The view of human nature is bleak; the central tragedy is that David himself is corrupted into avarice and false relations of clientage by concern for his loved ones.

The way in which the author smuggled this sequel into the world, as a brief appendix to a reprint of the original, seemed to one of her friends a kind of career suicide. James Harris remarked 'Mrs Fielding has just published a 3d volume of David Simple; the world thinks it a meer [*sic*] 3d volume and not a new story, and thus the book stops with the booksellers' (see Bree 1996: 15). The unknown reviewer in the *Monthly*, who dealt with the volume perfunctorily in the 'Miscellaneous' section, concurs with this view. But to her relation Lady Mary Wortley Montagu *Volume the Last* suggested something different; she mistakenly attributes three anonymous works to Sarah Fielding by way of praising what she understands to be a new determination to publish for glory rather than profit: 'Sally has mended her style in her last Volume of D Simple', she wrote to her daughter, 'The Art of Tormenting, the Female Quixote, and Sir C. Goodville are all sale work. I suppose they proceed from her pen, and heartily pity her, constrain'd by her Circumstances to seek her bread by a method I do not doubt she despises' (*Letters*, 3.66–7).

The realist conventions employed in *David Simple* were evidently not uncommercial enough for Sarah Fielding, and she sought out more rebarbative forms in which to communicate her raking vision of diseased human relations. She next joined with her friend Jane Collier, the true author of that curious satirical treatise *Essay on the Art of Ingeniously Tormenting*, to write *The Cry* (1754). It omits such standard devices as plot, naturalistic dialogue, and even individual characters. The eponymous *Cry* is an extraordinary conception, 'composed of all those characters in human nature, who, tho' differing from each other, join in one common clamour against Truth and her adherents'.[19] They—the plural is employed for the Cry—engage in debate with the heroine Portia in a dimension outside time and place, reviewing the history of her connections with her suitor

---

[19] Sarah Fielding and Jane Collier, *The Cry: A New Dramatic Fable*, 3 vols (London: R. and J. Dodsley, 1754), 'Prologue to Part the First', 1.20.

Ferdinand and others. The conventionality of the ending, which only takes up a few pages, doesn't detract from the remarkable nature of the project as a whole, to establish a form of anti-novel which would sweep aside embodied characterization the better to explore 'the labyrinths of the human mind' (1.14).

As one can imagine, *The Cry* was not a big seller, although it received a respectful notice in the *Monthly Review*. It is worth noting the remarkably welcoming attitude of the first review journal to works by both Sarah Fielding and Charlotte Lennox, given its general bias against feminocentric fiction (including Richardson's). These two female authors seem to have been protected by their connections with Fielding himself and with Samuel Johnson respectively, and by their own canny referencing of revered male literary precursors. The *Monthly Review* could find no fault with *The Female Quixote*, filling nearly twelve pages with extracts and citing Henry Fielding's judgement that in some respects it improved upon Cervantes. But this was a decade when, in spite of the continuing prevalence of masculine tastes and prejudices, women writers were being celebrated more widely than ever before in a cluster of works including George Ballard's *Memoirs of Several Ladies of Great Britain* (1752), John Duncombe's *The Feminead* (1754), Colman and Thornton's anthology *Poems by Eminent Ladies* (1755), and Thomas Amory's *Memoirs of the Lives of Several Ladies of Great Britain* (1755) and his semi-autobiographical paean to female genius, *The Life of John Buncle* (vol. 1, 1756). Feminist scholarship sometimes shares the economism—the notion that commercial success translates into cultural influence—of many of the most influential histories of the development of the eighteenth-century novel; see for instance Catherine Gallagher's insistence on the 'reciprocal shaping of the terms "women," "author," and marketplace"' (1994: xiii), or the tendentious title of a key collection of essays on female novelists of the 1750s, *Masters of the Marketplace* (Carlile 2011). Female authors certainly received some encouragement to enter the literary marketplace, but whether they achieved mastery there is another matter. It is unclear in Sarah Fielding's case that this was even an objective.

Much could be said about Samuel Richardson's role in mediating with the marketplace on behalf of women, and on subscription publishing as a halfway house between the patronage system and the market, which enabled several key female-authored novels to see the light of day. Richardson did his best to salvage *The Cry*. He sent copies to friends and canvassed their opinions (lukewarm), and suggested a revised edition (Eaves and Kimpel 1971: 203). When Sarah Fielding again flew in the face of commercial wisdom by reviving an abortive plan from 1748 to write a fictional work based on classical history, Richardson was ready to offer his services as printer and coordinate a successful subscription.

Like *The Cry*, *The Lives of Cleopatra and Octavia* (1757) shows Sarah Fielding's dissatisfaction with the mimetic feigning expected in conventional prose fiction. It is not a novel, but rather belongs to the subgenre of 'Dialogues of the Dead', and this long-established form of historical fiction or fictional history licenses her undertaking (again, it was favourably reviewed). There is no suspense, no forward momentum, no plot as such; instead, retrospective reporting of a story the reader already knows, told twice. But it demonstrates a continuing fascination with the dissection of motive and character. *The History of the Countess of Dellwyn* (1759) and *The History of Ophelia* (1760) have the look of standard six-shilling two-volume novels. Sarah Fielding struck a good deal with the bookseller Andrew Millar in surrendering copyright of the *Countess* for £60. She may have returned to fictional conventions after a long detour exploring other possibilities, but the formidably learned dissertation which precedes the story shows her still reluctant to compromise on what she understands as her primary duty as a writer of fiction: not to entertain, not to promote sales, but to instruct on the most closely concealed and unpalatable aspects of human nature.

What was the legacy of the novel of the 1750s? Its hesitancies, regressions, false starts, and furious satire throw sharply into relief the game-changing triumph of *Tristram Shandy*. It is Sterne who, contrary to the initial fears of his bookseller Robert Dodsley and the gloomy predictions of Richardson, turns his combination of the wit of Henry Fielding and the sensibility of Samuel Richardson into a winning formula. Less spectacularly but more pervasively, the methods and moral tendency of *Sir Charles Grandison* come to provide a reliable model for the production of feminocentric fiction, underpinning the success of the epistolary mode from the 1760s to the 1780s; and eventually converted into a more flexible form with greater longevity by the genius of Frances Burney and Jane Austen. As for the lesson offered by the novel's brush with mortality, this remains elusive. Arguably it was at the moment when the genre appeared least welcome that it was best able to demonstrate its worth.

5

Tobias Smollett and the Ramble Novel

SIMON DICKIE

WHATEVER happened to transform the 'Age of Johnson' into an 'Age of Sensibility', one thing is certain. This newer version of the mid-eighteenth century leaves less room than ever for comic fiction. The Age of Johnson put Henry Fielding and Smollett front and centre: treated as narrative satirists, they were worth reading. Bawdy *romans à clef* and 'spy' novels like *Pompey the Little* (1751) or Charles Johnstone's *Chrysal* (1760–5) were likewise cast as strings of satiric episodes. More recently, however, satire has lost its accepted status as the primary literary energy of the age. Fielding's stock fell and Smollett's plummeted. Once thought almost unreadable, Samuel Richardson's *Clarissa* (1748–9) now presides over a cluster of newly canonized sentimental novels (which might have been tailor-made for recent critical preferences, each of them a fragmented and endlessly analysable commentary on class, gender, and historical change). The much-needed recovery of mid-century women novelists has had a complementary effect: since these authors were struggling for legitimacy after the scandal of Behn, Manley, and Haywood, they tended to work in more didactic and sentimental modes. Now rebranded as 'it' narratives, the spy novels have lately returned to favour, but not necessarily for their humour (see also Festa, Chapter 18).

In these circumstances, it may seem counter-intuitive to assert that the real money for mid-century booksellers lay with comic fiction. *Tom Jones* (1749) went through four authorized editions within the first year alone, a total of 10,000 copies. Compared to this, *Clarissa* was a disappointment. While the first four volumes sold briskly enough, the first impression of volumes 5–7 (3,000 copies) took two years to sell, with at least a quarter of purchasers never even completing their sets (Keymer 1994). The fashionable world, as Richardson's major biographers acknowledge, found *Clarissa* 'very moral and very long and was not inclined to welcome novels with unhappy endings' (Eaves and Kimpel 1971: 306). Even Smollett's *Roderick Random* (1748), so clearly a lesser achievement, sold 6,500 copies in less than two years. Closer attention to James Raven's statistics for these years brings further surprises. Sterne, Fielding, and Smollett all come before Richardson in Raven's list of best-selling authors (as do Haywood and Defoe). Not far behind are the big translations of Cervantes and Le Sage—both periodically reissued in large runs—and other French and Spanish texts that are only now gaining their rightful place in histories of British fiction. Early translations of *Lazarillo de Tormes, Guzmán de Alfarache*, and Quevedo's *El Buscón* went through multiple editions, as did the works of Rabelais, Sorel, and Scarron. And beyond these recognizable texts lie hundreds of now-forgotten comic novels, texts that were read for a season and then tossed aside. Raven counts 508 entirely new novels and a similar number of reprints for the two decades of his study, a total of almost 1,100 texts. A rough accounting of subgenres might put the proportion of comic fiction at 25 or 30 per cent—at least as much as the sentimental fiction we have learned so much about in recent years. The statistics also suggest that so much good work on women's fiction has cumulatively overemphasized their actual contribution to the genre. Between 1750 and 1770, at least, Raven finds that women authors can positively be identified for just 14 per cent of new fiction (1987: 14, 18, 2007b: 116).

Certainly contemporaries had no doubt that readers picked up novels for entertainment rather than morals or sentiment. Nothing but amusement would do, carped the critics; serious and useful works were scarcely read. The success of *Tom Jones*, the *Critical Review* complained in 1756, had 'fill'd half the world with imitating fools'.[1] 'The ridiculous' was so much the rage, bemoaned another mid-century essayist, 'that no sooner a droll rogue touches that foible, but he commands all our affections'. Moralists could put on their grave face, critics could complain, parsons could harangue from the pulpit, but it was all no use. Readers wanted a good laugh, and anyone who tried to stop them 'may as well think of stemming a floodtide in the river *Humber*'.[2] Fielding himself had turned towards sentimentalism with *Amelia* (1752), but his public scoffed and the book was a financial failure. 'Now the Humour, or Manners, of this Age are to laugh at every Thing', he complained—'and the only Way to please them is to make them laugh.'[3]

My task in this chapter is to flesh out this immensely unfamiliar image of mid-eighteenth-century fiction. Inevitably the earlier Fielding looms large—Fielding the 'English Cervantes', the greatest humorist of his age. But it seems infinitely more important to write about the second great comic novelist of these years. Tobias Smollett is now the least familiar of Raven's top six authors, and it is easy to see why. No author sits less comfortably with the current emphasis on the politeness and sensibility of mid-century British culture, and no author is less amenable to feminist perspectives. Smollett's fiction is full of cruel caricatures and nasty torments. He seems to delight in blood, shit, and vomit. But the cripples, the brawls, the misogyny, and emptied chamber pots were all

---

[1] *Critical Review*, 2 (October 1756), 276.
[2] 'A Censure on the Present Reigning Taste for Novels and Romances, and How to Cure It', *London Magazine*, no. 18 (May 1749).
[3] *The Covent Garden Journal and A Plan of the Universal Register-Office*, ed. Bertrand A. Goldgar (Middletown, CT: Wesleyan University Press, 1988), 58 (no. 7 [25 January 1752]).

too typical of mid-eighteenth-century humour. Closer attention to this most unlikeable author might help us understand some of the most confounding incidents in Frances Burney, Maria Edgeworth, Walter Scott, Charles Dickens, and early sentimental fiction. The present discussion begins with the least-read of Smollett's major novels, *Peregrine Pickle* (1751), a text that moves almost systematically through the everyday comic situations of its age. From this canonical text, it will move to the ephemeral comic fiction that Smollett's contemporaries were consuming in such quantities.

Peregrine Pickle and the Hostility to Sentiment

The rise and fall of Smollett's fortunes would itself make a fine case study of the changing preferences of eighteenth-century studies, and indeed of academic literary scholarship as a whole. The earliest real Smollett scholars—those who took up his cause in the early twentieth century—faced an uphill battle trying to rescue their author from the Victorian consensus that he was a coarse and brutal man who wrote dangerous and immoral books. Further difficulties came with the formalist standards then being codified by Henry James: Smollett's fiction was rambling and diffuse, full of digressions and needless attacks on personal enemies. He was a shameless padder and probably took money to include the brazen 'memoirs' of Lady Vane in *Peregrine Pickle*.[4] Smollett had neither the formal unity nor the intense psychological realism that readers now expected from a truly great novelist. And most important for present purposes, Smollett's sense of humour had become almost incomprehensible. Thus George Bernard Shaw's comments on *Humphry Clinker* (1771):

> Poverty in rags is a joke, yellow fever is a joke, drunkenness is a joke, dysentery is a joke, kickings, floggings, falls, frights, humiliations, and painful accidents of all sorts are jokes. Hen-pecked husbands and termagant mothers-in-law are prime jokes. The infirmities of age and the inexperience and shyness of youth are jokes; and it is first-rate fun to insult and torment those that suffer from them … *Humphry Clinker* may not have become absolutely unreadable; but there is certainly a good deal in this book that is now simply disgusting to the class of readers that in its own day found it uproariously amusing. (1891: 200–1)

All this on the kindliest of Smollett's novels (the only one Shaw knew).

Smollett studies long remained in a defensive posture, ever obliged to establish the moral and artistic worth of his fiction. Two particular arguments proved their mettle over the generations. First, Smollett's novels were conscious attempts to adapt the ethical functions of Augustan satire to the less formal medium of the novel (see, inter alia, Paulson 1967; Rousseau 1982; Beasley 1998). Here it helped that satire was itself such a

---

[4] Tobias Smollett, *The Adventures of Peregrine Pickle*, ed. James L. Clifford (Oxford: Oxford University Press, 1983), ch. 88; 432–539.

loosely defined genre, and that copia or plenitude were expected characteristics of satiric writing. If Smollett was at heart a satirist, ethical functions could be ascribed to almost all his humour, and even the memoirs of Lady Vane could be treated as a pointed satire on upper-class vice. A second argument treated *Roderick Random* and *Peregrine Pickle* as novels of moral education, coming-of-age narratives comparable to *Tom Jones* and looking forward to *David Copperfield* and the rest (Putney 1945; Boucé 1976).

With these and other justifications behind him, Smollett was one of the Big Five for most of the twentieth century. Paired with Fielding in the old *Cambridge History of English Literature* (1913) and the subject of a long chapter in McKillop's *Early Masters of English Fiction* (1956), he remained one of the 'Four Major Authors' in the mid-eighteenth-century volume of the *Oxford History of English Literature* (1979). Modern Language Association [MLA] statistics for Smollett and Richardson scholarship ran close throughout the 1960s and 1970s. There were scores of dissertations and recognized centres of Smollett studies at Yale, Princeton, and the Scottish universities. Smollett and Cervantes, Smollett and Johnson, Smollett and British empiricism, Smollett and Voltaire: generations of scholars patiently traced such connections. Why had Smollett abandoned his early aspirations as a poet? Was he closer to Swift or to Pope as a satirist? As with the two great Augustans, much labour went into identifying historical originals for fictional characters. The Whiggish doctor in *Peregrine Pickle* was Mark Akenside; Mr Spondy was Fielding; Garrick, Quin, Chesterfield, and Lyttelton all made their appearances. Such identifications buttressed the topical satire argument and produced serious-looking annotations for the editions. As befitted a major author, there was a long scholarly biography, competing editions of the letters, a volume in the *Critical Heritage* series, and dedicated sections in the big bibliographies. A bicentennial Smollett edition was announced in the late 1960s, although its first volume would not appear until 1988. Smollett featured on every survey course and there were student editions of all his novels. There was even a decent forgery scandal (1948–53), when the sometime Smollettian Francesco Cordasco came up with five letters to solve some long-standing mysteries in Smollett studies.

Then it all went downhill. Smollett's MLA statistics halved between 1980 and 2010, even as eighteenth-century fiction received more attention than ever. New generations of researchers were quite naturally wondering if such an envious and spiteful author was even worth reading. With Pope and Swift also in decline, satire no longer worked to justify widely differing genres. Above all, the rediscovery of early women novelists and the emergence of feminist criticism altered eighteenth-century studies almost beyond recognition. So much good work on Burney, Charlotte Lennox, Sarah Fielding, and Frances Sheridan has created a sort of replacement canon of mid-century fiction. Smollett has disappeared from most curricula and only *Humphry Clinker* remains consistently in print. Even more quickly than Oliver Goldsmith, Smollett sank into the undifferentiated mass of sources raided by broadly new historicist work. Smollett features prominently in recent studies of travel writing and the grand tour, of Enlightenment historiography, and of gender, sexuality, and the body. Always recognized as a Scottish author, Smollett remains central to studies of linguistic regionalism, the codification of standard English, and the emergence of an inclusive British identity after the union of 1707 (see also Keymer, Chapter 23). But even with these newer topics, the annual total of articles has dwindled to a trickle. John Richetti's new *Cambridge History of English Literature 1660–1780* (2005) gives just five index references to Smollett, only two of them to his fiction. A new volume of the Georgia Smollett comes out every few years, meticulously edited and annotated. But it is all a bit late.

One need not champion Smollett, nor revive the twentieth-century interpretations, to acknowledge his centrality to mid-century fiction. No author so instantly leads us to the long-buried comic strain in early British fiction. If this comedy is now alien or distasteful, all the more reason for striving to understand how eighteenth-century readers could enjoy it so much. And for these purposes, there may be no better place to start than the opening chapters of *Peregrine Pickle*, where one encounters all Smollett's signature characteristics: the general atmosphere of resentment and suspicion, the vicious pranks and delight in physical pain, and the linguistic gusto that made all his novels so good for reading aloud. The trio of naval characters bursts onto the scene like a travelling circus—all wallops, shrieks, and drunken curses. In Commodore Trunnion, the one-eyed braggart mariner who runs his house like a man-of-war, Smollett created one of the great eccentrics of British fiction, a figure much admired by Burney, Scott, Dickens, Thackeray, and many more. Trunnion provides a perfect victim for the book's earliest sequences of practical jokes, the work of Jack Hatchway (his one-legged former lieutenant) and Tom Pipes (his boatswain), both of them experts at getting the old man into a fit.

Also with the sailors comes the misogyny and the violence that so repels modern readers. This time the misogyny appears in appropriately nautical metaphors, which Smollett clearly delights in reproducing. Women were leaky vessels with desires as deep as the Bay of Biscay. They were painted galleys or hurricanes that blew from every side. Since Trunnion especially detests old maids—'devils incarnate sent from hell to torment mankind'—it is a huge joke for his old shipmates to trick him into marrying Mrs Grizzle Pickle, the hero's meddling and puritanical aunt, 'a squinting, block-faced, chattering piss-kitchen' as the commodore has described her (*Peregrine Pickle*, ch. 5; 20). Husbands and wives always hate each other in Smollett, and the Trunnion–Grizzle ménage is the first of many unlikely pairings. (Volume 2 is almost structured around the hero's encounters with the pitiful Mr Hornbeck, an aging cuckold who finds himself married to an oversexed oyster wench.) An early instance of the novel's spectacular violence comes in Trunnion's subjection to petticoat government, completed only when his wife hires a carpenter to build them a bed. A great brawl ensues, with Trunnion furiously defending his hammock and the carpenter taking a hammer to the old man's remaining eye, leaving him to be 'led about the house like a blind bear growling for prey' (ch. 9; 46). And so it goes on. Since Trunnion hates everything Hanoverian, Hatchway mischievously summons the local exciseman. After much confusion, the man is tied to the household whipping-post and flogged by Pipes (who never goes anywhere without his trusty cat o' nine tails).

Pranks like this were easy enough for modern critics to cast as satiric vignettes. Like lawyers, moneylenders, card-sharpers, and quack doctors, excisemen were regular targets in Tory satire. Satire was routinely described as an act of corporal punishment, and the lash was its most traditional emblem, so the critics had their precedents to cite. But consider the details: the exciseman is flogged until his skin is flayed off 'from his rump to the nape of his neck', while he 'bellowed hideously with pain, to the infinite satisfaction of the spectators' (ch. 16; 76). Such concluding formulas recur throughout the book; a constant reminder that a good joke in Smollett's world depends both on extreme pain and an audience to witness it. In their most spectacular trick against the new Mrs Trunnion, the sailors spike her medicinal brandy with jalap, a laxative of explosive force. After watching through their spy hole for several days, they finally see the lady take several large gulps before church on Sunday. Result? 'Her bowels were afflicted with such agonies, as compelled her to retire in the face of the congregation'. Fits of swooning and defecating reduce her 'to the brink of the grave' (ch. 14; 67). And as usual in Smollett, the initial joke soon accumulates further comic consequences, with the whole village assuming that Trunnion must have poisoned his wife (after all, everyone knew proverbially that the best wife was a dead wife).

The stage thus set, our hero makes his appearance. Peregrine Pickle is a comic functionary with ancient roots, the descendant of native trickster figures and the heroes of continental picaresque. (Alliterative character names link all Smollett's early protagonists to folk heroes like Tom Thumb and jestbook personas such as Merry Martin or Ferdinando Funny.) As with Tom Thumb or the German Till Eulenspiegel, this special status is signalled by portents surrounding his appearance in the world. Mrs Pickle spends her pregnancy inventing odd errands to tease her sister-in-law, a fanatical reader of contemporary gynaecology who resolves to satisfy every craving. Two pineapples, a fricassee of frogs from Boulogne, a neighbouring gentlewoman's favourite chamber pot, three black hairs plucked (very painfully) from Trunnion's beard—all are procured to protect the delicate foetus. It comes as no surprise, therefore, that Peregrine himself is mischievous from birth. He already knows how to terrify the household, summoning everyone with a shriek or pretending to be dead only to cackle at their concern. He quickly learns to torment his uncle Trunnion, standing on the old man's gouty toe, twisting his nose, and putting snuff in his rum. This early promise is soon fulfilled in that set piece of so much early modern comic narrative, the extended torment of a tutor or clergyman. Peregrine's victim is Mr Keypstick (keep-stick), a low-German schoolmaster. The nasty boy hides his wig, puts soot in the soup, and kills all the chickens by pushing needles through their heads (a trick that goes back to Till Eulenspiegel).

By no mere accident, Keypstick is also a shrunken hunchback. Little Perry strews his way with bean shells (the eighteenth-century equivalent of the slapstick banana skin) so that 'his heels slipped from under him, his hunch pitched upon the ground, and the furniture of his head fell off in the shock; so that he lay in a very ludicrous attitude for the entertainment of the spectators' (ch. 13; 58–9). Critics bent on treating Smollett as a satirist could point out that Keypstick was also illiterate and shouldn't be trying to run a school. Glossed in this way, the episode took its place beside other attacks on public schools, like Parson Adams's speech in *Joseph Andrews*. But here as everywhere else in this book, satiric purposes are secondary to an elemental comic situation: the sight of a furious little hunchback on the floor with no wig. The deformed and disabled are reliable figures of fun throughout Smollett's *oeuvre*, from *Roderick Random* to *Humphry Clinker*. Deafness, myopia, and missing limbs made anyone a standing joke; Hatchway's wooden leg creates comic mishaps throughout *Peregrine Pickle*. Illnesses of every sort were laughable. Diabetes, for example, was hugely funny because it required such constant urination. Smollett effortlessly improvises on the plight of a large matron forced to use a travelling urinal (the fold-up leather variety) in a stagecoach. 'Odds plague! you nincompoop', she cries at her unfortunate husband, 'you have fumbled so long about the pot, that I have drenched myself all over. I wish to God you had received the stream in your mouth' (ch. 86; 424).

As Pickle grows up, the raucous comedy alternates with amorous intrigues, followed by some richly deserved misfortunes and a final spell in Fleet Prison. Naturally all ends well, with Pickle rescued by the beautiful Emilia Gauntlet, who forgives him for trying to rape her in a London brothel. Punctuated as it is by the narrator's intermittent moralizing, this plot of youthful error and repentance enabled the most determined modern critics to treat *Peregrine Pickle* as a *Bildungsroman*. This argument was always a stretch, demanding a certain wilful blindness to the book's real energies. From his perspective outside the academy, Walter Allen more frankly acknowledged that there was little or no interiority. Pickle was little more than a 'joke-machine, a mechanism by which a headlong series of practical jokes are projected one after another' (Allen 1956). If these jokes have so often been explained away as something more respectable, it is because of the immense historical distance between eighteenth-century humour and our own, the gulf that struck Shaw in the 1890s and must now be wider than ever. Few people would now find it funny to burst in on others having sex or watch everyone trying to escape a burning house. Pickle skips for joy at both these things. He cudgels his rivals, knocks old men down stairs, and knows multiple ways of making people sick. Revenge is an open and intoxicating pleasure in Smollett, and Pickle never relents without driving his victims to their wits' end. Our last encounter with Mr Hornbeck finds him ducked in a canal and running about 'like a drowned rat, squeaking for assistance and revenge' (ch. 64; 319). Tossing people into ponds or rivers was doubly funny in early modern culture because almost no one could swim: they were terrified to death as well as soaked to the skin.

These were not rustic or pre-modern barbarities, the sort of amusements that polite urban culture was leaving behind. Writing in 1819, William Hazlitt more easily recognized how close so many of these incidents were to the London newspaper anecdotes of Smollett's day.[5] Two hack authors who come to blows in a bookshop, a French fop pulled by the nose, scaldings and plucked wigs at the Bedford Coffee House: this sort of thing was comically described in newspapers and excitedly recounted in letters from the city. Mid-century men about town competed with each other to enact more and more complex hoaxes, and Smollett repeats or elaborates on some of the most celebrated (Dickie 2011: 149–50). Two fraudulent lawyers are summoned to do business with each other. As revenge against 'an old peevish puritanical' landlady, Pickle publishes an advertisement in which she offers to buy a black tomcat. An angry crowd of forty gathers, each throwing their cat at the terrified old woman. Pipes and Pickle especially delight in fomenting brawls. Pipes punishes two insolent chairmen by getting into their chair with a heavy parcel (100 lbs). The chairmen trade accusations of laziness and soon come to blows. 'Peregrine, who followed at a distance, enjoyed the pleasure of seeing them both beaten almost to jelly' (ch. 93; 577). The jelly reminds us that a really enjoyable fight in this culture—the sort that made one rush to the window or stop the coach—produced a decent show of blood and went on until the loser could hardly move. Ferocious boxing and short-sword displays were also profitable parts of the London entertainment economy, practised at dedicated venues like John Broughton's amphitheatre in Tottenham Court Road. Always up for a good fistfight, Smollett's Tom Pipes seems to be named after a famous bruiser ('the neatest boxer I remember', a contemporary described the historical Pipes, one who placed his blows 'with surprising Time and Judgment').[6]

None of the novel's early readers seem to have objected to the violence. Many agreed that Smollett went too far with his attacks on contemporaries. Some of the most tasteless pranks attracted criticism, like the one about holes drilled in Mrs Trunnion's chamber pot. But few objected to the elemental nastiness of this book. When he revised *Peregrine Pickle* for the second edition of 1758, Smollett took out the perforated chamber pot and a few of the most spiteful lampoons (Buck 1925). Gone was his cruel parody of Lord Lyttelton's *Monody* to his wife (1747) and the lewd account of Peregrine's affair with a nun. Yet most of the vicious practical humour remained—all those bleeding noses and broken heads. The near-drownings are still there, too, as are the burns from roasting pans and falling joints of meat. A troublesome bailiff still falls into a fireplace, 'where his chin was encountered by the grate, which, in a moment, seared him to the bone' (ch. 97; 616). These scenes of brutal disorder long remained favourites for illustrators: Trunnion and Hatchway trading blows at a tavern, the great 'battle' at the college of authors, all the puking and upset tables at the feast in the manner of the ancients.

---

[5] William Hazlitt, *Essays on the English Comic Writers in Complete Works*, ed. P. P. Howe, 21 vols (London: J. M. Dent, 1930–4), 6.115–17.

[6] Captain John Godfrey, *A Treatise upon the Useful Science of Defence* (London: for the Author, 1747), 57.

More strikingly, given current critical preferences, few contemporary readers said anything about Smollett's starkly primitive misogyny. The cast of coquettes, adulteresses, and vindictive old maids was always problematic for academic readers (and always excused with a tip of the hat to Swift and Juvenal). With every year that passes, it all looks worse and worse. But in this, too, Smollett was typical of his age. His fiction rehearses mainstream early modern prejudices about women as carnal, deceitful, and irrational beings. Romance ideals are flatly set out in heroines like Emilia Gauntlet or Narcissa in *Roderick Random*, but Smollett's real imaginative energy goes into the negative portraits. Mrs Trunnion is one of many grotesque old women. Three long chapters of *Peregrine Pickle* collect the stories of scandalous ladies of fashion who consult Pickle's friend Cadwallader Crabtree during his time as a London fortune teller, including one who has conceived a child with her black footman.

Without being pornographic, *Pickle* also offers a chilling record of contemporary assumptions about sexual violence. Women of lower status are always available in this novel, for a few coins at most. Pickle himself is a 'dragon among the chambermaids' from beginning to end (ch. 90; 553). One long sequence finds him roaming about the countryside with Emilia's brother '[laying] close siege to every buxom country damsel that fell in their way' (ch. 34; 166). On another jaunt, Pickle buys a pretty beggar-girl from her mother, clearly for sexual purposes. And along the way come several explicit representations of rape. The hero's assault upon Emilia is a villainy for which he must atone, but the apparent clarity of this instance only points up the ambiguities of so many others. As in other early modern comic texts, rape in *Peregrine Pickle* is less about self-gratification than vengeance—against rival suitors or the victim herself. At one point during their early sex ramble, Pickle and Gauntlet decide to punish a recalcitrant farmer's wife who had rebuffed them both. Our hero easily imitates her husband's voice (trickster rapists are always accomplished mimics), and the pair burst in on her. With 'some seeming reluctance', the 'hale rosy wench' submits to Gauntlet while Pickle overcomes the housemaid (ch. 34; 166–70). Volume 2 ends with Pickle's 'punishment' of a lady of Bath who dared to prefer a brawny soldier to himself. It is as gruesome as any Jacobean bed trick: after hiring a pair of thugs to waylay his rival, Pickle sleeps with the lady himself and then completes his revenge by spreading the story about town. Presumably, this incident provided a satisfying sense of closure for readers obliged to wait for Volume 3.

At first sight, such episodes seem completely oblivious to the sentimental movement and the much-noted feminization of mid-eighteenth-century culture. If sympathies for paupers and invalids really were growing, Smollett shows scant recognition of them. Richardson may have created unprecedented first-person records of the trauma of sexual assault, but *Peregrine Pickle* perpetuates much more degraded representations of femininity and all the older comic treatments of rape. Just two years later, the narrator of Smollett's *Ferdinand Count Fathom* would openly declare his intolerance of sentimentalism, 'the moral sense so warmly contended for by those ideal philoso-phers'.[7] From this perspective, episodes like the burlesque of Lyttelton's *Monody* read like attacks on the movement's literary manifestations. Read aloud at the college of authors, the mock *Monody* attracts sharp criticism. Why indulge in 'imaginary sor-rows', the chairman asks its blubbering author, when everyone has 'real grievances' to cope with (*Peregrine Pickle*, ch. 102; 655)? Burying one's wife was supposed to be *fun*. On closer inspection, even Pickle's assault on Emilia Gauntlet turns out to have an explicitly anti-Richardsonian subtext. Although drugged like Clarissa Harlowe, Smollett's hero-ine easily repels her attacker. 'With a most majestic severity', Emilia denounces Pickle, opens the door, walks downstairs, and entrusts herself to a watchman 'who accommo-dated her with a hackney-chair, in which she was safely conveyed to her uncle's house' (ch. 82; 408). This episode draws on a long pre-sentimental tradition of more physical and resistant heroines (see Dickie 2010: 584). But it also implies, more disturbingly, that women knew how to repel a sexual attacker if they really wanted to. By 1751, Richardson had made sexual violence the great test case for emerging sympathies towards women. Smollett and other comic authors reacted by restating beliefs that 'real' rape—genuinely non-consensual sex—was impossible.

Over the course of his career, as we know, Smollett's attitudes would soften. By the time of *Humphry Clinker* (1771), he had evidently developed some benevolence and at least a selec-tive sympathy for women. *Clinker* works almost pedantically through the major set pieces of sentimental fiction. The penniless consumptive relieved by Matt Bramble, the black-smith's widow who has lost her senses, emotional reconciliations and reunions: such scenes waver between pathos and farce, but they are there nonetheless. The old misogyny, too, is now balanced by more rounded and sympathetic female characters like Lydia Melford. By adapting Richardson's multi-voiced epistolarity, Smollett allowed Lydia, alone of all his gen-teel young ladies, to speak in her own voice. Twenty years earlier, however, Smollett was relentlessly scornful of tender-heartedness or refinement. 'In their purifications', as he com-plained in *Ferdinand Count Fathom*, the right-minded critics of his age 'let humour evaporate, while they endeavour to preserve decorum' (ch. 1; 9). In this impatience with fine feelings and humourless moralizing, Smollett may have been typical rather than anomalous.

Ramble Fiction and its Readers

Rebarbative as they now seem, *Peregrine Pickle* and *Roderick Random* were in their time surrounded by dozens of brash comic novels very much like them. Every season

---

[7] Tobias Smollett, *The Adventures of Ferdinand Count Fathom* (1753), ed. O. M. Brack Jr, introd. Jerry C. Beasley (Athens, GA: University of Georgia Press, 1988), ch. 53; 259.

throughout the 1750s and 1760s brought ten or twelve new 'lives' and 'histories', each of them using a skeletal plot and a rudimentary central character to unify a string of broad comic incidents. Orphans, sailors, rascally apprentices, waggish students sent down for blasphemy: there were larky adventure novels about all these figures. There were also prize-fighters, fairground orators, dandy apothecaries, and a surprising range of trickster heroines. *Ramble novels*, these texts were often called, after the names of so many central characters and their careless progress through the world. And this term seems preferable to *picaresque*, which was not yet used in this period and too easily connotes the bleak survivalism of Defoe and his European predecessors. Ramble fiction is firmly rooted in the metropolitan culture of its day and altogether lighter in tone.

Among these long-lost novels are some spectacular best-sellers—texts like Edward Kimber's *Life and Adventures of Joe Thompson* (1750), which went through at least six editions before 1800, further reprints in the nineteenth century, and translations into French and German. We now know very little about Kimber (1719–69), but he was a prominent fixture in the mid-century literary world, the author of seven original novels and a translation from Crébillon *fils* (he was also a major contributor to the *London Magazine* and its editor from 1755). Kimber comes eighth on James Raven's hierarchy of top-selling novelists—just behind Richardson and ahead of Sarah Fielding, Lennox, and Goldsmith (1987: 14). Some of the earliest Irish novels are exercises in the ramble genre, most notably William Chaigneau's best-selling *History of Jack Connor* (1752 and four more editions), which soon entered the national folklore. Consider a few other titles from just one decade:

> *The Adventures of Shelim O'Blunder, The Irish Beau* (1751)
> *Adventures of the Revd. Mr. Judas Hawke* (1751)
> *Young Scarron* (1752)
> *The Female Rambler* (1754)
> *The Adventures of Jerry Buck* (1754)
> *The History of Jasper Banks, Commonly Call'd the Handsome Man* (2 vols, 1754)
> *The History of Will Ramble* (2 vols, 1755)
> *The Adventures of Dick Hazard* (1755)
> *Adventures of Jack Smart* (1756)
> *The History of Two Orphans* (4 vols, 1756)
> *The Adventures of a Rake. In the Character of a Public Orator* (2 vols, 1759)
> *The History of Tom Fool* (2 vols, 1760)

And on it went: *The History of James Lovegrove* (2 vols, 1761), *The Amours and Adventures of Charles Careless* (2 vols, 1764), *The Adventures of Jack Wander* (1766), *Adventures of a Kidnapped Orphan* (1767), and many, many more.

Where they are acknowledged at all, such texts are dismissed as *Tom Jones* knock-offs. This description is true up to a point. All go to Fielding for their high-written comic incidents. Kimber's *Joe Thompson* pays tribute by reversing the initial syllables of *Tom Jones*. But to cast them all as imitations is to obscure the variety and innovation of a hugely profitable subgenre. Like other types of fiction, ramble novels attracted talented authors who experimented with different sorts of protagonists and widely different narrative voices. Will Ramble is a fairly mainstream practical joker, skilled from an early age with firecrackers and itching powders. Dick Hazard is one of many ingratiating Irish rascals. *Jack Smart* and *Jerry Buck* are the lives of riotous London bucks (very close to *Peregrine Pickle* and packed with the same vicious torments, *Jerry Buck* went through three editions in 1754 alone). *Young Scarron* is a lively Anglicization of Paul Scarron's *Le Roman comique*, the story of the actor Bob Loveplay and his hapless troupe of strolling players in the north of England. *Tom Fool* is the deliriously silly story of a handsome simpleton by the comic orator George Stevens (running joke: 'You're a fool.' 'Thank you, Sir, I certainly am.'). Shelim O'Blunder is a hapless Irish fortune hunter, far too stupid to do much harm. Judas Hawke, by contrast, is an astonishingly depraved clergyman who reads pornography, prostitutes his wife for a living, and takes particular joy in literally terrifying nice people to death. These last texts might help us make better sense of books like *Ferdinand Count Fathom*, always the most confounding of Smollett's novels.

In narrative structure, the default setting was the picaresque *cum* romance formula of Fielding and Smollett. The same portents are there. Mrs Pickle's frog fricassee finds its analogues in the disgusting cravings of other expectant mothers (vile concoctions from the village alewife, unmentionable bits of pig). There are baffling pre-natal dreams and gatherings of village gossips to interpret them. Heroes are born in boats (like Lazarillo de Tormes) or moving carts (like Ferdinand Count Fathom). There are bungled baptisms and contemporary obstetric accidents of the sort made famous by *Tristram Shandy*. The childhood mischiefs are there, too: little turds on the housekeeper's Bible, wee-wee in the gin bottle, and corns or chilblains to be stood upon. Pickle's treatment of Mr Keypstick is also characteristic. Mr Surly, Dr Birch, Revd Tickletext: almost every text includes some self-righteous pedagogue whose function is to be tormented or inveigled into bed with a whore. And as in *Peregrine Pickle*, the adversarial attitude and the practical jokes continue into adulthood, now alternating with amours and misfortunes (a spell in debtor's prison is one obligatory episode) before the hero settles down with a suitable heiress (Miss Rich, Miss Charlotte Lovely) and her £10,000.

These patterns also lent themselves to comic 'lives' of public figures. A few years after the success of *Joe Thompson*, Kimber rolled out his familiar formula in *The Juvenile Adventures of David Ranger* (1757). *David Ranger* is a heavily fictionalized 'life' of David Garrick, thinly disguised under the name of his most celebrated comic role (Ranger in Hoadly's *Suspicious Husband*, 1747). Kimber's hero bears little resemblance to the historical actor (for extra fun, the book even turns him into an Irishman). What is interesting is how easily readers tolerated this blend of fact and fancy—how little they cared about consistency or formal realism. Little Davy is the child of a mother who behaves like a tragic queen and even scolds her servants in couplets. Almost as soon as he can walk, Davy is performing his exits from every room ('Farewell!') and practising Garrick's well-known death agonies on every carpet. The two long volumes of adventures that follow are entirely invented; only in its final chapter does the novel come closer to a *roman à clef*, with clear allusions to Lord Burlington and Garrick's marriage to Eva Maria Veigel (the 'most enchanting' Miss Tulip). A much brasher example of the same subgenre is Christopher Anstey's *Memoirs of the Noted Buckhorse* (1756), a fanciful 'life' of the prize-fighter John 'Buckhorse' Smith. By 1756, Buckhorse had retired from the ring, but he remained a familiar sight in Covent Garden, working as a pedlar and so fantastically ugly that provincial visitors came to gawk at him. Anstey himself would eventually become famous for his *New Bath Guide* (1766); *Buckhorse* sheds light on his apprentice years and situates ramble fiction alongside the jumble of odes, epistles, dialogues, and periodical essays with which aspiring authors tried to earn their living.

Like *Peregrine Pickle* and *Tom Jones* before them, ramble novels are packed with misogynist caricatures and unpleasant jokes about sexual violence. It is all the more peculiar, therefore, to find a large parallel body of comic novels about women. This general category has attracted greater attention in recent years, with cheerful 'lives' of actresses, pickpockets, female soldiers, and courtesans proving invaluable to feminist criticism. Still, this scholarship does not always convey the levity of so many feminocentric texts. Whore biographies, for example, drift insistently towards the ramble genre. Or consider *The Authentic Memoirs of Nancy Dawson* (*c.*1762), the story of a celebrated London dancer. The fictional Nancy is the daughter of a drunken basket-woman and a shiftless pimp, born in a stable near Clare Market. Her early feats include cursing other children during games ('B[la]st your eyes for a b[itc]h!') and getting wind when the local boys start fooling around with the butcher's daughter—'and when once she catched them in the fact, all came out'.[8] A consistently lively text, *Nancy Dawson* points us towards an unsuspected variety of female protagonists. An immense continuum stretches between criminals like Moll Flanders and the well-known sentimental heroines at an opposite extreme. Somewhere in the middle, one finds clusters of witty and independent women who are nevertheless not sexually compromised (characters such as *Clarissa*'s Anna Howe or the unforgettable Charlotte Grandison, so fond of remarking that her brother 'still kept his Maidenhead').[9] Feminized adaptations of *Tom Jones*—*The History of Charlotte Summers*

---

[8] *Authentic Memoirs of the Celebrated Miss Nancy D*ws*n* (London, [*c.*1762]), 9.
[9] For contemporary commentary on Charlotte Grandison, see Francis Plumer, *A Candid Examination of the History of Sir Charles Grandison*, 3rd edn (London: Dodsley, 1754), 49.

(1750), *Sophia Shakespear* (1753), and others—generate particularly memorable reporters of the social scene. Beset by her sex-crazed mother and a villainous quack named Potion, Sophia Shakespear is a plucky and endearing survivor.

These are all wildly heterogeneous texts—stuffed, like *Peregrine Pickle* and so many other early novels, with digressions and interpolations. There are passages of literary criticism and accounts of London actors. The action suddenly stops for five chapters about Abyssinia or some gloomy reflections on mortality. Didactic claims come and go, as they do in Smollett. But what really sticks in the mind is the raucous and often nasty humour of these books. Long after the volumes have gone back to the stacks, one can still hear the thuds and screeches. Mad bulls on the loose. Terrified old ladies tumbling into privies. Blind men led into walls. Who could forget the fight with a London coachman in *Nancy Dawson* ('one of the whores whipt off his wig, pissed in it, and knocked it in his face' [24])? There is vomit in the stew, vomit out the window onto a noisy ballad singer, vomit at the dinner table when someone convinces the vicar he has eaten a dead dog. Mortal terror is always hilarious: convincing someone that the ship was sinking or they had eaten something poisonous were prime jokes (and the second one would show up in *Humphry Clinker*). It is hard now to imagine getting someone arrested for a lark, yet this, too, was a mainstream practical joke. Pages and pages are devoted to elaborate acts of vengeance. Jerry Buck's revenge on his Oxford tutor involves hiring a prostitute to seduce and infect the man with a good clap. Nauseating as it is, this joke might just tell us something about eighteenth-century student wit.

Much of this comic filler was entirely standardized and repeated from one text to another: ramble fiction catered to a significant demand for more of the same. Nocturnal commotion at a coaching inn. Ferocious kitchen brawls—all curses, spitting, and volleys of half-picked pork bones. 'A Ludicrous Circumstance of Distress', 'Mischievous Contrivances', 'High Words Between the Ladies', 'An Alarm on the Road': such chapter titles promised readers specific and familiar forms of amusement, most of it entirely irrelevant to plot. Authors plagiarized without shame (*Jack Smart*, sniffed the *Critical Review*, simply lifted everything from a comic miscellany called *Laugh and Be Fat*). The most self-conscious novelists even apologize for having to repeat so many tired old conventions. 'We are obliged to introduce a Night Scene, for which we must beg the Reader's Pardon', begins Christopher Anstey's example of that set piece. If he left it out, no one would believe him.[10] But originality, a principle that looms so large in literary history and to which the imaginative force of early realist fictions is often ascribed, is manifestly less important than entertainment. Ramble novels therefore confound normative

---

[10] Christopher Anstey, *Memoirs of the Noted Buckhorse*, 2 vols (London: S. Crowder and H. Woodgate, 1756), 1.159.

expectations not just about the nature and functions of the early novel, but about reading and narrative in general. Plot is so rudimentary and characterization so shallow, that the usual motors of narrative are just not there. Ramble novels are almost without desire, as a narratologist might say. There is no hermeneutic plot, no great mysteries to be resolved. But the predictable comic episodes were evidently satisfying to the readers who bought them in such quantities.

Ramble novels were in no way distinguished—neither by the book trade nor by reviewers or readers—from texts now accepted as literary novels. *Joe Thompson* and *Sophia Shakespear* were published in the same duodecimo format, and sold for the same price of 3*s.* per volume, as the canonical fiction of the age. At 12*s.* for four volumes, the longer ramble novels cost as much as *Amelia* or Frances Brooke's *Emily Montague* (1769). At 6*s.* for two duodecimo volumes, *Will Ramble* and *Jack Smart* cost the same as *Pamela* or Sarah Fielding's *The Countess of Dellwyn* (1759). Who was reading these books and paying so much for them? One easily imagines a readership of idle young men— boozy templars like the young James Boswell, who kept himself 'well supplied' with novels throughout his first stay in London (1762–3).[11] It comes as no surprise to find that Laurence Sterne owned *The Adventures of a Valet* (1752), *David Ranger*, and John Cleland's *Memoirs of a Coxcomb* (1751), or that he read William Toldervy's unendurable *History of Two Orphans* (4 vols, 1756), which turns out to have demonstrable influences on *Tristram Shandy* (Keymer 2002: 30).

Much more unexpected is the evidence that these novels were read as much by women as by men. Increasingly empirical work on book-trade data is showing us just how wrong we were to infer male or female readers from a book's content. We now know that eighteenth-century men read romances, domestic fiction, and sentimental lyrics, just as eighteenth-century women read bawdy farces, low comic periodicals, and all the coars- est comic fiction (Fergus 2006). Most of the early ramble novels are there on the list of 200 books that George Colman attaches to his preface to *Polly Honeycombe* (1760)—the 'greasy' and 'much thumbed' 'Catalogue of the Circulating Library'.[12] Young ladies ran away with rascals because they were charmed by bluff male heroes like Dick Hazard and Jerry Buck, Colman suggests, not just because of all the foolish romances. Ramble fiction also looms large in surviving records of Lady Mary Wortley Montagu's reading. During her Italian years (1746–61), Lady Mary scoured the English newspapers for recent titles, which would then be shipped out by her dutiful daughter. She loved Smollett and Fielding, but she also ordered a striking proportion of the ephemeral fiction that appeared each year. *Joe Thompson, Dick Hazard, Jack Smart, Jasper Banks, Charlotte Summers, Sophia Shakespear,*

---

[11] *Boswell's London Journal, 1762–63*, ed. Frederick A. Pottle (New Haven: Yale University Press, 1991), 272–3 (4 June 1763).

[12] *Polly Honeycombe: A Dramatick Novel of One Act* (London: T. Becket and T. Davies, 1760), [v]–xiii.

Young Scarron: Lady Mary read all these books. 'Wiser people may think it trifling', she concedes to one of her daughter's routine objections, 'but it serves to sweeten Life to me'.[13]

This diverting, recreational consumption is only slowly gaining its rightful place in the history of reading. Probably it should always have been obvious that eighteenth-century people read rather like we do: intermittently and in bits and pieces, at the interstices of busy lives. Even so, the incongruities take some getting used to: *Jerry Buck* and *Will Ramble* were read alongside sermons, sentimental fiction, travel narratives, and London newspapers. One first-person record of these practices must stand for many. In March 1748, *Roderick Random* and *Clarissa* had just appeared within a few weeks of each other. In Caledon, Co. Tyrone, the Earl of Orrery and his family were reading them on alternate nights. '*Clarissa* kept us up till two in the morning', wrote the Earl to his friend Thomas Carew. '*Rhoderic* will keep us up all night, and he, I am told, is to be succeeded again by *Clarissa*, whom I left, adorable girl, at St Albans.'[14] Every bit as nasty as *Peregrine Pickle*—stuffed with all the standard burns, flesh-wounds, and rape jokes—*Random* was read alongside Richardson's feminocentric masterpiece, and in explicitly higher doses.

＊ ＊ ＊ ＊ ＊

Why read these texts now? Beyond their obvious interest as historical documents, ramble novels may also have much to tell us about the canonical fiction of their age, the texts that they both imitated and influenced. In a strict sense, as Pierre Bourdieu points out in his fascinating analysis of minor novelists around Flaubert, any critic who fails to explore the lesser publications around a major literary text is doomed to an 'unknowing poetics'— destined to take up the book with modern expectations rather than the norms of its own time (1993: 202). This is not to say that a fully 'knowing' poetics could ever be possible, or that anyone could read every minor novel around the accepted literary ones. Yet once approached from the comic archive, the odder moments of many canonical novels start to make sense. One sees, for example, how Fielding refined his comic raw material while his contemporaries retained or elaborated it. The baby Tom shows up in Allworthy's bed. His proleptic act is not an impish cackle, but a gentle squeeze of the old man's finger. Prosody and Tickletext have their equivalents in Thwackum and Square, but there is no puke, no soiled breeches, and Square makes his own way to Molly's garret. Here and everywhere else, Tom is the witness of comic humiliations rather than their agent. At the same time, after working through so many ramble novels, one begins to notice other less differentiated details—as in the heavy-handed vulgarity of the Seagrim family; or the stupefying gay-bashing episode in *Amelia* (which takes its place beside similar episodes in *Peregrine Pickle* and other texts).

---

[13] Lady Mary Wortley Montagu, *Complete Letters*, ed. Robert Halsband, 3 vols (Oxford: Clarendon Press, 1965–7), 2.473 (24 December 1750).

[14] *The Orrery Papers*, ed. Emily Charlotte Boyle, Countess of Cork and Orrery, 2 vols (London: Duckworth, 1903), 2.23.

Frances Burney, too, starts to look rather different. Captain Mirvan, the boorish practical joker in *Evelina* (1778), is openly indebted to the nautical characters in *Peregrine Pickle*. The taunting of Mme Duval, the old women's footrace, and the humiliation of Mr Lovel are all very close to ramble fiction. Other incidents easily come to mind. The hysterical Mrs Delvile bursting a blood vessel in *Cecilia* (1782). All those frenetic scenes in *Camilla* (1796)—the dogfight, the orchestra of tamed monkeys at Northwick Fair, the disastrous provincial *Othello* (straight out of *Young Scarron* and *Le Roman comique* before it). One easily thinks of other episodes in Lennox, Edgeworth, and, by way of the Juvenilia, in Jane Austen. And then one begins to notice odd comic traces in more overtly didactic or sentimental novels. Yorick's encounter with the dwarf in Sterne's *A Sentimental Journey* (1768). The enclosure of rescued freaks in Sarah Scott's *Millenium Hall* (1762). And what to make of the farcical rape accusation in Sarah Fielding's *The History of Ophelia* (1760)? This dire piece of comic business is a way of humiliating the nasty Mrs Herner, first when the alleged rapist insists that the lady had actually got into bed with him, and then when a candle comes in and the man announces that Mrs Herner was too ugly to rape anyway. Read alongside the forgotten comic fiction of the age, such scenes start to make an appalling kind of sense.

6

The Novelty of Laurence Sterne

JAMES CHANDLER

L
AURENCE Sterne was born in Ireland in 1713 to an English military family.[1] Almost immediately, the family moved to Yorkshire, where Sterne would spend most of the rest of his life. At twenty, he enrolled at Jesus College, Cambridge, where he was trained in Latitudinarian theology. He was ordained an Anglican priest in 1737—rather improbably, given his developing habits of licentiousness—and he then laboured in the relative obscurity of various English vicarages for more than two decades. His early writings consisted mainly of sermons. He won both immediate celebrity and lasting literary fame, however, with two works that he produced in the final decade of a life cut short by consumption: *Tristram Shandy*, serialized in nine volumes from 1759 to 1767, and the unfinished sequel, *A Sentimental Journey*, published just three weeks before his death, at the age of 54, in 1768. Though it rests on just these two late works, his claim to a place of real prominence in the history of the novel is nonetheless compelling.

Tristram Shandy dramatizes the hilarious efforts of the title character to tell the story of his life when he can scarcely get beyond an account of his birth. It introduces the memorably idiosyncratic duo of Walter Shandy, the narrator's obsessively pedantic father whose perfectionist hopes for his son are systematically defeated by circumstance, and his brother, Uncle Toby, the gentle military veteran whose 'amours' with the Widow Wadman are plagued by his compulsion to revisit the scene of a battle wound. The publication of volumes 1 and 2 of *Tristram Shandy* in December 1759 turned the obscure country parson into an international celebrity almost overnight. The successive appearance of later volumes in the 1760s fuelled the craze. 'Sterne's Popularity at one time arose to that pitch', wrote John Croft, a contemporary, that 'a Wager [was] laid in London that a Letter addressed to Tristram Shandy in Europe' would reach his hands safely. In the event, Croft goes on, 'the Letter came down into Yorkshire and the Post Boy meeting Sterne on the road to Sutton pulled off his hatt and gave it him' (see Ross 2001: 7).

---

[1] A version of this chapter has appeared in James Chandler's *An Archaeology of Sympathy: The Sentimental Mode in Literature and Cinema* (Chicago: University of Chicago Press, 2013).

A Sentimental Journey was written after most of the volumes of *Tristram Shandy* had appeared. Building on the popularity of its predecessor, Sterne set an example much emulated in popular culture ever since with the genre of the 'spin-off'. He took from *Tristram Shandy* a minor character, Parson Yorick, and made him the central character (and narrator) of a new work, an account of a journey to the Continent that is undertaken in order to prove a point about table manners. There are parallels with *Tristram Shandy*. For example, where Tristram has a difficult time getting beyond the circumstances of his birth, Yorick's tale is long detained in a carriage yard in Calais, where he is at pains to find a proper means of conveyance. Though *A Sentimental Journey* was thus something of a sequel to *Tristram Shandy*, Sterne didn't wish simply to repeat an earlier formula, his own or anyone else's. Just before embarking on this, his final novel, he promised his daughter in early 1767 that it would be 'something new, quite out of the beaten track'.[2] It was. And like many such innovative works, it immediately attracted a host of imitators. It was imitated in the way it structured its narrative not in numbered chapters but in a series of titled vignettes. It was imitated in its tone, in its humour, in its vocabulary, in its forms of characterization, even in its very characters: 'Yoricks' began popping up everywhere. Sterne's own text was repeatedly reprinted in English and translated into several languages. Even an unauthorized sequel by Sterne's friend John Hall Stevenson, *Yorick's Sentimental Journey Continued* (1769), went through multiple editions over the two decades after Sterne's death.

These two books earned Sterne high praise even from tough critics. Thomas Jefferson, who carried a copy of *A Sentimental Journey* with him on his own travels, claimed that Sterne's writings made up 'the best course of morality that ever was written'.[3] Though David Hume had reservations, he still regarded *Tristram Shandy* as the 'best Book, that has been writ by any Englishman these thirty Years'.[4] Edmund Burke, reviewing the book for the *Annual Register* in 1760, thought its originality more than redemptive of any blemishes: 'The faults of an original work are always pardoned; and it is not surprizing, that at a time, when a tame imitation makes almost the whole merit of so many books, so happy an attempt at novelty should have been so well received.'[5] Another admirer, Ugo Foscolo, the great Italian Romantic, covered much of the same ground as a soldier that Yorick did as a tourist, and eventually moved to England, where he embarked on a full translation of *A Sentimental Journey* (Vincent 1953: 9). Goethe, on rereading Sterne late in his life, found that his admiration 'has increased and is still increasing': 'I still have not met his equal in the broad field of literature' (Howes 1974: 435).

---

[2] Laurence Sterne to Lydia Sterne, 23 February 1767, Melvin New and Peter de Voogd (eds), *The Letters, Part 2: 1765–1768, The Florida Edition of the Works of Laurence Sterne*, vol. 8 (Gainesville: University Press of Florida, 2009), 536.

[3] Thomas Jefferson to Peter Carr, 10 August 1787, *The Writings of Thomas Jefferson*, vol. 6, ed. Andrew A. Lipscomb and Albert Ellery Bergh (Washington, DC: The Thomas Jefferson Memorial Association, 1905), 258.

[4] David Hume to William Strahan, 30 January 1773, *The Letters of David Hume*, ed. J. Y. T. Greig, 2 vols (Oxford: Clarendon Press, 1932), 2.269.

[5] Edmund Burke, review of *Tristram Shandy*, *Annual Register, or a View of the History, Politicks, and Literature, of the Year 1760* (London: R. and J. Dodsley, 1761), 247.

The novelty and originality of Sterne's work was widely acknowledged in an age caught up in praise for the novel and original. *Tristram Shandy*'s style, mode, characters, and trope became regular features of the literary landscape in Britain, Ireland, America, and even the Continent. 'Shandyism' was a term coined to capture the brave new world that had such beings as Uncle Toby, Walter Shandy, and the Widow Wadman in it. The unfinished sequel, *A Sentimental Journey*, effectively created a new subgenre in fiction. Its title formula was so new that the Germans had trouble translating it, but its transformation of the travel narrative would be widely emulated at home and abroad in myriad ways: faux sequels, for example, and imitations echoing Sterne's innovative title. Jean-Claude Gorjy's Sternean effort, *Le Nouveau voyage sentimental* (1784), was just one of many books so titled in France. In the transatlantic context, Sterne's fiction is an explicit subject of debate in one of the earliest American novels, William Hill Brown's *The Power of Sympathy*, 1789 (see Chandler 2008). The influence of Sternean sentimentalism reaches into the Victorian period, in spite of some worries about Sterne's moral character. Thackeray was outraged: 'There is not a page of Sterne's writing but has something that were better away, a latent corruption— a hint, as of an impure presence' (1853: 291). Yet Dickens's sentimental tour de force, *The Old Curiosity Shop* (1841), begins with an early approving reference to *A Sentimental Journey*, and Dickens unquestionably learned much from Sterne's idiosyncratic craft.

Through the Modernist period, indeed, Sterne's work was recognized as a literary-historical touchstone and a provocation to innovate. In Sterne's work, wrote Virginia Woolf in *The Common Reader*, '[we] are as close to life as we can be' (1932: 79). James Joyce paid Sterne his own distinct form of homage in the chapter of *Ulysses* (1922) that has come to be known as 'Oxen of the Sun'. In one of the longest and most virtuosic chapters of his long and virtuosic book, Joyce narrates an allegorical episode in a Dublin maternity hospital by re-enacting a nine-stage evolution of English prose from the medieval period to the moment of *Ulysses* itself. This evolution includes a three-page passage in imitation of Sterne's *Sentimental Journey*, unmistakably so:

> A sigh of affection gave eloquence to these words and, having replaced the locket in his bosom, he wiped his eye and sighed again. Beneficent Disseminator of blessings to all Thy creatures, how great and universal must be that sweetest of Thy tyrannies which can hold in thrall the free and the bond, the simple swain and the polished coxcomb, the lover in the heyday of reckless passion and the husband of maturer years. But indeed, sir, I wander from the point. How mingled and imperfect are our sublunary joys![6]

Joyce's dilation of the moment of giving birth at such enormous length might itself be said to reproduce the protracted account of his own birth by the title character in *Tristram Shandy*. Later, describing his first efforts with the book that became *Finnegans Wake*, Joyce

---

[6] James Joyce, *Ulysses* (New York: Penguin, 2000), 529.

wrote: 'I am trying to build many planes of narrative within a single aesthetic purpose. Did you ever read Laurence Sterne?' (see Ross 2001: 430). And beyond Joyce, beyond Woolf, Sterne's experimental impulses might be understood to inform later twentieth-century novelists as diverse as the John Barth of *Giles Goat-Boy*, the David Foster Wallace of *Infinite Jest*, and the J. M. Coetzee of *Diary of a Bad Year*.

How, then, do we begin to explain the reorientation achieved in Sterne's fiction? One starting point would be his own representations of his novelty. In Yorick's preface to his journey, the question of novelty is raised but only in the most enigmatic terms possible. This is perhaps no more than we should expect since, in good Shandean fashion, this preface appears not at the beginning of the book but as the seventh of the book's several dozen vignettes. It follows vignettes that tell of his reason for travelling and his arrival in Calais, and also those that deal with his disconcerting encounter with a Franciscan mendicant to whom he refuses alms almost as soon as he gets there. In the preface, waxing philosophical, Yorick stands back to produce for us a taxonomy of travellers, which includes Inquisitive Travellers, Vain Travellers, and Simple Travellers, and which eventually arrives at the category of 'Sentimental Traveller'. Apropos of this last category, the Sentimental Traveller, Yorick begins to boast that, since both his 'travels and [his] observations will be altogether of a different cast from any of [his] fore-runners', he 'might have insisted upon a whole nitch entirely to [himself]'. But then Yorick quickly renounces an exclusive claim to the category of 'sentimental traveller', for fear that he 'should break in upon the confines of the *Vain* Traveller, in wishing to draw attention towards me, till I have some better grounds for it, than the mere *Novelty of my Vehicle*'.[7] 'Vehicle' will prove to be a term of art central to the Latitudinarianism in which Sterne was trained at Cambridge, part of a semi-occult discourse on the immateriality of the soul. Even without knowing the history of this technical concept, however, it is clear that part of Sterne's fun in this formulation, and indeed in his play with vehicles and vehicularity everywhere, has to do with his chiastic joke about the relation between the novelty of his vehicle and the vehicle of the novel. Enfolded in this joke is the story that I seek to tell here.

Learning, Wit, and the Satirical Vein

It must be conceded at the outset that Sterne's claim to a place of innovative prominence in the history of the novel has had its challengers over the years, not only on moral grounds (long before Thackeray, Samuel Richardson thought Sterne's work 'execrable'[8]), or on

---

[7] Laurence Sterne, *A Sentimental Journey through France and Italy*, ed. Melvyn New and W. G. Day, *The Florida Edition of the Works of Laurence Sterne*, vol. 6 (Gainesville: University Press of Florida, 2002), 15.

[8] Samuel Richardson to Bishop Hildesley, January–February 1761, *Selected Letters of Samuel Richardson*, ed. John Carroll (Oxford: Clarendon Press, 1964), 341.

the grounds of narrative incoherence, but also on the grounds that his writings should not properly be understood as novels in the first place. There are many who would say that his relation to the novel is adventitious and that his two celebrated late works belong more properly to other traditions and species of prose writing. One might well make a similar claim about *Ulysses* itself: major innovations in fiction often raise the question of whether they are themselves novels. Joyce's own most pointed evocation of Sterne in *Ulysses*, the pastiche of *Sentimental Journey* in 'Oxen of the Sun', seems indirectly to raise such a question, for Joyce locates this passage in a sequence that includes imitations of Bunyan, Defoe, Sterne, Goldsmith, Sheridan, and Burke. Of these writers, only Defoe was primarily a novelist and, even so, his four celebrated works of fiction share space in his oeuvre with a large body of non-fictional prose. Joyce thus seems to leave the question of Sterne's genre identification as open as he leaves that of his own in this very book.

In recent scholarship, the debate about Sterne and his relation to the novel form has been fuelled by scholarly source hunting, perhaps because a writer with Sterne's pretensions to originality invites heightened attention to precedents and models (the great analyst of rhetoric in fiction, Wayne Booth, actually wrote his dissertation at the University of Chicago on the precedents for Sterne's fictional inventions (1950)). Those commentators on Sterne who would sooner place his work in the history of prose than in the history of the novel have found support for their views in the exhaustive reference-tracking research on display in the Florida edition of Sterne's works.[9] For what the ample glosses in this edition show is an enormous number of references to prose works in the tradition of satire and 'learned wit', reaching back to the Renaissance and beyond. This body of evidence seems to corroborate the view of D. W. Jefferson, who argued years ago that the primary frame of reference in which Sterne is to be read is that of Renaissance learned wit, and not that of the eighteenth-century novel (1951). In comparison with the many Renaissance references noted in the Florida edition, there are very few references to the fiction of Sterne's contemporaries. For example, the two giants of the novel in Sterne's mature lifetime, Richardson and Fielding, do not appear anywhere in these notes. It has thus even been suggested that Sterne's relation to the mid-eighteenth-century novel is an artifice of twentieth-century curricular choices on the part of English departments: Sterne tends to be taught, willy-nilly, in courses on the eighteenth-century novel, so the argument goes, and this creates, after the fact, a sense of his relationship to its history.

Some considerations recently laid out by Thomas Keymer in a lucid and compelling account of this controversy argue against those who would refuse to see Sterne's narratives as novels or even novel-oriented (2002: 15–36). One consideration advanced by Keymer is that Sterne's relation to the novel—what Fielding called 'the new species of

---

[9] Melvin New et al., *The Florida Edition of the Works of Laurence Sterne* (Gainesville: University Press of Florida, 1978–2009).

writing' in the mid-eighteenth century—would be less *marked* than his relation to the more distinct tradition of learned wit. That is, the conventions of the contemporary novel would probably have been part of the woodwork for Sterne and his readers in a way that learned Renaissance references would not have been. Sterne's 'intertextuality' with contemporary fiction may have been fuzzier, less explicit, but it can nonetheless be discerned in a careful look at, for example, his handling of characters. The celebrated introduction of Dr Slop the midwife in *Tristram Shandy* is for Keymer a case in point for establishing Sterne's reliance on, and refashioning of, eighteenth-century narrative conventions. A second consideration has to do with the key role of Cervantes, to whose *Don Quixote* there are many telling references in both of Sterne's late narrative works. Keymer rightly points out that references to the Renaissance learned wit of Cervantes do not so much distance Sterne from the mid-eighteenth-century novel as link him to it. From Fielding to Eliza Haywood to Tobias Smollett, the novel of that moment is frequently characterized by a marked engagement across a range of reactions to Cervantes' legacy and example.

In view of Keymer's arguments, it is fitting that Sterne's place in this *Oxford History of the Novel* falls near the beginning of the second volume. By 1750, certainly, a new species of prose writing had clearly achieved recognition under the name of the novel. We find ample evidence of this development in the various critical essays of that moment, not least Dr Johnson's important *Rambler* essay on the novel, which addresses the 'works of fiction, with which the present generation seems more particularly delighted'.[10] And when, for example, Horace Walpole commented unfavourably on *Tristram Shandy* in 1760, he had little trouble in labelling it. 'At present', he wrote, 'nothing is talked of, nothing admired, but what I cannot help calling a very insipid and tedious performance: it is a kind of novel.'[11] But accepting that Sterne's fiction was recognizable as a kind of novel, and that 'novel' was a term of recent origin, we still have to face the question of what kind of 'reorientation' he achieved in the young and still varied form, and of how other kinds of writing may have figured in Sterne's achievements.

One sort of writing that certainly matters to Sterne is the Scriblerian tradition of satire, especially in connection with the first several books of *Tristram Shandy*, where Sterne's investment in the novel form is less evident. Sterne's satirical gestures in the early volumes may well be understood as following the general formula for satire proposed in Alexander Pope's *Essay on Man* (1733–4): 'shoot Folly as it flies, | And catch the Manners living as they rise' (Epistle 1, ll. 13–14). Beyond this more general connection, one can note Sterne's specific efforts to send up philosophical pretence and academic pomposity,

---

[10] Samuel Johnson, *The Rambler*, no. 4, in *The Yale Edition of the Works of Samuel Johnson*, vol. 3, ed. W. J. Bate and Albrecht B. Strauss (New Haven: Yale University Press, 1969), 19.

[11] Horace Walpole to Sir David Dalrymple, 4 April 1760, *Horace Walpole's Correspondence with Sir David Dalrymple*, ed. W. S. Lewis, Charles H. Bennett, and Andrew G. Hoover (New Haven: Yale University Press, 1951), 66.

a key element in the major writings of the Scriblerians. In *Gulliver's Travels* (1726), Jonathan Swift satirizes the scientists and scholars who hold forth on the floating Island of Laputa, as men who lose sight of the world (and their wives) as they elaborate more and more recondite theoretical positions. It is not difficult to see Sterne's characterization of that modern man of system, the anxiously philosophical Walter Shandy, as a literary heir to Swift's academicians. This is a clear connection to Scriblerian satire.

More specifically still, one might point out that the instalment publishing format of *Tristram Shandy* made it possible for Sterne to emulate one of the most strikingly modern practices satirically mobilized in two of the greatest Scriblerian texts: Pope's *Dunciad* (1728) and Swift's *Tale of a Tub* (1704). This is the practice of incorporating into a work's ongoing publishing process the response of readers—public and private alike—to the work's earlier publication moments. Where Swift and Pope incorporated into scholarly footnotes and a variorum apparatus various responses to their own work, Sterne managed to include a similar range of responses (real or imagined) in the free-flow and highly reflexive gestures of Tristram's attempt to tell the story of his life. All three texts self-consciously exploit the expanded capacities of eighteenth-century book production, its readership, and its market to produce a text at once reflexive and proleptic.

The satirical vein of writing is thus important to Sterne, and likewise, the exercise of wit, closely associated with that mode. Yet Sterne's reorientation of the novel is ultimately better explained by way of the discourse of the sentimental than by the traditions of wit and satire. Indeed, wit itself is transformed in his adaptation of sentimental discourse. This discourse also provides the context in which Sterne's contemporaries and literary heirs understood his contributions. I focus here on two distinct lines in the sentimental that Sterne helped to bring together. The former line is one I trace back to the Earl of Shaftesbury's notions of reflexivity and early eighteenth-century ways of understanding the subject as spectator to himself and others. The latter line is one I trace back to Henry More's early Latitudinarian response to seventeenth-century debates about mechanism and materialism. It is in the bringing together of these two lines of discourse—roughly, sentiment and sensibility—that Sterne's reorientation of the novel is finally best understood.

The Impurity of Sentiment

As noted earlier, Sterne's use of the term 'sentimental' in *A Sentimental Journey* was so new in 1768 that the Germans had difficulty finding a translation for it. Traditional philological work on the emergence of the term *sentimental* traces it to the late 1740s. Phrases such as 'sentimental novel' or 'sentimental history' do not start to appear in English book titles until the mid-1750s, when the term enters a rapid phase of development. In the British Library, the first book to bear a title containing the word 'sentimental', *Reflections on Sentimental Differences in Points of Faith* (1752), is an exercise in religious syncretism aimed at bringing persons of learning and reason closer in respect to their religious sentiments. The adjective form here, in other words, pertains to the older sense of 'sentiment', whose genealogy has been traced, for example, by Isabel Rivers (2000). Yet already by 1754, in *The Friends: A Sentimental History*, the adjective form is being used in a new sense that pertains to a mode of writing and feeling ('a higher Finishing of Language, and more Delicacy of Sentiment').[12] It is possible that the appearance of sentiments culled from Richardson's *Clarissa* as an addition for the popular third edition of the novel in 1751 helped to shift the discourse, as had Richardson's massive cultural intervention in this novel's predecessor, *Pamela*. But there is no doubt that, starting in the 1750s, the word 'sentimental' was routinely associated with a new way of producing narrative, and by 1768, when Sterne coined a new phrase for *A Sentimental Journey through France and Italy*, that massively influential work, together with the book to which it was a sequel, established the term and the mode on a lasting footing (on the Sterne craze, see Erämetsä 1951: 18–63; extended in Banfield 2007).

Sterne's title was in play for him at least by early 1767, when, still hard at work on the later volumes of *Tristram Shandy*, he announced to a friend that he was 'going to publish a *Sentimental Journey* through *France & Italy*'. How would Sterne himself have understood the term? A few months later, he writes that the new book is 'fabricating at a great rate'. This book, he promises, 'shall make you cry as much as ever it made me laugh—or I'll give up the Business of sentimental writing—and write to the Body'.[13] In what sense, we must ask, is 'sentimental writing' opposed here to writing to the body? And what does this distinction have to do with Sterne's promise that the book will be as much involved in tears as in laughter?

Nearly thirty years after Sterne died, Goethe and Schiller had an exchange in letters of their own about the meaning of the sentimental, with Sterne's *Sentimental Journey* obviously very much on their minds.[14] Goethe did not agree with Schiller about much in these days, but he did nod to Schiller's recent work on the subject in the essay *On Naive and Sentimental Poetry* (1795). There, with powerful insight, Schiller had argued that while the naive poet might produce 'varied impressions', they nonetheless depend 'solely upon the various degrees of one and the same mode of feeling'. Not so with the sentimental poet, however, who inspires 'mixed feelings', and who is always involved with 'two conflicting representations and perceptions'.[15]

---

[12] William Guthrie, *The Friends: A Sentimental History*, 2 vols (London: T. Waller, 1754), 1.iii–iv.

[13] Laurence Sterne to Isaac Panchaud, 20 February 1767; to Hannah [no last name given], 15 November 1767: *The Letters, Part 2: 1765–1768*, ed. New and de Voogd, 8.533, 631.

[14] See, among others, Goethe to Schiller, 16 August 1797, in *Correspondence between Goethe and Schiller, 1794–1805*, trans. Liselotte Dieckmann, Studies in Modern German Literature, vol. 60 (New York: P. Lang, 1994).

[15] Friedrich Schiller, 'On Naive and Sentimental Poetry', in *Essays*, ed. Walter Hinderer and Daniel O. Dahlstrom, The German Library, vol. 17 (New York: Continuum, 1993), 204.

There is more to Schiller's definition, and I will return to it below, but this connection of the sentimental with the issue of 'mixed feelings' helpfully avoids the common but mistaken association of the sentimental with simplicity or sincerity. Certainly as Sterne elaborated it, the sentimental is, precisely, a complex and impure mode. This point can be illustrated throughout Sterne's work but perhaps nowhere more patently than in the most famous of all episodes in Sterne, indeed one of the most celebrated episodes in eighteenth-century sentimental culture: the fictional encounter with Maria of Moulines in the Normandy countryside as narrated in the ninth and last volume of *Tristram Shandy*, during the final leg of Tristram's tour of France. This tour clearly gave Sterne the idea for *A Sentimental Journey*, and the Maria episode is reprised there when Parson Yorick, a central character in *Tristram Shandy* and the narrator of *A Sentimental Journey*, recalls the episode in *Tristram Shandy* in order to explain why he seeks his own encounter with Maria. Taken together, these passages were among the most frequently anthologized of Sterne's vignettes. They appeared in many volumes promising a digest of 'The Beauties of Sterne', and provoked many illustrations over the coming decades, including two remarkable paintings executed by Joseph Wright of Derby.

Maria of Moulines is a shepherdess who has half-lost her senses on account of a wedding that never took place, having been blocked by a vindictive curate. She now sits by the roadside, in a somewhat dishevelled state, playing the same melody over and again on her wooden flute. The episode unfolds in stages, and its denouement comes with the only words that are spoken between Tristram and Maria during their brief face-to-face encounter. The visual description of Maria is quite straightforward:

> We had got up by this time almost to the bank where Maria was sitting: she was in a thin white jacket with her hair, all but two tresses, drawn up into a silk net, with a few olive leaves twisted a little fantastically on one side—she was beautiful; and if ever I felt the full force of an honest heart-ache, it was the moment I saw her—
>
> —God help her! poor damsel! above a hundred masses, said the postillion, have been said in the several parish churches and convents around, for her,—but without effect; we have still hopes, as she is sensible for short intervals, that the Virgin at last will restore her to herself; but her parents, who know her best, are hopeless upon that score, and think her senses are lost for ever.
>
> As the postillion spoke this, Maria made a cadence so melancholy, so tender and querulous, that I sprung out of the chaise to help her, and found myself sitting betwixt her and her goat before I relapsed from my enthusiasm.
>
> Maria look'd wistfully for some time at me, and then at her goat—and then at me—and then at her goat again, and so on, alternately—
>
> —Well, *Maria*, said I softly—What resemblance do you find?[16]

---

[16] Laurence Sterne, *The Life and Opinions of Tristram Shandy, Gentleman*, ed. Melvyn New and Joan New, *The Florida Edition of the Works of Laurence Sterne*, vols 1–2 (Gainesville: University Presses of Florida, 1978), 2.783.

One contemporary reviewer suggested that Sterne's 'excellence lay in the PATHETIC',[17] yet I want to insist that, here and elsewhere, his narrative turns on a kind of witticism. It is a wit in the technical sense developed by studies of rhetoric popular in his own moment: it involves the yoking of two disparate images.

Such forms of wit are Sterne's stock-in-trade, and he likes nothing better than to launch a chapter, such as the one about the Widow Wadman's seductive gaze toward Uncle Toby, with a digression that assumes the following form:

> An eye is for all the world exactly like a cannon, in this respect; That it is not so much the eye or the cannon, in themselves, as it is the carriage of the eye—and the carriage of the cannon, by which both the one and the other are enabled to do so much execution. (2.707)

The issue of visual resemblance posed in Tristram's remark to Maria is part and parcel of his reassuring invocation of the tradition of wit. It involves the linking of two conflicting representations or perceptions—in this case the juxtaposition of Tristram and the goat. Coming in a moment of tender pathos, the remark ('what resemblance do you find?') suggests that wit and the sentimental might be interlocking rather than antithetical modes.

It is because of the persistence of wit in this episode—the mixture of representations— that the remark carries a sense of ambivalence. Though it is softly spoken, it nonetheless strikes an odd tone. Sterne does not leave it to us to judge of the tone for ourselves. For Tristram immediately registers his consciousness of its oddity, and of the sense of ambivalence that seems to accompany it:

> I do intreat the candid reader to believe me, that it was from the humblest conviction of what a *Beast* man is,—that I ask'd the question; and that I would not have let fallen an unseasonable pleasantry in the venerable presence of Misery, to be entitled to all the wit that ever *Rabelais* scatter'd—and yet I own my heart smote me, and that I so smarted at the very idea of it, that I swore I would set up for Wisdom and utter grave sentences the rest of my days—and never—never attempt again to commit mirth with man, woman, or child, the longest day I had to live.
>
> As for writing nonsense to them—I believe, there was a reserve—but that I leave to the world. (2.784)

Tristram seeks to defend himself against the charge that his remark owes something to wit and yet he also seems to acknowledge that his very impulse of self-defence implies a certain sense of culpability about his having lapsed into pleasantry with a person so miserably circumstanced. His defence is that he meant only that man is a beast, but he seems to acknowledge that he has himself committed what the French postillion might have called a *bêtise*.

This seems to be the sort of moment in Sterne that Thomas Jefferson singled out when he praised Sterne as a moralist. On the one hand, Sterne's spontaneity and candour involve

---

[17] Ralph Griffiths, *Monthly Review*, 32 (February 1765), 138.

him in situations of embarrassment and worse. But what we might now call his emotional honesty enables him to acknowledge his errors and correct them. Looked at too quickly, one might imagine that this is all there is to it. But what is unmistakably peculiar about this acknowledgement of the *bêtise*, and of the mixed feelings that seem to have produced it, is that it reproduces pleasantry in the act of repentance for it. Tristram's account of his reaction to his sense of remorse is hyperbolic. He swears to 'never attempt again to commit mirth with man, woman, or child', but the oath itself seems, in its overstatement, to be something of a pleasantry. For evidence that it is, or that it proves to be, a pleasantry we need search no farther than the next sentence, in which the oath proves to have a reserve clause that permits nonsense. The idea that a solemn oath, taken in a moment of remorse, might have a reserve clause such as one might find in an ordinary commercial contract is, clearly, a witticism.

To leave the centrality of ambivalence to the episode beyond doubt, Sterne closes the chapter with a final repetition of the pattern:

> Adieu, Maria!—adieu, poor hapless damsel!—some time, but not *now*, I may hear thy sorrows from thy own lips—but I was deceived; for that moment she took her pipe and told me such a tale of woe with it, that I rose up, and with broken and irregular steps walk'd softly to my chaise.—What an excellent inn at Moulins! (2.784)

The shift from Tristram's sadness about Maria to his relief about the Inn is so abrupt that Sterne seems to be driving home a point about 'mixed feelings', about the complex structure of pathos in his narrative ethics.

If we return to Schiller we find remarks that are quite helpful in thinking through the problems raised in this exemplary sentimental episode. The explanation, according to Schiller, for the distinctive sense of 'mixed feelings' in sentimental writing (by contrast with the naive poetry) has to do with the defining practice of the sentimental poet. Such a poet, he writes, '*reflects* [Schiller's emphasis] upon the impression that objects make upon him, and only in that reflection is the emotion grounded which he himself experiences and which he excites in us'. The mixture of feelings, Schiller suggests, is a function of the *reflexivity* of the generative process.[18]

Schiller's comment resonates strikingly, I think, with the way in which Sterne has Tristram considering the significance of his comment, turning it over in his mind, pondering its implications for Maria and for himself. As we've already begun to see, however, in this sprawling and notoriously self-obsessed work of fiction a relatively simple act of reflection on Tristram's part proves to be part of a kind of hall of mirrors, a massive convolution of reflective performances and reflexive structures. That sense of recursivity is absolutely pervasive in Sterne, and is a well-known part of his legacy to culture down to

---

[18] Friedrich Schiller, *Naive and Sentimental Poetry and On the Sublime: Two Essays*, trans. Julius A. Elias (New York: F. Ungar, 1967), 115–16.

our own time. It is another crucial feature of his reorientation of the novel. It raises the question: how should we understand the relation between 'reflection' and mixed feelings in the sentimental mode?

Soliloquy and Sentiment

To answer this question, it helps to see Sterne's place in a larger history of sentiment. For example, although Sterne nicely exemplifies the connection between reflection and emotional ambivalence, he was in large part following a set of practices and principles established for the modern era chiefly by the Earl of Shaftesbury, a writer who would himself be saluted in the years of Sterne's celebrity as the chief of the sentimental school of philosophy. Shaftesbury classified the relevant set of practices and principles under the heading *soliloquy*, a distinctive kind of theatre of self-discovery that he traces back to the earliest poets but sees reincarnated in the conventions of the Elizabethan stage—in *Hamlet*, no doubt, paradigmatically (making another connection with Sterne's Yorick). He finds the injunction to soliloquy as far back as 'that celebrated Delphic inscription, "Recognize yourself!", which was as much as to say, "Divide yourself!" or "Be two!" For if the division were rightly made, all within would, of course, they thought, be rightly understood, and prudently managed. Such confidence they had in this home-dialect of soliloquy!'[19]

The argument is long and circuitous, but central to our purposes here is the fact that Shaftesbury accounts for the workings of 'soliloquy' with a recurring set of visual metaphors:

> We might here, therefore, as in a looking-glass, discover ourselves, and see our minutest features nicely delineated and suited to our own apprehension and cognizance...And—what was of singular note in these magical glasses—it would happen that, by constant and long inspection, the parties accustomed to the practice would acquire a peculiar speculative habit, so as virtually to carry about with them a sort of pocket-mirror, always ready and in use. In this, there were two faces which would naturally present themselves to our view: ...Whatever we were employed in, whatever we set about, if once we had acquired the habit of this mirror, we should, by virtue of the double reflection, distinguish ourselves into two different parties. And in this dramatic method, the work of self-inspection would proceed with admirable success (87–8).

In these metaphors of redoubled personae, duplicated faces, mirrored images, we arrive at a full account of how we monitor our emotional lives through 'self-discourse', and how we produce and negotiate mixed emotions through self-reflection. Shaftesbury's

---

[19] Anthony Ashley Cooper, 3rd Earl of Shaftesbury, *Characteristics of Men, Manners, Opinions, Times* [1711], ed. Lawrence E. Klein (Cambridge: Cambridge University Press, 1999), 77.

categories, in short, seem to provide in advance a key or legend for the sentimental corpus that Schiller analysed in retrospect nearly a century later.

Sterne, I maintain, navigated his sentimental travels according to some such scheme of reflection understood in this way. *Tristram Shandy* reoriented the novel form in part by taking it in the direction of the Shaftesburyan soliloquy. As an episode such as Maria of Moulines shows, and as Thomas Jefferson recognized, Tristram's is a discourse in which a dramatic process of acknowledging and correcting faults is clearly part of the point of the work. Tristram's reflexive narration recurringly divides him into two parties, thus in effect reproducing Sterne's own self-division, the one that arguably produces the character of Tristram Shandy in the first place. So when Tristram acknowledges the insensibility of his *petite bêtise* with Maria, he becomes two persons, the one who both poses the question and defends it, and the one who questions that defence, who 'second-guesses' that impulse in the first place, the one who swears never again to commit mirth with man, woman, or child. But the other Tristram resurfaces in that oath, and makes the joke about the reserve clause that it contains, and so the soliloquy continues. One finds a similar 'dramatic method', a similar duplicity of soul (so to speak), at the opening of *A Sentimental Journey* in the episode where Yorick refuses alms to a poor mendicant and then regrets his stinginess.[20]

To see just how Tristram Shandy's encounter with Maria of Moulines illustrates the visual dimension of the sentimental—the connection between reflection and mixed feelings—we must first look at how Sterne prepares us for the moment of Tristram's eventual *bêtise*. The episode is introduced abruptly:

> —They were the sweetest notes I ever heard; and I instantly let down the fore-glass to hear them more distinctly—'Tis Maria; said the postillion, observing I was listening— Poor Maria, continued he, (leaning his body on one side to let me see her, for he was in a line betwixt us) is sitting upon a bank playing her vespers upon her pipe, with her little goat beside her.
>
> The young fellow utter'd this with an accent and a look so perfectly in tune to a feeling heart, that I instantly made a vow, I would give him a four and twenty sous piece, when I got to *Moulins*—
>
> —And who is *poor Maria*? said I.
>
> The love and pity of all the villages around us; said the postillion—it is but three years ago, that the sun did not shine upon so fair, so quick-witted and amiable a maid; and better fate did *Maria* deserve, than to have her Banns forbid, by the intrigues of the curate of the parish who published them—
>
> He was going on, when Maria, who had made a short pause, put the pipe to her mouth and began the air again—they were the same notes;—yet were ten times sweeter: It is the evening service to the Virgin, said the young man—but who has taught her to play it—or how she came by her pipe, no one knows; we think that Heaven has assisted her in both; for ever since she has been unsettled in her mind, it seems her only consolation—she has

---

[20] Sterne, *A Sentimental Journey*, ed. New and Day, 6.7–11.

never once had the pipe out of her hand, but plays that *service* upon it almost night and day.

The postillion delivered this with so much discretion and natural eloquence, that I could not help deciphering something in his face above his condition, and should have sifted out his history, had not poor Maria's taken such full possession of me. (2.781–3)

Maria is not initially visible to Tristram. We know this because the postillion has to describe the source of the sound to him: ''Tis Maria...sitting upon a bank...with her little goat beside her.' We also know that, at the start, the chaise is close enough for the sound of the flute to reach Tristram with the chaise window closed, but not so close that he doesn't need to put it down to hear it better.

Visually, the unfolding of the chapter is quite precise in its account of the main stages of the episode. The details are few, but they are telling. Especially crucial, I suggest, is the emphasis on the line of sight, the apparently needless clarification on Tristram's part that, as he and the postillion approach Maria in the chaise, it is necessary for the postillion to lean to one side, 'for he was in a line betwixt us'. Why this precision in the narrative? One reason is that it helps establish a key relation between stage one of the episode, in the chaise, and stage two, after Tristram has leapt from the chaise to join Maria on the bank. Geometrically considered, the movement of the postillion out of the line of sight creates a triangle, albeit a very obtuse one, out of the three characters involved in this stage of the episode. In the second stage of the episode, after Tristram suddenly places himself between Maria and her goat, a new obtuse triangle has been created, with new lines of sight. But the perceiving subject of this new triangle, at least provisionally, is Maria, whose countenance betrays her oscillating, triangulating regard for both Tristram and her goat.

This consideration of spectatorship within the episode richly complicates the sense of how reflection might be said to operate there. Stage one of its unfolding fully establishes Tristram as an ingénu spectator (one, significantly, as will be discussed later on, located in a moving vehicle), and does so precisely enough to establish provisional lines of sight within a triangular drama. Stage two not only places him in a new triangle, with new sight lines, but it also reverses the angle of vision. In her oscillating regard for Tristram and her goat, Maria turns the spectator—Tristram himself—into a spectacle. Or at least he imagines himself a spectacle seen from where she sits. One might say that the sense of embarrassment that Tristram experiences in this moment—the embarrassment that leads to his *bêtise*—is a result in part of this sense of sudden exposure, his having left the enclosure of his vehicle (after the initial, tentative overture of the chaise window in response to the overture of Maria's performance on the flute) and launched himself onto the bank.

Tristram's reversal of role, from spectator to spectacle, is structurally pivotal to the episode in that it constitutes a specific kind of mirroring, a particular mode of reflection. Tristram, we might say, suddenly sees himself reflected in Maria's regard—reflected in his situation next to her goat. Further, this reversal of point of view, and the comparison that Tristram imagines Maria making in her oscillating gaze, creates a symmetry with the situation in stage one of the episode. For there, still in the chaise, Tristram had both Maria and the postillion in his field of vision (once the postillion shifts position). In this earlier instance, it is Tristram who seems to be making the implicit comparisons between the two figures, Maria and the postillion. Tristram says that the postillion's manner of expression had interested him so much that he 'should have sifted out his history, had not poor Maria's taken such full possession of me'. Once on the bank, crucially, Tristram imagines himself the *object* of a comparative reflection.

The Vehicular Hypothesis

Extending the work of Shaftesbury, who did much to transform the notions of theatricality and spectatorship for the eighteenth century, Sterne produced a new mode of writing in the direction of increased reflexivity and increased ambivalence, much as Schiller would register in his essay of 1795. For both Shaftesbury and Sterne, the kind of spectatorship at work in the soliloquy of sentiment can be said to have the structure of a double redoubling. An 'author' turns on himself to become a spectator to his own person, and in so doing he makes it possible to create a work in which others see themselves mirrored. There are many important differences between them, of course. One of the most signal of these is that Sterne constructs a world out of this mental theatre, one with quasi-empirical angles of reflection, relays of viewpoint—'sight lines'. To account for this development requires some attention to the philosophical development of 'moral sentiments' theory in the line of philosophical writing that extends from Shaftesbury to Sterne—especially Francis Hutcheson, David Hume, and Adam Smith, the first and last of them avowed disciples of Shaftesbury. Especially important, I contend, is the increasing emphasis in this tradition on the significance of 'point of view' in acts of reflection, individual or social, of which sentiments are composed.

Humean sentiments, as Annette Baier reminds us, are not 'raw feels' but rather what Hume calls 'impressions of reflection' (1991: 180). In the theory of ideas that Hume and Smith alike inherited from Hutcheson, an *impression* (which is affective) leaves behind a (cognitive) trace or image of itself that Hume calls an *idea* (like the image of the candle that remains after the candle itself has been removed). These ideas can return to strike us again, in memory or imagination, to create second-order affective experience. *The impression of reflection* is Hume's term for this second-order phenomenon, so crucial to Hume's moral-sense analysis. What is crucial for our purposes is to recognize that, since the original impression was registered from a point of view, the idea carries that point of view with it on its return, even as the position of the subject has altered.

Hume's friend Adam Smith adds a second dimension to this account in *The Theory of Moral Sentiments* (1759), positing a deep human capacity, cultivated in the daily life of commercial civil society, both to function as a sympathetic spectator for another person and to recognize that, as an agent, one performs before a social world of (likewise) potentially sympathetic spectators. In developing Hume's account of sympathy from within the framework of the Hutchesonian theory of ideas, Smith also attended to Hume's comments on the importance of the 'general point of view', as Hume most often called it, or alternatively the 'steady' or 'common' point of view. On this basis he elaborated the now-familiar notion of the 'impartial spectator', an internal principle of general perception that is able to counteract our egotism (as the weak spirit of benevolence cannot) because it carries the force of recognition, the sense of truly seeing ourselves, for example, in our own littleness within the world.

It is not a great step, I think, from the central ethical and aesthetic functions made possible by the redoubling mirrors of the self in Shaftesburyan soliloquy to the moral-sentiments function of the general point of view and impartial spectator in Smith. What Sterne does in the wake of Smith's account, as I've tried to suggest in my reading of Maria of Moulines, is to dramatize a soliloquy in which one moves among different points of view in a landscape of shifting sight lines. This sort of activity characterizes the figure whom, in *A Sentimental Journey*, Sterne labelled the 'Sentimental Traveller', a figure for whom 'moving' (shifting perspectives) and 'being moved' (registering new feeling) amount to the same thing. The work of this sort of sentimental sightseeing, as it were, is much as Schiller claimed: to blend feelings, to mix them (as Schiller says), by virtue of the juxtaposition (or superimposition) of, again in Schiller's words, 'two conflicting representations and perceptions'.

Such a logic, inherent in the way in which Sterne developed his narrative techniques over the course of writing *Tristram Shandy*, partially explains the conflation of levels Sterne effected in *A Sentimental Journey*, whereby it becomes impossible to distinguish travel in space from travel in feeling. Further background for this revised encounter is connected with Sterne's play with 'vehicles'. The former involves the new conceptual apparatus that Henry More developed in his response to the emergent philosophical materialism of Descartes, Hobbes, and Spinoza. A citation as early as the late 1640s of More's new coinage 'sensorium' is to be found in the *Oxford English Dictionary*. In his prose writings of the 1650s, More redescribed his theory of the sensorium in non-materialist terms as part of his refutation of Hobbes and others. More's concession to the new mechanistic materialism was the acknowledgment that, while the soul was distinct from the body, it was nonetheless housed or 'carried' in a highly subtilized form of matter that registered perceptual vibration and effected locomotion. This subtilized body, the sensorium, he also called the soul's 'vehicle', and he posited that this organ actually survived the death of the gross body.[21]

---

[21] Henry More, *The Immortality of the Soul* (London: William Morden, 1659).

This theory would be debated (and satirized) for a century and a half under the heading of 'the vehicular hypothesis'. Abraham Tucker devoted a hundred pages to 'the Vehicular State' in a quirky tract much admired by William Hazlitt, *The Light of Nature Pursued* (1768). Joseph Priestley kept the issue in play with his chapter 'Of the Vehicle of the Soul' in *Disquisitions Relating to Matter and Spirit* (1782). The mid-1790s moment for this strand of my story occurs in Mary Hays' *Memoirs of Emma Courtney* (1796)—a rough transcription of letters between herself and William Godwin—in which, in a passage for which Hays supplies a footnote to Tucker, Emma writes to her would-be lover as follows: 'I wish we were in the vehicular state, and that you understood the sentient language; you might then comprehend the whole of what I mean to express, but find too delicate for *words.*'[22]

Still more important, at least for the *literary* history of the sentimental, the vehicular hypothesis set the condition for Sterne's creation of the subgenre of the sentimental journey. Though no modern commentator seems to have noticed, Sterne's invention features long series of inside jokes about various kinds of vehicles, foregrounded early on when Yorick, well into his narrative but not his journey, steps into an unhitched chaise in a carriage yard in Calais to write his 'Preface in a Desobligeant'. Here he produces his taxonomy of travellers, in which he insists that the sentimental traveller should not be distinguished by virtue only of the '*Novelty of*[his] *Vehicle*'.[23] These jokes resolve in conclusions like the one Yorick draws in his encounter with Maria of Moulines, a reprise of the encounter in *Tristram Shandy*, to which Yorick makes reference. The whole controversy is made explicit in Yorick's comment: 'I am positive I have a soul; nor can all the books with which materialists have pester'd the world ever convince me of the contrary' (151). It is this declaration that leads Yorick into his famous paean: 'Dear Sensibility!...great SENSORIUM of the world!' (155). Sensorium: the very word that Henry More coined in the mid-seventeenth century as an alternate name for the vehicle.

Dickens is just one of many heirs of this tradition, especially in his most explicitly political novel, *A Tale of Two Cities* (1859), where we are initially introduced to the events of the French Revolution by a character pointedly named Mr Lorry, redundantly riding in a vehicle. This is a novel in which the connecting work of the English mail coach, the divisive work of the Marquis's murderous coach, and the answering murderousness of the revolutionary tumbrels on the French side all carry out Dickens's sentimental allegory of the two political cultures. Though decisively shaped by melodrama, Dickens's fiction shows that the sentimental legacy has left its mark on him in the vehicular journeys of the soul in *A Christmas Carol* (1843), for example, when Scrooge is spirited over the landscape. Further, *A Christmas Carol* makes explicit the sentimental-journey theme of materialism

---

[22] Mary Hays, *Memoirs of Emma Courtney*, 2 vols (London: G. G. and J. Robinson, 1796), 1.177–78. See also Mee, Chapter 11.

[23] Sterne, *A Sentimental Journey*, ed. New and Day, 6.15.

overcome when Scrooge famously tries to dismiss the Ghost of Marley, condemned to travel after death because he had not gone forth during his life, as a failure of his alimentary system: "'You may be an undigested bit of beef, a blot of mustard, a crumb of cheese, a fragment of an underdone potato. There's more of gravy than of grave about you, whatever you are!'"[24] This, perhaps, helps explain what Sterne meant when he wrote that if *A Sentimental Journey* were not properly understood, he would have to give up sentimental writing and write to the body.

The anti-materialism of latitudinarian vehicularity, then, is one important strand of the sentimental tradition that persists over the long Romantic period. Indeed, understood in these terms, the influence of Sterne's writings on the Romantic novel deserves a further word. Beyond England there is the influential duel in Ireland between Lady Morgan and Maria Edgeworth, whose rival Odyssean novels of journeys through Ireland, *The Wild Irish Girl* (1806) and *The Absentee* (1812), allude often to the sentimental as a category, and share many of Sterne's new premises for fiction, but debate their ethical and political implications in pointed ways. Like Sterne's, these sentimental journeys become tales of cultural travel, and the visitors to Ireland whose courses they chart enter a world of encounters—a negotiation of affective viewpoints—modelled on the various encounters of Sterne's narrators, Tristram and Parson Yorick.

Walter Scott dedicated the first of his globally influential Waverley novels to Sterne's early Scottish disciple, Henry Mackenzie. This novel brings the sentimental journey of Edward Waverley on both sides of the '45 Rebellion to a close with the execution of the rebel chieftain, Fergus Mac-Ivor, under whom he had briefly served. In both the trial scene at Carlisle, and in the insistently sentimental resolution that follows it, action is rendered as a relay of visual regard and space a network of feeling. Mac-Ivor exchanges glances with Edward as he is carried off for execution. Here is Scott's rendering of the following moment:

> the court-yard was now totally empty, but Waverley still stood there as if stupified, his eyes fixed upon the dark pass where he had so lately seen the last glimpse of his friend.— At length, a female servant of the governor, struck with surprise and compassion at the stupified misery which his countenance expressed, asked him, if he would not walk into her master's house and sit down?[25]

In this triangular relay of affective gazes—the servant of the governor who imprisoned Mac-Ivor before his death responding to his countenance with sympathy—we discover Scott's way of mediating the violent conflict of his grandfather's generation, his sentimental mixing of feelings by means of redoubled perception. The real action of this scene can be said to take place in a medium of crossing viewpoints, a space of sentiment.

---

[24] Charles Dickens, *A Christmas Carol and Other Christmas Books*, ed. Robert Douglas-Fairhurst (Oxford: Oxford University Press, 2006), 21.

[25] Walter Scott, *Waverley: or, 'Tis Sixty Years Since*, ed. P. D. Garside (Edinburgh: Edinburgh University Press, 2007), ch. 69; 350.

My claim, then, is that, elaborated philosophically by Smith and fictionally by Sterne, Shaftesbury's world of mirroring soliloquy develops into a newly articulated sense of social space. This is not the empty homogenous field that Benedict Anderson associated with novels of this period (2006: 24–6), but rather a medium itself defined by a field of virtual spectators and their 'views', as we say—that is, by various lines of sight, some of them crossing, some of them matching, some of them reciprocated, some of them not. This new social space was already emergent in, say, the novels of Samuel Richardson, whose interest in sight lines and earshot is markedly more pronounced in *Clarissa* than it was in *Pamela*. But Sterne raised it to a particularly acute level of self-consciousness.

Sterne's Reorientation of the Novel

I suggested at the start that Joyce's *Ulysses* is a novel that shares a number of features with Sterne's works in respect to its place in the history of the novel. In them, one might say, we find two Irish-born writers who transformed the novel by virtuosic miscellaneity of style and subject matter, and who transformed our very notion of literary travel in the bargain. I also suggested that Joyce's self-consciousness about literary history led him to acknowledge Sterne's contribution to English prose style in the episode that has come to be known as 'Oxen of the Sun'. Another episode in *Ulysses*, however, though it does not acknowledge the Sternean sentimental explicitly, comes perhaps closer to registering Sterne's long-term impact. The episode is 'Nausicaa', where Bloom encounters several young women at Sandycove strand in the early evening, and where he becomes fixated on one of them in particular, Gerty, who is perched, like Homer's Nausicaa, on the rocks above the beach.

Like most chapters of *Ulysses*, the style of the chapter does much of its work, and the style of this chapter is universally acknowledged by commentators to be 'sentimental', even from its opening words: 'The summer evening had begun to fold the world in its mysterious embrace. Far away in the west the sun was setting and the last glow of all too fleeting day lingered lovingly on sea and strand....'[26] Or from the introduction of Gerty: 'Gerty MacDowell who was seated near her companions, lost in thought, gazing far away into the distance, was in very truth as fair a specimen of winsome Irish girlhood as one could wish to see' (452). But what is involved in the stylistic performance of the Nausicaa section is more than a matter of syntax and diction. It is all about triangulated sight lines and the relation of body and spirit. A mass is being said nearby to the Blessed Virgin, 'Mary, star of the sea' (449). It is said of Gerty that 'her very soul is in her eyes' (456). But over the course of the chapter, Gerty knowingly exposes her 'transparent stockings' to the prurient eyes of the lingering passer-by, Leopold Bloom:

---

[26] James Joyce, *Ulysses* (New York: Penguin, 2000), 449.

She could almost see the swift answering flush of admiration in his eyes that set her tingling in every nerve. She put on her hat so that she could see from underneath the brim and swung her buckled shoe faster for her breath caught as she caught the expression in his eyes...Edy Boardman was noticing it too because she was squinting at Gerty, half smiling, with her specs, like an old maid, pretending to nurse the baby. (469)

The entire episode is articulated in the play of looks and looking. Fireworks go off overhead, metaphorizing Bloom's masturbatory emission: 'My fireworks. Up like a rocket, down like a stick' (483). But even after this assertion of the body's role, which leaves Bloom complaining of the stickiness in his pants, a note of sentimental soulfulness is sounded again: 'Their souls met in a last lingering glance and the eyes that reached her heart, full of a strange shining, hung enraptured on her sweet flowerlike face' (478).

Even the associative stream of consciousness that characterizes much of the narration in *Ulysses*, including 'Nausicaa' itself, once we move to Bloom's perspective on the episode on Sandycove Strand, might be understood as owing something to Sterne's narrative associationism. As Woolf wrote of Sterne a decade later, just a few years after she had rewritten Bloom's sentimental journey in Dublin as Mrs Dalloway's in London: 'In this preference for the windings of his own mind to the guide-book and its hammered high road, Sterne is singularly of our own age' (1932: 81). The remark is intended as a high compliment, and it can serve as yet another measure of Sterne's reorientation of the novel. Not even the broad field of the novel, however, offered horizon enough when Friedrich Nietzsche decided on his terms of praise for Sterne: 'the most liberated spirit of all time' (see Ross 2001: 430).

7

Sentimental Fiction of the 1760s and 1770s

HELEN THOMPSON

THE accession of George III on 25 October 1760 demarcates an era of domestic political turbulence and imperial reorganization. The end of the Seven Years' War (1756–63) with France, Austria, and Russia sealed Britain's conquest of Canada, the Ohio River valley, the land east of the Mississippi River, most of the Lesser Antilles, and the Carnatic and Bengal regions of India. The war nearly doubled Britain's national debt, leading the government to exact payment for its protection of the American colonies with import duties like the Stamp Act (1765). The ensuing crisis over Britain's right to tax subjects without direct parliamentary representation resonated with new forms of political dissent at home. These were focalized by the populist parliamentarian John Wilkes, whose arrest for seditious libel (1763) mobilized protest in 'extra-parliamentary' (Brewer 1976: 9) media including pamphlets, handbills, cartoons, graffiti, and ballads, as well as in venues like coffee houses, clubs, and societies. Both the American colonies and Britain experienced the convergence of calls for representational reform with the expansion of modes of political expression that fuelled the American Declaration of Independence (1776), resulting in the Americans' alliance with France (1778) and Britain's loss of the colonies (1783).

British sentimental fiction of these decades, as well as sentimental fiction translated from the French, seems disconnected from topical concerns like continental and overseas warfare, extra-parliamentary protest, and the representational crisis. Despite their paucity of concrete references to these events, however, sentimental novels of the 1760s and 1770s addressed them on another front. In his pamphlet *Thoughts on the Present Discontents* (1770), the MP Edmund Burke envisioned a House of Commons whose representational mandate derived neither from the expansion of the franchise nor from the popularization of politics enacted by Wilkes but rather from the members' capacity to 'feel with a more tender and a nearer interest every thing that concerned the people'.[1] Burke, whose

---

[1] Edmund Burke, 'Thoughts on the Present Discontents', in *The Writings and Speeches of Edmund Burke*, vol. 2, ed. Paul Langford (Oxford: Clarendon Press, 1981), 292.

notion of virtual representation was rejected by the American revolutionaries, invoked 'some sympathy of nature with their constituents' (292) to guarantee that the House of Commons acted in the name of a largely disenfranchised populace. With their central attention to the operations of sympathy, sentimental novels of the 1760s and 1770s explore the medium that Burke and his party championed to defend the 'tender' bond between government and 'people'. Marking a broadly diffused interrogation of the unifying force of sympathy, popular sentimental fiction by the Irish dramatist and novelist Hugh Kelly, the Irish novelist Henry Brooke, the English novelist and sometime resident in colonial Quebec Frances Brooke, the Irish novelist, poet, and physician Oliver Goldsmith, and the Scottish novelist Henry Mackenzie shows the pre-eminence of a distinctly British discourse of sentiment that counteracted the provincialism propounded by Wilkes and his movement as a 'swaggering and intolerantly Little English patriotism' (Colley 1992: 106). The overwhelming success of the first two volumes of Laurence Sterne's *Tristram Shandy* (1760), which went through six editions by the time of Sterne's death in 1768, galvanized sentimental fiction for the next two decades; at the same time, Tristram's blind spots, divagations, and impotencies anticipate the sentimental novel's tendency to question its own claims for the ameliorative powers of sympathetic feeling.

This chapter examines philosophical antecedents to the discourse of sympathy as we find it in sentimental fiction of the 1760s and 1770s. It then takes up the relation between sentiment and domestic authority as this was determined by sexual difference inside the home. Finally, the chapter discusses four novels that exemplify the self-reflexive tendencies of much sentimental fiction of the period. In its representations of how sentiment might rectify structural injustice, we encounter the sentimental novel's most urgent literary-historical reflection, on the equivocal political agency of feelings spurred by 'some sympathy of nature' with plantation slaves.

Sentimental Fiction, Lockean Empiricism, and Moral Sense Philosophy

In Oliver Goldsmith's *The Vicar of Wakefield* (1766), a friendly 'money-borrower'[2] accounts for the famed generosity of the vicar's new landlord, Sir William Thornhill:

> Physicians tell us of a disorder in which the whole body is so exquisitely sensible, that the slightest touch gives pain: what some have thus suffered in their persons, this gentleman felt in his mind. The slightest distress, whether real or fictitious, touched him to the quick, and his soul laboured under a sickly sensibility of the miseries of others. Thus

---

[2] Oliver Goldsmith, *The Vicar of Wakefield*, ed. Arthur Friedman (Oxford: Oxford University Press, 1974), ch. 3; 20.

disposed to relieve, it will be easily conjectured, he found numbers disposed to solicit: his profusions began to impair his fortune, but not his good-nature. (21)

In making this diagnosis, the money-borrower Mr Burchell illuminates the role of Lockean empiricism in the development of the sentimental novel. Sir William's susceptibility to 'the miseries of others' amplifies the defining conceit of John Locke's *An Essay Concerning Human Understanding* (1689): that because at birth the human mind contains no innate, essential, or ready-made ideas, 'The Senses at first let in particular *Ideas*, and furnish the yet empty Cabinet'.[3] For Locke, 'the Mind comes to be furnish'd' only after the sense organs are 'imprinted by external Things' (55); as opposed to a Platonic or Christian scheme whereby a person finds within himself knowledge that he has always possessed, Locke stipulates that ideas must be 'let in', admitted into the mind or 'yet empty Cabinet' by means of '[t]he Senses'. Unlike theorists of knowledge who insulate mind from body—for example, Nicholas Malebranche claims that ideas occasioned by the outside world are inserted into the mind by God[4]—Locke renders coextensive 'external Things', the sensory organs those things touch or move, and the mind that is subsequently 'imprinted'. Although Locke is not a materialist, his *Essay* establishes the indissolubly corporeal basis of empirical understanding: sensory 'Organs, or the Nerves which are the Conduits, to convey them [ideas] from without to their Audience in the Brain' (121). Lockean empiricism shapes the sentimental novel's formal, moral, and political development.

Insofar as it is engendered from the outside in, Thornhill's 'disorder' is most remarkable for its enabling figural pretence. Whereas readers of Locke's political writings have argued that he posits a possessive individual who owns external things as well as the capacities of his body, Locke's *Essay* and Goldsmith's *Vicar of Wakefield* describe a person who is not possessive but receptive. Thornhill models a hypersensitive case of empirical understanding that Locke illustrates with the mind's analogy to an empty cabinet as well as 'white Paper' (104) or a 'mirror' (118). As Locke states, 'the mind is fitted to receive the Impressions made on it' (118): while the cabinet figures the penetrability of a mind into which ideas enter, the 'Paper' and 'mirror' are sensitive surfaces exposed to the world, 'fitted to receive' stimuli that, in Goldsmith's version of Lockean analogy, 'touched [Thornhill] to the quick'. In sentimental fiction of the 1760s and 1770s, Thornhill's 'exquisitely sensible' uptake of ideas does not constitute a 'disorder' but rather the prototypical condition of the protagonist who is 'so nicely sensible, so delicately tender'[5] and so 'susceptible'[6] that he or she occupies a state of enhanced receptivity which, as Hugh Kelly concurs in his *Memoirs of a Magdalen* (1767), is 'piercingly exquisite'.[7]

[3] John Locke, *An Essay Concerning Human Understanding*, ed. Peter H. Nidditch (Oxford: Oxford University Press, 1975), 55.

[4] Nicholas Malebranche, *The Search After Truth*, trans. Thomas M. Lennon and Paul Olscamp (Cambridge: Cambridge University Press, 1997).

[5] Charlotte Lennox, *Sophia*, ed. Norbert Schürer (Peterborough, ON: Broadview Press, 2009), 67.

[6] Henry Mackenzie, *Julia de Roubigné*, ed. Susan Manning (East Linton, Scotland: Tuckwell Press, 1999), 3.

[7] Hugh Kelly, *Memoirs of a Magdalen: or, The History of Louisa Mildmay*, 2 vols (Dublin: Wilson, Exshaw, et al., 1767), 1.76.

However, the sensibility that Burchell describes is not indiscriminate, for Thornhill is predisposed to be 'touched' by the 'miseries of others'. With this specification of Thornhill's disorder as susceptibility to scenes that would not otherwise seem able to excite his interest—since they involve not family and friends but *'others'*—*The Vicar of Wakefield* reveals the vital point of contact between Lockean empiricism and moral sense philosophy as the latter was influentially formulated by Anthony Ashley Cooper, Third Earl of Shaftesbury, and Adam Smith. Writing a decade after his tutor Locke, Shaftesbury appropriates to moral ends the mental agency that Locke's *Essay* designates 'reflection': 'The Mind, receiving the *Ideas* . . . from without, when it turns its view inward upon it self . . . takes from thence other *Ideas*, which are as capable to be the Objects of its Contemplation, as any of those it received from foreign things' (127). Shaftesbury takes this Lockean 'turn' as the figure for moral conscience, which transpires when the mind serves as a stage on which a person becomes visible to himself: for Shaftesbury, conscience is rendered inescapable by a mental scenography in which somebody 'is by his nature forced to endure the review of his own mind and actions and to have representations of himself and his inward affairs constantly passing before him'.[8] It would be difficult to overstress the significance for eighteenth-century sentimental fiction of Locke's turn to reflection and Shaftesbury's staging of conscience, for a mind that 'turns its view inward upon it self' entails a simultaneously cognitive and figural aptitude for self-reflexivity whose eighteenth-century literary form is perhaps most fully realized by the epistolary novel.

Shaftesbury rewrites Lockean reflection to skew its figural tendencies even more decisively in the direction of theatre: the inner *'Ideas'* that Locke claims as 'Objects' of mental 'Contemplation' are rendered more decisively perceptible, more like ideas 'received from foreign things', in the form of 'representations' that pass, in peculiarly cinematic fashion, 'before him'. Indeed, Burchell notes that Thornhill is touched to the quick by either 'real or fictitious' distress: Shaftesbury thus anticipates a sentimental deployment of conscience whose key criterion is not an object's reality but rather the feeling it induces when transposed into the medium of representation. In sentimental novels of the 1760s and 1770s, moral stimuli are potentially fictitious representations whose historicity is trumped by their power to stimulate emotion in an observer who, Shaftesbury writes, has thereby been 'forced' to feel.

In his influential work of moral philosophy *The Theory of Moral Sentiments* (1759), Smith exploits the mind's figuration as a cavity, receptacle, or stage to resolve the dilemma: if Shaftesbury's conscience or 'self-system' (219) motivates a person's moralized response to his own thoughts and actions, then what compels that person's

---

[8] Anthony Ashley Cooper, 3rd Earl of Shaftesbury, *Characteristics of Men, Manners, Opinions, Times* [1711], ed. Lawrence E. Klein (Cambridge: Cambridge University Press, 1999), 208.

concern for the thoughts and actions of others? Smith begins *Moral Sentiments* by pointing to the solipsism threatened by a sensationalist epistemology in which impressions cannot pass out of the body that receives them, for even if 'our brother is upon the rack... our senses will never inform us of what he suffers'.[9] Smith overcomes the isolation portended by an internalized theatre of feeling with the claim that representations of others interest an observer just as much as representations of the observer's own self:

[I]t is by the imagination only that we can form any conceptions of what are his [the other's] sensations. Neither can that faculty help us to this any other way, than by representing to us what would be our own, if we were in his case. ... By the imagination ... we enter as it were into his body, and become in some measure the same person with him. ... His agonies, when they are thus brought home to ourselves, when we have thus adopted and made them our own, begin at last to affect us, and we then tremble and shudder at the thought of what he feels. (9)

Smith's affinity with Shaftesbury resides in the necessity of 'representing', which transforms the inaccessible feelings of the other into objects of one's own mental apprehension. While 'imagination' converts extrinsic feeling into perceptible 'conceptions', representation is that imported feeling's final medium. Representation thus serves to get one person's feeling inside another: while the prospect of 'enter[ing] as it were into his body' vividly underscores the fictionality of moralizing representation, it is Smith's reversed figuration of the process, entailing feelings 'brought home to ourselves', 'adopted ... and made ... our own', that iterates the constitutive premise of Lockean understanding, that ideas must be taken in. Smith offers a powerfully crystallized recapitulation of sentimental fiction's social mandate, whose cultural currency is reflected in *Tristram Shandy* when Tristram's sight of his uncle Toby's merciful treatment of a fly 'instantly set my whole frame into one vibration of most pleasurable sensation ... this I know, that the lesson of universal good-will then taught and imprinted ... has never since been worn out of my mind'.[10] What is indelibly 'imprinted' on Tristram's—and the reader's—mind is not moral doctrine but representation, not ethical rules but the spectacle of uncle Toby's benevolence.

As a model sentimental protagonist, the eponymous heroine of Frances Brooke's *The History of Lady Julia Mandeville* (1763) typifies the confluence of Lockean receptivity and proneness to feel for another that Brooke invokes under the heading of 'softness': 'As her mind has been adorned, not warped, by education, it is just what her appearance promises: artless, gentle, timid, soft, sincere, compassionate; awake to all the finer

---

[9] Adam Smith, *The Theory of Moral Sentiments*, ed. D. D. Raphael and A. L. Macfie (Indianapolis: Liberty Fund, 1982), 9.

[10] Laurence Sterne, *The Life and Opinions of Tristram Shandy Gentleman*, ed. Graham Petrie, introd. Christopher Ricks (Harmondsworth: Penguin, 1982), 131.

impressions of tenderness, and melting with pity for every human woe.'[11] The amenability to impression exemplified by Julia's 'soft' mind is continuous with her virtue; when her mind 'melt[s] with pity for every human woe', Julia demonstrates the collapse of sentimental reactivity and moral practice achieved not through self-discipline but rather through the ethico-physiological state of meltingness. Kelly's *Memoirs of a Magdalen* points to the ensuing legibility of virtue, which is evident not in language but in somatic signs like tears, when his ruined protagonist's mother explains to a sympathizing friend: 'She was pleased to see me touched; and, more than once kissing away the drops from my cheeks, declared she was never sorry to see a young lady miserable at a scene of distress, because those only could continue unmov'd, who were utterly destitute of humanity and understanding' (2.10). As Kelly repeats, the semiotics of sympathy entail moral virtue that an observer can 'see'. In *The Man of Feeling* (1771), Henry Mackenzie distils the extra-linguistic imminence of sentimental morality into its most concise algorithm: 'there is virtue in these tears'.[12]

Mackenzie's reduction of 'virtue' to the unadulterated materiality of a bodily fluid plays on Smith's claim that moral feeling 'is produced instantaneously and, as it were, mechanically' (145). Smith thus renders moral practice continuous with the extra-volitional process of sensory impression elaborated by Locke's *Essay*: 'all Sensation being produced in us, only by different degrees and modes of Motion in our animal Spirits, variously agitated by external Objects' (133). Effected by 'different degrees and 'modes of Motion' of 'variously agitated' animal spirits (the subtle but still material liaison between things in the world, nerves, and ideas), Lockean 'Sensation' models a mechanical process whose instantaneity and anteriority to conscious control Smith extends to the moral feeling excited by distressing representations. We have seen in Goldsmith's *Vicar of Wakefield* that Thornhill's sensibility entails not only his 'pain' and, presumably, his tears, but his charitable 'profusions'. Spontaneous charity, sentimental morality's pre-eminent world-directed act, is propelled in *The Man of Feeling* by its protagonist's still mechanical incarnation of sensibility: after he 'draw[s] a shilling from his pocket.... His fingers lost their compression' (61). By transferring the impetus for this man's gift to the mystified de-'compression' of his 'fingers'—and, with a recourse to quasi-occult causation that would not be lost on his readers, to gravity—Mackenzie grants unpremeditated charity the same agential and physical status as virtuous tears. Moved to charity by 'modes of Motion', sentimental fiction's receptive protagonist further dispossesses him- or herself.

---

[11] Frances Brooke, *Lady Julia Mandeville*, ed. E. Phillips Poole (London: The Scholartis Press, 1930), 42.

[12] Henry Mackenzie, *The Man of Feeling*, ed. Maureen Harkin (Peterborough, ON: Broadview Press, 2005), 82.

Sentimental Fiction, Love, and Domestic Power

On the control of the will over the ideas a person lets in, Locke's *Essay* stipulates that '*the Understanding can* no more refuse to have, nor alter, when they are imprinted, nor blot them out...than a mirror can refuse, alter, or obliterate....As the Bodies that surround us, do diversly [*sic*] affect our Organs, the mind is forced to receive the Impressions' (118). With the figure of a mind 'forced to receive the Impressions' that make up its initial stock of ideas, Locke anticipates the sentimental discourse not only of extra-volitional charity, but of extra-volitional love. In this capacity, we must reconsider the paradoxical influence upon sentimental fiction of Samuel Richardson, whose epistolary novels *Pamela; or, Virtue Rewarded* (1740–1), *Clarissa; or, The History of a Young Lady* (1748–9), and *Sir Charles Grandison* (1753–4) establish feeling's formal articulation as the personal letter. In *Pamela*, Locke's vision of a mind whose impressions are 'forced' upon it claims a highly local instrumentality: after resisting seduction by her aristocratic master with unprecedented rhetorical fluency, the servant Pamela succumbs to his offer of marriage by citing the influence of 'this strange wayward Heart of mine, that I never found so ungovernable and awkward before'.[13] To inoculate Pamela against the charge of self-interest, as well as to defuse the rationality of her prior objections to master–servant pairings, Pamela's 'wayward Heart' takes charge of her choice of husband because, Pamela explains, 'Love is not a voluntier [*sic*] Thing' (248). Richardson's formal innovation of writing to the moment thus transcribes in real time Pamela's impression by the irresistible mechanism of her own feeling: 'Fie upon it! my Heart begins to flutter again!...it is throb, throb, throb, like a little Fool' (342). Pamela's 'throb, throb, throb' marks the sentimental novel's continuity with the fiction of, most notably, Aphra Behn and Eliza Haywood; as in Behn's *Love-Letters Between a Nobleman and His Sister* (1685–7) or Haywood's *Love in Excess* (1719), Pamela's preference is compelled by amorous reflex that is not 'a voluntier Thing'.

By enabling Pamela's transcription of the experience of her own throbs, Richardson's epistolary novel anticipates further typographical and formal refinements of feeling's proximity to literary representation. Louisa Mildmay, protagonist of Kelly's *Memoirs of a Magdalen*, writes to her confidante about the 'sentimental libertine' (1.42) who ruins her on the eve of their marriage: 'That Harold too—but save me, Harriot—I must not suffer myself to think—of that—I cannot find an epithet to distinguish him by—my reason is impatient to brand him with the most detestable—but this infatuated bosom eternally beats in his behalf, and, though I strive to despise and abhor him, yet I feel I passionately love' (2.100). The immediacy of Louisa's feeling fragments her syntax into dashed ejaculations, which assume the rhythm of a series of cognitive throbs; this distinctly syntactic

---

[13] Samuel Richardson, *Pamela; or, Virtue Rewarded*, ed. Thomas Keymer and Alice Wakely (Oxford: Oxford University Press, 2001), 245.

mechanism assures the perdurability and exclusivity of the love with which Louisa's 'infatuated bosom eternally beats', facilitating her eventual union with a man who has refused to marry the woman he enjoyed one night too soon.

Kelly's vindication of the tendencies of Louisa's 'bosom' over those of her 'reason' shows the discrepancy between his deployment of amorous mechanism and that of the Richardsonian novel. As soon as Richardson began to revise *Pamela* for republication, he expurgated Pamela's throbs. Although Richardson realizes the confluence of Lockean epistemology and literary form, achieving the novelistic incarnation of Locke's cabinet, mirror, or paper in the form of letters written to the moment, *Clarissa* and *Sir Charles Grandison* repudiate amorous impression as a justification of feminine marital choice. *Clarissa* recapitulates the fatal lesson of a plot catalyzed by Clarissa's initial susceptibility to a man who looks like he should be good: 'Many a girl has been *carried*, who never would have been *attempted* had she showed a proper resentment when her ears or her eyes were first invaded.'[14] In *Grandison*, the discourse of amorous impression enables women's tolerance of masculine insult: 'with the thoughtless, is the beginning and progress of that formidable invader, miscalled *Love*; a word very happily at hand, to help giddy creatures to talk with, and look without confusion of face on, a man telling them a thousand lyes.'[15] With 'miscalled' love the 'invader' to blame for ladies' 'invaded' ears and eyes, Richardson rejects both the empiricist mechanism of amorous receptivity and love's sentimental figuration as entrance. Even though writing to the moment relays the immediacy of both impression and reflection, Richardson marshals the form to assist an anti-sensational justification of marital choice whose sources are metaphysical and Christian.

Richardson ranks as the novelist with the sixth-largest number of British editions printed between 1750 and 1769; number seven is the French author Marie-Jeanne Riccoboni (Raven 1987: 14). Riccoboni's popularity illuminates a split within the eighteenth-century deployment of epistolary form, a split, as Thomas Keymer suggests, 'between Richardson's own priorities and the trends his fiction impelled' (2005: 583). Indeed, Riccoboni's *Letters from Juliet Lady Catesby* (1759), translated by Frances Brooke, employs the personal letter to amplify the resistance of passion to words:

> My Lord improved me in the *French* Language and I instructed him in the *Spanish*: our Studies led us to Reflexions, of which our Sentiments were always the Foundation. The Secret of our Souls seemed every Moment ready to escape us; our Eyes had already betrayed it; when one day, reading an affecting Story of two tender Lovers, who had been cruelly torn from each other, the Book fell from our Hands, our Tears began to flow, and seized with I know not what Kind of Fear, our Eyes were fixed ardently on each other. He put one of his Arms round me, as if to detain me; I leaned towards him, and breaking

---

[14] Samuel Richardson, *Clarissa, or, the History of a Young Lady*, ed. Angus Ross (Harmondsworth: Penguin, 1985), 521.

[15] Samuel Richardson, *The History of Sir Charles Grandison*, ed. Jocelyn Harris, 3 vols (London: Oxford University Press, 1972), 3.111.

Silence at the same Time, we exclaimed both together, Ah! how unhappy were these Lovers!

A full Confidence followed this accidental Discovery of our Tenderness.[16]

It may be triggered by a 'Book', but this 'accidental' disclosure of feeling realizes a fundamentally anti-discursive mode of amorous communication. Located in 'Eyes', 'Tears', and 'Arms', the extra-volitional agency of amorous 'Discovery' subsumes the book. Rather than abstracting sentiment into discourse, the book materializes as one more cog in love's mechanical progress.

In its hostility to linguistic abstraction, Riccoboni's amorous plot echoes the elaboration of sentiment authored not by Richardson but by the political theorist, *philosophe*, and novelist Jean-Jacques Rousseau. Whereas Richardson promotes a pre-marital ethic that relies on philosophical, religious, and literary discourse—especially as this is deployed to debunk the libertine designs of would-be men of feeling—Rousseau fuses his defence of affective mechanism to a historico-political twist of Lockean empiricism that predicates virtue upon a person's or collectivity's resistance to the abstractions of modern culture. We can recall that the protagonist of Brooke's *Lady Julia Mandeville* possesses a melting mind that 'has been adorned, not warped, by education': as Julia repeats, 'I am not formed for deceit: artless as the village maid, every sentiment of my soul is in my eyes: I have not learnt, I will never learn to disguise their expressive language' (121). By ascribing Julia's incapacity for 'disguise' and 'deceit' to the 'education' that preserves her artlessness, Brooke draws upon eighteenth-century pedagogical thought, extending from Locke's *Some Thoughts Concerning Education* (1693) to Rousseau's *Emile* (1762), which asserts the power of early childhood education wholly to 'form' the initially empty minds of empiricist persons. Rousseau's signal disagreement with Locke is captured in Julia's comparison of herself to a 'village maid': while Locke insists that children can learn to reason, Rousseau seeks to naturalize the external forces that shape his fictional pupil Emile, thereby protracting Emile's likeness, Rousseau writes, to 'a savage made to inhabit cities'.[17]

For many authors, sentimental masculinity is nourished in isolation from novels, urban leisure, and philosophy and the resulting vices of affectation, fashion, and scepticism. Henry Brooke's *The Fool of Quality* (1766–70) envisions the extreme case of an aristocratic boy who, raised by peasants to 'run about, mother-naked, for near an hour, in a frosty morning',[18] is so unable to abstract his impressions into words that his mother declares him 'positively an ideot; he has no apprehension of persons or things' (1.47). Because he has been neither 'physicked into delicacy, nor flattered into pride' (1.43) and

[16] Marie-Jeanne Riccoboni, *Letters from Juliet Lady Catesby, To Her Friend Lady Henrietta Campley*, trans. from the French, 2nd edn (London: R. and J. Dodsley, 1760), 72–3.

[17] Jean-Jacques Rousseau, *Emile*, trans. Allan Bloom (New York: Basic Books, 1979), 205.

[18] Henry Brooke, *The Fool of Quality; or, The History of Henry Earl of Moreland*, new edn, 5 vols (London: Edward Johnston, 1777), 1.42.

because he seems to lack 'any kind of ideas' (1.47), juvenile Harry channels the 'sentiments', one tearful onlooker testifies, that 'heaven…inspires' (1.57): 'The language of true love is understood by all creatures, and was that of which Harry had, almost the only perception' (1.52). By linking illiteracy to an extra-discursive virtue that extends to 'all creatures', Brooke offers a potent but unsustainable deployment of Rousseauvian savagery, perhaps especially because little Harry manifests his goodness by beating up the effeminate, overly chatty young nobles with whom he is placed in contact. In *Evelina, or, A Young Lady's Entrance into the World* (1778), Frances Burney's avatars of foppishly *au courant* and crudely jingoistic masculinity similarly suggest that the Rousseauvian identity of virtue and resistance to discursive cultivation yields only dwindling returns. Burney's violent xenophobes parody an insular, English or Country version of Rousseauvian savagery; by equating masculine virtue and politeness, Burney endorses a cosmopolitan Court ideology that recuperates cultural sophistication in the name of heightened sensitivity to the state of the 'common good' (Pocock 1975: 487).

The affiliation of linguistic incompetence and even prelapsarian innocence claims a more durable half-life in the case of sentimental women. Before she is kidnapped by a nobleman, the protagonist of Sarah Fielding's *The History of Ophelia* (1760), necessarily writing after the fact, compares herself to the 'Animals' at her retired Welsh habitation, 'myself, then as ignorant of Evil, and almost as Dumb as they'.[19] What facilitates Ophelia's ability to forestall her abductor's sexual assault is his own sentimental receptivity to the virtue evident in her incomprehension of the meaning of the word 'rape': 'I could not suspect him of any ill Design against my Innocence; of all such Views I was totally ignorant, I knew not what they meant. The Shadow of such Schemes had never been represented to my Imagination, whose simple Purity received no Light from his Behaviour' (75). Fielding's equivocation of feminine 'Innocence' and 'ignoran[ce]'—which, Ophelia writes, qualifies her as a 'fair Savage' (81)—sustains a defence against libertine predation whose reliance upon 'simple Purity' defines this novel's divergence from *Pamela* and *Clarissa*. Unlike Pamela, the lower-class heroine of Riccoboni's *L'Histoire d'Ernestine* (1765; English trans., 1766) proves her suitability to become her wealthy admirer's wife because she lacks words: his 'presence', she writes, 'inspires I know not what delightful sentiment'.[20] Richardson's discursive, Puritan, and potentially de-sexed articulation of virtue, whose inability to justify women's marital subordination *Pamela* and *Clarissa* cannot quite repress, contrasts strongly with Ophelia's and Ernestine's extra-discursive, natural, and essentially feminized purity.

[19] Sarah Fielding, *The History of Ophelia*, ed. Peter Sabor (Peterborough, ON: Broadview Press, 2004), 44.

[20] Marie-Jeanne Riccoboni, *The Story of Ernestine*, trans. Joan Hinde Stewart and Philip Stewart (New York: The Modern Language Association of America, 1998), 38.

Rousseau's *Julie, ou La Nouvelle Héloïse* (1761; English trans., 1761) exemplifies the unstable construction of sexed nature in the sentimental novel. Translated into 'at least nine separate English editions' from 1761 to 1795, with a positive 'majority' of reviews praising such things as its 'elocution, fire, and sensibility' (Warner 1937: 809, 810), the epistolary novel *Julie* relates the irresistible, and briefly consummated, amorous attraction between Julie and her tutor St Preux. Six years after her father compels Julie to marry the more eligible Wolmar, St Preux returns from abroad to live with the family in virtuous harmony. Like *Emile*, which argues that sexed 'inequality is not a human institution' (361) but a natural one, *Julie* invokes feminine essence in exhortations like the following, written to Julie by her cousin Claire:

> What separates us from men, is nature itself which prescribes us different occupations; it is that sweet and timid modesty...it is that attentive and provocative reserve which, fomenting in men's hearts both desires and respect, serves so to speak as virtue's coquetry....That is why the most honest wives in general keep the most sway over their husbands; because with the help of that wise and discrete [*sic*] reserve, without caprice or refusals, they know within the tenderest union the art of keeping them at a certain distance, and never let them become sated with them.[21]

Remarkably, the 'nature' invoked by Claire to justify women's 'different occupations' mutates into her defence of the 'art' wives must practise to sustain their husbands' erotic appetite. Rousseau's 'nature' both precedes and enables culture, for Claire's advice is motivated by an institutional economy in which wives must captivate husbands who have legal and social sanction to stray. The circularity typified by wives whose 'sweet and timid reserve' is both sexed essence and post-marital expedient reveals the recursive construction—or, as Judith Butler (1993) might say, the constitutive iterability—of Rousseauvian femininity.

Nowhere does Rousseau depart further from the premises of Richardsonian writing to the moment than when Julie submits to a forced marriage. On the day of the ceremony, she writes to St Preux: 'At the very moment when I was ready to swear everlasting fidelity to another, my heart still swore an everlasting love to you.' But narrating her experience at the altar, Julie continues:

> The purity, the dignity, the holiness of marriage, so vividly set forth in the words of Scripture, those chaste and sublime duties so important to happiness, to order, to peace, to the survival of mankind...all this made such an impression on me that I seemed to experience within me a sudden revolution. It was as if an unknown power repaired all at once the disorder of my affections and re-established them in accordance with the law of duty and nature...

---

[21] Jean-Jacques Rousseau, *Julie, or the New Heloise*, trans. Philip Stewart and Jean Vaché (Hanover, NH: Dartmouth College Press, 1997), 411.

I could bear myself witness that no tender memory had profaned the solemn engagement into which I had just entered. (291–2)

Julie uses the language of Lockean empiricism to cite her 'impression' by the magnitude
of the commitment that her own thoughts must ratify. But when she testifies that she
retains 'no tender memory' of the man to whom she writes, she betrays an empirical
model of understanding that, as we have seen with Locke's mirror analogy, cannot efface
its ideas on command. *Julie*'s abrupt eradication of the 'everlasting love' that Julie 'swore'
to her correspondent on the previous page suggests that Rousseauvian sentiment and its
novelistic form may be less committed to the demands of empirical understanding than
to those of patriarchy.

The extra-epistolary utility of the 'unknown power' that submits Julie's willingness
to wed to 'a sudden revolution' opposes other, less sanguine renditions of the relation
between epistolary form and 'the law of duty', such as when the protagonist of *Julia de
Roubigné* (1777)—Mackenzie's own rendition of *Julie*—evokes her own forced marriage to
refer to herself as 'the silent ~~victim~~ [sic] of the scene, (why should I score through that word
when writing to you? yet it is a bad one, and I pray you to forgive it,)' (68). Frances Sheridan,
who dedicates her epistolary *Memoirs of Miss Sidney Bidulph* (1761) to Richardson, deploys
parenthetical disclaimers to deny—at the same time that they elicit—ideas of the man
whose love her mother has forced Sidney to disavow for another: 'I told her, my heart
was not engaged (as it really is not; for indeed...I do not think of [him]).'[22] Mackenzie and
Sheridan place extreme typographical pressure upon an epistolary form that would make
transparent the entirety of the mind's content. The parentheses and scorings of these
reluctant but virtuous brides-to-be manifest, in the stress they place upon the opaque
materiality of a letter that cannot otherwise communicate undutiful thought, an unspoken but palpable critique of women's lack of marital self-determination under patriarchy.

While Sheridan and Mackenzie exploit typography to gesture towards the intractable
resistance of the 'heart' to external command, Rousseau subverts the empiricist and—
insofar as Julie instantaneously loses her amorous 'memory'—narrative allegiances
of Richardsonian form, privileging instead discontinuous intensities of feeling whose
abrupt reversals permit Julie's instantaneous 'repair'. *Julie* thus illuminates another development in sentimental fiction of the 1760s and 1770s, the tension between present-tense
impression as opposed to narrative or lateral commitments that implicate sentiment in
structures impervious to feeling. The incompatibility of lateral and discontinuous modes
is captured in Julia de Roubigné's introduction to the letters that make up her novel: 'I
found it a difficult task to reduce them into narrative, because they are made up of sentiment, which narrative would destroy' (5). Mackenzie's episodic and fragmented *Man of*

---

[22] Frances Sheridan, *Memoirs of Miss Sidney Bidulph*, ed. Sue Townsend (London: Pandora Press,
1987), 74–5.

Feeling realizes sentiment's departure from narrative with a novel whose form reflects the dismemberment inherent in its source text, a 'bundle of papers' used prior to their supposed editor's transcription as a rifle's 'wadding' (48).

Aesthetics, Judgement, and Meta-sentimental Critique

Sentimental novels of these decades are highly aware of their philosophical, figural, and generic conventions; many of them intermittently subvert moralizing, sympathizing, or feminizing reflex, whether by amplifying the textuality of feeling's representation or by foregrounding feeling's improbable excess. These novels employ sentimental discourse as the vehicle of what might be called meta-sentimental critique to query the sentimental actor's powers of judgement and, inextricably, the resemblance of sentimental and aesthetic objects. The sympathetic person's ability to determine who or what elicits feeling, and the conversion of sympathy into deracinated sensation, are addressed in Sterne's *A Sentimental Journey* (1768), Goldsmith's *Vicar of Wakefield*, Mackenzie's *Julia de Roubigné*, and Sarah Scott's *The History of Sir George Ellison* (1766). But other, less obtrusively self-critical texts—even those that promote sentimental mechanism as public policy—broach the same liabilities.

Yorick, the protagonist of *A Sentimental Journey*, poses the problem of sentimental judgement when he insists that his innkeeper, Monsieur Dessein, feels for a rental carriage that sits unused in the coach-yard. Dessein begins by disclaiming:

> I have no interest—Except the interest, said I, which men of a certain turn of mind take, Mons. Dessein, in their own sensations—I'm persuaded, to a man who feels for others as well as for himself, every rainy night, disguise it as you will, must cast a damp upon your spirits—You suffer, Mons. Dessein, as much as the machine—[23]

By suggesting that what connects Dessein to the coach is his 'interest' in his 'own sensations', Yorick deploys a notion of sympathy that, as we have seen, predicates a person's responsiveness to the other's suffering on his ability to internalize it as his own. But Yorick pokes fun at Dessein's sympathetic introjection of dampness, since Dessein's capacity to 'feel[] for others' is no more, as Yorick deftly evokes it, than the potentially gratuitous capacity to feel 'for himself'. Of course, because Dessein can only suffer 'as much as the machine', he may not suffer at all, since feeling 'as much as' something inanimate means feeling nothing. Indeed, by feeling as much as the machine Dessein may, like the soulless protagonist of Julien Offray de la Mettrie's materialist manifesto *Machine Man* (1747; English trans., 1748), himself become a machine. Both versions of meta-sentimental

---

[23] Laurence Sterne, *A Sentimental Journey through France and Italy*, ed. Ian Jack (Oxford: Oxford University Press, 1984), 14.

critique—Dessein feels for machines with no feeling, or Dessein's feeling makes him a machine—challenge the moral agency of sympathetic suffering. As the pretext for feeling that becomes real only when it is Dessein's own, suffering is constitutively fictional; as indiscriminate reflex, sympathetic distress turns men into machines.

Goldsmith's *Vicar of Wakefield* also poses the problem of sentimental judgement. Rather than interrogating sympathetic mechanism, however, the vicar animates the pitfalls of Rousseau's equation of virtuous innocence and insulation from modern culture. Novels like Mackenzie's *Man of Feeling* offer as a litmus of virtue susceptibility to the artifices of various sharpers and pretenders; rather than manifesting stupid gullibility, Mackenzie's protagonist Harley inhabits a semantic universe untainted by hypocrisy, guile, sophistication, or any linguistic abstraction that would deviate from Locke's claim for the initial correspondence of words to sensory impressions. Vulnerability to the schemes of others is the sentimental flip-side of proneness to dispense charity, for both define a state of receptivity to linguistic representation uncompromised by the intimation that words can deceive. Goldsmith's vicar, however, illustrates at least one way in which sentimental credulity blurs into a less defensible suspension of judgement when, at a dance hosted by Sir William Thornhill's dissipated nephew, he observes some attendant 'ladies':

> [They] threw my girls quite into the shade; for they would talk of nothing but high life, and high lived company; with other fashionable topics, such as pictures, taste, Shakespear.... 'Tis true they once or twice mortified us sensibly by slipping out an oath; but that appeared to me as the surest symptom of their distinction, (tho' I am since informed that swearing is perfectly unfashionable.) (46)

The vicar's elision of 'fashion' and corruption levels 'Shakespear', 'pictures', and profanity; more gravely, his reliance on routine signs of 'distinction' renders him unable to evaluate its content. His failure to discern the shoddiness of a simulation of feminine virtue whose performers 'slip[] out an oath' converts Rousseauvian innocence into fecklessness, comically realized as the vicar's failure to differentiate the viciousness of these falsely elevated 'ladies' from his social aspirations for 'my girls'. As a subspecies of sentimental credulity, inapprehension of the snares that lead to feminine ruin results in the seduction and demise of the vicar's eldest daughter, although Goldsmith restores her to respectability in a twist whose flagrant wish-fulfilment—and whose antagonism to narrative continuity—the novel foregrounds as her resurrection from death.

An aphorism pronounced by Yorick in *A Sentimental Journey* transmits the meta-sentimental critique of moral mechanism: 'When the heart flies out before the understanding, it saves the judgment a world of pains' (16). As we have seen, Dessein's 'heart flies out' even before he determines the sentience of his object. In the vicar's case, the Rousseauvian equation of moral virtue and cultural illiteracy renders him unable to adjudicate feminine value. A related target of meta-sentimental critique is the encroaching autonomy of feeling, its detachability from historical or narrative context, which we find in Mackenzie's *Julia de Roubigné* when the eponymous protagonist seizes upon her family's lost fortune as an opportunity for sentimental representation:

> [I]n my hours of visionary indulgence, I have sometimes painted to myself a husband—no matter whom—comforting me amidst the distresses which fortune had laid upon us. I have smiled upon him through my tears; tears, not of anguish, but of tenderness;—our children were playing around us, unconscious of misfortune; we had taught them to be humble and to be happy;—our little shed was reserved to us, and their smiles to cheer it—I have imagined the luxury of such a scene, and affliction became a part of my dream of happiness. (16)

This passage hints at the perversely anti-historical force of a 'dream of happiness' sustained not despite but because of material 'distresses'. Poverty that inspires 'visionary indulgence' rather than physical discomfort foregrounds the fictionality of distress whose status as representation—as ideas that must be 'painted to myself'—dissolves even the vestigial reality that occasions it. A depoliticized appropriation of Rousseau's defence of agrarian simplicity, Julia's fantasy transforms poverty into the occasion for an even more rarefied experience of 'luxury'. Her projected 'husband—no matter whom' amplifies this scene's generic specification of shared 'tenderness', which might suggest not only that sentimental 'virtue is utterly stylized' (Mullan 1988: 120) but also that its catalyst, in this case poverty, is stylized likewise.

Painted to herself in stylized terms, the 'misfortune' that facilitates Julia's visionary indulgence resembles the aesthetic object theorized by Burke in his influential treatise *A Philosophical Enquiry into the Origin of our Ideas of the Sublime and Beautiful* (1757). This text's affinity with Smith's *Theory of Moral Sentiments* resides most clearly in Burke's description of sympathy 'as a sort of substitution, by which we are put into the place of another man, and affected in many respects as he is affected',[24] but Burke takes the additional step of claiming sympathetic mechanism as a source of aesthetic feeling, thereby affirming the indifference of fact, fiction, and internalized ideas as movers of a sensorium that cannot distinguish historical from novelistic objects: 'It is by this principle [of sympathy] chiefly that poetry, painting, and other affecting arts, transfuse their passions from one breast to another, and are often capable of grafting a delight on wretchedness, misery, and death itself' (91). Representations that 'transfuse...passions' provoke a 'delight' that overrides not only their prospective historicity but also their manifest content. The importance of the *Enquiry* as a hermeneutic for meta-sentimental critique lies in Burke's recovery of 'wretchedness, misery, and death itself' as entities whose pleasures proceed from the process of their transfusion into the spectator's 'breast'. Rather than narrative details, it is the mechanics of these scenes' internalization that dictate how they will be felt, as Burke

---

[24] Edmund Burke, *A Philosophical Enquiry into the Origin of our Ideas of the Sublime and Beautiful*, ed. David Womersley (London: Penguin, 2004), 91.

stipulates when he specifies that the sublime is produced when ideas 'strike the mind' (106), 'rush in upon the mind' (108), or 'stagger[], and hurry . . . the mind' (123).

Paralysis is one effect of the collapse of sympathetic and aesthetic impression. An equally cogent strand of meta-sentimental critique queries the moral agency of the action that does ensue, charity. In *The Theory of Moral Sentiments*, Smith suggests that because sympathy is engendered by representation, its objects must be vividly perceptible:

> Let us suppose that the great empire of China, with all its myriads of inhabitants, was suddenly swallowed up by an earthquake, and let us consider how a man of humanity in Europe, who had no sort of connexion with that part of the world, would be affected upon receiving intelligence of this dreadful calamity. He would, I imagine, first of all, express very strongly his sorrow for the misfortune of that unhappy people. . . . And when . . . all these humane sentiments had been once fairly expressed, he would pursue his business or his pleasure, take his repose or his diversion, with the same ease and tranquillity, as if no such accident had happened. (136)

The quick return of Smith's 'man of humanity' to an affectively neutral state does not cancel his claim to the 'exquisite sensibility' (9) that Smith cites to differentiate garden-variety sympathy from the heightened susceptibility that distinguishes a subset of more acutely feeling persons. Smith's rather lackadaisical sketch of the fate of 'that unhappy people' justifies this man's easy resumption of pleasure or business: as literally countless 'myriads', Chinese people refuse 'connexion' both because they are far away and because they cannot be brought into representational focus. Julia de Roubigné may dream of marrying no matter whom, but her fantasy husband still occupies her level of resolution (she imagines that she 'smiled upon him through my tears'); Smith's people, however, cannot be resolved into units of sentimental apprehension. As no more than numbers—as numbers that cannot, as symptom of a kind of quantitative orientalism, be counted—myriads mark moral sentiment's outer limit as the failure of abstract ideas to stimulate sympathy.

Remarkable historical evidence for the practical and formal parameters of charitable agency can be found in the anonymous *Histories of Some of the Penitents in the Magdalen House, as Supposed to be Related by Themselves* (1760). Written to promote the institution, in 1758, of London's Magdalen House for the Reception of Penitent Prostitutes, the text's four discontinuous plots fit ruined women's reform to Smithean representational scale. Although the text is formally akin to Sarah Scott's utopian novel *A Description of Millenium Hall* (1762), which is composed of vignettes detailing the causes of women's dependency and destitution, *Magdalen House* avoids the overarching critique of patriarchy that propels Scott's 'female Arcadia'.[25] After an adulterous wife in *Magdalen House* is held prisoner in a mouldering manor by the husband whom she was forced to marry, she remarks of her sons: 'I rejoiced in the sex of my children, as it saved me from all fears of their becoming

---

[25] Sarah Scott, *A Description of Millenium Hall*, ed. Gary Kelly (Peterborough, ON: Broadview Press, 1995), 223.

as forlorn and wretched beings as their mother.'[26] This reference to 'sex' marks the text's most cogent gesture toward structural or institutional complaint, for *Magdalen House* keys feminine penitence to each woman's assumption of privatized blame. The sources of *Magdalen House*'s four penitents' ruin are sentimental and personal, as in the case of the extreme innocence of one new arrival in London, who 'begged pardon for my vulgarity' of a brothel-keeper whose 'bold[ness]' (100) she has dared to point out. *Magdalen House*'s empiricist derivation of the ignorance of this 'young savage' (99) closely resembles that given by Sarah Fielding for her 'fair savage' Ophelia, underscoring the similarity of novelistic representation and history 'supposed to be related' by real penitents. As scenes whose vividness derives from a personalized scale of sentimental resolution, the episodes that vindicate these sufferers' claim to philanthropy prevent the abstraction of women's misfortunes into either structural critique or utopian corrective.

For Locke, abstract ideas herald a fall from the sense impressions that initially furnish the mind, as he explains of young children's inability to consent to simple logical propositions: 'For Words being but empty sounds, any farther than they are signs of our *Ideas*, we cannot but assent to them, as they correspond to those *Ideas* we have' (61). As 'empty sounds' that must be filled by sensory '*Ideas*', '*Words*' revert to emptiness when they are deployed as jargon, system, enthusiasm, or occult philosophy; indeed, the *Essay*'s defining political mandate is to advance a prophylactic epistemology resistant to such abuses. In *A Sentimental Journey*, Sterne dramatizes the repercussions of sentimental morality's empiricist bias. After sympathizing with a caged bird, Yorick decides 'to figure to myself the miseries of confinement' by using 'my imagination':

> I was going to begin with the millions of my fellow creatures born to no inheritance but slavery; but finding, however affecting the picture was, that I could not bring it near me...
> —I took a single captive, and having first shut him up in his dungeon, I then look'd through the twilight of his grated door to take his picture.
> I beheld his body half wasted away with long expectation and confinement, and felt what kind of sickness of heart it was which arises from hope deferr'd...
> ...As I darkened the little light he had, he lifted up a hopeless eye toward the door....He gave a deep sigh—I saw the iron enter into his soul—I burst into tears—I could not sustain the picture of confinement which my fancy had drawn—I started up from my chair, and calling La Fleur, I bid him bespeak me a *remise*, and have it ready at the door of the hotel by nine in the morning. (72–3)

As a variant of Smith's earthquake scenario, this episode inserts a novel expedient, Yorick's attempt to represent a 'single' sufferer. However, the paired impasses of 'I could not bring it near me' and, after Yorick's too successful effort, 'I could not sustain the picture ... my fancy had drawn' reveal that abstract distance and sentimental immediacy are mutually

---

[26] Anon., *The Histories of Some of the Penitents in the Magdalen-House, as Supposed to be Related by Themselves*, ed. Jennie Batchelor and Megan Hiatt (London: Pickering & Chatto, 2007), 167.

to blame for Yorick's imperviousness to the moral demands of 'slavery': he either feels nothing or he feels too much. Sterne's acutely meta-novelistic rendition of how Yorick makes himself feel asserts the near identity of sentimental and aesthetic agency. If Yorick is a spectator who 'beheld', he is first and foremost the artist who 'figure[s]' and 'draw[s]' or indeed, to recall Shaftesbury's mutually ethical and theatrical vision, he is the auteur who 'darkened the little light [the prisoner] had'. An internally generated 'picture' whose purpose is to provoke his own feelings, Yorick's moral auto-stimulation does not, Sterne makes clear, lead him outside the enclosure of his own fancy. As empirical reflection's final turn upon itself, the act of aesthetic or novelistic self-stimulation that renders slavery 'affecting' cannot reattach itself to the 'millions of my fellow creatures' who provide feeling's pretext. At stake in this scene is the capacity of sympathetic mechanism and its representational stimulants to elicit more than a privatized response. If Yorick's initial reference to the slavery of millions entails thought whose projected field of action is scaled not to individual but to structural or taxonomic redress, then this episode suggests that the requirements of sympathetic reactivity might impede its alliance with the necessarily depersonalized discourse that would, by the end of the eighteenth century, marshal ubiquitous human feeling in the name of human rights.

   Sarah Scott's *History of Sir George Ellison* and Mackenzie's *Julia de Roubigné* represent plantation slave ownership as a mode of domestic power justified by the identity of slaves, George Ellison proclaims, and 'my children'.[27] The novels' slave-owners, Ellison and Savillon (in Jamaica and Martinique, respectively), thus practise 'good usage' (Scott, 14) in accordance with the slaves' peculiar status as, Savillon writes, 'declared free, according to the mode prescribed by the laws of the island' (Mackenzie, 100). Ellison extends only qualified freedom to his slaves: he 'did not chuse to consider them slaves, except by ill behaviour they reduced him to the disagreeable necessity of exerting an absolute power over them' (14). As the dissimulation of still 'absolute power' in the premise that slaves will be moved spontaneously to obey, 'good usage' would transform forced subjection into the slaves' sentimental gratitude that their experience is no worse: Ellison's slaves 'threw themselves at my feet, embraced my knees, and lift[ed] up their streaming eyes to heaven' (11). Because, as Markman Ellis observes, 'the ultimate guarantee of Ellison's "gentle" regulations is the normative institutional violence of the system of chattel slavery that surrounds it' (1996: 106), this equivocation of absolute power and gratefully 'streaming eyes' shows the power of sentimental representation to elide 'institutional' complaint. But it also anticipates sentiment's appropriation by far more eloquent speakers than Scott's tearful objects, as when the eponymous narrator of *The Interesting Narrative of the Life of Olaudah Equiano* (1789), a memoir recounting Equiano's own slavery

[27] Sarah Scott, *The History of Sir George Ellison*, ed. Betty Rizzo (Lexington, KY: University of Kentucky Press, 1996), 14. For additional commentary, see Coleman, Chapter 24.

and manumission, compels the reader's sympathetic reaction to distress whose historical antecedents cannot be sublimated.

Scott, whose insistently utopian imagination clashes with her text's excursions into sympathetic causality, gestures toward an unsentimental modality of moral action when she qualifies Ellison's commitment to 'doing some good' with the caveat: 'As this was the constant fixed principle of his mind, it occasioned none of that eagerness and bustle by which starts of benevolence are generally distinguished' (78). Having affirmed the difference of sentimental 'starts' from 'fixed principle', Scott ends *The History of Sir George Ellison* by conceding the antagonism of humanitarian planning to the medium of her novel: 'To enter into more particulars of his beneficence might be tedious' (203). At the horizon of sentimental fiction lies the tedium of concretely reformist 'particulars', whose uneven historical fulfilment testifies to the limits and latent powers of moral feeling that must be stimulated by representation.

8

Bluestocking Women and Rational Female Fiction

BETTY A. SCHELLENBERG

I N a *New York Times* opinion piece entitled 'A Case of Mental Courage' (23 August 2010), American columnist David Brooks described the novelist Frances Burney's 1811 account of her mastectomy without anaesthesia as 'a sort of mental boot camp—an arduous but necessary ordeal if she hoped to be a person of character and courage'. Brooks elaborates:

> Burney's struggle reminds one that character is not only moral, it is also mental. Heroism exists not only on the battlefield or in public but also inside the head, in the ability to face unpleasant thoughts.
>
> She lived at a time when people were more conscious of the fallen nature of men and women. People were held to be inherently sinful, and to be a decent person one had to struggle against one's weakness. In the mental sphere, this meant conquering mental laziness with arduous and sometimes numbingly boring lessons. It meant conquering frivolity by sitting through earnest sermons and speeches. It meant conquering self-approval by staring straight at what was painful. (Brooks 2010)

While Brooks's account of eighteenth-century British culture is generalized for effect, in the service of his critique of what he calls the 'mental flabbiness' of contemporary American culture, his description captures the spirit of 'rational female fiction' as it was inherited and practised by Frances Burney. Through the rubric of rational female fiction, taken as anti-sentimental novels of moral cognition, social survival, and courtship, this chapter will examine views on the emerging novel developed by a loose network of mid-eighteenth-century women who came to be known as the Bluestocking circle, and the legacy of these views for succeeding women novelists. It will look at how Frances Burney's four fictional works can be seen as furthering, while revising, this legacy within an increasingly mainstream novel tradition, but also at how ongoing resistance to this generic mainstream resulted in consistently 'Bluestocking' forms of rational fiction in a primarily Scottish Enlightenment context.

A Bluestocking Theory and Practice of Fiction

To begin an exploration of rational female fiction with the first generation of British Bluestockings may seem unpromising, in that these women were rather unlikely to write what we would call novels (for an exploration of the first-generation Bluestockings' theory of the novel at somewhat greater length see Schellenberg 2010). When they did stray into fictional territory, they didn't take much pride in the fact; indeed, they were careful to distinguish themselves, even as readers, from mere consumers of novels and romances, 'destined to *eternal emptiness*', as Elizabeth Montagu puts it.[1] Yet, as Norma Clarke has illustrated in a discussion of the writings of Catherine Talbot, for many mid-century readers, the use of fiction in the periodical, the sermon, and the devotional manual was increasingly and explicitly endorsed as a tool 'approximat[ing] to the values of polite society: social, pleasant, bent on improvement, not specially earnest, and bookish in a relaxed sort of way' (2005: 460); this endorsement of fiction as device was matched by an ideally 'devotional attitude towards reading in general' (471). Thus the 'novel' that the first generation of Bluestockings—Catherine Talbot, Elizabeth Carter, and Elizabeth Montagu—ultimately accepted and assimilated into their literary horizons was not the novel they initially resisted, whether in the form of the amatory romances of Eliza Haywood or the materialist fantasies of Daniel Defoe, but rather, a deliberately constructed hybrid genre whose theory and practice were inseparable from their allegiance to a rational and benevolent Christianity. The fiction these women endorsed, moreover, was a mode that they helped to entrench, through their culturally influential patronage and modelling.

This mode of fiction reflects three interdependent constants which characterize intellectual women's writing about novels and other forms of literary 'entertainment'. These constants can be traced from Elizabeth Carter and Catherine Talbot's exchanges of the 1740s, to Sarah Fielding, Sarah Scott, and Elizabeth Montagu's statements through the middle decades of the century, to Frances Burney's thirty-five-year span as a publishing novelist beginning in 1778, to the work of Maria Edgeworth, Elizabeth Hamilton, and Susan Edmonstone Ferrier from their widening national perspectives. The first of these constants is a resistance both to absorptive reading and to writing that represents a frivolous or harmful use of intellectual powers—in more positive terms, an insistence that reading engage the mind and be disciplined by rational self-control. This refrain is consistent across decades of their commentary. On 1 December 1750 Carter expresses to Talbot her dislike of Charlotte Lennox's early poem *The Art of Coquetry*, although the poetry is 'uncommonly correct', because '[i]t is intolerably provoking to see people who

---

[1] Elizabeth Montagu, 'Dialogue XXVIII', in George Lyttelton, *Dialogues of the Dead* (London: W. Sandby, 1760), 319.

really appear to have a genius, apply it to such idle unprofitable purposes'.[2] An even younger Scott (then Sarah Robinson) appears to read fiction less for story than for ideas, perusing 'some of David Simple's life' (a reference to the 1744 *Adventures of David Simple*, by Sarah Fielding) in combination with 'the history of Florence & Lord Bacons Essays & the old Plays; Christianity not founded on argument Randolph's answer to it, Fontaines Tales; some of Mr. Harris on arts and happiness'.[3] Finally, as a very elderly woman, Scott rejects Ann Radcliffe's 1794 *Mysteries of Udolpho*, 'which no doubt is well written', because it has been 'too much for [her] weak nerves' (to Montagu, 18 February [1795] mo5519). She had admired Samuel Richardson's skill at 'cook[ing] up a madness' in his 1753–4 *Sir Charles Grandison* (to Montagu, [1754] mo5246), but in the 1790s she will not submerge *herself* in that madness; rather, she resumes control as reader by determining never again to read a novel of 'horrors'. This suggests that a category of rational female fiction challenges some of the fundamental chronological and ideological categories we work with in the history of the novel: the developmental line from 'realist fiction' and 'fiction of moral sentiments' to 'sentimental fiction', for example, or the distinction between politically engaged and domestic novels.

A second, related tenet of the Bluestockings' increasingly self-conscious working model of the novel was a requirement of verisimilitude, a capacious realism that enabled women to look squarely at the realities of female lives, but also represented a broad range of human nature and experience. Thus, still in her early twenties, Scott writes that she has refused to loan 'the Arcadia or any romance' to a young friend for fear it would 'deprav[e] her taste' for her lover, a country squire (to Montagu, May 1744 mo5184), and Montagu wonders of Sarah Fielding 'how ... a virtuous maiden who has lived in single blessedness [could] guess at all the arts of a Wanton Cleopatra?' (to Scott, [1757] mo5765). Yet Carter and Talbot were appreciative of Henry Fielding's 1742 *Joseph Andrews*; reading it at Talbot's recommendation, Carter recognizes it as 'a complete satire', containing a 'surprizing variety of nature, wit, morality, and good sense', as well as a 'spirit of benevolence', and finding it hard to believe that there were those (very likely including their later friend Richardson) who considered it 'a very immoral thing, and of the most dangerous tendency' (1 January 1743, *A Series of Letters*, 1.23–4).

Finally—and this is a less explicitly expressed tenet of the Bluestocking theory of the novel, but it arises out of the first two—the materials of everyday life were never enough; to be human was to consider, to bring a moral and self-disciplined imagination to bear on those materials. Thus a rational theory and practice of fiction, for these women writers

---

[2] *A Series of Letters between Mrs. Elizabeth Carter and Miss Catherine Talbot*, ed. Montagu Pennington, 2 vols (London: F. C. and J. Rivington, 1809), 1.367.

[3] Scott to Montagu [5 June 1744] mo5187. All quotations from the Montagu Collection are by permission of The Huntington Library, San Marino, California, and will be indicated in parentheses in the text.

and readers, served to work against appeals founded upon mere emotion or sensation on the one hand, and a reductive materialism on the other, through a sophisticated appeal to the imagination. While Scott, writing to her sister Montagu about her fictional utopia *A Description of Millenium Hall* (1762), disparages it as 'a thing like that [which] takes so very little time in writing' in contrast to 'a better thing [i.e. a work of history]' ([31 January 1763] mo5300), she also describes its desired effect on its reader as a movement of the mind and the will: 'shou'd it bring into any person's mind and inclination the means of doing one benevolent action, I shall be very happy' ([November 1762] mo5299). In her sequel to *Millenium Hall, The History of Sir George Ellison* (1766), Scott goes further theoretically by reframing the question of factuality—whether there might be a gentleman in Dorsetshire who actually matches the hero of her 'biography'—as a challenge to the moral imagination: she 'hope[s] that the county contains so many gentlemen who resemble Sir George, that several will be pointed [to] as the originals from whence his character is drawn'; failing that, 'If any one should object, that Sir George Ellison is too good to have existed any where but in imagination, I must intreat my censurer will, before he determines this point, endeavour to equal the virtue of Sir George'.[4] Moral possibility created by the novelistic imagination, in other words, is a fitting subject for empirical investigation: the reader cannot judge the realism of Scott's fiction without trying to replicate the social experiment carried out by Sir George. Thus the ideal use of the fictional imagination is to elaborate moral and social improvements which may in turn induce further imaginative activity; to paraphrase Scott, fiction's goal is to bring into readers' minds and inclinations the means of doing benevolent actions. This theory, in turn, underpins the notion of novel-writing and novel criticism as a vocation which begins to be articulated in the latter decades of the century by Frances Burney, Clara Reeve, Maria Edgeworth, and Elizabeth Hamilton.

Karen O'Brien has demonstrated in detail the allegiance of the early Bluestocking writers to a Latitudinarian Enlightenment philosophy articulated by thinkers such as Damaris Masham, Samuel Clarke, Catherine Cockburn, and Joseph Butler. Together with the leading divines Gilbert Burnet, Conyers Middleton, and Thomas Secker, who went out of their way to encourage their wives' and friends' intellectual and theological inquiries, these thinkers offered women a theology that affirmed their capacity for a rational understanding of moral truths. As O'Brien explains, these women found affirmation in arguments by moral philosophers that 'the private affections [were] the source of moral normativity in society', but they stopped short of 'sentimental irrationalism', 'remain[ing] committed to the notion that true virtue, though often prompted by affection, can only really be the quality of a self-reflective, rational being' (2009: 38). Like

---

[4] Sarah Scott, *The History of Sir George Ellison*, ed. Betty Rizzo (Lexington, KY: University Press of Kentucky, 1996), 4.

Alexander Pope in the third epistle of his *Essay on Man* (1733), they viewed the exercise of active benevolence in one's extended household, neighbourhood, and even broader spheres, 'neither as a delusion of egotism nor as a potential distraction from the duty to love God, but as the main business of a virtuous, socially purposeful life' (39).

All writing had the potential to serve as an expression of such benevolence, even the writing of fiction, despite its inferior status to true history; indeed, as Scott's statements quoted above suggest, it was in its extension of history that fiction, as fictional private history, found its vocation. Thus the genealogy of the realist novel, as the Bluestockings understood it, is quite different from that hypothesized by William Warner (1998) as an elevation out of its origins in amatory and romance narratives. This is not to suggest that Warner's account of the succession from an early eighteenth-century suspicion of all fiction to a concerted project of turning the novel to improving ends is inaccurate; indeed, this chapter traces a very similar pattern in the Bluestockings' own remarks on novels in relation to other genres. However, their reading response and critical commentary suggest that the modern novel for them did not evolve primarily, if at all, from what they understood to be 'the novel'. Rather than owing a direct generic debt to plot patterns of desire and transformation, writers such as Scott and the Bluestocking favourite Sarah Fielding blurred the lines between their fictions and the genres of history and biography. For Fielding, it is a given that readers are actuated by a desire to become 'acquainted with the various and surprising Incidents of Mankind'. From this common desire, she argues, can arise either an 'insatiable Curiosity for Novels and Romances', reinforced by a mind 'Infatuated with a Sort of Knight errantry' and 'pleasingly deluded' by 'false Coin, [that is]...rather calculated to deceive, than profit us', or a more healthy taste for the 'grateful Variety,...copious Instruction,...and know[ledge of] itself' offered to the mind by biography. In contrast to the 'false Coin' of novels and romances, biography, 'like current Gold, is of intrinsic Value, and may, with greater Certainty, be disposed of, or applied to our Service and Emolument' by 'inform[ing], and giv[ing] us juster Notions of ourselves'.[5] Again, reading about human experience inevitably activates the mind to exercise imagination; the question is whether the investment will be in counterfeit or real currency—whether this imagination will operate in a space of delusion or in the realms of human nature and action.

The Bluestockings were thus theoretically inclined to valorize fiction that they could approach through the model of instructive private history. In this respect they agreed with Samuel Johnson, whose famous *Rambler* No. 4 essay praises those works of fiction that 'exhibit life in its true state, diversified only by the accidents that daily happen in the world, and influenced by those passions and qualities which are really to be found

---

[5] Sarah Fielding, 'Introduction', *Lives of Cleopatra and Octavia*, 2nd edn (London: for the Author, 1758), i–vii.

in conversing with mankind'.[6] Their practice as readers and writers of fiction was nurtured through encounters with the novelist Samuel Richardson (and his fictions), who encouraged their sense of a calling to exercise their own intellectual gifts through conversational and written response to fiction, and ultimately, the writing of it themselves. Catherine Talbot, for example, became a particular advisor and even collaborator during the period of Richardson's composition of *Sir Charles Grandison*, and Elizabeth Carter's gradual incorporation into the corresponding circle of Talbot, Susannah Highmore, and Richardson shows her learning to discuss responses to reading, as well as her own writing experiences, in a manner that is not visible in her earlier exchanges with local friends or with her London publisher Edward Cave. Sarah Fielding, similarly, composed her 1749 work of novel criticism, *Remarks on Clarissa Addressed to the Author*, as an outgrowth of her mutually respectful relationship with Samuel Richardson, and Hester Mulso (later Chapone) gained a reputation as a poet and essayist through conversation and debate in this context. As some of the evidence above has suggested, these women's appreciation of Richardson's personal qualities of generosity, hospitality, and encouragement to them as authors and rational beings did not translate into unquestioning acceptance of his views of fiction or slavish imitation of his novels; nevertheless, Richardsonian discourse, as Emma Clery has shown, undoubtedly served as a powerful incentive for women in developing their intellectual and social potential through the vehicle of fiction, whether as readers or writers (2004: 138–54).

Frances Burney, the Moral Imagination, and the World

What was for the early Bluestockings an intense commitment to delineating a practical Christian calling for women was easily secularized by succeeding English women novelists because of its very practicality and engagement of this world. For these succeeding generations, an explicit focus on anatomizing and shaping the social order around them through their interventions became part of their claim to professional authority. Clara Reeve's spokesperson Euphrasia, for example, insists in *The Progress of Romance* (1785) that to have studied this generic tradition, culling its 'honey' to 'store in the common Hive', is to 'have performed the duties of a good citizen of the Republic of Letters'.[7] But it is the fiction of Frances Burney, in particular, that insists on invoking 'the World' as the vast social and moral stage on which her heroines, however reluctant, must act; it is in this sense that Margaret Anne Doody calls Burney's 'a deeply political imagination'

[6] Samuel Johnson, *The Rambler, vols 3–5 of The Yale Edition of the Works of Samuel Johnson*, ed. W. J. Bate and Albrecht B. Strauss (New Haven: Yale University Press, 1969), 3.19.

[7] Clara Reeve. *The Progress of Romance through Times, Countries and Manners*, 2 vols (Colchester: W. Keymer, 1785), 2.98.

(2007: 96). George Justice's summary description of *Camilla: or, A Picture of Youth* (1796), can be generalized to apply to all four Burney novels: they offer the reader 'a concentrated representation of [the heroine's] embodied life, in which the politics of being a powerless young woman in the late eighteenth century manifest themselves in the concrete, even realistic depiction of familial and public structures' (2002: 229). Samuel Johnson's and the monthly reviewers' comparisons to Henry Fielding notwithstanding,[8] the permission Burney felt for the ambitious scope of her novels must surely have arisen out of the sense of high calling, both realized and thwarted, of Bluestocking women she deeply admired, such as Elizabeth Carter, Hester Chapone, Elizabeth Montagu, and Hester Thrale, as well as the women novelists they furthered. For example, Burney's early letters and journals allude to Sarah Fielding's *Familiar Letters between the Principal Characters of David Simple* and Scott's 1775 *Agreeable Ugliness* (*Early Journals and Letters*, 2.4–5; 3.105–6). Her admiration of Montagu was tempered by various rivalries, but her respect and liking for Carter, and her pride at being considered a Bluestocking in company with Carter, were unequivocal (*Early Journals and Letters*, 4.136–7; 154; 161; 314). Just as scholars of the late eighteenth century such as Amanda Vickery (1998) and Lawrence E. Klein (1995) have convincingly challenged the rigidly gendered dichotomy of public and private spheres once so influentially claimed by Nancy Armstrong in *Desire and Domestic Fiction* (1987), recent Burney criticism has thoroughly dismissed any notion that 'the World' anatomized in her novels, as the imaginative realm of human nature and custom, is limited to a 'properly' feminine sphere.

The bookends that Frances Burney sets to her novel-writing career adopt the language of the mid-century Bluestockings while appropriating for a nascent novelistic tradition the place that her predecessors had assigned to biography and history. Thus the Preface of *Evelina, or, A Young Lady's Entrance into the World* (1778) situates the work as far as possible from 'the fantastic regions of Romance, where Fiction is coloured by all the gay tints of luxurious Imagination, where Reason is an outcast, and where the sublimity of the *Marvellous* rejects all aid from sober Probability', aligning itself with Rousseau, Johnson, Marivaux, Fielding, Richardson, and Smollett in the camp of 'Nature'.[9] At the other chronological extreme, Burney's preface to *The Wanderer; or Female Difficulties* (1814) elaborates on this novelistic 'nature', the product of the novel's unique species of imaginative realism: '[The Novel] is, or it ought to be, a picture of supposed but natural and probable human existence. It holds, therefore, in its hands our best affections; it exercises our imaginations; it points out the path of honour; and gives to juvenile credulity knowledge of the

---

[8] Francis Burney. *The Early Journals and Letters of Fanny Burney*, ed. Lars E. Troide et al., 4 vols (Montreal and Kingston: McGill-Queen's University Press 1998–2003), 3.114–15; *Monthly Review*, 67 (July 1782), 453.
[9] Frances Burney, *Evelina, or, the History of a Young Lady's Entrance into the World*, ed. Edward A. Bloom, introd. Vivien Jones (Oxford: Oxford University Press, 2002), 9–10.

world, without ruin, or repentance; and the lessons of experience, without its tears'.[10] This exercised imagination is represented as the answer to the problem posed by the *Evelina* preface: there, the desire of young ladies for the imaginative pleasures of novel-reading can only be held at bay with harmless fictions until 'the slow regimen of Time, and bitter diet of Experience' cures them of the 'distemper' (10), whereas by 1814, Burney is prepared to assert, like Jane Austen in *Northanger Abbey* (1818), that the imagination can in fact be harnessed, like the weakened viruses of an inoculation, to provide immunization against the most ruinous forms of 'knowledge of the world'.

The brief overview of Burney's rational fictions permitted in this chapter will focus on a seeming paradox in her version of the rational novel—her tendency to subject her heroines to a bout of madness. This pattern has been most fully examined by Julia Epstein in one of the earliest critical studies of the author. Epstein's title phrase, *The Iron Pen*, is taken from Camilla's bout of mad hallucinations at the climax of Burney's third novel, discussed below. Epstein reads this madness autobiographically, as embodying the impossible situation of Burney the female professional author, caught 'between silence and exposure, and ultimately, between narrative and its interpretations; [the iron pen] represents an industrial rather than a domestic image, a masculine rather than a feminine means of communication: it is a sign of profound discomfort' (1989: 20). In a more recent and equally suggestive analysis of what she labels 'the real madness of selfhood' in Burney's second novel *Cecilia, or Memoirs of an Heiress* (1782), Susan C. Greenfield resituates the motif within the eighteenth-century realist novel's concerns with madness as a response to new ideas about how the mind might work to create a kind of reality of the imaginary, the fictional, or the immaterial that was in tension with material reality and specifically with an equally unreal world of finance. For Burney's fiction, specifically, 'madness' is an extension of the sensibility, idealism, and rich imagination of her heroines' minds; this is what makes them attractive as heroines. In her second novel, madness, according to Greenfield, is 'all Cecilia has to escape the commerce that degrades her and everyone else'—'mind, for all its profound limitations, is the only redemptive alternative in the modern world' (2004: 62). If we posit Burney as the secular heir of a Bluestocking tradition which values the rationally guided imagination as the God-given source of benevolent action in the world, it is not difficult to see how Cecilia's psychic breakdown comments on a society whose venality and base materialism offer no points of contact for the enlightened mind, with its imaginative recognition of moral truths.

Yet it must be noted that Cecilia also emerges from her madness in a return to, and reconciliation with, that modern world. In the novel's famous conclusion, which Burney as

---

[10] Frances Burney, *The Wanderer; or, Female Difficulties*, ed. Margaret Anne Doody, Robert L. Mack, and Peter Sabor (Oxford: Oxford University Press, 1991), 8–11. For the comparable passage in Austen, see *Northanger Abbey*, ed. Barbara M. Benedict and Deirdre Le Faye (Cambridge: Cambridge University Press, 2006), vol. 1, ch. 5; 30–1.

famously insisted on as the foundation of her entire project ('if I am made to give up this point, my whole plan is rendered abortive, and the last page of any novel in Mr. Noble's circulating library may serve for the last page of mine'),[11] she asserts that a moderate happiness is made available to one who applies her powers of mind to a survey of this imperfect world:

> The upright mind of Cecilia, her purity, her virtue, and the moderation of her wishes, gave to her in the warm affection of Lady Delvile, and the unremitting fondness of Mortimer, all the happiness human life seems capable of receiving:—yet human it was, and as such imperfect! she knew that, at times, the whole family must murmur at her loss of fortune, and at times she murmured herself to be thus portionless, tho' an HEIRESS. Rationally, however, she surveyed the world at large, and finding that of the few who had any happiness, there were none without some misery, she checked the rising sigh of repining mortality, and, grateful with general felicity, bore partial evil with chearfullest resignation.[12]

While Cecilia's madness might, in this sense, be the purest representation by Burney of the challenge faced by the self-reflexive and benevolent imagination that will not console itself, for whatever reason, in the promise of happiness beyond human life, a similar tension operates to varying degrees for each of her heroines. Even Evelina, protagonist of Burney's more comic first novel, when trapped between the callous and grasping Branghtons of this world and the demands placed on her more comprehending mind, describes herself as moving in and out of control of her faculties, fainting from shock after saving the Branghtons' hapless lodger Macartney from suicide and 'half-frantic' and 'rav[ing]' at her cousins' misuse of her acquaintance with Lord Orville (*Evelina*, 249). Utterly disillusioned by Orville's apparent attempt (through a letter later exposed as a forgery) to take advantage of her, she exclaims, 'Never, never again will I trust to appearances,—never confide in my own weak judgment, . . . What cruel maxims are we taught by a knowledge of the world!' (256–7). Evelina's individual story is more optimistic than Cecilia's in enabling her to acquire worldly experience and judgement at the cost only of short-term illness and for the reward of Orville's hand in marriage, but as Vivien Jones has noted, 'this "happy" ending is hard won and remains precarious', and the unresolved presence of the licentious and sadistic Lord Merton in the family Evelina marries into 'speaks of the limits rather than the confident ascendancy of the sentimental community' (Jones 2002: xxxi, xxxiii). Nevertheless, both Evelina and Cecilia, while temporarily overwhelmed by a world so alien to their values, are dealt relatively good odds in engaging the complex and degenerate world around them because of their solid educations, reputable connections, and fundamentally good judgement. Burney's later heroines, by contrast,

---

[11] Francis Burney, *Diary and Letters of Madame D'Arblay*, 6 vols, ed. Charlotte Barrett, preface and notes Austin Dobson (London: Macmillan, 1905), 2.80–1.

[12] Frances Burney, *Cecilia, or Memoirs of an Heiress*, ed. Margaret Anne Doody and Peter Sabor (Oxford and New York: Oxford University Press, 1988), vol. 5, ch. 10; 941.

are placed in heightened positions of vulnerability that cast into stark relief the range of ineffective, self-indulgent, prejudiced, callous, and predatory behaviours that make up the society they are thrust into.

In *Camilla*, the eponymous heroine (and to a lesser extent her siblings and her foster brother/lover Edgar) encounters an almost surreal range of eccentric characters representing 'the [wild] wonders of the Heart of man; that amazing assemblage of all possible contrarieties'.[13] Burney's own letters describe the work in progress as 'of the same species as Evelina & Cecilia: new *modified*, in being more multifarious in the Characters it brings into action,—but all *wove* into *one*, with one *Heroine* shining conspicuous through the Group' (*Diary and Letters*, 3.129). This heroine finds the hidden motives of those she encounters, the 'perverseness of spirit which grafts desire on what is denied' (*Camilla* 7), beyond her comprehension, which renders it impossible for her to navigate her world successfully. After a lengthy series of errors whose consequences are far out of proportion to her moral culpability, Camilla, under the emotional force of guilt at hurting her family, allows her undisciplined imagination to veer into a solipsistic preoccupation with the remorse and forgiveness she would win from her estranged relations should she die an untimely death. Imagination succeeds to madness when her conscience resumes the 'reins' of her mind and reminds her of the further suffering she would inflict on her family thereby (872). Her return to mental health is effected by her reconnection with Edgar, whose 'anguish [at] her situation' leads Camilla to a kind of resurrection to the world and its social ties (878). Despite the somewhat lurid colouring of the novel's denouement, Camilla's adventures beyond the sheltered circle of her family and neighbourhood, at Tunbridge Wells and Southampton, could be pointed to as an education in life skills and judgement, as an ensuing discussion of Edgeworth's *Belinda* will note.

While the sources of the pressures on these heroines' minds are not identical, in each case the protagonist can be seen to stand in for the reader who must learn to follow 'the path of honour' through 'the World', by cultivating a rational, benevolent imagination. This condition holds despite the fact that Burney's idealistic heroines are faced with a world that is deeply flawed, in whose capacity for moral improvement they do not feel the optimism of the earlier Bluestocking women. In Doody's formulation, 'From *Cecilia* on, Burney seizes upon a central political paradox: the good society needs the good individual, but society is not good' (2007: 96). Nevertheless, even under the threat of a maddening dissonance between what they see and what they can imagine, they insist on the value of the goals of self-knowledge and knowledge of the world.

Returning to an even more extreme, yet still objectively caused, psychological distress, Burney subjects her final heroine, the mysterious Juliet Granville of *The Wanderer*, to

---

[13] Frances Burney, *Camilla, or a Picture of Youth*, ed. Edward A. Bloom and Lillian D. Bloom (Oxford: Oxford University Press, 1983), 7.

almost unremitting horrors of mind arising out of social and moral chaos in one nation, exacerbated by the callous and fragmented social order of another. In a study of the notoriously negative critical responses to Burney's *Wanderer* (and to Maria Edgeworth's *Patronage*, 1814), Mark Schoenfield has noted how the anxieties experienced by Juliet over the implications of her attempts at employment and her forced marriage in revolutionary France were dismissed by the *Edinburgh* and the *Quarterly* reviews as excessive delicacy, as 'imagined' obstacles, rather than as significant political, legal, and economic issues facing women (2002: 68–70). Observing that it is the heroine's difficult experiences with the excesses of a patriarchy she has internalized that have left her suffering from 'a paranoia indistinguishable from her material fears', Schoenfield argues that William Hazlitt, the *Edinburgh* reviewer, by satirizing these fears as 'obstacles, lighter than "the gossamer that idles in the wanton summer air"', which the author has raised 'into insurmountable difficulties', denies the novel a political reading (69). In thus wilfully misreading Burney's delineation of 'Female Difficulties' of the imaginative kind, the reviewers are at the same time repudiating a tradition that began with the Bluestockings' elaboration of a theory of the rationally guided imagination as a means of showing the reader herself and the world.

The Later Rational Tradition

Critics such as Clifford Siskin (1998) have identified a not unrelated shift by which the views of Hazlitt and other *Edinburgh* reviewers were influential in directing the mainstream of the domestic novel in the direction represented by Jane Austen's two or three families in a country village (193–203, 224–5). It can be argued, however, that the principal current of rational female fiction extends from *Evelina, Cecilia*, and *Camilla* not to Austen's circumscribed landscapes, no matter how considerable her debt to Burney, and not even to the heightened emotional register of Burney's own final novel, but rather to the fictions of some of Burney's and Hazlitt's most accomplished contemporaries who insisted on the capacities of both female characters and, through them, the societies they inhabited, to act upon rational and moral principles. Maria Edgeworth, Elizabeth Hamilton, and Susan Ferrier's respective 'courtship' novels *Belinda* (1801), *Memoirs of Modern Philosophers* (1800), and *Marriage* (1818), for example, use the occasion of a young woman's entrance into society to comment on a broad range of educational, social, moral, and political issues that would have been highly resonant for their contemporary readers. Like the early Burney and the first-generation Bluestockings before her, these writers continue to express self-consciousness about the novel genre, but their tendency to incorporate into their fiction defensive or even disparaging commentary on novels, and especially on stereotypically young, female readers of novels, signifies more than the 'ungenerous and impolitic' self-loathing roundly condemned by Austen in *Northanger Abbey* (vol. 1, ch. 5; 30). As Katherine Binhammer has argued in a discussion of female novel-reading in Mary

Hays and Hamilton, by the end of the eighteenth century, writers 'integrated' critical attacks on novel-reading into their own works in order to 'interrupt[] and revis[e] the model of reading [such attacks] assume' (2003: 2). In so doing, they 'construct the active female reader by shifting attention from *what* a woman reads to *how* she reads, and the *how* necessarily brings to the foreground questions concerning the cultural conditions of female education' (5). Thus the heroines of Edgeworth and Austen are directed in turn to *Cecilia* and/or *Camilla* as to resources which offer them 'the most thorough knowledge of human nature' and 'the happiest delineation of its varieties' *(Northanger Abbey*, vol. 1, ch. 5; 31). Like the young Sarah Scott selectively reading portions of Sarah Fielding's *David Simple* before her, Edgeworth's Belinda is referred specifically to one element of Camilla's experience—that of being drawn into costly clothing expenditures by the manipulative Mrs Mitten.[14] The implication is that effective reading was expected to involve acts of judgement—memory, generalization, and selective application in response to specific needs—rather than an unreflecting emotional identification.

Indeed, in a witty and significant turn, the reference to *Camilla* in *Belinda* has the heroine being teased by Lady Delacour, precisely the character whom Belinda must judge as like, yet unlike, Mrs Mitten. Embedded in a chapter in which we find that Belinda is, 'for the first time in her life . . . reason[ing] for herself upon what she [sees] and [feels]', the point is surely that to be a heroine is not, as Lady Delacour asserts, to refuse to 'open [one's] eyes, which heroines make it a principle never to do—or else there would be an end of the novel' *(Belinda*, ch. 5; 69; ch. 6; 83), but rather to proceed with one's eyes open, to learn from Lady Delacour's bitter experience without being tainted by it. Edgeworth's heroine, unlike the ignorant and ill-equipped Camilla, is repeatedly able to bring reason and vicarious experience—including the experience of preceding novel heroines—to bear in navigating social waters that are not entirely uncharted: marriages motivated by interest, the pressures of polite society towards hypocrisy, the threats posed by gossip, the problem of a first and second love. Belinda thus has an advantage over Burney's heroines, who struggle to maintain their grasp on good sense in societies that are themselves increasingly mad, careering towards destruction through the irrational channels of consumerism, sentimental self-indulgence, and, culminating in the world of *The Wanderer's* Juliet, solipsistic and materialistic repudiation of any higher good. In this sense, Edgeworth's social world, despite the instabilities resulting from flawed models of female education and pernicious radical philosophy, is one that is governed by certain laws of human behaviour, and therefore can be read and successfully engaged by the heroine as moral agent. Perhaps for this reason, any loss of wits, real or threatened, is firmly relegated to characters whose undisciplined imaginations prevent, rather than heighten, their perception of social

---

[14] Maria Edgeworth, *Belinda*, ed. Kathryn Kirkpatrick (Oxford: Oxford University Press, 1994), ch. 5; 72.

realities—characters like Lady Delacour, whose 'understanding, weakened perhaps by disease, and never accustomed to reason, [is] incapable of distinguishing between truth and errour; and [whose] temper, naturally enthusiastic, hurrie[s] her from one extreme to the other—from thoughtless scepticism to visionary credulity' (ch. 20; 270).

Clíona Ó Gallchoir has noted that Edgeworth relied on Scottish Enlightenment thought in her post-revolutionary writings as a means of insisting on the place of educated women in a rational public sphere that did not define itself against, but rather included, the domestic (2005: 32–7). In her study of *Women Writers in the Edinburgh Enlightenment* (2010), Pam Perkins explores in detail the influence of an Edinburgh-centred intellectual praxis on Elizabeth Hamilton, with whom Edgeworth felt a great affinity as a writer. Claiming that this 'Athens of the North' brought together philosophers, scientists, conjectural historians, reviewers, and literary women in a kind of intellectually focused sociability reminiscent of that of the first-generation English Bluestockings, Perkins demonstrates that, despite a tendency to use the term 'Bluestocking' and its derivatives pejoratively in turn-of-the-century Scotland as in England, there is a very real sense in which Hamilton embodied the Bluestocking legacy as it has been characterized in this chapter. In writings that blur the boundaries of fiction, history, moral philosophy, and educational theory, Hamilton insists throughout her authorial career on rational judgement as the basis of right conduct, whether that of a mother, an educator, an author, or what encompasses all of these, a contributing member of society. Critics have argued convincingly for Hamilton's reflection of Edinburgh philosopher Dugald Stewart's Common Sense moral philosophy and his emphasis on enlightened women's role in the creation of a morally strong commercial society (Price 2002; Rendall 2005: 334; O'Brien 2009: 204–5). Perkins observes that:

> Hamilton's writing…is, in significant ways, social. On the most basic structural level, much of Hamilton's work is underpinned by representations of intellectual debate (much of it parodic but some of it serious)….In effect, the books blur the distinction between domestic conversation and the public exchange and promulgation of philosophical and political ideas. (2010: 63)

It is by means of this conversational sociability that Hamilton draws readers into the uniquely active and rational form of engagement endorsed by rational female fiction. Hamilton's first major publication, the fictional *Translation of the Letters of a Hindoo Rajah*, published in 1796 just a month before Burney's *Camilla*, owes its most obvious debts to the oriental tale and the satirical fiction of the naive outside observer of a society. Yet it can also be seen as a 'translation' of the model of the young ingénue who comes to London to encounter a wide range of contemporary social types and issues, not the least of which, in terms of emphasis, is the issue of female education and the products of various approaches to it. The latter portion of the novel presents a spectrum of three intelligent sisters receiving, at one extreme, a 'masculine' education in all branches of knowledge, but without training in judgement; in a second case, a similar education that also includes high notions of duty, decorum, and Christian excellence; and at the opposite extreme, a boarding-school education in accomplishments, haughtiness, and excessive sensibility. Through an episode in which the sisters respond variously to an accident victim, Hamilton clearly ranks these alternative models, with 'masculine' knowledge valued above deliberate ignorance and selfish sensibility, but proving inferior to an education that not only prepares the female mind 'to fill its place in the scale of rational beings', but also disciplines both reason and 'brilliancy of imagination' so that 'benevolence becomes a principle of action'.[15] Hamilton's explicit emphasis throughout this work on 'the old system of Christianity, as it was taught by Jesus Christ and his Apostles' (*Translation*, 241), together with her deployment of a detached, episodic structure of satiric vignettes, harkens back as well to the values and methods of mid-century Bluestocking works such as Sarah Scott's *Description of Millenium Hall* and Sarah Fielding's *David Simple*.

In her 1800 novel *Memoirs of Modern Philosophers*, Hamilton uses a spectrum of female educational methods and ensuing courtships as the central structuring device of her text—a debt to the conception of *Camilla*, with its comparative focus on the characters and educations of four young girls. As signalled by the title, and reflecting the model of intellectual debate highlighted by Perkins as fundamental to Hamilton's novels, the 'social' landscape to be navigated by her trio of heroines is essentially one of the mind: they not only participate in intellectual debates with mentors, suitors, and intimate female friends, but their very social survival depends on their ability to distinguish specious from true logic, an overheated imagination from one guided by reason, and above all, transcendent moral truths from unmoored, self-serving philosophies of the moment. Harriet Orwell, Hamilton's model of female exemplarity at the centre of the text and of the moral spectrum, is carefully distinguished, as a rationally judging, morally and emotionally disciplined woman, from the intellectually gifted yet morally indiscriminate philosopher Bridgetina Botherim on the one side and the extremely sensitive, emotionally driven Julia Delmont on the other. It is no accident that Harriet is the educational product of her tolerant and reasonable clergyman father and is beloved by a dissenting minister's son, Henry Sydney, whose recent excursion to Scotland inspires him to enthusiastic praise of Scottish Presbyterianism and its educational and moral influence in the lowland villages he visited. The characters of Bridgetina and Julia are the product of undisciplined and indiscriminate reading in both radical philosophy and novels, and as a result they ignorantly reject, as prejudice and enthusiasm, the very Christian moral standard that would 'allay[] the ferment of imagination' and keep it subject to steady reason.[16] By the time they throw themselves into the wider social world in the form of impulsive elopements to

---

[15] Elizabeth Hamilton, *Translation of the Letters of a Hindoo Rajah*, ed. Pamela Perkins and Shannon Russell (Peterborough, ON: Broadview Press, 1999), 220–2, 274–8.

[16] Elizabeth Hamilton, *Memoirs of the Modern Philosophers*, ed. Claire Grogan (Peterborough, ON: Broadview Press, 2000), 164.

London, they are victimized on the streets and in private spaces by self-serving sharpers; Harriet Orwell, on the other hand, visiting London under the guidance of the enlightened Bluestocking Mrs Fielding, finds there a cultural and social landscape that calls forth her admirable traits of judgement and charity. Janice Thaddeus has noted that the 'central theme' of this novel, as indeed of all Hamilton's writing, is 'the interaction of character and environment' (1995: 279); with reference to Hamilton's *Letters on the Elementary Principles of Education* (1801), Thaddeus adds that Hamilton's (like Edgeworth's) specific contribution to this theme is to assert 'that character can change environment, that those who are aware of their socially constructed personalities are free to change their condition' (279)—an assertion embodied in Hamilton's popular final novel, *The Cottagers of Glenburnie* (1808). In this respect again, Hamilton returns full circle to the spirit of the English Bluestockings, in the belief she shares with them in the power of 'domestic politics' (Thaddeus's term, again)—the belief that women possessed a unique asset in their intimate, practical knowledge of varieties of human nature, which they could use to powerful moral ends if they would apply rational analysis to those observations.

Hamilton was not the only female novelist committed to surveying a wide social landscape from an explicitly rational, Christian, and Scottish perspective. *Marriage* (1818), Susan Ferrier's first work of fiction, juxtaposes the stories of a mother—Lady Juliana, an ill-educated and impulsive English heiress who marries her Scottish lover, travels with him to rural Scotland, returns to London with one of her twin daughters, and dispatches her husband to permanent oblivion in India while she lives in fashionable discontent in London—and her abandoned daughter Mary, raised in Scotland by a wise and loving aunt who is similarly half English, half Scottish. This aunt, who as a young woman experienced both London's 'frivolity of beauty, . . . heartlessness of fashion, and . . . insipidity of elegance' and Edinburgh society's contrasting 'exalting enjoyment produced by a communion of intellect',[17] has educated Mary in the 'purest principles of religion' (vol. 2, ch. 1; 158) and therefore in the rational judgement and firm moral framework that enable her to negotiate the pitfalls of English high society when her mother is shamed into receiving her as a marriageable young woman. Like Edgeworth's Belinda and Burney's Evelina and Cecilia before her, Mary is forced by the inadequacies of those who should be her guides—beginning with a French-novel-reading mother completely lacking in self-knowledge, judgement of character, moral reflection, or maternal affection—to chart her solitary course; unlike those heroines, her deliberations are guided by the unfashionable Christian precepts of her Scottish upbringing.

Binhammer has suggested that 'escalating attacks on the novel' at the end of the eighteenth century 'paradoxically asserted the novel's centrality to literary production and

---

[17] Susan Ferrier, *Marriage*, ed. Herbert Foltinek, introd. Kathryn Kirkpatrick (Oxford: Oxford University Press, 1997), vol. 1, ch. 14; 89.

ultimately had the positive effect of differentiating certain kinds of novels from others and certain scenes of reading from others' (2003: 3). In turning an initial uneasiness about fiction to a theory of the novel that valorized rational self-control, a capacious realism, and the individual exercise of a benevolent moral imagination, the mid-eighteenth-century Bluestockings endorsed, and sometimes themselves wrote, fiction that insisted on the sort of 'mental courage' later exhibited by Frances Burney in submitting to the surgical knife without anaesthetic. In doing so, they established novel-writing as a serious vocation for later women writers such as Burney, Maria Edgeworth, Elizabeth Hamilton, and Susan Ferrier. Together these novelists claimed for their own sex a heroism that began, in Brooks's words, 'inside the head, in the ability to face unpleasant thoughts' and to 'conquer[] self-approval by staring straight at what was painful'. Though such heroism might at times set a female protagonist apart from the society around her, and even push her to the brink of madness, its promised reward for readers, female as well as male, was knowledge of a world very like their own, the possibility of doing some good in it, and knowledge of themselves.

9

The Novel of Sensibility in the 1780s

CAROLINE FRANKLIN

Of love take first a due proportion—
It serves to keep the heart in motion:
Of jealousy a powerful zest,
Of all tormenting passions best;
Of horror mix a copious share,
And duels you must never spare;
Hysteric fits at least a score,
Or, if you find occasion, more;
But fainting fits you need not measure,
The fair ones have them at their pleasure;
Of sighs and groans take no account,
But throw them in to vast amount;
A frantic fever you may add,
Most authors make their lovers mad...

From Mary Alcock, 'A Receipt for Writing a Novel' (1799)

In her very first review for Joseph Johnson's rationalist *Analytical Review* Mary Wollstonecraft protested: 'An analysis of novels will seldom be expected, nor can the *cant* of sensibility be tried by any criterion of reason; ridicule should direct its shafts against this fair game.'[1] The object of her impatience, *Edward and Harriet, or the Happy Recovery; A Sentimental Novel*, By a Lady (1788), was one of several 1780s novels which wore their hearts on their sleeves. A few examples suffice: *Anna: A Sentimental Novel* (1782); John Murdoch, *Pictures of the Heart, Sentimentally Delineated in the Danger of the Passions* (1783); *The Sentimental Deceiver: or History of Miss Hammond. A Novel, in a Series of Letters* (1784); *Novellettes Moral and Sentimental*, ed. T. Potter (1785). Laurence Sterne's use of the previously rare adjective 'sentimental' in *A Sentimental Journey* (1768) had popularized its use in book and magazine titles, while the 1783 edition of Chambers's *Cyclopaedia* cited Beattie's observation that the word 'sentiment' was now being used not as 'a formed opinion, notion or principle' but 'an internal impulse of passion, affection, fancy or intellect'.

---

[1] *The Works of Mary Wollstonecraft*, ed. Janet Todd and Marilyn Butler, 7 vols (London: Pickering and Chatto, 1989), 7.19.

The word 'sensibility' had likewise been unusual before the mid-century, having originally denoted the capacity to feel physical sensations rather than emotions. Pejorative
connotations of naivety, artifice or excess are sometimes implied in titles containing the
word, such as: *Unfortunate Sensibility; or, The Life of Mrs. L******. Written by Herself* (1784);
Anna Thomson, *Excessive Sensibility; or, The History of Lady St. Laurence* (1787); and *Female
Sensibility; or, The History of Emma Pomfret* (1783; first published 1778 under a different
title). Yet sensibility was usually viewed as a desirable and pleasurable quality; as the poet
William Cowper averred in a letter to Mrs Margaret King on 19 June 1788 'sensibility is the
sine quâ non of real happiness'.[2]

The philosophy of John Locke, Anthony Ashley Cooper, third Earl of Shaftesbury,
Adam Smith, and Francis Hutcheson had influenced the first wave of epistolary novels
of sensibility beginning in the 1740s. These explored the interaction between emotion
and reason in producing moral actions. Response to stimuli was minutely examined,
especially the relationship between the psychological and physiological manifestations
of feelings. Later in the century, and, in particular during the late 1780s when the novel
enjoyed a surge in popularity, the capacity for fine feeling became increasingly valued
for its own sake rather than moralized. Just over 40 per cent of novels published in the
1780s were epistolary, and the decade also saw the proportion of named women authors
overtaking that of men for the first time. An expanded readership reflected increasing
literacy amongst women, the bourgeoisie, and the young. The 'enthusiasm' of the religious revival produced a secular counterpart in the cult of sensibility, whose novels often
urged the reform of society and discussed difficult issues such as poverty, slavery, and
colonialism. These novels 'mix freely a large number of varied discourses' (Ellis 1996: 8):
the history of ideas, religion, aesthetics, civic humanism, sexuality, and popular culture.

In place of the earlier novels' stylistic emphasis on structure and closure, 'a literature
of process' was inaugurated by Sterne (Frye 1956: 145) which was fragmentary, playfully
digressive, and revelled in satirically exploiting the failure of typographic marks to register emotion. Jean-Jacques Rousseau had influenced *A Sentimental Journey*, and Henry
Mackenzie's *The Man of Feeling* (1771) and *Julia de Roubigné* (1777). German sentimentalism, especially Johann Wolfgang von Goethe's *Die Leiden des jungen Werthers* (1774), first
translated as *The Sorrows of Werter: A German Story* (1779), offered a yet more sensitive,
effeminized, melancholy young man to this controversial series of male-authored novels
challenging traditional masculinity.

Self-consciously 'false' sensibility was denounced and parodied in this fiction which
on the one hand manipulated the reader's emotions, and on the other might humiliate
him/her by insouciantly depicting the pages of a novel being used as wadding for a gun.
For the debate over whether sensibility 'ought to be cherished or repressed', as William

---

[2] *Private Correspondence of William Cowper*, ed. John Johnson, 2 vols (London: Colburn, 1824), 2.143.

Enfield put it,[3] had begun long before the 1790s, though the 'Revolution Debate' undoubtedly politicized the question. However, it would be naive to accept the binaries implied by such a question, or to imagine that there was an incremental tide of silliness which provoked a definitive reaction. For self-parody as well as self-criticism was programmed into the DNA of the genre whose most energetic debunkers were often also its practitioners. So Goethe wrote the satirical 'Der Triumph der Empfindsamkeit' (1778); Mackenzie deplored the moral relativism which pervaded the sentimental novel;[4] and sentimental dramatist Richard Cumberland feared that *Clarissa* would inflame the passions of female readers (Williams 1970: 332). Samuel Jackson Pratt, whose *Emma Corbett* (1780) drenched handkerchiefs on both sides of the Atlantic, had the year before authored *Shenstone-Green; or, The New Paradise Lost* (1779), which validated 'masculine common-sense' and stigmatized sensibility as 'emasculating, morally suspect and socially corrosive' (see London 1999: 141). As Michael Bell argues, 'The longer-term positive impact of sensibility depended on its assimilating the critique it provoked' (2000: 105).

Sensibility should be seen as a long-lasting literary movement rather than an ephemeral fashion. It has been detected in Anglo-American political drama 'as early as the Exclusion Crisis of 1679–81' (Ellison 1999: 16) and certainly survived as the mid-nineteenth century lachrymosity of Charles Dickens and Harriet Beecher Stowe. It put paternal authority and conventional modes of masculinity under question. Neo-classical drama staged dilemmas where a man of authority must choose between civic sacrifice and family love, and novels followed suit by asking if a bourgeois gentleman should embrace the materialistic outlook of an entrepreneur or the Horatian ideal of retirement and benevolence.

The American Revolutionary War

Sensibility is usually linked with subjective interiority. However, the central principle of David Hartley's theory of the human mind—associationism—developed from the idea that the self is externally constituted. The power of sympathy directed the gaze of the sensible self 'outward, not inward', towards society (Wahrman 2004: 187). At the time of the American Revolution, sensibility offered 'to help forge the social bonds of the new republic' (Knott 2009: 237) and to enable its citizens to achieve self-transformation. It promised British Whiggery self-refinement suitable to a meritocracy and channelled patriot energies towards philanthropic causes. Sensibility dramatized the homosocial emotionalism binding republican masculinity in oppositional circles on both sides of the Atlantic.

---

[3] 'The Enquirer No. 9', *Monthly Magazine*, 9: 2 (October 1796), 706–9.
[4] Henry Mackenzie, 'On Novel Writing', *The Lounger*, no. 20 (18 June 1785).

The American Revolutionary War galvanized popular fiction. The first novel to turn the conflict into a family melodrama became a publishing phenomenon which went through five editions by 1783 and was translated into German in 1781 and French in 1783. The epistolary *Emma Corbett; or, The Miseries of Civil War* (1780), was published anonymously by Samuel Jackson Pratt, though he used the pseudonym Courtney Melmoth in miscellaneous writing on humanitarian causes. The excessive theatricalism of Pratt, who had been both a clergyman and an actor, and failed in both pursuits, gave vent to collective mourning over the fissure which had opened up between the new nation and its parent country. Old wounds festering after the 1660 restoration of the monarchy and later the 'Glorious Revolution' of 1688 were reopened by American republicanism.

To juxtapose the role of patriot with that of a parent, as Pratt does in *Emma Corbett*, was to image colonialism in terms of human generation. This extended the patriarchal metaphor of the king as father of the nation. It also drew on organicist discourse, which likened the state to a body whose parts and members have different functions. Though both patriarchalism and the image of the body politic dated from classical times, these concepts had been extensively debated in the pamphlet wars of the seventeenth century. Now, sensibility endowed the corporeal metaphor of the parent nation with a new vitality. In *Emma Corbett*, the result was to anthropomorphize the British desire for imperial consolidation. Through sensationalist juxtaposition of the physical barbarities of war with emotional scenes of mourning, British shock at the amputation of its American limb was insistently replayed in imagery of dismemberment.

Within the breast of the agonized British father, Charles Corbett, rages a secret sympathy: for 'my massacred America', where his son is reported to lie dead after defending family property against a British army which grotesquely made use of the 'tomahawk…and the scalping knife' in its unnatural attack.[5] Charles thinks of himself as American and the new nation is dearer to him than his actual daughter, Emma, whom he virtually drives away when he tyrannizes over her—ironically, just as Britain had treated its colony. He refuses to let Emma marry his adopted son, the loyalist Henry Hammond, who, impelled by patriotic duty, sets off to fight the American revolutionaries. As a woman, Emma does not voice political opinions but 'Her approbation is the animating trumpet' (1.62) inspiring humanitarian ideals amongst the male characters. She condemns imperial war over property and learns surgery to ameliorate the carnage when she journeys to the American battlefields in search of Henry.

Male rivalry drives the plot, for the young men, Henry Hammond and Edward Corbett, had quarrelled over their opposing political beliefs. When the former departs

---

[5] Samuel Jackson Pratt, *Emma Corbett; or, The Miseries of Civil War*, 3 vols (Bath: Pratt and Clinch, and London: R. Baldwin, 1780), 2.193.

for America, Charles unsuccessfully urges the suit of his middle-aged nabob friend Sir Robert Raymond for Emma's hand. The latter is a cosmopolitan who abjures patriotism and party loyalties, avowing attachment to all mixtures of colours of 'SPECIES' (1.167). Raymond's disinterestedness perhaps alludes to Thomas Paine's point that the majority of Americans were not of British descent, but constituted a racial and cultural mix. Emma herself dyes her skin with berries and takes on the guise of a Native American when seeking her lover amongst the wounded. This signals to the reader the way she symbolizes America, whose 'youth, her bravery and her misfortunes' are chivalrously proclaimed by Emma's long-lost brother, facially disfigured by horrific wounds.

Though republican masculinity was conventionally expressed through neo-classical stoicism, Emma reads 'A Military Fragment', a friend's father's memoir which suggests that martial manliness is not natural but inculcated through gendered upbringing. Six sons were brought up to become soldiers. Despite their 'effeminate' faces inherited from their mother, they lost all their 'delicacy' after the first 'virgin engagement' (2.58) in battle. Two mutilated brothers survived a lifetime of military hardening and hardship: the colourfully named Julius Carbine and his brother Nestor. The former gestures with his stump while telling their story, indicating the depth of emotion language cannot fully communicate. The single tear which is all Nestor can now shed is produced by the memory of his wife's death. When it lands on his auditor's daughter, the latter accidentally transfers it to the cheek of the narrator in a stylized enactment of the sympathy the reading process is intended to generate. This reminds the reader that 'The tear of Sensibility' was all the praise the author wished for in his preface (1.v). However, self-ironizing is never far from the tear-sodden page of the novel of sensibility. We remember that this novel is gratefully dedicated to an appositely named Dr Delacour who has cured the Shandean writer of his delusional 'enthusiasm' for literary composition—but not before the story was completed.

Imitators of Pratt made America ubiquitous in fiction, though 'by 1785, types of war stories were becoming quite varied' (Heilman 1937: 100), often incorporating topographical description. Examples include Catherine Parry's *Eden Vale. A Novel* (1784), *The Liberal American. A Novel, in a Series of Letters, by a Lady* (1785), Mrs Johnson's anonymous *Francis, the Philanthropist: An Unfashionable Tale* (1786), and *The American Hunter, A Tale, from Incidents which happened during the War with America* (1788). Many novels featured an American war episode in addition to other exotic locales either within Britain or abroad. This was because post-1776 fiction now had imaginatively to realign England's relationship with various colonial spaces. The North and South Americas, the West Indies, India and Africa functioned as lands of opportunity where magical transformations of rank and wealth resolved the plot. Yet they could now be imagined as possible scenes of revolution, or as holding secrets of many a British villain's guilty past: from rape and pillage to gluttony and sloth.

Sensibility and the Novel of Ideas

British oppression of its American colonies calls out for the male reader's chivalric protectiveness in *Mount Henneth, A Novel* (1782) by Robert Bage, who was bolder than Pratt when representing America as a woman. Anticipating William Blake in *Visions of the Daughters of Albion* (1793), he made literal the metaphor of colonialism as rape and problematized the sexual politics of this. A middle-aged Derby paper-maker, Bage was a member of Enlightenment intellectual circles in the Midlands. The epistolary *Mount Henneth* was the first of a string of successful anonymous novels, three more of which appeared in the 1780s: *Barham Downs* (1784), *The Fair Syrian* (1787), and *James Wallace* (1788).

Bage varied the tone of the novel of sensibility, heightening the effect of its emotionalism by including fewer scenes of high drama and adventure and setting these off by social comedy and lively dialogue. He used fiction to stimulate sympathy for the oppressed and air social questions, and thus instigated the philosophical novel of ideas or 'Jacobin novel' (see also Mee, Chapter 11). The publisher Lowndes paid £30 for *Mount Henneth*, which went into three editions. Walter Scott selected it for *Ballantyne's Novelist's Library* in 1824, probably unwilling to endorse the more radical later fiction such as *Man As He Is* (1792). Even in the early twentieth century, George Saintsbury felt it necessary to warn readers off Bage, who possessed 'only talent and was not quite a gentleman' (1913: 144).

The British protagonist of *Mount Henneth* bewails the loss of his property when he is bankrupted by the American War. However, America in the form of Camitha Melton is seized by Captain Suthall, an English privateer, along with the American ship she was aboard, and her body claimed as his rightful property which he could sell as 'a slave to the plantations' to defray the costs of her subsistence.[6] When he attempts to prostitute her in Britain instead, the Madam of the brothel boasts that she can make two hundred pounds out of her the first month. Miss Melton 'acknowledged neither his power, nor his right' (1.136) and cried out for her liberty so the Captain had her held down while he attempted to rape her. She however stabs him with a pair of scissors and then escapes—though only to further captivity in debtors' prison. Suthall's purely mercantile view of the woman's body emphasizes the link between slavery, prostitution, and colonial exploitation of the young nation. The eventual reunion between Miss Melton and her missing father signals the restoration of the republic's self-determination as a future nation based on blood and birth.

Bage is not content with a single exemplum for political discussion. This fable of the British loss of America is contrasted with the backstory explaining how wealthy Mr Foston obtained his fabulous fortune. Unsurprisingly, the nabob's career in the East India Company coincided with its most notorious plundering of the subcontinent. Indeed, as the novel unfolds, it is apparent that Bage juxtaposes three geographical areas, each of

---

[6] Robert Bage, *Mount Henneth, A Novel*, 2 vols (London: T. Lowndes, 1782), 1.135.

which represented a different stage or type of imperialism: Wales, India, and America. India teaches the callow and dissipated young Writer how shallow is his smug Christian religiosity and contempt for Hinduism and Islam. When Foston is robbed and has to journey back to Calcutta he has to depend on the charity of the Indian peasants and learn survival from them. As a Lieutenant under Robert Clive, Foston saves a Persian merchant and his daughter, Caralia, from allies of the British in warfare over the possession of Calcutta, whom he names 'Mahrattoes' (soldiers of the Mahratta or Maratha empire in the south-west), who had entered their house, brutally attacked the family, and raped the women. When it is proposed that she marry her rescuer, Caralia asks Foston if he does not view her as having been dishonoured. She knows it is not just Indian culture which holds this view, as she has noticed that English novels do not 'permit a lady to live and marry, and be a woman after this stain' (1.233). Foston sharply distinguishes between 'honour' of the spirit and the violation of the body by another. The couple discuss the difficulties a 'mixed marriage' will doubtless encounter, but they do wed. After ten years of happy marriage Caralia dies. Foston brings his Anglo-Indian daughter Julia home to Britain to make her a 'princess' (1.69) by buying her a dilapidated castle with her merchant grandfather's immense fortune. Foston and his friends set up an ideal society in the poverty-stricken county of Cardiganshire, where the castle is a reminder of English subjugation of the Welsh in the Middle Ages. 'Every man amongst us, should be a man of business, of science and of pleasure' (2.304), declares Foston. They plan to invest surplus colonial wealth in the mother country: bringing the litigious Welsh peasants both law and trade, teaching the women to spin flax and the men to make glass and build ships, and to create 'a thriving colony' there (2.306).

British involvement in India became a frequent theme of late 1780s novels, published at the time of the impeachment of Warren Hastings. Phebe Gibbes' novel of sensibility, *Hartly House, Calcutta* (1789), is epistolary in form but gives only one correspondent's letters: those of the young lady Sophia Goldborne communicating to her intimate female friend in England her detailed impressions of the way of life in British Bengal. Gibbes thus combined the effect of a travel journal with a thought-provoking novel of sensibility. This is not limited to 'costume' alone: the protagonist communicates what she has learned about Eastern notions of a spiritualized nature, and introduces to the reader 'some of the tenets of Hinduism in an easily assimilable form' (Franklin 2007: xxv), which Gibbes had undoubtedly gleaned from the writings of Sir William Jones. Sophia will eventually marry a fellow Briton, but this is saved for a surprise ending. The main purpose of the novel is to show the curious and intelligent Sophia, whose name means wisdom, learning the highest respect and admiration for this religion. The book goes further than humanitarian benevolence for the natives: it challenges racial and cultural prejudice. For Sophia falls in love with her devout Brahmin tutor, mourning his loss when he dies unexpectedly.

Exotic tales of sensibility *Paul et Virginie* (1788) and *La Chaumière Indienne* (1790) were published by Rousseau's follower, the botanist Jacques-Henri Bernadin de Saint-Pierre, who had travelled widely and who eloquently depicted the innocence and goodness of natural man. The former was translated into English in 1795 by the radical poet Helen Maria Williams, whose own *Julia, A Novel* (1790) had been much influenced by Rousseau's *Julie, ou La Nouvelle Héloïse* (1761) and Goethe's *Werther.*

Gender, Internal Colonization, and Britishness

The interrelationship between travelogue and novel did not always produce exoticism. The popularity of the picturesque tour and fascination with the varied areas of Britain led to regionalism in the novel. This began with descriptions of the Celtic fringes in late eighteenth-century fiction. However, awareness that the centre had impoverished those peripheries in the course of establishing centralized nationhood imparted an ironic edge to such decorative settings. In a discussion of 'Internal Colonialism and the British Novel', Janet Sorenson comments that the dialogic form of the novel is 'reflective of the equally heterogeneous yet unified entity of the nation' (2002: 55). Moreover, in a century bookended by Acts of Union defining the United Kingdom, it would be surprising if the benefits and losses incurred by Anglicization and modernization were not explored in fiction.

Perhaps because the novel was itself of doubtful legitimacy, with its hybrid origins in romance, journalism, and travel, the orphan protagonist seemed particularly appropriate for exploring the multifariousness of Britain and its internal boundaries in an age of empire. The principality of Wales had become shorthand for a refuge, a feminine space far from urban sophistication. It didn't even possess a capital such as Edinburgh or Dublin. Andrew Davies comments: 'Of the twenty Wales-related sentimental novels and novels of sensibility identified between 1780 and 1830, the majority have female central focalisers and almost all are socially displaced orphans' (2001: 64). Many were published in the 1780s, including: William Godwin, *Imogen; A Pastoral Romance from the Ancient British* (1784), Catherine Parry, *Eden Vale* (1784), Anna Maria Bennett, *Anna; or, Memoirs of a Welch Heiress* (1785), Richard Graves, *Eugenius: or, Anecdotes of the Golden Vale* (1785), Mrs H. Cartwright, *Retaliation; or, The History of Sir Edward Oswald, and Lady Frances Seymour* (1787), *Powis Castle* (1788), Mr Nicholson, *Catharine; or, The Wood of Llewellyn* (1788), Charlotte Smith, *Emmeline, the Orphan of the Castle* (1788), Mary Wollstonecraft, *Original Stories* (1788), and Elizabeth Ryves, *The Hermit of Snowden: or Memoirs of Albert and Lavinia* (1789).

Anna Maria Bennett's *Anna* went into four editions by 1805 and was twice translated into French. The whole impression of this anonymous first novel, told in the third person, had sold out on its first day of publication. As Anna shares the author's name and the word 'memoirs' emphasized her claim the story was 'taken from real life',[7] it was

---

[7] Anna Maria Bennett, *Anna; or, Memoirs of a Welch Heiress*, 4 vols (London: William Lane, 1785), 1.ix.

probably imagined to contain autobiographical revelations. Mrs Bennett was a colour-ful character, and the preface of her second racy novel, *Juvenile Indiscretions* (1786), also stated she had fictionalized her own experience, though earning a ticking-off from the *Critical Review* for overstepping that 'propriety and decorum which we expect in a female's conduct'.[8]

Bennett entertained the reader with sharp social comedy, spiced with vernacular speech; surprising him/her with twisting plots unravelling mysteries of birth and blood and other transformational romance motifs familiar from folk tales. An extraordinarily popular novelist, who was associated with William Lane's Minerva Press and circulating library, the leading fiction publisher of the decade, she was also well-regarded by critics such as S. T. Coleridge and Mary Wollstonecraft. She prepared the way for Charlotte Smith and Charles Dickens.

Anna cleverly conflates rags-to-riches romance with characters bearing recogniz-able names or identities, but the main object is to critique the gentry's involvement in the industrialization of Wales and to indict male libertinism, rather than indicate a *roman à clef*. The emphasis on names 'becomes itself a textual marker of an anxiety focused on the relationship between changing inheritance patterns, that is, weakened kinship and emergent Britishness' (Rhydderch 1997: 6). Moira Dearnley notes that 'family names in the novel—Edwin, Herbert, Mansel, Turbville [*sic*] are those of the gentry in eighteenth-century Glamorgan, while Anna's ancestral estate, Trevannion, brings to mind the great estate of Y Fan...inherited by the Countess of Plymouth, formerly Elizabeth Lewis in 1734' (2001: 132). The most vivid passage in the novel is the realistic portrait of Llandore with its distinctive South-Walian limewashed walls and a nearby ironworks: probably conflated with the novelist's birthplace, Merthyr Tydfil, near the foundries at Cyfarthfa, Dowlais, and Hirwaun. At Llandore Castle, Anna meets Mrs Herbert who has inherited the ironworks from her grandmother, just as the actual Charlotte Herbert's 'daughter-in-law Alice owned part of the land on which the [Dowlais] ironworks was built' (Dearnley 2001: 224). Sarah Prescott notes that Mrs Herbert's brother-in-law, the traditional landowner Sir William Edwin, is a literary reincarnation of Sir Watkin Williams Wynn (third baronet) and suggests it is his family which is put forward as an 'ideal vision' (2008: 135). They are certainly solvent and charitable, for Sir William prudently left his own and his wife's estate to the latter's careful management while restricting himself to carrying out the pub-lic duties of Tory knight of the shire. However, Lady Cecilia is caricatured for her overweening pride in blood and rank, their son Hugh is a rake, and their daughter a coquette; and their house in Grosvenor Square, where Anna endures the demeaning role of a lady's companion, is a byword for dissipation and luxury. Anna's tormentor,

---

[8] *Critical Review*, 62 (July 1786), 69.

the libertine nabob Patrick Gorget, Lord Sutton—recently 'graced with the favour of a virtuous Prince' (*Anna*, 2.137)—is the Edwins' honoured guest. The character, whose name cleverly yokes associations of greed and military insignia, may gesture towards Robert Clive, who received an Irish barony in 1762 and who controlled political seats on the Welsh border. (His eldest son married Lord Powis's daughter, Henrietta of Powis Castle.)

It is the Edwins' cousin Charles Herbert whom Anna chooses to marry and whose family she will redeem from bankruptcy. Mrs Herbert's ironworks are mortgaged owing to her effete husband's neglect. He spends his time womanizing at Bath while his young partner Mr Wilkinson, a lower-class technological genius but also a man of feeling, runs the business for a share of the profits. Mr Wilkinson falls in love with Anna, yet behaves with noble dignity when she rejects him. The character presumably alludes to the pioneering ironmaster John Wilkinson who produced a steam engine for Boulton and Watt, was a friend of Crawshay, brother-in-law of Priestley, and became a folk hero of the working people. The plot plays with the possibility that the orphan heiress, who represents Wales, might accept this entrepreneur (another long-lost foundling) or will be captured and prostituted by the wealthy nabob colonialist. Fears of Welsh despoliation or decline are eventually submerged in dreams of future wealth. Both bourgeois newcomers Anna and Wilkinson marry Herbert gentry, in a wish-fulfilment union of entrepreneurial drive plus capital (Anna inherits £60,000) with the cachet of the gentry. The younger generation are modernizers who reconcile the absurd Welsh patriotism of Sir William and Lady Edwin 'to the British establishment and its Monarchy' (Aaron 1994: 73). The hope for the future of Wales is that the rustic beauty spot of Llandore will be transformed into the iron capital of the world (as Merthyr Tydfil was), while retaining a paternal duty of care to the workers and Wales's distinct heritage (Anna learns Welsh in order to bring charity to the peasants).

In the epistolary *Agnes de-Courci, A Domestic Tale* (1789), Bennett shocked some reviewers by sentimentalizing Jacobitism and also by making a failed marriage rather than courtship the object of attention. The mysterious General Moncrass, a Catholic, is descended from the Stuarts and most of his family was destroyed in the Jacobite rebellion. He has at last been able to return from exile to claim their forfeited estates and extols Scotland as the land of Ossian and is likened to Sterne by his niece. The malicious gossip surrounding his secret discovery and protection of his twin sister, an apostate nun, and his niece causes a separation between him and his wife, as well as a series of lovers' entanglements both comic and tragic. Bennett exploits the capacity of the Richardsonian epistolary form to view a predicament from various perspectives. She also makes use of the double mother/daughter plot instigated by Burney's *Evelina, or, A Young Lady's Entrance into the World* (1778). The story of the elder Agnes's escape from the nunnery and discovery that she had been duped by a libertine perhaps influenced M. G. Lewis's *The Monk* (1796) and Walter Scott's long poem *Marmion* (1808).

Though Catholics themselves are portrayed positively, the institution of the Church is the source of Gothic horror, for the erring nun had been threatened with being 'shut up forever between four walls, without light or sustenance'.[9] An eloquent speech proclaiming religious toleration is, however, put into the mouth of the virtuous heroine (4.156). Though Catholics are welcomed into the British fold, the novel's plot registers uneasiness at the repercussions. For the restoration of Jacobite estates and the return of Agnes trigger the disinheritance of English Lady Mary and her daughter Julia. Even when Agnes renounces the inheritance, the sensational discovery that the lovers—hero of sensibility, Harley (named in tribute to Mackenzie's Man of Feeling), and the saintly Agnes—had the same father destroys their union and all ends in Wertherian suicide and madness.

Women Writers and Sexual Politics

Women writers such as Bennett made the novel of sensibility their own in the 1780s, adapting the genre towards social critique. Whereas male novelists of the 1770s experimented with a new type of masculinity, women set their orphaned heroines to wander through society, particularly inspired by French novels such as Marivaux's *Vie de Marianne; ou, les Aventures de la Comtesse de* *** (1731–41), three English translations of which had been in circulation by 1746, including that of Mary Collyer (Letellier 2002: 507). The idea of a woman of feeling does not challenge gender stereotyping because women are conventionally assumed to be emotional. Indeed, Starr points out that: 'sentimentalism can be a powerful agent for the socialization of a woman' (1994: 195). Thus the female-authored novel of sentiment borrowed from the conduct book tradition as well as courtship comedy to evolve towards the *Bildungsroman*, as we will see.

Female sentimental novelists occasionally combined the didactic with the sensational in stories in which heroines of sensibility are portrayed as sexual beings. Mrs H. Cartwright's *The Platonic Marriage: A Novel, in a Series of Letters* (1786) earned the sarcasm of the reviewers for its tale of a young man hopelessly in love with his grandmother-in-law. Mary Wollstonecraft portrayed a silly character enjoying this titillating novel in her own *Mary, A Fiction* (1788). Nevertheless, Cartwright exaggerated in order to problematize the age disparity between spouses that most took for granted at the time. Harriet Lee's *The Errors of Innocence* (1786), tells of a protagonist whose feminine capacity for pity leads her astray when she marries a man she believes to be on his death-bed, only to find, when he miraculously recovers, that she has been tricked.

---

[9] Anna Maria Bennett, *Agnes de-Courci, A Domestic Tale*, 4 vols (Bath: S. Hazard, 1789), 4.22.

More frequently, women novelists were inspired by Richardson's *Clarissa* (1748–9) when representing sexual violence and male libertinism in their courtship fiction. Teacher Elizabeth Helme prided herself on 'exposing vice' in the preface of her first novel, *Louisa; or, The Cottage on the Moor* (1787). However, her melodramatic story of attempted rape was shocking enough to trigger such popularity that it went into four editions in the year of publication, and was translated into French (1787), German (1789), Russian (1790), and Spanish (1823). The publisher's advertisements stoked the excitement by claiming the tale was based on actual events and by informing the public of the lengths to which he had to go to satisfy the demand for copies.

Reviewers noted that the novel was well written, and, for the fourth edition, Helme signalled its claim to literary merit by appending poetic epigraphs from Edward Young's *Night Thoughts* to the chapter headings. This may have been the first time poetry had featured in a novel in this way. The novel adopted a feminocentric—not to say feminist— structure in which one woman gives sanctuary to another in the eponymous cottage, picturesquely situated on the moors near the Lake District. Both are orphans, both are victims of paternal figures who turn out to be sexual predators. Each tells her story to the other, so that they offer each other friendship and support. The book may have had an influence on the female literary tradition: the name of the villain, Darnford, was used by Mary Wollstonecraft in her unfinished, posthumously published novella, *Maria; or, The Wrongs of Woman* (1798), and the scene of a female wanderer taken into a cottage on the moors owned by a woman named Maria Rivers brings Charlotte Brontë's *Jane Eyre* to mind.

The poet Charlotte Smith was eager to extend this genre's capacity for social critique, not merely in castigating aristocratic libertinism but in indicting the materialism and philistinism of the gentry, professional, and mercantile classes. It is significant that Smith's earliest prose publications were eye-catching translations from the French. *Manon Lescaut, or, the Fatal Attachment* (1786) was rapidly withdrawn after the outraged protest of critic George Steevens that two English versions of the Abbé Prévost's controversial novel already existed. It was followed by *The Romance of Real Life* (1787), a selection of curious legal cases culled from the thirteen volumes recounted by Gayot de Pitaval. Both Smith's translations offered sensational stories pitting the power of sexuality against society's laws, which went on to inspire operas, dramas, ballets, and films right up to the present day. Smith dared not publish anything as scandalous as *Manon Lescaut* under her own name. As it was, reviewers, even including the future feminist Mary Wollstonecraft, were shocked by her lenient depiction of adulteresses in her courtship fictions *Emmeline, the Orphan of the Castle* (1788) and *Ethelinde, or The Recluse of the Lake* (1789).[10] Rival sonneteer Anna Seward abhorred Smith's 'boundless vanity' in describing Mrs Stafford, in

---

[10] *Analytical Review*, 1 (July 1788), 327–33.

the former, as having 'first-rate talents'.[11] For Smith's prefaces referred to her own status as a lone mother, separated from a feckless husband, and readers connected the autobiographical allusions surrounding Mrs Stafford with the 'feminist' agenda of these feminocentric novels. Both books were successful critically and commercially: *Emmeline* went into three editions and *Ethelinde* had two London and one Irish editions. Judith Phillips Stanton notes: 'In her most profitable year, 1789, she earned £470—£180 for the subscription edition of the sonnets and £290 for *Ethelinde* and the third edition of *Emmeline*' (1987: 393). However, she felt aggrieved that her publisher Cadell had returned a money order she had made in advance of her payment.[12]

Formally Smith was innovative. Steeped in tourist literature, she was the first English novelist to use the concepts of the sublime and picturesque in landscape description (Fry 1980: 86). She also infused the novel of sentiment with poetry written by the characters. Her third-person adventurous narratives juxtaposed scenes in different parts of the country, and in different ranks of society. She knew upper-class life from her girlhood experience, as Wollstonecraft surmised, but also had an ear for diverse idiolects, so could orchestrate dialogue demonstrating the variety of identities and affiliations of modern society. In her liberalism and frank espousal of entertainment over didacticism, Smith paved the way for the popular fiction of the next century: the romances of Charles Dickens and Harriet Beecher Stowe which cast the spell of sensibility over a mass readership in order to crusade for causes.

Smith refused to take the novelized conduct-book approach of moralistic writers such as Frances Burney, who teaches the reader via the socialization of her young protagonists in *Evelina* (1778) and *Cecilia, or Memoirs of an Heiress* (1782). Charlotte Smith idealized rather than ironizing her heroines: by implication, she proclaimed women as heroic models of humanitarian sensibility. In *Emmeline*, it is the male aristocrat, Delamere, who, having been allowed to run wild, has no control over his passions and whose idea of love is to force himself on his illegitimate cousin and to control her through moral blackmail. Initially he seems a Richardsonian threat when he breaks the lock on the heroine's bedroom door, but Smith refuses to let the heroine remain a victim for too long. While Delamere remains immature and pathetic, Emmeline gains strength of character through exercising independent judgement in helping other women. Smith daringly waits until halfway through the book before the alternative male lead makes his entrance. Instead of courtship we see the orphan experiencing the hard facts of women's lives: nursing her dying foster-mother; befriending Mrs Stafford when fleeing debtors; assisting Lady Adelina during childbirth following an adulterous relationship with her brother-in-law.

---

[11] Letter to Mrs Hayley, 11 January 1789, in *Letters of Anna Seward between the Years 1784 and 1807*, 6 vols (Edinburgh: Constable, 1811), 2.215.

[12] *The Collected Letters of Charlotte Smith*, ed. Judith Phillips Stanton (Bloomington and Indianapolis: Indiana University Press, 2003), 20.

Though initially Emmeline allows Delamere to foist an unwanted engagement on her, she is given a second chance when he repudiates her after crediting some malicious gossip. Her own choice is the worthy naval captain, Godolphin, who had chivalrously proclaimed his sister Adelina's child as his own to shield her from ostracism. Walter Scott commented that at the time he read the book he was shocked, for conventionally the lady should be 'faithful to her first affection' (Williams 1968: 184). The daring story of Godolphin's sister Adelina reinforces the message about the foolishness of early marriages implied by the experience of Mrs Stafford and Charlotte Smith herself and, together with the Delamere entanglement, warns the young reader against passivity.

Smith based her plot on property law, for Emmeline was apparently illegitimate, but discovered to have been defrauded of her inheritance by her uncle for nineteen years. First Burney in *Evelina* and now Smith added a feminist twist to the bastard figure earlier utilized by Daniel Defoe and Henry Fielding. Originally the bastard alluded to the fact that since 1688 the apportioning of power through strict lines of genealogical descent had been abandoned in Britain (Schmidgen 2002: 101).

Following the examples of Horace Walpole's *The Castle of Otranto* (1765) and Clara Reeve's *The Old English Baron* (1778), *Emmeline* takes the castle as setting. Walpole's theme of usurpation and the decline of a noble house was susceptible of a political interpretation, especially in a tale written by the Prime Minister's son. The castle might be thought to allude symbolically to the realm of Britain. The ruinous 'castle of the state' image had then featured in Book 5 of William Cowper's popular poem *The Task* (1785). Now Smith placed a female orphan within the political metaphor of the decaying castle, and postulated Cinderella bypassing the prince's offer of marriage and asserting her own claim. This medieval backdrop, image of the orphan's dispossession, underlines the pointlessness of women relying on chivalry and protection by men. Influenced by Gray and Gilpin, Smith makes it Pembroke Castle so she can have Emmeline referred to as 'Welch' yet also be of Scottish descent for good measure. This imparts a Jacobite shading to the symbolic setting.

In *Ethelinde* (1789), again told in the third person, Smith reprised her unique combination of provincial genre painting and condition-of-Britain critique. Her landscape description, as contemporary reviewers noticed, was 'steeped in literary allusion and shot through with quotation' (Sodeman 2009: 139). Probably influenced by Thomas West's *A Guide to the Lakes in Cumbria, Westmoreland and Lancashire* (1778), which itself referenced Gray and West's earlier work on Furness Abbey, Smith set her story in a fictional Grasmere Abbey. The lakeside locale epitomized picturesque landscapes but, importantly, Smith's imperfectly modernized Gothic building, half-ecclesiastical and half-secular, elaborated further the 'castle of state' symbolism. It specifically targeted those local gentry who had been the backbone of stable government since the Tudors dissolved the monasteries and formed the modern secular state. Ethelinde's cousin, Sir Edward Newenden, has not been near the ancient house and estate for four years, and his spoilt wife, complete with Indian servant, symbolizes their modern love of metropolitan luxury. National power and much greater wealth is indicated by the grander, aristocratic mansion of Abersley, owned by Ethelinde's obnoxious uncle, Lord Hawkhurst. Feeling utterly alienated there, humiliated by her dependent role as a poor relation, the despairing Ethelinde calls upon her dead father, who is buried in the family vault. 'She figured to herself her father standing there and beckoning to her to follow him',[13] and is heartened by the thought that his spirit wishes to comfort her. In fact, patriarchal wisdom and authority prove to be a phantasm. Ethelinde's father and brother, both in the military, had been responsible for dissipating the family fortunes through gambling.

The worthy but disinherited are symbolized by the poet and sensitive idealist Charles Montgomery who lives with his mother in a cottage near a waterfall at Grasmere on an income of £200. (This description may well have influenced the young Wordsworth in making his home in Grasmere in the 1790s.) Their Welsh surname is again twinned with Scottish descent, as Mrs Montgomery belonged to the Douglas family and her husband was a Catholic and Jacobite who fought for the French against Ethelinde's father in the battle of Minden during the Seven Years' War. 'How much superior is Mrs Montgomery in her cottage to the most affluent among them, surrounded by splendour!' (1.209) thinks the heroine on hearing their story, having fallen in love with the handsome Charles. Both Ethelinde's brother Chesterville, and lover Montgomery, have to try to mend their fortunes through colonialist careers—in the army in the West Indies and India respectively, though Montgomery aims to become 'the protector of the people among whom he proposes serving' (2.74). While Chesterville succeeds in marrying an heiress, Montgomery hates being 'sent to extort from the helpless natives of another hemisphere—gold' (4.268).

After five volumes of separation and gloom, Smith eventually satisfies her reader with the return of Charles and a modest income sufficient to marry Ethelinde but not to compromise his principles. However, the dream of love in a cottage is subjected to ironic treatment by the hard-headed characters. The heroine's unfeeling brother derides 'inviolable friendship and everlasting love' as 'stuff that you have picked up from the novels and story books you are eternally reading' (5.195). Ethelinde is also claimed as a soulmate by the ridiculous Clarinthia Ludford, who confides her own plan for a novel of sensibility in Smith's masterstroke of metafictional mockery.

> My heroine falls in love with a young man; quite a divine creature of course, who is obliged to go as Ambassador to Tripoli.... She ... determines to hire herself into the family of the Tripoline Ambassador here, to learn the language and accompany her lover as his valet de chamber. This plan, by the help of walnuts to change her complexion, and a pair of black mustachios, she accomplishes ... then she meets with an amazing number of adventures in France ... (2.167)

---

[13] Charlotte Smith, *Ethelinde, or The Recluse of the Lake*, 5 vols (London: T. Cadell, 1789), 5.212.

The Novel of Sensibility and the Female *Bildungsroman*

As the decade came to a close, the ubiquity of the novel of sensibility blurred its distinctiveness as a recognizable subgenre, and it became absorbed into most types of prose fiction. It also generated the new Romantic forms of the *Bildungsroman* and the Gothic novel. Debates over education had particularly inspired women's writing: they novelized conduct books and imagined the upbringing and courtship of a young girl. It was therefore female fiction which particularly focused on the socialization of an individual, as in Frances Burney's *Evelina* and *Cecilia*. Jean-Jacques Rousseau's *Emile, or Education* (1762), however, argued that girls should be brought up to please men, and set the parameters of the *Bildungsroman* as definitively masculinist.

Mary Wollstonecraft's *Mary, A Fiction* (1788) was both inspired by Rousseau's educational theories (quoting him in her epigraph) and determined to refute them by producing the portrait of a female genius. Wollstonecraft deliberately avoided the word 'novel', which denoted entertainment, as hers was a philosophical fiction intended to generate ideas about education. Wollstonecraft adopted the objective third-person narration that the pedagogical view of a young protagonist demands, but combined it with indirectly subjective accounts of the neglected child communing with sublime nature in solitude, 'making verses, and singing hymns of her own composing'.[14] By giving the heroine her own name she was signalling the autobiographical nature of the novel. Inspired by Rousseau's *Confessions*, the novel was influenced by the rise of life writing, developing into a quasi-*Künstlerroman*.

Wollstonecraft boldly abandoned plot to concentrate on a psychological character study. She illustrated Rousseau's premise that the neglect of the little child's formal instruction is a blessing in disguise in that it allows originality to flower. However, lack of encouragement is not equivalent to child-centred education, and results in a tortured female genius such as Mary rather than an independent Emile. Wollstonecraft demonstrates that, because sons are more valued than daughters, lack of maternal love makes for a lonely childhood leading to Mary's lifelong melancholia and insecurity in human relationships. Mary is certainly 'a character different from those generally portrayed' by Richardson, Rousseau, or their followers, as Wollstonecraft claimed in her 'Advertisement'. However, though not idealized as a moralist, Mary remains a passive prey to her emotionalism. She channels sensibility into romantic friendship, religious sublimity, and acts of benevolence, yet lacks the dynamism to shape her own life. Marriage is destiny for literary heroines, and Mary's capacity for choice is therefore further restricted when a match is arranged. Wollstonecraft daringly attempted to devalue the importance of marriage by demonstrating that her heroine's relationships

---

[14] Mary Wollstonecraft, *Mary, A Fiction* (London: J. Johnson, 1788), 28.

with women and friendships with both sexes continued to be more crucial to the married Mary's personal, intellectual, and artistic life. However, the sensibility which characterizes Mary's mother, her hyper-feminine friend Ann, and the man of feeling, Henry, is insistently linked to fragility of body, illness, and absence or death. Ultimately, the novel is torn between a fatalistic providential universe and the progressive individualism of the *Bildungsroman*.

The Gothic Romance

In the middle of the eighteenth century, authors of novels of sensibility such as Samuel Richardson had been eager to discriminate between the novel and the romance. The latter was tainted by its association with female and/or French authors and with the Catholic past. The second half of the eighteenth century saw a revaluing of the medieval and early modern romance by Richard Hurd in *Letters on Chivalry and Romance* (1762), Elizabeth Montagu, *An Essay on the Writings and Genius of Shakespear* (1769), James Beattie, *Dissertations, Moral and Critical* (1783), and Clara Reeve, *The Progress of Romance Through Times, Countries and Manners* (1785). By the end of the 1780s the age of Catholicism and feudalism seemed so safely consigned to the past that historical romances began to appear. The most successful was Sophia Lee's *The Recess; or, A Tale of Other Times* (1783–5), which was regularly reprinted in the next twenty years and was translated into French and German. A feminocentric novel of sensibility, it revealed the horrifying incarceration of two (fictional) daughters of Mary, Queen of Scots: their womblike and tomblike prison had obvious symbolic resonance. The sisters are the only correspondents so that the claustrophobic epistolary narrative has the urgency of first-person spontaneity combined with dialogic drama.

Ann Radcliffe's first attempt at Gothic romance, *The Castles of Athlin and Dunbayne* (1789), followed suit in that the most horrific secret that is uncovered is the secret imprisonment for fifteen years of two ladies, mother and daughter, in a concealed apartment in the masculine domain of the Castle of Dunbayne: 'for there the virtues were captive, while the vices reigned despotic'.[15] This human brutality is much more terrifying than fear of the supernatural. The patriarchal Gothic villain, the Baron, has usurped the female heirs of their rightful wealth and property. Not only has he broken the aristocratic and masculine code of honour and chivalry appropriate to his own time, but he obviously lacks the modern capacity for sensibility.

---

[15] Ann Radcliffe, *The Castles of Athlin and Dunbayne. A Highland Story* (London: T. Hookham, 1789), 91.

In 1786 a very different Gothic fiction had appeared: William Beckford's [*Vathek*]. *An Arabian Tale.* This imitation of an oriental tale recounted a caliph's life of indulgence. The narration of ever more spectacular sins, excess, luxury, eroticism, conspicuous consumption, and sadistic violence obtains a disturbing effect simply by refraining from any attempt to judge the protagonist or manipulate the reader's emotion. By implication, it ironizes and subverts the bourgeois, feminized, and moralistic form of the modern novel of sensibility, as would M. G. Lewis's *The Monk* (1796) and the works of the Marquis de Sade. However, parodic black comedy was only one side of Gothic. Under the spell of Ann Radcliffe, the genre of the novel of sensibility would be spirited away to other times and climes, face fears of supernatural and preternatural sublimity, and survive within tales of terror until the new century.

10

Early Gothic Novels and the Belief in Fiction

DEIDRE LYNCH

SHAKESPEARE'S Macbeth attempts to defend the consternation he betrayed when the spectre of the murdered Banquo, visible to him alone, entered his banqueting hall and occupied his seat at the table. The question he asks at this point is one that narrative fiction of the late eighteenth century also posed again and again, sometimes in verbatim terms: 'Can such things be? | And overcome us like a summer's cloud, | Without our special wonder?' (III.iv.109–11). Later eighteenth-century authors working in this still disreputable form, who had reason to doubt their own cultural credentials, regularly mined the plays of Shakespeare for chapter epigraphs, as though these requisitions on the national canon might summon, Emma Clery has said, a high-culture fairy godmother to christen their low-culture form (1995: 113). The novelists whom we nowadays classify as *Gothic* showed particular zeal in appropriating passages from those dramas of Shakespeare—*Macbeth, Julius Caesar,* and *Hamlet* particularly—that included ghosts in their cast lists. In 1794 Ann Radcliffe made Macbeth's question the epigraph for the tenth chapter of *The Mysteries of Udolpho*; in 1796 the lines appeared on the title page of *The Mystery of the Black Tower* by John Palmer, Jun.; in 1799 they provided the epigraph for chapter 17 of volume 2 of Anne Ker's *The Heiress di Montalde* ('a wretched imitation of Mrs. Radcliffe's manner', according to one wearied reviewer).[1] Another frequently recycled Shakespearean passage was the question with which Brutus gauges the ontology of the ghost of the murdered Caesar, when the spectre appears to him in his tent on the eve of battle:

> I think it is the weakness of mine eyes
> That shapes this monstrous apparition.
> It comes upon me. Art thou anything?
> Art thou some God, some Angel, or some Devil
> That mak'st my blood cold, and my hair to stand? (IV.iii.276–80)

---

[1] *New London Review*, 2 (October 1799), 388–9.

Radcliffe transcribed these lines also, the first two for the epigraph for the sixth chapter of the second volume of *Udolpho*, the remaining three for the third chapter of *The Italian* (1797).

In Shakespeare's dramas, as in the late eighteenth-century prose fictions that requisitioned his texts as paratextual announcements of coming narrative attractions, ghosts are dubious figures, who divert the speech of the plays' 'real' characters into an interrogative mode. The question of whether one sees a ghost or simply *thinks* that one is seeing it perplexes the ghost-seer, who even if he or she is supposed to be a figure from the benighted past is nonetheless granted sufficient rationality to wonder—as the patrons of the Jacobean stage or novel-readers of Enlightenment Britain might well do themselves—whether ghosts can be something other than the individual's psychological projections, whether they really exist outside the mind at all. The ghost undermines the naturalistic tenets of a modern ontology which maintains that the realms of spirit and matter never intersect and that the dead never walk.

In comparable fashion the idea of the Gothic novel has, since the late eighteenth century, challenged the metaphysics of modern literary history. The history of the novel, according to a historiographic scheme well established by the close of the century, is the story of a modern form's increasing refinement of the mimetic powers that separate it from the extravagances and outlandish stereotypes of the old romance. The novel is the form, ostensibly defined by its ambitions to verisimilitude, that has learned to sustain readerly curiosity without violating common sense and nature and so dispenses with supernatural marvels and horrors. (In 1815 the critic William Gifford, writing about *Pride and Prejudice*, instanced that definition, and the gender and class politics with which it would often be intertwined, as he asserted that the Gothick-y things which Jane Austen's novel omitted—it had, Gifford said, 'No dark passages; no secret chambers; no wind-howlings in long galleries; no drops of blood upon a rusty dagger'—might 'now be left to ladies' maids and sentimental washerwomen': see Southam 1968: 8.) Marvels and horrors belonged to a pre-modern time before the novel, and before modern rationality debunked the delusive belief systems that had flourished during dark ages of superstition and religious zealotry. Since the late eighteenth century its announced allegiance to the familiar lives of ordinary people has underwritten the novel's bid to become a serious literary form, in keeping with the axiology which holds that only probabilistic pictures of human nature, an 'observance of real life', can number 'among the permanent sources of amusement' (as a dismissive review of *The Italian*, generally thought to be Samuel Taylor Coleridge's, warns).[2]

Put otherwise, a Gothic Romance or even 'a Gothic Story' (subtitle of both Horace Walpole's *The Castle of Otranto* and Clara Reeve's *The Old English Baron*) may be one thing, but a Gothic *Novel* is something else again. Though that term has been retrospectively

---

[2] Review of *The Italian*, *Critical Review*, 23 (June 1798), 166.

applied to a body of macabre, sensational, ghost-infested fiction from the late eighteenth century only since the early twentieth, in its suggestion of a perverse hybridizing of the outmoded and the up-to-date it aptly captures the transgressiveness these fictions represented for their original critics. Gothic novels: *Can such things be?* To think that they can, to think that there can be modern novels that turn on occurrences—hauntings, sorcery, miracles—which elude rationalistic explanation, flouts standard schemes of cultural progress. Umbrage over this violation informs the critical animus that Coleridge, like Gifford, voices as a reviewer of the popular fiction of his day. That same animus has meant that until recently scholars of late eighteenth-century fiction have been on the defensive, obliged to explain, in the light of readers' and writers' enthusiastic embrace of improbabilities and of opportunities to regress from modern reason, how it was that the rise of the realist novel that began so promisingly in the 1740s ended up stalling so soon afterwards.

Implicitly contesting Coleridge's account of where literature might discover truly 'permanent' sources of readerly pleasure, the American author Lev Grossman has taken stock of a contemporary literary landscape that is overbrimming with fantasies about magicians, wizards, and vampires, proposing in an interview that it is fiction obeying the laws of mundane reality that is actually the 'aberration': "'what we're seeing now is a bit of a correction...literature going back to business as usual'".[3] It is true that the Gothic conventions developed in the late 1700s have proved astonishingly durable. Grossman's reference to 'business as usual', however, might lead one to underestimate the difficulties writers such as Walpole and Radcliffe had to negotiate in arranging for the spirit world of their ancestors to be accommodated within the modern cultural pantheon. At the same time, we might also think about their relationship to realism as being rather more equivocal than Grossman's binary opposition might suggest. '[R]ealism, however commonplace or precisely mimetic, is, after all, a representation, and thus the illusion of reality.' Redescribing in this manner the realist riposte to Gothic mysteries famously delivered by Jane Austen's *Northanger Abbey*, Sonia Hofkosh states that it follows that 'the realist may be considered as much a magician as a natural historian' (2009: 101). With their accounts of terrorized ghost-seers and victims of magical delusion—individuals who find themselves (like Shakespeare's Brutus and Macbeth) questioning their eyes and believing in what they know does not exist—late eighteenth-century Gothic novels, this chapter will suggest, served as a forum in which the reading public could come to terms with the pliable epistemological dispositions on which realist art depends—and on which aesthetic experience more generally depends, since it demands that we suspend our scepticism and consent to be enchanted by mere representations. As we shall see, these books characteristically arrange for their characters to pass back and forth between real and aesthetic

---

[3] As quoted in John Barber, 'J. K. Rowling's Sorcerer Apprentices: How Literary Magic is Entrancing the Masses', *Globe and Mail*, Toronto, Friday, 30 September 2011. Grossman's novels include *The Magicians* (2009), *The Magician King* (2011), and *The Magician's Land* (2014).

experience. They arrange for a 'real' experience of the supernatural to be counterpointed by the illusions of immediacy engendered by works of mimetic art (the statues of saints, portraits of dead relations, and absorbing old romances that litter the dilapidated abbeys and castles that house these characters). These arrangements and the commitment to self-reflexivity they instance made the Gothic a kind of training ground for new receptive competencies that were all the more useful as fiction came to saturate the field of entertainment, as a commodity 'furnished from the press, rather as a regular and necessary supply, than as an occasional gratification'.[4]

Gothic novels tirelessly thematize their own position within the cultural history of reading. More directly than the contemporary fictions that aspired to be life-like and observe the norms of probability, they foreground that peculiar mental gymnastics that since the eighteenth century has enabled us to participate in a secular culture industry 'which invites the subtle and supple deployment of belief', and whose consumers necessarily are adepts at 'accept[ing] one set of propositions in relation to the domain of fiction, and another in relation to the everyday world' (During 2002: 65, 50). In this sense, by helping to define the frontiers of the fictive, the Gothic mode did not interrupt the rise of the novel, but instead completed it. At the same time, as we shall also see, this fiction aligned itself with the history-writing of the eighteenth century, often by means of the packaging that presented it to the public as 'A Tale of Other Times' (another significant subtitle, this one for Sophia Lee's *The Recess*, 1783–5). Frequently finding its most significant intertexts in travelogues and historical works such as David Hume's *History of England* (1754–62), early Gothic fiction, even while treating 'such things' as cannot 'be', was also situated in perverse proximity to what Mary Poovey (1998) has called the matrix of the 'modern fact'. It accompanied its characteristic plot—the storyline tracing how family secrets are brought to light and lineages clarified—with meditations on the preservation and intergenerational transmission of documents from the past.

Counterfeit Antiquities

Initially, in fact, *The Castle of Otranto* (1765)—at once the template for subsequent instances of the Gothic mode and, as Ina Ferris demonstrates in Chapter 16, a prototype for the new historical romance—presented itself as a contribution to the knowledge of the medieval past and of the old books that were the historian's sources. It only afterwards pretended to model a new kind of fiction. Walpole's first step had been to ventriloquize contemporary antiquarian scholarship. His book's first, pseudonymous edition originally appeared on Christmas Eve 1764 as a translation of a much older Italian work, 'printed at Naples,

---

[4] Anna Letitia Barbauld (ed.), *The British Novelists*, 50 vols (London: F. C. and J. Rivington et al., 1810), 1.38.

in the black letter, in the year 1529'; this old book had somehow found its way into 'the library of an ancient catholic family in the north of England', laying the ground for its eighteenth-century publication. This story of the Castle's usurpation and of the supernatural means by which divine Providence restores the line of succession and returns the property to its legitimate owners is implausible, the translator, one 'William Marshal', admits in this 1764 Preface and perhaps, he implies, little to the refined taste of his contemporaries, since in his own modern day even 'romances' have had to expel '[m]iracles, visions, necromancy, dreams, and other preternatural events'. However,

> That was not the case when our author wrote; much less when the story itself is supposed to have happened. Belief in every kind of prodigy was so established in those dark ages, that an author would not be faithful to the *manners* of the times who should omit all mention of them.[5]

Fidelity to historical fact here becomes a way to sidestep rather than resolve the question of whether the preternatural is reality or fiction. Ghosts might not exist, and heaven might not ever have communicated with this world by means of a gargantuan helmet that falls fatally from the sky (the portent that notoriously launches *Otranto*'s over-the-top plot). But look into the past and you will find that the *belief* that such things were certainly existed. This tricksy passage holds out the incredible as the very hallmark of authentic historicity. The Preface in general shifts artfully between the beliefs of an eighteenth-century audience, those of the characters involved in the story, which William Marshal dates to the era of the Crusades, and those of the author, who writes at some moment in between the medieval and the modern, and who, though he 'is not bound to believe' 'every kind of prodigy' as his characters do (4), is compelled by his scholarly scruples to do these beliefs justice. Pre-empting objections to how the weird events that his story recounted deviated from common sense, Walpole took shelter behind the argument, then emerging in the discussions of medieval and Elizabethan culture being produced by scholars such as Thomas Warton and Richard Hurd, that readers needed to cultivate a historical sense: 'what we hear censured in their writings as false, incredible, and fantastic, was frequently but a just copy of life . . . there was more of truth and reality in their representations, than we are apt to imagine', declares one of Hurd's spokesmen in his 1759 'Dialogue on the Golden Age of Queen Elizabeth'.[6] If we concur, then we will also agree that the norms of *vraisemblance* that would condemn *Otranto*'s improbabilities as unworthy of readerly attention should be trumped by a regard for historical context. The preternatural becomes an appropriate feature of its contents when context is factored back in.

[5] Horace Walpole, *The Castle of Otranto*, ed. W. S. Lewis (Oxford: Oxford University Press, 1982), [3], 4.

[6] Richard Hurd, *Letters on Chivalry and Romance with the Third Elizabethan Dialogue*, ed. Edith J. Morley (London: H. Frowde, 1911), 56.

In the second edition of 1765, however, Walpole did an about-face. This edition revealed that what had been presented as Gothic, a product of 'the darkest ages of christianity', was, more precisely, Neo-Gothic. (Complicating matters further, this was the edition in which *Otranto* acquired that subtitle 'A Gothic Story'; it became Gothic at the very moment that revealed its contemporaneity.) A second Preface furnished for this new edition renounced the pretence that the book was a contribution to a collective research project (the first Preface had ended by suggesting that further investigation of 'the Italian writers' might bring to view 'the foundation on which our authors has built', 6). The book now represented, instead, the manifesto of a maverick rebelling against his contemporaries' orthodox identifications of realism, literary modernity, and literary morality. Modern fiction has been 'cramped' by its 'strict adherence to common life' (7), Walpole explains, and this calls for a remedy. He has therefore struck out a new route and concocted 'a new species of romance' (12); cheekily, Walpole here reminds 'the public' that they had already, in receiving the first edition, 'applauded the attempt' (8). He has blended 'the two kinds of romance, the ancient and the modern' (7)—keeping the naturalistic characterization of the latter, but emulating the former, in which 'all was imagination and improbability', by 'leaving the powers of fancy at liberty to expatiate through the boundless realms of invention' (7). As redefined in Walpole's new preface, the primary business of the modern novelist should be to unleash the imagination.

Later, a new generation of writers, with particular fervour during the 1790s, would build on Walpole's contention that fictions of the supernatural were especially conducive to those sensations of imaginative transport that their contemporaries had recently begun to celebrate as encounters with 'the sublime'. Edmund Burke's account in the *Enquiry into . . . the Sublime and the Beautiful* (1757) of how terror 'is productive of the strongest emotion of which the mind is capable' had made it possible to have a taste for terror, to preserve, that is, one's identity as person of taste while seeking out the experience of 'artificial' terror. (Burke had also acknowledged outright how incongruous such raptures were with the protocols of the age of reason: 'the great power of the sublime' is 'that far from being produced by them, it anticipates our reasonings, and hurries us on by an irresistible force'.)[7] But before tracing how 'romance' became recuperated for its imaginative extravagance and as a source of the sublime, it is worth noting that the second preface to *Otranto*, with its claim about the extension of the dominion of 'fancy', never entirely displaced the first, with its claim about the extension of historical knowledge. In *Otranto*'s later editions, the 1764 preface was consistently retained alongside that of 1765. The virtue of this arrangement, one supposes, was how it enabled the readers of these editions, now undeceived and in on the hoax, to admire Walpole's performance as a kind of literary

---

[7] Edmund Burke, *A Philosophical Enquiry into the Origin of our Ideas of the Sublime and the Beautiful*, ed. James T. Boulton (Notre Dame and London: University of Notre Dame Press, 1968), 39, 57.

conjuring trick—a droll contribution to the Christmas revels of his circle (the latter seems at many moments to have been Walpole's own view of his creation). Regarded as a hoax, *Otranto* predicts the pseudo-documentary pretences that will often distinguish later Gothic fictions—James Hogg's 1824 *Private Memoirs and Confessions of a Justified Sinner* and Edgar Allan Poe's 1845 'The Facts in the Case of M. Valdemar' are signal instances, both presenting themselves as the records of investigations, antiquarian and medical respectively, of 'real' remains. And when his book is so regarded, Walpole also comes across as a cleverer version of the literary counterfeiters of the 1760s and 1770s, contemporaries like James Macpherson and Thomas Chatterton, who at this time were responding a tad overeagerly to British literary culture's enthusiasm for the archival recovery projects that promised to salvage the sources of national genius from historical oblivion. *Otranto* resembles Macpherson's *Fragments of Ancient Poetry Collected in the Highlands of Scotland* (1760), which claimed to be the remnants of an epic by a third-century Celtic bard, but was not, and Chatterton's *Poems, Supposed to Have Been Written at Bristol, by Thomas Rowley, and Others, in the Fifteenth Century* (1777), which claimed to be authored by a medieval monk, but was not. Yet Walpole arguably outmanoeuvred both Macpherson and Chatterton, who were soon excoriated for their abuses of the public trust. For one thing, he managed to turn the tables, so that the honours that *his* book paid to the national canon became apparent at the very moment that (in the second preface) he abandoned his scholarly and documentary pretences and announced that he had instead opted for untrammelled fictionality (in opting, as this second preface explains, to reindulge the wild imaginings that were the essence of the old romance). As he asserted in 1765, in this experiment with modern romance he had actually had his eye on the example of Shakespeare's dramas all along ('I ... shelter my own daring under the cannon of the brightest genius this country ... has produced', 12).

The way that Walpole's extensive prefatory apparatus delays readers at the threshold of his story bespeaks, as recent commentators often note, the obstacles hampering the launch of a fantastic fiction. That Walpole felt this apparatus was needed suggests the defensive footing on which the would-be author of a supernatural fiction was necessarily placed in the late eighteenth century. But, as we are beginning to see, the movement taking readers from the first Preface to the second also models in miniature a dynamic that was basic to the Gothic novel in its early days, when Gothic novelists appear to have been particularly intent on exploring the context dependency of meaning and, by extension, the transvaluations that occur when one shifts between things as they were and things as they are and things as they are inside books exclusively. Variations on the lessons of Walpole's two prefaces—i.e., that it is one thing to read a text as a history and another to read it as fiction, that the terrors of one age can become for another the sources of aesthetic pleasure—quickly became the Gothic's stock in trade. In Radcliffe's fictions and those of her imitators, for instance, scenes get rapidly shifted and worlds get multiplied (Otto 2011: 97). The protagonist's displacement in space doubles as a kind of time travel between civilized and savage eras, an occasion on which we gauge the differences between one historical time and another that is further back in the past. As a Radcliffean heroine like Emily St Aubert is wrested from the peaceful existence she has led in a villa in the south of France to a rather more anxious existence in a warlord's castle in the Appenines, and as she exchanges the up-to-date refinements of the sixteenth century for something more barbarous and antiquated, the reader of *The Mysteries of Udolpho* (1794) discovers alongside her how the impossibilities of one culture—the things that in that context only the childish or foolish entertain—may be the probabilities of another. The castle of Udolpho is a place where, says Annette, Emily's maidservant, "'I can almost believe in giants again, and such like'" (fairies and ghosts are also up for re-evaluation, she adds).[8]

It is not only, in other words, *Otranto*'s combination of a threatened virgin, a predatory aristocratic tyrant, and a castle whose ruinous dark passages witness this pair's flight and pursuit that proved generative for Walpole's successors, though its character types and plot motifs were indeed frequently recycled. The first Preface's trope of scholarly retrieval stuck too; likewise Walpole's interest in the mechanisms of cultural transmission and decontextualization that make the past available for the present's fictionalizing. Later writers' expression of their interest in such matters took various forms. Clara Reeve's *The Champion of Virtue: A Gothic Story* (1777), retitled in its second edition as *The Old English Baron*, abandoned for that second edition the pretence of being a modern edition of a document recovered from the past, instead overtly presenting itself as a contribution to a new-minted tradition of hybridized fiction: Reeve's second Preface (1778) advises readers that 'This Story is the literary offspring of the Castle of Otranto', and states that the intention here, too, has been to unite 'the most attractive and interesting circumstances of the ancient Romance and modern Novel'. But notwithstanding this explicit avowal of the fact of Reeve's authorial invention, her readers still hear intermittently from an editorial voice that means to keep us informed about the condition of the manuscript that is its charge: this 'editor' notes the different hands in which the manuscript is written and the depredations that 'time and damp' have made on its legibility.[9] The novel chronicles the struggles of the noble Edmund, raised as a peasant but in truth (as supernatural interventions instruct him) the rightful master of Castle Lovel. But at moments this history of Edmund's origins recedes behind the history of the origins of the modern printed text that we are reading. Radcliffe's *A Sicilian Romance* (1790) opens with a Preface in which our author poses as a peripatetic antiquarian, who on a visit to a dilapidated castle 'still to be seen' on the northern shore of Sicily has been granted the sight of an old manuscript housed in the library of a nearby friary: it tells the 'solemn history' that once unfolded

---

[8] Ann Radcliffe, *The Mysteries of Udolpho*, ed. Bonamy Dobrée, introd. Terry Castle (Oxford: Oxford University Press, 1998), vol. 2, ch. 5; 231.

[9] Clara Reeve, *The Old English Baron: A Gothic Story*, ed. James Trainer (London: Oxford University Press, 1967), Preface, 3; 27.

within the now deserted castle's walls.[10] On its first English appearance in 1786, William Beckford's *Vathek* was accompanied by extensive notes 'Critical and Explanatory' that occupied a full third of the volume—as if this narrative, as its 1786 title, 'An Arabian Tale, From an Unpublished Manuscript', deceptively suggests, were really most appropriately read as a culturally representative document and as if extra provision had to be made for such a reading to occur. (These notes were furnished by one Samuel Henley, whom Beckford, then in exile on the Continent, and writing in French, had charged with his book's English translation and publication. Henley made the most of his acquaintance with the new orientalist scholarship then sponsored by the East India Company.) Framed by this apparatus and the pseudo-contextualization of the tale that it appears to provide, Beckford's wild story of the Caliph Vathek's perverse appetites and dealings with dark powers became even more bizarre, a paradoxical combination of romance excess and historical reference (Watt 2008: 130).

Sophia Lee's Advertisement to *The Recess*, still another book presented as a document from the past that has been rediscovered and pieced together by a modern editor, similarly presents conundrums in the very section of the book in which readers expect their reading matter to declare its true nature and generic affiliation. Lee both suggests in that Advertisement that these memoirs she introduces might record a true story, that they might really be written by the secret daughters of Mary, Queen of Scots—for 'the narrative is stamped with probability'—and then goes on to state that 'the reign of Elizabeth was that of romance'. Those truly acquainted with history know that it is romance, she seems to say, taking away with one hand what she has granted with the other.[11] Over the course of their turbulent lives, her royal heroines (or royal pretenders) hover on the edge of public acknowledgment, never quite leaving the shadows and assuming their rightful place in public history but thereby, through that liminality, further troubling history's secure opposition to fiction.

Romance Nations

As well as pillaging Hume's *History* for details of the plotting and counter-plotting that surrounded Tudor succession crises, Sophia Lee was a student of Hurd's and Warton's scholarship on the early sources of the national canon. Her comment about the romance of the Elizabethan age recapitulates, albeit in slippery terms, their argument, and Walpole's argument, that the imagination had been less fettered in the past. In time past, as Warton put it at the start of his *History of English Poetry* (1774–81), 'the gloom of ignorance and

---

[10] Ann Radcliffe, *A Sicilian Romance*, ed. Alison Milbank (Oxford: Oxford University Press, 1993), 1.

[11] Sophia Lee, 'Advertisement', *The Recess; or, A Tale of Other Times*, ed. April Alliston (Lexington, KY: University Press of Kentucky, 2000), n.p.

superstition' formed, whatever its drawbacks, a congenial habitat for 'those spectres of illusive fancy, so pleasing to the imagination'.[12] The uncouth romances of Dark Ages England that were informed by that 'illusive fancy' and that had kindled the imagination of a Shakespeare, a Spenser, and a Milton had also necessarily been the casualty of history's onward march, Warton admitted ruefully. (An Anglican clergyman, he could not afford to regret outright the Reformation.) Though it makes it sound as though the cultural revolutions that brought the age of romance to an end and ushered in 'much good sense, good taste, and good criticism' were a raw deal, Warton's *History* finally comes down on the side of progress (*History of English Poetry*, 2.463). The terms in which he and his fellow romance scholars conformed with the conventional Whiggish narrative of cultural refinement and progress were sufficiently equivocal, however, as to leave other writers plenty of loopholes. When they braved critical opprobrium and exploited those loopholes, the aficionados of the medieval preternatural could take encouragement, as we have seen, from the era's discussions of an aesthetics of the sublime. Patriotism, too, provided an alibi: promoting the romances of chivalry, reclaiming these sources of the native canon despite their lapses from *vraisemblance* and neo-classical precepts of taste propounded by French critics such as Boileau and Voltaire, was in the late eighteenth century a way to mark Britain's distinction as a nation blessed with special imaginative powers.

In 1783, in his 'Dissertation on Fable and Romance', James Beattie inventoried the features in their domestic life that would have caused credulity and superstition among the bygone 'Gothick nations'. One was that the winds howled eerily through the crevices of their castle walls, which were reared in 'a rude but grand style'; their lives were customarily led in earshot of 'the grating of heavy doors on rusty hinges of iron; the shrieking of bats, and screaming of owls'. (Furthermore, 'The world was then little known'.)[13] That Beattie's inventory might easily double as a passage of novelistic scene-setting registers how contemporary romance scholarship provided (generally unwittingly) a high-culture justification for the otherwise suspect enterprise of those novelists who revoked the boundary between romance and novel and refocused fiction on weird events that should not happen. The essayist Nathan Drake in 1798 argued for the preserving of the mythology of spectre and fairy that he called the 'vulgar Gothic' because this superstition was poetic par excellence, 'formed…to surprize, elevate, and delight'; it is to such superstition 'that Shakspeare, beyond any other poet, owes the capability of raising the most awful, yet the most delightful species of terror'.[14] Drake confined himself, tastefully, to

---

[12] Thomas Warton, 'On the Introduction of Learning into England', *History of English Poetry*, 4 vols (1774–81; repr. London: Routledge/Thoemmes, 1998). I quote from one of the 'Dissertations' that open the first volume and which are unpaginated.

[13] James Beattie, *Dissertations Moral and Critical* (London: W. Strahan and T. Cadell; Edinburgh: W. Creech, 1783), 540–1.

[14] Nathan Drake, *Literary Hours, or, Sketches Critical and Narrative* (London: T. Cadell and W. Davies, 1798), 88, 93, 90.

the high end of the literary market. Poetry was for him the ideal medium of that preservation. But an essay from 1773 that Drake acknowledges, 'On the Pleasure Derived from Objects of Terror', by the brother and sister John Aikin and Anna Letitia Aikin, did include prose fiction, the *Arabian Nights* and Walpole's 'Gothic Story' explicitly, in an enthusiastic vindication of the taste for wildly fanciful reading matter. The conventional arrangement in which the fictionality of fiction was tolerated on the grounds that readers may extract from verisimilar stories lessons for their own lives was set aside by the Aikins. Instead, an early Romantic account of imaginative transcendence supplied the place of the usual moral arguments by which the recourse to fiction was justified: 'where the agency of invisible beings is introduced' into a narrative, 'our imagination darts forth, and explores with rapture the new world which is laid open to its view, and rejoices in the expansion of its powers'.[15]

Manifestly fictional fictions, romances *represented* magical events. The fragmentary tale the Aikins appended to their essay by way of putting its theories into practice features, for instance, a spooky blue flame that seems to move of its own accord and a coffin whose inmate sits upright and embraces the knight-errant who has mysteriously been led into her presence. But the very reading of such fictions, the Aikins implied, was likewise magical: an occasion for heightened experience and ecstatic transport, as that reference to 'the new world' suggests. The Gothic novel, it has been said, sits astride a major shift in the response of readers to literature, a shift from catharsis to aesthesis, from reading for instruction and information, to reading in search of sensation and escape (Richter 1996: 112; Bray 2009: 156). The Aikins' readiness to vindicate reading matter that aims more at readers' astonishment than their moral improvement bears this out.

Just prior to the moment that new, proto-cinematic forms of entertainment like Philippe de Loutherbourg's sound-and-light show, the eidophusikon (1781), began to usher audiences into high-tech immersive environments engaging all their senses, bookish experience too had begun both to be associated with, and even praised for, its capacity to displace real reality altogether by installing a virtual one in its place (Otto 2011: 81). Thus, detailing in 1762 the 'Emotions Caused by Fiction', Henry Home, Lord Kames, described at length the acts of mind by which readers contrive to blur the distinction between the reality compelling their belief and the books which do the same: this description recast illusion as a near-normative component of literary experience. The reader that he profiled was a figure who while reading was moved by a magic, even divine, force, as he found himself placed as if before the objects depicted in his book, experiencing their 'ideal presence'

---

[15] J. and A. L. Aikin, 'On the Pleasure Derived from Objects of Terror, with Sir Bertrand, A Fragment', *Miscellaneous Pieces in Prose* (Belfast: James Magee, 1774), 60. Tradition ascribes 'Sir Bertrand' to John Aikin, the essay introducing it to Anna Letitia Aikin, who is better known by her married name, Anna Letitia Barbauld.

and losing 'the consciousness of self, and of reading, his present occupation'.[16] When a skilful writer endows them with eidetic vividness, even fictions—as much as reports on things that really are—can feel as if they present rather than merely *represent*: so Kames, a devout believer in fiction, proposes. When this happens, their images 'convert' the reader into 'a spectator' (Marshall 2005: 49). Enthusiastic endorsements of this account of reading abound in the late eighteenth-century Gothic and contribute to the mode's self-justifying vindication of a modern romance. One such involves the hero of Francis Lathom's *The Castle of Ollada* (1795), who is determined to delve into the rumours about this castle's haunted state and who will eventually discover not ghosts but a gang of counterfeiters and, in a secret apartment, a long-imprisoned woman who turns out to be his aunt. When Lathom's protagonist takes time off from ghost-busting with an absorbing book, 'a history of Charlemagne', 'the warmth with which he re-fought the battles of that great hero, in a short time took entire possession of his thoughts'.[17] Journeying across the Alps, Radcliffe's Emily St Aubert recalls her study of history, and not only thinks of how her journey repeats that of Hannibal's armies, but sees those troops in 'the eye of fancy': 'she perceived the gleam of arms through the duskiness of night, the glitter of spears and helmets' (*Udolpho*, vol. 2, ch. 1; 166). Emily is seeing things.

Artful Priests and Enslaved Minds

Still, from *Otranto* on, Gothic novels obtained many of their frissons from stories of people who believed in the *wrong* ways: superstitious devotees and bigots, a deluded populace under the yoke of priestcraft, and/or youthful enthusiasts who tremble with merely ideal terrors because, like the hero of *The Italian*, their 'ardent imagination[s]' have seduced them away from 'plain reasoning, or . . . the evidence of the senses'.[18] The etymological and representational connections linking romance to the Church of Rome were deliberately exploited by Gothic writers, who gravitated towards benighted, priest-ridden settings—often Italy, Spain, or Germany's Black Forest—and cast them both as mystery's natural habitat and as fertile ground for a lamentable incredulity. Part of the writers' intention, clearly, was to use these settings to lend their writing atmosphere, and many furnish their English readers with opportunities for armchair tourism. (These readers appear to have taken in their stride the contradiction between that engagement with a world elsewhere

---

[16] Henry Home, Lord Kames, *Elements of Criticism*, 3 vols (London: A. Millar; Edinburgh: A. Kincaid and J. Bell, 1762), 1.107, 112.

[17] Francis Lathom, *The Castle of Ollada*, ed. James D. Jenkins (Chicago: Valancourt Books, 2006), vol. 2, ch. 2; 75.

[18] Ann Radcliffe, *The Italian, or, The Confessional of the Black Penitents*, ed. Frederick Garber (Oxford: Oxford University Press, 1981), vol. 3, ch. 10; 397.

and the fact that at every turn in their books they would have encountered familiar snippets of English literature, either as the ornamental verse epigraphs that signalled those
books' affiliation with a native literary tradition or as material prompting the characters'
own exercise of literary taste. In *The Romance of the Forest* (1791), set in seventeenth-century
France and Switzerland, Radcliffe even arranges for her heroine, in the rare intervals of
calm in a story organized around her successive abductions and a plot against her life, to
study 'the best English poets' and write a poem of her own in homage to *A Midsummer
Night's Dream.*)[19] But this choice of Continental settings also placed the Gothic in close relation with a tradition of Protestant polemic devoted to detailing the myriad ways in which
Catholic doctrine systematically erred beyond the limits of reasonable religion. Following
the Reformation, that Church and its opponents differed over whether dead souls could
pass over into the world of the living, with Protestants denying the doctrine of Purgatory
that had formerly served to make sense of reports of ghost-seeing. They differed too over
whether any actual miracles had occurred since the establishment of the early Church,
with Protestants maintaining that in modern times God had been able to dispense with
the preternatural since Scripture in itself was a sufficient foundation for faith. Much plotting in Gothic fiction of the 1790s is geared to exposing how the apparitions and miracles
that engender terror and wonder in the characters, and, in a different way, in us, originate not with divine Providence but rather with the machinery of Continental priestcraft,
whose adepts dazzle and delude the senses of the credulous multitude so as to quell dissent
and maintain a very un-English uniformity of belief. (That Europe's credulous multitudes
were, after 1789, enthralled rather more by new doctrines of political revolution than by
the romancing of the Church of Rome likely confirmed as much as it challenged the ideas
of national character underpinning such plots.)

Exploring in his philosophy of mind the causes of belief, sketching an example of how
the association of ideas operated to enliven our thoughts about things we could not see
and assisted in commanding our assent to their existence, David Hume had had recourse
back in 1739 to 'the devotees of that strange superstition', as he calls the Catholic faith,
who say in excuse of their 'mummeries' that

> we shadow out the objects of our faith…in sensible [i.e., material] types and images and
> render them more present to us by the immediate presence of these types, than 'tis pos-
> sible for us to do merely by an intellectual view and contemplation.[20]

As portrayed in the Gothic, however, the Catholic visual culture that caters to this feature of our minds' operations is generally a system of fraud. It depends on sleight of hand

---

[19] Ann Radcliffe, *The Romance of the Forest*, ed. Chloe Chard (Oxford: Oxford University Press, 1991),
vol. 1, ch. 5; 82, and vol. 2, ch. 17; 284–5.

[20] David Hume, *A Treatise of Human Nature*, ed. Ernest C. Mossner (Harmondsworth: Penguin, 1969),
149.

and optical illusion. Friedrich Schiller's much-imitated *The Ghost-Seer*, which launched an English craze for German stories when translated in 1795, pivots on the nefarious attempts to secure the conversion to the Church of Rome of a German prince sojourning in Venice. One such attempt involves making the prince believe that he has really seen a ghost, but he subsequently learns—through the agency of an enigmatic figure who is terrifying in his own right—how the apparition was purpose-built to ensnare him, by someone using phosphorus, magnets, and a magic lantern. Matthew Lewis's *The Monk* (1796) has, in a Madrid convent, its statue of St Clare, the kind of 'sensible . . . image' that Hume had had in mind, and which has, furthermore, 'for time immemorial . . . been famous for performing miracles'.[21] Her marvellous animation, Lewis's denouement reveals, is an illusion originating with artfully concealed levers and the deluded senses of timorous nuns. The latter ascribe the groans in her vicinity to the ghost of a thief who had tried to steal the statue's ruby ring and now hovers eternally around the scene of his impiety: so construed they testify to the saint's supernatural power. The denouement reveals them instead to be those of one of their sister nuns, Agnes di Medina, pleading for release from the subterranean prison in which she has been buried alive to expiate her violated vow of chastity: they evidence, that is, very real human abuses of power.

The impulse to debunk their characters' chimerical fears has some peculiar aspects in these books. In the course of conveying the lesson that ghosts are merely fabrications, Gothic texts do not so much banish the terrors in which they have trafficked, as redirect them. We may no longer fear seeing a spectre, but we have been left with an impression of a world governed by cruelty or honeycombed with plots and conspiracies against our sanity. The bad faith with which Lewis pursued his free-thinking project of demystification is even trickier still, a fact that registers the young man's determination to outdo his novelistic predecessors for sheer outrageousness (or for camp, as Robert Miles observes in Chapter 13). Even as in his subplot Lewis endorses scepticism about the supernatural, and exposes the human trickery behind the statue that seems miraculously to come alive, he also asks us to believe that the principal plot of *The Monk*—which traces the eponymous protagonist's abandonment of all religious and moral scruples as he falls under the spells of a mysterious seductress—was scripted by the real devil in advance. ('Know, vain Man! That I long have marked you for my prey', the devil says as he discloses to Ambrosio the Satanic sting operation by which he has been entrapped (vol. 3, ch. 5; 440).) Like many Gothic protagonists whose lot it is to be sacrificed to the foreordained storyline set up by a family curse or ancient prophecy, this Monk is, in multiple ways, a victim of plotting.

Provokingly, these books often extend to the psyches of their own readers the investigation of that mental vulnerability that makes possible the reigns of terror of wily priests

---

[21] Matthew Lewis, *The Monk*, ed. Howard Anderson (Oxford: Oxford University Press, 1967), vol. 3, ch. 3; 364.

and abbesses. While underscoring the aspects of auto-hallucination involved in the kind of reading act that Kames depicts, the books slyly place priestly trick and the 'illusions of the page' (*Romance of the Forest*, vol. 2, ch. 14; 208), superstitious delusion and absorptive aesthetic illusion, into apposition rather than opposition. (The theological overtones of 'convert' in Kames's discussion of reading matter that 'converts' readers into spectators, foretold such linkages (Marshall 2005: 43–4).) In Walpole's first Preface, his translator alter ego, William Marshal, speculated about the authorship of the ancient story of Heaven's revenge on the usurpers of the duchy of Otranto and imagined some 'artful priest' who, subverting comfortable notions of history as linear progress, had turned modernity's own weaponry against modern rationality and had used the newly invented printing press to disseminate with new efficacy just the 'ancient errors and superstitions' that print was supposed to have banished (*Otranto*, [3]). Such monkish propaganda might 'enslave a hundred vulgar minds' ([3]). Subsequently outing himself as that selfsame artful priest, and so showing off how easily he could shunt confessional polemic into the world of entertaining fiction, Walpole founded a genre that is consistently self-conscious about playing a double game. Gothic narrative, which commentators of the 1790s associated with an unprecedented and alarming power of moving its audience, both tells the story of the deleterious effects of credulity on its characters and plays on its readers' readiness to believe. Frantically turning its pages, our volition suspended by our drive to know what will happen next, tortured by the narrative digressions that sadistically prolong our time on the rack of suspense, in our interactions with the book we have reason to see ourselves as the doubles of the victims of plotting *inside* the book.

Aesthetic Education

When the audience of *Otranto* or *Udolpho* confront within these novels a real belief in ghosts—something that the protagonist who is our proxy does each time that she indulges the domestic servants around her in their idle chatter—that credulity both resembles and contrasts with our own willingness to let ourselves be swayed by the powers of aesthetic illusion. It is as though for the Gothic novel, belief in fiction, which is belief only in the figurative sense, 'cannot exist without poaching on its opposite' (Russett 1998: 165). 'Where did the charm exist?' Emily St Aubert asks plaintively in a scene of reading that makes her status as our proxy conspicuous, as she finds that 'the visionary scenes of the poet' no longer absorb her as they once had (by this stage in the narrative she is a prisoner of Udolpho, held there against her will until she signs over her inheritance to her wicked uncle): 'Was [the charm] in my mind, or in the imagination of the poet?' (vol. 3, ch. 5; 383). The presence in *Udolpho* of such questions, posed within a narrative that right up to its conclusion equivocates as to whether spectres too are, or are not, only 'in' the 'mind', testifies to how programmatic early Gothic novels were about taking the measure of the 'emotions caused by fictions' and about assessing the differences separating the ostensibly consensual illusions that are at stake in aesthetic response from reactions to other sorts of objects, real and unreal.

The novels pursued this project, as well, in their preoccupation with visual representations. They gauge in some detail beholders' responses to the spooky portraits and statues that are to be found in nearly every nook and cranny of the standard-issue haunted mansion or ruined abbey. In *Otranto*, for instance, the responses elicited by the portrait and statue of 'Alfonso the Good' (the dead ancestor whose spirit presides over the catastrophes the novel unfolds) run a gamut of possibilities. They variously endow these works of art with too much spirit and animation and too little. When the novel's chatty servant takes notice rather crudely of how her young mistress, Matilda, in the wake of her meeting with the brave young peasant who resembles these representations, has taken to gazing at the portrait and saying her prayers in front of the statue, even though Alfonso is '"no saint by the almanack"' (ch. 2; 39), Matilda replies that, though she admits this show of admiration is uncommon, '"I am not in love with a coloured pannel"' (ch. 2; 39). What or whom is she in love with, then? Matilda's response is both one of those denials that affirm and a repudiation of art as such. Walpole, an impassioned collector of pictures himself, underscores that it is the proper nature of works of art to make viewers, whether pious idolaters or art-lovers, act as if they are engaging not with dead matter but with living persons. At the start of *The Monk* Ambrosio must talk himself into a proper response, a compound of piety and aesthetic taste, to the painting of the Virgin Mary on the wall of his cell and proves no more convincing than Matilda in *Otranto*: 'It is not the Woman's beauty that fills me with such enthusiasm; It is the Painter's skill that I admire, it is the Divinity that I adore!' (vol. 1, ch. 2; 41). Gothic writers further probe the boundaries demarcating the aesthetic when they arrange for the supernatural to erupt into the mundane world in the form of representations that come literally rather than figuratively to life. Thus in *The Monk* the devil gets his claws into Ambrosio by having his 'subordinate but crafty spirit' approach him in the form of a human being who also is the original of his adored painting (vol. 3, ch. 5; 440). When the unfortunate Agnes di Medina sketches the spectre known as the Bleeding Nun, elaborating on superstitious legends circulated by servants in her household, her picture is inadvertently necromantic and raises the ghost, who then usurps Agnes's place in the arms of her lover: that origin makes that 'real' ghost a copy of a copy of something that has no real-world referent.

In the Radcliffean *The Nocturnal Minstrel*—which Eleanor Sleath published with Minerva Press in 1810, just as the spell that Gothic stories, romances, and tales of other times had cast on the public appeared at last to be dissolving—a certain Earl Ormond, volunteering to watch all night in a chamber reported to be haunted, tries to entertain himself with 'the history of St Dunstan, and several other persons of like religious eminence'. The saint's legend, normally devotional reading, constitutes for this well-educated sceptic of the fifteenth century, the narrator informs us, 'what he perhaps thought, but dared not call, sacred romance'.[22] Almost a half-century after Walpole modelled how an after-life as fiction might be bestowed on a work written as a history, novelists continued to rehearse the experiments with genre and context initiated by *The Castle of Otranto*. They remained committed to exploring the aesthetic education enabling the modern, sceptical reader to have faith in his or her book and to read on, as if believing that such things as miracles and ghosts could really be.

---

[22] Eleanor Sleath, *The Nocturnal Minstrel; or, The Spirit of the Wood*, 2 vols (London: A. K. Newman, 1810), 2.7.

11

The Novel Wars of 1790–1804

JON MEE

THE French Revolution profoundly shaped the English novel in the 1790s. Originally the Revolution was welcomed by sections of the reading public, many of whom regarded it as bringing France into line with the liberty under law perceived as the British system of constitutional monarchy. Opinion began to change significantly after Edmund Burke's attack on the Revolution in *Reflections on the Revolution in France* (1790). The pamphlet was the first of a series that warned the propertied classes against men of talents—Jean-Jacques Rousseau providing the prime example—who lacked the ballast to steady their own wilful imaginings without the authority of Church and King. A host of pamphlets and books from Thomas Paine's cheap and popular *Rights of Man* (1791–2) to William Godwin's *Enquiry Concerning Political Justice* (1793) rebutted Burke's faith in time-tested precedent as mere Gothic prejudice. The early years of the 1790s were dominated by this pamphlet war now known as 'the Revolution controversy' (Butler 1984).

Accounts of the novels written in the decade after Burke's assault on the Revolution are now routinely organized around the two poles of 'Jacobin' and 'Anti-Jacobin' fiction. Certainly the novel in this decade did find itself shaped by the 'war of ideas' (Butler 1975), but—like the pamphlet war itself—it was neither conducted as a straightforward exchange of fire between two distinct ideological camps, nor was it untouched by developments in the novel as a form. Questions of literary medium and political perspective were not neutral in relation to each other. William Godwin's unpublished essay 'History and Romance', for instance, implied that the novel provided a distinctive kind of historical knowledge, oriented towards lived experience rather than chronology or the deeds of great men, precisely the kind of orientation Burke thought Jacobin philosophers neglected in their visionary enthusiasm for change.[1] In Godwin's eyes, the novel or 'romance' was uniquely adapted to communicating philosophical issues in an accessible and persuasive

---

[1] 'Essay of History and Romance', in William Godwin, *Educational and Literary Writings*, ed. Pamela Clemit: vol. 5 of *Political and Philosophical Writings of William Godwin*, gen. ed. Mark Philp, 6 vols (London: Pickering and Chatto, 1993), 290–301.

form, but also to giving a deeper sense of the affective nature of human intercourse. From a more traditional perspective, however, the novel was surrounded by questions of status. In this regard, anxieties about presuming to act in the name of the state felt by many of those who wrote in defence of the status quo were exacerbated by using a form not readily associated with traditional values, but nor were those writing on the other side of the question necessarily confident about their medium either. In her *Memoirs of Emma Courtney* (1796), Mary Hays implicitly dissociated her own intervention in the medium from her heroine's 'avidity for books': 'I subscribed to a circulating library, and frequently read, or rather devoured—little careful in the selection—from ten to fourteen novels in a week'.[2] Assumptions such as these often reinforced a tendency among those committed to reform to think of all forms of linguistic mediation as vitiated by the effects of social rank and hierarchy. Language itself is under pressure in 'Jacobin' novels from a dream of communication as rational transparency or the open commerce of the heart. If the popularity of the novel as a medium was part of the attraction for those with a political point to make, it also created an additional layer of anxiety in relation to their authority to intervene in public culture as novelists whatever their ideological point of view.

'Jacobin' Novelists 1792–6

Early in the 1790s a group of novels were published with a distinctly progressive agenda by writers most of whom were known to each other socially. These included Eliza Fenwick's *Secresy* (1795), William Godwin's *Things as They Are; or, The Adventures of Caleb Williams* (1794), Thomas Holcroft's *Anna St. Ives* (1792) and *Adventures of Hugh Trevor* (1794–7), Elizabeth Inchbald's *A Simple Story* (1791) and *Nature and Art* (1796), and Charlotte Smith's *Desmond* (1792). Godwin's diary and Wollstonecraft's correspondence show that from 1796 at least Mary Robinson was also in contact with this cluster of writers.[3] Many of their values are obviously present in her fifth novel *Walsingham* (1797), not least in its emphasis on woman as a 'thinking and an enlightened being' elaborated later in her *Letter to the Women of England* (1799).[4] To this group of novels written mainly in the metropolis might be added Robert Bage's *Man As He Is* (1792) and *Hermsprong* (1796). Bage was a product of the provincial Enlightenment associated with figures like Erasmus Darwin and

---

[2] Mary Hays, *Memoirs of Emma Courtney*, 2 vols (London: G. G. and J. Robinson, 1796), 1.26.

[3] Godwin seems to have taken tea with Robinson on 9 February 1796, and then saw her regularly over that spring and into the next year. See Godwin's diary, MS Abinger e. 7, Bodleian Library, University of Oxford. Some time late in 1796, Wollstonecraft wrote to Robinson to accept a dinner invitation on behalf of herself and Mary Hays. See Mary Wollstonecraft, *Collected Letters*, ed. Janet Todd (Harmondsworth: Penguin, 2004), 387.

[4] Mary Robinson, *Letter to the Women of England, on the Injustice of Mental Subordination* (London: Longman, 1799), 12.

Joseph Priestley, a group very much networked into the intellectual ferment of London. Metropolitan booksellers like Joseph Johnson and the Robinson brothers played a crucial role in these networks, whether by publishing novels, especially the Robinsons, or bringing them together with other writers in sociable gatherings. (Publishers were not rigidly ideological: the Robinson brothers, for instance, published both of the 'conservative' Elizabeth Hamilton novels discussed later in this chapter.) Describing this group as 'Jacobin' is to accept a smear that opponents applied to the reform movement in general, implying that it was a conduit for French republicanism and atheism, which is not very helpful in any accurate description of the politics of the novels under consideration here, but speaks to the difficulty of maintaining any position critical of the status quo in the febrile atmosphere of literary culture after 1792.

Nearly all the members of this group of novelists were sympathetic to political reform in some degree and certainly wished for what they perceived as a more rational reordering of the social hierarchy, not least by making it more open to people of talents like themselves. Most of them were from the middling sort. Several had associations with religious nonconformity, especially Rational Dissent, although Inchbald was a Catholic. Many had already made literary careers for themselves prior to the French Revolution. The reputation of Charlotte Smith as a major poet gained by her *Elegiac Sonnets* (1784), for instance, had been followed with the success of a series of sentimental novels in the 1780s. Less of a celebrity author, Bage had also published several novels in the 1780s, as had Godwin much less successfully. Holcroft and Inchbald were already important figures in the theatre.

These novelists were 'Jacobins' much after the sense explained by Richard Dinmore (Junior) in 1796. Dinmore was a participant in the vibrant radical culture of Norwich well known to Godwin and several other of the novelists discussed here. He sharply distinguished their English 'Jacobin' principles from 'the proceedings of that fell monster Robespierre'.[5] These 'principles of pure English growth' included 'equality, without which...there can be no liberty,' but clearly distinguished from any 'desire, forcibly to equalize all property' (6–7). Whatever the specifics of their politics individually, few of the novelists were active members of the popular political associations (virtually impossible, anyway, for the women), with the exception of Holcroft, who joined the Society of Constitutional Information in 1792. Most, like Eliza Fenwick, married to a London Corresponding Society member, were part of the penumbra of sociability that surrounded them in London and provincial centres like Derby and Norwich. Godwin, whose *Political Justice* (1793) was perhaps the most important intellectual influence on the novels of the decade, was very much part of the same world, but actively wrote against political

---

[5] Richard Dinmore, Junior, *An Exposition of the Principles of the English Jacobins*, 2nd edn (Norwich: John March, 1796), 6.

associations and attacked his friend John Thelwall for addressing them.[6] Godwin's politics were predicated on a faith in the progressive possibilities of enlightened exchanges between educated readers. His validation of 'the collision of mind with mind' in *Political Justice* (3.15) imagined a limitless field of enquiry, with almost no subject off limits, but did not encourage it much beyond the relatively closed circles of his literary friends and acquaintances.

Brought up in the political environment of the popular debating societies of the 1780s and by 1794 the principal intellectual organizer of the London Corresponding Society, Thelwall believed that Godwin failed to realize that 'the closet would be as fruitless as the tomb, if it were not for the materials that debate and conversation furnish'.[7] This riposte was not simply exercising the contempt of the activist for the intellectual. Thelwall himself had always been eager to succeed as a man of letters. His Shandean prose medley *The Peripatetic* (1793), written while he was defending London's radical clubs from the magistracy's attempts to close them down, was an exploration of the relationship between sympathy and politics common to most Jacobin novels. Thelwall later wrote at least one novel, *The Daughter of Adoption* (1801), under the pseudonym John Beaufort, his reputation as a Jacobin still strong enough to make it difficult for him to get a public hearing. In the 1790s, literary publications associated with the LCS tended to oscillate between familiar forms of satirical poetry and versions of pastoral classicism that implied cultural competence on the part of those bidding for inclusion in the public sphere. In this regard, the novel as a cultural form still associated with the unsophisticated reader would have been a dubious ally for those aiming to assert their cultural literacy.

The 'Jacobin' novels of 1792–6 had a great deal in common with the sentimental novelists of the 1770s and 1780s, not least in their tendency to couch their explorations of the workings of human sympathy in epistolary form. Where they differed was in exploiting the format to create a space for more explicitly political attacks on the empty forms of social convention (including the cult of sensibility). Many of the plots, with important exceptions, including *Caleb Williams*, to which I will return, focus on a romantic triangle, placing a woman between two suitors, often under the authority of an uncaring or despotic parent. Often one of the suitors is a seducer, usually a pale imitation of Samuel Richardson's Lovelace, as with Coke Clifton in Holcroft's *Anna St. Ives*. The other is a version of Henry Mackenzie's 'man of feeling', but with the emphasis on stoical self-command over a naturally impassioned personality. A generous sympathy validates the authenticity of the hero and heroine's responses to their world and each other, but it is constantly being indexed for its rationality in contrast with the emotional self-indulgence associated

---

[6] See the 'Of Political Associations' section of *An Enquiry concerning Political Justice*, ed. Mark Philp, and *Considerations on Lord Grenville's and Mr. Pitt's Bills* (1795) in *Political Writings II*, ed. Philp: vols 3 and 2, respectively, of *Political and Philosophical Writings of William Godwin*.

[7] John Thelwall, *The Tribune*, 3 vols (London: for the Author, 1795–6), 2.xiv.

with the cult of sensibility. In *Anna St. Ives* the hero and heroine debate the relative merits of acting upon their love for each other. Anna at first determines to repress her passion and marry the rake Clifton in order to reform him. Frank Henley, the son of her father's landscape gardener, argues that they ought to be together not just in the name of the truth of their affections, but also to 'exert their powers for the welfare of society'.[8] For their critics, like George Walker in *The Vagabond* (1799), these *'political romances'* were simply falling into the trap long associated with prose romance in general. The 'heated . . . imaginations' of their authors were giving visionary impossibilities 'which never were, and never will be practical'.[9]

The heroes and heroines of the Jacobin novel speak a language of the heart focused on sincerity rather than the display of affection. In this regard, indiscriminate novel reading of the kind Emma Courtney indulges in as she descends into gloomy isolation often features as a form of self-indulgence, although the Rousseau of *Julie, ou La Nouvelle Héloïse* and 'the divine Sterne', as Holcroft described the author of *Tristram Shandy* in *Anna St. Ives* (1.2), sometimes appear as prototypes of natural sensibility transcending social convention. Eliza Fenwick's *Secresy* (1795) begins with Caroline Ashburn pleading with the guardian of her young friend Sibella to allow her more intercourse with the world: 'Gladly would I divise [*sic*] a means by which to induce you to lay aside this prejudice against us, and in the language of reason, as from one being to another, discuss with me the merits or defects of your plan.'[10] Where the guardian wishes to educate his ward in seclusion (somewhat after the plan of Rousseau's *Emile*), Caroline is a Wollstonecraftian advocate of the merits of rational conversation for women out in the world. Later, Caroline tells Lady Barlowe that Sibella only 'wishes for communication, for intercourse, for society; but she is too sincere to purchase any pleasure by artifice and concealment' (1.128). The novel's love plot ends tragically, as in Hays's novel, because the hero and heroine can find no adequate means of communication under current social arrangements. Caroline is one of several female characters in these novels who complicate the love-triangle plot by offering a 'rational' perspective on the thwarting of 'romance' narrative by social structures and conventions; another is Miss Campinet in Bage's *Hermsprong*. Their very rationality seems implicitly to debar them from a central role in the romance plot.

Frequently these novels seek epiphanies of sincerity, sometimes modelled after the exchange of the tear-soaked handkerchief between Yorick and Maria in *A Sentimental Journey* (1768). What is omitted is Sterne's delight in the libidinal possibilities of such scenes, repressed, as in *Anna St. Ives*, in the name of a higher ethical imperative. The debate on the question of obedience to paternal authority that had surrounded Richardson's *Sir*

---

[8] Thomas Holcroft, *Anna St. Ives*, 7 vols (London: Shepperson and Reynolds, 1792), 1.176–7.
[9] George Walker, *The Vagabond*, 3rd edn, 2 vols (London: G. Walker, and Hurst, 1799), 1.ix.
[10] Eliza Fenwick, *Secresy; or, The Ruin on the Rock*, 3 vols (London: for the Author, 1795), 1.3.

Charles Grandison (1753–4) tends to be decided decisively in favour in the autonomy of rational judgement in the younger generation, with an emphasis on the equality of the intellectual capacities of the sexes. In this regard, nearly all these 'Jacobin' novels narrate a preference for domesticity as a natural order. The dangers of the Gothic castle associated with the aristocracy, as in Fenwick's Gothic-tinged *Secresy*, develop a logic implicit in the novels of Ann Radcliffe into a more explicitly radical account of the corrupting power of patriarchy. Political romances of this kind may offer love between men and women as a metonym for free society, but in the process often insulate their protagonists from the claims of any more collective or historical sense of identity. In formal terms, these tendencies tend to operate so as to render dialogue into a version of formal debate (Kelly 1976: 163–4). Readers expecting the naturalism of the nineteenth-century novel may find these aspects of the Jacobin novel stiff and unrewarding. Perhaps more fairly, complicating triumphalist accounts of fiction's victory over the philosophical dialogue as a genre, the novels might be regarded as an experimental development. For some time, eighteenth-century criticism had been exploring the idea that the philosophical dialogue ought to remake itself into a more affective form oriented towards engagement of the reader's sympathies. Hazlitt, sympathetic to Holcroft's politics, still judged his fiction a failure because his characters remained 'pure creatures of the understanding, mere abstract essences, which cannot kindle too warm a glow of enthusiasm in the breast'.[11] Where dialogue tends towards the formal statement of principles and, especially, mutual transparency, these novels appear to perpetuate a dream of reason. Language seems an obstruction rather than material for creating values. Jane Austen's sense of conversation as a complex arena, where the motives of the participants are not always fully known even to themselves, rarely informs them. Where distinctive speech patterns appear, they are often satirical either of the complacent cant of the aristocracy, again as in Holcroft's Coke Clifton in *Anna St. Ives*, or of the irrationality or concupiscence of the lower classes, as in the local traders in Smith's *Desmond*, whose only concern in the franchise seems how best to sell their vote. Unfortunately for the didactic purposes of the novelists, these excursions into linguistic variety can serve to make these speakers the centre of readerly interest, as Hazlitt noted in his *Life of Holcroft* (2.3–4), compounding the Lovelace-paradox that makes the rake the centre of narrative engagement. In this regard, Holcroft's skills as a playwright often appear, with some few exceptions (Kelly 1976: 163–4), to conflict with his novelistic aims.

Similarly, these novels split from sentimental precursors in Mackenzie and Sterne in their relative inattention to the psychology of association. Most Jacobin novelists were committed to some version of the idea that error was produced by environment rather

---

[11] Thomas Holcroft (and William Hazlitt), *The Life of Thomas Holcroft, Written by Himself*, 2 vols (London: Constable, 1925), 2.6.

than inherent evil. Change the conditions, reform society, and human improvement will follow. Ironically then, environment often appears in these novels as a rather uniform external influence that is to be superseded in the name of right reason to leave the protagonists free, usually to enjoy their love for each other, even if it is imagined as radiating out to set an example to the world. In novels such as *Anna St. Ives*, the operations of circumstance in forming character are rarely described in any detail nor understood with much subtlety. Hazlitt thought Holcroft's characters 'machines put into action, or vehicles of certain general sentiments to operate in particular situations', more like the failure of *Sir Charles Grandison* than Richardson's achievement in *Clarissa* (*Life of Holcroft*, 2.4, 7).

Caleb Williams and Hermsprong

Perhaps the two most obvious exceptions to these generalizations are Godwin's *Caleb Williams* and Bage's *Hermsprong*. Godwin's novel develops an interest in psychology that quickly won it a reputation as a major innovation in the novel, although this was partly because of a desire (with which Godwin to a certain extent colluded in his later years) to play down its political motivations. For Hazlitt, *Caleb Williams* brilliantly overcame the failings of novels like *Anna St. Ives* in its faithfulness to 'the possible workings of the human mind'.[12] Godwin started the novel soon after the success of his major philosophical work *Political Justice* (1793), widely accepted among intellectuals at the time as the defining text of the reform movement. Godwin's book has none of the vernacular zing that made Paine's *Rights of Man* the major influence on the popular reform societies. Indeed its aim is to argue that mind can transcend social conventions of any kind to perceive justice disinterestedly on the basis of rational utility. For Godwin, even associations for reform were dubious if they clouded the independent intellect with the echoing passions of noisy assemblies. Yet he was not insensitive to the role of the affections in human perception, and his decision to write a novel revealed his understanding that the road to truth had to be fitted to human imperfections.

In the preface he restored to the second edition of 1796, Godwin opposed his novel to the 'refined and abstract speculation' of *Political Justice*, presenting it as 'a study and delineation of things passing in the moral world'.[13] Committed to the idea that 'the spirit and character of government intrudes itself into every rank of society', Godwin's novel is predicated on the assumption that this is a 'truth highly worthy to be communicated to persons whom books of philosophy and science are never likely to reach' (1.vi). The minute particularity of the novel allows for exposure 'of the modes of domestic and

---

[12] William Hazlitt, *Complete Works*, ed. P. P. Howe, 21 vols (London: J. M. Dent, 1930–4), 6.130.
[13] William Godwin, *Things as They Are; or, The Adventures of Caleb Williams*, 2nd edn, 3 vols (London: G. G. and J. Robinson, 1796), 1.[v].

unrecorded despotism' (1.vi). Gothic plots of dark deeds in distant places are brought home to the heart of the nation. 'History and Romance', probably written when the second edition of *Caleb Williams* was in preparation, was even more explicit on the appropriateness of the novel as a medium for such a task. Acknowledging that the novel as a genre had been 'exposed to more obloquy than any other' because of the association with the unselective tastes 'of women and boys', Godwin nonetheless celebrates it as 'a nobler species of composition than history' (5.298). He identifies its greatest achievements with 'a delineation of consistent, human character, in a display of the manner in which such a character acts under successive circumstances, in showing how character increases and assimilates new substances to its own, and how it decays, together with the catastrophe into which by its own gravity it naturally declines' (5.301).

The description closely fits the course of *Caleb Williams*, whose hero's curiosity leads him on into destruction via a complex fascination with his pursuer that anticipates the relationship between Victor Frankenstein and the Monster in the great novel written by Godwin's daughter Mary Shelley. The aristocratic protagonist, Falkland, is no evil seducer, but a paragon of English civility of the sort celebrated by Burke, whose adventures on the continent, told in the first portion of the narrative, invoke the Italian adventures of Richardson's *Sir Charles Grandison*. A society based on inequality defended by warped institutions cannot but pervert even its best souls; so Falkland kills his boorish neighbour Tyrrel because of his overinvestment in a code of honour. When Caleb discovers this secret he becomes a standing threat to Falkland's reputation that must be extirpated. The plot of pursuit shows Caleb unable to find any redress in institutions of state, or, indeed, to find comfort in any community, whether construed as popular print media or the group of robbers he joins in the forest. As the novel goes on, so the possibility for the individual finding redress in any forum other than face-to-face personal accountability seems to disappear. In the original version of the novel's ending, Caleb fails to convince the court of Falkland's guilt. He dies a victim, his personality dispersed into the manuscript fragments that form the novel's last few pages. In the published revised version, Caleb's face-to-face denunciation of Falkland in the courtroom destroys his nemesis, but also leaves the hero isolated and consumed by guilt. In both versions, public institutions prove equally inadequate to a drama of individual psychology where pursuer and pursued have become caught in the same web of misperceptions.

If Godwin's novel turns into a powerfully darkening study of pathology, Robert Bage's *Hermsprong* is notable for the comic lightness of its philosophical and political debates in a style that seems to anticipate Thomas Love Peacock's novels of the 1810s. The issue of the natural affections is brought to the fore by making its hero a version of the noble savage. Hermsprong returns to the artificialities of English society having been educated among Native Americans, although, in a transformation scene true to the romance origins of most Jacobin novels, he turns out eventually to be an English aristocrat in disguise. The revelation takes place in a courtroom, like the denouement of *Caleb Williams*. In

Bage's novel, the hero seems able to step in with his 'unstudied, unimitated ease' and assert the autonomy of his rational goodwill.[14] Whereas Godwin's hero is the victim of social identity, Hermsprong enjoys a fantasy of endless reinvention. His critiques of English manners, 'you talk, and call it conversation' (2.155), produce not so much the alternative of rational transparency, 'the reciprocal communication of mind with mind' (1.107), a phrase that implies a rebuttal of Godwin's 'collision', but ironic deferral as he refuses to reveal his identity until the final courtroom scene. Liberty here seems to be primarily a kind of rational flirtation, where the hero remains disinterestedly aloof from social constraint before revealing himself to have been loyal to the King all along. Brought to court on a charge of sedition, it emerges that not only is Hermsprong the heir to the title of his chief accuser, but also that he has thwarted a wage riot: 'We cannot all be rich: there is no equality of property which can last a day' (3.196). Whereas the final encounter with the law in *Caleb Williams* provides only testimony to its inadequacy as a tribunal to judge personal relations, in *Hermsprong* it seems paradoxically only to confirm a liberal dream of the hero's autonomy and freedom from the various claims of identity placed on it by other characters in the novel (Nersessian 2011).

Hays and Wollstonecraft

One of the many devoted admirers recruited by *Political Justice* was Mary Hays. Impassioned by the doctrine of candour common to Godwin and many other Jacobin novelists, she wrote directly to the author to borrow a copy of the book she had heard widely praised. There followed a lengthy correspondence and friendship, until they were estranged after Wollstonecraft's death. Prior to meeting Godwin, Hays had already become a devoted admirer of Wollstonecraft's talents. Both women were to develop their own novelized explorations of the claustrophobia so brilliantly developed in the narrative technique of *Caleb Williams*, but with a feminist edge that showed how artificial social relations vitiated even the intimacies of the domestic sphere and any opportunity for women to relate to others on anything like a rational basis.

Early in her career as a writer, Hays had already published on the virtues of candour: 'the great bane to the pleasures of conversation is affectation, or the wish to appear to possess what nature has denied'.[15] Contrary to Godwin's insistence on disinterested benevolence, Hays—influenced by the philosophy of Helvétius—placed a stronger emphasis on the role of the affections in human relations. She insisted upon it in their correspondence: 'Man appears to me to be of one substance, capable of receiving from external impressions

---

[14] Robert Bage, *Hermsprong; or, Man as He is Not*, 3 vols (London: William Lane, 1796), 1.84.
[15] Mary Hays, *Letters and Essays, Moral and Miscellaneous* (London: T. Knott, 1793), 192.

sensible ideas, successively formed into various combinations & trains, carried on, by means of sympathy & association with mechanical exactness, in an infinite series of causes & effects.'[16] One consequence was that she tended to represent human relations, when allowed to flow unhindered, as an open-hearted intercourse, a mechanical relay of sympathy, centred, unlike Godwin's ideas of disinterestedness, on the individual physical body. By the same token, the pathology of the passions was a central concern of her writing. These issues are subjected to intense scrutiny in her novel *Memoirs of Emma Courtney* (1796), which caused a scandal by recycling letters and conversations with Godwin and William Frend. In the novel, Hays explores the desire for 'genuine effusions of the heart and mind' as distinct from 'the vain ostentation of sentiment, lip deep, which causing no emotion, communicates none' (2.14). One result of this kind of distinction could be an emphasis on the immediate role of the body in sympathetic communication. Compared with forms of social speech vitiated by the codes of politeness and their replication of false distinctions of hierarchy, the body might seem a more immediate conveyor of the truth of one's affections, but this response tended to bring with it a further anxiety about sex in tainting the purer feelings, one of the reasons Hays upbraided Godwin for his love of Sterne in their correspondence (399). At one point at least in *Emma Courtney*, the heroine expresses a preference for 'conversing [by letter] at a distance' with Mr Francis, because of his 'penetrating glance' (1.73, 85). The intense desire for a transparency of affection could find the body a further unwelcome obstacle in the desire for truthful relations between subjects.

The plot of *Memoirs of Emma Courtney* charts the development of an ardent young woman who is educated first through solitary reading and 'conversing only with books' (1.86). She then graduates to the sociable conversation at her father's table, an uneven mix of fashionable gallantry and literary talk. There she meets Mr Francis who provides her with the rational conversation for which she hungers. The literal and epistolary conversations with Mr Francis fulfil the notion of the medium's ability to give vigour and spark to intellectual life. Without it, her mind 'wanted *impression*, and sunk into languor' (1.89), an allusion to Wollstonecraft's *A Short Residence in Sweden, Denmark, and Norway* (1796), read by Hays as she wrote her novel. Emma also finds relief in the conversation of a neighbour, Mrs Harley (the surname of Mackenzie's hero in *The Man of Feeling*), but her incessant return to the virtues of her son Augustus so impresses Emma that her enthusiastic nature converts him into a version of Rousseau's St Preux or Emile. Gazing at Harley's picture in the library, she imagines a communion with it that allows her to 'read in the features all the qualities imputed to the original by a tender and partial parent' (1.112–13). 'Cut off from the society of mankind', as Emma puts it, she gives in to a tendency to 'reverie'

---

[16] Hays to Godwin, 1 October 1795, *The Correspondence of Mary Hays (1779–1843), British Novelist*, ed. Marilyn L. Brooks (Lewiston, Queenston, Lampeter: The Edwin Mellen Press, 2004), 400.

(1.113) associated with Rousseau (a pattern also explored in Wollstonecraft's travel book). When Emma actually encounters Harley, they do for a short while enjoy a happy form of domestic sociability: 'our intervals in study were employed in music, in drawing, in conversation, in reading the *belles letters*—in—"The feast of reason, and the flow of souls"' (1.139). Alexander Pope's line from the 'First satire on the second book of Horace' does its familiar eighteenth-century work in marking the desire for the circulation of polite senti-ment around society, but Emma seeks a more absolute sympathy, a form of transparent communion, not usually identified with the allusion to Pope. What she finds instead is misunderstanding, resistance, and outright rejection. Emma writes to Augustus Harley wishing 'we were in the vehicular state, and that you understood the sentient language; you might then comprehend the whole of what I mean to express, but find too delicate for *words*' (1.177).[17] Faced with the 'insipid *routine* of heartless, mindless intercourse' on offer to women, 'an ardent spirit, denied a scope for its exertions!' inevitably, so Hays implies, projects the sympathetic intercourse it desires onto its surroundings, finding reciproca-tion where none exists (1.168–9).

In Mary Robinson's fiction, especially *Walsingham* (1797), the same kind of critique is aimed particularly at the routines of fashionable life, which she knew much better than either Hays or Wollstonecraft. What these women novelists explored as a pathol-ogy of the passions subject to feminist critique was misrepresented in many anti-Jacobin novels as their credo. Novelists like Hays were represented as abandoning the realities of social relations as they operated in the world around them for the romance of pure communion and political equality. Godwin, Hays, and Wollstonecraft, especially after the passing of William Pitt's repressive legislation in the 'Two Acts' of 1795, lived in an atmosphere of paranoia about the government's power to restrict freedom of speech even in quasi-domestic situations. Pitt's system of spies and informers was taken to have pen-etrated not just the coffee house, but even into the home. This sense of claustrophobic relations of power striking into the deepest domestic relations plays a powerful part in *Maria; or, The Wrongs of Woman*. The novel was left unfinished at Wollstonecraft's death in 1797, but published by Godwin with his *Memoirs of the Author of the Vindication of Rights of Woman* (1798).

'Marriage had bastilled me for life' says Wollstonecraft's heroine.[18] Wollstonecraft's novel opens with the Bastille made domestic in both senses of the word. Cast into a London madhouse by her husband, Maria declines under both an English state tyranny and a despotic marriage pointedly distinguished from the exotic settings of the Gothic

---

[17] The idea of 'vehicular language', as Hays acknowledged in her notes (1.178), was taken from Abraham Tucker's *The Light of Nature Pursued* (1768–77). Tucker's book was abridged by Hazlitt a few years later. See also Chandler, Chapter 6.

[18] Mary Wollstonecraft, *Posthumous Works of the Author of Vindication of the Rights of Woman*, 4 vols (London: J. Johnson, 1798), 2.34.

novel: 'Abodes of horror have frequently been described, and castles, filled with spectres and chimeras, conjured up by the magic spell of genius to harrow the soul, and absorb the wondering mind. But, formed as such stuff as dreams are made of, what were they to the mansion of despair, in one corner of which Maria sat, endeavouring to recall her scattered thoughts' (1.1). The account of Maria's treatment at the hand of her libertine husband continues the Jacobin novel's critique of 'the misery and oppression, peculiar to women, that arise out of the partial laws and customs of society' (1.[7]). Where *Maria* departs from the kind of plot line laid down in *Anna St. Ives* is that the virtuous reformer who rescues the heroine turns out to be only another version of the man of feeling whose passions operate primarily for the satisfaction of his own desires. Like Bage's *Hermsprong*, Darnford is American-returned, but he seems only to have imbibed a sense of commercial self-interest there that he affects to despise. The Bastille of gender and perhaps even all social relations seems so deeply inscribed in the novel that there is no perspective beyond the sense of the world as 'a vast prison, and women born slaves' (1.14). The only partial exception may be the relationship Maria starts to form with her gaoler, the ex-prostitute Jemima, who seems to redeem the idea of the 'square-elbowed family drudge' disdained in *A Vindication of the Rights of Woman* (1792).[19] More generally, the novel has replaced 'political romance' with a sense of a dead end for any woman who has the kind of personality able to respond to Rousseau's *Nouvelle Héloïse* with the vivacious sympathy Maria shows.

Anti-Jacobin Novels

After 1795, a wave of anti-Jacobin novels operated as a form of cultural policing designed to counter the political principles of Godwin, but also aiming to curb what was more generally perceived as the feminization of culture widely identified with the novel itself. In these novels, the Jacobin romance plot that mapped politics on to Eros became a seduction plot, often ending in tragedy for the gullible girl who casts off traditional values in the name of 'the new light'.[20] For all that they presented a critique of sensibility in their fiction, the lives of Hays and Wollstonecraft, especially, were used as proof of the necessary consequences of casting aside traditional authority. Where the novels of Hays, Robinson, and Wollstonecraft present Rousseau's fiction, for instance, as a promise that is far from easily fulfilled or even as a snare set by predatory males, anti-Jacobin novelists repeatedly represented thinly veiled versions of the women novelists as gleefully sacrificing prudence to the libidinal ideology of *La Nouvelle Héloïse*. The details of Wollstonecraft's

---

[19] Mary Wollstonecraft, *A Vindication of the Rights of Woman* (London: J. Johnson, 1792), 145.
[20] See Mrs Bullock, *Dorothea, or A Ray of the New Light*, 3 vols (London: G. G. and J. Robinson, 1801).

unhappy love life presented in Godwin's *Memoirs of Wollstonecraft* (1798) were something of a godsend in this respect, and it was often cited directly by anti-Jacobin novelists. In Robert Bisset's *Douglas; or, The Highlander* (1800), Mr William Subtlewould—who also quotes directly from *Political Justice* in various places—even gives an account of his wife's pre-nuptial affairs. Sometimes the role of the sentimental seducer bifurcated into types of Godwin and Thelwall: the unworldly enthusiastic philosopher and the zealous popular agitator, as, for instance, in Walker's *The Vagabond*, where they appear as Stupeo and Citizen Ego respectively. As for the female characters, they tend to fall into two types (or some combination of them). Abandoning trust in parental authority and religious guidance, the independent judgement of the heroine is usually shown to be little match for the powers of seduction of the radical villains, as with the eponymous heroine in Mrs Bullock's *Dorothea, or A Ray of the New Light* (1801). Other heroines, more like the versions of Mary Hays in Charles Lloyd's *Edmund Oliver* (1798) and Elizabeth Hamilton's *Memoirs of Modern Philosophers* (1800), aggressively throw off constraints, actively preaching a doctrine of sexual liberation, largely unreciprocated by the objects of their desire. As these summaries suggest, radicalism in these novels appears less in terms of the popular associations for reform that were the primary objects of governmental repression, than as philosophical speculation degenerating into visionary enthusiasm. In this regard, although anti-Jacobin novels like Walker's *Vagabond* routinely claim to be placing 'absurdities' in 'a *practical* light' (1.ix), their energies are expended more in parody than in any attempt at faithfully delineating things as they are.

George Walker described his novel as 'an attempt to parry the Enemy with their own weapons' (1.vi). The trope captures the ambivalence felt by conservative novelists in using a medium so frequently identified with cultural decline. In *The Aristocrat* (1799), Henry James Pye's targets included not just radical philosophy but also 'novellism'.[21] Where 'romance and the earlier novels' had raised expectations of 'courage and modesty' to 'the highest pitch', in the fiction of the present time 'the sentimental philosopher takes the place of the warrior' and 'Platonic love no longer soothes the fair enthusiast' (1.54–5). A later digression acknowledges the necessity of the writer of fiction connecting 'probable events by circumstances, which though by no means either impossible or improbable, seldom really occur in ordinary life', but expresses a concern that novels such as *Caleb Williams* use the medium's disposition towards the ordinary to create a form whereby 'a probable series of incidents...shall make mankind dissatisfied with their natural or political situation, or plead an excuse for the breach of fidelity and chastity' (1.130–1). Pye's own earlier novel *The Democrat* (1795) had included a survey of British society wherein Le Noir, a French agitator, looks for support for his revolutionary schemes. His search is fruitless and scarcely confirms his hopes for a popular insurgency, but any sense of

---

[21] Henry James Pye, *The Aristocrat*, 2 vols (London: Sampson Low, 1799), 1.54.

innate loyalism in the British people is serially compromised by Le Noir's encounters with a host of disaffected individuals eager to complain. The strongest rebuke to Le Noir comes in the guise of an American Quaker, who blames the company for encouraging the Frenchman with their constant arguments on subjects they do not understand. The episode seems emblematic of a more general reluctance in these novels to trust in any populist repudiation of the revolutionary threat and a deeper anxiety about the conse-quences of the liberty of opinion that was supposedly a defining characteristic of British civil society. Few of the novels simply reproduce the sense of cultural superiority to be found in the writing of George Canning, William Gifford, and the elite activists associ-ated with the two *Anti-Jacobin* periodicals (Gilmartin 2007: 151).

Walker already had a career as a popular novelist before he wrote *The Vagabond*, and returned to it after his solitary foray into political fiction. His muted criticism of 'the destructive torpor of the rich' (1.xviii) in his preface suggests an ambivalence about his own role. Walker's reluctance to bring out a '*cheap* edition, which might be within the purchase of *all ranks*' (1.xv), and the justification that it could be consulted in the circulat-ing library just as easily as Thomas Paine's pamphlets, further suggest the kind of status anxiety that haunts many of these novels. When Pye tells those readers of *The Aristocrat* who feel sympathy for its radical characters 'to proceed no further, but immediately to shut the volume, and send it back to the circulating library' (1.25), he implies that novels might be part of the problem with civil society they were aiming to solve. Book clubs and circulating libraries were nearly always treated as objects of suspicion in the *Anti-Jacobin Review*. Faced with this uncertainty about the dissemination of knowledge, the state often acts as a kind of *deus ex machina* in the anti-Jacobin novel whereby the author's control steps aside in the interest of properly vested authorities (Gilmartin 2007: 166–7). Both *The Democrat* and a few years later Isaac D'Israeli's *Vaurien* (1797) used government enforce-ment of the Aliens Act (1793) as a plot device to deport 'patriots and philosophers... with a violent, but a salutary effort'.[22] The intervention of the state at climactic moments in the plots of these two novels serves to indicate the limits of their faith in the good sense of the private citizen as either political participant or the reader of novels.

Edgeworth, Hamilton, and Opie

If anti-Jacobin novels are complicated by ambivalent relations with their medium, a fur-ther obstacle for any simple binary account of the 'war of ideas' comes with those women writers, sometimes bracketed as conservative, who attempted to maintain an idea of the relative autonomy of female rationality in the face of the reaction against the feminism

---

[22] Isaac D'Israeli, *Vaurien: or, Sketches of the Times*, 2 vols (London: Cadell and Davies, 1797), 2.323.

of Hays and Wollstonecraft. Maria Edgeworth, Elizabeth Hamilton, and Amelia Opie all wrote novels that contained parodies of the enthusiastic feminist. Their novels and other writings may seem to place a woman's 'path of duty' outside 'the theatre of public life', as Elizabeth Hamilton placed it in her *Letters on the Elementary Principles of Education* (1801–2).[23] For Hamilton this 'marked [women] out as the mediators and peace-makers of society' (2.224), and in the process what may seem a retreat from public issues turns out to be a matter of primary concern to the welfare of the nation. The ambivalence of the novels in this regard is hardly surprising since Edgeworth, Hamilton, and Opie, each, in different ways, had connections with the Jacobin novelists.

Maria Edgeworth grew up under the strong influence of her father Richard Lovell Edgeworth, who had been a fervent Rousseauist, moving in the same circles of the Midlands enlightenment as Robert Bage. He made sure to provide his daughter with a rational education that included science as well as polite letters. For most of the 1790s, Maria was in Ireland with her family, relatively insulated from the intellectual wars of the 1790s, although not from the French landing of 1798. Edgeworth's Anglo-Irish situation inflected her perspectives on the ideological conflicts of the period, but did not weaken the commitment to an idea of rational improvement, open to women as well as men. Her later fiction, from *Tales of Fashionable Life* (1809–12) onwards, contained penetrating satires of aristocratic life in Britain and Ireland and then across Europe, arguably making her the pre-eminent novelist writing when Jane Austen appeared on the scene. *Belinda* (1801), her first full-length novel, is perhaps more circumspect, but the dangers facing its innocent abroad include unthinking obedience to authority figures as much as any criticism of the rage for innovation, as one might expect from a novel published by Joseph Johnson, friend and supporter of Wollstonecraft from early on in her career.

The novel takes the form of a series of letters between Belinda and her aunt Mrs Stanhope who packs her off to London in the hopes of her making a match. In the metropolis she falls under the influence of Lady Delacour, a slave to the fashionable world, who proves no more reliable a guide for Belinda than her fussy aunt. The true alternative is with the Percival family of Oakley Park who enjoy a rational domesticity at odds with the aunt's conventional piety and the glamorous superficiality of Lady Delacour, the precariousness of whose principles is indicated by her conversion to Methodism when she believes she is dying. Edgeworth offers a portrait of independence of mind carried too far in the travesty of Wollstonecraftian feminism provided by the character of Harriet Freke. Belinda navigates between these different models of feminine conduct to choose (and eventually reform) a hero, Clarence Harvey, who has been tempted by aristocratic worldliness. What this summary of the topography of Edgeworth's plot omits is her often

---

[23] Elizabeth Hamilton, *Letters on the Elementary Principles of Education*, 2 vols (London: G. and J. Robinson, 1801–2), 1.264, 255.

mischievous command of idiom, which catches the ear of conversational variety, and implies her heroine's own attentiveness to the social world. This attentiveness may make the heroine wary of Harriet Freke's idea of emancipation, but it also suggests a freedom to navigate on the grounds of one's own judgement, relatively free of patriarchal author-ity, and, as critics were soon to note of Edgeworth's novels, without the moral guidance of religion.

Elizabeth Hamilton's fiction may seem easier to categorize as anti-Jacobin than Edgeworth's, not least because it is more explicitly committed to a Christian moral-ity, but it is equally absorbed in the question of a rational education for young women. Edgeworth praised Hamilton for having 'thrown open, to all classes of readers, those metaphysical discoveries or observations which have been confined chiefly to the learned'.[24] Hamilton's first novel *Translation of the Letters of a Hindoo Rajah* (1796) satirized various aspects of modern Britain, but also makes a display of the orientalist knowledge Hamilton had gleaned from her brother, insisting 'where freedom of discussion is per-mitted, there scepticism and infidelity will be but little known'.[25] Such confidence in the liberty of opinion is unusual in anti-Jacobin fiction worried that improvement might be carrying a virus destructive of its benefits. Miss Ardent's masculine understanding is cen-sured for neglecting the domestic virtues, but it does *not* lead her down a primrose path of promiscuity. Hamilton's Indian observer, on the contrary, suggests it may be more of a risk to allow 'the powers of the mind to lie dormant' (2.329).

Hamilton's second novel, *Memoirs of Modern Philosophers* (1800) is a much more direct attack on the Godwin circle and contains a memorable parody of Mary Hays as Bridgetina Botherim, who has never 'read any thing but novels and metaphysics'.[26] The plot contrasts three female protagonists: Bridgetina; Julia Delmond, who elopes with the seductive phi-losopher Vallaton; and Harriet Orwell, destined to marry the clergyman Henry Sydney, but only after waiting patiently for their fortunes to improve. If the character of Julia Delmond parodies Wollstonecraft in her love for Vallaton, who quotes Godwin directly at various points, then the portrait is not without sympathy. In a discussion of *Rights of Woman*, Henry describes Wollstonecraft as a 'sensible authoress' betrayed by her feeling nature into arguments that 'superficial readers' mistake as an intention to 'unsex women entirely' (1.196). This position is very different from the demonization of Wollstonecraft found elsewhere in prose and verse satire. Moreover, Harriet Orwell is shown to be quite able to debate matters of principle, backing up active work for the relief of the poor with a philosophical justification that makes her powers of rational deliberation explicit.

---

[24] See Elizabeth Benger, *Memoirs of the Late Mrs Elizabeth Hamilton*, 2nd edn, 2 vols (London: Longman [etc.], 1819). 1.225.

[25] *Translation of the Letters of a Hindoo Rajah*, 2 vols (London: G. G. and J. Robinson, 1796), 2.245.

[26] *Memoirs of Modern Philosophers*, 3 vols (Bath: G. G. and J. Robinson, 1800), 1.4.

As the unmarried Amelia Alderson, Opie had enjoyed very strong links with Norwich radicalism, and knew Godwin and Wollstonecraft personally. She had attended the Treason Trials in 1794, and provided a commentary to her father, later destroyed, sympathetic to the radical defendants, but in *Adeline Mowbray* (1805) she provided a sharp satire on the Godwin–Wollstonecraft circle. Her heroine becomes a disciple of the philosopher Glenmurray, obviously based on Godwin, whom she forces to live up to his theoretical contempt for marriage (as Godwin had not done when he and Wollstonecraft married). Complicating this familiar narrative of the seduction of a young woman by radical ideas is the fact that the locus of the novel's Christian morality is not a representative of Church and State, but another Quaker, Mrs Pemberton. Opie converted to Quakerism herself in the 1820s, to the surprise of many who remembered the brilliant conversationalist of the 1790s, but her change of faith was not simply a withdrawal from the world. In *Adeline Mowbray*, Mrs Pemberton combines elegance with unadorned Quaker dress and manners. This might be seen as meliorating any tinge of enthusiasm associated with the sect, but it also functions as a sign of the novel's idea of her moderation that also plays out in a sympathetic response to Adeline. For it is Pemberton who reunites Adeline with her mother at the end of the novel.

Opie always had reservations about the strenuous rationalism of Wollstonecraft in *Vindication of the Rights of Woman*. She had responded to *A Short Residence in Sweden, Denmark, and Norway* with pleasure, telling Wollstonecraft that 'the cold awe which the philosopher had excited, was lost in the tender sympathy called forth by the woman'. Not that this response simply trumps the rational virtues with feeling, for she praises Wollstonecraft as someone 'who had alternately awakened my sensibility, & gratified my judgement'.[27] The satire of the Godwin–Wollstonecraft relationship in *Adeline Mowbray* may be cruel, but it continues and develops an exploration of the role of female judgement that does not simply reinscribe domestic obedience. These were issues that continued to exercise women novelists like Hannah More in *Coelebs in Search of a Wife* (1808) and Jane Austen in the novels that followed *Sense and Sensibility* (1811). As they moved on from dealing with the Revolution controversy explicitly, these women novelists continued the exploration of the interplay of sympathy and judgement in the world of circumstance that Godwin had seen as intrinsic to the novel as a form, even if from significantly different political perspectives.

---

[27] Alderson to Wollstonecraft, 28 August [1796], MS. Abinger c. 41, Bodleian Library, Oxford.

12

The National Tale

CLAIRE CONNOLLY

THE designation 'national tale' was first used in the early years of the nineteenth century by Irish and Scottish novelists who sought, in the context of a centralizing British state, to draw attention to the cultural specificity of the worlds represented within their fictions. From the 1990s onwards, cultural critics began to return to the term, animated by new devolutionary pressures on the political framework of the United Kingdom. Even as the national tale plays a role in imagining and reimagining Britishness, the fictions may also be seen to adumbrate national futures outside of the framework of Union. Irish crises exert special pressure on the form of the novel in this period: the 1798 and 1803 rebellions and the campaign for Catholic emancipation all play key roles in the development of the national tale.

Edmund Burke's declaration (in conversation with Frances Burney) that the closing decades of the eighteenth century were 'the age for women!'[1] is borne out in the development of the trends in novel-writing in Ireland and Scotland (at least until 1814). Yet despite what Seamus Deane describes as 'the senior role of women' in the nineteenth-century Irish novel (2006: xviii), few critics have chosen to foreground gender in their conceptualization of the national tale. Writers such as Maria Edgeworth, Sydney Owenson (later Lady Morgan), and Christian Isobel Johnstone reimagined the resources of the sentimental novel and drew energy from debates about feminization and domesticity. Maria Edgeworth may have mocked Bluestocking culture in her unpublished play *Whim for Whim*, and Jacobin feminism in *Belinda* (1801), but in fact is highly alert to advanced thinking on women's education and its public consequences. National tales more generally display a self-reflexive interest in genres that belong to both private and public worlds: biography, letters, diaries, anecdotes all address a wider culture of politicized emotions that crosses the four nations. To this extent, the national tale builds on developments in eighteenth-century aesthetics pioneered by such Irish and Scottish thinkers as

---

[1] *Memoirs of Doctor Burney, by his Daughter Madame D'Arblay*, 3 vols (London: Edward Moxon, 1832), 2.236.

Burke, David Hume, and Adam Smith, which connected private responses (located in the culturally particular world of the senses) to universal standards (represented in the abstractions of taste). The language used by these theorists to imagine embodied emotions becomes, in the novels, a way of writing about oppressed national cultures.

Histories, Themes, Theories

Rather than directly addressing large political themes, national tales engage the public sphere via plots drawn from the details of private life (romantic love, marriage, elopements, adultery, orphanhood, as well as conversation, dinners, dancing, and tea-drinking). Such domestic details help to create believable national worlds that are all the more credible because represented as divided and conflicted. Gender is at once integrated within and helps to articulate a set of powerful and interrelated divisions: between periphery and centre, past and present, nation and empire. The kinds of social and psychological details which had been realized within fiction since the early eighteenth century are mined for their specific cultural meanings. Landscape is significant, and the national tale draws energies from late eighteenth-century Gothic and sentimental fictions. Domestic interiors are equally important, especially as the genre develops in the nineteenth century, and they allow writers to depict a differentiated and stratified society which encompasses courts, castles, drawing-rooms, cottages, one-room cabins, and isolated caves. Together, land, house, and family come to serve as a microcosm of the national culture: national tales imagine their fates as inextricably linked, most often via the figure of a heroine whose qualities embody those of her place.

Notable also is the development of a culturally sensitive form of realism, within which place can be seen to shape characters who are in turn judged according to national expectations and stereotypes. Maria Edgeworth's *Ormond* (1817) opens with a discussion of the problematic division of male from female company in the context of an Irish country house. As the men rejoin the women in the drawing room, Sir Ulick O'Shane (a bad landlord and a corrupt banker) complains: 'What! No music, no dancing at Castle Hermitage to-night; and all the ladies sitting in a formal circle, and petrifying into perfect statues!'. The wife of the rakish Sir Ulick frostily retorts by asking how else the women should behave 'when the gentlemen are at their bottle'. The assembled men, we are told, are all 'veterans of the old school of good fellows, who at those times in Ireland—times long since past—deemed it essential to health, happiness, and manly character, to swallow, and show themselves able to stand after swallowing, a certain number of bottles of claret per day or night.'[2]

---

[2] Maria Edgeworth, *Ormond*, ed. Claire Connolly (Harmondsworth: Penguin, 2000), ch. 1; 3.

The novel suggests a close connection between the depiction of national cultures and representation of divided genders. Sir Ulick's comments on the women echo the 'fears' of the Bluestocking writer Elizabeth Vesey, who expressed her 'horror... of a circle, from the ceremony and awe which it produced'. Such stiffly circular gatherings impeded the flow of sociability, which, Vesey thought, was better served by a more 'zig-zag path of communication'.[3] Just as the women are petrifying into statues under the influence of dated and rigid ideas of conduct, so the men's behaviour belongs to a past time. This *'rear-guard'* of men group together in sullen drunkenness and shrink from the network of sociable interactions; instead they are characterized by what they consume. Edgeworth's earlier novel *Castle Rackrent* (1800) similarly addressed cultural progress via consumption. The novel's closing lines attempt to 'determine, whether an Union will hasten or retard the amelioration of this country', before finally asking 'Did the Warwickshire militia, who were chiefly artisans, teach the Irish to drink beer? or did they learn from the Irish to drink whiskey?'[4] While the question has often been cited as a comment on the complexities of cultural exchange, critics remain unsure as to how to decipher its meanings: as humorous aside, proto-deconstructive account of the way in which difference produces meaning, or dark prophecy of military violence to come?

The manner in which compressed intellectual and political content finds expression within a highly worked image of cultural exchange is characteristic of the national tale, where such representations are rarely static. These images draw from life in the sense that all realism does; but also use and develop the full range of somatic, economic, and social meanings with which Romanticism was to endow that term. In the case of Edgeworth in particular, it is worth nothing how many strange specimens are framed within her fictional morphology; in *Ormond*, above, the Bluestocking point of view is voiced by the representative of a crooked Anglo-Irish oligarchy. Edgeworth's national tales do not neatly arrange their intellectual content along gendered or national lines but rather proceed via an 'interdisciplinary commitment to experiment and practical observation' (Chandler 2011: 94). The fictions not only represent but also model such modes of enquiry, which is why national tales foster and sustain so many devices and themes associated with scrutiny and investigation: letters, reports, diaries, interviews, and histories as well as disguise and secrets are all integral to the narrative dynamism of the national tale.

Even as it represents stultifying social formality, then, *Ormond* advances the liveliness of the form of the national tale. The opening exchange is rendered in brisk dialogue, which serves at once to condense and animate a complex set of intellectual and political debates. As the *British Critic* in 1817 remarked of *Ormond* and its companion novel

---

[3] *Memoirs of Doctor Burney*, 2.264.

[4] Maria Edgeworth, *Castle Rackrent*, ed. Jane Desmarais, Tim McLoughlin, and Marilyn Butler, in *The Novels and Selected Works of Maria Edgeworth*, gen. ed. Marilyn Butler and Mitzi Myers, consulting ed. W. J. McCormack, 12 vols (London: Pickering and Chatto: 1999–2003), 1.54.

Harrington: 'all is nature, all is vivacity, all is life'.[5] In this vignette of separated genders and divided time frames, *Ormond* serves to introduce some of the most significant features of the national tale form, as well as drawing attention to some less recognized aspects of its meanings.

In *Ormond*, a discussion that would not be out of place in many early nineteenth-century British women's novels is depicted in the specific context of 'Irish disturbances' and 'Irish dirt' (*Ormond*, ch. 1; 6). Details of the particularities of national life fill the pages of *Ormond*, as they do many other Irish, Scottish, and Welsh novels of the late eighteenth and early nineteenth centuries. Its hero, Harry Ormond, wants 'A place of my own . . . a comfortable house and estate, on which I could live independently and happily, with some charming amiable woman' (ch. 19; 170). He has to choose between the different models presented by Sir Ulick's corrupt Anglo-Irish estate, the quasi-feudal Gaelic world of King Corny on the Black Islands, and the benevolently managed nearby Annaly estate, all filtered through his experience of pre-revolutionary Paris and its cosmopolitan community of philosophers, courtiers, and diplomats. From an initial focus in the Irish midlands, the narrative span of *Ormond* reaches out and across to Dublin, the sea coast, Paris, America, and India, forming a national tale that can also be described as 'a panoramic, geopolitical bildungsroman' (Trumpener 1997: 62). Yet Harry's desire for 'a place of my own' remains strongly marked by the Irish experience of dispossession: the process whereby lands originally held by the native Irish passed into English and Anglo-Irish hands via centuries of conquest and colonization.

Edgeworth's own family came into their Irish lands following the Cromwellian conquest of Ireland: her ancestors were granted 600 acres of land at Mastrim, County Longford, later renamed Edgeworthstown. In the novel, Harry Ormond eventually marries Florence Annaly, whose surname echoes the name of the medieval lordship of Annaly, which became County Longford in 1553. The narrative might be said to restage historical Irish conflicts as convenient plot solutions in the present: Harry, who was nursed in an Irish cabin as a baby, comes to acquire lands long lost to the Gaelic peasantry; while Edgeworth, in the process, puts right the historic wrongs done by her own family. Yet the narrative treatment of land and inheritance is much more nuanced than such a summary would suggest. The genesis of the novel gives evidence of Edgeworth's sense of the losses and pains attendant upon Irish history. Among her manuscript sketches for *Ormond* are her notes for the 'histy of K of the B. Islands'. The Black Islands in the novel represent a kind of Gaelic stronghold presided over by the feudal figure of King Corny. They exist in counterpoint to the shady dealings of Sir Ulick and the benevolently managed Annaly estate. Yet in the manuscript note we find a markedly negative account of the Annaly family. The benevolent landowners of *Ormond* are described as coming from 'the

---

[5] *British Critic*, 8 (August 1817), 166.

unfriendly Islands'. This may refer to the novel's setting on the shores of a large inland lake in the Irish midlands, but also suggests tensions between Britain and Ireland. The wider resonances build in the manuscript notes, which go on: 'Old storys English settlers', suggesting a high degree of awareness of the successive waves of English settlement of Irish land and the 'old storys' of loss and injustice. At one point the Annaly name is rendered 'Any=lies', in an indictment of the legitimacy of their claim to their estate. Such densely woven historical and topographical contexts allow the novel to depict a history of possession and dispossession which dates back at least to the early eleventh century and which directly involves Edgeworth's own family.[6]

The complex relationship between the treatment of such pressing political themes as land ownership and the details via which such tensions are realized in fiction creates a structuring dynamic within the national tale form. Despite their recurrent interest in specific details from Irish history, national tales have often been described in terms of a kind of attempt at colonial control via culture. Kevin Whelan, for instance, imagines Irish novels as 'desperately struggling to encompass the wildly divergent class divisions of pre-Famine Ireland within one fictive frame' (2000: 189). The suggestion that fictions exert themselves in a doomed effort to contain a hectic culture is characteristic of a particular kind of Irish postcolonial criticism, within which national tales are not only criticized for their effort to imagine forms of political union, but further censured for their failure to achieve aesthetic unity. Maria Edgeworth's fictions, for example, have been characterized in terms of 'a striking nervousness surrounding matters of representation' (O'Connell 2006: 22) while the conclusion to *The Wild Irish Girl*, Sydney Owenson's three-volume novel of 1806, has been described not only as 'improbable' and 'unlikely' (Haslam 1987: 19), but as 'inadequate to its epoch' (Andrews 1987: 16).

A more developed understanding of the novels' depiction of the densely textured realities of national life requires a fuller apprehension of 'the unsettled nature' of early nineteenth-century realism (Galperin 2003: 5). National tales emerged alongside parallel developments in domestic fiction, the historical novel, and works of religious and moral instruction; while also drawing energy from, and sometimes debating with, government reports, parliamentary speeches, travel writing, folklore, and antiquarian scholarship. Positioned on such a spectrum, national tales may be connected with explicitly regulatory and didactic writing, certainly, but can also be seen to exist at a distance from such material. Their reliance on and interrelationships with such related literary modes as drama, poetry, and song are notable also, and have yet to be fully explored.

The factual mode developed within national tales is perhaps most associated with descriptions of past reality, as in *Ormond*'s semi-anthropological account of the 'old school of good fellows'. Other narrative devices that are used to develop the impression of reality

---

[6] Maria Edgeworth, 'Notes for hist.Y of K of the B. Islands', MS. Eng.misc.c.896, Bodleian Library.

include footnotes and glosses, often containing extraneous information about national history, manners, and culture. Edgeworth's pioneering use of notes in her one-volume novel *Castle Rackrent* resulted in a fiction notably fragmented in its narrative texture. *Castle Rackrent* is comprised of a Preface by a distant 'editor' figure; the 'Memoirs of the Rackrent Family', written by their seemingly naive Irish steward and interspersed with learned notes; and an editorial glossary containing mini-essays and other digressions on Irish linguistic practices and Irish popular culture. Stephen Cullen's earlier Irish novel, *The Castle of Inchvally: A Tale—Alas! Too True* (1796) also included footnotes on aspects of national life, though these are distributed unevenly through the three volumes of the novel. The information contained in Cullen's novel is miscellaneous in nature: there are notes on Irish history, including, for example, a brief disquisition on the iniquities of colonial land practices, some polemically anti-Catholic material, and an account of the chemical composition of phosphorus.

The Castle of Inchvally shares with Edgeworth's fiction the orientation of its notes towards an English reader who is imagined to be in need of education or better information on the topic of Ireland. At the centre of Cullen's tale is 'the confiscated property of an old respectable Catholic family' and among the earliest notes is one explaining the process whereby Protestants could claim or 'discover' Catholic lands: 'An English reader will certainly be unable to comprehend what is here meant by the appellation "Discoverer", unless it be explained to him; and, when it is explained, will find ample room for the exercise of his faith in believing that men could be got to do, or men got to suffer, such unqualified wrong.'[7] The notes not only provide historical information, however, but also disrupt the reading experience, by forcing readers to move between narrative levels and spaces. The narrative incorporation of extra-fictional material has the potential to open up spaces of cultural mediation, within which rival perspectives can compete or be accommodated. The notes to *The Castle of Inchvally* offer a highly sympathetic account of Catholic dispossession; yet their potential effect is thwarted by a plot that depicts the world of contemporary Catholicism, replete with deceitful illusions and supernatural trappings, as dangerously vital.

The balance between the narrative aspects of the text and the surrounding notes is destabilized still further in *The Wild Irish Girl*. The novel combines a dispossession plot with a love story, and sees the eventual marriage of Glorvina, representative of the dispossessed native Irish, to a man whose ancestors had been granted land belonging to hers in the seventeenth century. Even as it develops the romantic relationship between these two figures, the novel stages an encounter with the deep Irish past. Conversations between Glorvina and her lover are not only triangulated via a cast of characters from contemporary Irish life (notably a priest figure), they are also routinely diverted via the

---

[7] Stephen Cullen, *The Castle of Inchvally; A Tale—Alas! Too True*, 3 vols (London: J. Bell, 1796), 1.107–8n.

notes into digressions on Irish plant life, history, poetry, and legends. The novel yields evidence of Owenson's research, and bears the mark of a particular kind of extractive reading: the result is a love story that is also a compendium of knowledge about Ireland. One of her key sources is Geoffrey Keating's *Foras Feasa ar Éirinn* (1634), a Gaelic history whose title translates as 'foundation of knowledge about Ireland'. Like Keating's history, which gathered the existing evidence for ancient Irish learning and traditions and transmitted it to the modern world of post-conquest Ireland, Owenson's novel has value as a kind of repository or encyclopedia of sources and stories.

The information-rich notes characteristic of the national tale have aesthetic as well as documentary value. They draw on and inform, but are distinct from, the thematization of cultural misunderstanding between Britain and Ireland. In the case of both Owenson and Edgeworth, their observations on popular practices are cited as among the earliest anthropological accounts of Irish culture. One of the longest of the notes in *The Wild Irish Girl* tells the story of the 'Bard of the Magilligans', a Jacobite harper sometimes described as 'the last of the bards'. Owenson's information about Dennis Hampson of Garvagh in County Derry (1697–1807) comes from the Derry antiquarian, George Vaughan Sampson, author of *Statistical Survey of the County of Londonderry* (1802), mediated by the assistance of another scholar, William Patterson MD, a Derry physician. The footnote, which spreads over five pages of the third volume of the 1806 edition, includes a letter from Sampson containing stories about the harper's life and music. Among these is an account of Hampson's playing Jacobite songs for Bonnie Prince Charlie, in Edinburgh in 1745. At the end of the letter, Owenson reports how 'in February 1806, the author, being then but eighteen miles distant from the residence of the bard, received a message from him, intimating that as he heard she wished to purchase his harp, he would dispose of it on very moderate terms'. There is pathos in the image of the elderly, impoverished, and lonely harper who would sell his instrument, but a measure of brash promise also in the suggestion that Owenson herself might be the natural inheritor of a tradition of Irish music and song. In *Castle Rackrent*, a rather shorter glossary entry on tea-drinking below stairs shares this quality of authorial self-fashioning. The note concludes in a manner that suggests the careful and deliberate crafting of the writer's role: 'But why should not we have *low life above stairs*, as well as *High life below stairs*' (1.66). As with a short story, these notes bring into view aspects of life on the economic margins and encapsulate an entire social world via a small selection of carefully chosen details.

Genre, Styles, Modes

Telling as such details are, they acquire shape and meaning within a set of emerging fictional protocols for the depiction of cultural difference. Indeed, one definition of the national tale is simply as 'a female-authored genre launched by Edgeworth and Morgan' (Ferris 2008b: 236). Ferris further notes the coincidence of the emergence of the national tale with what she calls 'a distinctive Irish line of English-language fiction' (235). Yet important antecedents to the national tale exist in Ireland, Scotland, and Wales, most often in the shape of sentimental and Gothic fictions with an interest in distinct regional landscapes and the particularities of vernacular speech as marked by the languages spoken across the islands. The novels of the 1780s and 1790s are characterized by crossing of regional and national borders: Regina Maria Roche's *The Children of the Abbey* (1796) presents an especially interesting case of a text in which 'the characters...spend the whole novel crossing back and forth from one periphery to another, from Ireland to Wales to Scotland to Ireland to Scotland to Ireland' (Trumpener 1997: 17). In Ireland, *The Fair Hibernian* (1789) and Mrs. F. C. Patrick's *The Irish Heiress* (1797) both link national politics with domestic plots. Scottish examples include *Duncan and Peggy: A Scottish Tale* (1794) and *Albert; or, The Wilds of Strathnavern* (1799), both by Elizabeth Helme. In Wales, many sentimental novels of the 1780s include lengthy accounts of Welsh scenery coupled with an emergent interest in industrialization (see Franklin, Chapter 9). Anna Maria Bennett's *Anna; or, Memoirs of a Welch Heiress* (1785) uses the standard eighteenth-century plot of an imperilled heiress who overcomes treachery and deceit in order to discover her true identity, yet also asks readers to comprehend Anna's story within such specifically South-Walian contexts as Methodism, gentry professionalism, and the growth of the iron industry. One chapter is entitled 'A Family Picture by a Discarded Servant'. While subsequent chapters serve to correct the servant's perspective on the family fortunes, what is notable is Bennett's interest in the literary possibilities of spreading narrative point of view across class and nation.

There are, however, a number of difficulties in attempting to disaggregate an Irish, Scottish, or Welsh aspect to the overall picture of the novel in this period, given increasingly close political and cultural connections across the islands in the aftermath of the 1801 Act of Union. In the case of Ireland, the number of novels actually published on the island in the early nineteenth century was tiny, certainly until the 1820s. The extension of the Copyright Act of 1710 to Ireland in 1801 all but killed off an Irish publishing industry that was reliant on markets for cheap reprints in Ireland, Britain, the American colonies, and the West Indies. The anonymous *False Appearances*, Sydney Owenson's *St. Clair; or, The Heiress of Desmond* (both dating from 1803), and Sarah Isdell's *The Vale of Louisiana: An American Tale* (1805) represent rare examples of Dublin-published novels in the immediate post-Union period. John Connor of Cork, who had commercial connections with the Minerva Press in London, published local author Anna Milliken's *Plantagenet* (1802) and *The Rival Chiefs* (1804). The Scottish publishing industry, on the other hand, enjoyed a 'golden age' in the second decade of the nineteenth century, while publishers of Scottish origin such as John Murray II played a key role in the London book trade, at least until the booksellers' crash of 1826.

The publishing history of the earliest national tales ties them closely to London publishers, in particular to the radical publishers Joseph Johnson and Richard Phillips. Johnson, a Unitarian, published William Godwin, Mary Wollstonecraft, Thomas Paine, and Mary Hays, as well as Edgeworth. Phillips, who published Sydney Owenson's *The Wild Irish Girl* (1806), was imprisoned in 1793 for selling Thomas Paine's *Rights of Man* in Leicester; in London he chiefly published popular works of instruction, aimed at the lower classes, as well as novels such as John Thelwall's *The Daughter of Adoption* (1801) and Godwin's *Fleetwood: or, The New Man of Feeling* (1805). Phillips advertised *The Wild Irish Girl* almost as a travel book, 'in which are delineated the State of Society, the Domestic and Moral Habits, the Manners, Amusements, and Grievances of the PEASANTRY and YEOMANRY of IRELAND'; the novel's publication was announced alongside John Carr's *Stranger in Ireland*.[8]

Michael Gamer (2001) locates Edgeworth's fictions within a 'literary and generic tradition' that he calls 'romances of real life'. Other relevant formal paradigms for the national tale include the trend for fashionable fiction, itself related to the special strand of scandalous novels that cluster around the separation of the Prince and Princess of Wales in 1806–7. Mary Anne Clarke's account of the Duke of York's trial before both Houses of Parliament on charges of political corruption and her own appearance before this formidable court contained a virulent attack on one of the prosecutors, the soon-to-be *Quarterly* reviewer John Wilson Croker, as a 'ludicrous Irishman', a 'peeping Tom' with social aspirations and a thick brogue.[9] Garside notes that 1807–8 constitute 'the highpoint for a special kind of acerbic scandal fiction' (2000: 42), of which the pseudonymous Charles Sedley's *Winter in Dublin* (1808) is an often-noted example. *A Winter in Edinburgh* (1810) transplanted the novel of scandalous fashionable life to Scottish society. The satirical talents of Irish poet and novelist Eaton Stannard Barrett are evident in *The Heroine, or Adventures of a Fair Romance Reader*, which mocked existing trends in novel-writing and was published by Henry Colburn in 1813.

The years between 1808 and 1814 yield clear evidence of a set of titles with a distinct interest in national customs. Novels include Elizabeth Gunning's *The Exile of Erin* (1808); Charles Robert Maturin's *The Wild Irish Boy* (1808); Henrietta Rouviere Mosse's *The Old Irish Baronet; or, Manners of My Country* (1808); Theodore Melville's *The Irish Chieftain, and His Family* (1809); John Agg's *MacDermot; or, The Irish Chieftain* (1810); Ann Mary Hamilton's *The Irishwoman in London* (1810); and Maturin's *The Milesian Chief* (1812). Elizabeth Hamilton's *Cottagers of Glenburnie* (1808) is an important precursor to Walter Scott's *Waverley* (1814), while the early 1810s saw a number of significant Scottish examples of the national tale, including Honoria Scott's [pseud?] *The Vale of Clyde* (1810); Kate Montalbion's

---

[8] *Dublin Evening Post*, 10 June 1806.
[9] Mary Anne Clarke, *The Rival Princes; or, A Faithful Narrative of Facts relating to Mrs. M. A. Clarke's Political Acquaintance with Colonel Wardle, Major Dodd, &c. &c. &c. who were Concerned in the Charges against the Duke of York*, 2 vols (London, 1810), 1.275–85.

[probably Catharine Bayley's] *Caledonia; or, The Stranger in Scotland: A National Tale* (1810); and Sarah Wigley's *Glencarron: A Scottish Tale* (1811). Analysis of these novels can help to develop Trumpener's distinction between the national tale's 'thick evocation of place' and the historical novel's 'plot of loss and growth through historical change'. While the publication patterns represented here may be broadly illustrative of the tendencies described by Trumpener, individual novels also provide key instances of what happens as 'one genre crystallizes out of another' (1997: 131). The Scottish female-authored national tales discussed above, for example, quickly lost ground to *Waverley*, as several Scottish women authors themselves noted. Christian Isobel Johnstone's Advertisement to her Scottish national tale *Clan-Albin* (1815) is at pains to point out that 'the first half' of her novel 'was not only written but *printed*' before the appearance of Scott's novel, while Mary Brunton, author of *Discipline* and Mary Johnston, author of *The Lairds of Glenfern*, made similarly defensive remarks (see Duncan 2007: 37). The relationship between national tale and historical novel is best characterized in terms of 'an ongoing interplay and friction between two successive, related and increasingly enmeshed generic forms' which themselves feed into and inform later developments in nineteenth-century realism (Trumpener 1997: 131). A novel such as Charles Dickens's *A Tale of Two Cities* can be seen to answer the question of 'what could a mode of fiction that exported marginal United Kingdom cultures to the metropolis offer to a later fiction celebrated for its capacious and intensive scrutiny of *English* society and devoted to the location of *Englishness*?' (Buzard 2005: 42).

Yet national tales do not simply cede ground to historical novels or die away only to re-emerge as ghostly residues in Victorian realism. They possess distinct generic characteristics that include close connections with both Gothic and sentimental modes. Charles Robert Maturin's early Gothic romance, *Fatal Revenge* (1807), signals an interest in national identity: Maturin not only assumes the pen name of Dennis Jasper Murphy, but also offers specimens of Irish poetry alongside observations on its merits. In the preface to *The Wild Irish Boy* (1808), Maturin announces himself to be 'an Irishman, unnoticed and unknown', while later novels concerned themselves with the intricacies of Dublin society (*Women; or, Pour et Contre*, 1818) and with an imagined rural rebellion (*The Milesian Chief*, 1812). *Melmoth the Wanderer* (1820) represents a marked departure, inaugurating a tradition of Irish Gothic while working to unpick the affective bonds that are central to the national tales of Edgeworth and Morgan.

Julia Wright suggests that national tales are involved in a 'sentimental tradition' which they in turn reform and adapt, from the 1780s through to the 1820s (2007: 64–72). The different national routes taken by sentiment require careful tracking, however: they constitute a culturally specific and geographically diffuse phenomenon which is at the same time highly concentrated within individual narratives. The career of Owenson (Lady Morgan from 1812) is instructive here. Her first novel, *St. Clair*, is remarkably similar to *The Wild Irish Girl*: a stranger arrives in the wilds of the West of Ireland, and falls in love with the daughter of a chieftain. Like *The Wild Irish Girl*, the novel consists of a series of letters, from the Englishman to his friend in London. But in *St. Clair*, the setting, scenery, and location are almost accidental. Unlike *The Wild Irish Girl*, where the landscape heaves with political meaning, the terrain of *St. Clair* possesses scant historical significance (although a revised edition of the novel, appearing in 1812, sought to remedy this). This is in marked contrast to Morgan's two subsequent novels following the success of *The Wild Irish Girl*: *Woman: or, Ida of Athens* (1809) and *The Missionary: An Indian Tale* (1811), where we see the kinds of connections made possible by the association of heroine with homeland. The title of *Woman: or, Ida of Athens* announces its heroine's national significance. In it, Greece is 'love's region' while England is 'the most commercial, opulent, but least picturesque country in the world'.[10] It plots revolution in Greece in terms of Ida's passion for a rebel leader: 'in love's hour, the vicissitudes of an age are registered' (3.3). Later novels retain this interest in 'the related metaphors of gender and geography' (Leask 1992: 126) but embellish plots of national difference with narratives that stress the ambiguities of subjective identity. *O'Donnel* (1814), *Florence Macarthy* (1818), and *The O'Briens and the O'Flahertys* (1827) all feature irresolute and mysterious protagonists whose motives are difficult for readers to fathom. Reviewing Lady Morgan's novel of Belgian independence, *The Princess; or, The Beguine* (1835), Christian Isobel Johnstone remarks that it is as if Lady Morgan had 'forgotten how to paint any character that the reader can either love at first sight, or approve upon reflection'.[11]

Johnstone's own novel *Clan-Albin: A National Tale* (1815) mixes sentimental and domestic modes within an enclosed Highland space that is traumatically evacuated by the key characters over the course of the novel. Set in the 1780s, the novel tracks the interlinked experiences of Highland clearances, military service overseas, and emigration to Upper Canada. The novel also bears the impress of its own moment, depicting as it does a 'Highland Arcadia' that is strongly marked by post-Waterloo demobilization, rural migration, and the passage of the Corn Laws (Duncan 2007: 82). National tales are thus enmeshed in the history of their periods in ways that problematize the Scottian model of historicized distance. The case of Edgeworth's novel *Patronage* (1814) provides a useful parallel here. A domestic novel that is also an ambitious fiction of contemporary English political life, *Patronage* tests the limits and capacities of the national tale. Marilyn Butler remarks that a contemporary reader would have 'assumed comfortably that he or she was reading a story of the closing phase of the Napoleonic Wars, after the French armies had been driven out of Germany', yet also points out that Edgeworth draws a longer seventeenth- and eighteenth-century history into her text, with allusions to 'the Jacobite politics of the first half of the eighteenth century' evoking a sense of contested national pasts (Butler 1999: xii). The novel received markedly negative reviews, which

---

[10] Sydney Owenson, *Woman: or, Ida of Athens*, 4 vols (London: Longman [etc.], 1809), 2.181, 4.63.
[11] *Tait's Edinburgh Magazine*, n.s., 2 (February 1835), 85–114 (113).

criticized Edgeworth's lack of specialized professional knowledge in the areas of law, politics, and diplomacy. Ferris suggests that these reviews of 1814 erect hitherto invisible 'gender boundaries' around Edgeworth's fiction, and are part of the masculinization of the novel (1991: 67–8). National as well as gendered boundaries make their presence felt, however: Sydney Smith in the *Edinburgh Review* likens Edgeworth in England to a tourist in an unfamiliar land, sending back just the kind of hasty impressionistic judgement of which she herself despairs in her Irish fiction.[12] *Patronage* belongs on a spectrum that stretches from the national tales of Owenson and Maturin through the historical novels of Scott and on to the English fictions of Jane Austen.

Patronage further suggests just how difficult it is to disentangle the national tale from its contemporary moment, even as that moment itself shifts with new generations of readers. Thomas Bartlett has shown how the very title of *Castle Rackrent* 'soon became shorthand for all that was bizarre and burlesque amongst the Irish governing elite'. When Charles Abbot, Chief Secretary in the immediate post-Union period, was travelling around Ireland 'on the mandatory getting-to-know-the-country tour', he confided to his Viceroy, Lord Hardwicke, that he had 'dined one day at a thorough Castle Rackrent, but pray never say so' (Bartlett 2000). Ellen O'Connell Fitz-simon, eldest daughter of Daniel O'Connell and herself the author of *Darrynane in Eighteen Hundred and Thirty-Two, and Other Poems* (Dublin, 1863), characterized *Castle Rackrent* as a novel of 'revolting unpleasantness' while finding it 'overcharged in its details . . . crudely and coarsely drawn'.[13] An emphatically nationalist judgement on the world depicted within the novel shades into emergent Victorian expectations of narrative propriety in women; together, these forces restrict the remit and reputation of the national tale.

Such involvement in shifting contexts and readerships makes the politics of the national tale particularly difficult to pin down. Lady Morgan's novel *O'Donnel* (1814) allows us to see how different kinds of political energies and campaigns intersect in the shaping of the Irish national tale. Set in the 1810s, the novel's hero is the descendant of the earls of Tyrconnell, an O'Donnel who has been disposed of his ancient lands and who is barred from public office or military service because of his Catholicism. O'Donnel instead performs valiantly in the service of the Austrian and French armies but returns to Ireland to voice criticisms of the penal laws in a manner highly consonant with the cause of Catholic Emancipation as it developed in the years after the 1798 rebellion. Morgan's preparation for the novel involved reading such '"Rebelly" books' as the four-volume *An Impartial History of Ireland*, written by the exiled United Irishman Denis Taaffe.[14] Elsewhere, however, Morgan refers to the novel's 'emancipating tendency' and the novel clearly joins

---

[12] *Edinburgh Review*, 22 (January 1814), 416–34 (434).
[13] 'Irish Novels and Novelists', *Dublin Review*, 4 (April 1838), 495–543 (498).
[14] W. Hepworth Dixon (ed.), *Lady Morgan's Memoirs: Autobiography, Diaries and Correspondence*, 2 vols (London: William H. Allen & Co., 1862), 1.516.

with contemporary demands for Catholic Emancipation, significantly in a decade in which the Catholic Association had become internally split and politically stalled.

The *Augustan Review*'s suggestion that Morgan's Irish veteran of the Napoleonic Wars is a 'transplanted' *Thaddeus of Warsaw* helps us see, via Jane Porter's Polish romance with its 'ambitious war scenes' and splendid military detail (Maxwell 2008: 74), the many ways in which war in Europe was mediated by and in turn helped to shape the national tale.[15] The focus in Lady Morgan's novel on the military prowess and martial virtues of O'Donnel is echoed in the depiction of the protagonist of Francis S. Higginson's highly coloured and derivative romance, *Manderville; or, The Hibernian Chiliarch* (1825). *Manderville* is set in the seventeenth century and against the backdrop of an imaginary Jacobite rebellion in the north of Ireland. To this setting the author, who writes as a retired Army officer, liberally adds details of Volunteer parades of the 1780s (the rebels' green and gold uniforms), United Irish symbolism from the 1790s (their Jacobite flag displays a gold harp upon a green field), and battle manoeuvres suggestive of the Peninsular wars.

In 1827, a review of Gerald Griffin's *Holland-Tide* commented that 'The Irish and Scotch divide the department of novels as they do the army, the good things in India and in other British dependencies; that is to say, pretty equal between them.'[16] This comparison between the Scottish and Irish dominance of the fiction market and forms of military and colonial service assumes a link between the kinds of work done by novelists, the military, and colonial administrators, and supports a reading of the national tale as a wartime genre. The genre may have grown up as a way of framing the Irish question for the British public, but even that Irish question is itself one shaped by the exigencies of conflict overseas: 'Britain's Irish policy from 1778 onwards was influenced by the increasing demands of war' (Bew 2007: 52). Furthermore, despite the association of national tales with the literary expression of a distinct national identity, they may also be considered as stabilizing an enlarged sense of a Britishness, which, in the face of the threat from Napoleonic Europe, draws energy, scale, and substance from the representation of regional and national difference.

In *Clan-Albin*, discussed above, the Highland characters are forced to choose between military service overseas and emigration to Canada. The novel imagines a world shaped by 'modern imperial war, waged on a planetary scale' on the one hand, and 'colonial dispersal' on the other. Both war and migration reshape 'communal frameworks' within 'empire-wide networks of sentimental allegiance' (Duncan 2007: 99). Yet such networks of allegiance can overlap with and contradict one another. In both Scott's 'The Highland Widow' (part of *Chronicles of the Canongate*, 1827) and Hamilton's *Cottagers of Glenburnie*, aspects of the plot turn on the presumed reluctance of Highland men who have enlisted

---

[15] *Augustan Review*, 10 (1815), 518–21 (520).
[16] *London Magazine*, 7 (1827), 399.

in the British Army to undergo regimental punishment for desertion. These tales suggest that modern military expectations of obedience and submission clash with an honourable but independent tradition of Highland armed service. In Hamilton's novel, the conflict between traditional Highland martial habits and what Scott calls 'the restraints imposed by discipline on ordinary troops'[17] frames the McClarty family's reaction to news that their son Sandy was 'aff to be a sodger'. His father comments: 'Here's Sandy done for himsel' wi' a vengeance! He, too, wad do naething but what he liked! see what he'll mak o' it now, but to be tied up to a stake, and lashed like a dog!—a disgrace, as he is, to us a'! I would rather he had ne'er been born!'[18] Sandy remains 'a wilfil' lad' (*Cottagers of Glenburnie*, 160) but has his threatened court martial for desertion mitigated and is instead dispatched to the East Indies. In 'The Highland Widow', however, the son does not share his mother's fears of proper forms of punishment; instead, the tale depicts submission to army discipline as a painful, confusing, and traumatic aspect of a Scottish modernity that must turn its back on a proud past.

A relevant factor here is both Irish and Scottish involvement in Britain's overseas campaigns on land and at sea. An estimated 130,000 Irishmen served in the army during the Napoleonic Wars, and in 1830 'an estimated 40 per cent of the non-commissioned members of the British army was Irish-born' (Kinealy 1999: 4), at a point when 'the Irish represented less than a third of the total population of the United Kingdom' (Alvin Jackson 2005: 35). In the later nineteenth century, the army was 'up to 75 per cent Irish or Irish and Scottish combined' (Pittock 2008: 236). In the case of Irish fiction, many traces of wartime are found in the national tale, most notably in accounts of the economic depression and agrarian unrest which followed the large-scale demobilization in the wake of the British naval victory at Trafalgar and the eventual end of the Napoleonic War. Gerald Griffin's 'Card-Drawing' features a combatant, Duke Dorgan, who has served aboard the HMS Trafalgar and been with Nelson at his death, as he returns home to Ireland. There, he finds himself on trial for murder. The tale, one of Griffin's *Tales of the Munster Festivals* (1827), is notably concerned with the distinction between different types of death; in particular the difference between fatalities suffered in the normal course of military service and the execution of Irish men and women who are unfairly treated by British justice ('judicial murder'). In the same decade, the novels of John and Michael Banim contain striking accounts of Irish violence and its punishment at the hands of a cruel and corrupt army.

Such representations build on and draw from the incorporation of military life within fiction: an attempt, perhaps, to give linguistic shape to the affective charge of war and to

---

[17] Walter Scott, 'The Highland Widow', *Chronicles of the Canongate*, ed. Claire Lamont (Edinburgh: Edinburgh University Press, 2000), ch. 11; 98.

[18] Elizabeth Hamilton, *The Cottagers of Glenburnie [1808]*, ed. Pamela Perkins (Glasgow: Association for Scottish Literary Studies, 2010), ch. 9; 136.

register its 'wayward power' (Favret 2010: 11). The fictions of Edgeworth and Scott are notable for their use of the technical language of combat in everyday situations: their narratives serve to normalize war via language. The *Oxford English Dictionary* definition of 'freelance' to mean 'a type of military adventurer . . . who offered his services to states or individuals for payment' derives from Scott's *Ivanhoe* (1820). Edgeworth and Jane Austen are credited in the same source for the first use of 'manoeuvring' outside of its specific military context, while Edgeworth's novel of the same title explicitly extends the meanings of manoeuvring into the field of sexual relations. In *Ormond*, images from military engineering are used to describe Sir Ulick's corrupt scheming, while in the same novel a reference to 'the delightful mail coach roads' reminds us that Charles Bianconi's coaching monopoly across Ireland depended on the post-Waterloo demobilization and the availability of cheap horses. Irish writers more generally are at the forefront of the advance of military and naval fiction as a key subgenre of the 1830s and 1840s. William Hamilton Maxwell and Charles Lever made their reputations with dashing tales of military and naval life, novels which can be seen to have learned much from the generic innovations of the national tale. Military fictions, national tales, and historical novels meet on the contentious territory of statehood, empire, history, and culture: there, they inflect, influence, and constitute one another's themes and methods, while also shaping one of the most pressing questions to emerge from within the national tale: whether such fictions express distinct national agendas or promote imperial unity.

Above all, it is the issue of the readership of national tales that makes such questions difficult to answer. Anne Grant remarked of *Castle Rackrent* that a full appreciation of Edgeworth's novel will only emerge from a mixture of knowledge and detachment: 'one must have lived in Ireland, or the West Highlands which contain much rackrent; but one must not have lived always there, as, in that case, the force of these odd characters would be lost in their familiarity.'[19] Yet many readers of national tales encountered the worlds represented there only in print. Whether involved or detached, the composition, attributes, and attitudes of the readership of the national tale remain a key area for further research.

Politics, Reputations, Afterlives

Genres are tied to their time and place, Franco Moretti argues, in ways that make certain literary forms appear 'normal' in a given period (2005: 18–19). The writing and reading of national tales constitutes a pervasive cultural phenomenon in early nineteenth-century

---

[19] *Memoir and Correspondence of Mrs Grant of Laggan*, ed. J. P. Grant, 3 vols (London: Longman [etc.], 1844), 1.229–30.

Ireland, Scotland, and Wales. The Gaelic scholar John O'Donovan wrote the plot for a romantic tale while working for the Ordnance Survey of Ireland, while the poet and folklore collector Jeremiah Joseph Callanan penned a now lost manuscript novel based on a legendary tale concerning Lough Ine, near Skibbereen, in County Cork. Daniel O'Connell, the leader of the Irish Catholic nation in the first decades of the nineteenth century, admired both Henry Mackenzie's *The Man of Feeling* and William Godwin's *Caleb Williams*; his biographer says of *Caleb Williams* that its 'doctrine... suffused his public conduct all his life' (MacDonagh 1988: 39). O'Connell also began writing a novel of his own (probably in 1796), which sought to connect sensibility with rational improvement against the backdrop of the American War of Independence. Nothing of the planned novel survives but O'Connell retained a keen interest in the fiction of his own time. He admired Walter Scott above all others but also read both Edgeworth and Morgan aloud to his family. His daughter recalls receiving the novels 'scarce dry from the press': 'Even now we cannot peruse a page of *Florence Macarthy* without in fancy hearing that full-toned and mellow voice give new point to the sarcasm—new energy to the indignant burst of national feeling.'[20] O'Connell maintained a strong suspicion of Edgeworth, however, believing that a character in *Ormond* was based on himself and that an incident from *Patronage* was derived from one of his legal cases.

Whether Daniel O'Connell was correct in thinking that Edgeworth drew from his life for her fictions or not, the presence of disputable information of this kind is central to the role and reputation of the national tale. What Ina Ferris calls 'the cultural power of modern fact' manifests itself in complex ways within the fictions, as evident in the negative reaction to *Patronage* discussed above (2009b: 489). Sydney Smith remarked of Edgeworth that 'If she has put in her novels people who fed her and her odious father she is not trustworthy' (see Butler 1972: 257). Morgan too was criticized for introducing recognizable individuals into her novels; in her case, there are close links between such intrusions of reality and the publishing industry within which national tales were produced and circulated. Scott advised Maturin to remove defensive references to critical commentary on his work from the preface to *Women*, telling the Irish novelist that: 'We take up a novel for amusement, and this current of controversy breaks out upon us like a stream of lava out of the side of a beautiful green hill; men will say you should have reserved your disputes for reviews or periodical publications, and they will sympathize less with your anger, because they will not think the time proper for expressing it' (see Idman 1923: 144).

The problem that Scott identifies arises in relation to the fictional cultivation of reality and the proximity of the national tale to other, more news-oriented genres. National tales imagine the world that they depict in vividly detailed ways, even when some aspects of those societies seem to exist only to be reformed or abolished within the narrative.

[20] 'Irish Novels and Novelists', 501.

The commitment to cultural specificity results in such formal innovations as footnotes, glosses, lists, as well as narrative shifts in voice, time, and space. The distance between past and present allows readers to apprehend an unfolding history, yet national tales more often offer compelling scenes such as the one quoted at the outset of this chapter than they deliver any steady narrative of progress. It is from such a contrast between static, often highly visual effects and the more steady-paced, linear movement of history, that the national tale derives its energy. Katie Trumpener conceives of the national tale's mode as primarily spatial, in contrast to the temporal axis of the historical novel (1997: 131), yet most national tales feature some mixing of modes. These axes of comparison can be further developed, additionally, to attend to the aesthetic mode of fictions that are often pictorial in their mode of address.

National tales exploit the narrative space of the scene, in order to frame a set of cultural pictures whose address may be secure but whose effects are unpredictable: as Lady Morgan puts it in *The O'Briens and the O'Flahertys* (1827), 'Men ... are always more readily convinced through their sensations, than their reason—for arguments are words, but images are facts; and a scene got up, is always well worth a case stated.'[21] Such scenes, however, are notably dependent on highly achieved, intransitive moments in narrative. Scott read Griffin's *Tales of the Munster Festivals* and tempered his admiration for these 'diverting' fictions with criticism of their 'one fault, that the crisis is in more cases than one protracted after a keen interest has been excited' by the introduction of narrative digressions and 'scenes of mere amusement'.[22] The narrative cultivation of static pictures, where readers might expect swift transitions from one action to the next, has close connections to the dramaturgy of the romantic stage. Gerald Griffin was himself a playwright and his *Tales* explicitly draws attention to drama as a mode to be imitated and aspired to, from within the texture of prose fiction.[23]

The reading experience of protracted or prolonged scenes is matched in the narrative inscription of arrested or psychologically intense states; these increasingly came to dominate the national tale as it was developed in the hands of such novelists as Maturin, James Hogg, John Galt, Griffin, and the Banims. In the Irish and Scottish novels of the 1820s, individuals are as likely to be stalled as swept along by the forces of history. Katie Trumpener charts this movement in terms of 'the transformation of an allegorically flattened national character, over the history of the genre, into one torn apart by the contradictions of uneven development'. As the novel 'moves from the unchanging national world towards the dislocations of the historical novel', she says, 'the national tale (as a genre centered on an allegorical equation of personal and cultural identity) becomes the

---

[21] Lady Morgan, *The O'Briens and the O'Flaherties*, 4 vols (London: Colburn, 1827), 4.266.

[22] *The Journal of Sir Walter Scott*, ed. W. E. K. Anderson (Edinburgh: Canongate Books, 1998), 498 (entry for 13 March 1828).

[23] Gerald Griffin, *Tales of the Munster Festivals*, 3 vols (London: Saunders and Ottley, 1827), 1.8.

birthplace of a new literary schizophrenia' (1997: 142). Gothic plots of doubled or trauma-tized identities are not the only issue of the national tale, however. A culturally sensitive focus on affective states characterized by forms of internal division remains a hallmark of these novels. Meanwhile, the national tale's movement between private and public life continued to attract the attention of women as both writers and readers. George Yeats [Mrs W. B. Yeats] wrote to her 'dear Willy' in 1932 that Edgeworth's style seemed to her 'the grandmother and grandfather of all the Virginia Woolf's [sic] and Stella Bensons and of all those modern novelists who seem to write with the astonished eyes of an imaginary child'.[24] Not only Woolf and Benson, but Elizabeth Bowen in Ireland, Catherine Carswell in Scotland, and Margiad Evans in Wales all generated distinctive local modernisms that owed much to the national tale's shaping of social relations in the dynamic movement between sexuality and politics.

---

[24] George Yeats to W. B. Yeats, 25 January 1932, in Anne Saddlemyer (ed.), *W. B. Yeats and George Yeats: The Letters* (Oxford: Oxford University Press, 2011), 290.

13

Gothic and Anti-Gothic, 1797–1820

ROBERT MILES

FROM 1797 to 1820 the story of the Gothic would seem to be one of rise and fall. Glancing back at an adulthood misspent as a Gothic novelist, the Irish writer Charles Robert Maturin ruefully noted that the fashion for terror was already 'out' in 1807, the year of his first 'Gothic', *Fatal Revenge; or, The Family of Montorio*.[1] The bibliographic record supports the claim. The Gothic reached its apogee in the late 1790s, when it secured a third share of the novel market, after which it withered, poisoned by a steady drip of parodies. Indeed, from 1797 onward, the Gothic seems inseparable from an anti-Gothic shadow that materialized in myriad forms, from ad hoc animadversions found in the reviews mocking the genre's formulaic character, to full-blown parodies. If Keats was 'snuff'd out by an article', the Gothic perished from a veritable army of scoffing Henry Tilneys.

Although correct in substance, the story requires qualification in every particular, starting with the numbers. While the quantity of novels advertising themselves as products of the 'terror-system' declined during the first two decades of the century, the Gothic did not peter out: it migrated downmarket, into chap-books, bluebooks, and magazines; it clogged the shelves of circulating libraries; and it sustained itself, post-1820, by embedding itself in other 'genres' (Potter 2005). Share of the expensive novel market is only one way to gauge a genre's penetration; other measures suggest that while Gothic lost prestige, it continued to gain readers.

The drift downmarket ultimately led to a literary-historical myth. Critically we still live in the periodic architecture bequeathed by the Victorians. It was the Victorians who formulated this period as Romantic, conceived as a poetic renaissance in which Literature emerged, renewed by a vigorous encounter with sublimity, nature, and the transcendental. Capital 'L' 'Literature' requires its lower-case opposite to make sense and for Victorian critics Gothic was the ideal candidate, being, by repute, formulaic, founded on base emotions, such as horror and lust, and devoted to quenching its readership's unsophisticated

---

[1] Charles Robert Maturin, Preface, *Women; or, Pour et Contre*, 3 vols (Edinburgh: Constable, 1818), 1.iv.

thirst for stimulation. As in all such gambits, the genre's status was associated with that of its lowest putative consumers and producers: women and servants. And just as the Victorians thought of poetry as the acme of the high, being a strenuous, uplifting, minority taste, so they considered entertaining prose as the epitome of the reverse.

This myth has been latterly debunked. That the Gothic novel was the exclusive domain of women writers and readers now seems an implausible claim. While the picture, and evidence, is complex, the gist can be summarized as follows: while women were more likely to rush into Gothic novel writing, either explicitly or implicitly admitting authorship, male authors were wanting mainly in lacking courage to own up. As the novel form gained in prestige, especially after the boost provided by *Waverley* (1814) and the open secret of Walter Scott's authorship, so the proportion of purely 'anonymous' novels tends to fall, while the percentage of declared or identified male authors rises, including in the field of the Gothic (see also Garside, Chapter 2). Just as the authorship figures complicate the myth of the Gothic as a female ghetto, so does the evidence regarding readership. For every John Thorpe affecting superiority, there were closet male readers, such as Henry Tilney, avidly seeking hair-raising sensations.[2] Nor could one say that the genre was in decline, aesthetically, given that three of its masterpieces appeared late in the period: *Northanger Abbey* (1818), *Frankenstein* (1818), and *Melmoth the Wanderer* (1820). Finally, it was not even the case that Gothic was a modifier that attached itself exclusively, or even mainly, to prose: during the Romantic period, the Gothic taste pervaded poetry and drama as thoroughly as ever it did the novel.

The last point raises an especially tricky question: what was allegedly rising and falling? When the Victorians began referring, retrospectively, to the schools of Radcliffe, Godwin, and Lewis as the 'Gothic', they did so as if there were a clearly identifiable genre, something that rose and fell. In contradistinction, Gothic writing during the period is trans-, sub-, and multi-generic. It occurs, more or less uniformly, across the major genres of novel, drama, and poetry. Putting aside the tale, which the Gothic dominated, and restricting our view, artificially, to extensive prose fiction, we quickly perceive that the Gothic is a variety of the novel, one of its subgenres best labelled 'romance'. And when we narrow our focus even further, to any extended prose work founded on the terror system, it becomes apparent that the form is hybrid, containing many different generic strands, including satire, pastiche, pastoral, novel *and* romance, lyric, epic, and so on. At the same time, against this picture of baffling heterogeneity, we have to put the equally significant fact that the Gothic was indeed formulaic: somewhere in the mix one finds the usual ingredients of castles, heroines in distress, tyrannical aristocrats, enraged fathers, missing mothers, ghosts, hobgoblins, bad weather, hooting owls, mouldering manuscripts,

---

[2] Jane Austen, *Northanger Abbey*, ed. Barbara M. Benedict and Deirdre Le Faye (Cambridge: Cambridge University Press, 2006), vol. 1, ch. 14; 107–8.

half-buried corpses, banditti, secret tribunals, torch-lit caves, etc. etc. (to use the flourish much favoured by contemporary parodies).

In looking at the Gothic novel during the Romantic period we need always to remind ourselves that our object is not the Gothic per se, but a particular generic manifestation of a much larger taste, style, or cultural movement. The organizing principle of Thomas Love Peacock's 'anti-Gothic' work, *Nightmare Abbey* (1818), is that the popular embrace of a glamorous, obfuscating transcendentalism, and a Gothic aesthetic of mouldering abbeys and hooting owls, are two sides of the same Romantic coin. Where Victorian critics separate Romantic from Gothic, Peacock sees them as indissolubly joined. Having recognized the Gothic novel's affinity with larger currents of Romantic-era literature, we need to note that during this period the novel was inherently unstable and hybrid. As moderns we tend to view the history of the novel through the lens of the current dispensation, evident in most contemporary bookstores, where we have, on one side, a large category of self-consciously literary works conformable to the conventions of 'realism', often designated simply as 'novels', and on the other, numerous divisions of sub-literary genre-writing, such as mystery, horror, detective, romance, and science fiction. This organization is not a product of nature but of two hundred years, and more, of literary history. During the Romantic period, the modern order was in the process of being formed, with the novel very much in flux, as Deidre Lynch indicates in Chapter 10 in this volume. Most Romantic-era novels, including Austen's, are multi-generic in that they incorporate aspects of previously popular genres. Driving this instability was an intense competition to commandeer the market, to become (as Walter Scott, the era's canniest operator, would put it) the founder of one's own 'school' of fiction (Williams 1968: 110). Two countervailing forces were thus at work: a restless search for novelty, for innovation in the novel form, and the tendency to pile in, once a winning formula was identified. Often, the two forces went together in the same author. Thus Charles Robert Maturin, who imitated Radcliffe in his first novel, *Fatal Revenge*, Lady Morgan in his next two, *The Wild Irish Boy* (1808) and *The Milesian Chief* (1812), both being variants of her innovation, the Irish national tale, and Walter Scott in his last, the historical romance *The Albigenses* (1824), even as Maturin ultimately proved an innovator with the *sui generis Melmoth*. Accordingly, one can best and most accurately represent the Gothic novel during our period as the proliferation of several schools, above all, of Radcliffe, Godwin, Lewis, and Schiller. To put matters in this way is to bring home the diversity of the 'Gothic novel'.

The School of Radcliffe

Of all the schools, the Radcliffean was by far the largest, most copied, and parodied. Scott's characterization of Ann Radcliffe as 'the first poetess of romantic fiction' (Williams

1968: 103) is especially apt, as it captures the conspicuously cross-generic nature of her art, where she combines the outlook, and even verse form, of poetical romance, with the emerging techniques of the modern novel. The heroine of sensibility is necessary, as she is the generative centre of poetic sentiment in the romance, through her tendency to produce or elicit lyric effusions, as well as through her overdeveloped capacity for 'seeing things', as Deidre Lynch puts it (193). Radcliffe further mixes poetry and romance through her pioneering technique of attaching snippets of fashionable verse to her chapters, as epigraphs (Price 2000: 92). Her famed landscape descriptions, drawing upon the picturesque Claude Lorrain and the sublime Salvator Rosa, offered endless opportunities for Radcliffe to indulge her appetite for poetic prose. Finally, in classic generic terms her novels are romances, being equidistant between the anarchic spirit of festive comedy and the austere one of tragedy.

The school of Radcliffe casts the longest shadow, reaching into our present: as Norman Holland and Leona Sherman argue, the modern Gothic romance 'formula' found in Mills and Boon and Harlequin has its origin in her novels. Their description is wonderful in its economy: 'The image of the woman-plus-habitation and the plot of mysterious sexual and supernatural threats in an atmosphere of dynastic mysteries within the habitation has changed little since the eighteenth century' (1977: 279).

'Dynastic mysteries' nicely encapsulates the double impulse of much early Gothic, as Deidre Lynch shows in her chapter. On the one hand the genre develops through its obsession with intergenerational haunting, which we may take as a figure for the ambiguous survival of archaic information into the present, whether through curses, stories, wills, autobiographies, diaries, histories, or documents relating to property; on the other, it obsesses about the credibility of this material and whether it is worthy of belief. For critics of the female Gothic, Radcliffe's importance lies, in part, in her ability to dramatize the lesson that such fantastical material may contain symbolic matter otherwise suppressed by the novel's modern adhesion to the discipline of induction. But it also lies in the fact that the Radcliffe formula proved so potent. In her nod to the Gothic novels pouring from popular presses, such as Minerva, Jane Austen references three of Radcliffe's most conspicuous imitators in *Northanger Abbey*: Eliza Parsons, Regina Maria Roche, and Eleanor Sleath. While this school of romance dominated the Gothic, then as now, it failed to produce a successor capable of emerging from Radcliffe's shadow until the advent, mid-century, of the Brontës.

The School of Lewis

Although useful, 'Gothic/anti-Gothic' is an artificial distinction, for many works are both at once, such as M. G. Lewis's *The Monk* (1796). Lewis revolutionized the Gothic by dwelling transgressively on what Radcliffe dismissively called 'horror', by which she meant a graphic poetic, rather than, as she preferred, a suggestive one.[3] In his 'minute' description of libidinous and violent material,[4] from Matilda's erotic body to Ambrosio's broken one, or from Agnes's clutching the worm-eaten corpse of her infant to Ambrosio's subterranean rape of his sister, he systematically broke the norms of what was permissible to depict in polite letters, to the extent that he was reviled in a press campaign, and forced by a legal one to expurgate his text. Lewis summarily dismissed Radcliffe's explained supernatural in favour of unrestrained supernatural mayhem, largely setting the agenda for future Gothic works. And yet *The Monk* is also anti-Gothic, or what amounts to the same thing in 1796, anti-Radcliffe, in its satiric assault on sensibility, which scarcely receives more respect in Lewis's text than it habitually does in the Marquis de Sade's: where sensibility should be an incitement to empathy and benevolent affect, it simply incites desires of an unpleasant, Freudian, kind. To put matters another way, as Susan Sontag (1964) noted, the Gothic has its origins in 'camp,' in a particular form of modern sensibility that relishes pastiche with its subtle assaults on the prestige and gravitas of 'originality', together with the cultural norms originality supports. Without doubt the 'campiest' moment of Lewis's romance is Ambrosio's encounter with one of Satan's superior minions: an epicene youth, 'perfectly naked', bathed in pink fairy lights.[5] It is hard to imagine any reader taking this image seriously while also maintaining a simple belief in the moral authority of revealed religion.

The school of Lewis is always outrageous in this fashion; indeed, the mark of belonging to it is a willingness to take matters to an extreme. In the hands of male imitators, such as William Henry Ireland in, for instance, *The Abbess* (1799) or *Gondez, the Monk* (1805), or Edward Montague in *The Demon of Sicily* (1807), this generally means exploring the boundaries of pornography. In the case of his most extraordinary female follower, Charlotte Dacre, the boundary crossing of her best-known novel, *Zofloya; or, The Moor* (1806) includes 'nymphomania' (Craciun 1997: 21–2), female violence of an unprecedented kind, and interracial desire. While each of these works has unique features, they all conspicuously model themselves on the formula of *The Monk*, none more so than *Zofloya*, which also features an antagonist (Victoria de Loredani) led down the garden path by a libidinous, shape-shifting devil who equivocates with proscribed desires. As the case of Lewis's most conspicuous imitators seems to indicate, his model appealed to writers well beyond the pale of polite society: thus Dacre, daughter of the notorious 'Jew King', an infamous moneylender, friend alike to the shadier members of the Prince Regent's set and diehard Jacobins, and himself notorious for his outré family arrangements. If her Jewish, Bohemian upbringing wasn't handicap enough, Dacre lived with the raffish newspaper

---

[3] Ann Radcliffe, 'On the Supernatural in Poetry', *New Monthly Magazine*, 16: 1 (January 1826), 145–52.
[4] S. T. Coleridge, *Critical Review*, n.s., 19 (February 1797), 194–200.
[5] Matthew Lewis, *The Monk*, ed. Howard Anderson (Oxford: Oxford University Press, 1967), vol. 2, ch. 4; 277.

editor Nicholas Byrne, bearing him three illegitimate children. Ireland, for his part, was the infamous Shakespeare forger, son of the arriviste and parvenu Samuel Ireland, collector, art critic, and author of fashionable travel books, and Amelia De Coppinger, alias Mrs Freeman, a cast-off mistress, it seems, of the Earl of Sandwich. While Lewis himself was a product of high society (his father was a senior mandarin in the civil service with large holdings in Jamaica), he suffered the embarrassment of his mother, who eloped with his music teacher, and the enduring scandal of his homosexuality, a serious matter in an age of escalating executions for sodomy. Like Horace Walpole before him, Lewis was careful to keep within the extensive bounds of aristocratic permissiveness, but also, like Walpole, he clearly had a 'camp' sensibility that delighted in sporting at the edge. His imitators, without any respectability to lose, often went over it.

The School of Godwin

In writing on 'The Novel Wars of 1790–1804' in this volume (Chapter 11), Jon Mee explains William Godwin's extensive influence as a 'Jacobin' novelist. As a philosopher he won renown as a champion of progressive values, with rational self-interest and benevolence pitched against Burke's Gothic system of entrenched privilege and prejudice. As a novelist he led the way by finding a form that combined philosophical ideas with 'psychology', or as Godwin calls it in his essay 'Of History and Romance', 'a genuine praxis upon the nature of man'.[6] In the Godwin school of Gothic fiction the needs of characterization, and the needs of philosophy, are locked in a productive tension.

As Mee notes, in the 1796 preface to the second edition of *The Adventures of Caleb Williams* (1794) Godwin makes his theme clear by asking a question: how does the system of government tyranny pervade and pervert everyday life? How is it that otherwise well-intentioned and well-disposed individuals come to act in ways that are against their own rational self-interest, extending, even, to monstrous acts of violence? In short, how is violence reproduced in modern society? The short answer is 'Gothic', a word that encodes an important political ambiguity. As Burke notoriously argued in *Reflections on the Revolution in France* (1790), the Gothic spirit of the pan-European past, embodied in the cult of chivalry, was a glorious thing; it made modern manners, and our country, 'lovely', worthy of respect, and therefore functional, a view typically rebutted by 'Jacobins' as 'mere Gothic prejudice'.

Godwin is explicit on the point: Falkland has internalized Burke's 'love of chivalry'.[7] As Mee observes, this act of internalization becomes the focus of Godwin's

---

[6] William Godwin, 'Of History and Romance', in *Caleb Williams*, ed. Maurice Hindle (London: Penguin, 1988), 367.

[7] Godwin, *Caleb Williams*, ed. Hindle, vol. 1, ch. 2; 12.

psychological study. Falkland lives out chivalry's Gothic spirit in conspicuously generous ways, until the very source of his virtue turns septic, poisoning his life and his actions. The decisive moment is the insult administered to him by his brutish neighbour, Tyrrel, who scorns the resort of gentlemen, duelling, and simply kicks Falkland across the floor of a public house—a humiliation the diminutive Falkland revenges through the ignoble means of assassination. The same exquisite sense of honour commands his silence as his neighbour and son are hanged for the offence, even as it exacts a fatal price from his tortured conscience. The point Godwin is driving at is that the 'love of distinction'[8] embedded in Burke's cult of chivalry is at the same time a deep love of self, a factitious desire produced by the commercial system of overproduction and luxury, a love that actually runs counter to our rational self-interest, even as it serves as a deep well of envy, malice, and ultimately violence. No man, within this system, is able truly to know himself. Thus Caleb Williams, who, in probing his master's secret, is ostensibly motivated by the electric bonds of sympathy: a revolutionary force for good as feeling overleaps the artificial distinctions of rank to cement empathy and brotherhood. However much Caleb might rationalize his motives as a desire to understand and thus alleviate his master's suffering, Caleb, too, is infected with the modern system of tyranny, evident from the selfish motives he keeps from himself, but which become increasingly manifest in a doubling between himself and his master. In a perverted system, the magic of affective doubling simply reproduces the perversion inherent within it.

As a philosopher essaying a genuine praxis upon human nature, Godwin is far too alert to the nuances of his story to suppress evidence contradictory to his theory. His narratives thus founder on a contradiction inherent within his method: if the 'spirit and character of the government intrudes itself into every rank of society', manifesting itself in the 'modes of domestic and unrecorded despotism by which man becomes the destroyer of man' (*Caleb Williams*, Preface, 3) how is man ever to commandeer his rational self-interest? If he is the prisoner of 'opinion'—of an 'ideology' Karl Marx would later classify as a 'false consciousness'—how is he ever to extricate himself, save by lifting himself up by his own bootstraps? It is a chicken-and-egg question, an infinite regress. The answer implicit in Godwin's aesthetic is that while the means of extrication are not available to his characters, as he pursues a genuine praxis, they are available to readers as they absorb the lessons of Godwin's philosophical fable. However, within the realm of his fictional worlds, Godwin's narratives run counter to the philosophy enunciated in his *Enquiry Concerning Political Justice* (1793). Notoriously, Godwin illustrated the moral conclusion of his necessitarian philosophy—whereby our actions are predetermined by a thousand previous ones,

---

[8] William Godwin, *An Enquiry Concerning Political Justice and its Influence on General Virtue and Happiness*, 2 vols (London: G. G. J. and J. Robinson, 1793), 2.824.

in a chain—by saying that the 'assassin cannot help the murder he commits, any more than the dagger' (*Enquiry*, 2.690). There is a distinction: 'The man differs from the knife, just as the iron candlestick differs from the brass one; he has one more way of being acted upon. This additional way in man is motive; in the candlestick, is magnetism' (*Enquiry*, 1.309). It is in the genesis of our motives that Godwin locates his doctrine of necessity. Just as a perverted system will produce corrupt motives, so will a rational one infallibly produce—in the uncorrupted youth—'motives' arising out of man's natural capacity for benevolence. In his *Enquiry* Godwin imagines readers changing through the awakening of their reason; in his fictions, no such transformation is possible for his characters, locked as they are in the iron chain of necessity. In illustrating this 'iron chain' Godwin reproduces two central Gothic tropes: live burial and the dead hand of the past. Thus, even as Godwin labours in the hope of freeing the reader from inherited 'mind-forg'd manacles', his narratives seem to offer vivid proof of the delusiveness of all such hope: as sure as Falkland's spies, the past reaches into the present to lock characters within their mental prisons.

The same contradiction comes to dominate the work of his American follower, Charles Brockden Brown. One might question Godwin's influence on Brown given the propinquity of Godwin's early work (the *Enquiry* in 1793 and *Caleb Williams* in 1794) with Brown's (*Wieland* in 1798, *Edgar Huntly* and *Ormond*, both 1799, and *Arthur Mervyn*, 1799–1800). In fact, the Atlantic world had a remarkably cohesive print culture, with Godwin penetrating intellectual circles in Philadelphia every bit as deeply as London during the same time frame (Kafer 2004: 66–72). The traffic flowed in both directions, with Minerva publishing *Ormond* (1800), *Arthur Mervyn*, and *Edgar Huntly* (the latter two both 1803). *Wieland*, itself a major influence on Godwin's 1817 novel *Mandeville. A Tale of the Seventeenth Century in England*, was published by Colburn in 1811.

The Enlightenment creed of *Edgar Huntly*'s eponymous hero is meant to sound Godwinian. It tended to 'deify necessity and universalize matter; to destroy the popular distinctions between soul and body, and to dissolve the supposed connection between the moral condition of man, anterior and subsequent to death'.[9] Like Godwin, Brown sets out to write a genuine praxis on the nature of man by anatomizing, and pulling apart, the chain of associations anterior to the formation of a 'motive'. His main device for doing so, again following Godwin, is a series of embedded first-person narratives (a technique later employed by both Mary Shelley and Maturin). Through these first-person narratives Brown aims to slow down, and so make available for readerly contemplation, the delusive chains of thought that engulf his protagonists in a moral maze, a conceit literalized in *Edgar Huntly* as the curious topography of Norwalk, a remainder of the 'Old West' within

---

[9] Charles Brockden Brown, *Edgar Huntly; or, Memoirs of a Sleep-Walker*, ed. Norman S. Grabo (Harmondsworth: Penguin, 1988), ch. 13; 125.

strolling distance of Philadelphia, which owing to its curious terrain of convoluted valleys, caves, and cliffs, constitutes a holdover of the recent past, of panthers, Indians, and bloodshed: a 'labyrinth' that is at once an atavistic expression of the frontier, a dreamscape, and a model of the human mind itself. Thus, even as Brown ostensibly labours in the cause of Enlightenment rationality, of understanding the sources of modern error, thus escaping the past, his 'accomplish'd horrors', as John Keats called them,[10] serve only to underline the impossibility of doing so.

In the first flush of Brown's 'rediscovery' during the middle of the last century, there was a tendency to attribute the sudden irruption of pessimism into Brown's novels to something quintessentially American: a Calvinist legacy of always falling back on the 'power of blackness', on the radical frailty of human powers unassisted by grace. But if we see Brown in the context of a wider Atlantic culture, he appears simply modern. Stephen Behrendt puts the point well: 'The emerging "modern" novel whose roots we see in the late eighteenth and early nineteenth centuries is "realistic" precisely to the extent that it moves toward a world-view characterized by unresolved inconsistencies, contradictions, ambivalences, and "dead ends" of all sorts' (2009: 201).

When the Gothic is modern, it is modern in precisely this way, of which there is no better example than Mary Shelley's *Frankenstein; or, The Modern Prometheus* (1818), another multi-generic work. *Frankenstein* is late Gothic and early science fiction; it is also a classic example of a philosophical romance where the supernatural is permitted because it becomes the occasion of a modern parable. In many ways its most obvious progenitor is her father's *St. Leon: A Tale of the Sixteenth Century* (1799), which also features a protagonist forever alienated from his family, and humanity, through his dabbling in alchemical mysteries. As with Brown, Shelley follows Godwin in using embedded first-person narratives to complicate her fable, in the process creating a series of disturbingly interchangeable identities: thus Walton echoes Frankenstein in his blind enthusiasm and reckless scientific ambition, even as the murderous monster comes to impersonate the voice of domestic longing and persecuted humanity. Like the quotations from Milton's *Paradise Lost*, the point of these mobile identifications is to create irresolvable irony: in the story, who is the creator, and who the created? Frankenstein and his monster are evidently both at once, even as another, blasphemous possibility is discreetly invoked (where man stands to God as the monster does to Frankenstein: an imperfect creature aggrieved with his vainglorious, selfish, and incompetent maker). Such unstated connections, of which Brown, incidentally, was a particular master, multiply the interpretative possibilities even as no single one leads to an 'answer'.

---

[10] John Keats, letter to Richard Woodhouse 21, 22 September 1819: *Letters of John Keats: A Selection*, ed. Robert Gittings (Oxford: Oxford University Press, 1979), 297.

The School of Schiller

Frankenstein's immersion in alchemical mysteries is set in Ingolstadt, one of the novel's key allusions. Ingolstadt was the home of Adam Weishaupt, the alleged founder of the Illuminati, a radical sect of freemasons dedicated to reviving the Gnostic lore of the Rosicrucians; they were also, apparently, committed revolutionaries, sworn enemies of monarchies across Europe, and libertines with a cunning plan: to indoctrinate the cream of European nobility in their fierce materialist creed by severing the connections between these young men and their kith and kin, establishing new relations based on the stern codes of the Illuminati policed by the secret society's fatal tribunals. By turning the future leaders of Europe against family, church, and nation, the Illuminati supposedly aimed to take a stranglehold on the continent, turning it, irreversibly, in the direction of their rational, Enlightenment ideals, and on course for bloody revolution. Fear of the Illuminati and other radical freemasons fed a European-wide paranoia. The Scottish writer John Robison issued his *Proofs of a Conspiracy* in 1797, shortly supported by the Abbé Barruel's monumental *Memoirs Illustrating the History of Jacobinism* in 1798–9, a work strongly encouraged, from its inception, by Edmund Burke (Deane 1988: 11). Both offered conclusive proof that the French Revolution was the work of Jacobins seeded in France by the German illuminati; worse, these secret societies had set up cells across the Continent, including Britain, and were even now hatching plots.

Such sensational material was bound to find its way into the Gothic novel, which it did, through Friedrich Schiller's seminal *Der Geisterseher* (1787–9). First translated into English in 1795 as *The Ghost-Seer*, few tales of the period can claim to be as influential as Schiller's. *The Ghost-Seer* relates the events that unfold around a young and impressionable German prince after encountering a mysterious Armenian while visiting Venice. The Armenian appears to have preternatural insight into the Prince's affairs, dropping canny hints as to hidden dangers and coming to his aid when the 'Sicilian' is on the verge of hoodwinking the prince through a demonstration of his 'supernatural' powers. The character of the Sicilian is based on Count Cagliostro, the notorious freemason and Egyptian adept. The Armenian lifts the veil, revealing the mechanisms of the Sicilian's cheap tricks: exploding powders, magnets, and a magic lantern. Only in the denouement do we learn that the exposure was part of an elaborate sting designed to deliver the Prince irrevocably into the Armenian's power. A member of the Inquisition, the Armenian conspires to convert the Prince back to Catholicism. The Inquisition targets the Prince's 'fondness for the mysterious',[11] using his credulity to bind him to the Armenian. *The Ghost-Seer* was written prior to the Revolution, but was much imitated, in Germany, in its immediate

---

[11] Friedrich Schiller, *The Ghost-Seer; or, Apparitionist*, trans. D. Boileau (London: Vernor and Hood, 1795), 45.

aftermath; in the process, the core story was fused with Barruel's paranoid material; the conspiracy, hoodwinking, and political transformation were now in the cause of the Illuminati, rather than the Inquisition. Two of the most notorious stories of conspiracy and skulduggery, featuring the Illuminati, were both translated into English by Peter Will: Cajetan Tschink's *The Victim of Magical Delusion; or, The Mystery of the Revolution of P—l; A Magico-Political Tale* (1795), and Isabella Thorpe's favourite in *Northanger Abbey, Horrid Mysteries* (1796), by Karl Grosse. Radcliffe's *The Italian* nods its respect to Schiller through the character of Schedoni, whose appearance is based on the Armenian (Norton 1998: 127), and through the character of Vivaldi, who like the German Prince, has a fatal fondness for the marvellous. Banditti-infested caverns also derive from Schiller, via his 1781 drama, *The Robbers* (*Die Räuber*), but in the post-Revolutionary period bandits are frequently Illuminati to boot, as in the case of Percy Bysshe Shelley's two adolescent tales, *Zastrozzi* (1810) and *St. Irvyne* (1811).

Anti-Gothic

Thinking generically about a work means relating its constituents to the 'aim or aims of the generic structure' (Cohen 1991: 88). Given the diversity of the main schools of the Gothic in the period 1797–1820, enumerating constituents does not get us very far: we can observe that each work features a castle, or live burial, or incest, but this still leaves the interpretative work to be done, which we begin by determining the genre's underlying aim, or aims. Predictably enough, criticism has provided a wide variety of answers, from a primal ontological angst to the horror of the primal scene, which is to say, from philosophical (Brown 2005) to psychoanalytical explanations (Punter 1980). However different these approaches might be, they all begin with affect, with the premise that the fundamental aim of a Gothic work is to instil terror, or horror, in the reader. However useful these approaches might be in understanding the motive forces that have sustained Gothic writing for over two hundred years, they do not really help us in grasping the relation between the Gothic and the antithetical works it provoked over our much shorter period, where the motive was often politically tinged. A much better place to begin is with the obvious characteristics of the work that founded the Gothic's several schools, Horace Walpole's *The Castle of Otranto* (1765). *Otranto*'s core trope is legitimacy, and its leading textual or tonal feature is pastiche.

The several schools belong to a single genre, then, in that all of them deploy the typical constituents of the Gothic in the service of broadly similar aims that reach back to Walpole: they narrate the discontents of modernity in broad, quasi-allegorical strokes, nowhere more so than in the predominating, highly elastic trope of body/castle/house/nation, and they do so in a radical, self-reflexive fashion. At the centre of this exploration is the haunting absence of 'legitimacy'. The period 1797–1820 was, politically, reactionary, as Britain recoiled from the Revolution and wars with Napoleonic France. In this context, the theme of legitimacy was politically charged. The theme could be couched in several ways, of which the most dominant was the 'dead hand of the past', meaning the power of feudal remnants to reassert themselves in the present, such as a brutal patriarchal order, a superstitious religious one, or a violent political system. The point was not so much that the past had an uncanny power to live on, corrupting the present, but that the contrast between the 'feudal' and the 'modern' threw both into doubt as models of political legitimacy (in Behrendt's terms, both prove a 'dead end').

There are two ways in which a work may be 'anti': it may be against or different from; contra or 'antithetical to'. Parodies fall into the first category, the novel into the second. Parodies worked against the Gothic largely by emptying the genre of its 'aims', or ideological content, leaving behind a senseless, formulaic husk. The antithetical novel bled the Gothic of its prestige through quite different means. One can restate the opposition, with Deidre Lynch (in her earlier chapter), as that between romance and novel; between works requiring a tincture of 'the marvellous', as Nathaniel Hawthorne was later to argue,[12] and those steadfastly tied to the 'method of induction'[13] and probability.

On the face of it, the parodies were the more damaging of the two. The Gothic no sooner secured market dominance, than it invited satire, doubtless owing to its formulaic and outré character, which made it an easy target. So while the major parodies appear at regular intervals during the first two decades of the century, they draw their impetus from the late 1790s. Thus *La Nuit anglaise* (1799) by Louis François Marie Bellin de la Liborlière, a parody of the English Gothic novel (and French reader) loosely translated as *The Hero; or, The Adventures of a Night* (1817) by Sophia Shedden, Matthew Lewis's younger sister. Internal evidence strongly suggests that Eaton Stannard Barrett's *The Heroine, or Adventures of a Fair Romance Reader* (1813) was based on Liborlière's work. *The Monk* provoked an immediate riposte: *The New Monk*, by R. S. Esquire (1798). *The New Monk*'s enthusiast is Joshua Pentateuch, a canting London Methodist, rather than Madrid priest, while his painted object of hypocritical desire is a juicy joint of mutton. *St. Leon* was immediately followed by *St. Godwin* (1800), by Edward Dubois, in which Godwin's self-conceit as the age's leading philosopher is expertly skewered through selective misquotation from his published oeuvre, including, fatally, his *Enquiry*. As this last example reminds us, in the case of Godwin, at least, 'Anti-Gothic' and 'Anti-Jacobin' are more or less the same category (see Grenby 2001). The contention that the late 1790s was the formative period for anti-Gothic parody is further supported by the compositional history of Austen's *Northanger Abbey*, which bears the marks of its gestation in the dates of the

---

[12] Nathaniel Hawthorne, *The House of the Seven Gables*, ed. Milton R. Stern (Harmondsworth: Penguin, 1986), Preface, 1.

[13] Hugh Murray, *Morality of Fiction; or, An Inquiry into the Tendency of Fictitious Narratives, with Observations on Some of the Most Eminent* (Edinburgh and London: Longman [etc.], 1805), 10.

'Horrid Novels' breathlessly recommended by Isabella Thorpe (all first appearing in the period 1793–8). Thomas Love Peacock's *Nightmare Abbey* is a notable exception in having a much later provenance.

Eaton Stannard Barrett's *The Heroine* (1813) was one of the period's most successful novels; according to an obituary notice of 1820, it 'made the nearest approach to the success of the "Waverley Novels"' (see Reiman 1979: v). *The Heroine* and *Northanger Abbey* display remarkable similarities, but it seems highly unlikely that Barrett could have influenced Austen's anti-Gothic work as she had completed a version as early as 1803; more plausible is that as satirists they spied the same targets, leading to similar jokes, especially as both draw on Charlotte Lennox's *The Female Quixote* (1752) and Cervantes's original, for inspiration.

The heroine, the self-styled 'Cherubina' Wilkinson ('Cherry' being too prosaic) is determined, quixotically, to live out a life patterned on the best authorities: the Gothic romances that have addled her mind. Like Catherine Morland in *Northanger Abbey*, Cherubina is much disobliged by the affectionate common sense of her father, a prosperous landowner Cherubina dismissively dubs 'the Farmer', a man no more 'addicted to locking up' his daughter than is Mr Morland (*Northanger Abbey*, vol. 1, ch. 1; 5). And like Catherine, Cherubina discovers an innocuous scrap of paper in mysterious circumstances, into which she outrageously over-reads: in her case, that she is the dispossessed daughter of Thomas De Willoughby, a relative of Nell Gwyn, and the rightful inheritor of Gwyn Castle. She further determines that 'farmer Wilkinson' has been suborned to murder her, the better to secure the property of the usurper. Cherubina immediately sets upon the road intent on seizing Gwyn Castle, establishing her rightful claim, and turfing out its illegitimate occupant, the present Duchess. Cherubina is both a fantasist and a girl of parts: a deluded being incapable of distinguishing between life and art, or the world and books, and an ever-resourceful ingénue who rises above the threats engulfing her. Through ingenious legal advice she rescues Jerry Sullivan, an Irish navvy, from committal as he is arraigned for theft before extricating herself, through her quick wits, from the machinations of a scheming street girl. At the same time she is easily gulled when a bit-part Covent Garden actor styles himself Lord Altamont Mortimer Montmorenci, having ascertained her status as an heiress and the drift of her lunacy. There then ensues a series of madcap adventures as she escapes the wiles of the various thieves, charlatans, and libertines who besiege her, as an easy mark, for her body and/or money, even as she resourcefully sets about establishing her claim to Gwyn Castle by taking up residence in one of its dilapidated outbuildings, protected by a phalanx of Irish labourers rounded up by Sullivan, her faithful lieutenant and erstwhile Sancho Panza.

In short, Cherubina is less a fictional character, and more a vehicle for satire. As in *Northanger Abbey*, Radcliffe is the principal target. In recounting his 'melancholy memoirs', Montmorenci makes a delightful hash of her work: 'on a beetling rock, lashed by the Gulf of Salerno, stood Il Castello di Grimgothico'. We hear of the banditti, Stiletto,

Poignardi, and Daggeroni, of 'long corridors, tall spiral staircases, the suites of tapestried apartments...', not to mention abductions, imprisonment and 'picturesque scenery'.[14] The parody echoes Henry Tilney's, when he imagines Catherine undergoing Gothic adventures in the abbey of her dreams (*Northanger Abbey*, vol. 2, ch. 5; 162–4). Or rather, both parodies reduce Radcliffe to a series of plot elements, in the process excising those aspects of her 'poetical' romance form that tend towards the heroine's subject formation and her pivotal position as the locus of a transcendent sensibility.

By stripping sensibility out of his parody Barrett reduces the Radcliffean heroine to a mere comic cipher, at once echoing the critics' complaint against Radcliffe (too eager to get into virtue-endangering scrapes while displaying an unfeminine appetite for the gruesome) while negating her counterbalancing virtue: a centre of self ostensibly equal to the hero's but actually much superior to it, as it proves the generative locus of value within the novel. In the process Barrett questions the 'legitimacy' of the Radcliffean heroine, the power of her novels to question gender stereotypes.

Austen was too appreciative of the efforts of a sister novelist to subject Radcliffe to the same treatment. Indeed, the narrator of *Northanger Abbey* goes out of her way to quarantine Radcliffe from the taint of the abysmal, German, 'horrids', not least by having her hero come to Radcliffe's defence, praising her above all others as the master of the hair-raising affect. Even so, *Northanger Abbey* is decidedly split on Radcliffe. The gentle mockery of book-fed heroines—and the constant equation of the Gothic with what Austen terms the 'unnatural and overdrawn' (vol. 2, ch. 7; 186), evident above all in Henry Tilney's Radcliffean parody—naturally takes a toll, even if the famous turning point of the novel is not as anti-Radcliffe as some critics maintain. The point, ostensibly, is the famous 'Dear Miss Morland' speech (vol. 2, ch. 9; 203) in which Henry takes Catherine to task for imagining General Tilney another 'Montoni' (vol. 2, ch. 8; 192) addicted to assassination, or like the father in Radcliffe's *A Sicilian Romance*, prone to burying supernumerary wives in effigy while keeping them imprisoned somewhere on the premises (vol. 2, ch. 8; 193), when newspapers, roads, and the 'age' lay everything open in England's home counties, beset as they are with neighbourhoods of voluntary spies (vol. 2, ch. 9; 203). Catherine's response is one of Austen's early bravura pieces of free indirect speech, in which the reader is invited to spy the irony of the heroine categorically swearing off Radcliffe and all her works (vol. 2, ch. 10, 205–6). Her problem all along has not been her authorities, but an absence of self-generated critique. Austen is too much of a realist to imagine that characters can change at the drop of a hat, or homily, no matter how withering; thus Catherine, who simply replaces one authority (Radcliffe) with another (Henry). And just as the one proves fallible, so does the other. When she hears a mysterious scratching at her

---

[14] Eaton Stannard Barrett, *The Heroine*, introd. Michael Sadleir (London: Eakin, Mathews & Marrot, 1927), 84–5.

door, late at night, in the abbey, she does not take alarm, as she should, falsely reassured as she is by Henry; thus she finds herself a real-life romance character when she least expects it, turfed out upon the road by the General in a fit of pique at her lack of fortune, a lone, young, vulnerable girl, on a road teeming with villains (to judge from the local press). This is the true turning point of the novel, the moment when Catherine really does begin to think for herself, concluding, in spite of Henry, that 'in suspecting General Tilney of either murdering or shutting up his wife, she had scarcely sinned against his character, or magnified his cruelty' (vol. 2, ch. 15; 256).

Austen takes a balanced view of Radcliffe's symbolic truth, according some weight to the view that a patriarchal world is also a dangerous one for female subjectivity. But that is precisely the problem for Radcliffe's school of poetic romance. *Northanger Abbey* is a powerfully anti-Gothic work, not in its parody, where it is even-handed, but in being antithetical to the Gothic mode; it is not realism that Catherine awakens into so much as it is the 'realist novel'. When Catherine comes to understand that the General is 'not perfectly amiable' (vol. 2, ch. 10; 206), she ceases to view the world through the lens provided by Gothic romance. Barrett's heroine comes to a similar understanding, to be sure; the difference is that Austen models the difference at the level of form, where inductive particulars and probability determine representation, or, in this case, the heroine's judgement, at the expense of the 'poetic' techniques pioneered by Radcliffe.

Walter Scott's *Waverley* is also anti-Gothic in both senses. In the first chapter the narrator gently scoffs at the schools of Radcliffe ('A Tale of Other Days') and Schiller ('a Romance from the German') as passé,[15] and he parodies both, with Waverley undergoing a comic inversion of what Ellen Moers termed Radcliffe's 'travelling heroinism' (1976: 126) when he is taken on mountain adventures, including an ironic rendering of the Schilleresque cavern of banditti, led by the cattle-rustler, Donald Bean Lean, all the while not quite realizing he's been abducted. But *Waverley* is also anti-Gothic in further developing a form, 'the historical novel', fundamentally at cross-purposes with the Gothic's aims. Scott's subject is not the past, but 'history'. Instead of the past serving as an uncanny well, empty or 'exploded', yet seeping into and poisoning the present, Scott illustrates a Burkean process in which the present emerges out of the past, as a continuous growth. The Gothic frequently turns on moments when the past proves inescapable, a subterranean stone labyrinth, to use the genre's favoured, recurring image. In Scott, the past is tinged with nostalgia, something generally absent in Gothic. In the Gothic the past is only ambiguous to the extent that its transcendence by the present is uncertain; in Scott ambiguity is its core value, as we both thank the past for delivering us into our present and lament our loss. In the Gothic, history is like an alien force that battens upon the present, a succubus fattened

---

[15] Walter Scott, *Waverley; or, 'Tis Sixty Years Since*, ed. P. D. Garside (Edinburgh: Edinburgh University Press, 2007), ch. 1; 3–4.

on fatherly sins. In Scott, it resembles Hegel's ascending gyres, as past conflict and difference produce, dialectically, a higher unity. This is certainly so in his two most influential romances from the period, *Waverley* and *Ivanhoe* (1820), which tackle Scottish and English history respectively. Both follow the same formula, worked out through the marriage plot: ancient conflicts are reconciled, symbolized by the union of the principals at the expense of an excluded other (thus the ancestral enmity of the English and Lowland Scots is resolved through the marriage of Waverley and Rose Bradwardine, at the expense of the Highland Flora, just as Saxons and Normans reconcile through Ivanhoe and Rowena, at the expense of the Jewish Rebecca). This distance from the Gothic is nicely summed up by Archibald Alison, in an 1848 *Blackwood*'s essay on the 'Historical Romance', when he praises Scott for helping the modern reading public fall in love with feudalism, an accomplishment one could not attribute to the Gothic with its need to make the feudal frightful.[16] Given Scott's prestige, and the influence of his own school, the Gothic was squeezed, as Scott fully intended.

Despite the proliferation of titles suggesting otherwise—*Headlong Hall* (1816), *Melincourt* (1817), *Crotchet Castle* (1831)—only one of Thomas Love Peacock's novels, *Nightmare Abbey*, is meaningfully Gothic, and even then it is *sui generis*. Formally, Peacock's books are not really novels at all, if by a novel we mean a work built around character or a theory of personality—on the belief that individuals are, indeed, individual, with unique histories, where they change and learn in a manner peculiar to themselves as circumstances and company alter. As Marilyn Butler argues, *Nightmare Abbey*'s structure is neo-classical in that it depends upon the reader's familiarity with the Classics, to which frequent allusion is made, not as slavish imitation, but by way of citing underlying ideas (1979: 108). It is these ideas, rather than characters, that drive Peacock's fictions. For a beleaguered 'radical' such as Peacock, neo-classicism also meant a return to simplicity, to nature, and to an essential humanism, a task made all the more urgent by the recent European turn to formal religion, mysticism, and apolitical inwardness. Against this essentially German spirit, crystallized in the self-conscious Romanticism of August and Friedrich Schlegel, and the opacities of Kantean philosophy, now advancing influentially in England (embodied in *Nightmare Abbey* as the Coleridgean Mr Flosky), Peacock set a politically engaged Hellenism. His texts, then, eschew the cult of personality, the gloomy egotistical inwardness that disfigured the present age, and allusively advance ideas through a comic structure that is part dialogue, and part operatic score, inspired, it seems, by a love of Mozart. The purpose of this new form was to render intelligible '*opinion*—that is, a familiar contemporary controversy' (Butler 1979: 19) by setting it out dialectically, as rich matter for inference.

---

[16] Archibald Alison, 'The Historical Romance', *Blackwood's Edinburgh Magazine*, 58: 359 (September 1845), 347.

Peacock's form was a response to the central dilemma of the second-generation Romantics, who were old enough to have been shaped by the Enlightenment ideal of a rational public sphere—a 'republic of letters' sustained by civic humanist ideology—and young enough to experience its decline, undone by the commercial imperatives of popular literature, and undermined by high literature's inward lyrical turn. In this context, Peacock's treatment of the Gothic was bound to differ. The political fault-line dividing the various schools of the Gothic had been between those who regarded the Gothic taste as a harmful feudal holdover (Godwin and Wollstonecraft) and those who saw it as more or less the reverse (Burke, Scott, and the anti-Jacobins). But that was twenty years earlier; now the Gothic was simply another emanation of modern, solipsistic fashion. Hence *Nightmare Abbey*'s hero, Scythrop, who is, in himself, the epitome of the Gothic taste. In true Gothic style Scythrop is raised by his widowed father, Mr Glowry, a misanthrope who has retired to his property, an isolated, dilapidated abbey in the fens of Lincolnshire, surrounding himself with servants of a suitably gloomy countenance (Raven, Crow, Skellet), and naming his only son after a maternal ancestor who had committed suicide, 'Scythrop' being Greek for 'of a sullen countenance'.[17] Disappointed in love like his father, Scythrop's haunt, while at home, is the ivy-smothered, owl-infested south-eastern tower and terrace. Much of the parody is aimed at Godwin's *Mandeville* (1817), nicknamed 'Devilman' by Peacock, which provided the model for Glowry, Scythrop, and their fen-surrounded abbey.

Despite his misanthropy, Glowry opens his house to a motley crew of great men, including the transcendental poet and philosopher, Mr Flosky; the 'Manichean Millenarian', Mr Toobad; a fashionable young aristocrat, Mr Listless; a man of science, Mr Asterias, the Ichthyologist; and the fashionable poet, Mr Cypress, who has perfected the modern poetic system of gloom and misanthropy. The plot is fashioned around a classic triangle: Scythrop falls in love with his penniless cousin, the light, frolicsome Marionetta, a marriage opposed by his father, who wants to prevent the same calamity happening to his son as to himself, of having nothing material to compensate him when his love turns sour, as it naturally will; and the mysterious 'Stella', a self-conscious 'Goth', who has fetched up in Scythrop's secret apartment 'mantled in the folds of a black cloak' (ch. 10; 402). Judging by his 'physiognomy' that Scythrop 'may be trusted', Stella unveils herself, revealing 'a female form and countenance of dazzling grace and beauty, with long flowing hair of raven blackness, and large black eyes of oppressive brilliancy, which strikingly contrasted with a complexion of snowy whiteness' (402). Stella is eventually revealed to be Celinda, Mr Toobad's daughter, and Scythrop's 'intended': in true Gothic fashion, the fathers in the case had arranged the marriage for financial reasons, which Celinda, also in

---

[17] Thomas Love Peacock, *Nightmare Abbey*, in *The Complete Novels*, ed. David Garnett, 2 vols (London: Rupert Hart-Davis, 1963), 1.356, n. 2.

true Gothic fashion, had declined, fleeing until she finds herself, by miraculous chance, domiciled with her intended in the secret compartment of his mouldering tower.

Readers often find it difficult to see past the alleged *roman à clef*, where Scythrop is the young Shelley, Marionetta Shelley's first wife, the tragic Harriet, and 'Stella' Shelley's second, Mary; and where the various visiting luminaries map onto, for instance, Samuel Taylor Coleridge (Flosky), Lord Byron (Cypress) and Sir Lumley Skeffington (Listless). While these references help one's reading by adding the expansive views to be had from matching type with token, they are only a part of a larger play of ideas, one very much detached from celebrity gossip, which Peacock deplored.

The references to the Gothic exemplify the play of ideas. When Stella appears, she is compared explicitly to Geraldine, from Coleridge's *Christabel*:

> I guess 'twas frightful there to see
> A lady so richly clad as she,
> Beautiful exceedingly. (ch. 10; 402)

The joke works on numerous levels. She is so clad, because she is, literally, rich—an heiress; like Geraldine, she is not what she seems, not a true, freethinking Goth on the Wollstonecraft or Dacre model, but a conventional miss who will eventually pair off with the impenetrable Mr Flosky (a coupling that contains its own Gothic joke, for if Flosky is Coleridge, and Stella Geraldine, Flosky incestuously mates with his own intellectual offspring); and finally, it makes the point that Gothic has become mere fashion, a style, one whose Romantic glamour belies the Godwinian principles Stella delphically utters. Similarly, we are told that Scythrop had become 'troubled with the *passion for reforming the world*' (ch. 2; 362), that he 'built many castles in the air, and peopled them with secret tribunals, and bands of illuminati' and 'slept with Horrid Mysteries under his pillow' (362–3). Scythrop dreams Gothic thoughts of the Schiller kind, just as Catherine Morland dreams hers through Radcliffe, and, as much as Miss Morland's, Scythrop's reveries are politically ineffective, being, indeed, Gothic 'castles in the air'. At the same time Peacock slyly alludes to Shelley's two first novels, the Schilleresque *St. Irvyne* and *Zastrozzi*, both swarming with Illuminati, making the point, in passing, that such novels are similarly lacking in serious political content, being, indeed, juvenilia. Finally, Scythrop's desire to possess both his mistresses (his inability to give one of them up being his undoing) recalls not just Johann Wolfgang von Goethe's *Stella*, with its similar theme, but the infamous 'double arrangement' of the highly successful anti-Jacobin satire *The Rovers* (1801), which pilloried Schiller's *Die Räuber*.

In an ensuing soliloquy, Scythrop makes the central point:

> A few to think, and many to act; that is the only basis of a perfect society. So thought the ancient philosophers: they had their esoterical and exoterical doctrines. So thinks the sublime Kant, who delivers his oracles in language which none but the initiated can comprehend. Such were the views of those secret associations of illuminati, which *were* the terror of superstition and tyranny ... (ch. 2; 363: my italics)

'Were' indeed: but no more. Superstition and tyranny have come again in the monarchies springing up across Europe, supported by the mystic hocus pocus of Romantics, like Coleridge, whose signature position, vis-à-vis the public sphere, was that the masses were not to be trusted, just enlightened clerks, such as himself, whom the 'many' must follow. Once tuned into Peacock's critique, it becomes easy to see how the 'sublime Kant' is a severe oxymoron (how severe may be gathered from a withering footnote in which Peacock equates political apostasy with the mysteries of Burkean sublimity, ch. 10; 402–3n). In effect, Peacock has recurred to a root meaning of the word 'Gothic', signifying Saxon or German, and by it he means (regardless of any ostensive progressive purposes) the school of German Romanticism as it was being fashioned in England via Thomas De Quincey, Coleridge, and later, Thomas Carlyle.

As Marilyn Butler notes, *Nightmare Abbey*'s crisis happens in high comic style: stooping at Scythrop's locked door Glowry hears a strange female voice, and a low grating sound, of something heavy being closed (1979: 135). Admitted by Scythrop to the now otherwise deserted room, Glowry reprehends his son for his behaviour given his declared love for his cousin, Marionetta, which the hidden Stella overhears, bringing her into the room in a towering jealous rage, along with the rest of the cast, drawn by the hubbub, including an aghast Marionetta. In the denouement the offended girls in turn refuse Scythrop, Marionetta taking up with Listless in fashionable Berkeley Square, and Stella running off to Germany with Flosky, the 'true transcendentalist' (ch. 15; 432). In the novel's final dialectical movement the synthesis is simply implied at the level of form: the opposite of fashionable Romantic inwardness (whether Coleridgean, Byronic, or Gothic) is the sprightly, Hellenic structure of classical comedy; and with this realization, Scythrop drops the pistol with which he was to cut a final, Wertheresque dash, and instead reaches for the Madeira in true Epicurean fashion.

In Peacock's Romantic/Gothic critique, both sides are associated with the decay of the republic of letters and the growth of a fashionable, apolitical inwardness. In 1818 this was a highly unusual view made possible by Peacock's radical Hellenism, his familiarity with popular Gothic works, and by his knowledge of modern German literature and philosophy. As such *Nightmare Abbey* was a highly rarefied work, outside the mainstream of Gothic novels and parodies alike. However, in one respect *Nightmare Abbey* is very much like the other novels from the end of the Gothic's first phase that still command a readership: it is a highly deviant work.

But this is only to be expected. Once a genre has established itself, one of two things tends to happen: either it is incorporated into other genres, as a 'mode', or writers are moved to a radical act of reimagining in order to refresh the genre, often, in the process, starting a new one. As we have already seen, such is the case with Mary Shelley's *Frankenstein*, which is as much science fiction as it is Gothic. Its mode is also complex and ironic, with events filtered through a series of first-person narratives, one encased within the other, a technique reaching back through Godwin to Walpole. It is also a technique found in two of the Gothic's late masterpieces: *Melmoth the Wanderer*, and James Hogg's *Confessions of a Justified Sinner* (1824). These are, to an extent, *sui generis* works, falling outside the mainstream of the four main schools of Gothic writing. Or rather, they are if one judges simply from their constituent parts. As regards the genre's aims, they are deeply Gothic, nowhere more so than in their form, which internalizes the Gothic principle of live burial, or broken communication; to recur to Behrendt's phrasing, to read these texts well is always to find oneself led up an interpretative 'dead end'. This is especially true of Hogg's *Confessions*, which deals with and, indeed, thematizes the irresolvable ambiguity that flows from irreconcilable truths. And, of course, both works recur to the Gothic's deep, sectarian roots.

It is also significant that both works emanate from the 'periphery', a trend that continues with the best mid-century Gothics produced in America (by Nathaniel Hawthorne, Herman Melville, and Edgar Allan Poe), Ireland (Sheridan Lefanu), and Yorkshire (the Brontës). It is not simply that Maturin's Dublin and Hogg's Edinburgh are provincial capitals; even within these comparatively marginal elites, they were marginal figures, something they turn to account in their works, literally so in Hogg's case, insofar as he ends his novel with a dispute about 'margins', which is to say boundaries, markers, and territory. Although numerous vernacular voices intrude into Hogg's narrative, including Hogg's own, in the persona of his *nom de plume*, the Ettrick Shepherd, there are two main ones: the 'objective' editor, who is the historian narrating the events outlined in the mouldering manuscript—and confession—recently found in an ancient unmarked grave from the Scottish borders; and the author of the manuscript, the justified sinner, suicide, and sneaking Calvinist hypocrite, Robert Wringhim. The novel's temporal setting is crucial; the events described are set in the early 1700s, a point after which the sectarian heat generated by fractious presbyterians and convenanters will begin to wane, while the secular Enlightenment starts to wax, reaching a zenith around the time of the book's present, that is, the early 1820s, and typified by the editor. No reader could sympathize with the backstabbing Wringhim, but as one reads on, it becomes apparent that the editor's poise as an objective historiographer is another unreliable voice, one encoding the worldly values of Enlightenment Edinburgh.

The reader is left with a neither/nor: neither the sanctimonious hypocrisy and violence of the Wringhims, nor the heedless, boisterous superiority of the confident Colwans. The historiography of Scotland's cosmopolitan centre was essentially Whiggish, whether Scottish 'stadialism' or Walter Scott's 'historical romance', in that both schools of history stressed 'progress'. The last thing Hogg is doing is offering a nostalgic backward glance at the good old days of sectarian murder; but he is concerned with what has been left out of this confident Whiggish history, with what doesn't fit its dominant storylines (hence the editor's blind spot regarding Wringhim). When the obviously highly sophisticated Hogg represents himself in his own novel as an apparently dim yokel wilfully ignorant of the contents of his own letter, one knows a complex game is afoot. Perhaps the least that can be said about it is that Hogg is alerting us to his deep wariness of the editor, or other similar suspicious personages from the capital, who Hogg knows will get the local culture wrong as they take their Enlightened, anthropological look at it; hence the quibbles about boundaries and property lines, as the narrative skirts around what is lost, left out, and traduced, by modern 'mapping'. One way of thinking about Wringhim is that he represents the kind of sectarian strife and violence modern Scotland needed to throw down, and 'abject', in order to erect its modern institutions and identity. As Hogg asserts in his letter to *Blackwood's Magazine* on the matter, nothing could be more repellent than Wringhim's grave.[18] For modern Scotland such abject material is disgusting indeed: hence the air-blighted nature of Wringhim's corpse, which quickly turns putrid once exposed to the light of day. Hogg's game is to ensure that the truth of Wringhim's story—the kind of material 'air-brushed' out of official history—is allowed to mature in the reader's mind, surrendering its own discomfiting truth. Hogg has used the narrative grammar of the Gothic to think through the lack of legitimacy of, not so much Edinburgh castle, Scotland's ancient seat of authority, but of the intellectual elite operating in its shadow, the architects, after all, of the celebration of all things Scots, orchestrated by Walter Scott, for the King's visit in 1822, one of the first, great, kitsch festivals of the modern heritage industry.

---

[18] James Hogg, *The Private Memoirs and Confessions of a Justified Sinner*, ed. P. D. Garside (Edinburgh: Edinburgh University Press, 2001), 166.

14

Evangelical Fiction

ANTHONY MANDAL

The various impressions received by good and by bad dispositions from the profession of methodistical or evangelical tenets, form a curious chapter in the history of our modern manners.... [Evangelicalism] is making way amongst us with strength, and will one day have its influence on the fate perhaps of nations.[1]

Walter Scott's observations in 1818 encapsulate both the concern with which evangelicalism was regarded and a recognition of its seismic influence on social mores in early nineteenth-century Britain. According to Boyd Hilton (1988), the evangelical revival ushered in an 'Age of Atonement' that dominated British thinking from 1795 to 1865, with its focus on private salvation realized through discourses of economic responsibility and national duty. The influence of Anglican evangelicalism was not confined solely to the theological and philosophical arenas: it gained a great deal of potency because of its popular appeal within the power-broking stratum of Britain. Sam Pickering has suggested that the evangelical influence on an emergent readership of middle classes, the professional elites, and the landed gentry is not to be underestimated, and that 'evangelical readers constituted the largest segment of the reading public in the early nineteenth century' (1974: 346). In this context, it is unsurprising that the emergent literary genre of the period—the novel—became a powerful tool in effecting the evangelicals' mission to improve the moral condition of the nation. At the same time, the troublesome reputation of fiction, particularly during in the wake of the French Revolution, caused fundamental problems for evangelical writers, who remained anxious about the genre and their association with it. Nevertheless, these authors were able to blend populism with propriety through a careful traversing of theological, national, and generic boundaries, contributing significantly to the rehabilitation of the novel during the opening decades of the nineteenth century.

---

[1] Walter Scott, review of C. R. Maturin's *Women*, in *Edinburgh Review*, 30 (June 1818), 253–4.

The Religious and Social Background

The Romantic era was one marked by religious controversy, witnessing a shift, in Kevin Gilmartin's words, 'from natural supernaturalism to literary sectarianism' (2008: 621). On the one hand, more rationalist or 'scientific' models of belief were articulated in various quarters: from the persistent challenge of deism ('natural religion'), which had emerged at the turn of the seventeenth and eighteenth centuries; through the latitudinarianism that dominated eighteenth-century Anglicanism, which culminated in William Paley's famous 'argument from design' in 1802; as well as the spread of rational dissent, particularly in the form of Unitarianism. On the other hand, a desire towards a Christianity grounded in the numinous explains the widespread appeal of religious 'enthusiasm', notably through the evangelical proselytizing of Methodism and, in more extreme forms, in the premillennial fervour of Edward Irving and Joanna Southcott. Such upheavals ultimately resulted in greater toleration beyond the Established Church, leading first to the 1828 repeal of the Test and Corporations Acts and culminating with the Catholic Relief Act in 1829. As Robert M. Ryan observes: 'For a period of approximately three decades, the decades in which Romantic poetry flourished, religion in England seemed to abandon its character as a guarantor of social stability and to become, as it had during the sixteenth and seventeenth centuries, a force for potentially revolutionary change' (1997: 18).

In such a period of protean theological shifts, it is unsurprising that the concept of an 'evangelical revival...is as slippery as it was ubiquitous' (Hilton 2006: 175). Nevertheless, the roots of evangelicalism as a recognizable phenomenon within the Church of England can be traced back to the 1730s, under the leadership of clergymen such as Thomas Haweis, Thomas Wills, and George Burnett. Their evangelicalism was driven by a fervent Calvinism which led them to perceive that the Established Church had drifted towards a faith grounded more in Enlightenment rationalism and benevolism than in revelation and Scripture. The publicly expressed criticism of the Anglican Church voiced by evangelical divines in the first half of the century did much to alienate the influential ranks of British society. By the last third of the century, however, the good-natured rationalism of contemporary Anglicanism was perceived to have failed as an ethical system in many quarters, particularly by a more moderate breed of evangelicals, who called for Christians to recognize the fallen nature of humanity and seek salvation through grace. Particularly noteworthy was their anxiety that many Anglicans had slipped into a 'nominal' kind of Christianity, which led them to observe the practices and ordinances of the church while ignoring the living faith that should inform their daily lives. In sharp response to these problems, the evangelicals advocated a simplified return to the gospels as the creedal basis of communion.

It was during the 1780s that such demands coalesced into something more tangible, inspired by the ministry of John Newton, and transformed into a social force with the emergence of the Clapham Sect in 1792. So named because its key members resided in the village of Clapham, this group led by William Wilberforce and Henry Thornton associated with, rather than condemned, the Establishment, within whose ranks they found many powerful converts. A close friend of Wilberforce and evangelical propagandist, the former Bluestocking Hannah More was careful in making the distinction between belonging to an imperfect society and being governed by it: 'the mischief arises not from our living in the world, but from the world living in us; occupying our hearts, and monopolizing our affections.'[2] Among the demands of evangelicals were the abandonment of plurality (clergymen holding more than one living at the same time), a return to Scripture as the foundation of Anglican orthodoxy, and perhaps most famously the abolition of the slave trade. Britain's participation in the slave trade was a fundamental grievance for the evangelicals, who were seeking salvation not only at the individual level but also at the national. Consequently, domestic and continental crises—war with France, the insanity of the monarch, Luddite agitation—were interpreted as warnings of the need for a systemic shift in the cultural ethos, away from decadence and towards rectitude. As part of its reformist agenda, Anglican evangelicalism promoted a hegemonic patriarchalism that drew upon a coalition of the landed gentry and the emergent middle classes, complemented by a variety of evangelical fictions that attempted to locate the appropriate domain for a newly perceived 'female sphere', which supplemented, but did not encroach upon, that of the male. The emergence of evangelicalism can be understood as part of a broader turn-of-the-century *zeitgeist* that sought to recondition the country into a nation of middle-rank propriety and serious faith.

The success of evangelicalism in effecting social change was due, in no small part, to the sophisticated and sustained use it made of print, most particularly in the immediate wake of the French Revolution. The 1780s and 1790s saw the appearance of didactic primers on moral behaviour, followed by the establishment of religious periodicals in the 1800s (such as the moderate *Christian Observer* and the more trenchant *Evangelical Magazine*). Hence, it is unsurprising that evangelical writers would turn their gaze upon the expanding novel genre shortly thereafter. Much of the groundwork had already been laid in pamphlet form with a different audience in mind: under More's direction, the *Cheap Repository Tracts* (1795–7) had sought to steer the working classes away from incipient radicalism (see also Jarrells, Chapter 26). The pamphlets, consisting of simple fables that emphasized social conformity mediated through religious zeal, achieved an unprecedented circulation: over two million copies had been disseminated by March 1796. The *Tracts* established a successful model for further evangelical forays into fiction aimed at supposedly impressionable members of British society (namely, the poor, children, and

[2] Hannah More, *Thoughts on the Importance of the Manners of the Great to General Society*, 2nd edn (London: T. Cadell, 1788), 96–7.

women): both Rowland Hill's *Village Dialogues* (1801) and Legh Richmond's *Annals of the Poor* (first collected in 1814) sold in huge numbers.

Despite such successes, evangelicalism was nothing if not controversial, with continued hostility being directed at the movement from the more traditional parts of British society. High Churchmen were angered by the evangelical critique of traditional Anglican prerogatives and what they perceived to be its emphasis on passion over reason, while latitudinarians were alienated by its strictures on scriptural orthodoxy and condescending attitude towards other parts of the Church. In particular, what grated upon fellow Anglicans was the evangelicals' emphasis on the 'Invisible Church' of true Christians (which included Nonconformists, Quakers, and Methodists) over the 'Visible Church' of the often nominally Christian Establishment. V. Kiernan distinguishes between two eighteenth-century views of Anglican theology: 'One was of religion as the formulary of an established society, its statement of faith in itself; the other as a catastrophic conversion of the individual. . . . One was fixed on this world, the other on the next' (1952: 46–7). While partly true, this model is qualified in evangelical fiction, which is grounded in rural paternalism, local communities, and close interchange between a circle of like-minded neighbours and friends. Indeed, this chapter will demonstrate that while the evangelicals used a charged discourse of salvation, damnation, and grace, they did so in order to maintain the status quo.

Evangelicalism, Moral–Domestic Fiction, and the Literary Marketplace

Although evangelicalism had made noteworthy incursions into the general literary marketplace, it was not until the opening decades of the nineteenth century that its writers staked a more sustained claim through its experiments with fiction. In order to understand why evangelical novels emerged during the early nineteenth century, it is worth briefly considering the state of the novel at this time. The 1800s witnessed an increase of 10 per cent in the production of new works of fiction from the already abundant previous decade: 778 titles, as compared to 701 in the 1790s (Garside, Raven, and Schöwerling 2000; Garside et al. 2004). In addition to the seeming excess of fiction that was appearing, certain types of title troubling to more conservative readers were being published with alarming frequency, especially scandal fictions and Gothic novels. Alongside tales depicting the excesses of the fashionable set, such as T. S. Surr's *Winter in London* (1806) and the pseudonymous Charles Sedley's *The Faro Table; or, The Gambling Mothers* (1808), writers like Germaine de Staël (*Delphine*, 1802; *Corinne*, 1807) and Charlotte Dacre (*Confessions of the Nun of St. Omer*, 1805; *Zofloya; or, The Moor*, 1806; *The Libertine*, 1807) wrote melodramatic, pan-European tales of passion that featured powerful women who revived earlier associations of fiction with scandal and immorality. Indeed, evangelical fiction can be understood as a response to such controversial titles, making a substantial impression on the novel within a fairly short period (from the late 1800s to the late 1810s).

When considering evangelical influences on the novel, it is important to distinguish between two types of didactic fiction, the 'evangelical' and the 'moral–domestic', which overlap while nevertheless remaining discrete. In their earliest forms, evangelical works such as More's *Coelebs in Search of a Wife* (1808), Henry Kett's *Emily, A Moral Tale* (1809–11), and Harriet Corp's *A Sequel to The Antidote to the Miseries of Human Life* (1809) were programmatic in nature, subordinating fictional praxis to didactic imperatives: the evangelical idea is the unifying concept of these works, with its emphasis on religious rectitude, the importance of the community, and appropriate models of female domesticity. The plot structure is relatively static, consisting of a series of sketches and observations rather than a truly developed plot, the aims of which are to inculcate appropriate moral lessons. In later, 'polite' (that is, moderate and genteel) evangelical novels by authors such as Mary Brunton, Laetitia-Matilda Hawkins, Barbara Hofland, and Elizabeth Lester,[3] the plot is as important as the moral, as it leads to a fuller investigation of the heroine's mental state, measuring her character against various criteria of proper feminine behaviour. Works of this second sort continued through the Regency period, before dispersing more generally into mainstream fiction or being redirected towards a juvenile audience.

While moral–domestic fiction shared similar didactic aims to those of evangelical works, concerning itself with its protagonists' spiritual and moral well-being, the proselytizing elements were less explicit and the focus was on establishing appropriate behavioural models in the domestic sphere. These moral–domestic novels were written both by previously anti-Jacobin novelists (for instance, Frances Jacson and Jane West) and by a newer generation of writers, perhaps motivated by the evangelical phenomenon if not actually a part of it (such as Amelia Opie and Maria Benson). However, distinctions between 'evangelical' and 'moral–domestic' fiction should not be treated as absolute, and instead the terms can be seen as overlapping parts of a continuum, which itself emblematized homely life, specifically that of women, emphasized fundamental Christian virtues, and focused on the inner life of the heroine.

With few exceptions, virtually all mainstream evangelical fiction was written by women, although contemporary readers would not necessarily have been aware of the gender make-up of evangelical fiction, since the bulk of these works was published anonymously. Under the influence of evangelicalism, anonymity would have been seen as a fitting approach, because it was the didactic message of the novel rather than the fame of the author which should endure. Despite such attempts at self-erasure, contemporary records indicate that the provenance of a number of these anonymous works was an open

---

[3] For the reattribution of a number of works previously identified as by 'Mrs Ross' to Elizabeth Lester, see Garside (1998) and Garside, Raven, and Schöwerling (2000: vol. 2).

secret: reviews of *Coelebs* make it clear that More was its author,[4] while Brunton complains that everyone had recognized her as the author of *Self-Control* (1811).[5] Brunton's protestations notwithstanding, it is clear that, despite its conservative agenda, evangelical fiction provided a discursive space within which women were able to explore issues of female agency while simultaneously attempting to correct the troubled reputation of contemporary fiction.

Key Authors and their Works

Hannah More's *Coelebs* (1808) set the tone for much of the fiction in its wake. More's rejection of the genre at the end of the previous century, as 'one of the most universal as well as most pernicious sources of corruption among us', had been somewhat trenchant.[6] Nevertheless, it is clear that she subsequently felt a call to counteract this deficiency by reintroducing faith into fiction, as noted in a letter of December 1809 to Sir William Pepys:

> I thought there were already good books enough in the world for good people; but there was a large class of readers whose wants had not been attended to;—the subscribers to the circulating library. A little to raise the tone of that mart of mischief, and to counteract its corruptions, I thought was an object worth attempting.[7]

Coelebs tells the story of Charles, an Edinburgh graduate who visits various circles of acquaintance seeking a suitably Christian wife following the death of his beloved father. During his encounters, Charles meets a variety of social 'types', including votaries to fashion, nominal Christians, and the truly devout Stanleys, whose daughter Lucilla is a paragon of demureness and silent intelligence. Despite its popularity, leading to a twelfth edition by the end of 1809, *Coelebs* is rather programmatic in its use of an intrusive first-person narrator, operating more as a series of domestic vignettes with accompanying moralizing commentary, conducted mostly through staged scenes that rely heavily on dialogue. As one reviewer put it: 'We have no objection to see religious topics gravely and seriously discussed; but as the true repository of all religion is the heart, we are apt to think that when religion makes the sole or principal subject of discussion, it is apt to degenerate into a mere jargon of words.'[8] However, the portrayal of Lucilla, while idealized and conservative, is less constrained than might be assumed, offering a nuanced

---

[4] See, for example, *British Critic*, 33 (May 1809), 481.

[5] Alexander Brunton, 'Memoir', in Mary Brunton, *Emmeline. With Some Other Pieces* (Edinburgh: Manners and Miller, and Constable; London: John Murray, 1819), xlv.

[6] Hannah More, *Strictures on the Modern System of Female Education*, 5th edn, 2 vols (London: Cadell and Davies, 1799), 1.191.

[7] William Roberts, *Memoirs of the Life and Correspondence of Mrs Hannah More*, 2nd edn, 4 vols (London: Seeley and Burnside, 1834), 3.313–14.

[8] *Critical Review*, 3rd ser., 16 (March 1809), 263.

portrait of dutiful femininity. Patricia Demers observes that 'Lucilla . . . does much more than parrot pieties. Adroit at parrying the narrator's pompous talk, she conveys humility but not self-abasement. . . . While Coelebs drones on in his generally censorious mode, Lucilla is down-to-earth and thoughtful' (1996: 93).

Writers influenced by More's example were able to blend didacticism with plot more convincingly; and, while *Coelebs* can be understood as the inspiration for polite evangelical fiction of the 1810s, no work more clearly emblematizes this moment than Mary Brunton's *Self-Control* (1811). The novel offered a tale of seducing villains and virtuous heroes, fashionable society and persecuted innocence, culminating in an abduction that leads to Canadian misadventures—all the while attempting to provide in its heroine a model of female perseverance, piety, and charity. At the same time, Brunton constructs a sophisticated third-person narrative that redeploys romantic sensibility into religious sensitivity, particularly through its introspective and heavily psychologized focus on the plight of the strong-willed but sympathetic Laura Montreville. Strictly speaking, the Presbyterian Brunton was not part of the Anglican evangelical movement; however, her expressed aim in writing *Self-Control* was clearly evangelical: 'If my book is read, its uses to the author are obvious. Nor is a work of fiction necessarily unprofitable to the readers. When the vitiated appetite refuses its proper food, the alternative way may be administered in a sweetmeat.'[9]

The publishing history of *Self-Control* demonstrates the commercial viability of evangelical fiction in the Regency literary market. Publication was initially handled by the Edinburgh firm of Manners and Miller, and then taken up by their London partner Longmans once public demand for the novel became clear. Published between February and May 1811, three editions totalling 3,000 copies had sold out by the following November.[10] A fourth edition appeared in February 1812, although the take-up was much slower, and it was not until 1821 that the entire run of 1,250 copies was sold—three years after Brunton's death. Two decades after its initial publication, *Self-Control* was published as part of Bentley's Standard Novel series in 1832, a fact which suggests that the novel was valued enough to be included as canonical reading for a new generation of readers.

While the commercial success of *Self-Control* was overwhelming, the critical response was far more mixed. The *Eclectic Review*, a conservative dissenting journal, played down the novel's commercial profile, recommending instead its didactic qualities: 'Self Control cannot boast of leading the way, either in point of time, or of merit, and can only deserve a subordinate notice; but it is evidently written with good intentions, and maintains a constant reference to correct, devotional principles.'[11] Elsewhere, Brunton's pietism led

[9] Mary Brunton, 'Dedication to Joanna Baillie', *Self-Control. A Novel*, 2 vols (Edinburgh: Manners and Miller; London: Longman [etc.], 1811), 1.vi–vii.
[10] Figures for *Self-Control*'s print runs are taken from the Longman Archives at Reading University, Impression Books 4 (fol. 150) and 5 (fol. 102).
[11] *Eclectic Review*, 8 (June 1812), 612–13.

to some extreme responses: in particular, the *Critical Review* railed against the novel's 'Evangelical cant', which made it necessary 'for some self-controul on our parts, in order to subdue feelings of disgust'.[12] While the *Critical* was antagonized by the novel's religiosity, the *Edinburgh Christian Instructor* felt that the heroine's misplaced affection for the villain vitiated the didactic elements: 'her narrative will either prove uninteresting in the perusal, or immoral in its tendency'.[13]

Around the same time as Brunton's novel was causing such controversy, Laetitia-Matilda Hawkins' *The Countess and Gertrude; or, Modes of Discipline* (1811) appeared. Born in 1759, the daughter of attorney and musicologist Sir John Hawkins, she commenced her literary career with the publication of *Constance* (1785) and continued to write novels up to the 1790s. Aside from one translation in the mid-1800s, however, Hawkins published no original fiction for eighteen years, until the appearance of *The Countess and Gertrude*.[14] Excepting the 1806 translation, Hawkins' prior works had been anonymous, so she met being named on the title page of *The Countess and Gertrude* with a certain trepidation: 'When we set out on the system of what is jocularly called *we-gotism*, we knew not that our name would be demanded:—it is with the utmost repugnance, with no confidence in our own powers, and with a just deference for the public opinion, that we submit ourselves to view'.[15] Like all of Hawkins' fiction, this work is an education novel, and is built on the dynamic between the titular characters, who represent the opposing forces of fashionable life (the Countess) and religious rectitude (Gertrude). Unlike her eighteenth-century fictions, however, this novel eschews exotic or melodramatic accoutrements in favour of a more quotidian setting. Lady Luxmore takes the orphaned Gertrude Aubrey under her wing, but plays the role of bad fairy, attempting to misdirect her ward into a life of dissipation, abetted by various works of imaginative fiction. Despite such lures, Gertrude resists temptation and treads the paths of Christian virtue. *The Countess and Gertrude* is a strongly Anglican tale that follows an eighteenth-century didactic model, combining satire and Christian discourse in equal parts. Unlike *Self-Control*, Hawkins' tale secured the praise of the *Critical Review*, which noted that its author 'has delighted us with her sterling sense, charmed us by her vivacity, and amused us by her anecdote. She has done even more; she has made us reverence her for her rational and her cheerful notions of religion.'[16]

In a similar manner to Hawkins, Amelia Alderson Opie made a transition in her literary career—from writer of domestic melodramas to author of strongly didactic

---

[12] *Critical Review*, 3rd ser., 24 (October 1811), 160.

[13] *Edinburgh Christian Instructor*, 3 (October 1811), 267.

[14] For the recent attribution of five early novels to Hawkins, previously thought to be written by Eliza Kirkham Mathews, see Fergus (2007).

[15] Laetitia-Matilda Hawkins, *The Countess and Gertrude; or, Modes of Discipline*, 4 vols (London: Rivingtons, 1811), 1.xxix–xxx.

[16] *Critical Review*, 4th ser., 2 (July 1812), 63.

fictions. Early in life, she had mixed with the radical dissenting circle based around the Norwich home of her father, Dr James Alderson, whose acquaintances included William Godwin, Thomas Holcroft, and Mary Wollstonecraft. After an inconspicuous debut with the anonymous *Dangers of Coquetry* (1790), Opie achieved commercial success with her best-selling melodramas, *The Father and Daughter* (1801) and *Adeline Mowbray, or The Mother and Daughter* (1805). As the evangelical revival took root in fiction, she began to publish works that amplified the didactic resonance of her fiction while playing down its more sentimental components (although melodrama still continued to appear in her narratives). *Temper, or Domestic Scenes* (1812) was more heavily driven by its moral imperatives than her previous novels, while also making use of Opie's typical blend of melodramatic incident and comic scenes. Despite a successful print run of 3,000 copies across three editions within sixteen months,[17] reviewers were less impressed than purchasers: the *Critical Review* compared it unfavourably with Opie's earlier fictions, describing its plot as 'too near that in the novel of Evelina', while the *Monthly Review* observed that Opie 'might have excited greater interest if she had treated the subject less didactically'.[18] Unperturbed by such criticisms, Opie went on to write increasingly moralizing fictions, such as *Tales of Real Life* (1813), *Valentine's Eve* (1816), *New Tales* (1818), and *Tales of the Heart* (1820). By 1824, however, Opie converted to Quakerism and seemingly limited herself to writing works of a thoroughly didactic nature aimed at children.[19]

An immediate contemporary of Opie, Barbara Hofland ranged across various modes of writing over five decades, publishing a large number of works for an adult audience alongside her children's fiction. Despite experiments with different styles, genres, and milieus, she remained an author with a decidedly didactic focus, whose works consider appropriate models for filial duty, parental responsibility, and religious rectitude. Born in 1770, Hofland made her first forays into the literary marketplace in the mid-1790s with the publication of periodical verses, but it was not until a decade later that she began publishing in earnest, starting with a collection of *Poems* in 1805, which sold over 2,000 copies. Her fictional output commenced with *The History of an Officer's Widow* (1809), which no doubt drew upon her own experiences of the privations and demands of widowhood. This was the first of a trilogy aimed at older children and young adults, being followed by *The History of a Clergyman's Widow and her Young Family* (1812) and *The Merchant's Widow and her Family* (1814). Occasionally, Hofland departed from her typically domestic focus, in novels such as *Iwanowna; or, The Maid of Moscow* (1813), but even these works aimed to inculcate Christian principles in their readers. More indicative of Hofland's output are

---

[17] Figures taken from Longman Archives, Impression Books 4 (fol. 186v) and 5 (fol. 78).

[18] *Critical Review*, 4th ser., 1 (June 1812), 625; *Monthly Review*, 2nd ser., 68 (June 1812), 217.

[19] But see Garside, Raven, and Schöwerling (2000: 2.586—entry 1824: 73) for the tentative attribution of a novel, entitled *Much to Blame*, to Opie, published after her conversion.

such titles as *Patience and Perseverance* (1813) and *A Father as He Should Be* (1815), as well as her later, one-volume moral tales such as *Integrity* (1823), *Moderation* (1825), and *Self-Denial* (1827). Hofland's work was typically well received by reviewers, who praised her ability to render interesting moral protagonists and sustain readers' interest. An apposite summary of her reception in the periodicals is offered in the *Critical Review*'s judgement of *A Father as He Should Be*:

> There are in her present work, notwithstanding the common place introductions of the hero and heroine, several domestic scenes arranged with considerable judgment. Again, there are others which are better adapted for romance. Most of the characters are well imagined; the moral is good, and the tale a lesson for married men in their grand climacteric, who are not absolutely incorrigible.[20]

Later moral–domestic works in the Regency period were greeted with less excitement than those of More, Brunton, and Opie, although some noteworthy titles did appear, such as Frances Jacson's *Rhoda* (1816), Elizabeth Lester's *The Quakers* (1817), Anne Raikes Harding's *Correction* (1818), and Andrew Reed's *No Fiction* (1819). Alongside these titles appeared more heavily didactic works that are more like sketches than fiction, such as Jane Taylor's *Display. A Tale for Young People* (1815) and Olivia More's *The Welsh Cottage* (1820).

Evangelical fiction was significant enough to draw a high degree of attention from contemporary novelists. The increasing evangelical fervour in the Church of Ireland during this time put more moderate Anglicanism under severe pressure, uniting writers such as Maria Edgeworth, Sydney Owenson, and C. R. Maturin in their assaults on the evangelicals, despite their own differences. Edgeworth's *Ormond* (1817) lampoons evangelicalism through the character of Mrs M'Crule, a malicious busybody who stirs up Irish sectarian divisions and attempts to inflame anti-Catholic feeling among her peers. In *Florence Macarthy* (1818), Owenson satirizes the evangelicals through a minor character, Mrs Magillicuddy, an intolerant, 'elected agent of salvation'. Maturin's *Women; or, Pour et Contre* (1818) interrogates religious enthusiasm (particularly Methodism and Calvinistic evangelicalism) through the central figure of the orphaned and tragic Eva.

Perhaps the best-known reaction to the evangelicals was that of Jane Austen: it was certainly ambivalent, and seems to tip between respect for their aims and irritation with their methods. Early in 1809, Austen had expressed unease with *Coelebs*: 'My disinclination for it before was affected, but now it is real; I do not like the Evangelicals.'[21] Austen's next sentence mitigates the severity of her initial response, introducing a

---

[20] *Critical Review*, 5th ser., 2 (July 1815), 105.
[21] Deirdre Le Faye (ed.), *The Letters of Jane Austen*, 3rd edn (Oxford and New York: Oxford University Press, 1995), 170.

degree of facetiousness that relates more to the commercial success of More's novel than its religiosity: 'Of course I shall be delighted when I read it, like other people, but till I do, I dislike it.' Similarly, Austen's comments on *Self-Control* praise Brunton's morality and decorous style, while critiquing its lack of 'anything of Nature or Probability' (234, 282–3). Her mixed reaction to Hawkins' *Rosanne; or, A Father's Labour Lost* (1814) echoes this: 'Mrs Hawkins' great excellence is on serious subjects...but on lighter topics I think she falls into many absurdities; and, as to love, her heroine has very comical feelings. There are a thousand improbabilities in the story' (289). Although Austen had accepted by the mid-1810s that religion and fiction could be blended, she also seems to have recognized that evangelical writers found it difficult to achieve the more rigorous everyday realism now demanded in modern fiction. Of course, her most thoroughgoing exploration of, and debate with, evangelical fiction takes place in her third published novel, *Mansfield Park* (1814). Through her heroine Fanny Price, Austen deconstructs the evangelical ideology of approved femininity (that of silence and submissiveness), while simultaneously endorsing the evangelicals' attack on fashionable education. Consequently, the novel admits the wisdom of evangelicalism while questioning its feasibility: Fanny's depiction in *Mansfield Park* establishes that women on the periphery of society cannot be the agents for social change that the evangelicals wanted them to be. For Austen, the evangelical paradox emerges from the tension between the lack of power women have as autonomous individuals and the social obligation upon them to function as signifiers of unimpeachable morality (for a fuller exploration of Austen's negotiation with evangelicalism in *Mansfield Park*, see Mandal 2007: 91–130).

Themes and Motifs

Many of these novels eschew subtitles altogether, preferring a simple generic description, such as 'a tale' or 'a novel'. The use of 'tale' on title pages conveys a simplicity and concision appropriate for the generic affiliations of these didactic narratives. Indeed, numerous moral–domestic narratives were published as anthologies of short stories (for instance, Opie's various collections of *Tales*) or as one-volume novellas (many of Hofland's works fall readily into this category). As noted earlier, the term 'novel' carried far more problematic connotations, so that 'evangelicals were initially loath to apply it to a Christian work' (Rosman 1977: 306). While it might therefore seem surprising that evangelical writers would employ such a troublesome term themselves, authors like Mary Brunton were actively seeking to recuperate the genre for moral purposes: 'Why should an epic or a tragedy be supposed to hold such an exalted place in composition, while a novel is almost a nickname for a book? Does not a novel admit of as noble sentiments—as lively description—as natural character—as perfect unity of action—and a moral as irresistible as either of them?'[22] Simply put, these works of fiction described themselves as 'novels' in order to draw 'novel readers' towards proper, pious material. Having been provided with a template by More, writers such as Brunton and Hofland were appropriating the 'novel'—both as a term and as a genre—for their own, moral purposes.

A fundamental characteristic of evangelical and moral–domestic novels is their self-affirming simplicity. Their title pages employ austerely brief titles that embody the underlying principle of, or a key moment in, the work itself: *Duty, Self-Control, Temper, Conduct, Discipline, The Acceptance, The Decision, The Times,* and *The Ordeal.* Key phrases in titles or subtitles signified domesticity ('cottage sketches', 'domestic scenes'), analytical insights ('comprehending observations', 'the most important subjects', 'sketches moral and religious'), communality ('active retirement', 'family mansion'), veracity ('founded on facts'), religiosity ('a serious novel', 'a religious tale'), and intended audiences ('a tale for the female sex'). A further layer of intricacy is developed in the intertextual relationship between the titles of some of these works and their evangelical progenitor, *Coelebs*: as with the anonymous *Caroline Ormsby; or The Real Lucilla* (1810) and Elizabeth Sandham's *Lucilla; or, The Reconciliation* (1819), both of which look back to Lucilla Stanley, *Coelebs's* exemplary 'heroine'.

Moral–domestic fictions avoid the peripatetic topographies of sentimental fiction or the vertiginous precipices of Gothic romance, instead being girded firmly within small, provincial communities. These parochial locales are often juxtaposed with anonymous urban spaces, and, although the metropolis is not always programmatically portrayed as the seat of vice (the Clapham Sect was after all based in London), it is certainly the source of discomfort. In *Coelebs*, the evangelically governed Stanley Grove in Hampshire is contrasted favourably with the bustle of London; Kett's *Emily* compares the rural purity of Cumberland to the fashionable inanities of the capital; *Self-Control's* Laura is forced to endure all sorts of trials in London when financial pressures compel her to leave an idyllic existence in the Highlands. At its heart, evangelical fiction often deals with the conflict between the evanescent values of the fashionable world and enduring morality, typically centring on young female protagonists who have been displaced to the margins of society, by poverty or the malice of others. Such dependence is mitigated by the heroine's philosophy of righteous abstinence, resulting in personal and economic prosperity. The generally domestic settings of these novels fix them in the present day, within a closed world of counties and villages. Interestingly, melodrama and death sometimes occupy these novels in surprising combinations, and the extent to which these are deployed effectively depends on the author's talents: novels which connect melodrama to morality include Opie's works, Brunton's *Self-Control*, the anonymous *The Ordeal* (1813), and Lester's *The Quakers* (1817). On the whole, however, these tales avoid too much 'incident',

---

[22] Letter to Eliza Izett, 15 April 1814: 'Memoir' in Brunton, *Emmeline* (1819), lxxiv.

preferring a more measured approach, through which unambiguous moral lessons can be provided to the reader.

Heroines in evangelically influenced fictions either begin as exemplars of rectitude and correct judgement (for instance, in *Coelebs*, *Self-Control*, and *The Countess and Gertrude*), or from erroneous beginnings must learn certain moral 'lessons', which will make them proper Christians (as in *Emily*, *Temper*, and *Discipline*). They must avoid the sirens of the temporal world—vanity, accomplishments, gambling—and follow the examples set by mentor figures. The question of social propriety in young women manifests itself in the conflict between hollow 'accomplishments' and serious principles. 'Accomplishments' carry markedly pejorative connotations in evangelical fiction. *Coelebs* is especially antagonistic: before he sets out on his quest for a partner in life, Charles's mother warns him, 'I call education, not that which smothers a woman with accomplishments, but that which tends to consolidate a firm and regular system of character'.[23] Charles himself makes a similar avowal: 'I detest the term *accomplishments*, since it has been warped from the true meaning in which Milton used it' (1.193). Here, accomplishments signify those artificial qualities acquired by young women in order to compete in the marriage market, as well as other supposedly frivolous pursuits, such as amateur dramatics, modern languages, and ostentatious musical ability. Moral–domestic novelists compare such acquisitions unfavourably with the 'serious' (in other words, Christian) qualities of piety, charitableness, filial submissiveness, and moral sensitivity, often combined with an appreciation of poetry, nature, and historical or didactic writings. In Margaret Roberts's *Duty, A Novel* (1814), Ellen Herbert, a clergyman's daughter, firmly states: 'I possess no accomplishment of any kind: in truth, I am a plain unlessoned girl, unschooled, unpractised. Happy in this, I am not yet so old but I may learn.'[24] In Kett's *Emily*, the heroine is advised by her father to '[s]eek a pleasure in doing your duty, and you may depend upon me you will find it, for the ways of Religion *are ways of pleasantness, and all her paths are peace*.'[25] These evangelically directed texts are predicated on educating their heroines (and thereby, their readers) in order to improve one's internal principles of mind, rather than to increase an individual's external value as a marriageable commodity.

Despite this focus on domesticating their heroines, evangelical writers understood the paramount role of feeling in religion, while at the same time being suspicious of passion, especially when it tipped into 'enthusiasm', a religious feeling that almost bordered on the sexual. Jon Mee comments on this tension: 'If through Methodism and the Evangelical movements...affect came to play an increasing role in eighteenth-century religion,

---

[23] Hannah More, *Coelebs in Search of a Wife (1808)*, 7th edn, 2 vols (London: Cadell and Davies, 1809), 1.14.

[24] Margaret Roberts, *Duty. A Novel, by the Late Mrs. Roberts*, 3 vols (London: Longman [etc.], 1814), 1.51.

[25] Henry Kett, *Emily, a Moral Tale*, 3 vols (London: Rivingtons, 1809–11), 1.50.

that role was carefully [i]nvigilated to make sure that it did not degenerate into enthusi-asm' (2003: 13). *Self-Control* treats such feeling with suspicion, and is alert to its excesses; however, that ultimate discourse of feeling—sensibility—becomes associated in Brunton's novel with moral rectitude. This disjunctive relationship is exemplified in Laura, who causes her would-be seducer Hargrave to reflect on 'her charms; and her manner, so void of all design,—the energy—the sometimes wild poetic grace of her language—the shrewdness with which she detected, and the simplicity with which she unveiled, the latent motives of action, whether in herself or in others' (1.80). At times, this evangelical pattern of femininity becomes a somewhat paradoxical, if not unsettling, one. Lucilla, the unimpeachable hero-ine of *Coelebs*, treads this problematized borderland of gender with appropriate scrupulos-ity: 'To see her so full of sensibility, without the slightest tincture of romance, so feeling, yet so sober-minded, enchanted me' (2.202–3). Evangelical fiction eschews the sentimentalist's instinctual effusiveness, imposing silence (even worse, duplicity) as the appropriate trait of feminine virtue. Such a myth of womanly purity sublimates female desire whilst stimulat-ing that of the male, and demureness is both demanded and distrusted. One way around this problem is through the evangelical reconfiguration of sentimental benevolism, which is secular, private, and instinctive, into a religious sympathy grounded in faith, communal values, and self-reflection.

Such preoccupations with appropriate models of femininity are complemented by an equally rigorous consideration of the suitable occupation for a gentleman in his society. This question typically focuses on the relationship between the landlord and his estate, and his engagement with the surrounding community. In expanding the conservative Burkean nation/family paradigm it reconfigures the private as inherently political, in keeping with the evangelicals' belief that the health of a nation is ensured not by sweeping reforms at the parliamentary level but by improvements in the moral behaviour of the individual citizenry. (Although this did not stop the evangelicals from effecting legislative change when neces-sary, the most obvious instance being the abolition in the British Empire of the slave trade in 1807 and of slavery in 1833.) Improvement should not be motivated by ephemeral trends and for the purposes of vain showiness—a concept that parallels the discourse surround-ing feminine 'accomplishments'. Rather, it should embed the landlord more fully within his community, functioning as a beacon of morality. Similar views are held about the appropri-ate function of a clergyman, who should be equally integrated in provincial life, assisting the landowner in the moral governance of the nearby residents. In *Temper* (1812), Opie's clergy-man–mentor, Mr Egerton, understands how dangerous social dislocation can be, when he realizes how sorrow has led him to neglect his pastoral duties: 'He had allowed the powers of his mind to droop, unstimulated by the influence of collision; and had suffered hours, pre-cious hours, to be wasted in the languor of unavailing regret, which he might have employed to amuse, to instruct, and to enlighten his fellow-creatures.'[26]

---

[26] Amelia Opie, *Temper, or Domestic Scenes (1811)*, 3rd edn, 3 vols (London: Longman [etc.], 1813), 1.166.

The motifs of the improving landlord's estate and the clergyman's role are repeatedly employed to promote engagement between the gentry and the adjacent moral landscape. This dynamic is fundamentally conservative, as existing hegemonic structures are not only vindicated, but they are also ascribed greater potency: as the custodians of morality, improving landowners become powerful forces for Christian morality. Kett's *Emily* concludes with its protagonists inheriting their parents' desire to improve: Emily's husband Edward, 'following the useful steps of his father, but with enlarged means of doing good, acted as a magistrate and undertook the care of a neighbouring church'; while '[i]nfluenced by a similar motive, Emily established a school for the education of the indigent girls of the parish' (2.325). The final arrangement of the morally governed estate implies a paternalistic vision, one which synthesizes private domestic action with national moral improvement: just as *Coelebs*'s Mr Stanley arranges his world around Stanley Grove, so the governing classes should ground their political vision within the ordinances of the Church.

Evangelical fiction often sets up a paradigmatic contrast between such benevolent patriarchs and morally feckless counterparts, who enjoy the privilege and prestige of rank while eschewing its concomitant responsibilities. Perhaps the most vividly rendered portrait of a dissolute aristocrat appears in *Self-Control*, in the figure of Laura's dissipated suitor, Colonel Hargrave, 'the undoubted heir of a title, and of a fine estate' (1.78). Although a prospective inheritor, Hargrave is rootless and cares nothing for improvement, of either his estate or himself. His rootlessness parallels his lack of moral understanding, as he wanders the country both in search of Laura and to evade the consequences of his various seductions. Moral–domestic fictions repeatedly castigate itinerancy as one of the social ills of the times: 'Those who go "to play a part" at a distance from home, are the most amusing set; and the *contretems* [sic] they are fated to experience, are sometimes to an observer of manners, most whimsically ludicrous'(*Countess and Gertrude*, 1.141). At the beginning of *Self-Control*, Laura proposes a test to Hargrave: he must part from her for two years and return a reformed Christian. He fails the task, however, and his adultery with a married woman and her subsequent pregnancy result in national scandal. Hargrave's self-imposed social exclusion leads to desperation and moral degeneration, culminating in his abduction of Laura to the Canadian wilderness: 'Laura perceived through the dusk, that they were on a barren moor. Waste and level it seemed to spread before her; but the darkness prevented her from distinguishing its features or its boundaries' (2.413). In the novel's melodramatic conclusion, Laura manages to escape Hargrave's clutches by stealing away on a canoe and shooting the Canadian rapids; upon discovering her flight, Hargrave commits suicide. His inability to discharge an essential obligation to contribute to the communal good leads ineluctably to self-destruction.

The interlinked evangelical concerns of religion, education, and social improvement are articulated within the discourse of 'domestic economy'. This term encapsulates the entire evangelical project: that religious duty and regulation of the self culminate in moral autonomy. Boyd Hilton perceptively distils the transactional basis of evangelical theology:

> Reduced to essentials [evangelicalism] was a *contractual* religion. Evangelicals took from Anselm and Calvin the idea that sin constituted a *debt* owed by humans to their divine banker. Individuals stood in a *commercial relationship* with God, whose ultimate *merchandise* was Heaven. Christ, by his sacrifice, had *redeemed* that debt on behalf of all true believers. (2006: 183)

At its most transparent, domestic economy subscribes to a business model that correlates expenditure of time and money with their practical benefits. The evangelical approach to charity favoured considered action rather than heedless extravagance: for instance, in *Self-Control*, we are told that 'Hargrave's fine eyes had been seen to fill with tears at a tale of *elegant* distress: he could even compassionate the more vulgar sorrows of cold and hunger to the extent of relieving them, provided always that the relief cost nothing but money' (1.81). In *Temper*, the charity of Emma Castlemain is based on an impulse to outdo her grandmother, and she gives away her expensive silver shoe-buckles. This not only results in Emma literally getting stuck in the mud when her shoes fall off, but, rather more seriously, in the arrest for theft of the woman to whom she unthinkingly gave them. Instead, careful regulation of both expenditure and charity function as key components of a domestic economy in which considered motives must precede impulsive generosity, and the use of money for charity cannot replace social responsibility. The social analogue of such domestic economy is the evangelical principle of practical and social piety. Ellen Herbert in *Duty* defines herself through her usefulness to the community, something which clearly emerges from vital religion: '*she never felt any thing a task, any thing a business: her duties were amusements, and her amusements were instructions*' (1.56–7).

Underlying the evangelical concern with domestic economy and social utility is the more fundamental act of self-regulation, which underpins one's place in the Christian schema and redirects the excesses of 'enthusiasm' towards restraint. As David Spring suggests, this 'almost feverish self-scrutiny . . . made for a training of the will and in consequence for spiritual action in the world', and was itself based on the discourse of the marketplace, reflecting the professional and trade origins of many of its key members (1961: 39). In *Emily*, the heroine's father admonishes her that 'Christianity is not designed to destroy, but to regulate our desires—not to lessen, but to increase our real pleasures' (1.49). Similarly, in *Self-Control*, we are told that 'Laura had long been accustomed, when assailed by any adverse circumstance, whether more trivial or more important, to seize the first opportunity of calmly considering how far she had herself contributed to the disaster' (1.39). This act of self-discipline has a strong evangelical precedent, being voiced directly by Wilberforce: 'There is a call on us for vigorous and continual resolution, self-denial, and activity. . . . Scrutinize yourself rather with rigorous strictness'.[27] This is not an end in itself, but a Christian methodology, which—like the improved estate—culminates in one's fuller contribution to the moral good of the community, just as a lack of self-regulation is shown to be a form of unregulated moral itinerancy. In this context, Eileen Cleere (2007) persuasively argues that the evangelical deployment of appropriate femininity—encapsulated by domestic economy and careful expenditure of the self within a scrupulously governed estate—should be read ultimately as an act of the purposeful reconfiguration of the nation at the levels of gender, class, and religion.

Legacy

The apparatus of evangelically directed novels—the simple, morally laden titles, the occasional use of the prestigious octavo format, and delicately illustrated frontispieces—moved them away from eighteenth-century circulating-library items towards artefacts for individual purchase and personal edification. The legacy of evangelicalism to fiction was the purging of many of its excesses and the legitimization of the novel from the mid-1810s onwards. At the same time, the evangelical heyday was short-lived. Exhausted perhaps by the phenomenal success of its early years, later didactic fictions made nowhere near the same impression as that of *Coelebs* and *Self-Control*, despite the rising quantities of such novels.

Nevertheless, evangelically inspired narratives continued into the 1820s and beyond in a variety of guises. At a general level, much of the religious impetus became less overtly pietistic, and was quietly reabsorbed into a broader didactic tradition that had existed since the birth of the novel. Other novels still retained the triple-decker form, but became more severely evangelical: authors who continued to publish fictions of this kind well into the 1820s include Hofland, Lester, and Harding. Conversely, collections of shorter moral tales, written in a similar vein to those earlier anthologies by Opie, gained increasing significance in the 1820s, providing another route for the continued articulation of evangelical discourse (see Killick 2008: 73–115). A final strand, tangible from the 1820s onwards, signals an essential refocusing of the evangelical novel towards a younger audience, through the use of simplified moral fables with a much sharper polemical focus. These single-volume works were generally released by publishers specializing in this field, such as Francis Westley, Houlston and Son, and John Hatchard. Typical examples include Olivia More's *The Welsh Cottage* (1820), and works by Anglo-Irish evangelical writers such as Selina Bunbury's *The Pastor's Tales* (1826) and Charlotte Tonna's *The Rockite, an*

---

[27] William Wilberforce, *A Practical View of the Prevailing Religious System of Professed Christians, the Higher and Middle Classes in this Century, Contrasted with Real Christianity* (London: Cadell and Davies, 1797), 92, 268.

Irish Story (1829). Of particular note is the output of the prolific evangelical writer Mary Sherwood, whose *History of the Fairchild Family* appeared in three instalments (1818, 1842, 1847) and remained in print as a key work of children's literature until the 1930s. These moralistic works were bought by parents for their adolescent children, and had moved almost retrogressively into a simplified form far more comparable to Hannah More's *Cheap Repository Tracts* of the 1790s than to the multi-volume circulating-library fictions of Brunton, Hawkins, and Opie.

Despite the often negative reception that evangelical fiction endured from both periodical reviewers and other authors, these works—which had begun with More's *Coelebs in Search of a Wife*—achieved incontrovertible popularity, helping to make religious fiction best-selling material throughout the Regency period. In many ways, Brunton's *Self-Control* exemplifies the various trends that characterized the mode generally: it was a female novel published anonymously (and therefore modestly) that moved paradigmatically into the literary mainstream; responses were mixed, but it was a commercial success. And it was this commercial success that was the key to the evangelicals' programme for social improvement, as fictions like Brunton's fulfilled More's legacy by redirecting readers' appetites from scurrilous to improving fiction. In order to meld didacticism with fiction, evangelical novels sometimes perplexed contemporary readers, blending often antithetical components: sermons and sensibility, domesticity and melodrama, piety and sexuality, rigid gender politics and psychological sophistication. Despite their potential for self-contradiction, these novels were nonetheless successful in their aim to reshape the troubled topography of fiction, both in the immediate context of the 1810s and more diffusely over succeeding decades. In making evangelicalism more palatable through the form of the novel, that very form itself was made more acceptable through the efforts of these religious and didactic writers. Novels such as *Coelebs* and *Self-Control* not only garnered favour in religious quarters, they also began to make fiction a less 'pernicious' genre after all.

15

Jane Austen's Domestic Realism

VIVIEN JONES

JANE Austen's status within histories and canons of the novel has been simultaneously assured and ambivalent since soon after her death in 1817.[1] Wherever a canon, however small, of 'great' novelists is invoked, her name is securely among them (including in this volume where, alongside Sterne and Scott, Austen is one of the very few individual writers afforded a dedicated chapter). But, uniquely, she is at once hyper-canonical and supremely susceptible to what Deidre Lynch describes as the 'double play' always likely to attach to the feminine and the female writer (1996: 161). A major technical innovator working within the deceptively simple confines of domestic realism, and now hugely popular, Austen tests the hierarchies of cultural definition. This ambivalent status was already at work during her lifetime in Walter Scott's seminal review of *Emma* in the *Quarterly Review* and was reinforced by the impact of his own career as a novelist on dominant critical opinion about the aesthetics and gendering of fiction. And it's an ambivalence which is still operative two hundred years later as rewritings and sequels, screen adaptations, and online fan sites constantly reinvent Austen's status as a (cult) classic.

Austen's writing career, beginning in the 1790s, spans a period of unprecedented canon-making in the history of the British novel—an activity to which she famously contributed in *Northanger Abbey* with an uncharacteristic intervention in the authorial voice. Significantly, the examples offered there in illustration of the novel's 'genius, wit, and taste' are all by women, with Frances Burney's *Cecilia* (1782) and *Camilla* (1796) and Maria Edgeworth's *Belinda* (1801) named as works 'in which the greatest powers of the mind are displayed, in which the most thorough knowledge of human nature, the happiest delineation of its varieties, the liveliest effusions of wit and humour are conveyed to the world in the best chosen language'.[2] Yet by the 1820s, canon-making was resulting in

---

[1] Austen's work was republished in Bentley's Standard Novels in 1833; her reputation was firmly established with the publication of James Edward Austen-Leigh's 1870 *Memoir* of his aunt.

[2] Jane Austen, *Northanger Abbey* (begun 1798; posthumously published 1818), ed. Barbara M. Benedict and Deirdre Le Faye (Cambridge: Cambridge University Press, 2006), vol. 1, ch. 5; 31. All references are to *The Cambridge Edition of the Works of Jane Austen*, gen. ed. Janet Todd (Cambridge: Cambridge University Press, 2005–8).

what Clifford Siskin has called 'the Great Forgetting': a masculinization of fiction-writing from which Austen, of all female novelists of this period, emerged as the most success-ful long-term survivor (1998: 193–227). Scholarly remembering of the non-survivors by feminist and other literary historians in the last quarter of the twentieth century has done much to redress our understanding of Austen's immediate fictional context—as evidenced throughout this volume. But the question of her peculiar combination of popu-larity and canonical status remains. This chapter seeks to define the nature and quality of Austen's originality and to account for her very particular position in the historical canon, in part through an examination of her relationship with those writers and genres which proved less enduring.

In an important sense, that relationship was one of rejection—or, perhaps more accu-rately, of seamless absorption of popular forms within her rigorously unassuming real-ist aesthetic. Key to Austen's originality is the way in which her novels transcend any attempt to reduce them to versions of the contemporary fictional subgenres in which she was nonetheless immersed. (The Austen family were, famously, 'great Novel-readers & not ashamed of being so'.[3]) As the tribute in *Northanger Abbey* makes clear, Austen's ambi-tion is to join that very select group of (female) writers—in Ina Ferris's terms, the 'proper' novelists (Ferris 1991: 35), or, to use one of the categories of this volume, the writers of 'rational female fiction'—whose work was making the critical running at the turn of the nineteenth century. Self-schooled in fictional conventions and clichés through the writ-ing of her exuberant early parodies, now collectively known as the 'Juvenilia', the mature Austen ruthlessly eschews any phrase or situation that might themselves be susceptible to parodic ridicule or vulnerable to the contemporary periodical press's scorn for the predictability and excess of the 'ordinary' novel. And though the fictional and political context in which she drafted her 1790s novels (*Sense and Sensibility, Pride and Prejudice, Northanger Abbey*) is very different from that in which she wrote and published *Mansfield Park, Emma,* and *Persuasion,* this strategy is evident across all her fiction.

It is this writerly discipline which Scott is in part responding to when, in his anony-mous review of *Emma,* he recognizes Austen as the supreme exemplar of what we would call the new domestic realism: she 'stands almost alone' in the 'originality' and 'preci-sion' with which she 'cop[ies] from nature as she really exists in the common walks of life'; because of the 'knowledge of the world' and the 'peculiar tact' and eye for 'minute detail' with which Austen presents her narratives of 'common occurrences', the reader 'never miss[es] the excitation which depends upon a narrative of uncommon events'.[4] Scott recognized Austen's originality at a moment when other commentators could still

---

[3] *Jane Austen's Letters,* ed. Deirdre Le Faye, 3rd edn (Oxford and New York: Oxford University Press, 1995), 26.

[4] Walter Scott, review of *Emma, Quarterly Review,* 14 (October 1815), in Southam (1968: 58–69, esp. 64, 63, 67, 68, 63).

see her as unsurprising: just one of the more competent exponents of female-authored moral fiction, her 'sweet and unambitious creations' with their capacity to 'tranquilliz[e] every discordant emotion' largely indistinguishable from those of the conservative moralist Frances Jacson, their 'mild influence' welcomed as balm after Sydney Owenson's more dangerous and 'dazzling brilliancy'.[5] There is nevertheless an evident continuity between this overtly patronizing account of decorous female literature and Scott's more discriminating appreciation. With the benefit of retrospect, perhaps, Scott's review has been seen as the 'foundationally diminishing' precursor to a persistent strain in Austen criticism which damns her with praise for her precise miniaturism and, in making her the doyenne of 'minute detail' and 'common occurrences', admits her to the canon under a false distinction which puts her 'domestic' fiction, however perfectly executed, into an unequal, implicitly gendered relationship with the fiction of 'uncommon events'—in other words, with the emergent national historical novel as practised by Scott himself (Johnson 2001: 176).

But that was to come. As Austen began to write seriously in the 1790s and then, from 1811, to be published, the relationships between gender and respectability, and between gender and quality in the dominant critical discourse were more fluid than critics once assumed, or than they later became. Austen worried (only partly ironically) when Scott, whose poetry she loved, turned to writing fiction ('Walter Scott has no business to write novels, especially good ones.—It is not fair' (*Letters*, 277)), and the *Northanger Abbey* intervention makes clear her sensitivity to the 'only a novel' school of criticism—a sensitivity which is as much about genre as it is about gender. But though reviewers of new fiction were scathing about poor work, they were also ready to praise good fictional writing—regardless of the sex of the author. And, as Peter Garside's chapter on Authorship in this volume demonstrates, after a period dominated by men, novels by women came to outnumber those by male writers during the last two decades of the eighteenth century and by the 1810s, when Austen was publishing, had overtaken them by a significant margin. The partial evidence offered by sheer numbers is reinforced by the evaluations of contemporary canon-makers. In the 1790s and early 1800s, as Austen drafted and revised *Sense and Sensibility, Pride and Prejudice,* and the work that would become *Northanger Abbey,* an emergent critical consensus had Fielding, Richardson, Smollett, Burney, and Radcliffe as the writers who 'form[ed] an era in the history of British novels'.[6] In 1810, just a year before *Sense and Sensibility: A Novel,* 'By a Lady', entered the booksellers' lists, Anna Letitia Barbauld published her influential fifty-volume collection, *The British Novelists.* Eight of Barbauld's twenty-one authors were women, responsible for twelve of the

---

[5] 'On the Female Literature of the Present Age', *New Monthly Magazine and Universal Register,* 13 (1820), 271–5, 633–8 (637).
[6] Samuel P. Miller, *A Brief Retrospect of the Eighteenth Century,* 2 vols (New York: T. and J. Swords, 1803), 2.164–5.

twenty-eight novels reprinted, and her introductory essay, 'On the Origin and Progress of Novel-Writing', affirmed that 'we have more good writers in this walk living at the present time, than at any period since the days of Richardson and Fielding. A very great proportion of these are ladies'.[7] Indeed, the living novelists included by Barbauld—Elizabeth Inchbald, Frances Burney, Ann Radcliffe, and Maria Edgeworth—were all women, a contemporary female canon reflected in *Northanger Abbey*.

This is the critical environment which helped shape Austen's professional aspirations and which informs her proud characterization of a genre distinguished by 'genius, wit and taste' and her assertive defence of the seriousness and sophistication of its female writers and readers. And as Austen would have been the first to acknowledge, it is a critical environment made possible in the last quarter of the eighteenth century by the achievement of Burney, whose spectacular critical success with *Evelina* (1778) and then *Cecilia* (1782) spawned a host of imitators, established a woman writer as the heir of Richardson and Fielding, and helped restore the novel's popularity as a genre, as well as lending it a fragile new respectability. It is no coincidence that the first of only two occasions on which Austen's name is known to have appeared in print was when 'Miss J. Austen, Steventon' was listed among the subscribers to Burney's third novel, *Camilla*, in 1796; and the *Northanger Abbey* intervention boldly positions what Austen at one time expected to be her first novel in relation to the aesthetic and professional status enjoyed by Burney, who in 1796 was declared by the *Critical Review* to be 'without a competitor'.[8]

Begun in 1798, sold as 'Susan' to the publisher Crosby 'in the spring of 1803' (Le Faye 2004: 144), then eventually bought back and revised as 'Catherine' in 1816, *Northanger Abbey* was finally published only after Austen's death, making it uncertain precisely when she wrote her defence of fiction in the form in which we now know it. Clearly, any revision must post-date the publication of *Belinda* in 1801 and the inclusion of Edgeworth registers Austen's sense of her as a successor and rival to Burney. But the tribute to both Burney and Edgeworth is also quietly barbed, betraying something of Austen's ambition. At least as significant as its championing of women readers and writers is the way in which Austen's celebration of fiction defends the generic label, 'novel'. This is the serious modern genre which, she asserts, is most responsive to changing tastes and has successfully superseded earlier forms—most notably periodical writing—in its ability to combine pleasure and instruction. She condemns 'that ungenerous and impolitic custom so common with novel writers, of degrading by their contemptuous censure the very performances, to the number of which they are themselves adding' (*Northanger Abbey*, vol. 1, ch. 5; 30). Indeed, it may be that the whole passage was stimulated by a review of *Belinda*

---

[7] Anna Letitia Barbauld, 'On the Origin and Progress of Novel-Writing', *The British Novelists*, 50 vols (London: F. C. and J. Rivington et al., 1810), 1.58–9.

[8] Review of *Camilla*, *Critical Review*, n.s., 18 (September 1796), 26. The other occasion on which Austen's name appeared in print was again as a subscriber, to Thomas Jefferson's *Two Sermons* (1808).

in the *Critical* which, commenting on Edgeworth's prefatory 'Advertisement', expressed a similar concern at the readiness of fiction writers to deny their chosen genre: 'Is it at all necessary to discard the title of novel from its own rank and place, because many bad novels are in existence?' Apparently fearful of contamination from the 'folly, error, and vice ... disseminated by books classed under this denomination', Edgeworth followed Burney in 'not wishing to acknowledge a Novel', preferring instead to describe *Belinda* as 'a moral tale', just as Burney had chosen to describe hers as 'memoirs' or the novelist as the 'historian of human life'.[9] By contrast, all of Austen's work published in her lifetime appeared free of any apologia and under the simple, confident category: 'A Novel'.

The *Northanger Abbey* defence could, of course, be the work of the mature Austen, emboldened by success in 1816 as her reputation began to outstrip that of Burney following the indifferent critical reception in 1814 of Burney's last novel, *The Wanderer*, and Scott's review of *Emma*. But even without the evidence of the dates of the novels cited, Austen's brief foray into critical polemic reads much more like an early manifesto, the very nature of which betrays a narrative method still in the process of refinement. Ironically, Austen's statement of intent breaches her own rigorous aesthetic, the disciplined consistency of narrative voice and point of view which would become such a fundamental feature of her originality, underpinning her claim for admittance into the ranks of 'genius, wit and taste'.

Austen's only other surviving pronouncements on the art of fiction come from her letters: most famously, those to her niece Anna and nephew James Edward who submitted their own attempts at novel-writing for her scrutiny; but also in all too rare comments on the work of her contemporaries. Common to them all are the Austenian imperatives of probability and knowability, and most revealing are the commentaries in 1814 on drafts of Anna's novel 'Which is the Heroine?'—not so much the overquoted commitment to '3 or 4 Families in a Country Village', but the unsparing subjection of every detail to the credibility tests of consistent behaviour or authentic idiom. 'Remember, [Mrs F] is very prudent;—you must not let her act inconsistently'; 'I have only taken the liberty of expunging one phrase of his, which would not be allowable. "Bless my Heart" ... is too familiar & inelegant'; 'Henry Mellish I am afraid will be too much in the common Novel style—a handsome, amiable, unexceptionable Young Man (such as do not much abound in real Life)'; or, perhaps most tellingly, 'I wish you would not let him plunge into a "vortex of Dissipation". I do not object to the Thing, but I cannot bear the expression; it is such thorough novel slang' (*Letters*, 275, 277). This horror of 'thorough novel slang' is at the heart of Austen's innovative realism, the unprecedented 'precision' which Scott

⁹ *Critical Review*, 2nd ser., 34 (February 1802), 235; Maria Edgeworth, 'Advertisement', *Belinda*, 3 vols (London: Joseph Johnson, 1801), 1.5–6; Frances Burney, *Camilla, or a Picture of Youth [1796]*, ed. Edward A. Bloom and Lillian D. Bloom (Oxford: Oxford University Press, 1983), 7.

recognized. Her distinction here between dissipation as acceptable subject matter and 'vortex' as unacceptable jargon is crucial. This is an aesthetic, not a moral judgement; it is the credo of a committed realist, not the counsel of a female novelist cravenly urging propriety.

The point is worth emphasizing if we are to appreciate fully Austen's achievement within a broader history of the novel in this period. Grand narratives which use Austen as supreme exemplar of the novel's slow progress to a measure of respectability, and which emphasize her role as epitomizing the decorous, female-authored, moral domestic novel within that process, risk collusion with those 'foundationally diminishing' aspects of Scott's judgement of her fiction (Johnson 2001: 176). This is also true of those still influential readings which, often in the service of a narrative about female oppression, lament Austen's 'domestication' from the feisty experimentation of the Juvenilia to what is seen as the social conformism of the mature novels. There, it is suggested, 'her movements became constricted and she spoke in an altered tone', constraining her heroines and limiting the possibilities for heroism within the conventional courtship plot, a plot which is identified as both socially and politically conservative (Doody 1997: 98; Kaplan 1992; Poovey 1984: 172–207). Austen's social and political instincts were undoubtedly anti-revolutionary, and it is certainly possible to align her novels with various contemporary subgenres. But a proper recognition of the workings of her ambitious realist aesthetic should give pause to any hasty categorization. Austen's fiction remains independent of the historically determined appropriations made of it by subsequent critics. Austen sought to transcend the 'common Novel style' and the associated judgements of her contemporaries through a rigorous commitment to describing things as they are. Modern criticism's efforts of recovery and mapping mean that we have a much clearer understanding of the contours and variety of Austen's fictional context, but both her novels and the subsequent critical uses made of her reputation continue to challenge our retrospective taxonomies.

The Earlier Fictions: Austen and the 1790s

Northanger Abbey, *Sense and Sensibility*, and *Pride and Prejudice* were first conceived during the 1790s. In the increasingly reactionary atmosphere which followed Britain's declaration of war on revolutionary France in 1793, a fictional commitment to 'things as they are', the alternative title of William Godwin's *Caleb Williams* (1794), with its claims to accuracy and transparency, is dominantly associated with political partisanship. The phrase nevertheless also provides an apt definition of Austen's programme as a serious novelist precisely because it helps draw attention to the complex and much debated relationship between aesthetics and politics as it is played out in her fiction. Throughout the decade, as Jon Mee demonstrates in detail in Chapter 11, fiction's claims to authenticity were mobilized on both sides of what Barbauld, looking back in 1810, recognized as a 'war of systems' (1.59). Many novels shaped their representation of 'life and manners' and decided the fate of their characters in order to argue from and for a particular ideological position, and the fate of female characters took on a special prominence as Mary Wollstonecraft and others extended the revolutionary language of rights explicitly to women. In this highly politicized context, any novel might be read in partisan terms and women writers came under particular scrutiny. Female patriotism became narrowly identified with domestic duty and, as Harriet Guest has noted, patriotism was 'more prominent than learning' as the mark of critical acceptability (2000: 175). Any attempt to place Austen within the novel's and women novelists' growing claims to seriousness in this period must necessarily take account of this shifting and increasingly febrile critical and political atmosphere. It provides the background against which Austen wrote several of her early experimental pieces: in which she drafted 'Elinor and Marianne' (1796) and began to revise it into *Sense and Sensibility* (1797); completed 'First Impressions' (1796), the early draft of *Pride and Prejudice*, which was rejected in 1797 by the publisher Cadell; and in which she wrote *Susan* (1798–9), which became *Northanger Abbey*.

Ever since Marilyn Butler (1975, 1986) provided her invaluable corrective to the patronizing dismissal of Austen's fiction as, in George Steiner's words, 'almost extraterritorial to history' (1975: 9), it has been impossible to ignore the political resonances at work in the novels' engagement with the '3 or 4 Families', members of the porous but still comparatively narrow social group which provide their dominant subject matter. For the young Austen, with Burney as her role model and mindful of the precariousness of the female writer's reputation, seriousness and professionalism were associated with an avoidance of reductive labels, whether of genre or political partisanship—a position which would have been confirmed by Burney's publication of *Camilla* in 1796, with its studied focus on contemporary manners rather than contemporary politics and its definition of the novelist as an 'investigator of the human heart in its feelings and changes' (*Camilla*, 7). But it is a mistake simplistically to equate that non-partisan creative principle with a doctrinaire anti-Jacobinism or even a default conservatism; and/or to take it as the sign of a compromising submission to a reactionary version of femininity—or, on the other hand, to want to claim Austen as our contemporary by identifying her fiction with a subversively progressive version of gender politics. Austen's instincts were conservative; her family's political affiliations were proudly Tory; but within those allegiances, she espouses a sceptical empiricism, the aesthetic principle of which is truth and the fictional manifestation of which is complexity.

In her Juvenilia, Austen's sceptical investigations focus primarily on genre and the novelistic conventions she inherited. Her instrument is a comic daring which relies for its effects on a sophisticated readership. Produced largely between 1787 and 1793, and dismissed by her anxious Victorian descendants as 'clever nonsense', these very far from 'childish effusions' have long been recognized as a significant part of Austen's *oeuvre*.[10] Writing for the private entertainment of a family circle of unashamed 'great Novel-readers' gave Austen the freedom to experiment, testing the boundaries not just of fictional acceptability—and what might be acceptable coming from a woman's pen in particular—but of the reality on which fiction depends for its plausibility. Delightedly exploiting the novelist's power to imagine anything, the early writings revel in the arbitrary and the unexpected, drawing attention to power's attendant responsibilities precisely by ignoring them. In these stories, intimacy between families is measured by their readiness to 'kick one another out of the window on the slightest provocation' ('Frederic and Elfrida'), and heroines are liable to 'partak[e] too freely of . . . claret' ('Jack and Alice') or, in a yet more extreme fantasy of independence, to have murdered their parents ('A Letter from a Young Lady').[11]

As Austen's editors have shown, the Juvenilia abound with references to, among many others, Samuel Richardson (in particular *Sir Charles Grandison*), Sarah Fielding, Henry Fielding, Charlotte Lennox, Frances Brooke, Frances Burney, Laurence Sterne, Oliver Goldsmith, Henry Mackenzie's *Man of Feeling*, and Charlotte Smith's *Emmeline*, as well as, in other genres, Alexander Pope, Samuel Johnson, Richard Brinsley Sheridan, and Hannah Cowley; and they parody a variety of popular fictional modes (epistolary fiction, moral tales, libertine narratives, travel fiction, Gothic and exotic motifs). Even more pervasively, the idioms and tropes of popular fiction are deftly reproduced and ridiculed, particularly the distorted femininity and emotional hyperbole of sensibility. Heroines lament the ways of men with exquisite bathos ('Oh! cruel Charles to wound the hearts and legs of all the fair' ('Jack and Alice', 25)); or accept offers of marriage from two suitors in the space of an hour only to drown themselves from remorse, victim to overenthusiastic feminine compliance ('Frederic and Elfrida'); or—in some ways the most interesting— they are simply young women to whom very little happens ('The Beautifull Cassandra'; 'A Collection of Letters'). Formulaic fiction and the self-absorbed forms of femininity which it creates are exposed as equally absurd. Clara Reeve's influential distinction between the novel and the romance provides a useful implicit measure here. In describing her burlesques as 'A Novel', Austen implicitly invokes Reeve's definition: 'a picture of real life and manners, and of the times in which it is written'.[12] The effect is to raise questions about where 'real life' might reside; or, more precisely, to test the boundaries of what fiction, its readers, and its publishers will tolerate as both 'real' and entertaining, according to laws of probability which are in turn partly dictated by decorum. There is an immediate comic incongruity in Alice, the drunken heroine. But, like the cruelty and violence

---

[10] Caroline Austen, letter (1869); James Edward Austen-Leigh, *A Memoir of Jane Austen* (1870) (in Sutherland 2002: 186, 42).

[11] Jane Austen, *Juvenilia*, ed. Peter Sabor (Cambridge: Cambridge University Press, 2006), 6, 25, 222.

[12] Clara Reeve, *The Progress of Romance, through Times, Countries, and Manners*, 2 vols (Colchester: Keymer, 1785), 1.111.

in other stories, the joke also works more subtly, appealing to a knowledge of life which recognizes that though young women readers might indeed occasionally 'drink a little too much' (26) and talk nonsense, such behaviour in a heroine is unthinkable. Similarly, unforeseen vicissitudes of fortune pervade the Juvenilia ('alas! the House had never been their own and their Fortune had only been an Annuity on their own lives!' ('Love and Freindship', 118–19)). Used arbitrarily, such reversals offer yet another burlesque instance of the novelist's power to dictate circumstances, but the subject matter is painfully close to a recognizable actuality.

Entertaining, but ultimately limited and limiting, burlesque provided Austen with a training ground rather than a lasting professional mode. But its motifs are clearly evident in her 1790s novels, and particularly in *Northanger Abbey* and *Sense and Sensibility*. Less exuberant than the Juvenilia, perhaps, her serious fiction is far more innovative, as Austen undertakes to realize 'real life and manners' rather than simply invoke them as a given. Catherine Morland may not drink to excess like Alice, but the daring representation of her flawed eligibility as a heroine in the opening chapter of *Northanger Abbey* is something entirely new.

> She had a thin awkward figure, a sallow skin without colour, dark lank hair, and strong features;—so much for her person;—and not less unpropitious for heroism seemed her mind. She was fond of all boys' plays, and greatly preferred cricket not merely to dolls, but to the more heroic enjoyments of infancy, nursing a dormouse, feeding a canary-bird, or watering a rose-bush.... She could never learn or understand any thing before she was taught.... The day which dismissed the music-master was one of the happiest of Catherine's life.... her proficiency... was not remarkable, and she shirked her lessons... whenever she could. What a strange, unaccountable character!—for with all these symptoms of profligacy at ten years old, she had neither a bad heart nor a bad temper;... hated confinement and cleanliness, and loved nothing so well in the world as rolling down the green slope at the back of the house.
>
> ...At fifteen, appearances were mending; she began to curl her hair and long for balls... Her love of dirt gave way to an inclination for finery, and she grew clean as she grew smart...
>
> ...provided that nothing like useful knowledge could be gained from them, provided they were all story and no reflection, she never had any objection to books at all. But from fifteen to seventeen she was in training for a heroine; she read all such works as heroines must read... (vol. 1, ch. 1; 5–7)

Still unusual when it appeared posthumously at the end of 1817 (dated 1818), this frank, nuanced account of a recognizable rural girlhood as it modulates into the contradictions of adolescence would indeed have been unprecedented if completed, as large parts of it might well have been, as early as 1798. But, as with any genuinely innovative writing, Austen's work is in constant, conscious touch with its predecessors and contemporaries. The radicalism of this portrait depends not just on an unusual openness about Catherine's limited appetite for education (in itself a significant comment on the dominant moral discourse which expected women to conform to impossible ideals of perfection); it also works through more precise echoes of equivalent, but rather different, presentations of the heroine in the work of writers Austen nevertheless admired. So, unlike Catherine's 'thin, awkward figure' and 'unpropitious mind', the 'form' of Burney's eponymous heroine in *Cecilia* 'was elegant, . . . her countenance announced the intelligence of her mind'; Charlotte Smith's Monimia in *The Old Manor House* (1793) has 'luxuriant' rather than 'lank' dark hair; and though the portrait of Burney's Camilla is more qualified, her beauty less 'complete' than that of her cousin Indiana, her 'form and mind' are nevertheless 'of equal elasticity'. Even Edgeworth's Belinda, educated like Catherine 'chiefly in the country', 'had early been inspired with a taste for domestic pleasures'. The heroines of both Gothic and rational fiction are typically intellectually impressive and artistically accomplished. Smith's Emmeline has 'a kind of intuitive knowledge', and comprehended every thing with a facility that soon left her instructors behind her'; and Emily St Aubert, in Radcliffe's *The Mysteries of Udolpho* (1794), far from giving up music lessons at the first opportunity, spends her time practising 'elegant arts, cultivated only because they were congenial to her taste, and in which native genius . . . made her an early proficient'.[13] Though Gothic fiction in general and Radcliffe's novel in particular are *Northanger Abbey*'s most obvious referents, Austen's new heroinism also rewrites Burney's complex but still conventionalized protagonists. It is also, of course, a self-conscious development from Charlotte Lennox's *The Female Quixote* (1752), which Austen much admired, where the clever but misguided Arabella's 'Fondness for Reading' is dangerously and paradigmatically fixated on Romances.[14]

Throughout Austen's novels, the references extend well beyond fiction, and there is a possible unexpected echo of Mary Wollstonecraft in Catherine's preference for cricket over dolls or other stereotypically feminine 'enjoyments'. In *A Vindication of the Rights of Woman* (1792), Wollstonecraft attacked Rousseau's assumption in *Emile* (1762) that children's play will follow gendered lines: 'I will venture to affirm, that a girl, whose spirits have not been damped by inactivity . . . will always be a romp, and the doll will never excite attention unless confinement allows her no alternative.'[15] Whether or not the explicit parallel with Wollstonecraft is intended, the sentiment is certainly shared. It provides a valuable example of the way in which, for the alert reader, Austen's sceptical intelligence

---

[13] Frances Burney, *Cecilia (1782)*, ed. Peter Sabor and Margaret Anne Doody (Oxford and New York: Oxford University Press, 1988), 6; Charlotte Smith, *The Old Manor House*, 4 vols (London: J. Bell, 1793), 1.31; *Camilla*, 15; *Belinda*, 1.10; Charlotte Smith, *Emmeline, The Orphan of the Castle*, 4 vols (London: T. Cadell, 1788), 1.5; Ann Radcliffe, *The Mysteries of Udolpho (1794)*, ed. Bonamy Dobrée (Oxford: Oxford University Press, 1980), 3.

[14] Charlotte Lennox, *The Female Quixote*, ed. Margaret Dalziel (Oxford: Oxford University Press, 1989), 7.

[15] Mary Wollstonecraft, *A Vindication of the Rights of Woman, The Works of Mary Wollstonecraft*, ed. Janet Todd and Marilyn Butler, 7 vols (London: Pickering, 1989), 5.112.

introduces live political issues into her fiction, subordinated always to her novelistic agenda. Enlightenment debates about the proper education of girls and, beyond that, about the relative effects of nurture and nature ('neither a bad heart nor a bad temper') underpin the challenge of establishing a 'not remarkable' girl as a therefore remarkable (anti-)heroine.

In her treatment of Marianne and Elinor Dashwood in *Sense and Sensibility*, Austen pushes unspectacular heroinism further. Choosing a high-risk strategy which anticipates Fanny Price in *Mansfield Park*, Austen locates the dominant point of view with Elinor's quiet, introspective intelligence and relegates her superficially livelier, but in fictional terms more conventional sister to a supporting role. In all her fiction, the choice of hero-ine is of course key to Austen's critical engagement with popular genres and modes, and a recurrent motif is the way in which she gives only comparatively minor roles to the accomplished or beleaguered young women who for other writers would be obvious heroine material (Jane Fairfax in *Emma* or Mrs Smith in *Persuasion*, for example). But in *Northanger Abbey* and *Sense and Sensibility* that dialogue with other fiction is conducted at a more explicit level than in Austen's later work. The uses of reading become the mat-ter of the plot as Catherine Morland and Marianne Dashwood follow the tradition of *The Female Quixote* in demonstrating the dangerous consequences of reading badly or solipsistically, expecting their lives to conform to the tropes of fiction: for Catherine, the assumption that General Tilney, as a latter-day Gothic villain, might have murdered his wife; for Marianne, misplaced pride in her own unusual capacity for the refined sensibil-ity associated with heroines. The consequence for Marianne is all too predictable as she becomes emotionally subject to the attractive but sexually irresponsible Willoughby and life becomes a (more commonsensical) version of the familiar eighteenth-century seduc-tion narrative.

Austen's domestic realism tests contemporary fictional commonplaces with a level of subtlety impossible in burlesque. As always, her critique is of forms of excess, but it would be a gross misreading to assume that Gothic in *Northanger Abbey*, or sensibility in *Sense and Sensibility* are simply being dismissed. Austen's project in both novels is to explore the ways in which life might, indeed, imitate fiction—in less spectacular, though not necessarily less alarming, ways. In *Northanger Abbey*, Catherine's instinctive mistrust of General Tilney, the judgement of an ordinary girl who has a good 'heart', turns out to be accurate. Though not guilty of the wife-murder of her Gothic imaginings, he is capable not only of a gross breach of social responsibility in summarily dismissing Catherine from Northanger on discovering she is not an heiress but, more fundamentally, of day-to-day cruelty toward his own daughter. As we learn almost in passing in the concluding chapter, Eleanor Tilney was subject to the 'evils' and 'habitual suffering' of isolation and parental tyranny at Northanger before being freed by her marriage—a marriage engineered, of course, through the arbitrary power of the novelist working on behalf of romantic fulfilment (vol. 2, ch. 16; 260).

Eleanor's intelligence, quiet good sense, and experience of 'habitual suffering' would qualify her as a Burney heroine. In *Northanger Abbey* she is relegated to a small but vital role. As the foil to both Catherine's naivety and Henry Tilney's masculine complacency, she is a pivotal figure of female rationality who helps the reader connect the exaggerations of Gothic with the actualities of domestic existence. Henry's much-quoted response on discovering Catherine's fears about life at Northanger is to dismiss them out of hand: 'Dear Miss Morland . . . Remember the country and the age in which we live. Remember that we are English, that we are Christians.' Similarly, when Catherine, anticipating the publication of the latest Gothic novel, announces that something 'more horrible than any thing we have met with yet' will 'soon come out of London', Eleanor assumes she must refer to the likelihood of political violence and puts her faith in the government to take 'proper measures', whilst Henry dismisses his sister's interpretation as chauvinistically as he does Catherine's Gothic terrors: 'Forgive her stupidity. The fears of the sister have added to the weakness of the woman' (vol. 2, ch. 9; 203; vol. 1, ch. 14; 113–15). But the threat of invasion by France in 1797–8, when the novel was first written, or of strikes and demonstrations about political reform in 1817–18, when it was published, might well have led readers to sympathize with Eleanor's anxiety, whether or not they agreed with her loyalist confidence. Eleanor emerges as the measured voice of (female) sense, and Austen's dialogue with contemporary fiction again displays its indirect but firm engagement with urgent contemporary issues.

In *Sense and Sensibility*, that engagement is conducted through an analysis of the effects of different female behaviours. The stark contrast signalled in the title has led some commentators to assume a programmatic, almost punitive, and certainly conservative preference in the novel for a narrow interpretation of sense, identified with Elinor, over Marianne's self-indulgent and potentially revolutionary sensibility. But, as with her complex appraisal of Gothic in *Northanger Abbey*, Austen escapes easy categorization, moving beyond the dismissive parodies of sensibility in her Juvenilia to test its positive as well as negative consequences when put into everyday action. The novel's point of view is with Elinor whose 'disposition was affectionate, and her feelings were strong', but who also 'knew how to govern them'; Marianne is 'sensible and clever . . . every thing but prudent'.[16] Thus it is made clear at the outset that the sisters have both reason and feeling in common. The differentiator is prudence, a capacity for circumspect self-discipline. Again echoing Wollstonecraft (whose wish was for women 'to have power [not] over men; but over themselves' and who advocated an '*active* sensibility'), but also more conservative commentators on female education and behaviour such as the Evangelical Hannah More (for whom an 'early habitual restraint' was 'peculiarly important to the future character

---

[16] Jane Austen, *Sense and Sensibility (1811)*, ed. Edward Copeland (Cambridge: Cambridge University Press, 2006), vol. 1, ch. 1; 7.

and happiness of women'), Austen's novel addresses the pragmatics of restraint and constraint.[17]

It does so, again, through a reworking of fictional tropes. The novel begins with an explanation of the Dashwoods' financial circumstances and disinheritance, a common enough mode of scene-setting, but recounted here with an unusually precise level of legal and familial detail. The particularity establishes the novel's realist credentials and anticipates its narrative focus, through Elinor, on just how it feels to be dependent. In choosing Elinor as heroine, Austen sets herself the realist's ultimate technical challenge: to make the frustration and boredom of unavoidable social interaction interesting. Marianne's emotional vicissitudes would be the expected focus in a more conventional novel of sensibility; instead, the reader's primary interest is directed to Elinor's internalized emotional intelligence as she manages the impact of Marianne's behaviour: 'it was impossible for [Marianne] to say what she did not feel, however trivial the occasion; and upon Elinor therefore the whole task of telling lies when politeness required it, always fell' (vol. 1, ch. 21; 141).

The plot not chosen—for either of the sisters—is that of sensibility and seduction, the formulaic subject of Eliza Haywood's popular early fiction, raised to classic status in Richardson's *Clarissa* (1748–9), and replayed in numerous popular novels. In this paradigmatic eighteenth-century cultural myth, the naive heroine's ill-judged feelings make her prey to seduction and, at worst, abandonment and ruin by a fatally attractive, usually aristocratic libertine. In all of Austen's novels in which it plays a part, the seduction plot involves someone other than her heroine (with the comic exception in *Northanger Abbey* of John Thorpe briefly manoeuvring Catherine into his well-hung gig). In *Pride and Prejudice*, for example, it is Lydia's story, and it recurs in *Mansfield Park* with the elopement of Julia and adultery of Maria Bertram. In *Sense and Sensibility*, it provides a tragic backdrop in the story of Colonel Brandon's ward Eliza, a stark reminder of Willoughby's 'libertine practices' and a warning of the fate that, in a different novel, Marianne might have suffered (vol. 3, ch. 11; 396). Just as *Northanger Abbey* explores the familiar experiences of social and sexual bullying which lend authenticity to the extremes of Gothic fiction, *Sense and Sensibility* is clear-sighted about the financial constraints and compensating fantasies that make young women vulnerable to sexual predators, whilst suggesting that in most women's experience, this takes a less extreme—though no less significant—form.

In describing her heroines, or in self-consciously eschewing the full-blown tragic melodrama of Gothic or the seduction plot, Austen's fiction signals its commitment to a new realism. But the imperative of the ending re-establishes fictionality. Austenian realism comes in the contradictory, and some would argue inherently conservative, form

---

[17] Wollstonecraft, *Vindication*, 131; *The Wrongs of Woman: or, Maria* (1798), *Works*, 1.144. Hannah More, *Strictures on the Modern System of Female Education*, 2 vols (London: Cadell and Davies, 1799), 1.142.

of comedy. Financial difficulties and previous entanglements are swept away as the writer's arbitrary power is put at the service of romance, reconciliation, and happiness. The 'tell-tale compression of the pages' requires Catherine to be married off in 'perfect felicity' to Henry Tilney (*Northanger Abbey*, vol. 2, ch. 16; 259); Marianne escapes ruin, in large part due to the protection of her female family; and Edward Ferrars is honourably extricated from his involvement with Lucy Steele so that Elinor's self-discipline might be rewarded and her pent-up sensibility released into 'tears of joy, which at first she thought would never cease' (*Sense and Sensibility*, vol. 3, ch. 12; 408). Comedy imagines romantic fulfilment in spite of economic barriers; and, in the socially conventional but pointedly gendered concluding image of *Sense and Sensibility*, an ideal community based on sisterly affection.

Like the authorial intervention in *Northanger Abbey*, the narrative voice which effects this ending is among the most directive in all Austen's fiction. Though the sympathetic focus of *Sense and Sensibility* is with Elinor, her point of view is still narrated from the perspective of an omniscient author who, as in burlesque, makes evident their power over events. It is in *Pride and Prejudice*, the most mature of the works first drafted in the 1790s, that Austen fully transcends that apprenticeship and perfects the mode of free indirect narration which was to be her most distinctive contribution to the development of the novel.

Two rather different examples help illustrate Austen's technical achievement, as well as her continuing dialogue with her literary peers and predecessors. From the novel's famous opening lines—'It is a truth universally acknowledged, that a single man in possession of a good fortune, must be in want of a wife'—the witty authorial voice entertains, but also challenges a sophisticated reader to decide whose point of view they are hearing and where, precisely, 'truth' might lie. The ventriloquized Johnsonian idiom claiming universal truth is bathetically reduced to a parochial truism, as the universe shrinks to 'a neighbourhood'—or, of course, to the imagined neighbourhood of novel readers. In a subtle redefinition of narrative authority which deftly establishes the novel's preoccupations, the effect is simultaneously to acknowledge and to disavow the shaping power of female financial dependency and the function of marriage; and, at the metafictional level, to question the part played by popular romantic fiction in a socio-economic system where personal affection and happiness are mere unspoken adjuncts to material expectations.

More typically, Austen's free indirect narration moves subtly and seamlessly between the authorial voice and the idiom and point of view not of a community of opinion, but of an individual character—most often in *Pride and Prejudice* that of Elizabeth Bennet:

> She began now to comprehend that he was exactly the man, who, in disposition and talents, would most suit her. His understanding and temper, though unlike her own, would have answered all her wishes. It was an union that must have been to the advantage of both...

But no such happy marriage could now teach the admiring multitude what connubial felicity really was.[18]

At this moment of crucial realization, the coincidence between Elizabeth's point of view and that of her author is particularly close, but still distinguishable. In a modulation characteristic of Austen's method throughout the novel, the first sentence could be read as in the authorial voice, but the tension between the idiom of rational analysis and the betrayal of emotion in the unqualified idioms of romantic love ('exactly the man'; 'most suit her'; 'answered all her wishes') alerts the reader to a shift into Elizabeth's consciousness. And that shift becomes more evident in the affectionately mocking representation of Elizabeth's still unbowed pride as she regrets the lost opportunity to provide 'the admiring multitude' with a model of marital bliss. The further irony, of course, is that by the end of the novel Elizabeth and Darcy will indeed provide an example of 'connubial felicity'. In explicit contrast to her fears that Lydia and Wickham can 'justly' expect 'neither rational happiness nor worldly prosperity', Austen's protagonist achieves both (vol. 3, ch. 7; 339).

It is in the endings of her novels, in the reward of her heroines with both emotional and material fulfilment, that Austen comes closest to the forms of popular fictional excess eschewed by her rigorous domestic realism. Free indirect narration helps justify this risky but hugely pleasurable conjunction of realism with romance: through enlisting the reader's complex sympathies, but also through the knowing, flexible ventriloquism of the narrative voice, a self-effacing but constant reminder that we are, after all, reading a novel.

Conceived in the 1790s, the reconciliatory endings of *Sense and Sensibility* and *Pride and Prejudice* speak also to the moment of their publication through their depiction of a social order restored and reinvigorated by female influence and the workings of romance. Both Elinor and Elizabeth achieve 'rational happiness'—a term which invokes not simply a philosophical quest as fictionalized in, for example, Johnson's *Rasselas* (1759), but also the new femininity promulgated by Wollstonecraft and echoed by Elizabeth. Austen's deft appropriation of this politicized vocabulary is clearly illustrated in two key scenes from *Pride and Prejudice* in which Austen's modern romance heroine demonstrates her autonomy in choosing a husband, confronting the power and prejudice of the old order in the form of Mr Collins and Lady Catherine de Bourgh. Desperate to persuade Lady Catherine's creature, Mr Collins, that 'no means no', Elizabeth invokes a Wollstonecraftian opposition: 'Do not consider me . . . as an elegant female . . . but as a rational creature speaking the truth' (vol. 1, ch. 19; 122).[19] She resists Lady Catherine herself by asserting her individual right to 'act in that manner, which will . . . constitute my

---

[18] Jane Austen, *Pride and Prejudice (1813)*, ed. Pat Rogers (Cambridge: Cambridge University Press, 2006), vol. 3, ch. 8; 344.

[19] 'My own sex, I hope, will excuse me, if I treat them like rational creatures . . . I wish to shew that elegance is inferior to virtue' (Wollstonecraft, *Vindication*, 5.75).

happiness', invoking her social status as a 'gentleman's daughter', where 'gentleman' is defined by moral respectability rather than mere birth (vol. 3, ch. 14; 396, 395). In making this rational 'gentleman's daughter' the mistress of Pemberley, Austen's romantic comedy puts 1790s Enlightenment ideals at the service not of revolutionary change, but of a gender-inflected vision of gradualist reform.

The Later Novels: Austen in the Napoleonic Period

Having revised two of her 1790s fictions for publication (the third, *Susan*, later *Northanger Abbey*, had already been sold to a publisher and was unavailable to her), Austen embarked on new writing. She did so in a changed literary environment and in an atmosphere of political uncertainty at home and abroad, as the war with Napoleonic France dragged on. Following the publication of *Pride and Prejudice* in 1813, Austen suggested that her novel was 'rather too light & bright & sparkling', in need of 'a critique on Walter Scott, or the history of Buonaparte' (*Letters*, 203). Disingenuous though it might be, Austen's playful remark nevertheless betrays a characteristically sharp awareness that, for some commentators at least, the seriousness of fiction might be measured by the extent to which it acknowledges contemporary debates. All of her novels engage with their immediate context, albeit indirectly, but Austen's later novels address the condition of England in a more explicit and sustained way. They also register shifts in popular fictional taste which can be attributed at least in part to a national mood shaped by a long war and its attendant insecurities. The effect is most obvious in *Mansfield Park* (begun 1811; published 1814) where, in choosing for her title the name of an estate, a socio-economic microcosm of the nation, Austen signals a new level of ambition. But in her other two mature novels Austen's domestic realism is similarly used as a vehicle through which to reflect on the moral health of Britain and its governing classes: in *Emma* (1816), with its anatomy of social and commercial manoeuvres in a microcosmic English village; and in Austen's novel of the peace, the posthumously published *Persuasion* (1818), which celebrates the navy, seen as so crucial in Britain's eventual defeat of Napoleon. And the pattern appears to continue in the acerbic, unfinished *Sanditon*, set in 'a young and rising bathing-place'.[20] In each case, Austen's intervention in fictional debates on the state of the nation is conducted through her critique of popular novelistic conventions.

In *Mansfield Park*, Austen's rigorous realism engages with versions of heroism and new forms of novelistic excess introduced into domestic fiction by the interventions of

---

[20] Jane Austen, *Sanditon*, in *Later Manuscripts*, ed. Janet Todd and Linda Bree (Cambridge: Cambridge University Press, 2008), 142.

Evangelical writers. Hannah More's dull but influential *Coelebs in Search of a Wife* was published in 1808 and went through ten impressions in six months; it was followed in 1811, just as Austen began to draft *Mansfield Park*, by Mary Brunton's hugely popular *Self-Control*. Where Brunton 'connect[s] melodrama to morality', as Anthony Mandal puts it in this volume (266), More's text is a barely fictionalized conduct book in which the protagonist's search for a marriageable model of feminine perfection provides the occasion for men to talk at length about women's shortcomings. '[P]ictures of perfection as you know make me sick & wicked', Austen wrote, discussing 'Novels & Heroines' with her Evangelically inclined niece, Fanny Knight (*Letters*, 335). Fanny Price, Austen's most experimental (and least popular) heroine, is very far from being a picture of perfection, but her restrained, forbearing nature is symptomatic of a newly sombre note which strikingly distinguishes *Mansfield Park* from *Pride and Prejudice* and which has sometimes been mistaken for an unproblematic endorsement of More's Evangelical patriotism. But just as *Pride and Prejudice* engages with Wollstonecraft's ideas yet is not itself Wollstonecraftian, *Mansfield Park* is manifestly the product of the first decade of the nineteenth century during which Evangelicalism had such a pervasive cultural effect, but it is very far from being in any straightforward sense an Evangelical novel.

Austen nevertheless shares something of the agenda epitomized by More and described by Linda Colley (1992: 237–81), putting women and domesticity at the centre of national moral reform. *Mansfield Park* depicts a crisis of absent authority in a family whose wealth has been built on slavery and, in Austen's depiction of the Crawfords, the dangerous temptations of a secularizing modernity. Echoes of More's preoccupations in *Coelebs* recur. The insubstantial education and pastimes of the Bertram sisters, memorizing 'all the Metals, Semi-Metals, Planets, and distinguished philosophers' and 'making artificial flowers or wasting gold paper', recall in more recognizable terms the comprehensive but superficial education of Miss Rattler in More's novel: 'what little time I can spare from these *principal* things ['varnishing, and gilding, and japaning'], I give by odd minutes to ancient and modern history, and geography, and astronomy, and grammar, and botany'.[21] Mary Crawford's dismay on learning during the walk at Sotherton that Edmund is to be a clergyman ('A clergyman is nothing') occasions a conversation contrasting churchgoing habits in London with those in the country which repeats the reflections of More's protagonist on the issue (*Mansfield Park*, vol. 1, ch. 9; 107–8; *Coelebs*, 1.27–8). In Austen's version, however, with Fanny the miserable witness to Edmund, infatuated with Mary's metropolitan challenge, sexual rivalry gives narrative momentum and an unpredictable edge to socio-moral debate.

---

[21] Jane Austen, *Mansfield Park (1814)*, ed. John Wiltshire (Cambridge: Cambridge University Press, 2005), vol. 1, ch. 2; 21, 16; Hannah More, *Coelebs in Search of a Wife*, 5th edn, 2 vols (London: T. Cadell and W. Davies, 1809), 1.334–5.

In all three of her mature novels, Austen articulates her socio-political analysis through the complexities of desire and her heroines' claims to happiness. In *Mansfield Park*, she draws explicit attention to this fictional discipline, to the requirements of psychological probability which underpin her critique of the didactic modes of her contemporaries and, ultimately, give credibility to her comedic romance endings. This differentiation from rival novelists is clearly signalled as Henry Crawford prepares to seduce Fanny:

> although there are doubtless such unconquerable young ladies of eighteen (or one should not read about them) as are never to be persuaded into love against their judg-ment...I have no inclination to believe Fanny one of them, or to think that with so much tenderness of disposition...she could have escaped heart-whole from...such a man as Crawford, in spite of there being some previous ill-opinion of him to be overcome, had not her affection been engaged elsewhere. (vol. 2, ch. 6; 269–70)

The 'unconquerable young ladies' include Lucilla Stanley, More's paragon of femininity in *Coelebs*, whose resistance to seduction is uninteresting because entirely unconflicted; and, more immediately, Laura Montreville, Mary Brunton's heroine in *Self-Control* (1811), who sets her flawed suitor Colonel Hargrave a two-year test of moral rectitude which he spectacularly fails by abducting her to the wilds of Canada. Ever alert to popular fiction's absurdities, Austen described *Self-Control* as 'an excellently-meant, elegantly-written Work, without anything of Nature or Probability in it', and its North American episode as 'the most natural, possible, every-day thing [Laura] ever does' (*Letters*, 234). Though Brunton does convey a sense of Hargrave's attractiveness, Laura's real struggle is with an open boat on a Canadian river rather than with her moral reason. Fanny's otherwise precarious resilience, by contrast, is fuelled not by abstract moral certainty but by the fact that she is in love with Edmund, the emotional realization of her moral conviction. This is what motivates her most heroine-like moment, when she dares to defy Sir Thomas Bertram's insistence that she accept Henry Crawford's offer of marriage.

In this climactic scene, Fanny opposes not just the social orthodoxies represented by Sir Thomas's authority, but the new mantras of Evangelical reform as it bore down on women. Accusing Fanny of 'that wilfulness of temper, self-conceit, and...independence of spirit, which prevails so much in modern days, even in young women, and which in young women is offensive and disgusting beyond all common offence' (vol. 3, ch. 1; 367), Sir Thomas echoes Hannah More's fulminations against the way in which 'not only sons but daughters have adopted something of that spirit of independence, and disdain of control, which characterize the times'.[22] Through Fanny, the heroine least likely to assert 'disdain of control', Austen tests the emotional simplifications of Evangelical fic-tion against the demands of realism, and the absolutism of the Evangelical agenda against

---

[22] More, *Strictures*, 1.134.

the more traditionally Anglican pragmatics of a liveable morality. Unlike Elizabeth Bennet at Pemberley, Fanny does not become mistress of Mansfield. By the end of the novel her influence has started a process of moral renewal, but as the wife of a clergyman she remains under the 'view and patronage' of the estate and its future (vol. 3, ch. 17; 548), rather than at the heart of the 'comfort and elegance of the family party' like Elizabeth (*Pride and Prejudice*, vol. 3, ch. 18; 426). Austen's programme of conservative reform reasserts traditional relationships between gentry and church and endorses change which, unlike the impatient ambitions of the Crawfords, is 'acquired progressively' (vol. 1, ch. 6; 67). But happiness in this wartime novel is hard-won. Austen's comedic ending can offer only 'tolerable comfort' and Fanny's romantic fulfilment is achieved 'in spite of... the distress of those around her' (vol. 3, ch. 17; 533).

In complete contrast to Fanny Price, Emma Woodhouse, 'handsome, clever, and rich', starts from a position of some social power and 'a disposition to think a little too well of herself'.[23] Casting herself as author, rather than protagonist, of the domestic novel's marriage plot, Emma 'always declares she will never marry' (vol. 1, ch. 5; 41), preferring instead to make matches for other people: successfully, in the case of her former governess; dangerously, as she influences the feelings and social aspirations of her protégée, Harriet Smith. The novel's most obvious narrative irony is to prove Emma wrong about both herself and others. But its real narrative interest lies in the unprecedented effects of Austen's free indirect narration: the precision with which it establishes the changing yet claustrophobic social environment of Highbury, the reason at least in part for Emma's overactive imaginings; and the sympathetic intimacy between the authorial voice and her fictional author-*manqué* which, unlike the more overt moralism of other contemporary fictions, demands that the reader engage in a constant process of fine judgement.

As Austen was writing *Emma*, during 1815, Napoleon was finally defeated and the long war with France ended. Like Mansfield Park, the 'large and populous village' of Highbury, 'almost amounting to a town', can be read as microcosmic of the nation, and Emma herself, for whom Highbury affords 'no equals' (vol. 1, ch. 1; 5), as Austen's realist response to the idealized heroines of overtly nationalist tales. This gives a new resonance to Scott's distinction in his review of the novel between the scenes of 'higher life' through which Maria Edgeworth 'embod[ies] and illustrat[es] national character' and Austen's focus on 'the paths of common life' (Southam 1968: 64). In contrast to Edgeworth (or Scott himself), Austen's novel both evokes and inculcates a sense of shared (national) identity precisely through the reader's recognition of the familiar, a recognition made all the more powerful through the tactful intimacy of free indirect narrative. During the

---

[23] Jane Austen, *Emma (1816)*, ed. Richard Cronin and Dorothy McMillan (Cambridge: Cambridge University Press, 2005), vol. 1, ch. 1; 3.

quintessentially English strawberry-picking at Donwell Abbey, for example, the view of Mr Knightley's estate is described as: 'sweet to the eye and the mind. English verdure, English culture, English comfort, seen under a sun bright, without being oppressive' (vol. 3, ch. 6; 391). The novel's most explicit moment of nationalist feeling—experienced as the collective consciousness of the otherwise 'scattered' party—immediately modulates into Emma's concern that the landscape might have the power to reignite Harriet's feelings for Robert Martin, Mr Knightley's tenant farmer. For the reader, who recognizes the appropriateness of those feelings in spite of Emma's manoeuvring on Harriet's behalf, the effect is to make Harriet's eventual marriage to Mr Martin representative of a social order ideally supported by such a landscape.

Harriet's happy ending depends, of course, on Emma's own—itself representative of what is seen by the novel as an ideal social union, in this case between established wealth (Emma's thirty thousand pounds) and inherited land (Mr Knightley's visually rich but financially more precarious estate). Emma's recognition that 'Mr Knightley must marry no one but herself!' (vol. 3, ch. 11; 444) is also the moment at which she sees the folly of her vicarious ambitions for Harriet. Like other Austen heroines, Emma's moment of self-knowledge is the moment at which she understands her own desires. When Mr Knightley makes his feelings known, Emma defines herself as the heroine of her own narrative rather than the author of Harriet's. In his eyes at least, her hero-inism takes on a national dimension: '"I have blamed you, and lectured you, and you have borne it as no other woman in England would have borne it"' (vol. 3, ch. 13; 469). Emma's private response is to acknowledge her sense of guilt by invoking an even more extreme version of heroic forbearance, against which, like Fanny Price or any other heroine of realist romance, she is inevitably wanting: 'as to any of that heroism of sentiment which might have prompted her to entreat him to transfer his affection from herself to Harriet, as infinitely the most worthy of the two . . . Emma had it not' (vol. 3, ch. 13; 469–70).

Through the subtle wit of her free indirect narrative, Austen once again critiques the excesses of contemporary fiction as her novelizing heroine tests its conventions by turning them on herself. Imagining Jane Fairfax's 'dangerous pleasure' in being loved by her friend's husband (vol. 2, ch. 8; 237), Emma had indulged not just in 'thorough novel slang' (*Letters*, 277), but in irresponsible moral speculation, missing the real drama of Jane's clandestine engagement to Frank Churchill. Plotting an ambitious marriage for Harriet, casting her as one of the upwardly mobile, or unexpectedly noble, orphans who have lead roles in the Gothic novels of which Harriet is so fond—Ann Radcliffe's *The Romance of the Forest* (1791), for example, or Regina Maria Roche's *The Children of the Abbey* (1796)—she had put her protégée's happiness at risk. She must acknowledge both as deeply misguided and accept the more mundane narrative of marriage to a social equal to which Harriet and herself belong. Emma's novelizing is born of boredom, and speaks eloquently of the limited opportunities for an intelligent woman in a society like that of

Highbury. But though the novel is acutely aware of what Emma notes as 'the difference of woman's destiny' (vol. 3, ch. 8; 417), it engages only briefly and indirectly, through Jane Fairfax's almost becoming a governess, with the question of what life choices might or might not be open to women—the question addressed in Frances Burney's *The Wanderer* (1814), or more radically in the 1790s novels of Mary Wollstonecraft and Mary Hays. Instead, the trajectory of romance moves Emma from frustrated imaginings to 'perfect happiness' (vol. 3, ch. 19; 528). In the shifting but still narrow world of Highbury, where Augusta Elton's brash self-confidence must be accommodated and where the Coles, 'of low origin, in trade', now mix with 'the superior families' (vol. 2, ch. 7; 223–4), *Emma's* marriage plot endorses 'English comfort' based in a still recognizable social hierarchy which tolerates rather than embraces change.

Persuasion, very differently, engages directly with change and with the ways in which historical events bear down on the individual. Completed in 1816, a year of international peace but also of social unrest triggered by the post-war slump, the novel is set in 1814–15, during the 'Hundred Days' respite from hostilities following Napoleon's initial capture and exile. Changes of fortune are immediately evident, setting the domestic plot in motion. Sir Walter Elliot's profligacy exacerbates the economic difficulties already experienced by landowners, necessitating retrenchment, and it is the consequent letting of Kellynch Hall to Admiral Croft and his wife that brings Mrs Croft's brother, Captain Wentworth, back into Anne Elliot's life. Like Captain Wentworth, and many other navy officers, the Crofts have accrued 'a noble fortune . . . made during the war',[24] but Austen's shift of attention from the established gentry to this newly affluent professional group is announced also, and most importantly, as a shift of values. The Crofts' relationship of loving equality enacts a new sexual politics, for example: Mrs Croft has been 'almost as much at sea as her husband', and she echoes Wollstonecraft and Elizabeth Bennet in her dismissal of the idea that women are 'all fine ladies, instead of rational creatures' (vol. 1, ch. 6; 52; vol. 1, ch. 8; 75). And the novel closes with a very precise form of praise for the navy. This national institution, the focus of patriotic celebration, is 'if possible, more distinguished in its domestic virtues than in its national importance' (vol. 2, ch. 12; 275)—a conclusion which, in its association of public achievement with the private virtue which is the territory of moral domestic fiction, defines Austen's novelistic engagement with historical process.

That engagement is deftly put into action through the contrast between Anne Elliot's compulsive reading of 'navy lists and newspapers' (vol. 1, ch. 4; 32), which gives her access to the changing fortunes not just of Captain Wentworth but of the nation, and that of her father, poring narcissistically over the Baronetage with its records of a narrow familial

---

[24] Jane Austen, *Persuasion (1818)*, ed. Janet Todd and Antje Blank (Cambridge: Cambridge University Press, 2006), vol. 1, ch. 3; 19.

past. Motivated by 'attachment and regrets' (vol. 1, ch. 4; 30), Anne's reading is a particularly poignant reminder of women's mediated relationship with public events, and of the difference between her own experience and that of Captain Wentworth in the years that have intervened since Lady Russell persuaded her to break off their engagement. Time and action have fulfilled Anne's expectations of Wentworth, changing him into a man of fortune, but meanwhile her 'bloom had vanished' (vol. 1, ch. 1; 6). In an elegiac reversal of the familiar Austen plot, 'She had been forced into prudence in her youth, she learned romance as she grew older' (vol. 1, ch. 4; 32). Romance—including its pleasures and dangers. Anne's eventual happiness is measured by the 'quick alarm' attendant on being a sailor's wife (vol. 2, ch. 12; 275).

In *Persuasion*, her last completed novel, Austen reasserts realist romance as a way of scrutinizing the gendered nature of historical change, and the rewards and pitfalls of constancy—as well as the uses of reading and, by implication, novel-writing. At the climax of the novel, Captain Wentworth is convinced of Anne's continuing affection when he overhears her defending women's capacity for 'loving longest, when existence or when hope is gone'. Anne's conviction is based in experience; she rejects any evidence to be found in books, on grounds familiar from contemporary proto-feminist arguments: 'Men have had every advantage of us in telling their own story. Education has been theirs in so much higher a degree; the pen has been in their hands' (vol. 2, ch. 11; 256, 255). Austen's own female-authored novel stands as the implicit exception to her heroine's rule. Much earlier in her career, in *Northanger Abbey*, Austen had defended the (female) novel's capacity to display 'the most thorough knowledge of human nature' (vol. 1, ch. 5; 31). At the premature end of her writing life, she maintains by example her critique of fiction, or any kind of writing, which fails that test.

* * * * *

The disposition of topics in this volume reflects the remapping of Austen's contemporary fictional landscape which began with the recovery of 'forgotten' women's fiction by feminist literary historians in the last quarter of the twentieth century, and which has established a taxonomy of subgenres in opposition to which, though she might not recognize their labels, Austen defined her realist method. This detailed topography allows us an even more precise appreciation of Austen's originality. Beyond parody, but wittily in touch with contemporary fiction's excesses, beyond partisanship, but harnessing the language of polemical debates to illuminate ordinary experience, Austen set a rigorous standard for (domestic) realism. In an age which came to be dominated by Scott, her subtle, equally serious engagement with the processes of historical change was often overlooked, and it is one of the ironies of her lasting popularity that it too often takes the form of twee fetishization of an idealized past. Much more exciting are those adaptations which seek to reproduce Austen's complexity, either through their representation of her contemporary world, as in Patricia Rozema's 1999 film version of *Mansfield Park*, or through translation into a modern post-feminist environment, as Amy Heckerling does so wittily with *Emma* in *Clueless* (1995) (see Macdonald and Macdonald 2003; Jones 2010). For all those who engage with Austen, whether as adapters of her work or as literary historians, the continuing challenge, if we are to do justice to her subtly understated realism, is to bring a properly historicized attention to bear on the allusive intelligence at play in her free indirect narratives.

16

Historical Romance

INA FERRIS

I N 1762 there appeared an anonymous novel titled *Longsword, Earl of Salisbury. An Historical Romance*, generally attributed to the Irish historian and antiquary Thomas Leland. Based on medieval chronicles and featuring William Longsword, illegitimate son of Henry II, Leland's work inaugurated the modern historical romance in Britain. It is not that the novel itself was particularly influential—in fact it made little noise—nor was it by any means the first to use a historical setting (fictions set in the historical past had long existed). But *Longsword* brought into the novelistic genre the new and intense fascination with the medieval past that lay behind the late eighteenth-century romance revival, a revival that was to prove momentous not only for the course of British literary history but also for the formation of national feeling across European cultures. The romance revival, at once a sentimental and scholarly enterprise, directed attention to the long-derided 'Dark Ages', deploying medieval settings for a variety of purposes across a broad range of historical and imaginative genres, from paintings and poems to ballad collections and theatrical reconstructions. Much of this activity was sparked by the remarkable Ossian phenomenon generated by James Macpherson's publication in the early 1760s of controversial 'translations' (as he termed them) of third-century bardic verse from Gaelic into English. An international hit with the publication of the first volume, *Fragments of Ancient Poetry* (1760), the Ossian texts sounded a new note in European literature. Macpherson invested an obscure historical era and a peripheral geographic space with poetic glamour as the site of a lost heroic culture, and evoked a mood of cultural mourning that resonated widely, popularizing the strangely elegiac trope of the modern poet as ancient bard. The Ossian phenomenon was a supremely literary event, shot through with motifs of sublimity and sentiment; at the same time, it was equally an intervention in historiography. Macpherson presented his texts as an antiquarian act of historical recovery, underscoring the new prominence of the medieval past and literary culture in the construction of national histories that was underway across Europe.

Indeed, as controversy over the authenticity of the Ossian texts mounted in Britain, Macpherson's antiquarian claims became ever more insistent. Where *Fragments of Ancient*

Poetry authorized itself primarily through a preface written by the respected professor Hugh Blair and was not heavily annotated, *Fingal, an Ancient Epic Poem, in Six Books* (1762), published just two years later, included a lengthy preface by Macpherson himself, along with 'A Dissertation Concerning the Antiquity, &c. of the Poems of Ossian the Son of Fingal', and the text of the poem was anchored in an elaborate stratum of footnotes. Nor was this foregrounding of scholarly argument and annotation simply self-defensive: Macpherson was claiming oral forms as the ground for a native literary history. During the same time span that Macpherson was collecting his Ossian materials, Thomas Percy was gathering and constructing the ballad collection that would prove one of the most influential poetic collections in English, *Reliques of Ancient English Poetry* (1765). Like Macpherson's Ossian poems, Percy's collection (whose title echoes Macpherson) recovered ancient poetic modes as at once a source of new literary effects and the foundation of a national literary history. The important point is that the medieval past was becoming doubly available to the eighteenth-century reading public: on the one hand, it functioned as a source of imaginative pleasure, part of a literary culture of sentiment; on the other, it emerged as the object of properly historical inquiry, in this respect part of historiography's reconfiguration of its own method and parameters of inquiry under the impetus of an emergent interest in forms of living ('manners') in the past.

Moving beyond history's traditional focus on political and military matters of state, late eighteenth-century historiography began to expand its purview to unofficial spheres of social, cultural, and private life typically cultivated by informal genres such as memoirs, biographies, and novels (see O'Brien 2005a; Phillips 2000; Rigney 2001). The 'matter' of history was being increasingly redefined, and this had two key effects that bear on the question of historical romance. First, the 'reframing' (Phillips 2000) of the historical field generated a marked reciprocity among the different historical genres in the literary field, as they borrowed material and tactics from one another; second, it led to a splintering albeit not displacement of 'general' history, as new branches of history writing took shape, notably that of literary history as a distinct form of history (see London 2010). Especially when it came to remote periods for which there was little conventional historical documentation, literary productions came to be understood as historical documents, valuable as an index to 'customs and manners' of the time. Percy, for example, concluded the Preface to the *Reliques of Ancient English Poetry* with a justification for his 'rescuing from oblivion some pieces (tho' but the amusements of our ancestors)' on the grounds that such pieces 'tend to place in a striking light their taste, genius, sentiments, or manners'.[1] Hence romance now denoted not only the realm of 'fancy' but a superseded literary form of renewed interest in the rethinking of the national past. Sitting astride both significations, the mixed genre of historical romance, experimenting with different uses

---

[1] Thomas Percy, *Reliques of Ancient English Poetry*, 3 vols (London: J. Dodsley, 1765), 1.ix.

of the historical past, participated in intellectual currents that were putting history and fiction in an increasingly fluid relation. But the blurring of generic boundaries did not mean their erasure: history and the novel remained formally distinct and (more significant) continued to occupy different positions in the generic hierarchy (O'Brien 2005b). Even as different forms of historical romance emerged in the later eighteenth and early nineteenth century, all sat uneasily in the literary field. As a genre straddling higher and lower reaches in the hierarchy, historical romance appeared a markedly unstable and awkward amalgam, the subject of continuing debate and definition but generally relegated to the category of the 'common novel' churned out for circulating libraries. From within this dubious position, however, it opened up new fictional zones and expanded the dimensions of novelistic representation, relocating the novel in the literary field in ways that would ultimately lead to the genre's ascension to literary and cultural centrality by the first third of the nineteenth century.

Beginnings: Romance Revival Fictions

When historical romances emerged in tandem with the romance revival of the 1760s, they did so primarily as a sport. The Advertisement to *Longsword* set the tone. It announced the historical provenance of the story, declaring that the outlines and some details derived from 'the antient English historians', but it immediately admitted that the author had taken 'liberties' with the historians' accounts. To take such 'liberties' in a novel, however, was no great matter, for 'the reader who looks only for amusement will probably forgive it: the learned and critical (if this work should be honoured by such readers) will deem it a matter of too little consequence to call for the severity of their censure'. The author (anonymous but a professor of history at Trinity College, Dublin) makes clear he knows he is trifling. Moreover, even as Leland refused to be bound by historical protocols, he equally refused to answer to the fictional convention that 'pieces of this kind should convey one useful moral'. Brushing aside fiction's traditional didactic alibi, he declares that readers are capable of discerning any moral the story might contain without authorial help: 'if any thing lies at the bottom, worth the picking up, it will be discovered without his direction'.[2] Entering the arena of the historians in a mood of relaxation, the historical romancer thus approached the past as a zone in which the 'liberties' of fiction could find free play. Leland's tale draws on standard romance plots and tropes, revolving around the motifs of usurpation, secrecy, betrayal, and persecution that became the staples of historical romance. Sluggish and stilted, *Longsword* is not a memorable narrative and did

---

[2] *Longsword, Earl of Salisbury. An Historical Romance*, 2 vols (London: W. Johnston, 1762); all quotations are from the Advertisement.

not achieve much success, but Leland's reorientation of novelistic fictions from contemporary life and manners into the byways of official history was a consequential move, and it marked out what would become the generic terrain of historical romance.

This terrain overlaps with that of Gothic romance, and it is no accident that Horace Walpole's *The Castle of Otranto*, published shortly after *Longsword* late in 1764, is itself a romance revival novel. While best known as the founding text of Gothic fiction (see Lynch, Chapter 10), Walpole's work initially masqueraded as a 'found' antiquarian text printed in Italy in 1529 from an earlier manuscript, now translated into English by one William Marshal, Gent. If few readers were fooled by this hoax, the original Preface is an important part of the story of historical romance, for its positioning of the text as an edited historical document places the past in quite different terms than does the better-known preface to the second edition. The antiquarian editor of the first preface casts his authorship as the transmission of a remote past largely opaque to modern understanding, one so alien to current sensibilities that its literary remains can be presented to the reading public only as 'a matter of entertainment'. He thus operates out of a historicist model for which the past is cut off from the present, but such distance and alterity, he claims, only heighten an obligation of fidelity to 'the *manners* of the times'. This argument is less serious than canny, preparing readers for the exuberant display of supernatural phenomena in the tale to follow, as the editor figure explains that while his own modern self may not believe in such things, 'he must represent his characters as believing them'.[3] In general terms historicism tended to turn the past into a detached object available for modern study, imitation, and reproduction; for Walpole, however, its detachment from the present effectively transferred it to the free-floating zone of romance. Reframing *Otranto* in the preface to the second edition, he dropped any mention of chronology to place his 'trifle' (as he called it) within a history of literary genres, defining it as an attempt to blend the pleasures of old romance with the modern novel's commitment to probability and 'common life'. Suggestively, however, the preface is governed less by this idea than by an acute chafing at the constricted space of modern fiction wherein 'the great resources of fancy have been dammed up'.[4]

Walpole's primary motive in *Otranto*, according to this second preface, is to release 'the powers of fancy', leaving them 'at liberty to expatiate through the boundless realms of invention' (vi). To reinforce the point, he added the new dedicatory sonnet to Lady Mary Coke, which declared that 'Blest with thy smile, my dauntless sail | I dare expand to fancy's gale' (iii). 'Fancy's gale' expands through the conjuring up of a pre-modern past represented most dramatically in the novel by the topos of the castle with its

---

[3] *The Castle of Otranto, A Story. Translated by William Marshal, Gent. From the Original Italian of Onuphrio Muralto, Canon of the Church of St. Nicholas at Otranto* (London: Thomas Lownds, 1765), v.

[4] *The Castle of Otranto, A Gothic Story*, 2nd edn (London: Bathoe and Lownds, 1765), vi.

subterraneous passages and supernatural inhabitants. In *Otranto* the past is transformed into a dreamscape in which rational dimensions of time explode: an unpredictable zone wherein Walpole subjects his modern hero and heroine of sentiment to a disorienting loss of bearings, ultimately restored but never fully recovered. Reframed in its second edition, the novel approaches the past as a salutary liberation from and expansion of a narrow present. Where the antiquarian editor of the first preface embraced a progressive modern order, relegating the medieval world to superseded 'Dark Ages', the authorial voice of the second preface stands at a critical distance from such an order. Placed in juxtaposition, the two prefaces underline both the commonality and divergence of Gothic and historical romance. These two forms cohere as expressions of a desire for a broader novelistic canvas than that offered by prevailing forms of fiction, and they converge in looking to the past for novelistic room. But the prefaces foreshadow their eventual separation into distinct modes by the end of the century, when historical romance became ever more inflected by a historicist-antiquarian sense of the past as historical difference while Gothic fiction increasingly abandoned any pretence at historical reference to transform the past into a tropological literary space.

Walpole's experiment with 'a new species of romance' did not coalesce into what we have come to call Gothic fiction until the 1790s, but it produced a direct descendant in the 1770s that gave a more earnest turn to romance revival fictions. Clara Reeve's *The Champion of Virtue. A Gothic Story*, published in 1777 but better known by its revised title, *The Old English Baron*, not only alludes to the subtitle Walpole assigned *Otranto* in the second edition but presents itself as 'the literary offspring of the Castle of Otranto, written upon the same plan, with a design to unite the most attractive and interesting circumstances of the ancient Romance and the modern Novel'.[5] For Reeve, as for Walpole, romance represents a liberation of fictional impulse, but in her case liberation means an idealizing power freed from responsibility to history's sorry record of human nature. Romance by contrast displays 'only the amiable side of the picture'; hence it can work to an ethical end by stimulating readers to emulate the virtues and values so displayed. Although her preface asserts that her work offers 'a picture of Gothic times and manners', Reeve is not much interested in history-likeness, and she includes few period details; nor does she embrace Walpole's symbolic terrain and dark mood, let alone his over-the-top supernatural effects of which she was highly critical. In her hands historical romance, almost completely stripped of historicity, turns the past into a transparent screen on which to throw into sharp relief modern English virtues and values, explicitly working to consolidate a sense of national identity for its own time. Domesticating Walpole's plot of usurpation and restoration, *The Old English Baron* brings it home to an English setting ostensibly feudal but remarkably compatible with a genteel middle-class eighteenth-century world of property, goods,

---

[5] *The Old English Baron: A Gothic Story* (London: Edward and Charles Dilly, 1778), iii.

domesticity, and sociability. One of the benevolent barons of the title, for example, takes satisfaction at the end of the novel in reflecting that he has done his duty 'as a citizen, a husband, a father, a friend' (209). The novel's lost and dispossessed hero rises in the world on the basis of virtue and 'merit' (a reiterated term) before he comes into his aristocratic title and inheritance, and the novel is punctuated by recurring scenes of male sensibility, as characters weep and sigh and throw themselves into one another's arms. In short, the old English baron emerges as the ideal modern English gentleman, sentimental-style.

Take-off: Secret Histories

While romance revival novels set out new threads for historical fiction, its take-off as a popular genre in the latter decades of the eighteenth century following the success of Sophia Lee's *The Recess; or, A Tale of Other Times* (published in two parts in 1783 and 1785) owed much to its alliance with the older, more dubious tradition of secret history. Marking yet another conjunction of history and fiction, secret histories took the form of 'behind-the-scenes' history, making use of informal documents such as letters, memoirs, and dispatches that exposed the private motives and machinations behind public events. In contrast to the genres of the romance revival, those linked to secret history focused on periods closer to the present and more intimately linked to political history. The term itself derives from an ancient manuscript, Procopius's scandalous revelations about the court of Justinian, *Anecdota*, written around 550 but not published until the early seventeenth century when an edition was printed under the title *Arcana Historia*, translated into English in 1674 as *The Secret History of the Court of Justinian*. In the late seventeenth and early eighteenth centuries secret histories proliferated in France and England both in the form of histories (or what purported to be such) and in the form of novels and romances presenting themselves as 'memoirs' or as the 'true secret history' of a known historical event or person (see Bannet 2005; Mayer 1997; Maxwell 2009). In England the Stuart line became a favourite subject, generating the production of rival secret histories either supporting or discrediting Stuart claims. Polemical and often spurious, secret histories had a shady reputation; nor was their status enhanced by the ease with which novelists such as Eliza Haywood and Delarivier Manley appropriated the subtitle 'secret history' in the early eighteenth century for their scandal fictions. But over the course of the century secret history also began to acquire a less provocative and salacious antiquarian register to refer to the publication of private and informal documents from the archive (see Ferris 2008a), as in James Macpherson's chronological compilation of mostly unpublished Jacobite documents, *Original Papers; Containing the Secret History of Great Britain, From the Restoration, to the Accession of the House of Hanover* (1775). Exposing a submerged line of national history, Macpherson's collection straddles the line between a scholarly compendium of archival materials and a political secret history. The key point is that, whichever register it assumed, secret history always stood at a distance from official history. No matter how dubious its processes or motives, it thus represented a locus where the past could be contested and rewritten either by pointing to what had been overlooked or hidden or by speculating on what might have been.

Lee's *The Recess* placed itself squarely in this tradition. Its Advertisement identified the source of the narrative as a secret document (a manuscript whose provenance could not be revealed), and it explicitly dissociated itself from the viewpoint of historiography: 'History, like painting, only perpetuates the striking features of the mind; whereas the best and worst actions of princes often proceed from partialities and prejudices, which live in their hearts, and are buried with them.'[6] Taking advantage of long circulating rumours that Mary Queen of Scots had secretly married the Duke of Norfolk in captivity and become pregnant, the novel posits the existence of twin daughters from this marriage, Matilda and Ellinor. Raised in secret in the recess of the title, the daughters themselves eventually end up in secret marriages to the earls of Leicester and Essex respectively, enduring a breathless series of trials and disasters as they encounter persecution by Elizabeth and James I. The novel thus belongs to the category of 'pretender novels' that coalesced in France and England between 1680 and 1740, most of which focused on actual pretenders; but it takes its cue from the variant represented by Abbé Prévost's *Le Philosophe Anglois ou Histoire de Monsieur Cleveland* (1731–9), which imagines an illegitimate son of Oliver Cromwell. As in Prévost the narrative is first person, bringing the represented experience closer to hand than in the third-person accounts characteristic of romance revival novels. Each sister writes her story as a letter, retrospective in form but charged with the immediacy of testimony. The dramatic shape of both life stories is sanctioned by Lee's assertion in the Advertisement that 'the reign of Elizabeth was that of romance', a formulation in which romance refers less to a literary genre than to a historical condition: an era when the rules of probability that now obtain did not pertain. Collapsing the distinction Reeve had made between romance and history, Lee invokes romance as precisely history's genre.

Her plot builds on the historical reputation of Elizabeth's court as a nest of caprice and intrigue, marked by the spectacular rise and fall of careers. Here all manner of evil and chicanery thrives; passions run wild; madness erupts. As the novel subjects the virtuous but naively passionate heroines to repeated imprisonment, nick-of-time rescue, betrayal, and entrapment, it ratchets up standard motifs of sentiment and sensibility to an extraordinary pitch. In the end Ellinor dies insane, while Matilda pens the final lines of the narrative in exile and despair, anticipating the grave that will soon enclose her. Distress, anguish, and lament dominate the mood, prompting more than one contemporary reviewer to long for respite from the misery. As the *Monthly Review* put it: 'The

---

[6] *The Recess; or, A Tale of Other Times*, 3 vols (London: T. Cadell, 1785).

gloom of the *Recess* gathers a deeper and still deeper shade till the heart sinks under the oppression of melancholy.'[7] The reviews generally treated *The Recess* primarily as a fiction of sensibility, commenting only casually and mildly on the whole notion of 'interweaving fictitious incident with historical truth'.[8] Their minimal interest reflects Lee's own. Unconcerned with historical reconstruction, she approached the past not as an object of mimesis but as a subject of speculation, prying open history's narrative to reflect on the turns the past might have taken in the passage from 'then' to 'now'.

This does not mean that *The Recess* engages in theoretical or critical reflection; rather, its mode of reflection is precisely novelistic, as in the memorable image of the recess itself. As 'the space of rejected tradition and also, equally, the space of novelistic invention' (Maxwell 2002: 169), the recess is a suggestive emblem not just for Lee's own project but for that of the mode of historical romance her novel helped to consolidate. A hidden place, the recess is a set of rooms located almost fully underground, formed out of the ruins of a deserted convent on monastic land seized from the Church during the Reformation. It is connected to parts of the now aristocratic estate through a series of subterraneous passages, linked in this way to the mansion built on the remnants of the destroyed St Vincent's Abbey (whose name lingers on in the name of the estate). It has served as refuge for those expelled by the state (Catholic monks turned it into a hidden monastery), as well as for those with transgressive desires (a brother and sister who narrowly avoided an incestuous union). It now hides the unacknowledged royal daughters, serving as their shelter but also their enclosure, the place where, Matilda writes, they were 'entombed alive' (1.9). With its layered history, the recess tropes historical process in non-linear terms, figuring it as palimpsest rather than progress. Like a palimpsest the recess foregrounds willed human effort rather than impersonal systems: the erasure and replacement of one order by a rival order that nonetheless never quite succeeds in forgetting or destroying what has been suppressed. By turning the spotlight on what continues to exist underground and in the ruins, Lee's image of the recess unsettles the historical settlement, writing historical time as the friction of forms that cannot cohere. Elizabeth and her kingdom come to appear strangely vulnerable despite the court's formidable power, disturbed by residual, even illusory processes as embodied in the two heroines.

By focalizing Elizabeth's reign through the recess, Lee inflects an era central to England's national myth with a certain scepticism, and it may not be precisely a mistake that this respected schoolmistress (notoriously) gets wrong the date of the Armada. Nor is it incidental that women authors were prominent in the alternative or supplementary 'histories' that sprang up in the wake of Lee's success. Many of these were opportunistic imitations aimed at supplying the demand in the literary market Lee had tapped, and

---

[7] *Monthly Review*, 75 (August 1786), 135.
[8] *Gentleman's Magazine*, 56: 1 (April 1786), 327.

they simply adopted her most striking device, as do Rosetta Ballin's *The Statue Room: An Historical Tale* (1790), with its fiction of a secret daughter of Henry VIII, and A. Kendall's *Tales of the Abbey* (1800), which features a secret son of the Earl of Essex. But others responded more alertly to the implications of Lee's positioning of her narrative in history's gaps and erasures, making explicit a notion of fiction she had left largely unstated. Jane West, for instance, explains her decision to focus on the historically shadowy figure of Alice De Lacy, Countess of Lincoln, in *Alicia De Lacy; An Historical Romance* (1814) by arguing that the role of literature is to give 'enlarged portraits of those whose miniatures only were exhibited by history'.[9] The historical Alice De Lacy achieved notoriety in the early fourteenth century when her marriage to the powerful 2nd Earl of Lancaster broke down amid tales of abduction and adultery. Despite her eruption into the historical record, however, little was actually known about De Lacy, and West declares herself licensed to 're-cast' her character. At the same time, she attempts to reconcile the fictional character she has invented (a shallow but virtuous young woman) with the dubious woman depicted in the historical narrative. West's solution is Gothic: she invents a ruthless double, who masquerades as Alicia after the latter has been abducted and reported dead. Acknowledging the 'romantic' nature of this fiction, West contends it is nonetheless one that 'the annals of those times shews to be not improbable' (1.xiv). While 'not improbable' does not translate into 'probable', the motif of impersonation scrambles the line of historical story, as false and true claimants to the name of Alicia De Lacy inhabit the same stage at the same time, culminating in a scene where the authentic Alicia (disguised as a glee-maiden to gain entry into the king's court) finally reveals herself only to be denounced as an imposter by the fake Alicia.

A similar sense of fiction as legitimately released in history's interstices and silences shapes Anna Maria Porter's *Don Sebastian; or, The House of Braganza. An Historical Romance* (1809). 'It has been my aim', Porter announces in her Preface, 'to keep as close to historical records, as was consistent with a work wherein imagination is allowed to make up for the deficiencies of actual tradition'.[10] In her case imagination has even more scope than in that of West, for the fate of Don Sebastian, king of Portugal, presumed killed at the disastrous Portuguese defeat at Alcazar in 1578, was never certainly known. Uncertainty bred rumour, along with a series of pretenders to the throne; it also generated a long-lasting myth of Sebastian as The King Who Will Return in both Portugal and Brazil. Porter's sprawling, episodic novel accounts for his disappearance from history by having Don Sebastian taken into slavery in North Africa on his way back to Portugal after the battle of Alcazar. In slavery he marries the Muslim daughter of his master by whom he has

---

[9] Jane West, *Alicia De Lacy; An Historical Romance*, 4 vols (London: Longman [etc.], 1814), 1.vii.

[10] Anna Maria Porter, *Don Sebastian; or, The House of Braganza. An Historical Romance*, 4 vols (London: Longman [etc.], 1809), 1.iv.

a daughter, who is raised in Europe under another name but aware of her royal father. After twenty years of trials and wanderings in the New World and the Old World (in the course of which Sebastian comes to value domestic ties and an obscure life), he returns to reclaim his throne, but his goal is thwarted by European high politics. Thirty more years of wandering ensue before the aged Sebastian returns once again, this time more happily, to witness his descendants not only mounting the throne of Portugal through a fortuitous marriage but throwing off the yoke of Spanish rule in the process. Sebastian himself, however, dies unknown. Porter's novel thus ends up endorsing dynastic history even as it urges a middle-class argument about the superior value of private life and domesticity, but the figure of the lost king in the shadows haunts her text, imbuing both orders with a sense of fragility and chance. If the past in historical romance is a place where anything can happen, so permitting the release of fancy sought by Walpole, *Don Sebastian* defines it as also a place where anything might happen, turning attention instead to the contingency that is the condition for fancy's liberation.

Generic Consolidation: National Romance, Antiquarian Romance

Romances in the mode of secret history are premised on the privilege of fiction: the demands of story typically trump those of history. By the turn of the nineteenth century, however, the authors of fictional secret histories felt compelled to acknowledge historical protocols, as Sophia Lee had not. Both Porter and West, for example, took pains to establish their historical credentials. Porter's Preface to *Don Sebastian* highlights her reading of historiographic texts (from those of 'general history' to antiquarian collections) and details her familiarity with travel writings produced in the period in which she set her scenes. For her part, West stresses that the 'liberty' of fiction for which she contends in *Alicia De Lacy* is conditional on the novelist's paying proper attention to 'the manners and *costume* of those times' (1.viii); moreover, she exhibits her own command of historical knowledge by appending a substantial set of historical notices to the end of the novel. Such paratextual moves point to a rhetoric of historical specificity that became more prominent in historical romance as it coalesced into a recognized 'species of composition' between 1790 and 1810 (Stevens 2009; Schöwerling 1989). The number of novels set in a determinate historical past significantly increased in the 1790s, which saw a proliferation of subtitles like 'An Historical Tale', 'A Tale, Founded on Facts', and 'An Historical Novel'. This interest in historical settings answered both to a popularization of history in these years and to national anxieties generated by war with France abroad and powerful unrest at home. Political turbulence was the impetus behind the emergence of national romance at this time as an explicitly patriotic inflection of historical fiction in which the past was summoned to answer present political purpose. In the agitated and polarized climate of Britain during the war years political import and allegory were virtually inescapable, all the more so when national history came into view. Thus the anonymous author of *The Minstrel; or, Anecdotes of Distinguished Personages in the Fifteenth Century* (1793) found it necessary to preface her story of the struggle over the English throne in the time known as The Anarchy not by defending its historical accuracy or invoking fiction's privilege but by declaring her political principles: 'It is, perhaps, as ridiculous in the obscure writer of an insignificant novel, to profess that in her fictitious discussions she meditates no injury to the existing government of her country, or its rulers, as it would be in a mole, digging her dark mansion under the base of a mountain, to protest she had not the least intention to overturn it.'[11] The 'general alarm', however, prompts her to declare that while a liberal 'friend to freedom' in France, she is a firm opponent of radical overthrow at home. Invasion fears framed Henrietta Rouviere Mosse's medieval tale, *A Peep at Our Ancestors. An Historical Romance* (1807), whose opening extols the Saxon Harold, 'bravely fighting to defend his rights' against the Norman invader, William. Lest readers miss the contemporary point, Mosse invokes the current European situation when 'an *invader*' seeks to conquer unknown worlds but trembles 'at the power of *one* unsubdued country, whose *heroes dare* to meet his countless hosts'.[12] A few years later, Jane West's *The Loyalists: An Historical Novel* (1812), set in the English civil wars of the seventeenth century, opens with an impassioned chapter on the imperilled state of the nation that advances a straightforwardly pragmatic model of historical fiction (rather different from the one governing *Alicia De Lacy*) as a 'vehicle' directed at 'conveying instruction to the present times, under the form of a chronicle of the past'.[13]

The most prominent of such national romances was Jane Porter's *The Scottish Chiefs. A Romance* (1810). Translated into several languages and going into numerous editions on both sides of the Atlantic, Porter's novel showcased William Wallace, the storied Scottish patriot executed by Edward I, as 'one of the most complete heroes that ever filled the page of history'.[14] The novel's success stems in large part from the fact that Porter sought less to inculcate 'instruction' in West's sense than to animate or renovate national feeling by exploiting the powers of romance. While her preface gestures vaguely in the direction of unidentified 'old British historians' and 'Scottish annals' as sources, her allegiance is more accurately indicated by her choice of an epigraph from Ossian on the title page: 'There comes a voice that awakes my soul. It is the voice of years that are gone; they roll before me with all their deeds'. Summoning up the heroic 'voice' of Wallace, *The Scottish Chiefs* immediately establishes him in unambiguous terms, casting him against

---

[11] *The Minstrel; or, Anecdotes of Distinguished Personages in the Fifteenth Century*, 3 vols (London: Hookham and Carpenter, 1793), 1.i.

[12] Henrietta Rouviere Mosse, *A Peep at Our Ancestors. An Historical Romance*, 4 vols (London: Lane, Newman & Co., 1807), 1.2.

[13] Jane West, *The Loyalists: An Historical Novel*, 2nd edn, 3 vols (London: Longman [etc.], 1812), 1.8.

[14] Jane Porter, *The Scottish Chiefs, A Romance*, 5 vols (London: Longman [etc.], 1810), 1.v.

the craven Scottish nobles who signed a 'bond of submission' to the 'ruthless conqueror' in 1296, 'purchasing life at the price of all that makes life estimable—-Liberty and Honour' (1.1). 'The spirit of one brave man remained unsubdued', the narrator declares, as Wallace retires to his glen, disgusted at the pusillanimity of the Scottish leaders (1.2). Jolted out of this retirement by the shocking murder of his wife by an English official, he leaps into action (and into history) to revenge her death. The moment marks not simply private vengeance but the launch of national resistance: 'From this hour may Scotland date her liberty, or Wallace return no more!' (1.125). Porter's dramatic, fast-paced opening sequence establishes the contours of her patriot-hero, and the rest of the narrative puts him on display in a series of spectacular scenes, rousing speeches, and effusions of sentiment.

Contemporary reviewers were fully alert to the novel's contemporary resonance. 'The state of Scotland in the time of Wallace', noted the *British Critic*, 'bore a striking resemblance to the state of Spain, when her patriot sons first unsheathed their swords against the present tyrant of the continents of Europe.' Indeed, the reviewer wishes for a Spanish translation of the novel, so that it might circulate through the peninsula, 'where so many patriots are without such a leader as Wallace, contending for the independence of their country against a tyrant more fell than our first Edward'.[15] Such a wish testifies to the performative charge of Porter's novel: *The Scottish Chiefs* does not just summon an exemplary figure from the remote past for present contemplation but summons readers into a participatory relationship with this figure. Setting up Wallace as a popular hero, Porter brings into her conservative historical romance a post-revolutionary understanding of the nation as a 'people' rather than a kingdom or state. Thus even before his decisive intervention, she highlights Wallace's understanding of the nation as located in those who inhabit the land rather than in the kingdom's official sites or documents. Informed that Edward I has destroyed 'the archives of the kingdom' and (even worse) that some Scottish chiefs have followed suit with their own records, Wallace dismisses the loss of the annals as of little consequence: 'Scotland's history is in the memories of her sons' (1.25). When he himself embarks on active resistance, it is to the peasants of his valley that he first appeals, literally summoning them with the call of a bugle, addressing them as 'Scotsmen!', and urging them to recall 'the spirits of your fathers' who died for freedom (1.123, 125). In a scene that fuses the sentimental tropes of Celtic romance with more ambiguous images of the revolutionary mob, the peasants grab whatever weapons lie to hand, and follow Wallace. Porter's own authorship locates itself in much the same way, making the point of her reliance on informal 'traditions' in her portrait of Wallace; suggestively, the only written

---

[15] 'Miss Porter's *Scottish Chiefs, a Romance*', *British Critic*, 37 (May 1811), 247, 255.

source she actually specifies in the preface is a fifteenth-century Scots poem celebrating Wallace by the semi-legendary Blind Harry.

Writing Wallace as a charismatic figure in this way, Porter invests him with an erotic charge: the patriot-hero as object of desire (see Dennis 1997). Staged as an attractive body and typically placed in elevated stations, Wallace is exhibited as the cynosure of adoring eyes and hearts, while both genders frequently remark on his comely locks, countenance, and form. Regularly bounding over chasms and scaling rocks, he merges the virile power associated with ancient codes of masculinity with the refined sentiment of a modern man of sensibility, attracting everyone's attention but most particularly that of the women he encounters. Indeed, regretted one reviewer, this Wallace is represented 'as a finished fine gentleman, and the idol of every female heart'.[16] Those female hearts included that of the author, who could not in the end bring herself to consign Wallace to the ignominious brutal death recorded by history. The novel rewrites his final hours to give him a second marriage and a triumphant natural death on the scaffold, eluding the hangman's rope.

Romance flourishes of this sort intensified a deepening critique of historical romance as the undermining of historical discourse. Critics saw the problem as endemic, inherent in the very mix of history and fiction constitutive of the genre, a mix repeatedly cast as misleading young or inexperienced readers by inducing in them a confusion of categories. Clara Reeve had worried about this issue decades earlier in *The Progress of Romance* (1785), troubled that fictions based on 'true history' blended truth and fiction so closely together 'that a common reader could not distinguish them'.[17] Such misgivings, muted in the late eighteenth century, became louder when the rise in the publication of historical fictions at the end of the century converged with a widespread conviction that a rapid influx of new entrants was expanding the reading public far beyond familiar parameters. 'To mingle real with fictitious characters will give a wrong bias to the minds of those not deeply read in history', argued a reviewer of *Alicia De Lacy*, 'and lead them to believe the fictitious part of the work a recital of historical events.'[18] This line of critique assumed fiction to be the more powerful discourse, making a deeper mental impression than historical discourse. The *British Critic* was typical in claiming that when historical truth and romantic fiction were mingled, it was almost impossible for anyone 'to prevent the fictitious from, in some measure, involuntarily identifying itself in their memory with the real one, and thus forming a confused and unfaithful picture'.[19] No longer able to separate chronicle from fable, readers lost purchase on the difference between the fictional and the real—and not

---

[16] *Scots Magazine*, 72 (April 1810), 279.
[17] Clara Reeve, *The Progress of Romance, through Times, Countries and Manners*, 2 vols (Colchester: W. Keymer, 1785) 1.64.
[18] Review of *Alicia De Lacy, Critical Review*, 5th ser., 2 (July 1815), 103.
[19] Review of *Alicia De Lacy, British Critic*, n.s., 2 (November 1814), 550.

only, it was feared, in relation to the past. At the same time another, opposing critique was also being formulated, this one taking its stand by contrast on aesthetic rather than episte-mological grounds to argue that historical romances undermined fiction. Propelling this line was the heightened emphasis on historical 'keeping' that was making itself felt in fic-tion. In a bid for authenticity historical romances had begun to include extended descrip-tions of manners and customs, along with mundane period details, often punctuated with smatterings of archaic phraseology. Such procedures, critics argued, blocked imagi-nation and were fatal to narrative unity. Indeed, the very choice of a historical subject, contended the *British Critic* in the review just cited, operated as itself 'a heavy clog upon the fancy'. Historical romance was thus seen as an impossible 'species', made up of fun-damentally incompatible elements: 'We consider the words "historical" and "romance" as at hostility with each other, and utterly irreconcileable.'[20] When yoked together, both genres lost out: history was compromised, fiction constrained. The particular target in this line of critique was antiquarian romance, routinely charged with undermining the pleasure of novel reading by interrupting the narrative with intrusive period detail. As one reviewer complained, directing his remarks at Joseph Strutt's *Queenhoo-Hall* (1808), 'all the interest which we ought to have had in the characters and in the fable is exchanged for that afforded by a glossarial dictionary'.[21]

Antiquarian romance, a variant of historical fiction that emerged along with national romance at the turn of the century, typically circumvented the criticism directed at secret histories and national romances by avoiding the representation of well-known historical figures like Wallace and Elizabeth I (or keeping them in the background). Instead, it focused on fictional characters embedded in a concrete historical milieu, transferring attention from the world of state politics to the social world of everyday life and manners, generally of the chivalric sort. Strutt himself had made his reputa-tion as an engraver and antiquarian with a series of pioneering studies of the customs, dress, sports, and pastimes of English people from the Middle Ages to the Tudor period. He turned to fiction out of the desire to reach a broader audience, convinced that the novel represented a '*medium* of conveying much useful instruction imperceptibly, to the minds of such readers as are disgusted at the dryness usually concomitant with the labours of the antiquary'.[22] Strutt himself, however, was no novelist. His narrative, set in the time of Henry VI, is a loose, episodic work telling of several courtships pursued in and around Queenhoo-Hall, lurching abruptly between the chivalric world of the baronial hall and the carnivalesque world of the vassals in the village below. Character and plot receive only cursory attention in comparison with the specificity with which

---

[20] Review of *Alicia De Lacy*, *British Critic*, n.s., 2 (November 1814), 550, 549.

[21] 'Strutt's Queenhoo Hall, &c.', *Critical Review*, 3rd ser., 14 (August 1808), 407.

[22] Joseph Strutt, *Queenhoo-Hall, A Romance*, 4 vols (Edinburgh: John Murray and Archibald Constable, 1808), Preface.

Strutt describes sports, food, clothes, and other period details. The difficulty lies not just in his lack of narrative skill but in the pictorial and static nature of Strutt's antiquarian imagination. Unable to bring the various elements of the narrative into dynamic relation, *Queenhoo-Hall* breaks apart into set pieces.

Antiquarian romances typically dissolved in this way, but the potential of a more synthetic (if still not fully synthesized) narrative in this mode is adumbrated in the little-known *The Borderers. An Historical Romance, Illustrative of the Manners of the Fourteenth Century* (1812) by Elizabeth Strutt (no relation to Joseph). The novel focuses on the complicated intertwined lives of two families from the borders (one Scottish, the other English), and it relies on the standard romance plots of usurpation, unhappy love, and fraternal rivalry. Its own narratorial processes are distinctly antiquarian, starting with a preface that quotes a long passage from the antiquarian journal *The Topographer for the Year 1790*. Displaying her learning in an apparatus of notes and epigraphs, Strutt also prints ballads and songs in the main text, and provides detailed period descriptions (e.g. clothes, buildings, banquets, forms of combat) throughout her story. In contrast to *Queenhoo-Hall*, however, the whole is animated by a narrative dynamic governed by a historical intuition, albeit not quite realized, that cultural clashes and differences rooted in particular localities are the motor of historical experience. Inhabiting the 'debatable' zone of the borders, the two families shift around in the same territory at the same time, but they possess differing customs and values that are a function of the distinct national histories of England and Scotland. Moreover, *The Borderers* exploits the doubled signification of a border as at once a site of crossing and clashing, depicting the collisions that mark limits as well as the traversals that test boundaries. Cross-cultural romances, conversions, cross-dressing—these are prominent motifs, as in the story of Eupheme, a heroine not fully within her time or place. Possessing a refined sensibility at odds with those around her, she knows that 'I must be every thing to myself… for no other person will ever enter into my feelings'.[23] A 'borderer' in her marginality, she seeks to become a border crosser, assuming a male identity in the process, and she ends badly because the time is not right for someone like her. In *The Borderers* later eighteenth-century historical romance almost turns into the nineteenth-century historical novel. In a prescient gesture, Strutt's preface invokes as a model Walter Scott, the poet of 'border history'. Had she realized her ambitions for her novel, Strutt writes in a graceful compliment, she would have dedicated the work to Scott 'as a slight tribute of admiration for the abilities of him who has illustrated border history, with the fire of the poet, the extended views of the historian, and the minute research of the antiquary' (1.v–vi).

---

[23] Elizabeth Strutt, *The Borderers. An Historical Romance, Illustrative of the Manners of the Fourteenth Century*, 3 vols (London: A. K. Newman, 1812), 1.138.

Two years later *Waverley* would appear, synthesizing antiquarian romance with realist fiction and historical theory with national romance to initiate a new phase not just in the history of historical fiction but in that of novel writing *tout court*. Even Scott's extraordinary success, however, failed to entirely legitimate the practice of historical fiction. The genre continued to provoke debate and critique for the rest of the nineteenth century (as it still does), underlining that one function of this peculiar mixed form is to keep open not only the question of history but (perhaps more crucially) that of generic distinction itself.

17

Walter Scott and the Historical Novel

IAN DUNCAN

Impact

Early in July 1814 an anonymous novel in three volumes titled *Waverley; or, 'Tis Sixty Years Since* appeared under the imprint of Archibald Constable, a prominent Edinburgh bookseller who was not well known, before now, for publishing novels. Constable had risen to the top of his trade by publishing the first of the great critical quarterlies, *The Edinburgh Review*, and several volumes of Scottish ballads and metrical romances (*Minstrelsy of the Scottish Border, The Lay of the Last Minstrel, Marmion*) which had made their author, Walter Scott, wartime Europe's most popular poet, rivalled in recent years only by Byron. Scott was of course the author of *Waverley*. He had taken hesitant first steps into the new genre: recent scholarship indicates he began writing *Waverley* in 1808, laid it aside after the opening chapters, resumed it in 1810–11, and sped through the second and third volumes in the heady aftermath of the allied victory over Napoleon, in the spring and early summer of 1814.

The new novel's critical reception, while warm enough, scarcely anticipated the conflagration to come. By the end of the year *Waverley* had gone into a third printing and sold 4,000 copies. A second novel 'by the Author of "Waverley"', *Guy Mannering*, sold out the whole of its Edinburgh stock on the day it was published, in February 1815. Three years later (January 1818) a fifth 'Waverley novel', *Rob Roy*, was issued in an unprecedented print run of 10,000 copies, with 3,000 more called for by the end of the month. The career of the 'Great Unknown' (as he came to be called, his anonymity an open secret) had taken off. The apparently unstoppable rush of novels continued until Scott's death in 1832: twenty-seven separate titles in all, in a range of editions and formats. According to William St Clair, 'the "Author of Waverley" sold more novels than all the other novelists of the time put together' during the Romantic period; as late as the 1860s he was still, 'by several orders of magnitude, the author whose works had sold the largest number of copies in the English-speaking world' (2004: 221, 245–6, 418–20). That success was not confined to English, or even to literature. In Scott's lifetime translations of his novels appeared in most of the European literary languages, and retellings and adaptations proliferated across the genres of print into the theatrical, pictorial, musical, touristic, monumental, ceremonial, and other media and symbolic practices of nineteenth-century public life.

So immense a phenomenon reshaped the field of British fiction publishing. Scott's high sales guaranteed standard formats for the novel for the remainder of the century, from the guinea-and-a-half, three-volume octavo sets of first editions (fixed with *Kenilworth*, 1821) to the author's uniform stereotyped edition in five-shilling monthly-issue 'small octavo' volumes (1829–33), for which Scott revised his texts and added historical notes and introductions. This, the so-called 'Magnum Opus' edition, set the pattern for reprint editions in the Victorian period (such as Bentley's *Standard Novels*) and established the revised, collected edition as the major bibliographic platform for novelists who aspired to serious literary stature (see Millgate 1987).

In addition to shaping the material form of the novel as a book, Scott's success transformed the cultural status of the novelist, investing a figure that had lurked at the margins of respectability with professional dignity, official honours, and critical prestige. Raised to the baronetcy by George IV, to whom his collected works would be dedicated, Scott was one of the nation's eminent men, cultural viceroy (in effect) of the Tory administration in Scotland, in addition to his official jobs as Sheriff-Depute of Selkirkshire and Clerk at the Edinburgh Court of Session. At the same time, he took care to separate his public roles from his identity as a novelist. Scott's experiments with the role laid out a morphology of authorship for the nineteenth century. He had entered the literary field as an antiquarian editor, curating a literary heritage (*Minstrelsy of the Scottish Border*, 1802), before recasting himself as wartime national minstrel, reviving an ancient poetic form and function for a modern public. Turning in 1814 to the unequivocally market-based genre of the novel, Scott developed the standard practice of anonymous authorship into an elaborate game played between himself and his readers. Enlivening the novels' prefaces and introductory chapters with a masquerade of avatars (the Author of 'Waverley', Jedediah Cleishbotham and Peter Pattieson, Laurence Templeton, Jonas Dryasdust, Captain Clutterbuck, and the rest), Scott presented himself to the world as a dispersed, corporate, cybernetic being, comprising the functions of editor, compiler, informant, translator, promoter, and critic, rather than as a unique creative source. Part quarrelsome crowd, part machine, this author-entity sought to command the alienation of person from function that was the basic condition of commercial literary production, by turning it too into an aspect of his own fiction-making.

In vain: Scott and his publishers came down in the financial crash of 1825–6, which revealed the secret identity of the Author of Waverley as a partner in the printing firm of Ballantyne & Co. In the wake of his ruin he reassembled himself as a fully personified figure, 'Sir Walter Scott', and devoted the last half-dozen years of his life seeking to reclaim his authorial role: formally and commercially, through the Magnum Opus edition, as well as ethically, through the honourable struggle to repay his debt rather than seek refuge in bankruptcy. Chronicling that struggle in the *Journal* he began keeping on the eve of the crash, Scott bequeathed a new figure, at once inspirational and cautionary, to the Victorian age: the author as hero.

Scott set the novelist at the centre of national life not just because he sold vast numbers of books or because he flourished amid powerful networks of Tory patronage, but, above all, because his writing renovated the form of the novel, charging it with a fresh cultural potency. 'His works (taken together) are almost like a new edition of human nature', William Hazlitt, a political opponent, paid tribute: 'This is indeed to be an author!'[1] Scott's career-turn from Last Minstrel to Great Unknown sealed the ascendancy of the novel in the nineteenth-century genre system. By 1819, as his reputation reached its zenith, reviewers could claim that the novel had taken over the epic function of representing 'the different modes of national existence . . . in modern times'.[2] Scott made the novel a modern epic form by making it national, and he made it national by making it historical. In doing so he endowed the novel with the aura of philosophical dignity attached to history, the most prestigious of the Enlightenment human sciences, especially in Scotland. The historical novel became the 'classical' form of the novel as such throughout the nineteenth century, retaining popularity and prestige well after the major Victorian novelists had absorbed Scott's techniques for a historicism trained on modern conditions. The combination of history and *Bildungsroman* inaugurated in *Waverley* would provide a model for aspiring national literatures across Continental Europe, its imperial frontiers, and its colonial (and former colonial) satellites, well into the next century.

Historical and national themes were not in themselves new to the novel. In the 'Postscript' to *Waverley* Scott paid tribute to the pioneering representation of regional manners by Maria Edgeworth, who had explored Enlightenment theories of social and moral progress in her Irish tales. Recent scholarship has drawn attention to precursors Scott did not acknowledge, and whose prior achievements his triumph would eclipse (Garside 1991, 1999; Trumpener 1997: 128–57). These include authors of Jacobin and anti-Jacobin novels, which harnessed the political debates of the 1790s to explore the relations between private and public life in an age of revolution. Two of them, Charlotte Smith's *Desmond* (1792) and Jane West's *The Loyalists* (1812), share the 'uncontaminated name', Waverley, of Scott's protagonist. Dissident practitioners of the Irish national tale, notably Sydney Owenson and Charles Robert Maturin, brought those debates to bear on the ideologically charged categories of nation and empire. Owenson's *The Wild Irish Girl* (1806) models the unionist marriage-plot developed in Edgeworth's *Ennui* (1809), broken apart in Maturin's *The Milesian Chief* (1812), and then soldered again in *Waverley*, in which

---

[1] William Hazlitt, *Lectures on English Poets and The Spirit of the Age* (London: Dent, 1967), 230.
[2] 'Thoughts on Novel Writing', *Blackwood's Edinburgh Magazine*, 4 (January 1819), 394–6.

a young English gentleman travels to the Celtic hinterland and learns to admire its culture under the sentimental tutelage of a native heiress.

As for historical fiction, its modern genealogy stretches back into late seventeenth-century France, with the form taking root in Britain in the second half of the eighteenth century and ramifying into subgenres of antiquarian and national romance in the Romantic period (Maxwell 2009; also Ferris, Chapter 16). And while the period settings of English Gothic fiction, from Horace Walpole to Ann Radcliffe, could not be called 'historical' in any scientific sense, Scott drew on their symbolic associations (with the threatening resurgence of an imperfectly superseded pre-modernity) as well as the genre's formal techniques, such as antiquarian framing, narrative involution and suspense, and a dissociation of the protagonist's agency from the plot. Most of these precursor forms were written by women, who dominated the early nineteenth-century fiction market. Indeed, the novel's association with female authors and (presumptively) female readers was routinely invoked as an index of its degraded cultural status. Scott's intervention in the field, binding fiction to history, was accordingly viewed not only as a 'philosophical' elevation of the form but as a reclamation of novel-reading, as well as novel-writing, as a properly masculine enterprise (Ferris 1991: 79–104).

History

In his major study of the genre, György Lukács argued that Scott's foundation of 'the classical form of the historical novel' owed little or nothing to literary precursors, and that the onset of new historical conditions—the opening of vistas of mass experience and popular consciousness through the French Revolution and Napoleonic Wars—made the new form of representation possible (1983: 23–5). While the scholarly recovery of prior traditions and practitioners has adjusted the first of these claims, Lukács was right to emphasize Scott's originality and its epoch-making impact—even if originality is to be characterized in terms of synthesis rather than of creation *ex nihilo*.

Scott made the novel historical: not just by setting its action in a determinate period and intermixing invented with documented characters and incidents, but by a mimetic 'inundation' of the novel's world with the dynamic, transformative currents of historical time (Maxwell 2009: 29). *Waverley* and its successors render the whole of human life—social forms, institutions, manners, morals, psychology, culture—as historically saturated, evolving, and interconnected. The novel's historical field includes the ethnographic data of daily life as well as the chronicle of public events, the lives of common folk as well as of social elites. Scott was the first European novelist to represent not just the middle ranks but the labouring poor and those on the margins of national society—vagrants, outlaws, ethnic outsiders such as Highlanders, Jews, and Gypsies—as leading their own lives, in something like their own terms, with their distinctive histories, languages, and outlooks.

His most ambitious novels, such as *The Heart of Mid-Lothian* (1818), unfold the dynamic extensions (and pleats and rifts) of an entire, variegated social world across national space and historical time. *The Heart of Mid-Lothian* follows the entwined stories of the Deans and Butler families from the aftermath of the seventeenth-century civil wars through the first half of the eighteenth century, from turbulent Edinburgh and its rural outskirts, along the Great North Road to London, and then to the edges of the West Highlands; its cast of characters includes dairy farmers, bonnet-lairds, schoolmasters, Presbyterian and Anglican ministers, lawyers and clerks, artisans, shopkeepers and innkeepers, the Duke of Argyle, Queen Caroline, and a host of smugglers, rioters, robbers, prostitutes, luna-tics, and wild and semi-civilized Highlanders. Scott bequeathed to nineteenth-century fiction a vivid polyphonic mix of languages, styles, and discourses, including popular speech, as the formal medium of this representation. The Waverley novels invigorate their reader with passages of regionally differentiated vernacular Scots, a stylized pidgin English ascribed to Highlanders, legal, criminal, religious, antiquarian, and military jar-gons, interpolated poems, songs, and swathes of scriptural quotation, and an encyclope-dic array of literary styles and genres. 'History' manifests itself to the reader through the densely sedimented, richly palimpsestic textures of Scott's prose.

Scott brings history to bear with unprecedented precision on the details of scene and char-acter. In a striking set piece—marking a critical threshold of his protagonist's adventure—the narrator of *Waverley* pauses to analyse the 'mixed and peculiar tone' of the character of the Highland chieftain Fergus Mac-Ivor, 'which could only have been acquired Sixty Years since':

> Had Fergus Mac-Ivor lived Sixty Years sooner than he did, he would, in all probability, have wanted the polished manner and knowledge of the world which he now possessed; and had he lived Sixty Years later, his ambition and love of rule would have lacked the fuel which his situation now afforded.[3]

The reflection echoes one of the early monuments of eighteenth-century Scottish histori-ography, Thomas Blackwell's *Enquiry into the Life and Writings of Homer* (1735). 'Homer had the good Fortune to see and learn the Grecian Manners, at their true Pitch and happiest Temper for Verse', Blackwell observes:

> Had he been born much sooner, he could have seen nothing but Nakedness and Barbarity: Had he come much later, he had fallen either in *Times of Peace*, when a wide and settled Polity prevailed over *Greece*; or in *General Wars*, when private Passions are buried in the common Order, and established Discipline.[4]

This dialectical relation between history and character, signally developed by David Hume in his *History of England* (1754–62), would be realized in full by Scott, who

---

[3] Walter Scott, *Waverley*, ed. P. D. Garside (Edinburgh: Edinburgh University Press, 2007), ch. 19; 98.
[4] Thomas Blackwell, *An Enquiry into the Life and Writings of Homer*, 2nd edn (London: [J. Oswald], 1736), 35.

combined the novel's amplified techniques for rendering character with the principles of Enlightenment philosophical history. According to those principles, historical events and the ethical field of character are both shaped by large-scale modes of economic and social organization, which change over time. The motor of history consists not in the rise and fall of dynasties or parties but in impersonal, irresistible tides of structural transformation: the decay of feudalism and of absolutist conceptions of sovereignty, the break-up of traditional ways of life, the long-durational onset of what could now be recognized (from the vantage point of eighteenth-century civil society) as modern conditions.

This evolutionary history provides an overarching scheme for the great series of novels of Scottish life that occupied the first phase of Scott's career as novelist, from *Waverley* through the third series of *Tales of My Landlord* (1819). Scott cast his third novel, *The Antiquary* (1816), as the capstone of a trilogy of 'fictitious narratives, intended to illustrate the manners of Scotland at three different periods. WAVERLEY embraced the age of our fathers, GUY MANNERING that of our own youth, and the ANTIQUARY refers to the last ten years of the eighteenth century.'[5] The statement encourages readers to align the novels along the developmental or progressive plot of modern national history, from the final conflict between old and new regimes in 1745 to the global crisis (the war with revolutionary France) that gave birth to the present. The 'Author of "Waverley"' would make a comeback in 1818, revisiting the historical and anthropological themes—Jacobite insurrection, the fate of the Gaelic clans—of his first novel, and rewriting its romantic plot of a poetic young Englishman's drift northwards into entanglement with outlaws, rebels, and fiery women, in *Rob Roy*. Meanwhile Scott adopted a new set of authorial avatars for the first two series of *Tales of My Landlord* (*The Black Dwarf* and *Old Mortality*, 1816; *The Heart of Mid-Lothian*, 1818). The series' masterpieces, *Old Mortality* and *The Heart of Mid-Lothian*, extend the backwards reach of national history and draw their imaginative energy from the ideological challenge posed by the Covenanters (late seventeenth-century Presbyterian radicals) to the moderate political settlement of the 1688–9 Revolution and the Act of Union: exploring the revolutionary phase of militant Presbyterianism in *Old Mortality* and its gradual, painful, but eventually successful domestication in *The Heart of Mid-Lothian*. *The Bride of Lammermoor* (1819) crowns a third set of *Tales of My Landlord*, as well as the miraculous five-year run of Scottish historical novels, with its doom-laden plot of botched courtship and reconciliation set in the unsettled period around the 1707 Act of Union, when the old world of an independent feudal Scotland has broken up but the new regime has yet to deliver a stable civil society; the novel's protagonists, calamitously askew from a progressive history, fail to anchor themselves to the past or bind themselves to a future.

---

[5] Walter Scott, *The Antiquary*, ed. David Hewitt (Edinburgh: Edinburgh University Press, 1995), 'Advertisement', [3].

Following the cue given by Scott in the 'Advertisement' to *The Antiquary*, commentators have been tempted to rearrange all the great Scottish historical novels of 1814–19 along the axis of a grand narrative of the making of modern Scotland: one which traces the country's emergence from the chaos of seventeenth-century dynastic and sectarian warfare and its gradual integration into the temperate, prosperous, depoliticized order of late eighteenth-century British civil society. Scott's novels thus disclose the past as 'the prehistory of the present', in Lukács' phrase, 'giving life to those historical, social, and human forces which, in the course of a long evolution, have made our present-day life what it is and as we experience it' (1983: 53). The past is historical because the present is; and it comes fully to bear upon the novel's reader. Civil society affords its inhabitants both cognitive detachment and moral release from the contending fanaticisms—dynastic, ethnic, sectarian—of the pre-modern era, as these become topics of critical retrospection in the print media of history and historical fiction. Scott's novels project civil society as the horizon of their reading, in that civil society provides the historical conditions for reading, and reading (in turn) reconstitutes civil society as a liberal continuum of reflection, conversation, and shared enjoyment.

Scientific practitioners of Scottish philosophical history, notably Adam Smith, Adam Ferguson, John Millar, and Lord Kames, secured this national history within a universal scheme of stadial development. In his Glasgow jurisprudence lectures, Smith argued that human societies progressed along a fixed sequence of stages based on modes of economic subsistence, from hunting through herding and farming to commerce. The last of these stages, 'commercial society', afforded the complex internal subdivisions—including the separation between civil society and politics—that constitute the socio-cultural order of modernity. Progress, while inevitable, is uneven, not just across different regions of the world but within imperial and national borders. It was no coincidence that stadial history took hold in Scotland: the commercial and university towns of Glasgow and Aberdeen were only a few hours from the Highlands, where 'a character... blending the wild virtues, the subtle policy, and unrestrained license of an American Indian, [could be found] flourishing in Scotland during the Augustan age of Queen Anne and George I', as Scott wrote in the 'Magnum' introduction to *Rob Roy*.[6]

Scotland's destiny was one of acceleration into this modern order through the Revolution settlement and Union with England. Looking back at the 1745 rising, the author of *Waverley* observes that the 'gradual influx of wealth, and extension of commerce, have since united to render the present people of Scotland a class of beings as different from their grandfathers, as the existing English are from those of Queen Elizabeth's time' ('Postscript', 363): two hundred years of social evolution compressed

---

[6] Walter Scott, *Introduction and Notes from the Magnum Opus: Waverley to A Legend of the Wars of Montrose*, ed. J. H. Alexander and others (Edinburgh: Edinburgh University Press, 2012), 216.

into two generations. The novels insist on, if (sometimes) to palliate, the violence that is the crucible of this formation. Scott follows Shakespeare (as the title page epigraph of *Waverley* announces) in making civil war the topos of historical fiction. His own modernizing move is to make the fate of cultures, more than of dynasties, at stake in the clash of regimes—and to give the losing side the bias of human interest and feeling. The difference of extinguished ways of life, rendered with an anthropological solidity and vividness, yields a world-historical pathos.

An influential recent tradition of criticism has argued that Scott's novels popularize an imperialist, unionist historiography: their evocation of regret for the vanquished clans, and for other peoples and traditions lost in the march to modernity, justifies the hard sentence of historical necessity by cloaking it in a melancholy antiquarian aestheticism. In *Waverley*, thus, the failure of the 1745 rising confirms the anachronistic character of Stuart absolutism and its 'organic' base of support, the old Perthshire gentry and Highland clans. Scott draws on stadial history to cast *Waverley's* Scottish excursion as a journey back in time, rewriting ethnological difference as historical anteriority. The novel renders clearly—and critically rather than symptomatically—the sacrificial logic that makes the archaic character of clan life, doomed to extinction, the condition of its fascination for the modern reader. The Mac-Ivors are executed for treason, while our hero survives and prospers: once Jacobitism and the clans are destroyed as political and social realities, civil society can reclaim them, sublimated into aesthetic and sentimental capital. Empire renews itself ideologically by cannibalizing primitive virtues of loyalty and bravery (Kidd 1993: 256–67; Makdisi 1998: 70–99; Buzard 2005: 81–98).

Fiction

Even as they invoke the imperial logic of stadial history, however, Scott's novels mount a resistance to it in the local experience of reading—in the felt quality of these works as historical novels, rather than as novelized histories. Contemporary readers were variously dazzled, delighted, bewildered, and annoyed by the unprecedented heterogeneity of the novels' linguistic texture: an explosion of dialects, styles, and jargons, with forms of vernacular Scots predominating in the 'Scotch novels' following *Waverley* (achieving unprecedented density and virtuosity in the *Tales of My Landlord*), and the pastiche of antique styles taking hold in *Ivanhoe* (1820) and the series of romances set in remote historical periods which followed it in the early 1820s, such as the glittering Elizabethan fantasia *Kenilworth*. Overwhelmingly in the works with pre-1700 settings, Scott mines these languages from historical, antiquarian, ethnographic, literary, and other documentary sources. These include state papers, legal charters, trial reports, memoirs, letters, travelogues, and 'secret histories', as well as the expansive archive of European literary traditions opened in the late Enlightenment: traditional Scottish lyrics and ballads, Norse heroic and French courtly love poetry, medieval chivalric romance, Chaucer, Froissart, Ariosto, Shakespeare and the lesser English dramatists, Dryden and Swift, Spanish and French picaresque novelists, Robert Fergusson, 'Ossian', Schiller, and Wordsworth.

Spilling across the narrative, unsettling any sense of the novel as the transcription of a single voice, this impasto of literary citation is more miscellaneous and dynamic than anything found in earlier British fiction (such as the quotations and epigraphs from Shakespeare, Milton, and Collins that punctuate Radcliffe's Gothic romances). And it does more than buttress the novel's newly won classical gravity, although it surely does that. The twin epigraphs to the *Tales of My Landlord* series, from Robert Burns's 'On the late Captain Grose's peregrinations thro' Scotland' and from *Don Quixote*, signal what Scott is up to: adjusting the default setting for the tradition in which he is writing, the English novel, within a larger European frame of 'international literary space', and at the same time injecting the Scottish poet's satirical reply to an English antiquary (the ethnographic subject writes back) to hybridize that tradition from within. Far from rehearsing his work's assimilation to an English master-tradition, Scott restructures 'English' around local and cosmopolitan poles. The novel becomes fully British—transcending English—by being at once Scottish and international (see Crawford 1992).

The novel's mixed stylistic textures not only serve a mimetic purpose, rendering a historical and regional diversity of human communities, which it curates as though in a print museum. Through them, also, the novel enacts a powerfully reflexive turn upon its own conditions and operations. The insistence of literary citation urges upon the reader a continuous awareness of the novel itself as both formal medium and historical object. In *Waverley*, this citational insistence works together with the novel's combination of narratives of national history and *Bildungsroman* to produce a third narrative layer, that of a literary history of which the novel itself and our act of reading are the products. The early chapters associate the undisciplined growth of Waverley's imagination with 'romance', a mode of reading (rather than a canon of texts) attuned to a scene's aesthetic atmosphere at the expense of its historical meaning. As the story proceeds, the pattern of citations trains the reader, alert to the hero's foible, to interpret romance historically. Thus, the aura of Macpherson's *Ossian*—a factitious translation posing as an ancestral heroic revival—fatally compromises Flora Mac-Ivor's performance of 'Highland minstrelsy' at the end of the first volume, while Waverley's involvement in the 1745 rising is persistently associated with the Italian Renaissance courtly romances of Boiardo, Ariosto, and Tasso—works that, even as they narrate a series of enchanted distractions from epic ambition, are themselves debased (if enchanting) modern substitutes for epic. The Jacobite adventure, in short, is no authentic epic—reclaiming a national destiny—but a glamorous delusion investing the outworn politics of Catholic absolutism. The veteran Jacobite, the Baron of Bradwardine, sounds the only remaining genuine epic note; his quotations from Virgil (*'Fuimus Troes*—and there's the end of an auld sang', ch. 65; 323) recall a vanishing Scottish Tory humanist tradition in the elegiac conditions of defeat and exile.

In a much commented-on scene late in *Waverley*, the narrator subjects the hero to a disciplinary renunciation of romance: 'he felt himself entitled to say firmly, though perhaps with a sigh, that the romance of his life was ended, and that its real history had now commenced' (ch. 60; 301). History, the genre of experience, would appear to have conquered romance, the genre of illusion. That is not what happens in the novel, however, which resumes the protocols of romance to reward Waverley with an improbable exemption from historical causality and with a conventional comic finale, even as it keeps open an ironical and critical distance between his progress and our reading of it. Not 'real history' but historical fiction, in short, maintains its privilege as the modern heir of both epic and romance. Scott's narrator alternately dons the masks of historian and novelist—the latter making swaggering intrusions into his tale:

> I...hold it the most useful quality of my pen, that it can speedily change from grave to gay, and from description and dialogue to narrative and character. So that if my quill displays no other properties of its mother-goose than her mutability, truly I shall be well pleased; and I conceive that you, my worthy friend [the reader], will have no occasion for discontent. (ch. 19; 97)

Dispensing with the apologetics of earlier practitioners, the Author of *Waverley* revels in the mixed, inconstant, 'wavering' character of his art. What was a liability in his hero is in him virtuosity.

It is the double valence of fiction and history, the dialectical bond between them, that constitutes Scott's originality—his unprecedented, indeed unmatched achievement in the history of the novel. Far from sinking one term in the other, the combination releases the full potential of both. The century that followed would be the high epoch of the novel in Great Britain and Europe as well as the high epoch of historiography. Scott's novels historicize not just their mimetic content—scene, event, character—but their own production and our reading of them; and in doing so they affirm the work of fiction as the medium of that historical cognition. Once again, Scott realizes Scottish Enlightenment philosophical principles, this time the account of the imagination's role in the formation of knowledge developed by David Hume. His *History of England* provided the model of a 'Moderate' historiography, with its national narrative of Whig progress tempered by Tory sentiment and its aesthetics of 'historical distance' (Phillips 2000: 34–7). Hume's *Treatise of Human Nature* (1739–40) dissolves the metaphysical foundations of reality (relations of continuity in space and time, of cause and effect) and covers the resulting 'abyss of scepticism' with a sentimental commitment to 'common life', everyday social intercourse, which the philosopher and his readers may intermittently recognize as an imaginary construction of reality ratified by custom. Our acceptance of reality is in the strict sense a work of fiction, not one entertained solely (quixotically) by our selves but sustained and reproduced by social consensus.

Waverley, in these terms, narrates not only the emergence of modern civil society through the final defeat of an ancient regime, and the moral and literary analogues of this progress, but a Humean dialectic of Enlightenment in the movement from metaphysical illusion through melancholy disenchantment ('the romance of his life was over') to an at once sentimental and ironical reattachment to common life. Reflexively insistent on their fictional status, Scott's novels activate scepticism rather than belief as the mode of their readers' (although not necessarily their protagonists') relation to history, which includes, in the logic of metafictional reflection, the reader's own historical situation. After Hume, Scott makes fiction the technique of a liberal ideology—one that stakes its modernity on the claim of having superseded primitive modes of ideological identification (superstition, fanaticism) through a capacity for critical detachment and reflection on its own conditions. Double consciousness, not false consciousness, is the novel's gift to its reader.

The 'Waverley Novels'

At its close *Waverley* strikes a precarious equipoise, comic yet melancholic, between the imperatives of history and romance. That equipoise is unsettled in the novels that follow, as they play experimentally with different centres of literary gravity. *Guy Mannering* is set (mainly) in the early 1780s, at the height of the Scottish Enlightenment and Scotland's integration into the globalizing circuits of empire; focused on the wild Galloway coast, the plot ranges across a succession of other, archetypally 'Romantic' sites—India, the Lake District, the Scottish Border, Edinburgh. Weaving these settings into the greater cosmos of *Guy Mannering*, Scott establishes a template for the modern conception of romance (theorized by twentieth-century critics such as Northrop Frye) as a universal, immemorial genre, repairing the gaps of world space and historical time (Duncan 1992: 113–35). In *The Antiquary*, conversely, Scott sets going a hyper-intricate machinery of plot in order to suspend it: creating a kind of meta-Waverley novel, an allusive meditation on the sources and contexts of his art, in which nothing happens—or rather, sensational events (manslaughter, infanticide, incest, a discovery of buried treasure, a French invasion, the defeat of a Roman invasion, the creation of an epic poem) turn out not to have happened. The dense narrative accretion of non-eventfulness bears an apotropaic force, meant to ward off the era's great historical event, its true epic theme—Jacobin revolution—from national life. Here Scott's insistence on his work's fictional character exuberantly realizes the logic of a Humean 'moderate scepticism' at the service of things as they are.

In contrast Scott's next full-length novel, *Old Mortality*, undertakes his most rigorous commitment of the work of fiction to the logic of historical causality. The novel discloses that logic as providential in the scale of national destiny (issuing in the 'Glorious Revolution') but fatal for the characters on the ground: the novel's embattled protagonist, Henry Morton, finds himself inhabiting what Ina Ferris (2009a) has called 'the time of the remnant', spectrally adrift from the official chronology of a progressive history. Set in the abyss of civil war, *Old Mortality* tracks the radicalization of a regional insurgency towards the apocalyptic horizon of revolution. After a succession of crises, shocks, and reversals, the final chapter flashes forward to the present day and the scene of reading. Dressmaker Miss Martha Buskbody, connoisseur of 'the whole stock of three circulating libraries in Gandercleuch and the next two market-towns',[7] persuades the editor of *Tales of My Landlord* to redact his story according to novelistic convention. Scott's Romantic irony erects a protective barrier between our banal, pacified present and the late-seventeenth-century escalation of rival fanaticisms.

Old Mortality develops the core relation of character to historical action explored in *Waverley*, in which a 'mediocre' hero is caught between opposing sides in a civil war. The explicitly thematic reprisal of *Waverley* in *Rob Roy* more thoroughly disrupts the relation between the narrative logics of romance and history. Balancing the official protagonist's passive relation to historical action, the titular outlaw's foothold outside the linear time of history grants him reservoirs of preternatural strength. Exerting occult control over the plot, Rob Roy embodies a primitive vitality that will not fade away into the past (like the Jacobite nobles) but shadows the modern imperial order: the wild Highlander as secret sharer of 'economic man'. In a notable experiment, Scott gives the story to the first-person narration of the 'Waverley hero', Frank Osbaldistone, whose weakness as an agent is matched by his weakness as a narrator, continuously interrupted by other speakers, wiser or wittier or simply more talkative than he, and failing to control the meaning of his story even in half a century's retrospect (see Millgate 1985: 149–50). Scott's experiment reflects on the instability of the impersonal narrative elsewhere in the novels, prone to slippages among its various editorial and authorial personae, citationally and stylistically yielding to other discourses, even on occasions losing its grip over key events and crises—such as this spectacular formal implosion in *The Bride of Lammermoor*:

> I have myself seen the fatal deed, and in the distinct characters in which the name of Lucy Ashton is traced on each page, there is only a very slight tremulous irregularity, indicating her state of mind at the time of the subscription. But the last signature is incomplete, defaced, and blotted; for, while her hand was employed in tracing it, the hasty tramp of a horse was heard at the gate, succeeded by a step in the outer gallery, and a voice, which, in a commanding tone, bore down the opposition of the menials—the pen dropped from Lucy's fingers, as she exclaimed with a faint shriek—'He is come—he is come!'[8]

The narrator wrenches us out of the scene, to index its historical source, an original act of writing, only to fall back under the story's deadly momentum—in which, as ever, the

---

[7] Walter Scott, *The Tale of Old Mortality*, ed. Douglas S. Mack (Edinburgh: Edinburgh University Press, 1993), 'Conclusion', 349.

[8] Walter Scott, *The Bride of Lammermoor*, ed. J. H. Alexander (Edinburgh: Edinburgh University Press, 1995), ch. 32; 246.

hero arrives too late. The mutability of the author's pen, celebrated for its comic prowess in *Waverley*, yields a peculiarly modern, ironized, hollowed-out form of tragedy.

After the third series of *Tales of My Landlord*, comprising *The Bride of Lammermoor* and *A Legend of Montrose*, the appearance at the end of 1819 of *Ivanhoe*, a romance of the medieval English greenwood, marked a deliberate turning point in the Author of Waverley's career. The novels that follow shift their historical settings from later seventeenth- and eighteenth-century Scotland to more remote periods and/or locations: the Scottish Borders at the time of the Reformation, in *The Monastery* (1820) and *The Abbot* (1820); Elizabethan, Jacobean, and Civil War-era England, in *Kenilworth*, *The Fortunes of Nigel* (1822), and *Woodstock* (1826); France and Switzerland in the age of Louis XI, in *Quentin Durward* (1823) and *Anne of Geierstein* (1829); India during the Mysore Wars, in 'The Surgeon's Daughter' (1827); the Welsh marches, Palestine, and Constantinople during the Crusades, in *The Betrothed*, *The Talisman* (both 1825), and *Count Robert of Paris* (1832). This shift is sometimes characterized as an abandonment of the historical realism of the Scottish novels, sustained by an organic continuity with a recent, local past (a 'prehistory of the present'), for a more blatant reliance on 'romance', fictional conventions, and formulae, bolstered with antiquarian data gleaned from books. *Ivanhoe* is the first of the Waverley novels to call itself (in the subtitle) 'A Romance'; in the 'Dedicatory Epistle' Scott's avatar, Laurence Templeton, reflects on the vastly enlarged historical distance that separates the English author from national antiquity, and the corresponding absence of a connective tissue of historical memory.

Scott however turns this absence to account, filling it with brilliant invention: *Ivanhoe* is one of his strongest works and arguably the most consequential of all of them for the century that followed, giving the modern public its vision of the Middle Ages as well as the English their story of national origins. The dynamic, critical impetus of the Scottish author's address to English national formation has only recently begun to attract critical attention. *Ivanhoe* discloses a mélange of colonizing, colonized, and otherwise alien tribes, castes, creeds, and races in the place of an 'organic' England. The novel vexes the national promise of Saxon–Norman reconciliation, extended in the closing chapters, at various levels: in the prominence it awards the Jewess Rebecca, the tale's authentic bearer of Christian and chivalric virtues despite (or rather because of) her gender and her adherence to her faith, whose exile diminishes the English future from which she is shut out; and in its invocation of the historical record against its comic resolution, reminding readers that King Richard (exhibiting 'the brilliant, but useless character, of a knight of romance') will once again abandon his country and waste himself in the Crusades. Romance carries a creative, critical, and expansive rather than residual force in Scott's fiction; it is the medium that shapes the data of history, tradition, and invention into a collective story, into national myth; and *Ivanhoe* offers a resplendent demonstration of that shaping.

Rivals

Scott's triumph boosted the expansion of the British fiction industry in the decade after Waterloo. Still more decisively, it drove a belated Scottish rise of the novel, in which national rivals as well as imitators flourished. The proportion of British fiction titles produced in Scotland had risen from 0.5 per cent in the first decade of the nineteenth century to around 4.5 per cent by the early 1810s; after *Waverley* it increased threefold, reaching 15 per cent (fifty-four out of 359 titles) in the peak years of 1822–5 (Garside 2000: 76, 89–90; Garside et al. 2004). Scott's popularity, fame, and prestige made him an inescapable presence in the Scottish literary field, a centre of gravity that shaped the aspirations and careers of other authors. The most significant Scottish novelists before *Waverley* were women, who developed a moralized domestic variant of the Irish national tale: Elizabeth Hamilton, Mary Brunton, Christian Isobel Johnstone, and Susan Ferrier (who began writing *Marriage* in 1810, although it was not published until 1818). This female-authored tradition petered out after 1815, effectively displaced by the historical novel (and discouraged too, no doubt, by the militantly masculine character of the ascendant reviewing culture), although Johnstone's later novel *Elizabeth de Bruce* (1827) marshals a later, more critical strain of the Irish national tale to disrupt the Scottish fictionalizing of national history. Some of the Scottish novelists in Scott's shadow were little more than mechanical imitators (e.g., Thomas Dick Lauder, whose *Lochandhu* (1825) and *The Wolfe of Badenoch* (1827) were among the few non-Scott novel titles published by Constable and his successor, Robert Cadell). Others however defined their practice in opposition to Scott's, forging alternative ideological and aesthetic principles upon which to base their originality, even as they drew upon his achievement.

The post-war surge of Scottish fiction rode a larger swell of Edinburgh-based publishing, the basis of the city's brilliant literary ascendancy (rivalling London) between the founding of *The Edinburgh Review* in 1802 and Scott's death thirty years later. One of the great centres of the eighteenth-century Enlightenment, Edinburgh played a leading role in the general expansion of print production and formal innovation that constituted the literary field of European Romanticism after 1800. Edinburgh booksellers, beginning with Constable, reoriented Scottish literary production from the curricular genres of the Enlightenment human and natural sciences to the commercial genres that would dominate nineteenth-century publishing, giving them their definitive forms and associations: periodicals, including the quarterly review (the *Edinburgh*) and monthly and weekly magazines (*Blackwood's Edinburgh Magazine*, 1817; *Chambers's Edinburgh Journal*, 1832); popular poetry, including the national ballad anthology and ballad-based metrical romance; and prose fiction, including the magazine tale and fictional memoir as well as the historical novel.

The Edinburgh periodicals were arguably the most consequential of these new formations, since they took it upon themselves to regulate the literary market, evaluating its products and defining the terms in which they were judged. The Scottish rise of the novel was closely enmeshed with them. Scott's publisher Constable was the proprietor of the *Edinburgh Review* (and Scott himself an early contributor); Scott's synthesis of romance with philosophical history and his professionalization of anonymous authorship charged his novels with the rhetoric of 'literary authority' fashioned by the *Edinburgh* in its campaign to relocate the intellectual projects of Enlightenment in the industrial print market (Ferris 1991: 19–59). In the post-war decade William Blackwood emerged as Constable's chief Edinburgh rival, politically as well as commercially (founding *Blackwood's Edinburgh Magazine* as a Tory counterblast to Constable's Whig periodicals). Blackwood briefly acquired Scott in 1816, when he published the first series of *Tales of My Landlord*; after Scott went back to Constable, Blackwood set himself up as the main broker of Scottish fiction not written by Scott. Blackwood's stable of authors, which included John Galt, James Hogg, Susan Ferrier, John Gibson Lockhart, John Wilson, and D. M. Moir, comprised a distinctive corporate profile of self-consciously 'national' fiction, variously comic, sentimental, and sensational, focused on regional and provincial manners. All these authors (except Ferrier) were contributors to *Blackwood's Magazine*, which became the leading forum for experiment and innovation in non-novelistic prose fiction by the 1820s, not only in Scotland but throughout the English-speaking world.

The miscellaneous format of *Blackwood's*, scrambling the codes of genre and mixing fictional and non-fictional articles, incubated the modern short story as well as more volatile forms of anecdote, sketch, serial, fictitious memoir, and satirical symposium (the famous 'Noctes Ambrosianae'). The most original of the Blackwood authors, Hogg and Galt, made these non-novelistic forms the basis for their own experiments in national and historical fiction. After a series of attempts at book-based genres (biography, travelogue, drama, the novel), Galt enjoyed a breakout success with a *Blackwood's* serial, part epistolary fiction and part topical travelogue, 'The Ayrshire Legatees' (1820–1), which he followed up with a sequel, 'The Steam-Boat' (1821–2), and a pair of fictional memoirs, *Annals of the Parish* (1821) and *The Provost* (1822) (published in single volumes rather than as serials). Impelled by Scott's success, Galt went on to write a series of three-volume novels, two of which, *The Entail* and *Ringan Gilhaize* (both 1823), challenge the aesthetic hegemony of the Waverley novels with their radically different approaches to the fictionalization of Scottish history.

Meanwhile Hogg, who had produced tales and sketches for his own weekly miscellany *The Spy* in 1810–11, contributed short fiction to *Blackwood's* from its inception ('Tales and Anecdotes of Pastoral Life', 1817) through the mid-1820s ('The Shepherd's Calendar', 1823–5). A two-volume set of his 'cottage tales', *The Brownie of Bodsbeck*, along with Ferrier's three-volume satirical national tale *Marriage*, marked Blackwood's effective debut as a publisher of book-length Scottish fiction in 1818. The titular novella in *The Brownie of Bodsbeck* takes on the same historical topic—the late seventeenth-century persecution of the Covenanters—as Scott's *Old Mortality*, published two years earlier. *The Brownie* did not do very well, in sales or critical reception; another two-volume collection, *Winter*

Evening Tales (1820), fared better. Once again, the precedent of Scott's success proved irresistible (complicated in this case by the personal friendship between the two authors), and Hogg resumed his reckoning with the national historical novel in a series of ambitious experimental fictions: *The Three Perils of Man: War, Women, and Witchcraft* (1822), a medieval 'Border Romance'; *The Three Perils of Woman: Love, Leasing, and Jealousy* (1823), an interlinked 'Series of Domestic Scottish Tales'; and his acknowledged masterpiece, *The Private Memoirs and Confessions of a Justified Sinner* (1824).

Scott's predominance ensured that *The Brownie of Bodsbeck* was received as a response to *Old Mortality*, although Hogg claimed (plausibly) he had written it earlier. With *Old Mortality* Scott's fictionalization of national history became controversial, as his treatment of militant Presbyterianism, a source of the modern Scottish tradition of popular democratic politics, proved far more divisive than his treatment of Jacobitism. Radical and evangelical reviewers rejected the novel's claim on a principled Whig Moderatism, the prototypical ideology of modern civil society, struggling to be born between revolutionary and reactionary extremes. They took exception to Scott's depiction of the Covenanters, champions of Scotland's civil and religious liberties, as uncouth, murderous zealots, prototypes of Jacobin terrorists. *Old Mortality* provided an ideological flashpoint for rival projects of national historical fiction as well as for dissenting reviewers (see Ferris 1991: 37–94; Rigney 2001: 31–52). Hogg stresses the natural piety of rural communities, resistant to political mobilization, in *The Brownie of Bodsbeck*; five years later, in *Ringan Gilhaize*, Galt distinguishes the heroic epoch of the Scottish Reformation from its traumatized seventeenth-century remnant. More striking than their management of historical content are the formal strategies with which Galt and Hogg challenge the procedures of Scott's historical novel. *The Brownie of Bodsbeck* defies the retrospective, rationalizing logic of Enlightenment history, realized in a unified plot and an impersonal English narration, in favour of a simulation of irregular oral recitation in which local, rustic actors take over and tell their stories in their own words. *Ringan Gilhaize* fuses family tradition, personal memoir, and national and religious history into a virtuoso monologue through which Ringan transmits the life stories of his grandfather, his father, and himself, and with them the spiritual legacy of the Reformation. Ringan's narration renounces Humean tenets of fictionality for a story that rests on the strong term of belief, faith: keystone of a historical agency that suffers a tragic fall from revolutionary collectivism, as the story unfolds, to a survivor's vengeful obsession.

Tales of My Landlord set the agenda for the characteristically Blackwoodian fiction that flourished in the early 1820s. Scott characterized his work as a collection of 'Tales, illustrative of ancient Scottish manners, and of the Traditions of their Respective Districts'; regional tradition, as well as the looser format of the 'tale' (see also Jarrells, Chapter 26), became the preferred media for Hogg's and Galt's experiments in historical fiction. Hogg grounded his writing in the popular traditions of the Scottish Borders, while Galt thought of his works as comprising a series of 'Tales of the West' with North Ayrshire and Clydeside settings, a topography socially and culturally distinct from Edinburgh. Together Hogg and Galt gave the miscellany-based form of the tale its most ambitious contemporary development, the first-person fictional memoir, rooted in local patterns of experience and discourse. Their characteristic works, radically divergent in other respects, promote regional dialects of vernacular Scots to the main vehicle of narration, in contrast to Scott's standard technique, which frames Scots speakers within a third-person, insistently literary English narrative.

Galt took care to distinguish his fictional experiments from Scott's, characterizing *Annals of the Parish* and *The Provost* as 'theoretical histories of society' rather than 'novels or romances', on the grounds that they lacked a 'consistent fable' or unifying plot.[9] These imaginary autobiographies of a naive rural minister and a venal small-town politician renounce the Scott model of plot-intensive romance for an alternative fictional development of Enlightenment scientific history: an annalistic, anecdotal narration of historical change, from the period of the Seven Years' War through the wars with revolutionary and Napoleonic France, as it unfolds in the micro-political domain of provincial society. Galt forges a fictional medium that registers the vibrations of an emergent political economy of world empire within the textures of local, everyday life, and within the faultlines of ordinary psychology, with unprecedented sensitivity (see Trumpener 1997: 153–6).

While these works exhibit the virtue Galt claimed as his 'originality', his most ambitious achievements are the three-volume historical novels published in 1823. No less forcefully—and more subtly—than *Ringan Gilhaize*, *The Entail* engages with the early series of *Tales of My Landlord*, this time recasting Scott's most formidable work, *The Heart of Mid-Lothian*. Like Scott's novel, Galt's (narrated by an impersonal editorial figure) brings to bear upon a multi-generational family chronicle a legal crux that lays open a general moral crisis in eighteenth-century Scottish society: here, the eponymous entail, encoding a life-denying obsession with patrimony and 'gear'. Scott's novel, while recalling the Covenanting troubles and looking ahead to the aftermath of 1745, focuses on a crisis in the lives of the Deans sisters in the late 1730s; Galt's novel extends its scope more evenly across three generations, interweaving the tragic and ironic course of family history with a continuous and subtle notation of economic and social change in and around Glasgow, Scotland's commercial metropolis, across the eighteenth century.

Galt challenges the dialectic at work in the Waverley novels with a strong development of one of its terms, empirical social history, and a rejection of the other, antiquarian romance. Hogg, in contrast, affirms the potency of vernacular storytelling in opposition to top-down teleological schemes such as that of Enlightenment stadial history. The novella-length picaresque autobiography 'Renowned Adventures of Basil Lee' (in *Winter*

---

[9] John Galt, *Literary Life and Miscellanies*, 3 vols (Edinburgh: Blackwood, 1834), 1.226; see also *The Autobiography of John Galt*, 2 vols (London: Cochrane and McCrone, 1833), 2.219–20.

Evening Tales) reproduces its miscellaneous origins (an earlier version had appeared in *The Spy*) as an internal formal principle; dispatching its feckless protagonist through pastoral misadventures in the Borders, anti-heroic exploits in the American War of Independence, ghost-hunting on the Isle of Lewis, and imbroglios in the Edinburgh marriage market, shifting the gears of genre along the way, the tale blithely flouts the gravitational imperatives of 'nation' and 'history'. Hogg's attempts at multi-volume, novel-magnitude narratives in the early 1820s retain this miscellaneous internal structuration. *The Three Perils of Man* wraps a prolix, tonally unstable historical romance (later extracted and reprinted as *The Siege of Roxburgh*) around a ferociously comic performance of proto-postmodern magic realism, in an extended adventure in the castle of the warlock Michael Scott, which devolves, in turn, into a succession of interpolated tales. The romance as a whole refutes the Enlightenment historiography that Hogg takes to be informing Scott's contemporary antiquarian fictions (*Ivanhoe, The Monastery*): far from fading into an anthropological anteriority under the rubric of 'superstition', legendary wizards and demons occupy the same world as historical barons, monks, and peasants.

Hogg takes this formal disaggregation several steps further in *The Three Perils of Woman*. Instead of a continuous, progressive narrative, the work falls into a sequence of 'Circles' which trace a chronological retrogression from love intrigues in present-day Edinburgh to misadventures set around the 1745 rising. In a disturbing reversal of the trajectory of *Waverley*, *Perils of Woman* renders the developmental path of the Scottish novel, from domestic national tale to historical romance, as a cultural, psychological, and formal meltdown. No point of repose, of final mediation or reflection, is offered the reader. The final chapters, set in the desolated Highlands after Culloden, veer recklessly between the harrowing and the ludicrous.

Limits

The Author of Waverley did not stand aloof from these rival developments. In 1824, after the procession of romances with various 'Gothic' settings, Scott returned to Scotland for a problematic experiment in the female-authored national domestic tale, *Saint Ronan's Well*, a work that modulates uneasily between satire and melodrama. Scott then reclaimed his signature form of Scottish historical novel in one of his finest works, *Redgauntlet; A Tale of the Eighteenth Century*. The historical retrospect of *Redgauntlet* comprises an anthology of eighteenth-century genres—letter, journal, folktale, popular song, Gothic romance, family chronicle, law case, criminal autobiography, stage comedy—as well as of themes and motifs from the Scottish novels of 1814–19, as Scott rewrites the plot of Jacobite rebellion enmeshed with family romance he had developed in *Waverley* and *Rob Roy*. In the summer of 1765 a last attempt at Jacobite insurrection falls apart into anticlimax and non-event, a failure to re-enter history which is confirmed in the plot's historiographic status as Scott's own fictional invention. *Redgauntlet* reaffirms—with superb virtuosity—the aesthetic of Romantic scepticism inaugurated ten years earlier in *Waverley*. This reaffirmation, mediated through the novel's insistently miscellaneous and discontinuous formal texture, rebuts the aesthetic and ideological challenge of Galt's *Ringan Gilhaize*, with its fantasy of the transmission of historical memory through an unbroken narrative voice. (Scott burlesques *Ringan Gilhaize* in the inset story of the Redgauntlet family curse; Galt returned the compliment with a burlesque of this episode, in a chapter called 'Redgauntlet', in his next novel *Rothelan*, 1824: a disappointingly listless chronicle-romance.)

Hogg's terrifying and sardonic *Private Memoirs and Confessions of a Justified Sinner*, published in the same month as *Redgauntlet* (June 1824), has also been read as a reply to Galt's fable of terrorist declension of the Covenant, as well as a critical deconstruction of the historical novel in its Scott-authored and Blackwoodian phases (Kelly 1989: 260–73; Garside 2004; Mack 2006: 69–70). The outrageous force of Hogg's work comes in part from its yoking together of incompatible strains of Romantic fiction—the Jacobin-Gothic first-person narrative of a criminalized outcast developed by William Godwin and Mary Shelley and the national historical novel of Scott. Hogg splits his tale between the contending forms of imaginary memoir, its subjective horizon intensified into psychopathic delirium, and fictitious history, curated by an enlightened but increasingly vexed and baffled modern editor. Far from resolving into a 'moderate' synthesis, antinomies and antagonisms swarm through the text, in a virulent formal as well as thematic proliferation. The tale tears itself in two between irreconcilable narrations and irreconcilable realities, while divisions and doublings splinter across the domains of psychic, familial, religious, and national life. The major public event of the period in which it is set, the Treaty of Union, is never once mentioned in this story in which union of any kind, at any level, is revealed as an impossible or annihilating condition.

Like *Redgauntlet*, *Confessions of a Justified Sinner* reflects on its status as a 'tale of the eighteenth century' ten years after *Waverley*. Where *Redgauntlet* reaffirms the Humean model of historical romance and its ideological domain, the liberal habitus of civil society, *Confessions of a Justified Sinner* opens a metaphysical abyss—the suicide's grave of the final pages—that swallows not only its wretched protagonist and uncomprehending 'Editor' but its author and reader too. (The 'James Hogg' who makes a cameo appearance as the 'Ettrick Shepherd' gruffly refuses to have anything to do with the editor's antiquarian project.) Hogg's novel proved too wild and perverse for post-Enlightenment Edinburgh, and it would not find a receptive public until the second half of the twentieth century.

Hogg retreated from novel-length to shorter, magazine-based fiction forms, less perhaps out of a failure of artistic nerve than because of the general slump in book-based literary genres that followed the 1825–6 financial crash. Those booksellers that survived the crash preferred magazine and part-issue formats for publishing new fiction, along with relaunching older titles, to the risk of expensive three-volume novels. In any event the Scottish historical novel suffered a notable decline through the late 1820s. By the time of Scott's death in 1832 the tradition was effectively extinct; Hogg, Galt, and the other Blackwood authors had reverted to miscellany-based genres, and no new talents appeared on the horizon, or if they did (Robert Chambers, Thomas Carlyle) it was to abandon fiction for other kinds of writing.

If *The Private Memoirs and Confessions of a Justified Sinner* marks one imaginative limit of Scottish Romantic historical fiction, Scott's last Crusader novel *Count Robert of Paris* marks another. Routinely dismissed as commercially driven, imaginatively exhausted productions, inferior to the great novels of Scotland's long eighteenth century, Scott's late romances await reassessment. While some (*Woodstock*, 1826; *The Fair Maid of Perth*, 1828) develop aesthetic and ideological themes already well established in Scott's writing, others strike out in new directions, with a startling experimental thrust. Both tendencies are represented in his last completed works, published as a set, the Janus-faced *Tales of My Landlord, Fourth Series* (*Count Robert of Paris* and *Castle Dangerous*, 1832). One of them, *Castle Dangerous*, looks backwards and inwards. Scott superimposes the beginnings of his career in Border minstrelsy upon its imminent dissolution, in the representation of the eponymous castle as at once an enchanted archive (haunted by the original Scottish minstrel, Thomas the Rhymer) and an obscene mass grave and rubbish dump, 'the Douglas Larder'. The author summons his own dying body onto the page, dismissing once and for all the masquerade of avatars, in a disconcerting 'Envoi'.

Count Robert of Paris, in contrast, looks forwards and outwards, to a post-national arena of world history and the disintegration of the Enlightenment idea of a universal human nature. In his prefaces to *Waverley* and *Ivanhoe* Scott had invoked that idea as the scientific basis of historical fiction: 'It is from the great book of Nature, the same through a thousand editions, whether of black letter or wire-wove and hot-pressed, that I have venturously essayed to read a chapter to the public' (*Waverley*, ch. 1; 6). *Count Robert of Paris*, more aptly characterized as a work of anthropological science fiction than a historical novel, imagines a monstrous confusion of the categories of cultural, sexual, racial, and species difference in its eleventh-century Constantinople, the decadent capital of post-classical world empire. The bizarre cast of characters includes an orang-utan, the subject of heterodox speculation on the natural history of man from Jean-Jacques Rousseau's *Discourse on the Origin of Inequality* (1755) to the *Zoological Philosophy* of Jean-Baptiste Lamarck (1809). Edinburgh had become the key British site for the reception of advanced scientific thought from the Continent, including Lamarck's transmutationist zoology, by the late 1820s. Even in his last years, ailing and distracted, Scott kept his fiction open to the intellectual currents of the age—including those that were eroding the philosophical foundation of his art.

Part III

Generic Variations and Narrative Structures

18

It-Narratives and Spy Novels

LYNN FESTA

I N the 1750s and 1760s, the taciturn world of inanimate objects stirred to life and began to speak. Coins, clockwork, coaches, garments, pens, pets, and pests, all assumed a speaking part in a series of immensely popular tales recounted from the point of view of inanimate things or animals. Cached in pockets or borne about the body, unnoticed by habit or unobtrusive in their ubiquity, the things in these novels of circulation move from battlefield to boudoir, from the Royal Exchange to the writer's garret, visiting the dens of thieves and counterfeiters and paying homage to kings. As they flit between the intimate recesses of domestic life and the public spaces of the court, the marketplace, the coffee house, and the theatre, these peripatetic narrators trace the broader patterns of circulation that structured the commercial society of eighteenth-century Britain, describing the history, private lives, and true character of the people they encounter on their travels, and delighting readers with the scandalous revelations they purvey. This popular appetite for the adventures and ruminations of coins and clothing, of lap-dogs and air-balloons was complemented by a resurgence of interest in 'spy narratives', which recorded the exploits of Europeans and exposed the follies of their customs and manners from the perspective of an invisible rambler or foreign observer. Although slighted in narratives of the rise of the novel that emphasize formal realism and psychological depth, such subgenres play a significant role in the mid-eighteenth-century history of prose fiction in their representation of the print market's response to the shifting relations between persons and things wrought by commercial expansion, social mobility, and the burgeoning imperial engagements of Great Britain at mid-century.[1]

At first glance, both tales told by things and spy narratives seem like literary oddities— at best a Grub Street whimsy or sociological curiosity. Yet the immense and enduring popularity of texts like Francis Coventry's *The History of Pompey the Little: or, The Life and Adventures of a Lap-Dog* (1751) and Eliza Haywood's *Invisible Spy* (1755), both reprinted

---

[1] See especially the essays collected in Mark Blackwell's *The Secret Life of Things* (Lewisburg: Bucknell University Press, 2007) (Blackwell 2007).

eight times before 1800, and Charles Johnstone's *Chrysal, or, The Adventures of a Guinea*, which doubled from two to four volumes between 1760 and 1765 and went through some twenty editions in the course of the century, suggests a cultural and literary influence that ought not to be lightly dismissed. Seven new book-length it-narratives and numerous short magazine pieces were published in the decade following the success of *Pompey the Little*, with a curious lull in the 1760s when few new contenders entered the ring against *Chrysal*. The uptick in it-narratives from the 1770s onward coincides with a dwindling number of picaresque and ramble narratives, as the 'Life and Adventures' of persons are supplanted by the 'Life and Adventures' of animals and things. More than a dozen new narratives of circulation were published in each of the last three decades of the eighteenth century in books and in periodicals, as journals such as the *Westminster Magazine* and the *Rambler's Magazine* sought to capitalize on the trend by serializing it-narratives across multiple issues. In addition, earlier successes were reprinted or translated throughout the period. Susan Smythies's 1753 *The Stage-Coach* saw a Dublin edition in 1754 and London reprints in 1789 and 1791, while the 1760 *Adventures of a Black Coat* had Dublin, Boston, and Edinburgh editions in 1762, 1767, and *c*.1780, respectively. *The Adventures of a Hackney Coach* was published in London and Dublin in 1781, with a second London edition in 1783, a Philadelphia edition in 1783, and a German translation in 1788. Such abundance created a glut: 'Every thing has had its adventures, from a Bank Note to a Shilling, from a Coach to a Sedan, from a Star to a Gold-headed Cane', the *Critical Review* complained in a review of *Phantoms; or The Adventures of a Gold-Headed Cane* (1783). 'This mode of conveying political censures, private scandal, or general satire, is almost exhausted; and the spirit and good sense which animated the imaginary Chrysal, was lost in the Hackney Coach, and scarcely breathe in the "Phantoms".'[2] It is perhaps due to market saturation that the speaking objects and animals increasingly addressed younger readers in the final decades of the century. Mary Ann Kilner's *The Adventures of a Pincushion* (*c*.1780) and her *Memoirs of a Peg-Top* (*c*.1790) were among the first of the didactic fictions narrated by thimbles, toys, pets, and birds marketed by publishers of juvenile fiction like Thomas Boreman, John Newbery, and John Marshall.

The period between the 1750s and the late 1780s when it-narratives and spy chronicles thrived has historically been a canonical sinkhole, interrupting the smooth narrative path that conjoins the achievement of Richardson and Fielding to Jane Austen and the nineteenth-century realist novel. In teleological accounts of the rise of the novel, prose fictions are valued principally for their formal or psychological realism: the detailed, verisimilitudinous representation of daily reality and the nuanced depiction of interiority designed to connect actions to character, binding plot to psychology. Object and spy narratives are decidedly lacking on these fronts. Their exploitation of eccentric points of

---

[2] *Critical Review*, 57 (March 1783), 234.

view challenges narratives that affiliate the rise of the novel with the emergence of the modern individual possessed of interiority and psychological particularity. More conceit than autonomous character, the principal 'personage' of these stories furnishes the thread on which the various scenes, nested stories, and digressions can be strung. 'This mode of making up a book, and styling it the Adventures of a Cat, a Dog, a Monkey, a Hackney-coach, a Louse, a Shilling, a Rupee, or—any thing else, is grown so fashionable, that few months pass which do not bring one of them under our inspection', the *Critical Review* noted in 1781. 'It is indeed a convenient method to writers of the inferior class, of emptying their common-place books, and throwing together all the farrago of public transactions, private characters, old and new stories, every thing, in short, which they can pick up, to afford a little temporary amusement to an idle reader.'[3] Understood as marketable but ephemeral novelties designed to amuse or distract, these tales simultaneously exhibit a kind of ruthless generic opportunism, a willingness to exploit any available resource to fill up a page, and display a hospitable readiness to accommodate any and all comers, so many literary strays. Their virtual disappearance from the canon stems in part from their heterogeneous form: they are a veritable grab-bag of prose genres customarily sidelined in conventional accounts of the novel, containing elements of oriental tales, picaresque narratives, political satire, secret histories, nonsense and jest books, beast fables, allegories, mythical stories of metamorphosis, and the periodical essay. As such, they deviate from the emerging critical consensus toward the end of the century that sought to consolidate the domestic, realist, and nationally-based novel over and against other, 'lesser' fictional forms.

Disdained as the money-grubbing bastard offspring of a respectable family tree, these sprawling, digressive, self-referential narratives bear a genetic resemblance to earlier forms of prose fiction. The excoriating political critique and *à clef* revelations featured in narratives such as Tobias Smollett's *The History and Adventures of an Atom* (1769) place them in a lineal descent from Swiftian prose satires and the *chroniques scandaleuses* of Delariviere Manley and Eliza Haywood, while the episodic, accumulative structure and intercalated tales proclaim the it-narratives' kinship to picaresque narrative and the oriental tale. Charles Gildon's *The Golden Spy* (1709), usually considered to be the earliest British it-narrative, explicitly signals its debt to the *Arabian Nights* in its sub-title, *British Nights Entertainments*, while the eponymous narrator of the 1753 *Travels of Mons. le Post-Chaise, Written by Himself* insists that he has 'as much Right to enquire into the Causes of Things, as any of *Aesop*'s Birds or Beasts had'.[4] Like the ramble narratives by Smollett and Edward Kimber that enjoyed a vogue during these decades (see Dickie, Chapter 5), spy chronicles and it-narratives feature wandering protagonists whose unrestrained mobility enables them to offer a picture of the differentiated ranks, occupations, identities,

---

[3] *Critical Review*, 52 (December 1781), 477–8.
[4] *The Travels of Mons. le Post-Chaise, Written by Himself* (London: J. Swan, 1753), 4.

and languages of the increasingly fragmented society of late eighteenth-century Britain. Often no narrative trajectory dictates the overall story arc; no marriage plot corrals characters into enforced sociability. Individual episodes are cut off arbitrarily when the corkscrew abruptly changes hands or the passenger descends from the coach. The serial, episodic format, with its seemingly accidental accumulation of incident and anecdote, strains conventional ideas of formal unity or even of plot coherence typically associated with the novel.

If the it-narrative seems at first glance to be the mongrel spawn of earlier prose forms—an unviable mutation subsequently winnowed out in the Darwinian evolution of the domestic realist novel—it may conversely be understood as the avatar of the experimental techniques that characterize modernity, indeed postmodernity. With their nested tales, elaborate paratextual apparatus, and frequent metafictional turns, these narratives contain the kind of reflexivity about the acts of reading and writing, the print marketplace, and the materiality of the book usually associated with Laurence Sterne's *Tristram Shandy* (1760–7) and *A Sentimental Journey* (1768). Indeed, seen in relation to these tales, Sterne's innovations in novelistic technique seem less the absolutely original products of his idiosyncratic genius than more accomplished examples of the playful but unsystematized generic experiments of the period. The narratives themselves deliberately blur the line between high and low culture, producing a kind of primitive counter-canon through allusions both to exalted predecessors (including Apuleius, Cervantes, Le Sage, Fielding, Sterne) and to Grub Street *confrères*. In turn, their reflexivity about their debased status within the literary marketplace casts in relief the emerging outlines of a canonical form of the novel.

These narratives draw heavily on the Spanish and French picaresque and quixotic traditions—Cervantes's *Don Quixote* (1605, 1615), Le Sage's *Gil Blas* (1715–35) and *Le Diable boiteux* (1707), all three freshly translated by Smollett in the late 1740s and 1750s—and libertine accounts such as those offered by Crébillon fils's *Le Sopha* (published and translated 1742; eighteen editions by 1801) and Diderot's *Les Bijoux indiscrets* (1748; English trans. 1749). Spy narratives—which include pseudo-ethnographic accounts offered from the perspective of a foreign visitor such as Oliver Goldsmith's Chinese Lien Chi Altangi in his *The Citizen of the World* (1762; serialized 1760–1)—proclaim their debts to Marana's immensely popular *Turkish Spy* (first published in French in 1684 and in English in 1687; by 1770 it was in its twenty-sixth edition) and Montesquieu's *Lettres persanes* (1721; first English trans. 1722), as well as their innumerable imitators.[5] These texts thus invite us to recognize the degree to which the British novel was bound to Continental traditions in the middle

---

[5] In addition to Haywood's *Invisible Spy* and Goldsmith's *Citizen of the World*, spy narratives include Ned Ward's *The London Spy* (1698–1700); Charles Gildon's *The Golden Spy* (1709); George Lyttelton's *Letters from a Persian in England* (1735); *The German Spy* (1738); Jean-Baptiste de Boyer, marquis d'Argens's *The Jewish Spy* (1738; English trans. 1739) and his *Chinese Letters* (1739; English translations in 1741 and

decades of the century. Even as the globe-trotting itineraries of the object-narrators—the 1785 *Aerostatic Spy*, for example, visits America, Africa, Turkey, India, Persia, and Europe—remove these narratives from the domestic and national settings increasingly given pride of place in the late-century English novel, the foreign provenance of these texts' literary precursors has helped to exclude them from the national canon and thereby from their shaping role in narratives of the novel's development.

The Vantage Point of Things

The it-narratives' experiments in perspective, their emphasis on consumer culture, their interest in the circulation of objects and persons in an increasingly complex and diversified society, all reflect the transnational flux of markets and the accelerating social and geographic mobility of populations during this period (Brewer and Porter 1994; Berg 2005). The ascendancy of these tales in a period of extraordinary commercial and military activity is unsurprising. When the Seven Years' War (1756–63)—a global conflict fought on the soil of Europe, the Americas, coastal Africa, and Asia—concluded with the defeat of the French, the British found themselves in possession of an immense empire encompassing swathes of North America, India, and the Caribbean. The years preceding the loss of the colonies in the American Revolutionary War (1775–83) were marked both by heady triumph and by a pervasive anxiety that too much had fallen into British hands too quickly. The expansion of global commerce fostered consumption on a wider scale, but also generated disquiet about the stability of individual and collective identities, as the influx of foreign goods and the appetite for novelties changed the literal and metaphorical constitution of bodies politic and personal. Thus *The Adventures of a Rupee* (1782) exalts the British Empire under King George—'Great monarch, into whatever country your free born subjects move, they shall carry in their hands both victory and law!'—while *Chiron: or, The Mental Optician* (1758) bewails the fact that the '[p]oor honest English walnut-tree, the produce of our glorious country, must now give place to every maggot of a whimsical brain, which, in obedience to the fashion of the times, he calls Chinese-work'.[6] It-narratives oscillate between the jubilant celebration of Britain's commercial prosperity and lamentations about the deleterious effects of trade on the moral and social order, pitting the sociable exchanges fostered by commerce against the rapacious self-interest inculcated by the market. In these texts, what stands as a bulwark

---

again under the title *The Chinese Spy* in 1751); Godard d'Aucour's *Mémoires turques* (1743); and Ange Goudar, *L'espion chinois* (1765; English trans. 1766).

[6] Helenus Scott, *The Adventures of a Rupee* (London: J. Murray, 1782), 231–2; *Chiron: or, The Mental Optician*, 2 vols (London: J. Robinson, 1758), 2.54.

against the disaggregation of society into isolated individuals and divisive interests is nothing but the thready insistent voice of a thing.

Unfettered by the constraints of human rank and birth, the coin, the tye-wig, and the louse travel from hand to hand (or head to head), moving fluidly up and down the social scale. Thus the eponymous narrator of *The History of a French Louse, or, The Spy of a New Species, in France and England* (French, 1779; English trans. 1779) migrates from the head of a courtesan to a parliamentary clerk, to a countess, to a washer-woman, to the queen, and thence to the notorious Mlle D'Eon, offering up-close-and-personal accounts of Benjamin Franklin's dinner conversation and the negotiations for French aid for the American Revolution. In addition to allowing the common reader to rub elbows with celebrities and aristocrats, the narratives grant a behind-the-scenes glimpse of the duplicitous practices of quacks, sharpers, merchants, and politicians. Even the unsavoury revelation in *The Adventures of a Bank-Note* (1770–1) that the secret ingredient in the pastry-cook's pie is dog does not quell the banknote's delight in its own mobility: 'Who would not be a bank note to have such a quick succession of adventures and acquaintance?' it inquires.[7]

As both instrument and embodiment of exchange, it-narrators proffer a distinctive view of the mobile commercial society of mid-century Britain. At a moment in which the division of labour and the expansion of markets extended social and economic relations beyond the immediate purview of the individual, it-narratives suggest that things possess a perspective on society not available to the individuals or groups of which it is composed. In the atomistic commercial culture of mid-century, objects alone establish bonds between otherwise dissociated individuals, making visible the material relations that conjoin and even constitute the social order. Thus the narrator of *The Adventures of an Air Balloon* [1780?] carries two musicians, a sharper, and an old servant before lifting Doctor Johnson to new heights, but these individuals have no connection to one another apart from their encounters with the narrator. Indeed, sometimes people drop out altogether, as the lady's slipper confides in the shoes, and the black coat 'whose venerable rents confest a life of business, and a length of years' offers sage moral advice to a 'gay white coat' closeted with him.[8] At times, the narratives seem a sinister anticipation of Karl Marx's commodity fetishism, in which 'the social character of men's labour appears to them as an objective character stamped upon the product of that labour' and social relations among persons take on the 'fantastic form of a relation between things' (1906: 83). Objects—above all, money—mediate all human relations in these accounts: 'a man who possesses ten thousand pounds a year', the narrator of *The Adventures of a Watch!* (1788) observes, 'cannot be a fool; for every one laughs at his jokes, feels his affronts, and sympathises with his—gold'.[9]

---

[7] Thomas Bridges, *The Adventures of a Bank-Note*, 4 vols (London: T. Davies, 1770–1), 2.25. The pie incident is at 1.163.

[8] *The Adventures of a Black Coat, As Related by Itself* (London: J. Williams, 1760), 1.

[9] *The Adventures of a Watch!* (London: G. Kearsley, 1788), 185.

The story these narratives tell involves not the ascendancy of the modern autonomous individual, but the supplanting of people by objects and systems that supersede their control. The narratives document the dwindling agency of individuals, their inability to grasp, let alone control, the systems into which they have been drawn—a revelation that flies in the face of Enlightenment theories of the social contract, of a polity willed into being through the consent of the governed, and of liberal economic principles grounded in the freedom of self-possessed and possessive individuals. Although we tend to think of society as human—it is made up of (and made up by) people—the personified object suggests that it is knitted together not by sociable relations among people but by the impersonal traffic of things. Only an individual endowed with some extraordinary prosthesis such as the preternatural looking-glass of *Chiron: or, The Mental Optician* that enables the bearer to have 'all England under my eye' (1.12) or accompanied by a Virgil-like guide to the underworld of the human heart can attain both a comprehensive purchase point on the otherwise ungraspable totality of society and detailed insight into the acts and motives of discrete individuals.

Possessed of a belt of invisibility and a wonderful tablet that magically 'receives the impression of every word that is spoken', the narrator of Eliza Haywood's *The Invisible Spy* (1755) fills out the backstories behind various salacious tales of adultery, rape, and seduction.[10] Bearing the traces of Haywood's careers as playwright, actor, journalist, and successful amatory novelist, *The Invisible Spy* is notable for its extensive use of dramatic dialogue, its topical references to current events (the passage of the Jewish Naturalization Bill in June 1753 and its repeal six months later, Lord Hardwicke's Marriage Act, the Elizabeth Canning scandal), and its incorporation of correspondence from readers in imitation of Addison and Steele's periodicals, *The Spectator* and *The Tatler*, and Haywood's own *Female Spectator*. The fact that the Invisible Spy withholds all identifying marks (including gender, although the chapter headings use the pronoun 'he') reinforces the resemblance of the spy to the anonymous Spectators male and female, although the spy's delight in the ingenious and subversive contrivances of its heroines suggests that accounts of Haywood's market-driven 'reformation' to conservative domestic moral fiction may be overstated. Like the it-narrators, Haywood's spy delights in the 'power to pluck off the mask of hypocrisy from the seeming saint;—to expose vice and folly in all their various modes and attitudes', but also endeavours to 'rescue injur'd innocence from the cruel attacks begun by envy and scandal, and propagated by prejudice and ill-nature' (1.23). Even as the spy offers withering exposés of the vices of cheating spouses, scheming society ladies, tyrannical fathers, and abusive husbands, it also cautions against too readily crediting the 'general whisper', defending women against misogynistic ridicule and

---

[10] 'Exploralibus' [Eliza Haywood], *The Invisible Spy*, 4 vols (London: T. Gardner, 1755), 1.10.

vindicating the virtue of the unjustly maligned: 'the Invisible Spy is a witness for her, that her inclinations were virtuous' (3.105).

The spy's invisibility is shared by the objects; it is because they are unobtrusive that people act such terrible scenes before them. Although the nature of the object is essential to the machinery of the text—it is because coins intrinsically circulate that they are able to tell the stories of such a diverse array of people—the things disappear, or at least our consciousness of them does. It is surprisingly easy to forget whether one is reading the story of a pin or a needle, a sedan chair or an air balloon, in part because we tend to assume that the traits associated with subjectivity—language, consciousness, thought, spirit—are immaterial. Reminders of an object's materiality surface primarily when its physical well-being is menaced or when it is misused. We recall that the narrator of the *Travels of Mons. le Post-Chaise* is a vehicle when he is dismissed from the dauphin's service for being 'too dangerous to be intrusted with the Royal Weight', a blow that 'would certainly have broke my Heart, had it been made of any Thing else but Oak' (5). Once introduced as a narrative device, the object tends to recede into the background, resurfacing at intervals like a prosy master of ceremonies to dislodge one human speaker from the stage and shuffle another one on. When granted a voice, things use it to talk about us.

And what they have to say is hardly flattering. The things loathe their owners, and can hardly wait to unmask their hypocrisy, their base motives and petty connivances, their vices and their crimes. The Waistcoat describes a lord's seduction of those who yielded themselves 'in Expectation of his Sincerity being as real inwardly as my Embroidery render'd him brilliant outwardly', while the Tye-wig laments its role in allowing charlatans to pass themselves off as professionals: 'Had nature furnish'd the inside of my master's head, as well as art by my means did the outside', the tye-wig observes of a law student, 'he by this time might have been a judge.'[11] Alternately the reluctant accomplices or innocent victims of their owner's nefarious schemes, the objects expose the gap between the exterior signs of rank and status and the 'real' value of their owners, debunking the deceptive nature of outward appearances and depressing the thrusting pretentions of social-climbing parvenus by revealing their 'true' origins. People are thus held hostage to—and by—their possessions. The chaise designed to proclaim that one has finally arrived might instead reveal one's true origins; the coin meant to confirm its owner's philanthropic bona fides might prefer to recount the dishonest ways it was acquired. The experience of reading *Chrysal*, Henry Mackenzie remarked, was 'like looking on a Collection of dry'd Serpents; one trembles at the Idea of Life in Creatures so mischievous to Man'.[12] At a moment in which access to credit and the increasing availability of luxuries

---

[11] *Memoirs and Interesting Adventures of an Embroidered Waistcoat* (London: J. Brooke, 1751), 6; 'The Genuine Memoirs and Most Surprizing Adventures of a Very Unfortunate Tye-Wig', *The Nonpareil; or, The Quintessence of Wit and Humour* (London: T. Carnan, 1757), 109.

[12] Henry Mackenzie, letter of 2 January 1771, in *Letters to Elizabeth Rose of Kilravock on Literature, Events, and People, 1768–1815*, ed. Horst W. Drescher (Edinburgh: Oliver and Boyd, 1967), 67.

to a broader body of consumers enabled members of the lower and middling classes to purchase the outward insignia of a higher social station, these narratives attest to the shifting relationship between property and personality, between what one has and who one is. In these texts, clothes *do* make the man; money *does* talk.

The narratives' interest in the way material things fabricate identity reflects the waves of Britons uprooted by agricultural enclosure and by broader economic changes, who found in the diversity and bustling anonymity of the metropolis new possibilities for self-invention but also immense risk. Both it- and spy narratives demurely promise to arm credulous country mice against the duplicitous ploys of city rats, even as they offer their readers a voyeuristic tour of the less savoury haunts of the urban underworld. In *The Midnight Spy* (1766), the street-smart Urbanus escorts the country-born Agrestis on a tour of the taverns, stews, playhouses, courtrooms, and watch-houses of the metropolis to bestow upon him the interpretive know-how necessary to avoid the traps laid for the innocent abroad. 'Surely,' exclaims Agrestis, ''tis not common for persons here to assume an appearance thus different from their characters? What! is this London world in a mask? How then are we to judge of mankind?'[13]

With their magical powers of seeing through deceptive outer appearances, the humans, animals, and things that spy upon others present the reassuring message that there is a decipherable truth to be found at the heart of each person. These narratives are committed not to a psychological exploration of the mysterious vicissitudes of the self, but to the didacticism of a crude moral progress. The bank-note and the black coat are never puzzled by the characters they encounter: they unmask hypocrisy with their immediate access to the 'truth' of the person who employs them, proffering serial portraits of characters understood as social types. The waistcoat meets Mr Threnody, a poet, Mr Blushless, a brothel-frequenting gamester, and Strutt, a coxcomb; the Corkscrew encounters the aptly named Lucy Lightaires, Mr Groveling, Captain Fearless, and Muckworm. The names of subjects in these stories are predicates; jealous people do jealous things in a tautology of character that fuses identity to act, admitting no distinction between characterological cause and effect. Nor do the objects themselves possess much personality; the central figure is more estranging device than interiorized subjectivity to be developed. There is no subjective 'surplus'—no gap between who one is and what one does—to carry the objects beyond their narrative role. Although they may, like their human counterparts, have social-climbing ambitions or a moral agenda, things never change. The coin never aspires to become a ring or a candlestick; at best, it wishes to belong to a better master.

Perversely, the personified narrator's lack of personality—the absence of character development; the fact that its point of view cannot (always) be fastened to a human

---

[13] *The Midnight Spy, or, A View of the Transactions of London and Westminster* (London: J. Cooke, 1766), 13.

analogue—constitutes one of the it-narrative's contributions to the history of the novel. For although some of the it-narrators are only able to recount the acts that they witness and the speeches they overhear, others possess the capacity to know and transcribe the thoughts and history of their owners. Thus the spirit of Johnstone's *Chrysal* possesses the 'power of entering into the hearts of the immediate possessors of our bodies, and there reading all the secrets of their lives', giving the first-person narrator the ability to enter into the consciousness of multiple third-person characters.[14] This rapid transfer between first and third person in this and other texts might, as Nicholas Hudson (2007, 2008) has argued, be understood as a fledgling version of Jane Austen's free indirect discourse and of the non-focalized or omniscient narration of the nineteenth-century novel. The literal 'objectivity' of the objects seems to promise a neutral, authoritative standpoint. Although the things prefer moral over immoral owners, the British over other nations, and high life over the low, they are ostensibly exempt from the schemes and appetites, the petty prejudices and niggling obligations of everyday life. This (presumed, tautological) objectivity licenses them to pass judgement on all ranks in a levelling appraisal of the moral qualities of king and commoner alike, as a kind of neutral touchstone for national identity and a vantage point from which the complexity and totality of society can be grasped. And the need for such a vantage point, aloof from the partial perspective of the individual, becomes even more urgent in an age of empire.

The Object Lessons of Empire

It-narratives promise to make readily intelligible a social and economic system whose growing complexity superseded immediate and easy comprehension. Once commercial networks expand beyond local transactions and systems of credit project beyond the temporal present, the capacity to grasp the workings of the world in one comprehensive glance is no longer available to the unassisted eye. At a moment in which the increasingly elaborate global networks of capital and credit had superseded straightforward relations of cause and effect—in which gold 'imp'd' by credit could, as Alexander Pope put it, pocket states and waft armies to distant shores (*Moral Essays*, Epistle 3, ll. 41–4)—the systemic causality that structures the market can no longer be understood through analogies with individual behaviour. Neither perspective nor agency can be lodged with any certitude in the individual. The personification of things in these narratives attributes to objects what might be called—what might be personified as—the will of systems: it explains the currents of global commerce through the animation of a particular object, begging the question of causes by attributing desire and autonomy to the effects.

---

[14] Charles Johnstone, *Chrysal; or, The Adventures of a Guinea*, 4 vols (London: T. Becket, 1760–5), 1.6.

Perhaps the most influential and popular it-narrative of the century, Charles Johnstone's four-volume *Chrysal, or, The Adventure of a Guinea*, offers a sprawling account of the pere-grinations of a coin from its discovery in Peru, its Atlantic crossing, and its subsequent progress through Britain and the war-torn Continent in the course of the Seven Years' War. Like other it-narrators, Chrysal recounts the stories of the people it encounters: the avaricious Traffick, the dissolute son of a virtuous British merchant; a rapacious countess and her stock-jobbing Jewish sidekick, Aminadab (but one instance of the text's pervasive anti-Semitism); William Pitt and the King of Bulgaria. The sheer length of the text—some 1,000 pages in four volumes—allows Johnstone to present a uniquely sweeping vision of the globe, drawing attention to the broader systemic forces that bind empire and metro-pole together: 'Whenever *England* is at war with any of her neighbours', Chrysal declares, 'the effects are felt to the extremities of the globe' (3.7). *Chrysal* depicts the transnational circulation of goods as a zero-sum economy, with the centripetal migration of wealth to the metropole ostensibly counterbalanced by its centrifugal diffusion through British generosity: 'if [Britain's] commerce collects the produce of every climate under heaven', the King of Bulgaria observes upon spying Chrysal in a pile of coins, 'its munificence does also diffuse its riches as far' (2.167–8). The agency of people is supplanted not only by the things, but also by abstract qualities and systems: it is 'commerce' rather than merchants and armies that 'collects produce', while 'munificence' usurps the place of individuals in the redistribution of wealth.

Despite Chrysal's celebration of Britain's imperial progress, its vision of virtuous com-merce is revealed to be more aspiration than reality. Whereas other narratives tend to depict corruption as the discrete acts of immoral characters, in *Chrysal* fraud and vice have become systemic. It is not just the individual, but also the very structures of the state, of law, of religion, and the stock market that are rotten. Thus a charitable institu-tion is condemned not merely for the hypocrisy of its individual members but because the wealth that sustains the benevolent association itself produces and perpetuates the suffering the charity is purportedly designed to relieve; peculation in the army and navy is less the product of individual venality than business as usual. Such endemic corrup-tion supersedes the agency of a single actor and is best made intelligible from the non-human perspective of the spirit of gold as the animating force underlying all. '[W]hen the mighty spirit of a large mass of gold takes possession of the human heart', Chrysal declares, 'it influences all its actions, and overpowers, or banishes, the weaker impulse of those immaterial, unessential notions called *virtues*' (1.7). In a world in which persons are animated by forces beyond themselves, the object alternately becomes an agent or marks the spot where the agency that governs the individual becomes obscure.

If it-narratives decipher the mysterious processes by which a commodity acquires value and comes to structure social relations through the biography of the familiar, known thing, they also instil or perpetuate the myth that the commodity *can* be used to decipher broader economic processes, that the engines that move the world economy *can* in fact be realigned with individual experience. Thus *The Adventures of a Silver Penny*—one of the numerous it-narratives addressed to children from the 1780s onward—dilates upon the history of an object's production in order to help its readers imagine the way their deeds affect distant populations. 'That nice silver spoon, with which you eat your milk for breakfast, and the pretty silver cup, out of which you drink your beer at dinner time, originally came from that distant place [the Peruvian mines]', the penny announces. They 'were dug out of the bowels of the earth, at the expense of the death of thousands, and the slavery of many more'.[15] The second-person address and the strategic use of the present tense call the reader to immediate account, overcoming the temporal and geographical gap separating colonial suffering from metropolitan luxury by conjoining the daily practice of drinking milk to the distant but coeval suffering of others. The familiar household object turns out to be the melancholy token of others' labours and losses, converting the silver spoon or cup into an affective touchstone able to conjure feeling and a sense of moral accountability in the reader. These texts thus participate in a sentimental literary tradition that sought to excite humanitarian sensibility through the selective recognition of other living beings as objects of sympathy.

Despite the fact that the silver penny condemns the exploitation of others, the tale's overall narrative trajectory—the penny's metamorphosis from valuable ore mined in Peru to English currency to historical artefact in the British Museum—helps to naturalize the metropolitan reader's proprietary claims over the spoils. Given particularity through its story, the penny becomes less fungible commodity to be exchanged than crafted object, gift, personal possession, object of use. The emotional investment of the reader in the object's story performs a kind of labour of appropriation, creating a bond that is, at depressingly infrequent intervals, reciprocated by the objects. When they fall into the hands of a good master, the things seek to linger there. The coat clings to its virtuous owners, while the pin laments its separation from the humane and charitable Miss Hartley: 'Never did I quit a residence with such regret, and never, alas! shall I meet such another.'[16] At such moments, personal property becomes interpersonal, as the circulating object perversely becomes the guarantor of the possibility of an absolute propriety wrought out of affection and consolidated by the virtue of the owner. As long as the proprietor is good, the object welcomes use; no shadow of resentment mars the relation of person to thing. That the watch is elated to have fallen into the hands of William Trueman, that the coin yearns to remain with the honest minister of state, creates the comforting fiction that—provided we are virtuous—our things *want* to be owned by us.

Object narratives thus produce the kind of emotional relation to things that can be found in sentimental novels such as Sterne's *A Sentimental Journey*, where stories associated

---

[15] *The Adventures of a Silver Penny* (London: E. Newbery, 1786), 10.
[16] *The Adventures of a Pin, Supposed to be Related by Himself, Herself, or Itself* (London: J. Lee, 1790), 90.

with objects or animals—a monk's snuff box, a starling, the crown Sterne's travelling parson Yorick bestows upon a servant girl—transform potentially indifferent things into the shared vehicles of a commonly held feeling and the inalienable vessels of personal history. These texts offer tutorials in intellectual and sentimental appropriation, schooling readers in the ways to make commodities into properties of the subject, personal effects in both senses of the term. In the process, they raise a set of questions about the kind of property people can take not only in things, but also in books and the figures they encounter therein. These books about commodities reflect on their own commodification, interrogating the intellectual and physical labour invested in the production of the book, the material and textual object held in the reader's hands.

Print Matters

Almost every object spends some time in the presence of a hack writer—Squire Tag-Rime, Mr Tellagain, Mr Quarto—documenting the terrible life of a Grub Street author. Once fallen into the hands of the hack-writing Mr Eitherside, the narrator of the 1806 serialized 'Adventures of a Pen' describes itself as 'at once the packhorse of the public and the slave of the press, the hireling of booksellers and the drudge of letters . . . obliged to contradict my own maxims so violently, that I was quarreling with myself, and controverting my own words, under twenty different characters at the same time'.[17] Enslaved to the will of others, Mr Eitherside is dictated to by the market in the same way that the narrating pen dictates to its amanuensis. Although the text is the product of an authorial hand, it gives objective form to thoughts and ideas that are not the author's own, making person and thing alike the (writing) implements of the print market. The human author in these narratives becomes a kind of it-narrator: a text-transcribing mechanism, a 'secretary', as the Bank-note puts it, 'or more properly . . . a machine' (1.3). Together, writer and object crank out material at a relentless pace. It is not its fault that its narrative has become sloppy, the Bank-note in his Adventures observes: 'my bookseller rather hurries me, or more properly speaking, hurries the person I inspire with my knowledge' (1.164–5). If at times it is difficult to distinguish the hack-writing described in the text from the hack-written product that is the text, it is because the it-narratives foreground the connection, flaunting their derivative nature. *The Adventures of a Watch!* is typical both in offering a catalogue of precursors ('lap-dogs, fleas, lice, bank notes, guineas, nay even Birmingham halfpence') and in its shrugging admission of unoriginality: 'why not adopt the example?' (1, 2). In their subjection to literary fashion and market demand, hack-writers become as much commodities as their ventriloquized things. These dispiriting

---

[17] 'Adventures of a Pen', *The European Magazine and London Review*, 50 (October 1806), 277–8.

accounts of alienated authorial labour cast a dim light on visions of the print market as a promoter of public culture and civic virtue.

More flea market of prose than exalted marketplace of ideas, the publishing arena into which the it-narrators enter is a fight to the death, in which the cultural aspect of storytelling is couched exclusively in terms of profit and loss, and in which the rival proprietary claims of writers, publishers, booksellers, and readers call into question how—and how much—a book or text can be claimed for one's own. Even as language is simultaneously personal and communal, and coins are simultaneously possessed and exchanged, the text is both the issue of the author's subjectivity and an object to be sold: a commodity whose value is derived from both material and immaterial qualities. These narratives thus echo contemporary debates about intellectual property, copyright, piracy, imitation, plagiarism, originality, and authorship: what rights do authors possess over their work? What kind of property does the printer, stationer, bookseller, or reader acquire upon purchasing a text? How can the ostensibly inalienable and apparently immaterial ideas of the author be converted into an alienable commodity in the form of a book? And what exactly—sentiment? language? physical copy?—is being bought and sold?

What seems to be the direct transcription of the prose of the world proves to be filtered through multiple levels of human mediation that themselves become the objects of the it-narrative's reflexive self-consciousness. The framing paratext typically offers explanatory notes from the editor and the publisher, discussions of the material form of the manuscript (often mangled or fragmentary) as well as an explanation of the circumstances under which it came to hand. Thus the preface to *Chrysal* describes at length its publisher's efforts to reconstitute the complete manuscript from the scraps used by various shops to wrap goods and foodstuffs, while the 'large parcel of paper entirely spoiled, being scribbled all over' that proves to be *The Adventures of a Cork-Screw* is retrieved from the personal effects of its recently deceased transcriber.[18] These narratives by things are themselves things in the form of printed artefacts, as much physical object as text. Indeed, in the 1779 'Adventures of a Quire of Paper', letters, newspapers, books, are almost never read. They are used (or misused) for mopping up messes, wrapping up meat, curling hair, as if the paper itself is more valuable than the authorial labour inscribed upon it. What is produced by the quire's circulation is not a reading public unified by ideas or speech, but a sequence of individuals fleetingly connected by a thing—less an imagined community of readers than an ephemeral cluster of consumers. Although the fact that *we* are reading the Quire's tale perhaps mitigates its bleak message about the possibilities of human communion, print matter in these texts often turns out to be just matter.

The texts likewise remind us of the literal as well as ideational labour involved in the production of language, ideas, text. If the author's interpellation (through direct address,

---

[18] *The Adventures of a Cork-Screw* (London: T. Bell, 1775), x.

mystical inspiration, or dream) by the narrating object often suggests that language is a gift divinely bestowed—Chrysal is *an incorporeal substance in the form of a spirit* from which a 'celestially harmonious' voice sounds (1.2–3, 1.2)—the texts also at times equip their narrators with the physical apparatus of speech. In the dream vision of a writer featured in a 1753 issue of *The Adventurer*, the half-penny 'erected itself upon its rim, and from the royal lips stamped on its surface articulately uttered the following narration'.[19] When the pen endeavours to revolt against its master's barbarous plans—the 'ink had froze with horror to the nib'—the owner 'deepen[s] the slit of my tongue' in what suggestively figures an act of human torture.[20] Rather than magically transferring the powers of a person to a non-human entity, the personified things invite us to linger over what personifications normally mystify. The move from person to thing to the rhetorical figure of the person does not erase the essential difference between person and thing by conferring the powers of the former upon the latter; it reveals the consequences of failing to recognize that difference. And that revelation proves to be an important part of the ethical project of these narratives, as they seek to expose the exploitative and dehumanizing relations not only between authors and the market, but also between masters and their human servants, apprentices, workers, and slaves.

The Thresholds of Humanity

If things take on the qualities of persons in these narratives, it is because persons have taken on the qualities of things in the world beyond the text, where the instrumental use of the bodies of labourers, servants, and soldiers converts them from man to machine, as in Chrysal's description of the efforts of injured soldiers to get 'the mangled remains of their mutilated carcasses, carried like other worn-out instruments of the war, to their respective countries' (2.119). Alternating between scolding remonstrance, baleful indictment, and woeful cry, objects decry the inhumanity of man to man—and to woman. The exchange of women as commodities in marriage and in prostitution is a staple in these narratives. The prostitute Lucy Lightaires is passed around in much the same way as the inanimate narrator of *The Adventures of a Cork-Screw*: she was, the corkscrew notes, 'at different times the property of the peer, the squire, the tradesman and others' (76). The gold ring describes the repeated sale of a maidenhead, while the Rupee encounters a young chimney sweep who has sold his teeth for transplantation to a lady of quality. His sister, a fellow-sufferer, the boy notes, finds little comfort in the fact that 'her teeth are at court, while she lives at home on slops, without any hope of a husband'.[21] The fact

---

[19] *The Adventurer*, 43 (Tuesday, 3 April 1753), in *The Adventurer*, 2 vols (London: J. Payne, 1752–4), 1.255.

[20] 'Adventures of a Pen', *The European Magazine and London Review*, 50 (July 1806), 26.

[21] 'Adventures of a Gold Ring', *The Rambler's Magazine*, 1: 3 (April 1783), 128–30; Scott, *Adventures of a Rupee*, 215.

that commercial markets overreach—that individuals are obliged to alienate not only their time and labour but also, and potentially irretrievably, aspects of themselves—suggests the precariousness of the division between the commodified object, up for sale, and the purportedly inalienable subject, not to be exchanged. In personifying things, the object narratives stage the non-correlation in eighteenth-century legal thought between 'human' and 'person', in which the category of the person includes non-human entities—offices, bridges, institutions, as well as the abstract and disembodied aggregate of corporations—but may also exclude human beings such as slaves, the poor, women under coverture. The houseless heads and unfed sides of the poor naked wretches featured in these narratives serve as reminders of the disenfranchisement of broad swathes of humanity who did not possess legal or political personality during the eighteenth century.

If the hazy threshold between persons and things is at the heart of it-narratives, the distinctions between human and animal and between animal and thing come to the fore in the tales narrated by the lapdog, the cat, the mouse, the louse, the flea. Possessed of sentience but not speech, able to move by their own locomotion and capable of suffering, animals dwell in a kind of no-man's land between person and thing. Debates about whether animals possessed souls or were mere machines were a familiar feature of the post-Cartesian landscape, and philosophical and scientific discussions in the wake of John Locke sought to pin down the evasive feature—language, reason, consciousness, laughter—that might distinguish the human from other living creatures. Although most of the narratives do not explicitly take up philosophical, scientific, and medical debates about whether matter can possess life, thought, and activity, and steer clear of the explosive religious questions regarding the materiality and immateriality of the soul, they may be understood in the context of mid-century controversies over the properties of living matter raised by Julien Offray de la Mettrie's materialist *L'Homme machine* (1748; trans. 1749) or David Hartley's associationist *Observations on Man* (1749). At a moment in which both mechanistic and vitalist philosophy threatened the eighteenth-century understanding of human distinction, the casual conferring of the capacities of speech and consciousness upon animals and things raised volatile questions that were political as well as philosophical. Jeremy Bentham's much-quoted 1789 protest against the fact that animals, like slaves, stand 'stand degraded into the class of *things*' crystallizes some of the concerns raised by the object and animal narrators about the threshold of different kinds of being: 'the question is not, Can they *reason*? nor, Can they *talk*? but, Can they *suffer*?'[22] For although not all the animals speak in these narratives—*Pompey the Little* and *The Adventures of a Cat* (1760) are both narrated in the third person—all of them, without

---

[22] Jeremy Bentham, *An Introduction to the Principle of Morals and Legislation* (London: T. Payne, 1789), 308, 309n.

exception, suffer. In the experience of these animals, the trait that best distinguishes humanity is inhumanity.

When they acquire a voice, animals use it to describe the brutality of people. The spirit that addresses the dreamer in John Hawkesworth's 'Various Transmigrations of a Flea' (1752) recounts its metempsychosis from tortured puppy (as pet) to blinded bullfinch (as songbird) to impaled beetle (as toy) to worm (as fishing bait) to lobster (as food). Each incarnation betrays the cruelty that characterizes—or rather gratui-tously supersedes—humanity's instrumental usage of all creation; the story concludes when the author crushes the flea that proves to have been its narrator. When trapped with his brothers by two young boys, the narrator of Dorothy Kilner's *The Life and Perambulation of a Mouse* (*c*.1785) describes how '[o]ur little hearts now beat quick with fear of those tortures we expected to receive'.[23] The sustained ventriloquism of an animal's viewpoint is ostensibly designed to foster sympathetic identification with the plight of another, instructing juvenile readers in the rudiments of humane behaviour in an effort to reconcile the interests of mice and men. More often it exposes the casual cruelty of the workaday world, the imperviousness of humans to emendation. The narratives' sustained engagement with the opacity of others yields neither sympathy nor understanding.

Although animals are frequently beaten, maimed, or killed in these tales, they also serve as the satiric lash. The dog's life in Coventry's *Pompey the Little* appertains to the degraded humans as much as to the canine hero, as the bestial aspect of humanity is held up for ridicule and lament. Pompey the Little's behaviour is simultaneously a mocking echo of human comportment ('he quickly became a great Admirer of Mr. *Garrick*'s acting at the Play-house, grew extremely fond of Masquerades, passed his Judgment on Operas') and superior to it (the editor marvels that having 'lived near two Years with a Lady of Quality...his Morals were not entirely corrupted'[24]). Alternately satiric observer and parodic shadow, the lapdog is both a diminutive copy of his owners and a mirror held up to the culture that passes for nature, inviting self-reflexivity and social critique through a defamiliarizing (cross-species) perspective on the world.

The anthropomorphizing aspect of these narratives does not necessarily yield an anthropocentric point of view. 'The Mysteries' revealed by the narrating guinea coin in Gildon's *Golden Spy*, the narrator notes, 'are not to be expos'd to unhallow'd Eyes, for fear the Sense of Things should destroy all confidance betwixt Man and Man, and so put an end to Humane Society'.[25] To steep oneself, however provisionally, in 'the Sense of

[23] Dorothy Kilner, *The Life and Perambulation of a Mouse*, 2 vols (London: John Marshall, [1790?]), 1.42.
[24] Francis Coventry, *The History of Pompey the Little: or, the Life and Adventures of a Lap-Dog* (London: M. Cooper, 1751), 52, 270.
[25] Charles Gildon, *The Golden Spy: or, A Political Journal of the British Nights Entertainments* (London: J. Woodward, 1709), 116.

Things'—to glimpse the perspective of the object—is to relinquish the grid that social-izes the world, to court the dissolution of one's place at its centre. The fanciful delights of imaginatively steeping oneself in a radically 'other' perspective may also slip over into an ontologically perilous cultivation of an alien perspective—the non-social, non-human, antagonistic view harboured within the animal or the thing. In these texts, things and animals acquire the human capacity for speech in order to speak for—and against—a humanity that cannot, or perhaps will not, speak for itself.

19

Philosophical and Oriental Tales

ROS BALLASTER

To the mind, as to the eye, it is difficult to compare with exactness objects vast in their extent, and various in their parts. When we see or conceive the whole at once we readily note the discriminations and decide the preference; but of two systems, of which neither can be surveyed by any human being in its full compass of magnitude and multiplicity of complication, where is the wonder, that judging of the whole by parts, I am alternately affected by one and the other as either presses on my memory or fancy? We differ from ourselves just as we differ from each other, when we only see part of the question, as in the multifarious relations of politicks and morality: but when we perceive the whole at once, as in numerical computations, all agree in one judgement, and none ever varies his opinion.[1]

So speaks Nekayah, the princess of Abissinia, who in Samuel Johnson's *The Prince of Abissinia* [*Rasselas*] (1759) has joined her brother Rasselas in escaping from the unchanging retirement of the happy valley in which they have been raised in order to discover how to live. On their arrival in Cairo, the pair divide the task between them, preferring to confer with each other because the scepticism of the wise genius Imlac, who has travelled with them, tends to dampen their enthusiasm. Rasselas investigates the courts, while Nekayah examines life among the humbler inhabitants. He points out Nekayah's inconsistency in interpreting her observations: in one instance she concludes that celibacy is worse than marriage, in another that marriage is a bleaker prospect (67–8). Nekayah's response alerts the reader to the difficulty at the heart of the 'philosophical tale', a difficulty with which these protagonists consistently wrestle: that the attempt to draw general (philosophical) conclusions from observable incidents rendered in (aesthetic) narrative form leads to logical inconsistency. Far from building up a composite picture of life's opportunities, Rasselas and Nekayah find themselves drawing alternating and often contradictory conclusions about where pleasure and fulfilment may lie.

This is the challenge of the linked and overlapping modes of the philosophical and oriental tale (set in Abyssinia and Egypt, *Rasselas* is, after all, both). The reader approaches these modes in expectation that they will explicate a philosophical (whether moral,

[1] Samuel Johnson, *The History of Rasselas, Prince of Abissinia*, ed. J. P. Hardy (Oxford: Oxford University Press, 1988), ch. 28; 68.

political, or religious) viewpoint. But the vehicle (narrative) of this explication seems resistant to the tenor (philosophical meaning). Individual stories demonstrate particularity, peculiarity, indeed eccentricity, rather than generality. While fiction seems a method to convey a general truth, the attraction of narrative lies in the errant pressure of 'memory or fancy' (as Nekayah identifies). While an oriental setting might appear to provide the opportunity to reveal the universality of human nature, it all too often promotes curiosity about alterity and strangeness. Antoine Galland's composite 'translation' of a Syrian medieval manuscript and oral tales, the *Mille et Une Nuits* (1704–17), translated from the French as *Arabian Nights Entertainments*, had already made apparent this paradox at the heart of the myth that stories can reform and educate their auditors. The sultan Schahriar is not educated by the content of Scheherazade's stories, but rather kept waiting for the next instalment. There is no causal connection between his decision to defer and eventually cancel his sentence of execution on each new wife, and the nature of the stories Scheherazade tells. Indeed, the teller must take care to hide the didactic elements of the story, in case the despot takes offence; speaking truth to power *requires* subterfuge, the substitution of a fiction for an evident truth. Nevertheless, Schahriar seems a particularly obtuse auditor who cannot see the connection between the many tales that advocate deferred judgement and reveal the dangerous consequences of overly swift or absolute interpretation; he proves addicted to the experience of hearing a story and the pleasure of seriality itself rather than a discerning consumer of content. The philosophical-oriental tales of the later eighteenth century, still profoundly influenced by the ever expanding and changing sequence of the *Entertainments* and its imitators, often appear to be more concerned to please their readers through the rapid substitution of one extraordinary narrative incident with another than communicating a persuasive truth.

The only reliable 'cure' offered by the eighteenth-century philosophical and oriental tale to the kind of individual eccentricity that often results in the indulgence of personal vice and political despotism lies in the experience of community itself: the individual finding himself in a loving community, the story finding itself placed among equally eccentric tales. This is most clearly demonstrated in the recovery of the astronomer befriended by Rasselas's group. Forty years of solitary communion with the stars has led him to believe that he has power over the weather. Months of gentle companionship, especially from the women of the company, bring him to recognize his delusive association of ideas.

But the sum of parts does not form a conclusive whole. *Rasselas* and Voltaire's *Candide* (1759) both conclude not with a philosophical truth but with a retreat into an uneasy and temporary concord of individuals. Thus Candide instructs a ragtag collection of individuals on a Turkish farm (including his old tutor Pangloss, and Candide's once lovely and now ugly and bad-tempered mistress Cunégonde and her elderly serving-woman) to 'take care of our garden';[2] Rasselas, Nekayah, and the latter's maid, Pekuah, determine

---

[2] Voltaire, François Marie Arouet de, *Candid: or, All for the Best* (London: J. Nourse, 1759), 132. Cunégonde is named as Cunegund in this first English translation.

that their ambitions are unattainable fantasies of power and decide to retire to the happy valley once more in the company of Imlac and the astronomer.

The philosophical fictions of the second half of the eighteenth century did not just identify a conflict between a philosophic and an aesthetic purpose in the treatment of the synecdoche of part to whole; they also made visible a tension within philosophy itself. This tension resulted from the increasing investment in natural philosophy and empirical investigation, which came to challenge the humanist assumption of design (that parts in a sequence are designed to produce an order derived from a divine system). As Michael B. Prince helpfully summarizes:

> [D]esign was as influential in its eclipse as in its preservation. Design is a hypothesis about order. It assumes the creation of a set that includes or at least accounts for all things. But it is manifestly impossible to include all things in a set, since sets work through a dialectic of inclusion and exclusion. (2005: 402)

The irresolute conclusions of temporary concord rather than eternal unity propounded by philosophical tales are themselves philosophical conclusions, which demonstrate the kind of empirically based sceptical enquiry advocated by the most influential philosophers and moralists of the period: John Locke, Joseph Addison, David Hume. The only critic yet to have provided a book-length study of the philosophical tale, Frederick Keener, presents this conclusion with great clarity:

> In the end the tales are unending, emphasising throughout and afterward the fallacies of mindless idealization, disseminating doubts about the allure of the romantic and novelistic, single-minded ideal, going about the business of promoting inner and outer concords when practicable. (1983: 41)

This chapter provides a historical account of developments in the philosophical and oriental tale after the moment of the extraordinary synergy of *Rasselas* and *Candide*, which both appeared in early 1759. (The simultaneous publication on 22 February of a print run of 2,000 distributed from Voltaire's printers in Geneva to five European cities, including London, was carefully orchestrated in anticipation of the swift censorship from Paris that followed: see Pearson (1993: 111). Johnson's *Rasselas* was published in London in April 1759 having been composed in January of that year swiftly in order to earn money from his printer William Strahan to defray the cost of Johnson's mother's funeral.) *Rasselas* and *Candide* take both the philosophical and oriental strands in eighteenth-century fiction in new directions before we see a mutual decline in the early nineteenth century, when they are displaced by more 'national' modes of the novel. The burden of the present argument is not that these modes are forms of resistance to the novel's rise to aesthetic dominance in the field of prose fiction. Rather it proposes that the philosophical and the oriental tale offer alternative means of exploring the same preoccupations as those that drive the more familiar realist and domestic fiction of the second half of the eighteenth century (characterized by the work of Henry Fielding, Samuel Richardson, Tobias Smollett, and Frances Burney): a fiction that self-consciously explores relations between reader and text, between disciple and mentor, between past and present generations. Where philosophical and oriental tales differ from the domestic realist fictions (themselves hugely various in their manifestations) is in exploring these relations on the level of form and plot rather than the level of character. It is not that character is insignificant in these tales but that it tends to demonstrate the universality of the human mind and its responses to external stimulus rather than to promote our belief in the plausibility or authenticity of persons through individualizing marks or impressions.

Critical discussions of these types of fiction have argued that the philosophical imperative serves to erase differences between the cultures in which oriental tales are purportedly located. In these 'oriental' systems of political or domestic economy, European readers can see a universal human psychology play itself out without the interference of a known context. Martha Pike Conant (1908) distinguished four traditions in her study of the oriental tale: imaginative, moralistic, philosophic, and satiric. For her, the philosophic tradition is a minor one manifested in a handful of texts from Addison's 'Vision of Mirza' (*Spectator* no. 159, 1708) to Oliver Goldsmith's short tale, included in a collection of his essays of 1765, entitled 'Asem; or, the Man-hater'. My own *Fabulous Orients* (2005) argues, by contrast, that meaningful distinctions, based on varying degrees of first-hand encounter with eastern territories, were drawn between different kinds of oriental locales in the fictions of the eighteenth century. In particular, a powerful distinction is drawn between the luxury, excess, and sensuality associated with Islamic Turkey and Persia and Mughal India, and the wisdom, restraint, and authority invested in Brahman India and Confucian China.

Beginnings

Rasselas and *Candide* can be situated in a well-established tradition of philosophical and oriental tales produced in and between Britain and France in the late seventeenth and eighteenth century. A series of texts had established a repertoire of conventions that made the mode recognizable to its eighteenth-century readers and encouraged them to seek out a philosophical 'conclusion' in such tales. 'The History of Hayy ibn Yaqzan' is a medieval Arabic tale about the development of a child to intellectual transcendence (through his contact with the natural world on an uninhabited island). It was authored in Muhammadan Spain by the philosopher and statesman Abu Bakr Ibn Tufail, and was available in Latin (from 1671) and then English translation (from 1674). A less obviously 'oriental' philosophical tale of reach and influence was *Les aventures de Télémaque* (1699, translated into English as *The Adventures of Telemachus* in the same year) by Fénelon, Archbishop of Cambrai and tutor to Louis XIV's infant grandson. This prose epic, about the instruction of Ulysses's son under the guardianship of Minerva disguised as an elderly male 'Mentor', was a scathing critique of Louis XIV's absolutist autocracy, resulting in the author's banishment from Versailles. The 'mirror for princes' tradition of the philosophical and oriental tale received new impetus in the publication of a translation (via a Persian source) of an ancient Sanskrit story cycle, under the title *Les Fables de Pilpay* (1698, translated by Joseph Harris into English in 1699 and corrected and enlarged in 1747). The Indian sage, Pilpay (also referred to as Bidpai), delivers a variety of animal and human fables designed to instruct the prince in the principles of wise government.

Other French critiques of Louis XIV and French absolutism proved important sources of oriental and philosophical tales. Giovanni Paolo Marana's *Letters Writ by a Turkish Spy* (1687–96) consisted of seven volumes containing over six hundred letters by a fictional Arab informant, Mahmut, who passes as a Moldavian instructor in oriental and classical languages, while sending reports to the Istanbul seraglio concerning European, and especially Parisian, state affairs from 1637 to 1682. Charles-Louis de Secondat de Montesquieu's *Lettres persanes* (1721), translated by Charles Ozell as the *Persian Letters* in 1722, was another oriental series of letters, this time from two exiled Persian aristocrats, Usbek and Rica, describing France in the period of Philippe d'Orleans' troubled Regency after the death of Louis XIV in 1715. Most successful of all was Antoine Galland's twelve-volume *Mille et une Nuits*. The enthusiastic reception of Galland's first few volumes spawned imitations such as François Petis de la Croix's *Les Mille et un Jours* (translated as *Persian Tales* between 1714 and 1715). These sequences feature female tale-tellers: Scheherazade, the brave new wife deferring her husband's sentence of execution by recovering his interest in her stories before dawn each day; and Sutlememe, the nurse who tells the princess of Kashmir stories of loyal husbands in an attempt to persuade her to marry. The 'philosophical' aspects of such sequences are not explicit in these eighteenth-century renderings. Rather, they inject into the oriental tale a new energy and humour, offering stories set in a variety of eastern locales incorporating elements of magic and comedy.

1759: The Tale Turns

This overview of the history of the emergence and convergence of philosophical and oriental tales in the first half of the eighteenth century alerts us to the variety of their manifestations. Their repertoire encompasses: a central protagonist, whether observer and auditor of tales or character within them (and sometimes both), who undergoes an educational experience; a sequence of events that often involves travel from one space to the other and sometimes the contrast of oriental and occidental cultures or norms; a 'genius' character, usually an older man, who provides instruction and advice to a protagonist in order to prepare him, rarely her, for future government; conscious archaism and extravagance of style, often manifested in the speech of characters, claimed to be characteristic of the oriental tale-teller; a critique of despotism, often expressed through complaint about the oppression and confinement of women.

If we return to *Candide* and *Rasselas*, however, we see a marked failure in confidence in the agency of philosophical truth and the explanatory capacity of a philosophical system. Both tales translate the critique of political despotism, still evident on the level of plot in both works, into a relentless series of proofs that all systemic thinking is a form of despotism best resisted through practical scepticism. Voltaire's tale explicitly criticizes the Leibnizian 'optimism' in the assertions of Candide's sage advisor/tutor Pangloss that everything is for the best and that there is a design behind apparent evil and suffering. Candide encounters and himself inflicts suffering, violence, and cruelty at every point in his travels from western Europe to South America to Constantinople, relentlessly (mis)applying his tutor's truism that everything is for the best despite the evidence that stacks up against it. Unlike Candide, Rasselas does not travel with a system or hobby horse, unless we count his pursuit of a single satisfactory mode of living as a hobby horse in itself. But he too encounters disappointment, violence, arbitrary passions, and an inability to live up to ideals in his journey from Abyssinia to Cairo and back.

The publication of these works so close to each other at this moment in history, as Carol Watts (2007) has identified, is symptomatic. They voice a shared pessimism and exhaustion after several years of violent conflict in Europe, in which both France and England had been entrammelled since the outbreak of the Seven Years' War in 1756 (when Voltaire's onetime friend, Prince Frederick of Prussia, invaded Saxony). Not only do they offer fictional representations of those conflicts and voice complaints about the pursuit of 'absolute' solutions to an inevitable and ongoing state of rivalry, they also critique the easy solutions offered in the oriental and philosophic tale of instruction through or by fiction. All that characters can learn from the series of tales they hear or the experiences they undergo in the course of these tales is that humankind consistently fails to transcend the senses. The pursuit of a total system of living produces characters who fail to live themselves, just as reading tales can be seen not as a means to reform a way of living but rather as a form of vicarious living. Rasselas, we should remember, is an inveterate procrastinator; having determined to escape the happy valley, he spends twenty months imagining the world beyond without devising a practical means of escape (ch. 4; 10). Imlac calls the attention of Nekayah and Rasselas back to the task of living when he finds them so busy debating the finer points of marriage and celibacy, that they are failing to see the most magnificent and instructive sight of Egypt, the pyramids. '[W]hile you are making the choice of life, you neglect to live' (ch. 30;

73) he complains. However, true to the principle that no single voice can deliver a single truth for all to live by, *Rasselas* also mocks the easy narrative device of the sage truth-teller or 'genius' by leaving Imlac's an increasingly marginal and questionable voice within the tale. His wisest choice is often the decision *not* to speak. In this way we see him keep silent when Rasselas, Nekayah, and Pekuah, after an encounter with a bitter elderly man in the course of an evening walk, refuse to accept that old age will only bring disillusion; Imlac, we are told, 'had no desire to see them depressed . . . and remembered, that at the same age, he was equally confident of unmingled prosperity' (ch. 45; 109).

Rasselas and *Candide* subvert and convert the familiar elements of the oriental and philosophic tale. They question the capacity of story to reform. The heroes of these tales are not extraordinary young princes destined to rule, nor do they illustrate the development of the intellect abstracted from all social relations (as does Hayy ibn Yaqzan). The 'geniuses' who are provided as companions are at best deluded and at worst rank hypocrites; readers of the texts find themselves more often aligned with an ironic narrator observing the self-delusions of all the characters than with either the genius or the ward. The woundings and mutilations that are evidence of providential judgement or the effect of magical powers in the *Arabian Nights Entertainments* are explicitly replaced with accounts of extreme physical violence and torture in a time of war in *Candide*, or the relentless depression of the encounter with real life as opposed to soaring imagination in *Rasselas*.

Finally, we can observe that these two tales reserve a special place for women as the most effective proponents of the practical scepticism advocated. Nekayah, Pekuah, Cunégonde, and the princess of Palestrina are fellow-travellers with the male protagonists, often more capable of accommodating the disappointments when idealizations fail. The oriental and philosophic tale of the preceding decades was either an entirely homosocial affair, especially preoccupied by the relation between male genius and his young male tutee, or it pitted female against male in an epistemological conflict, such as that between the despotic eye of the sultan and the reforming tongue of his queen in the *Arabian Nights Entertainments*. English writers of the eighteenth century traditionally characterized the Orient as a region where political despotism was mirrored in a domestic tyranny that treated women as sensual slaves rather than affective companions.

Rasselas is particularly unusual in its presentation of central female characters who do not seek fulfilment through marriage and who are also not sought in this way. Even when Pekuah is abducted by nomadic Arabs, it appears to be for ransom and no sexual motive is canvassed. Johnson depicts women conversing with men about topics other than love and marriage—an uncommon representation, in the novel of the period. This provides one reason for the continuing popularity of the tale among those female as well as male imitators to whom we now turn.

1760s: Imitations and Developments

During the first five years of the 1760s, several oriental and philosophical tales were published that clearly sought to capitalize on the success of *Rasselas*. Johnson's successor as compiler of the parliamentary debates for *The Gentleman's Magazine*, John Hawkesworth, published *Almoran and Hamet* in 1761, dedicating this fevered tale of rivalry between twin male heirs to the throne of Persia to the new King George III. The tale is a thinly veiled allegory and compliment to George, whose character if favourably represented was close to that of the virtuous twin, Hamet: shy, devout, and domestic. George's devotion to his counsellor-friend, Lord Bute, whom he swiftly made Prime Minister, estranging William Pitt from power, is evidently mirrored in Hamet's loyal advisor Omar (by comparison with the evil genius that drives his active, aggressive, and despotic twin, Almoran). *Almoran and Hamet* concerns the conflict between two brothers whose father has left them in equal control of his kingdom. A genius provides the envious twin, Almoran, with the power to adopt the appearance of others; he uses this power to substitute for his brother in the courtship of a lovely commoner, Almeida, and to attempt to seize power from Hamet once the people have expressed a preference for the latter to be their single sovereign. Almoran's overreaching receives fit punishment. He pronounces the mystic words given to Hamet as a protective charm only to find a genius appear who announces (in a return to the argument for providential design) that 'I have been appointed to perfect virtue, by adversity; and in the folly of her own projects, to entangle vice'.[3]

So too a 1762 tale by John Langhorne, *Solyman and Almena*, melds political reference with preconceptions of philosophical and oriental design. This work by a Dagenham curate was dedicated to the Queen, previously Princess Charlotte of Mecklenburg-Strelitz, who married George III on 8 September 1761 having made the King's acquaintance only a few hours before the ceremony. However, Langhorne does not proceed by political analogy between oriental and occidental states (in order to contrast eastern despotism with western contractual monarchy), but by an equally strong tradition in such tales of bringing the oriental hero into contact with occidental wisdom to produce a fiction of reformed government. The Mesopotamian and devoutly Zoroastrian king Ardavan opens the tale with an invocation to providence to protect his son and heir Solyman who has determined, like Rasselas, to leave the peaceful valley in which he has been brought up, here called Irwan. Solyman defends the oppressed, sending a pair of eloping lovers to the protection of his father in Irwan and arranging the escape of a political exile from Ormus to Europe. Early in the tale, Solyman befriends an English merchant at Ispahan with whom he travels. In India he is attracted by the lovely music played by his neighbour, Almena. The feeling

---

[3] John Hawkesworth, *Almoran and Hamet*, in *Oriental Tales*, ed. Robert Mack (Oxford: Oxford University Press, 1992), ch. 18; 112.

is reciprocated and Solyman persuades Almena to leave with him, fearing that she may become a victim of *sati* (burning on her husband's funeral pyre) should she marry a man of her own culture. However, when they flee, Almena is taken captive in a sea skirmish between rival Indian kings off the peninsula. Solyman finds Almena imprisoned in the harem of an evil governor whom he kills and is rewarded by the king of Kanara with the person of Almena, despite the king's own attraction to her. The tale concludes with the marriage of Solyman and Almena and a poem in praise of eternal providence.

While Hawkesworth's tale is of political intrigue and violence delivered in highly wrought tragic language, Langhorne's is a romance filled with poetical descriptions of landscape and oriental edifices touched by light and beauty. Solyman's simple Zoroastrian admiration for the wonders of nature and the expressive arts, and his power to win the love of virtuous persons of a variety of races and cultures, is a device to promote the principle of a Christian monarchy that seeks connection with other cultures through trade rather than military power, as demonstrated in the strong bonds forged between the English merchant and oriental hero.

The oriental 'pagan' religions of Zoroastrianism and Hinduism—as well as the Confucian philosophy of China—often feature as alternatives to a despotic Islam for the Christian European writer of oriental tales in the later eighteenth century (seeking to represent English trade as an alternative and successor to Muslim territorial expansion in the context of newly won territories in India following the Seven Years' War). Two longer and more complex tale sequences of the 1760s take this direction: James Ridley's *Tales of the Genii* (1764) and a work entitled *The Bonze, or, Chinese Anchorite* (1769), ostensibly translated from the Chinese of Hoamchi-Vam by one Monsieur d'Alençon. Ridley was, like Langhorne, a jobbing Oxbridge-educated clergyman. On his retirement (due to ill health) from a chaplaincy in a marching regiment, Ridley wrote and published a sequence of tales ostensibly delivered by a wise Muslim scientist, Horam, to an English ambassador at Bombay. Horam claims to have composed the stories in an attempt to correct the vices of Osmir, son to the Mughal emperor, Aurengzeb (reigned 1658 to 1707). They consist of nine tales delivered by a council of genii to two children, Patna and Coulor, all designed to provide guidance on how to uncover the truth behind false appearances and how to recognize the signs of divine favour. Ridley's tales identify moral similarities in the monotheisms of East and West. Providentialism was understood to be a theosophy shared by Christianity and Islam, and Ridley presents these tales of virtue and salvation in an Islamic framework as prefiguring the values that Christian rule in India will bring to perfection. English Christianity is here understood as the rightful successor to Muslim rule in India—so long as it abjures the despotism and acquisitiveness that the narrator Horam identifies as the downfall of the Mughal Empire.

Theories of transmigration in Hinduism and Buddhism were also to prove popular vehicles for exploring the development and perfectibility of the devout hero, as *The Bonze* illustrates. Two Englishmen in China, Captain Wilford and Mr Theodore Johnson, discuss the ancient Chinese belief in transmigration and, to provide evidence, Johnson introduces his friend to a eunuch hermit named Confuciango who is also, remarkably, a convert to Anglicanism. Confuciango narrates his experiences at the fall of the Ming dynasty in the mid-seventeenth century. His sister, Philasanga, beloved wife of the Prince Zangola, is killed by the rebel leader, Li, while Confuciango and Zangola flee to travel through China disguised as bonzes (mendicant Buddhist priests). Zangola dies of grief at the loss of his wife, and then revisits Confuciango as an angelic presence to tell him a variety of stories. Some of these concern the biblical fall, apocalypse, and final day of judgement; others detail Zangola's various reincarnations (as an eastern monarch, a negro prince, and a European wife unhappily imprisoned in a Turkish seraglio—as well as a variety of animal incarnations from mite to leopard to turtle dove). Finally, Zangola departs to live on Venus where he has rediscovered the soul of Philasanga (a topical reference to the discovery of the atmosphere of Venus in 1761 by the Russian polymath, Mikhail Lomonosov). This obscure novel shares with Ridley's more coherent fiction a proselytizing commitment to the reformed English Protestant church, a tendency to satirize Catholicism as a form of pagan idol worship, and an optimism that English Protestant humanism will speak to the moral principles underpinning the ancient philosophies of the Orient, here those of Hindu India and China (Confucius). Ridley and the obscure French 'translator' of Hoamchi-Vam's *The Bonze* (referred to as 'Monsr. d'Alenzon' on the title page) continue with the pragmatic and opportunist use of the oriental narrator (found in Marana and Montesquieu) to critique despotism and promote Christian mercantilism as the new form of universal government.

Two short tales of the 1760s demonstrate the continuing attraction of another objective of the oriental tale: to promote simple moral truths by presenting to readers a tale whereby the central character is reformed through a fictional vision: Oliver Goldsmith's 'Asem; or, the Man-hater', published as number 16 of his *Essays* (1765), and Frances Sheridan's short fiction, *The History of Nourjahad* (1767). Goldsmith tells us that Asem has retired to a cave at the foot of a mountain in Tauris in disgust at the ingratitude of those friends he supported generously when he was affluent. Asem is about to take his own life by drowning when a genie approaches him across the waves and spirits him to a world designed by the prophet Muhammad in which perfect reason prevails and there is no vice. He is disappointed to discover a world without arts, without friendship, and a population terrorized by wild animals that lives at subsistence level in great unhappiness. Asem decides that the world designed by Allah, which incorporates countervailing vice with virtues, is better than the rational universe imagined by his prophet. He heads back to his native town and engages in commerce repairing his fortune and happiness.

Frances Sheridan, like others before her, presents her experiment in the oriental tale as a text designed to instruct a potential monarch, on this occasion George III's eldest son, also called George. Unusually, however, the tale focuses on the correction of the errant counsellor rather than monarch. Shemzeddin, the young king of Persia, tests his close friend Nourjahad by asking him to confide his fondest wish. He is disappointed when Nourjahad cites vast wealth and immortality. A 'guardian genius', a lovely young boy, visits Nourjahad to offer him a choice that night of fulfilling his wish or enjoying once again the sultan's favour. Nourjahad chooses the treasure and embarks on a life of luxury. However, he finds himself prey to the genius's curse that when he succumbs to evil he will fall asleep for many years and find his world changed around him. After a succession of traumatic rewakenings, he finally repents but, in exercising his new-found benevolence, breaks an order from Shemzeddin's newly ascended son, Shemerzad, that no one can do business in the city for twenty days as a sign of respect to the dead king. Nourjahad is willing to embrace his punishment of death. The execution is averted, however, by the disclosure that he has been the victim of a trick orchestrated by Shemzeddin. It has been only fourteen months since the visit from his 'genie', a part played by a lady called Mandana who had fallen in love with Nourjahad and sought Shemzeddin's assistance to win his love. Shemzeddin concludes the tale with the moral: 'Let this dream of existence then be a lesson to thee for the future, never to suppose that riches can ensure happiness, that the gratification of our passions can satisfy the human heart; or that the immortal part of our nature, will suffer us to taste unmixed felicity, in a world which was never meant for our final place of abode.'[4] Nourjahad is given Mandana for a wife and becomes the Sultan's first minister, a role he conducts virtuously so 'that his name was famous throughout the Eastern world' (194).

In both Goldsmith's and Sheridan's tales an encounter with a carefully designed fiction provides the means to restore a character to active engagement in the 'real world'. This is the special magical effect of the oriental-philosophical tale which, while it energetically promotes engagement with the real, recognizes the power of fiction to effect that engagement. Readers of the tale, like protagonists within it, find themselves transported by the 'arts' of fiction to other worlds which restore them renewed (if only by scepticism) to the real world.

1780s: Metatextual Reflections

In the mid-1780s the conventions of the oriental and philosophical tale were sufficiently established for three authors to produce versions that are newly playful and self-conscious in their treatment of genre. Clara Reeve, Horace Walpole, and William Beckford exaggerate fantastic and extreme content to cast doubt on the claims that the fiction is a vehicle for moral truth, and rather reveal the pleasures of transgression, extremity, and manipulation that it serves. These publications also coincide with evident critical

---

[4] Frances Sheridan, *The History of Nourjahad*, in *Oriental Tales*, ed. Mack, 194.

interest in debating the history of the genres of prose fiction as the novel comes to increasing aesthetic dominance. Thus, the Professor of Moral Philosophy at Marischal College, Aberdeen, James Beattie, gives the oriental tale considerable attention in his influential essay 'On Fable and Romance', but complains that the tradition of the oriental tale is geared only toward the entertainment of its consumer: the 'Eastern prince . . . at a loss for expedients to kill the time . . . does not desire, that they should be probable, or of an instructive tendency: it is enough if they be astonishing'.[5]

Clara Reeve is equally concerned to place the oriental tale in relation to the tradition of moralized romance. *The History of Charoba, Queen of Ægypt* stages a battle between embodiments of the narrative genres discussed explicitly in the critical work to which it was appended, *The Progress of Romance* (1785). In the latter, Euphrasia, at the prompting of Sophronia, defends the genre of the romance from the attacks of a male critic Hortensius who considers the 'Genus' to contain 'trash' and to be 'a kind of writing . . . generally exploded'.[6] In the accompanying tale, the Egyptian Queen Charoba prevents her suitor, the foreign giant Gebirus the Metaphequian, from forcing her into marriage by persuading him to use the stones he has brought to dam up the Nile to build a palace in her honour on its banks; each night she conjures sea spirits or genii to dismantle the work he has completed during the day. The buildings erected and dismantled in the tale (*Charoba*) appear to be a narrative construction equivalent to the metaphor deployed in the critical text by Hortensius to describe Euphrasia's preparatory arguments which he says are 'laying a deep foundation', while he is puzzled as to 'what kind of building you will raise upon it'; she answers that she 'propose[s] to trace Romance to its Origin, to follow its progress through the different periods to its declension, to shew how the modern Novel sprung up out of its ruins' (8).

The battle in both critical and narrative text is won, however, not through the force traditionally deployed in epic, but through stratagem, specifically the kind of dilatory verbal agency associated with the romance and with Scheherezade. Charoba has been blessed by Abraham as a result of her generosity to him and Sarah with 'subtilty to deceive her enemies'.[7] Gebirus plans to marry Charoba in order to gain possession of Egypt. It is only when he enlists the assistance of a sea nymph in love with one of his shepherds that he acquires the magic lore to circumvent the magic woven by Charoba and her clever nurse. When Gebirus has completed his city, Charoba is forced to take more drastic action having 'meant only to weary out the King, and to reduce him to an impossibility' (207). First his troops and then Gebirus are poisoned when they confront the Egyptian queen. On

---

[5] James Beattie, 'On Fable and Romance', in *Dissertations, Moral and Critical* (London: W. Strahan and T. Cadell, 1783), 509.

[6] Clara Reeve, *The Progress of Romance and the History of Charoba, Queen of Egypt, 1785* (New York: Facsimile Text Society, 1930), 130.

[7] Clara Reeve, 'The History of Charoba, Queen of Egypt', in *Oriental Tales*, ed. Mack, 198.

his death bed, Gebirus asks Charoba to engrave his dying words on a pillar of the palace he has built. Romance overcomes epic and points toward the advent of the novel with the latter's attention to female speech and agency, and its preference for the representation of domestic rather than dynastic conflict. Moreover, oriental tale (*Charoba*) and critical discourse (*Progress of Romance*) illustrate and complement each other; both defeat the force of a masculinity that masks its aggression as courtship through a wily appearance of cooperation.

A similar metatextual turn is evident in the work of two contemporaries otherwise very different from the earnest and popular professional writer of fiction, Reeve. Neither Horace Walpole nor William Beckford apparently sought wide circulation or public attention for their playful experiments with the oriental and philosophical tale in the mid-1780s. Horace Walpole's six *Hieroglyphic Tales* appeared in an edition of seven copies, including proofs from his press at his Gothic castle-home of Strawberry Hill, designed apparently as gift copies to a variety of friends who appear transformed into fairytale, oriental, or philosophical characters within the tales (which were composed between 1776 and 1772). Walpole conjures references to the significant modish crazes of the late eighteenth century. In 'The King and his Three Daughters', the enthusiasm for all things Egyptian is mocked when a mummified three-legged Egyptian prince, comically and obscenely named Quifferiquimini, sets a court fashion for cadaverous looks and clothes marked with hieroglyphics when he comes to France to court a (dead) older princess (much preferred to her younger sister who, bizarrely, speaks with a Yorkshire accent). In 'A New Arabian Nights Entertainment', the unlikely Scheherazade is a Dutch merchant's daughter who passes as a princess, marries a surprisingly short, despotic, insomniac giant, and suffocates him with the help of his grand vizier—having successfully sent him to sleep with her 'short account of the troubles that have agitated Europe for the last two hundred years, on the doctrines of grace, free-will, predestination, reprobation, justification, &c.'.[8] She promptly takes the throne herself and marries a new husband each night, but dispenses on the surety of his good behaviour with both the requirements for diurnal storytelling and execution. In 'Mi Li. A Chinese Fairy Tale', Walpole plays with the dual reputation of China as the home of an extreme Confucian rationalism and an eccentric, wayward aestheticism as displayed in fanciful imported porcelain work. A Chinese prince seeks out his destined bride, identified by a fairy oracle as a girl with the same name as her father's dominions, by taking a ship to England. He finds her at Henry Conway's estate in Henley where he meets Conway's ward, Caroline Campbell, daughter of the Governor of South Carolina. The modern estate garden along the lines of William Chambers' 1772 *Dissertation on Oriental Gardening* complies with a series of unlikely requirements Mi Li receives in a dream: that his bride is to be found where there is a bridge over no water, a tomb 'where nobody ever

---

[8] Horace Walpole, *Hieroglyphic Tales, 1785* (London: Pallas Athene, 2010), 7.

was buried', ruins 'that were more than they had ever been', and an underground passage containing dogs with eyes of rubies and emeralds and a menagerie of Chinese pheasants (58–9). Walpole's collection is a hilarious, extravagant verbal concoction: a print version of the hybrid simulacrum of architectural styles he created at Strawberry Hill. In the short postscript he comes closest to a direct statement of his intent, describing the tales as 'an attempt to vary the stale and beaten class of stories and novels, which, though works or inventions, are almost always devoid of imagination' (71). History, he complains, proves more inventive. The clue to the collection may lie in the English pronunciation of the mock-Chinese name of one of its heroes (Mi Li is 'my lie'). Walpole's 'lies' draw attention to the potential of fiction and especially its capacity to debunk and mock authorities clerical, political, and philosophical, as the 'Hieroglyphic Tales' do throughout.

William Beckford was rumoured to be the most wealthy commoner of England, an enthusiastic collector of art and oriental manuscripts, with tastes for the Gothic and the comical very close to those of Horace Walpole. Beckford intended to publish the tale of *Vathek* (which he composed originally in French) with several other associated tales (known as the *Episodes*), but it first appeared as a single tale in an English translation with learned footnotes produced by Beckford's one-time tutor, Samuel Henley. The crazed despotic oriental ruler, Vathek, finds himself at the novel's conclusion in the company of his mistress, Nouronihar, in the caves of 'Eblis', a place of eternal punishment where sinners find their hearts permanently on fire. There they are told first-person tales by other vicious characters, which explain the punishment they all share. Beckford had composed *Vathek* in French by 1783, and Henley embarked on a translation into English which Beckford corrected. After a scandal concerning his relationship with a thirteen year-old male relative, Beckford retired to his estate at Fonthill, where his wife died in May having given birth to a second daughter. In late summer 1786, Beckford learnt that Henley had published the translation with a series of footnotes. In November, Beckford published the text in French without footnotes in Lausanne. Thirty years later, in 1816, a third edition revised by Beckford was published in English and French in response to a revival of interest, due to a series of admiring references to *Vathek* in Lord Byron's narrative poems. This later edition had footnotes trimmed back from the elaborate learnedness of Henley which had always been out of keeping with the mocking and playful manipulation of traditions in oriental and occidental narrative within the tale itself.

Like Walpole, Beckford was a collector and an antiquarian, and his 'oriental' tale also combined personal references with scholarly ones. The author's homoerotic passion for a young man that had attracted such scandal is fictionalized in the representation of the lovely boy Gulchenrouz who, when he dresses like his cousin, Nouronihar, 'seemed to be more feminine than even herself'.[9] The rivalry for Nouronihar's

---

[9] William Beckford, *Vathek with The Episodes of Vathek*, ed. Kenneth W. Graham (Peterborough, ON: Broadview Press, 2001), 102.

affections between Gulchenrouz and Vathek is returned to in the most notorious of the drafted 'episodes', the story of Firouz and Alasi (in a version which only existed in manuscript until Kenneth Graham's edition of *Vathek with the Episodes of Vathek* in 2001); here, the evil blasphemous boy-prince Firouz blazes a trail of destruction resulting in the disfigurement of Alasi's affianced, haughty, and virtuous Princess Roubadah.

Beckford mixed ostentatious learning with the kind of childish contempt for decorum and morality displayed by Firouz in the first Episode and Vathek in the main tale. It is worth noting that the name Gulchenrouz is a variant of the 'Gulshan-i Raz' or 'Mystic Rose Garden', a fourteenth-century collection of poems in Persian by Mahmud Shabistari in the Islamic mystical tradition of Sufism, whereas the character of Vathek is based on an account in Barthélemy d'Herbelot's *Bibliothèque Orientale* (1697) of the Abbasid ruler, al-Wathick Bi'llah (ruled AD 842–7), famous for his terrible one-eyed stare, and for his excesses with women, food, and drink. Despite these learned references, in *Vathek* itself both learning and morality are compromised and uncertain. Beckford's later revisions suggest he was not happy with the ethnographic and antiquarian annotation Henley superimposed on his work. The concluding 'moral' of *Vathek*—delivered after the display of the wicked, who are left in eternal revolutions (Vathek's monstrous mother, Cariathis) or eternal unsatisfied *burning* of the heart (Vathek and Nouronihar)—is unconvincing in its very assertiveness as the conclusion of a tale that has taken impish delight in the representation of despotic excess:

> Such was, and such should be, the punishment of unrestrained passions and atrocious deeds! Such shall be, the chastisement of that blind curiosity, which would transgress those bounds the wisdom of the Creator has prescribed to human knowledge; and such the dreadful disappointment of that restless ambition, which, aiming at discoveries reserved for beings of a supernatural order, perceives not, through its infatuated pride, that the condition of man upon earth is to be—humble and ignorant. (148)

Indeed, Beckford's tale might be seen as a conscious parody of the conservative, pessimistic advocacy of restraint in Samuel Johnson's *Rasselas*, which opens with the solemn invocation:

> Ye who listen with credulity to the whispers of fancy, and persue with eagerness the phantoms of hope; who expect that age will perform the promises of youth, and that the deficiencies of the present day will be supplied by the morrow; attend to the history of Rasselas prince of Abissinia. (1)

Walpole and Beckford are more inclined to shout than whisper fancy; they remind us that fancy is not an unruly presence to be kept in check by sceptical reason but precisely the stock in trade of the philosophical and oriental tale. They make their readers self-consciously aware of the attractions and pleasures of the wayward and the eccentric, and expose the moral truism as an empty, arbitrary, if necessary, gesture of conclusion.

After 1790: Domestic and National Revision

By the end of the eighteenth century, both the oriental and philosophical tale seem to have exhausted their appeal. Two tales, both by women, Ellis Cornelia Knight's *Dinarbas* (1790) and Maria Edgeworth's 'Murad the Unlucky' (1804), are the final expressions of a mode rapidly overtaken by the meteoric rise of new forms of fiction that absorbed many of its elements and techniques. The Gothic of Ann Radcliffe, Matthew Lewis, and others (along with the historical novels of Walter Scott and national tales of Sydney Owenson and Maria Edgeworth) also deployed conscious archaism in speech and narration, fantastic sometimes supernatural elements, a critique of an outdated despotism and its conquest by a more accommodating mix of opposed cultures (occidental and oriental, northern and southern, colony and colonizer). But these later writers brought such elements closer to home, situating their tales in the past centuries of mainland Europe or the present of Britain's liminal territories, Scotland and Ireland. Oriental narratives such as Elizabeth Hamilton's *Letters of a Hindoo Rajah* (1796) and Phoebe Gibbes's *Hartly House, Calcutta* (1789) shift to an ethnographic and imperial—rather than a philosophical—emphasis, and the new centre of attention among oriental territories is India, where British imperial power had enjoyed rapid and sudden growth.

By contrast with the excess and extravagance of the Gothic tale, *Dinarbas* and 'Murad' are restrained, moralized narratives. Ellis Cornelia Knight had met Samuel Johnson in her youth and wrote her fifty-chapter tale of the continuing adventures of Rasselas and his company on their return trip to the happy valley, in conscious imitation. Like Beckford, she challenges the pessimistic conclusions of her model, but in a very different way: by arguing that when the powerful come in contact with the real lives of others, they will be able to identify and practise real virtue. Happiness need not be an impermanent fiction if it is grounded in sociable relations of mutual respect. Whereas sociability proves a temporary relief from unhappiness in *Rasselas*, *Dinarbas* represents it as an absolute cure and a destination that compensates for all ills. Rasselas and Nekayah find themselves in the fortress home of Amalphis at the border of Abyssinia. They become attracted respectively to Amalphis's daughter, Zilia, and son, Dinarbas. Without revealing their true identities, they win returning affection. In the course of the novel, Rasselas is taken prisoner, Dinarbas is thought dead and miraculously revives, Rasselas succeeds in defeating his two brothers in their attempts to seize the throne from his father, and finally all the couples are married. Along the way, the themes raised in Johnson's original are revisited: the advantages of travel in broadening the mind, the responsibility of a good monarch, the nature of happy marriage. Despite the oriental setting, Knight's tale bears strong resemblance to the realist domestic novel of the mid-eighteenth century such as Sarah Fielding's *The Adventures of David Simple* (1744), in which two couples similarly attempt to forge virtuous friendship and marriage in a hostile environment.

Likewise Maria Edgeworth's tale 'Murad the Unlucky', first published in her *Popular Tales* (1804), a collection of sketches and short stories, proffers a sociable sensibility as the philosophical virtue to be prized above all others in the oriental tale. Murad, teller of the tale, believes fate has destined him and those he loves always for disaster, while his prudent and socially responsible younger brother, Saladin, appears to bring benefit wherever he goes. The tale proves that it is prudence and scepticism, rather than providence, that bring about social happiness and universal profit. While Edgeworth here retains the educational purpose of the oriental tale, the troubled issue of an errant 'fancy', which had preoccupied these fictions from the early eighteenth century onwards, is now quietly shelved. Content and form work in tandem to promote a sceptical prudential reading practice that brings the oriental and philosophical tale into line with the aims of the domestic realist novel. Yet these tales also lack the detail of character and complexity of narrative voice that make the domestic realist novel of the later eighteenth century, as practised elsewhere by Edgeworth herself, so complex and stimulating. The empirical philosophy that appears to have prompted eighteenth-century authors to turn to the oriental and philosophical tale to demonstrate its principles has, by this point, become embedded and naturalized in the domestic realist novel. Nonetheless, the most impressive realist authors of the nineteenth century—Charles Dickens, Wilkie Collins, Charlotte Brontë—continue to refer to and recall the (lost) enchantments of the oriental tale.

20

Epistolary Fiction

NICOLA J. WATSON

Heyday

The heyday of epistolary fiction, the novel told entirely or mostly in letters, stretched from the 1750s until the late 1790s, before it suffered abrupt decline and extinction. According to James Raven, 10 per cent of all new novels published in Britain between 1750 and 1760 were in letters (1987: 12). By the mid-1760s, this proportion had risen to a quarter. By 1767, a full third of the new crop of novels were epistolary, and during the 1770s and 1780s over 40 per cent of novels appeared in letter form. In seven of the years between 1776 and 1784, at least half of new fiction was epistolary (Raven 2000: 32). Raven notes that this vogue for epistolary fiction, whether of British or foreign origin, was magnified by extensive reprinting; Raven's count of British editions published between 1750 and 1769 of Marie-Jeanne Riccoboni, Jean-Jacques Rousseau, Jeanne Marie le Prince de Beaumont, and Frances Brooke comes to fifty editions. Between 1750 and 1800 Samuel Richardson's novels, *Pamela* (1740–1), *Clarissa* (1748–9), and *Sir Charles Grandison* (1753–4), went through no fewer than fifty-four editions between them (Raven 1987: 12, 14, 15). In the magazines, too, epistolary fiction was prominent throughout the period. The novel in letters, in short, was the dominant form of fiction.

This pre-eminence is attributable to the century's well-documented investment in letter writing as the prime way of constituting the social and sociability, whether conceived as the private domain of the family or as the wider public sphere. A letter-writing and letter-publishing culture flourished in relation to economics, politics, religion, housekeeping, medicine, travel, and, especially, questions of conduct; and, as Clare Brant has put it, 'print culture expanded in large part because letter writing expanded. There was an expansion of *writing* culture, part of which ended up in print' (2006: 335). A new middle-class culture of writing was in the making, and letter writing and the depiction of letter writing played its own part in constructing that culture.

This culture of letters is conveyed by the frontispiece and title page of a letter-writing manual first published around 1780. *The New English Letter-Writer, or Whole Art of General Correspondence* describes an ideal writing and reading constituency by depicting its prospective readership in its frontispiece. This engraving shows a well-to-do family seated together in a large and well-furnished library, all busily writing and reading letters ranging from love letters to a will, and is captioned: 'The Father, Daughter, Youth and Blooming Fair, | Make our New Work the object of their care'. The lengthy subtitle of *The New English Letter-Writer* advertised its contents as 'a | Series of the most important, instructive, and interesting | Entire New Letters, | on Every Occurrence in Life'. It would supply models for letters on 'Trade, Affection, Love, Courtship, Marriage, Friendship, Instruction, History, Commerce, Industry, Prosperity, Prudence, Gratitude, Generosity, Misfortunes, Consolation, Prodigality, Virtue, Vice, Piety, Wit, Mirth, Folly, Pleasure, Humanity, Memory, Morality, Education, Happiness, Business, Sickness, Death, Integrity, Oeconomy, Affluence, Politeness, Fidelity, Riches, Duty and concerns of Parents, Children, and other relations, Masters, Mistresses, Illustrious Persons, Officers, Soldiers, Seamen, Schoolmasters, Scholars'; it also undertook to advise on 'notes of compliments', petitions, wills, and other legal correspondence. One of the legacies of letter-writing culture to epistolary fiction was this sense of the vast range of subject matter that might appropriately form the topic of a letter. Thus it was possible and even desirable to flag up the incorporation of all sorts of material in a novel besides the fictional. *The History of Charles Wentworth Esq. in a series of letters* (1770), attributable to Edward Bancroft, boasted that it was *Interspersed with a variety of important reflections, calculated to improve morality, and promote the oeconomy of human life*. Similarly *The History of Mr. Cecil and Miss Gray. In a Series of Letters* (1771) was advertised as including 'interspersed original Remarks on the French Nation'. The subtitle to Phebe Gibbes's *Friendship in a Nunnery; or, The American Fugitive* (1778) promised all sorts of further information: *a Full Description of the Mode of Education and Living in Convent Schools, both on the low and high pension; the manners and characters of the Nuns; the Arts practised on young minds; and their baneful effects on society at large*. At the same time *Letters from Henrietta to Morvina* described itself as educational travelogue, being *Interspersed with Anecdotes, historical and amusing, of the different courts and countries through which she passed*.

One of the striking characteristics of *The New English Letter-Writer* is the way that each series of letters it includes tends to turn into a mini-fiction. From letter writing it was a very short step to fiction. Richardson's first foray into writing was a letter-writing manual, and he was not the only one to move from writing private letters into publishing them as fictional. Although publication forced such letters to operate as fiction, in that they were no longer functioning strictly as letters between private correspondents or their immediate families, the line between private and public circulation was blurred, and the fictionality of these letters was typically elided because it was perceived as detracting from their authenticity and thus their power as real-life models. *A Series of Genuine Letters, between Henry and Frances* (1757–70) by Elizabeth and Richard Griffith, was very much what it claimed to be—a real correspondence—and owed its celebrity to this. In the earlier part of the period, epistolary novels therefore often sited themselves very uncertainly as fictional, preferring to describe themselves as originating in real life or as consisting of 'original' letters whether they did or not. A survey of titles published between 1770 and 1799 reveals a consistent strategy of advertising epistolary fiction as based on facts, whether collections of genuine letters, or as 'founded on facts' or 'real characters'. Some novels carried prefaces claiming that the letters had been collected up and edited by a well-wisher, for the edification of a wider public. In the cases of Richardson's *Clarissa*, Jean-Jacques Rousseau's *Julie: ou, La Nouvelle Hélöise* (1761, translated into English that year), and Johann Wolfgang von Goethe's *Die Leiden des jungen Werthers* (1774, translated as *The Sorrows of Werter*, 1779), readers responded to these novels as though they were non-fictional, identifying or even corresponding with the characters as real people. Other titles, such as *The History of Sir Charles Dormer and Miss Harriet Villars: In Which are Exemplified, from a Late Catastrophe in Real Life, the Contrast of Virtue and Vice, and the Dangerous and Fatal Consequence Arising from Confidants and Intermeddlers in Family Affairs* (1770), *Les Delices du Sentiment; or, The Passionate Lovers: In a Series of Letters which Have Recently Passed between Two Celebrated Characters* (1781), or *False Friendship; or, Nature in Masquerade. A Novel. Founded in Truth. Consisting of Letters which Have Actually Passed between Persons in Fashionable Life, upon the Most Affecting Subjects* (1799), made the same claim to authenticity in promising the racy delights of sex and scandal in high life. It was only by the 1790s that this claim had become too conventional automatically to entice. In 1794, reviewing *Caroline Merton*, the *Critical Review* dismissed its claim to veracity as a threadbare fiction: '*Founded on fact* is an assertion which we are seldom disposed to credit, and we would advise young writers especially, to drop it.'[1]

The explosion in fiction writing was probably rendered possible by the familiarity of the form of letters; Raven argues that it may have seemed 'an easy form to adopt for the inexperienced or unimaginative writer' (2000: 30). In his study of contemporary magazine culture, Robert Mayo estimates that as much as half of the original material included in magazines was produced by a young, female, and amateur readership (1962: 306). Such fiction typically sold itself to its reader through the assertion that the author was one of them, that this was an extension into the realm of the virtual of a middle-class social circle already constituted by letter writing. Authors advertised themselves as genteel, amateur, and non-commercial, and by far and away the most popular assertion of this came in the anonymous byline, 'by a Lady'. *The Rock; or, Alfred and Anna* (1798), attributable to Mrs Barnby, was advertised as 'by a young lady, her first literary attempt'. One novel claimed to be by someone now beyond the realms of commerce, 'a lady, now deceased'. The sense that telling a story 'in a series of letters' could be readily achieved by female amateurs seems also to have extended on occasion to the less well-educated. Possibly inspired by the fictional example of Pamela herself, the servant-girl whose letters caught

---

[1] *Critical Review*, n.s., 12 (December 1794), 473.

her a baronet for a husband, one or two titles appeared such as *The Feelings of the Heart: or, The Letters of a Country Girl. Written by Herself, and Addressed to a Lady of Quality* (1772). Critics also register a sense that much novel writing is amateur, youthful, and opportunistic. The *Monthly* commented sardonically of *Edwin and Julia: A Novel, in a Series of Letters, by a Lady* (1774) that 'Ev'ry love-struck swain . . . and every melting nymph who sighs . . . is qualified to write a love-story which shall pass for a pretty novel; at least with the help of a friend, *to spell it, and put it together*'.[2]

Despite the presence of so many anonymous ladies scattered across title pages, it is possible to overstate the importance of female authorship of fiction in the period. Recent scholarship has qualified and complicated the literary historical hypothesis developed by feminist scholarship in the 1980s that the late eighteenth-century novel was authored predominantly by women (see Raven 2000: 42–9; also Garside, Chapter 2). One might expect that letter fiction, associated conventionally with female authorship, might perhaps show a preponderance of women writers, but the statistics offer a salutary corrective to this view. Even counting all the epistolary fictions that claim on their title pages (truthfully or not) to be 'by a Lady' and adding them to those novels by known female authors gives only 145 novels actually or putatively authored by women between 1770 and 1800. That represents a third of the total of 435 new epistolary titles over those thirty years. Even if allowance is made for the large number of additional anonymous authors, the figure would still be unlikely to be more than half. It is equally possible to overstate the importance of a female readership for epistolary fiction. Although the reader of fiction was comprehensively satirized at the time as female (as in the figure of Lydia Languish in Richard Brinsley Sheridan's *The Rivals*, 1775), there is little hard evidence to suggest an overwhelmingly female readership.

Any plausible claim for the feminocentrism of epistolary fiction of the second half of the century therefore rests not on quantitative evidence for a predominantly feminine authorship or readership but on its characteristic mode and subject matter. The form of letter fiction has attracted much attention from feminist critics in particular for its interest in depicting female subjectivity in the potentially subversive act of constituting itself through writing. As the heroine of Charles Brockden Brown's *Jane Talbot* (published in Philadelphia 1801, first British edition 1804) writes: 'I have always found an unaccountable pleasure in dissecting, as it were, my heart; uncovering, one by one, its many folds, and laying it before you, as a country is shown on a map.'[3] Indeed, epistolary fiction is overwhelmingly organized around women's stories told largely by themselves, whether described as their 'history', their 'memoirs', or more simply, their correspondence. Of the 435 epistolary novels published between 1770 and 1800, for example, fully 193, or nearly

---

[2] *Monthly Review*, 52 (April 1775), 361.
[3] Charles Brockden Brown, *Jane Talbot* (Boston: Goodrich, 1827), 89.

half, specify a female protagonist in their titles, and the majority of these give a name to the woman in question. In the early part of the period such names may include the mildly allegorical ('Constantia' or 'Felicia'), but the tendency in the 1770s is to give female protagonists both first and second names in a bid for social realism. In 1772, for example, a reader would have been able to choose between *Genuine Memoirs of Miss Harriet Melvin and Miss Leonora Stanway, The History of Miss Dorinda Catsby, and Miss Emilia Faulkner*, or a translation of Madame Riccoboni's *Lettres d'Elisabeth-Sophie de Vallière* (as *Letters from Elizabeth Sophia de Valiere to her friend Louisa Hortensia de Canteleu*). (By the 1780s, this documentary realism was increasingly shadowed by a practice of using first names to signal the exemplary function of the character as a heroine; 1788 saw, for example, the publication of *Augusta; or, The Dependent Niece; Beatrice, or The Inconstant; Juliet; or The Cottager; Sophia; or, The Embarrassed Wife*; and Elizabeth Helme's *Clara and Emmeline; or, The Maternal Benediction*.)

The mass of this fiction explored very similar fictional territory—the description, and often critique, of modern domestic life among the gentry refracted through plots concerned with the possible fates of young women in the marital marketplace. Reviewing *The Correspondents* in 1775, the *Critical* commented approvingly on it as a notable exception to this rule, in so doing usefully laying out the reviewer's sense of the general run of novelistic narrative at the time:

> In this novel, no female laments that the tyranny of her parents prevents her from eloping with the dear dear man she loves; no cooing turtle pours forth her soul in tender epistles, which the faithful chambermaid conveys to the favourite swain; no rake triumphs over, and forsakes, the fair one he has deceived; in short, no intrigue is carried on; and, for that reason alone, a true novel reading girl would not give sixpence for the book.[4]

Such novels generally belong to the sentimental strain of fiction both in subject matter and language. A series of pathetic and sentimental 'effusions of the heart' describe the heroine's progress through a series of 'distresses' ranging from social embarrassment at one end of the spectrum (the anonymous *The Delicate Objection: or, Sentimental Scruple*, 1775) to sexual misdemeanour, incarceration, and rape at the other (as in Frances Brooke's celebrated *The History of Lady Julia Mandeville*, 1763). The heroine is conducted eventually to either a happy marriage or a tragic death. This story organizes the exploration and exemplification of the moral and social consequences of different courses of (mostly) female conduct in private life, advising against, variously, ill-considered friendships (*The Fatal Friendship*, 1770), moral pliability (*The Fatal Compliance*, 1771), amatory precipitation (*The Advantages of Deliberation; or, The Folly of Indiscretion*, 1772), marrying solely for money (*The Mercenary Marriage*, 1773), and the imprudent management of prospective husbands (*The Way to Lose Him; or, The History of Miss Wyndham*, 1773). Above all, novels

---

[4] *Critical Review*, 39 (April 1775), 341.

advise against forming 'unfortunate attachments' unsanctioned by family, a preoccupation signalled in the title of *Emma: or The Unfortunate Attachment* (1773). Taken in the mass, this fiction is concerned to describe the proper relation between the authority of the patriarchal family and female subjectivity, as the titles of *The Undutiful Daughter; or, The History of Miss Goodwin* (1771) or *The Test of Filial Duty* (1772) both suggest. It considers in particular the dangers that a modern cultivated female subjectivity might pose to itself and to the established social order, exploring sexual transgressions which might at the extreme breach class lines, as in William Combe's *Original Love-letters, between a Lady of Quality and a person of inferior station* (1784).

This strain of mainstream feminocentric epistolary fiction acknowledged Richardson as its origin and impetus, and the two novels that probably exerted the most pull on the fiction of the period right across Britain, France, and latterly Germany, were *Clarissa* and *Sir Charles Grandison* which gave birth to innumerable reworkings and rethinkings of their plots from first publication onwards in England and beyond. Those fictions that followed the line of *Clarissa* (the story of a young woman pursued and eventually raped by the libertine Lovelace who is revenged through staging a lengthy and sanctified death) subjected their heroines to lengthy sorrows and distresses before conducting them to the grave. Alternatively, they arranged to circumvent the ghastly inevitability of Clarissa's death by reforming the figure of the rake. This, essentially, is the strategy of Hugh Kelly's very popular *Memoirs of a Magdalen; or, The History of Miss Louisa Mildmay* (1767) which engineers the rescue of the heroine by her rakish lover (who originally rather fancies himself as Lovelace) from an even more unprincipled suitor; and saves her from undeserved incarceration in a house of correction to marry her first lover, now reformed, with the approval of all her friends and relatives. Frances Burney's *Evelina* (1778) equally flirts with the possibility that Evelina will be abducted, but ultimately reduces the Gothic extremities of *Clarissa* to the agonies of social embarrassment resolved successfully in a marriage which owes more to the ideals expressed by the plot of *Sir Charles Grandison*. Burney's denouement marries an English woman to the ideal English gentleman.

Nor was Richardson's influence confined to Britain. In America, the huge popularity of *Pamela* and *Clarissa* informed the early fiction of the republic. Hannah Webster Foster's *The Coquette* (1797), for instance, retold a celebrated (and true) story of a well-born widow who died in a public inn giving birth to an illegitimate baby, very much in the terms and language of *Clarissa* (see Verhoeven 1996). In France, Richardson's exploration of the limits of women's sexual and emotional freedom within the patriarchal family inspired Rousseau's *Julie: ou La Nouvelle Héloïse*. Set in the environs of Lake Geneva, the first half is concerned with the passion of a tutor, St Preux, for his pupil Julie, followed by her virtuous repudiation of him to conform to her father's choice of husband. The second half details the setting-up of a moral marital domestic idyll which eventually comes to incorporate the former lover, and culminates in the fortuitous death of Julie at the moment when it begins to seem that she has unsuccessfully repressed her earlier passion. Translated into

English, it caused a sensation in Britain, as much for its dangerous moral tendencies as for the beauties of its epistolary language. Clara Reeve remarked that:

> It is a dangerous book to put into the hands of youth, it awakens and nourishes those passions, which it is the exercise of Reason, and of Religion also, to regulate, and to keep within their true limits. On this account I have often wished that the two first Volumes of *Eloise* [sic] could be abridged and altered, so as to render them consistent with the unexceptionable morals of the two last.[5]

The further host of epistolary imitations, sequels, and responses that followed in Rousseau's wake variously endeavoured to celebrate passion or to regulate it. Sequels included *Letters of an Italian Nun and an English Gentleman* (1781), sometimes attributed to William Combe; novels importantly indebted to it included Henry Mackenzie's popular and influential *Julia de Roubigné* (1777), which concluded its story of a Rousseauistic trio of lovers by killing off the sentimental hero. Exported to Germany, Rousseau's novel inspired Goethe's *Die Leiden des jungen Werthers*. The story of another fatal passion, this is told not in the letters of a community of friends but solely through the solipsistic letters of the agonized protagonist, whose unrequited love for Charlotte, further thwarted by her dutiful marriage, eventually drives him to suicide. Apart from generating a fashion for both yellow waistcoats and suicide amongst young men of the time, the novel inspired a large number of consciously Wertheresque fictions throughout the 1780s and 1790s across Europe and America. In Britain, these included William James's *The Letters of Charlotte, during her connexion with Werter* (1786) which gave the other side to Goethe's one-sided correspondence. In America the hero of William Hill Brown's *The Power of Sympathy* (1789) kills himself, leaving a copy of *Werther* by his bedside (see Chandler 2008). In this way it is possible to trace Richardson's influence spreading through Europe and then returning into anglophone writing in other, emphatically foreign, versions, and to watch the way that, over the course of some fifty years, Richardsonian letter fiction mutated from the sociable through the forbidden and into the frankly pathological.

Although the vast mass of epistolary fiction conforms generally to this sentimental mainstream, it is worth noting that it proved entirely possible to extend the technical capabilities of letter fiction beyond it (for detailed taxonomies of the technical resources of epistolary fiction see Altman 1982; Bray 2003: 27). Towards the end of the century, in particular, authors experimented with using letters for a surprising variety of types of fiction. Tobias Smollett's *The Expedition of Humphry Clinker* (1771) is made up of letters written home while travelling around Britain by members of the same party about the same places and events but coloured by the very different perspectives of master and servant, male and female, young and old. As such, it represents a particularly original

---

[5] Clara Reeve, *The Progress of Romance, through Times, Countries and Manners*, 2 vols (Colchester: W. Keymer, 1785), 2.17–18.

combination of the sentimental with the picaresque, the feelings of the heart with social satire. Letter fiction was also pressed into service within historical romance (the most celebrated of these being Sophia Lee's *The Recess*, 1783–5, a novel which has entered the modern scholarly canon, and the least competent of which is probably Rosetta Ballin's *The Statue Room*, 1790, which has not), the Gothic (in the shape of, for example, Henry James Pye's *The Spectre*, 1789), and the satiric (a category which includes Oliver Goldsmith's *The Citizen of the World*, 1762, and Charles Johnstone's *The Pilgrim: or, A Picture of Life. In a Series of Letters, written mostly from London by a Chinese Philosopher, To his Friend at Quang-Tong...*, 1775; as well as Elizabeth Hamilton's late *Translation of the Letters of a Hindoo Rajah*, 1796, in the same vein). They lent themselves to the mildly pornographic in *The Rich Young Country Squire... A Novel chiefly in the Luscious Taste* (1787), to gossip about high life in *The Rattle; or, Modern Life* (1787), and to philosophical-cum-political comedy of ideas in Robert Bage's *Barham Downs* (1784). In the 1790s, they were co-opted to serve in what Marilyn Butler (1975) has termed 'the war of ideas', and debates sparked by the French Revolution enlivened the correspondence of Thomas Holcroft's *Anna St. Ives* (1792), Charlotte Smith's *Desmond* (1792), and Mary Hays' *The Memoirs of Emma Courtney* (1796). In the opening decades of the nineteenth century Sydney Owenson experimented with the form in her early regional fiction, *St. Clair; or, The Heiress of Desmond* (1803) and *The Wild Irish Girl* (1806).

If epistolary fiction dominated the market by virtue of sheer quantity, it was prominent, too, in the canon of the novel then emerging. In 1785, when Clara Reeve published *The Progress of Romance*, her influential literary history of the novel, the reading list she appended of recommended 'Books for Young Ladies' specified no novels other than 'Richardson's Works'. But in the main body of the book, she identified a number of epistolary works which 'deserve a place in every good young woman's closet': Brooke's *The History of Lady Julia Mandeville* and *The History of Emily Montague* (1769), Oliver Goldsmith's *The Citizen of the World*, Frances Sheridan's *Memoirs of Miss Sidney Bidulph* (1761), John Langhorne's *Letters between Theodosius and Constantia* (1763), *Letters from an English lady at Paris, in which are contained the memoirs of Mrs Williams* (1770), Richard and Elizabeth Griffith's *Letters of Henry and Frances*, and Charles Jenner's *Letters from Altamont in Town to his Friends in the Country* (1776). Reeve's choices are endorsed and extended by two less morally prescriptive and indeed frankly commercial contemporary collections directed at the general reader. *The Novelist's Magazine*, publishing novels in serial parts between 1779 and 1788, selected, in addition to *Pamela* and *Clarissa*, *Letters between Theodosius and Constantia*, and added three other older perennial popular favourites: Mary Collyer's *Letters from Felicia to Charlotte* (1744), the translation of Madame de Grafigny's *Lettres d'une Péruvienne (Letters of a Peruvian Princess)* (1748), and Kelly's *Memoirs of a Magdalen; or, History of Louisa Mildmay*. In the 1790s *Cooke's pocket edition of novels, or Novelist's Entertaining Library* reiterated Reeve's judgement by including *The Citizen of the World*, but amplified her selection with *Humphry Clinker* and Grafigny, Kelly, and Langhorne.

Decline

By the 1790s, however, the production of new epistolary fiction was definitely on the wane. While there is plenty of evidence of republication and consumption of favourite epistolary classics whether in the original or in translation, the decline in production is spectacular in its suddenness. In 1791 only a fifth of new novels were written in letters, and this decayed further to only a tenth of the total between 1797 and 1799. Between 1800 and 1829, the database *British Fiction 1800–1829* (Garside et al. 2004) includes perhaps nineteen titles of full-scale epistolary fiction of a total of 2,272 works of fiction published; that is to say, over these thirty years, the proportion of new fiction written in letters had declined to less than 1 per cent. Garside notes of this period that '[o]nly seven titles . . . contain the once potent phrase "In a Series of Letters", which had introduced more than one hundred new novels between 1770 and 1790' (2000: 53). The preface to Ann Mary Hamilton's novel, *The Irishwoman in London, A Modern Novel* (1810), revealingly suggests that this precipitous decline may have been as much the result of the bottom dropping out of the market as a failure of writers' interest in the form; Hamilton notes that her novel had originally been epistolary but that 'Immediately after disposing of it, the Author left town, and the Publisher conceiving it not so saleable, altered it from Letters to Chapters'.[6] The reviewers had long been unenthusiastic: the *Monthly* sighed as early as 1790 that 'we are indeed so sickened with this worn-out species of composition, that we have lost all relish for it'.[7] Authors who had established careers in writing letter fiction occasionally hung on (one thinks here of Charlotte Smith's last novel *The Letters of a Solitary Wanderer*, 1800–2), but most new authors simply abandoned it. The suddenness of its fall from favour is marked in two writing careers. Germaine de Staël writes *Delphine* (1802; English trans. 1803) in letters but *Corinne* (1807) in the third person, even though it is a rewriting of *Sir Charles Grandison*. Jane Austen's output in the nineties included a considerable amount of epistolary fiction, including *Lady Susan*, the first draft of *Sense and Sensibility*, and arguably that of *Pride and Prejudice*. But by the 1810s, although the letter continues to play an important part in her fiction, she has adopted her own variants of third-person omniscient narration within which the letter is embedded and managed.

By the 1810s, although letter fiction would survive and even flourish within hybrid forms, pure epistolary fiction was definitively obsolete on the British literary scene. Among the many novels that bear witness to this, Walter Scott's *Guy Mannering; or, The Astrologer* (1815) stands out. Set mainly in the early 1780s, it exploits the obsolescence of the form to convey period flavour. It contains within itself a pastiche of the epistolary fiction of that decade, featuring the correspondence of a heroine, called with a particular

---

[6] Ann Mary Hamilton, *The Irishwoman in London: A Modern Novel*, 3 vols (London: J. F. Hughes, 1810), 'Advertisement'.

[7] *Monthly Review*, n.s., 2 (August 1790), 463.

eye to Rousseau, Mackenzie, and sentimental convention, Julia. In conformity with the conventions that the *Critical* sent up in 1775, she pours forth letters lamenting the tyranny of her father which divides her from the man she loves. Her forbidden intrigue, however, is swiftly overtaken by a plot concerning the ruin of an ancient and proud family brought about by a smuggler and a lawyer. In hindsight the general run of late eighteenth-century epistolary fiction had now resolved itself into a formula, burlesqued at length by Charles Robert Maturin in 1818:

> The heroine must be exquisitely, *unimaginably* beautiful.... She must be an orphan (if a foundling so much the better), left mysteriously in the care of some opulent and noble family who most unaccountably...suffer her to board and lodge with them, and water her geraniums till the decisive age of sixteen, though conscious that the noble and enamoured heir of the family has been in love with her from their mutual cradles...the heroine is distracted by the ambition of the father, the pride of the mother, and the jealous insults of the sisters, not forgetting a snug misery of her own arising from the persecutions of some desperate baronet...Persecuted by love and hatred, she flies, flies over mountains without a stain on her white satin slippers.... She must be run away with five or six times before she reaches the end of her journey...and it is on such occasions that she displays that extraordinary contrast of physical debility and mental independence, of fragility and hardihood, that constitutes the very essence of a novel heroine...she can tramp in her silk stocking feet...straight up Piccadilly, and then new troubles begin...just as she is about to be fully committed [for debt to jail]...the hero enters...clasps her to his bosom, maugre the bailiff's followers, swears that nothing shall divide them...; in the struggle, her wig or her handkerchief (we forget which) drops off, and her *mole cinque-spotted*, or strawberry-mark, or something equally conclusive and satisfactory, is discovered, by which she is proved to be a duke's daughter...her noble family in the same breath recognize her, and give their consent to her marriage: her disappointed lovers, one and all, pair off with the "sweet friends," into whose sympathising ears her epistolary sorrows had been poured through five volumes.[8]

If epistolary fiction now seemed formulaic, threadbare, and longwinded, it was also associated with old-fashioned French taste. In 1827 Étienne de Jouy prefaced his epistolary novel, *Cécile: ou, les Passions*, with an argument for the superiority of both the subject matter and the form of epistolary fiction as practised by Richardson and Rousseau over historical romance as practised by 'the Author of Waverley'. The *Monthly's* review of de Jouy nevertheless caustically dismissed the epistolary, once regarded as the most natural, graceful and realistic fictional mode, as 'unnatural', 'cumbrous', and downright implausible:

> Perhaps so unnatural and cumbrous a machinery of fiction as the epistolatory [*sic*] never was invented. The ungraceful appearance of egotism which it entails upon the favourite personages of the story, the troublesome necessity of frequent repetition, the unavoidable

---

[8] Charles Robert Maturin, 'Novel-Writing', *British Review, or London Critical Journal*, 11 (February 1818), 40–4.

interruptions which break the continuous flow of events, the awkward transfer of the narration from one writer to another, and the absurdity of supposing the whole business and minute details of life to be represented in an eternal interchange of letters—all these inconveniences completely dissipate the illusions of fiction, and destroy that air of reality which is its principal charm.[9]

Jouy's view that the vogue for Scott was responsible for the fall into disfavour of epistolary fiction makes for too simple a piece of literary history. Still, Scott had already experimented with pastiching and exploiting the form in *Guy Mannering*, and he would repeat this effect at more length in 1824 with the almost simultaneous publication of volumes 6 to 8 of the deluxe collected edition of novels, *Ballantyne's Novelist's Library*, devoted to Richardson, and his latest novel, *Redgauntlet*. As the disconcerted *Monthly* noted, this last represented a marked departure: 'On opening the first volume, we were struck with dismay to observe that it was entirely occupied with letters, and that the correspondence was carried on solely between two young gentlemen... '.[10] The two projects were not, of course, unconnected; a year spent editing Richardson and reflecting upon his place within the national history of the novel had prompted in Scott an experimental and a historicist turn, by which the first volume of *Redgauntlet*, set in the 1760s, would be written in a pastiche of a mode associated largely with Richardson's *oeuvre*.

The experiment did not find favour with this reviewer: 'it was', he continued, 'with real satisfaction that we discovered, on opening the second volume, that the author had abandoned the epistolary style' (198). The reviewer felt that this decision required neither apology nor explanation; nonetheless, Scott provided one, addressed explicitly to the reader. It is an obituary for letter fiction, summarizing the now commonplace contemporary view of its inadequacies. He starts by sending up its claim to authenticity, pointing out the inconveniences that arise either from its reality or from its pretensions to it: 'a genuine correspondence of this kind, (and Heaven forbid it should be in any respect sophisticated by interpolations of our own!) can seldom be found to contain all in which it is necessary to instruct the reader for his full comprehension of the story.' Scott notes how unsuited it is technically to the demands of pacy narrative: 'it must often happen that various prolixities and redundancies occur in the course of an interchange of letters, which would only hang as a dead weight on the progress of the narrative.'[11] Volume 2 went on to experiment with the first-person journal, a form more associated with the Gothic, before resolving into third-person narration. Segueing from modes of narration associated with the period being depicted into modern modes of narrative, *Redgauntlet* effectively constructed in miniature a literary history of the development of the British novel. Third-person narration superseded first person, and the novel abandoned the close-up of 'writing to the

---

[9] *Monthly Review*, n.s., 5 (August 1827), 541.

[10] *Monthly Review*, 2nd ser., 104 (June 1824), 198.

[11] Walter Scott, *Redgauntlet*, ed. G. A. M. Wood, with David Hewitt (Edinburgh: Edinburgh University Press, 1997), vol. 2, ch. 1; 125.

moment' for a grand historical overview. This narrative has shaped conventional literary history ever since.

A number of explanations have been advanced for the sudden fall from favour of the epistolary mode. The most long-standing of these reiterates this story of technical exhaustion. By this account, Richardson took epistolarity as practised earlier in the century by the likes of Aphra Behn and Eliza Haywood to new heights of narrative sophistication, dramatically expanding the technical resources of epistolary fiction. In the following decades lesser writers slavishly imitated him, but, lacking his peculiar genius, they reproduced only the drawbacks of the form—prolixity, repetition, vast length, otiose sentimentality, and a near-fatal retardation of plot. This view has been expressed influentially by scholars such as Frank Gees Black, who argued that Richardson's 'ingenuity' 'left comparatively little for his followers beyond tame imitation', 'hodge podges', 'servile copies', 'ineffective burlesques', and 'impudent prostitutions' (1940: 1). A variant and extension of this explanation is the more specific suggestion that the sensational and relatively fast-moving Gothic fiction which became immensely popular in the 1790s under the aegis of Ann Radcliffe simply ousted the leisurely redundancies of the letter form. Black noted the difficulties inherent in adapting the reflective and retrospective epistolary to Gothic in producing enough surprise, speed, and suspense (47); more recently, Garside remarks that 'one suspects that the mechanics of the epistolary form had become an impediment to a readership eager for the thrills and escapades available in newer direct narrative modes, notably the Gothic novel' (2000: 54).

Other scholarship suggests that this decline might be attributable to the increasing cultural acceptance of the novel as a form. Clifford Siskin argues that anxieties about the novel's generative power gradually waned, so that the novel began to be seen as 'a primarily reflective, rather than inherently productive tool—that was increasingly understood to depict, not construct or change, the details of English life', while at the same time attention shifted away from the widespread vogue for writing to the figure of the celebrity author (1996: 434–7). Fiction had perhaps become so successfully naturalized by the end of the century that it no longer needed to describe and excuse itself as a collection of real letters. It is certainly the case that later in the century title-pages suggest that epistolary fiction comes to identify itself more securely as novelistic. In 1770, of a total of fourteen epistolary fictions, only two described themselves as novels; in 1785, fourteen of twenty so described themselves. In this version of events, the novel simply grows up, becomes professionalized, and sheds epistolarity as a now unnecessary alibi. Others have argued that the demise of epistolary fiction can be connected to the political upheavals of the 1790s. Did epistolary fiction acquire a distinctively radical tinge in that it valorized subversive sentimental feeling rather than patriarchal and monarchical authority (Watson 1994)? Was it that the letter fell under suspicion in an era of anxiety over spies and their correspondence (Favret 1993)? Was it that the form was no longer able to manage contemporary anxieties of individual self and identity (Bray 2003)? Did it fail because of a global collapse of the Enlightenment ideal of transnational cosmopolitanism in the face of global warfare (Cook 1996) or because it was unsuited to a new sense in the wake of the French Revolution of the epic grandeur of the nation (Beebee 1999)?

These various explanations are not necessarily mutually exclusive; they can be bound together in the general hypothesis that after 1790 there was a change in the conception of contemporary fiction's work in the negotiation of readerly subjectivities and, in particular, the regulation of the relation between private feeling and public authority. There was, in consequence, an abrupt termination to the cycle of reiteration and contestation evident over the previous thirty years of fiction. In effect, so this argument might run, the work of fiction shifted over the wartime years, accounting for the rise of first Gothic and then its second cousins, regional and historical novels. Letter fiction might well have come to be perceived as technically exhausted once it was no longer well-matched to the contemporary project of mainstream fiction. It was suited to the self-conscious depiction and examination of a feminized private subjectivity, interested in the depiction of the ebb and flow of sociability played out in a limited and specific class context, and in describing the flow of communication across the spaces between comparable and separated persons, cosmopolitan and pan-European in outlook, and, despite a few exceptions, concerned with stories of contemporary life. Conversely, it was not suited to the portrayal of public historical events, to painting a panorama of a society from top to bottom, to chronicling the minutiae of the local, to depicting the past—in short, it was not suited to the newly national and often self-consciously masculinist preoccupations of the wartime novel (on which, see Trumpener 1997, Ferris 1991). With the definitive move in fiction away from the exploration and elaboration of a pan-European and feminized culture of sensibility to the panoramic and diachronic depiction of nation, and, increasingly, empire, third-person retrospective narration moved into the ascendant.

Canons

Although the letter itself would remain active and important within hybrid forms from 1800 onwards, the epistolary generally came to denote the past. Richardson's fiction—inefficient, slow, extravagant—stood for everything that was not modern. As *Blackwood's Magazine* put it in 1824:

> Who reads Richardson?... The merit—the perfection, we may say, of a few particular conceptions, and of some scenes in these immense volumes, is undeniable; but how few, now-a-days, will wade, or ought to wade, through such a heap of lumber as Clarissa Harlowe, merely that they may be able to understand the sublime catastrophe; or to endure the interminable prosing of the Cedar Parlour in Grandison, for the sake of Clementina's Shakespearian madness...[12]

[12] *Blackwood's Edinburgh Magazine*, 15 (April 1824), 408.

What then did the nineteenth century choose to preserve and display upon its library shelves? What was still being read in the opening years of the new century?

One piece of evidence is the self-improving reading list that Mary Wollstonecraft Shelley was working her way through in 1817 and 1818 while touring the continent, on the eve of drafting *Frankenstein* (1818), itself organized within an epistolary framework. It included a number of epistolary fictions: Italian translations of both *Pamela* and *Clarissa* (suggesting not so much that these novels were only available to her in Italian because she was abroad, but perhaps rather that she knew the novels so well that this seemed a good way of improving her Italian), *Lettres d'une Péruvienne, Julie, Anna St. Ives, Letters of a Solitary Wanderer, The Wild Irish Girl*, and Mackenzie (perhaps *Julia de Roubigné*). More evidence is furnished by Leigh Hunt's whimsical essay 'A Novel-Party', first published in the periodical *The Examiner* (no. 9, 18 July 1825). This imagines an occasion at which characters from the previous century's novels attend an evening party together, amuses readers with the incongruities of their dress and demeanour, and classes the fiction of the previous century into categories of guest. 'A Novel-Party' depends for its effect on Hunt's readers being familiar with all of the novels to which he refers, even if only by reputation. The guests he describes include the Grandisons, Pamela, Mr and Mrs Humphry Clinker, and Evelina. Clarissa and Lovelace are mentioned, but are not actually in attendance, because they properly belong 'in the region of romance' rather than the novel. Hunt also includes figures from two more epistolary novels: Louisa Mildmay and Desmond.

Taken together, Shelley's reading list and Hunt's essay suggest that many of the favourites of the previous century were still in circulation. But this snapshot of which epistolary fictions were still visible on the cultural horizon in the early decades of the nineteenth century is to some extent belied by the very short list of epistolary classics which survived in three collections of the early nineteenth century—William Mudford's *The British Novelists* (1810–16), Anna Laetitia Barbauld's *The British Novelists* (1810, revised 1820), and Scott's *Ballantyne's Novelist's Library* (1821–4). Between them, they preserved only eight epistolary novels: *Pamela, Clarissa*, and *Sir Charles Grandison; The History of Lady Julia Mandeville; Humphry Clinker; Julia de Roubigné; Evelina*; and *Barham Downs*. Startlingly, only *Humphry Clinker* appeared in all three collections (for more detail, see Gamer 2008). This much-reduced list of the previous era's epistolary fiction that would cumulatively be promoted to the status of classic is borne out elsewhere. John Dunlop's *The History of Fiction: Being a Critical Account of the Most Celebrated Prose Works of Fiction* (1814), for example, singled out only Richardson's works, *Evelina*, and *Humphry Clinker*. One reason for this reduction in the number of titles is the increasingly national agenda of such collections and histories, which tended to exclude French fiction. In fact, the persistence of *Evelina* and *Humphry Clinker* may be in large part attributable on the one hand to their deviation from the sentimental tradition and on the other to their congruence with a newly national agenda. *Humphry Clinker* was both a 'Scotch novel' and a novel which toured Britain—as such, akin in some respects to Scott's project. *Evelina*, on the other hand, was perceived as especially English: in 1818 Maturin singled out *Evelina* for attention and further commended all Burney's novels because they 'impress us with an indescribable sense of their *nationality*—they could not have been written by any but an English woman' being 'inveterately untranslateably English'.[13]

Attending in this way to the canons of epistolary fiction that were successively constructed from the late 1770s onwards—canons which increasingly sought to isolate a moral, British tradition as distinct from a European perspective in which Richardson might instead feature as a colleague of Rousseau—can usefully provide the outlines of possible reading lists for the modern reader. But the modern reader has to decide whether to consider the period's epistolary fiction according to its own assessments or according to the verdict of nineteenth-century posterity. Even in the twenty-first century it remains hard comprehensively to reverse the judgement of conventional literary history against letter fiction, for this would require reversing the relative desirability of narrative and sentiment. It would require being able to sympathize with Mackenzie's remark in his introduction to *Julia de Roubigné* that it had been mostly impossible and undesirable to reduce the letters to narrative 'because they are made up of sentiment, which narrative would destroy'.[14]

[13] *British Review*, 11 (February 1818), 45.
[14] Henry Mackenzie, *Julia de Roubigné, A Tale. In a Series of Letters*, 2 vols (London: W. Strahan and T. Cadell, 1777), 1.x.

21

Celebrity and Scandalous Fiction

CLARA TUITE

The Scandal of Fiction

For much of the eighteenth century, and for many eighteenth-century readers, the novel genre was itself a scandal—and all novels scandalous—identified as it was with a range of scandalous factors: lower-class and women readers; cheaper and more widely available print matter; an unregulated flow of reading materials; a shift in the technique and location of reading; a new mobility and transportability through which novel reading became associated with solitary interactive pleasures; and a new inclusiveness by which the everyday and the ordinary came to figure as the customary subjects of fictional representation.

The scandalous status of the early novel genre is enthusiastically rehearsed by moralists and pedagogues in the anti-novel discourse that accompanied the emergence of this new cultural technology. Anxieties about print—paradoxically, so material yet so virtual—fuelled this anti-novel discourse, which fixated on the potential of print fiction, like pornography, 'to move the body', as Richard Dyer subtly suggests (1992: 121). Somewhat more luridly, the clergyman Vicesimus Knox claimed that '[novels] often pollute the heart in the recesses of the closet, inflame the passions at a distance from temptation, and teach all the malignity of vice in solitude'.[1] As the headmaster of an elite boy's boarding school, Tonbridge School (attended, incidentally, by Jane Austen's father), Knox had professional reasons to worry about vice in solitude and the interactive possibilities of the novel genre. Knox was writing in 1778, three years after Jane Austen was born, and forty-three years before Archbishop Richard Whately was to claim in a review of Austen's fiction that 'the times seem to be past when an apology was requisite from reviewers for condescending to notice a novel'.[2]

---

[1] Vicesimus Knox, 'On Novel Reading', *Essays, Moral and Literary*, 3 vols (1778; New York: Garland, 1972), 1.96.

[2] Richard Whately, 'Review of *Northanger Abbey and Persuasion*', *Quarterly Review*, 24 (January 1821), 352–76 (352).

In this context, not even chaste novels were chaste. As Jean-Jacques Rousseau wrote in the Preface to *La Nouvelle Héloïse* (1761), one of the most influential novels of the eighteenth century, which details a pupil's seduction by her tutor and the *ménage à trois* with her husband that ensues, 'Never did a chaste maiden read Novels'.[3] These words, which served simultaneously as warning, provocation, and seduction, were echoed across the Channel, by novel-writers and anti-novel moralists alike. Even Rousseau's most ardent fans (and they were legion) expressed their admiration in terms of a paradoxical repudiation of the genre: 'I feel myself to be a better person ever since I read your novel, which I hope is not a novel' (quoted in Darnton 2001: 248). How the novel itself strives to become a 'better' genre—less scandalous and more polite—offers one way of reconsidering the development of the genre in the eighteenth century.

What evolved with the so-called 'rise of the novel' was a form of realism that would later come to stand in for the novel genre itself. As the formal features of realism were being consolidated at mid-century, other fictional genres came to be marginalized under the increasingly stigmatized generic label of romance: scandal fiction, *chroniques scandaleuses*, erotic fiction, pornography, secret histories and what William Warner calls 'the novel of amorous intrigue' (1998: xiii). Scandal fiction needs to be understood as part of this newly anachronistic repertoire of romance genres. Whilst these romance genres lay at the outskirts of the emergent bourgeois novel, they can be seen, nevertheless, to enact central features of the modern realist novel, and to participate vitally in mainstream currents of the novel.

The traditional story of the rise of the novel is also complicated by the emergence of celebrity culture. The premium placed on authorial presence in celebrity culture works against the realist decorum of authorial discretion. In the early eighteenth century, novel authorship is associated with the notoriety of hackdom and anonymity rather than heroic authorial fame, but this starts to change from the 1750s with the move to greater specific generic definition, refinement, and respectability. Once authorship is understood as a form of publicity, it becomes a more complex and varied phenomenon. Another paradox then that marks the culture of fiction from around 1750 is the ambivalent status of the celebrity author who could, as typified by Rousseau, both urge a new kind of sincere communion with his adoring readers while fleeing those very same readers when they sought him out in the flesh.

The novel's refinement of generic codes was accompanied by institutional controls that defined polite literature through systems of censorship. Our period is marked by a shift in the economy of literary production from a patronage to a market economy. Censorship is therefore connected with developments in licensing laws that move away

---

[3] Jean-Jacques Rousseau, *Julie, or the New Heloise*, trans. Philip Stewart and Jean Vaché (Hanover, NH: University Press of New England, 1997), 4.

from a conception of the author as the punishable subject of printed obscenity towards a conception of the author as someone with an economic interest in the commodity that they produce. Nevertheless, the two forms are interconnected.

Pre-publication censorship of published works ended in 1695 with the lapsing of the Licensing Act (although it continued for theatrical performances). After 1695, censorship occurred indirectly through regulatory measures in copyright and libel laws, whereby all manner of printed materials that represented sexual activity (including novels, para-medical texts, and adultery trials) could be tried at the King's Bench for obscene libel. The pivotal piece of legislation in this regard was the 1710 Statute of Anne, which sought to regulate the press by way of economic controls.

A defining event was the 1727 case of *Rex v. Curll* against the pirate publisher, Edmund Curll, for publishing in 1724 *Venus in the Cloister*, a translation from the French, and *A Treatise of the Use of Flogging in Venereal Affairs* (1718), originally published in Latin by John Henry Meibomius. This case established the foundation of the English law for obscene libel as a misdemeanour within common law that survived until 1959 with the repeal of the Obscene Publications Act of 1857. However, Curll's work was also targeted for its political opposition, demonstrating the close imbrication between obscene and sedi-tious libel that obtained at this time. The *Treatise* was republished in 1761 as 'The Use of Flogging, as provocative to the pleasures of love. With some Remarks on the Office of the Loins and Reins', moving away from Curll's paramedical framing of the original transla-tion and thereby enhancing the work's erotic potential within the emerging English por-nographic speciality of flagellation which peaks in the *Bon Ton Magazine* of the 1790s and the titles published by George Cannon in the 1830s. As Nicola Parsons observes, 'the lapse of pre-publication censorship does not result in increased openness', but rather 'creates secrecy and subterfuge' (2009: 31). In this context, *roman à clef* modes of fiction thrived, before the bourgeois realist genre started to define itself against such modes.

In the 1740s, as Karen O'Brien points out, 'the novel enjoyed something of a rebirth as a realist genre, self-consciously distanced from its previous incarnations as romance, politics à *clef*, and feminized erotic fantasy' (2005b: 403). A seminal form of this romance and politics à *clef* was the 'secret history' of Delarivier Manley's *The New Atalantis* (1709), a Tory exposé of members of the Whig cabinet, who appeared thinly disguised by alle-gorical names and in 'disabilly', or *déshabille*, enmeshed in scandalous love intrigues, and whose real identities were unmasked via a 'key'.[4] This particular form of scandal fiction combined scandals of politics with scandals of the bedroom.

To trace the endurance and transformation of these scandal genres from 1750 to 1820 is to trace the residual power of some of the more atavistic novelistic forms and genres, and of the earliest defining impulses and generic features of this vital new form of print culture.

---

[4] Delarivier Manley, *The New Atalantis*, ed. Rosalind Ballaster (Harmondsworth: Penguin, 1992), 23.

These genres raise questions about the way the history of the novel genre has been told. They maintain the fascination with novelty, news, and reportage: with the heightened charge of the collision between fact and fiction, private and public, the sentimental and the sexual, the corporeal and the intellectual, the sophisticated and the vulgar; and with the exposure of 'real' life. These genres force a particular kind of close encounter between reference and figuration, reportage and invention, sense and sensation.

The genre of the Atalantis had a rich and varied life after the 1740s, when the term 'Atalantis' became a kind of shorthand for the *roman à clef* or for any scandalous text which employed dashes to stand in for the proper names of the real personages it represented: simultaneously advertising and concealing these identities. This technique was taken up in pornographic writing with *Kitty's Attalantis* (1766), a form of whore's biography that presented accounts of well-known prostitutes in London. In 1823, Lord Byron's narrator ironically invoked the 'Atalantis' as a point of contrast with *Don Juan*—'For I disdain to write an Atalantis' (*Don Juan* XI.87, 693)—in a customary gesture of disavowal that functioned more to license the comparison than to disown it. For Byron's text—as much as Manley's—thrives on the satirical exposure of contemporary behaviour through *roman à clef* techniques.

One way of registering how scandal fiction might figure in a revised history of the novel is to consider scandal fiction as embodying everything that the polite novel sought to repudiate or disavow: criminality; sexuality; sensation; vulgarity; voyeurism; reflexivity. For just as the novel genre itself is a scandal for much of the eighteenth century, the increasing respectability of the novel genre from the 1750s is predicated upon the move away from forms such as *romans à clef* and *chroniques scandaleuses*. A notable feature of these genres, as their names attest, is the close connection between English and European forms, with much importation and cross-fertilization. What we notice is how the English novel starts to define itself as a national genre against the scandalous excesses of the French or Italian novel—which it often does while exploiting and purveying these foreign excesses. This is particularly the case with the most scandalous forms of fiction: pornography and erotic fiction.

Erotic Fiction, Libertinism, and the Sentimentalization of Pornography

The first important context for modern pornography and erotic fiction is sixteenth-century Italian Renaissance humanism and its central text of Pietro Aretino's *Ragionamenti* (1534–6) or *Dialogues*, an anti-clerical satire which presents fictional dialogues between women about the best profession for women—nun, wife, or prostitute. The first English translation of the *Dialogues* appeared in 1658 as *The Crafty Whore: or, the Mistery and Iniquity of Bawdy Houses*. As Lynn Hunt notes, the 1740s saw 'a major recasting of pornographic writing' after a period of stagnation that followed the high moment of the mid-seventeenth century's *L'Ecole des filles* and *L'Académie des dames* (1993: 31). In the English context, John Cleland has long been considered 'the most skilful eighteenth-century English pornographer' (Jacob 1993: 178). And the diversity of Cleland's *oeuvre* testifies not only to Cleland's entrepreneurialism but also to the porousness of the novel form at this moment, as it took infusions from a range of genres such as the criminal and whore biography. Cleland's main contribution to English pornography was *Memoirs of a Woman of Pleasure* [*Fanny Hill*] (1749), a key text in the efflorescence of European pornographic writing that occurred in the 1740s with *Histoire de Dom Bougre, portier des Chartreux* (1741), *Le Sopha* by Crébillon fils (1742), and Diderot's *Les Bijoux indiscrets* (1748) and *Thérèse Philosophe* (1748).

Cleland's *Memoirs* is probably the single most read European pornographic novel of all time (Hunt 1993: 21), as well as a vital protagonist in the development of the realist novel as a bourgeois form. First published in November 1748, it was withdrawn from publication on 24 November 1749, after the author, printer, and publisher were found guilty of producing an obscene book. Cleland's novel thereby offers a benchmark for evaluating the terms in which the new literary marketplace was defining itself as a polite, middle-class space in opposition to the popularly obscene.

A feature of early modern pornography and erotic fiction is the preponderance of female narrators, which Cleland's novel continues through the first-person epistolary voice of its main protagonist, the young prostitute Fanny Hill. This device facilitates eavesdropping, enabling intimate access to female experience for the male reader. Like Aretino in his *Dialogues*, Cleland features the voyeuristic sexual initiation of its heroine. In one memorable scene, Fanny Hill watches two men having sex. Whilst she fantasizes 'due vengeance' for them, it is Fanny herself however who suffers the consequences as she attempts to escape the premises unseen and raise the house against the men:

> All this, so criminal a scene, I had the patience to see to an end, purely that I might gather more facts, and certainly against them in my full design to do their deserts instant justice...burning as I was with rage, and indignation, I jump'd down from my chair, in order to raise the house upon them, with such an unlucky impetuosity, that some nail or ruggedness in the floor caught my foot, and flung me on my face with such violence, that I fell senseless to the ground.[5]

This moment is critical not only for its explicit representation of sexual relations between men, but also for the narrative complexity with which this representation occurs. It bristles with the irony of double entendre whereby Fanny's 'burning' with rage is also her burning with voyeuristic desire. And it features the dramatic irony and comic slapstick of Fanny falling flat on the ground, as though her desire for vengeance is thwarted by

---

[5] John Cleland, *Memoirs of a Woman of Pleasure*, ed. Peter Sabor (Oxford: Oxford University Press, 1985), 159.

an inanimate object: 'some nail'. This conjunction of the powers of random detail and chance with a narrative omnipotence that parodies divine intervention (and through which the text itself works against its first-person narrator) embodies a particularly modern novelistic energy and complexity.

At the time, 'due vengeance' for homosexual acts between men was meted out through hanging or the violent public punishment of the pillory (see Crompton 1985: 158–71). In Cleland's novel, we see a symbolic subversion of this punishment, and a satirical exposure of the voyeuristic impulse that animates it: not only do the two men escape 'due vengeance'—as the text imagines a world in which sexual relations between men goes unpunished—but the would-be punisher is herself tripped up and thrown on the floor. In the history of censorship, silences are often eloquent sites of meaning. Hence, the very absence of this homosexual scene in the censored version of the novel, published in 1750 after the prosecution in 1749, testifies to its scandalous potency.

The eighteenth-century novel remediated elite masculine cultures of Enlightenment humanism, libertinism, and materialism. In *Memoirs*, Cleland's materialist libertinism represents innocence as corporeal pleasure and offers an empiricist celebration of learning through the senses. Here, pornography activates pastoral conventions that represent innocence dialectically as sexual initiation. Dramatizing the moment at which sexual innocence is transformed into experience, Fanny's body becomes 'the sweet seat of the most exquisite sensation, which had been, till that instant, the seat of the most sensible innocence' (11). The *Memoirs'* Enlightenment materialism deploys an eroticized language of sensibility, as in the description of Fanny's kiss from Phoebe as a kiss that 'seemed to exhale her soul through her lips' (12). Here, a spiritualization of the senses works against religion in favour of humanist materialism. Such etherealization of corporeal experience enhances the text's lyric intensity and rhetorical digression, moving the text away from the corporeal pleasure principle of pornography's drive 'to move the body' toward the more open-ended pleasures of linguistic and aesthetic absorption.

Despite its sexual explicitness, the *Memoirs'* high literariness distinguishes it both from other contemporary whore's biographies in English and earlier classics of European pornography. Unlike Aretino, for example, who recommended explicit language that everyone could understand—'Speak plainly and say "fuck", "prick", "cunt", and "ass" if you want anyone except the scholars at the University of Rome to understand you'[6]—Cleland used suggestive euphemisms such as the 'soft laboratory of love' and 'systems of manliness' (116, 64). This exuberant aestheticizing of sexual practices and body parts displays a euphemistic virtuosity; and the extraordinary lyricism of Cleland's writing of the body

---

[6] Pietro Aretino, *Aretino's Dialogues*, trans. Raymond Rosenthal (London: George Allen & Unwin, 1972), 43.

confounds the distinction between the polite and the obscene, the sentimental and the pornographic.

Cleland also adopted the paramedical genre (see Wagner 1988: 8–46), with his 1755 translation of Giovanni Bianchi's *The True History and Adventures of Catherine Vizzani* (1755), a conjectural biography of the *cause célèbre* and 'passing' woman, Catherine Vizzani, who lived as a man and was only discovered to be a woman on her deathbed. The translation, like the original, and like Boccaccio's *Decameron*, with which the original was compared, was quickly censored.

In any discussion of the history of censorship, special attention must be given to the asterisk. As Paula Findlen writes, 'The second edition [of Cleland's *Memoirs*] discovered the beauty of the asterisk to omit anything that was best left to the imagination' (2009: 246). Both insistently material and illimitably metaphorical, one particular beauty of the asterisk is its rhetorical capacity to commit by omission or omit by commission. Experimentation with the asterisk is one way in which eighteenth-century novels enact a fascination with the novelty of print culture and explore the profoundly ambivalent ontological status of print as both material and virtual.

Sterne's ****

Laurence Sterne's novels are exemplary in this regard. They lovingly proliferate typographical excess in a range of devices such as rows of asterisks, dashes, diagrams, blank pages, blacked-out pages, and marbled page—'(motley emblem of my work!)'—all of which draw attention to the materiality of print and to the constructed (rather than mimetic) nature of the novel form.[7] Sterne's fondness for mixing up typefaces in what is called 'circus make-up' suggests the proximity of print culture to popular entertainment: such special effects are the tricks of the trade of writing fiction in popular print-cultural form (Pinkus 1968: 82).

Sterne's 'obscene asterisms'[8] simultaneously embody, materially replace, and stand in for the sexually unspeakable. They also enact the peculiarly British empiricist problematization of language as an interruption of sensation and experience, first elaborated in John Locke's *An Essay Concerning Human Understanding* (1690). As Sterne writes in *Tristram Shandy* (1760–7), 'Well might Locke write a chapter on the imperfections of words' (354). One of Sterne's great innovations is to join these two concerns within the novel form so that a serious empiricist exploration of the limits of language goes hand in hand with an exploration of the limits of what may and may not be said in polite discourse.

---

[7] Laurence Sterne, *The Life and Opinions of Tristram Shandy Gentleman*, ed. Graham Petrie, introd. Christopher Ricks (Harmondsworth: Penguin, 1982), 232.

[8] *Monthly Review*, 32 (February 1765), 125.

A leading example occurs in an episode of *A Sentimental Journey* (1768) entitled 'The Case of Delicacy', where Sterne's narrator, Yorick, is called upon to share his room at a one-bedroom inn with an unknown lady traveller and her *fille de chambre*. How to comply with this request while preserving all due 'delicacy' is the drama that ensues. Much like the curtains of the bed-chamber in the little inn at Savoy—which are first judged to be 'of a flimsy transparent cotton, and . . . too scanty to draw close', but later 'deemed a sufficient barrier on the side of Monsieur'—Sterne's fiction materially embodies as it dramatizes 'The Case of Delicacy'.[9] Sterne preserves delicacy by parodying it, subjecting it to the double entendre which is produced by translating 'the case of delicacy' as 'the manner in which the lady and myself should be obliged to undress and get to bed' (124). The double entendre of 'undress and get to bed' suggests how delicacy can also be construed as obscenity, and how perilously and pleasurably close the delicate can come to the coarse.

Sterne's parody of delicacy enacts the tensions between the polite and the vulgar that are played out in the novel genre's development from scandal to respectability. At a meta-textual level, 'the case of delicacy' is also the case that Sterne prosecutes for the novel genre as a legitimate space for reflection on the complex aesthetic, epistemological, ethical, social, and sexual questions that the issue of delicacy raises. For delicacy is, as the novel suggests, a highly complex and multifaceted entity. And as to *how* 'the lady and myself should be obliged to undress and get to bed—there was but one way of doing it, and that I leave to the reader to devise; protesting as I do it, that if it is not the most delicate in nature, 'tis the fault of his own imagination—against which this is not my first complaint' (124). This strategic shifting of blame to the reader is also an invitation to that reader to supply what's missing with her own imagination. Sterne's narrator thereby rehearses the age-old strategy of combining censoriousness and scandalousness, and of disavowing libidinous authorial intention by projecting it onto the reader.

If Sterne's novels tell a story of British empiricism's suspicion of the word, they do so by poignantly inhabiting and reflecting upon the space between words and things, language and feelings. And they exploit the full symbolic potential of that space and its intervening printed signs. As Ronald Paulson suggests, 'Verbal structures—by which we mean all non-perceptual or directly experiential structures—conceal rather than communicate, and contact is possible only by the sympathy that occasionally breaks through them' (1975: 49). In this sense, the asterisk that cheekily announces the sexual double entendre and hidden meaning is also an eloquent marker of the pathos of language's failure to communicate. And if one of Sterne's recognitions is that language fails to communicate, his novels nevertheless seek to register this as sociably and congenially as they can. Both the pregnant silences and visual effusions of typographical signs that supplement

---

[9] Laurence Sterne, *A Sentimental Journey through France and Italy*, ed. Ian Jack (Oxford: Oxford University Press, 1984), 123.

language are forms of eloquence in Sterne's work; in these ways Sterne manages to say the unsayable.

In *Tristram Shandy*, the narrator highlights the significance of 'that ornamental figure in oratory, which Rhetoricians stile the *Aposiopesis*' (120) and which is the breaking off in the middle. This technique also enables Sterne to speak the unspeakable; and his narrator comments reflexively on precisely this function: 'Make this dash,—'tis an Aposiopesis.—Take the dash away, and write *Backside*,—'tis Bawdy. Scratch Backside out, and put *Covered way* in, 'tis a Metaphor;—' (120). The most spectacular example of such eloquent silence is the closure of the incident in *A Sentimental Journey* which ends ambiguously in mid-sentence 'So that when I stretch'd out my hand, I caught hold of the Fille de Chambre's' (125).

So there is delicacy in Sterne, but also bawdy and Rabelaisian grotesque. As Arthur Cash suggests, 'English libertines made of Rabelais a patron anti-saint' (2001: 297). Sterne is a particularly important figure in the development of the novel for remediating the libidinal energies of earlier forms of popular picaresque fiction within the more aesthetically self-conscious form of realist fiction that developed from the 1750s. Paradoxically, Sterne's heightened aesthetic complexity enabled a more pointed integration of popular bawdy into the novel form through the sophisticated reflexivity by which this bawdy was simultaneously produced and disavowed.

Authorial Celebrity

Bawdy notwithstanding, it was the scandal of a particular kind of authorial celebrity that compounded what many saw as the primary affront of Sterne's fiction. This affront was also Sterne's innovation. As Claire Brock observes, identifying the emergence of the celebrity author with Rousseau and Sterne, the 1760s brought

> a dramatic change, a deliberate authorial conflation of fictional character with writer in a bid for audience affection and empathy. Sterne even began to write to his admirers in the eccentric style of his character, Tristram Shandy, presenting an enticing *melée* of author and creation to his public. (2006: 9)

Sterne's innovation is dramatized by the fact that Sterne's narrator Yorick, the Parson, was often taken to be Sterne himself, who was also a parson: 'Laurence Sterne, commonly known by the name of Yorick', as *The Sentimental Magazine* put it in 1774.[10] Yorick makes his first appearance as the protagonist of *Tristram Shandy*, reappearing in *A Sentimental Journey*, the full title of which is *A Sentimental Journey through France and Italy. By Mr. Yorick*.

---

[10] *The Sentimental Magazine; or, General Assembly of Science, Taste, and Entertainment* (January 1774), 4.

The leading sentimental novelist Samuel Richardson expressed his scandalized disapproval of *Tristram Shandy* in a letter to Mark Hildesley, the Bishop of Sodor and Man: 'Who is this Yorick? you are pleased to ask me. You cannot, I imagine have looked into his books: execrable I cannot but call them.'[11] Richardson objects to the slippery identification between protagonist and author that Sterne cultivates, lamenting the new licence of the author to act as it were 'in character'. As Richardson continues, 'it is almost singular to disapprove: even the bishops admire, and recompense his wit, though his own character as a clergyman seems much impeached by printing such gross and vulgar tales' (341). In fact, as celebrity culture developed, such scandalousness functioned less to 'impeach' than to add interest both to the author's 'character' and to the fictional characters that the author produced. When Daniel Defoe referred to the early eighteenth-century pirate-king and pornographer Edmund Curll as 'scandalous in his Fame', he was making a distinction between heroic fame and notoriety that would become intriguingly and profitably blurred by the end of our period.[12]

Nevertheless, censorious suspicion attended the reception of Sterne's celebrity persona by later readers and contemporaries alike. That utterly respectable British literary celebrity, Walter Scott, attacked what he saw as Sterne's scandalous fondness for publicity. Reading Sterne through the lens of Rabelaisian satire, Scott argues that Sterne's style of satire is a kind of faux-Rabelaisianism, a simulacrum of satire, a form of satire for publicity's sake. Whereas Rabelais was 'compelled to adopt this Harlequin's habit' so that he might 'vent his satire against church and state', Scott argues, 'Sterne assumed the manner of his master, only as a mode of attracting attention, and of making the public stare'.[13] While the early Augustan *Martinus Scriblerus* was a satire on science and learning, 'Sterne, on the contrary, had no particular object of ridicule; his business was only to create a person' (xix). Fiction, as it evolves after 1750, is precisely about the creation of persons and imaginative characters, as Catherine Gallagher notes (2006: 353). Hence, Scott's point of critique—that there is no real satirical object in Sterne, but rather the 'business... only to create a person'—marks a dramatic development in the history of fiction by lamenting the absence of reference that came before. Here, in place of that 'scandalous referentiality' that marks the *roman à clef* (Gallagher 1994: 101), Sterne's work involves a scandalous *absence* of referentiality. The public is 'made to stare', but there is nothing to see—no direct satirical object or 'real' person to attack.

The Victorian satirical novelist, William Thackeray, wearily disapproved of Sterne's double entendres and celebrity persona: 'Some of that dreary *double entendre* may be

---

[11] *Selected Letters of Samuel Richardson*, ed. John Carroll (Oxford: Clarendon Press, 1964), 341.

[12] Daniel Defoe, Letter on Curll's *Onanism Displayed*, in *The Weekly Journal*, no. 69 (5 April 1718).

[13] Walter Scott, 'Prefatory Memoir to Sterne', *Ballantyne's Novelist's Library*, vol. 5 (London: Hurst, Robinson, & Co., 1823), xvii.

attributed to freer times and manners than ours, but not all. The foul Satyr's eyes leer out of the leaves constantly: the last words the famous author wrote were bad and wicked' (1853: 292). In this intensely corporeal figuration of authorial presence, in which 'satire' has morphed into 'satyr', Thackeray's censorious scowl palpably twists his own leaves in recoil from the 'leering' author.

For Samuel Taylor Coleridge, Sterne's fictions flaunted '[a] sort of *knowingness*... a sort of dallying with the devil'.[14] Clearly legible here as an intertextual presence is Byron's spectacular scandalous celebrity, suggesting how much Byron had created his precursors in the minds of his contemporaries. Indeed, as Sterne writes back to his critics—and forward in high-Byronic satirical style:

> But for the chaste married, and chaste unmarried part of the sex—they must not read my book! Heaven forbid the stock of chastity should be lessen'd by the Life and Opinions of Tristram Shandy—yes, his Opinions—it would certainly debauch 'em! God take them under his protection this fiery trial, and send us plenty of Duennas to watch the workings of their humours, 'till they have safely got through the whole work.—If this will not be sufficient, may we have plenty of Sangrados to pour in plenty of cold water, till this terrible fermentation is over.[15]

With superlative devilish 'knowingness', Sterne here parodies the moralizing anti-novel discourse exemplified by Vicesimus Knox.

This parodic scene of censored reading supervised by Duennas anticipates Juan's drama of censored reading in the Spanish Canto (I) of Byron's *Don Juan* (1819). *Don Juan's* own dramas with censors and pirates are themselves defining events in the history of censorship. The attempts of Byron's publisher, John Murray, to block piracies of Byron's work demonstrate the fraught entanglement of the legal jurisdictions of libel, copyright, and criminal law within systems of censorship. In the case of Dugdale *v.* Murray, it was the pirate and pornographer himself, William Dugdale, who argued that *Don Juan* was 'immoral, and licentious', and therefore not worthy of the protection of copyright (see St Clair 2004: 324–5). Lord Eldon found in Dugdale's favour, decreeing that blasphemous books could not be protected by law, which effectively gave open slather to the pirates of *Don Juan*. Censorship was often frustrated by such tantalizing contradictions between criminal and intellectual property law.

Sterne's prose has always been identified as a chief precursor of Byron's digressive style, not least by Byron himself, who wrote of *Don Juan* that 'I mean it for a poetical T[ristram] Shandy—or Montaigne's Essays with a story for a hinge'.[16] William Hazlitt's disparaging demurral—'[*Don Juan*] has been called a *Tristram Shandy* in rhyme: it is

---

[14] Samuel Taylor Coleridge, Lecture IX, 'On the Distinctions of the Witty, the Droll, the Odd, and the Humours' (1818), in *Literary Remains*, 2 vols (London: William Pickering, 1836), 1.141.

[15] Laurence Sterne, to Dr Noah Thomas, 30 January 1760, in *A Collection of the Letters Written by the late Rev. Mr. Laurence Sterne, to his most intimate friends* (London: Joseph Wenman, 1790), 24.

[16] Byron to Douglas Kinnaird, 14 April 1823, *Byron's Letters and Journals*, ed. Leslie A. Marchand, 12 vols (London: John Murray, 1980), 10.150.

rather a poem written about itself'—effectively underscores the similarity (however counter-intuitively), for *Tristram Shandy* is also a novel written about itself.[17] Our period is bookended by Sterne's *Tristram Shandy* and Byron's *Don Juan* (1819–24), both of which dramatize a particular kind of scandalous textual self-reflexivity and celebrity author persona. Sterne and Byron both pre-empt censorious readers by making their imagined responses part of the drama and dialogic complexity of their texts. They also illuminate the developing career of literary celebrity from the 1750s to the 1820s through quite distinctive modes of authorial celebrity. In the figures of Yorick and Don Juan, respectively, Sterne and Byron elaborate a highly reflexive figure within the text, and one that is also a 'transtextual' authorial persona, moving across and outside the text or between the text and the world of the 'extratextual' beyond the text.

Sterne's experiments with voice, narration, and multiple and changing addressees work to draw attention to narrative constructedness, as does his emphasis on typography. These experiments in textual self-reflexivity and transtextuality give Sterne a foundational place in the consideration of celebrity and fiction and 'the aesthetics of authorial presence' that marks celebrity culture (English and Frow 2006: 52). Sterne pioneered strategies of publicity such as the writing of 'puffs' and fake letters of recommendation for his novels written by friends. On account of these techniques, as Tom Mole suggests, Sterne's career is perhaps best thought of as being poised on the cusp of modern celebrity, straddling patronage and commerce, as his 'success relied on ceaselessly collecting subscriptions' from a known readership rather than the anonymous readership of the modern audience (2007: 9).

Mole cites Scott's reflections on the impact of Byron's *Childe Harold's Pilgrimage* (1812–18) to mark the difference between Scott's generation and Sterne's:

> Reading is indeed so general among all ranks and classes, that the impulse received by the public mind on such occasions is instantaneous through all but the lowest classes of society, instead of being slowly communicated from one set of readers to another, as was the case in the days of our fathers.[18]

This distinction between 'instantaneous' recognition and what is 'slowly communicated from one set of readers to another' is fundamental to the specificity of celebrity culture. Scott here articulates the difference between traditional heroic modes of fame and newer modes of celebrity in terms of temporality. But this transition is also pivotal for changes in the affective and evaluative registers of fame. Modern celebrity, as distinct from traditional fame, involves the ambivalent combination of fame with notoriety, a form of scandalous celebrity (see Tuite 2007: 78). This difference marks a significant qualitative

---

[17] William Hazlitt, 'Lord Byron', in *The Spirit of the Age: or Contemporary Portraits* (London: Henry Colburn, 1825), 43.

[18] Walter Scott, 'Review of *Childe Harold's Pilgrimage, The Prisoner of Chillon, a Dream*, and other Poems', *Quarterly Review*, 16 (October 1816), 172–208 (175).

distinction between the respectable Scott and the scandalous Byron, who was, after all, Scott's contemporary.

Rousseau was a vital mediating figure between scandalous fiction and celebrity, and between Sternean and Byronic forms of authorial celebrity. His *Confessions* (written 1764–70, published posthumously 1781, 1788) capitalized on the moral ambiguities of self-disclosure in the same way *La Nouvelle Héloïse* had capitalized on the moral ambiguities of sensibility and fiction. Indecent the *Confessions* may have been, due to its sexual explicitness, but its novel effects of sincerity and full and frank disclosure provided ample compensation for many devoted readers. Rousseau anticipated modern celebrity by 'going Garbo' and refusing interviews two centuries before the actress famously declared 'I want to be alone' (strictly speaking, a line spoken by of one of Greta Garbo's characters and later integrated into Garbo's off-screen persona). No one was apparently more surprised than Rousseau himself that the author's elusiveness only increased his attraction: 'The ruder I was to people the more they persisted'.[19] Thus, a star celebrity turn was born.

The 1790s: Jacobin, Sentimental, and Gothic Scandal

As an Enlightenment hero of the French Revolution, Rousseau was a crucial figure for English Jacobin novelists of the 1790s such as Mary Hays, William Godwin, Elizabeth Inchbald, Charlotte Smith, Helen Maria Williams, and Mary Wollstonecraft. Wollstonecraft's ambivalent relationship with Rousseau swerved between a lifelong attachment ('I have always been half in love with him'[20]) that celebrated Rousseau as an icon of sensibility and genius, and the feminist revulsion at Rousseau's misogynistic belittling of women that informed her eloquent defence of female education in *A Vindication of the Rights of Woman* (1792). When Wollstonecraft and Godwin started courting in 1796, she loaned him a copy of *La Nouvelle Héloïse*. And when in introducing *Mary, A Fiction* (1788) she claims the most powerful fictions are those 'where the soul of the author is exhibited', it is Rousseau she conjures as the master exhibitor and as her ideal vision of a new kind of authoriality that enraptures the reader through extravagant feats of self-revelation.[21]

William Godwin's *Memoirs of the Author of The Rights of Woman* (1798), published after Wollstonecraft's death in 1797, attracted fame and notoriety as a scandalous memoir on account of its frank sexual revelations. Godwin also published Wollstonecraft's *Posthumous Works* (1798), which included Wollstonecraft's love letters to another man,

---

[19] Jean-Jacques Rousseau, *The Confessions*, trans. J. M. Cohen (Harmondsworth: Penguin, 1953), 242.
[20] Mary Wollstonecraft to Gilbert Imlay, 22 September 1794, *Collected Letters of Mary Wollstonecraft*, ed. Ralph M. Wardle (Ithaca and London: Cornell University Press, 1979), 263.
[21] Mary Wollstonecraft, *Mary and The Wrongs of Woman*, ed. Gary Kelly (London: Oxford University Press, 1976), 'Advertisement', n.p.

Gilbert Imlay, the American revolutionary and father of Wollstonecraft's daughter, Fanny Imlay; it also included the radical sentimental-Gothic novel *The Wrongs of Woman*, a fictionalized account of the relationships with Imlay and Godwin, which offers a dark vision of marriage and explores the role of fantasy in women's emotional lives. All of this led to scandalized outrage and the widespread vilification of Wollstonecraft in popular squibs, caricatures, and attacks such as George Canning's in the *Anti-Jacobin* (1797–8) and Richard Polwhele in *The Unsex'd Females* (1798).

Another compelling feminist figure of scandal (and friend of Mary Wollstonecraft) was Mary Robinson (1758–1800), actress, poet, novelist, and memoirist. In *A Letter to the Women of England, on the Injustice of Mental Insubordination* (1799), published under a pseudonym in the wake of the public outrage over Godwin's *Memoirs*, Robinson made a feminist appeal for female celebrity and public recognition for women. She also defended herself against the relentless public vilification she endured in the 1780s as the lover of the Prince Regent. Robinson started her career in the 1770s as a teenage theatrical sensation, and caught the eye of the Prince Regent in 1781 playing the part of Perdita in *The Winter's Tale*. Targeted by scandal sheets such as *The Rambler's Magazine*, which covered the affair obsessively, and by the satirical and pornographic *Memoirs of Perdita* (1784), Robinson was 'assailed by pamphlets, by paragraphs, and caricatures, and all the artillery of slander', as she wrote in her posthumously published *Memoirs* (1801) completed by her daughter, Maria Elizabeth Robinson.[22] Nevertheless, an often canny manipulator of her own image and an astute theorist of fame, Robinson undertook a comparative critique of celebrity and notoriety in her late essay 'Present State of the Manners, Society &c &c of the Metropolis of England', published in *The Monthly Magazine* for August 1800.

Another key site of scandalous fiction in the 1790s was the homegrown Gothic genre. Initiated late in 1764 by Horace Walpole's *The Castle of Otranto*, Gothic evolved from antiquarian romance into an exhilarating, explosive, and sensational form charged with anarchic political and libidinal energies. In particular, Matthew Lewis's *The Monk* (1796), read as an allegory of the Terror, recast the libertine Enlightenment critique of institutional religion through a sensational attack on Catholic sexual hypocrisy and repression. Lewis's form of so-called masculine Gothic combined sexual explicitness, violence, and outré supernaturalism (as against Ann Radcliffe's feminine Gothic of psychological interiority and the 'explained supernatural'). The novel met with scandalized calls for suppression on charges of obscenity and blasphemy, and 'M. G. Lewis, Esq., M.P.' was thereafter known as '"Monk" Lewis', becoming inextricably linked in the public imagination with the novel's protagonist, the fallen monk Ambrosio, and one of the most notorious literary figures of England.

---

[22] Mary Robinson, *Memoirs of the Late Mrs. Robinson*, 2 vols (London: R. Phillips, 1801), 1.178.

Charlotte Dacre reworked the resources of Lewis's masculine Gothic to explore feminine erotic obsession in her Gothic novels, *Confessions of the Nun of St. Omer* (1805), *Zofloya* (1806), *The Libertine* (1807), and *The Passions* (1811). Dacre crafted her own celebrity persona through the pseudonym 'Rosa Matilda' that indexed the diabolical *femme fatale* of Lewis's novel. This heady concoction of female-authored violence and eroticism was both popular and deeply scandalous. As *The Annual Review* declared of *Zofloya*: 'there is an exhibition of wantonness of harlotry, which we would have hoped, that the delicacy of the female mind, would have been shocked to imagine'.[23] In her poem 'To the Shade of Mary Robinson' (1806), Dacre paid tribute to another *scandaleuse*, celebrating 'Thy fame sounding loud in thine *enemies'* ears!'[24] However, having started her career as a radical, Dacre later attacked feminist figures such as Mary Wollstonecraft in *The Passions*, and turned apologist for the Prince Regent.

The Regency: Silver-Fork Scandal and Celebrity

The Prince Regent and the Royal family were themselves the source of many scandal sheets, squibs, and scandal fictions during the 1800s and the Regency period, named after the Prince of Wales, Prince Regent, from 1820 George IV. Gothic and scandal fictions were the specialty of the publisher J. F. Hughes, who published Dacre's first novel, *The Nun of St. Omer*, as well as a range of scandal fictions that exploited interest in the separation between the Prince and Princess of Wales and the 'delicate investigation' of the Princess in 1806 on account of her adoption of two mysterious children. As Peter Garside notes, in '1807–8, Hughes announced his "royal" titles alongside a growing body of "scandal" fictions claiming to unfold the mysteries of high life, not least the secret origins of "illegitimate" children' (1987: 249).

A prominent author of Hughes's stable was the pseudonymous Charles Sedley, who authored *A Winter in Dublin* (1808), but it was T. S. Surr's *A Winter in London* (1806) that initiated the so-called 'season' fictions that represented the fashionable London social season of balls, parties, and sporting events in all their sensational excess. The sensation of *Winter in London*'s 'season' is the discovery on a shipwreck of the royal foundling, Edward. High-life is the site of scandal in this genre that develops toward the melodrama of the mid-nineteenth-century novel of adultery: '"Thou art the fruit of crime, the offspring of adultery!"', says Edward's stepfather, having chanced upon Edward on a walk in Richmond Park.[25] The Whig hostess (and keen Rousseauvian) Georgiana Cavendish,

---

[23] *The Annual Review*, 5 (1806), 542.

[24] Charlotte Dacre, 'To the Shade of Mary Robinson', in *Zofloya; or The Moor*, ed. Adriana Cracuin (Peterborough, ON: Broadview Press, 1997), Appendix C, 276.

[25] T. S. Surr, *A Winter in London*, 3 vols (London: Richard Phillips, 1806), 1.103.

Duchess of Devonshire, makes an *à clef* appearance in *A Winter in London* as an inveterate gambler and—in a nicely self-reflexive touch—victim of a blackmailer, forced to pay out to prevent the publication of a libellous memoir about herself.

This kind of scandal fiction initiated the fascination with the material minutiae of high-life that was soon to be intensified in the silver-fork genre (see Sadoff 2012). The silver-fork or fashionable novel, which emerged in the mid-1810s and continued until the mid-1830s, was a vital subgenre in the development of new middle-class readerships for the novel and the recognizably modern culture of literary celebrity that developed during the Regency.

Henry Colburn was the main publisher and arguably inventor of the silver-fork novel. Like Hughes, he specialized in titles that blurred the boundaries between fiction and scandalous memoir. He pioneered a range of publicity techniques that intensified the association between text and author and engaged the author's biography in ways that enhanced the selling power of the novels, such as the planting of gossip about the author. As Edward Copeland notes, Colburn 'promoted the novels as aristocratic *romans à clef* written by authors who were themselves members of fashionable society' (2009: 434). Colburn also revived the early eighteenth-century scandal genre of the key, with his 'Key to Fashionable Persons Figuring in the Novel' that accompanied some novels. Silver fork's most famous practitioners were social and literary celebrities such as Lady Caroline Lamb, Robert Plumer Ward, Theodore Hook, Edward Bulwer Lytton, Benjamin Disraeli, and later, during the 1830s and 1840s, Catherine Gore. Set usually in the West End of London, the silver-fork novel was the novel of social and cultural high-life that documented and romanced for middle-class aspirants the lives of the 'exclusives' and the *beau monde*.

The silver-fork novel reworks the allegorical cryptographic and *roman à clef* novelistic methods pioneered by the fictions of Delarivier Manley. It shares this earlier preoccupation with the private lives of the rich and powerful, and the engagement with court and political culture, particularly in the close connection between fiction and court culture that revolved around the Prince Regent, and in relation to the reform platform of the Whig party (see Copeland 2009: 434–5). This is dramatized most clearly through the figures of Caroline Lamb and Benjamin Disraeli, silver-fork authors with direct connections to that new political culture. Silver fork mixes the pulling power of social, political, and authorial celebrity, and cultivates a mode of glamour based on the interpenetration of political, social, economic, and cultural power. Fashion and politics are closely related in the silver-fork novel for the practical reason that the social season was a slave to the rhythm of the parliamentary sessions.

Regency silver fork specializes in scandalous Whig ladies—whether as characters, structuring absent personages outed by keys, or authors themselves. The Duchess of Devonshire's niece, Caroline Lamb, was both the most elite of Colburn's silver-fork authors and the most scandalous. Lamb's most famous and notorious novel *Glenarvon* (1816) represents a revival of the earlier form of *roman à clef* political fiction of Manley's

New Atalantis (1709), attacking as it did the members of the high Whig establishment, many of whom Lamb was herself related to, not the least of them her husband, William Lamb, cuckolded by Byron in the affair that *Glenarvon* writes up in *à clef* form, and her mother-in-law, Lady Holland, who appears as 'The Princess of Madagascar'. As Byron's close friend, John Cam Hobhouse, wrote, 'The hero is a monster, and meant for B.; . . . The new Atalantis over again' (Broughton 1909–11: 1.338). A dazzling *mélange* of Gothic novel, political melodrama, Irish nationalism, and scandalous memoir, *Glenarvon* offers an effusive, innovative, and mixed-genre version of what becomes refined in the 1820s as a more polite and loyal—and far less scandalous—form of silver fork.

Glenarvon is remarkable for its combination of *roman à clef* satire and allegory ('real' targets) with compelling fictional and maximum transtextual authorial presence. Part of the thrill of *Glenarvon* was its power to shock from within the circles of social power—a form of power that Lamb shared with Byron and with which she heroically met him and stood her ground against him. Lesser, more socially slavish examples of silver fork, by those not born or self-made to rule, tend to document high-life from a more abject and voyeuristic perspective within a middle-class celebrity culture of aspiration.

Appearing just after Byron had left England in scandalous exile, *Glenarvon* is also significant for mediating the celebrity culture of Byronism, and for initiating the genre of Byronic silver fork, which includes Edward Bulwer Lytton's *Pelham* (1828), Benjamin Disraeli's *Vivian Gray* (1826)—advertised in Colburn's *New Monthly Magazine* as 'a sort of *Don Juan* in prose'—and Catherine Gore's *Cecil* (1841). Byronism also opened out onto the world of pornographic novels, often in very material ways, as through the endpapers of William Benbow's 1822 pirated edition of *Cain* (Byron's biblical drama and Satanic allegory of free speech, which Francis Jeffrey claimed argued '*con amore*, in the name of Lucifer').[26] These endpapers advertised pornographic works, many of which were published in expensive octavo formats to cater to the elite reader's market: 'On the 1st of February was Published, price 8s. No. 2, of the Rambler's Magazine, and Man of Fashion's Companion; or, The Annals of Gallantry, Glee, Pleasure, and the Bon Ton.'[27] Benbow's *Rambler's Magazine* of 1822 and 1824 crossed pornography with fashionable fiction and scandal sheets, and 'revived a late eighteenth-century genre of similarly titled "bon ton" or "galanterie" miscellanies which had recounted stories and scandals of fashionable libertines' (McCalman 1998: 210).

The term 'silver fork' was coined by William Hazlitt in a review of Theodore Hook, one of the Tory silver-fork novelists. By deriding Hook (the son of a composer, songwriter and organist at Vauxhall Gardens) for his admiration of the aristocracy 'because they eat their fish with a silver fork', Hazlitt draws attention to the aspirationalism of the

---

[26] Francis Jeffrey, unsigned review of *Sardanapalus, The Two Foscari* and *Cain, Edinburgh Review*, 36 (April 1822), 413–52 (438).

[27] Advertisement, *Cain, A Mystery*, 'By the author of Don Juan' (London: W. Benbow, 1822).

silver-fork genre, on the part of both readers and authors.[28] Hook was the founder and editor of *John Bull*, the abusive Tory and Regent-supporting scandal sheet produced to attack the Queen and her supporters during the Queen Caroline scandal of 1820, when the already deeply unpopular Prince Regent further galvanized popular support against him by laying charges of adultery against Caroline in an attempt to exclude her from his coronation. Hook wrote *John Bull* in debtor's prison, where he was when Colburn suggested that he write a fashionable novel, which resulted in *Sayings and Doings* (1824). After his release from prison, Hook became a fashionable supporter of the Tory party, and *John Bull* was displaced in the 1820s by other more scurrilous and vicious scandal sheets such as the *Age* and *Satirist*.

Colburn's other claim to fame was as the first publisher of the diaries of Samuel Pepys. Written in cipher, the diaries include an account of Pepys's masturbatory reading in 1668 of that 'mighty lewd book' *L'Ecole des filles*, and had languished in Magdalene College Cambridge since the early eighteenth century until published by Colburn in 1825.

During the growing conservatism of the 1820s, when the market for radical literature dried up, many radical publishers turned to pornography. A notable innovation was the crossover between political radicalism and pornography represented by publishers such as William Benbow and William Dugdale. In this late libertinist literature, as Iain McCalman details, 'a concern with philosophical freedom has been displaced by interest in deception and perversity. . . . Anything from the French libertinist canon—"classic" or "hack"—was eagerly translated or plagiarised, then published under new titles and pseudonyms to suit English tastes' (1998: 209). Work by earlier eighteenth-century libertines such as Rochester, Wilkes, and Cleland was revived in the 1820s through new editions and plagiarisms by Dugdale and others.

Dugdale's prolific output of pornography eventually provoked the passage of the Obscene Publications Act of 1857 (see McCalman 1999: 656). For the first time, this law made the sale of obscene material a statutory offence, giving the courts power to seize and destroy offending material. Now, by providing a singularity lacking in a long history of imbrication between obscene, blasphemous, and seditious libel, the law turned obscenity into a specific offence and genre.

A significant figure for Regency celebrity culture is Edward Bulwer Lytton, for the dissemination of Byronism, dandyism, and for his pioneering of popular fictional forms such as silver-fork and Newgate crime novels. He crossed both of these genres in *Paul Clifford* (1830), which features a dandy highwayman hero, and derives some of its own fame—or notoriety—from the most clichéd opening line ever of a novel: 'It was a dark and stormy night'. Mixing social and political concerns, Bulwer Lytton writes in his 1840 Preface that an object of the novel was 'to show that there is nothing essentially different between

---

[28] 'The Dandy School', *The Examiner*, 18 November 1827.

vulgar vice and fashionable vice—and that the slang of the one circle is but an easy para-phrase of the cant of the other'. If the novel's opening line is a cliché, its closing line is a forthright plea against the death penalty: 'The very worst use to which you can put a man is to hang him'. This crossing of silver-fork genre involves a crossing too of the social topography from West End to East End (see Moretti 1998: 79–86; and Copeland 2001).

T. S. Surr re-entered the field in the 1820s with a form of silver fork that crossed the fash-ionable novel with the emergent genre of crime fiction, demonstrating a new fascination with the criminal underworld that would develop into the fully fledged crime and detec-tive fiction of the Victorian period. *Richmond* (1827) represents the policing of this under-world, tracing the life, from early boyhood, of a Bow Street policeman as 'partly regular and partly adventurous'.[29] It is a kind of refigured picaresque, with the law enforcement officer featuring as adventurer (and a very fashion-conscious one at that: 'My only objec-tion was the scarlet waistcoat; which, although not quite so bad and low as a livery, was still a badge I could have gladly dispensed with' (1.312)). In this early nineteenth-century crossing of fashionable novel into crime fiction, the novel genre re-engaged with the themes of criminal life that had so fascinated readers of the early eighteenth-century novel. This fascination continued with the emergence of crime fiction as an influential genre from the mid-nineteenth century. An accompanying culture of scandalous celeb-rity mediated between crime and transgression.

Scandal fiction and celebrity culture both founded their enduring appeal on their insight into how multiple social and fictional worlds might be crossed: the high and the low; the polite and the obscene; the voyeuristic and the discreet; the fashionable and the criminal (or merely scandalous); the public and the private; the reported and the reflex-ive. Indeed, by showing how they might be crossed, they suggest these worlds are not so much opposed, as, more often than might be supposed, quite intimately related.

---

[29] T. S. Surr, *Richmond; or, Scenes in the Life of a Bow Street Officer*, 3 vols (London: Colburn, 1827), 1.311. Also sometimes attributed to Thomas Gaspey.

Part IV

===

Contexts

22

All in the Family: Consanguinity, Marriage, and Property

THE utter indifference of heroes and heroines to money or property and their democratic perception of human value in the poorest of their fellow creatures—coupled with their own innate natural dignity and obvious breeding—are forms of idealization that marked the fiction of the period under consideration here. Jane Austen sent up this formula in her juvenile 'Evelyn', written in 1792 when she was sixteen, about characters who act with absurdist generosity. In her sketch, a Mr Gower comes to the sweet village of Evelyn and is welcomed into the house of Mr and Mrs Webb—whom he has never seen before and to whom he has no introduction—where he is fed venison pie, sandwiches, fresh fruit, ices, soup, and jellies and cakes. When he is asked what more he desires, he replies "'Give me then your house and Grounds; I ask for nothing else." "It is yours," exclaimed both at once; "from this moment it is yours."' (233).[1] Austen, keenly aware of the economic lining of the social fabric, exaggerates this unrealistic response to emphasize the cliché of fictional characters who seem to have been invented as living rebukes to the growing capitalist ethos.

Eighteenth-century fictional protagonists are impractical to a fault; they never act to maximize their material well-being, they do not think about the future, but always act according to their highest moral lights. Their material generosity is exceptional; they disdain to fight with their siblings or any other family members over questions of inheritance. They do not require dowries or fortunes with the women and men they plight their troths to. Heroes are always falling in love with perfectly lovely, dowerless young damsels and marrying them, sometimes clandestinely, for which they are frequently disinherited by their ambitious and materialistic parents. The same is true of heroines, despite the trickiness of depicting a decent, respectable young woman falling in love with a man unknown to her family—and of a seemingly lower social class.

---

[1] For this and other texts of Austen juvenilia, page numbers refer to the edition *Juvenilia*, ed. Peter Sabor (Cambridge: Cambridge University Press, 2006).

Lydia, in Tobias Smollett's *The Expedition of Humphry Clinker* (1771) is a good example of this latter formula. The innocent niece of Matthew Bramble, the leader of this family expedition, she is addressed by a young man who is an actor in a strolling company, of whom she knows nothing. Nonetheless, he is well-spoken, claims to be a gentleman, and treats her with trembling respect. He calls himself 'Wilson'; the manager of the acting company reports that he had been with the company about six months, had never accepted a salary (again, that disinterestedness), and was well-respected by his fellow actors. Throughout the novel, this 'Wilson' turns up at odd times trying to see and speak with Lydia and exciting and alarming her. It turns out, of course, that he is hardly the impecunious actor he at first seemed, but the only son of her uncle's old college friend, Charles Dennison. Not only is he worthy of her regard but sufficiently well off materially to be a proper suitor. So Lydia's attraction to this youth is justified and precedes their proper introduction in the same way that the poor maidens with whom the fictional heroes in other novels fall in love always prove to be well-born after all.

In Charlotte Lennox's *Henrietta* (1758), the youngest son of the Earl of —— is smitten with the beautiful daughter of a supplicant to his father. He follows the mother and daughter home and comes to know the daughter's gentle ways and the mother's cultivated mind. Despite his father's fury, he marries the maiden in the presence of her dying mother in order to protect the young woman and to allow her mother to die in peace. Inevitably, he is disinherited; and it is the daughter of this union, with her aristocratic birth and sentimental poverty, who is the protagonist of the novel. In Robert Bage's *Hermsprong; or, Man as He Is Not* (1796) Lord Grondale's daughter, Caroline Campinet, resigns her right to her portion gladly in order to evade marriage with Sir Philip Chestrum, whose weak mind appals her and whose rent rolls hold no attraction for her.

Indifference to money in marriage is key in sentimental novels; marriage for love without consideration of wealth is proof of noble moral status, the *sine qua non* for a hero or heroine, the sign that they are worthy of our regard. They are thus the antithesis of the aggrandizing ethic that supposedly characterized property owners in this era of the amassing of great estates. As an irritated father in Susan Ferrier's *Marriage* (1818) tells his daughter outright:

> I'll suffer no daughter of mine to play the fool with her heart, indeed! She shall marry for the purpose for which matrimony was ordained amongst people of birth—that is, for the aggrandisement of her family, the extending of their political influence—for becoming, in short, the depository of their mutual interest. These are the purposes for which persons of rank ever think of marriage.[2]

---

[2] Susan Ferrier, *Marriage*, ed. Herbert Foltinek, introd. Kathryn Kirkpatrick (Oxford and New York: Oxford University Press, 1997), vol. 1, ch. 1; 2.

The angry speaker exhibits the stereotypical attitude of the older generation in fiction of this period, the purely venal approach to marriage that the idealized hero or heroine must set him or herself against.

These caricatures represented the extremes of attitudes about land and money in a period in which people were experiencing the temptations of capitalism on a new scale for the first time. Just when marriage choices turned on questions of money versus love, or at least compatibility, in the world of the novel—where the 'right' decision was to ignore wealth and property, not to mention the advice of one's family and friends, and to marry where one's heart directed one—marriage in the 'real world' was the primary means of circulating capital, of moving it from one family to another. According to Amy Louise Erickson, 'Most of the capital—in all European societies—was both accumulated and transferred by means of marriage and inheritance' (2005: 2). In other words, it was in precisely the same period in which mobility and the flexibility of the marriage market rendered it the most important avenue to wealth and property that novelists were creating fictional characters who married for love and disdained material considerations. At the very least this tells us that one cannot extrapolate from fiction to historical reality; the relation of fiction to 'real life' is not simply mimetic but rather must be understood as a complexly refracted reaction to the hard facts of 'real life'. Fiction must thus be understood variously as compensatory, nostalgic, wishful, consoling, or deliberately myth-making—as imaginative projections as much as imitative representations of life.

Marrying for Love

Daughters in novels are always being sacrificed on the altar of Mammon. In order to thwart their romantic choices or to prevent their dowries from going out of the family, their fathers try to marry them to rich men. Fathers seek to control their daughters' lives and sexuality in order to command whatever wealth and property they might possess. They seem to feel that their daughters do not count as independent persons in their own right, but that whatever their daughters possess ought to be at their service. In Richardson's *Clarissa* (1748–9), for example, a novel whose influence on fiction of the period can hardly be overestimated, Clarissa's troubles begin with the reading of her grandfather's will and the announcement that she is his legal heir and stands to inherit his estate. As James Thompson observed, inheritance makes trouble for female characters; while it may be 'enabling or authorizing for male protagonists' it is inevitably 'disabling for female protagonists' (1996: 174). Certainly Clarissa's grandfather's bequest is an unusual one for an unmarried woman and much resented by her brother and father, whose plans for the family include accumulating enough property to buy her brother a title. Their pressure on her to marry the repellent Mr Solmes springs from the highly advantageous material terms that Solmes holds out to them: his willingness to forego Clarissa's inheritance and his promise to leave his own fortune to the Harlowe family rather than to his own family make him the ideal suitor for their daughter/sister, whom they consider merely a pawn in their larger plan for the family's fortunes. How could a woman hold property when she *is* property?

Thus the plot of *Clarissa* begins with two clichés of subsequent fiction of the period: that women have difficulty holding onto their property independent of men—whether fathers or brothers or husbands—and that parents favour marriages contracted for the purpose of accumulating property rather than for 'love' (attraction, compatibility). As the novel unfolds, the crisis that drives Clarissa from her father's house and into the orbit of the unscrupulous Lovelace is her resistance to being sacrificed by her family for the sake of an ever-larger estate. Many later novels follow this pattern in which repellent suitors are encouraged by the parents of the heroine because they agree to waive her dowry. *Hermsprong* has already been mentioned. Two lesser-known examples of some interest are Anne Dawe's *The Younger Sister; or, The History of Miss Somerset* (1770) and the anonymous *Anecdotes of a Convent* 'by the Author of Memoirs of Mrs. Williams' (1771).

It would be tedious to catalogue all the novels fuelled by generational conflict in which parents press their sons and daughters to marry advantageously while the younger generation holds out for marriage with 'love' or at least where there is no repugnance (see Perry 1999 for characteristics of a cluster of thirteen novels by women in the late 1760s and early 1770s that imitated *Clarissa*). Susan Ferrier's *Marriage* (1818) plays with this formula by creating a heroine manqué in the vain and heartless Lady Juliana Douglas who elopes with a handsome Scotsman rather than marry the old, ugly Duke of L ——, the rich man that her father proposes. But not being a proper heroine, she soon regrets her romantic impulse and the loss of jewels, coaches, horses, mansions, and all the rest of the trappings of the *beau monde*. Ferrier further tweaks the convention by introducing in the same novel Alicia Malcolm, who marries sensibly when she cannot wed her first love. Although she cannot conceive a child—perhaps a sign of the passionlessness of this union—her rational and sensible match nonetheless gives her peace and contentment. In the more typical formulaic plot line, however, the reader is encouraged to favour the impractical love matches of the younger generation in opposition to their parents' decrees, although authors often redeem these hopelessly idealistic unions by producing a fortune in the last volume—often from the East or West Indies—to support the young couple in their extremity and romance.

Jane Austen's juvenile 'Love and Freindship' (1790) mocks the conventional formula with young characters who refuse—absurdly— to marry where their parents dictate. In Letter 6th, a 'noble' youth relates how his father,

> 'seduced by the false glare of Fortune and the Deluding Pomp of Title, insisted on my giving my hand to Lady Dorothea. No never exclaimed I. Lady Dorothea is lovely and Engaging; I prefer no woman to her; but Know Sir, that I scorn to marry her in compliance with your Wishes. No! Never shall it be said that I obliged my Father.' (108)

Our hero then marries his Laura, whom he has just met, and when asked by his sister how he expects to support her, i.e. feed her, he replies 'dost thou then imagine that there is no other support for an exalted Mind (such as is my Laura's) than the mean and indelicate employment of Eating and Drinking?' 'None that I know of so efficacious', she replies, deliciously (111).

In her mature novels, of course, Austen placed her characters in more difficult moral situations with more complex dilemmas. Edward Ferrars in *Sense and Sensibility* (1811) refuses to give up Lucy Steele when his mother demands that that he break the engagement in order to marry a wealthier woman—but he no longer loves Lucy Steele and would like nothing better than to get out of his engagement to her. His moral fibre is proved by his fidelity to his word despite his present feelings. Frances Burney, too, gave her own twist to the dilemma about marrying for love versus marrying for property and rank that generated the conflict in so many contemporary novels. Her novels complicate the issue with her heroines' problems of identity. For example, the heroine of *Evelina* (1778) does not have a legitimate name and hence her birth and class status—and her suitability as a match for Lord Orville—are equivocal. The heroine of *Cecilia* (1782), on the other hand, cannot relinquish her name without forfeiting her fortune but must find a husband who will take her family name and give up his own. Mortimer Delvile's mother threatens to abjure him if he complies with this requirement, crying 'How will the blood of your wronged ancestors rise into your guilty cheeks, and how will your heart throb with secret shame and reproach, when wished joy upon your marriage by the name of *Mr Beverley*?'[3] Thus Burney turns up the heat on the intergenerational conflict concerning marriage choice that stands behind so many fictional plots.

On a metaphysical level, this formulaic plot might be interpreted as the conflict between the claims of self—the 'new' individual following his or her own heart's desire—and the claims of society, the individual's obligations first to his or her family and extended kin group and then to the larger community into which he or she was born. That is, heroes and heroines are torn between their own desires and the plans and choices of their families and advisors. Or, at a more literal level, this plot may reflect the subtle shift in kin priorities that was occurring in the course of the eighteenth century, the increased importance of the family created by marriage and the diminished importance of one's family of origin. The consanguineal family—the family into which one was born—was becoming less salient than the family that one created by marriage, the affinal family. The order of personal loyalties was changing. Women, in this new dispensation, were becoming more significant as wives and mothers than as daughters and sisters. Fathers' responsibility for the personal happiness of their daughters became less compelling as it came to be felt that these young women were 'chickens brought up for the tables of other men'—rather

---

[3] Frances Burney, *Cecilia, or Memoirs of an Heiress*, ed. Peter Sabor and Margaret Anne Doody (Oxford and New York: Oxford University Press, 1988), vol. 4, ch. 6; 677.

than scions of the family, bearers of the family blood and lineage.[4] Similarly, brothers increasingly felt more responsible for their own wives than for their blood sisters as the ideology of kin responsibility was relocated to the marital unit (see Perry 2004 for a full working-out of this paradigm shift).

Novels of the period reflect the friction between these two configurations of family, the affinal and the consanguineal; many plot lines can be interpreted as the conflict between these two forms—and a contest as to which family a man owed his primary loyalty. If the cries of daughters fall on deaf ears in their families of origin in the novels of the period, and if their parents are willing to marry them off in a way most advantageous to their own marriage-created unit—it may be a sign of this shifting precedence. Thus, beyond noticing which characters display noble rather than mercenary motives, and who does and who does not act to maximize his or her financial self-interest in marriage choices, one might trace other patterns of conflict over money and property in the novel in order to pinpoint which relations in contemporary life were strained by the evolving social and economic structures. If the drama in eighteenth-century fiction is quintessentially about property relations in families, the stock characters and clichéd situations of these dramas can shed light on the pressure points within actual families in that period.

Brothers and Sisters

Attitudes of brothers towards their sisters, for example, are a touchstone of their moral character in the fiction of the later eighteenth century, when inheritance law was funnelling property into ever larger estates to be held by the eldest son and limiting the share of the estate to which daughters and younger brothers were entitled. In life, unmarried sisters often depended on their brothers for financial support and occasionally for an establishment. They relied on their brothers for legal advice and public negotiation, for mobility and escorted travel, for social and sexual protection. Men moved more easily in the world; they could carry weapons for self-defence, and their economic resources were usually greater than sisters of whatever age. Especially if there was no father, brothers were supposed to protect and look after their sisters' interests; it was a vestigial obligation from an earlier time increasingly observed in the breach rather than in the observance.

The problem was that despite their social and economic dependence, sisters had no legal leverage to compel this protection and these services from their brothers because theirs was, after all, a sibling relation and not a child–parent relation. Brothers had very little motivation other than conventional humanitarian reasons, or old-fashioned sentiments about family honour, to arrange for their sisters' comfort, when their money might

---

[4] James Harlowe says this in Samuel Richardson, *Clarissa, or, the History of a Young Lady*, ed. Angus Ross (Harmondsworth: Penguin, 1985), 77.

instead be spent on their own business or pleasure. Despite the convention that brothers, in the absence of fathers, were responsible for their sisters, there was very little economic incentive for them to take this responsibility seriously. Many brothers must have viewed their sisters as responsibilities they never chose, rivals for family resources and a debt to the future, occasion for both resentment and guilt. In families with property, the need to provide daughters with dowries created further tension between brothers and sisters because it was from his inheritance that her portion was to be subtracted. Good brothers in fiction paid this debt willingly and even augmented it; bad brothers tried to evade it.

It is noteworthy that the first thing the exemplary Sir Charles Grandison does upon returning home after his father's death, in Richardson's novel, is to restore his sisters' rightful portions. As Sir Charles's mother explains to them on her deathbed, in a lesson that many wise older women articulate in eighteenth-century fiction,

> 'I am afraid there will be but a slender provision made for my dear girls. Your papa has the notion riveted in him, which is common to men of antient families, that daughters are but incumbrances, and that the son is to be everything... Your brother loves you: He loves me. It will be in *his* power, should he survive your father, to be a good friend to you.—Love your brother.'[5]

In the context of this somewhat outmoded moral code with regard to dependent sisters, the extent to which brothers voluntarily undertook to protect and to care for their sisters became a measure of their moral fibre. In Jane Austen's fragment, 'The Watsons' (1805), Emma Watson's brother, Robert, 'carelessly kind, as became a prosperous man and a brother' is morally suspect from the start, a judgement in which the reader is confirmed by his subsequent behaviour.[6] Austen demonstrates his lack of consideration in this scene in which he pays more attention to 'a doubtful half crown' than to a sister he has not seen for years, and it exposes his selfish heart from the outset. The degree to which a brother exhibited his care and concern for his sister was a moral litmus test in eighteenth-century fiction, a convention for reading a man's real character. A family obligation from an earlier era, it came to be idealized in fiction as it was eroded in life by competing demands of conjugal families and the cash requirements of the new economy.

In *Pride and Prejudice* (1813), when Mrs Reynolds the housekeeper shows Elizabeth Bennet and the Gardiners around the rooms at Pemberley and praises Darcy's treatment of his sister, it is a tribute well understood by those versed in the novel conventions of the period. 'Whatever can give his sister any pleasure, is sure to be done in a moment', she tells them. 'There is nothing he would not do for her.'[7] This is an even more powerful

---

[5] Samuel Richardson, *The History of Sir Charles Grandison* [1753–4], ed. and introd. Jocelyn Harris (Oxford and New York: Oxford University Press, 1996), 315.

[6] Jane Austen, *Later Manuscripts*, ed. Janet Todd and Linda Bree (Cambridge: Cambridge University Press, 2008), 120.

[7] Jane Austen, *Pride and Prejudice*, ed. Pat Rogers (Cambridge: Cambridge University Press, 2006), vol. 3, ch. 1; 276.

endorsement than her assurance that she had never had a cross word from him or that he was very kind to his tenants, for it reveals the strength of his affection as well as his sense of duty. Most of the significant novels before Austen—whether by Eliza Haywood, Mary Collyer, Sarah Fielding, Samuel Richardson, Tobias Smollett, Frances Burney, Elizabeth Hamilton, or Sarah Scott—reveal the moral qualities of their male protagonists by how they treat their sisters. 'Cherchez la soeur' ought to be a critic's first rule in judging a man in these novels. Grandison, the perfect hero, acts immediately upon his father's death to give his sisters what is due them by custom. It is not simply the impulse to protect innocent sufferers that motivates him, but a clear instinct for justice. When he restores his sisters' rightful portions he is not acting out of charity but out of rectitude. He acts quickly and decisively to make them comfortable and independent, giving them each £10,000 irrevocably free and clear. One assumes from the complex and detailed circumstances—narrated with care and at great length—that readers found much of interest in this example of how Grandison legally provided for his unmarried sisters.

Similarly, in Charlotte Smith's *The Old Manor House* (1793), the idealized Orlando gives each of his sisters £5,000 as soon as he comes into his illegally detained inheritance. That Lord Orville in Frances Burney's *Evelina* disapproves of his sister's suitor for moral rather than financial reasons shows the reader at once that he is a good man and a caring brother. And when the deracinated Evelina wishes out loud she had the protection of a brother and Lord Orville offers to act the part of one, it is a further sign of his moral rectitude. Matthew Bramble, in Smollett's *Humphry Clinker*, puts up with his sister Tabitha Bramble—with her flirtations and complaints and her irritating dog, Chowder—and he gives her an establishment, a home. His forbearance with her is consistent with his other kindnesses—as a landlord, a friend, and an uncle. When the eponymous heroine, Henrietta, in Lennox's novel, is reunited with her brother after a long separation, it is understood that he will protect and support her. She, who has been cast adrift for several years, supporting herself as a maid, a lady's companion, and a milliner, finally finds a safe harbour when she is reunited with her only brother. And when he is made the heir to their aunt's fortune, subject only to a relatively small dowry to be given to Henrietta on her wedding day, he vows to give her a more substantial fortune when he comes into his estate—although Henrietta's prospective husband, disinterested as a proper hero usually is, requires no substantial dowry with her. His father, however, 'loves money', and requires a hefty dowry with Henrietta before he will give his consent to his son's marriage.[8] In the protagonists' generation, then, we have a round-robin of generosity: Henrietta's brother who gives up his inheritance and her betrothed who would willingly forego it.

Northanger Abbey (1818), with its array of brothers, perhaps displays most systematically Austen's treatment of brotherly love as an important moral diagnostic. All the brothers in

---

[8] Charlotte Lennox, *Henrietta*, ed. Ruth Perry and Susan Carlile (Lexington, KY: University of Kentucky Press, 2008), 256.

Northanger Abbey display their truest selves in relation to their sisters, as one might have expected in a novel so intensely self-conscious about the conventions and clichés of fiction. John Thorpe's swaggering selfishness is apparent from his first insolent greeting of his mother and sisters. After boasting about his horses and his gig, the only subjects on which he has anything to say, and offering to drive Catherine around, he assures Isabella that 'I did not come to Bath to drive my sisters about'.[9] His address to his mother and sisters is equally engaging: 'Ah mother! How do you do... where did you get that quiz of a hat, it makes you look like an old witch', he says to her, and then 'bestow[s] an equal portion of his fraternal tenderness' on his two younger sisters by observing how ugly they looked (vol. 1, ch. 7; 44). John neither protects, supports, instructs, advises, nor in any way empathizes with his sisters; his boorishness towards them is of a piece with the rest of his behaviour.

Henry Tilney, a loving and companionable brother by comparison, talks things over with his sister Eleanor, reads novels with her, educates her, and tries to keep her company as much as his duties at Woodston allow. 'I am always sorry to leave Eleanor', he tells Catherine, aware of how lonely life must be for her, immured at Northanger Abbey (vol. 2, ch. 5; 161). Their older brother, Captain Frederick Tilney, on the other hand, chafes under familial obligation much as he resists any responsibility in his flirtation with Isabella Thorpe. 'How glad I shall be when you are all off' (vol. 2, ch. 5; 158) he whispers to Eleanor as they prepare to leave Bath and return to Northanger. The contrast tells the reader at once which is the good brother and which the bad brother, even without Austen's hints about Captain Tilney's Gothic potential.

Eldest Sons

More than just another bad brother, Frederick Tilney, as the beneficiary of primogeniture, is another stock character in fiction of the period—a selfish, pleasure-seeking, spendthrift eldest son. He evades his responsibility to his family, bristles at his fathers' remonstrances about his debts, and is concerned only for his own pleasure. To represent the eldest son this way became a convention of the genre. Tom Bertram in *Mansfield Park* (1814) is another good example of the type. Now eldest sons may have always behaved thus, but the shift in the way families managed their fortunes in the course of the eighteenth century may have contributed to the force of this representation. A new device for managing inheritance, a legal invention of the late seventeenth century called the strict settlement, increasingly used in marriage contracts in the eighteenth century, helped families concentrate their wealth in one branch and limit the leaching of resources to

---

[9] Jane Austen, *Northanger Abbey*, ed. Barbara M. Benedict and Deirdre Le Faye (Cambridge: Cambridge University Press, 2006), vol. 1, ch. 7; 42.

other branches. Its function was to assist the accumulation of larger and larger estates, and to leave them in the male line, without permitting the present incumbent to sell or mortgage any part of his family estate. The strict settlement did this by designating provisions for the as yet unborn children of the coming union and ensuring that the property jointly owned by the new couple would be entailed on male offspring born to them. The strict settlement thus limited what could be left to daughters and younger sons out of the estate, no matter how they might be favoured by their parents, and thus insured the consolidation and accumulation rather than the distribution of a family's wealth. That accumulated wealth was then left to the eldest son, usually at his majority, making his parents life-tenants in their property and making *him* independent of their favour. The strict settlement put eldest (or only) sons beyond their parents' power to enrich or impoverish and thus created the material basis for the thoughtless and selfish behaviour they often display in eighteenth-century fiction.

James Harlowe, Clarissa's brother in Richardson's novel, is another good example of this type of headstrong young man, domineering and self-centred, hardly even polite to his parents, being the Harlowes' only son and thus the heir to the carefully constructed family estate. Like the profligate Colonel Hauton in *Patronage* (1814), whom Maria Edgeworth describes as being like 'a thousand other young men of the same class' and 'generally thought a sociable, good-natured fellow', except that he had 'more exclusive and inveterate selfishness' than many,[10] these young men are given everything by their families but do not bestir themselves to help their siblings. A subplot in the anonymous *Anecdotes of a Convent* (1771) refers to the 'inhuman partiality' that a set of parents felt for their son and how, in order to enrich him, they determined 'never to give a shilling to his sisters during their lives, and at their death, to leave them a small annuity, which was at their decease to devolve to their brother or his heirs'.[11] The brother of Maria Venables in Mary Wollstonecraft's posthumously published *Maria; or, The Wrongs of Woman* (1798) is another such relation who thinks that all the money in the family should be his; it is with some difficulty that the heroine manages to 'prevent the whole property of the family from becoming the prey of my brother's rapacity'.[12] Sarah Fielding's *The Adventures of David Simple* (1744) refers bitterly to brothers of the type that, 'having got the Possession of all the Estate of the Family … allow their Sisters enough out of it to keep them from starving in some Hole in the Country, where their small Subsistence just serves to keep them the longer in their Misery, and prevents them from appearing in the World to *disgrace their*

---

[10] Maria Edgeworth, *Patronage*, 4 vols (London: J. Johnson & Co., 1814), 1.69–70.

[11] Anon., *Anecdotes of a Convent*, 3 vols (London: T. Becket and P. A. De Hondt, 1771), 1.129–30.

[12] Mary Wollstonecraft, *Mary, A Fiction and The Wrongs of Woman*, ed. Gary Kelly (London: Oxford University Press, 1976), vol. 2, ch. 10; 150.

Brother, by their Poverty'.[13] Thus are eldest sons (or only brothers) represented as heedless of the needs of their younger—or female—siblings in much contemporary fiction.

This devaluing of women in their role as sisters within their families of origin is also visible in novels in contests between sisters and wives for the resources and affection of the man who was brother to one and husband to the other. Jane Austen dramatized this conflict acutely in that remarkable second chapter of *Sense and Sensibility* in which Mr John Dashwood is convinced by his selfish wife to disregard the deathbed vow that he made to his father to protect and support his stepmother and sisters. Austen, who keenly felt her place in her family as a sister and a daughter (and who was never called upon to reassign these loyalties to a new conjugal family nor to compete with a husband's sisters for his love and support because she never married), is always aware of what a man owes his sisters—his consanguineal family—and this scene is a good example of this concern.

In Austen's novel, the sequence begins with the land itself, the estate of Norland, inhabited at the outset by a single man and his constant companion and housekeeper, his sister. When this sister dies in the opening chapter, the old gentleman invites his nephew—presumably a sibling's child—Mr Henry Dashwood, together with his wife and daughters, to live with him. The estate is to pass to Henry Dashwood after the old gentleman dies, and then to Henry Dashwood's son by a previous marriage, John Dashwood, whom Henry Dashwood urges to look after the interests of his stepmother and sisters. Norland is duly inherited by his son John, bypassing the female protagonists—Mrs Dashwood and her daughters Elinor, Marianne, and Margaret—who will inherit *no land*.

Thus Austen sets up an opposition between John Dashwood's obligation to his conjugal family, his wife and child, and his duty to his consanguineal family, his blood kin—already somewhat attenuated by their being only a stepmother and half-sisters. Norland, once the site of a family constructed by siblinghood—where the old gentleman lived with his sister—has become the private domain of a nuclear family, and John Dashwood's wife makes his stepmother and sisters feel unwelcome in what had been their home. They are 'degraded' to the condition of visitors; their claims as consanguineal kin are very much secondary to hers as a conjugal spouse.

Next we watch her whittle away her husband's intended largesse to his blood kin of £1,000 apiece to £500 apiece to an annuity of £100 per annum for his stepmother to an occasional gift of £50 to presents of game or fish in season. Their dialogue is punctuated by venal remarks on Mrs Dashwood's good health and probable longevity and reflections on their toddler son's adult requirements and necessities in excess of the income of more than £4,000 a year that he already stands to inherit. Austen plays this scene for laughs, but when one considers that the reduced income of the Dashwood women was probably about what she and Cassandra and their mother had to live on after her father, George

---

[13] Sarah Fielding, *The Adventures of David Simple*, ed. Linda Bree (London and New York: Penguin, 2002), 141.

Austen, died—and that this income was partly constituted by the voluntary contributions of Austen's brothers—the calculations of this comic scene take on more of an edge (Le Faye 2004: 146–7).

Elizabeth Hamilton's *Cottagers of Glenburnie* (1808) depicts another such unfeeling brother, Lord Lintop. 'He was, indeed, of a cold and reserved temper, and had a very narrow heart. Much inclined to avarice, except upon his own pleasures, and they were all of the selfish sort.'[14] This is a standard image of an eldest son on whom the family estate is entailed; he has no one to answer to and no one to please, and he knows from an early age that he is entitled to inherit the estate. When his father dies without having made a will, he comes into 'all', and soon evicts his stepmother and stepsisters. 'I thought it a sad thing to see her and her children turned out, as it were, of her own house, and obliged to go to seek a place to lay her head', writes the narrator of the tale, Mrs Mason. She goes on to tell us that Lord Lintot was prejudiced against 'my lady', because she was a stepmother, although she had, 'from the time he was a boy, done all in her power to gain his affections'. But he had been turned against her when in the nursery by a maid who used 'to threaten him with a stepmother as a monster—and he never got the better of the impression' (ch. 5; 94).

Stepmothers

Fiction abounds with stepmothers who favour their own undeserving daughters, who waste the fortunes of their new husbands, and who victimize and exploit the clear-seeing daughters of these second husbands. Most of these plots turn on greed and selfishness— the stepmother trying to aggrandize all and without compassion for the bereaved family into which she has married. Such is the story of Camilla and Valentine in Sarah Fielding's *The Adventures of David Simple*. After their mother dies, their father becomes infatuated with Livia, whose fortune is small because 'all the Estate that is in the Family is gone to the eldest Son; who, as he is married, and has Children of his own, cannot be expected to do much for her' (126). Urged to make himself happy by his loving children, he marries this woman, who then baits and manipulates his son and daughter and misrepresents them to their father in order to drive them from the house so that she will be free to spend his money. Her greed and extravagance so reduce his fortune that he is obliged to stay indoors for fear of meeting his creditors. Eventually he is delivered from his predicament by her death and on her deathbed she confesses how she had misrepresented his children's behaviour to him because she thought her interest opposed to theirs (276–7).

[14] Elizabeth Hamilton, *The Cottagers of Glenburnie*, ed. Pam Perkins (Glasgow: Association for Scottish Literary Studies, 2010), ch. 5; 93.

Miss Almon's tale in Sarah Scott's *The History of Sir George Ellison* (1766) recounts how her stepmother brings into their house a collection of crude and brutal people and subdues her father's resistance to this new and unpleasant way of life. She runs away when a servant tells her of overhearing her stepmother 'bargaining with your lover for your person'—arranging for her to be sexually taken for a financial consideration.[15] In *Millenium Hall* (1762), Sarah Scott again tells the tale of a young woman victimized by a scheming stepmother in her story of Miss Melvyn. Sent out of the way to boarding school because her vain stepmother wants to avoid comparison with her beauty, she is later married off to a repugnant suitor when her stepmother convinces her father that she is in a secret relationship with a farmer's boy. A cruel stepmother in Mrs Woodfin's *The Auction* (1760) favours her own daughter and treats her stepdaughter so badly that the poor displaced girl is forced to flee from the house. Although she loses contact with her father and has many adventures, eventually there is a tearful and sentimental reunion with her one remaining parent.

Usurping Heirs

In some novels, the eldest son is the victim rather than the villain in plots in which all the family property is settled upon one heir. In this formula, the younger son—through connivance and treachery—succeeds to the family fortune at the expense of his older brother. Perhaps the most violent of these tales of family fraud is Clara Reeve's *The Old English Baron*, originally titled *The Champion of Virtue* (1777). Set in the Middle Ages, its Gothic atmosphere inspired by Horace Walpole's *Castle of Otranto* (1765), the chain of events begins with a knight returning from the crusades, waylaid and murdered by his younger brother, his body in its bloodied armour hidden in a trunk at the bottom of the stairs in the castle. The younger brother's acts are motivated by his desire to possess both the estate and the wife of his older brother. There is a traditional ballad, 'Fause Footrage', with this same plot, in which the pregnant widow manages to escape the clutches of the villain and to give birth to a son away from the surveillance of her captor. In Reeve's novel, the widow dies soon after giving birth; but in the ballad the she is held prisoner by the usurper. In both, however, the noble son is found and reared by a labourer and his wife in the village and lives to avenge his father's murder. In the old ballad, the son does so by simply killing the usurper. The mechanism in the novel for this adjustment is a longer, more complicated, and curiously peaceful sequence of retributive justice.

---

[15] Sarah Scott, *The History of Sir George Ellison*, ed. Betty Rizzo (Lexington, KY: University of Kentucky Press, 1996), 159.

The villain is driven away from the castle, the scene of his murder, by ghosts that haunt his sleep. He rents the castle to his brother-in-law, the Baron Fitz-Owen, who in due course notices the boy from the village who is bright, handsome, brave, and gifted beyond his station. He invites him to be a companion to his sons and their cousins and he educates all the lads together. Our hero, Edmund Twyford, the labouring-class lad who is really the son of the murdered knight, discovers his true identity by the revelations of his father's ghost who still inhabits the castle. An old retainer of his father's, Joseph, also still in the castle, offers his services. The church is also on his side—Father Oswald believes in him and helps him. Edmund eventually proves his claim against his usurping uncle, marries Fitz-Owen's daughter, and re-establishes the proper lineage of the family. A cross between *Hamlet* and a sentimental novel, *The Old English Baron* was the second Gothic novel published in England, twelve years after Walpole's *Otranto*, but without the sexual heat or the breathless fright of Radcliffe's later Gothic novels (see also Ferris, Chapter 16).

Sarah Fielding's *The Adventures of David Simple* contains perhaps the earliest of these plots about a usurping younger brother. This novel begins with two brothers: David, 'who was of a sober prudent Disposition', able to save his money and happy to supply his younger brother Daniel, who is much more profuse in his spending (7). David is honest and generous; Daniel grasping and cunning. When their father falls ill, Daniel finds a way to forge a will making himself sole heir and executor, which he replaced for the original one. David's perplexity when this forged will is read has more to do with wondering how he had disobliged his father than with regretting the money he had lost. Being a proper eighteenth-century hero, he never suspects his brother nor grudges him the lion's share of their father's estate. But Daniel treated him so badly after this that he leaves the house with but a half a crown in his pocket, 'a Shilling of which he gave away in his Walk to a Beggar, who told him a Story of having been turned out of doors by an unnatural Brother' (16). Sick at heart and ill, David is rescued by his uncle who learns about the forged will from a servant and helps to reinstate David into his inheritance. All this happens within the first three chapters, and it motivates David to 'travel through the whole World' in search of a true friend.

Robert Bage's *Hermsprong* (1796) harbours another such a story at its centre. Our hero's father, who is a second son, rivals his younger brother for the love of a young woman, Miss Debank, but is betrayed by this youngest brother who debauches the young woman in question and falsely dishonours his rival with their wealthy grandfather. The betrayed brother is enjoined never to return to his native land, never to claim his alliance with the family, and to change his name. All this he does, raising his son—our hero, Hermsprong—among the Indians of North America. Meanwhile, the oldest son of this family dies, and the treacherous, selfish, youngest son succeeds to the family estates since his older brother is exiled. All is made right by the death of this wicked brother upon the public disclosure of his evil deeds, and the marriage between his daughter and our hero, who are first cousins.

First-Cousin Marriage

First-cousin marriage was never frowned upon in English society at this time; indeed, it was common enough among the aristocracy as a means of keeping the property in the family. That first cousins—the children of siblings—could marry shows a belief that the relation was understood not to transcend generations; the sibling tie was altered by adulthood and marriage. In Jane Austen's fiction, for example, there is not the slightest hint of impropriety in first-cousin marriage. The thing that mattered, rather, was whether or not the cousins were maternal first cousins or paternal first cousins, i.e. whether the marriage conferred the advantage of combining two fortunes as is the case in paternal first-cousin marriage among the rich. In *Mansfield Park*, for instance, although Sir Thomas Bertram has initial doubts about taking Fanny Price into his household because of her possible intimacy with his sons—'cousins in love &c'—as the novel progresses the match between Edmund and Fanny is increasingly the only one that makes any moral or psychological sense. That Fanny and Edmund are maternal cousins means that no material advantage will accrue from the marriage—such as keeping a title or estate in the family—although the union will strengthen consanguineal bonds and consolidate family feeling. Austen's other fully approved first-cousin marriage is also between maternal cousins—Charles Hayter and Henrietta Musgrove in *Persuasion* (1818)—whereas the possible paternal first-cousin matches in that novel (William Elliot with either Elizabeth or Anne) are tainted by social ambition and venal desire for the accumulation of wealth. In other words, maternal and paternal first-cousin marriages had very different social and fiscal implications because of the concentration of wealth and title in the male line; they thus carried very different moral valences. Maternal first-cousin marriage did not profit from this fact of inheritance, however; maternal first cousins were no better off marrying each other than anyone else in the world.

Conclusion

Thus the plots and characters of English fiction of this period can be illuminated by an awareness of property law and the customary disposition of property within families. That material greed as well as rivalries and competitions springing from even more primitive sources should be represented as occurring within families in the fiction of the day should surprise no one who has ever lived in a family. What is noteworthy are the excesses of innocence on the one hand and of rapaciousness on the other. One finds good characters who seek nothing for themselves and are generous to a fault, and bad characters whom nothing can touch but their ruthless desire for material wealth. Perhaps these dichotomies are nowhere so vividly portrayed as in Sarah Fielding's *The Adventures of David Simple*, which imagines a small band of friends operating with complete love and trust within a world seething with cruelty and selfishness.

The novel is a moral picaresque in the order of Voltaire's *Candide* or Samuel Johnson's *Rasselas*, but pre-dating both by fifteen years. As suggested, it tells the story of a man who travels the world to observe human nature, to seek virtue, and to discover the best way to live. Although he is the kindest and most generous of men, the perfidy of his brother is the condition on which the story of David Simple's adventures is founded. He finds society a stew of family-centred bitterness, filled with caricatures of the most egregious selfishness and exploitation—stepmothers who poison their new husbands against their children, brothers who forge wills, parents who force their children to marry for riches and against their inclination, sisters who hate one another for their beauty or who compete for wealthy suitors. In one metaphoric example, David comes across three sisters who have cut up a beautiful carpet rather than allowing any single one to possess it. Every sort of distortion of family feeling caused by greed and avarice makes its appearance to the horrified David Simple; the novel is a compendium of stories about families squabbling over property, their intense feeling for goods and money bringing them into conflict and poisoning daily life. The novel seems to count the ways that property can turn family members against one another.

Eventually the few good people who find one another form a community and live in peace. Although the first volume ends with David's death, his honest optimism and faith in the future make his last hour with Cynthia a real pleasure for her. Total disillusionment about the possibility of happiness on earth lies in wait in the second volume; but at the end of the first volume, love's happiness and the pleasures of friendship are still very much in evidence.

This text of 1744, a relatively early eighteenth-century novel, splits the characters into good and evil, dividing the world into black and white, and keeping them separate and far apart. But as the century wore on, more and more authors of fiction created characters with more plausibly mixed moral qualities, until by the end of the century a clever reader like young Jane Austen could apprehend and choose to burlesque extreme generosity in a fictional hero as an amusingly outworn convention. Moral traits such as attitudes towards wealth and property were embedded in characters a reader might recognize as more or less like his neighbour, rather than as a caricature of an attitude. The property issues that fuelled the plots of eighteenth-century fiction—unequal inheritance, forced alliances based on wealth, the transfer of women's wealth to their husbands or male relatives—these things did not begin to change legally until later in the next century.

But the outrage about them faded and the way that writers treated these scenarios in fiction evolved; they became naturalized, and treated as simply the way things were. No longer the spur for action, they became the givens of society, the background conditions for other kinds of moral dilemmas, which tended to be about the authenticity or fulfilment of the self rather than the justice of prevailing social arrangements for property within families. But in the fiction of between 1750 and 1820 one can still read the human responses to material inequities that tore families apart and made them accomplices of an economic system that put property before family loyalty.

23

Fictions of the Union

THOMAS KEYMER

A T the culmination of her influential essay 'On the Origin and Progress of Novel-Writing', originally prefixed to her multi-volume anthology *The British Novelists* (1810), Anna Laetitia Barbauld makes an arresting claim for the nation-building potential of the novel genre. An English author of Scots descent, married to the grandson of Huguenot refugees, and thus a living embodiment of the new Britain, Barbauld looks back to a renowned Scots patriot of the previous century to make her point:

> It was said by Fletcher of Saltoun, 'Let me make the ballads of a nation, and I care not who makes the laws.' Might it not be said with as much propriety, Let me make the novels of a country, and let who will make the systems?[1]

In some ways, this was a defence of the novel genre—and, implicitly, a rationale for Barbauld's inclusions and exclusions in *The British Novelists*—bolder than Jane Austen's more or less contemporaneous defence in *Northanger Abbey* (1818). Where Austen focuses on generalities and universals—'the most thorough knowledge of human nature' and 'the happiest delineation of its varieties',[2] things to be explored through minute attention to domestic and interior life—Barbauld emphasizes instead the public function of novels, and of the canon enshrined in her anthology. She does so a century after the British nation had been formally inaugurated by the 1707 Act of Union between England and Scotland (the much earlier annexation of Wales to England had been sealed by Tudor legislation), and just a decade after union with Ireland had taken effect. Her clear message is that in creating and sustaining a sense of overarching united nationhood, the 'systems' binding these composite entities—the principles and mechanisms underlying these unions—might be less efficacious than works of fiction, with their vivid and compelling dramatizations of shared interests, affiliations, and histories.

---

[1] Anna Laetitia Barbauld (ed.), *The British Novelists*, 50 vols (London: F. C. and J. Rivington et al., 1810), 1.62.

[2] Jane Austen, *Northanger Abbey*, ed. Barbara M. Benedict and Deirdre Le Faye (Cambridge: Cambridge University Press, 2006), vol. 1, ch. 5; 31.

Yet significant irony is embedded in Barbauld's claim by her choice of authority, Andrew Fletcher of Saltoun (1653–1716), a politician once praised by Tobias Smollett— with just a hint of accompanying amusement—as 'a man of undaunted courage and inflexible integrity, who professed republican principles, and seemed designed by nature as a member of some Grecian commonwealth'.[3] Fletcher had indeed made the comment invoked by Barbauld, writing in his *Account of a Conversation Concerning a Right Regulation of Governments* (1704) that 'if a man were permitted to make all the ballads, he need not care who should make the laws of a nation'. But he took care to attribute this comfortable maxim to an unnamed acquaintance, and in his own voice denounced the street balladry of the day as in practice infamous and lewd: 'in this city the dramatick poet no less than the ballad-maker has been almost wholly employed to corrupt the people, in which they have had most unspeakable and deplorable success.'[4] In effect, Fletcher was debunking his friend's dictum for its naivety about the nature of popular entertainment and the hardscrabble realities of urban life. More important, he made this judgement about the London of 1703, and the contribution to its social disorders of both ballads and plays, in the context of a passionate argument for a strictly limited, federal union of equal sovereign states, with minimal transfer of power from Edinburgh to London. 'All other coalitions', he insisted, 'are but the unjust subjection of one people to another' (214). By this point in the political process, Fletcher clearly recognized that some form of Anglo-Scottish union had become inevitable, and was devoting his formidable energies to limiting the damage. A classical republican who looked to Sparta for his ideals of civic virtue and was steeped in the principles of Machiavelli, he distinguished himself in the Edinburgh parliament of 1703–6 as a trenchant and unyielding opponent of incorporating union, which would place Scotland, he maintained, 'under the miserable and languishing condition of all places that depend upon a remote seat of government' (214). Yet it was an incorporating union that was duly enacted, and inherited a century later by Mrs Barbauld. The paradox is that she rests her case for the nation-building role of *The British Novelists* on a last-ditch attempt by her chosen authority to prevent the British nation from being formed.

It is hard to believe that this paradox was lost on Barbauld, who may have found Fletcher's words in a much earlier essay about novels by Hugh Blair,[5] but no doubt knew about their original context from her friend David Erskine, Earl of Buchan, author of a life of Fletcher. Nor, at a time when vernacular ballads in English, Welsh, Scots, and Gaelic were increasingly being recovered and valued as witnesses of cultural heterogeneity, can she have missed the contradiction involved in likening a form displaying

[3] Tobias Smollett, *A Complete History of England*, 4 vols (London: J. Rivington and J. Fletcher, 1757–8), 4.262.

[4] Andrew Fletcher, *Political Works*, ed. John Robertson (Cambridge: Cambridge University Press, 1997), 179.

[5] Hugh Blair, *Lectures on Rhetoric and Belles Lettres*, 2 vols (London: W. Strahan and T. Cadell, 1783), 2.303.

difference and diversity to a form promoting common identity. Perhaps she felt, after a century of strengthening political union, and with it social, economic, and cultural union, that early hostility to the 1707 settlement was now irrelevant: not only Fletcher's hostility, grounded as it was in austere republican theory, but also that of his allies such as John Hamilton, Baron Belhaven, who drew instead on a flamboyant rhetoric of hallowed bloodlines and traditional fealty to 'our *Ancient Mother* CALEDONIA' (see Davis 1998: 32). If proto-nationalists like Fletcher and Belhaven were on the wrong side of history regarding the union, moreover, they were also on the wrong side of the novel, for a century at least. With the exception of Smollett's disruptive masterpiece *The Expedition of Humphry Clinker* (1771), one would search in vain through the fifty volumes of Barbauld's anthology (which contained twenty-eight works by twenty-one authors) for any sustained treatment of the social and cultural consequences of 1707: for sustained treatment, that is, of a theme that in the wake of Walter Scott's *Waverley; or 'Tis Sixty Years Since* (1814) would shortly come to dominate new fiction.

Yet Barbauld herself can scarcely be blamed for the omission. As her introduction makes clear, numerous factors constrained her selection, including copyright considerations and public demand for the inclusion of popular favourites. More interestingly, Barbauld was a pioneering taxonomist of narrative form, and she based her choices in part on a desire to represent the range of techniques and perspectives developed in the novel since Defoe and Richardson, and thus on formal as much as thematic variety. That said, the simplest explanation for the absence from *The British Novelists* of novels about Britain as opposed to England, or more generally about the jostling diversity of united nationhood, with all the stresses, strains, and strengths entailed, is that few compelling candidates were there to be found. In the aftermath of the Jacobite rising of 1745, which sought alongside the primary goal of dynastic change to dissolve the union, obscure romances were published such as *Ascanius; or, The Young Adventurer* (1746), an instant *roman à clef* about Bonnie Prince Charlie's escape after Culloden for which the Anglo-Welsh bookseller, Ralph Griffiths, was arrested and briefly detained. The union remained available thereafter as a topic for throwaway jokes of more or less derogatory kinds, as when an obese, mean-minded alderman in John Shebbeare's *Lydia* (1755) leaves the narrator 'amazed at such Colossal Bodies and Pigmy Souls, a monstrous Union like that of *Scotland* with this Kingdom, something poor and scurvy with something fat and sawcy'.[6] For the most part, however, Robert Crawford's observation that 'the Union of Parliaments in 1707...had very little effect on literature written in England' (1992: 45) holds true for eighteenth-century fiction, which in its exploration of national identity typically avoids the issue of being British as opposed to English, and offers little interrogation, or even sustained representation, of ethnic, cultural, and linguistic diversity in the larger nation.

---

[6] John Shebbeare, *Lydia, or Filial Piety*, 4 vols (London: J. Scott, 1755), 2.199.

Of course, predictable cameos of fortune-hunting teagues, bare-arsed sawneys, and mendacious taffs, with assorted English yokels and cits, are a routine feature of minor satirical novels from the mid-century onwards. But representations of this kind, derived from the theatrical repertoire of the day, rarely amount to much more than farcical interludes. Outside the work of Smollett, the most thoughtful novels of cultural difference and interaction—as in the triangulated ethnography of Frances Brooke's *The History of Emily Montague* (1769), which compares the Huron, French, and English populations of newly conquered Lower Canada—were focused on the overseas empire for which union paved the way, not on the diverse homeland. The wide-ranging, ambitiously historicized analysis of social and cultural conflict and modernization that was to characterize the novels of Scott—and in general 'the Scotch novels' which, as the *London Magazine* announced in 1820, had now ushered in 'an era in our literary history' (see Duncan 2007: 33)—is nowhere to be found in the eighteenth century. It has been argued that significant pre-*Waverley* subgenres such as the national tale were later obscured by Scott's nineteenth-century popularity and by twentieth-century formulations about historical fiction by György Lukács and others, and that in this context 'most of the conceptual innovations attributed to Scott were in 1814 already established commonplaces of the British novel' (Trumpener 1997: 130). If so, however, the commonplaces in question were very recent, and concentrated in the work of Anglo-Irish writers responding in novels such as Sydney Owenson's *The Wild Irish Girl* (1806) and Charles Maturin's *The Milesian Chief* (1812) to political turbulence and national crisis surrounding the United Irishmen rebellion of 1798 and the ensuing union with Britain. In Britain itself, novelists made only the most rudimentary moves in this direction before *Waverley*, and though historical novels were written, most were historical in the strictly limited sense of being set in the past, without anticipating Scott's ambition to explain the present in terms of progress through stages of social organization and conflicts inherited or reconciled. Between 1800 and 1813, no more than a dozen new novels were published directly from Scotland, mainly in a conservative tradition of didactic domestic fiction and, to the extent that they touched on national issues, displaying none of the dissident charge that animated some Irish works (Garside 2000: 76–9; Duncan 2007: 34). More characteristic of Scottish-authored fiction in this regard (and the most recently written example in Barbauld's anthology) was John Moore's *Zeluco* (1789), a Gothic novel set in Italy and Cuba, which raises the union only to marginalize it in a farcical episode when two Scots servants, one a veteran of the '45, the other a staunch Whig of Covenanter stock, squabble about the consequences of 1707 and end up fighting a drunken duel over the honour of Mary Queen of Scots.

Among the writers of national tales, the most important precursor as Barbauld put together her anthology was Maria Edgeworth, whom Scott more than once credited as pioneering a regionally specific, historically attentive fiction of national character and consciousness that broke ground in theme and method for his own novels (see Ferris 1991: 106). Yet when Scott praised Edgeworth, in a somewhat Barbauld-like formulation of 1829, for having done more in her novels 'towards completing the Union [with Ireland], than perhaps all the legislative enactments by which it has been followed up' (see Ferris 2002: 12–13), he had in mind her national tales such as *Ennui* (1809) and *The Absentee* (1812), with their mobilization of interest in, and sympathy for, indigenous Ireland, and their reformist commitment to progress and integration within the new political framework. Edgeworth is the only writer of the nineteenth century represented in *The British Novelists*, but she appears as the author of *Belinda* (1801), primarily a novel of metropolitan society, and one more engaged, like *Emily Montague*, with the implications of colonialism abroad than with the anatomy of four-nations Britain. (The most provocative aspects of this engagement, in *Belinda*'s dual plots of courtship between English women and West Indian men, were toned down in revisions undertaken specifically for republication by Barbauld.) Also included as a makeweight was Edgeworth's *The Modern Griselda* (1805), a satirical novella about fashionable marriage set in London and rural Devon, marked by traditional elements of country–city satire but lacking the alertness to national identities and interactions of Edgeworth's more ambitious works.

Jacobitism, the Union, and the Novel

A good way to gauge this collective oversight in eighteenth-century fiction is to consider the earliest writer in Barbauld's collection, Daniel Defoe. On the face of it, Defoe was perfectly placed to write a novel exploring the implications of the 1707 union, not least because he had been a key player on behalf of the English government in the fraught negotiations in Edinburgh surrounding its passage, and a tireless pamphleteer in the unionist cause. In his journalism, satire, and polemics of the period, his usual strategy was to ignore Fletcher, not least because the radical Whig principles from which Fletcher began were so close to his own (both men, indeed, had participated in the abortive Monmouth rebellion of 1685). Instead Defoe targeted the mystical rhetoric—'the Cant of the old Times', he calls it in a letter[7]—associated with Belhaven. As Leith Davis has noted, 'Defoe recognized that in order to promote a new imagining of the nation, it was necessary to dispel residual notions of Scottish national identicality and mythical belonging' (1998: 34). He set about the task by drawing on an alternative vision of melting-pot, hybridized identity that he had previously articulated in *The True-Born Englishman* (1701), a verse satire written to rebut xenophobic attacks on William III, the Dutch prince who had successfully displaced the Stuart monarchy three years after the Monmouth debacle. In the best-known couplet from this poem—'A *True-Born Englishman*'s a Contradiction, | In Speech an Irony, in Fact a Fiction' (ll. 372–3)—what matters is not some idealized, imaginary past of ethnic purity,

---

[7] *The Letters of Daniel Defoe*, ed. George Harris Healey (Oxford: Clarendon Press, 1955), 142 (5 November 1706).

but the energies inherited in the present from the 'Amphibious Ill-born Mob' (l. 187) of Celts, Romans, Saxons, Normans, and other races in whom the English take their multiple, and still expanding, origins. In this context of heterogeneous modern identity—the context of a mongrel race 'In eager Rapes, and furious Lust begot, | Betwixt a Painted Briton and a Scot' (ll. 336–7)—Belhaven's blood-and-soil traditionalism could be dismissed as fanciful and bogus. In its place, Defoe looks pragmatically forward to the only circulating lifeblood that really mattered, the lifeblood of trade, which would now, as the commercial provisions of the union began to kick in, enrich and modernize Scotland. 'Here a Country Improv'd, there a Country to Improve', he enthused with Whiggish fervour in 1706: 'here a Nation grown opulent by Trade, there a Nation, which let into Trade, will be in time as Rich and Opulent, and in Proportion, as much improv'd as they.'[8]

Yet it was only after his retirement as a novelist, in his monumental *Tour thro' the Whole Island of Great Britain* (1724–6), that Defoe undertook a comprehensive examination of the new nation, with a focus in particular on its burgeoning economic life. By contrast, his novels take England and the wider world as their canvas, with scant attention along the way to the Celtic fringe. The example selected by Barbauld, *Robinson Crusoe* (1719), may have been partly inspired by the sufferings of a Scottish mariner (Alexander Selkirk), and Crusoe's ordeal may partly allegorize the oppression of both English and Scottish dissenters under the restored Stuart monarchy of 1660–88 (which is almost exactly the span of his castaway years). But *Robinson Crusoe* has nothing at all to do with the political consequences of the union, or with the implications of the union for national identity, unless we read more than seems warranted into Crusoe's anxieties about the trackless 'other side' of his island, with its marauding savages and inviting resources. Moreover, although Defoe was elsewhere a penetrating observer of urban crisis, as in the traumatized London of *A Journal of the Plague Year* (1722), he never drew on memories of Edinburgh in the turbulent union years as a setting for his fiction, as James Hogg would do to such sinister effect a century later in *The Private Memoirs and Confessions of a Justified Sinner* (1824).

Only in the relatively obscure *Colonel Jack* (1722) does Defoe send one of his protagonists north of the border, and then only briefly, in episodes set before the union was enacted. Crossing the Tweed to escape retribution for his crimes in England, Jack experiences Scotland as a place of regeneration, and at the close of the novel attributes his acquisition of moral and religious knowledge to his sojourn in Edinburgh. Yet he also notes that his Scots-born sobriety was too shallow to last, and that 'with my leaving that Country, it soon left me too'.[9] Earlier, Defoe's emphasis falls not only on the anomaly of the lawless border zone either side of the Tweed, where divided legal jurisdiction persisted after the union, but also on the mutual hostility of its populations. Soon after Jack's

---

[8] *Political and Economic Writings of Daniel Defoe, Volume 4: Union with Scotland*, ed. D. W. Hayton (London: Pickering & Chatto, 2000), 66.

[9] Daniel Defoe, *Colonel Jack*, ed. Samuel Holt Monk (London: Oxford University Press, 1965), 308.

arrival in Edinburgh, 'an unhappy, ill-natur'd *Scotch-man*, perceiv'd by our Speech, that we were *English-men*', and threatens Jack and his companion with public whipping (100). Later episodes revive the theme of conflict when—with motives rendered uncertain by his enigmatic narrative voice—Jack enlists in the failed French endeavour of 1708 to land the Pretender in Scotland, and then narrowly avoids disaster in 1715 when his wife dissuades him from joining an improvised force of English Jacobites in support of the invading Scots. When the union was formally enacted, Defoe may have rejoiced as a journalist that England and Scotland would now 'become one Nation, one Kingdom, one People, United in all our Civil Interests' (*The Review*, 10 May 1707). But when he later considered the situation as a novelist, it was division and discord that continued to strike him.

For John Kerrigan, Defoe's involvement in the union debates, and the contested identities he encountered in the process, shaped his novels not so much in their overt content as in 'the powers of empathy and analysis that later informed his fiction, including, palpably, *Colonel Jack*' (2008: 348). But this direct experience of Scotland was not shared by novelists of the next generation, whose own powers had little of a four-nations or 'archipelagic' dimension. There is nothing distinctively Scottish about the hero of Eliza Haywood's *The Agreeable Caledonian* (1728), and although Haywood was later arrested for another fictionalized account of Charles Edward Stuart's wanderings, *A Letter from H —— G—g, Esq., One of the Gentlemen of the Bed-Chamber to the Young Chevalier* (1749), the primary impulse of this work is most likely parodic. More formidable novelistic responses to the '45 were produced by Richardson and Fielding, to the extent, at least, that the power struggles in which the protagonists of both *Clarissa* (1748–9) and *Tom Jones* (1749) are embroiled are amplified by political overtones. In both these works, however, emphasis falls most often on theoretical issues about authority, legitimacy, and self-determination that the Jacobite rising had made urgent, or on glancing analogies between private and public conflicts, not on the underlying question of Anglo-Scottish relations. *Clarissa* was planned and partly drafted before the '45 broke out, but heavily revised prior to publication, and throughout the novel the recent crisis colours the heroine's predicament, caught as she is between the corrupt authority of her nouveau-riche father and the arbitrary will of a seductive aristocrat who speaks in terms of prerogative and ancient birthright. Though recognizing her father's entitlement 'to prevent a headstrong child, as a good prince would wish to do disaffected subjects, from running into rebellion, and so forfeiting everything',[10] Clarissa flees his house in an episode poised ambiguously between elopement and abduction, only to suffer imprisonment and rape—a familiar metaphor of political subjugation since Lucretia—at Lovelace's hands. Yet for all the hints and shadows that haunt this personal drama of resistance and tyranny, *Clarissa* never reaches a level of allegorical equivalence, and when Richardson wishes to associate his anti-hero with Stuart absolutism, he does

[10] Samuel Richardson, *Clarissa, or, The History of a Young Lady*, ed. Angus Ross (Harmondsworth: Penguin, 1985), 65.

so by having Lovelace echo *The True Briton*, an English Jacobite periodical of the 1720s, or by having him drink at the Cocoa Tree, a London coffee house for disaffected Tories. Nothing beyond the surname of Lovelace's brutal accomplice, the brothel-keeper Mrs Sinclair, marks her as Scottish, and this name was plainly selected as a moral, not national or political, indicator—the clear thing about Sinclair being her sin, not her membership of a Highland clan (which, in any case, was no longer actively Jacobite, and supplied a key government commander at Culloden).

Richardson's indifference to, or at least his inability to write about, the Jacobite rebellion as specifically a crisis of the union is unsurprising. As a leading master printer, he must have interacted daily with the Scots who were an increasingly conspicuous presence in the London book trade, but he had no personal experience of life outside England, and indeed (he once told an Irish correspondent) had never seen the sea, 'and hardly any Rocks but the Inland ones at Tunbridge' (Eaves and Kimpel 1971: 73). The more cosmopolitan Henry Fielding had broader experience to draw on, and in *Tom Jones* he blazed the trail for a long line of novelists from Scott to Robert Louis Stevenson and John Buchan by incorporating the Jacobite rising as a critical backdrop to his main action. But Fielding was plainly by now embarrassed about the intermittently Scotophobic rhetoric that he had employed as a journalist during the rebellion, notably in his pro-ministerial organ the *True Patriot*, and in its references to Jacobitism *Tom Jones* combines a comic, irenic tone with obvious efforts to minimize the national dimensions of the conflict. When the Jacobite invaders are abruptly introduced as 'Banditti' in Book 7 of the novel (the belatedness is sometimes taken as evidence that Fielding, like Richardson, began work before the rebellion broke out), they sound more like romance brigands than real Scots, a far cry from the kilt-clad, claymore-wielding savages of Fielding's most paranoid *True Patriot* leaders, for which he apologized when winding up the journal in 1746.[11] In the novel as a whole, some of Fielding's most egregious villains are Hanoverian loyalists, while his Jacobite characters are endearing buffoons, represented not as marauding clansmen but as English nostalgists, like the deluded patriot who celebrates rumours of a secondary invasion—'Ten thousand honest *Frenchmen* are landed in *Suffolk*. Old *England* for ever!' (578)—or Squire Western, a Tory backwoodsman who names his favourite horse after the Pretender and governs his daughter by Stuart principles of absolute power. It was for Fielding's characterization of Western that Barbauld thought *Tom Jones* an anachronism in the modern, commercial, imperial nation to which she addressed *The British Novelists*: estates like his were now often possessed by self-made men who 'bring down the habits of mercantile life from the brewery or the warehouse'; as for Western's rural sports, 'there are more of his majesty's subjects at this moment hunting

---

[11] Henry Fielding, *Tom Jones*, ed. Martin C. Battestin and Fredson Bowers (Oxford: Clarendon Press, 1974), 368: see also Henry Fielding, *The True Patriot and Related Writings*, ed. W. B. Coley (Oxford: Clarendon Press, 1987), 308–9 (no. 33, 10 June 1746).

the tiger...in India, than there are hunting foxes at home' (*British Novelists*, 1.xxiii). Though Jacobitism was soon to be revived thematically by Scott, it was little more for Barbauld than a historical curiosity—as it may eventually have been for Charles Edward himself, who ended his life resigned to exile and listing *Tom Jones*, somewhat bizarrely, among his favourite books (McLynn 1991: 520). Within a generation, and most conspicuously in the global theatre of the Seven Years' War (1756–63), the Highlanders who had once threatened Fielding's England were now at the cutting edge of British military supremacy, confirming as a long-term consequence of Anglo-Scottish union the new pre-eminence of Great Britain as an imperial power.

Smollett's Civil Dissensions

Why was the novel genre so slow to address a question at the very heart of the national life? One answer is that for all the technical innovations of the period, not least Fielding's effort to endow the genre with the public reach of epic, novels still lacked the formal resources necessary to tell complex stories of national evolution, and would only later absorb these resources from the philosophical historiography of the Scottish Enlightenment, with its characteristic plot of stadial development. So long as the issue of political union remained entangled with that of Jacobitism, it may also have been too close to the national bone for direct analysis in fiction, as would only become possible once the Jacobite threat was safely extinct—'*Tis Sixty Years Since*, in Scott's famous subtitle—and the bloodshed a distant memory. Nor should we underestimate the persistence of censorship as a constraint on expression in the eighteenth century. Although both Haywood and Griffiths were able to talk their way out of trouble without real difficulty in the 1740s, it was not until Scott's day—as, famously, in the tartan pageantry of the 'King's Jaunt' to Edinburgh in 1822—that the iconography of Scottish Jacobite culture was completely freed of seditious connotation.

Yet perhaps the most persuasive explanation for the novel's delayed reaction as a genre is a more general lag in perception, the full implications of 1707 only coming to be grasped when made conspicuous or actualized by practical crises and their outcomes in later decades. In his postscript to *Waverley* and his *Quarterly Review* essay of 1816 on the *Culloden Papers*, Scott identifies the post-rebellion legislation of 1746–8, not the union of 1707, as the decisive watershed in the national life, and for Kerrigan 'Culloden and its aftermath brought about the real shift in perspective' (2008: 352). No less significant than the '45 and the modernizing campaign to which it led was the toxic political atmosphere of the Seven Years' War, partly conducted under a controversial Scots-led ministry and culminating in the dizzying acquisition of a global empire. Both contexts emerge as crucial in *Humphry Clinker*, the only Smollett novel in Barbauld's collection, which in its sustained treatment of national heterogeneity opened up new terrain for the genre, yet in ways that indicate the ongoing difficulty, even after so long, of writing fictions of the union, or of reconciling responses, in the manner of Scott, within a single celebratory view.

Smollett was perfectly placed to write the novel of united nationhood that his precursors had not produced. Years before his birth in 1721, his Whig grandfather had been among the commissioners appointed on the Scottish side to frame the articles of union, and Sir James Smollett went on to represent the family's home county of Dunbartonshire in the Westminster Parliament. As the youngest child of a fourth son, Smollett had no prospect of following his grandfather (whom he remembered with cordial hostility) down the corridors of power, but as an author he was often in the forefront of political controversy, notably when Anglo-Scots relations were at issue, and in a manner typically at variance with the Whig family tradition. In the immediate wake of Culloden, his early poem 'The Tears of Scotland' (1746) was guarded and ambiguous enough to be reprinted in both Jacobite and anti-Jacobite miscellanies, and at one level Smollett's poem is a rebuke to Jacobitism for provoking a crisis of allegiance and civil war between fellow Scots in which 'The sons, against their fathers stood, | The parent shed his children's blood' (ll. 35–6). With this focus on internal division, the poem anticipates Smollett's later accounts of Scotland, irrespective of union with England, as in itself composite and heterogeneous—a land 'originally inhabited by two nations that widely differed from each other in language, garb, manners, customs, and disposition', and still divided along the Highland line by 'a national and rancorous prejudice' between Gaelic Highlander and Anglophone Lowlander.[12] That said, the primary drift of 'The Tears of Scotland' is oppositional, with emphasis on the gratuitous slaughter of defeated rebels and the harrying of the Jacobite clans by government forces: 'Yet, when the rage of battle ceas'd, | The victor's soul was not appeas'd', writes Smollett with bold reference to 'Butcher' Cumberland, the Hanoverian general: 'The naked and forlorn must feel | Devouring flames, and murd'ring steel!' (ll. 37–40).

Two years later, Smollett's first novel *Roderick Random* (1748) was cast in the voice of a protagonist 'born in the northern part of this united kingdom',[13] and with this emphasis on the redefinition of Scots as 'North Britons' it confronts the tensions of united nationhood, and specifically of hyphenated Scoto-British identity, on an expansive scale. A picaresque work that follows its hero across three continents, *Roderick Random* is also a narrative of assimilation in which the roguish protagonist, his origins and identity blurred by strategic suppression of his accent, finally completes his integration by marrying an English bride. Here was a familiar emblem of national union from the debates of 1707 (Smollett may have been reminded of it by the posthumous publication of Jonathan Swift's 'Story of an Injured Lady' (1746), a bilious allegory in which England jilts loyal

---

[12] Tobias Smollett, *The Present State of All Nations*, 8 vols (London: R. Baldwin, 1768–9), 2.1–2.

[13] Tobias Smollett, *The Adventures of Roderick Random*, ed. Paul-Gabriel Boucé (Oxford: Oxford University Press, 1979), 1.

Ireland for a slatternly Scottish bride), and this emblem was frequently resumed in early nineteenth-century national tales, and in novels such as *Waverley*. In Smollett's hands, however, the wedlock-as-union trope is accompanied by characteristic hints of disharmony, from the sense of disdain and doom conveyed by the unflattering name of Roderick's bride, to a closing intimation that Narcissa will soon tire of Scotland. Later novels are no less equivocal in their representation of British identity, not least *Sir Launcelot Greaves* (1762), first serialized in Smollett's own monthly *British Magazine* between 1760 and 1761. With his Arthurian name, the quixotic hero of *Sir Launcelot Greaves* embodies an ancient ideal of British virtue while observing and lamenting—like his woeful Cervantic prototype, Sir Launcelot *grieves*—the erosion of this ideal in the modern nation. On witnessing the disorder and corruption of electoral hustings, he despairs that compatriots he took for 'free-born Britons and fellow-citizens' turn out to be 'a pack of venal, infamous scoundrels', Whig and Tory alike.[14]

Its notes of satirical disillusion notwithstanding, the *British Magazine* was one of several publications in which Smollett signalled his embrace of overarching British identity during the Seven Years' War, when Whig opposition to the Tory ministry of the Earl of Bute revived anti-union feeling in England, most rancorously in the *North Briton* (1762–3), a radical weekly by John Wilkes and the bludgeoning verse satirist Charles Churchill. Their immediate target was Smollett's pro-Bute *Briton* (1762–3), which fought back with vigour, and in one of his best-aimed counterblasts Smollett caricatured the divisive rhetoric and sneering Scotophobia of Wilkes's leaders while neatly insinuating that the British Empire that was now being won was a direct consequence of the union. Writing in the splenetic voice of an English bigot, he protests that state institutions have become infested by ambitious Scots, to the point that 'our army cannot be recruited, nor our navy manned, nor our manufactures proceed, nor our navigation be carried on, without employing that generation of vipers' (*Briton*, 15 January 1763). Yet the pugnacious eloquence of Smollett's journalism belied a thin skin, and in 1763 he 'fled from my country as a scene of illiberal dispute', as he angrily recalled in the opening letter of his *Travels through France and Italy* (1766), 'where a few worthless incendiaries had . . . kindled up a flame which threatened all the horrors of civil dissension'. He was back in Italy again by 1769, and for all the sensory immersion of his last novel in the sights, sounds and smells of modern Britain, *Humphry Clinker* seems to have been completed and revised in a Tuscan villa where Smollett died, asthmatic and consumptive, three months after the novel appeared in London.

Central to the achievement of *Humphry Clinker*, and to its exploration of British identity as complex, contested, and plural, is its virtuoso handling of narrative form. To eighteenth-century ears, the very term 'narrative' was a Scotticism—'to *narrate*, to speak in the Scottish phrase', says Lovelace in *Clarissa* (1025)—of the kind for which Smollett

---

[14] Tobias Smollett, *Sir Launcelot Greaves*, ed. Robert Folkenflik and Barbara Laning Fitzpatrick (Athens, GA: University of Georgia Press, 2002), 76.

was notorious, and in this case there is a direct link between the novel's self-consciousness about narration and its self-consciousness—Scottish in bias, detractors insisted—about nation. Where Smollett's previous novels had been formally straightforward, presented as first-person memoir or authorial retrospect, *Humphry Clinker* distributes its narrative between five distinct epistolary voices, which in their recurrent disagreements—this is not polyphonic but cacophonous narration—imply intense scepticism about the capacity of stable perspectives and linear stories to represent the modern nation. Not only do these narrators fail to achieve consensus about the world they witness and describe; they are even inconsistent within themselves, and at one point the most prolix of the five, a prickly Tory squire named Matthew Bramble, acknowledges that humans perceive and judge 'imperfectly through the mist of prejudice'. His own opinion of any phenomenon depends more on fluctuating internal well-being than on the phenomenon itself, he adds, and 'like mercury in the thermometer, rises and falls according to the variations of the weather'.[15] As befits a work that explicitly celebrates the Edinburgh Enlightenment of Hume and Smith, *Humphry Clinker* constantly implies the discontinuity of identity, the relativity of perception, and the inaccessibility of objective reality except via the subjective conduits of sense and feeling. Perspectives uneasily converge towards the conclusion, but this is above all a novel of conflicting viewpoints, used by Smollett to represent and articulate divided feelings about the state of the nation. Where fifty years later Scott could abandon letter narration partway through *Redgauntlet* (1824), able to reduce his material instead to the clarity of authorial overview (see also Watson, Chapter 20), for Smollett the epistolary form was an essential resource for voicing contradictions that were not yet resolved.

No less important than multiple-correspondent fictions such as *Clarissa* in the generic background of *Humphry Clinker* is the eighteenth-century literature of domestic tourism. With its perfunctory and conventional plot—'its principal defect is the want of events', complained the *Gentleman's Magazine*[16]—the novel lays emphasis more on environment than action. In this respect Smollett's full title, *The Expedition of Humphry Clinker*, is worth keeping in mind, less for its reference to the oddly marginal eponym (who is expeditious by nature, and expedited by the plot from his predicament as a penniless vagrant) than for its emphasis on excursion or travel. If the work has a single unifying action, it is the wide-ranging tour that Bramble undertakes with his household in pursuit of well-being, which he finally, albeit precariously, achieves not from the dubious treatments he undergoes but by absorption from the diverse energies of the nation around him. Setting out from rural retirement in Wales (significantly, Smollett's narrators are Anglicized Welsh gentry, participant-observers who approach the issues of 1707 as representatives of a prior

---

[15] *The Expedition of Humphry Clinker*, ed. Thomas R. Preston (Athens, GA: University of Georgia Press, 1990), 74.

[16] *Gentleman's Magazine*, 41 (July 1771), 317.

union), the group moves through the health resorts of England with a stop in London, then north into Scotland, penetrating the Highland line before returning home by way of the new industrial cities and two representative rural estates, the first destroyed by flashy bad taste and Whiggish display, the second a Tory haven of benevolent stewardship and settled hierarchy. Like Defoe in his *Tour*, though here in fusion with, not abandonment of, the novel form, Smollett moves finally beyond fiction as such towards a systematic exercise in social geography, a robust documentation of the united Britain in all its thriving diversity.

There are two large differences, however. Defoe's *Tour* grounds itself in a secure epistemology through which the world can be perfectly perceived and described, and presents itself is a definitive fixing of Great Britain to the permanence of print. In particular, Scotland—the least familiar, most intriguing section of the work for most readers—will be rigorously documented 'as it really is, and as in Time it may be'.[17] This last phrase reasserts the progressivist, Whiggish emphasis of the *Tour*, with its insistent keyword 'Improvement'. Throughout the work, Defoe is indifferent to rural tranquillity, scornful of picturesque backwaters, alarmed by untamed nature; instead he celebrates the spread of prosperity through industry, trade, and their corollaries: urban expansion, demographic growth, and the ascendancy of commercial values. His subject is 'the Improvement, as well in Culture, as in Commerce, the Encrease of People, and Employment for them...also the Encrease of Wealth' (1). Applied to Scotland, this perspective involves applause for the early economic fruits of union, alongside anticipation of the more extensive post-1750 modernization on which Scott would later look back in his *Waverley* postscript. As Defoe writes, 'it is no Reflection upon *Scotland* to say they are where we were, I mean as to the Improvement of their Country and Commerce; and they may be where we are' (690).

In this context, the significance of Smollett's kaleidoscopic narrative form becomes clear, as does the Tory cast of his response—or at least his lead narrator's response—to Defoe. By distributing his narrative among competing letter-writers, whose failure to agree about the truth and nature of things allows the environments of Bath or London to appear, adjacently, in bafflingly different ways, Smollett relinquishes the positivist ambition of objectively describing the world, and instead describes those more unstable and uncertain things, subjective perceptions of the world. The objectivity claimed by Defoe no longer seems attainable; perception can never transcend the vagaries of feeling and sense; partiality is the inescapable condition of all experience and discourse. The relativity of perceptions is often cited to explain the incompatible reports of narrators who experience the world 'through the falsifying medium of prejudice and passion' (*Humphry Clinker*, 318), and in these conditions nothing, certainly nothing as complex as a diverse

---

[17] Daniel Defoe, *A Tour thro' the Whole Island of Great Britain*, ed. G. D. H. Cole (London: Peter Davies, 1927), 690.

nation, can be described from one perspective 'as it really is'. As Smollett questions the confident epistemology of Defoe, moreover, so he questions Defoe's confidence in progress. In the prosperous resorts of southern England, Bramble finds only decadence, corruption, and the debilitating effects of fashion and commercial modernity. 'All these absurdities arise from the general tide of luxury, which hath overspread the nation, and swept away all', he laments in a characteristic image of ruinous inundation (36). Pockets of sanity survive this riot of improvement, but they survive most of all in Bramble's memory. The evaporation of traditional, pre-commercial virtues is nowhere more obvious than when he visits the once flourishing estate of his old friend Baynard, now 'improved' into a chaos of conspicuous consumption and arid display, and soon to be lost to circling creditors.

In Scotland, however, the traditionalist cast of Bramble's vision takes on more nuance, and in the emergent manufacturing heartland of Paisley and Glasgow he is able to celebrate a virtuous commercial culture, grounded in production, not consumption, and not yet declined into the fashionable excesses of consumerism and credit that run riot south of the border. Smollett would probably have known Defoe's *Tour* in the less strenuously Whiggish posthumous editions that were updated under the editorship of Richardson in the mid-century, but there remains a sense of pointed resistance in the novel to Defoe's notion that post-union Scotland should improve itself into the condition of England; rather, the Scotland of *Humphry Clinker* represents a happy medium between traditional society and commercial modernity to which England should seek to return. When Bramble eventually comes to adopt Defoe's lexicon of 'improvement', it is specifically in the context of his praise for manufacturing Glasgow, its population activated by 'a noble spirit of enterprise' that has not yet tipped over into luxury and excess (239). Albeit after a lapse of several decades, Scotland has come to reap the harvest of 1707, leading Bramble to celebrate 'the happy effects of the union, so conspicuous in the improvement of their agriculture, commerce, manufactures, and manners' (265). Yet Smollett then disrupts the celebration by introducing the dissenting voice of Lieutenant Lismahago, a veteran of Ticonderoga (the American victory that sealed the reputation of Scots regiments as the shock troops of empire) who nevertheless continues to deplore the subsuming of Scotland within Britain. Though elsewhere a butt of ridicule, and plainly a fortune-hunter, Lismahago here becomes the mouthpiece for a long and eloquent critique of 1707. At one level he represents a *reductio ad absurdum* of the classical republican case for austere independence, a caricature Fletcher of Saltoun for whom economic benefit is beside the point: 'The Lacedaemonians were poorer than the Scots, when they took the lead among all the free states of Greece, and were esteemed above them all for their valour and their virtue' (265). He is undercut by Smollett when citing the Darien venture of 1698–1700 to argue that 'before the union, there was a remarkable spirit of trade among the Scots'—the Darien expedition being a disastrous attempt to found an independent empire that in its failure helped precipitate the union (to the dismay of Fletcher, who had promoted Darien among his compatriots as 'the only means to recover us from our present miserable and despicable condition').[18] Yet the practice of insinuating cogent argument into the voice of a buffoon, so enabling authorial disavowal of controversial material, is a long-established technique. Where as a historian Smollett had used flat descriptive neutrality to address 'that treaty of union which was so eagerly courted by the English ministry, and proved so unpalatable to the generality of the Scottish nation',[19] as a novelist he renders the controversy active in competing voices, so articulating deeply felt contradictions that could not be resolved into a single thesis.

Similar contradictions emerge at the extremity of the tour, when Smollett's narrators finally enter the western Highlands—those once lawless tribal areas, cradles of Jacobite insurgency. Observing the defeated and demoralized clansmen of the region, Bramble continues to perceive them as a threat—'We have lived to see four thousand of them, without discipline, throw the whole kingdom of Great Britain into confusion' (246)—and applauds the statutes enacted after the rising (the Proscription and Heritable Jurisdictions Acts are specifically noted) to modernize their feudal culture out of existence. Confronted by pre-commercial simplicity at its most extreme, he now abandons his primitivist illusions about Ossianic virtue, and instead looks eagerly to Whiggish remedies—property, improvement, fishery, manufacture—as the best security against future insurrection. Yet as Smollett wrote, the most widely resented part of the post-Culloden legislation was just a decade from repeal (the ban on Highland garb was lifted in 1782), and in the voice of Bramble's nephew he presents a more sympathetic view of the Highlanders, and one that anticipates not *Waverley* so much as Hogg's *The Three Perils of Woman* (1823), with its grim account of the defeated clansmen as 'poor wrecks of the spoil of an extirpated people'.[20] For Jery Melford (Bramble's nephew), they are objects of pity who, their traditional tartan under prohibition, 'now lounge along in loose great coats . . . and betray manifest marks of dejection'. With a shrewd sense of forcible modernization and the eradication of culture as a means of political control, he adds that 'the government could not have taken a more effectual method to break their national spirit' (233). With a dizzying flourish of absurdity, Smollett also adds a third view, that of the Welsh servant Win Jenkins, to whom the clansmen are simply 'a parcel of selvidges that lie in caves among the rocks, devour young children, speak Velch, but the vords are different' (252). Yet this is a meaningful joke, and of a piece with Jery's observation that everything he sees, hears, and feels now 'seems Welch', and that the Gaelic Highlanders and 'Sassenagh' Lowlanders of Scotland are to one another, 'in their looks, garb, and language, as the mountaineers of Brecknock are from the inhabitants of Herefordshire' (232–3). The Britain of the novel is a diverse union

---

[18] Fletcher, *Political Works*, 38.
[19] Smollett, *Complete History*, 4.315.
[20] James Hogg, *The Three Perils of Woman*, ed. Antony Hasler and Douglas S. Mack (Edinburgh: Edinburgh University Press, 2002), 362.

of prior entities that were always already diverse, and the resulting nation is legitimized and strengthened by complex affinities across the boundaries of each constituent unit.

In the same spirit, the novel concludes in not one but three marriages that cut across differences of nationality and rank, and demand to be seen, like the hero's wedding in *Roderick Random*, as emblems of larger comedic resolution, harmonizing national rivalries in personal unions. Yet Smollett is never one for banal celebration, and he ends *Humphry Clinker* in a riot of disruptive malapropism that destabilizes the superficial concord of the novel's ending. Nothing escapes the semantic havoc of Win's concluding letter (as Fielding puts it when using the same technique, 'there was more eloquence in the false spellings, with which it abounded, than in all Aristotle'[21]), and her botched words subvert her companions' celebrations of consensus and sociability. She ends by announcing the tourists' amicable parting of ways; now 'our satiety is to suppurate', she says, to live in future 'upon dissent terms of civility' (337). For a novelist who had earlier cited the horrors of 'civil dissension' as his reason for leaving Britain, the replacement of decency by dissension, society by satiety, separation by suppuration, are not reassuring jokes.

Vindicating the Scots

The internal conflicts of *Humphry Clinker* were replicated in its contentious reception. Some reviewers saw the Tory Bramble as Smollett's ideological mouthpiece, a simplification that still persists in modern readings despite various clever ironies that undercut his position. (Bramble's complicity in the consumerism he deplores is one of the novel's running jokes, as when he excoriates the craze for imported luxuries while sending to London for American ginseng, fretting that it might be inferior to the Asian alternative.) Other readers, including Horace Walpole, who called *Humphry Clinker* 'a party novel, written by the profligate hireling Smollett, to vindicate the Scots and cry down juries', looked instead to Lismahago's voice for authentic, authorial meaning.[22] The *Universal Magazine* worried that the novel would 'tend rather to widen than heal the breach that at present subsists betwixt the South and North Britons, whom every lover of his country would wish to see united without distinction or difference',[23] and more than one newspaper carried a spoof advertisement for 'A Dissertation tending to prove, that the cities of London and Bath are filthy, stinking, disagreeable, hateful places, filled with a *Mob of impudent Plebeians* . . . and that Edinburgh, and the whole kingdom of Scotland, is superior to every other part of the world for elegance, cleanliness, politeness of manners, learning, magnificence, good

[21] Henry Fielding, *The Journal of a Voyage to Lisbon, Shamela, and Occasional Writings*, ed. Martin C. Battestin (Oxford: Clarendon Press, 2008), 377.
[22] For Walpole's remark, see his *Memoirs of the Reign of King George the Third*, ed. G. F. Russell Barker, 4 vols (London: Lawrence and Bullen, 1894), 4.218.
[23] *Universal Magazine*, 49 (November 1771), 257.

living, and universal plenty…By TOBIAS SMOLLETT' (*Middlesex Journal*, 18–20 July 1771). Why ever, this notice continued, did Smollett not choose to live in Scotland himself?

In this context, it is unsurprising that other Scottish novelists downplayed their nationality, notably Henry Mackenzie, whose best-selling sentimental novel *The Man of Feeling* (1771) drew for its narrative form on the Ossianic fragments of James Macpherson but remained emphatically English in character and setting. There is little counterpart in fiction of the period to the creative use of vernacular Scots by poets such as Allan Ramsay and Robert Fergusson, and most novelists sought to blend into the neutral background of standard English, or, like Jean Marishall in *The History of Alicia Montague* (1767), were upbraided by reviewers when they failed to do so. (Marishall makes up for her Scotticisms with the integrationist enthusiasm of her protagonists, reporting that 'a firm and lasting union betwixt *England* and *Scotland* was toasted in a bumper every day after dinner').[24] And though Scotland became an increasingly popular setting for fiction as a growing vogue for domestic tourism drew the two solitudes together, some novels were no more convincing than *The Unfortunate Caledonian in England*, anonymously published in 1781, which made one reviewer suspect that 'the Author, instead of *having never left Scotland* till January 1st 1779, was, probably, never in it'.[25] As Robert Burns complained a few years later, there was a marked disparity between the harsh realities of life in rural Scotland and the pastoral projections of fiction ('a Novel-Writer might perhaps have viewed these scenes with some satisfaction, but so did not I', he recalls of his Ayrshire childhood),[26] and the ideological turn of literature following the French Revolution did little to promote the development of more rigorous or nuanced representation. Ann Radcliffe's debut novel *The Castles of Athlin and Dunbayne* (1789) set off a modest vogue among English writers for medieval Scottish settings, though they typically addressed the subject in presentist spirit, as in Radcliffe's own representation of the Earl of Athlin as a polished, sentimental proto-Whig, contrasted with the barbarous laird of feudal Dunbayne. In this minor subgenre—to which Radcliffe herself did not return—even the most unpropitious figures could be co-opted in the celebration of modern, pan-British values. In *William Wallace; or, The Highland Hero* (1791), written amidst early enthusiasm for the French Revolution by Henry Siddons (teenaged son of the actress Sarah Siddons), Wallace is applauded for stalwartly resisting the tyranny of an unmistakably Norman Edward I. In her Napoleonic-era *The Scottish Chiefs* (1810), another romance to cast Wallace in the hero's role, Jane Porter celebrates in the marital union of 1328 between the royal houses of Scotland and England the seeds of political union centuries later. In an unlikely compliment to the increasingly erratic George III, she rejoices that destiny has now at last 'consolidated their rival nations

[24] Jean Marishall, *The History of Alicia Montague*, 2 vols (London: for the Author, 1767), 2.166.
[25] *Monthly Review*, 67 (August 1782), 152.
[26] *The Letters of Robert Burns*, ed. G. Ross Roy, 2 vols (Oxford: Clarendon Press, 1985), 1.137 (August 1787).

into one, and by planting the heir of Plantagenet and Bruce upon the British throne, hath redeemed the peace of the land, and fixed it on lasting foundations'.[27]

From Scott's point of view, the one significant novel of these years was *The Cottagers of Glenburnie* (1808), in which Elizabeth Hamilton, a conservative Edinburgh-based author with strong links to Ireland, had depicted 'the rural habits of Scotland . . . with striking and impressive fidelity'.[28] A dimmer view would have been taken by Burns, however, of Hamilton's didactic motive in this work, which was, she cheerfully acknowledged, 'to shame my good country folks into a greater degree of nicety with regard to cleanliness, and to awaken their attention to the source of corruption in the lower orders' (see Shields 2010: 105). With its overpowering rhetoric of hygiene, and a plot that subjects local manners and dialect to the modernizing forces of politeness and reform, *The Cottagers of Glenburnie* has none of the relish for filth and chaos that characterizes *Humphry Clinker*, nor for the clashing energies of diverse traditions, which it seeks to erase in the name of a salutary, modern, shared British identity. Perhaps it was only as external threats to this identity receded with the defeat of Napoleon a few years later that the searching fiction of competing and compound identities inaugurated by Smollett could at last be resumed in earnest.

---

[27] Jane Porter, *The Scottish Chiefs*, ed. Fiona Price (Peterborough, ON: Broadview Press, 2007), 42.

[28] Walter Scott, *Waverley*, ed. P. D. Garside (Edinburgh: Edinburgh University Press, 2007), 'Postscript', 364.

24

Imperial Commerce, Gender, and Slavery

DEIRDRE COLEMAN

T HE intersection of two mid-eighteenth-century legal decisions frames the arguments of this chapter. The first was the Marriage Act of 1753 which entrenched the
principle of *coverture* whereby the wife's person and identity were 'incorporated
and consolidated into that of the husband; under whose wing, protection, and *cover*, she
performs every thing'.[1] The other was Judge Mansfield's decision in 1772 to free James
Somersett, a slave brought to England, abused, and threatened with deportation by his
West Indian owner. In his ruling in Somersett's favour, Mansfield declared that slavery
was odious and unknown to English common law. Starting with Sarah Scott's *The History
of Sir George Ellison* (1766), this chapter charts the twinned emergence in the British novel
of a critique of plantation slavery and commercial imperialism with a proto-feminist
questioning of the 'commerce of the sexes'. The discourses of racial and sexual oppression
resonate with one another, helping to establish connections between inequalities at home
and the sufferings of distant others. It has been argued that novelistic representations of
violence and suffering are central to an 'imagined empathy' which in turn assisted the
development in the eighteenth century of humanitarian sentiment (Hunt 2007). In the
novels discussed below, we see a series of mutually illuminating narratives in which gender oppression at the metropolitan centre is juxtaposed with racial oppression in the colonial periphery. While it might be charged that the mid-eighteenth-century novel failed
to grant full humanity to the enslaved and that it was somewhat instrumentalist in its
handling of slavery reform, it can be demonstrated that the versatility of the figure of slavery, as seen in Scott's novel—the shuttling back and forth between the sufferings of commodified white women and black slaves—enabled fuller characterization (including the
voices) of the colonized and enslaved, as well as the more explicit imagining of colonial

---

[1] William Blackstone, *Commentaries on the Laws of England*, 4 vols (Oxford: Clarendon Press, 1765–9),
1.430. See also Clery, Chapter 4.

violence depicted in Phebe Gibbes's *Hartly House, Calcutta* (1789) and Robert Bage's *Man As He Is. A Novel* (1792).

The exchange in Jane Austen's *Emma* (1816) between Mrs Elton and Jane Fairfax on the possible equivalences of the 'governess-trade' and the 'slave-trade' is only the most famous instance of the complex role played by gender within various dimensions of human difference, such as race and class.[2] The non-human animal also plays an important role in thinking about human difference, as can be seen in the lap-dog incident in *The History of Sir George Ellison*, or in Bage's *Man As He Is* where an invidious comparison between dogs and black people triggers rape, suicide, and murder. Finally, the enlarged focus on analogous processes of commodification and exchange, from the circulation of women in the chattel economy of marriage to the ownership of black slaves, was accompanied by a critique of chivalry as a retrograde, Gothic code brimming with outmoded and erroneous notions of loyalty, honour, and gallantry. Familiar as one of the central platforms from which Mary Wollstonecraft and other women writers launched their feminist critiques, chivalry as a discourse and practice is also aligned with pro-slavery apologetics and colonial exploitation.

Sarah Scott, *The History of Sir George Ellison* (1766)

In Jane Austen's *Mansfield Park* (1814), when the urbanite Mary Crawford complains about the difficulties of hiring a cart and horse to transport her harp from London to Northamptonshire, Edmund Bertram gently remonstrates with her, arguing that the farmers and their labourers were in the midst of a 'very late hay harvest' and that 'the importance of getting in the grass' must take precedence over all other activities. Inducted in the 'true London maxim that every thing is to be got with money', Mary Crawford is unmoved by Edmund's argument, referring mockingly to the 'sturdy independence' of country customs.[3] The clash between the needs of the local farming community and individual egotism recalls an episode in *The History of Sir George Ellison*, when the eponymous hero altruistically dismisses the labourers working on his elegant garden so that they can help the farmers bring in the harvest.[4] Ellison's prioritizing of the needs of agriculture ahead of his own private interests puzzles his first cousin, Sir William Ellison, who asks: 'While you are providing for the happiness of others, who is to provide for yours?' Ellison's answer, inspired by Alexander Pope's *Essay On Man* (1733–4), is that 'self-love

---

[2] Jane Austen, *Emma*, ed. Richard Cronin and Dorothy McMillan (Cambridge: Cambridge University Press, 2005), vol. 2, ch. 7; 325.

[3] Jane Austen, *Mansfield Park*, ed. John Wiltshire (Cambridge; Cambridge University Press, 2005), vol. 1, ch. 6; 68–9.

[4] Sarah Scott, *The History of Sir George Ellison*, ed. Betty Rizzo (Lexington, KY: University Press of Kentucky, 1996), 50–1.

and social are the same'; they cannot be differentiated (51). Pope's happy axiom, beloved of so many female writers in this period, has of course no resonance for the selfish and materialistic Mary Crawford.

Ellison's sacrifice of his labourers for the greater good of the countryside occurs in Book One where we also learn about his business dealings in Jamaica, including his marriage to a wealthy West Indian slave-owner, and his implementation of ameliorative reforms on the plantation into which he has married. In order to achieve amelioration Ellison first resolves 'to withdraw his whole attention from commerce' (13). He then abolishes whips and torture, believing that obedience and loyalty will come through paternal kindness rather than through terror. The ironic upshot is that his experiment in kindness and benevolence ends in increased commercial success. Thanks to happier and healthier slaves, productivity and profits rise dramatically. The clear message is that benevolence and commercial self-interest (which does not recognize itself as such) go hand in hand together. The message is not lost on Ellison's fellow slave-owners, for he notes with satisfaction that 'the condition of the slaves' is 'much mended in the greater part of the island' (36).

Despite Ellison's disgust with the cruelty of West Indian plantation slavery, there is nothing sentimental about the novel's characterization of the slaves; in fact the slaves are presented in contradictory ways. On the one hand they are described as 'naturally faithful and affectionate' but they can also be resentful and revengeful (17). Mindful of the 'ferocity of their tempers' (36) and wary of an 'excess of lenity' (14), Ellison has no intention of dissolving the slaves' bonds of obedience to him, or even of abolishing punishment. On the contrary; he wants to soften and rationalize the punishment regime in order to further tighten his control over his slaves. Procuring a greater quantum of happiness for them may be a noble aim, but there is also the calculation that 'the greater their happiness, the more they would fear incurring his punishments' (17). Those who do offend risk being sold to another owner and thus subjected to the system's more routine barbarities. From these examples it is clear, as Markman Ellis puts it, that Scott's novel 'seeks to transform the peculiar asymmetries of power endemic to the slavery economies, but without destroying the ideology or economy of slavery' (1996: 87).

The History of Sir George Ellison is a key text for exploring the interlocking themes of imperial commerce, gender, and slavery. For what is so striking in this (and other) novels is the complex transferability of the figures of slavery and commerce to a number of other dimensions, most especially those of sexuality, marriage, and class. This metaphorical richness is evident from the very outset where we read that Ellison is so intent on making his fortune in Jamaica that he is 'perfectly indifferent' to women, worshipping instead the fair form of Commerce, bedecked with the 'gums of Arabia, the gems of India, and in short the various riches of different climes' (8–9). When he does marry, it is to a rich widow, but she is not a 'fair form of Commerce', her dowry consisting of a slave-run plantation managed by a brutal overseer. In a remarkable slide which moves from Ellison's 'marriage into slavery' to a direct conflation of marriage and slavery, the narrator comments that 'perhaps few have more severely lamented their being themselves enslaved by marriage, than he did his being thus become the enslaver of others' (10). Especially bitter for Ellison is his reflection that his wife has doubly enslaved him—sexually and racially—by making him 'that slave which he would suffer no one to be to him' (22). Of course plantation slavery is invisible to Ellison's Jamaican friends; they can only see his sexual enslavement. His unpleasant neighbour Mr Reynolds even reminds him that only 'women and negroes were made to be slaves' (23). To all this mockery about his wife's exercise of 'arbitrary power' over him (35), Ellison responds jokily about the gratitude he owes to her for her large fortune, arguing that 'long application to merchandize had taught him to see every thing in the light of traffic; and his wife had bought him at so great a price, that he thought she had a right to make the best of the purchase' (23). A merchant himself, he is entitled to joke about the way in which a market-based economy confuses affective relations, but in terms of the marriage market he can only be seen as a flawed figure, with an excess of good nature his one 'great weakness' (15).

Ellison's sojourn in Jamaica comes to an end when his wife dies suddenly, freeing him up to return home with his son. The language of slavery does not, however, end with his departure from the West Indies but continues until the novel's comic ending where Ellison, in love with Mrs Tunstall, cannot contain his joy when he learns that her husband has drunk himself to death. Nature, we read, could not 'be entirely enslaved; like the generous subjects of a free country, she may be governed by laws, and influenced by wisdom, but she will not submit implicitly to arbitrary rule' (167). For most of this novel, however, the figure of slavery is not about self-government, nor is it generally comic. Instead, the figure of slavery is put to serious political use, dramatizing the material and psychological oppression experienced by financially dependent, vulnerable women. There is the beautiful Miss Almon, for instance, who, when urged by Ellison to start a new life in Jamaica, refuses the offer because she assumes the object of her travel is to win herself a husband—a 'making a traffic of her person' which she regards as nothing less than a 'kind of prostitution' (164). Later, the same negative interpretation would be applied to the poor orphan, Cecilia Wynne, shipped out to 'Bengal or Barbadoes or wherever' for a husband and a 'maintenance' in Austen's burlesque *Catharine, or The Bower* (1792).[5]

There are also the tales of mortifying economic dependency narrated to Ellison by the women living at Millenium Hall. (Four years earlier Scott had published her now best-known novel, *A Description of Millenium Hall, and the Country Adjacent: Together with the Character of the Inhabitants* (London, 1762), to which *Ellison* in some respects offers a sequel.) There is Mrs Alton who is made 'a slave, and yet reproached as a burden' by her sister-in-law, a mistreatment which forces her to adopt the humiliating self-defence of

---

[5] Jane Austen, *Juvenilia*, ed. Peter Sabor (Cambridge: Cambridge University Press, 2006), 256.

keeping 'an account of debtor and creditor in generosity' (105). Other women describe themselves as oppressed by wealthy benefactors whose lavish bounty and gift-giving take the form of ritualized aggression. As one woman remarks, 'a giving hand, and a generous heart are distinct things' (113). Furthermore, obliged to receive benefactions, poor and dependent women have no power 'to make a proper return', leaving them 'enslaved by gratitude and cowardice' (111, 114). The last of the novel's inset narratives understands poverty according to its impact on class. For the lower classes of society—those 'born and bred in indigence'—the evils of poverty are more or less unvarying because they are 'chiefly corporeal'. For those of superior education and of a higher rank, however, 'the mind is the seat of greatest sufferance', and it is this mental suffering which makes genteel women less fit to deal with poverty's many and different 'sources of mortification and anxiety' (114–15). This rumination on poverty and class is strikingly similar to Austen's discussion of slavery in *Emma* (1815). When the silly and vulgar Mrs Elton leaps on Jane Fairfax's cautious reference to 'the sale—not quite of human flesh—but of human intellect' as a reference to the slave trade, Jane is quick to deny the analogy because of the enormous difference in guilt involved in the conduct of each trade: 'I did not mean, I was not thinking of the slave-trade . . . governess-trade, I assure you, was all that I had in view'. Having said this, however, Jane then goes on to add the equivocation: 'as to the greater misery of the victims, I do not know where it lies' (*Emma*, vol. 2, ch. 17; 325). The variable impact of poverty in class terms finds its racial parallel in the differences between black bodies and white minds.

To some extent George Ellison is modelled on the character of Uncle Toby in Laurence Sterne's *Tristram Shandy* (1760–7). Just as Uncle Toby is horrified at the thought of killing a fly (see also Thompson, Chapter 7), Ellison experiences 'compunction' at the thought of destroying the many spiders living in his recently purchased English house. In a reversal of sexual norms which at the same time confirms class arrangements, the act which sentimental delicacy prevents Ellison from executing is achieved 'by the potent hand of a stout char-woman'. Notably, while reflections on the spiders' 'rights of long possession' made Ellison hesitate at first, no sooner are the long-standing tenants exterminated than, in the economy of property ownership, he refers to them as 'usurpers' (45). A similar equivocation can be seen in the principles informing Ellison's plantation reforms. At the heart of these is an acute sensitivity to the cruelties inflicted by white owners on their slaves, 'as if the difference of complexion excluded them from the human race, or indeed as if their not being human could be an excuse for making them wretched' (10). The possibility of the slaves 'not being human' follows (and calls into question) the first half of the proposition. A similar equivocation emerges in the scene in which Ellison declares to his wife that the slaves are their fellow creatures, and that the 'present difference' between black and white is 'merely adventitious, not natural'. He then carefully adds that this innate sameness and equality will only become manifest in the afterlife: 'when you and I are laid in the grave, our lowest black slave will be as great as we are' (13). In other words, the argument that all people are by nature equally free and independent, with certain inherent natural rights, does not apply to slaves in the here and now, but only in some otherworldly space, in the post-social arena of the dead.

Readers today might find Sarah Scott's novel somewhat hard-nosed in its attitude towards slavery, but for her contemporaries she led the way in true sentiment concerning the equality of black and white people. It is even possible that she inspired Sterne's vignette of the 'poor negro girl' in *Tristram Shandy*.[6] So famous did this sentimental episode become that Thomas Clarkson, in his *History of the Abolition of the Slave Trade* (1808), included Sterne in his roll call of honour to those who championed the cause of black people. According to Clarkson it was Sterne who 'in his account of the Negro girl in his Life of Tristram Shandy, took decidedly the part of the oppressed Africans. The pathetic, witty and sentimental manner, in which he handled this subject, occasioned many to remember it, and procured a certain portion of feeling in their favour.'[7] That Sarah Scott should also have been included in Clarkson's honour roll can be seen in the comment made by the African man of letters, Ignatius Sancho, to Sterne in 1766 that only he and 'the humane author of Sir George Ellison' had 'drawn a tear in favour of my miserable black brethren'.[8]

Whereas Markman Ellis recuperates sentimental novels, arguing that they could still, despite their equivocations, make 'a radical statement' about slavery's morality (1996: 94), George Boulukos is less sympathetic. Focusing on the 'grateful slave', Boulukos argues that this trope 'enabled the transition, at its most dramatic between 1770 and 1790, to a raced view of humanity throughout the British Atlantic world' (2008: 7). Once we distinguish between a true commitment to anti-slavery and a more general reorganization and reform of plantation slavery, it will be obvious (he argues) that many eighteenth-century sentimental novels accepted slavery and the colonial economy 'without question' (118). Zeal for reform springs from instrumentalist rather than sentimental motives, the aim being to modernize management techniques and improve slaves' productivity. According to this instrumentalist agenda, 'reformers improve slaves' lives only in order to enslave them more securely' (117). Furthermore, sentimental depictions of slave reform 'loudly insist that they are recognizing African humanity, but in fact they are carefully circumscribing it' (138). Unlike Ellis, Boulukos is not at all interested in the rhetorical slipperiness of the figure of slavery—its deployment in the service of other relations of dominance and subordination, such as the chattel economy of marriage or the plight of daughters subject to tyrannical paternity.

---

[6] Laurence Sterne, *The Life and Opinions of Tristram Shandy, Gentleman*, ed. Graham Petrie, introd. Christopher Ricks (Harmondsworth: Penguin Classics, 1967), 578.

[7] Thomas Clarkson, *History of the Rise, Progress and Accomplishment of the Abolition of the African Slave Trade*, 2 vols (London: Longman [etc.], 1808), 1.60–1.

[8] *Letters of the Late Ignatius Sancho, An African*, ed. Vincent Carretta (London: Penguin, 1998), 74.

Henry Mackenzie, *Julia de Roubigné* (1777)

In some respects the second (and final) volume of Henry Mackenzie's sentimental novel, *Julia de Roubigné*, fits well with Boulukos's more severely moralistic argument about scenes of amelioration in the late eighteenth-century sentimental novel. This volume opens with the sentimental hero Savillon on the slave island of Martinique, disgusted to learn that, in slavery, 'profit is the only medium of opinion...morality has nothing to do in the system'.[9] Living on his uncle's sugar plantation, he reflects that trade in general is not conducive to what he prizes most, 'a delicacy and fineness of sentiment' (103), so much so that he must 'unlearn' long-standing feelings: 'I must accommodate sentiment to conveniency, pride to interest, and sometimes even virtue itself to fashion' (92). And yet, with the optimism characteristic of the sentimental hero, Savillon refuses to believe that honesty and goodness are entirely absent from the island. In an echo of Sarah Scott's *Ellison*, he concludes that 'self-interest' is 'the parent of social obligation' (92) and to this end devises an experiment in free labour. Struck by the 'shocking' treatment of the negroes, Savillon believes he will 'undoubtedly profit' by substituting other motives for work 'than those of punishment and terror' (96-7). Adhering to the twinned motivations of self-interest and profit, Savillon is drawn to an enslaved African prince in his uncle's possession called Yambu whose 'untractable stubbornness' had rendered him almost worthless. Determined to 'improve his price', Savillon tells him he is free, and that he can do whatever he pleases (98). This freedom is, however, immediately constrained when Yambu is told that he cannot realize his first desire, which is to return to Africa. Plantation work must continue, Savillon argues, for without sugar there can be no food and clothing. Finally, Savillon gives a negative spin to freedom by presenting it as careless of loyalty and proper duty. To one of Yambu's faithful retainers Savillon teasingly remarks: 'Your master...is now free, and may leave you when he pleases', a statement the prince 'warmly' rebuts: 'Yambu no leave you' (100). In the end, the only difference brought about by Savillon's experiment is that Yambu and his people will no longer in name be slaves but free labourers, a principle eagerly embraced by Yambu who declares, in what is apparently the first use of African dialect in the history of the novel: 'Chuse work, no work at all' (99). Despite the rhetoric of freedom, however, ownership of the slaves is only intensified by their liberation, with Savillon noting triumphantly at the end of his experiment that 'they work with the willingness of freedom, yet are mine with more than the obligation of slavery'. Furthermore, just as ownership is, paradoxically, intensified by freedom, so too is output. The slaves, 'under the feeling of good treatment, and the idea of liberty', almost double the output of those still 'subject to the whip of an overseer' (100). Finally, as can be seen in the phrase 'idea of liberty', the slaves' conception of liberty is something

---

[9] Henry Mackenzie, *Julia de Roubigné*, ed. Susan Manning (East Linton, Scotland: Tuckwell Press, 1999), 92.

of a phantom, a point underscored by Savillon's ambiguous remark that Yambu is 'free, according to the mode prescribed by the laws of the island' (100).

In a novel in which the oppressive stasis of epistolary sentiment conflicts with the forward momentum of narrative, Savillon oscillates between the rhetoric of a 'merchant' and that of a 'man'. The merchant observes the high costs of purchasing slaves in the first place, and the despondency, sickness, and mortality which quickly follow, all of which 'make the machine...of a plantation extremely expensive in its operations'. The man, on the other hand, observes many 'fellow-creatures groaning under servitude and misery...[in] a theatre of rapine, of slavery, and of murder!' (101). The interest of this passage lies in Savillon's ability to hold together the perspectives of both man and merchant; in other words, his desire to ameliorate slavery is not, as Boulukos would argue, the outcome of instrumentalist rather than sentimental motives. But while his meditations on slavery, ownership, and freedom might do little to challenge the colonial economy, the racial oppression he identifies on the island resonates with the plight of his beloved, Julia de Roubigné, explored in Volume One. In introducing the novel, Susan Manning even goes so far as to claim that 'Julia has a less "free" mind than Yambu' (xiv). The fearful and dutiful only child of a proud father who has fallen on hard times, Julia's story is (in her own words) 'the story of sentiment' (39). Writing to her intimate friend Maria, she often fails as a narrator, confessing that 'our feelings speak for themselves, before we can tell why we feel' (38). 'Bewildered in sentiment' (39), Julia lives unhappily in a claustrophobic family group in which, contradictorily, 'every one's look seemed the spy on another's' (20) and yet all 'are afraid to think of one another's thoughts' (9). In love with the poor Savillon but courted by a wealthy Count, Julia shrinks from the 'adultery of the heart' (42) which will be incurred by marrying a man she does not love. In the end, her fear of her father's vengeance, born of his stern idea of honour, weighs more heavily in the balance, and she consents to the Count's marriage proposal.

With the classical figure of Iphigenia in mind, Julia sacrifices herself to a proud and tyrannical father who cannot come to terms with the poverty into which he has been plunged. To the Count who has provided financial and legal assistance, she gives her hand as a debt of gratitude. As we saw in the life stories told to George Ellison by the women of Millenium Hall, gratitude is closely bound up with relations of dominance and subjection. Caught between two powerful men, her father and her suitor, Julia describes herself as a 'silent ~~victim~~' [sic] (68). While she might score through the word as a 'bad' one, she bemoans her lot as a wretch, not of vice, but of virtue (for the scoring-through of 'victim', see also Thompson, 140). That she is impaled on an outmoded, masculinist code of honour can be seen in the rich Count's 'peculiar delicacy' in handling her father's injured pride. Desirous of obtaining a strip of ground owned by Julia's father, the Count strategically 'never made the proposition of a purchase, but only requested that he might have leave to open a passage through an old wall...that he might enjoy a continuation of that romantic path, which the banks of the rivulet afforded' (18). The cleverness of the Count's manoeuvre can be seen in the fact that he gets what he wants, but does so in such a way that Julia's father is granted 'the power of conferring an obligation' (18). This delicate negotiation around property is clearly an allegory of the chattel economy of marriage in which Julia is trapped. Determined to enjoy her, the Count pursues Julia along the not so 'romantic path' of her entrapment between gratitude to him and fear of her father. Chivalry helps him win Julia in the end, but it is a pyrrhic victory. That the Count's courtship and marriage are entirely about the commodification of Julia can be seen most clearly near the end of the novel when, believing Julia to be an adulteress, he jealously rails: 'I purchased her consent, I bribed, I bought her; bought her, the leavings of another'. Oblivious to the violence of his commodification of Julia, the Count can only see her in terms of the honour code between men. In the end she is nothing more than 'the leavings of another' (136).

In sacrificing herself to the Count, Julia must surrender her earlier illusion that affections enjoy a realm of 'native freedom' (77). As she learns from her dead mother's reflections on marriage, love is all about power but, like chivalry itself, it is a power which is all the more formidable for disguising itself. In marriage, her mother advises,

> The idea of power on either side, should be totally banished from the system; it is not sufficient, that the husband should never have occasion to regret the want of it; the wife must so behave, that he may never be conscious of possessing it . . . it must never be forgotten, that the only government allowed on our side, is that of gentleness and attraction; and that its power, like the fabled influence of imaginary beings, must be invisible to be complete. (148)

These observations about the power dynamics of marriage recall Savillon's experiment in plantation management. Adopting the persona of the good, benevolent master, Savillon banishes the *idea* of power only to bind Yambu and his people more powerfully to his will. That nothing is ever quite as it seems in this novel can be seen in Savillon's characterization of his love for Julia as 'despotic under the semblance of freedom' (87). Love's despotism is fully displayed at the end of the novel, when the jealous Count, consumed by an Othello-like rage, murders his wife for an adultery she did not commit.

Robert Bage, *Man As He Is. A Novel* (1792)

Robert Bage's *Man As He Is* first appeared late in 1791, the same year in which William Wilberforce introduced the first parliamentary bill to abolish the slave trade. The year 1791 also witnessed the first of a series of slave revolts on French Saint-Domingue, uprisings which would result in the declaration of the free republic of Haiti and turbulence within the three empires of France, Britain, and Spain. Although the work appeared twenty-five years after Scott's novel, Bage returns to the ameliorative experiment of free labour in an inset narrative told by Fidel, the faithful and loyal black servant of the heroine, Miss Colerain. Fidel, whose slave name encodes 'fidelity', once belonged to Miss Colerain's father who, on a visit to Jamaica, is so horrified by the cruelty of slavery that he is determined to learn more about the workings of this arcane system. Befriending Fidel, Colerain asks him numerous questions, including 'if good usage would make de black people work well as bad', to which the answer is an enthusiastic 'yes'.[10] Since the white planters have no idea as to how to begin this experiment, Colerain gives Fidel the management of a little plantation, stating 'it was probable I might be of singular use to de black people, if I could shew the planters dat it was deir interest to use deir negroes kindly' (4.210). Like Yambu, Fidel proves to be a successful plantation manager, achieving great efficiencies in manpower through 'ver little sickness' (4.211). Baptism, escape to England, and marriage to his beloved Flowney are to be his rewards for transforming slavery into a non-violent mode of production, but the entire project fails when Flowney commits suicide after being serially raped by the 'young masser' Benfield and his valet Stukely.

Fidel's harrowing tale of murder, rape, torture, and suicide comes right at the end of Bage's lengthy novel. Spoken entirely in faux-dialect, Fidel's narrative is unusual for its focus on the sufferings of a slave woman. It also sits oddly within this satirical and light-hearted romp of a novel, with its flaccid, perambulatory, and digressive structure, dotted throughout with playfully flirtatious appeals to its 'twenty thousand fair readers' (4.80, 196). The tale is elicited from Fidel by the aristocrat Sir George Paradyne, the novel's wealthy and amiable but somewhat dissolute hero who, on account of disappointed love, has withdrawn from the world and become 'enamoured of death' (4.197). After numerous jokes at his hero's expense, the narrator suddenly plunges us into Fidel's tale of suffering and loss, a tale prompted by Sir George's somewhat idle curiosity about his black servant's earlier life, now that the 'slave trade was at this time become a popular topic' (4.201).

Whereas Yambu's voice in *Julia de Roubigné* is only heard in snatches, Fidel is completely in charge of his story, a likeable figure who gives us his full history from point of sale onwards. At the outset Fidel reveals his true name of Benihango. A native of Benin, at twelve years old he is sold by his father to a Liverpool slave trader in exchange for a gun, a transaction which he explains thus: 'It was not that he did not love his Benihango, but he had six children at home, and never a Birmingham musket' (4.201). After a 'very good voyage' to Jamaica, in which the 'heat and stench' kill only 'twenty-seven, out of two hundred and three' (4.202), Fidel's ironic minimizing of suffering continues with his description of his first master as 'kind hearted' for only delivering a whipping once a week, and not insisting on it 'being bloody'. Furthermore, 'I do ver believe he would not have take the pleasure in de whip, if he did know a better vay to send a profitable cargo of the sugar into dis England' (4.203–4). Fidel's ironic, Gulliver-like, and slightly pedantic narrative

---

[10] Robert Bage, *Man As He Is. A Novel*, 2nd edn, 4 vols (London: William Lane, 1796), 4.210.

then gives way to the following exchange with Sir George, in which the oppression of West Indian slavery suddenly appears as analogous to the oppression of romantic love:

> 'How long were you in Jamaica?' Sir George asked.
> 'Thirteen years,' answered Fidel.
> 'Were you much oppressed?'
> Fidel with great simplicity answered, 'I was in love.'
> 'In love!' said Sir George.—'What has that to do with oppression?'
> 'It oppress you, Sir George, do it not?'
> 'Me!' said Sir George.
> 'You will please me pardon, sir. I no ought to speak to you in dis way,' said Fidel.
> 'Speak freely,' said Sir George. (4.202)

But instead of Fidel's oppression in love operating as a bridge connecting his life in Jamaica to Sir George's aimless existence, a chasm opens up in the narrative between the self-centred aristocrat's failure to capture his beloved, and the train of events which leads to Fidel's loss of Flowney.

At the heart of Fidel's narrative lies a debate about the humanity of black slaves, an issue raised in Sterne's and Sarah Scott's novels as well as in numerous seventeenth- and eighteenth-century British portraits of African servants and grooms, many of whom are depicted in close juxtaposition with domestic dogs or with exotic pets such as monkeys. The debate can also be seen in the developing body of racial science towards the end of the eighteenth century, with African skulls lined up alongside the skulls of monkeys and dogs at the lower end of a hierarchy topped by the European (Kriz 2008: 87). Indicative of the temper of the period in which Bage was writing is Thomas Jefferson's *Notes on the State of Virginia* (1787), a text which describes blacks as inferior to whites in all respects, closer to brute animality in their strong bodily smell, their deficiencies in reason and imagination, and their insensitivity to grief. On the topic of love Jefferson states that, compared to whites, blacks are 'more ardent after their female' as well as driven more by 'eager desire' than 'a tender delicate mixture of sentiment and sensation'. This lower, sensual desire means that Africans produce no poetry since 'Love is the peculiar oestrum of the poet'.[11] Fidel's narrative gives the complete lie to such generalizations, and of course the point is driven home even more emphatically by the novel's implicit comparison between the black man's true love for Flowney and Sir George's somewhat more fickle love for Miss Colerain.

Fidel's cruel master, young Benfield, triggers the debate around the human status of blacks by referring to his slaves as dogs. Fidel, whose own slave name is uncomfortably close to the popular dog name 'Fido', comments somewhat bitterly that, if slaves were dogs then they would be a lot better treated, to which young Benfield replies 'dogs were a superior species of animal to negroes, and had better understandings'. Piqued by this,

---

[11] Thomas Jefferson, *Notes on the State of Virginia* (London: John Stockdale, 1787), 231, 234.

Fidel responds with Swiftian precision: 'Den I did look angry at him, and I did say, if God did give de white men more understanding, it was de tousand pities dey could not see how to make de better use of it' (4.205). Just as Gulliver is regarded by the Houyhnhnms as an even lesser Yahoo on account of his reason, so too does Fidel mock Benfield in direct proportion to his supposed superiority. This exchange, in which the white man is so clearly outwitted by the black man, immediately results in an ugly altercation. In the end, Fidel believes that Benfield rapes Flowney in 'revenge'.

Freed as a young slave for saving his master from drowning, Fidel has learnt to read and write, immersing himself in his master's newly imported books from England. Bage's characterization of Fidel as a well-read former slave is striking for its analysis of acculturation, in particular what literacy means in terms of the internalization of white codes of behaviour, cues no doubt taken from Olaudah Equiano's popular and highly influential autobiography, *The Interesting Narrative of the Life of Olaudah Equiano* (1789). But whereas for Equiano the trope of the 'talking book' represents white Christian culture, for Fidel the attainment of literacy amounts to an induction into the chivalric code rather than the Bible: 'I learned great deal of English manner, especially of de delicate points of de love and de honour' (4.205). In terms of the history of the black voice finding itself in eighteenth-century writing, it is rather odd that Fidel should speak the language of romantic chivalry, but this fits well with Bage's politically progressive opposition to chivalry and the honour system, a theme which runs throughout the novel. For just as slavery is a barbaric system which does not belong in the modern age, so too is the chivalric code a relic from a more primitive past. To this end Bage makes many satirical tilts at Edmund Burke's *Reflections on the Revolution in France* (1790), arguing that chivalry and 'the empire of prejudice and passion' must give way to the age of truth and reason. Instead of despotism which, in an earlier period of misery and violence, demanded 'fawning servility and slavish obedience', modernity transforms 'that *generous loyalty to rank*, into attachment to peace, to law, to the general happiness of mankind, that *proud submission* and *dignified obedience* into an unassuming consciousness of natural equality, and that *subordination of the heart* into an honest veneration of superior talents, conjoined with superior benevolence'. Instead of the knight-errant, it is now legal justice which 'redresses wrongs, protects damsels, and punishes the base miscreants who oppress them' (4.64–6). All the italicized phrases are taken from Burke's *Reflections*.

Fidel is able to lend his master's books to Flowney because she has learnt English from her mistress. That her education in English has also centred on 'de delicate points of de love and de honour' can be seen in Fidel's account of Benfield's unsuccessful attempt at seducing the beautiful Flowney:

> He did cast de eye of love—as he did call it—upon my poor Flowney, and as I have read of the Turkish bashaw, he did trow the handkerchief to her; for de poor black women tink it honour to be taken notice of by white man; especially masters. But Flowney read a great much of her mistress books, and was Christian, and tought it was great sin, and

besides all dis, loved me dearly. So she refused to gratify Masser Benfield. So his dignity was insulted. So he did resolve to revenge it, and also take revenge upon me, for he did hate me vast much. (4.211–12)

Flowney knows better than to succumb to Benfield's oriental-style blandishments, thanks to the Bible and to her mistress's conduct books, but her refusal leads to her rape and suicide. Determined to avenge Flowney's death, Fidel falls back on the chivalric code which he has internalized through his reading. If he is going to avenge Flowney, he insists on doing it 'wid honour' (4.217), so he challenges the valet Stukely to a duel. Stukely knows nothing of honour, of course, and fires before taking his ten steps backwards, a cowardly act which leads Fidel to shoot him dead. Fortunately, the scene is witnessed by two white servants who (unlike black witnesses) are able to testify on Fidel's behalf. These white servants show unshakeable solidarity with Fidel, shedding tears as they hand him over to the law, a move designed to keep him safe from summary execution by Benfield and his fellow planters.

Fidel's long and melancholy tale is told in two instalments, breaking off immediately after Flowney's rape and suicide, with Sir George rising from his seat and pacing the room whilst Fidel retreats to his chamber, overwhelmed by emotion. During this interruption the novel's principal love plot resumes, propelled forward by Sir George's discovery of a mysterious and anonymous billet-doux, which appears to be addressed to him. Fidel then resumes his tale for a few more pages, petering out with an inconclusive court case against young Benfield, and his departure from Jamaica for England. 'So ended the tale of Benihango' the narrator tells us, adding that Sir George made a 'very extraordinary comment' on it by adding a codicil to his will 'bequeathing Fidel fifty pounds a year for life'. That the narrator intends us to see this act for what it is—perfunctory and shallow—is obvious in the narrator's comment that 'however occupied by the past afflictions of Mr. Fidel', Sir George was much more occupied by his mysterious note (4.220).

Despite being mocked at one point by his pupil as a prematurely aged 'splenetic moralizer' (1.69), Sir George's tutor, Mr Lindsay, is the narrator's principal mouthpiece. In what is a recurrent theme throughout the novel, Lindsay complains that, in becoming more refined, the nation has become less equal under an excess of wealth. In the process, 'manly manners' such as firmness of nerve and strength of constitution have been exchanged for the manners of women: 'In short, we have lost tobacco; but we have made it up to the revenue in pomades, in essences, and in hair-powder' (1.239–40). Although Lindsay agrees to some extent with the prevailing orthodoxy 'that diffusion of wealth through the whole body of a society … has humanized our manners, purified our religion … rendered the nation happy, strong within, terrible without, and unbounded in its resources', he sees a number of vices arising out of this new wealth, chief of which is the 'vague term, honour' (1.196). Then follow vanity, pride, luxury, the current political status quo, the fashionable world (the 'bon ton'), excessive delicacy, coxcombry, and 'court puppies' (1.57). Championing manliness, democracy, and the rights of man, Lindsay is wary of the oppressions of romantic love, likening the yoke of marriage to that of slavery, and recommending that divorce be more widely instituted. Another character who has been wronged in marriage like- wise wishes for a time when 'the commerce of the sexes shall be pure and unmixed, flowing from the heart, unshackled, unrestrained' (1.241). Sir George, defending him- self against his tyrannical mother and pompous uncle, claims: 'I will be no man's slave, and no man's property' (4.154). Similarly, when it comes to love he declares: 'I bear no chains but those of love, and even those I shall break, if they gall'. Looking around at the neck chains of so many around him, he boasts that he is cured 'of all pas- sion for slavery, political or hymeneal' (3.46–7).

The alignment of colonial oppression with the oppressions engendered by the 'empire of love' is pointed in Bage's novel, if not quite so skilfully deployed as the juxtaposed stories of Julia and Yambu in *Julia de Roubigné*. Nevertheless, there is a curious and disturbing mini-narrative about colonial India and 'the commerce of the sexes' which might be said to foreshadow Fidel's Jamaican tale. This is the story of Sir George's sister, who marries an extremely rich but reclusive and unpredictable East Indian nabob, Mr Birimport, described as suffering from the disease of 'hypochon- driacism' (2.130). Accordingly his moods are capricious and his politics unpredictable. At one minute he delivers a panegyric on Warren Hastings, India's first Governor General, currently enduring a seven-year trial in London on charges of corruption. At another moment he denounces him 'in the blackest colours' (2.126). In the words of one acquaintance, Birimport acquired in the East a 'habit of command, which he can scarce remember to lay aside when speaking to free people' (2.127). One such free per- son is his Scottish valet, Mr Macreith, who sarcastically complains that time spent in India has spoiled his master's 'eye-sight, so that he canno ken the deefference between a free mon and a slave' (2.128). Birimport tyrannizes over his domestic household like an Eastern despot, treating his valet like a chattel and resenting him for his independ- ent thinking. Eventually, retreating into madness and misogyny, Birimport demands that everyone around him behave like unthinking automata, performing his behests to the letter. This includes his loyal, patient, and obedient wife, to whom he is a tyrant and jailer, the man who keeps her 'cooped up in a cage' (3.19) whilst subjecting her to his insane, misogynist outbursts.

Sexual Inequality, Racial Oppression, and the Feminist Imagination: Phebe Gibbes, Mary Hays, Mary Wollstonecraft, and Elizabeth Inchbald

Colonial commerce and the marriage market of Warren Hastings' India had come together a few years earlier in Phebe Gibbes's *Hartly House, Calcutta* (1789), a comic novel in which the giddy heroine, Sophia Goldborne is (as her surname suggests) wafted from England to India on buoyant currents of the 'all-creative power of gold'.[12] Eager to dissociate herself from the so-called 'fishing fleet' of young marriageable women travelling to the colonies in search of husbands, Sophia nevertheless rejoices in her high market value. With a scarcity of marriageable young women in Calcutta she enjoys cutting a figure about town as a sexualized commodity and the 'property' of her father. In letters home to her girlfriend Arabella, she jokily declares her intention of returning to England a 'nabobess' (84), and revels in the pageantry of 'Eastern pomp, splendour, and magnificence' (13), describing splendid scenes of nabobs on bejewelled thrones, mounted on elephants. A champion of the East, Sophia is receptive to Hindu culture, admires her young Bramin tutor, and marvels at the country's peaceable manners where Hindu diamond merchants travel unmolested with their valuables while Europeans wade 'through the blood of millions, to bring home gems of inconsiderable value' (58). At times ashamed of being a European, she adopts the orientalized pose of 'we Asiatics' (86). The only negatives about India are the high mortality rates and a hot climate which sometimes leaves her feeling like 'a kind of state-prisoner, enfeebled and fettered by vertical suns' (13). But transformative 'all-creative' gold is always at the rescue, lifting her mood from negative to positive and turning oppressive heat into soft, exotic breezes, and exquisite scents.

For the British in Calcutta, India is a 'land of commerce' with East India Company employees making vast fortunes (145). Although Sophia champions Warren Hastings and the 'prosperous flights of commerce' achieved by the Company since its establishment in 1600, she concedes that corruption is all-pervasive, with the 'Phaetons' of commerce sometimes losing their wheels (82). Nevertheless, the volatile sexual and commercial public sphere of Calcutta presents a realm of liberty for European women, a 'land of gallantry and politeness' (131) for married and unmarried alike, where 'stays are wholly unworn' (20) and flattery forms 'the daily incense of the sex' (89). The language of chivalry and honour abounds. Women 'live only to be adored' (86) while the slightest provocation becomes a 'fatal point of honour' for gallants who duel under certain well-known 'trees of destruction' (124). Edmund Burke's much publicized depiction of Britain's colonial relationship with India as sexualized and unstable, swinging dangerously between protective courtship and violent rape, was no doubt influential in Gibbes's adoption of the language of chivalry. Sophia even alludes to the Hastings impeachment in London, launched the year before with Burke's horrifying account of the rapes at Rangpur. Just as Bage's novel ends with colonial violence—the rape of Flowney by two white men—Gibbes concludes her novel with an account of the brutal rape of a young Indian girl by a British army officer. Astonished that 'the man whose profession it was to protect, thus brutally and barbarously destroyed!', Sophia fears that such 'fiend-like acts' are 'much

[12] Phebe Gibbes, *Hartly House, Calcutta*, ed. Michael J. Franklin (Oxford: Oxford University Press, 2007), 5.

oftener perpetrated than detected; for the grave complains not, and gold can unnerve the arm of justice' (158). And while she trusts that the new Governor will deliver the deserved punishment, the legal case against the white rapist remains (as in Fidel's case) unresolved, back in the colony.

In Mary Hays' *Memoirs of Emma Courtney* (1796), a much more sombre novel than *Hartly House*, we see the symbolic value of slavery fully entrenched in a narrative charting the history of a young woman who, whilst herself enslaved by passion, complains bitterly of the ways in which social customs 'have enslaved, enervated, and degraded woman'.[13] The grand conception of 'woman' in the singular recalls Wollstonecraft's *A Vindication of the Rights of Woman* (1792), itself a text littered with references to women as 'abject slaves', the metaphor meant, she tells us, 'in a political and civil sense'.[14] For Wollstonecraft slavery comes in many different guises: 'the slavery of marriage' (248), the coquettish slave, the slave of sensibility, and the slave of fashion. Enervated, like men, 'by the relaxing pleasures which wealth procures', women are also 'made slaves to their persons' (235). Nor is the key analogous oppression obscured: 'Is sugar always to be produced by vital blood? Is one half of the human species, like the poor African slaves, to be subject to prejudices that brutalize them, when principles would be a surer guard, only to sweeten the cup of man?' (235). True to the spirit of Wollstonecraft's critique, Hays also keeps West Indian slavery in view, presenting her reader near the start of Volume Two with Mr Melmoth, once an amiable youth but now, after seven years in the West Indies, a 'haughty, opulent, purse-proud Planter' who believes that slaves, servants, and women have nothing to do with thinking (vol. 2, ch. 5; 108). Such an alteration in character can also be seen in Elizabeth Inchbald's *A Simple Story* (1791) where Dorriforth turns into the cruel Lord Elmwood, owner of a 'very large estate in the West Indies'.[15] In Hays' novel the topic of slavery is discussed across several pages, with the hero Augustus Harley championing 'gradual emancipation' as well as pleading 'the cause of freedom and humanity with a bold and manly eloquence, expatiating warmly on the iniquity as well as impolicy of so accursed a traffic' (vol. 2, ch. 5; 112). In the background the West Indians complain about the insubordination of their English servants. This is precisely the kind of mixed discussion, spanning the worlds of empire and home, which (to Fanny Price's disappointment) is missing from the drawing room of *Mansfield Park*. And notably, wherever the oppression of women or slaves is mooted, a critique of chivalry is not far away. In Hays' novel chivalry is represented by the figure of Mr Montague, 'a gallant knight . . . calculated for

---

[13] Mary Hays, *Memoirs of Emma Courtney*, ed. Eleanor Ty (Oxford: Oxford University Press, 1996), vol. 1, ch. 13; 39.

[14] Mary Wollstonecraft, *Vindication of the Rights of Woman*, in *Political Writings*, ed. Janet Todd (London: William Pickering, 1993), 156, 263.

[15] Elizabeth Inchbald, *A Simple Story*, ed. J. M. S. Tompkins, introd. Jane Spencer (Oxford: Oxford University Press, 1988), vol. 3, ch. 1; 196.

the defender of distressed damsels' (vol. 1, ch. 13; 39), who, whilst married to the heroine, seduces the maidservant and ends up shooting himself.

Conclusion

When Ignatius Sancho thanks Sterne for drawing a tear on behalf of his 'miserable black brethren', then urges him to give in addition 'one half hour's attention to slavery, as it is at this day practised in our West Indies', he is not advocating a course of action to redress the structural and institutional iniquities of slavery. Instead he hopes Sterne's gift of a half hour will ease the yoke '(perhaps) of many—but if only of one—Gracious God!—what a feast to a benevolent heart!' (*Letters*, 74). Sancho's effusiveness here, which peters out into what Ellis has described as 'the shoals of the pathetic and the little' (1996: 128), needs to be seen in the context of the earlier, ameliorative period when, as Helen Thompson argues in this volume, the sympathy aroused for fictional slaves translates into an 'equivocal political agency' (see 130). The same limitations might also be argued of the later period, when the abolitionist movement was at its height, for in important ways the dilemma was the same: how to reconcile egalitarian principles on the one hand, and racial difference on the other. The chief difference between the novels of the 1760s and the 1790s is that the violence of slavery is depicted much more graphically—the outcome, no doubt, of a print and visual culture which was saturated with the atrocities of slavery.

There can be no doubt that the eighteenth-century novel engaged with imperial commerce and slavery, but it did so by mapping these issues onto its inherited repertoire of love dilemmas and gendered power struggles, adding new bite to the depiction of women's struggles for autonomy and independence. Relations between the sexes under patriarchy, like racial relations between black and white under slavery, embody the logic of domination. The advice of Julia de Roubigné's dead mother, that she should aim for complete power over her future husband by ensuring the domination was 'invisible', mirrors Savillon's reformist schemes which aim at strengthening rather than ameliorating the chattel status of his slaves. Julia's dead mother may aspire to transform, through her advice, the asymmetries of power endemic to patriarchy, but she does so in such a way as to preserve the system's ideology.

Part V

Alternative Forms of Fiction

Narrative Forms of Fiction

25

Fiction in the Magazines

GILLIAN HUGHES

MAGAZINE fiction before 1820 has been viewed as irredeemably derivative and ephemeral. The field was charted by Robert D. Mayo almost fifty years ago, not least with his impressive catalogue of 1,375 items of prose fiction in excess of five thousand words taken from almost five hundred different periodicals of the period (Mayo 1962). Notions of the canon, however, are now wider than they were and there is more interest in the typical as well as in the best fiction of the period. More attention is given to the overall readership for fiction and the conditions and context in which it was published and experienced, while women's fiction in particular has become a prominent field of study.

Novelists themselves read magazine fiction, which formed part of the cultural context from which their work developed and in which it may be understood: specific strands of eighteenth-century magazine fiction share ground with the writings of Jane Austen, for instance, or anticipate the subject matter of the Brontës. The emergence of the profession-ally written tale in the 1820s can be seen as meeting a growing desire for more sophisti-cated magazine fiction and as providing for the needs of those who were attempting to produce it.

Magazines, Proprietors, and Editors

As the name suggests, magazines were thought of as storehouses rather than originators, and the eighteenth-century ideal was one of comprehensiveness, *multum in parvo* ('much in a small space'), with many brief articles on a variety of subjects making up the typi-cal monthly miscellany such as the long-running *Gentleman's Magazine* (1731–1907), the *Universal Magazine* (1747–1815), or the *European Magazine* (1782–1826). The editor's chief equipment was in many cases a letter-box (for the receipt of readers' contributions) and a pair of scissors and a pot of paste (for compiling a suitable selection of materials from other periodicals and newspapers and recently published books). Most fiction was very brief, and magazines included novels chiefly in the form of abridgements, adaptations, and extracts from volume publications, since these were safely outside copyright protection. 'The Affecting History of Caroline Montgomery', for instance, was taken from Charlotte Smith's *Ethelinde* (1789) in the year of publication and given in two parts in the *Universal Magazine*, while the next three years saw its reappearance in a further seven magazines (Mayo 1962: 448–9—entry 66). Although eighteenth-century magazines were wont to emphasize the originality of at least a portion of their contents and to criticize rival magazines that reprinted them without due acknowledgement, editors and proprietors acknowledged that their fiction legitimately passed into and out of the magazine from a wider publication context. When a reader of the *Universal Magazine* complained that 'Albertina; a Tale, from the German' was plagiarized from *Caroline of Lichtfield* (1786), the editor immediately responded, 'on the contrary, the Author of that work has founded his Novel, without acknowledging the Circumstance, on the German original of *Albertina*, extending it by a number of Incidents, like the Variations in a favourite Tune'.[1] The *European Magazine* was unusual, under a variety of publishers, in providing fresh translations of foreign fiction, which were often copied. Translated fiction was generally prominent in magazines, initially largely from the French but (with the fashion for the Gothic and the dawning of Romanticism) increasingly also from the German after 1800. The *Town and Country Magazine* (1769–95), which was published by its editor Archibald Hamilton (subsequently with George Robinson also), added to the standard fare of the general miscellany magazines a series of thinly disguised scandal tales, 'Histories of the Tête-à-têtes', about the aristocratic or famous.

Short fiction also dominated most of the popular women's magazines: the long-running *Lady's Magazine* (founded in 1770) owned by George Robinson (also an important publisher of novels); the *Lady's Monthly Museum* (founded in 1798) published by Vernor and Hood; and rather later the *La Belle Assemblée* (founded in 1806) of John Bell. The bound volumes of these magazines presented an attractive appearance, partly to sell as Christmas and New Year's gifts. Several engravings were included in each issue, and sometimes advertised separately at high prices, as with the subsequent annuals of the 1820s and 1830s designed for the same market. The firm of Robinson, owners of the *Lady's Magazine*, happily enjoyed a family connection with the engraver Charles Heath. The costume plates made these magazines particularly welcome to 'friends on the Continent, in the East or West Indies, the United States, &c.', not otherwise able to keep abreast of the latest fashions in dress.[2] It was desirable for gift-volumes to be relatively self-contained, and the editor of the *Lady's Monthly Museum* stated openly, 'Novels, Tales, or Romances, so calculated

---

[1] *Universal Magazine*, 85 (November 1789). In this chapter editorial comments are taken from the paragraphs addressed to correspondents in the relevant issue (generally on the unnumbered verso of the contents page), unless otherwise referenced.

[2] 'Preface', *La Belle Assemblée*, 3rd ser., 1 (1825).

as not to engage more than three or four pages, will be most acceptable'.[3] The magazine's
1798 prospectus declared that 'every article in continuation shall be finished within the
same volume, that the attention may neither be distracted by distant combinations, nor
the pocket taxed by the necessity of pursuing unending narratives'.[4]

Proprietors could make a significant income from magazines. George Robinson's
Lady's Magazine and *Town and Country Magazine* at their peak each sold 'about 14,000 copies, monthly' (Rees and Britton 1896: 38–9). Robinson made an annual profit of something
like five thousand pounds a year from the two magazines, but he did so very much at the
expense of his editors and authors. John Huddlestone Wynne, an early editor of the *Lady's
Magazine*, for instance, lived hand-to-mouth working on a variety of newspapers and periodicals, some of which literally paid him by the inch for his writing. The newly founded
Lady's Monthly Museum vaunted in 1798 its 'chief Contributors', 'Ladies of established
Reputation in the literary Circles', but paid them very badly.[5] Mary Susanna Pilkington,
for instance, received only twenty-four guineas annually for editorial duties as well as
regular articles and frequently asked in vain for her salary to be increased to reflect her
continued commitment. In 1810, shortly before her final illness, she transferred her services to the *Lady's Magazine*, though writers for it were mostly amateur and unpaid.

Genre and Topicality

It is often difficult to distinguish fiction from biography or even history in miscellany
magazines, since, unlike poetry, it did not appear in a discrete section and by no means
all magazines gave sources for their material. Essays often included fictional examples
illustrating the effects of good or bad conduct, and history commonly included passages of invented dialogue and descriptive scene-setting. The publication of Helen Maria
Williams's biographical and topical *Letters from France* (1790–6) was eagerly greeted by the
Universal Magazine as containing 'many new Anecdotes relative to the French Revolution,
and the present State of French Manners'.[6] Popular extracts like 'The affecting History of
Monsieur and Madame Du F ——' (Mayo 1962: 521—entry 619), written as biographical
and historical narratives, read as topical prose fiction.

A similarly indefinite border shades drama into prose fiction. Theatricals were a staple
topic of conversation in London society, and lack of information about them an obvious
embarrassment to country-dwellers. Provincial readers could consult a series of pamphlets published in London by W. Reeve in the 1750s with titles such as *The Story on which*

[3] *Lady's Monthly Museum*, 1 (September 1798).
[4] This prospectus may be conveniently viewed on microfilm, *The Eighteenth Century* (Woodbridge,
CT: Research Publications, 1983), reel 486, no. 37.
[5] 'To the Fair Patronesses of the *Lady's Monthly Museum*', *Lady's Monthly Museum*, 1 (1798).
[6] Prefatory note to 'August and Madelaine: A Real History', *Universal Magazine*, 91 (July 1792), 25.

the New Tragedy, Call'd, The Roman Father, Is Founded. With some Account of The Author, and His Writings, 1750 (Raven 1987: 62—entry 51), or they might consult a monthly magazine. Magazines provided prose summaries of the plots of theatrical novelties, along with biographical sketches of actors (often with portrait engravings) and verse extracts. A note following 'The True Patriot: A Dramatic Tale' in the September 1775 issue of the *Universal Magazine* informed the reader:

> The above story is the foundation of a Drama, by the celebrated Metastasio, from whom the ingenious Miss Moore has taken the general plan of her new Tragedy, now performing at Bath, called the Inflexible Captive, the Prologue and Epilogue of which may be seen in our Magazine for August last.[7]

Magazine fiction is only separated out with difficulty from its surroundings, and the most apparently conventional story reads differently in context. 'The Fall of Amerath; or, The Fate of Tyranny: An Oriental Tale' was published in the October 1791 issue of the *Universal Magazine*, which also contained part of a serial commentary on the 'Affairs of France'. The two-part 'History of Captain Winterfield' in the imitative *British Magazine and Review* (1782–3) of March and April 1783 (probably written by the publisher, James Harrison) was accompanied by an engraving showing a soldier being attacked by an Indian, combining dramatic confrontation with the topicality of the American War. In one passage the survivors of a shipwreck are revived by 'the process recommended by the Humane Society (with which every man of humanity ought to make himself thoroughly acquainted)'. A footnote directs that man to the February issue of the *British Magazine*, where suitable directions were provided.[8] Harrison's story is thoroughly embedded in the culture of the general miscellany magazine, and unsurprisingly proved so popular that it was reprinted a dozen times in other periodicals (Mayo 1962: 513—entry 565).

Magazines designed chiefly for women embody consumerism as much as topicality, with their engraved music, embroidery patterns, and descriptions and plates of the latest fashions. In fiction such as the five-part 'Virtuous Love Rewarded' in the *Lady's Magazine* of 1809–10 the costliness of the aristocratic heroine's wedding outfit features largely in her happy ending:

> She wore, over a dress of white sarsanet, a beautiful robe of Brussels lace. An elegant set of pearls, together with the portrait of her Augustus, (a present of Lady Cleveland's) which, surrounded with costly diamonds, hung suspended from her necklace, completed the sumptuousness of her attire.[9]

Pretentious Mrs Elton in Jane Austen's *Emma* (1816) judges the success of a marriage in the same crudely material terms, denigrating Emma's wedding to Mr Knightley because of

---

[7] *Universal Magazine*, 57 (September 1775), 140.
[8] 'The History of Captain Winterfield', *British Magazine and Review*, 2 (April 1783), 282.
[9] 'Virtuous Love Rewarded', *Lady's Magazine*, 41 (March 1810), 110.

the absence of white satin and lace veils. Jane Austen's earlier satirical fiction also shows her awareness of this linkage of sentimentalism and conspicuous consumption, so characteristic a feature of the women's magazines.

Authors

It was rare for a celebrated author to contribute to an eighteenth-century magazine, even anonymously. Many editors and proprietors drew upon a freely available repertory of fictional pieces 'once of known origin, but now largely forgotten' (Mayo 1962: 229), and were reluctant to pay for original fiction. This tended to be the work of amateurs, who would be content to be paid in flattery and the gratification of seeing their work in print, or of hack writers paid only a small rate of remuneration. Even the popular *Lady's Magazine* allowed selected contributors only 'four guineas per sheet for poetry, and three guineas and a-half for prose' (Grant 1836: 2.331). According to a surviving receipt dated 18 February 1791, George Robinson paid Joseph Trapp twelve guineas for his translation from the French (of F. G. Ducray-Duminil) of 'Alexis, or The Cottage in the Woods';[10] this was serialized in the same magazine in thirty-one parts between March 1791 and July 1793 and, although described in the receipt as a four-volume novel, never apparently published in volume form (Raven 2000: 23, n.30). This modest payment is comparable to the prices given by Robinson for novels by relatively unknown authors: low payments for fiction were common both inside and outside magazines.

The cult of amateurism was reinforced by the traditional prestige of the essay periodical, morally improving reading that combined didacticism with illustrative and amusing case histories and examples of the moral faults or virtues under discussion. Henry Mackenzie, author of *The Man of Feeling* (1771), was the leading member of a circle of Edinburgh lawyers and professional man who produced *The Mirror* (1779–80) and *The Lounger* (1785–7). His periodical tales, which were frequently reprinted and imitated in miscellany magazines, were less obviously didactic, appealing to a readership of social equals to exercise their literary taste and refined moral judgement. The three-part 'Story of La Roche' in nos 42–4 of *The Mirror*, for instance, describes how an atheistic philosopher living in France (based on David Hume) through his encounter with an old clergyman and his daughter comes to value the effects of religion on minds of sensibility. In Mackenzie's 'Story of Albert Bane' in no. 61 of *The Lounger* friendship survives the political oppositions of the 1745 Jacobite rising and is consummated in a marriage. Walter Scott's subsequent dedication of *Waverley* (1814) to Mackenzie signals a similar masculine gentility.

---

[10] Literary Assignments of George Robinson, Manchester Central Library, MS f.091 A2, fol. 211.

Editorial communications to authors of fiction were generally made through the 'To Correspondents' paragraphs of the miscellany magazines, and while it is clear from these that both sexes wrote fiction it is hard to determine the proportion of each gender. The use of initials and pseudonyms by anonymous authors could be deliberately misleading: a male author might adopt a female pseudonym in writing for a women's magazine, or a female author choose a male pseudonym in writing for a general magazine for its added gravitas. Michael Gamer describes in Chapter 29 how popular and influential reprint series of older novels now out of copyright protection, notably James Harrison's serially published *Novelist's Magazine* (1779–88), helped to create a widely accepted canon of classic fiction centring on the work of Fielding and Smollett and in which the work of female novelists was strikingly underrepresented. The underlying assumption was that those novels that had stood the test of time and become monumental were predominantly the work of male authors.

An increasing emphasis on delicacy in magazines intended for family readership, however, might favour female authors. Harrison's canon included Dr William Dodd's *The Sisters* (originally published in 1754), in which Lucy eventually falls into prostitution: Dodd, who was chaplain to London's Magdalen Hospital, gives a horrific account of her treatment by two clients who make her dance naked about a hired room in a tavern, first threatening her body with a red-hot poker and then laying her on the fire. Such novels, together with the salacious 'Histories of the Tête-a-têtes' of the *Town and Country Magazine* are survivors of an old-fashioned masculine tradition of fiction increasingly regarded as coarse.

Writing was an important part of female self-education, both as penmanship and as composition, and practice was provided by letter-writing. The middle-aged spinster Jane Oakwood in Catherine Hutton's novel 'Oakwood House', serialized in *La Belle Assemblée* from 1811–13, recalled that in her youth she and her friends in neighbouring villages 'corresponded with each other daily, and generally were the bearers of our own letters ... '.[11] In her memoirs the governess Nelly Weeton objected to her pupil Mrs Pedder spending her evenings playing cards, noting, 'I have several times represented how much more profitably our evenings might be passed in reading, writing letters to each other, &c. &c.'.[12] Epistolary fiction in particular echoed such female employments, which also strengthened reader–author identification. Writing for the magazines could be an opportunity for a woman to display her culture and accomplishments: one fictional would-be author, for instance, decided not to delete a quotation from her story, as 'it fills up a line, and *shews that I read Byron*'.[13]

---

[11] 'Oakwood House ... Letter XI', *La Belle Assemblée*, 2nd ser., 7 (March 1813), 113.

[12] *Miss Weeton: Journal of a Governess 1807–1811*, ed. Edward Hall (London: Oxford University Press, 1936), 254.

[13] 'Sketches from My Diary. No. I', *La Belle Assemblée*, 3rd ser., 4 (July 1826), 20.

Not unnaturally, inexperienced amateur writers failed to adhere to professional standards of legibility, punctuality, and reliability. The writer of the four-part 'Interesting History of the Monmouth Family' in the *Lady's Magazine* of 1780 reveals lack of confidence in offering what is almost exclusively plot summary, which the author noted 'in the hands of an ingenious writer, might, by adding some well wrought incidents, furnish out an agreeable novel'.[14] The dilatory authoress of 'The History of Aurelia', whom the editor of the *Lady's Magazine* referred to as Sophy, was urged in February 1775 not 'to precipitate the *catastrophe* of her story'. Nevertheless she resolved a complicated love plot in a single episode by which the heroine's lover became suddenly acceptable to her father when an uncle not previously mentioned in the tale died and he inherited a large fortune and a neighbouring estate.[15]

There are very few indications, however, that the women's magazines could serve as a starting point for the professional novelist. The title page of C. D. Haynes's *The Foundling of Devonshire* (1818) described her, exceptionally, as 'Author of Castle Le Blanc', a serial novel published in the *Lady's Magazine* between 1816 and 1819 (Garside, Raven, and Schöwerling 2000: 2.463—entry 1818: 35). The sisters Catherine and Eliza Yeames, however, produced a number of serials and short fictions for the *Lady's Magazine* without apparently achieving volume publication at all and later applied to the Royal Literary Fund for assistance (Mayo 1962: 300). Amateurs such as 'Elizabeth Caroline Litchfield' continued to be paid for successive fictions with flattery alone. Serials such as 'The Forest of Alstone' and her poetry in the pages of the *Lady's Magazine* gave her celebrity within the magazine itself in the late 1780s and 1790s, where several poems by enthusiastic readers written in her honour were printed.[16] She remained unknown, however, outside the magazines.

Some magazine fiction itself suggests the economic insecurity of the authors of it. The protagonist of a cautionary letter in the *Lady's Monthly Museum* of 1801 seeks in vain to follow up her notable success as a magazine writer by volume publication, noting 'I began to think I must take my novel back, and boil my tea-kettle with it'. Her marriage prospects having been destroyed by her efforts at professional authorship in London, she is eventually relieved from the anxiety of labouring piecemeal for bare subsistence by securing from an employer a small but regular weekly pension for her magazine contributions and other literary hack work.[17] 'The Novelist.—A Fragment' in the *Manchester Magazine* of December 1816 recounts the destruction of a young clerk as he progresses from reading to writing novels, from employment in a respectable counting house to suicide in his scribbler's garret.[18] The handsome payments made by the *Edinburgh Review* from 1802 for

---

[14] *Lady's Magazine*, 11 (August 1780), 416.

[15] *Lady's Magazine*, 6 (February 1775); 'The History of Aurelia', *Lady's Magazine*, 6 (May 1775), 237–8n.

[16] See, for example, 'Lines Addressed to Veritas, on reading his to Miss E. Caroline Litchfield', *Lady's Magazine*, 24 (July 1793), 383.

[17] 'Letter to the Old Woman', *Lady's Monthly Museum*, 7 (November 1801), 293.

[18] *Manchester Magazine*, 2 (December 1816), 544–6.

long review articles appear to have had no immediate knock-on effect on the profession-alization of magazine fiction.

Readers

James Raven suggests that £50 annually might have been the book purchaser's minimum income, and that around 1780 only about 150,000 households came into this category (1992: 58). A new periodical was more affordable than a new three-volume novel: in 1807, for example, a new magazine cost between 1s. 6d. and 2s. 6d. (Sullivan 1983: xvi), whereas a new novel typically cost 13s. 6d. (Garside 2000: 93). Where the average edition for a new novel consisted of about 800 copies (Raven 1992: 35–6), between 1,750 and 5,000 cop-ies may have been produced of the more popular miscellany magazines of 1797 (Altick 1957: 392), with the *Lady's Magazine* outselling these. Although novels could be borrowed through membership of book clubs and circulating libraries, so too could magazines: the taste of readers was probably shaped by and reflected in magazines more powerfully than is often admitted.

The magazine readership certainly included the rural and urban elite. As David Allan notes in Chapter 3, the *Gentleman's Magazine* was present in Cathedral libraries at Lincoln and Lichfield, while it was clearly a reader of leisure who informed the editor of the *Lady's Monthly Museum* that 'it is a diurnal practice with me constantly to peruse (during the time of breakfast) either a pamphlet, or a periodical publication'.[19] However, there was also a strong element of a socially aspiring rather than a socially established class among the readership of women's magazines. Jan Fergus (1986) has argued that the *Lady's Magazine* in particular enlarged the provincial readership of magazines to include the wives of farmers and tradesmen. Grant remarked that its circulation was 'principally among dress-makers, to whom its plates of fashions are a strong recommendation' (1836: 2.332). It was also bought by governesses such as Nelly Weeton who had, with her widowed mother, kept a small school in order to assist her brother to become an attorney, and then was engaged as a governess-cum-housekeeper in Ambleside at a salary of thirty guineas per year (*Journal*, 261).

Both the miscellany magazines and the women's magazines were committed to an educational role. The *British Magazine*, for instance, felt that the magazine should encourage 'young Genius' and therefore included in the issue of June 1783 a school-boy's poem on the death of his pet rabbit.[20] In its prefatory address to the public the *Lady's Magazine* of 1775 returned thanks to 'the *governesses* of *boarding-schools*, who have kindly introduced our work into their seminaries, and, not less kindly, have furnished

---

[19] Letter to the Editor, *Lady's Monthly Museum*, 3 (November 1799), 340.

[20] *British Magazine and Review*, 2 (June 1783).

us with several pieces from their fair pupils', while the engraved frontispiece to the volume for 1780 showed ladies on their way to the temple of Wisdom 'carrying in their hands the Lady's Magazine, as a kind of ticket to obtain their entrance'.[21] The *Lady's Monthly Museum* was 'Adapted for Families and Boarding Schools', according to its 1798 prospectus: readers were subsequently reassured that contributions were scrupulously screened before publication to render them 'agreeable, but not injurious, to the young'.[22] An important element of the target readership of the women's magazines was juvenile.

The average subscription period to a magazine may have been quite short. Jan Fergus has argued that short subscriptions, particularly for new magazines, were not unusual: her analysis of the records of one Midlands bookseller indicates that only twelve of their sixty-two female subscribers to the *Lady's Magazine* in the late 1770s continued for two or more years (1996: 207), so that many subscribers lasted for a shorter period than that taken to complete a serialized novel. A work serialized in brief instalments over several years could strain the attention of the reader, who might also be confused by the appearance in a single issue of instalments of several different fictions. The *Lady's Magazine* for May 1793, for example, contained instalments of 'The Rival Princesses', 'Gonzala de Cordova', 'Alexis; or, The Cottage in the Woods', and 'Grasville Abbey'. One of the protagonists of 'The Correspondence of Caroline' in *La Belle Assemblée* of November 1820 recalls the bewilderment of a previous generation:

> Do you not remember, my dear, how we used to quiz our aunt Delmore, who used to get through *The Unhappy Attachment*, in a series of letters, with about twenty other novels, in the course of two or three years, through the medium of one of the old Magazines; and how much she used to be perplexed in giving the *dénôument* of one story, which in reality belonged to another.[23]

The magazine reader, however, was accustomed to fragments in the form of the extracts from new novels that allowed him or her to reflect on the desirability of a possible future loan or purchase or simply to demonstrate awareness of the work in conversation. The poems of Ossian and the novels of Sterne also made fragments increasingly acceptable. Sometimes the women's magazines were read annually rather than monthly, borrowed from libraries or received as gifts. An advertisement at the end of the *Lady's Monthly Museum* of 1801 noted that such bound volumes (which generally included a helpful index) 'are much in vogue, not only as elegant Presents to Female Friends, but also as Parental Rewards for Filial Virtue, and Prizes for Scholastic Merit and Diligence'.

---

[21] 'Address to the Public', *Lady's Magazine*, 6 (1775) and 11 (1780).

[22] *Lady's Monthly Museum*, 7 (October 1801).

[23] 'The Correspondence of Caroline. Letter IX', *La Belle Assemblée*, 2nd ser., 22 (November 1820), 203.

Serialization and Full-Length Novels

The two groundbreaking serialized novels written specifically for and first published in eighteenth-century magazines were both written by authors whose literary reputation was well-established before they entered on the conduct of a magazine and who had an interest in that magazine's commercial success. Previous to the appearance of *The Adventures of Sir Launcelot Greaves* in the *British Magazine* in twenty-five instalments between January 1760 and December 1761, Smollett had achieved a secure reputation with both novels and his translation of *Don Quixote* (1755). His contributions were expected to secure the success of the *British Magazine*, which was protected from unauthorized reprinting and piracy by Royal Licence partly on the grounds that he had 'been at great Labour and Expence in writing Original Pieces himself' for it (Knapp 1949: 221). The novel had been carefully shaped for periodical publication, with semi-autonomous chapters or instalments that nevertheless generally contained a reference to what could be expected to follow: it is clear that Smollett had a plan governing the outline and direction of the story. Charlotte Lennox was known as an actress, novelist, and translator before the commencement of the *Lady's Museum* in 1760, a magazine advertised as 'By the Author of the Female Quixote'. The serialization of her original novel 'Harriot and Sophia' was its key attraction, and the eleven monthly instalments were subsequently subdivided into forty-one chapters for publication as a two-volume novel (Mayo 1962: 288–90). Several of the instalments conclude with a misunderstanding that is only cleared up in the following one: at the end of the ninth part, for instance, Sophia learns that Harriot is living in the London house Sir Charles once offered to her if she would become his mistress and fears his affections have turned towards her sister, but at the start of the tenth part she hears that the house now belongs to Lord L ——, to whom Sir Charles has sold it. Despite the involvement of Smollett and Lennox, the *British Magazine* lasted only eight years and the *Lady's Museum* less than one.

Unless authors were also editors they had little or no opportunity to exercise control over the production of their work. Novels seem to have been portioned out into monthly instalments by the magazine editor rather than the author. George Moore's *Grasville Abbey* had been written in twenty chapters, for instance, but appeared in the *Lady's Magazine* in forty-seven monthly parts between March 1793 and August 1797 (Garside, Raven, and Schöwerling 2000: 1.722—entry 1797: 58).[24] The author of the 'Tale of Moorad' was informed by the editor of the *Lady's Magazine* in February 1808 that 'we have inserted this month as much of it as we had room for' and that though 'larger portions' might appear in future issues 'the variety we always wish to present to our readers will not permit us to promise entire compliance with the wish of the author'.[25] Under

[24] See also Mayo's Introduction to the facsimile edition of *Grasville Abbey* (1797), 3 vols (New York: Arno Press, 1974), 1.xiii.

[25] *Lady's Magazine*, 39 (February 1808).

such conditions it was impossible for novelists to utilize the gaps between instalments of magazine serials as Victorian novelists would do, to create suspense or suggest the passage of time.

Volume Publication and Anthologies

Few original magazine serials were thought worthy of a subsequent appearance in volume form, and those that have been traced before about 1810 (besides the pioneering attempts by Smollett and Lennox already noted) are almost exclusively Gothic novels appearing in the *Lady's Magazine* during the 1790s and early 1800s. The last of the forty-seven instalments of George Moore's *Grasville Abbey* (1797) advertised its imminent three-volume publication by Robinson. A. Kendall's *Derwent Priory* was published in twenty-two parts between January 1796 and September 1797, and then separately brought out by Robinson in two volumes the following year, flagged on the title page as 'First Published Periodically; Now Republished, with Additions'. *The Monks and the Robbers* was abandoned by its original author after only three episodes in the *Lady's Magazine* of 1794 and resumed in 1798 by another author, 'A. Percy'. It was concluded only in May 1805, though appearing very irregularly after 1801. It was not until 1808 that it was republished by Robinson in two volumes.

These are rare instances. It is possible, however, that there may be more that have not yet been identified, since on occasion the title of a novel was changed between magazine and volume publication. After 'The Two Castles' had appeared in the *Lady's Magazine* in eleven parts between June 1797 and November 1798, it was published by S. Fisher of London in 1799 as *The Castles of Montreuil and Barre* (Garside, Raven, and Schöwerling 2000: 1.780—entry 1799: 35). Publishers other than Robinson were perhaps more likely to change the title in order to obscure the fact that a novel had previously appeared in a magazine owned by a competitor.

Within the *Lady's Magazine* itself the demand for competent and sophisticated serial novels tended to outstrip supply. On 2 February 1803, while he was out for the evening, Samuel Hamilton's printing office and warehouse off Fleet Street burned down, destroying most of his stock and a number of novels produced for George Robinson.[26] These were mostly novels of a kind that might be read only once by an individual purchaser or borrower rather than added to an individual or family book collection for repeated perusal, consumables rather than collectables, and therefore judged hardly worth reprinting. Robinson used survivors as copy for serials in his magazine, commissioning engravings to accompany them. *The Algerine Captive* (first published in Britain by

---

[26] 'Alarming Fire', *The Times*, 3 February 1803.

Robinson in 1802) was serialized in 1804 and *The Batavians* (1799) as 'The Dutch Patriots of the Sixteenth Century' between 1811 and 1815. The popular Gothic novelist Catherine Cuthbertson's *The Romance of the Pyrenees* (1803) was quickly serialized between 1804 and 1806, featuring prominently in advertisements for the magazine itself, and additionally promoted as 'no longer to be procured but in the Lady's Magazine'.[27] Since this novel achieved a fifth edition by 1822 and was even translated into French (Garside, Raven, and Schöwerling 2000: 2.168—entry 1803: 27), Robinson presumably delayed volume republication to add some desirable fictional sparkle to a magazine that was by then lagging behind readerly expectations.

Since magazines avoided literary property issues by focusing on amateur, translated, excerpted, and abridged fiction, the way was clear for compilation volumes of shorter fiction taken from the magazines produced for the Christmas and New Year's gift market. William Lane, founder of the popular Minerva Press, published two volumes of *Lane's Annual Novelist* in 1786, described as 'A Collection of Moral Tales, Histories, and Adventures Amusing and Instructive Selected from the Magazines & other Periodical Publications'. Its Preface deplores the fact that when the 'anonymous scattered pieces' in magazines have been read they are 'thrown by with the number which contains them, and are lost to remembrance and praise'.[28] Lane's work comprised a selection of tales largely taken from the *British Magazine*, *European Magazine*, and *Universal Magazine*, and an intention was expressed to publish occasional sequels, though none apparently appeared. It was, however, the precursor of a number of subsequent anthologies that were heavily dependent on magazine fiction, such as James Harrison's *New Novelist's Magazine* (1786–8), a weekly periodical of shorter fictions, many drawn from magazines. Subsequent periodicals mixing magazine fiction with detached episodes from novels and translations from French and German had suggestive titles like *The Gleaner* (1805–6) or *Harvest Home* (1807–8).

Monthly compilations of Gothic chapbook fiction such as the *Tell-Tale, or Universal Museum* (1803–5) published by Ann Lemoine were more likely to disguise the origins of their stories in previous magazines or as compressions of Gothic novels: about a third of the fiction of the *Tell-Tale* fits this category, while a substantial proportion of the rest was written by little-known authors such as Sarah Wilkinson, then at the start of her writing career as the author of around fifty Gothic bluebooks. The subsequent spectacular success of the literary annuals of the 1820s and 1830s was to be founded not on derivative material but on original poetry and prose fiction by well-known or aristocratic authors accompanied by luxury steel-plate engravings.

---

[27] 'The Romance of the Pyrenees', *Lady's Magazine*, 35 (February 1804), 87n.
[28] *Lane's Annual Novelist*, 2 vols (London: W. Lane, [1786]), 1.ii.

Education, Escape, and Reflecting Readers' Lives

The educational role of magazine fiction partly derived from the moralistic essay periodical such as the *Spectator* or *Rambler*. A black mark is plainly awarded to the heroine of 'Eleanor Thomas—A Nouvellette' in February 1818 for her lack of interest in the 'tales of instruction and morality, of entertainment and profit' of *La Belle Assemblée*, which she neglects in favour of 'the decorative part' of the magazine which will help her 'to embellish her person'.[29] A tale the following June explains that they prepare 'the junior readers' to acquire a 'taste for information in history, geography, and elegant researches concerning the wonders of nature', and that they are factually accurate.[30] Gothic fiction was more contentious, for it was often considered to be both immoral and devoid of useful information: the publication of 'Shabraco. A Romance' in the *Lady's Monthly Museum* in 1798 caused a controversy between the boarding schools and the author (Mayo 1962: 264). Gothic fiction, on the other hand, was a staple of the *Lady's Magazine*. The escapism of the Gothic was, no doubt, welcome to many female readers of modest income leading lives of economic and social constraint as governesses, dressmakers, companions, or even schoolgirls. Such lives were much less often explored in the women's magazines than fantasies of aristocratic splendour or Gothic excess, but some magazine stories do describe the lives of lower-middle-class women, albeit generally en route to an affluent happy ending.

Harriet, the heroine of 'The History of an Humble Friend' (published in twenty-one parts in the *Lady's Magazine* from 1774 to 1776), for instance, has been abandoned as a five-year-old child at a boarding school. (The author's embittered comment that 'Girls, in general, are, I believe, put to a boarding-school, in order to be out of the way' evoked an embarrassed editorial aside.[31]) She is partly student and partly servant. As her kindly governess constantly urges her to cultivate the well-connected among her schoolfellows, she visits them during the holidays but is treated harshly. Subsequently Harriet is employed firstly as an assistant teacher, then as a companion—as such, her musical talents are exploited and she is subjected to the caprices of her employers and the attempted seductions of their male connections. Miss Haywood of 'The Governess' (published in thirty-one parts in the *Lady's Magazine* from 1778 to 1780) is a more confident protagonist, and her first-person narrative is invariably forthright and sometimes humorous. She reorganizes the neglected household of one employer, the Bluestocking Mrs Classic, and mocks another, Mrs Manning, who dotes upon her various pets and instructs Miss

---

[29] *La Belle Assemblée*, 2nd ser., 17 (February 1818), 75.
[30] 'A Tale Descriptive of the Regions to be Explored in the Expedition to the North Pole', *La Belle Assemblée*, 2nd ser., 17 (June 1818), 262–3.
[31] 'We have inserted these remarks on *Boarding-Schools* to shew our *impartiality*, but differ from the author in opinion', *Lady's Magazine*, 5 (October 1774), 521.

Haywood to teach a pet monkey along with her neglected children, since 'the last governess had taught the parrot both French and Italian'.[32] Miss Haywood eventually marries the man of her choice following the unexpected arrival of her wealthy brother from India. The readers of such tales were well prepared to read in the subsequent novels of the Brontë sisters about the trials and ultimate triumph of governesses and companions and the endurance practised by unwanted girls of genteel background.

The economics of the love plot feature as largely in such magazine fictions as they do in Jane Austen's. In the epistolary novel 'Harriet Vernon; or, Characters from Real Life' (published in twenty-nine parts in the *Lady's Magazine* from 1807 to 1809) the sisters of a wealthy but miserly merchant, George Vernon, have their marriage prospects hampered by his refusal to move in society or provide them with reasonable fortunes. Young Mr Wilson, though he behaves considerately to the elderly wife he married for money, is tormented by her emotional insecurity. Mr Beaumont loves Harriet Vernon, but plans nevertheless to marry an affected Bluestocking with twenty thousand pounds. The financial disinterestedness of the protagonists is tested before a happy ending can result: Maria Vernon, for instance, must resist the temptation of marriage to the worthy and wealthy Colonel Ambrose before she can marry her brother's clerk, Charles Wentworth.

New Developments

After the turn of the century there were signs of a desire for more sophisticated magazine fiction that would appeal to an experienced readership. John Bell's new magazine, *La Belle Assemblée*, founded in 1806, attempted to appeal to older women as well as to girls. At half a crown it was relatively expensive, but was beautifully laid out and included hand-coloured fashion plates and superior engravings, as well as a dedicated advertising supplement featuring luxury goods aimed at a female market (Morison 1930: 61–4). After 1815 and the opening of the continent to British travellers *La Belle Assemblée* reported on French drama and fashions as well as English ones, while an editorial on novel-writing in December 1810 noted, 'Change of place is now so frequent, that there are few of those qualified to write works of fancy who have not travelled beyond the limits of the fireside'.[33]

Catherine Hutton's 'Oakwood House', published in thirty-three parts between January 1811 and October 1813, has the independent middle-aged spinster Jane Oakwood as a protagonist, who communicates many of Hutton's own insights and experiences to the reader. Hutton typifies the desired older reader of *La Belle Assemblée*: she was the daughter of the Birmingham bookseller William Hutton and a member of Joseph Priestley's congregation, travelled extensively in northern England and Wales, and had a wide circle

---

[32] *Lady's Magazine*, 11 (September 1780), 482.
[33] 'Novels and Romances', *La Belle Assemblée*, 2nd ser., 2 (December 1810), 358.

of correspondents that included the novelist Robert Bage (Hill 1994). Although Hutton subsequently claimed that her novel had been written previous to being 'cut into shreds' for serial publication,[34] it effectively enfolds many of the features of the magazine itself. Jane Oakwood recollects encounters with O'Brien the Irish giant, Borowlaski the Polish dwarf, and the fat man Daniel Lambert; she amuses herself by composing absurdities constructed by reading across two columns of a newspaper; and she recalls attending performances by the actress Mrs Siddons. Each of these topics might well have formed a magazine article, and indeed Jane Oakwood's remarks on Mrs Siddons appeared in the August 1812 issue of *La Belle Assemblée*, at a time when the magazine was featuring a series of illustrated accounts of famous actresses. (An article on Mrs Siddons in this series had appeared in April 1812.) Mrs Oakwood is also a discriminating critic of novels. She accords limited praise to Owenson's *The Wild Irish Girl* (1806), for instance, praising Owenson's descriptions of Irish manners but deploring her 'rage for words': 'When I tell you she talks of the *sylphid elegance of spheral beauty being united to the symmetrical contour which constitutes the luxury of human loveliness*, I need say no more'.[35] 'Oakwood House' participates in, yet sharpens and intellectualizes, typical magazine culture for the more sophisticated readership *La Belle Assemblée* was seeking to attract. It also moves the magazine novel northwards from metropolitan London and displays an interest in regional customs, prefiguring the later regionalization of the novel by George Eliot and Thomas Hardy: Mrs Oakwood visits places of historical and topographical interest in Yorkshire and the Lake District, introduces passages in dialect, and describes local events such as the cushion dance and a hiring fair.

Hutton's recognition as a novelist, however, was not the result of her work for *La Belle Assemblée*. It was only after the appearance of her first volume-publication novel *The Miser Married* in 1813 that 'Oakwood House' was published separately in three volumes by Longmans in 1819 as *Oakwood Hall* (Garside, Raven, and Schöwerling 2000: 2.480–1— entry 1819: 43). Prevailing conditions of anonymity mean that the true extent of Hutton's early contributions to *La Belle Assemblée* is unknown and there appears to be no record of her payments for it. Hutton's partial record of her professional contributions dates from the 1820s and 1830s after conditions had changed.[36]

James Hogg was another author who failed to make his name by writing innovative periodical fiction in the 1810s. Having had little success as a Borders farmer and shepherd, Hogg came to Edinburgh in 1810 and attempted to turn literary man. He found, however, that the city's magazines and newspapers would accept his work only as that of an amateur, and so decided to produce his own eight-page weekly, *The Spy* (1810–11).

---

[34] Catherine Hutton, *Oakwood Hall, A Novel*, 3 vols (London: Longman [etc.], 1819), 1.vi.

[35] 'Oakwood House . . . Letter XI', *La Belle Assemblée*, 2nd ser., 7 (March 1813), 114.

[36] Among Hutton's papers in Birmingham Central Library, MS 168 includes a number of draft manuscripts, cuttings from *La Belle Assemblée*, and lists of her contributions, mostly subsequent to 1824.

Hogg's earlier book of ballad imitations, *The Mountain Bard* (1807), had included substantial prose notes retailing Borders legends and customs, and he now combined sketches of country life and supernatural tales with depictions of public scenes in Edinburgh, mixing the characteristics of the essay periodical with those of the miscellany magazine. The physical limits of *The Spy* prohibited the appearance of novel-length fiction and meant that some of Hogg's tales had to be divided between several issues: one entitled 'Story of a Berwickshire Farmer' ends with what reads as a plot summary for a possible continuation,[37] and Hogg did subsequently extend this and a number of other stories from *The Spy* for his *Winter Evening Tales* (1820). Hogg's fiction and that of his contributors focuses attention on farmers, local lairds, schoolmasters, and ordinary citizens. The protagonist of James Gray's 'Life of a Profligate Student' is the son of a country minister, while that of Thomas Gillespie's 'The Scots Tutor' comes from a peasant background and subsidizes his own university studies by employment as a family tutor. After recounting his early progress in classical literature, for instance, he owns that 'excepting once, when dispatched with a basket of gooseberries to a widow lady, a distant relation of my mother's, I had never in my life set my foot on a carpet' (379). Hogg's 'History of the Life of Duncan Campbell' recounts the wanderings of a homeless boy and his supernatural encounters, while 'Description of a Peasant's Funeral' has a more ethnographic slant. In 'Story of the Ghost of Lochmaben' a spirit appears to bring spiritual reassurance and to urge legal justice, combining folk morality with the providentiality of the *Methodist Magazine*. Like Hutton's, Hogg's work moved magazine fiction northwards, in this case to Edinburgh and the Scottish Borders, fashionable territory in the age of Scott's narrative poetry.

When the ambitious Edinburgh publisher William Blackwood decided to begin his own periodical in the spring of 1817 he initially made the mistake of adopting the financial practices relating to the conventional miscellany magazine while hoping to achieve the brilliance and *éclat* of his publishing rival Archibald Constable's *Edinburgh Review*, which paid its contributors handsomely. In his initial arrangements with his editors there was apparently no mention of who was to pay the contributors. Hogg as a trusted supporter urged Blackwood, when plans were underway to revitalize the somewhat lacklustre periodical that resulted, to 'affix a price to the writers per sheet', adding, 'There is a charm in this to writers from the highest to the lowest the idea that their labours are not entirely thrown away'.[38] Blackwood began to pay a professional minimum of ten guineas per sixteen-page sheet for original fiction as well as non-fiction, with remarkable results.

During the 1820s original fiction by Scottish authors such as James Hogg, John Galt, and David Macbeth Moir appeared regularly in *Blackwood's Edinburgh Magazine* and was subsequently reprinted in volume form, with its magazine origins deliberately flagged as

---

[37] *The Spy*, ed. Gillian Hughes (Edinburgh: Edinburgh University Press, 2000), 43.
[38] *The Collected Letters of James Hogg*, ed. Gillian Hughes et al., 3 vols (Edinburgh: Edinburgh University Press, 2004–8), 1.300 (letter of 24 September 1817).

an attraction to the reader and a guarantee of quality. Galt's *The Ayrshire Legatees* (1821), for example, was first serialized in the magazine and then issued as a single-volume novel. Such works were structured in self-standing yet related episodes that build into a single narrative, facilitated by the lengthening of the typical magazine tale or instalment from the three to four pages desired by the earlier *Lady's Monthly Museum* to around eight to ten pages. The correlation of instalment and chapter became more straightforward, and a complete novel could appear in the magazine within a reasonable time. Hogg's supernatural tales and sketches of Borders life could also be published without being artificially divided: *The Shepherd's Calendar*, for instance, appeared serially in *Blackwood's Edinburgh Magazine* before being published in two volumes by Blackwood in 1829.

Other magazine proprietors followed Blackwood's lead. A notice at the start of *La Belle Assemblée* for 1827, for instance, declared that all its literary and arts material was now written expressly for the magazine. During the 1820s magazines increasingly paid adequately for fiction, and the result was the rise of the magazine tale. Some of the early tales of Mary Russell Mitford subsequently included in *Our Village* (1824) were first published in the *Lady's Magazine*. Most of the component parts of Allan Cunningham's *Traditional Tales of the English and Scottish Peasantry* (1822) had previously appeared in the *London Magazine*. Anonymity gradually faded, as editors capitalized on the recognizable names of their affiliated tale-writers: Hogg's tales in *Blackwood's* were flagged as his by the use of his *nom de plume* the Ettrick Shepherd, while from 1829 onwards *La Belle Assemblée* published Catherine Hutton's contributions as by 'The Author of "The Miser Married", &c.'.

It became possible for a writer like Hogg to achieve a strong identity within the pages of the magazines. As a result he was much in demand as a contributor to the fashionable annuals of the later 1820s and 1830s: in a letter of 23 February 1835, he estimated his income from magazines and annuals as 'from one to two hundred pounds annually' (3.256). During the 1820s, however, magazine fiction was still predominantly short fiction: 'Oakwood House' remained the only novel by Hutton serialized in *La Belle Assemblée*, for example, while even into the 1830s novels such as Samuel Warren's controversial *Passages in the Diary of a Late Physician* (1832), originating in *Blackwood's*, retained a characteristically episodic structure. The long-delayed professionalization of their fiction during the 1820s, however, prepared the magazines to become the training ground for Victorian novelists such as Dickens and Thackeray.

26

Short Fictional Forms and the Rise of the Tale

ANTHONY JARRELLS

In the presence of the novel, all other genres somehow have a different resonance.

Mikhail Bakhtin, 'Epic and Novel' (1981: 39)

After Novels

In *Before Novels*, J. Paul Hunter argues that the novel did not emerge out of or displace a single genre—romance—but rather engaged with and imitated a broad field of writing that included journalistic texts, didactic writing, 'rhetorics of advice', romance, 'perspective narratives', private histories, and personal diaries (1990: 86–7). Genres such as these not only provided materials for the early novel to draw on and colonize, he suggests, they also prepared the very field of reading in which the novel could emerge. But what, we might ask, became of these many different kinds of writing after the 1750s, the moment for Hunter when there appeared a 'broad consciousness among readers and potential writers that a significant and lasting form'—the novel—'had been created' (22)? Did they continue to exist and to exert an influence on the novel? Did the novel register their continued presence and did they in turn register the influence of this new, increasingly dominant form?

The answer to these questions is 'yes'. But while literary historians in large part have agreed that the novel was an established genre by the 1750s, one effect of this consensus has been to leave off studying the many other forms that continued to fill out its broader cultural contexts. Clifford Siskin has coined the term 'novelism' to describe 'the now habitual subordination of writing to the novel', a subordination that obscures a more inclusive 'history of writing' (1998: 172–3). Any such history of the years that comprise this volume would have to include not only the many different forms the novel took, but also the myriad other fictional forms that existed and in some cases thrived *after* novels took their place in the busy market of British print culture. James Raven, for instance,

highlights the 'extraordinary variety of narrative forms' that flourished in the later decades of the eighteenth century, naming among them 'fables, romances, biographical and
autobiographical memoirs and histories, satirical tales and narratives in letters' (2000: 15).
The novel has long been understood to be imperialistic in its tendencies: its 'greedy maw',
says Hunter, 'takes what it wants where it can find it' (57). But being written into the narrative of the novel's rise should not mean being devoured by literary history, too. This
chapter thus will examine some of the short fictional forms that persisted in as well as
alongside the novel, including chapbook and bluebook abridgements, religious tracts,
and what would come to be called—by the end of the period covered here—the tale.
Together, these forms highlight the dynamic field of writing that comprised the years
that span the novel's rise and canonization. In addition, they suggest that the novel itself
inspired experimentation and mixing among non-novelistic forms even as these forms
pushed it to refine and consolidate its own formal boundaries.

The Literary Market in Fiction

William Godwin's *The Adventures of Caleb Williams* (1794) is a striking example of a novel
that mixes various styles—Gothic Jacobin, domestic realism—while also drawing upon
shorter forms such as the tale, the periodical essay, and the chapbook adventure. One
scene in particular highlights this mixing, in a sense dramatizing late eighteenth-century
competition among genres. The scene comes late in the novel when Godwin's eponymous hero arrives in London. Still on the run from the law and in need of employment,
Caleb decides upon literature because it allows him to work unobserved. His first productions, 'of the poetical kind', are rejected at the newspaper office to which they are first
directed. The editor at the magazine where he sends them next is more open but says he
is interested in productions of a different kind. '[I]f the gentleman would try his hand in
prose', he explains, 'a short essay or a tale, he would see what he could do for him'. Caleb
finds success initially by writing in the style of Addison's *Spectator*. Doubting his resources
'in the way of moral disquisition', however, he turns to the editor's other genre of choice:
the tale. 'By a fatality, for which I did not exactly know how to account,' he writes, 'my
thoughts frequently led me to the histories of celebrated robbers . . .'.[1]

Of course, by this point in the novel Caleb is himself a celebrated robber. As he is making
his way into London, for instance, he finds that a tale about his recent misdeeds and escapes
is already circulating around the countryside, acquiring 'historians and commentators'
(vol. 3, ch. 5; 245). And after settling in London, he encounters 'The Most Wonderful and
Surprising History and Miraculous Adventures of Caleb Williams', a 'halfpenny legend'

---

[1] William Godwin, *Things as They Are; or, The Adventures of Caleb Williams*, ed. Maurice Hindle
(London: Penguin, 1988), vol. 3, ch. 8; 267–8.

(vol. 3, ch. 11; 283) being hawked on the city streets. Indeed, Caleb's own history is an extended apology of sorts for a celebrated robber, one that must compete with these other accounts of his life and character. Famous for his daring escapes from jail, Caleb encounters a new kind of prison in such accounts, which limit his movements and his ability to make connections with other people. To escape, he pens a history of his own, one he hopes will 'appear to have that consistency which is seldom attendant but upon truth' (vol. 1, ch. 1; 5) and that will trump the others by being more authoritative, more authentic. Caleb succeeds, in part, by assimilating the competing accounts of his life into the structure of his own narrative, which includes his experiences in London writing tales about robbers as well as the tales that other people have written about him. His history also contains biographies (of his employer, Squire Falkland, and of Falkland's enemy, Barnabas Tyrrel), moral essays on the state of the nation's prison system, and a more general allegory of the 'arbitrary power' (vol. 3, ch. 8; 263) that Godwin witnessed first-hand in the famous government 'terror' of the 1790s. In bringing all of these forms together into a single, coherent narrative, Caleb's 'full and authentic report' does exactly what Ian Watt says that eighteenth-century novels do: it tells the story of a supposedly real person whose character develops over a consistent period of time and across a realistically defined space (1957: 32).

One such realistically defined space is the London print market. Godwin was familiar with the scene. Prior to writing his *Enquiry Concerning Political Justice* (1793) and *Caleb Williams*—the works that made him famous—he worked as a Grub Street hack, translator, and journalist, writing a *Life of the Earl of Chatham* in 1783 and summaries of the year's events for the *New Annual Register* starting in 1784. He also wrote three popular novels: *Damon and Delia* (1784) and *Imogen* (1784) for the circulating libraries (Thomas Hookham and William Lane's, respectively), and *Italian Letters* (1784) for the publisher George Robinson. Historically, Caleb's own stint as a writer would have been made possible by a host of miscellaneous and periodical publications that emerged in the wake of the 1774 *Donaldson v. Becket* ruling that ended the common-law practice of perpetual copyright. The Donaldson ruling resulted in 'an explosion of reading' (St Clair 2004: 348) and a 'rejuvenated' print market (Raven 2000: 88) as works formerly protected by copyright became available for reprinting and for wider circulation. Anthologies, cheap reprints, novel-in-part series, circulating libraries, and book clubs all flourished in this 'less regulated market' (Raven 2007a: 241). The sheer quantity of new venues and vehicles of print brought genres into proximity as never before.

Given Caleb's duties in the novel, one such venue that comes to mind is the *New Novelist's Magazine*, published by James Harrison from 1786 to 1788. *The New Novelist's Magazine* offered an 'entertaining library of pleasing and instructional histories, tales, adventures, romances, and other agreeable and exemplary little novels'.[2] The lead tale

---

[2] Title page for *The New Novelist's Magazine; or, Entertaining Library*, vol. 1 (London: Harrison and Son, 1786) (vol. 2, 1787).

in the first volume of *The New Novelist's Magazine* was in fact an original work written by Harrison and titled 'The Criminal'. Like *Caleb Williams*, 'The Criminal' tells the story of a young man accused of stealing from (and possibly murdering) a worthy gentleman, and it presents a picture of a community enraged against the heartless wretch who could insult someone so 'universally beloved'. 'The minds of even the most enlightened', says the narrator, 'possessed therefore no room for compassion.... There was, indeed, hardly an eye that did not scowl at him with indignant abhorrence' (1.3). But where *Caleb Williams* develops its central character over a long period of time and across multiple settings, 'The Criminal' centres on the more circumscribed spectacle of a courtroom scene and on a dramatic discovery that follows the jury's verdict. The supposed criminal's story competes only against the initial evidence (things in his possession) and the impression of guilt such evidence suggests. In the end, this story tempers the outrage of the crowd and allows time enough for the real criminal to be discovered. Caleb's story, on the other hand, competes with the evidence mounted against him (things in his possession) as well as with the many stories that circulate about him—the various 'adventures' to which the original title gives way (*Things as They Are; or, The Adventures of Caleb Williams*). Unlike 'The Criminal', which ends abruptly, only to be followed by another tale, Caleb's story ends only after ensuring that no other tales can follow. It vindicates him, finally, but at the expense of turning him into a 'murderer' ('Postscript', 336)—of his employer, Falkland, and, one imagines, of the other accounts of his life. Caleb's consolation is that 'the world may at least not hear and repeat a half-told and mangled tale' (337).

But as the popularity of Harrison's *New Novelist's Magazine* attests, eighteenth-century readers had not yet given up their interest in reading half-told and mangled tales. For Caleb, the difference comes down to truth. For scholars of the novel, it often has come down to quality. However, to read a novel like *Caleb Williams* in relation to the genres it explicitly engages is not necessarily to read the former against the latter—the individual instance of quality against the quantity of the literary market. It is to read the literary market in the fiction itself—to explore, that is, how different genres borrowed from each other, registered one another, and changed to accommodate shifts or developments in form and popularity. Mary Poovey describes such an approach as 'historical description', distinguishing it from 'interpretation' or more traditional close reading (2008: 343–52). Historical description enables the scholar to read across multiple generic surfaces—rather than deeply into one—in order to see how specific combinations of features and forms helped writers 'differentiate among kinds of writing' (344). The approach is spatial rather than hierarchical, a way of reading that accounts for what Franco Moretti calls the 'collective system' (2003: 68) of the novel and that explains how and why certain forms thrived (or failed to thrive) when they did.

Harrison's *New Novelist's Magazine*, for example, is both compared to its predecessor, *The Novelist's Magazine* (1779–88), and subtly differentiated from it. As Harrison writes in the Advertisement:

> The plan of the former [*The Novelist's Magazine*] comprehends all the larger novels and romances of eminence, foreign as well as English, from Clarissa, in eight volumes, to Voltaire's Sincere Huron, in one; at prices often more than two hundred per cent. less than the very same works are usually sold for, even without copper plates: and the design of the latter is, to serve up to the public, on terms proportionately advantageous, an elegant collection of the many beautiful little tales and stories scattered throughout innumerable miscellanies.

The repetition of the word 'novelist' in the two publication titles highlights a deliberate attempt at association. *The Novelist's Magazine*'s circulation peaked at around 12,000 an issue, so there was a clear incentive to capitalize on its success and on a seemingly limitless public appetite for novels. But in using qualifying adjectives such as 'little' to describe these new 'novels' and by using a separate generic description—'tales'—Harrison also differentiates his product in ways that go beyond temporal newness. *The New Novelist's Magazine* is likened to a miscellany: among its contents are original compositions like Harrison's; many previously published works or excerpts of works by Samuel Johnson, Eliza Haywood, Henry Mackenzie, and Laurence Sterne; a wealth of oriental tales; new translations of works from the Continent; and even a couple of essays, including a lecture by James Fordyce on parental indiscretion and David Hume's 'On Impudence and Modesty', here newly classed as 'an allegory'. Like *Caleb Williams*, then (and like *The Novelist's Magazine*), *The New Novelist's Magazine* featured a mix of genres and styles. But unlike *Caleb Williams*, or the novel generally, *The New Novelist's Magazine* did not assimilate these distinct genres into one coherent narrative, form, or series. Half-told and mangled tales were standard fare and would remain so for some time to come.

Chapbooks, Bluebooks, and Tracts

The novel may be the obvious place to look for the kinds of mixing that took place following *Donaldson v. Becket*, for the novel is a genre that benefited enormously from the explosion of reading that marks these years. But as the varied contents of Harrison's *New Novelist's Magazine* suggest, shorter forms, too—or 'little novels'—participated in the new possibilities for mixing and combining. And these forms were everywhere. As Robert Mayo notes, '[t]he century is usually thought of as belonging in large part to the novel, but approached through the magazines it is an age of tiny tales and diminutive narrative sketches . . .' (1962: 4; see also Hughes, Chapter 25). The novel borrowed from the fictional forms that surrounded it, as discussed above; but so too did these tiny tales and diminutive sketches borrow from the novel as they struggled to compete in a fiction market defined more and more by the presence of novels. They borrowed its realism and forms of storytelling (tales such as 'The Criminal' read like abbreviated novels); and they borrowed its most popular examples for abridgements, redactions, and characters. Indeed, with so much fiction appearing in periodical form, it becomes difficult to discern the contours of the late eighteenth-century novel from the forms that filled out its broader contexts. Readers of the period did not seem to mind the confusion, as long as they got a steady supply of fiction. If such an attitude does not yet signal the subordination of all writing to the novel, it does suggest that the novel was now dominant enough to make inroads into the forms it had formerly drawn upon for materials.

One of these forms was the chapbook. In the Romantic period, William Wordsworth sang the praises 'Of Jack the Giant Killer, Robin Hood | And Sabra in the Forest of St George!' (*The Prelude*, bk 5, ll. 366–7)—all chapbook heroes he associated with the powerful form of imagination that grew out of childhood reading. But by the period of Wordsworth's own childhood, the chapman's inventory included more modern characters such as Robinson Crusoe and Moll Flanders, too. Usually 8, 12, or 24 pages in length, and with a woodcut illustration, chapbooks provided readers with short tales of criminals, heroes, and strange or supernatural adventures. They were, in Margaret Spufford's words, 'crude, unsubtle, earthy, uncompassionate, but full of movement and violence, sex, vivid imagery and better or worse jokes' (1982: 249). The content and the form of chapbooks may have appealed largely to a poor, labouring-class audience; but they were also read by children and by writers such as Wordsworth's contemporary, Walter Scott, who admired their 'directness' and who found in them a model for mixing 'real historical figures' and 'imagined characters from low life' (St Clair 2004: 347). Novelists well before Scott—or Godwin—also mined the chapbook form. Defoe, for instance, drew heavily on the popular print forms of his day, including chapbook adventures. It is no wonder, then, that novels like his *Robinson Crusoe* (1719) were in turn adapted, abridged, and imitated in later eighteenth-century versions of these same popular forms.

Outwardly, later eighteenth-century chapbooks continued to look largely the same as the 'little books' that had been peddled in the English countryside 'at least from the 1570s onwards' (Spufford 1982: xix). But as novels by Defoe or Tobias Smollett found their way into chapbook lists, the contents, styles, and narrative voice of chapbook stories changed. One example of this is the 'bluebook' Gothics popular in the first decade of the nineteenth century (discussed further below). Another is the religious tract literature written by Evangelical writers such as Hannah More and Legh Richmond. Between 1795 and 1798, More's Cheap Repository of Moral and Religious Tracts printed and distributed tales, ballads, allegories, and Sunday readings, each selling for a penny with discounted bulk prices to encourage the wealthy to distribute the tracts throughout their parishes. Two million tracts were printed and distributed in the first year alone. The short tales issued by the Cheap Repository combined fictitious narrative with conduct-literature morality and sought to inculcate frugality, temperance, domestic felicity, and contentment with the political system. One of More's stated targets in publishing the tracts was the radical pamphlets circulating around the nation and raising fears of violent revolution. '[I]t was judged expedient', she explains, ' . . . to supply such wholesome aliment as might give a new direction to [the common people's] taste, and abate their relish for those corrupt and inflammatory publications which the consequences of the French Revolution have been so fatally pouring upon us.'[3] A second, more general, target was what More took to be the degraded state of popular literature at the end of the eighteenth century. In the Advertisement to her *Cheap Repository Shorter Tracts*, she writes that '[t]he great object had in view in publishing them, has been to supplant the multitude of vicious tracts circulated by hawkers, and to supply instead of them, some useful reading, which may be likely to prove entertaining also'.[4]

In a sense, the *Cheap Repository Tracts* are moral tales disguised as chapbooks. Their 'attack' on popular literature and culture, as Susan Pederson argues, 'was concealed in a product that was not, at first glance, distinguishable from a chapbook' (1986: 106). But with their thoroughly modern content and middle-class morality, More's tracts represent a radical revision of the chapbook tale. Even typical chapbook fare like an account of a criminal is framed by a message and a narrative voice that aim to instruct rather than merely to amuse. 'I have thought it my duty to print this little history,' says the narrator of 'Tawney Rachel; or, The Fortune Teller', 'as a kind of warning to all you young men and maidens not to have anything to SAY TO CHEATS, IMPOSTERS, CUNNING WOMEN, FORTUNE-TELLERS, CONJURERS, AND INTERPRETERS of DREAMS' (*Cheap Repository Tracts*, 101). Still, though the message or moral may be explicit, the tales themselves offer close, careful descriptions of everyday life and provide characters with a psychological depth not to be found in typical chapbook renderings of Robin Hood or Simple Simon. 'The Cheapside Apprentice', written by More's sister, Sarah, is told in the first-person voice of an apprentice whose time running errands after hours for his master's fashionable wife and 'lounging about the purlieus of the playhouse' (2) has led to his ruin. Descending into worldly decadence, he seduces his master's daughter and ends up in prison for forgery. He repents eventually, although too late to save his life. A separate editorial voice interjects to explain that a note titled 'Written the night before my execution' was found in the apprentice's coat pocket after his death sentence is carried out. The note contains the warning that begins the tale—to thoughtless men entering trade; but such a warning is really superfluous by this point: the narrative itself has already detailed the effects of turning from righteousness.

If More seems adept at deploying the very form she hopes to eradicate, she evinces a similar intelligence about the field of print culture more generally. Kevin Gilmartin argues that More's tracts move beyond a Romantic-era conservative culture's fundamental distrust of print, associated as it then was with radical politics, in order to enlist print itself in the cause of reform. In a tale like 'The History of Tom White the Postilion', for instance, he notes a 'shift from conventional parable to a more ambitious fictional

---

[3] Hannah More, *Tales for the Common People. The Works of Hannah More, in eight volumes* (London: T. Cadell and W. Davies, 1801), 5.vii–viii.

[4] Hannah More, *Cheap Repository Shorter Tracts* (London: F. C. Rivington, 1800), iv–v.

synthesis of the whole machinery of moral reform...' (2007: 59). One way to account for this ambitious fictional synthesis is to understand it as a product not of popular chapbook literature or radical pamphlets but rather of another form that More distrusted: the novel, a genre whose impact on her tracts can be seen in their use of dialogue, in the details they provide of common life, and in their consistent emphasis on domesticity. After they were published in tract form, many of More's tales were republished in bound collections with titles such as *Tales for the Common People* and *Stories for Persons of the Middle Ranks*. Thus they took their place in the bookshop, competing not just with popular forms like the chapbook and the ballad, but also with the novel, a genre whose higher class of readership did not make it above the need for reform. In 1808, More published a novel of her own, *Coelebs in Search of a Wife*, which, like her tracts, is also a moral tale in disguise. 'The novel reader will reject it as dull,' says the fictional Coelebs, in his Preface; and he is not wrong.[5] His account does not feature 'striking events' (vi) or present love as 'an ungovernable impulse' (viii), as novels were thought to do. Its aim, rather, is 'to shew how religion may be brought to mix with the concerns of ordinary life' (ix–x).

More's formula of using fictional narratives to mix religion with the concerns of ordinary life was imitated by Legh Richmond, whose 'The Dairyman's Daughter', 'The Negro Servant', and 'The Young Cottager' were published first serially in the *Christian Guardian* starting in 1809, then quickly issued through the Religious Tract Society, and finally in book form as *Annals of the Poor* in 1814. Richmond's narratives, 'given from real life and circumstances',[6] were among the most successful of Religious Tract Society publications. And as Gary Kelly notes, *Annals* was 'the most frequently reprinted book during the Romantic period' (1990: 165). Given its mixture of novelistic description, epistolary depth, and graveyard-school meditation upon the landscape and elegiac pathos, it is easy to see why (Richmond's title, 'Annals of the Poor', is taken from a line in Thomas Gray's 'Elegy Written in a Country Churchyard': 'the short and simple annals of the poor'). More sometimes divided her tales over two or three tracts. But Richmond extends his stories out over seven or eight parts, occasionally to lengths well over 100 pages. This allowed for a higher order of generic mixing; and it allowed, as well, for a higher order of narrative complexity. Richmond's clergyman-narrator intermixes sermon-like monologues with multiple perspectives, characters, and plotlines.

'The Dairyman's Daughter' tells the story of a young woman's conversion. It begins with a letter from this young woman—Elizabeth—asking if Richmond will preside over the burial of her sister. The letter is included in the narrative because as Richmond explains, 'epistolary communications...afford genuine portraits of the mind' (66). We come to know the clergyman-narrator's character through his reflections on the letters he

---

[5] Hannah More, *Coelebs in Search of a Wife. Comprehending Observations on Domestic Habits, Manners, Religion, and Morals*, 2nd edn, 2 vols (London: T. Cadell and W. Davies, 1809), 1.v.

[6] Legh Richmond, *Annals of the Poor* (London: J. Hatchard and Son, 1831), 2.

receives from Elizabeth and through his dialogues with her. We come to know Elizabeth's character through her letters, via an account provided by her father (to Richmond), and from her own retelling of her conversion and life. 'The Dairyman's Daughter' is made up of eight parts, most of them organized around a visit (to the funeral; to Elizabeth's sister's employer, where Elizabeth is filling in following her sister's death; to Elizabeth's parents' house) and around a letter from Elizabeth to Richmond. The parts can be read separately as individual tracts, each one offering a reflection upon the 'operations of divine grace' as Richmond discovers them among 'God's real children' (2), the poor. But when read together, they develop a complicated story of friendship, conversion, and death (Elizabeth dies of consumption), one that assimilates multiple strands of dialogue, reflection, and character development into a single coherent narrative.

Less formally complex but equally interesting in terms of changes and developments in chapbook literature are the bluebooks, or 'shilling shockers', that adapted, redacted, and sometimes simply plagiarized Gothic novels. These bluebooks—called such for their disposable blue wrappers—sold for sixpence or a shilling and were usually 36 or 72 pages, representing one or two gatherings in 18mo form. Although they resembled chapbooks, they differed from them in that they were not hawked on the streets or carried in chapmen's packs but rather sold in bookshops or obtained through circulating libraries (Potter 2005: 43–4). In form, however, they did what eighteenth-century chapbooks did with the novels of Defoe and Smollett: they abridged, redacted, and reprinted them. Thus Matthew Lewis's novel, *The Monk* (1796), was adapted in *Raymond and Agnes; or The Bleeding Nun of the Castle of Lindenberg* (1797); Clara Reeve's *The Old English Baron* (1778; first published 1777 as *The Champion of Virtue*) supplied the plot for *Edmund and Albina; or Gothic Times* (1801); and Charlotte Dacre's *Zofloya the Moor* (1806) became *The Daemon of Venice, an Original Romance* (1810). Titles appeared separately as individual bluebooks and were also bound together in chapbooks such as *Tales of Wonder* (1801), which contained four tales in fifty pages, or *Romantic Tales* (1802), which featured three tales written by Isaac Crookenden, whom Frederick Frank calls 'the most notorious counterfeiter of the Gothic age' (1987: 65).

To fill out standard length requirements, additional one- or two-page tales—or a fragment of another tale or novel—were sometimes added on to the end of a bluebook. So attached to *The Haunted Castle; or, The Child of Misfortune* (1801), for instance, is a one-page story called 'Ivar and Matilda'. Ivar is a thirteenth-century knight who wants to marry the fortuneless but beautiful Matilda. When he presents her to the king, however, a crafty prince, Reginald, who also has eyes on Matilda, has Ivar banished and Matilda imprisoned. While Matilda stays busy resisting Reginald's several attempts at her virtue, Ivar becomes a monk. But one day when he is out wandering he hears a shriek from a tower. 'Advancing eagerly', explains the narrator, 'he heard a voice nearly exhausted—"Mother of God! Save Matilda"—while, through a chink in the barrier that now separated them, he saw the virgin, with dishevelled hair and throbbing bosom, about to be sacrificed to the lust and violence of Reginald'.[7] Fortunately for Matilda, the old knightly rage that Ivar has been concealing beneath his monk's habit returns instantly. He rushes in, plunges a sword into Reginald's bosom, and then escapes with Matilda through a 'subterraneous' passage to the seaside and onto a boat bound for Ireland. This summary of what is fairly typical bluebook fare highlights the concentration of action and violence that drew so many readers—a young Percy Shelley among them—to these redacted Gothics. With all of this in a single page one can only imagine what might happen in thirty-six. One thing that usually did not happen was character development. Nor is there much of the lyrical ruminating upon natural scenes that featured in Ann Radcliffe's novels. As Frank explains, 'the Gothic chapbook strips away all of the complications of the immense Gothic plot in order to jar the reader with supernatural shocks. These little Gothics are shortened and plagiarized novels devoted not to the story or to the moral but to spectacular special effects' (1987: 20).

Shortened and plagiarized they may have been. Yet these little Gothics were not completely devoid of formal innovation or narrative complexity. A number of bluebooks, such as Crookenden's *The Revengeful Turk; or Mystic Cavern* (1802), are set in the East and contain the tale-within-a-tale structure and mix of the natural and supernatural that readers would have associated with the *Arabian Nights Entertainments*. Translated into French starting in 1704—and soon after into English—*Les mille et une nuits* inspired multiple editions, a host of imitation oriental tales, and a general craze for the East (see also Ballaster, Chapter 19). As Johnson, Maxwell, and Trumpener (2007) explain, *Les mille* 'also shaped a wide range of experimental texts that deployed literary embedding, whether or not they featured orientalizing motifs' (247). The tales in Ann Lemoine's chapbook collection, *English Nights Entertainments* (1802), for instance, are not set in the East. But as the series title suggests, they draw upon the framing devices and tale-within-a-tale structure of their Arabic-French counterpart. Under the main heading 'Romances and Gothic Tales' are five tales, each with a separate title but all connected by plot or association. In 'Ruins of an Abbey', the first in the grouping, the daughter of a baron driven by financial losses to restore an old, haunted abbey, becomes a kind of local historian of the place, and in particular of a nun imprisoned and murdered there long ago. The daughter, Rosaline, finds in the deep recesses of the abbey a cell and a coffin, inside of which is a manuscript: 'the Story of the Unfortunate Anna' (the next tale in the sequence). In a nod to the bluebook form, the tale proceeds—out of necessity—to redact the longer history of the nun: as the narrator explains, 'many of the lines were totally extinct, and only here and there a few that could be distinguished'.[8] The omissions are marked by ellipses; what remains are merely a few main

---

[7] *The Haunted Castle; or, The Child of Misfortune. A Gothic Tale* (London: Ann Lemoine, 1801), 48.
[8] *English Nights Entertainments. Consisting of a Selection of Histories, Adventures, Lives, & by the most Celebrated Authors* (London: Ann Lemoine, 1802), 13.

plot points. A second account of the same history is found; this one, 'The Bleeding Nun of St. Catherine's' (the next tale), is penned by monks and better preserved. But it, too, contains places where 'all traces of writing were lost in mildew and obscurity' (15). Lemoine's tales, then, not only deploy *Arabian Nights*-style literary embedding, they highlight their own gaps—indeed, the gaps of the genre itself.

Frank sees in the bluebook form a 'literary link' (1987: 20) between the three- and four-volume Gothic novels of the eighteenth century and the short 'tale of terror' that would become a staple of *Blackwood's Edinburgh Magazine* (founded in 1817). The latter tales condensed the horror and terror of the Gothic novel into original, focused, and often highly stylized short fictions. Their impact on the short story can be seen in the work of Edgar Allan Poe, who imitated and sometimes parodied the tale of terror's 'exaggerated intensity' (Morrison and Baldick 1995: xiii); and in general they were part of a burgeoning Romantic genre, the tale, that comprised part of the short story's own 'distinctive reading context' (Hunter 1990: 86). *Blackwood's*, for instance, promoted a whole range of short fictional forms under the denomination 'tale', including tales of terror, regional tales, fictional autobiographies, sketches, narrative essays, mock-journalism, and parodies. As it rose in both popularity and prominence in the early years of the nineteenth century, the tale brought the features of the novelistic and the non-novelistic into more subtle relation than did bluebooks and Evangelical tracts—albeit still not, as in *Caleb Williams*, to be assimilated or made necessarily to cohere.

Toward a Time of Tales

James Raven's publishing statistics for the second half of the eighteenth century show that the spike in novel sales beginning in 1780 was accompanied by a similar spike in the publication of fiction in magazines (1992: 34). But as noted in the previous section, boundaries between novels, little novels, tales, and redactions can be difficult to make out in these years. This would change in the Romantic period as a distinct genre of short fiction—the tale—took shape out of what Tim Killick describes as 'a multitude of disparate precursory influences' (2008: 11). 'Instead of compressed novels and stories that read like extracts from romances,' he explains, 'short fiction began to pursue its own narrative strategies' (31). It is fair to say that where the short fictional forms discussed above show signs of registering the impact of the novel, the Romantic tale, although clearly influenced by the novel, was also popular enough to influence in turn its more established sibling. Indeed, if we look at generic descriptions used by authors and publishers, the Romantic period was quite literally on the way to becoming a time of tales. Collections of short tales were on the rise from the 1810s. And as Peter Garside notes, starting in 1820 (and continuing through that decade), the word 'tale' became the most popular generic title used for fictional works, surpassing both 'romance' and 'novel' (2000: 50–1).

But 'tale', like 'novel' a century earlier, was a loose designation. Many novelists, for instance, called their works 'tales' in order to escape the novel's associations with frivolity, exaggeration, political radicalism, and immorality. And a tale could refer very generally—as it still can—to a story or narrative: thus any novel could be a tale. But the word also gained several specific associations in the Romantic period, and these associations helped define the tale as a distinct genre even as they proved attractive to novelists. One of these was with the didactic—with 'moral tales' such as those written in the eighteenth century by Jean-François Marmontel, or, later, by educational writers, including More and Maria Edgeworth. A second association was with the oral, or with talk. In her 1832 preface to the Bentley Standard Novels edition of *Canterbury Tales* (1797–1805), Harriet Lee says that she and her sister and co-writer, Sophia, titled the work 'merely in badinage . . . as being a proverbial phrase for gossiping long stories'.[9] Interestingly, Ann Lemoine published a chapbook collection of four Gothic bluebooks called *Canterbury Tales* in 1802. The title page epigraph, which reads, 'When aught that's wonderful is told, | It shall for ever hence be call'd | A Canterbury tale', adds the further suggestion of marvellous talk—as in a 'tall tale'. The word's association with the oral would be significantly deepened after Scott's *Tales of My Landlord* (first series 1816) explicitly linked orality to tradition and local history. As he explains in the Dedication to the first volume in the series, these tales were meant to be 'illustrative of ancient Scottish manners, and of the traditions of [his fellow countrymen's] respective districts'. Scott did not create the tale's association with the local or the regional single-handedly: in calling his new series 'tales' he drew upon the national tales of Edgeworth and Sydney Owensen. But his popularity was such that his use of the word was a leading factor in the genre's rise.

The word 'tale' may have been employed by writers hoping to avoid the associations—if not the devices—of the novel. Yet it was also a genre in its own right, one that shared some features with the novel but which had features of its own to set it apart. Clara Reeve made the tale a subgenre of the novel in the *Progress of Romance* (1785), a book now well known for its attempts to distinguish between the novel and the romance and for arguing that the latter 'sprung up' from the 'ruins' of the former.[10] Late in her dialogue, Reeve's spokeswoman, Hortensius, turns to 'tales and fables', which she calls 'another species of the same genus of writing [novels and stories original], which will make some variety in our progress' (2.54). Like Harrison, Reeve is not entirely clear about where tales fit in the generic spectrum. She places them under the 'genus' of the novel, but the terms she uses to describe tales make them sound more like romance—at least as Reeve defines it. That is, the tales she describes 'treat of fabulous persons and things' more than they give 'a picture of real life and manners' (1.111); they are a kind of romance-after-novels, or romance

---

[9] Harriet and Sophia Lee, *The Canterbury Tales* (London: Bentley, 1832), viii.

[10] Clara Reeve, *The Progress of Romance, through Times, Countries and Manners*, 2 vols (Colchester: W. Keymer, 1785), 1.8.

highly conscious of the presence and popularity of novels. Appended to the *Progress of Romance* is Reeve's own oriental tale, *The History of Charoba*, which she provides as an example of early Egyptian romance. In Reeve's account and example, the tale appears to be a mixed form, one that allows for marvellous events even as it offers descriptions of real life and manners. English editions of the *Arabian Nights* would highlight a similar kind of mixing. In his *Tales of the East* (1812), for instance, Henry Weber points to the *Nights'* 'superabundance of the marvellous' while claiming, too, that the individual tales 'give perfect insight into the private habits, and domestic comforts and deprivations of the orientals'.[11]

The same confusion about the tale is evident in Leigh Hunt's anthology, *Classic Tales, Serious and Lively* (1806–7). But Hunt and his fellow editor, Thomas Reynell, go farther than Reeve does in suggesting that the tale is a genre in its own right. The first writer introduced in this five-volume collection is Henry Mackenzie, some of whose *Lounger* and *Mirror* tales had also appeared in *The New Novelist's Magazine*. Hunt explains that although there are places of 'delicate pathos' in novels such as *The Man of Feeling* (1771) and *Julia de Roubigné* (1777), Mackenzie's 'want of experience, which made him an imitator in his essays, made him an imitator in his novels'.[12] 'It is only as a writer of tales', Hunt states, 'that Mackenzie can claim any originality at all' (1.4). *Classic Tales* features two works by Mackenzie, both of them tales: 'Louisa Venoni' and 'The Story of La Roche'.

Hunt's emphasis on the tale leads him to a rather unorthodox grouping of writers and texts—at least compared with the two anthologies of the novel that appeared just a few years later: Anna Barbauld's *The British Novelists* (1810) and Walter Scott's *Ballantyne's Novelist's Library* (1821–4). Along with Mackenzie, Hunt includes works by Voltaire, Johnson (his *Rambler* stories, not *Rasselas*), Marmontel, and John Hawkesworth, who is described as 'an English miscellaneous writer...whose talents are in nothing more conspicuous than in the few moral tales which are interspersed in his works'. *Classic Tales* bills itself, in fact, as the 'only uniform and distinct collection of the moral tales of Hawkesworth' (4.219).

The confusion in these early attempts to distinguish the tale points not only to the multitudinous character of eighteenth-century fiction, but also to a key marker of the genre's identity: its unique mix of romance and novelistic features. Hunt's co-editor, Reynell, describes Marmontel's tales as 'a mixture of nature and romance; in which the fable is romance, and the characters are in nature' (3.226). And later masters of the genre, such as James Hogg, used the tale to mix minute descriptions of rural life with accounts of marvellous and miraculous events, as if stories of old—like the supposedly

---

[11] *Tales of the East: Comprising the most Popular Romances of Oriental Origin; and the best Imitations by European Authors*, 3 vols (Edinburgh: John Ballantyne & Co., 1812), 1.i–ii.

[12] *Classic Tales, Serious and Lively*, ed. Leigh Hunt, 5 vols (London: John Hunt and Carew Reynell, 1806–7), 1.9.

outdated forms of the communities attached to them—still shadowed the modern, post-Enlightenment world of Hogg's urban readership. Of course, the novel, too, was a mixed form. To distinguish the kinds of mixing that featured in the tale, it is necessary to note not only what was mixed—the natural and the supernatural in Hogg; journalism and the rural sketch in Hogg's fellow *Blackwood's* writer, John Galt—but also how such materials were mixed. In other words, it is necessary to show what the tale does or does not do with the various forms it draws from. Unlike the novel, for instance, which increasingly came to synthesize and assimilate its disparate materials and discourses, the tale remained open to the forms and content that surrounded it and in many cases made no attempt at synthesis.

The Romantic tale, then, can be characterized as a genre that moves beyond the 'little novels' of eighteenth-century magazines, reprints, and redactions but which maintains the miscellaneous character of that same period's fictional output. Many tales in fact advertised themselves in just these terms. In his 'Address to the Reader' in *Tales of a Traveller* (1824), Washington Irving compares the contents of his volumes to the contents of 'an ill packed travelling trunk': memories, fictions, history, and descriptions of specific places become jumbled and confused following the bumps and shifts of travel. And in *Chronicles of the Canongate* (1827), which at one point was provisionally titled 'The Canongate Miscellany', Scott's author-persona, Chrystal Croftangry, originally entertains the idea of 'sustaining a publication of a miscellaneous nature, as like to the Spectator, or the Guardian, the Mirror or the Lounger', but decides in the end to publish in book form. Chrystal's first thought regarding his miscellany is to set up 'shop' as an antiquarian. However, 'as antiquarian articles interest but few customers', he proposes 'also to have a corresponding shop for Sentiment, Dialogues, and Disquisitions'—or as he describes it, 'a sort of green-grocer's stall set up in front of my ironmongery wares, garlanding the rusty memorial of ancient times with cresses, cabbages, leeks, and water purpy'.[13]

Scott turned to the short tale partly for financial reasons: as Claire Lamont explains, his creditors had claims on a new novel and *Chronicles*, a two-volume collection of Tales, was clearly enough not a novel ('Essay on the Text', 293). That he could do so in 1827, after drawing upon (and promoting) the tale's associations for years in his novels, suggests just how established the genre had become. As noted above, this was partly due to Scott's own success as a writer of historical fiction. But partly, too, it was due to the work of writers such as Hogg and Galt, who, in reacting against both the formal features and the progressive historicism of the Waverley novels, gave to the tale what Ian Duncan describes as 'its most striking formal development' (2007: 35). Scott had written and published short fiction throughout his career—including for *Blackwood's Magazine*. But the tales he wrote

---

[13] Walter Scott, *Chronicles of the Canongate*, ed. Claire Lamont (Edinburgh: University of Edinburgh Press, 2000), ch. 5; 51.

for *Chronicles of the Canongate* and those he published soon after in *The Keepsake*, a literary annual, show him explicitly engaging with a form mastered by his competitors. This engagement is most evident in the tales' formal, geographical, and temporal borders, which, in their open-endedness, challenge the kinds of novelistic resolution readers expected from the Author of Waverley and often resist what Scott calls 'a natural conclusion' (*Chronicles*, 285).

Like Scott, Galt and Hogg also developed elaborate framing devices to hold their disparate materials together without assimilating them into one coherent narrative. A fictional correspondent who listens in while a group of small-town residents gathers to listen to—and comment on—letters sent by a family from the same town on excursion in London; a cloth-merchant travelling by steamboat and repeating for his audience the different tales he hears from passengers getting on and off the vessel; a shepherd chronicling the events, characters, and legends of a rural parish in the Scottish Borders: such are a few of the ways different tales, parodies, sketches, and journalistic accounts are held together in their work. But stand-alone collections of tales well before the genre's heyday had also used framing devices to do just the same. Some are quite basic and simply emphasize the didactic nature of the collection. In the Advertisement to Mary Linwood's *Leicestershire Tales* (1808), we are told that '[t]he author of the following tales, by exhibiting vice in its inevitable deformity, and virtue in its never-changing loveliness, hopes to impress upon the youthful mind a sense of the advantages and importance of moral rectitude'. And in *London Tales; or, Reflective Portraits* (1814), dozens of tales—some only a paragraph or two—are brought together in two volumes 'to shew to minds, not yet troubled with the strong propensies of our nature, the mournful effects that sometimes arise from yielding to the passions under circumstances which render indulgence a crime'.[14]

More elaborate framing devices were used for more ambitiously conceived collections. In *Canterbury Tales*, Harriet and Sophia Lee introduce a traveller (as Chaucer did before them) who is stranded at an inn on account of snow and who proposes to the six other stranded passengers that 'each of the company would relate the most remarkable story he, or she, ever knew or heard of'.[15] The character and nationality of each teller go some way toward accounting for the kind of tale he or she tells. This design also allowed the Lees to keep adding to their collection and for parts of it to be removed or anthologized elsewhere. *The Canterbury Tales* still reads like the compressed, short novels of the eighteenth century (and this perhaps explains their inclusion in Bentley's Standard Novel series); but the dramatic rise of the tale that occurred between the 1790s

---

[14] Mrs Roche, *London Tales*, 2 vols (London: John Booth, 1814), 1.iii. Sometimes attributed—falsely—to Regina Maria Roche.

[15] Harriet Lee, *Canterbury Tales for the Year 1797* (London: G. G. & J. Robinson, 1797), xix. Vol. 2 (by Sophia Lee) was published in 1798 and vol. 3 (both Harriet and Sophia) in 1799. Two additional volumes were added in 1804 and 1805.

(when the collection was first published) and the 1830s (when it was reissued) must have inspired Harriet to claim her place in the genre's history. She describes her tales as 'professedly adapted to different countries' and as 'abruptly commencing' or 'breaking suddenly' from one kind of writing to another (1832 edn: viii). Both features became more pronounced as the tale came into its own as a form. The latter feature in particular highlights what the tale held on to that the novel didn't: an openness to surrounding content and the lack of a need, as yet, to fully assimilate the various parts or features that comprised it.

As it appeared in stand-alone collections, magazines, and literary annuals, the tale pushed the novel to consolidate its boundaries even as it developed its own mix of features to challenge the novel on its established ground. But in the end, as with *Caleb Williams's* fuller, more complete account of 'things as they are', the novel won out in its generic competition with half-told and mangled tales. Such tales, as the subtitle of an 1820 collection of *Tales* by Mary Anne Grant claims, may have been *Founded on Facts*—on discrete instances or places, many of which did not need to be connected to a larger whole. But what writers like Scott did so well was to assemble these facts, instances, and places into something that resembled history—'blending them', as Godwin wrote in 'Of History and Romance' (*c*.1797), 'into one continuous and indiscernible mass'.[16] Indeed, as readers came to expect the kinds of consistency and closure delivered by the novel, short fictional forms such as the tale, in order to compete at all, had to become more adept at finding images and tensions suitable for similar resolution in smaller form. The result was what we now call the short story proper. There was nothing inevitable about this. As with the mixed form of novel in the late eighteenth century, the Romantic-period tale suggests multiple possible futures for short fiction.

But taking a longer view, two things become clear. The first is that many of the short fictional forms that existed before novels continued to circulate and sometimes to thrive well after the novel became an established genre. These forms competed with the novel in the expanded fiction market of the late eighteenth century, drawing on its features or reacting against them, but becoming in the process part of the novel's collective system. It is also clear, however, that short fictional forms such as the tale would never be the same after novels, especially in the Romantic period when the novel became—in Duncan's words—the 'ascendant genre of national life' (2007: 28). This ascendancy was not without its setbacks: after the market crash of 1826, when three-volume novels were deemed risky investments by nervous publishers, the shorter tale was an obvious fit for the new miscellanies that flourished in London, Edinburgh, Dublin, and Philadelphia. But it was not long before the tale's solid place in the literary market gave way to the more controlled forms of the serialized novel and the short story. Indeed, even so established a tale writer

---

[16] Godwin, 'Of History and Romance', in *Caleb Williams*, ed. Hindle, 368.

as John Galt felt the pressure. The short fiction he published in the 1830s—in *Stories of the Study* (1833) and in *Fraser's Magazine*—is not at all like the compressed novels of the later eighteenth century. Nor, however, does it resemble the loose, disorderly fictions he wrote for *Blackwood's* a decade earlier. Instead, Galt's later stories aim for what Edgar Allan Poe would call a 'single effect', assimilating their materials in ways similar to the novel, but on a smaller scale.

27

Children's and Juvenile Literature

M. O. GRENBY

Children and the Novel

In January 1783, Mrs Chapone, Mrs Delaney, Mrs Thrale, and the dowager Duchess of Portland discussed the novel *Cecilia, or Memoirs of an Heiress*, published a year earlier, in the presence of its author, Frances Burney. Burney reported the duchess to have exclaimed, '[I]t should be the *study of Youth!* ... And it ought to be put in every *Nursery*, it is so innocent and so pure, and if *I* had the care of any young people, it should be the first Book I would put in their Hands.'[1] What an inhabitant of the nursery would have made of the novel's five-volume account of a young woman's entrance into London life, and her protracted courtship, is open to debate (although the basic plot of an orphan adrift in a hostile world would remain a staple of much children's fiction). And there can be little doubt that the 67-year-old Duchess's opinions were governed less by contemporary pedagogic practice than literary enthusiasm (she had read *Cecilia* three times in six months). But her views should nevertheless remind us that books written solely for young people were not necessarily what sprang to mind in the later eighteenth century as the most suitable reading matter for children. This is something that many histories of children's literature omit. Certainly, it was during the later eighteenth century—and, as we shall see, the 1780s in particular—that fiction especially for the young first became established as a separate, and thriving, literary form in Britain. But this is by no means to say that this new product suddenly became ubiquitous.

Many pre-Victorian children didn't encounter children's fiction at all. A substantial number, of course, were largely disconnected from literary culture by indigence or illiteracy. But lots of those young people who did consume books continued to use material designed primarily for adults. For instance, in the 1740s, the decade often held to have witnessed the birth of modern children's literature, the young Edward Gibbon (born 1737) was reading Pope's Homer, Dryden's Virgil, Ovid's *Metamorphoses*, and the *Arabian Nights*

---

[1] Frances Burney, *Journals and Letters*, selected by Peter Sabor and Lars E. Troide (London: Penguin, 2001), 202.

Entertainments, before, at eleven, being given access to his grandfather's library, where he devoured the collection of poetry, romances, histories, and travels. In some families, little had changed by the early nineteenth century. Elizabeth Barrett (later Browning, born 1806) was reading 'adult' novels by the age of six, Pope's Homer at eight and, shortly afterwards, Dante, Voltaire, Wollstonecraft, Kant, Spinoza, and de Staël. Clearly these were precocious children, but the same absence of books designed specifically for the young is noticeable in probably the majority of recorded childhoods in this period, even (perhaps especially) in much less bookish and prosperous families.

What confuses the matter is that the distinction could be very blurred between literature for adults and literature for 'young gentlemen and ladies' (properly supposed 'to be *Children*, till they are *fourteen*, and *young persons* till they are at least *twenty-one*', according to Sarah Trimmer, herself a successful children's author and an important, if severe, critic of juvenile literature).[2] What would now be called 'crossover' works were common: titles originally aimed at adults that were quickly appropriated by or for young readers. Notable examples include John Bunyan's *Pilgrim's Progress* (1678–84) and Jonathan Swift's *Gulliver's Travels* (1726), or the many chapbook tales and fairy stories that continued to circulate despite warnings about their unsuitability. As the Duchess of Portland's avid approval of *Cecilia* shows, it could be argued that the eighteenth-century novel as a whole should be regarded as a kind of 'crossover' product. Mid-century novels, notably those of Samuel Richardson, were often held up as appropriate, morally improving reading for young adults. But against this, very strenuous cautions against youthful novel-reading were constantly appearing, especially later in the century, in parenting manuals, pedagogic treatises, and conduct books. More relaxed commentators were prepared to permit the young to read novels so long as responsible adults selected proper titles and were on hand to explain moral lessons. But the deplorable long-term ill effects of, in particular, girls' unsupervised novel-reading were frequently depicted, often actually in novels, both adults' and children's. Indeed, this anxiety about the effect of fiction on the *young*, as well as the female, was central to the development of the anti-novel tradition as it evolved from *Don Quixote* to novels like Charlotte Lennox's *The Female Quixote* (1752) and Jane Austen's *Northanger Abbey* (1818).

But if these warnings against novel-reading were common, did children and young people actually heed them? The available evidence—letters, journals and memoirs, inscriptions and marginalia, records of book circulation—presents a mixed picture (see Grenby 2011: 111–16). Some children recorded having their access to novels strictly forbidden or rationed: Charlotte Yonge (born 1823), for instance, when about eleven, was allowed one chapter of a Walter Scott novel per day, 'provided I first read twenty pages of Goldsmith's *Rome* or some equally solid book' (Sanders 2000: 216). Others seem to

---

[2] Sarah Trimmer, *Guardian of Education*, 1 (1802), 65–6.

have suffered no such restriction. Ann Radcliffe's Gothic novels were evidently popular with girls much younger than Austen's seventeen-year-old Catherine Morland. The celebrated child diarist Marjorie Fleming (born 1803) was perhaps not especially unusual in reading Radcliffe's *Mysteries of Udolpho* (1794) when she was seven, alongside books more clearly designed for children by Maria Edgeworth and Sarah Trimmer. Boys read 'adult' fiction too. Jan Fergus has pointed out that the pupils at Rugby School and Daventry Academy were the local bookseller's best customers for novels (2006: 183–93). Children's use of circulating and subscription libraries was far from unknown. Proprietors could be apprehensive, the library rules demanding that an adult stand surety for any books borrowed, but some eager young readers record borrowing a good deal of fiction. The apprentice cutler Joseph Hunter (born 1983), when only fourteen or fifteen, borrowed *The Mysteries of Udolpho* and the same author's *The Italian*, Horace Walpole's *The Castle of Otranto*, Elizabeth Inchbald's *Nature and Art*, and what he called 'a very silly love tale': Martha Hugill's *The Castle of Mowbray*.[3]

Abridgements of novels intended for the young were not uncommon either. As early as 1756, *The Paths of Virtue Delineated* was providing in under 250 pages 'the history in miniature of the celebrated Pamela, Clarissa Harlowe, and Sir Charles Grandison' for 'the youth of both sexes, for whose use it is solely intended'. Although these abridgements could be conscientiously justified—for children were 'too apt to be disgusted' when moral truths were 'inculcated by dictatorial wisdom' while fiction's 'living pictures affect the minds of youth by an irresistible charm'—some publishers were no doubt motivated as much by the chance to bring down the price of novels and thus extend the market.[4] In the 1770s, for example, R. Snagg was printing six- or nine-penny versions of the novels of Richardson, Fielding, Smollett, Lennox, and others, all cut down to under a hundred duodecimo pages.

The Rise of the Novel for Children

Despite the residual presence of so much 'adult literature' in children's lives, it is undoubtedly the case that a new, commercialized children's literature began to flourish in Britain in the second half of the eighteenth century. This 'rise of children's literature' was due partly to the same things as led to the 'rise of the novel' as a whole: technological advances, demographic developments, changing literacy rates, socio-economic shifts, and so on. But some factors were more specific. Historians are now sceptical about the idea that

---

[3] 'Journal of Joseph Hunter', British Library Add. MSS 24,879, fols 5r-v, 17r-v, 26r, and 29v. See also Colclough, Chapter 30.

[4] *The Paths of Virtue Delineated; or, The History in Miniature of the Celebrated Pamela, Clarissa Harlowe, and Sir Charles Grandison* (London: for the Booksellers, 1768), iv–vi.

modern childhood was newly 'invented' in the eighteenth century, but all sorts of evidence—from sermons and conduct books to poetry and portraiture—clearly shows that childhood and parenthood (particularly motherhood) were being accorded much more value, represented as both personally fulfilling and nationally important. A concomitant willingness to invest both emotionally and financially in children was obviously essential to the foundation of children's literature.

Equally crucial was the gradual alteration in attitudes to the mainstream novel. In the early part of the century novels were expected to provide moral education for readers of all ages. As Felicity Hughes points out, the words 'young people' or 'our youth' appear in virtually every review or essay on the novel until at least the mid-eighteenth century, and the 'debate on the relative merits of Richardson and Fielding seems to have revolved around the question of which novel was more appropriate for the moral, social and literary education of British youth' (1978: 543). Hughes argues that the novel continued to be understood as an educative medium, and that audiences and critics demanded that it remain suitable for young people, until the cultural ruptures of the 1880s. Perhaps. But it is certainly the case that some later eighteenth-century novels were becoming less unambiguously moral, more experimental, and, even simply in physical terms, more suited to an adult audience—something exemplified by the work of John Cleland, say, or Laurence Sterne. This coincided with the rise of the novel for children. Put topographically, if the novel for adults vacated its ground, space was left for a new product which could fulfil its moralistic and didactic functions.

Sarah Fielding, sister of the author of *Tom Jones*, friend of Richardson, and herself already the author of the 'Moral Romance' *The Adventures of David Simple* (1744), appears to have been among the first to exploit this opening. Her *The Governess; or, Little Female Academy* was published in 1749, explicitly 'Calculated for the Entertainment and Instruction of Young Ladies in their Education'. It may have been inspired by the second part of Richardson's *Pamela* (1741), which was largely concerned with children's education and included a scene in which Pamela encounters girls from a flourishing boarding school rather like the one depicted in *The Governess*. But by extending this into the first full-length novel for children (and the first of a long line of school stories) Fielding broke new ground, establishing the principle that an extended piece of fiction could effectively be used as an instructive tool for children. After an initial set piece—'An Account of a Fray, begun and carried on for the sake of an Apple: In which are shewn the sad Effects of Rage and Anger'—the novel settles down to present a series of instructive stories, divided into two sorts. Each of the nine girls, aged seven to fourteen, takes a turn to give an account of her life up until arriving at the school. Interspersed are moral stories, mostly allegorical but involving princesses, giants, dwarves, and fairies. The 'Governess', Mrs Teachum, is seldom actually present, but she carefully monitors the girls, employing the oldest as her agent and demanding regular reports. The girls' accounts of themselves read rather like confessions, or transcripts of sessions on the psychoanalyst's couch. Inexorably the girls internalize the values of the generally unseen but omnipresent Mrs Teachum, losing their wild, passionate individuality, and becoming polite, reasonable, and obedient. The final inset fable tells of a contest to find the happiest bird. The eagle grants the prize to the dove, precisely because she has not attended the debate, preferring to stay at her nest, caring for her fledglings and waiting for the return of her mate. 'Now, my good children', says Mrs Teachum, 'if you will pass thro' this Life with real Pleasure, imitate the *Dove*'—superfluous advice, for they 'had all in their own Minds forestalled the *Eagle's* Judgment'.[5] The girls have been trained to become paragons of nubilty and maternity.

Fielding's novel is a little more slippery than this, however. Acclamation of the bourgeois domestic ideal, into which the girls are apparently being propelled, is undermined by several things. Its fragility is shown by the death of Mrs Teachum's husband and two daughters, and the sudden collapse of the bank which keeps her whole fortune, all of which is briefly described at the very start of the novel. The fact that Mrs Teachum's pupils all come from problematic families, and live in exile at her boarding school, hardly offers an endorsement of bourgeois domesticity either. Nor do the unhappy families living near the school that the pupils sometimes encounter. One of the inset tales—'The Story of Cælia and Chloe'—can be read as an assertion of the importance of female solidarity in countering the disruptive effects of male intrusion, even when the intruder is the eligible bachelor Sempronius. His attempts to decide between Cælia and Chloe set them, temporarily, against each other, but their friendship is soon healed. Indeed, it is difficult not to read the all-female community of Mrs Teachum's school as a utopian alternative to the lives of confined and submissive domesticity into which the girls are being hurried.

Seldom noticed by modern readers of *The Governess* are the sources of the inset stories. These are introduced either as tales that Mrs Teachum has collected for the edification of her pupils, or as manuscripts given to her pupils by relatives which they then share with their classmates. None of these, apparently, are published titles. Likewise, Pamela had invented stories for the children in her care in the second part of Richardson's novel. The use of such 'homemade' texts should not surprise us. They were the precursors of published children's literature. But we should be clear that many children continued to encounter fiction in manuscript form even after commercial children's books had become widely available.

Probably the most notable example of this kind of home-produced literature is contemporary with *Pamela* and *The Governess*: an astonishing collection of hundreds of alphabet, syllable, and lesson cards, most of them delightfully illustrated and decorated, produced in the 1740s by Jane Johnson, wife of an independently wealthy Buckinghamshire vicar (now held in the Lilly Library at Indiana University, Bloomington). These were for the use of her children, some of whom feature in the one piece of extended fiction that Johnson wrote

---

[5] Sarah Fielding, *The Governess; or, Little Female Academy. Being the History of Mrs. Teachum, and Her Nine Girls. With Their Nine Days Amusement* (London: A. Millar, 1749), 236.

and illustrated, called 'A Very Pretty Story to Tell Children When They Are About Five or Six Years of Age' (1744). A great many other homemade children's stories have no doubt been entirely lost, but a few survive, showing that the tradition continued well into the nineteenth century. Among the most notable is 'Stories for Miss Cecilia-Charlotte-Esther Burney, aged five years', a delightful manuscript 'book', written in 1793 by Sophia and Frances Burney (nieces of Frances Burney d'Arblay) and illustrated by their uncle Edward (now held by the Pierpont Morgan Library, New York). Also remarkable is the recently rediscovered 'Maurice, or The Fisher's Cot', written in 1820 by Mary Shelley for Laurette Tighe, the daughter of her friend Lady Mountcashell. Shelley's father, William Godwin, from 1805 the proprietor, with his second wife Mary Jane Clairmont, of a children's book publishing house called the Juvenile Library, declined to print 'Maurice'. But prefaces and dedications to many children's books that *were* published testify that they originated in stories written out by relatives for individual children. Such prefaces apologizing for intruding a private production on the public became conventional, but nevertheless, it would seem likely that even into the nineteenth century, many children's first encounters with fictional texts would have been with personalized stories devised within their households, only a small proportion of which were subsequently published.

That Fielding's *Governess* was not apparently regarded as something entirely original or daring when it appeared in 1749 may be connected with the pre-existence of this tradition of home-produced fiction for children. Also already in existence by 1749 were the first of many collections of short stories for children, such as *A Christmass-Box* (1746) by 'Mary Homebred', which included such simple but not unpalatable moral tales as 'The meanly proud Girl', 'The Undutiful Child', and 'The Advantages of Truth'. At just a few pages each, these were not children's novels but they were an important springboard. Certainly it was sometimes novelists who wrote them. 'Mary Homebred' was actually Mary Collyer, author of the successful Richardsonian novel *Letters from Felicia to Charlotte* (1744–9). Collyer's reasons for writing children's fiction are made clear in one of Felicia's letters, in which a footnote puffs *A Christmass-Box* as the sort of text a caring parent ought to use. Such a book as this, we are told, could 'dress up morality, and the sublimest truths of natural religion, in the easy language of infancy'.[6] Collyer's oldest child (of eight) was born in 1743, so she may simply have been publishing material created first for domestic use. We should note also, though, that her bookseller husband was insolvent in the late 1740s, and, as Collyer put it in another of her works, 'It is in order to contribute to the support and education of my children, I have taken up the pen'.[7] This combination of pedagogic and commercial imperatives would remain characteristic of children's novel authors throughout the period.

---

[6] Mary Collyer, *Letters from Felicia to Charlotte*, vol. 2 (London: J. Payne and J. Bouquet, 1749), 282.

[7] Mary Collyer, *The Death of Abel. Attempted from the German of Mr. Gessner* (London: R. and J. Dodsley, 1761), iv.

Clearly there was a demand for this new product. *The Governess* was a success, going into a fourth edition in 1758. Other, similar works followed, such as Jeanne Marie le Prince de Beaumont's *The Young Misses Magazine* (1757), a collection of instructive stories, many of them fairy tales, linked with instructive dialogues between several 'Young Ladies of Quality' and their governess, Mrs Affable. John Newbery included what can be thought of as miniature novels in his *Lilliputian Magazine*, a periodical advertised in 1751 and 1752 but apparently surviving only in the form of a book combining the first three issues. Incident enough to fill a full volume of a standard novel was crammed into four or five pages. In 'An Adventure of Master Tommy Trusty; And his delivering Miss Biddy Johnson, From the Thieves who were going to murder her', for example, the heroine is kidnapped as a result of the pride she takes in her clothes, taken to a wood outside London, and rescued, in the nick of time, by one of her playmates who impersonates a posse of horsemen. Newbery did not experiment with more sustained narratives until the 1760s, when he published *The Renowned History of Giles Gingerbread* (1764) and *The History of Goody Two-Shoes* (1765), the latter sometimes attributed to Oliver Goldsmith. *Giles Gingerbread*, at a penny for thirty pages, was still essentially a miscellany of instructive material linked by a clunky frame story. Much the same could be said of *Goody Two-Shoes*—it is fundamentally a Cinderella story, showing how the literacy that we see Margery Meanwell acquiring and passing on to others leads to social elevation when she catches the eye of the local magnate. But with its continuous plot developed over 150 pages, with its more fully rounded protagonist, and costing sixpence, it was a more sophisticated item. Margery foils a robbery; proves that the church is not haunted; is accused of witchcraft. Several sagacious tame birds, and a dog that saves Margery's pupils from the collapse of their school building, add interest. The appended story of Margery's brother Tommy neatly rounds off the narrative. Deposed, with his sister, from early affluence by the machinations of Sir Timothy Gripe and Farmer Graspall, he goes abroad, is cast away 'on that Part of the Coast of *Africa* inhabited by the *Hottentots*', makes a fortune by solving a riddle in '*Prester John's* Country', and returns at the moment of Margery's wedding to bestow a vast dowry on her.[8]

Also worth noticing is *Goody*'s politics. The 'Introduction', written, the 'Editor' acknowledges, 'for Children of six Feet high', explains that Sir Timothy Gripe has just become Lord of the Manor of Mouldwell. He allows one man, Farmer Graspall, to take control of all the twelve farms in the parish, deposing the previous honest tenants and ruining the labourers who had happily worked for them. Only Margery's father continues to stand up for their rights, but he is soon defeated by Gripe and Graspall. Nobody remains to prevent their 'tyranny' and they successfully 'reduce the common People to a State of Vassalage' (12). This is the angry social protest of Goldsmith's celebrated narrative

---

[8] Anon., *The History of Little Goody Two-Shoes; Otherwise Called, Mrs. Margery Two-Shoes. With the Means by which She Acquired her Learning and Wisdom, and in Consequence Thereof her Estate* (London: J. Newbery, 1766), 145.

poem *The Deserted Village* (1770). In a more general sense *Goody*, along with much other children's fiction of the period, is a hymn to new, radical bourgeois values. Margery's rise to wealth and status through her assiduity and good sense powerfully articulates an eighteenth-century middle-class ideology. And a close reading of individual episodes reveals a critique of both plebeian and aristocratic practices. Commenting on the funeral of the local dignitary Lady Ducklington, for instance, the narrator attacks the pride and vanity of the elite, even in death, bitterly complaining that the money 'squandered away' on the funeral 'would have been better laid out in little Books for Children, or in Meat, Drink, and Cloathes for the Poor' (46). But the poor are equally condemned for their foolish belief that Lady Ducklington haunts the church after her funeral. Margery shows that the noises they have heard are nothing but a dog. While she educates the poor out of their superstitions, she symbolically exorcizes the spectre of aristocracy, all the while endorsing her own middle-class ethics.

As much as it now seems rather simplistic to talk about the mid-eighteenth-century novel as a form which intrinsically asserts the values of the middle class, many of the early landmark novels written for children do clearly emphasize the importance of rising above an improvident and irrational plebeian culture and of reforming the upper classes. Thomas Day's *The History of Sandford and Merton*, published in three volumes between 1783 and 1789, is the best articulation of the latter trend, enacting a fantasy of the infiltration and rectification of the social elite. The frame narrative, surrounding a set of inset stories that Day had appropriated from various sources, describes the education of Tommy Merton, the pampered and ignorant son of a rich, slave-owning family just returned from Jamaica, and Harry Sandford, son of an industrious farmer. They first meet when Harry, fully at home in nature, for this is the most Rousseauvian of texts, appears in the nick of time to remove a large snake from Tommy's leg. Impressed with Harry, Tommy's parents decide that their son should be educated, with Harry, by the clergyman Mr Barlow. He instructs the boys using a combination of practical life lessons, the fables that punctuate the narrative, and some blunt lectures. Barlow continually attacks the decadence of the upper classes and praises the diligence, plainness, self-reliance, and philanthropy of yeomen like Farmer Sandford. Sometimes this leads to genuinely radical sentiments: 'the rich do nothing and produce nothing', he tells Tommy at one point, 'and the poor every thing that is really useful'.[9] This is not an attempt to undermine social hierarchy, but rather a call for the elite to refashion themselves according to the values of the middle classes, which Tommy, after one or two relapses, duly does. To modern critics, concerned with the politics of gender, Day's book can also seem to voice concerns about British masculinity. Contemporaries were very aware of this too, Day's 1791 biographer being clear that *Sandford and Merton* was written 'to guard the rising generation against

---

[9] Thomas Day, *The History of Sandford and Merton, a Work Intended for the Use of Children*, 3 vols (London: John Stockdale, 1783–9), 3.89.

the infection of... effeminacy' by contrasting the 'manly virtues in young *Sandford*' with 'the feebler character of young *Merton*, a boy bred up in... effeminate indulgence'.[10]

Day uses Harry, meanwhile, as an agent of satire, rather like Montesquieu's Usbek in *Lettres persanes* (1721). In the Mertons' home he annoys his hosts by being wholly unimpressed by their finery. Why should silver plates and cups be valued, he asks, if cheaper items will not only serve as well but will relieve their anxiety about damage and theft? But should he not like 'a coach to carry you about', asks Mrs Merton, as if in direct reference to the 'Coach and Six' ostentatiously promised by Newbery in both *Giles Gingerbread* and *Goody Two-Shoes* as the definitive symbol of wealth and prestige. Harry's rather Puritanical answer—'I don't want to ride, because I can walk wherever I chuse' (1.26)—exposes a fracture between the ideological positions of John Newbery and Thomas Day. Though we might call both purveyors of 'bourgeois' values, Newbery's claim that education will, or should, lead to social mobility is absent from *Sandford and Merton*. Patient industry brings its own rewards in Day's fiction, but he clearly disagreed that affluence should be in itself the object of a child's ambition, mistrusted the idea that wealth could be suddenly acquired, and resisted Newbery's promise that education and enterprise could disturb the prevailing social order.

The Children's Novel

In other ways too, *Sandford and Merton* represents a new turn in children's fiction. It has been claimed that its origins lie in stories written for the private use of the children of his friend Richard Lovell Edgeworth (Blackman 1862: 119). But Day's preface tells a different story. He explains that, being unable to find suitable books for his own adopted child, he had carefully selected various passages from Plutarch's *Lives*, Xenophon's histories, Defoe's *Robinson Crusoe*, Henry Brooke's novel *The Fool of Quality* (1766–70) and other such sources. He had planned to publish such an anthology, but decided that this method was 'defective, as the objects would overwhelm the tender mind of a child by their variety and number'. The result was his determination to produce 'a continued narrative; so that every story might appear to rise naturally out of the subject', and linked by characters who 'speak and behave according to the order of nature'. Further, Day 'endeavoured to throw into it a greater degree of elegance and ornament than is usually met with in such compositions; preserving at the same time a sufficient degree of simplicity to make it intelligible to very young children'. 'It is to them I have written;', he concluded, so 'it is from their applause alone I shall estimate my success' (1.vi–ix).

---

[10] James Kier, *An Account of the Life and Writings of Thomas Day, Esq.* (London: John Stockdale, 1791), 80–2.

Several things were new here, all of which contributed to the establishment of the children's novel. The determination to write primarily for children, not their parents or teachers, was one. The emphasis on literary quality, as being equally important as educational utility, was another. A third was Day's conviction that children should be presented with situations familiar to them. But what most set apart the children's literature of the 1780s from that which had gone before was the disillusionment with anthologies, abridgements, and adaptations. William St Clair (2004) claims that these increasingly dominated the literary marketplace following the ending of the de facto system of perpetual copyright in 1774, particularly in the children's market. Purely in numerical terms this may have been so, but a countervailing trend was a pronounced enthusiasm for more coherent narratives. Probably the most successful children's title of the 1770s was *A Father's Instructions; Consisting of Moral Tales, Fables, and Reflections* (1775–7, with a third part in 1800). It was a compilation of narratives, anecdotes, experiments, and verses, some original and some borrowed, assembled by the Unitarian physician Thomas Percival. It merely gestured towards a linking narrative through the use of recurrent characters who occasionally requested or related the stories. By contrast, the most successful children's books of the 1780s put a premium on both cohesiveness and originality.

Characteristic here were the moral tales written by Dorothy Kilner and her friend Mary Ann Maze, afterwards Kilner (she married Dorothy's brother in 1774). Between them they pseudonymously published more than a dozen children's novels in the 1780s and 1790s, contributing to, or rather helping to form, a number of emerging genres. *The Adventures of a Pincushion* (c.1780) and *Memoirs of a Peg-Top* (c.1790), both by Mary Ann, were it-narratives, or novels of circulation, in the tradition of those recently written for adults. Dorothy's *The Life and Perambulation of a Mouse* (c.1785) and *The Rational Brutes; or, Talking Animals* (1799) helped to establish the animal story as a core children's literature subgenre, while her *The Village School* (c.1795) and *First Going to School, or, The Story of Tom Brown, and his Sisters* (1806) did the same for the school story. Others, such as Dorothy's *The Holyday Present, Containing Anecdotes of Mr & Mrs Jennett, and their Little Family* (c.1780) and Mary Ann's *Jemima Placid, or, The Advantages of a Good-Nature* (c.1783), were family stories, relating the minor incidents of domestic life—sibling quarrels, broken toys, ornaments broken, rivals reconciled. The Kilners were only two among many women writers who, in the 1780s and 1790s, produced this largely new kind of sustained moral tale. Others included Sarah Trimmer, whose avian story, *Fabulous Histories* (1786), later published as *The History of the Robins*, remained in print for over a century; the bookseller Lucy Peacock (*Martin & James, or The Reward of Integrity*, 1791); and Mary Pilkington, who specialized in biographies, both fictionalized and factual (*Biography for Girls*, 1798; *Memoirs of Celebrated Female Characters*, 1804). Elizabeth Kilner, Mary Ann's niece, produced *A Puzzle for a Curious Girl* (1801–2), in which the heroine strives to find out what article her mother has secretly purchased. Although she is continually reprimanded for it, the reader cannot help but share her curiosity, so that the moral tale doubles as a mystery story. Compilations of short pieces bound together by frame narratives did remain popular too. These included Mary Wollstonecraft's *Original Stories from Real Life* (1788) and *Evenings at Home* (1792–6) by John Aikin and his sister Anna Laetitia Barbauld. Maria Edgeworth published her stories in various collections, some of them unconnected, others tracing the gradual development of a single character. As she wrote more stories she shuffled them between these collections, demonstrating an increasingly nuanced awareness of the importance of matching particular stories to particular readers.

With their focus on manners, personal development, domestic tribulations, interpersonal relations gone awry and then resolved, these children's stories were not dissimilar to the novels of Frances Burney or Jane Austen say, although of course they did not revolve around courtship and they ended in morals not marriages. Their authors were generally anxious to point out that the work emerged from their own actual experiences of childcare: often true, no doubt, but also a rhetorical strategy to deflect the criticism they feared of what might be thought their 'unqualified' entrance into print, and perhaps also an assertion that only those directly involved in childcare had the qualifications necessary to produce this kind of writing. But regardless of whether or not these novels did come out of lived experience, in a generic sense they were ostentatiously exercises in realism, even when an element of fantasy was (usually apologetically) introduced, as in the tales of talking animals. They dealt with the ordeals of ordinary children's lives: a boy getting into a fight about a stolen kite; a girl so excited about attending a ball that she vomits on her friends in the carriage taking her there. They often introduced harsh social realities: beggars, gypsies, servants, slaves. And even if most of the actual readers of these books did not live in comfortable houses, set in spacious grounds, in semi-rural environments, with devoted if firm parents who were always attentive to their well-being, the books were designed to present an idyll that was recognizable and realizable, unlike the world of fairy tales.

Realism, a 'domestic' morality, and sustained narrative were also features of the fiction being published by those who took over John Newbery's business (he had died in 1767). The best of these were probably those written by Richard Johnson. His *Letters Between Master Tommy and Miss Nancy Goodwill* (1770) might be called an epistolary novel for it comprised a series of letters written between a girl and her brother, away at school. They swap gossip, factual information, and stories. His *Juvenile Trials* (1771) was also innovative, describing an elaborate and rather Foucauldian children's game in which children learn to discipline themselves, putting their friends on trial 'for Robbing Orchards, Telling Fibs, and other Heinous Offences' as the book's subtitle puts it. The 1770s, though, seem to have seen a slump in the production of children's books before an upsurge in the 1780s—a pattern that neatly matches the recent identification of a temporary dip in the number of novels published for adults in the same period (Raven 2000: 26–7). Moreover, the moral tales that came to dominate children's literature from the 1780s were qualitatively different in a number of important ways. First, while Johnson was a male 'hack' writing for money (his account books survive, showing that he was paid £5 5s. for *Letters Between Master Tommy and Miss Nancy Goodwill*, for instance, and another £1 11s. 6d. to revise it in 1775), the dominant authors of the 1780s and 1790s were amateurs, predominantly female, publishing reluctantly, so they said, only to share their pedagogical expertise. Second, the moral tales of the 1780s and beyond were more substantial and better-produced, and thus more expensive. Or rather some of them were, for as the century progressed, children's literature became more stratified both in terms of the age of the intended audience and the books' cost. Whereas Newbery's early publications had done double duty as spelling books and fiction for those who could already read, by the 1780s the 'children's novel' was quite distinct from the collections of simple, short stories, and dialogues used to teach infant literacy, such as Anna Laetitia Barbauld's *Lessons for Children* (1778–9) and Ellenor Fenn's *Cobwebs to Catch Flies* (1784). There were also distinct categories within the 'children's novel'. When, in 1793, John Marshall, the dominant children's publisher after Newbery, issued a catalogue of his 'Publications for the Instruction and Amusement of Young Minds' his titles ranged from 3s. per volume (*The Conversations of Emily*) to some at as little as a penny (*A New Instructive History of Miss Patty Proud, or The Downfal [sic] of Vanity*). Bindings varied too, providing a useful index of the diversification of intended markets. Newbery and some of his competitors had pioneered the use of brightly coloured but fairly cheap 'Dutch floral boards', used across his range to make his wares attractive to young consumers. From the 1780s John Marshall adapted this ploy, offering his penny, twopenny, and fourpenny publications in 'gilt paper'. His sixpenny books could be had in this binding too, but were also sold for ninepence bound in red leather, the format in which he offered all his shilling and two-shilling books. But more expensive titles were sold simply in sheets so that purchasers could custom-bind them themselves.

As much larger numbers of children's novels appeared over the next decades, issuing from an increasing number of publishers, the basic formula established in the 1780s remained fairly standard. The novels could be shorter or longer, more or less sophisticated, but the teaching of simple moral and developmental lessons—to control one's temper, not to complain of trivial hardships, not to waste time—through realistic stories of family life remained at the core of many children's reading experiences. Some authors did begin to give more agency to their young protagonists and to add elements of adventure, perhaps even in exotic settings far from the home. It is young Ludovico, for instance, the eponymous hero of Barbara Hofland's *The Son of a Genius; a Tale for Youth* (1812) who, rejecting his father's 'artistic' self-indulgence in favour of industry and integrity, manages to secure the well-being of his family. The same author's *Young Crusoe; or, The Shipwrecked Boy* (1828) was one of many early nineteenth-century Robinsonades, following J. D. Wyss's *Swiss Family Robinson* (first published in English in 1814), that paved the way for the adventure stories of the next generation, such as James Fenimore Cooper's *Leather-Stocking Tales* (from 1823) and Captain Marryat's sea stories (from 1829), popular with children from the first though not initially intended for them. Other forms of fiction were available too. Charles and Mary Lamb had produced *Tales from Shakespear*, in 1807, and, from 1823, British children were also able to enjoy *German Popular Stories*, the first translation of the fairy stories collected by the Brothers Grimm. In fact, having first been translated for adults in the early eighteenth century, collections of Charles Perrault's and Madame d'Aulnoy's fairy tales, along with a few classics of the indigenous British tradition, had been available throughout the preceding fifty years in various anthologies and redactions. Often, publishers had done what they could to conform the fairy story with the moral tale, as in *Fat and Lean or The Fairy Queen, Exhibiting the Effects of Moral Magic* (*c*.1820), one of a whole series of slim books actually marketed as 'Moral Fairy Tales' published in the 1820s by A. K. Newman, successor to William Lane at the Minerva Press.

The major development in children's fiction of the early nineteenth century, however, was the arrival of huge numbers of Evangelical titles. The records of both the Society for the Propagation of Christian Knowledge (SPCK) and the Religious Tract Society (RTS) make it clear that many million copies of tract-length and, increasingly, book-length fictions were published in the 1810s and 1820s, although the heyday of these societies was in the following decades. At first these titles were designed equally for adults and children, but works specifically for the young were printed in increasing numbers. Commercial publishers successfully competed with the subsidized societies too. F. Houlston and Sons of Wellington, Shropshire, became a leading name in Evangelical fiction chiefly on the back of one author, Mary Martha Sherwood. In the 1790s she had written novels for adults for the Minerva Press, but from India, where she had accompanied her military husband, she sent *Little Henry and his Bearer* back to her sister who sold it to Houlston for £5. Published in 1815, it became the first of her many hugely successful Evangelical stories. These novels can seem serious and severe, and if memoirs testify to their ubiquity in Victorian Britain they can also sometimes reveal readers' resentment of the overt piety. But in fact they were only marginally different from the more secular children's fiction of the time. Both Evangelicals, like Sherwood, and rationalists, like Day and Wollstonecraft, hoped to effect social renovation through the education of a rising generation. Both made 'conversion' central to their narratives, even if the rationalists' dramatization of a child's gradual maturation contrasted with the more sudden religious conversions favoured by Sherwood and others. And both generally stuck to the educative family model, as pioneered in the moral tales of the 1780s. Indeed, the form was perfected by Sherwood in her enormously successful *History of the Fairchild Family* (1818, with two further parts in 1842 and 1847) in which kind, if strict, parents take every opportunity to draw out religious lessons from their children's everyday experiences.

By the end of the period under discussion in this volume, then, the impression one gets of the market for children's fiction is that it was very vigorous, hugely expanded, but also somewhat disorderly, and rather deceitful. In 1824, the RTS was claiming that although it had published 1,688,760 children's books in the previous year, still greater efforts were needed to protect children from the 'Romances, Novels, Plays, Farces and Tales of a very improper description'. Their strategy was deliberately to mimic this kind of popular fiction, drawing readers in with the similar appearance and titles of their wares, but, under these false colours, providing them with wholesome, pious narratives instead. Also in 1824, though, the Sunday School Union Catalogue expressed alarm that squalid publishers were doing exactly the same thing in reverse, deliberately trying to trick consumers into buying 'very exceptionable' material under 'specious and deceptive titles' of the sort used by religious reward books (Bratton 1981: 38, 59–60).

Separate but Similar

If there was confusion between the pious and profane, it could also be difficult to distinguish between books for adults and children. On the one hand, the division between the two was becoming more obvious and entrenched. By the beginning of the nineteenth century, children's literature had its own, separate institutions: publishers specializing in children's books (John Marshall styled himself 'The Children's Printer'), bookshops designed exclusively to sell children's books (as depicted in Eliza Fenwick's *Visits to the Juvenile Library*, 1805), lending libraries, both charitable and commercial, catering especially for children. There were essays, annotated catalogues, and review journals advising parents on what to purchase for their children, most notably Sarah Trimmer's *Guardian of Education* which appeared monthly, then quarterly, from 1802 until 1806. The labels used by publishers could be distinctive too. The term 'novel', for example, was almost never used for material aimed at children, probably in deference to those many commentators who noisily deplored the spread of novel-reading to new constituencies—women, the poor, the young—thought to be unable to resist fiction's addictive hold or discriminate real life from its seductive fantasies. 'Romance' was of course also deemed inappropriate.

On the other hand (and quite apart from the significant amount of cross-reading that was always going on), there could be little to differentiate between those books designed for children and those for adults. At the lower end of the market, by 1800, traditional 'adult' chapbooks had been joined by a new species of children's chapbook: that is to say cheap, short pamphlets containing moral stories and educational or devotional material instead of—or alongside—the ballads, romances, and severely abridged novels that had formed the staples of popular literature. At the top of the range too, works for adults and for children could be difficult to distinguish. They could cost the same and be similarly bound. They could both be illustrated by a handful of high-quality engravings, rather than the multitude of cheap woodcuts that had been used to enliven the children's books of an earlier generation. Although many children's novels were composed only of a single volume, these could run to the same length as a volume of a standard 'adult' novel. Either might be labelled 'a history', 'a tale', or 'the adventures of'. Even the designation 'a moral tale', apparently so characteristic of the children's fiction of the period, was inde-terminate. Maria Edgeworth used the term for her 1801 collection of stories for 'young people', *Moral Tales*, and, in the same year, offered the first of her society novels, *Belinda*, in its 'Advertisement' as 'a Moral Tale—the author not wishing to acknowledge a Novel'. Even experts in the field could credibly profess to be confused by the intended audience of certain titles. Writing in her *Guardian of Education* about *The Dog of Knowledge; or, Memoirs of Bob, the Spotted Terrier* (1801), Sarah Trimmer claimed that if she had not 'learnt from the dedication, and from the prefatory advertisement, that this Book was written for young people, we should have ranked it among *Novels*' (that she made the distinction is interest-ing in itself).[11]

Indeed, children's fiction was produced in pretty much the same range of genres as the novel for adults. Epistolary, evangelical, and sentimental children's novels were common; so too it-narratives and Robinsonades and, naturally, *Bildungsromans*. George Walker's picaresque *The Adventures of Timothy Thoughtless: or, the Misfortunes of a Little Boy Who Ran away from Boarding-School* (1813) provides a good example of the latter, its title nodding to Eliza Haywood's *The History of Miss Betsy Thoughtless* (1751). Unjustly beaten for purloin-ing a book, the self-absorbed protagonist flees the safety of his school, erroneously believ-ing he can thrive on his own in the world. He soon discovers otherwise, losing all markers of his identity when he is robbed, and becoming a beggar, ballad-seller, and chimney sweep before eventually being rescued, much chastened, by his parents. Oriental tales were written for the young (such as Jane Porter's *The Two Princes of Persia*, 1801); so too his-torical fiction, even before Walter Scott. Some authors, such as Elizabeth Sandham (*The History of Britannicus and his Sister Octavia*, 1818), urged their books' potential for instill-ing factual knowledge and emphasized the efficacy of historical incidents, if engagingly related, in forming the reader's character. *The Beautiful Page, or Child of Romance: Being the History of a Baronet's Daughter, Intended as an Instructive Lesson for Youth* (1802) was more complicated, turning from historical novel (it tells the story of Matilda, a god-daughter of Elizabeth I) to moral tale (her wilfulness is cured after she is sent away to a remote and dismal house with only a governess and her tutors) to 'anti-novel' in the manner of Lennox's *Female Quixote* (reading romances makes Matilda think she has been confined against her will and, dressed as a page, she escapes to have a series of comical adventures). Indeed, a number of metafictive children's novels were attempted, though usually with a pronounced didacticism. A year after *Northanger Abbey* was published, Jefferys Taylor's *Harry's Holiday; or, The Doings of One Who Had Nothing To Do* (1818) described a boy overly influenced by his reading of *Robinson Crusoe*. He admires its hero because, cut adrift of adult authority, Crusoe can do as he likes. His father makes a 'castaway' of Harry, freeing him from all rules and duties. Naturally, Harry quickly repents his desire to have his own

---

[11] Trimmer, *Guardian of Education*, 1 (1802), 327.

way and be marooned from society, and comes to appreciate the social contract that binds the family together.

Some authors were even prepared to attempt children's fiction in modes widely deemed unsuited to the young. The anonymous *The Castle on the Rock: or, The Successful Stratagem* (1808), for example, is a fairly standard, if rather short, Gothic novel, centring on the incarceration of two women who refuse to consent to be the mistress of a wicked count. It comes as a surprise to find it was published by John Harris, a successor to Newbery, 'at the Original Juvenile Library'. Eleanor Sleath, author of *The Orphan of the Rhine* (1798), one of the seven 'horrid novels' named in *Northanger Abbey*, was responsible for a more coherent attempt to introduce the Gothic to children. Her *Glenowen, or The Fairy Palace* (1815), also published by Harris, tells of two young orphans abandoned in a picturesque Welsh village. A ghostlike stranger is seen; mysterious gifts appear; the children are summoned to an eerie mansion. Eventually, all is explained as the ministrations of a benign lady, once betrothed to the children's father, who has encouraged their belief that she is a fairy so that she may aid them anonymously.

Some children's authors even sought to use their work to engage with current political events and debates. The slave trade was frequently reprehended, and children might be shown joyously boycotting slave-produced goods or urging legislators to act. Slavery was a matter of deep conviction for many authors, especially some of the Dissenters who produced so much of the children's literature of the 1780s and 1790s. But the campaign was also useful for teaching children about difference, empathy as the driver of maturity, sensibility and its proper limits, and privilege and its responsibilities. In the wake of the French Revolution, it has been argued, a number of authors deployed their children's books in the 'war of ideas'. Aikin and Barbauld's *Evenings at Home* in particular has been identified as providing a 'radical education' (Levy 2006). From the 1790s, a substantial number of children's émigré novels were published, following the fortunes of aristocratic children forced to flee France during the Terror. They were popular because they offered the possibility of exciting adventure: young protagonists were separated from their parents and forced to fend for themselves in a hostile world. They had a self-contained moral lesson too: that children, no matter how privileged, might be deprived of their comforts at any moment and so needed to cultivate 'that true wealth of which all the revolutions in the world cannot rob them; namely, virtue, peace of mind, knowledge, talents and industry', as Madame de Genlis, herself an émigrée, put it in 'The Children's Island'.[12] At least one critic, though, has read them as propaganda: 'a juvenile literature that complements the antiJacobin novels directed at adults' (Craciun 2005: 148). Certainly, they show that not every author was willing to comply with the orthodox positions, shared by

---

[12] Stéphanie Félicité, comtesse de Genlis, *A New Method of Instruction for Children* (London: T. N. Longman and O. Rees, 1800), 220.

commentators as different as Rousseau and Trimmer, that the young should be kept free from political indoctrination.

Ultimately, perhaps the only thing present in fiction for adults but almost never in children's novels was courtship and sex. It had not always been so. Presumably talking of romances, fairy tales, or abridged novels, Dorothy Kilner complained in about 1780 that it was 'much to be lamented... that almost the whole catalogue of entertaining books for children, turn chiefly upon subjects of *gallantry, love*, and *marriage*', which were 'Subjects, with which no prudent parents would wish to engross the attention of their children, of six, seven, eight, or even a dozen years of age'.[13] She might even have been talking about *The Governess* or *Goody Two-Shoes*, which certainly discuss marriage and could occasionally include moderately sexual language (in *Goody Two-Shoes* we read of pirates 'who took his Daughter [and] attempted to rob her of her Chastity', 30). Such stuff was quickly eradicated. In 1790, Mary Wollstonecraft complained that she had wished to say 'something of chastity and impurity' in her writing for children, and had hoped 'to speak to children of the organs of generation as freely as we speak of the other parts of the body', but, knowing that some subjects were off-limits in children's literature, had been forced to reconsider.[14]

Further blurring the distinction between fiction for adults and children, there is ample evidence that, just as children read novels intended for adults, so many adults read children's literature. This was in accordance with prescribed practice. Educationalists recommended that parents and teachers made a prior check of any book to be given to children, and children's reading was supposed to be supervised by their elders. A concurrent dual audience was often acknowledged in the text. Sherwood's *The Little Woodman* (1818), for instance, explicitly addresses parents alongside children: 'Fathers and mothers, you should lead your children to love God while they are little, and while their hearts are tender. And you, little children, lose no time, but give yourselves up to God before you become hard and stubborn, like William's brothers.'[15] The very title of one text (an exception to the rule that children's books were not labelled 'novels') makes the same point: *The Brothers; a Novel, for Children. Addressed to Every Good Mother* (1794). But adults could choose to read children's books for their own satisfaction too. Some children's titles were routinely included amongst the stock of circulating libraries. *Sandford and Merton*, to take the most notable example, sat alongside 'adult' novels in over 50 per cent of circulating library catalogues. Such titles could be reviewed as works of general literature in the major periodicals. Diaries record adult reading of children's books. In 1783, for example, when over thirty, Frances Burney read Arnaud Berquin's

---

[13] Dorothy Kilner, *Dialogues and Letters. On Morality, Œconomy, and Politeness for the Improvement and Entertainment of Young Female Minds* (London: John Marshall, 1780?), xi.

[14] Mary Wollstonecraft, *Elements of Morality, for the Use of Children; with an Introductory Address to Parents. Translated from the German of the Rev. C. G. Salzmann* (London: J. Johnson, 1790), xii.

[15] Mary Martha Sherwood, *The Little Woodman, and His Dog Cæsar* (Wellington: F. Houlston and Son, 1818), 10–11.

Ami des enfans together with her father.[16] By 1830, Mary Russell Mitford was apologizing for her decision to include stories 'composed purposely for children' in *Sketches of Rural Character and Scenery* by explaining that 'as the Author has herself, in common with her wisers and betters, a strong propensity to dip into children's books when they happen to fall in her way, she by no means thought it necessary to omit them'.[17] A number of critics have identified the 'children's book for adults' as a phenomenon of the later nineteenth century: that is to say titles notionally published for the young but primarily popular with grown-ups, or even perhaps deliberately intended to induce in them 'childish' sentiments (Nelson 2008: 137–8, 147–8). Evidently, though, the children's novel had a dual audience even from its inception.

By 1820, then, the novel for children was establishing itself as a distinct entity, but had not quite disconnected itself from the mainstream. Separate institutions were being developed. Publishers and authors were becoming increasingly aware of their audiences' diverse needs and were nuancing their work accordingly. But children's fiction was still shadowing the novel for adults, imitating its genres, and sharing its concerns. Its consumers were crossing the notional divide between adults' and children's fiction freely, and in both directions. Such cross-reading would never cease. But over the following decades, the formal and thematic differences between fiction for children and for adults would gradually reify to produce more enforceable zones of cultural and commercial demarcation.

---

[16] *The Diary and Letters of Madame d'Arblay, Edited by her Niece*, 7 vols (London: Henry Colburn, 1842–6), 2.281.

[17] Mary Russell Mitford, *Our Village: Sketches of Rural Character and Scenery. Fourth Series* (London: Whittaker, Treacher, & Co., 1830), 'Preface'.

28

The Novel and the Stage

GILLIAN RUSSELL

ACCORDING to William Wordsworth, writing in the Preface to the 1800 edition of *Lyrical Ballads*, the rapid urbanization of British society and the proliferation of information or 'intelligence' had led to a disturbing 'tendency' in 'the literature and theatrical exhibitions of the country': 'The invaluable work of our elder writers, I had almost said the works of Shakespear and Milton, are driven into neglect by frantic novels, sickly and stupid German Tragedies, and deluges of idle and extravagant stories in verse' (1.xix). Wordsworth's claim that the founding fathers of the British literary tradition were being overwhelmed by the enfeebled but irresistible force of low-grade literature is widely recognized as a foundational statement in British Romanticism, establishing the terms of that movement's enduring preoccupation with questions of cultural hierarchy, value, and genre. Less often recognized, particularly for studies of the novel, are the implications of Wordsworth's linking of the novel and the drama as part of the same pernicious 'tendency'.

The extent to which the development of the novel in this period interacts with that of the stage, not to mention other forms of print media, has received comparatively little attention in literary history. This partly reflects the differentiation of literary genres that took place in the nineteenth century and its subsequent academic institutionalization which has resulted in the novel and the drama constituting distinct fields within literary studies. This development was reinforced by the 'rise' of the novel to the status of a legitimate literary genre, one indeed regarded as central to modern global culture, and, conversely, the 'decline' of the prestige of theatre and drama, particularly that of the period 1750–1950. The latter view, which has been tenacious, is in the process of revision, highlighting the need for a re-examination of the novel and the theatre of the Georgian period as contiguous and in many respects symbiotic cultural phenomena. Novels and plays were the products of the same cultural, political, and social contexts: they were performed, circulated as texts, and interpreted in relation to and often in dialogue and competition with each other. Yet modern literary history continues to treat them as if they belonged in worlds apart. Wordsworth's grouping of 'frantic' novels with the fashion for

German drama in the 1790s is one example of how contemporaries saw the novel and the stage as linked—in this case, at the centre of the proliferation of print genres and reading audiences. The late eighteenth and early nineteenth centuries are therefore of tremendous significance for the long-term history of the novel and the drama as they represent the period when the affiliation between the novel and the stage begins to erode, leading ultimately to the generic distinctions that prevail today. Restoring that affiliation also enables us to identify the importance of the relationship of the novel and the stage to genres which have had a long-lasting and pervasive impact on modern culture—that is, Gothic and melodrama. To examine this history in the detail it deserves is beyond the scope of a chapter such as this: what follows outlines some of the ways in which realigning the novel with the stage can potentially illuminate both genres and also cultural history more broadly.

The Stage and the Novel / the Novel and the Stage

Which comes first, the novel or the stage? For most of our period the theatre took precedence as the dominant force in Georgian public culture, its ideology and practices extending beyond the strictly literary to permeate politics, fashion, the visual arts, and philosophy. The potency of the theatre as a mode of representation and a form of sociality was reflected in long-held suspicions of play-going and of acting as immoral and vicious, often linked with prostitution, and in anxieties about the playhouse as a dangerous forum for political expression. From 1737 under the terms of the Licensing Act all plays were subject to censorship prior to production, a condition which Elizabeth Inchbald characterized in 1807 as 'despotic government' in contrast to the 'free' agency of the novelist.[1] The censorship of texts was combined with the monitoring of the theatre through a system of licences and patents which controlled the construction of playhouses and what kind of plays could be performed in them. It was this complex pattern of regulation, combined with the 1737 Licensing Act, which divided theatre in London between the 'legitimate drama', identified with the authority of writers such as Shakespeare and the royal theatres of Covent Garden and Drury Lane, and the 'illegitimate' theatre practised in venues such as Sadler's Wells. The latter was identified with forms such as pantomime which relied on the communicative power of gesture, spectacle, and music rather than the words of the privileged dramatic text. In spite or because of this system of control, however, the theatre thrived and developed in this period. By the early nineteenth century there were more playhouses in towns throughout Britain than at any other period in history. This network of playhouses was supplemented by a

---

[1] Elizabeth Inchbald, 'To the Artist', *The Artist*, 1 (1807), no. 14, 16.

vital tradition of itinerant performers or strollers who staged plays in barns, fairground booths, or the open air. In addition, Georgians of all classes were keen amateur performers, their theatricals ranging from artisan acting clubs in taverns to lavish semi-public occasions at the country houses of the elite. Far from a period of atrophy for the stage, 1750–1820 therefore represented a high watermark in its history, the theatre being a dominant force in Georgian public culture and social life.

Men and women of this period would have understood the term 'stage' primarily to mean the material space of the theatre and the performances taking place within it, both on stage and in the auditorium. Georgian playgoers were notoriously demonstrative and attending the theatre was as much a sociable as it was a cultural activity. Play-going was an opportunity to socialize and network with others, to assert one's place in the idea of the public embodied by the theatre audience. Importantly, the idea of the stage also included the wide range of print media associated with it. The penetration of theatre into all aspects of British cultural life after 1750 was facilitated by print: conversely, print exploited the fascination with theatre. The print culture of the Georgian theatre ranged from books of the play to paratexts such as prologues and epilogues, often published separately, to the playbills that advertised particular performances and even the tickets that facilitated access. 'Dramatic intelligence' was also widely disseminated in newspapers and journals, a number of which were dedicated to the stage. Acting luminaries such as David Garrick and Sarah Siddons were multi-media stars, the subjects of extensive commentary in the newspaper and periodical press and, as we shall see, novels; their images retailed in the form of paintings, engravings, graphic satire, and ceramics. The fact that many writers were both playwrights and novelists is a sign of their gravitation towards the fame, prestige, and also the considerable financial rewards of writing for the stage. It is also an indication that authorship itself had not yet been defined or delimited by genre. It was still possible to work in a variety of kinds of literary endeavour, a crossover practice that the dominance of genre in literary historiography had tended to neglect. There are very few analyses of how the novels of writers such as Walpole, Goldsmith, Burney, Godwin, Holcroft, Inchbald, Edgeworth, M. G. Lewis, Galt, Mitford et al. relate to their work as dramatists and vice versa.

Within this spectrum of theatre-related print, the book of the play was similarly diverse, ranging from editions of 'illegitimate' farces and afterpieces, suggesting a market for textual records of such productions, to prestige scholarly editions of the works of Shakespeare, designed for the libraries of gentlemen. The latter kind of text, however, represented a fraction of the broad range of play texts, most of which related to the theatre repertory. It was possible to buy books of the play at the theatre and some playgoers were accustomed to reading them in the course of a performance. Richard Brinsley Sheridan's tragi-melodrama *Pizarro* was a publishing as well as a theatrical sensation when it was first staged in 1799. Sheridan's play, an adaptation of August von Kotzebue's *Die Spanier in Peru*, was an example of the 'sickly and stupid' German drama condemned by Wordsworth. By 'German Tragedies', therefore, he was not just referring to the theatre but also to a literary phenomenon that was being avidly consumed by readers.

The Georgian theatre, therefore, did not exist in a sphere that was separate from print and reading but was embedded in and constructed by the same contexts of textual production and dissemination that were influencing the novel. This is apparent in the history of the commercial or circulating library. Fashionable centres such as Bath had many of these establishments but even small towns had their printers who lent books as part of a diversified trade, a penetration of print closely linked with the development of the theatre in such towns. The interest in play-reading is indicated by the fact that many of these circulating libraries stocked drama in addition to the novels with which they are traditionally associated. According to Paul Kaufman, of a total of 5,158 books listed in the 1755 Catalogue of Thomas Lowndes more than a fourth are plays in contrast to fiction which accounts for only a tenth, while the 1780–6 Catalogue of James Sibbald's Edinburgh Circulating Library 'gives no less than 1019 plays out of a total of 3855 works, as compared with 888 novels', a pattern repeated at other institutions (Kaufman 1969b: 565, 567; also Allan, Chapter 3). This suggests the material contiguity of novels and plays, located in close proximity on the duodecimo-size shelves of circulating libraries, or jumbled together in pockets or on the parlour table or the shelves of libraries and closets. Not only could the customer of a circulating library borrow a play text together with a novel, but as centres of information for local communities—publishing and distributing newspapers in which theatre performances and new novels were promoted—these institutions were often bound up with the business of the local theatre. The fact that they sold tickets for plays and distributed playbills reinforced the connection between novel reading and play-going as interrelated aspects of urban sociability and polite culture.

This connection is also reflected in the history of reading practices in this period. The development of 'closet' drama—plays designed for reading rather than performance—has been interpreted as a reaction against the perceived decline in the quality of serious drama, as the building of larger theatres, especially after 1794, led to an increased emphasis on spectacle. But it has proved a perennial problem for scholars to detach even the most literary of 'dramatic poems' from the idea if not the practice of theatrical performance. Rather than regarding closet drama as inherently anti-theatrical, it can be viewed as an aspect of how, by means of the spread of print, Georgian men and women were learning to read and write dramatic literature in complex and diverse ways. Drama could be read novelistically, as much as the novel could be 'staged' in the mind of its readers. Sometimes that staging was not confined to the mind: it was the practice in gentry families, such as that of Jane Austen, to read novels aloud to a group, thereby creating an intimate theatre of the reader and audience and drawing attention to the dramatic qualities of the narrative, particularly the nuances of direct speech and dialogue.

'An Ever-green Tree, of Diabolical Knowledge': Staging the Novel

It was the theatre rather than the novel itself which first tried to represent the impact of the novel as a cultural phenomenon. George Colman's *Polly Honeycombe*, an afterpiece subtitled 'A Dramatic Novel of One Act', first staged in 1760, and Richard Brinsley Sheridan's comedy *The Rivals* (1775), both feature novel-mad heroines who are addicted to the wares of the circulating library. In *The Rivals* Sir Anthony Absolute declares that 'a circulating library in a town is, as an ever-green tree, of diabolical knowledge', a comment that has subsequently become a commonplace in accounts of such libraries and in histories of the novel.[2] It formed the title of Devendra Varma's 1972 study of the circulating library and surfaced again in David Allan's *A Nation of Readers* in 2008: 'The colourful opinion of Sir Anthony Absolute [which Allan goes on to quote] has brooked particularly large in subsequent discussion of the phenomenon' (2008: 119). Not only has the opinion of this fictional character been influential in perpetuating the idea that giddy young girls were the main consumers of novels, a view that Jane Austen tried to contest in *Northanger Abbey* (1818), but, as indicated before, it has led to the mistaken idea that circulating libraries were mainly devoted to purveying low-grade fiction. An underlying assumption, though this has rarely been explicitly articulated, is that the view of Sheridan's character stands for a generally hostile response to the novel by the theatre as a whole.

Both *Polly Honeycombe* and *The Rivals* are deserving of more attention from historians of the novel, not the least for how they represent the novel as a commodity and a material object. The prologue to Colman's play marks the transition from the old-fashioned 'Folios' of the romance to the convenient 'Two Neat Pocket Volumes' of 1760.[3] The eponymous heroine then enters—the scene direction is 'Polly, *with a book in her hand*'— declaring 'Well, a novel for my money' (141). The 'problem' of young girls and modern fiction is thereby staged concretely rather than abstractly as a matter of the power of print to realize desire in the form of the exchange of a thing—the novel—for money. As in *The Rivals*, *Polly Honeycombe* includes a jeremiad by the heroine's father against the institution which he believes has led her astray. At the end of the play he declares 'a man might as well turn his daughter loose in Covent Garden, as trust the cultivation of her mind to A CIRCULATING LIBRARY' (159), but the emphasis signalled by the capitalization in the printed text is incapable of marking closure. In the play as a whole prose fiction is depicted as the epitome of multiplying forms of writing and representation including the newspaper press, the stock market, and the law—the commerce of print and the print of commerce—which Honeycombe is ultimately incapable of resisting. The epilogue to the play, spoken by Polly on behalf of 'we Girls of Reading', announces her father's defeat:

---

[2] Richard Brinsley Sheridan, *The Rivals*, ed. C. J. L. Price (Oxford: Oxford University Press, 1968), 41.
[3] George Colman, *Polly Honeycombe, A Dramatic Novel of One Act*, in Richard W. Bevis (ed.), *Eighteenth Century Drama: Afterpieces* (Oxford: Oxford University Press, 1970), 139.

'Let us to arms!—Our Fathers, Husbands, dare!
NOVELS will teach us all the Art of War:
Our Tongues will serve for Trumpet and for Drum;
I'll be your Leader—General HONEYCOMBE!' (161)

In the context of the Seven Years' War, then in progress, these lines license the novel as the epitome of the commercial strength, with all its feminized unpredictability, that would make the British Empire great. The theatre in this respect plays the role of monitor and also mediator of cultural change, seeking to situate itself both within and also above the maelstrom of texts that was driving the mid-century economy. By representing novel reading and the novel itself as a material object on stage, the theatre was engaging in a complex act of containment. It appropriated the energy of the novel as a circulating medium as well as reminding audiences that the theatre was still the pre-eminent venue to which contemporary society needed to come in order to recognize itself.

A similar emphasis on the materiality of the novel and on novel reading as a somatic experience is apparent in Sheridan's *The Rivals*. The novel-mad heroine Lydia Languish is discovered, like Polly, '*with a book in her hand*' (33), waiting for the return of her servant Lucy who has been searching the many circulating libraries of Bath on her behalf. Novels in *The Rivals* are convenient, portable, and ubiquitous commodities. Lucy takes a number of them from '*her cloak, and from her pockets*' (34), though she has to disappoint her mistress because *The Memoirs of Lady Woodford* was unobtainable as 'Lady Slattern Lounger...had so soiled and dog's-eared it, it wa'n't fit for a Christian to read' (34). Lady Lounger, according to Lydia, is renowned for 'her most observing thumb' and 'cherishes her nails for the convenience of making marginal notes' (34). When Sir Anthony Absolute is announced, Lydia frantically orders Lucy to hide the evidence of her reading:

'Fling *Peregrine Pickle* under the toilet—throw *Roderick Random* into the closet—put *The Innocent Adultery* into *The Whole Duty of Man*—thrust *Lord Aimworth* under the sofa—cram *Ovid* behind the bolster—there—put *The Man of Feeling* into your pocket—so, so,—now lay *Mrs. Chapone* in sight, and leave *Fordyce's Sermons* open on the table.' (39)

This scene dramatizes the transformative power of print and of the novel in particular, which literally penetrates every nook and cranny of the 'private' space over which Sir Anthony Absolute pretends control. It reveals novel reading to be a social performance which women, and men too, could use to stage versions of themselves. (This comedy of book panic also has a meta-dimension in that, like *Polly Honeycombe*, it demonstrates the capacity of the theatre to mediate the power of the novel.) The fact that Sheridan refers to actual novels of the period—now canonical works such as those of Smollett and Mackenzie as well as the forgotten *Memoirs of Lady Woodford* (1771)—suggests either Lydia Languish's lack of discrimination or the tendency of readers to resist categories of literary value. 'High' and 'low' novels rub together, the play implies, because they belong to the same mechanisms of production and circulation and the same social world, analogous to how the theatre itself catered to multiple tastes in the one social body.

The Rivals can be seen to realize the nightmare of the 'diabolical knowledge' of female reading engendered by the novel, particularly in Lady Lounger's propensity to read with her 'observing thumb', treating the book as a kind of prosthetic. Alternatively, it represents an acknowledgement of female reading communities and the canny servants who facilitate their desires: in the play as a whole, moreover, it is the leading male characters of Captain Absolute and Falkland who are shown to have the more dangerous imaginations in their willingness to play with identity and to doubt the faith of the women who love them. Like Colman's *Polly Honeycombe*, then, *The Rivals* recognizes the affinities between the novel and the stage, as much as it makes fun of an art form and a commodity that was competing with the theatre for public attention.

'I Almost Wished to Have Jumped on the Stage': Novelizing the Theatre

The theatre's engagement with the novel as a cultural artefact or commodity was reciprocated by the novel's preoccupation with theatre. This is apparent not only at the level of the novel's deployment of the figurative meanings of theatre in relation to concepts of character, the nature of social 'performance', and the questions of the 'real' and the 'fictive'. The novel also importantly engages with the materiality of theatre, particularly play-going as a sociable activity. Accounts of visits to the theatre and descriptions of actors and performances occur in a number of texts of this period, particularly the novel of manners or the society novel. As a trope such episodes have received little attention from critics, partly because of the tendency to treat drama and theatre metaphorically in approaches to the novel, reflecting a lack of interest in and knowledge of the theatrical culture with which writers of this time were closely familiar. The trope of play-going in the Georgian novel is notable for its referencing of actual plays, playhouses, and performers: an art form and cultural institution that was regarded with suspicion on account of its shameless reliance on pretence was often used to enhance the reality effect of these narratives. The topical immediacy of the eponymous heroine's encounter with London society in Frances Burney's *Evelina* (1778), for example, is validated with reference to David Garrick's performance as Ranger in Benjamin Hoadly's comedy, *The Suspicious Husband*. This was one of Garrick's most celebrated roles, which he had performed as part of his farewell season before retiring in 1776, two years before the publication of *Evelina*. Garrick's 'natural' style—'I could hardly believe he had studied a written part', comments Evelina—is the model of the hero Lord Orville's successful performance of gentlemanly authenticity.[4] Evelina is so impressed that she 'almost wished to have jumped on the

---

[4] Fanny Burney, *Evelina, or, The History of a Young Lady's Entrance into the World*, ed. Edward A. Bloom, introd. Vivien Jones (Oxford: Oxford University Press, 2002), 27.

stage' (28) to join the marriage dance that concludes the comedy, proleptic of the comedic outcome of the novel itself.

Drury Lane theatre and another actual play, Congreve's *Love for Love*, play an important part later in the novel as the venue and pretext for Evelina's education in performing before the eyes of the 'world', also enabling Burney to stage a debate between the doughty English chauvinist Captain Mirvan and the fop Lovel on the relative merits of the theatre and the opera, on public culture as a commodity, and on the intrinsic value of play-going as a sociable activity. 'I have no time to read playbills,' declares Lovel, 'one merely comes to meet one's friends, and shew that one's alive' (82). The reference to the playbill indicates engagement with the theatre not primarily in terms of its literary value but as a multifaceted cultural and social formation, in which print culture, in the broadest sense, was thoroughly implicated and materially present. As such, Burney asserts the capacity for the novel to act as a cultural and social formation of comparable if not greater complexity than the theatre. She uses theatre to experiment with how the novel might appropriate the kind of framing function or suprageneric authority associated with the stage, outperforming playwrights such as Colman and Sheridan at their game of projecting and thereby controlling the potency of the novel.

Burney's *Evelina* is echoed in another enthusiastic playgoer, Laura Montreville in Mary Brunton's *Self-Control* (1811), who is also initiated into the world by means of witnessing a star performer, in this case Sarah Siddons acting the role of Mrs Beverly in Edward Moore's tragedy *The Gamester*. Laura is overwhelmed by Siddons' performance, acting, as in *Evelina*, being constructed as an elevated form of expression and communicative power. She subsequently becomes a Siddons-obsessive, sketching more than twenty portraits of the actress in the days following. In Maria Edgeworth's *The Absentee* (1812) there is a similar rapt involvement in the theatre by a woman, Lady Isabel, daughter of the pushy Lady Dashfort, who is the object of scrutiny by the hero Lord Colambre. Lady Dashfort's excessive sociability at the Dublin theatre, as she talks with 'masculine boldness . . . stretched from box to box', is contrasted with Lady Isabel's absorption in the playbill, a 'performance' about which Lord Colambre is uncertain whether it signifies 'nature' or 'art': 'If this be acting, it is the best acting I ever saw. If this be art, it deserves to be nature.'[5] Edgeworth uses a realistic evocation of social behaviour in the contemporary theatre, indicated by Lady Dashfort's putting herself about in the boxes and the reference to the textual paraphernalia of play-going in the form of the playbill, in order to ground as well as catalyse her romance. The novel locates the theatre at the fulcrum of a social world that is immured and conditioned by performance at every turn. As a reworking of the trope of play-going in *Evelina*, from the perspective of the hero rather than the heroine,

---

[5] Maria Edgeworth, *The Absentee*, ed. W. J. McCormack and Kim Walker (Oxford: Oxford University Press, 1988), ch. 6; 97, 98.

The Absentee also indicates how fully assimilated as well as how structural to the novel of manners this trope had become.

Another aspect of the tendency of late eighteenth-century novels to go to the theatre was that it distinguished the genre from the competing form of the playbook. Texts of plays could not evoke the experience of play-going—the crush of bodies in boxes and lobbies, the thrill of the sociable encounter, the magic of a star performer—in the same way as a detailed fictional narrative. By materializing theatre in this way, the novel was able to accrue to itself the power to represent an important aspect of why theatre mattered in late Georgian society. Two significant dimensions of this trope are the kinds of play-going represented by private theatricals and by encounters with strolling players. Of the former, the failed attempt to stage *Lovers' Vows* in Jane Austen's *Mansfield Park* (1814) is the best-known example, the subject of an extensive and ongoing critical commentary. Less well known are other similar episodes in the novels of Austen's peers, Frances Burney and Maria Edgeworth, such as Lionel Tyrold's efforts to 'get up' a play in the attic room in Burney's *Camilla* (1796), the private performance of *The Provoked Wife* in her *The Wanderer* (1814), and the staging of *Zara* in Edgeworth's *Patronage* (1814). Both writers also deploy the fashion for private theatres as a sign of rampant, even tragic, decadence: in Burney's *Cecilia* (1782) the headlong rush to perdition of the Harrels is indicated by their extravagance in building their own private theatre, while the heroic failure of Anglo-Irish civility in Edgeworth's *Castle Rackrent* (1800) is pinpointed by Lady Isabella Rackrent's attempt to make a theatre out of a barrack room. *Mansfield Park* is, however, the most sustained and complex treatment in the novel of the Georgian obsession with private theatricals, part of an engagement with theatre as a whole in Austen's fiction which is undergoing critical re-evaluation. This revision has led to a recognition that Austen's representation of theatre and theatricality is not only moral and philosophical but also embedded in the cultural politics and material conditions of the theatre of her time. This is apparent in the *Lovers' Vows* episode of *Mansfield Park*, the meanings of which as an exploration of family and national politics, public and private selves, publicity and print culture, only become fully clear in relation to the historical phenomenon of private theatricals as a whole (see Russell 2007).

The representation of the strolling player in fiction relates to the stroller as a version of the 'picaro'. Some picaresque novels, such as Thomas Mozeen's *Young Scarron* (1752) and Thomas Holcroft's *Alwyn: or The Gentleman Comedian* (1780), take the actor's life as a model. The strolling player as a type of the wanderer, trading in role-playing and experiencing mercurial transformations from privilege to destitution and back again, structures or haunts the novel's own investments in purposeful mobility and meaningful change. In Oliver Goldsmith's *The Vicar of Wakefield* (1766), the protagonist Parson Primrose encounters a group of travelling players with whom he engages in discussion about the state of the theatre, particularly the taste for spectacle and 'attitudes' at the expense of the beauties of Shakespeare's poetry. Later Primrose goes to see the strollers perform Nicholas Rowe's tragedy *The Fair Penitent* in a barn, discovering to his dismay that one of the leading actors is his errant son, George. In an excursus into the genre of the stroller's tale, George narrates how he found himself in this position, having failed to make a career in London and on the Continent because he was thwarted by corruption and the arbitrary use of privilege. The stroller's tale can therefore be seen to act as a counter-narrative to the novel's increasing investments in the value of mobility and self-transformation: the stroller's tale takes another path altogether, the form of which is not always clear nor its outcome finite. It is important to note, however, that while they might seem archetypal, the strollers in *The Vicar of Wakefield* are also specifically situated. The players represent the kind of troupe that readers of the time might easily have encountered, performing a well-known play, *The Fair Penitent*, while the discussion they have with Primrose marks them as sophisticated professionals, confounding any sense of them as provincial bumpkins. This strategy accentuates the value of the novel as a commentary on the contemporary world, capable of assuming the theatre's own prerogative to act as a mirror of society, as well as harnessing, in the figure of the stroller, the more universal meanings of theatre—its capacity to mark the boundaries between what is and what might be, between what is within and what is without.

This dual strategy, on the one hand representing the contemporary theatre and in particular play-going in a way that enhances the 'reality effect' of the novel and its authority as a mode of social commentary, while at the same time mobilizing the potency of the stage as a place for dreams, is also apparent in Thomas Holcroft's *The Adventures of Hugh Trevor* (1794–7). Holcroft uses the political and sentimental education of the eponymous hero to mount a critique of the major institutions of British society—the church, the universities, the law, and also the republic of letters. An important forum for that education is the theatre, Holcroft's novel representing the most sustained treatment of the trope of play-going in the late eighteenth-century novel. Trevor initially views the London theatre as a site of wonder, embodied by the genius of Sarah Siddons (acting in *The Fair Penitent*), but eventually is convinced that it is as venal and shallow as the rest of society. The most important reference to the stage in the novel, however, takes the form of Trevor's encounter with Belmont, a gentleman with whom he had become acquainted in the metropolis and encounters again, Belmont telling him that in the interim he had been '*vagabondizing*', that is, acting in a company of strolling players.[6] Belmont characterizes strolling as a 'peculiar kind of magic' or necromancy, capable of making a barn seem like a temple or king's palace: its chief exponent is a 'certain sorcerer called Shakspeare' (210, 211). Belmont's stroller's tale is designed to seduce both Trevor and the reader, the figure of theatre in this sense standing for the magic of literary invention itself, embodied by Shakespeare, its greatest representative.

---

[6] Thomas Holcroft, *The Adventures of Hugh Trevor*, ed. Seamus Deane (London: Oxford University Press, 1973), vol. 3; ch. 6; 210.

However, Holcroft counteracts this effect by having the first-person narrator, Trevor, 'inform the reader of a secret, of which I myself at that time and long continued to remain utterly ignorant' (vol. 3, ch. 7; 219), i.e. that 'Belmont' is actually Wakefield, the man who persecuted Trevor's mother and continues to act as his enemy. This twist is melodramatic in that it gives the reader privileged knowledge which the narrator did not possess at that time as well as transforming at a stroke the character of Belmont who had seemed plausible into one whom we must now regard with suspicion. This is melodrama in a novelistic rather than a theatrical sense, however. If the narrative of *Hugh Trevor* is to remain viable, the reader has to trust this turn of events and also the first-person narrator, both credibly authoritative and also crucially ignorant, who is now revealed to us. The theatre in the form of strolling therefore functions as a way for Holcroft to compare theatrical and novelistic codes of representation. In the form of the twist concerning Belmont/Wakefield the magic of the theatre's capacity to invent and transmute 'reality' is countered by the fiction-making of the novel which Holcroft suggests is of a different order, requiring, above all, the reader's commitment to the novel working in the service of credible 'truth', however strange that truth might be, rather than necromantic fantasy.

Gothic Novels / Gothic Theatre

The 1790s as a whole is an important decade for the contiguity of the novel and the stage, particularly in relation to the emerging trans-genres of Gothic and melodrama. (By 'trans-genre' I invoke Michael Gamer's definition (2000: 4) of Gothic as 'an aesthetic' and a 'site that *moves*, and that must be defined in part by its ability to transplant itself *across* forms and media from dramatic and poetic modes, and from textual into visual and aural media'.) It is noteworthy that the more protean trans-genres of Gothic and melodrama emerged at the same time as the generic difference between the novel and the drama was beginning to be asserted. The 1790s is the decade when Gothic fiction takes off, while the first formal stage melodrama is widely acknowledged to be Holcroft's *A Tale of Mystery* of 1802. The 1790s is also the decade when the balance of the relationship between the stage and the novel begins to shift in favour of the novel. Until that period the theatre had cultural dominance, a perspective from which it is able to scrutinize and, as we have seen, 'stage' the novel in plays such as *The Rivals*. With the rise of the Gothic novel and, in particular, the exceptional success of writers such as Ann Radcliffe, the theatre begins to regard the novel differently, as a genre with which it is no longer competing from a position of advantage.

The nature and significance of this shift should not be exaggerated, however. The novel and the stage remained closely bound up with each other, particularly when they shared the idiom of Gothic. This is apparent in Horace Walpole's *The Castle of*

Otranto (1765), the first Gothic novel, which is overtly dramatic in its structure and textual presentation, following the five acts of tragedy and deploying parenthetical 'scene' directions in an extensive use of dialogue. Writing in 1811, Walter Scott noted Walpole's 'dramatic talent', reserving particular praise for the novel's 'grand catastrophe': 'The moon-light vision of Alphonso dilated to immense magnitude, the astonished group of spectators in the front, and the shattered ruins of the castle in the back-ground, is briefly and sublimely described.'[7] This was a reference to the celebrated *coup* of Walpole's novel when the 'form' of Alfonso erupts like a volcano to destroy the house of Otranto. The passage in the text, which suggests the machinery of the stage masque, is read by Scott in terms of the staging practices of the early nineteenth-century theatre, as it would appear in perspective view and could indeed have been realized in the larger theatres after 1794 when spectacular effects of real water, sophisticated pantomime transformations, and parades of animals became customary. In the theatre of the 1760s, however, the scale of such effects was impossible, an indication of how the Gothic novel anticipated and also influenced the development of spectacular theatre, the lens through which Scott read this text. *The Castle of Otranto* was also groundbreaking for showing how the novel could develop its own distinctive theatricality, exceeding in imaginative effect that which the Georgian stage was ever capable of achieving. Scenes such as the enormous helmet that crushes the heir of Manfred, and the form of Alfonso 'dilated to an immense magnitude', echo but also challenge or even mock the sister arts of theatre. They are in many respects proto-cinematic. In his emphasis on 'dilation', which Scott reproduced in his discussion of the novel, Walpole was exploring the capacity of prose fiction to expand the senses, to create an imaginative experience that would surpass the spectatorial and aural dimensions of experiencing a play in the theatre.

The exercise of outperforming theatre is also apparent in *The Mysterious Mother*, the tragedy which Walpole wrote and printed privately in 1768, four years after *Otranto*. The novel and the play are in effect companion texts. The play's central theme of a mother's incestuous love for her son rendered it unproducible in the public theatre. By choosing to represent such a taboo subject in the form of drama rather than as a novel, Walpole was affirming the intense theatricality of 'private' life. *The Castle of Otranto* and *The Mysterious Mother* therefore highlight how print culture and the development of reading audiences were creating new conditions for the reception of both prose fiction and the drama that confounded distinctions between the two. Both texts cannot simply be described as anti-theatrical—they use print and reading practices such as reading out loud to take theatricality in new directions, some of which would inevitably leave the theatre behind.

---

[7] Horace Walpole, *The Castle of Otranto* (Edinburgh: John Ballantyne & Co., 1811), xxxi, xxx.

'To Dramatize': Modern Adaptation

The Castle of Otranto was adapted for the stage by Robert Jephson as a tragedy, *The Count of Narbonne*, first performed in 1781: not surprisingly, many of the novel's extravagant effects were not attempted. However, this did not affect the success of the play which remained in the repertory into the nineteenth century. Readers and playgoers were able to view Walpole's novel and *The Count of Narbonne* as related but also distinct works of art—the fact that Jephson's tragedy was based on *Otranto* was not a condition defining its reception. This is signalled by the fact that the titles of the two works are different, as is also the case with the many stage versions of Gothic novels that were produced in the 1790s. Ann Radcliffe's *Romance of the Forest* (1791) was adapted by James Boaden as *Fountainville Forest* in 1794, while M. G. Lewis's controversial *The Monk* (1796) was the basis of *Aurelio and Miranda* (1798), also by Boaden. In 1796 Drury Lane staged *The Iron Chest* by George Colman the Younger based on William Godwin's *Things as They Are; or, The Adventures of Caleb Williams* (1794). Colman's play derived from but was also radically different from the novel, in part because conditions of censorship meant that Godwin's critique of the political and social order in the wake of the treason trials of 1794 could not be represented. The topical immediacy of Godwin's depiction of the social system as Gothic in its paranoid secrecy and self-loathing was countered in Colman's play by setting the action in the past, a displacement accentuated by the scenic design with its emphasis on the Gothic picturesque of forests and ruined abbeys. The play is Gothic in setting rather than content. It clearly vindicates the Caleb Williams character, named Wilford, in a scene in which the brother of Mortimer, the equivalent of Falkland, the gentleman who persecutes Caleb, discovers a paper in which Mortimer admits the crime of murder. In contrast to *Caleb Williams*, which is ultimately sceptical of the power of writing and of the print media to illuminate truth, Colman's play relies on the credibility of the written record. Theatrical modes of representation—the 'reality' signified by the iron chest of the title and the brandished paper—are used to affirm the validity of providential, natural justice, significantly located not in the apparatus of the state or social class, but in the core social unit of the family, Mortimer's guilt being discovered by his brother, to whom there is no equivalent in Godwin's novel. In its performance of the possibility of natural justice and the transparency of 'truth', *The Iron Chest* is a political romance or comedy as opposed to the tragic melodrama of *Caleb Williams*.

That Colman was doing something new is clear in newspaper commentary describing *The Iron Chest* as a 'Play, as it is now become the fashion to term a Serio-Comic Drama'[8] rather than the conventional tragedy or comedy. The emergence of the modern genre of the 'play' can therefore be partly ascribed to the impact of the novel on dramatic writing

---

[8] *True Briton*, 14 March 1796.

in this period. These newspapers, while acknowledging the play's indebtedness to *Caleb Williams*, were also prepared to accept the validity of *The Iron Chest* as a work of art in its own right, capable of also reaching a wider audience than an expensive novel costing 10*s*. 6*d*. By 1808, however, when Elizabeth Inchbald was writing her comments on the play for *The British Theatre*, a twenty-five-volume collection of plays for which she wrote prefaces, the relative status of the two genres was changing. A playwright and actress herself, as well as a novelist, Inchbald was committed to the theatre: nonetheless she represents the novel and the stage as fundamentally different, the 'finer details' of *Caleb Williams* being impossible to represent 'in action': 'the dramatist was here compelled merely to give the features of the murderer's face; whilst the novelist portrayed every shade of his countenance, every fibre that played in forgetful smiles, or was convulsed by the pangs of remembrance.'[9] The novelist enabled the reader to see into character in a way that was impossible in the theatre in which seeing meant something different—the 'real' signified by Mortimer's written confession or what Inchbald described as 'the assassin's dagger reeking' (21.5)—as opposed to the intangible, 'finer details' of interiority. It was the novel's capacity to represent the latter, and the British public's increasing desire to 'see' in this way, encouraged by critics such as Inchbald, that gave it an advantage over the theatre.

The 1790s therefore represent an important transitional period between traditional modes of literary borrowing and modern practices of adaptation centred on the novel. This is signified by the coining of the term 'dramatize' which the *Oxford English Dictionary* dates to this period, citing one of its earliest uses as Walter Scott's reference in 1810 to a theatrical adaptation of one of his poems. The term was also current earlier than this date, used in relation to *The Iron Chest*: one newspaper remarked that 'the popular novel of *Caleb Williams* has been recommended to every "tiny scribbler of the stage" as a good subject to dramatize'.[10] 'To dramatize' indicated the new position of the theatre vis-à-vis the novel, as the former was compelled to seek its inspiration from and compete with the commercial success and increasing legitimacy of prose fiction. The expansion of print culture and the related diversification and multiplication of reading audiences created a permeability between cultural practices and genres, the 'crisis' in hierarchy and value that so worried Wordsworth. This permeability is reflected in trans-genres such as Gothic and melodrama and in more hybrid dramatic writing as the shape of tragedy and comedy blurs and mutates. In this general dissolution the category of the literary emerges as a means of determining value: the novel and poetry become the dominant literary genres, the novel accruing to itself the role that theatre had in mediating the complexity and immediacy of the social world, partly, as I have been suggesting, by making play-going one of its subjects.

---

[9] Elizabeth Inchbald, *The British Theatre*, 25 vols (London: Longman [etc.], 1808), 21.4.
[10] *Whitehall Evening Post*, 12 March 1796.

However, this development does not necessarily mean that the permeability between the stage and the novel, a condition of a highly diverse print culture and a manifold reading public, was broken or ended. The symbiosis of the novel and the stage was, if anything, amplified by the cultural phenomenon that was Walter Scott in the nineteenth century. The popularity of both his poetry and his novels was seized upon by dramatists and theatre managers, capitalizing on a commercial and critical success that exceeded by far that of the fashion for Gothic novels in the 1790s. The keenness of the stage to attach itself to the Scott 'brand' is indicated by the use of the titles of his novels in the numerous dramatizations mounted in London and throughout the English-speaking world. Five versions of *The Heart of Mid-Lothian* (1818) were produced in 1819, while in the following year there were seven dramatizations of *Ivanhoe* (1820): at one point five 'Ivanhoes' were being performed in London at the same time.[11] In many cases the minor or illegitimate theatres of the metropolis, particularly the Surrey and Coburg theatres south of the Thames, took the lead in dramatizing Scott's novels as melodramas. As manager and dramatist at the Surrey theatre, Thomas Dibdin was adept at producing versions of Scott's novels, many of which were regarded as more successful than their competitors at the major theatres of Covent Garden and Drury Lane. The *London Magazine* described Miss Taylor in the role of Jeanie Deans at the Surrey as 'one of the most perfect pieces of character we ever saw acted.... There is a seeming hardness in the original draught of the character, which we were never reconciled to, till Miss Taylor taught us to understand it better.... We shall read the novel twice the oftener, for her commentary on it'.[12] Jeanie Deans represented an important innovation in fiction—a lower-class woman as heroic in her own right and idiom. Stage melodrama and the Surrey theatre in particular served to amplify that achievement, as indicated by the *London Magazine* reviewer reading Miss Taylor's Jeanie Deans back into the Jeanie Deans of the novel. This in turn led ultimately to the elevation of melodrama as a legitimate art form. Together, *The Heart of Mid-Lothian* the melodramatic novel and *The Heart of Mid-Lothian* the novelistic melodrama created new possibilities for the representation and articulation of lower-class subjectivity that would have long-term implications for nineteenth-century culture in general.

The Scott phenomenon is important in other respects. It signalled the consolidation of the British public as primarily a reading public, and the breakthrough of the novel as a literary genre of nation-making power, as well as a coveted fashionable commodity. While the theatre played a supplementary role in this phenomenon, reflecting its waning literary status, the Scott craze on stage was important in reinforcing the sense of his novels as cultural events that in this case literally brought together a public. Those who saw *The Heart of Mid-Lothian* at the Surrey could feel themselves participating in the community for his fiction as vicarious readers, even if they could never have afforded the

---

[11] Nicoll (1955: 93); *Literary Chronicle and Weekly Review*, 2: 53 (20 May 1820), 326.
[12] *London Magazine*, 2: 10 (October 1820), 442.

novel or were even illiterate: conversely readers of *The Heart of Mid-Lothian* could go to the theatre to extend or affirm their experience of the book and the imagined community created by the sensation of Scott's fiction. This suggests how by 1820 the novel and print culture in general had reconfigured the cultural landscape. The 'novel' had become a cultural complex, including the theatre and visual art, its impact extending beyond the book to other forms of representation such as, later in the nineteenth century, the cinema. Novel 'reading' had become similarly diverse, not only capable of constituting the reading public, but also no longer strictly limited to the form of the book itself.

Considering the novel in relation to the stage therefore brings into relief two important dimensions of the novel's history. On the one hand, it served as one of the ways in which literary value was defined as a response to the expansion in print culture, the proliferation of reading audiences, and the convergence of media. The novel was transformed from being at the centre of the problem of modern culture, according to Wordsworth, to becoming part of the solution to that problem by being elevated as the literary genre, with poetry, which best represented the spirit of the age. This 'rise' was commensurate with the 'fall' of the theatre, or at least, the hardening of the distinction between drama as literature, made synonymous with Shakespeare, and what were pejoratively termed theatrical 'amusements'. However, at another level, the 'problem' which Wordsworth identified did not go away: as the dramatizations of Scott suggested, the novel and the stage continued to sustain each other, as they would also do in the case of Dickens. Moreover, the novel and the stage remained affiliated as part of a cultural formation, what I have called the novel 'complex', in which the novel, while central, functions primarily in a dynamic, expansive relationship with other media. It is only in the twenty-first century when the cultural and economic reach of the novel complex is greater than ever, as evident in the current status of Jane Austen or J. K. Rowling, that the significance of the Scott craze as a foundational event can be properly recognized.

Part VI

Assimilation and Cultural
Interchanges

29

Assimilating the Novel: Reviews and Collections

MICHAEL GAMER

Waverley and the *History of Fiction*

In 1814, there appeared the first book-length history of prose fiction written in English, *The History of Fiction: Being a Critical Account of the Most Celebrated Prose Works of Fiction, from the earliest Greek Romances to the Novels of the Present Age*, written by the Edinburgh advocate John Dunlop. Printed by James Ballantyne of Edinburgh and published by the firm of Longman, Rees, Hurst, and Brown of London, the treatise provides a comprehensive account of prose fiction that spans millennia, national boundaries, and literary traditions. Published in three large octavo volumes each numbering over 400 pages, the study is meant to be imposing, a self-consciously weighty treatment of a genre derided by reviewers and critics for over a century for its lightness.

Dunlop had some reasons for apprehension in this undertaking. For one thing, *The History of Fiction* was the debut work of its author. He thus understandably based a number of his claims and his organizational principles on established models like Thomas Warton's similarly titled *History of English Poetry* (1774–81), which in one of its chapters had argued for romance as a non-indigenous literary development. As Warton had four decades earlier, he proposed tracking his chosen genre's progress from its origins to the present day. Like Clara Reeve's *Progress of Romance* (1785), however, Dunlop posited an even grander vision that emphasized prose fiction's international history and roots in ancient culture. His final chapter, moreover, provided a sweeping assessment of recent British fiction: identifying 'Serious' and 'Comic' modes founded in the works of Samuel Richardson and Henry Fielding, and discovering a new type of novel, the 'Romantic', embodied in the works of Ann Radcliffe and her imitators. In this way, *The History of Fiction*'s publication constituted an entrée for Dunlop and prose fiction into the world of serious literature. It is no wonder that the book's formidable title and appearance mirrored its monumental scope, since both were designed to signal prose fiction's growing cultural importance and prestige.

Three months after Dunlop's study appeared, James Ballantyne completed the print-ing of another work foundational to the history of fiction, a novel: *Waverley; or,'Tis Sixty Years Since* (1814). Though anonymous, its author was reputed to be another Edinburgh advocate-turned-writer, Walter Scott, author of four best-selling metrical romances, some well-received editions, and two translations. Different as these two texts are, com-paring them shows the extent to which Dunlop and Scott shared more than just a printer. *The History of Fiction* testifies Dunlop to have been a methodical scholar and an able clas-sicist with a taste, like Scott, for medieval tales of chivalry, particularly those of Italy. Scott's relationship with Dunlop testifies to these sympathies, and shows Scott providing the younger writer with letters of introduction and advice for revising his work.[1] Like his older compatriot, Dunlop hoped to have his literary activities rewarded through politi-cal patronage (shortly after publishing *The History of Fiction*, he became sheriff-depute of Renfrewshire, a post held until his death in 1843). And, like Scott, he cared deeply about the novel's prestige. Though they do so in fundamentally different ways, both *Waverley* and *The History of Fiction* speak eloquently about the novel and its history. Both seek to raise its cultural status, portraying the writer of fiction as at once an antiquarian collec-tor of historical facts and a moral philosopher. Dunlop's own theories about the psycho-logical and social functions of fiction at times even recall Scott's first chapters on Edward Waverley's romance-reading, especially his contention that fiction has the power to 'raise the mind by accommodating the images of things to our desires'.[2] For Scott, however, the point is that Waverley reads with desire but without the exertion necessary to transform the romances of his adolescence into books of real instruction.

Here the resemblances between the two books most likely end, and not merely because of their differing audiences. In spite of sharing a desire to raise the prestige of prose fiction, *The History of Fiction* and *Waverley* occupy fundamentally different posi-tions in their relation to the novel's history, not to mention to literary tradition gener-ally. Scott's opening chapters, even as they invoke the novel's recent past, do so not to honour that tradition but to assert *Waverley*'s own claims to innovation against it. Unlike Dunlop, Scott invokes literary history in order ostentatiously to reject it. He may adopt a philosophical tone similar to that of *The History of Fiction* in surveying the current state of the novel, but here learned discourse serves as a vehicle for irony, signalling his break with prevailing modes of British fiction. For, in its treatment of the history of the novel, Scott's project is anything but scholarly. Rather, it rejects past fictional models while ironically invoking a detailed historical setting and mock-antiquarian tone. Far

---

[1] See Walter Scott to Richard Heber, 11 March 1815, in *The Letters of Walter Scott*, ed. H. J. C. Grierson, 12 vols (London: Constable & Co., 1932–7), 12.354 and 354n. In an 1816 'Advertisement' to the 2nd edn of the *History of Fiction*, Dunlop publicly thanked both Heber and Scott for their help.

[2] John Dunlop, *The History of Fiction: Being a Critical Account of the Most Celebrated Prose Works of Fiction, from the earliest Greek Romances to the Novels of the Present Age*, 3 vols (London: Longman [etc.], 1814), 1.vi.

from canvassing fiction's origins or carefully mapping the pedigree of his hero Edward Waverley, Scott proclaims the newness of both his plan and his title character. With showmanship and humour, his opening chapter's rapid survey of novelistic genres— from 'Tales of other Days' and 'Romance[s] from the German' to 'Sentimental Tales' and 'Tale[s] of the Time'—ends in a total break, much in the same way that *Waverley* itself calls up the scene of the 1745 Jacobite rising to emphasize modern Scotland's distance from its former, more romantic self.

Dunlop's and Scott's differences—rendered more compelling by shared backgrounds, assumptions, and goals—aptly introduce two starting points for considering the novel's assimilation into British culture between 1750 and 1820. First, their contrasting agendas remind us that formal histories and theories of genres (the kind embodied in the *History of Fiction*) almost always happen last or at least late in the game, even when a critical treatise also happens to be the first of its kind in a given language. At once scholarly, synthetic, and belated, works like Dunlop's are most frequently acts of establishment, intended to create retrospective order out of the chaos of culture. Second, Scott's self-conscious debut, staged as a competition with other contemporary novelistic traditions, represents a different kind of cultural assimilation. It illustrates how genres can continuously 'theorize' and 'historicize' themselves, doing so through not only the posturing of authors but also the activities of publishers, reviewers, librarians, anthologizers, and other energetic readers, all of whom improve on existing accounts of the novel or invent new ones. Put another way, between 1750 and 1820 the vast majority of theories and histories of the novel were introduced not through formal critical studies like *The History of Fiction*, but rather through an array of other publications that helped constitute print culture in these years. Of these other acts of publishing, this essay focuses on the activities of eighteenth-century literary reviews and anthologies, particularly on large reprinted collections of novels published after 1774, when the legal case *Donaldson v. Becket* abolished perpetual copyright in Britain.

The Rise of the Review

The periodical and the novel are creatures of the same publishing boom. Both came of age in the eighteenth century during a sustained expansion of the British book trade that continued well beyond 1800. As a result, the earliest critical responses to British fiction were usually published in newspapers and magazines for a general audience. To read these early essays—often no more than a paragraph in length—is to be struck by just how early and how established specific cultural anxieties about fiction were in the novel's history.

As early as 1692, for example, newspapers like the *Athenian Mercury* were actively questioning the intellectual and moral effects of reading romantic fiction, declaring the activity dangerous to class stability and the social fabric.[3] By mid-century, in the wake of the popular debate sparked by Samuel Richardson's *Pamela: or, Virtue Rewarded* (1740–1), commentators had sought to explain more fully fiction's impressive power to move, instruct, or debauch its readers. *Pamela* had been a sensation; with it and Richardson's next novel, *Clarissa* (1748–9), Richardson succeeded in inspiring not only a new school of fiction but also a formidable rival in the form of Henry Fielding, whose *Shamela* (1741), *Joseph Andrews* (1742), and *Tom Jones* (1749) positioned themselves against Richardson's epistolary practice and with the more picaresque tradition of Cervantes and Le Sage. Given these developments, we should probably not be surprised that the same decade that witnessed the novel's coming of age as a genre—one not yet established but now meriting serious critical attention—should also have marked the launching of the first 'serious' literary review.

Founded in 1749 by the publisher and bookseller Ralph Griffiths, the *Monthly Review* (1749–1845) was nothing less than groundbreaking in its format and effect on British literary culture. In providing only reviews of new publications, it filled a gap in British periodical writing by offering evaluative accounts of books as they were published. Griffiths's Advertisement for his new periodical was succinct and pointed: with so many books being published each month and with their title pages frequently misrepresenting their contents, readers needed 'an account… which should, in virtue of its candour, and justness of distinction, obtain authority enough…to be serviceable to such as would choose to have some idea of a book before they lay out their money or time on it'.[4] Implied in these sentences were three pledges. The first two, disinterestedness and expertise in reviewers, remain conventions of literary reviewing today. The third, covering every book published—whether through longer reviews (for weighty or significant books) or short notices (for more ephemeral publications)—became a reality only with time. Yet, it was the combination of these promises that led to the *Monthly*'s unprecedented success and that induced one of its reviewers, the novelist Tobias Smollett, to found the *Critical Review* (1756–1817) seven years later. There, in the Preface to his own opening issue, Smollett vowed to review 'every material performance' with disinterestedness and fairness.[5] His promises show just how quickly the *Monthly* had established codes of reviewing that remained dominant through the end of the century.

In spite of their vows of fairness, both the *Monthly* and *Critical*, as 'serious' literary Reviews, were generally unfriendly to fiction, treating novels most often as needing regulation and correction. An early *Monthly* review of Tobias Smollett's *The Adventures of Peregrine Pickle* (1751) typifies these early notices. Lamenting that 'serious and useful works are scarce read', the reviewer condemns, in order, 'lewd or profane' works,

---

[3] 'Quest. 2. Whether 'tis lawful to read Romances', *Athenian Mercury* (17 December 1692), 1.
[4] 'Advertisement', *Monthly Review*, 1 (May 1749).
[5] 'Preface', *Critical Review; or, Annals of Literature*, 1 (1756).

'worthless frivolous pieces', and 'that flood of novels, tales, romances, and other monsters of the imagination'.[6] This expressive trio of genres anticipates the argument that
follows. '[R]omances and novels', the reviewer continues, 'turn upon characters out of
nature, monsters of perfection, feats of chivalry, fairy enchantments, and the whole train
of marvellous-absurd', and as such 'transport the reader unprofitably into the clouds,
where he is sure to find no solid footing, or into those wilds of fancy, which go for ever out
of the way of all human paths' (356–7).

These pronouncements typify how reviewers theorized the novel in the eighteenth
century. Ranging in tone from the merely negative to the condemnatory, the remarks
should suggest to us that, in spite of the popular and artistic successes of a host of novelists in the first half of the century, little had changed between the attitudes of critical
readers and reviewers of the mid-eighteenth century and those of the *Athenian Mercury*
six decades earlier. I say 'should suggest' because what follows is not a negative review
of Smollett's novel. Rather, the reviewer prints two substantial extracts of the work, and
then grudgingly praises the character of Peregrine as represented 'with great uniformity
of principle', and (more vaguely) as 'too natural to be perfect' (363). As such, the review
structurally enacts what we might call an emerging disjunction between popular taste
and the critical judgement of the Reviews. Its lengthy initial condemnation of fiction—
lumping the generality of novels with lewd and scandalous publications—smacks of anxious self-consciousness, as if the act of praising an individual novel required a certain
quantity of general abuse for the genre as a whole to maintain the reviewer's authority
and credibility.

With notable exceptions, this general pattern among reviewers remained largely
unchanged for much of the eighteenth century. The cause lay most likely not in the sameness of the fiction—far from it—but in the cultural position taken up by the Reviews themselves. In the interest of bolstering their cultural authority, the *Monthly* and the *Critical*
during these decades made it an institutional practice to assert their intellectual independence and to deny their status as booksellers' vehicles. They did so most effectively by
downplaying their own contingent status as periodical publications and instead presenting themselves as creators of permanent knowledge. This rhetorical stance allowed the
Reviews to place themselves at once outside popular opinion and above the day-to-day
contingencies of traditional newspapers and magazines. More important, it enabled them
to deflect and otherwise deny the newness of their own mode of writing, literary criticism. Reading early reviews of fiction, one imagines from their tone that popular fiction
is a new phenomenon and that the literary review is as established as the most venerable
of government institutions, whereas the opposite is more true: that the novel is the older

---

[6] *Monthly Review*, 4 (March 1751), 355–64 (355).

and more established genre, and that the professional review as a specialized kind of writing stands less than a decade old.

Policing the Novel

Amidst this veneer of permanence, the hostility of Reviews to the novel becomes far more understandable, particularly when we remember that periodicals were just as subject to the literary marketplace as other publications. Reviews, after all, had a narrow line to walk as publications, since the long-term financial health of a Review required it to anticipate broad shifts in popular taste even as it sought to mould that taste. Faced with a work of quality written by a fellow *Monthly* reviewer, the *Peregrine Pickle* reviewer understandably chooses a critical position from which the *Monthly* might remain separate from popular taste while not fully opposing it. In this light, fiction's growing popularity presented for Reviews both an opportunity and an uncomfortable quandary, since their pledge to review all publications responsibly required them to review newly published fiction, however grudgingly. To notice such publications, these early reviewers complained, was to bestow cultural respectability where it was not deserved; still, to ignore them altogether was to shirk an important cultural duty and risk irrelevance. It is no wonder, then, that the *Monthly* and the *Critical* tended to project onto novels the very traits—popularity, ephemerality, disposability—that they most wished to deny about themselves.

By establishing the Review as a fundamental part of book production and reception, Griffiths and Smollett permanently changed print culture in Britain. Most directly, other periodicals were forced to take up the habit of reviewing at least desultorily and to make it part of their corporate identities. Founded in 1731, the influential *Gentleman's Magazine* may have helped shape the editorial voices of the *Monthly* and *Critical*, but these two Reviews in turn changed the organization of that older publication, which began experimentally adding 'remarks' to its 'List of Books' as early as 1751 and permanently adapted the practice in 1765.[7] Other magazines quickly followed suit. Modelled on the *Gentleman's*, the venerable *London Magazine* (1732–85) began adding periodic critical comments to their monthly 'Catalogue of Books' as early as November of 1759.[8] The new *Town and Country Magazine* (1769–95), meanwhile, did so from its opening issues, making its 'Account of New Books and Pamphlets' a regular feature. This general expansion of periodicals means that, for much of the second half of the eighteenth century, nearly every novel published could expect to be reviewed at least once, with the majority receiving at least two reviews after the founding of the *Critical Review* in 1756. The result of

---

[7] See, for example, *Gentleman's Magazine*, 21 (July 1751), 334; and *Gentleman's Magazine*, 35 (February 1765), 99.

[8] See, for example, *London Magazine*, 28 (November 1759), 630.

these activities was to establish a continuous and accelerating critical discourse on the novel's tendencies and history.

Novelists, in turn, were forced to adjust to the reality of reviewing by anticipating possible criticisms. Some even sought to short-circuit reviewer responses by providing their own histories of fiction or theories of reading. Gender also entered into the relationship, despite the customary anonymity of reviewers: in part because the majority of professional reviewers were male and in part because the Reviews habitually assumed a masculine voice of learned rigour. These roles were so firmly established that even female reviewers assumed this institutional voice. Thus, we find a *Monthly* reviewer like Elizabeth Moody, while anonymously reviewing *The Denial; or, The Happy Retreat* (1790), referring to her anonymous reviewer-self as one 'of the harder sex, as men, and of the still harder *race as critics*' even while she classes *The Denial*'s author, James Thomson, as a practitioner of popular fiction written by 'Ladies':

> Of the various species of composition that in course come before us, there are none in which our writers of the male sex have less excelled, since the days of Richardson and Fielding, than in the arrangement of a novel. Ladies seem to appropriate to themselves an exclusive privilege in this kind of writing; witness the numerous productions of romantic tales to which female authors have given birth.[9]

The only thing more striking than Moody's representation of herself as a member first of 'the harder sex, as men' and then of 'the still harder *race as critics*' is the way that Thomson's sex carries less significance than *The Denial*'s gender. Such a reversal points to a different kind of cultural assimilation of the novel, one that seeks to locate novel readers and novel writers within a specific, feminized demographic.

In other words, Frances Burney's justifiably famous 'To the Authors of the *Monthly* and *Critical* Reviews', with which she opened *Evelina* (1778), is merely one of many responses by novelists after 1750 to the new reviewing regimen that sought to dismiss their art. Faced with the prospect of reviewer anonymity, Burney's Preface recasts her reviewers as men of honour—as 'Authors' and as 'Gentlemen', who, rather than treating her 'trifling' work with contempt, should instead offer it protection. 'Without name, without recommendation, and unknown alike to success and disgrace', she queries, 'to whom can I so properly apply for patronage, as to those who publicly profess themselves Inspectors of all literary performances?'[10] Such a question winningly removes the Reviews' mask of disinterestedness and anonymity while exploiting the very biases of gender and education that have led reviewers, in Burney's portrait of them, to treat novels as 'frivolous amusement[s]' deserving 'contempt'. Instead, she argues, 'As Magistrates of the press, and

---

[9] *Monthly Review*, n.s., 3 (December 1790), 400–2 (400).

[10] Frances Burney, *Evelina, or, A Young Lady's Entrance into the World*, 2nd edn, 3 vols (London: T. Lowndes, 1779), 1.vi.

Censors for the Public . . . you are bound by the sacred ties of integrity to exert the most spirited impartiality' (1.vi).

With the Whig *Monthly* and the predominantly Tory *Critical* seemingly encompassing the Republic of Letters, Burney could still manage, in 1778, to imagine the Review as a coherent though corporate identity. Her decision to present herself as an informed hero- ine requiring the patronage of enlightened 'Gentlemen' stems, of course, from the uni- form persona projected by the Reviews themselves. Over the next decades, however, this sense of cohesion was steadily eroded by new periodicals such as the *New Review* (1782–6), which aimed at reviewing foreign publications, and the *English Review* (1783–95), which advertised itself not only as reviewing 'every book and pamphlet which shall appear in England, Scotland, Ireland, and America' but also as providing extensive coverage 'of literature in France, Italy, Germany, and Spain'.[11] The next decades in turn produce a small avalanche: first with additional monthlies like Joseph Johnson's *Analytical Review* (1788–99), the Anglican *British Critic* (1793–1843), the reactionary *Anti-Jacobin Review* (1798–1821); and later with the introduction of quarterlies like the *Edinburgh* (1802–1929), *Quarterly* (1809–1967), and *Westminster* (1824–1914) Reviews.

As these additions occur at the same time that the number of new novels is increasing dramatically, the portrait that emerges is rich and at times surprising. Most immediately arresting in Tables 29.1 and 29.2 are the production figures, which show the number of new novels published in Britain at mid-century tripling in four decades.[12] This increase occurs, moreover, in spite of a significant fall in production during the late 1770s and early 1780s, a fairly tumultuous time for the business of books. A likely contributing fac- tor to this sudden drop is *Donaldson v. Becket* (1774), the House of Lords case that fuelled a boom in reprinting by ending perpetual copyright in England. By reducing the term of copyright throughout Britain to no more than twenty-eight years, *Donaldson* opened up a lucrative market in reprinting older books overnight, and English booksellers and print- ers duly shifted their attention away from printing new books for nearly a decade. Thus, after 1775 the number of new novels published dropped to less than half of pre-*Donaldson* levels and did not recover itself for several years, when in 1784–5 production nearly dou- bled and then after 1788 increased dramatically again.

Taken together, the two tables confirm that growing numbers of new novels at first did not daunt the Reviews' drive to cover all publications. The average number of reviews

---

[11] 'Preface', *English Review*, 1 (January 1783), 3.

[12] In compiling this information, I have drawn on the bibliographic work of Antonia Forster, Peter Garside, James Raven, Rainer Schöwerling, and William S. Ward for assistance. The figures given for the number of new novels reviewed and the total number of reviews are my own, and were compiled from the collections of periodicals at the University of Pennsylvania and the British Library. As such, they represent minimum figures for a given span of years, meaning that almost certainly there exist additional reviews I have not been able to discover. Given the intensive nature of the work, I provide figures for the first three years of each decade.

Table 29.1. Reviewing new fiction, 1750–1820

Years	New Novels Published	New Novels Reviewed	% New Novels Rev'd	Total Reviews of New Novels	Reviews per New Novel
1750–2	65	45	69%	45	1
1760–2	74	64	86%	137	2.14
1770–2	141	131	93%	403	3.08
1780–2	68	53	78%	148	2.79
1790–2	206	184	89%	522	2.84
1800–2	217	155	71%	446	2.88
1810–12	238	95	40%	299	3.15

Table 29.2. Production of new novels and number of novels reviewed, 1775–90

Year	1773–4	1775–6	1777–8	1779–80	1781–2	1783–4	1785–6	1787–8	1789–90
New Novels Published	74	48	34	42	44	48	87	131	145
New Novels Reviewed	70	45	31	32	39	45	81	125	136
% New Novels Reviewed	95%	94%	91%	76%	89%	94%	93%	95%	94%

received by each new novel rises quickly from 1.0 for 1750–2 to 3.08 for 1770–2, and then stays fairly steady at that level for the next decades. While no periodical managed to review every published work, the steady expansion of publications printing reviews meant that relatively few novels could slip into the world unnoticed. As might be expected, celebrity authors and established writers received significantly more scrutiny, usually half-a-dozen notices in various forms. As policing mechanisms go, the view that emerges from these tables is one of equilibrium: that the market for novels expanded at roughly the same rate as that of periodicals; and that reviewers, in spite of their constant complaints about the increase of novels, maintained a fairly vigilant level of surveillance.

The sudden drop of coverage of new novels after 1800–2, therefore, is especially striking, and points to fundamental changes in reviewing as the nineteenth century turned. As with the sudden drop in the production of fiction in the later 1770s, one can point to a likely cause in this case as well: the founding of the *Edinburgh Review*, which transformed reviewing practice in Great Britain. First appearing in October of 1802, the *Edinburgh* was a quarterly rather than a monthly review, meaning that it appeared every third month and featured articles of greater length than its rivals. This format caught on immediately, in part because of the depth of its criticisms and in part because of the novelty of its critical persona, which rejected the even-handedness of other Reviews in the name of strong, energetic, and informed opinion. Such an editorial stance proudly boasted of its own exclusivity. As Marilyn Butler puts it succinctly, 'It [the *Edinburgh*] did not set out to serve the general public by extracting the contents of many books, but selected drastically in order to influence a more elite stratum of opinion...[and] break the mould of existing review culture' (2010: 137–8). Such practices sharply contrasted with the inclusiveness of the established monthly Reviews, which traditionally had provided a place for less prestigious genres like the novel to be noticed with at least some show of disinterestedness. Instead, the *Edinburgh* and its heirs embraced interested opinion, brutally attacked specific authors and ideas in the name of higher principle, and had little time for more plebeian literary forms: individual issues rarely boast more than one review of a novel per issue, and often ignore fiction altogether. With circulations hovering at three times those of other Reviews, the *Edinburgh*'s formula could not help but be influential. As a result, during the first two decades of the nineteenth century, review articles became longer and reviews of fiction fewer and farther in between. By the beginning of the Regency, we find the number of reviews of new novels declining sharply, from a peak of 522 for the three-year period 1790–2 to 299 for 1810–12.

It is worth noting, however, that many of these patterns emerge even before the advent of the *Edinburgh* and other quarterly Reviews. The *Monthly Review*, for example, began to abandon its ideal of programmatically reviewing all new works of literature as early as the mid-1790s, when it began to ignore novels published by the less prestigious Minerva and Hookham presses. Their decision to do so was likely facilitated by the founding of the *British Critic*, which in a fervent show of duty had vowed to review all popular works as a safeguard to preserving decency. Presented with such pledges of moral scrutiny, it becomes tempting to see eighteenth-century Reviews as a kind of novel police: with late eighteenth-century novelists seemingly incapable of policing themselves and requiring the institutional management of the Reviews, only to have this system of programmatic surveillance begin to break down because of internal changes in reviewing practice and the publishing industry. Examining Table 29.1 a final time, we find a noticeable falling away of the Reviews' pledge of total coverage at the beginning of the 1800s, just before the founding of the *Edinburgh*. The advent of more openly partisan critical opinion made famous by the *Edinburgh*, moreover, also occurs earlier, through the founding of the *British Critic* and the *Anti-Jacobin* in the 1790s.

In this sense, the data regarding reviewer behaviour in Tables 29.1 and 29.2 can tell us much about the history of criticism about the novel and its assimilation into British literary culture. At the very least, they point to the emergence of different categories of fiction in the final decades of the eighteenth century: 'literary' works worthy of reviewing; provincially published works usually not reviewed; and 'popular' works published by circulating librarians like Lane and Hookham of too low a stature to be worthy of serious consideration. Of course, such divisions between metropole and province, and between high and popular culture, have always been with us; as the *Monthly*'s review of *Peregrine Pickle* testifies, a constant project of eighteenth-century criticism of the novel was to define the criteria by which a small and select collection of standard English fiction might be separated from the greater mass of novels published each year. Still, the sudden legibility of this culture gap in the practice of British Reviews shows how fluid such divisions could be and how rapidly they could change—not merely among reviewers but also among the builders of collections of fiction.

Select Collecting: Reprinting the Novelistic Canon

As commentators from Barbara Benedict (1996) to Thomas Bonnell (2008) have reminded us, reprinting and canon-building are far from the same activity, since few of the acts of valuation involved in reprinting a text necessarily overlap with those we associate with canonization. An essentially economic decision involving risk and return, reprinting presupposes only a publisher's willingness to print based on the expectation of some kind of profit, usually taking the form of a belief that customers will buy. Canonization, in contrast, almost always involves the activity of distinguishing between texts, where the decision to prefer one to another usually depends on registers of value other than saleability. In case of the novel, these registers frequently are underwritten by arguments about the genre's history and characteristics. For this reason, scholars usually have associated the early canonization of the novel not with the activities of publishers but rather with those of early reviewers and critics, those separators of wheat from chaff who reserve their highest praises only for the choicest specimens of British fiction.

To look to the rich world of eighteenth-century publishing, of course, is quickly to realize the artificiality of such a split. Critics labour in hope of profits as much as any novelist, and reviewing as an institutional practice has served the producers of books from its outset. Ralph Griffiths may have been the creator and editor of the *Monthly Review*, but he also was a publisher and bookseller—which meant that his journal regularly reviewed the books he was producing. (In a similar manner, the *Critical Review* reviewed the works of its editor, Tobias Smollett.) These interested reviews, sometimes called 'puffs', might have drawn criticism because they brought profit motives in collusion with the critical act of impartial judgement, but such conflicts of interest were to a degree inevitable where publishers owned the Reviews, newspapers, and magazines that noticed their books.

We can make similar observations about the production side of eighteenth- and early nineteenth-century print culture when we consider anthologies and collections, since such books are not merely reprinted but also repackaged as exemplary works. Simply put, any publisher's anthology or collection of some 'genre X' cannot help but posit through its choice of texts a theory of what 'X' is, usually supported and formalized by a prefatory critical essay on the subject. As with the publisher who reviews his or her own books, here profit motive and critical act combine seamlessly, since the critical duty of selecting elite specimens of a given genre also underwrites the marketing and sale of a given set of volumes. In the case of the novel, these acts of reprinting and anthologizing have a long history, and even the earliest collections doubled as vehicles for theorizing fictitious narrative and recounting its history. Changing copyright laws also matter, particularly after *Donaldson v. Becket* (1774) made it possible to reprint novels on scales large enough to market them as coherent canons of British fiction.

Of course, 'Select collections' of novels, as I call these large and uniformly printed multi-volume anthologies of fiction, existed long before *Donaldson*. The name is taken from an early eighteenth-century collection of fiction published by Samuel Croxall in 1720. Its full title—*A Select Collection of Novels in Four Volumes; written by the most Celebrated Authors in several Languages; many of which never appear'd in English before; and all New Translated from the Originals, by several Eminent Hands*—nicely captures the dual urges of 'selection' and 'collection' at work in the multi-volume anthologized collection, not to mention its pre-1774 reliance primarily on newly translated foreign texts unprotected by British copyright laws. As the term 'select collection' implies, such publications claim to represent a category of object, in this case 'novels'; but, in doing so, they make two different and somewhat contradictory claims about the exemplarity of the collection contained within their volumes. On the one hand, Croxall's title foregrounds the idea that his collection can represent the novel's identity by collecting and reprinting specimens of the genre. Here, the collection has the power to capture what is typical (exemplary), since, by assembling suitable works of fiction together, readers can form a theory of the Novel more generally. On the other hand, as the term 'select' affirms, Croxall also claims to have assembled only the finest specimens; whether typical novels or not, they represent here what is best (exemplary) about a species.

In this sense, *A Select Collection of Novels* does everything in its power to claim an elite status for its assembled contents. As part of his collection's packaging, Croxall provides additional prefatory materials, including elaborate frontispieces and dedications for each volume. The aim here is to raise the prestige of the novels contained therein through these paratextual additions. A similar logic governs Croxall's decision to reprint Pierre Daniel Huet's then-famous *Treatise on the Origin of Romances*, since its prominent place in the collection confers on it a representative significance. Thus, the defining characteristics bestowed by Huet on the most unexceptionable romantic fiction—'Instruction and Entertainment...that no Novel shou'd have a Place, which...does not inspire Disinterestedness, Generosity, Fidelity, Constancy, with the like Virtues'—also become for Croxall 'the reigning Perfections of this Collection'.[13] Here, critical essays do more

---

[13] Samuel Croxall, *Preface, A Select Collection of Novels*, 4 vols (London: Croxall, 1720), 1.iii.

than bolster the reputation of a collection; they help to shape how that collection puts forward a 'theory' of its genre in its most ideal terms.

These implied arguments govern the formal dynamics of most anthologies and multi-volume collections, which change little throughout the eighteenth and early nineteenth centuries. Scanning through the catalogues of booksellers, we find dozens of select collections published over the decades, from Dodsley's *A Select Collection of Old Plays* (1744) to Joseph Ritson's authoritative *A Select Collection of English Songs* (1783). During these same years we find several collections of novels. Most, including *The Novelist; or Tea-Table Miscellany* (1766) and *A Collection of Novels, Selected and Revised by Mrs. Griffith* (1777), model themselves on Croxall even after the *Donaldson v. Becket* decision. For, while *Donaldson* enabled publishers such as John Bell to create ambitious collections like *A Select Collection of Oriental Tales* (1776), *Bell's British Theatre* (1776–8), and *Poets of Great Britain Complete* (1777–82), it did not inspire an analogous, uniformly printed multi-volume collection of novels in these years. Instead, what emerged were a few failed collections modelled on older models and a highly successful serial, *The Novelist's Magazine* (1779–88), which proved to be the first post-*Donaldson* publishing venture to produce a recognizable novelistic canon through select reprinting.

This venture, as orchestrated by its publisher James Harrison, from its beginning was a reprint series, a 'periodical' only in the sense of its appearing serially in instalments. With the novel occupying a less prestigious position than other literary forms, it is hardly surprising that Harrison took a more cautious approach to collecting and republishing British fiction in unabridged form than publishers had taken with other genres. Thus, his Prospectus, entitled 'A Pleasing Publication', opens by trumpeting *The Novelist's Magazine*'s low cost alongside fiction's popular appeal, promising that each volume will contain 'interesting HISTORIES, ADVENTURES, MEMOIRS, and other NOVELS'.[14] It is only after making these initial claims that the Prospectus shifts its emphasis to the collection's select nature. As Bell had done with his editions of British drama and British poetry, Harrison calls his readers' attention to his use of 'superfine paper' and 'most beautiful Type purposely contrived for this Publication'. Every number, moreover, is to be 'embellished with a truly elegant and original *Copper-plate*, designed and engraved by the first Artists in the Kingdom'. Clothed in the finest paper, typefaces, and illustrations, Harrison's proposed texts take on the status of art objects: *The Novelist's Magazine* will only contain the best works, those 'scarcest and most approved...which have at any Time appeared in the English Language'.

Harrison's Prospectus understandably aims at inclusiveness in its definition of the 'Novel', encompassing a broad spectrum of subgenres under that term. It also actively ruminates on 'the Power of this Species of Literature', insisting on its global history and

---

[14] James Harrison, *Prospectus for The Novelist's Magazine* (London: Harrison & Co., 1779).

proposing to supplement English texts with 'Elegant and New TRANSLATIONS from the French, Spanish, German, and Italian'. With each new number containing an expensive frontispiece, Harrison needed to achieve high circulation quickly; his choice of texts over the first volumes reflects this drive for high sales. As a result, unlike select collections in other genres or the treatises of critics like Warton, Reeve, or Dunlop, *The Novelist's Magazine* does not attempt to organize its contents by period, genre, or nation. Indeed, during its first three years of publication (1779–82), Harrison's only critical act lies in the choosing of works. These choices, however, display a remarkably coherent and particular sense of the novel's nature and history. As we shall see from subsequent anthologies and collections of novels, Harrison's emerging canon arguably did more to define the English novel and its history than any British publication of its time.

He accomplished this feat of assimilation, furthermore, without accompanying critical essays: the first volume commences immediately with John Hawkesworth's *Almoran and Hamet* followed by Henry Fielding's *Adventures of Joseph Andrews* and *Amelia*. The second and third volumes repeat this pattern of moving between exotic tale and homegrown history. The former begins with John Langhorne's *Solyman and Almena, an Oriental Tale* followed by Oliver Goldsmith's *The Vicar of Wakefield, a Tale*, Tobias Smollett's *The Adventures of Roderick Random*, Francis Ashmore's *Zadig*, and Alain René Le Sage's *Devil upon Two Sticks*; the latter opens with Sir Charles Morell's *Tales of the Genii* before moving to Fielding's *History of Tom Jones*. Each volume appears intentionally heterogeneous, opening with some form of foreign or oriental 'tale' followed by a homegrown English novel, and then alternating where necessary. Over its first nine volumes, the series constructs a bifurcated but international canon of fiction, inscribing Harrison's promise of pleasing variety but along fairly narrow generic and national lines. The emerging publishing formula combines an assortment of 'tales', usually foreign in their origin, with English novels, here centred on what we now call the novel of Fielding and Smollett. As novelistic canons go, this one is tightly cohesive and remarkably consistent; it was also both influential and popular.

Part of the power of any collection lies in its ability to represent a larger whole through a comprehensible assemblage of component parts. Certainly Harrison's selections comprise part of a more comprehensive marketing plan; yet they also constitute a fairly comprehensive history of fiction, isolating specific seventeenth-century precursors and tracing their genealogies through the present day. Consisting of twenty-eight works of fiction, Harrison's first nine volumes (1779–82) place a pointed and consistent premium on masculine adventure deriving itself from the picaresque realism of Cervantes and his heirs, providing little in the way of epistolary fiction and few dissenting and women writers. Whether these titles constitute an actual canon of fiction is in a sense immaterial; what matters is that they point to one. In grouping texts and connecting them through titling, generic tags, and placement within a given volume, Harrison's emerging collection foregrounds certain traditions of fiction as standard while ignoring others, and what emerges is a discernible theory of the English novel's nature, core texts, and influences.

That these choices were self-conscious is best seen through Harrison's periodic special Advertisements, such as the one that announced that all of volumes 10 and 11 would be devoted to the publication of Samuel Richardson's *Sir Charles Grandison*:

> The Publishers of the Novelist's Magazine flatter themselves they need make no apology for inserting, in a work which has received such marks of universal approbation, a production which has very deservedly been esteemed, by men of the first literary and moral characters, the most perfect of its kind that ever appeared in this or any other language.[15]

Here is palpably different language from the original 1779 Prospectus, one pointing not to the pleasure of readers but the 'approbation' of critics of 'the first literary and moral characters'. This statement is then followed by quotations from five men most famous for their critical and literary achievements outside of fiction—Warton, Samuel Johnson, Lord Lyttelton, Jean-Jacques Rousseau, and Diderot—who stand as models for prospective readers: 'those who read Sir Charles Grandison will need no guide to direct them to its beauties' (2). The scene of reading constructed in Harrison's original prospectus of 1779 is here replaced by the praise of learned critics and by readers who need no guidance to discover the 'beauties' of a writer of such canonical 'merit'. Such terms point not just to a gap between common readers and critics, but also to the existence of an accompanying body of critically approved fictional works requiring a different language to sell them to the public. To judge by the contents of volume 12—which commences with Charlotte Lennox's *The Female Quixote* before moving to Fielding's *A Journey from this World to the Next*, Edward Kimber's *Life and Adventures of Joe Thompson*, and Robert Paltock's *Life and Adventures of Peter Wilkins*—Harrison was only too pleased to revert to his earlier formula of masculine adventures and quixotic realism after publishing Richardson's final work.

After *The Novelist's Magazine*

Harrison ended *The Novelist's Magazine* in 1788 after twenty-three volumes and sixty novels. In nine years of publication, he achieved sales exceeding not only other contemporary select collections but also popular periodicals, including the *Gentleman's Magazine* and *Monthly Review*. His influence on the history of the novel can be felt in literary reviews' increasingly historical and comparatist notices of fiction after 1780, and in the sheer number of volumes of *The Novelist's Magazine* held in library collections and still available for

---

[15] James Harrison, 'Advertisement' for *Sir Charles Grandison* for *The Novelist's Magazine*, vol. 10 (London: Harrison, 1783), 1.

sale by antiquarian booksellers. In a genre notorious for flooding the market with new productions, Harrison almost single-handedly filled his country's bookshops and circulating libraries with reprints of standard British fiction. Still, the effects of his venture register most clearly in the repeated attempts of booksellers to duplicate his publishing success in the years that followed by privileging the same authors in their own collections. Both *The Novelist* (1792–3) and *Hogg's New Novelist's Magazine* (1794) failed to attract readers in spite of their obvious echoes of Harrison, while William Mudford's *The British Novelists* (1810–16) spluttered to a halt five volumes into what had become a *de rigueur* reprinting of Fielding, Goldsmith, Smollett, and Sterne. Even Leigh Hunt's *Classic Tales, Serious and Lively* (1806–7) enjoyed at best moderate success, chiefly by reprinting shorter works that had appeared in *The Novelist's Magazine* and *New Novelist's Magazine* (1786–8).

We find the most compelling proof of Harrison's influence as a theorist and historian of the novel in two collections of standard novels published, respectively, by Anna Barbauld (1810) and Walter Scott (1821–4). Of the two, Scott's collection most closely resembles Harrison's production model, particularly in Scott's desire to publish serially and to print in double columned, large octavo format. His reliance on Harrison's model may be explained in part by the fact that he first began planning his collection in 1808–9, before Barbauld's was announced. As might be expected, Scott's early plans for a collection of fiction were much grander than what finally found its way into print; as the correspondence from those years makes clear, however, Harrison's model constituted more than just a mode of publishing. Scott's letters to the publisher John Murray II show him determined not only to base his own collection on Harrison's but also to find in that collection a fully developed and hierarchized novelistic canon:

> I have been also turning over in my mind the plan of the Novels & Romances...beginning with the Novels of Richardson. Fielding & Smollett will lead the van with a very short memoir of each of their lives & a prefatory Essay on the peculiarities of their stile. These will be followd by a good selection of novels of less name.... To give the selection some appearance of arrangement, it will be necessary to separate the Translations from the original Novels, to place those of each author together—which I observe is neglected in Harrison's series—and to keep the Novels, properly so-called, separate from Romances and Tales. I have little doubt that 20 volumes of 700 pages will hold all the Novels, &c. that are worth reprinting, but I will be a much better judge when I see the catalogues. Should we find on strict selection that a volume or two more will be necessary, we can throw the Tales into a separate division.[16]

Scott's proposed organization and critical apparatus show him seeking to bestow a sense of collectedness—the 'appearance of arrangement'—as a way of bringing out principles already inscribed in Harrison's choice of texts. Here again formal critical histories of the novel come last, after the work of cultural assimilation has been largely completed, since

---

[16] Walter Scott to John Murray, 30 October and 2 November 1808, *Letters of Scott*, ed. Grierson, 2.114 and 2.119.

Scott's proposed Lives and Preface for the series merely render explicit principles present but implicit in Harrison's collection.

Negotiations with Murray eventually broke down, and Scott's idea lay dormant for over a decade. What is most striking about the *Ballantyne's Novelist's Library* (1821–4), the ten-volume series begun over a decade after Scott first wrote to Murray, is the tenacity with which Scott clung to his original scheme and Harrison's model. Though organized by author, its finished contents still essentially follow the trajectory of Harrison's series, devoting a volume to Fielding and two to Smollett before moving on to works by Alain Le Sage and Charles Johnstone, followed by Oliver Goldsmith, Samuel Johnson, Henry Mackenzie, Horace Walpole, and others. The presence of Harrison's publishing model extends even to a similar ambivalence over Richardson: Scott's desire to '[b]egin with the Novels of Richardson' yet 'lead' with Fielding & and Smollett reproduces Harrison's own division between economic profitability and cultural authoritativeness. Writing to Hurst, Robinson & Co. in 1822 (Constable 1873: 3.198–9), Scott put the matter even more bluntly: 'Having printed Smollett and Fielding, Richardson undoubtedly comes next in order. But then his works are so insufferably long, that they will take a great deal of room in the proposed edition—while, on the other hand, a collection of novels without Richardson would be very incomplete. What are you to say of Defoe?' As with *The Novelist's Magazine*, Richardson appears in *Ballantyne's Novelist's Library* only at this midpoint—*after*, rather than before, 'a good selection of novels of less name'.

Rather than collapsing under the magnitude of his early ambitions, Scott's proposals to Murray during the winter and spring of 1808–9 most likely failed because of unlooked-for success from an unforeseen quarter, in the form of Anna Barbauld's *The British Novelists*, published in fifty volumes in 1810. Announced at the same time as Mudford's *The British Novelists* and as Scott was beginning to prepare materials for Murray, Barbauld's collection trumped its rivals because of its richly authoritative editorial apparatus and its innovations in formatting and publication. Breaking with the traditional double columns and royal octavo format, it adopted the larger print and pocket size of earlier poetic and dramatic collections. Its timing and mode of publication also were groundbreaking, its fifty volumes advertised and appearing as a single collection rather than as a serial. In this way, *The British Novelists* exhibited to its audience for the first time a single body of fiction—fully theorized in its chronologies and boasting an authoritative critical introduction—whose claims to exemplarity could not be mistaken.

As Dunlop's *History of Fiction* would do four years later, Barbauld's 'On the Origin and Progress of Novel-Writing' (1810) presented a global history that sought to counter long-standing critical prejudices against fiction by arguing for its historical, aesthetic, and pedagogical importance. Asserting a 'good novel [to be] an epic in prose, with more of character and less (indeed in modern novels nothing) of the supernatural machinery', Barbauld argues that fiction's broad appeal renders it deserving of the highest cultural standing, with the novel now occupying the position once held by the ancient epic. Such a narrative is broadly historical and inclusive until it approaches the present day: British writers contribute to a long-standing tradition originating in ancient Greece even as they break from that tradition to invent the 'modern novel' early in the eighteenth century. Distinguished by its genius for 'natural painting', this modern English novel originates in Daniel Defoe's *Robinson Crusoe*, '*unique* in its kind' and functioning as a kind of prophetic precursor to the novels of 'Richardson, Fielding, and Smollett'.[17] Defoe thus functions in Barbauld's essay as a kind of conduit, at once the inheritor of a tradition of world fiction and an original genius of native growth providing the origins of the modern novel. Nourished on Hanoverian soil, the modern novel becomes in Barbauld's representation at once organic and locally grown, its flourishing state suggesting a similar state of health for the British nation.

Overlapping Histories, Contending Canons

Given the historical sweep and inclusive rhetoric of Barbauld's essay, the contending canon it offers is all the more remarkable for how it differs from its predecessors. Comparing its list of titles to earlier collections like Harrison's or even to the later *Ballantyne* series, *The British Novelists* offers a qualitatively different body of fiction, leading with Richardson and devoting a majority of the volumes to epistolary, female, and liberal and dissenting writers. In spite of its smaller number of titles, it features writers found in no other collection, among them Frances Burney, Frances Brooke, Maria Edgeworth, Elizabeth Inchbald, John Moore, and Charlotte Smith. (Of these, Scott had planned to include the novels of Smith, but ultimately was unable to do so.) Barbauld even differs in her selections of authors also printed in other collections, as when she chooses to print Smollett's epistolary masterpiece, *The Expedition of Humphry Clinker*, rather than the more picaresque earlier works. What emerges is a canon markedly different not only from earlier collections like Croxall and Harrison but also contemporary ones like those of Hunt, Mudford, and Scott: all fully theorized and historicized through a magisterial prefatory essay and some two hundred pages of biographical notices on each writer. Fielding is certainly present, as are tales like *Rasselas* and *Almoran and Hamet*, but the general drift is clear, a narrative of origins and progress plainly present. So also is Barbauld's desire to posit a novelistic tradition that differs from her predecessors—one beginning with Defoe, continuing through the epistolary fiction of Richardson, and culminating in the novels of Burney, Radcliffe, and Edgeworth—as a new and distinctly British variety of narrative art.

In this sense, both Barbauld's and Scott's collections confirm Homer Obed Brown's notion (1997) that the novel experienced many 'rises', and many accompanying episodes

---

[17] Anna Letitia Barbauld, 'On the Origin and Progress of Novel-Writing', *The British Novelists*, 50 vols (London: F. C. and J. Rivington et al., 1810), 1.37–8.

of self-assessment and assimilation, between 1750 and 1820. We find these moments in both individual reviews and authors' prefaces, in publisher's collections and the critical treatises that introduce them: each mode of writing more than capable of constructing compelling accounts of the novel. Thus, in the work of reviewers and essayists, we discover competing accounts of the history of fiction as well as emerging critical consensus on several issues, from the origins of fictitious narrative to its effects on readers. And in canons of Harrison, Barbauld, and Scott we find the same practices of grouping English fiction, the same separation of supernatural and romantic 'tales' from epistolary and picaresque fiction, as is later codified in Dunlop's categories of 'Romantic', 'Serious', and 'Comic' modes of fiction.

Yet, such moments of coalescence, of course, are themselves always contingent. Dunlop's *History of Fiction*, after all, was revised with the help of Scott after it received mixed reviews, and Scott himself over the next decades was to become an important shaper of the novel's identity in spite of the relative failure of *Ballantyne's Novelist's Library*. In this sense, the triumph of Barbauld's collection during the Regency hardly ended the attempts of Scott and others to define the British Novel and its history. Scott may have lost the battle over reprinted collections of fiction, but in many senses he was to have the final say in how his contemporaries thought about the novel's history. For, at the very time that Barbauld's *British Novelists* was effectively scooping Scott's plans to publish his own, very different collection of fiction with Murray, Scott himself was penning the opening chapters of *Waverley*, that groundbreaking work that not only distanced its author from other contemporary novelists but also celebrated many of the same romantic, picaresque, and adventuring conventions that Scott had so admired in *The Novelist's Magazine*. Put another way, I am convinced that one of the accidental survivors of this failed venture of Scott and Murray—and of the Regency drive to anthologize the British novel—was *Waverley* itself: most probably begun late in 1808, picked up and set aside in 1810, and eventually found in 1813 and finished in 1814.

30

Readers and Reading Practices

STEPHEN COLCLOUGH

Reading the Evidence

On 1 January 1803 the twenty-four-year-old bookseller's assistant William Upcott recorded his intention to 'keep an exact journal of my actions and studies' in order to 'assist my memory' and 'set a due value on my time'. Taking a 'review' of his actions at the end of the first month he noted that his reading had been 'various but not extensive—little pleasure attending with as little profit'.[1] That Upcott wished to 'profit' by his reading suggests that like many of his contemporaries he believed in an ideology of self-improvement. Thomas Augst has argued that the diaries kept by 'ordinary' middle-class men were part of a culture in which 'young men sought both to make particular moments of time useful as the capital of character and to measure their progress against a temporal framework of development'. Upcott's reference to 'profit' certainly suggests that he was 'managing the self as though it was an enterprise' (Augst 2003: 55–6). His journal is filled with accounts of moments of reading snatched during his busy working life and, as in this instance, he often felt disappointed by the slow development of his cultural capital. Amongst the books that Upcott consumed during January 1803 were three very different works of fiction—Smollett's *Ferdinand Count Fathom* (1753), Marmontel's *Moral Tales* (1764), and M. G. Lewis's *The Monk* (1796). Both Smollett and Marmontel were read hastily during periods of inactivity in the shop and he seems to have found little 'pleasure' or 'profit' in either, whereas Lewis's Gothic novel was the subject of a fascinated rereading in his own room late one night.

This chapter begins with this example in order to confirm that it is possible to recover information about non-professional readers in the period 1750–1820. Upcott's journal is also a useful reminder that readers from this period didn't only consume recently authored texts. His selection of a new copy of Smollett from the shop in which he worked

---

[1] 'Diary of William Upcott', British Library Add. MSS 32558, end paper; fol. 13. Further references are given as dates in the text.

reveals that he benefited from the reprinting and repackaging of earlier texts which both James Raven (2007a) and William St Clair (2004) suggest typified British print culture in this period. The selection of Marmontel and Smollett suggests a particular interest in fiction on Upcott's part, but his journal also records shared readings of the Bible, newspapers, and poetry, and a fascination with satirical prints. Like most novel readers, fiction was only one component of his cultural diet. His near contemporary, Mary Russell Mitford, is famous for her rapid consumption of novels, but the twenty-two titles that she read in January 1806 also included travel writing and poetry (Pearson 1999: 13). That much of Upcott's other reading took place in the company of male friends while fiction was read silently and alone suggests that he thought of novel reading as a different kind of activity. Case studies of individual readers are important because they help to reconstruct the social, cultural, and personal contexts in which novel reading took place. As John Brewer has argued, they 'restore the voice of the reader' to a debate that is sometimes overdetermined by the negative images of novel reading (especially *female* novel reading) that appeared in an array of different texts including some novels at this time (1996: 227).

The present account pays particular attention to readers such as Upcott, Mitford, Thomas Turner, and Joseph Hunter, who left extensive accounts of their reading in a range of autobiographical texts including letters and journals.[2] The Sussex mercer and draper, Turner, and the Sheffield-based apprentice to the cutlery trade, Hunter, recorded their experience of reading novels alongside other quotidian events in journals similar to that constructed by Upcott. To listen to these readers is not, however, to drown out other voices, including those of the anti-novel discourse that, as Brewer demonstrates, played an important role in shaping how Anna Larpent (wife of John Larpent, Inspector of Plays in the Office of the Lord Chamberlain) constructed herself as novel reader (1996: 232–41). The 'reader's reader' is thus every bit as constructed as the novelist's or the reviewer's and, as I hope is already clear, journals of the sort kept by Upcott had their own generic codes and restrictions that in part determined the way in which they depicted themselves. Of necessity, this chapter draws upon recent work on the history of reading that pays attention to the way in which particular sources defined specific reading practices. The relative lack of surviving novels with annotations and the infrequent appearance of extracts from novels in commonplace books suggest that they tended not to be subjected to two of the dominant practices associated with scholarly reading although there are important exceptions (Jackson 2001; Allan 2010). Of course, not all readers kept journals and, as Leah Price has argued, different techniques of recovery are needed to reveal the experience of those who consumed texts 'without creating others' and to throw light on those aspects of the reading experience about which autobiographical records remain silent (2000: 156).

---

[2] The *Reading Experience Database* <www.open.ac.uk/Arts/RED/> and the *British Fiction 1800–1829* database (Garside et al. 2004) are making it easier than ever before to analyse and compare records of individual responses.

Individual readers rarely mention the size, price, or other material qualities of novels that are the subject of the new bibliographies of fiction. This chapter's focus on reading diaries is thus informed by recent work on the discourses surrounding reading, the protocols of reading embedded in texts, and the reading practices associated with commercial libraries, which taken together provide a complex picture of the bibliographic world in which individual readers encountered novels.

Literacy, 'the Old Canon', and the 'Reading Revolution'

Recent accounts of reading in the eighteenth century have tended to take an optimistic view about its spread, with literacy rates at mid-century of about 40 per cent for women and 60 per cent for men being used as evidence of widespread print consumption. As Barbara Benedict argues, readers now 'belonged not merely to the traditional elite' but included 'many servants and labourers and, of course, women of all ranks' (2004: 4). Indeed, literacy rates for men and women appear to have remained fairly static throughout this period; but, as Alan Richardson suggests, the visibility of lower-class readers in the contemporary discourse of reading reflects a mixture of optimism about the spread of print culture and anxiety about how a growing population might use their reading skills. Coleridge's reference to books being present 'in every hovel' in *The Statesman's Manual* (1816), Richardson suggests, is actually a reflection on a world in which only about half of all lower-class males were literate (2005: 397). Similarly, David Vincent (1989) has noted that surveys from the 1830s and 1840s record that poorer working-class readers tended not to own new books. This kind of information suggests that it is important that we resist the temptation to imagine that novel readers were everywhere. However, there is enough evidence to suggest that some working-class readers (especially skilled artisans and servants) were able to acquire and read fiction. The Colchester tailor, Thomas Carter, grew up in a house containing few books and his first experience of the novel did not occur until as an apprentice his master gave him access to a 'little library' including Goldsmith's *The Vicar of Wakefield* (1766).[3] St Clair (2004) puts forward a very powerful argument that it was not illiteracy but the 'censorship of price' that kept many working-class readers unaware of the latest developments in modern culture. Servants sometimes took advantage of hearing the latest novels read aloud (as in Thomas Turner's household in the 1750s) or borrowed them from circulating libraries. However, the majority of working-class people in this period probably only encountered fiction in the form of chapbooks or the (relatively) cheap reprint series that began to be produced after changes in copyright law in the 1770s.

---

[3] Thomas Carter, *Memoirs of a Working Man* (London: Charles Knight & Co., 1845), 74–5.

As Upcott's reading suggests, reprints were a very important part of the reading culture of the late eighteenth century. From the mid-1770s onwards almost everyone who was a member of 'the reading nation' was familiar with the novels included in series, such as Cooke's Select Novels (St Clair 2004). Beginning with *Tom Jones* in 1794, Cooke's Novels were available in both serialized 6*d.* 'numbers' and complete. The nine numbers of Fielding's novel amounted to 4*s.* 6*d.*, whereas shorter novels, such as the *Vicar of Wakefield*, cost as little as 1*s.* or 6*d.* for the complete text. They were advertised as 'cheap and elegant pocket novels', small enough 'that a volume may be carried in each pocket without the least encumbrance'.[4] Printed as 'octo-decimo or eighteens', these books were smaller (and cheaper) than most contemporary novels which appeared in duodecimo or octavo and usually cost 3*s.* 6*d.* or 4*s.* per volume. Imagined as portable 'travelling companions' that could be read while on the road or out in the open air, the 'old canon' helped spread the novel to new reading constituencies and extended the possibilities of reading outside or in private.

In 'On Reading Old Books' William Hazlitt noted that the second novel he ever read as a teenager was Cooke's edition of *Tom Jones* that 'came down in numbers once a fortnight'. He recalls that part of the pleasure of reading a serialized text was the anticipation of the next issue: 'the sixpenny numbers of this work regularly contrived to leave off just in the middle of a sentence, and in the nick of a story'.[5] Serialization was not unique to the old canon. Some new fiction was serialized in magazines, and although novels tended not to end in mid-sentence when borrowed by volume from a circulating library there was sometimes a significant wait for the next volume. Anthologies of prose, particularly collections of 'beauties', may also have left the reader wanting more. Illustrations were a particularly important feature of old canon novels. Cooke's adverts proudly announced that *Tom Jones* included eleven illustrations.[6] Hazlitt's recollection of the 'eagerness' with which he 'used to look forward' to seeing the 'prints' contained in a new number resists the traditional anti-novel discourse that condemned fiction's erotic appeal, by describing a reading strategy in which the young male reader turned first to the illustrations in order to gaze upon them with an 'enthusiastic delight' that was part erotic fantasy and part anticipation of the 'story and adventures' that these images suggested (141). This essay also provides evidence of the pleasures of rereading the familiar: 'I retrace the story and devour the page'. Hazlitt's suggestion that rereading a favourite episode transported him back in time effectively enough to remember 'the feeling of the air, the fields, the sky' on the day he got the book, shows an underlying concern with reading as a form of daydreaming (141, 139).

---

[4] Advertisement in the *Sun*, 19 February 1794.
[5] William Hazlitt, 'On Reading Old Books', in *Table Talk, or Original Essays* (Paris: Galignani, 1825), 133–57 (139–40).
[6] See *St James's Chronicle*, 1 January 1795.

Perhaps just as pertinent to the recovery of actual reading practices is Hazlitt's reflection on the fact that a text subjected to regular rereading could be opened at any page. For the rereader of the old canon there was nothing novel about the novel. Indeed, in an essay that argues that some readers paid a form of excessive attention to novels in order to prolong the time spent with them, Deidre Lynch has noted that retracing the familiar was an important part of early nineteenth-century culture. The sheer length of a long novel, such as *Tom Jones*, could easily transform it into a 'habit' or regular ritual. Lynch argues that the history of reading overlooks 'the pleasures of familiarity' and those readers who made a 'favourite fiction interminable', at its peril (2009: 98–102). Of course, public avowals of rereading the old canon may have been employed in order to accrue cultural capital by signalling a personal distaste for modernity, and Hazlitt's essay is dismissive of the latest works from the Ballantyne and Minerva presses. As his 'enthusiastic delight' on first reading confirms, however, old canon reprints did not have to be consumed reverently, or habitually. As with any other novel, the reader could delight in every word, or skip and skim, particularly if searching for a favourite episode. Coleridge's annotated *Tom Jones*, for example, reveals both a close reading of individual passages and a concern for the novel as genre. His most extensive comments defend the novel against Fielding's supposed immorality by condemning the 'cant which can recommend Pamela and Clarissa Harlowe as strictly moral, though they poison the imagination of the young with continual doses of tinct. lyttae'.[7] Coleridge in his annotations places *Tom Jones* at the heart of contemporary debate about the moral effects of novel reading upon young readers.

Coleridge's playful reversal of Richardson's accepted role in the morality debate suggests that to reread old novels was not to retreat from contemporary culture. References to older texts within modern culture could also bring them to the attention of new readers. In 1798 Joseph Hunter (1783–1861) became interested enough in Sterne's work to borrow a copy of *Tristram Shandy* (1760–7) because his guardian had been reading William Combe's *Fragments in the Manner of Sterne* (1797). Sterne was the subject of much debate in the monthly reviews and Hunter noted that it was currently 'the fashion to cry [him] down as the greatest plagiarist'.[8] Hunter was not alone in making sense of Sterne in the context of the plagiarism debate of the late 1790s. As H. J. Jackson points out, Edmund Ferrer's copies of *The Sentimental Journey* (1768) and *Tristram Shandy* include notes from William Jackson, whose essay on Sterne's 'Thievery' appeared in 1798, alongside his own compendium of linked passages. His marginalia reveals a 'devoted reader' legitimizing the work of a favourite author. That many of the links, such as a note to Johnson on Burke from Boswell's *Life* (1791), could not have been known by Sterne allows us to get very close

---

[7] *The Collected Works of Samuel Taylor Coleridge: Marginalia II—Camden to Hutton*, ed. George Whalley (London: Routledge & Kegan Paul, 1984), 693.

[8] 'The Journal of Joseph Hunter', British Library Add. MSS 24,879, fol. 19r. Further references are given as dates in the text.

to the mind of a reader who delighted in making connections *between* texts (2005: 90–2). Both Ferrer and Hunter consumed *Tristram Shandy* as part of a cultural diet that included a wide range of contemporary texts with which it could be compared. For those readers who gained access to the latest productions of the press, new and old novels were frequently read together, in much the same way that Upcott moved from a rereading of *The Monk* to a first attempt at *Ferdinand Count Fathom* in January 1803.

The cheap reprint series allowed new constituencies of readers to access fiction, but the latest works were reserved for relatively wealthy bourgeois and upper-class readers who could afford to buy new fiction—or who paid to access it via commercial or subscription libraries. Throughout the period covered by this volume, the discourse of reading often associates novel reading with other forms of consumption, especially by women, but, as Deidre Lynch has noted, the discourse of reading 'character' that emerged during the Romantic period often relates to private libraries well-stocked with new novels that allowed the owner to meditate on his or her own interiority (1998: 144). If books were increasingly accepted as commodities from the 1770s, some readers found it relatively easy to get hold of contemporary novels by mixing renting and buying. In 1797–8 Joseph Hunter gained access to fifteen novels by combining membership of a subscription library with renting from a local circulating library and borrowing from friends. However, even with some novels available to rent at a few pence per night, access to new titles and the possibility of reading numerous novels back-to-back was still largely reserved for relatively wealthy readers during this period.

Critical Discourse: Reading the 'Gothic' and 'Highland' Subgenres

The period after 1770 saw the emergence of many new subgenres, including the domestic novel and the national tale. This section explores how readers responded to two of these subgenres, the Gothic romance and the Highland tale, and asks to what extent these responses were influenced by contemporary critical discourse. Michael Gamer's study of the reception of Gothic argues that reviewers tended to create fixed categories of Gothic writer (young, female), Gothic reviewer (male, even if actually female), and Gothic reader (young, usually young *and* female) that had 'little to do with the actual demographic of gothic's readership' (2000: 36). Reviewers quickly established a set of strategies for dealing with Gothic texts that involved the repetition of the notion that what the *Monthly Review* christened 'the marvellous' could only be enjoyed 'by a young and unformed mind'.[9] However, as Gamer argues, it would be wrong to dismiss these reviews as merely misinformed about Gothic's actual readership as Gothic writers, reviewers, and readers are

---

[9] *Monthly Review*, 81 (December 1789), 563.

'mutually produced' from each others' discourse. Austen's *Northanger Abbey* (1818) is just one of the novels from this period that responded critically to this reception by exploring the stereotype of the young female Gothic reader (2000: 38). Catherine Morland's own investment in this stereotype is explored through her surprised response to Henry Tilney's revelation that he has read 'all Mrs Radcliffe's works, and most of them with great pleasure'.[10] There is much evidence to suggest that actual female readers responded in a range of different ways to Radcliffe's writing. Frances Burney, Elizabeth Carter, Anna Seward, Maria Edgeworth, and Mary Wollstonecraft all 'enjoyed Radcliffe or found in her novels a useful language, not always parodic, for describing [their] own circumstances'. The wealthy young diarist Susan Sibbald even lived up to the stereotype of the naive female reader by enacting her own version of Radcliffe's 'explained supernatural' when she recalled that a terrifying sound heard during an 'all-night reading' of the *Mysteries of Udolpho* (1794) was discovered to emanate from a very real servant (Pearson 1999: 100). If Sibbald was entirely caught up in the supernatural elements of *Udolpho*, other female readers were resistant to its charms. Hester Thrale disliked Radcliffe's fiction and Elihu Hubbard Smith was frustrated by the way in which her 'writing...raises expectations, which it never gratifies' (see Price 2000: 98).

How did non-professional readers respond to the Gothic and to what extent was their response influenced by contemporary stereotypes of the Gothic reader? In March 1797, Joseph Hunter recorded that Radcliffe's *The Italian* (1797) was much in demand amongst the 113 members of the Sheffield Subscription Library. They had undoubtedly been encouraged by that month's *Monthly Review* which suggested that Radcliffe was one of the best authors of 'the modern Romance'.[11] Asked by the librarian to read the first volume as quickly as possible, Hunter returned it the following day, but had to wait several days for the next. As Leah Price has argued, the pace of reading was something that particularly concerned Radcliffe's reviewers who thought that the inclusion of passages of verse in her novels was designed as 'a series of textual speed-bumps' to slow the reader down. However, most reviewers of *Udolpho* also assumed that the majority of readers would ignore them as they 'eagerly and anxiously' pursued the 'thread' of the narrative.[12] Reviewers made this assumption about the *imagined* novel reader, Price suggests, because they favoured a slow-paced mode of reading threatened by fashionable novels. Price's own suggestion that Radcliffe used verse to replace 'immediate gratification by the discipline of delay' is particularly useful for thinking about this author's role in legitimizing the novel. However, unusually for a critic who argues for skimming as the novel readers'

---

[10] Jane Austen, *Northanger Abbey*, ed. Barbara M. Benedict and Deirdre Le Faye (Cambridge: Cambridge University Press, 2006), vol. 1, ch. 14; 107–8.

[11] *Monthly Review*, n.s., 22 (March 1797), 282–4.

[12] *Monthly Review*, n.s., 15 (November 1794) 278–83; *Critical Review*, n.s., 11 (August 1794), 361–72; *British Critic*, 4 (August 1794), 120.

modus operandi, Price assumes that readers were disciplined by Radcliffe's text in a way that the reviewers deemed unlikely (2000: 96–8). Unfortunately, even the most conscientious diarist tends not to record how they responded to the protocols of reading embedded in texts, but Upcott's description of rereading *The Monk* suggests that like Price's ideal reader he halted at the inscribed poems (19 January 1803). By contrast, Hunter's stop-and-go progress through *The Italian* was dictated more by the library context than its internal structure. However, after completing the second volume Hunter did feel the need to record that 'the scene between Schedoni and Spalatro...when they are going to murder Helena' could 'not easily be equalled' (27 March 1798). Hunter's notes on this novel provide a very immediate response to a text that had not yet been widely reviewed, although it is significant that he chose a scene that the *Monthly Review* considered of 'the greatest genius'.[13] Although little is revealed of how Hunter made sense of Radcliffe's disciplinary strategies, these diary entries demonstrate that his reading was framed by an awareness of both the kinds of critical discourse (including scene selection) applied to Radcliffe's work and the demands of other library members.

Hunter chose to read Radcliffe's *Udolpho* for a second time in August 1798. Disappointed at first that it had lost 'half its interest' he nevertheless went on to complete all four volumes and added an unusually long account to his journal (13–22 August 1798). His suggestion that his own criticism should not 'detract from the merits of a work' praised even by 'the graver part of mankind' indicates that he was aware of the novel's reception. After referring to some of its faults, including the 'veiled image' that so beguiled Austen's imagined reader, Hunter goes on to describe himself as one of 'that class of readers who delight in the Marvellous' (3 September 1798). If Gothic reviewing threatened to associate readers with 'the "stupidity" of female "nonsense"', as Gamer suggests, Hunter chose to read this discourse against the grain by celebrating his enjoyment of the 'Marvellous' and thus constructing himself as a Gothic reader (2000: 42). Anna Larpent's novel reading was also deeply indebted to the critical language of the Reviews. Her description of Charlotte Smith as 'a wild leveller' in her summary of *Desmond* (1792) shows that she could confidently manipulate the anti-radical discourse of the monthlies (Brewer 1996: 229). However, Hunter's diary shows that it was possible to rebel against the 'regulatory' anti-Gothic, anti-radical discourses of the reviews, but that such a rebellion was constructed within the very terms of the contemporary critical language to which it was opposed. By contrast, William Upcott's rereading of *The Monk* 'for the fourth time at least' makes no mention of the reviews which condemned this book as 'totally unfit for general circulation' and he fails to place the text within a specific genre (such as 'the Marvellous').[14] Given Upcott's attempt 'to set a due value on my time', it is surprising that

---

[13] *Monthly Review*, n.s., 22 (March 1797), 283–4.
[14] *Monthly Review*, n.s., 23 (August 1797), 451.

he gives so much space to documenting an evening 'loitered' away in the company of a novel full of 'too many improbabilities'. Upcott justified his time by turning Antonia into a figure of female innocence (even though such an interpretation is difficult to sustain) and emphasizing that he frequently reflected on some 'beautiful lines' of verse included in the novel's second volume (19 January 1803). That Upcott used similar reading strategies to Hunter, including the isolation of key scenes, suggests that novel readers approached texts in a similar fashion even if they did not have access to the latest reviews.

Ina Ferris has argued that despite the continued categorization of novel reading as an ephemeral, feminine activity during the early nineteenth century, 'a new and newly powerful critical discourse' that took the novel much more seriously emerged at this time. 'In an important way, the scene of novel reading was shifting from the sofa to the study' as the novel was re-gendered. Ferris sees Scott's Waverley series as the culmination of this period of transformation, but as her work makes clear the 'modern historical novel' was dependent upon the creation of a number of new 'serious' novelistic genres (the national tale, the domestic novel, the evangelical novel) created mainly by female authors (2009b: 474, 476, 484). How did readers respond to the 'Highland' tale? Christian Isobel Johnstone's anonymously published *Clan-Albin: A National Tale* (1815), set in a small Highland community after the Clearances, was certainly recognized as part of this genre. John Gibson Lockhart, who had heard about rather than read the novel, connected it to both Scott's *Waverley* (1814) and Johnstone's *The Saxon and the Gael* (1814). Similarly, Anne Grant praised the way in which it captured 'Highland feelings and manners', whereas Mary Russell Mitford thought it 'a pretty thing—only too Highlandish'.[15] The success of *Waverley* produced many imitations and it is in this context that Mitford thought of Johnstone's text as generic. If in this instance familiarity led Mitford to condemn with faint praise, she was later to suggest that one of the pleasures of reading Scott's Waverley novels was the feeling of 'intimate...familiarity' that returning to the same genre and the same author provoked.[16]

Silent, Sociable, and Partial Reading

If Ferris discerns a move from 'sofa to the study', Richard Cronin has argued that British literary culture after Waterloo began to embrace a form of reading pleasure dependent 'on its speed'. Particularly associated with periodicals, this was 'characteristically a solitary

---

[15] *The Life and Letters of John Gibson Lockhart*, 2 vols (London, 1897), 1.74; *Memoir and Correspondence of Mrs Grant of Laggan*, ed. J. P. Grant, 3 vols (London, 1844), 2.121–2; Mitford, 'The Literary Pocket Book', British Library C.60.b7, 14 December 1819.

[16] Mary Russell Mitford, *Recollections of a Literary Life* (London, 1852), 230. For a discussion of reading series, see Lynch (2009: 97).

kind of reading'. Cronin suggests that Scott's novels were a part of this cultural shift, with *Redgauntlet* (1824) embracing, in the novelist's own words, 'the laudable practice of skipping' (2009: 120–1). However, several of the actual readers studied here appear to have been reading silently, and at some speed, at least twenty-five years before the moment that Cronin detects this shift. William Upcott consumed *Count Fathom* silently and alone while minding the shop, noting that when not interrupted he could get through about six (short) chapters in one hour; Joseph Hunter sped through a volume of *The Italian* in an evening. Both seem to have preferred reading novels silently and alone, whereas other genres—such as newspapers and plays—were consumed communally. Most historians of reading now accept that there was no rapid transition from a world in which most books were read aloud to one in which they were consumed silently. Evidence for reading from the period 1800–29 included in the *British Fiction 1820–1829* database suggests that novel readers adapted their reading to the occasion—on some occasions reading silently (either in company or alone), at others vocalizing the text for an audience of listeners, or being a part of such an audience.[17] Cronin is thus identifying a new critical discourse that approved of the speed-reading practices that a previous generation of critics had condemned, rather than a new mode of reading.

During the 1820s, magazine writers such as Charles Lamb were particularly keen to promote a sociable form of silent reading in which men and women read together 'without interruption or oral communication' (Cronin 2009: 120). Mapping the spaces in which silent reading takes place and tracing what de Certeau has called the 'wild orchestration' of the silent reader's body will help historians of reading to differentiate and understand the difference between silent reading (in which the eye of the reader controls the text) and reading aloud, in which the text 'imposes its own rhythm' upon the reading body (2011: 137). Something of this 'wild orchestration' of the silent reader's body is captured by Austen when she describes her nephew 'intent over [Anna Maria Porter's] "Lake of Killarney" [1804], twisting about in one of our great chairs' and ignoring his brother playing close by.[18] The lone, silent reader sitting close to a window for light, or a blazing hearth for warmth, is often depicted in visual representations of the English country house. However, as James Raven has argued, the design of fashionable domestic libraries that were such a feature of middle-class homes from the mid-eighteenth century onwards often reflected a taste for shared reading and the performance of texts (1996: 199).

Social reading is often depicted in novels. Mr Collins's refusal to read aloud from a circulating-library novel in Austen's *Pride and Prejudice* (1813) brilliantly evokes his snobbery. It is also something of a private joke. Austen's family were 'great Novel-readers' (*Letters*, 26) who regularly read aloud together (for Austen's own reading, see Stabler 2005 and Halsey 2011). For example, in January 1808 a reading of de Genlis's *Alphonsine* (1806)

---

[17] Garside et al. (2004). The Database contains 'anecdotal' evidence from ninety-three sources.
[18] *Jane Austen's Letters*, ed. Deirdre Le Faye, 3rd edn (Oxford and New York: Oxford University Press, 1995), 151.

involving two guests, James Austen and his wife Mary, was abandoned after just twenty pages because they 'were disgusted' by 'indelicacies which disgrace a pen hitherto so pure'. As a result, this text was 'changed' for Lennox's *The Female Quixote* (1752) with which Austen was already familiar. She recorded her own 'amusement' in finding it as good as she remembered while at the same time noting that although 'Mrs F.A.' took pleasure in the text, Mary seemed not to care for books at all (*Letters*, 115–16). This letter suggests that some family groups policed reading aloud, rejecting any novel that seemed inappropriate for communal consumption. A novel already read by one of the group could at least be guaranteed free of 'indelicacies' even if it was not of interest to everyone. Indeed, Austen is particularly revealing about the different levels of response that such a collective reading could generate. Delighted by a text that she already knew, Austen's familiarity allowed her to concentrate as much on the audience as the text, not all of whom shared her enthusiasm. Letters and diaries documenting the reading aloud of novels as a form of 'after-dinner' entertainment suggest that a mixture of new and familiar texts were consumed in this way. Of course, reading aloud could be used to police novel reading and to discourage private consumption. Lucy Newlyn has argued that some groups engaged in this practice as a reaction against the commodification of print and the fast pace of silent reading (2000: 19–20). However, reading aloud was not necessarily opposed to the proliferation of print, and in households like Austen's may well have acted as a public sign of their participation in modern culture. Brewer notes that 'almost every member of Anna Larpent's household read aloud to others and, when the family went on visits in the summer, they formed part of reading circles in which guests took turns to read'. On 1 July 1780 the Larpent household heard readings from a volume of history, a comic drama, and a novel. Anna chose to read from Pierre Marivaux's *Marianne* (1743) while some of her female friends were sewing, but she also returned to the same novel in mixed company as part of the after-dinner entertainment (Brewer 1996: 241–2).

H. J. Jackson has noted that historians of reading have tended to concentrate their efforts on recovering reading aloud in groups while ignoring 'habits of reading in pairs or alone' (2005: 55–6). That the shared reading of novels in pairs was an unremarkable practice in the early nineteenth century is suggested by Lamb's description of an encounter with a 'familiar damsel', who, after discovering him at 'ease upon the grass' reading Richardson's *Pamela* (1740–1), is 'determined to read in company'. Lamb is mainly concerned with being discovered with a novel that deals with seduction, so it is not entirely clear how they read (aloud to each other, or turning the pages together in silence?), but the fact that her departure after they had 'read on very sociably for a few pages' is not judged as strange suggests that such casual textual encounters were not unusual at this time.[19]

---

[19] 'Detached Thoughts on Books and Reading', in *The Norton Anthology of English Literature: Volume D—The Romantic Period*, ed. Jack Stillinger and Deirdre Shauna Lynch (New York: Norton, 2006), 505–10 (509).

Naomi Tadmor's work on the diaries kept by the Sussex mercer and draper Thomas Turner between 1754 and 1765 suggests that the shared reading aloud of novels was used to instigate and promote friendship with other men of a similar social status. Indeed, to become one of Turner's 'select' friends shared business *and* intellectual interests were essential. Turner was introduced to Sterne's *Tristram Shandy* by his 'worthy friend' the innkeeper Thomas Tipper who read part of it aloud on 14 September 1762. Turner was familiar with a number of contemporary novels including Smollett's *Peregrine Pickle* (1751), from which he transcribed passages on friendship into his diary in 1755. He catches something of Sterne's playfulness when he refuses to align it with other novels: 'In the even Mr Tipper read to me part of a—I know not what to call it but Tristram Shandy'.[20] Turner's shared reading was not restricted to novels, but it is important to note the way in which this mode of reading combined the public and the private to produce bonds of intimacy with his friends. Tipper's reading was a private act in the sense that it took place in Turner's home and that only the two men were present, but it strengthened bonds of sociability that were important in their public lives as businessmen. Both Turner and his wife Peggy also read aloud to each other (sometimes in the presence of a servant maid or their nephews) and the regular though intermittent consumption of texts was part of the pattern of their domestic life. Tadmor notes that most of the texts owned or borrowed by the Turners were 'not read in a linear way from beginning to end', or, like *Tristram Shandy*, 'were not read throughout'. To read intermittently meant that 'parts of texts were read on one evening and parts of other texts were read on the next' (Tadmor 1996: 168). One text consumed in this intermittent fashion was Richardson's *Clarissa*. Read aloud by Peggy on 15 October 1755, Turner dipped into the seventh volume in December, the novel having been neglected in favour of other reading materials, including poetry and religious works. When Peggy eventually 'finished' reading it aloud some weeks later, Turner recorded that he found the text emotionally 'moving' even though he combined listening to it with writing business letters (169). Turner's diaries are important to the history of reading because they reveal the various ways in which reading aloud operated to strengthen and confirm familial ties and bonds of friendship while at the same time confirming that women sometimes took charge of reading aloud.

Of course, historians of reading need to be careful not to idealize sociable reading as in some way superior to the isolated individuality of silent reading. Some readers, like Austen's sister-in-law, may well have been bored listening to a novel for which they had no enthusiasm, and, as Austen acknowledged, the way in which a text was read impacted on the listener's interpretation. She was particularly disappointed with her mother's 'too rapid' reading of *Pride and Prejudice* (*Letters*, 203). Many of the examples discussed in this

---

[20] *The Diary of Thomas Turner 1754–1765*, ed. David Vaisey (Oxford: Oxford University Press, 1985), 258.

section reveal that a shared reading was often a partial reading as co-participants or listeners became distracted by other matters (such as letter writing), or chose to leave having sampled only a few pages. Jan Fergus's investigation of circulating library borrowing records suggests that the intermittent 'non-linear' reading of novels was commonplace in the second half of the eighteenth century, especially amongst readers who rented novels from circulating libraries (2006: 108–11). Such 'browsing' may feel familiar to twenty-first-century readers who 'browse' online, but any comparison with our own modes of accessing texts risks eroding what is distinctive about 'partial' reading after 1750. Partial reading may well announce a disregard for formal rules, but it also signals a textual economy in which novels were as often public as private property.

'The Greatest Pleasure in Reading': The Language of Response 1800–20

The 'anecdotal records' section of the *British Fiction 1800–1829* database (Garside et al. 2004) provides an unparalleled resource for comparing and analysing the interpretive strategies deployed by an extended community of readers during this period. Largely dependent upon the published autobiographical records of professional writers, the database reveals the language of response deployed by a community united by their easy access to contemporary literary culture, as much as by ties of friendship, family, place, or ideology. Perhaps not surprisingly, one of the commonest ways of writing about novels amongst this group was to describe the amount of pleasure that they provoked. In September 1804 Lady Stanley wrote to Louisa Chilton informing her that 'The Limerick Gloves' from Maria Edgeworth's *Popular Tales* (1804) was her 'delight'. Similarly, Mary Russell Mitford found 'Rosanna' from the same collection 'particularly delightful'.[21] Correspondence between novel readers, such as Mitford and Sir William Elford, often included recommended reading. On 26 September 1819 Mitford thanked Elford for advocating Catherine Hutton's *The Welsh Mountaineer* (1817) because his account of the book was 'exactly to [her] taste'. 'Have you seen?' is one of the most common phrases in letters from this period, with readers often going on to describe a book that they considered delightful. Mary Brunton was so pleased with Jane Taylor's *Display* (1815) that she recommended it to Mrs Izett with the words 'it is worth its price, I assure you'.[22] These word-of-mouth recommendations were important to a novel's success and show how some texts became fashionable talking points amongst this important community of

---

[21] *The Early Married Life of Maria Josepha, Lady Stanley*, ed. Jane H. Adeane (London: Longmans, 1899), 276; *The Life of Mary Russell Mitford*, ed. G. A. L'Estrange, 3 vols (London, 1870), 1.108–9.

[22] *Life*, 2.72–3; Mary Brunton, *Emmeline. With Some Other Pieces* (Edinburgh: Manners and Miller, and Constable; London: John Murray, 1819), xcii.

readers. Indeed, some letter writers reflected upon books that they read because everyone else was talking about them. Henry Mackenzie reported that he had 'glanced over the whole' of Edgeworth's *Patronage* (1814) in a letter that suggests it was being talked about by 'every body' in Edinburgh.[23] That this book was particularly in fashion during 1814 is suggested by Austen's reference to Cassandra Austen's *not* reading it as a vanity (*Letters*, 271). Similarly, both Sydney Smith and Henry Crabb Robinson entered into conversations, or responded to letters concerning Edgeworth's novel, despite not having read it.[24] To be aware of this text and its reception was thus an important aid to conversation amongst those who enjoyed the fashion for novels. That *Patronage* was in fashion is confirmed by the fact that it went through three editions in the first year after publication. Something of the panic that readers felt about being seen as unfashionable, is suggested by Anne Grant's fear that she might not see Edgeworth's *Tales of Fashionable Life* (1809) 'till all the world' had become 'tired of it'.[25]

If readers enjoyed communicating their sense of 'delight' in some books, they also enjoyed showing their displeasure. As Mitford noted, 'next to reading with an enthusiastic admiration and delight', such as she felt for *Pride and Prejudice*, 'the greatest pleasure in reading is to be critical and fastidious, and laugh at and pull to pieces' (*Life*, 2.60). Henry Crabb Robinson's diary suggests a reader who took great pleasure in the negative. Having been 'seduced' to read aloud from Anna Maria Porter's *Recluse of Norway* (1814), he complained that the 'style' was 'wretched, the characters coarsely drawn, the sentiments commonplace, and the descriptions, though lively and spirited, incorrect and monotonous'. Dorothy Wordsworth also protested against 'the badness of the style' of this novel and like Crabb Robinson found the second volume less interesting than the first.[26] Writing in the 1810s, these readers shared a critical vocabulary that allowed them to communicate their responses to fellow novel readers with little fear of being misunderstood.

Deidre Lynch has put forward a powerful argument for a post-1770s reading practice in which 'new techniques for reading' (such as 'the silent scanning' deployed in 'close reading') and an insistence on prolonging a text through rereading were tied together with the 'notion that sharing a space of sensibility with a fictitious character could occasion a therapeutic recovery of one's real feelings'. Lynch draws on contemporary accounts of 'character' and reviews of 'the new style of novel' or the 'Burney School' as evidence of a concern with interiority as one of the 'new techniques of the self' emerging at this

[23] *Literature and Literati: The Literary Correspondence and Notebooks of Henry Mackenzie: Volume I*, ed. Horst Drescher (Frankfurt: Peter Lang, 1989), 257.

[24] *The Letters of Sydney Smith*, ed. Nowell C. Smith, 2 vols (Oxford: Clarendon Press, 1953), 1.244; *Henry Crabb Robinson on Books and Their Writers*, ed. Edith J. Morley, 3 vols (London: Dent, 1938), 1.136.

[25] *Memoir and Correspondence of Mrs Grant of Laggan*, ed. J. P. Grant, 3 vols (London: Longman [etc.], 1844), 1.230.

[26] *Crabb Robinson on Books and Writers*, 1.162; *The Letters of William and Dorothy Wordsworth: The Middle Years. Volume II*, ed. Ernest de Selincourt (Oxford: Clarendon Press, 1937), 638.

time (1998: 129, 125, 143). The letters of several early nineteenth-century readers certainly reveal a fascination with 'character'. In response to Elford's recommendation of Hutton's *Welsh Mountaineer*, for example, Mitford confirmed that she would acquire a copy because she cared 'nothing for story, and all for character'. Dorothy Wordsworth and Crabb Robinson were equally interested in 'character', the latter praising *Pride and Prejudice* for 'the characters and the perfectly colloquial style of the dialogue'. Scott documents a rereading of the same novel ('for the third time at least') that is focused on everyday life and character.[27] However, as Lynch implies, such accounts of the 'close reading' of character are socially produced, often conjuring a bad reader or bad text as the Other against which the self of the reader was constructed. Sarah Harriet Burney, for example, associated skimming with 'common novels' read with 'carelessness and haste' in a letter apologizing for keeping Edgeworth's *Patronage* for too long because of the combined quality of the writing and 'the thickness of the Volumes'. Mary Berry thought it legitimate to finish Caroline Warren's *Conrade* (1806) by 'galloping over half the pages' because she could not 'regularly wade' through a text that constructed characters as either 'pious' or 'profligate'.[28] The search for 'character' thus legitimated forms of 'bad' reading. Berry 'galloped' through the second half of Warren's novel but she did not abandon reading it altogether. However, if some readers thought it perfectly legitimate to skim a novel that failed to give 'the characters' any depth, others admitted to the rapid consumption of books that they found intellectually satisfying. Jane Austen confessed to having 'torn through' the final volume of Eaton Stannard Barrett's *The Heroine* (1813), enjoying it as a 'delightful burlesque' on the Gothic style (*Letters*, 256). Henry Mackenzie judged the merit of Edgeworth's *Patronage* by 'glancing' over the whole book and close reading 'a considerable part' (*Literature and Literati*, 257). This anecdotal evidence suggests that readers in this community shifted confidently between different modes of reading, so that novels might be studied closely for the umpteenth time or skimmed at speed, read aloud to an after-dinner party, or perused alone in the library (as well as in many other combinations and spaces).

Conclusion: 'Excessive Delight'

From the recording of a baffled enjoyment of *Tristram Shandy*, through the conjuring up of the 'excessive' teenage delights taken in the illustrated novel, and on to the pleasures of dismissing emergent new genres as 'too Highlandish', the evidence presented here

---

[27] *Life of Mary Russell Mitford*, 2.72–3; *Crabb Robinson on Books and Writers*, 1.227; *The Journal of Sir Walter Scott*, ed. W. E. K. Anderson (Edinburgh: Canongate Books, 1998), 132 (entry for 14 March 1826).

[28] *The Letters of Sarah Harriet Burney*, ed. Lorna Clark (Athens, GA: University of Georgia Press, 1997), 179; *Extracts of the Journals and Correspondence of Miss Berry from the Year 1783 to 1852*, ed. Theresa Lewis, 3 vols (London: Longmans, 1865), 2.346–7.

suggests just how much pleasure readers gained from novels. Hazlitt's concentration on the unique material aspects of Cooke's novels (their serialized 'numbers' and illustrations) provides a useful reminder that readers engaged with fiction in a number of different forms during this time and that each textual context subtly altered the kind of reading that it was possible to produce. Similarly, anecdotal accounts of reading aloud help us to recognize reading as a material act, which brings the body as well as the mind into play, and it is worth remembering here those everyday gestures of reading, such as cutting open the pages with a 'long, smooth white paper-knife', or hurrying to the library for the next volume, that were such an important part of the novel reader's experience during this period.[29]

---

[29] 'On Reading and Readers', *New Monthly Magazine*, 14: 82 (November 1820), 533–9 (538).

31

The Global British Novel

WIL VERHOEVEN

N an important sense, the British novel always was a global phenomenon. While the novel as such has its roots in sixteenth- and seventeenth-century (mainly French and Spanish) romance, the British novel owes its emergence and subsequent rise to global supremacy during the eighteenth and nineteenth centuries to the expansion and ascendancy of the British Empire. The British novel initially evolved in conjunction with the proliferation of printed accounts of real or imagined journeys to exotic territories in Britain's trading empire. From the late seventeenth century onwards, British merchants involved in trade with the British colonies in America and the West Indies began to amass vast fortunes, fuelling significant changes in the socio-economic fabric of British society and permanently altering the balance of political power. Ian Watt's thesis that the novel was a cultural artefact determined by an emerging bourgeois world view arguably remains one of the most convincing accounts of the genesis of the novel form in Britain. However, Watt's paradigmatic argument limits the British novel form to a cultural institution functioning primarily on the national stage, more particularly on the English stage. What is missing from Watt's conception of the rise of the novel as the formal expression of bourgeois consciousness in Britain is a consideration of the wider historical process of the globalization of the British novel. That is to say, like the British middle class whose values it embodied, the British novel rose in tandem with the burgeoning of the British Empire, which, in turn, evolved with the spread of colonialism and global capitalism.

As Immanuel Wallerstein (1976) has argued, in the course of the sixteenth, seventeenth, and eighteenth centuries the international division of labour segmented the world into core, peripheral, and semi-peripheral regions of economic activity. Buttressed by strong central governments, extensive bureaucracies, and large mercenary armies, economic activity in the core regions—notably the Dutch Republic, England, and France—concentrated on higher-skilled, capital-intensive production of manufactured goods, cloth, furniture, and luxuries. Lacking strong central governments and self-sustaining economies, regions at the periphery—including the West Indies and the American colonies—exported raw materials to the core and relied on coercive labour practices.

Directly or indirectly deriving much of its wealth from the new economy, the New World came to loom large in the consciousness of Britain's emerging middle class. As a marker of middle-class identity, the British novel, and with it a prescriptive sense of 'Britishness' (or, more narrowly, of 'Englishness'), were duly exported to the American colonies, and subsequently to the imperial territories elsewhere on the globe.

But if the rise of the British novel was inextricably bound up with the making of British national culture, this process was predicated on the evolving history of Britain's relations with its overseas possessions, particularly with its North American colonies. While Britain's imperial history inevitably involved efforts to appropriate, assimilate, and domesticate the new, the strange, and the foreign, this process was crucially dialectical in nature. That is to say, the geographical, ethnographical, historical, and topographical narratives of America that began to appear in ever-growing numbers in the course of the seventeenth century were as much narratives of self-exploration and self-critique as they were narratives of appropriation and exploitation. Existing in close symbiosis with those empiricist narratives of scientific inquiry and speculation, the middle-class British novel operated within the same transatlantic dialectic. In this way, by defining itself vis-à-vis its American colonies, the British Empire generated a sociopolitical discourse that allowed it to pose critical questions about itself and about its relations to the transatlantic 'other'. Negotiating with the evolving idea of 'America' thus changed and shaped British society perhaps as much as it changed and shaped the colonies themselves.

This has important repercussions for the way in which we study the form, dissemination, and reception of the global English novel and its concomitant modes of Britishness. Thus, gauging the cultural and ideological impact of the British novel outside of metropolitan Britain involves much more than measuring the popularity of British novels in peripheral regions, for instance by collecting data on export and import volumes, circulating library catalogues and loan details, monitoring translations and foreign reviews, and so on. If the globalization of the British novel through exports and translations reconceptualized and restaged peripheral spaces—thereby instantiating and perpetuating certain kinds of cultural hierarchies—those spaces and those places unmistakably 'wrote back'. Hence, any analysis of the British novel's universal and imperial aspirations would crucially involve an engagement with local forms of resistance as well as resistant forms of local literary production. As A. L. Kroeber puts it, whenever a cultural novelty—such as the British novel—begins to exert its influence over local cultures, it encounters some kind of antipathy, due to 'the presence in the recipient cultures of material and systems which are, or are felt to be, irreconcilable with the invading traits or system' (1964: 143). Such opposition to the 'civilizing' agenda of the British bourgeois novel in the (semi-) peripheral zones would typically manifest itself in a range of oblique modes and structures of resistance aimed at subverting, appropriating, decentring, and 'nativizing' the British literary form as well as notions of Britishness.

In recent years the critical paradigm of global or world literature has offered valuable new insights into the dynamic relationship between the western European novel form and local realities elsewhere in the world. Building on groundbreaking bibliographical research carried out by Richard Sher (2007), James Raven (2002b), Peter Garside (2000), and others, theorists of world literature such as Pascale Casanova (2004), David Damrosch (2003), Franco Moretti (1998, 2000), and Mariano Siskind (2010), have sparked lively academic debate about the global ubiquity of the novel from the 1750s until the present day. Siskind, for example, has reminded us how in the second half of the eighteenth century, as it began to travel from the colonial metropolis to the peripheries and rise to a position of global hegemony, the European novel was still conceptualized in terms of 'a visual reality . . . that elevated the fiction of bourgeois ubiquity to a foundational myth of modernity' (2010: 337). Thus, in a 1784 essay, Immanuel Kant asserted that because it was the hegemonic form of the bourgeois imagination, the novel could be instrumental in generating discourses of globalization by conjuring up images of the world as a social totality represented by rising bourgeois culture and class consciousness. 'It is admittedly a strange and at first sight absurd proposition', Kant mused, 'to write a *history* according to an idea of how world events must develop if they are to conform to certain rational ends; it would seem that only a *novel* could result from such premises.'[1] Kant's concept of the globalization of the novel offers a useful tool to explore the historical parameters of the spread of the bourgeois novel from western Europe to the literary periphery. However, Kant's radical proposition tends to present the rise of bourgeois totality as an autonomous and unchallenged development and thereby obscures the ways in which local realities in the peripheries resisted and interacted with the western bourgeois form and content.

Franco Moretti has since sought to remedy this blind spot in Kant's thesis. Taking as his starting point the key premise of the world-system school of economic history that international capitalism is a system which is simultaneously 'one, and unequal', Moretti developed a concept of a world literary system (of interrelated literatures) which is 'one, not uniform' (2000: 64). According to Moretti's initial 'law of literary evolution', in cultures that belong to the periphery of the literary system, 'the modern novel first arises not as an autonomous development but as a compromise between a western formal influence (usually French or English) and local materials' (58). However, upon further reflection, Moretti found that while from 1750 onwards the novel arose just about everywhere in the periphery 'as a compromise between West European patterns and local reality', the 'formal compromise' that this encounter produced, took on different forms in different locations (64, 61). Not only was the local reality different from place to place, the pressure exerted by western European forms was also uneven. World literature was, indeed, a global system, but a 'system of *variations*' (64).

---

[1] Immanuel Kant, 'Idea for a Universal History from a Cosmopolitan Purpose' (1784), in *Kants gesammelte Schriften, herausgegeben van der Preussischen Akademie der Wissenschaften zu Berlin*, 29 vols (Berlin: G. Reimer, 1910–), 8.29.

If the pressure exerted by the system or 'core' of Anglo-French world literature was not uniform, nor was the resistance of local realities against that pressure. Such resistance rarely took on the form of outright rejection; rather, it was a matter of selective response and strategic negotiation between local reality and the foreign form. For instance, there is evidence to suggest that in some peripheral zones, notably in Latin America, local elites discovered in the translated or adapted narratives of modernity imported from the core the possibility of imagining postcolonial identities for themselves, which were independent of the colonial metropolis (see Siskind 2010: 339). Indeed, such resistance was also at work when the novel travelled to the 'peripheries' within the core itself. Thus, James Raven was struck by the 'often more problematic provincial work' within the genre of the novel, with regional novel adaptations often being radically reduced to as little as forty pages of the original (1987: 5). More strikingly, in eighteenth-century France, the *bibliothèque bleue*—perhaps the 'greatest publishing venture of the European provinces'—saw 'les petits romans' (between twenty-four and forty-eight pages) taking on their fully fledged rivals, 'les grands romans', in an attempt to woo a non-bourgeois readership of semi-literate readers (Moretti 1998: 169). Dismissed by one commentator as 'the dust bin of western culture', these little (often single-sheet) paperbound 'editions' of the classics of European literature and learning were churned out in vast quantities in assembly line print shops and peddled across the countryside (Hall 1996: 46). Yet for countless French peasants these little rags were their only connection to the distant culture of the learned and the cosmopolitan.

The history of the globalization of the British novel in the eighteenth and nineteenth centuries is therefore by necessity a history of negotiations and compromises between the foreign British form at the core of the literary system and the various local realities in the peripheral zones. Consequently, the following discussion of the British novel's transmission to America, the West Indies, India, and Europe will focus on variations in the dynamic interaction between the core's formal influence and local resistance; between hegemonic ideology and local *mentalités*; and between global markets and local material practices.

North America

When Updike Underhill, the hero of Royall Tyler's *The Algerine Captive*, returned to his native America in 1795 after an absence of seven years, the first thing that struck him was 'the extreme avidity, with which books of mere amusement were purchased and perused by all ranks of his countrymen—not merely in sea ports but also in inland towns and villages'.[2] When he left New England, Underhill goes on to say,

---

[2] Royall Tyler, *The Algerine Captive, or, The Life and Adventures of Doctor Updike Underhill—Six Years a Prisoner Among the Algerines* (Walpole, Newhampshire: Printed by David Carlisle, 1797), v.

books of biography, travels, novels, and modern romances, were confined to our sea ports; or, if known in the country, were read only in the families of clergymen, physicians, and lawyers.... On his return from captivity, he found a surprising alteration in the public taste. In our inland towns of consequence, social libraries had been instituted, composed of books, designed to amuse rather than to instruct; and country booksellers, fostering the new-born taste of the people, had filled the whole land with modern travels, and novels almost as incredible... (v–vii).

Underhill, or Tyler, is quite right in pointing out, as he goes on to do, that the relatively high literacy rate in New England was a major cause for the rapid increase of the secularization and feminization of the reading public's taste during the last three decades of the eighteenth century. Moreover, fundamental changes that took place in the marketing and dissemination of print in the same period had a significant impact on the demographics of the reading public. Booksellers began to adopt market strategies similar to those used by present-day publishers, including advertisements, trailers, and cross-listings. This radically redefined the relationship between booksellers and readers as one between producers and consumers of print, particularly of popular fiction. An even greater impact on the reading public's taste and hence on the consumption of print was the exponential rise in the number of circulating libraries in the second half of the century. This was particularly the case in the 1790s, when the number of circulating libraries tripled, while the population only doubled. Robert Winans has calculated that the percentage of fiction in booksellers' catalogues rose from 9 per cent in the period 1754–65 to 12 per cent in the period 1791–1800; at the same time, the percentage of fiction in the catalogues of circulating libraries rose from 10 per cent to over 50 per cent (1975: 270–1). Even though no loan records for circulating libraries are available, these data would support Winans' thesis that 'the American reading public in the late eighteenth-century was largely a novel-reading public' (268).

But what novels did Americans read? The wrong ones, is the short answer—at least according to Updike Underhill. 'While this love of literature, however frivolous, is pleasing to the man of letters', he observes, 'there are two things to be deplored. The first is that, while so many books are vended, they are not of our own manufacture.... The second misfortune is that... the English Novel... paints the manners, customs, and habits of a strange country' (*Algerine Captive*, ix–x). He therefore calls for a declaration of literary independence by urging that American authors from now on write their own novels and that they write about American manners, not English ones. Updike was far from alone in believing that in literary terms, America remained a colony of Britain. As David Simpson put it: 'It was to prove more difficult to declare independence from Samuel Johnson than it had been to reject George III' (1986: 33). It is one of those ironies of decolonization, as Edward Watts has convincingly argued, that through cultural mimicry and self-marginalization, the early Republic tried to 'restabilize the community by recreating the only standard of legitimacy the populace had ever known: that of the colonizers' (1998: 13). Thus, for several decades after political independence had been secured, literature produced in America would, at best, aspire to imitate British literary models, rather than commit itself to local subjects and subjectivities. Despite Updike Underhill's call for the institution of an indigenous, American novel tradition, the example of the eighteenth-century British realistic novel—novels written by Defoe, Fielding, Smollett, Richardson, Burney— would continue to loom large in libraries and booksellers' catalogues, at least until the 1820s. The history of the eighteenth- and early nineteenth-century novel in America is therefore by no means simply the history of American novels.

More significant than America's postcolonial cultural inferiority complex was the impact that the forces of transatlantic free-market capitalism had on the North American market for print in general, and for fiction in particular. In comparison to their European colleagues, American printers had several obstacles to overcome in their struggle for commercial survival, causing the domestic American print market to descend into 'a primal scene of rivalry' (Green 2000: 253). Their main disadvantage was a chronic lack of capital. Type-founding, for instance, did not gain a foothold in North-America till towards the end of the century, and as a result American printers remained dependent on type imported from Europe. An even bigger bottleneck was the production of paper, dependent as it was on a constant supply of rags, ropes, and similar flax- or hemp-based material to produce paper. Because paper was the largest cost in printing (up to half the total cost) and often had to be paid for in advance, much of a printer's capital would be tied up in the production of a book, as opposed to an issue of a newspaper (rarely more than a single sheet of paper folded once, thus making four pages), an almanac (usually a sheet and a half folded three times), or a pamphlet (usually two or three folded sheets).

The shortage of type and the cost of paper were not conducive to the production of relatively voluminous yet ephemeral books, such as novels, whether they were written by American or by British authors. Hence Franklin's decision to print and publish an American edition of Samuel Richardson's *Pamela* less than two years after the first British publication (in 1740) was an unprecedented venture. In the event Franklin gambled that novel's boundless popularity among European readers would for once warrant his investment of money and time in the republication of a two-volume novel. However, the size of the project put such a strain on his presses and his pocket book that it would take him more than two years (from 1742 to 1744) to produce the two-volume novel—by which time the domestic market had been well-nigh saturated by imported copies. Significantly, no other unabridged British novel would be reprinted in America until the Revolution, after which the war effort caused the near complete collapse of the print market for novels. Needless to say, despite its extraordinary readership throughout the eighteenth century, Richardson's *Clarissa* (1748–9)—with roughly one million words one of the longest novels in English—was only reprinted in America in abridged editions (all from the 1790s), which typically retained a mere 5 per cent of the original text.

Yet the significance of Richardson's truncated 'American' *Clarissa* goes far beyond the economics of the marketplace. In fact, the enormous popularity of abridged editions of *Clarissa*, as well as of *Pamela*, constitutes a salient case of America's resistance to British ideology. The editions of *Pamela* that appeared in America during the 1790s were reduced in size to no more than a handful of letters and were only about 27,000 words in length; the abridged editions of *Clarissa* were somewhat longer, at roughly 41,000 words. Leonard Tennenhouse has convincingly argued that this brevity of the American editions was fundamentally dictated by a postcolonial process of cultural reproduction, which made it incumbent upon readers in the early republic to retain a sense of Englishness. It is striking that during the reduction and adaptation process, the abridged Richardson 'dispenses with all but the most necessary verbal performances in order to concentrate on the conduct of the female body' (Tennenhouse 2007: 58). Crucially, the American *Clarissa* includes no personal record of her rape by Lovelace. By recasting 'the heroine's rape from an assault on her sensibility into a devastating physical experience', the American *Clarissa* renders the tragedy of the heroine into an unfortunate calamity, but one which can and has to be overcome (61). As in the English *Clarissa*, the heroine finally expires, yet, by intimating that if she had lived, marriage to an English gentleman could have been part of her recovery, the abridged edition leaves open the possibility of the social redemption of the heroine: 'What counts for an American readership... is not so much the loss of purity as one's fidelity to an idea of a home one imagined to be English' (63).

When the Peace of Paris of 1783 reopened trade between the new United States and Europe, book production in America was also restarted; but type, paper, and capital remained in short supply. These shortages continued to hamper domestic book production all through the 1790s and even during the early decades of the nineteenth century. The passing by Congress of the federal Copyright Act of 1790 ironically exacerbated the squeeze on the market, because it simply raised the production cost of books written by American authors. Faced with these pressures on the American print market, American printers and booksellers had always endeavoured to meet the growing demand for fiction by engaging in a large-scale import of cheaper books printed in Europe. In fact, in eighteenth-century America, book selling was synonymous with book importing. Consequently, most of the books eighteenth-century American readers read were imported books. Thus, it has been calculated that in the five years immediately following the Declaration of Independence the total annual shipment of books to the mainland American colonies may have amounted to more than 120,000 volumes, or approximately 4 per cent of the total British annual output (Raven 1997: 21). In practice this meant that the Anglo-American book trade was determined much less by the perceived quality of a text than by the mechanics of the commodity market in general. Demand and supply, cost base, and profit margins ultimately determined what books ended up on the book-shelves of readers and circulating libraries in America—far less so their aesthetic quality, scholarly content, canonical status, or even national pride.

The book trade between Britain and America was sluggish until the middle of the eighteenth century. The demand for books at that time was generally low in what was still an overwhelmingly agricultural and thinly populated society. Though literacy rates were relatively high in some regions, notably in Puritan New England, these readers tended to limit their consumption of print to a confined canon of religious works. The supply side of the trade was equally weak. London traders were discouraged by the high risks and costs of transatlantic shipping and the modest and uncertain profit margins. In the final analysis it was the entrepreneurial structure of the London publishing world that imposed the most serious constraints on the transatlantic book trade. The heavily capitalized publishing business in London was dominated by an exclusive fraternity of booksellers. So long as they refused to sell to the colonial retailers at a whole-sale price that was significantly below that of the going 'gentleman's price' in London, the American trade remained weak. A few booksellers operating on the margins of the London monopoly, particularly James Rivington and William Strahan, attempted to undercut London book prices using a variety of market strategies. These included the trade in pirated editions with false London imprints and in 'rum books'—unmarketable titles and random single volumes that were sold in batches with a few attractive titles mixed in as bait.

The only significant pressure on the London book tycoons came in the course of the 1760s and early 1770s from competitors who, because they either refused to recognize English copyright law (the Scots) or were outside of the jurisdiction of English law altogether (the Irish), could undersell their London rivals. This led to a marked increase in the transatlantic book trade. After the War of 1812, a steep rise in the demand in America for cheap books, especially novels, induced American booksellers to join the lucrative market of pirated books and cheap reprint editions. As a result a cut-throat competition emerged amongst American printers and booksellers. Particularly fierce was the rivalry between Mathew Carey in Philadelphia and the Harper brothers of New York, with each side trying to beat the other by cornering the market first. In 1836, for instance, Carey and Hart booked all the seats on the mail stage to New York in order to transport freshly printed copies of Edward Bulwer Lytton's *Rienzi, the Last of the Roman Tribunes* (1835) to the shops there, before the Harpers could begin distributing their own pirated edition of the novel. The unprecedented popularity of Walter Scott's Waverley Novels gave a vast additional impetus to the importation and reproduction of British novels in America. Each new title was reprinted almost simultaneously in Boston, New York, and Philadelphia, often within days of the first copy arriving in America. Mathew Carey's reprint trade in Waverley Novels was considerably boosted by the transmission of advance proof sheets from Edinburgh through the agency of Joseph Ogle Robinson, who operated first out of Leeds and later from London, with the tacit support of Scott's publisher, Archibald Constable. In 1822, for instance, Mathew Carey printed 1,500 copies of Scott's *Quentin Durward* within just twenty-hours after receiving the advance proof sheets from Edinburgh.

Although some American book traders managed to get a stake in the lucrative piracy and reprint market, even the more successful American importers were only small players in the transatlantic book trade. After the Act of Union (1801) joined Ireland and Britain into a single kingdom, this trade was dominated even more than before by London book concerns such as William Lane's Minerva Press. While Britain witnessed a sharp rise in the number of cooperative bookselling firms and partnerships from the 1780s onwards, in the United States such a consolidation in the market did not take place till considerably later, particularly between 1800 and 1840. As a result of this uneven competition, of the hundreds of colonial and early Republican printer-booksellers, only Mathew Carey's business survived into the nineteenth century. This meant that for much of this period, American readers continued to read what the London printers were able and willing to supply.

Needless to say, the overwhelming predominance of the English novel on the American literary marketplace made it both commercially and artistically virtually impossible for American authors to compete with their transatlantic counterparts—or even to get their work published in the first place. No early American author was more aware of the precarious condition of domestic literary production and consumption, and no author did more to amend the situation, than Charles Brockden Brown. A prominent member of the 'Friendly Club', New York's first successful attempt to form a coterie for serious literary discussion and criticism, Brown threw himself into a frenzy of literary activity. In the three years between 1798 and 1801 he produced no less than six romances and two epistolary novels. In addition to this, he wrote poetry, short stories, essays, political pamphlets, and edited two magazines, which he filled with many products from his own pen. Brown's ambition was unmistakable: he wanted to help establish and institutionalize a national literature in the United States and become America's first professional man of letters. Thus in the address 'to the public' prefacing his novel *Edgar Huntly*, Brown claims the status of a 'moral painter' who, by 'calling forth the passions and engaging the sympathy of the reader', aspires to 'exhibit a series of adventures, growing out of the condition of our country'.[3] Consequently, Brown defiantly dismisses earlier, English (and German) models of the novel, which were dominated by what he calls 'Puerile superstition and exploded manners; Gothic castles and chimeras'; instead, he asserts that 'incidents of Indian hostility, and the perils of the western wilderness,

---

[3] Charles Brockden Brown, *Edgar Huntly, or, Memoirs of a Sleep-Walker*, 3 vols (Philadelphia: Printed by H. Maxwell, 1799), 1.3, 4.

are far more suitable; [and] for a native of America to overlook these, would admit of no apology' (1.4).

Yet the ambitious American author, who in December 1798 had proudly sent a copy of his first novel to Vice-President Jefferson, had by 1801 abandoned all hope of declaring America's literary independence. Not long after, in a review essay entitled 'A Sketch of American Literature, 1806–7', published in the first issue of the *American Register*, Brown gives us a summary as well as sobering account of the state of American letters at the beginning of the nineteenth century. Although in his assessment 'America is probably as great a mart for printed publications as any country in the world', Brown comes to the conclusion that in terms of the volume of original publications 'the American states, are, in a literary view, no more than a province of the British empire', bearing in this respect 'an exact resemblance to Scotland and Ireland'.[4] In the final analysis, Brown reluctantly concedes, the volume of 'original publications' in America is not so much determined by the presence or absence of 'original genius' as by the blunt dynamics of the marketplace: as the inhabitants of Bristol, York, Edinburgh, and Dublin get their cloth from Manchester, their hardware from Birmingham, and their books from 'the great manufactory of London', so do the citizens of Baltimore, Philadelphia, New York, and Boston (174).

However, it was not the economics of the printing and trading of books alone that made Brown decide to abandon his literary ambitions: after all, the market dynamics of demand and supply, no less than the catalogues of the circulating libraries, merely reflected the literary taste of the general reading public. That popular readership in late eighteenth-century America was predominantly female, and that readership's prevailing taste was *not* for novels promoting neoclassical moral instruction and public virtue: the female reader with leisure time to kill went for sentimental and Gothic romances. After a visit to Hocquet Caritat's circulating library in New York—with upwards of 30,000 volumes one of the biggest in America at the time—the English traveller John Davis observed in 1802:

> Novels are called for by the young and the old; from the tender virgin of thirteen, whose little heart went pit-a-pat at the approach of a beau, to the experienced matron of three score, who could not read without spectacles. . . . [The library's] shelves could scarcely sustain the weight of *Female Frailty*, *The Posthumous Daughter*, and the *Cavern of Woe*; they required the aid of the carpenter to support the burden of *Cottage on the Moor*, the *House of Tynian*, and the *Castles of Athlin and DunBayne* or they groaned under the multiplied editions of the *Devil in Love*, *More Ghosts*, and *Rinaldo Rinaldini*.[5]

---

[4] Charles Brockden Brown, 'A Sketch of American Literature, 1806–7', *The American Register, or General Repository of History, Politics, and Science*, 1 (1806–7), 174.

[5] John Davis, *Travels of Four Years and a Half in the United States during 1798, 1799, 1800, 1801, and 1802* (Bristol: Printed by R. Edwards, 1803), 204n.

It is evident, then, that late eighteenth-century America, like Britain for that matter, had succumbed to a heavy bout of novel-mania. The phenomenal increase in the trade and consumption of sensationalist fiction triggered an equally extraordinary, indeed often hysterical barrage of censure. The sentimental and the Gothic novel had jumped the genre boundary of 'polite entertainment' and now had to be disciplined and brought back into line, along with other types of inflaming fiction, notably that promiscuous novelistic innovation called the 'political novel'. In the discourse of their critics, novels and readers were anxiously pathologized in a way that perversely confirmed that fiction is the heart, or sinews, of the body politic. Thus, reviewers on both sides of the Atlantic would claim that novels could 'captivate the feelings', 'inflame the passions or corrupt the heart' (see Orians 1937: 198). Presumed by many to be preying on the young and the unsuspecting (women in particular), novels were said to poison the mind and render vice amiable, with the ultimate effect of sapping public virtue and unstitching the fabric of society. Again and again, critics represented the impact of novels as polluting, staining, poisoning, or deforming the individual and the nation. In America novel-mania was regarded by many as a sure sign that the free press had spun out of control. In order to safeguard the nation's moral fibre, the press, and especially the novel, needed to be severely disciplined. A member of the Belles-Lettres Society of Dickinson College at Carlisle, Pennsylvania, even went so far as to argue that since novels threatened the welfare of the nation, Congress should eradicate them by slapping a punitive tax on them.[6]

The careers of budding American novelists like Charles Brockden Brown suffered fatal collateral damage from the widespread backlash against the popularity of the English novel. It was just about the most unpropitious time to attempt to become the nation's first professional man of letters and to give the fledgling Republic a literary voice of its own. In his earnest ambition to serve the entire nation, Brown was ignored by all: the literary elite considered his work un-English and hence bizarre; the general public thought it was dull and unpalatable; and the moralists hated it merely because it was fiction. Unsurprisingly, all of Brown's novels fell stillborn from the press and not one of them was ever reprinted in America during his lifetime. Abandoning his literary vocation, Brown was left to lament: 'Book-making . . . is the dullest of all trades, and the utmost that any American can look for, in his native country, is to be reimbursed his unavoidable expenses.' Ironically, Brown's only remaining hope to reach an audience for his American tales was to get a foothold in the English literary market: 'The saleability of my works will much depend upon their popularity in England, whither Caritat [his publisher and agent] has carried a considerable number of Wieland, Ormond and Mervyn.'[7]

---

[6] Anon., *Observations on Novel-Reading: In an Essay Written by a Member of the Belles-Lettres Society of Dickinson College, at Carlisle in the Year 1789 . . .* (Philadelphia: Printed by Thomas Dobson, 1792), 57–8.

[7] William Dunlap, *The Life of Charles Brockden Brown*, 2 vols (Philadelphia: Parke, 1815), 1.100 (Brown as quoted there).

The West Indies and India

While for much of the eighteenth century print culture in America was dominated by an intense struggle between a lingering mimicry of English literary standards and a budding literary nativism, such systemic rivalry was unknown in the West Indies and India. On the contrary, for many settlers in the British colonies in the Caribbean and East Indies (India, China, and south-east Asia), reading English books was primarily a way to preserve their national identity and maintain their cultural connectedness to the colonial metropole.

Book importations into the West Indies in particular were quite considerable during the eighteenth century. This was largely due to the emergence of the planter class on the Caribbean sugar islands. With well-heeled West Indian planters increasingly taking on the airs of English gentlemen, an indigenous patrician culture took root, which made the possession of a well-stocked library well-nigh a necessity. Giles Barber (1976) has computed that between 1700 and 1780 the West Indian colonies imported books from Britain to a value of £53,580. This sum represented about a quarter of total exports to the New World, and exceeded those to New England, as well as those to the East Indies. Of the West Indian book imports, over 40 per cent was taken up by Jamaica alone, which made the island's book imports roughly comparable to imports into New York and Pennsylvania during the same period. Barbados was good for 30 per cent of total imports into the West Indies, followed by Antigua with 10 per cent and St Kitts with just over 6 per cent.

The inventories of the contemporary Jamaican booksellers and advertisements in the West Indian newspapers suggest that initially during the eighteenth century the merchant trade was dominated by books of a utilitarian nature, notably medical and law books, history, biography, and political treatises. However, judging from circulating libraries' catalogues, by the end of the century a taste for English Gothic and sentimental novels had began to colonize West Indian planter society. As the sugar economy first began to falter following the abolition of the slave trade in 1808 and then entirely collapsed with the abolition of slavery itself in 1834, sugar planters left the islands in droves. With their exit the market for polite literature went into a sharp decline. The history of circulating libraries in the West Indies chronicles this decline. Catering in particular to the 'friends of polite literature', circulating libraries had been established in Jamaica as early as 1779—in Kingston, by William Aikman—and in 1784 in Montego Bay, by James Fannin (Cave 1980: 55–6). (Fannin also printed his own, pirated editions of such classics of the sentimental mode as *Yorick's Letters to Eliza*, and Goethe's *The Sorrows of Young Werther*.) Yet both libraries soon failed for lack of subscribers. A similar fate was met by most of their successors in Kingston and Montego Bay, as well as by similar initiatives set up by printers in Port of Spain, Grenada, and other towns during the 1820s and 1830s. English book exports to the West Indies would not recover from the downturn. In 1838 St George's Library Society at Buff Bay, Jamaica, had seventy-nine members left. According to the 1844 census, the population of St. George's was 8,800, of whom not more than 400 were white. With books falling prey to the country's climate and insect population as quickly as their dwindling readership did, the British novel had a relatively short shelf life in the West Indies during the first half of the nineteenth century.

Although the life expectancy of British readers and books was generally equally short there, the fate of the English novel in India could not have been more different. If book exports to the West Indies were sizeable within the American hemispheric context, they were dwarfed by the staggering export numbers involved in the Indian book trade, particularly from the 1790s onwards. During the 1790s the value of book exports to India was over £150,000; in the first decade of the nineteenth century the value of exports more than doubled to over £340,000. By 1830 the total value of books exported from Britain to India since the early 1790s had exceeded £1.2 million (Shaw 2009: 573, Table 29.1). The vast majority of these book exports were conducted through private trade, although frequently shipped on vessels belonging to the East India Company.

Roughly until the middle of the eighteenth century the majority of English books travelled to India as the personal belongings of employees of the East India Company, which from 1600 until 1833 enjoyed a monopoly on the trade between Britain and Asia. The Company itself also regularly exported batches of Christian literature to its settlements—or 'factories'—in India out of concern for the spiritual well-being of its employees. These initial shipments, which formed the nucleus of factory libraries, were usually placed in the care of the local chaplain. The factory collections were often expanded and diversified by bequests and by purchases of books from Company employees. The surviving 1729 catalogue of the Madras factory library, for instance, lists 1,235 works, supplemented by 640 books that belonged to the Madras chaplain. Although predominantly containing Christian literature, the collection also offered secular reading, including some works of prose and poetry.

By the 1750s the significance of factory libraries for the circulation of English books in India began to diminish. There were a number of reasons for this. As books increasingly began to be imported for their exchange rather than their use value, a growing number of Company employees were able to acquire or build their own private collections. Learned societies and educational institutions, such as the Bombay Literary Society, the Hindoo College, and the Asiatic Society of Bengal, also formed their own libraries. However, the most significant force behind the rapid dissemination of English books across India at the end of the eighteenth century was the establishment of commercial circulating libraries in several of the major settlements.

The sharp rise in the demand for English books was met by an increasingly vigorous commercial import trade. This trade was mainly carried out by the captains and officers on board the East Indiamen, who were allowed to ship freight-free a certain amount of speculative cargo. That these moonshine book traders were quite savvy about the prevailing literary taste of Anglo-Indian readers is inadvertently revealed by John Shore,

First Baron Teignmouth (who would later serve as Governor General of India from 1793 to 1798). Unequivocally dismissive of what by the early 1770s was evidently already a craze for popular English novels, Shore observed:

> The libraries brought out by the captains and mates of Indiamen into this country for sale, though very voluminous, consist mostly of novels, and such books as are termed, by the London shopkeepers, 'light summer reading', and such as are sent, at stated seasons, in large cargoes, to Bath, Tunbridge Wells, and such places. I had the good luck, last year, to furnish myself, at a very cheap rate, with some Latin and Greek Classics; which one of the captains, ill judging of the mart to which he brought them, imagined to have sold at a high premium.[8]

Many of those imported British novels ended up on the shelves of the circulating libraries that were founded in the three presidency capitals—although none of them appears to have been able to sustain more than one circulating library at any given time. The first circulating library was established by John Andrews in Calcutta in 1774, followed by the Bombay library, which opened in 1790, and the Madras subscription library, which was founded in 1792. Almost invariably founded by local printers who were keen to diversify their business activities, most circulating libraries in Calcutta, Bombay, and Madras doubled up as bookselling and stationery shops.

During the early decades of the nineteenth century bookselling in India became an increasingly sophisticated affair, with traders targeting different audiences with specific books and customized editions. Condensed editions of classic English titles, notably the 'Regent's Pocket Classics', were not only cheaper but also eminently portable, and hence popular among the lower orders in the East India Company. High-ranking British administrators could choose from a range of luxury editions printed on fine paper and elegantly bound in superb imported leather. By 1830 the importation of English-language books was no longer confined to books printed in Britain. Cheap American reprints began to find their way into India. Thus, from New York came the 'Family Library' series, which had been launched by John and James Harper in New York in 1830. From Paris came the editions of major British authors that Galignani had been producing from the early 1820s onwards and were disseminating across Europe and the globe from what allegedly was the first English bookshop on the Continent. Among the Galignani imprints that reached India was a condensed edition of Walter Scott's novels in six octavo volumes.

The vogue for cheap novels from Britain apparently began to dominate public life in major Indian towns, particularly Calcutta, the capital of British India and a key trading centre for the East India Company. The poet and travel writer Emma Roberts recorded in her account of a tour through India that

---

[8] John Shore, First Baron Teignmouth, *Memoir of the Life and Correspondence of John Lord Teignmouth. By His Son, Lord Teignmouth*, 2 vols (London: Hatchard, 1843), 1.45–6.

Immense consignments of books sometimes come out to Calcutta, through different mercantile houses, which are sold by auction, and are often knocked down for a mere tri-fle.... [C]ertainly, in the streets of Calcutta...books are thrust into the palanquin-doors, or the windows of a carriage...by natives, who make a point of presenting the title-pages and the engravings upside down. Some of these books seem to be worthy of the Minerva press in its worst days; and it is rather curious that novels, which are never heard of in England...are hawked about in the highways and byeways of Calcutta.[9]

Clearly the logistical challenges of the transcontinental book trade were formidable, and not all shipments safely reached India. Yet, from Roberts's anecdotal evidence we may gather that, despite occasional losses at sea before ships reached Calcutta, for the London book tycoons the Indian market for cheap British novels was a highly lucrative one: 'At the Cape of Good Hope, the beach is said sometimes to be literally strewed with novels; an occurrence which takes place upon the wreck of a ship freighted from the warehouses of Paternoster Row' (1.11).

The European Continent

Popular myth has it that the start of James Fenimore Cooper's literary career was the result of a self-imposed challenge to improve upon the fashionable English novel of domestic manners. Allegedly he was so dissatisfied with the (unidentified) sentimental novel he had been reading to his wife, that he threw the book down in disgust, saying: 'I could write you a better book than that myself' (see Spiller 1931: 73). However, it is indicative of the prescriptive force of the contemporary English novel that the education and marriage of young ladies was to be the theme for his debut novel, *Precaution* (1820). Having married into the well-established De Lancey family, one of the great New York dynasties, Cooper apparently saw nothing dissonant about a patriotic American gentleman farmer trying his hand at writing a 'civilizing' English middle-class novel. Even though he would go on to become the first successful practitioner of the American historical novel (notably in his Leatherstocking Tales), Cooper evidently found it hard to dissociate himself entirely from the English model of the national-historical tale—earning him the somewhat dubi-ous sobriquet of 'the American Scott' (see the title of Dekker 1967).

Cooper was by no means the only author to feel the imperial might of the global British novel. Katie Trumpener has aptly designated the Romantic period as one of a far-reaching 'literary devolution' (1997: 16), in which transperipheral circuits of influence linked England, Scotland, Ireland, and Britain's overseas colonies. The result was that after a long period of cultural infatuation with translated French and German fiction, the British

---

[9] Emma Roberts, *Scenes and Characteristics of Hindostan, With Sketches of Anglo-Indian Society*, 3 vols (London: W. H. Allen & Co., 1835), 1.10–12.

novel finally achieved export surplus over imported titles by the early 1820s. Increasingly in the first half of the nineteenth century exported novels ended up in circulating libraries, homes, and private collections across the European Continent. In Germany this trend had already started in the second half of the eighteenth century. Admiration for the English literary masters was increasingly used as a weapon to combat French dominion in matters of taste and foster a domestic, German literary tradition. As a wave of Anglomania swept through the nation, German readers adopted the English novel as a form of German self-expression. Among the largest receptacles of English prose fiction in Europe was the library at Castle Corvey near Höxter in Westphalia, Germany. The Corvey library was largely the creation of Victor Amadeus, Landgraf of Hesse-Rotenburg (1779–1834), who amassed over 74,000 volumes in all, including 35,000 volumes in German, 20,000 in French, and 15,000 in English. Among the last, the Romantic-era fiction collection is virtually unsurpassed in scope and depth. But the real measure of the rise of the English novel's popularity and impact on the European Continent is not the number of volumes that were exported to Europe, but the number of translations, adaptations, and conscious or unconscious imitations that were produced there. Sales of those far outstripped the import of English novels in the original language and editions.

Bibliographical research has revealed that in France alone at least 630 translations of English novels were published during the period between 1700 and 1805 (Streeter 1936: 1). However, there is considerable variability in the actual numbers due to the fact that throughout the eighteenth century both the 'novel' and the 'translation' were loosely circumscribed categories. Thus, among the English 'novels' that were translated into French were romances, utopias, allegorical fables, and juvenile literature. Conversely, particularly during the first half of the eighteenth century, French 'translations' of English novels included adaptations, imitations, and abridgements. Indeed, complete and accurate translations were the exception rather than the rule during this period. Notoriously, in his idiosyncratic translations of *Pamela, Clarisssa*, and *Sir Charles Grandison*, Abbé Prévost took astonishing liberties with Richardson's epistolary novels. Pruning, omitting, and collapsing letters as he saw fit, he even changed the ending of *Sir Charles Grandison*—all for the purpose of rendering Richardson's language and plots more agreeable to what he considered was France's refined and supreme literary taste. Until the 1750s, roughly, the dissemination of French translations of English novels suffered from the marginal status that the domestic novel had in France. Being a hybrid form of prose writing, the novel was generally regarded as an undesirable form of literary expression and was only deemed fit for idle entertainment. That said, the English novel had a formidable sponsor in Voltaire. As a result, the 'genre anglais', as it was known, attracted a steadily growing readership in France.

French being the lingua franca of polite middle-class society on the Continent, there was a vast market in Europe for French-language printing, including translations and adaptations of English novels. Because its printers and publishers enjoyed a relative freedom of the press, the Dutch Republic became a major hub for the production and dissemination of French translations of English novels across the entire Continent. The Republic's prominent position in the pan-European print market was further enhanced by its liberal stance towards religious minorities. From the late seventeenth century onwards, Dutch French-language reviews such as the *Nouvelles de la République des Lettres* (1684–9), the *Bibliothèque universelle* (1686–93), and the *Histoire des Ouvrages des Savans* (1687–1709) had been exploring the rich store of English literature for the benefit of readers across Europe, where at that time the English language was well-nigh unknown. The most notable translator of this period was Justus van Effen (1684–1735), who acted as a patron for English literature in Europe. Well-read in both English and French and across several disciplines, van Effen made two trips to England in 1715 and 1727, during which he made his acquaintance with some of the period's key literary figures. His association with Joseph Addison and Richard Steele resulted in the launch of several French- and Dutch-language imitations of the *Spectator*, among them the *Hollandsche Spectator* (1731–5). The author of numerous translations and adaptations of English literary texts (for the most part into French), it was van Effen who introduced readers on the Continent to Swift's *Tale of the Tub* (trans. 1721)—a work that had generally been regarded as untranslatable—as well as to Defoe's *Robinson Crusoe* (trans. 1720–1). While in the course of the first half of the eighteenth century the reading public in continental Europe had thus become familiar with the works of Jonathan Swift, Daniel Defoe, Tobias Smollett, and Henry Fielding, it was the novels of Samuel Richardson that lifted the popularity of the English novel on the Continent to an unprecedented level of appreciation.

The impact of Samuel Richardson's novels on the globalization of the English novel can hardly be overstated. Going through five editions in the first year and translated into most European languages, *Pamela* was one of the first international media hypes. At a time when English novels were still rarely reviewed in European literary magazines, *Pamela* was the notable exception. The novel immediately led to intense discussions in literary magazines, drawing rooms, and coffee houses all across Europe—and, indeed, the American colonies. Fashionable ladies displayed copies of the novel in their drawing rooms and held fans decorated with scenes from the novel. It became a play, an opera, and even a waxwork. In an age generally suspicious of sentimental prose fiction, ministers both in England and on the Continent recommended the novel from the pulpit. Yet the novel's detractors were almost as numerous as its fans—and by no means less volatile. Critics of the novel censured the book's 'immoral' agenda, reflected particularly in what they saw as the unashamed hypocrisy of its heroine, whom they regarded as a sly minx. Unsurprisingly, the satirical retorts that appeared on the heels of the novel's first publication—notably Henry Fielding's *An Apology for the Life of Mrs Shamela Andrews* (1741) and Eliza Haywood's *The Anti-Pamela; or Feign'd Innocence Detected* (1741)—were as popular on the Continent (in French translations) as they were in England itself. A Danish observer even spoke of society being divided into 'two different parties, Pamelists and

Antipamelists.... Some look upon this young Virgin as an Example for Ladies to follow.... Others, on the contrary, discover in it, the Behaviour of an hypocritical, crafty
Girl... who understands the Art of bringing a Man to her Lure' (see Keymer and Sabor
2005: 8). Yet, paradoxically, as deeply divided as it was over the virtues or otherwise of the
novel's socially ambitious heroine, Europe's bourgeois reading public unwittingly found
itself more intensely engaged than ever before in articulating a collective value system
for their emerging class.

But it was only with the extraordinary literary and popular success of *Clarissa* that the
English novel became truly transnational. Whereas *Pamela*, in its European translations,
was still primarily interpreted as a narrative of national, English morality, with the translations of *Clarissa* 'the national identification of the novel was expressed in cosmopolitan
terms such as order, manners, and moral purpose. The more the novel seemed to transcend national particularism, the more the translation system allowed nationalization,
at least as long as nationalization could be conflated with civilized virtues' (McMurran
2010: 125). Widely read as a sentimental novel of the human heart, *Clarissa* represented a
new cosmopolitanism that appealed to the universalizing ambitions of the burgeoning
middle class. However, it is important to be aware that this cosmopolitanism was more
strictly understood in terms of class than of gender or morality. What had particularly
upset and outraged the more genteel readers of Richardson's first novel was that Pamela
was a working-class girl with social aspirations beyond her station. The literary controversy that erupted in response to Pamela's meteoric rise in the world, then, was at heart
a reflection of an increasingly self-conscious and assertive middle-class insisting that the
boundaries of class be preserved and guarded against social upstarts. By contrast, the rape
and subsequent demise of Clarissa Harlowe unleashed a massive outpouring of sympathy
and public anger among the novel's bourgeois readership, less because of her personal
ordeal than because she was perceived as one of their own, who met her tragic fate at the
hands of a rakish member of the class they were seeking to displace.

During the decades following their first appearance on the Continent, Richardson's
novels would come to saturate the consciousness and moral imagination of Europe's middle classes. Accordingly, an endless stream of new editions, retranslations, and adaptations continued to feed the craze for the English novel in general and for Richardsoniana
in particular. Thus, one of the most successful adaptations of Richardson, *De Historie
van Mejuffrouw Sara Burgerhart* ('The History of Miss Sara Burgerhart'; 1782), written
by the Dutch collaborators Betje Wolff and Aagje Deken, found its way across Europe
after it was translated into French (Lausanne, 1787) and German (Berlin, 1796). Wolff
and Deken, who had started to live together following the death of Wolff's husband in
1777, established a highly successful writing partnership, producing further Richardson
imitations, including *Historie van den Heer Willem Leevend* (1784–5) and *Abraham Blenkaart*
(1787). Sympathizing with the patriotic cause, Wolff and Deken lived in France during
the height of the Revolution, where they wrote another popular Richardsonian novel of

manners, *Cornelie Wildschut* (1793–6). Even more astonishing was the dissemination of *De Kleine Grandisson, of de Gehoorzaame Zoon* ('Young Grandison, or The Obedient Son'; The Hague, 1782) by Margareta Geertruida de Cambon-van de Werken. Although the story is unrelated to Richardson's novel, this first Dutch epistolary children's novel became an international bestseller, with more than eighty new editions and reprints within a century after its first appearance (including translations into French, German, Swedish and—ironically—into English). De Cambon would duly produce a companion volume, *De Kleine Klarissa* ('Young Clarissa'; The Hague, 1790). The latter represented an extraordinary case of literary reappropriation—or repatriation—later appearing in an abridged English translation published by Charles Dilly, as *Letters and Conversations between Several Young Ladies, on Interesting and Improving Subjects* (1795).

In Germany, too, there was a sustained demand for novels written—or which proclaimed to have been written—in the manner of Richardson. Sometimes this involved the translation of novels that had failed to make any lasting impression upon readers in England itself. A salient example of this phenomenon is the rapid translation into German and subsequent republication in Germany during the 1750s and 1760s of all three of the novels published in the 1750s by Susan Smythies, comprising *The Stage-Coach* (1753), *The History of Lucy Wellers* (1754), and *The Brothers* (1758). In other cases the sustained interest in Richardsoniana involved more straightforward imitations, such as *The History of Sir William Harrington. Written Some Years Since, and Revised and Corrected by the Late Mr. Richardson*, sometimes attributed to Anna Meades, and Sophia Briscoe's *Miss Melmoth; or, The New Clarissa* (both published London in 1771). It is often hard to tell from such cases of 'literary sampling' where commercial opportunism ended and genuine literary taste began. Yet it is evident that throughout the eighteenth century the English novel was as popular as it was in Europe because it offered 'a particular cultural experience' of (what was perceived to be) 'Englishness' (Raven 2002a: 720). This sentiment was especially strong during the 1770s and the second half of the 1780s, when German translations of novels by Tobias Smollett, Henry Mackenzie, Richard Graves, and Henry Brooke appeared either in the same year as the English original or the year after (718: Table 1).

Literary trends and tastes in the second half of the eighteenth century were increasingly fluid and transnational. Thus, the contemporary, pan-European penchant for sentimental novels led to Johann Wolfgang von Goethe's *Die Leiden des jungen Werthers* (1774) reappearing in London as *The Sorrows of Werter: A German Story* (1779). However, the most significant example of this cultural counterflow from the German to the English literary marketplace concerned the exploding demand in England during the 1790s for the German *Schauerroman* or Gothic novel. Such was the craze for German ghost and ghoul stories that new arrivals were frequently offered to readers as translations 'from the German', even when they had been produced by local English hacks (Raven 2002a: 732). Conversely, in the latter half of the eighteenth century many original novels were published in Germany under the guise of English translations. Steeped in local history, custom, and prejudice, the Gothic novel by and large remained confined to the realm of national literatures. However, by its very nature having a much more universal appeal, it was the sentimental novel that emerged during the last decades of the eighteenth century as the first, truly borderless, pan-European bourgeois novel. The high point of the appeal of the sentimental genre across Europe was marked by the publication and translation of Laurence Sterne's *Tristram Shandy* (1760–7) and *A Sentimental Journey* (1768).

By the late 1760s Richardson's star had by no means set in Europe, yet it was about to be eclipsed by the rise of Laurence Sterne. Reviewers and readers across the Continent hailed Sterne's talent and creation as innovative and universal. Voltaire deemed Sterne superior to Rabelais and in Russia Sterne's *Sentimental Journey* made him the most popular and most influential English author during the last years of Catherine the Great's reign. In Germany, Sterne's period of literary activity in the 1760s happened to coincide with the heyday of British literary supremacy there. Sterne's exploration of the secret recesses of the heart was precisely what the German soul needed, at a time when German literature and the arts were moving into full 'Sturm und Drang' mode. During this upsurge of pre-Romanticism (roughly from the later 1760s to the early 1780s), writers and artists were keen to explore their individual subjectivity and give free rein to extremes of emotion in order to escape from what they saw as the constraints of rationalism imposed by the Enlightenment. Goethe praised Sterne as 'the most beautiful mind that ever lived; who reads him feels free and beautiful; his humour is inimitable'—adding that Sterne was 'a model in nothing' but 'a guide and an inspiration ... in everything'.[10] Goethe's own *Werther*, which first appeared in 1774, owed much of its immediate popular appeal, its author acknowledged at the time, to the sentimentality of Sterne. Imitations of Sterne began to appear in large numbers, and Sterne cults sprang up all over the country. In Marienwerder, near Hanover, an English landscape park was laid out, which included a poetic cemetery with graves for all of Sterne's famous characters (Thayer 1905: 89). Such extremes of sympathetic sensitivity inevitably elicited several satirical attacks on Sterne and the vogue for the sentimental in general. Yet, despite such criticism, Sterne's popularity in Germany continued virtually unabated into the nineteenth century and German Romanticism. In 1825 Arthur Schopenhauer proposed undertaking a new German translation of 'the immortal Tristram Shandy', a novel he read 'over and over again'.[11] Heinrich Heine regarded Sterne to be 'of equal birth with Shakespeare'.[12]

While Sterne's reputation on the Continent amounted to something of a pan-European mania, the same cannot be said for Jane Austen's reception in Europe—at least during the

---

[10] Johann Wolfgang von Goethe, *Goethes Werke. Herausgegeben im Auftrage der Großherzogin Sophie von Sachsen*, 143 vols (Weimar: Böhlau, 1887–1919), 42: 2, 197, 205.

[11] Arthur Schopenhauer, *Mensch und Philosoph in seinen Briefen*, ed. Arthur Hübscher (Wiesbaden: F. A. Brockhaus, 1960), 99.

[12] Heinrich Heine, *Die romantische Schule* (Hamburg: Hoffman and Campe, 1836), 266.

nineteenth century. In fact, prior to the publication in 1870 of *A Memoir of Jane Austen*, James Edward Austen-Leigh's idealized portrait of his aunt, Jane Austen's presence in Europe was relatively limited. Although by 1824 all of Austen's novels had appeared in at least one language (French, German, Danish, and Swedish), her work received only sixteen translations during the entire nineteenth century (Mandal 2009: 424, Table 37.1). In countries like Russia, Spain, and Italy, very few readers were aware of Austen's work, which was not translated there until well into the twentieth century. It is true that some readers in Europe became familiar with Austen's work in English editions, either produced in Britain or through cross-Channel joint ventures, such as Richard Bentley's 'Standard Novels', which were published and disseminated on the Continent in collaboration with the Galignani brothers of Paris. Yet the fact remains that Austen's European presence during the nineteenth century did not even begin to approach the late twentieth-century Austenmania, nor was there anything like a Janeite phenomenon (see Mandal and Southam 2007: xxi–xxiii).

On the contrary, there are signs of a deliberate resistance to the aesthetics of Jane Austen's work on the continent—oddly, even among her translators. While today's extraordinary, global popularity of Austen's novels is to a significant degree determined by the (perceived) sense of 'Englishness' that is ingrained in her work, many nineteenth-century readers in mainland Europe felt that Austen's novels were not 'English' enough. Thus, Austen's characteristic use of irony to expose social hypocrisy did not go down well with European readers, who associated 'Englishness' with morality, polite manners, and sensibility, not with witty social satire. Hence, there was a tendency among Austen's early translators to 'Anglicize' her novels, particularly by realigning Austen's originals with the genre of the sentimental novel. For instance, when the Swiss-French sentimental novelist Isabelle de Montolieu undertook to translate *Sense and Sensibility* (*Raison et sensibilité*, 1815) and *Persuasion* (*La Famille Elliot, ou l'ancienne inclination*, 1821), she eliminated Austen's quintessential ironic humour and scenes of domestic realism and replaced them with episodes of heightened emotion, while enhancing the pathetic quality of existing scenes. Emilia Westdahl's Swedish translation of *Persuasion* (*Familjen Elliot: skildringar af engelska karakterer*, 1836) similarly introduces a number of scenes of heightened emotion, which is perhaps not very surprising since Westdahl's translation closely follows Montolieu's *La Famille Elliot* (Mandal 2009: 427).

The example of Austen's translation into French and Swedish flags an important trend in the European reception of the British novel during the nineteenth century. With an increasing number of English-language novels being translated into one European language through the mediation of a prior translation into another European language (often French), we are no longer talking about a 'translation' in the stricter sense of the word, but rather about an 'adaptation' or an 'appropriation'. Speaking particularly to the case of Spanish 'translations' of English originals, Mari Carmen Romero Sánchez has observed that:

Spanish editions of English novels had a double filter: they were translations of French translations, adaptations adapted again to suit Spanish tastes. Hence we have a double modification: the change from the original English to the French taste, and then, again, to the Spanish one, with the additional impositions of censorship and social demands. Furthermore, French and Spanish readers of the moment preferred simple stories, without the English moral concepts or additional subplots usual in English novels: books like *Tom Jones* were cut to be brief and have a proper moral according to the beliefs and thoughts of the Spanish and French. . . . It is likely, then, that Austen was not translated from French to Spanish because of her ironical point of view; maybe her irony obscured the moral perspective desired (but not understood) by Spanish editors at the time (Sánchez 2008).

However, if Jane Austen remained essentially unrecognized in Europe during the nineteenth century, this neglect can be attributed to a significant degree to the boundless popularity on the Continent of Walter Scott's work. The growing nationalist climate that was sweeping across much of mainland Europe made Scottish historical themes and plots chime much better with audiences in Flanders, Finland, Greece, and Denmark than English ones. As a result, for many readers on the Continent, the 'English novel' was synonymous with Scott's novels.

Scott's tales about Scotland's burgeoning national consciousness did not exactly arrive on the Continent in a cultural-historical vacuum. Much of Europe had for some time been enthralled with the antiquarianism of the Ossian phenomenon. Although some questioned their authenticity, *The Works of Ossian*, James Macpherson's 1765 collection of pseudo-Gaelic epic poems, had won international acclaim and were universally hailed as the Celtic equivalent of Homer. Translations and imitations appeared all across Europe. In France alone fourteen editions of *Ossian* were published between 1776 and 1848. In Paris Jean-François Le Sueur's opera *Ossian, ou les bardes* was the talk of the town in 1804. Napoleon was so enamoured with Macpherson's poetry that he commissioned Ingres to paint 'The Dream of Ossian' on the ceiling of his bedroom in the Quirinal Palace in Rome. *The Works of Ossian* was reportedly one of the only two books the Emperor carried with him on his campaigns in Egypt and Russia (the other book being a copy of Goethe's *Werther*). In Germany *Ossian* poems resonated especially with the authors associated with the 'Sturm und Drang' movement. The first German translation appeared as early as 1768 (based on an even earlier Italian edition by Cesarotti). Herder wrote a rave review of the poems in 1773. It was also Herder who encouraged Goethe to attempt a new, less polished translation of *Ossian*. Goethe's translation of Ossian's 'Songs of Selma' would later feature prominently in a climactic scene in *Die Leiden des jungen Werthers*.

If primitive, unspoiled Scotland had struck a sympathetic chord with European sentimentalists, Walter Scott, conversely, had by the 1790s become thoroughly spellbound with German Romanticism, particularly with the works of Goethe and Schiller. In 1799 Scott translated *Götz von Berlichingen*, Goethe's tale about a chivalrous medieval German knight. This translation would mark the point of departure for Scott's own series of narrative poems, historical novels, and medieval romances. It was this close literary and cultural kinship between Scotland and Germany that paved the way for the success of Scott's novels in Germany during the course of the nineteenth century.

Scott's fame in Europe only took off with the appearance there of his historical novels (see Pittock 2006). In fact, Scott was widely regarded on the Continent as the inventor of the genre of realist historical narrative. Goethe, for one, considered Walter Scott 'to be the master of this subject'. According to Goethe, Scott 'took advantage of choosing important, but little known regions, half-missing occurrences, peculiarities in manners, customs and habits, put them up ingeniously and in this way provided his small half-true worlds with interest and applause'.[13] It was precisely this aspect of Scott's historical novels, particularly of his Scottish novels, that constituted them—in Goethe's phrase—as 'Weltliteratur'. By representing specific historical subjects in specific historical locations and situations, Scott's Scottish novels enabled readers from other spatiotemporal localities to understand the cultural identity of Scottish people. Equipped with this knowledge, such readers were subsequently also able to reflect upon their own cultural identity. This intercultural learning process was at the heart of Goethe's concept of 'world literature'. It was probably also because they functioned as 'Weltliteratur' that for nearly a century Scott's Waverley Novels were among the most popular and widely read novels in all of Europe. Without the revolutionary example of Scott, as György Lukács has argued, it is unlikely that we would have had the social-historical novels of Fenimore Cooper, Balzac, Hugo, Dumas, Fontane, Manzoni, Gogol, Pushkin, or Tolstoy—or at least the way in which they were executed. Penetrating through the accidental phenomena of social life to disclose the essences or essentials of a condition, the new historical consciousness at work in Scott's novels allowed him to realize the vital 'world-historical' forces peculiar to a particular socio-historical context (1983: 39). In significant ways, therefore, Scott's historical romance represents the epitome of the global British novel in the nineteenth century.

---

[13] *Goethes Werke*, 42: 2.126.

32

Foreign Imports

JENNY MANDER

R EFLECTING, in 1785, on a time when the English novel had been greatly over-shadowed by foreign imports, Clara Reeve did not have to cast her mind back very many decades.[1] The prevalence of imitations and translations of foreign novels had been a matter of significant critical concern throughout the first half of the eighteenth century and contemptuously identified by many a censorious reviewer as a corrupting influence on both the morals and letters of the nation. By the middle of the century, however, there was a strong sense that the English novel had come of age; and as British novelists progressively consolidated their position both at home and abroad, readers became decreasingly dependent on foreign fiction. Nonetheless, non-native fiction remained a convenient focus for multiple anxieties relating to the genre of the novel and its commercialization. For while the overall picture for 1750–1820 as regards imported imaginative literature was one of general decline, many foreign novelists continued to compete successfully for the attention of the British public. Furthermore, during the twenty years between 1790 and 1810—a period of widespread European turmoil during which Britain was almost continuously at war with France—there was a marked resurgence in translation activity. As a result, at the turn of the nineteenth century more foreign fiction was in fact circulating in Britain than at any previous point in the history of the English novel.

In what is to follow, the production statistics relating to translated fiction will be the initial focus of discussion. The second and third sections will offer a more differentiated mapping of the shifting geographical contours of this imported body of literature and foreground the role played by specialist booksellers and publishers in the introduction of foreign novels to the British public. Subsequent sections will then turn to consider in more detail some of the most popular foreign titles and authors.

---

[1] Clara Reeve, *The Progress of Romance, through Times, Countries and Manners*, 2 vols (Colchester: W. Keymer, 1785), 1.117. For the exact quotation, see Raven, Chapter 1, 5.

Translation Statistics

Notwithstanding the rising confidence in the maturity of the English novel, between 1750 and 1769 nearly 22 per cent of all new novels published in Britain (or fifty titles) were still translations. However, over the next three decades this share of the market continued to shrink: between 1760–9 translations fell to 16 per cent (forty-five titles); 1770–9 to 11 per cent (thirty-six titles); 1780–9 to 10 per cent (forty-one titles). The fact that translated titles rose very slightly at the end of this period is to be explained by the gradual expansion of the overall market. The deceleration in translation activity which is a feature of this period 1750–89 coincided with a more general malaise affecting novelistic production that has been linked to the deaths of Fielding, Richardson, Sterne, and Smollett. Contrary to what has sometimes been suggested, the gap left by this vibrant generation of British novelists was not filled by bad translations of mediocre French authors. It appears that in the absence of a buoyant domestic market, the interest in translations also declined, at least from a quantitative perspective. The slump in translations was particularly marked between 1776–85 during which period there were only ever one, two, or (in 1783 alone) three translations in any particular year from the French and no more than three genuine translations from any other source throughout.[2]

A connection between domestic production and translation activity is also suggested by the statistics for the following period 1790–1809. As the number of novels written by British authors increased, so translations rose to occupy 15 per cent of the market in new fiction. 1790–9 saw the publication of 106 translated titles; in the following decade 116 English versions of foreign novels were presented to the British public. Thus, as has already been observed, this period straddling the end of the eighteenth and the beginning of the nineteenth century was one of unprecedented richness as regards translated fiction. At this juncture, political hostilities seem to have stimulated rather than stifled interest in literary activity on the Continent. The sudden spike of twenty new translations from the French in 1803 following the brief period of peace sealed by the Treaty of Amiens in 1802 is an indication of the sort of delays that might affect the supply of new fictions in times of war. But the soaring figures for the decade as a whole bear witness to the fact that the cross-Channel trade in novels was nonetheless successfully maintained.[3]

Napoleon's Continental Blockade (1806–14) on the other hand had a more profoundly disruptive effect on the import of foreign fiction to Britain. From around 1810 the number of translations fell sharply. Not only did Napoleon's foreign policy directly

---

[2] Statistical information for the eighteenth century in this chapter is mainly dependent on the figures as tabulated in Raven (1987: 21) and Raven (2000: 58). For some further adjustments, see also Raven (2007b: 120–2).

[3] Statistical information for the early nineteenth century is based primarily on Garside (2000: 41, Table 1).

compromise the importation of French and German novels; the disruption of trade with Continental ports also restricted the supply of the rags used to make paper, significantly pushing up the costs of book production. In these circumstances, economic considerations appear to have played a major role in reshaping the market, encouraging at least booksellers at the top end to concentrate more on premium products, thus curtailing the publication of ephemeral trifles—a category into which much translated fiction typically fell. The figures are striking: over the decade 1810–19 only thirty-four foreign novels were put into English, forming barely 5 per cent of the overall total of new titles. If, following Napoleon's abdication, the number of translated titles did not return to previous levels, part of the explanation must be that while foreign imports were interrupted, new and more conspicuously indigenous novelistic fashions began to emerge: in the context of mounting public enthusiasm for subgenres such as the national tale and the historical romance Britain would appear to have turned her back on foreign novelists.

The Geographical Contours of Translated Fiction

Until the 1790s, the vast majority of translated fiction was from the French. Of the 172 translations published 1759–89 only twenty-five were from other languages. This preponderance of French authors is easily explained by the fact that for most of the period in question France remained the main producer and exporter of prose fiction in Europe. The number of French translations was also greatly facilitated, however, by the well-established history of Anglo-French commerce in books and widespread knowledge of the French language among the reading population at large in addition to a sizeable French-speaking expatriate community. Those who could read in French not only constituted an immediate market for the sale of French fiction, they also represented a large potential pool of translators. The fact that British novelists such as Smollett, Frances Brooke, Edward Kimber, Sophia Lee, and Charlotte Smith, were able and inclined to turn their hand to producing translations of French novels—even if financial motivations were often primary—also meant that they were able to bring a superior literary sophistication and prestige to their versions.

There was no dearth of interpreters of Italian and Spanish texts during this period. If, however, only a handful of translations was made from new Spanish and Italian novels this was because southern Europe, having played such a key role in the early history of the European novel, had entered a long period of stagnation. Neither Italy nor Spain would reestablish an international reputation for its imaginative prose fiction until well into the nineteenth century. Nonetheless, earlier Italian and Spanish classics continued to be widely read in new editions and new translations. Thomas Hookham's circulating library catalogue of 1785, for example, advertised 'novels' by

Boccaccio, Ariosto, and Tasso, as well as numerous titles by Miguel de Cervantes.[4] *Don Quixote* (original Spanish edition, 1605 and 1615; first English translation, 1620) was available from Hookham in three competing eighteenth-century versions, including the most recent translation by Smollett (*The History and Adventures of the Renowned Don Quixote*, 1755). The success of Smollett's version (which ran to thirteen editions within a few years), and that of other competing English translations that continued to sell well, secured the sixteenth-century Spanish author's place as one of the best-selling novelists in eighteenth-century Britain.

An ongoing interest in the East during this period was manifest in a scattering of English translations from genuine Middle Eastern and Indian sources, such as *The Loves of Camarupa and Camalata, an Ancient Indian tale*, translated by William Franklin in 1793 from the original Persian via a Hindustani text. The tales attributed to 'Inatulla of Delhi' were even translated twice: first by Alexander Dow (*Tales, translated from the Persian of Inatulla of Delhi*, 1768), and again in 1799 by Jonathan Scott, another East India Company man, who, under the new title, *Bahar-Danush; or, Garden of Knowledge. An Oriental Romance*, promised readers a more faithful rendition. Many of the so-called 'oriental' tales published during this period claiming to be translations were, however, of dubious authenticity. Most were homegrown productions seeking to perpetuate the vogue for oriental fictions unleashed by the first English publication of *The Arabian Nights Entertainments* back in 1706 (see also Ballaster, Chapter 19).

As regards those tales purporting to originate in northern Europe—a region producing very few novels until the nineteenth century—bogus translations again outnumbered genuine instances. Mary Ann(e) Radcliffe's claim that her *Radzivil*, published by William Lane in 1790, was 'translated from the Russ of the celebrated M. Wocklow' is not, for example, to be given much credence. Pseudo-translations of this sort are nonetheless indicative of the growing interest in such regions, giving rise to a trickle of genuine translations from the beginning of the nineteenth century: those from the Russian included Nikolai Karamzin's *Russian Tales*, translated by John Battersby Elrington in 1803; and from the Danish, Peter Frederik Suhm's *Signe and Habor* (first published in *The Lady's Magazine*, 1803).

Very occasional translations were made from other languages such as Dutch. The only source language, however, to rival French at any point between 1750 and 1820 was German. German novelists began to establish a literary reputation in Continental Europe from the middle of the eighteenth century, long before they were widely appreciated in Britain. Nonetheless, those following literary affairs in France would have been aware of the growing number of German novels translated into French and it is revealing in this regard that a number of the earliest English translations of German novels were made via a French intermediary version. The size of the expatriate German-speaking community

---

[4] Thomas Hookham, *A New Catalogue of Hookham's Circulating Library . . . Consisting of near forty thousand volumes in English, French, and Italian . . .* (London, 1785).

in London was not insignificant. However, it played very little role in the introduction of German fiction to Britain. The focus of its bookselling and translation activities lay elsewhere, chiefly in devotional and scientific literature. It was not until the 1790s that Peter Will, Minister of the Reform Congregation, was regularly announced as the translator of popular German novels. Likewise, it was not until the final decade of the eighteenth century that British writers like Wordsworth, Coleridge, and Matthew 'Monk' Lewis travelled to Germany to learn the language and better appreciate its literature, or that the Nonconformist literary critic, William Taylor 'of Norwich', published his influential series of articles on German authors. Prior to this point, notwithstanding the Hanoverian accession in 1714, there were very few non-native speakers of German in these islands and little curiosity regarding German imaginative literature. It is true that one or two translations of German novels enjoyed considerable individual success and these titles will be discussed later on. Real evidence of sustained public interest in German fiction did not, however, begin until 1789.

1790–9 saw the publication of thirty-nine new translations, with a marked surge notable from 1794; between 1800 and 1809 a further thirty-eight German novels were put into English. The extraordinary nature of this influx of seventy-seven titles from the German during this twenty-year period can be even better appreciated when compared to the figure of nine titles for the years 1770–89 and the even smaller number for the years 1750–69. However, it is important to recognize that the sudden flood of German translations did not alone account for the overall growth in the numbers of translated fictions during this turn-of-the-century period that has already been highlighted. While some critics initially welcomed the new type of German novel as a refreshing change from the familiar supply of French fiction, the flood of German translations should not be understood as the effect of a more profound cultural realignment between Britain and Germany. Notwithstanding British antipathies towards the French Revolution, France continued to be the main supplier of translated fiction—and by some considerable margin. Overall, against the seventy-seven German titles there were some 130 productions derived from French sources. In only four particular years between 1790 and 1809 did German translations outnumber those from the French.

The sudden fall in translation figures from around 1810 affected French and German novels in roughly equal measure (German and French titles during the 1810s fell by 76 and 70 per cent respectively). If anything, the supply of German fiction was more significantly disrupted: no German translations were published in 1810, 1814, 1815, and 1817, whereas only in 1814—a particularly bad year for translated fiction—was there not a single French translation either. Arguably, it also took longer for the tradition of translating from the German to recover from the effects of the Continental Blockade. All of this suggests that the first rise of the German novel in Britain was built on what proved to be but a passing fad. A German visitor to England had already observed with great regret in 1802 that the introduction of German literature to Britain had been excessively shaped by the huge success on the London stage of the sort of sensationalist drama associated with the name of August von Kotzebue. He argued that it was on account of the British enthusiasm for these sentimental Gothic plays that 'herds of wretched translators introduced a heap of ridiculous German novels to the attention of the public'.[5] He also noted that not only had such fiction established the reputation of German literature as immoral and dangerous but also that the public was already beginning to tire of these trifling products (which included several translations of Kotzebue's own novels). The German visitor was not wrong. As will be further discussed below, the 'German school' of Gothic fiction rapidly became the object of critical contempt and there was no renewal of serious interest in German fiction until the 1820s, when numbers of translations in German regularly matched those from French. By this point, however, translations of all foreign fiction were much more selective and represented barely 5 per cent of all new novels.

Specialist Foreign-Language Booksellers and Publishers

Foreign novels were not only read in English translation. Especially in the case of French, they also circulated in large numbers in the original language. One indication of the extent to which novels were read in languages other than English is found in the catalogues to private collections where, for example, it appears that French-language editions of Jean-Jacques Rousseau's *Julie, ou la Nouvelle Héloïse* (already circulating in 1760 although the date on the first edition is given as 1761) greatly outnumbered those of William Kenrick's much-praised English translation: *Eloisa: or, A Series of Original Letters*, 1761 (see Warner 1934: 233). Long lists of untranslated French (and to a much lesser extent, Spanish and Italian) stock contained in many of the circulating libraries offer another measure of the polyglot capabilities of the reading public for much of this period. The 1767 catalogue of John Noble's fashionable circulating library, for example, offered subscribers a choice of 1,013 items in French, over half of which were prose fiction.[6] Thomas Hookham's 1785 catalogue boasted some 3,297 'Livres françois', of which once again very many were novels; he moreover promised to obtain any work in either French or English that was not already listed. Foreign holdings were similarly emphasized in the catalogues of the circulating libraries of Thomas Lowndes and John Bell amongst yet others.[7]

The latest fashionable French fictions were generally available in London almost as soon as in Paris and increasingly in other parts of Britain. It is interesting to note, for

---

[5] C. A. G. Goede, *A Foreigner's Opinion of England* (London, 1808): quoted in Stockley (1929: 8).

[6] *Catalogue of the Large and Valuable Collection of Books (both English and French) in John Noble's Circulating Library...* (London, 1767).

[7] *A New Catalogue of Lownds's [sic] Circulating Library, Consisting of above ten thousand volumes (English, Italian and French) etc* (London, [1758]); *A New Catalogue of Bell's Circulating Library: consisting of above fifty thousand volumes (English, Italian, and French)...* (London, [1777]).

example, that in 1796, W. Berry, a bookseller and stationer in Edinburgh, announced the launch of a library consisting solely of French books, claiming his to be 'the first attempt in this country to establish a circulating library of foreign books'.[8] The vast majority of these foreign-language editions was imported. A small percentage was nonetheless printed domestically. However, the imprint 'Londres' is often misleading in relation to novels dating from this period. The English capital was often given as a fictitious place of publication in the case of clandestine works that were printed on the Continent and not primarily intended for a British market; alternatively, it appeared in the imprint of novels that were printed outside Britain but for sale by a London bookseller. With the exception of classic works from the past, French editions of novels were rarely printed in Britain until the arrival of a new wave of French émigrés after 1789.

It is not surprising that a number of London booksellers specializing in French fiction were themselves of French descent. Paul Vaillant, trading in the Strand until his retirement in 1768, was the third generation of a Huguenot family that had continuously maintained a bookselling business in London since fleeing Saumur after the Revocation of the Edict of Nantes in 1685. His catalogue boasted 'books in most languages' and included twelve pages of French novels that he had imported from France or the Low Countries.[9] Vaillant was not only a bookseller of French texts; he also published in the French language. Typically, however, the only novels he published in the original French were by authors from much earlier in the century such as Fénelon and the abbé Prévost. Instead, like other specialist booksellers, Vaillant chose to expand his market by publishing French fiction in translation. His publication of Jean-François Marmontel's *Bélissaire* (1767) in English as *Belisarius* showed just how successful such a venture could be, running to numerous editions within a few years. Of note is the fact that Arthur Murphy, the translator, had little share in the profits, even though he took Vaillant to court. Notwithstanding the fact that translators held the same legal rights as authors, the publisher successfully made the case that Murphy had renounced his entitlement to the copyright in choosing to withhold his name from the title page—something he had done lest he be regarded as a hack writer. The 1775 case of *Murphy v. Vaillant* provides a particularly stark picture of the double bind faced by translators during this period should they seek professional recognition for their labours (see McMurran 2010: 69–70).

The Strand had an early concentration of foreign booksellers and continued to be a centre for specialist modern-language bookshops in the later eighteenth century. Jean Nourse is one name that must be mentioned in this context. Trading until 1780, Nourse published over two hundred titles in French. Although the main focus of his publishing activity was

---

[8] *Cabinet littéraire, or a Catalogue of a Circulating Library, consisting of French books only*, at W. Berry, *bookseller and stationer* (Edinburgh, 1796).

[9] *Catalogus liborum apud Paulum Vaillant, bibliopolam, Londini venales prostantium: or, A catalogue of books in most languages and faculties, sold by Paul Vaillant, Bookseller in the Strand* (London, 1762).

scientific literature, not fiction, he played a key role in introducing the British public to the pedagogic fiction of Jeanne Marie le Prince de Beaumont. Between 1754 and 1767 he published five of her novels in French-language editions (all have London imprints but are presumed to have been printed on the Continent); he also brought out three English translations of her novels. It can be noted that in 1751 he also published the first English version of Claude-Prosper-Jolyot de Crébillon's libertine novel, *Les Égaremens du cœur et de l'esprit* (1736–8), translated by Michael Clancy as *The Wanderings of the Heart and Mind*.

Thomas Becket and Peter Abraham de Hondt operated another bookselling business on the Strand and were important agents of continental fiction. Relatively few of their own publications were in French. They nonetheless acquired the reputation in the 1760s and 1770s as one of the leading importers of fashionable French fiction; furthermore, they published in translation some of the most influential novels of the period, not least Rousseau's *Eloisa* (in conjunction with R. Griffiths) and Marmontel's *Moral Tales* (1764; *Contes moraux*, 1761), which sold very well despite a partial translation by Miss R. Roberts having been published only the previous year (*Select Moral Tales. Translated from the French, by a Lady*, 1763). Another well-received French translation brought out by Becket and de Hondt was Marie Anne Louise Elie de Beaumont's *History of the Marquis de Roselle* (1765; *Lettres du marquis de Roselle*, 1761). It was Becket and de Hondt's prominence as purveyors of French novels that led David Garrick to persuade his good friend, Marie-Jeanne Riccoboni to leave to them the translation and marketing of most of her novels in Britain. This was perhaps a mistake. Between 1764 and 1778, Becket and de Hondt published six translations of Riccoboni's novels; none, however, enjoyed the same success as the one that had been translated so well by Frances Brooke and published in 1759 by R. and J. Dodsley: *Letters from Juliet Lady Catesby, to her friend, Lady Henrietta Campley* (*Lettres de Milady Juliette Catesby à Milady Henriette Campley, son amie*, 1759). Unsurprisingly, having established a successful position as a publisher and dealer in translations of French novels, Becket was also one of the first to test the market with German translations (e.g. Marie-Sophie von La Roche's *Memoirs of Miss Sophy Sternheim*, 1776—also discussed below).

In the 1780s, principal publishers of translated fiction included Thomas Hookham and George Robinson. The latter was responsible for the appearance of English versions of best-selling titles by Madame de Genlis (*Veillées du château*, 1782; *Tales of the Castle: or, Stories of Instruction and Delight*, 1785) and Isabelle de Montolieu (*Caroline de Lichtfield*, 1786; *Caroline of Lichtfield*, 1786). Both had been taken from the French by Thomas Holcroft, who had gone to Paris as the correspondent of the *Morning Herald*. Robinson's much-respected firm also published over fifty works in the French language. In the 1790s these included some fiction by Genlis and, more intriguingly, an edition of Pierre Choderlos de Laclos's *Les Liaisons dangereuses* (see also below). In all cases, the London imprints for Robinson's French novels appear to be genuine. By this time, the market leaders in translated fiction—French and German—were J. Bew, Vernor and Hood, and above all William Lane and his Minerva Press that supplied cheap fiction to many of the circulating libraries (see Grieder 1975: 39).

Of note, however, is the fact that the Minerva Press published almost exclusively in English. On the other hand, when A. Dulau and partners set up their business in Soho in around 1795, they specialized almost exclusively in foreign-language publications. Their titles suggest that they were aiming at a different public altogether: that of the native-speaking French population in London, recently augmented by a new wave of Revolutionary exiles (see Shaw 2003: 138–9). Dulau & Cie did not attempt to encroach on the existing trade in translations; instead—almost certainly in a bid to expand their customer base—they published language-learning tools: dictionaries, grammars, and annotated editions of novels. Their 1799 edition of *Bélisaire*, for example, was sold as a 'Nouvelle édition, avec la signification des mots les plus difficiles en anglois au bas de chaque page'. Their publication of Genlis's *Les petits émigrés* that same year was similarly presented as a 'Nouvelle édition, avec ses notes grammaticales'. These publications were often undertaken with other 'libraires français' such as Thomas Boosey and J. Deboffe, and were printed for them on London presses associated with names such as T. Baylis of Greville Street and Bye and Law of Clerkenwell.

The specialist business of Dulau survived well into the twentieth century. By contrast, almost all the ventures of German specialist booksellers in London were short-lived. Furthermore, as noted above, the German booksellers played virtually no role in the introduction of German fiction to Britain in either original language editions or translations. The catalogue, for example, of Carl Heydinger, one of the most prominent and best-connected German booksellers from the late 1760s to his death in 1778, was virtually devoid of novels.[10] Novels were also peripheral to the ventures of James Remnant, Henry Escher, and Constantin Geisweiler, each of whom opened up German bookshops in the 1790s in response to the growing signs of interest in German letters. Prose fiction was likewise, by design, sparsely represented in the first German circulating library—the *Deutsche Lese-Bibliothek*—which opened in Charing Cross at around this same time (see Jefcoate 2002 and 1987). Novels were again explicitly avoided in the *German Museum*, a specialist periodical founded by Geisweiler in 1800 with the aim of introducing British readers to the very best of German writing. It may be noted that Geisweiler was part of a consortium of booksellers (that included Dulau) which published two German grammars adapted for English speakers in 1799 and 1800. He also attempted in the manner of Dulau to exploit German prose fiction for the purposes of language learning and (again with a consortium) published an annotated selection of tales, fables, and poetry in the German language made by George Crabb (1778–1851) that included a small dictionary and other aids for translation.[11] In general, however, it appears that those who wanted

---

[10] Charles Heydinger, *Catalogus librorum latinorum, graecorum, hebraicorum, &c ex omni scientiarum genere...* (Londini [London], 1773).

[11] George Crabb, *An Easy and Entertaining Selection of German Prose and Poetry. With a small dictionary and other aids for translating* (London: for the Author, 1800).

to learn the German language were not readers of novels. Hence German fiction was introduced to Britain in translation by other London booksellers for whom the novel was a more central part of their business.

Richardson à la française

Many French novels that found favour in Britain after 1750 were modelled on the sentimental fiction of Samuel Richardson. Nonetheless, although ostensibly cast in the mould of *Clarissa* (1748–9), they continued to be informed by earlier currents of French writing. Elie de Beaumont, for example, conspicuously aligned her well-received *History of the Marquis de Roselle* (which, as we have seen, was published by Becket and de Hondt, 1765) with the English master, adopting his epistolary style and tone of didactic sentimentality, even incorporating a eulogy of *Clarissa* within the correspondence. Responding in kind, *The Gentleman's Magazine* found the translation indeed worthy of such a comparison.[12] Beneath the surface, however, the female protagonist—an actress who cultivates a duplicitous mask of chastity to win a rich husband—has more in common with Prévost's manipulative Manon Lescaut (see also below) than Clarissa Harlowe. Moreover, Elie de Beaumont's subtle understanding of the theatrical nature of female virtue owed a considerable debt to the tradition of psychological analysis honed by Pierre de Marivaux and the more libertine fiction of Crébillon.

The ongoing yet covert influence exerted by the *roman libertin* through the practice of translation is worthy of note. The moral value of the English domestic novel had of course been elevated very much in contradistinction to the perceived immorality of earlier French translations and their English imitations, such as the amatory bodice-rippers of Eliza Haywood written in the 1720s. Consequently, translations of French libertine fiction after 1750 were typically excoriated in the British periodical press and rarely, if ever, ranked amongst the most popular titles. The case of Crébillon is instructive in this regard. The English version of his erotic political satire, *Le Sopha* (1742; *The Sopha*, 1742), had simply confirmed British prejudices regarding the French novel and its English imitators such as Haywood, who had translated the work with William Hatchett. Crébillon's earlier masterpiece, *Les Égaremens du cœur et de l'esprit* (1736–8), however, was not seen in English dress until 1751 when (as already noted) it was translated by Michael Clancy as *The Wanderings of the Heart and Mind*.

The success in Britain of Clancy's translation paved the way for translations of further works of the now 'celebrated Crébillon'. Under the title of *The Happy Orphans: An Authentic History of Persons in High Life* (1759), Edward Kimber offered an 'improved'

---

[12] *Gentleman's Magazine*, 35 (March 1765), 125.

version of Crébillon's *Les Heureux orphelins* (1754), itself a cynical adaptation, even parody, of Haywood's *Fortunate Foundlings* (1744) in which she attempted to realign her writing with the new moral novel of Richardson. The libertine tendencies of Crébillon's *The Night and the Moment* (1770; *La Nuit et le moment*, 1755) were, however, simply too conspicuous and the tale was condemned as dangerously foreign, displaying French manners that it was hoped would 'never be imitated... by those of the same class in this country'.[13] Similarly, when a translation of Laclos's *Les Liaisons Dangereuses* (1782) was printed under the title *Dangerous Connections* for Hookham's circulating library in 1784, critics wasted no time in declaring the novel 'delusive and dangerous' and 'a daring outrage on every law of virtue and decorum'.[14]

Far closer to the spirit of Haywood's exploration of the moral authority of female sensibility was the writing of Marie-Jeanne Riccoboni, who gained a reputation in Britain as one of France's best novelists. Once again, into the familiar 'English' framework of the sentimental epistolary novel, Riccoboni wove multiple 'French' threads drawn not least from her attentive reading (and continuation) of Marivaux's novels. Her fiction is shaped by a vision that female happiness and fulfilment can only be secured through the elusive prospect of a marriage founded on mutual love. Thus, for all their intelligence and assertiveness, her sensitive heroines invariably suffer as a result of inevitable male inconstancy and must find solace in their own strength of character and in the support of female friends. The forbearance of Juliet Catesby—the heroine of the novel translated to great acclaim by Mrs Brooke in 1759—is ultimately rewarded when she is finally able to marry the man she loves. Riccoboni does not, however, always provide such happy endings. Having learnt of her husband's infidelities, the heroine of *The History of the Marquis de Cressy* (1759; *L'Histoire de M. le Marquis de Cressy*, 1758) finds no better solution than to drink poison: her errant husband is left to rue his actions; she is left dead.

Fictional suicide typically aroused anxiety if not downright condemnation. The natural death of Rousseau's Eloisa (the name used throughout Kenrick's 1761 translation of *Julie, ou la Nouvelle Héloïse*) proved no less morally problematic. Rousseau's novel was a phenomenal success in Britain as elsewhere in Europe and the first volumes of Kenrick's translation were already sold out by the time the remaining volumes were available a couple of months later (see Warner 1937: 803–4). Deliberately free and far more restrained than the original, Kenrick's version nonetheless had the quality of idiomatic English and remained without competition: by 1800 it was in its tenth edition and a vast and diverse readership had entered into the emotional life of the Swiss author and his fictional characters in an unprecedented way. In the later words of Helen Maria Williams, hundreds of sentimental pilgrims were even inspired to travel to the Alps and 'with Heloise in hand, run over the rocks and mountains to catch the lovers' inspiration'.[15]

[13] *Critical Review*, 29 (May 1770), 396.
[14] *Critical Review*, 56 (June 1784), 473–4; *Monthly Review*, 71 (August 1784), 149.
[15] Helen Maria Williams, *A Tour of Switzerland*, 2 vols (Dublin: P. Eyme, 1798), 2.118.

Such antics could not fail in due course but to arouse censure on the part of paternalistic critics. Initially, however, the tale of Eloisa's illicit romance with her tutor was applauded. As long as the first part of Rousseau's novel was read as firmly embedded within the subsequent story of Eloisa's moral redemption, set in the idyllic rural community of Clarens, the novel could even be read as offering superior moral instruction to *Clarissa* for 'it hath taught us the means of retrieving the esteem of mankind, after a capital slip in conduct'.[16] Popular reception, however, suggested that many readers chose to identify not with Rousseau's heroine as virtuous wife and mother but as Saint-Preux's passionate lover. Eloisa's final tear-jerking letter, written on her death bed, in which she confesses to have never fully extinguished her former feelings for Saint-Preux, poignantly drew attention to the destructive tensions between female sexual desire and social duty. It was far from evident that the novel convincingly demonstrated the successful triumph of the latter over the former or its moral necessity.

As time passed, concerns regarding the suspect nature of the *philosophe*'s moral teaching were increasingly voiced, especially in the wake of the French Revolution when Edmund Burke famously condemned the novel as 'an unfashioned, indelicate, sour, gloomy, ferocious medley of pedantry and lewdness; of metaphysical speculations, blended with the coarsest sensuality'.[17] Others, however, began to explore the tension between female duty and desire in Rousseau's novel in more radical ways, offering various reworkings, as in Helen Maria Williams's *Julia* (1790) or Charlotte Smith's *Desmond* (1792). The direction of some of these later responses had already been anticipated in the novels of the prolific Pierre Henri Treyssac de Vergy. Adventurer, spy, scandalmonger, pamphleteer, and novelist, the self-styled 'Councellor of the Parliament of Paris', De Vergy was one of most productive novelists of the period, publishing at least five titles in the brief period 1769–72, possibly more (see Sutherland 1943: 306–7). He was also one who knew how to cater successfully to popular taste. He wrote in English for the British market; his identity as a foreigner, however, was never forgotten by the critical press and when the libertine tendencies of his fiction became too pronounced, it was expressly underlined. His first novel, *The Mistakes of the Heart* (1769), was received with reasonable warmth and it was approvingly noted of 'this sprightly Frenchman' that he was 'a professed imitator of our Richardson, and of Richardson's imitator, the celebrated citizen of Geneva'.[18] In certain subsequent novels, however, riding roughshod over conventional morality, he more emphatically endorsed the pursuit of strong passions and was duly castigated for taking his interpretation of Rousseau's philosophy of nature too far. So blatant were the 'licentious principles' underpinning *The Lovers* (1769–72)—possibly his most popular work

---

[16] *Critical Review*, 12 (September 1761), 205.

[17] Edmund Burke, *A Letter to a Member of the National Assembly [1791]* (Oxford and New York: Woodstock Books, 1990), 40.

[18] *Monthly Review*, 40 (June 1769), 511.

with the general public and in which he exploited the recent story of the elopement of Lady Sarah Bunbury—that he was emphatically cast aside as a 'foreign Scandal-monger' and 'shameless Scribbler'. Even his worst critics, however, were forced to acknowledge occasionally that he was not devoid of literary talent and that he was 'no mean proficient in the study of the female mind'.[19]

A more pragmatic response to the question of female happiness was found in the work of Jeanne Marie le Prince de Beaumont, who had risen to international fame through her 'Magazines', which she had written for young women while working as a governess in London (1748–63). Her characterization was judged unrealistic and the highly derivative nature of her plots also drew critical comment, as did her obvious Catholicism. One critic observed: 'There is not an incident that ever fell from the pen of Scudery, Behn, Richardson, Fielding, and all the numerous tribes of romancers and novelists, which does not present itself.'[20] Much less conventional, however, is her determination not to allow her heroines to become the victims of male passion (see Stewart 1993: ch. 2). Thus when she reworks Richardson's novel in *The New Clarissa* (1768), she not only excises those details troubling to her Catholic morality, she also guides her young protagonist along the path of happiness. Her Clarissa does not have to die for her virtue; she instead marries the man who helps her escape an unreasonable father and goes on to enjoy a fulfilled and meaningful life on her husband's country estate, growing vegetables and undertaking charitable works. Far more successful than Rousseau's Eloisa (another obvious model), Le Prince de Beaumont's heroine achieves happiness independently of passionate love. Indeed, in other novels by her, such as *The Virtuous Widow; or, Memoirs of the Baroness de Batteville* (1766; *Mémoires de Madame la baronne de Batteville, ou la veuve parfaite*, 1766), when the heroine is finally able to marry the man she had once passionately loved, she declines.

Moving beyond romantic dreams and erotic desire was likewise integral to the pedagogic project represented by the hugely popular fictional works of Madame de Genlis. Holcroft's translation of *Tales of the Castle* (1785) was in its eighth edition by 1806 and received almost unanimously positive reviews. Judgements were more reserved in the case of *Adelaide and Theodore* (1783; *Adèle et Théodore*, 1782), translated, according to a prefatory notice in the second edition of 1784, 'by some Ladies, who through misfortunes, too common at this time, are reduced from ease and opulence, to the necessity of applying, to the support of life, those accomplishments which were given to them in their youth, for the amusement and embellishment of it'. The closely choreographed education given here by Mme d'Almane to her daughter was considered impracticable. Concern was also voiced by the 'use of *falsehood*, as well as fiction, as the instrument of instruction'.[21] However, a crucial part of the legacy given to Adelaide by her mother is precisely the

---

[19] *Monthly Review*, 41 (December 1769), 480; 45 (July 1771), 73.
[20] *Critical Review*, 21 (June 1766), 432.
[21] *Monthly Review*, 70 (May 1784), 338, 345.

ability to penetrate such fictions and so move beyond the romantic dreams of youth and, like Le Prince de Beaumont's Clarissa, find personal fulfilment outside the structures of romance. At the end of the novel, Adelaide is a strong individual and productive citizen, running a school where poor girls are taught a useful trade.

It was through the shorter form of the moral tale that a number of French novelists exercised their greatest impact in Britain. Genlis's *Tales of the Castle* was little more than a collection of short moral tales knitted together within a frame narrative and many were reprinted separately in anthologies or in magazines. Le Prince de Beaumont also produced a collection of *Moral Tales* (1775; *Contes moraux*, 1774). Several were reprinted in the *Lady's Magazine*. Voltaire was of course the master of the short satirical tale and his international reputation guaranteed that his *contes* were all quickly translated; with the notable exception of *Candid[e]: or, All for the Best* (1759), very few of these translations were republished separately. The self-proclaimed inventor of the sentimental moral tale was Voltaire's *protégé*, Marmontel. Various translations of the latter's *Contes moraux* (1761; augmented 1765) had established his reputation in Britain even before Murphy's translation of *Belisarius* had been published by Vaillant. Moreover Marmontel's moral tales remained in fashion from the early 1760s well into the nineteenth century and they enjoyed more success in British magazines than the works of any other foreign writer (see Mayo 1962: 373). Like many of the other most popular foreign novelists in Britain, Marmontel's tales were self-consciously influenced by the sentimental didactic fiction of Richardson (whose novels he had reviewed for the *Mercure*). His tales provide the reader, however, with far more practical counsel. In 'The Happy Divorce' ('L'Heureux Divorce'; first English translation by Miss Roberts in *Select Moral Tales*, 1763) a dissatisfied wife is reconciled with her husband having learnt from experience that she had been running after illusions and that happiness is to be found in the silence of the passions. A similar moral emerges from the very popular 'Shepherdess of the Alps' (first English translation in the same collection). When she falls in love a second time, the shepherdess of the title must recognize that first love is not in fact sacred and that her youthful passion for an officer did not justify his dereliction of duty leading to his subsequent disgrace and suicide. Exploiting the codes of sentimental fiction, Marmontel—like Le Prince de Beaumont and Genlis—offered instruction as to how to find happiness within the realms of the possible.

German Sentiment and Satire

The influence of Richardson was no less conspicuous in the German novels translated into English in the earlier decades of the period in question. It was no coincidence that the first of these was by Christian Fürchtegott Gellert, who was also responsible for translating Richardson into German. In common with most German fiction at this time, *Das Leben der schwedischen Gräfin von G**** (1747–8) was also greatly shaped by French

fiction. Beasley (1972) records an early English translation, *The Life of the Countess of G
——. Translated from the German by a Lady*, printed in 1747 for B. Law (presumably not
including the second part of the novel yet to be published). In March 1752, *The Monthly
Review* announced a translation of the same work published by Dodsley under the title
The History of the Swedish Countess of G ——. Notwithstanding a translation seeming 'to
come from some foreigner, whose ignorance of the *English* idiom ought to have prevented
his undertaking a task he was but ill qualified for', the reviewer cautiously welcomed the
work as the first of its kind to come from Germany with sufficient vivacity to recommend
itself to 'less flegmatic nations'. Even so, he warned that it would be viewed as 'a tedious,
heavy, low performance' to those who do not make due allowance for 'the peculiar manners and notions' of the German people.[22] The novel is narrated in part by the Countess
and in part through interspersed letters, and champions Enlightenment sensibility and
the education of women. Negotiating bigamy, incest, murder, and suicide, it also engages
with a series of heterogeneous moral issues from religious tolerance to the adoption of
children (which Gellert appeared to promote over familial ties). It attracted sufficient
interest in Britain for further editions to be published in 1757 and 1776.

The combined influence of Richardson and Rousseau (and the wider English and French
traditions in which both were located) also shaped the first novel written by a female
novelist to be translated from German into English: Sophie von La Roche's *Geschichte des
Fräuleins von Sternheim* (1771). Two competing translations were published in 1776. The
first (*The History of Lady Sophia Sternheim*) was the undertaking of the bookseller, publisher, and translator, Joseph Collyer, who with his wife Mary, played an important role in
the early introduction of German authors to Britain, including Salomon Gessner (whose
pastoral writing exerted a lasting influence into the nineteenth century) and the poet,
Friedrich Klopstock. The reviewer, William Enfield, however, considered the second
translation by Edward Harwood (*Memoirs of Miss Sophy Sternheim*), printed for Thomas
Becket, 'a more pleasing form'.[23] Both translations promoted the work on the title page
under the name of La Roche's much better-known cousin and one-time fiancé, Christoph
Martin Wieland, whose involvement had been that of editor. Collyer also stressed the
novel's affinities with *Clarissa*. Richardson's novel was undoubtedly a model for La
Roche, but as in Le Prince de Beaumont's *New Clarissa* (which the German novelist had
very probably read) she introduces significant differences, above all in the importance
attached to women's education and to their mutual support. La Roche's Sophy refuses
to let her life be ruined by the English aristocrat who deceives her and breaks her heart.
Assisted by a network of older women, she instead learns to master her emotions and is
able to assume a valuable role within society. It is undeniable that the novel promotes a
framework of exemplary womanhood in which female virtue prevails. Nonetheless, the

[22] *Monthly Review*, 6 (March 1752), 232.
[23] *Monthly Review*, 55 (October 1776), 319.

sentimental narrative also engages profoundly with the complexity of female desires and offers a refreshing instance of active self-determination.

La Roche's feisty heroine was very different from the self-effacing Lotte of *Die Leiden des jungen Werthers* (1774), which took Europe by storm a few years later. The first English translation of Johann Wolfgang von Goethe's tragic love story—as *The Sorrows of Werter: A German Story* (1779), published by Dodsley—was made (either by Daniel Malthus, the father of the economist, or Richard Graves) not from the original but from a French version (generally thought to be Aubrey's version of 1777 but possibly that of Deyverdun 1776). At least eight further translations were published before 1815, many leading to multiple editions. The story was a runaway best-seller, triggering a wave of imitations in prose, on the stage, in verse, even in the form of porcelain figurines and waxworks. Influenced not only by the epistolary fictions of Richardson and Rousseau but also by other English works from *Hamlet* to *The Vicar of Wakefield* and *Ossian*, Goethe's novel offered a tempestuous physical and emotional landscape that was readily accessible to English taste. Its phenomenal success had little to do with its literary merit or more subtle psychological insights and sociopolitical contours; it was read straightforwardly as an intensely sentimental tale of tragic love. There is little evidence for the popular legend that the novel provoked a spate of copycat suicides, but critical opinion was quick to suspect that it might have a corrupting influence and, in the words of one reviewer, lead readers 'into the same destructive abyss'.[24]

Goethe's novel was without doubt the best-known and most widely read German novel of the eighteenth century. But it was an isolated success. Moreover, it did not immediately open up the British market to German fiction: there were no further translations from the German until 1786 and another gap until 1789. The only German novelist who enjoyed any sustained reputation in Britain prior to the period of the French Revolution was Wieland. The latter had the distinction of being the only novelist to be promoted by Carl Heydinger who was involved in the publication of two of his titles in 1773, both probably translated by John Richardson 'of York': *History of Agathon* (*Geschichte des Agathon*, 1766–7) and *Reason Triumphant over Fancy: Exemplified in the Singular Adventures of Don Sylvio de Rosalva* (*Der Sieg der Nature über die Schwärmerei oder die Abenteur des Don Sylvio von Rosalva*, 1764). Wieland's prose fiction no doubt commended itself to the German bookseller on account of its more philosophical nature and marked divergence from the fashionable sentimental fiction that was generally eschewed by the resident German community. On account of his humour, Wieland had more in common with Sterne, as was noted by more than one critic.[25] Indeed, in *Reason Triumphant over Fancy* the extravagant world of the sentimental romance was the object of critical satire and much informed by the *anti-roman* of the Jesuit, Guillaume-Hyacinthe Bougeant, *Voyage merveilleux du prince Fan-Férédin dans*

---

[24] *Critical Review*, 61 (May 1786), 359.
[25] See, for example, *Monthly Review*, 50 (March 1774), 177.

la Romancie (and may explain—at least indirectly—why this work dating back to 1735 should be translated for the first time in 1789: *The Wonderful Travels of Prince Fan-Férédin, in the Country of Arcadia*).

Wieland's ironic response to romantic fancy and quixotic readers can of course be situated within a much broader critical tradition that accompanied the rise of romance across Europe, beginning in sixteenth-century Spain (if not before). But it was also characteristic of a more specifically German reaction to the vogue for sentimental fiction and its identificatory modes of reading that included the writing of Johann Musäus. His collection of German fairy tales (*Volksmärchen der Deutschen* (1787–8)—which may in fact have been edited by Wieland—enjoyed a warm reception when they were translated into English by Coleridge's friend Thomas Beddoes in 1791 under the title *Popular Tales of the Germans*. The satirical laughter previously directed by Musäus at Richardson in his parodies of *Grandison* (never translated) was now turned to the 'Gothic' imaginary landscape of German folklore. The connection was not lost on one reviewer who declared the *Popular Tales* to be a welcome diversion from the tedium of the fictions supplied to the circulating libraries on which he was perennially called to opine, in offering 'a very singular display of the most risible absurdities of the Gothic Romance'.[26]

French and German Gothic Novels

Others also welcomed the growing number of translations of German Gothic novels that appeared to be consciously conceived in ironic opposition to 'tiresome love intrigues'—as was indeed declared the case by 'Lawrence Flammenberg' alias Carl Friedrich Kahlert in the preface to *The Necromancer: or The Tale of the Black Forest* (1794; *Der Geisterbanner*, 1792). In the words of one reviewer, such novels constituted 'a kind of antidote to the *deluge* of sentiments and gallantry, which, from time to time, have been translated from the French, and imitated in English'.[27]

The earliest vogue for Gothic fiction had indeed emerged from deep within the French sentimental tradition. Sophia Lee's *The Recess* (1783–5) drew its plot from the Abbé Prévost's *Philosophe anglais, ou Histoire de Monsieur Cleveland, fils naturel de Cromwell* (1731–9), recasting the protagonists as twin sisters in the time of Elizabeth I. Charlotte Smith turned to Prévost's *Histoire du chevalier des Grieux et de Manon Lescaut* (1731) which she reworked under the new title, *Manon L'Escaut; or, The Fatal Attachment* (1786), giving far more prominence to female psychology and introducing Gothic touches inspired by Burkean theories of the sublime (see Hale 2002: 64–5). Prévost's influence on English Gothic fiction was also extended indirectly through the popular reception given in

---

[26] *European Magazine*, 19 (May 1791), 351.
[27] *Analytical Review*, 7 (August 1790), 462.

Britain to his closest disciple, François Baculard d'Arnaud. John Murdoch first translated a selection of d'Arnaud's melancholic tales under the title *The Tears of Sensibility* (1773; from *Les Epreuves du sentiment*, 1772–3). Reprintings and new translations of individual tales also appeared very regularly in the British magazines. Even if editors cut some of the most macabre and violent episodes, readers of the *Universal Magazine* were nonetheless confronted with the prospect of two young lovers waking up in a cavern of corpses ('The Desert Island, or The Happy Recovery', April 1778; 'Makin' in *Suite des épreuves du sentiment*, 1776).

Baculard d'Arnaud's emotionally overwrought prose certainly opened up melodramatic sentimental fiction to ridicule. One reviewer, for example, observed sardonically in relation to *The History of Count Gleichen* (1786; 'Le Comte de Gleichen' in the third volume of *Nouvelles historiques*, 1777) that it fulfilled all the requirements of a modern sentimental novel, 'plentifully adorned with ahs! and ohs! with little real pathos, and less interest'.[28] Nonetheless, two important English Gothic writers found inspiration in his work. Sophia Lee's *Warbeck: A Pathetic Tale* (1786) was a translation of 'Varbeck' in volume one of the *Nouvelles historiques* (1774). Clara Reeve's *The Exiles; or, Memoirs of the Count de Cronstadt* (1788) was based on 'D'Almanzi' (from *Suite des épreuves du sentiment*, 1776). Furthermore, other novelists showed how 'Gothic' terror could be exploited within serious pedagogic projects. Genlis's *Adelaide and Theodore* (discussed above) includes, for example, an intercalated tale—the 'History of the Duchesse of C ——' (serialized separately in the *Lady's Magazine*, 1786)—in which the protagonist is locked up for nine years by her jealous husband in an underground vault. The fear induced by the prospect of subterranean incarceration is, however, used to drive home her moral instruction. Likewise, in her best-selling *Caroline of Lichtfield* (1786), Isabelle de Montolieu exploits Gothic motifs in the context of a sensitive exploration of a young woman's sexual anxieties. According to her father's wishes, Caroline is married to a man twice her age whom she finds physically repulsive. Before the marriage can be consummated, however, she must conquer the fears that his physical deformities arouse. This is achieved through a narrative in which she is gradually disabused of romantic illusions as peddled by sentimental fiction and learns to distinguish between fantasy and reality and recognize her husband's true merit.

The literary objective of both Genlis and Montolieu was to empower their female readers and the use of the Gothic in their texts was directed towards such ends. Later, in Genlis's *The Rival Mothers* (1800; *Les Mères rivales*, 1800), Genlis's use of Gothic terror did in fact become more closely associated with diminishing female agency, her earlier optimism having perhaps been shaken by her exile from Revolutionary France. Even so, the most notorious examples of the German school of terror (invariably written by men) were structured by dramatically different gender politics. Paradoxically, however, it was

---

[28] *Critical Review*, 62 (September 1786), 235–6.

the fiction of the prolific female German novelist, Christiane Benedikte Naubert that helped pave the way for their introduction to Britain.

The first of Naubert's novels to reach England was the sentimental *Heerfort and Clara*, translated by John Poulin in 1789 (*Heerfort und Klärchen*, 1779). English editions of two further novels followed in 1794: *Alf von Deulmen*, translated by Miss A. E. Booth (*Alf von Dülmen*, 1791) and *Herman of Unna* (*Hermann von Unna*, 1788). With regard to the latter, the *Critical Review* had no difficulty in identifying the particular dimension that would fascinate the British public, observing: 'The peculiar interest of this work, no doubt rests on the account, so novel and so striking, of the secret tribunal.'[29] Translations quickly followed of other German novels exploiting the plots and counterplots of Illuminati, Masonic societies, and other secret associations dedicated to international conspiracy and ritual sacrifice. The Lutheran minister, Peter Will, was responsible for putting into English in swift succession both Cajetan Tschink's *The Victim of Magical Delusion* (1795; *Geschichte eines Geistersehers*, 1790–3) and Karl Grosse's *Horrid Mysteries* (1796; *Der Genius*, 1790–4). The latter (also translated in the same year by Joseph Trapp under the title of *The Genius*) was published by William Lane and through its lurid portrayal of sex, violence, and barbarism contributed significantly to the association of his Minerva Press with sensationalist trash. Tschink's 'magico-political' tale on the other hand, which the *Critical* reviewer interpreted as a 'bold attack upon popular superstition',[30] was brought out by the far more respectable firm of G. G. and J. Robinson, indicating the broad appeal of the German Gothic novel during the mid-1790s.

The origin of most of these Gothic tales was widely recognized as Friedrich Schiller's *Der Geisterseher* (1787–9) which exploited under a thin veil of fiction the notorious adventures of the Italian Count Cagliostro, widely believed to be a member of the Illuminati—a secret transnational sect alleged to be plotting to bring down the monarchies of Europe and establish a new world order. Schiller's novel was profoundly inflected by his Enlightenment ideals and, in stark distinction to the often gratuitous sensationalism of its many imitations, offered serious reflection on the perennial philosophical themes of love and duty, and an insightful critique of the psychodynamics of power. However, by the time Schiller's novel was translated into English in 1795 as *The Ghost-Seer; or Apparitionist* the rumours regarding Cagliostro and the Illuminati had acquired dramatically new resonance on British soil in the context of William Pitt's Treason Trials of 1794. German Gothic fiction, although conceived in a different context, tapped into deep public fears in Britain—fears that were further encouraged by those in power who painted in vivid colours the prospect of revolutionary uprisings at home similar to those which had just convulsed France, justifying their heavy-handed crackdown on those perceived as political radicals.

---

[29] *Critical Review*, n.s., 14 (May 1795), 79.
[30] *Critical Review*, n.s., 15 (September 1795), 63–4.

Conservative opinion regarded with alarm the growing number of translations of German tales about Illuminati, for whom Jacobins or dissenting radicals could easily be substituted. In 1799, for example, Hannah More called upon 'those ladies who take the lead in society...to oppose with the whole weight of their influence, the irruption of those swarms of publications now daily issuing from the banks of the Danube'.[31] But it is possible that the vogue for such tales was also exploited by anti-Jacobin propaganda. In this regard it has been suggested that the Peter Teuthold who announced himself as the translator of Kahlert's *Necromancer*—one of the seven 'horrid novels' ridiculed by Jane Austen in *Northanger Abbey* (1818)—may have in fact been a conservative Englishman and that his sensationalizing version may have been deliberately designed to discredit German literature and political radicalism (see Conger 1980: 218).

The outrage provoked by Grosse's lurid *Horrid Mysteries*—another of the 'Northanger Seven'—had less to do with political considerations than an aversion to its violence and sexual immorality. This was the transgressive dimension of German Gothic fiction that was emphasized yet more subversively by Matthew Lewis. As previously noted, the latter was one of the earliest modern British novelists to be proficient in the German language and through his translations and adaptations he played an key role in defining the popular image of German fiction in Britain. He was also instrumental in wresting the Gothic novel from the feminized space of sentimental romance and giving it far more aggressively masculine contours. Lewis's brutal treatment of not only the bodies but also the aspirations of women was already patent in *The Monk* (1796), written before he was twenty and inspired by multiple German sources including Kahlert's misogynist *Necromancer*. A year after translating Johann Zschokke's *Bravo of Venice* (1805; *Abällino, der grosse Bandit*, 1794), Lewis turned to Benedikte Naubert's convoluted historical novel, *Elisabeth, Erbin von Toggenburg* (1789). Already from the new choice of title, *Feudal Tyrants, or, The Counts of Carlsheim* (1806), it was clear how Lewis was intent on quite literally transforming an earlier tradition of feminocentric Gothic fiction to give it a radically different character (see Brown 2005: 105–11). The subtitle of Naubert's novel (*Geschichte der Frauen von Sargans in der Schweiz*) clearly announced the focus of her narrative as being in the lives and stories of the women of Sargans. The original narrative is sensitive to the perennial abuse of women at the hands of men and to the mutual support women provide each other. Naubert's invocation of the supernatural is subtle and used to project female fears of male predation. Lewis, on the other hand, redirects the reader's attention from the very start to the male tyrants and allows their perspective to dominate his translation which becomes a gratuitously titillating melodrama.

---

[31] Hannah More, *Strictures on the Modern System of Female Education*, 5th edn, 2 vols (London: Cadell and Davies, 1799), 1.39.

The critical reaction to Lewis's translation indicates that by 1806 this was precisely what readers had come to expect of a German novel. The novelty had long since worn off. Too many translations and, above all, too many homespun and often inferior imitations had succeeded in turning 'German' fiction into a new topic for derision. Viewed thus, it is far from surprising that the unprecedented levels of translation activity from the German witnessed in the 1790s and 1800s did not survive the Continental Blockade: the fashion for German novels was already almost up. The *Critical Review* expressed incomprehension as to why Lewis might want to continue 'ransacking the repositories of German literature' to produce a work that was 'neither larger nor finer than has issued from the pen of many a teeming maiden in the sanctuaries of the Minerva Press'.[32]

Exile, Empire, and Nationhood

If the fashion for Gothic fiction was one response to the convulsions of the French Revolution, seeking refuge in the pastoral was another. One of the best-selling titles of the 1790s was Jacques-Henri Bernadin de Saint-Pierre's *Chaumière Indienne*, written two years after the fall of the Bastille and translated into English within the year by the children's author, Edward Augustus Kendall (*The Indian Cottage*, 1791). Informed by a sense of global complexity, the tale begins in London where the Society of Dilettanti engage twenty men of letters to go out across the world to gather information. The most important answers, however, are discovered in the secluded home of an Indian pariah who lives alone with his wife (who had refused to immolate herself according to custom on the funeral pyre of her first husband) and their infant child. The example of their hospitality, self-sufficiency, and freedom from social prejudice encourages the most learned of the English philosophers to abandon academic life and to pursue his quest for truth and happiness in the depths of the English countryside.

Elsewhere, the landscapes of paradise are more obviously colonial in inspiration. In François-Guillaume Ducray-Duminil's *Lolotte et Fanfan* (1788), for example, refuge is sought on a West Indian desert island. It is to this unspoiled tropical location, where the protagonists are cast away as infants, that they later return to found a new colony in which European distinctions of class and nationality might be left behind. The considerably abridged English version made by children's novelist and proprietor of the Juvenile Library, Lucy Peacock, under the title *Ambrose and Eleanor; or, The Adventures of Two Children Deserted on an Uninhabited Island*, 1796, was received with little enthusiasm in the critical press. A second edition was nonetheless already on sale the following year and the tale continued to have appeal on both sides of the Atlantic into the nineteenth century.

---

[32] *Critical Review*, 3rd ser., 11 (July 1807), 274.

More generally, however, the pastoral idylls conjured up by French and German novelists of this period proved unable to resist the destructive forces of European society and instead focused a sense of nostalgia for the putative simplicities of the past. In prison during the Terror, Helen Maria Williams, for example, turned to Bernadin de Saint-Pierre's *Paul et Virginie* (1788), set on the far-away Ile de France (now Mauritius) in the Indian Ocean. Although not the first, her translation, *Paul and Virginia* (1795), interspersed with her own prison sonnets, was the best-known English version of this very popular tale of two mothers who (with the help of their two black servants) withdraw from society and bring up their son and daughter as beneficent children of nature. The ultimate demise of the little community leaves little hope, however, for the future. Encounters with runaway slaves from the sugar plantations on the island highlight the gross inequalities on which Europe's colonial commerce was built and hint ominously at the inevitable rebellion which was already beginning to shake the New World by the time of the novel's translation into English. Virginie's death furthermore dramatizes the deadening structures of female oppression encoded in European attitudes towards women: she is dragged down to a watery grave by artificial notions of female virtue that give her an unnaturally pronounced sense of modesty such that she prefers to drown rather than cast off any of her clothes as her ship goes down.

Just as the 'natural' island of Mauritius offers no escape from European prejudice in Bernadin's novel, the wilderness of North America can likewise provide no happy ending to the two lovers in François-René de Chateaubriand's *Atala* (1802; *Atala, ou les amours de deux sauvages*, 1801)—a novel shaped by the author's own flight to the New World from Revolutionary Paris and his subsequent disillusionment.

One of the best-known foreign authors in Britain at the end of the eighteenth and beginning of the nineteenth century was the German novelist, August Lafontaine. Between 1797 and 1813 over twenty of his works were put into English—more than half for the Minerva Press. The title that established his immense popularity in Britain was *Clara Duplessis, and Clairant: The History of a Family of French Emigrants* (1797, translated by Mr Woodbridge; *Klara Du Plessis und Klairant*, 1794). Critical opinion was muted, one reviewer objecting that the plot had no direct connection with the French Revolution which provides the backdrop.[33] The novel does, however, indicate how historical context was beginning to assume a more active force within even the most traditional forms of sentimental fiction. The letters of Clairant, initially a supporter of the Revolution, provide insights into the unfolding of events in France, while those of his beloved Clara, forced to flee to Germany, describe the émigré community in Koblenz. Notwithstanding a brief moment of respite where the two lovers are reunited in a forest far from Clara's disapproving family, the relentless force of external events ultimately destroys their pastoral idyll and provokes the tragic ending.

---

[33] *Critical Review*, n.s., 21 (November 1797), 356.

Novels written by and about political exiles were of obvious interest to the expatriate French community in London and feature accordingly among the French language titles published in London during the 1790s. At the same time, the émigré novel offered a framework in which issues of much wider interest could be explored, such as the interplay between politics and sensibility on the one hand and the concept of national identity on the other. In this respect, the writing of Madame de Staël-Holstein was of enormous importance in Britain as elsewhere in Europe. The international reputation enjoyed by Staël as a result of her landmark treatise, 'On Literature Considered in its Relationship to Social Institutions' (1800), meant that the publication of her first novel *Delphine*, in 1802, was an event of some considerable public interest, and two English translations were published in quick succession in 1803. The tragic love story of the headstrong heroine and her irresolute lover, Léonce, culminating in his execution by a Revolutionary firing squad and her suicide, was met with a mixture of admiration and disgust. The novel was nonetheless tremendously popular. In many respects, *Delphine* was deeply informed by the sentimental tradition of epistolary fiction of Richardson, Rousseau, and Goethe, all of whom were singled out with admiration in the preface. Staël's originality, however, lay in the political perspective that she brought to the narration of women's lives, indicting the structures and values that left no place for free-thinking women like her heroine, or indeed herself (Napoleon recognized *Delphine* as a covert attack on his regime and ordered Staël to withdraw from Paris). Crucially, it was also to be found in the new importance she gave to public events and characters who not only belong to a social class or society but to a *nation* (Coulet 1987: 655).

The national framework within which Staël understood the formation of character emerged yet more powerfully in her celebrated second novel in which, it is often claimed, the French word *nationalité* was used for the first time. Inspired by her travels across Europe during her years of exile, *Corinne, ou l'Italie* (1807) was translated into English twice before the year was out (both under the title *Corinna, or Italy*). The work was not only a phenomenal success, it also announced a major shift in the understanding of literature and art as expressions of national culture. Into the narrative of another unhappy love story between the melancholic Oswald, Lord Nelvil, peer of Scotland, and the flamboyant Corinna, hailed as the poetic genius of her adopted sun-drenched Italy, Staël offered both a positive glimpse of what women could achieve in the right context and, opening up the format of the sentimental romance to a comparative study of Europe, she also introduced her readers to the artistic vitality and cultural specificity of the nation invaded by Napoleon in 1797. Three years later, the publication in England of her 'On Germany' did for that nation and its literature what she had done for Italy in *Corinna*. In 1818, *Blackwood's Edinburgh Magazine* declared as follows: 'The sciences have always owed their origin to some great spirit. Smith created political economy—Linnaeus, botany—Lavoisier, chemistry—and Madame de

Staël has, in like manner, created the art of analysing the spirit of nations, and the springs which move them.'[34]

The growing importance of the concept of the nation that historians typically date from the American and French Revolutions at the end of the eighteenth century would progressively subsume the genre of the novel. Over the nineteenth century narrative fiction, as the studies of Benedict Anderson (1983; revised 2006) and Homi Bhabha (1990) have powerfully argued, became tightly linked with the project of forging the 'imagined community' of the modern nation. The wide-ranging transnational geographies that were a characteristic feature of earlier prose fiction began to shrink in the context of tales rooted in local landscapes, Walter Scott's Waverley novels providing some of the most conspicuous examples. At the same time, novels (like other literature) were increasingly classified with respect to the nationality of writers and their native tongues, and attitudes towards translated fiction simultaneously began to alter. Anna Barbauld's *British Novelists* (1810) was, for example, indicative of this shift, expressly excluding from her collection anything written by non-British novelists, in sharp contradistinction to Clara Reeve who, twenty-five years previously, had begged leave 'to mention English and Foreign books indifferently' (*Progress of Romance*, 1.122). With the nationalizing of the novel, English and foreign fiction was no longer seen as belonging to essentially the same unbounded transnational field as had hitherto been the case. It is no coincidence that it was also from around this same time that the number of translated titles began to fall sharply as foreign fiction was increasingly perceived as culturally 'other'. It should not be forgotten, however, that the practice of translating novels over the course of the eighteenth century and into the early nineteenth played a vital role in creating the very context in which the indigenous novel could later triumph. Translations, as McMurran (2002) reminds us, were of primary importance in establishing a zone of cultural contact in which notions of national specificity could be experienced and articulated by translators, reviewers, and readers. Foreign imports were thus integral in more ways than one to the history of the naturalization of the 'English' novel.

---

[34] *Blackwood's Edinburgh Magazine*, 4: 21 (December 1818), 278.

Afterword

The Rise of the 'Rise' of the Novel

CLIFFORD SISKIN

- **1810**: *The British Novelists*, ed. Anna Laetitia Barbauld
- **1813**: The first reference to an 'English Department' in a school, the Belfast Academical Institution
- **1821–4**: *Ballantyne's Novelist's Library*, with introductions by Sir Walter Scott
- **1823**: The first designated 'Professorship in English Language and Literature' in England, in London University

Full disclosure: to write about the rise of the novel as part of the monumental collaborative effort we are calling the *Oxford History of the Novel in English* (*OHNE*) is to participate in the very phenomenon I am trying to describe. The appearance of these volumes will—certainly in the minds of the dozens of contributors, and, we hope, for many readers for decades to come—raise the profile of the novel. Our participation in that enterprise may at first appear to be yet more evidence for William Warner's observation that '"the rise of the novel" has been one of the most widely circulated narratives of English studies' for the last half-century (1998: 1). But a quick glance at the dates above suggests that we might want to scale up the history of this connection. The field of literary studies and the rise of the novel have been intertwined for a long time. In fact, *OHNE* is being published alongside two 200-year anniversaries: on the one hand, what Homer Brown calls the '"moment" of the novel's institution' in the canonizing efforts of the second decade of the nineteenth century (1997: x), and, on the other, the emergence of the English Department and the subject of 'Literature' in Britain.

Whether at this moment we think of both institutions as showing their age (e.g. 'death of the novel' and 'crisis' of the humanities) or their durability, these temporal intersections suggest that both their origins and their viability have to do with each other. This most recent intersection, for example, offers, at the very least, a timely and mutual boost: literary study gets a new story to tell in print and at length—whatever the crisis, there is still more to say—while the novel gets new 'life' in the telling. But does a longer-term view—the shared anniversary view—suggest that more has been—and is—at stake? Have the 'novel' and 'Literature' been conducting a primarily coincidental relationship or a more symbiotic one?

Scaling Up—Our Moment of 'Good Fortune'

Answering this question is where *OHNE* as a 'new' history—one that could *not* be written before—comes into play. We can, finally, scale up our history of the novel because we have, over the past two decades scaled up our scholarship. This is, importantly, the result of what Francis Bacon called the 'good fortune' of living in a moment of different 'resources' than one's predecessors.[1] For him, these were new seventeenth-century tools and methods such as print, gunpowder, the nautical compass, and new ways to access 'things as they are', such as 'induction'. Our fortunes today have been lifted by electronic media, networks, computable databases, and new ways to access things as they *change*, such as 'emergence'.

Augmented by this 'new organon', we have been, to borrow Bacon's word, advancing knowledge of the novel by scaling up our literary histories in two basic ways:

- ✓   Counting
- ✓   Zooming Out[2]

The turn to the quantitative tells us that the 'rise' of the novel was not a gradual development over the eighteenth century in numerical terms. From an annual rate of only about four to twenty new titles through the first four decades, and remaining—despite the popularity of *Pamela/Shamela*—within a range of roughly twenty to forty for the next three, new novel production peaked briefly to sixty in 1771 before a steep decline to well below forty during the latter half of that decade. In the later 1780s, however, the output jumped—more than doubled—to as many as eighty, and continued to increase at high points into the next century. That rise of the novel—the actual numerical rise of new ones—was not against the grain; as James Raven has shown, those figures parallel the dramatic rise in the overall *ESTC* publication totals (Raven 2000).

The generating of more raw data has gone hand-in-hand with new efforts to put that data to work. William St Clair, for example, has brought legal history, publication practices, and patterns to bear on what the counts tell us. He links the take-off in print that the numbers describe to the affirmation of limited-term copyright just as that last quarter-century began. *Donaldson v. Becket* (1774) not only 'rejuvenated' the print market

---

[1]   Francis Bacon, *The New Organon*, ed. Lisa Jardine and Michael Silverthorne (Cambridge: Cambridge University Press, 2000), 29.
[2]   See Siskin (1998: 15–17) and Johnson (1996: 50).

(Raven 2000: 88), as works formerly protected by copyright became available for reprinting, but also helped to fuel 'an explosion of reading' of new as well as old materials (St Clair 2004: 348).

Crucially—for literary studies—that explosion left a peculiar signature: as Trevor Ross has so shrewdly noted, old works now newly available became a particular kind of 'literature'. In the words of a contemporary, 'the Works of *Shakespeare*, of *Addison, Pope, Swift, Gay*, and many other excellent Authors . . . are, by this [decision] declared to be the Property of any Person'. Never before in English history, observes Ross, had it been possible to think that a canon—which had been a selection designed rhetorically in accordance with the practical needs of speakers and writers—might belong to the people of a nation, to its readers (1998: 297).

With that shift, 'literature', a word that referred through most of the eighteenth century to all kinds of writing—*Britannica* still defined it in the 1770s as simply 'learning or skill in letters'—came, in the space of a few decades, to signify a subset of itself. This second usage—let us call it Literature with a capital 'L'—narrowed and hierarchized those kinds of writing, admitting only certain texts within certain genres. It came to define, that is, the specialized subject matter that we house in Departments of English: English Literature.

As with the anniversary dates, then, our counts also suggest that any quantitative 'rise' in the novel went hand-in-hand with other kinds of rising. Not only did new novels increase only when total print output increased—the eighteenth-century novel never broke out numerically from other forms—but the new novel count rose only as 'Literature' arose, categorically and hierarchically, above literary output in general. Here, then, is where the second kind of scaling-up I mentioned earlier—'zooming out'—comes into play. With more than one rise to explain—as well as how those rises connect—we need a newly capacious history. We need, that is, to step out of the history of the novel and out of the history of the subject we call Literature into a history that can contain both.

Raymond Williams, whose *Keywords* first made the strong case for historicizing 'Literature', pioneered this kind of reframing in *Writing in Society* (1985). As the new organon began to remediate the old one—e.g. 'What we now have [in television] is drama as habitual experience: more in a week . . . than most human beings would previously have seen in a lifetime' (12)—Williams saw a need for a history adequate to this moment of change. This 'history of writing' (2–3) would begin with the formation of the norm now being disrupted: how were practices once new—'writing' was his shorthand for the interrelations of writing, silent reading, and print—'naturalized' *in* certain 'forms' and *by* the formation of 'Literature' itself? How, that is, did Britain become what we now call a 'print culture'?

To locate that becoming in the eighteenth century is not to deny that the printing press was invented much earlier and that its products had already been appearing in some quantity and with some force. But that is precisely the point: any claim to change must be an argument about continuity as well as discontinuity. This concept of change forms part of Ralph Cohen's theory of genre as historical rather than essential—an understanding that underlies my treatment of the 'novel' in this chapter. 'Since each genre is composed of texts that accrue', Cohen argues, 'the grouping is a process, not a determinate category. . . . A genre, therefore, is to be understood in relation to other genres' (Cohen 1986: 204, 207). This issue of change is where our new organon features—as 'induction' did in Bacon's—a new 'machine' for getting the mind's 'business done' (*New Organon*, 28). 'Emergence' has itself emerged across the disciplines as a powerful tool for analysing and articulating change outside of the standard model of 'development' versus 'rupture'. Rather than having to choose between tales of continuity or discontinuity, emergence negotiates a new relationship between them. Just as a flock is more than the sum of its birds, so the behaviour of a hive cannot be inferred from the actions of individual bees; based on the latter, one could never predict the former. The macro emerges, unpredictably, from the micro—higher-level complexity from lower-level simplicity—because more can be different.

As a 'machine' for making sense of change, then, emergence engages the quantitative—it foregrounds the factor of 'more'—but does not force it to be predictive. Instead, by loosening the standard knots of causation, it allows us to correlate changes of apparently different kinds. Emergence thus works well with the other tools that comprise our new organon—the counts and a newly capacious history that can comprehend them—and thus carries a number of possible advantages over concepts more routinely invoked in the study of large-scale literary and social phenomena.

Watt's 'Rise'—A Thought Experiment

No concept is more routine in the study of the novel than the one made famous by Ian Watt. *The Rise of the Novel* (1957) thus offers us a test of what we might have to gain from our new organon—a test that we can conduct in the form of an alternative history. What if Watt had in 1957 the 'good fortune' of having 'emergence' available as an alternative to 'rise' for his study of the novel?

As a familiar and fuzzy term for sweeping and often Whiggish developmental tales— think 'empires' and 'the middle class'—the term 'rise' may, in fact, have helped to make *The Rise of the Novel* an astonishingly influential and long-lived text. This may be for a number of reasons in addition to 'rise' being a familiar and accessible term. There are for example the eighteenth-century echoes, both of what was written back then ('rise' narratives such as *The Whole Birth, Life, and Glorious Rise, of John Duke and Earl of Marlborough*, 1707) and of what we assumed happened back then (the 'rise of the middle class'). And there is the additional irony, of course, of the vulnerabilities I name as keeping the book alive as a target of criticism. As user-friendly as 'rise' might be, however, it also comes with baggage—conceptual baggage that has invited the most persistent and telling criticisms of Watt's argument:

- 'rise' assumes or implies continuity, organic or otherwise; and
- 'rise' assumes or implies causality, often unilateral and triumphal, and, at times, teleological.

The cover designs in the University of California Press editions of *The Rise of the Novel*, for example, have consistently highlighted the organic and developmental connotations of 'rise': a leafy tree has morphed over the years into a close-up of the leaves themselves. But this book can't, in fact, be judged by its covers. The argument behind them is not one of continuous growth but the opposite: Watt's tale has become notorious, even among its admirers, for opening gaps in the novel's 'development', most conspicuously in his blanket dismissal, 'with only a few exceptions', of 'the fiction of the last half of the eighteenth century' (1957: 290).

Since Watt issues that dismissal in aesthetic terms—a fifty-year absence of 'intrinsic merit'—generations of readers have puzzled over when and how a rise of any kind might have occurred. If it was a qualitative rise, was it confined to just the first half of the century? Or was Watt primarily thinking in quantitative terms? The surprising answer is neither. The book ends with yet another aesthetic dismissal—this time of the 'fairly obvious technical weaknesses' and 'defects of art' of its protagonists from the first half of the century. The only type of positive quality Watt finds in all three main novelists—Defoe, Richardson, and Fielding—were the 'qualities of life' they expressed 'with a completeness and conviction which is very rare, and for which one is grateful' (301).

Gratitude for something rare is not an argument for a rise, especially when the gesture is made nostalgically across a half-century Watt urges us to forget. And what he wants us to remember does not settle the qualitative versus quantitative issue, since the question of what kind of 'life' those writers expressed raises yet another possibility: are we to understand his rise as primarily a sociological phenomenon? In the conclusion of his chapter on 'The Reading Public and the Rise of the Novel', Watt does claim that the life they 'express[ed]' from 'the inside' was 'the great power and self-confidence of the middle class as a whole' (59). However, in the 'Realism' chapter that is the book's theoretical foundation, Watt insists that 'what is probably the most original feature of the novel form' is its 'attempts to portray *all* the varieties of human experience' (emphasis mine, 11). The ambiguity of the overall rise arguments leaks into Watt's diction: is 'original' here an aesthetic claim or a historical one? Throughout the book, intermittent gestures toward identifying the form as an expression of a particular social class are trumped repeatedly by Watt's insistence on the novel's identification with the fully 'human': 'formal realism, in fact, is the narrative embodiment of a premise that Defoe and Richardson accepted very literally, but which is implicit in the novel form in general: the premise, or primary convention, that the novel is a full and authentic report *of human experience*' (emphasis mine, 32).

If, then, Watt's rise is not clearly keyed to a rise in 'qualities', either aesthetic or class-specific, was he making claims for a quantitative rise? Although not often credited for offering statistics, Watt did provide them—citing figures for the reading public and for print (36–7), as well as for 'works of fiction' (290). But the rise his numbers describe—a doubling of fiction in the last thirty years of the eighteenth century—has no purchase on an argument that explicitly ignores the entire second half of that same century. That disjunction is why Watt's turn to the quantitative has been rarely engaged by his readers: his numbers are themselves disengaged from any version of his thesis.

Ian Watt thus left us with a phrase—'the rise of the novel'—that is as perplexing as it is enchanting. We can't quite stop repeating it even—in fact, especially—as we critique it. The thought experiment I have proposed—breaking the spell by imagining Watt chanting a different tune—is not as far-fetched as it might at first sound. The keyword for change he used twice in the opening paragraph of the book's Preface was not 'rise' but 'emergence' (7). However, between 1938, when he began his study, and its publication in 1957, that term had not yet accrued the conceptual and multidisciplinary uses I have described. It was thus neither compelling nor useful enough to set the tune for the rest of the book's argument.

But what if it had been, at that point, load-bearing? Since emergence as it is used now engages change by positing 'more as different', then the quantitative issue of 'more' might not have floated free of the rest of the argument—and that argument might not have been embarrassed by a fifty-year gap. That gap opens in Watt because his 'rise' looks for developmental continuity, and when it does not find 'improved' versions of the earlier novels he admires, it finds nothing.

Emergence, on the other hand, not only keeps the quantitative in play; it also does not assume continuity. Instead, it tells us to expect change to take on the form of unpredictable difference. Difference of that kind is precisely what Watt's overall argument has needed, since even if we accept his notion that what he calls 'formal realism' (the use of spatial and temporal particulars) is 'implicit in the novel form in general' (32), the actual forms novels took changed substantially between the early eighteenth and nineteenth centuries. Both Fielding's and Richardson's experiments in generic mixing turned out, in fact, to be dead ends. Watt himself calls Fielding's epic recipe, 'sterile', 'retrograde', and of 'little importance in the later tradition of the novel' (259), while Richardson's epistolary models wane at precisely the moment, 1780s–1790s, that new novels take off in numbers—and, in the absences of these older models, in different formal directions.

Now imagine that Watt had at his disposal not only emergence's account of 'more' and 'difference', but also other parts of our new organon: the counts, as well as our means of making them, plus histories capacious enough to contain and connect them. In such a history, Watt could have compared counts and dates and then approached the problem of a 'rise' from different angles, such as the shared anniversaries of the novel and Literature. Their institution at the same time raises the issue of a 'rise' in its simplest relational sense, as describing a change of position. But positions *in* what? What did the novel rise *into*? Was it Literature? Was Literature already there waiting for it? Or was the eighteenth century's extensive discourse about the novel the medium for Literature's own rise?

The Fall of Watt's 'Rise'—a Prelude to New History

To answer these questions, let alone pose them, we need to make full use of our current good fortune—starting with an effort to put Watt's argument into a longer historical perspective. For the first forty years after publication, that argument was praised and patched, bruised and—some think—improved. In fact, one of our new tools, the Google Ngram Viewer, tells us that in their sample of scanned books, the appearance of the phrase 'rise of the novel' increased more than threefold between 1956, the year before publication of Watt's book, and 1996 when the frequency of the phrase reached its peak. However, at that point, something happened: the frequency fell precipitously, shrinking two-and-one-half-fold in just a dozen years (by 2008, the last year of Ngram's samples).[3]

What happened? Even while recognizing the limitations of the data and the many causes that may have been at work, one factor in particular deserves our attention because it is congruent with the cause of the rise. If the publication of Watt's book was the clear marker for the original take-off, then we should turn again to what was published to figure out the fall. Starting in 1996, the following books were published in rapid-fire order:

- 1996: *Cultural Institutions of the Novel*, ed. Deidre Lynch and William B. Warner
- 1996: *The True Story of the Novel*, Margaret Anne Doody
- 1997: *Institutions of the English Novel: From Defoe to Scott*, Homer Obed Brown
- 1998: *The Work of Writing: Literature and Social Change in Britain, 1700–1830*, Clifford Siskin
- 1998: *Licensing Entertainment: The Elevation of Novel Reading in Britain, 1684–1750*, William B. Warner

---

[3] For each year's figures, I have added the percentages for both the lower-case and upper-case versions of 'rise of the novel'. The upper-case version—most likely referring to the title of Watt's book—overtook the lower-case version within a year after the publication of the book. Ngram is a new and still crude tool; Google lists many of its significant limitations in the About note on the webpage. In addition to those issues, there are, of course, many potential factors in the 'rise' and 'fall' of the phrase besides the ones I identify and thus many alternative ways to interpret the data.

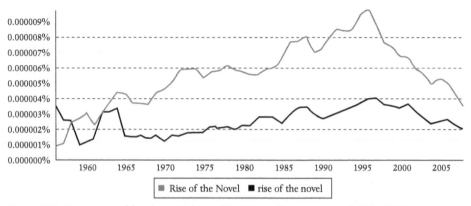

Figure 33.1. Frequency of the phrase 'R/rise of the N/novel' (case-sensitive), 1956–2008

What this cluster of books shared was the foregrounding of the need to zoom out. Although the histories they zoomed out to were different in kind and scale, each of these efforts focused on putting the novel and Watt's 'rise' into something more capacious.

There were, of course, precedents for this move, from Lukács's and Bakhtin's efforts to turn the novel into the generic hero of a rising modernity to the replacing of the novel into the history of sexuality (Armstrong 1987), philosophical and social dialectics (McKeon 1987), and patterns of print culture (Hunter 1990). But what distinguishes this late 1990s cluster, in addition to it being large and temporally tight, is that it came in the wake of two enabling changes—changes that enabled, that is, previously unavailable ways to zoom out. The first was the formation, described earlier, of a critical consensus on the historicity of the category of 'Literature', in general, and 'English Literature', in particular.[4] The second was the formation in the early 1990s of the World Wide Web. For Doody, for example, the historicizing of English Literature freed the history of the novel from a 'parochialism' that prevented a longer-term, multicultural view. I am not endorsing Doody's vastly expanded history as correct or better than those that came before or after; my purpose is to point to the historicity of her claims by linking them to the changes that enabled this entire cluster of books on the novel. For Warner, the 'media culture' of the Web—as well as the recognition that the 'modern literary system' began to 'take shape in the second half of the eighteenth century'—led him to a 'strategy for breaking the spell of 'the rise of the novel': 'inscribing the history of the novel *into* the history of (print) media' (emphasis mine, Warner 1998: xii, 278, xi). Rather than assuming that the novel must be treated as 'a type of literature', Warner scaled up into 'another story—that of the beginning of early modern print entertainment' (xiii).

[4] For a confirmation of the consensus see the two Forum sections in two issues of volume 21 of *Eighteenth-Century Life* (Terry et al. 1997a, 1997b).

Warner's monograph, as well as Brown's and Siskin's, were all anticipated by their contributions to the *Cultural Institutions of the Novel* volume. Instead of starting with the novel as the fully instituted object it is for us, and then describing that object's 'rise', that volume focused on what Brown called in his monograph the 'diverse, inchoate, singular acts of institution that could only much later be seen and instituted collectively as a more or less integral genre' (1997: xviii). Both Siskin—who explicitly invokes Williams's 'history of writing'—and Brown engage Watt's rise not as a explanation that can be made better but as something that needs to be explained: 'it is as necessary to "historicize" the discourse of the novel, particularly the discourse of the origins of the novel, as it is to historicize the novel itself' (Brown 1997: x). In Siskin's formulation, 'we must shift our attention outward from *the* novel as an object fated to "rise" to the discursive space I am calling *novelism*'—the 'discourse of and about novels' (1998: 173–4).

The fall of Watt's rise, then, is less about his argument falling *out* of favour and more about it falling *into* that space—into something larger of which it is a part. When we attend to this larger picture, we don't have to repeat after Watt but can explore what came before him. From that perspective, Watt's book can be seen as a recent vehicle for an argument with a very long history—a history long enough to play a constitutive role in the formation and instituting of the very object that the argument purports to be 'about'. In Watt's book, the rise is recited as a *critical* narrative, but the tale that he was retelling was, in the eighteenth century, *performative*. This can be understood as an act of 'prescription'—of writing working not to reflect but to pre-scribe—to write before—the real. This reversal of our conventional expectations is why, as Homer Brown observes, there is an 'anachronism' at the core of Watt's argument: 'the solution of the problem coming historically *before* "the whole tradition of the novel" shows it to be pervasive and continuing' (1997: 172). As his rise falls, the phenomenon highlighted by the title of this chapter—'The Rise of the "Rise" of the Novel'—comes into view, offering a history for *OHNE* that could not be written before.

How the 'Rise' Rose [I]: A Retrospective View

To grasp what is at stake in seeing Watt's rise as a retelling, we need only turn to Samuel P. Miller's *A Brief Retrospect of the Eighteenth Century*, written and published right as that century came to a close.[5] In 1803 the initial twists and turns are already in place—particularly

---

[5] Samuel P. Miller, *A Brief Retrospect of the Eighteenth Century: In Two Volumes Containing A Sketch of the Revolutions and Improvements in Science, Arts, and Literature during that Period* (New York: T. and J. Swords, 1803). Miller was an American. A three-volume edition was published in London in 1805.

the strange chronological assertion that many still strangely accept, that Fielding and Richardson constituted the 'golden age' of the novel for the eighteenth century, leaving its last fifty years in critical and literary historical limbo:

> The eighteenth century may be peculiarly and emphatically called the *Age of Novels*.... The earliest productions of Great-Britain in this department of writing may be considered as her best. FIELDING and RICHARDSON have never been exceeded, and probably not equalled, by any novelists since their day, either in their own or any other country. Each of these authors may be said to have invented a new species of fictitious writing, and to have carried it at once to the highest point of improvement which it has ever reached. (2.158–9)

What follow are a series of parallel constructions that turn Fielding and Richardson into Fielding/Richardson—a binary that defines 'the' novel in terms that echo through the centuries into Watt: e.g. 'The former succeeds better in describing *manners*; the latter in developing and displaying the *heart*'. But whatever their individual strengths and weaknesses, Miller values precisely what Watt writes he is grateful for: their skill at describing 'life'—their expression of 'sentiments' and 'knowledge of mankind' that brings them into comparison to 'Shakespeare' (2.159–60).[6]

In making that comparison, Miller is clearly participating in the instituting of the novel as a more respected form of writing. In fact, his decision to devote an entire chapter to 'Romances and Novels' in a 'Retrospect' that is supposed to cover *all* aspects of the eighteenth century in only two volumes, is itself a boost to 'fictitious narrative' (2.155). But the part of his argument that becomes Watt's rise—Fielding/Richardson (F/R) as origin and high point for the century—is just that, a part. The other part is to assert, with 'no hesitation', 'that, if it were *possible*, he would *wholly* prohibit the reading of novels':

> NO ONE WAS EVER AN EXTENSIVE AND ESPECIALLY AN HABITTAL [*sic*] READER OF NOVELS, EVEN SUPPOSING THEM ALL TO BE WELL SELECTED, WITHOUT SUFFERING BOTH INTELLECTUAL AND MORAL INJURY, AND OF COURSE INCURRING A DIMINUTION OF HAPPINESS. (2.179)

To get from his initial praise of the 'great work of this kind' (2.158) to this blanket dismissal, Miller took his argument where Watt later deigned not to tread: the second half of the eighteenth century. Although he finds no equal to F/R there, he does find what he needs to indict the novel: increasing numbers and a contemporary argument about the consequences.

Miller is at first quite positive about the proliferation of novels, novelists, and readers in those concluding decades, not only mentioning what Watt does not—the many women writers, the Gothic, oriental tales—but also praising them: 'Miss CHARLOTTE SMITH', he

---

[6] For an analysis of the role of Shakespeare in the instituting of the novel and of 'literature', see Jonathan Arac (2011: 3).

judges, 'holds an honourable place among the ingenious and moral novelists of the age' (2.164). But that praise turns out to be the fulcrum for his rejection of the novel once Miller brings into play an argument that was first published by Samuel Johnson at mid-century, a moment that Miller identifies as crucial for the novel. 'Fifty years ago', he argues, the question of whether novels form 'an *useful* kind of reading' was 'of little moment'. But, 'since that time, the case is, unhappily, altered; their number has increased, their character is so changed, and the task of discriminating among them has become so delicate and arduous' (2.172).

Miller turns for help to Samuel Johnson, whose *Rambler* essay (No. 4: Saturday, 31 March 1750) had managed to argue both that fiction writers were getting better and that the novel, therefore, was getting—in moral terms—worse: 'for the sake ... of following *nature*', those writers 'so mingle good and bad qualities in their principal personages, that they are both equally conspicuous'. The better they are at this 'promiscuous description', the more their readers 'lose the abhorrence' of the bad 'because they do not hinder our pleasure'. In other words, more novelists writing better novels means more danger. Using Johnson, Miller was thus able, unlike Watt, to discover much to admire in the later eighteenth century, but that meant, finally, that there was that much more to include in his remarkably choreographed dismissal of the entire genre. 'Were the whole number which the age produced divided into *a thousand* parts', Miller proclaims, it is probable that *five hundred* of these' would be a 'waste of time'. 'Four hundred and ninety-nine' of the remaining parts, he continues, 'may be considered as positively seductive and corrupting' and thus to be avoided even if ingenious. Of the one part left, only 'a single page would embrace all that could be with propriety recommended to the attention of the youthful mind'. But that single page poses, in turn, the problem of 'who is to make this selection', leaving the chapter to end with total 'prohibit[ion]' (2.174–9).

Between Miller and Watt, this argument ceases to be, to borrow Miller's phrase, 'useful reading'. By the early nineteenth century, the fear of writing—of its power to change people—was domesticated as society as a whole became comfortable with the new forms of print technology. What was left—left for Watt—was just the Golden Age story of F/R. In Miller's tale, as I have just shown, that was just one part of a history of the entire eighteenth century—a history that made quantitative and qualitative arguments about the entire period. Watt's retelling, in contrast, is radically partial, as if—in regard to the second half of the century—obeying Miller's prohibition against reading novels. But for Watt, the prohibition lifts with Austen, and so he supplements his rise story with a different kind of history—one that novelists and reviewers began to construct in the two decades immediately following Miller.

Those histories wrote up new novels in a new way—as 'singular' efforts departing from the past. Tales of imitative decline from F/R gave way to now familiar tales of ongoing improvement: the 'rise' of the creatively autonomous aesthetic object called the English novel. When, for example, Walter Scott, in a review published in 1816, and Richard Whately, in a review published five years later, wrote up Jane Austen's newness, they did so in a new way: not as a return to the Ancient heights of Fielding and Richardson, but as an emerging 'style', one that has 'arisen'.[7]

The burden of Watt's book was to suture, across a fifty-year gap, this type of rise to the F/R one. For him, Austen had to become the Great Tradition heir of Fielding and Richardson despite the absence of the intervening generations. One problem with doing so, however, was that—as noted earlier—both of the father figures turned out to be, in formal terms, sterile. But perhaps the greater problem has been that these histories actually are different in kind; they describe change in two incompatible ways. Together, their differences articulate a shift in narratives of knowledge from eighteenth-century tales of imitative decline from past masters (F/R) into Romantic claims of developmental innovation. Neither of these historically specific risings can or should be our history of the novel—they are, precisely, what we should be historicizing.

How the 'Rise' Rose [II]: Novelism in the Eighteenth Century

To put those risings into history, we need to turn back past Miller into the eighteenth century itself. Since he presents his retrospect not as a departure from conventional wisdom but as a report of it, we need to locate when and how that wisdom was formed. But the further we push back into the 1700s the more important it is to recognize that the focus of our attention cannot be 'the novel' as we know it. That object could not claim that definite article until the early nineteenth century. Miller himself notes the eighteenth century's plethora of terms for 'fictitious discourse', particularly the volatile interplay of 'romance' and 'novel'. The latter term, he drily notes, has been used 'without that accuracy of application which is desirable' (2.157). Even the notion of accuracy, however, is inadequate to this problem of 'the' novel, since the status of the object itself, and not just the term we desire to apply to it, was at issue.

Our turn back thus encounters the strange reversal I outlined earlier. The 'rise of the "rise"' in the eighteenth century is not about whether a given object did rise but about how a discourse of rising interpellated an object whose rise could be subject to ongoing debate. Cheryl Nixon, in her rich collection *Novel Definitions*, comprehensively documents how, from the early eighteenth century, 'the historicizing of the novel occurs side-by-side with the actual creation of the form'. The 'novel', she observes, was defined and redefined throughout the century by the ongoing construction of 'narrative[s] of its

---

[7] Sir Walter Scott, unsigned article in *Quarterly Review*, 14 (October 1815) and Richard Whately in *Quarterly Review*, 24 (January 1821); both reviews are reprinted in Southam (1968: 58–69, 87–105).

past'; the accumulation of those stories came both to describe 'the' novel and to create '"a rise of the novel" trajectory that', she notes with understatement, 'remains influential today' (2009: 44).

'Trajectory' is a particularly useful term for clarifying how and when we should find and use the word 'rise'. The phrase 'rise of——' was regularly used throughout the eighteenth century for many objects (individuals, war, cities, customs) but not 'the novel'. In part this was due to that object still being in formation, but there is also the simple fact that the novel did not, in any instantiation, rise in esteem during that century, securing critical approval only when fully instituted in the early nineteenth century. Its eighteenth-century trajectories were of intention and desire, of asking readers to engage with what they were reading as new and improved, and improving; they were not claims about a 'rise' having occurred.

When—and in what—were these trajectories articulated? Here is where the historicity of Literature again comes into play, for the formation of that disciplinary category gave institutional and professional force to our now habitual distinction between the creative and the critical. This binary has manifested itself since the early nineteenth century as not only a set of occupational distinctions but also of generic ones: we think of prefaces and afterwords, for example, as critical genres distinct from the creative, main text. But when we turn to the eighteenth century what are we to do with Laurence Sterne, as Joseph Bartolomeo points out, 'placing prefaces in the middle of novels' (1994: 19), Henry Fielding regularly interrupting his fiction with authorial addresses to the reader, and Jane Austen critically comparing the novel and the periodical in the middle of Chapter 5 of *Northanger Abbey*?

To up the ante, might we not profitably reclassify the eighteenth-century novel itself— written to amend the romance and read to recuperate the real—as, in all of its variations, a *critical* form? In the eighteenth century, writing (in Williams's sense as shorthand for the interrelated practices of writing, reading, and print) was as much an object of inquiry as a means: writing about writing produced more writing in a self-reflexive proliferation. One might argue that all writing became, in that sense, critical. To see 'criticism' only as a separate kind is thus to miss the historical point: it was a condition and product of the act of writing itself, as long as that act was still experienced as new (see Siskin 1998: 25). Certainly the amending and recuperating were not just performed by the part we partition off as 'creative': the 'story'. To recover more fully what was actually done and how, the creative/critical binary just gets in the way; we need, instead, a more inclusive rubric such as 'novelism'— a term embracing the full range of strategic forms and features with which stories mixed both inside and outside the printed volumes themselves, from prefaces, descriptive title pages, apostrophic turns to the reader, keys, and afterwords to advertisements, letters to editors, circulating library catalogues, and reviews.

If we insist on porting our own binaries into the eighteenth century, we will return, like the ancient mariner, repeating our own familiar tale. But if we don't want the 'trajectories' they mapped out back then to default into our 'rise of the novel', we can explore instead 'the advent of novelism'. In that discursive field, 'novel' is but one label—for what became only at the turn into the next century one kind—for efforts to generate new 'Species of Writing' (the term is Fielding's own) from a technology still seen as powerfully—and thus danger-ously—new (Siskin and Warner 2010: 9–11). The scope of that field and the intensity of that effort are now well documented in print in Nixon's collection, and, at a much larger scale, in electronic databases such as *Eighteenth-Century Collections Online*. These materials range chronologically from early eighteenth-century translations of seventeenth-century French sources—Delariviere Manley's prefatory description of 'Little *Histories*' taking the 'Place of *Romances*' (1705)—to William Godwin's fragment extolling Romance over History (1797). The message conveyed by this sweep and persistence of novelism is that efforts to set the trajectory of a new species were generative, but not in any directly linear way, of the par-ticular new species we now know as 'the' novel. From more and more novelism, something different *emerged*—different from any of the earlier experiments, even the most celebrated.

But the novel as we now know it was not all that emerged. If it was to be an improved 'species', one that would be better than others, within what framework could it be under-stood as better? Against what background could the trajectory be drawn? The inclusive eighteenth-century category of 'literature' could not support such hierarchical distinc-tions. What did form for precisely that purpose—and now shares an anniversary with 'the novel'—was 'Literature'. If all that was required to construct that sacralized subset of 'literature' were judgements of individual works, it would, of course, have formed earlier. But, as we can see in (Miller's) retrospect, it could not and did not until two con-ditions were met: the proliferation of print, including romances and novels, in the last decades of the century, and the instituting of a qualitative triage to manage that flow—a classificatory system for facilitating the critical operations of Literature.

As we saw in Miller's *Retrospect*, novelism was a primary discursive location for wor-rying about the effects of the 'many'; he explicitly cites the late-century proliferation as a watershed for his concern about the novel. And he manages that concern by dividing the many up into smaller groupings, using such phrases as 'belonging to a new and singular class' (2.164), 'productions of a singular kind' (2.166), and 'to this mixed class also belongs' (2.167). In foregrounding such classifications in 1803, Miller was once again following conventional wisdom from the century he was describing. In its latter decades, as Joseph Bartolomeo has argued, the discourse I am calling novelism, especially in the periodicals, exhibited an increasing 'awareness of genre' (1994: 134).

Both of Bartolomeo's terms need to be qualified. 'Awareness' suggests that these writ-ers had been in the dark about something that was already there. But the term 'genre' in its modern sense, as is still evident in Miller's persistent use of 'kind' and 'class', was not an eighteenth-century term, appearing only very rarely and only in the last decades of the century.[8] That was, of course, the very moment that novelism accelerated its efforts

---

[8] The online *Oxford English Dictionary* lists two eighteenth-century usages, both in the final decades.

to generate new species of composition, resulting not only in more individual texts but also more species. What Bartolomeo calls an 'awareness of genre' was the resulting focus on that proliferation of kinds and the need to manage it through increasingly systematic and hierarchical 'arrangement'.

One of his primary examples, an October 1796 review of Frances Burney's *Camilla* by William Enfield in the *Monthly*, captures the doubling at the core of this organizational imperative:

> Though few novels fall exclusively within any one of these classes [romantic, pathetic, and humorous], every good novel has a prominent character, from which its proper place in this arrangement may be easily discovered. (quoted in Bartolomeo 1994: 134)

Novelism's earlier focus on new 'species' with trajectories of improvement had, by the close of the century, become a placement procedure. All species were organized into a system of 'classes' and all trajectories were stabilized into a ranking of results. Every work had to find its 'proper place' in the former, and, once in place, be rated as 'good' (or not) within the latter. This was, in a very practical sense, a blueprint for the construction of Literature. The 'arrangement' of kinds was the scaffolding and the double placement— only the best examples of only certain kinds—the construction technique. Those kinds became the primary genres of our modern histories and anthologies of Literature—even when this required the wholesale reclassifying of earlier works. Thus the elevation of 'the novel' over all of the other kinds of prose fiction turned literary history into palimpsest, as our 'rise' narratives overwrote the title pages of Crusoe's *Adventures*, Clarissa's *History*, and *The History of the Adventures* of Joseph Andrews. The full list of overwritten kinds is much longer, including apologies, memoirs, romances, stories, tales, etc. As Anthony Jarrells points out in Chapter 26, we now realize that a comprehensive 'history of the years that comprise this volume would have to include not only the many different forms the novel took, but also the myriad other fictional forms that existed and in some cases thrived *after* novels took their place in the busy market of British print culture' (see 478).

The rise of the novel, as noted earlier, has been one of the most widely circulated narratives in the study of Literature. But when we track the rise of that rise, a very old and a very straightforward reason comes into view: Literature as a category to study was itself put into circulation by what I am calling novelism. The eighteenth century's extensive discourse of and about the novel was a primary medium not only for that genre but also for Literature's own rise. That is why, 200 years later, *The Oxford History of the Novel in English* matters, even for those with other generic predilections: a new history of the novel will be a necessary tool for anyone attempting to write a genuinely new literary history.

Bibliography

Aaron, Jane (1994). 'Seduction and Betrayal: Wales in Women's Fiction, 1785–1810', *Women's Writing*, 1.1: 65–76.

Allan, David (2008). *A Nation of Readers: The Lending Library in Georgian England* (London: British Library).

Allan, David (2010). *Commonplace Books and Reading in Georgian England* (Cambridge: Cambridge University Press).

Allen, Walter (1956). 'Introduction', *Peregrine Pickle* (London: Everyman's Library).

Altick, Richard D. (1957). *The English Common Reader: A Social History of the Mass Reading Public 1800–1900* (Chicago: University of Chicago Press).

Altman, Janet Gurkin (1982). *Epistolarity: Approaches to a Form* (Columbus: Ohio State University Press).

Anderson, Benedict (2006). *Imagined Communities: Reflections on the Origin and Spread of Nationalism* [1983], Revised Edition (London: Verso).

Andrews, Elmer (1987). 'Aesthetics, Politics and Identity: Lady Morgan's "The Wild Irish Girl"', *Canadian Journal of Irish Studies*, 12: 7–19.

Arac, Jonathan (2011). *Impure Worlds: The Institution of Literature in the Age of the Novel* (New York: Fordham University Press).

Armstrong, Nancy (1987). *Desire and Domestic Fiction: A Political History of the Novel* (Oxford: Oxford University Press).

Augst, Thomas (2003). *The Clerk's Tale: Young Men and Moral Life in Nineteenth-Century America* (Chicago: University of Chicago Press).

Backscheider, Paula R. (2005). 'Literary Culture as Immediate Reality', in P. R. Backscheider and C. Ingrassia (eds), *A Companion to the Eighteenth-Century Novel and Culture* (Oxford: Blackwell), 504–38.

Baier, Annette (1991). *A Progress of Sentiments: Reflections on Hume's Treatise* (Cambridge, MA: Harvard University Press).

Bakhtin, M. M. (1981). 'Epic and Novel', in Michael Holquist (ed.), *The Dialogic Imagination: Four Essays* (Austin, TX: University of Texas Press), 3–40.

Ballaster, Ros (2005). *Fabulous Orients: Fictions of the East in England, 1662–1785* (Oxford: Oxford University Press).

Banfield, Marie (2007). 'From Sentiment to Sentimentality: A Nineteenth-Century Lexicographical Search', *19: Interdisciplinary Studies in the Long Nineteenth Century*, 4. Available online at <http://19.bbk.ac.uk/index.php/19/article/view/459/319>.

Bannet, Tavor Eve (2005). '"Secret History": Or, Talebearing Inside and Outside the Secretorie', *Huntington Library Quarterly*, 68.1–2: 375–96.

Barber, Giles (1976). 'Books from the Old World and for the New: The British International Trade in Books in the Eighteenth Century', *Studies on Voltaire and the Eighteenth Century*, 151: 185–224.

Bartlett, Thomas (2000). 'Acts of Union', Inaugural Lecture delivered at University College, Dublin, 24 February.

Bartolomeo, Joseph (1994). *A New Species of Criticism: Eighteenth-Century Discourse on the Novel* (Newark: University of Delaware Press).

Battestin, Martin C. and Ruthe R. Battestin (1989). *Henry Fielding: A Life* (London and New York: Routledge).

Beasley, Jerry C. (1972). *A Check List of Prose Fiction Published in England, 1740–49* (Charlottesville: University Press of Virginia).

Beasley, Jerry C. (1998). *Tobias Smollett: Novelist* (Athens, GA: University of Georgia Press).

Beebee, Thomas O. (1999). *Epistolary Fiction in Europe 1500–1850* (Cambridge: Cambridge University Press).

Behrendt, Steven (2009). 'Response Essay: Cultural Transitions, Literary Judgments, and the Romantic-Era British Novel', in Miriam L. Wallace (ed.), *Enlightening Romanticism, Romancing the Enlightenment: British Novels from 1750–1832* (Burlington, VT: Ashgate), 189–206.

Bell, Michael (2000). 'Adam Smith and Friedrich Schiller: The Luxury of Sensibility and the Aetheticizing of Emotion', in Jürgen Schlaeger (ed.), *Yearbook of Research in English and American Literature*, 16: *Representations of Emotional Excess* (Tubingen: Gunter Narr Verlag), 105–15.

Benedict, Barbara M. (1996). *Making the Modern Reader: Cultural Mediation in Early Modern Literary Anthologies* (Princeton: Princeton University Press).

Benedict, Barbara M. (2004). 'Readers, Writers, Reviewers and the Professionalization of Literature', in Thomas Keymer and Jon Mee (eds), *The Cambridge Companion to English Literature 1740–1830* (Cambridge: Cambridge University Press), 3–23.

Berg, Maxine (2005). *Luxury and Pleasure in Eighteenth-Century Britain* (Oxford: Oxford University Press).

Bew, Paul (2007). *Ireland: The Politics of Enmity, 1789–2006* (Oxford: Oxford University Press).

Bhabha, Homi K. (ed.) (1990). *Nation and Narration* (London: Routledge).

Binhammer, Katherine (2003). 'The Persistence of Reading: Governing Female Novel-Reading in *Memoirs of Emma Courtney* and *Memoirs of Modern Philosophers*', *Eighteenth-Century Life*, 27: 1–22.

Black, Frank Gees (1940). *The Epistolary Novel in the Late Eighteenth Century: A Descriptive and Bibliographical Study* (Eugene: University of Oregon).

Blackman, John (1862). *A Memoir of the Life and Writings of Thomas Day* (London: John Bedford).

Blackwell, Mark (ed.) (2007). *The Secret Life of Things: Animals, Objects, and It-Narratives in Eighteenth-Century England* (Lewisburg, PA: Bucknell University Press).

Blain, Virginia, Patricia Clements, and Isobel Grundy (eds) (1990). *The Feminist Companion to Literature in English: Women Writers from the Middle Ages to the Present* (New Haven and London: Yale University Press).

Blakey, Dorothy (1939). *The Minerva Press 1790–1820* (London: Bibliographical Society).

Bonnell, Thomas (2008). *The Most Disreputable Trade: Publishing the Classics of English Poetry, 1765–1810* (Oxford and New York: Oxford University Press).

Booth, Wayne (1950). '"Tristram Shandy" and its Precursors: The Self-Conscious Narrator', unpublished PhD thesis, University of Chicago.

Botfield, Beriah (1849). *Notes on the Cathedral Libraries of England* (London: Charles Whittingham).

Boucé, Paul-Gabriel (1976). *The Novels of Tobias Smollett* [1971], trans. Antonia White (London: Longman).

Boulukos, George (2008). *The Grateful Slave: The Emergence of Race in Eighteenth-Century British and American Culture* (Cambridge: Cambridge University Press).

Bourdieu, Pierre (1993). *The Field of Cultural Production*, trans. Randal Johnson (New York: Columbia University Press).

Brant, Clare (2006). *Eighteenth-Century Letters and British Culture* (Basingstoke: Palgrave Macmillan).

Bratton, Jacqueline S. (1981). *The Impact of Victorian Children's Fiction* (London: Croom Helm).

Bray, Joe (2003). *The Epistolary Novel: Representation of Consciousness* (London and New York: Routledge).

Bray, Joe (2009). *The Female Reader in the English Novel, from Burney to Austen* (London: Routledge).

Bree, Linda (1996). *Sarah Fielding* (New York: Macmillan).

Bree, Linda (2010). 'Introduction', *Amelia by Henry Fielding* (Peterborough, ON: Broadview).

Brewer, John (1976). *Party Ideology and Popular Politics at the Accession of George III* (Cambridge: Cambridge University Press).

Brewer, John (1996). 'Reconstructing the Reader: Perceptions, Texts and Strategies in Anna Larpent's Reading', in James Raven, Helen Small, and Naomi Tadmor (eds), *The Practice and Representation of Reading in England* (Cambridge: Cambridge University Press), 226–45.

Brewer, John (1997). *The Pleasures of the Imagination: English Culture in the Eighteenth Century* (London: Harper Collins).

Brewer, John and Roy Porter (eds) (1994). *Consumption and the World of Goods* (New York: Routledge).

Brock, Claire (2006). *The Feminization of Fame 1750–1830* (Basingstoke: Palgrave Macmillan).

Brooks, David (2010). 'A Case for Mental Courage', *New York Times*, 23 August.

Broughton, Lord (1909–11). *Recollections of a Long Life*, ed. Lady Dorchester, 6 vols (London: John Murray).

Brown, Hilary (2005). *Benedikte Naubert (1756–1819) and her Relations to English Culture* (Leeds: Maney Publishing for the Modern Humanities Research Association and the Institute of Germanic Studies, University of London).

Brown, Homer Obed (1997). *Institutions of the English Novel: From Defoe to Scott* (Philadelphia: University of Pennsylvania Press).

Brown, Marshall (2005). *The Gothic Text* (Stanford: Stanford University Press).

Buck, Howard Swazey (1925). *A Study in Smollett: Chiefly 'Peregrine Pickle'. With a Complete Collation of the First and Second Editions* (New Haven: Yale University Press).

Burditt, Paul Francis (2005). 'The Novels of the 1750s: A Literary Investigation', unpublished DPhil thesis, University of Oxford.

Butler, Judith (1993). *Bodies that Matter: On the Discursive Limits of 'Sex'* (New York and London: Routledge).

Butler, Marilyn (1972). *Maria Edgeworth: A Literary Biography* (Oxford: Clarendon Press).

Butler, Marilyn (1975). *Jane Austen and the War of Ideas* (Oxford: Clarendon Press).

Butler, Marilyn (1979). *Peacock Displayed: A Satirist in his Context* (London, Boston, and Henley: Routledge & Kegan Paul).

Butler, Marilyn (1984). *Burke, Paine, Godwin, and the Revolution Controversy* (Cambridge: Cambridge University Press).

Butler, Marilyn (1986). 'History, Politics, and Religion', in J. David Grey (ed.), *The Jane Austen Handbook* (London: The Athlone Press), 190–208.

Butler, Marilyn (1999). 'Introductory Note', Maria Edgeworth, *Patronage*, Volumes VI and VII of *The Novels and Selected Works of Maria Edgeworth* (London: Pickering and Chatto), 6.vii–xxx.

Butler, Marilyn (2010). 'Culture's Medium: The Role of the Review', in Stuart Curran (ed.), *The Cambridge Companion to British Romanticism* (Cambridge: Cambridge University Press), 127–52.

Buzard, James (2005). *Disorienting Fiction: The Autoethnographic Work of Nineteenth-Century British Novels* (Princeton: Princeton University Press).

Carlile, Susan (ed.) (2011). *Masters of the Marketplace: British Women Novelists of the 1750s* (Bethlehem: Lehigh University Press).

Casanova, Pascale (2004). *The World Republic of Letters*, trans. M. B. DeBevoise (Cambridge, MA and London: Harvard University Press).

Cash, Arthur (2001). 'Sterne, Hall, Libertinism, and *A Sentimental Journey*', *Age of Johnson*, 12: 291–327.

Cave, Roderick (1980). 'Early Circulating Libraries in Jamaica', *Libri: International Journal of Libraries and Information Services*, 30.1: 53–65.

de Certeau, Michel (2011). 'Reading as Poaching', in Shafquat Towheed, Rosalind Crone, and Katie Halsey (eds), *The History of Reading* (London: Routledge), 130–9.

Chandler, James (1998). *England in 1819: The Politics of Literary Culture and the Case of Romantic Historicism* (Chicago: University of Chicago Press).

Chandler, James (2008). 'Placing *The Power of Sympathy*: Transatlantic Sentiments and the "First American Novel"', in Susan Manning and Francis D. Cogliano (eds), *The Atlantic Enlightenment* (Aldershot: Ashgate), 131–48.

Chandler, James (2011). 'Edgeworth and the Lunar Enlightenment', *Eighteenth-Century Studies*, 45: 87–104.

Clarke, Norma (2005). 'Bluestocking Fictions: Devotional Writings, Didactic Literature and the Imperative of Female Improvement', in Barbara Knott and Sarah Taylor (eds), *Women, Gender and Enlightenment* (Basingstoke: Palgrave Macmillan), 460–73.

Cleere, Eileen (2007). 'Homeland Security: Political and Domestic Economy in Hannah More's *Coelebs in Search of a Wife*', *ELH*, 74: 1–25.

Clery, E. J. (1995). *The Rise of Supernatural Fiction, 1762–1800* (Cambridge: Cambridge University Press).

Clery, E. J. (2004). *The Feminization Debate in Eighteenth-Century England: Literature, Commerce and Luxury* (Basingstoke: Palgrave Macmillan).

Cohen, Ralph (1986). 'History and Genre', *New Literary History*, 17.2: 203–18.

Cohen, Ralph (1991). 'Genre Theory, Literary History, and Historical Change', in David Perkins (ed.), *Theoretical Issues in Literary History* (Cambridge, MA: Harvard University Press), 85–113.

Colclough, Stephen M. (2000). 'Procuring Books and Consuming Texts: The Reading Experience of a Sheffield Apprentice', *Book History*, 3: 21–44.

Colley, Linda (1992). *Britons: Forging the Nation, 1707–1837* (New Haven: Yale University Press).

Conant, Martha Pike (1908). *The Oriental Tale in the Eighteenth Century* (New York: Columbia University Press).

Conger, Syndy McMillen (1980). 'A German Ancestor for Mary Shelley's Monster: Kahlert, Schiller, and the Buried Treasure of *Northanger Abbey*', *Philological Quarterly*, 59.2 (Spring): 216–32.

Constable, Thomas (1873). *Archibald Constable and His Literary Correspondents*, 3 vols (Edinburgh: Edmonston and Douglas).

Cook, Elizabeth Heckendorn (1996). *Epistolary Bodies: Gender and Genre in the Eighteenth-Century Republic of Letters* (Stanford: Stanford University Press).

Copeland, Edward (1995). *Women Writing About Money: Women's Fiction in England, 1790–1820* (Cambridge: Cambridge University Press).

Copeland, Edward (2001). 'Crossing Oxford Street: Silverfork Geopolitics', *Eighteenth-Century Life*, 26: 116–34.

Copeland, Edward (2009). 'Jane Austen and the Silver Fork Novel', in Claudia L. Johnson and Clara Tuite (ed.), *A Companion to Jane Austen* (Oxford: Wiley–Blackwell), 434–44.

Coulet, Henri (1987). 'Révolution et roman selon Mme de Staël', *Revue d'histoire littéraire de la France*, 4: 638–60.

Craciun, Adriana (1997). 'Introduction', *Zofloya; or, the Moor* (Peterborough, ON: Broadview Press), 9–32.

Craciun, Adriana (2005). *British Women Writers and the French Revolution: Citizens of the World* (Basingstoke: Palgrave Macmillan).

Crawford, Robert (1992). *Devolving English Literature* (Oxford: Clarendon Press).

Crompton, Louis (1985). *Byron and Greek Love: Homophobia in 19th-Century England* (Berkeley: University of California Press).

Cronin, Richard (2009). *Paper Pellets: British Literary Culture after Waterloo* (Oxford: Oxford University Press).

Cross, Nigel (1985). *The Common Writer: Life in Nineteenth-Century Grub Street* (Cambridge: Cambridge University Press).

Damrosch, David (2003). *What Is World Literature?* (Princeton: Princeton University Press).

Darnton, Robert (2001). 'Readers Respond to Rousseau: The Fabrication of Romantic Sensitivity', in his *The Great Cat Massacre* (Harmondsworth: Penguin), 215–56.

Davies, Andrew (2001). '"The Reputed Nation of Inspiration": Representations of Wales in Fiction from the Romantic Period, 1780–1829', unpublished PhD thesis, Cardiff University.

Davis, Leith (1998). *Acts of Union: Scotland and the Literary Negotiation of the British Nation, 1707–1830* (Stanford: Stanford University Press).

Deane, Seamus (1988). *The French Revolution and Enlightenment England, 1789–1832* (Cambridge, MA: Harvard University Press).

Deane, Seamus (2006). 'Foreword', in Rolf Loeber and Magda Stouthamer-Loeber, with Ann Mullin Burneham, *A Guide to Irish Fiction, 1650–1900* (Dublin: Four Courts Press), xvii–xxii.

Dearnley, Moira (2001). *Distant Fields: Eighteenth-Century Fictions of Wales* (Cardiff: University of Wales Press).

Deazley, Ronan (2004). *On the Origin of the Right to Copy: Charting the Movement of Copyright Law in Eighteenth-Century Britain (1695–1775)* (Oxford: Hart Publishing).

Dekker, George (1967). *James Fenimore Cooper, the American Scott* (New York: Barnes and Noble).

Demers, Patricia (1996). *The World of Hannah More* (Lexington, KY: University Press of Kentucky).

Dennis, Ian (1997). *Nationalism and Desire in Early Historical Fiction* (Basingstoke: Macmillan).

Dickie, Simon (2010). 'Fielding's Rape Jokes', *Review of English Studies*, 61.251: 572–90.

Dickie, Simon (2011). *Cruelty and Laughter: Forgotten Comic Literature and the Unsentimental Eighteenth Century* (Chicago: University of Chicago Press).

Donaldson, Ian (1970). 'The Clockwork Novel: Three Notes on an Eighteenth-Century Analogy', *Review of English Studies*, n.s., 21.81: 14–22.

Doody, Margaret Anne (1996). *The True Story of the Novel* (Rutgers: Rutgers University Press).

Doody, Margaret Anne (1997). 'The Short Fiction', in Edward Copeland and Juliet McMaster (eds), *The Cambridge Companion to Jane Austen* (Cambridge: Cambridge University Press), 84–99.

Doody, Margaret Anne (2007). 'Burney and Politics', in Peter Sabor (ed.), *The Cambridge Companion to Frances Burney* (Cambridge: Cambridge University Press), 93–110.

Duncan, Ian (1992). *Modern Romance and Transformations of the Novel: The Gothic, Scott, Dickens* (Cambridge: Cambridge University Press).

Duncan, Ian (2007). *Scott's Shadow: The Novel in Romantic Edinburgh* (Princeton: Princeton University Press).

During, Simon (2002). *Modern Enchantments: The Cultural Power of Secular Magic* (Cambridge, MA: Harvard University Press).

Dyer, Richard (1992). 'Coming to Terms: Gay Pornography', in his *Only Entertainment* (London: Routledge), 121–34.

Eaves, T. C. Duncan and Ben D. Kimpel (1971). *Samuel Richardson: A Biography* (Oxford: Clarendon Press).

Ellis, Markman (1996). *The Politics of Sensibility: Race, Gender and Commerce in the Sentimental Novel* (Cambridge: Cambridge University Press).

Ellison, Julie (1999). *Cato's Tears and the Making of Anglo-American Emotion* (Chicago: University of Chicago Press).

English, James F. and John Frow (2006). 'Literary Authorship and Celebrity Culture', in James F. English (ed.), *A Concise Companion to Contemporary British Fiction* (Malden, MA: Blackwell), 39–57.

Epstein, Julia (1989). *The Iron Pen: Frances Burney and the Politics of Women's Writing* (Madison: University of Wisconsin Press).

Erämetsä, Erik (1951). *A Study of the Word 'Sentimental' and of Other Linguistic Characteristics of Eighteenth Century Sentimentalism in England* (Helsinki: Academia Scientiarum Fennica).

Erickson, Amy Louise (2005). 'Couverture and Capitalism', *History Workshop Journal*, 59 (Spring): 1–16.

Favret, Mary (1993). *Romantic Correspondence: Women, Politics, and the Fiction of Letters* (Cambridge: Cambridge University Press).

Favret, Mary (2010). *War at a Distance: Romanticism and the Making of Modern Wartime* (Princeton: Princeton University Press).

Fergus, Jan (1984). 'Eighteenth-Century Readers in Provincial England: The Customers of Samuel Clay's Circulating Library and Bookshop in Warwick, 1770–72', *Papers of the Bibliographical Society of America*, 78: 155–213.

Fergus, Jan (1986). 'Women, Class, and the Growth of Magazine Readership in the Provinces 1746–1780', *Studies in Eighteenth-Century Culture*, 16: 41–56.

Fergus, Jan (1991). *Jane Austen: A Literary Life* (Basingstoke: Macmillan).

Fergus, Jan (1996). 'Provincial Servants' Reading in the Late Eighteenth Century', in James Raven, Helen Small, and Naomi Tadmore (eds), *The Practice and Representation of Reading in England* (Cambridge: Cambridge University Press), 202–25.

Fergus, Jan (2006). *Provincial Readers in Eighteenth-Century England* (Oxford: Oxford University Press).

Fergus, Jan (2007). 'Laetitia-Matilda Hawkins's Anonymous Novels Identified', *Notes & Queries*, 54.2 (June): 152–6.

Fergus, Jan and Janice F. Thaddeus (1988). 'Women, Publishers, and Money, 1790–1820', *Studies in Eighteenth-Century Culture*, 17: 191–207.

Ferris, Ina (1991). *The Achievement of Literary Authority: Gender, History, and the Waverley Novels* (Ithaca and London: Cornell University Press).

Ferris, Ina (2002). *The Romantic National Tale and the Question of Ireland* (Cambridge: Cambridge University Press).

Ferris, Ina (2008a). 'Scholarly Revivals: Gothic Fiction, Secret History, and Hogg's *Private Memoirs and Confessions of a Justified Sinner*', in Jillian Heydt-Stevenson and Charlotte Sussman (eds), *Recognizing the Romantic Novel: New Histories of British Fiction, 1780–1830* (Liverpool: Liverpool University Press), 267–84.

Ferris, Ina (2008b). 'The Irish Novel, 1800–1829', in Richard Maxwell and Katie Trumpener (eds), *The Cambridge Companion to Fiction in the Romantic Period* (Cambridge: Cambridge University Press), 235–50.

Ferris, Ina (2009a). '"On the Borders of Oblivion": Scott's Historical Novel and the Modern Time of the Remnant', *Modern Language Quarterly*, 70.4: 473–94.

Ferris, Ina (2009b). 'Transformations of the Novel—II', in James Chandler (ed.), *The Cambridge History of English Romantic Literature* (Cambridge: Cambridge University Press), 473–89.

Findlen, Paula (2009). 'Anatomy of a Lesbian: Medicine, Pornography, and Culture in Eighteenth-Century Italy', in Paula Findlen, Wendy Wassyng Roworth, and Catherine M. Sama (eds), *Italy's Eighteenth Century: Gender and Culture in the Age of the Grand Tour* (Stanford: Stanford University Press), 219–50.

Flanders, W. A. (1975). 'The Significance of Smollett's *Memoirs of a Lady of Quality*', *Genre*, 8: 146–64.

Frank, Frederick S. (1987). *The First Gothics: A Critical Guide to the English Gothic Novel* (New York: Garland Publishing).

Franklin, Michael J. (ed.) (2007). 'Introduction', *Hartly House, Calcutta* by Phebe Gibbes (Delhi and Oxford: Oxford University Press), xi–lvii.

Fry, Carroll Lee (1980). *Charlotte Smith: Popular Novelist* (New York: Arno Press).

Frye, Northrop (1956). 'Towards Defining an Age of Sensibility', *ELH*, 23.2 (June): 144–52.

Gallagher, Catherine (1994). *Nobody's Story: The Vanishing Acts of Women Writers in the Marketplace, 1670–1820* (Berkeley: University of California Press).

Gallagher, Catherine (2006). 'The Rise of Fictionality', in Franco Moretti (ed.), *The Novel*, 2 vols (Princeton: Princeton University Press), 1.336–63.

Galperin, William (2003). *The Historical Austen* (Philadelphia: University of Pennsylvania Press).

Gamer, Michael (2000). *Romanticism and the Gothic: Genre, Reception and Canon Formation* (Cambridge: Cambridge University Press).

Gamer, Michael (2001). 'Maria Edgeworth and the Romance of Real Life', *Novel*, 34.2: 232–66.

Gamer, Michael (2008). 'A Select Collection: Barbauld, Scott, and the Rise of the (Reprinted) Novel', in Jillian Heydt-Stevenson and Charlotte Sussman (eds), *Recognizing the Romantic Novel: New Histories of British Fiction, 1780–1830* (Liverpool: Liverpool University Press), 155–91.

Garside, Peter (1987). 'J. F. Hughes and the Publication of Popular Fiction, 1803–1810', *The Library*, 6th ser., 9: 240–58.

Garside, Peter (1991). 'Popular Fiction and National Tale: Hidden Origins of Scott's *Waverley*', *Nineteenth-Century Literature*, 46: 30–53.

Garside, Peter (1998). 'Mrs Ross and Elizabeth B. Lester: New Attributions', *Cardiff Corvey: Reading the Romantic Text*, 2. Available online at <www.cardiff.ac.uk/encap/journals/corvey/articles/cc02_n02.html>.

Garside, Peter (1999). 'Walter Scott and the "Common Novel", 1808–1819', *Cardiff Corvey: Reading the Romantic Text*, 3. Available online at <www.cf.ac.uk/encap/romtext/articles/cc03_n02.html>.

Garside, Peter (2000). 'The English Novel in the Romantic Era: Consolidation and Dispersal', in Peter Garside, James Raven, and Rainer Schöwerling (eds), *The English Novel 1770–1829: A Bibliographical Survey of Prose Fiction Published in the British Isles* (Oxford: Oxford University Press), 2.15–103.

Garside, Peter (2004). 'Hogg and the Blackwoodian Novel', *Studies in Hogg and his World*, 15: 5–20.

Garside, Peter et al. (2004). *British Fiction 1800–1829: A Database of Production, Circulation & Reception*. Available online at <www.british-fiction.cf.ac.uk>.

Garside, Peter, James Raven, and Rainer Schöwerling (2000). *The English Novel 1770–1829: A Bibliographical Survey of Prose Fiction Published in the British Isles*. James Raven, Antonia Forster, with Stephen Bending (eds), *Volume 1: 1770–1799*; Peter Garside, Rainer Schöwerling, with Christopher Skelton-Foord and Karin Wünsche (eds), *Volume 2: 1800–1829* (Oxford: Oxford University Press).

Gilmartin, Kevin (2007). *Writing against Revolution: Literary Conservatism in Britain, 1790–1832* (Cambridge: Cambridge University Press).

Gilmartin, Kevin (2008). 'Romanticism and Religious Modernity: From Natural Supernaturalism to Literary Sectarianism', in James Chandler (ed.), *The Cambridge History of English Romantic Literature* (Cambridge: Cambridge University Press), 621–47.

Grant, James (1836). *The Great Metropolis*, 2 vols (London: Saunders and Otley).

Green, James N. (2000). 'English Books and Printing in the Age of Franklin', in Hugh Amory and David H. Hall (eds), *The Colonial Book in the Atlantic World* (Cambridge: Cambridge University Press), 248–98.

Greenfield, Susan C. (2004). 'Money or Mind? *Cecilia*, the Novel, and the Real Madness of Selfhood', *Studies in Eighteenth-Century Culture*, 33: 49–70.

Grenby, M. O. (2001). *The Anti-Jacobin Novel: British Conservatism and the French Revolution* (Cambridge: Cambridge University Press).

Grenby, M. O. (2011). *The Child Reader, 1700–1840* (Cambridge: Cambridge University Press).

Grieder, Josephine (1975). *Translations of French Sentimental Prose Fiction in Late Eighteenth-Century England: The History of a Literary Vogue* (Durham, NC: Duke University Press).

Grossman, Joyce (2001). 'Social Protest and the Mid-Century Novel: Mary Collyer's *The History of Betty Barnes*', in Linda Troost (ed.), *Eighteenth-Century Women* (New York: AMS Press), 1.165–84.

Guest, Harriet (2000). *Small Change: Women, Learning, Patriotism, 1750–1810* (Chicago and London: University of Chicago Press).

Haldane, Elizabeth Sanderson (2004). *George Eliot and Her Times: A Victorian Study* (Kila, MT: Kessinger Publishing Co.).

Hale, Terry (2002). 'French and German Gothic: The Beginnings', in Jerrold E. Hogle (ed.), *The Cambridge Companion to Gothic Fiction* (Cambridge: Cambridge University Press), 63–84.

Hall, David D. (1996). 'The Uses of Literacy in New England, 1600–1850', in his *Cultures of Print: Essays in the History of the Book* (Amherst: University of Massachusetts Press), 36–78.

Halsey, Katie (2011). *Jane Austen and Her Readers* (London: Anthem).

Haslam, Richard (1987). 'Lady Morgan's Novels from 1806 to 1833: Cultural Aesthetics and National Identity', *Eire-Ireland*, 22.4: 11–25.

Heilman, Robert Bechtold (1937). *America in English Fiction 1760–1800* (Baton Rouge, LA: Louisiana State University Press).

Hill, Bridget (1994). 'Catherine Hutton (1756–1846): A Forgotten Letter-Writer', *Women's Writing*, 1.1: 35–50.

Hilton, Boyd (1988). *The Age of Atonement: The Influence of Evangelicalism on Social and Economic Thought, 1795–1865* (Oxford: Clarendon Press).

Hilton, Boyd (2006). *A Mad, Bad, & Dangerous People? England 1783–1846* (New York: Oxford University Press).

Hofkosh, Sonia (2009). 'The Illusionist: *Northanger Abbey* and Austen's Uses of Enchantment', in Claudia L. Johnson and Clara Tuite (eds), *A Companion to Jane Austen* (Malden, MA and Oxford: Wiley–Blackwell), 101–11.

Holland, Norman and Leona Sherman (1977). 'Gothic Possibilities', *New Literary History*, 8.2: 279–94.

Howes, Alan B. (ed.) (1974). *Sterne: The Critical Heritage* (London: Routledge and Kegan Paul).

Hudson, Nicholas (2007). 'It-Narratives: Fictional Point of View and Constructing the Middle Class', in Mark Blackwell (ed.), *The Secret Life of Things: Animals, Objects, and It-Narratives in Eighteenth-Century England* (Lewisburg, PA: Bucknell University Press), 292–308.

Hudson, Nicholas (2008). 'Introduction', *The History of Pompey the Little*, ed. Nicholas Hudson (Peterborough, ON: Broadview Press), 7–26.

Hughes, Felicity A. (1978). 'Children's Literature: Theory and Practice', *ELH*, 45: 542–61.

Hunt, Arnold (2001). 'The Sale of Richard Heber's Library', in Robin Myers, Michael Harris, and Giles Mandelbrote (eds), *Under the Hammer: Book Auctions Since the Seventeenth Century* (New Castle, DE and London: Oak Knoll Press and The British Library), 143–72.

Hunt, Lynn (1993). 'Introduction: Obscenity and the Origins of Modernity, 1500–1800', in Lynn Hunt (ed.), *The Invention of Pornography: Obscenity and the Origins of Modernity* (New York: Zone Books), 9–45.

Hunt, Lynn (2007). *Inventing Human Rights: A History* (New York: W. W. Norton).

Hunter, J. Paul (1990). *Before Novels: The Cultural Contexts of Eighteenth-Century English Fiction* (New York: W. W. Norton).

Idman, Nilo (1923). *Charles Robert Maturin: His Life and Works* (London: Constable).

Irwin, Raymond (1958). *The Origins of the English Library* (London: Allen & Unwin).

Jackson, Alvin (2005). 'The Survival of the Union', in Claire Connolly and Joe Cleary (eds), *The Cambridge Companion to Modern Irish Culture* (Cambridge: Cambridge University Press), 25–41.

Jackson, H. J. (2001). *Marginalia: Readers Writing in Books* (New Haven: Yale University Press).

Jackson, H. J. (2005). *Romantic Readers: The Evidence of Marginalia* (New Haven: Yale University Press).

Jacob, Margaret C. (1993). 'The Materialist World of Pornography', in Lynn Hunt (ed.), *The Invention of Pornography: Obscenity and the Origins of Modernity* (New York: Zone Books), 157–202.

Jefcoate, Graham (1987). 'The Deutsche Lese-Bibliothek and the Distribution of German Books in London 1794–1800', *The Library*, 6th ser., 9: 347–64.

Jefcoate, Graham (2002). 'German Printing and Bookselling in Eighteenth-Century London: Evidence and Interpretation', in Barry Taylor (ed.), *Foreign-Language Printing in London 1500–1900* (Boston Spa and London: British Library), 1–36.

Jefferson, D. W. (1951). '*Tristram Shandy* and the Tradition of Learned Wit', *Essays in Criticism*, 1.3: 225–48.

Johnson, Claudia (2001). '"Let Me Make the Novels of a Country": Barbauld's *The British Novelists* (1810/1820)', *Novel*, 34.2: 163–79.

Johnson, Rebecca Carol, Richard Maxwell, and Katie Trumpener (2007). '*The Arabian Nights*, Arab-European Literary Influence, and the Lineages of the Novel', *Modern Language Quarterly*, 68.2: 243–79.

Johnson, Steven (1996). 'Strange Attraction', *Lingua Franca*, 6.3 (March/April): 42–50.

Jones, Vivien (2002). 'Introduction', *Evelina, or the History of a Young Lady's Entrance into the World by Frances Burney*, ed. Edward A. Bloom (Oxford: Oxford University Press, 2002), ix–xxxiv.

Jones, Vivien (2010). 'Post-Feminist Austen', *Critical Quarterly*, 62.4: 65–82.

Justice, George (2002). *The Manufacturers of Literature: Writing and the Literary Marketplace in Eighteenth-Century England* (London: Associated University Presses).

Kafer, Peter (2004). *Charles Brockden Brown's Revolution and the Birth of the American Gothic* (Philadelphia: University of Pennsylvania Press).

Kaplan, Deborah (1992). *Jane Austen Among Women* (Baltimore and London: Johns Hopkins University Press).

Kaufman, Paul (1960). 'Coleridge's Use of Cathedral Libraries', *Modern Language Notes*, 75: 395–9.

Kaufman, Paul (1967). 'The Community Library: A Chapter in English Social History', *Transactions of the American Philosophical Society*, 57.7: 3–67.

Kaufman, Paul (1969a). *Libraries and Their Users* (London: The Library Association).

Kaufman, Paul (1969b). 'The Reading of Plays in the Eighteenth Century', *Bulletin of the New York Public Library*, 73: 562–80.

Kaufman, Paul (1973). 'Readers and Their Reading in Eighteenth-Century Lichfield', *The Library*, 5th ser., 28: 108–15.

Keener, Frederick (1983). *The Chain of Becoming. The Philosophical Tale, the Novel, and a Neglected Realism of the Enlightenment: Swift, Montesquieu, Voltaire, Johnson, and Austen* (New York: Columbia University Press).

Kelly, Gary (1976). *The English Jacobin Novel 1780–1805* (Oxford: Oxford University Press).

Kelly, Gary (1989). *English Fiction of the Romantic Period, 1789–1830* (London and New York: Longmans).

Kelly, Gary (1990). 'Romantic Evangelicalism: Religion, Social Conflict, and Literary Form in Legh Richmond's *Annals of the Poor*', *English Studies in Canada*, 16.2: 165–8.

Kerrigan, John (2008). *Archipelagic English: Literature, History, and Politics 1603–1707* (Oxford: Oxford University Press).

Keymer, Thomas (1992). *Richardson's Clarissa and the Eighteenth-Century Reader* (Cambridge: Cambridge University Press).

Keymer, Thomas (1994). 'Clarissa's Death, *Clarissa*'s Sale, and the Text of the Second Edition', *Review of English Studies*, 45.179: 389–408.

Keymer, Thomas (2002). *Sterne, the Moderns, and the Novel* (Oxford: Oxford University Press).

Keymer, Thomas (2005). 'Sentimental Fiction: Ethics, Social Critique and Philanthropy', in John Richetti (ed.), *The Cambridge History of English Literature, 1660–1780* (Cambridge: Cambridge University Press), 572–601.

Keymer, Thomas and Peter Sabor (2005). *'Pamela' in the Marketplace: Literary Controversy and Print Culture in Eighteenth-Century Britain and Ireland* (Cambridge: Cambridge University Press).

Kidd, Colin (1993). *Subverting Scotland's Past: Scottish Whig Historians and the Creation of an Anglo-British Identity, 1689–c.1830* (Cambridge: Cambridge University Press).

Kiernan, V. (1952). 'Evangelicalism and the French Revolution', *Past and Present*, 1: 44–56.

Killick, Tim (2008). *British Short Fiction in the Early Nineteenth Century: The Rise of the Tale* (Aldershot: Ashgate).

Kinealy, Christine (1999). *A Disunited Kingdom? England, Ireland, Scotland and Wales, 1800–1949* (Cambridge: Cambridge University Press).

Klein, Lawrence E. (1995). 'Gender and the Public/Private Distinction in the Eighteenth Century: Some Questions about Evidence and Analytic Procedure', *Eighteenth-Century Studies*, 29: 97–109.

Knapp, Lewis Mansfield (1949). *Tobias Smollett: Doctor of Men and Manners* (Princeton: Princeton University Press).

Knott, Sarah (2009). *Sensibility and the American Revolution* (Chapel Hill, NC: University of North Carolina Press).

Kriz, Kay Dian (2008). 'The Physiognomy and Pathology of "Black Humor": Caricature and the West Indies on the Eve of Abolition', in her *Slavery, Sugar, and the Culture of Refinement: Picturing the British West Indies, 1700–1840* (New Haven and London: Yale University Press), 71–115.

Kroeber, A. L. (1964). 'Diffusionism', in Eva Etzioni and Amitai Etzioni (eds), *Social Change: Sources, Patterns, and Consequences* (New York: Basic Books), 142–6.

Le Faye, Deirdre (2004). *Jane Austen: A Family Record*, 2nd edn (Cambridge: Cambridge University Press).

Leask, Nigel (1992). *British Romantic Writers and the East: Anxieties of Empire* (Cambridge: Cambridge University Press).

Letellier, Robert Ignatius (2002). *The English Novel 1700–1740: An Annotated Bibliography* (Westport, CT: Greenwood Press).

Levy, Michelle (2006). 'The Radical Education of *Evenings at Home*', *Eighteenth-Century Fiction*, 19: 123–50.

Little, Anthony J. (1976). *Deceleration in the Eighteenth-Century British Economy* (London: Croom Helm).

London, April (1999). *Women and Property in the Eighteenth-Century Novel* (Cambridge: Cambridge University Press).

London, April (2010). *Literary History Writing, 1770–1820* (Basingstoke: Palgrave Macmillan).

Lukács, György (1983). *The Historical Novel*, trans. H. and S. Mitchell (Lincoln: University of Nebraska Press).

Lynch, Deidre (1996). 'At Home with Jane Austen', in Deidre Lynch and William B. Warner (eds), *Cultural Institutions of the Novel* (Durham, NC: Duke University Press), 159–92.

Lynch, Deidre (1998). *The Economy of Character: Novels, Market Culture and the Business of Inner Meaning* (Chicago: University of Chicago Press).

Lynch, Deidre (2009). 'Canons' Clockwork: Novels for Everyday Use', in Ina Ferris and Paul Keen (eds), *Bookish Histories: Books, Literature and Commercial Modernity, 1700–1900* (Basingstoke: Palgrave Macmillan), 87–110.

Lynch, Deidre and William B. Warner (eds) (1996). *Cultural Institutions of the Novel* (Durham, NC: Duke University Press).

McBurney, W. H. (1960). *A Check List of English Prose Fiction, 1700–1739* (Cambridge, MA: Harvard University Press).

McCalman, Iain (1998). *Radical Underworld: Prophets, Revolutionaries, and Pornographers in London, 1795–1840* (Oxford: Clarendon Press).

McCalman, Iain (1999). 'Pornography', in Iain McCalman (ed.), *An Oxford Companion to the Romantic Age: British Culture 1776–1832* (Oxford: Oxford University Press), 655–6.

MacDonagh, Oliver (1988). *The Hereditary Bondsman: Daniel O'Connell, 1775–1829* (London: Weidenfeld and Nicolson).

Macdonald, Gina and Andrew F. Macdonald (eds) (2003). *Jane Austen on Screen* (Cambridge: Cambridge University Press).

Macdonald, Simon (2013). 'Identifying Mrs Meeke: Another Burney Family Novelist', *Review of English Studies*, 64.265: 367–85.

McKeon, Michael (1987). *The Origins of the English Novel 1600–1740* (Baltimore: Johns Hopkins University Press).

McKillop, Alan Dugald (1956). *The Early Masters of English Fiction* (Lawrence: University of Kansas Press).

McLynn, Frank (1991). *Charles Edward Stuart: A Tragedy in Many Acts* (Oxford: Oxford University Press).

McMurran, Mary Helen (2002). 'National or Transnational? The Eighteenth-Century Novel', in Margaret Cohen and Carolyn Dever (eds), *The Literary Channel* (Princeton: Princeton University Press), 50–72.

McMurran, Mary Helen (2010). *The Spread of Novels: Translation and Prose Fiction in the Eighteenth Century* (Princeton: Princeton University Press).

Mack, Douglas S. (2006). *Scottish Fiction and the British Empire* (Edinburgh: Edinburgh University Press).

Makdisi, Saree (1998). *Romantic Imperialism: Universal Empire and the Culture of Modernity* (Cambridge: Cambridge University Press).

Mandal, Anthony (2007). *Jane Austen and the Popular Novel: The Determined Author* (Basingstoke: Palgrave Macmillan).

Mandal, Anthony (2009). 'Austen's European Reception', in Claudia L. Johnson and Clara Tuite (eds), *A Companion to Jane Austen* (Oxford: Blackwell), 422–33.

Mandal, Anthony and Brian Southam (2007). *The Reception of Jane Austen in Europe* (London: Continuum).

Marshall, David (2005). *The Frame of Art: Fictions of Aesthetic Experience, 1750–1815* (Baltimore: Johns Hopkins University Press).

Marx, Karl (1906). *Capital*, trans. Samuel Moore and Edward Aveling (New York: Random House).

Maxwell, Richard (2002). 'Phantom States: *Cleveland*, *The Recess*, and the Origins of Historical Fiction', in Margaret Cohen and Carolyn Dever (eds), *The Literary Channel* (Princeton: Princeton University Press), 151–82.

Maxwell, Richard (2008). 'The Historical Novel', in Richard Maxwell and Katie Trumpener (eds), *The Cambridge Companion to Fiction in the Romantic Period* (Cambridge: Cambridge University Press), 65–88.

Maxwell, Richard (2009). *The Historical Novel in Europe, 1650–1950* (Cambridge: Cambridge University Press).

Mayer, Robert (1997). *History and the Early English Novel: Matters of Fact from Bacon to Defoe* (Cambridge: Cambridge University Press).

Mayo, Robert D. (1962). *The English Novel in the Magazines, 1740–1815* (Evanston, IL: Northwestern University Press).

Mee, Jon (2003). *Romance, Enthusiasm, and Regulation: Poetics and the Policing of Culture in the Romantic Period* (Oxford: Oxford University Press).

Millgate, Jane (1985). *Walter Scott: The Making of the Novelist* (Edinburgh: Edinburgh University Press).

Millgate, Jane (1987). *Scott's Last Edition: A Study in Publishing History* (Edinburgh: Edinburgh University Press).

Moers, Ellen (1976). *Literary Women* (New York: Doubleday).

Mole, Tom (2007). *Byron's Romantic Celebrity: Industrial Culture and the Hermeneutic of Intimacy* (Basingstoke: Palgrave Macmillan).

Moretti, Franco (1998). *Atlas of the European Novel, 1800–1900* (London: Verso).

Moretti, Franco (2000). 'Conjectures on World Literature', *New Left Review*, 1: 54–68.

Moretti, Franco (2003). 'Graphs, Maps, Trees—1', *New Left Review*, 24: 67–93.

Moretti, Franco (2005). *Graphs, Maps, Trees: Abstract Models for a Literary History* (London: Verso).

Morison, Stanley (1930). *John Bell, 1745–1831* (Cambridge: Printed for the Author).

Morrison, Robert and Chris Baldick (1995). 'Introduction', *Tales of Terror from Blackwood's Magazine* (Oxford: Oxford University Press), vii–xviii.

Mullan, John (1988). *Sentiment and Sociability: The Language of Feeling in the Eighteenth Century* (Oxford: Clarendon Press).

Mullan, John (2007). *Anonymity: A Secret History of English Literature* (London: Faber and Faber).

Neiman, Elizabeth (2012). 'The Female Authors of the Minerva Press and "Copper Currency": Revaluing the Reproduction of the "Immaculate-Born Minervas"', in Michael Rotenberg-Schwartz with Tara Czechowski (eds), *Global Economies: Cultural Currencies of the Eighteenth Century* (New York: AMS Press), 275–94.

Nelson, Claudia (2008). 'Adult Children's Literature in Victorian Britain', in Dennis Denisoff (ed.), *The Nineteenth-Century Child and Consumer Culture* (Aldershot: Ashgate), 137–49.

Nersessian, Anahid J. (2011). 'Romantic Liberalism and the Juridical Comedy: Robert Bage's *Hermsprong*', *Studies in Romanticism*, 50.4 (Winter): 639–59.

Newlyn, Lucy (2000). *Reading, Writing and Romanticism: The Anxiety of Reception* (Oxford: Oxford University Press).

Nicoll, Allardyce (1955). *A History of English Drama 1660–1900*, Volume IV: *Early Nineteenth Century Drama 1800–1850* (Cambridge: Cambridge University Press).

Nixon, Cheryl L. (ed.) (2009). *Novel Definitions: An Anthology of Commentary on the Novel 1688–1815* (Peterborough, ON: Broadview Press).

Norton, Rictor (1998). *Mistress of Udolpho: The Life of Ann Radcliffe* (Leicester: Leicester University Press).

O'Brien, Karen (2005a). 'History and Literature 1660–1780', in John Richetti (ed.), *The Cambridge History of English Literature, 1660–1780* (Cambridge: Cambridge University Press), 365–90.

O'Brien, Karen (2005b). 'History and the Novel in Eighteenth-Century Britain', *Huntington Library Quarterly*, 68.1–2: 397–413.

O'Brien, Karen (2009). *Women and Enlightenment in Eighteenth-Century Britain* (Cambridge: Cambridge University Press).

O'Connell, Helen (2006). *Ireland and the Fiction of Improvement* (Oxford: Oxford University Press).

Ó Gallchoir, Clíona (2005). *Maria Edgeworth: Women, Enlightenment and Nation* (Dublin: University College Dublin Press).

Orians, G. Harrison (1937). 'Censure of Fiction in American Romances and Magazines, 1798–1810', *PMLA* 52.1 (March): 195–214.

Otto, Peter (2011). *Multiplying Worlds: Romanticism, Modernity, and the Emergence of Virtual Reality* (Oxford: Oxford University Press).

Parsons, Nicola (2009). *Reading Gossip in Early Eighteenth-Century England* (Basingstoke: Palgrave Macmillan).

Paulson, Ronald (1967). *Satire and the Novel in Eighteenth-Century England* (New Haven: Yale University Press).

Paulson, Ronald (1975). *Emblem and Expression: Meaning in English Art of the Eighteenth Century* (London: Thames & Hudson).

Paulson, Ronald and Thomas Lockwood (eds) (1969). *Henry Fielding: The Critical Heritage* (London: Routledge and Kegan Paul).

Pearson, Jacqueline (1999). *Women's Reading in Britain, 1750–1835* (Cambridge: Cambridge University Press).

Pearson, Roger (1993). *The Fables of Reason: A Study of Voltaire's 'Contes Philosophiques'* (Oxford: Oxford University Press).

Pederson, Susan (1986). 'Hannah More Meets Simple Simon: Tracts, Chapbooks, and Popular Culture in Late Eighteenth-Century England', *Journal of British Studies*, 25.1: 84–113.

Perkins, Pam (2010). *Women Writers in the Edinburgh Enlightenment* (Amsterdam and New York: Rodopi).

Perry, Ruth (1999). 'Clarissa's Daughters; Or, The History of Innocence Betrayed', in Carol Houlihan Flynn and Edward Copeland (eds), *Clarissa and Her Readers: New Essays for the Clarissa Project* (New York: AMS Press), 119–41.

Perry, Ruth (2004). *Novel Relations: The Transformation of Kinship in English Literature and Culture, 1748–1818* (Cambridge: Cambridge University Press).

Phillips, Mark Salber (2000). *Society and Sentiment: Genres of Historical Writing in Britain, 1740–1820* (Princeton: Princeton University Press).

Pickering, Jr, Sam (1974). 'Evangelical Readers and the Phenomenal Success of Walter Scott's First Novels', *Christian Scholar's Review*, 3: 345–9.

Pinkus, Philip (1968). *Grub Street Stripped Bare* (Connecticut: Archon Books).

Pittock, Murray G. H. (ed.) (2006). *The Reception of Sir Walter Scott in Europe* (London: Continuum).

Pittock, Murray G. H. (2008). *Scottish and Irish Romanticism* (Oxford: Oxford University Press).

Pocock, J. G. A. (1975). *The Machiavellian Moment: Florentine Political Thought and the Atlantic Republican Tradition* (Princeton: Princeton University Press).

Poovey, Mary (1984). *The Proper Lady and the Woman Writer: Ideology as Style in the Works of Mary Wollstonecraft, Mary Shelley, and Jane Austen* (Chicago: University of Chicago Press).

Poovey, Mary (1998). *A History of Modern Fact: Problems of Knowledge in the Sciences of Wealth and Society* (Chicago: University of Chicago Press).

Poovey, Mary (2008). *Genres of the Credit Economy: Mediating Value in Eighteenth- and Nineteenth-Century Britain* (Chicago: University of Chicago Press).

Potter, Franz J. (2005). *The History of Gothic Publishing, 1800–1835: Exhuming the Trade* (Basingstoke and New York: Palgrave Macmillan).

Prescott, Sarah (2008). *Eighteenth-Century Writing from Wales: Bards and Britons* (Cardiff: University of Wales Press, 2008).

Price, Fiona (2002). 'Democratizing Taste: Scottish Common Sense Philosophy and Elizabeth Hamilton', *Romanticism: The Journal of Romantic Culture and Criticism*, 8: 179–96.

Price, Leah (2000). *The Anthology and the Rise of the Novel: From Richardson to George Eliot* (Cambridge: Cambridge University Press).

Prince, Michael B. (2005). 'A Preliminary Discourse on Philosophy and Literature', in John Richetti (ed.), *The Cambridge History of English Literature, 1660–1789* (Cambridge: Cambridge University Press), 391–422.

Punter, David (1980). *The Literature of Terror: A History of Gothic Fictions from 1765 to the Present Day* (New York: Longmans).

Putney, Rufus (1945). 'The Plan of *Peregrine Pickle*', *PMLA*, 40: 1051–65.

Raven, James (1987). *British Fiction 1750–1770: A Chronological Check-List of Prose Fiction Printed in Britain and Ireland* (Newark: University of Delaware Press).

Raven, James (1992). *Judging New Wealth: Popular Publishing and Responses to Commerce in England, 1750–1800* (Oxford: Clarendon Press).

Raven, James (1996). 'From Promotion to Prescription: Arrangements for Reading and Eighteenth-Century Libraries' in James Raven, Helen Small, and Naomi Tadmor (eds), *The Practice and Representation of Reading in England* (Cambridge: Cambridge University Press), 175–201.

Raven, James (1997). 'The Export of Books to Colonial North America', *Publishing History*, 42: 21–49.

Raven, James (2000). 'Historical Introduction: The Novel Comes of Age', in Peter Garside, James Raven, and Rainer Schöwerling (eds), *English Novel 1770–1829: A Bibliographical Survey of Prose Fiction Published in the British Isles* (Oxford: Oxford University Press), 1.15–121.

Raven, James (2001). 'The Book Trades', in Isabel Rivers (ed.), *Books and Their Readers: New Essays* (Leicester: Leicester University Press), 1–34.

Raven, James (2002a). 'An Antidote to the French? English Novels in German Translation and German Novels in English Translation', *Eighteenth-Century Fiction*, 14.3–4: 715–34.

Raven, James (2002b). *London Booksellers and American Customers: Transatlantic Literary Community and the Charleston Library Society, 1748–1811* (Columbia, SC: University of South Carolina Press).

Raven, James (2003). 'The Anonymous Novel in Britain and Ireland, 1750–1830', in Robert J. Griffin (ed.), *The Faces of Anonymity: Anonymous and Pseudonymous Publication from the Sixteenth to the Twentieth Century* (Basingstoke: Palgrave Macmillan), 141–65.

Raven, James (2007a). *The Business of Books: Booksellers and the English Book Trade* (New Haven: Yale University Press).

Raven, James (2007b). 'The Material Contours of the English Novel', in Jenny Mander (ed.), *Remapping the Rise of the European Novel* (Oxford: Voltaire Foundation), 101–25.

Raven, James (2009). 'The Book as Commodity', in Michael F. Suarez, SJ, and Michael Turner (eds), *The Cambridge History of the Book in Britain*, Volume V: *1695–1830* (Cambridge: Cambridge University Press), 85–117.

Rees, Thomas and John Britton (1896). *Reminiscences of Literary London from 1779 to 1853* (London: Suckling and Galloway).

Reiman, Donald (1979). 'Introduction', *All the Talents; The Second Titan War; The Talents Run Mad* (New York and London: Garland Publishing).

Rendall, Jane (2005). '"Women that Would Plague Me with Rational Conversation": Aspiring Women and Scottish Whigs, *c.* 1790–1830', in Barbara Knott and Sarah Taylor (eds), *Women, Gender and Enlightenment* (Basingstoke: Palgrave Macmillan), 326–47.

Rhydderch, Francesca (1997). 'Dual Nationality, Divided Identity: Ambivalent Narratives of Britishness in the Welsh Novels of Anna Maria Bennett', *Welsh Writing in English*, 3: 1–17.

Richardson, Alan (2005). 'Reading Practices', in Janet Todd (ed.), *Jane Austen in Context* (Cambridge: Cambridge University Press), 397–405.

Richetti, John J. (1969). *Popular Fiction before Richardson: Narrative Patterns 1700–1739* (Oxford: Clarendon Press).

Richetti, John J. (ed.) (2005). *The Cambridge History of English Literature, 1660–1789* (Cambridge: Cambridge University Press).

Richter, David (1996). *The Progress of Romance: Literary Historiography and the Gothic Novel* (Columbus: Ohio State University Press).

Rigney, Ann (2001). *Imperfect Histories: The Elusive Past and the Legacy of Romantic Historicism* (Ithaca and London: Cornell University Press).

Rivers, Isabel (2000). *Reason, Grace, and Sentiment: A Study of the Language of Religion and Ethics in England 1660–1780, Volume 2: Shaftesbury to Hume* (Cambridge: Cambridge University Press).

Rivington, Septimus (1919). *The Publishing House of Rivington* (London: Rivington).

Rose, Jonathan (2001). *The Intellectual Life of the British Working Classes* (New Haven and London: Yale University Press).

Rosman, Doreen M. (1977). '"What Has Christ to Do with Apollo?" Evangelicalism and the Novel, 1800–1830', in David Baker (ed.), *Renaissance and Renewal in Christian History* (Oxford: Blackwell), 301–11.

Ross, Ian Campbell (2001). *Laurence Sterne: A Life* (Oxford: Oxford University Press).

Ross, Trevor Thornton (1998). *The Making of the English Literary Canon: From the Middle Ages to the Late Eighteenth Century* (Montreal and Buffalo: McGill-Queen's University Press).

Rousseau, G. S. (1982). *Tobias Smollett: Essays of Two Decades* (Edinburgh: T & T. Clark).

Russell, Gillian (2007). 'Private Theatricals', in Jane Moody and Daniel O'Quinn (eds), *The Cambridge Companion to British Theatre, 1730–1830* (Cambridge: Cambridge University Press), 191–203.

Russett, Margaret (1998). 'Narrative as Enchantment in *The Mysteries of Udolpho*', *ELH*, 65.1: 159–86.

Ryan, Robert M. (1997). *The Romantic Reformation: Religious Politics in English Literature, 1789–1824* (Cambridge: Cambridge University Press).

Sadoff, Dianne F. (2012). 'The Silver Fork Novel', in John Kucich and Jenny Bourne Taylor (eds), *The Nineteenth-Century Novel, 1820–1880, Oxford History of the Novel in English, vol. 3* (Oxford: Oxford University Press), 106–21.

St Clair, William (2004). *The Reading Nation in the Romantic Period* (Cambridge: Cambridge University Press).

St Clair, William (2008). 'Publishing, Authorship, and Reading', in Richard Maxwell and Katie Trumpener (eds), *The Cambridge Companion to Fiction in the Romantic Period* (Cambridge: Cambridge University Press), 37–46.

Saintsbury, George (1913). *The English Novel* (London: Dent).

Sánchez, Mari Carmen Romero (2008). 'A la Señorita Austen: An Overview of Spanish Adaptations', *Persuasions Online*, 28.2 (Spring). Available online at <www.jasna.org/persuasions/on-line/vol28no2/sanchez.htm>.

Sanders, Valerie (ed.) (2000). *Records of Girlhood: An Anthology of Nineteenth-Century Women's Childhoods* (Aldershot: Ashgate).

Schellenberg, Betty (2005). *The Professionalization of Women Writers in Eighteenth-Century Britain* (Cambridge: Cambridge University Press).

Schellenberg, Betty (2010). 'The Bluestockings and the Genealogy of the Modern Novel', *University of Toronto Quarterly*, 79: 1023–34.

Schmidgen, Wolfram (2002). *Eighteenth-Century Fiction and the Law of Property* (Cambridge: Cambridge University Press).

Schoenfield, Mark (2002). 'Novel Marriages, Romantic Labor, and the Quarterly Press', *Prose Studies*, 25: 62–83.

Schöwerling, Rainer (1989). 'Sir Walter Scott and the Tradition of the Historical Novel before 1814—With A Checklist', in Uwe Böker et al. (eds), *The Living Middle Ages: Studies in Medieval English Literature and its Tradition* (Stuttgart: Belser), 227–62.

Shattock, Joanne (ed.) (1993). *The Oxford Guide to British Women Writers* (Oxford: Oxford University Press).

Shaver, Chester L. and Alice C. Shaver (eds) (1979). *Wordsworth's Library: A Catalogue* (New York and London: Garland Publishing).

Shaw, George Bernard (1891). *The Quintessence of Ibsenism* (London: W. Scott).

Shaw, David J. (2003). 'French Émigrés in the London Book Trade to 1850', in Robin Myers, Michael Harris, and Giles Mandelbrote (eds), *The London Book Trade: Topographies of Print in the Metropolis from the Sixteenth Century* (New Castle, DE and London: Oak Knoll Press and The British Library), 127–43.

Shaw, Graham (2009). 'The British Book in India', in Michael F. Suarez, SJ, and Michael L. Turner (eds), *The Cambridge History of the Book in Britain*, Volume V: *1695–1830* (Cambridge: Cambridge University Press), 560–75.

Sher, Richard B. (2007). *The Enlightenment and the Book: Scottish Authors and Their Publishers in Eighteenth-Century Britain, Ireland, and America* (Chicago: University of Chicago Press).

Sherbo, Arthur (2004). 'Susan Smythies', *Oxford Dictionary of National Biography*. Available online at <oxforddnb.com/view/article/72236>.

Shields, Juliet (2010). *Sentimental Literature and Anglo-Scottish Identity, 1745–1820* (Cambridge: Cambridge University Press).

Simpson, David (1986). *The Politics of the English Language, 1776–1850* (New York: Oxford University Press).

Siskin, Clifford (1996). 'Epilogue: The Rise of Novelism', in Deirdre Lynch and William B. Warner (eds), *Cultural Institutions of the Novel* (Durham, NC: Duke University Press), 423–40.

Siskin, Clifford (1998). *The Work of Writing: Literature and Social Change in Britain, 1700–1830* (Baltimore and London: Johns Hopkins University Press).

Siskin, Clifford and William B. Warner (eds) (2010). *This Is Enlightenment* (Chicago: University of Chicago Press).

Siskind, Mariano (2010). 'The Globalization of the Novel and the Novelization of the Global: A Critique of World Literature', *Comparative Literature*, 62.4: 336–60.

Skelton-Foord, Christopher (2002). 'Economics, Expertise, Enterprise and the Literary Scene: The Commercial Management Ethos in British Circulating Libraries, 1780–1830', in E. J. Clery, Caroline Franklin, and Peter Garside (eds), *Scenes of Writing, 1750–1850: Authorship, Commerce and the Public* (Basingstoke: Palgrave Macmillan), 136–52.

Skinner, John (2001). *An Introduction to Eighteenth-Century Fiction: Raising the Novel* (Basingstoke: Palgrave Macmillan).

Smiles, Samuel (1891). *A Publisher and His Friends: Memoir and Correspondence of the Late John Murray*, 2 vols (London: John Murray).

Sodeman, Melissa (2009). 'Charlotte Smith's Literary Exile', *ELH*, 76.1: 130–53.

Sontag, Susan (1964). 'Notes on "Camp"'. Available online at <interglacial.com/~sburke/pub/prose/Susan_Sontag_-_Notes_on_Camp.html>.

Sorenson, Janet (2002). 'Internal Colonialism and the British Novel', *Eighteenth-Century Fiction*, 15.1: 53–8.

Southam, B. C. (ed.) (1968). *Jane Austen: The Critical Heritage* (London: Routledge & Kegan Paul).

Spender, Dale (1986). *The Mothers of the Novel: 100 Good Women Writers before Jane Austen* (London and New York: Pandora).

Spiller, Robert E. (1931). *Fenimore Cooper: Critic of His Times* (New York: Minton, Balch, & Co.).

Spring, David (1961). 'The Clapham Sect: Some Social and Political Aspects', *Victorian Studies*, 5: 35–48.

Spufford, Margaret (1982). *Small Books and Pleasant Histories: Popular Fiction and its Readership in Seventeenth-Century England* (Athens, GA: University of Georgia Press).

Stabler, Jane (2005). 'Literary Influences', in Janet Todd (ed.), *Jane Austen in Context* (Cambridge: Cambridge University Press), 41–50.

Stanton, Judith Phillips (1987). 'Charlotte Smith's "Literary Business": Income, Patronage, and Indigence', *The Age of Johnson*, 1: 375–401.

Starr, G. A. (1971). *Defoe and Casuistry* (Princeton: Princeton University Press).

Starr, G. A. (1994). 'Sentimental Novels of the Later Eighteenth Century', in John J. Richetti (ed.), *The Columbia History of the British Novel* (New York and Chichester: University of Columbia Press), 181–98.

Steiner, George (1975). *After Babel: Aspects of Language and Translation* (London, Oxford, and New York: Oxford University Press).

Stevens, Anne H. (2009). *British Historical Fiction before Scott* (London: Palgrave Macmillan).

Stewart, Joan Hinde (1993). *Gynographs: French Novels by Women of the Late Eighteenth Century* (Lincoln: University of Nebraska Press).

Stewart-Murphy, Charlotte A. (1992). *A History of the British Circulating Libraries: The Book Labels and Ephemera of the Papantonio Collection* (Newtown, PA: Bird & Bull Press).

Stockley, Violet A. A. (1929). *German Literature as Known in England 1750–1830* (London: Routledge).

Streeter, Harold Wade (1936). *The Eighteenth Century English Novel in French Translation: A Bibliographical Study* (New York: Institute of French Studies).

Sullivan, Alvin (ed.) (1983). *British Literary Magazines: The Romantic Age, 1789–1836* (Westport, CT and London: Greenwood Press).

Sutherland, Bruce (1943). 'Pierre Henri Treyssac de Vergy', *Modern Language Quarterly*, 4: 293–307.

Sutherland, Kathryn (ed.) (2002). *J. E. Austen-Leigh: A Memoir of Jane Austen and Other Family Recollections* (Oxford: Oxford University Press).

Tadmor, Naomi (1996). '"In the Even My Wife Read to Me": Women, Reading and Household Life in the Eighteenth Century', in James Raven, Helen Small, and Naomi Tadmor (eds), *The Practice and Representation of Reading in England* (Cambridge: Cambridge University Press), 162–74.

Tadmor, Naomi (2001). *Family and Friends in Eighteenth-Century England* (Cambridge: Cambridge University Press).

Taylor, Richard C. (1993). 'James Harrison, *The Novelist's Magazine*, and the Early Canonizing of the English Novel', *Studies in English Literature*, 33: 629–43.

Tennenhouse, Leonard (2007). *The Importance of Feeling English: American Literature and the British Diaspora, 1750–1850* (Princeton: Princeton University Press).

Terry, Richard et al. (1997a). 'Forum', *Eighteenth-Century Life*, 21.1: 80–107.

Terry, Richard et al. (1997b). 'Forum', *Eighteenth-Century Life*, 21.3: 79–99.

Thackeray, William Makepeace (1853). *The English Humourists of the Eighteenth Century* (London: Smith, Elder, & Co.).

Thaddeus, Janice (1995). 'Elizabeth Hamilton's Modern Philosophers and the Uncertainties of Satire', in James E. Gill (ed.), *Cutting Edges: Postmodern Critical Essays on Eighteenth-Century Satire* (Knoxville: University of Tennessee), 265–84.

Thayer, Harvey Waterman (1905). *Laurence Sterne in Germany: A Contribution to the Study of the Literary Relations of England and Germany in the Eighteenth Century* (New York: Columbia University Press).

Thompson, James (1996). *Models of Value: Eighteenth-Century Political Economy and the Novel* (Durham, NC: Duke University Press).

Todd, Janet (ed.) (1987). *A Dictionary of British and American Women Writers 1660–1800* (London: Methuen).

Treadwell, Michael (1996). '1695–1995: Some Tercentenary Thoughts on the Freedoms of the Press', *Harvard Library Bulletin*, n.s., 7: 3–19.

Trumpener, Katie (1997). *Bardic Nationalism: The Romantic Novel and the British Empire* (Princeton: Princeton University Press).

Tuchman, Gaye with Nina E. Fortin (1989), *Edging Women Out: Victorian Novelists, Publishers, and Social Change* (New Haven: Yale University Press).

Tuite, Clara (2007). 'Tainted Love and Romantic Literary Celebrity', *ELH*, 74.1: 59–88.

Turner, Cheryl (1992). *Living by the Pen: Women Writers in the Eighteenth Century* (London and New York: Routledge).

Varma, Devendra P. (1972). *The Evergreen Tree of Diabolical Knowledge* (Washington, DC: Consortium Press).

Verhoeven, W. M. (1996). '"Persuasive Rhetorick": Representation and Resistance in Early American Epistolary Fiction', in A. Robert Lee and W. M. Verhoeven (eds), *Making America/ Making American Literature* (Amsterdam: Rodopi), 123–64.

Vickery, Amanda (1998). *The Gentleman's Daughter: Women's Lives in Georgian England* (New Haven: Yale University Press).

Vincent, David (1981). *Bread, Knowledge and Freedom: A Study of Nineteenth-Century Working Class Autobiography* (London and New York: Methuen).

Vincent, David (1989). *Literacy and Popular Culture: England 1750–1914* (Cambridge: Cambridge University Press).

Vincent, E. R. (1953). *Ugo Foscolo: An Italian in Regency England* (Cambridge: Cambridge University Press).

Wagner, Peter (1988). *Eros Revived: Erotica of the Enlightenment in England and America* (London: Paladin).

Wahrman, Dror (2004). *The Making of the Modern Self: Identity and Culture in Early Eighteenth-Century England* (New Haven: Yale University Press).

Wallerstein, Immanuel (1976). *The Modern World System: Capitalist Agriculture and the Origins of the European World Economy in the Sixteenth Century* (New York: Academic Press).

Ward, William S. (1972). *Literary Reviews in British Periodicals 1798–1820: A Bibliography*, 2 vols (New York and London: Garland Publishing).

Warner, James H. (1934). 'A Bibliography of Eighteenth-Century English Editions of J.-J. Rousseau, with Notes on the Early Diffusion of His Writings', *Philological Quarterly*, 13.2 (July): 225–47.

Warner, James H. (1937). 'Eighteenth-Century English Reactions to the *Nouvelle Héloïse*', *PMLA*, 52.3: 803–19.

Warner, William B. (1998). *Licensing Entertainment: The Elevation of Novel Reading in Britain, 1684–1750* (Berkeley: University of California Press).

Watson, Nicola J. (1994). *Revolution and the Form of the British Novel, 1790–1825* (Oxford: Oxford University Press).

Watt, Ian (1957). *The Rise of the Novel: Studies in Defoe, Richardson, and Fielding* (London: Chatto & Windus).

Watt, James (2008). 'Orientalism and Empire', in Richard Maxwell and Katie Trumpener (eds), *The Cambridge Companion to Fiction in the Romantic Period* (Cambridge: Cambridge University Press), 129–42.

Watts, Carol (2007). *The Cultural Work of Empire: The Seven Years War and the Imagining of the Shandean State* (Edinburgh: Edinburgh University Press).

Watts, Edward (1998). *Writing and Postcolonialism in the Early Republic* (Charlottesville and London: University Press of Virginia).

Weedon, Alexis (2003). *Victorian Publishing: The Economics of Book Production for a Mass Market, 1836–1916* (Aldershot: Ashgate).

Whelan, Kevin (2000). 'Writing Ireland: Reading England', in Glen Hooper and Leon Litvak (eds), *Ireland in the Nineteenth Century: Regional Identity* (Dublin: Four Courts Press), 185–98.

Williams, Ioan M. (ed.) (1968). *Sir Walter Scott on Novelists and Fiction* (London: Routledge & Kegan Paul).

Williams, Ioan M. (ed.) (1970). *Novel and Romance 1700–1800: A Documentary Record* (London: Routledge).

Williams, Raymond (1983). *Keywords: A Vocabulary of Culture and Society* (New York: Oxford University Press).

Williams, Raymond (1985). *Writing in Society* (London: Verso).

Wilson, Kathleen (1994). 'Empire of Virtue: The Imperial Project and Hanoverian Culture *c.* 1720–1785', in Lawrence Stone (ed.), *The Imperial State at War: Britain from 1689 to 1815* (London and New York: Routledge), 128–64.

Winans, Robert B. (1975). 'The Growth of a Novel-Reading Public in Late Eighteenth-Century America', *Early American Literature*, 9: 267–75.

Woolf, Virginia (1932). 'The "Sentimental Journey"', in *The Common Reader: Second Series* (London: Hogarth Press), 78–85.

Wright, Julia (2007). *Ireland, India and Nationalism in the Nineteenth Century* (Cambridge: Cambridge University Press).

Index of British and Irish Novels and Novelists, 1750-1820

General Index